Specialties of the HOUSE

Specialties of the

HOUSE

*A Country Inn and
Bed & Breakfast
Cookbook*

JULIA M. PITKIN

CUMBERLAND HOUSE

Nashville, Tennessee

Published by Cumberland House Publishing, Inc., 2200 Abbott Martin Road, Suite 102, Nashville, Tennessee 37215.

Book and jacket design by Bruce Gore, Gore Studios.

Distributed to the trade by Andrews and McMeel, 4520 Main Street, Kansas City, Missouri 64111-7701.

Library of Congress Cataloging-in-Publication Data

Pitkin, Julia M.
   Specialties of the house : a country inn bed & breakfast cookbook / Julia M. Pitkin
   p. cm.
   Includes index.
   ISBN 1-888952-00-8
   1. Cookery, American. 2. Hotels—United States—Guidebooks. 3. Hotels—
Canada—
   Guidebooks. I. Title.
TX715.P69 1996
641.5973—dc20   96-18008
                                      CIP

Printed in the United States of America
1 2 3 4 5 6 7 8—00 99 98 97 96

To Innkeepers Everywhere

Your hospitality is our inspiration.

CONTENTS

PREFACE

Specialties of the House is an unusual cookbook that provides a collection of more than 2,300 recipes served at some of the best country inns and bed and breakfasts in the United States and Canada. It also contains warm, inviting descriptions of the accommodations provided by each of the inns whose recipes appear in these pages. As you will quickly notice, in many ways the book is a *national* regional cookbook, for it includes every state, province, and region in the two countries. The many cultures and ethnic groups of the United States and Canada are reflected here in the food and accommodations provided by the inns. In communicating with innkeepers nationwide, we have been repeatedly struck by just how rich and culturally diverse the United States and Canada have become; and the "melting pot" certainly has reached our kitchens with gusto!

We have chosen to organize *Specialties of the House* alphabetically to make it as easy as possible to use. Beginning with Alabama, the inns in each state and province are presented alphabetically in the belief that this will help you find excellent inns and dining facilities near where you live, are traveling, or are thinking of traveling. Perhaps a description of one of the inns will capture your fancy and cause you to want to stay there the next time you are in its vicinity. To help you get a better opinion of what you might expect if you were to visit an inn, the recipes and descriptions appear together.

An exhaustive index (beginning on page 572) presents each recipe by its title and with its main ingredients (such as raspberries, shrimp, or asparagus) and food category (such as breads, soups, soufflés, cheese, or coffee cakes) where appropriate.

Limited space has certainly been the single most frustrating aspect of creating *Specialties of the House.* As large as the book is, we have still been forced not to include many excellent inns and recipes; making these decisions has not been a happy task. Before we invited inns to participate in the book, we carefully studied which ones were known for their fine food, relying on a variety of sources, including our own knowledge. We knew we had selected wonderful inns, but we were unprepared for the overwhelming response. Several inns sent us their entire cookbooks, telling us we could use as many recipes as we desired; others sent a dozen or more tempting recipes; most sent three to five. We could easily fill another volume as large as this one with the recipes we had to cut, most of which were certainly good enough to be included.

When we sent out our call for recipes, we specifically mentioned blueberry muffins as an item we probably wouldn't need; consequently, we received dozens of recipes for orange, pumpkin, rhubarb, raspberry, and other wonderful muffin recipes. The same was true with banana breads (more than forty were submitted), scones, overnight egg casseroles, and French toasts. In making our selections, uniqueness was the highest criteria. For instance, we were forced to weigh considerations of space along with just how unique another scones recipe was. We also tried to include as many inns as possible, enlarging the book from the original plan by more than one hundred pages. It would have been wonderful to include all the recipes and inns, but it was impossible to make them fit into one volume. We certainly do not wish to imply that because an inn or recipe does not appear in *Specialties of the House* we regard it as inferior in any way; I cannot think of one inn that responded that didn't sound as if it would be a wonderful place to stay.

ACKNOWLEDGMENTS

A project as large as *Specialties of the House* is seldom the work of only one person. I have been aided in my work by many persons who spent countless hours in fact-checking, typesetting, proofreading, and critiquing what they found on paper.

In the early stages of the project, Tonya Presley helped design the exquisite brochure through which we first contacted the inns, and Bruce Gore created the book's elegant design.

Others who worked on the book at one stage or another include George Knight, Alice Ewing, Ramona Richards, Janet Noble, Ray Jones, Leslie Peterson, and Jill McNeese. Those whose dedication and participation went far beyond the call of duty were Suzanne Chappin, Beverly White, Marti Molpus, Lori Murphy, and Stephen Woolverton, whose work at getting the project back on schedule must have tested our friendship on more than one occasion.

Finally, thanks goes to my husband, publisher at Cumberland House, for staying out of my hair as we assembled the book, even when asked to help. "Hey," he said, "this delegating thing has its advantages." Then he pitched in with the rest of us.

INTRODUCTION

Since colonial days, North Americans have had a love affair with country inns. Indeed, in those times, generally the only place available to the weary traveler was the inn with its pub, which also served as a restaurant, and sleeping quarters, usually all in one building. There were no hotels or motels or any of the amenities to which we have become accustomed. In a sense, then, the recent growth in popularity of country inns has been a return to our not-so-distant past.

Only in recent years have bed and breakfasts have gained popularity among the American public, particularly with those who are tired of the cookie-cutter experience available at most mainstream hotels and motels. Many fans of the usually smaller bed and breakfasts first encountered the inn experience at country inns; others have simply discovered—by word from a friend or just by accident—the delightful, personal bed and breakfast alternative on their own.

At a well-run bed and breakfast one can retire for the night in an atmosphere that reminds one of the ambience of an earlier era, where a personal welcome was the norm, service was not optional, and rooms were expressions of the innkeeper's individuality. Some have suggested this growing interest in inns is due to the high cost of foreign travel that has sent us exploring the small towns and back roads of our own country or that it is due to the hectic pace of urban life, which has instilled in us a desire to return to a quieter, more personal vacation or holiday experience. Whatever the reason, the country inns and bed and breakfasts of America have enjoyed extraordinary growth and support in the last twenty or so years.

My own experience with bed and breakfasts—and country inns—began with a telephone call. I was in my first editorial job at a small, regional publisher, and the person on the other end of the line asked me if I had any interest in publishing her bed and breakfast cookbook. I asked her about the book, of course, but I was even more fascinated with what she told me about country inns and bed and breakfasts. Like many other Americans, I was aware of such establishments, but I had never stopped to inquire about what they were.

To make a long story short, we not only published the cookbook, which I am proud to say has been very successful and is still in print, but in the middle of editing it, my husband and I spent our honeymoon in the carriage house at the delightful Shellmont Inn in Atlanta, Georgia, where Ed and Debbie McCord were our gracious host and hostess. We were hooked on the inn experience—particularly their helpful suggestions about the perfect places to eat for such an important occasion and about their advice regarding entertainment in the area—and we have yet to be disappointed whenever we are fortunate enough to stay at an inn during our travels.

But my experience with country inns and bed and breakfast books was not finished once the cookbook was completed, and before long I was editor of *The Annual Directory of American and Canadian Bed and Breakfasts*, which I edited for several years. Other inn cookbooks soon followed. When I left that publishing house in 1995, I began working on *Specialties of the House*. The result of a more than a year's planning and editing are in your hands.

I think all of us who have been associated with country inns and bed and breakfasts in any way have struggled to say something new about them. In reading through the introductions to the dozens of directories and other books that have appeared in recent years, I have been struck by how, at the end of the day, they all sound alike. There is, I believe, a good reason for that. Those who stay in the inns, as well as those who write about them, love the inn experience. Where else can we go where we know we will be welcomed as if we have just arrived home following a long absence? Where else will we find such gentility and ambience for such a reasonable price? And where else do we meet such interesting and thoughtful people?

Because, like others, I love the inn experience, I am so pleased to bring you the best of the best, recipes for the dishes that guests of these fine establishments ask for time after time. Enjoy.

—Nashville, Tennessee
  August 1996

Specialties of the
HOUSE

ALABAMA

The Victoria

1604 Quintard Avenue, P.O. Box 2213
Anniston, Alabama 36202
(205) 236-0503

*I*ncluding both a country inn and a hotel, the Victoria property provides relaxed elegance in the spacious surroundings of a turn of the century estate. At its heart is a classic Victorian mansion featuring handsomely appointed guest bedrooms decorated with period antiques, some of them original to the house. The hotel addition and exquisitely renovated guest house offer similar amenities. Museums, shopping, and other attractions, as well as the inn's private pool, offer opportunities for stimulation and relaxation.

Oven-roasted Portabella Mushrooms with Lobster in a Porcini Sauce served over Ground Grits

> 1   tablespoon olive oil
> ¼   yellow onion, medium diced
> 2   cups milk
> 1   cup heavy cream
> 1¼   cups enriched quick grits
> 1   ounce fresh grated Parmesan cheese
> ¼   cup white-grained mustard
>   Salt and pepper
>
> ....
>
> 1   tablespoon olive oil
> 2   ounces lobster claw and tail meat, cooked
> 3   ounces portabella mushrooms, cooked and sliced
> 3   ounces Porcini Sauce (recipe follows)

In a medium saucepan heat 1 tablespoon of olive oil and sauté the onion until tender. Add the milk and heavy cream. Bring the mixture to a boil. Gradually add the grits, making sure there are no lumps. When incorporated add the Parmesan and the mustard. Season with salt and pepper to taste. Set aside and keep warm.

In a medium saucepan heat 1 tablespoon of olive oil. Add the lobster and portabellas and sauté for about 30 seconds. Add the Porcini Sauce and sauté for another minute, then pour over the grits and serve.

MAKES 4 TO 6 SERVINGS.

Porcini Sauce

> 2   ounces dried porcini mushrooms
> ¼   cup red wine
> 2   tablespoons olive oil
> 1   carrot, medium diced
> 2   stalks celery, medium diced
> ½   medium onion, diced
> 2   tablespoons tomato paste
> ½   quart heavy cream

In a small bowl reconstitute the porcini in the red wine.

In a medium saucepan heat the olive oil. Add the carrot, celery, and onion, and sauté for 1 minute or until soft. Add the tomato paste the porcini, and the red wine, and cook until the red wine has evaporated. Add the heavy cream, stirring occasionally, until reduced by one-fourth or until slightly thickened. Strain and serve.

Fried Green Tomatoes

> ¼   cup olive oil
> ¼   cup balsamic vinegar
> ¼   cup diced red onion
> ½   cup halved cherry tomatoes
> 1   teaspoon minced garlic
> 2   teaspoons chopped fresh basil
>   Salt and pepper to taste
> ¼   pound rock shrimp, peeled and deveined
>
> ....
>
> 2   eggs
> 1   cup milk
> 3   cups Japanese breadcrumbs
> ¼   cup grated Parmesan cheese
> 1   medium-sized green tomato, sliced ¼-inch thick
> 2   cups all-purpose flour
> 1   tablespoon olive oil
>   Parsley for garnish

In a medium bowl mix the first 7 ingredients together and set aside.

In a skillet sauté the rock shrimp for about 1 minute. Add the cherry tomato vinaigrette, and heat through.

In a shallow dish mix the eggs and the milk together. In a separate shallow dish mix the breadcrumbs and Parmesan together. Dredge a slice of tomato in the flour. Then dip into the egg-milk mixture.

Place the tomato in the breadcrumb mixture, making certain everything is coated.

Heat 1 tablespoon of olive oil and sauté the tomato until brown on both sides. Repeat with the remaining tomato slices.

Place the warm cherry tomatoes and rock shrimp over the sliced tomatoes. Garnish with fresh Parmesan and parsley.

MAKES 2 TO 4 SERVINGS.

Riverview Bed & Breakfast

❧

Route 7 Box 123G
Florence, Alabama 35630
(205) 757-8667

As its name implies, all guest rooms at the Riverview offer spectacular views of the Tennessee River, as well as the Wilson and Wheeler TVA dams. A recently constructed contemporary home, it is well suited to its wooded setting, designed and decorated to blend with its surroundings. The B&B's two rooms promise privacy. Spacious decks and patios enhance enjoyment of the scenery.

Riverview Baked Bananas

4 to 6 bananas, peeled and sliced lengthwise
1   8-ounce jar orange marmalade
1   2-ounce package slivered almonds

In a well-buttered baking dish arrange the banana halves. Coat the top of the bananas with marmalade. Sprinkle with almonds. Bake in a 350° oven for 10 minutes or until bubbly.

MAKES 6 SERVINGS.

Breakfast Pizza

1   pound bulk pork sausage
1   8-ounce package refrigerated crescent rolls
1   cup frozen loose-pack hash brown potatoes, thawed
1   cup shredded sharp Cheddar cheese
5   eggs, beaten
¼   cup milk
½   teaspoon salt
½   teaspoon pepper
2   tablespoons grated Parmesan cheese
    Pimento (optional)
    Fresh oregano (optional)

In a medium skillet until cook the sausage until brown. Drain and set aside.

Separate the crescent dough into 8 triangles. Place with the elongated point toward the center of a greased 12-inch pizza pan. Press the bottom and sides to form a crust. Seal the perforations. Spoon the sausage over the dough. Sprinkle with hash brown potatoes and Cheddar cheese.

In a medium bowl combine the eggs, milk, salt, and pepper. Pour the mixture over the sausage mixture. Bake in a 375° oven for 25 minutes. Sprinkle with Parmesan cheese and bake an additional 5 minutes.

Garnish with pimento and fresh oregano, if desired.

MAKES 6 TO 8 SERVINGS.

Mentone Inn

❧

P.O. Box 290
Mentone, Alabama 35984
(205) 634-4836

The beaded, hand-polished wood paneling of this mountain top country inn suggest the roaring twenties, which is when it was built. However, guests are less likely to be doing the foxtrot than just relaxing or taking in the sights on Lookout Mountain. Desoto State Park, Cloudland, and the 600-foot-

---

Mentone Inn

deep Little River Canyon are all nearby and offer scenic spectacles on a grand scale rarely seen in the East. For the popular Rhododendron Festival in May and Colorfest in the Fall, plan your stay well in advance.

Zucchini Chocolate Chip Cake

1½   cups sugar
½   cup margarine or butter, softened
¼   cup oil
1   teaspoon vanilla extract
2   eggs
2½   cups all-purpose or unbleached flour
¼   cup sweetened cocoa
1   teaspoon baking soda
½   cup buttermilk
2   cups shredded zucchini
½   to 1 cup semisweet chocolate chips
½   cup pecans

Grease and flour a 9 x 13-inch pan. In a large bowl combine the sugar, margarine, oil, and vanilla until smooth. Blend in the eggs one at a time. In a separate bowl sift together the flour, cocoa, and soda. Add one-third of the flour to the egg mixture and mix well. Alternately add the flour and buttermilk until all ingredients are incorporated. Fold in the zucchini, chips, and pecans. Spread into the prepared pan. Bake in a 350° oven for 35 to 45 minutes or until a toothpick inserted in the center comes out clean. Cool completely.

Frost or garnish as desired.

MAKES 16 SERVINGS.

Lasagna Rosettes

2   10-ounce boxes frozen spinach
1   tablespoon chopped garlic
    Salt and pepper to taste
1   16-ounce carton ricotta cheese

1 16-ounce carton cottage cheese
1 tablespoon dried basil
1 egg, slightly beaten
1 16-ounce box lasagna, boiled and
  drained
  Marinara or white sauce

Thaw and drain the spinach well. In a food processor combine the chopped garlic, salt, and pepper and blend until spreadable.

In a large bowl mix together the ricotta and cottage cheeses, basil, and egg. On a work table lay 1 or 2 lasagna flat. Spread with some of the spinach mixture, leaving ½ inch at one end. Spread some of the cheese mixture on top. Starting at the filled end, roll up jelly roll fashion and seal with a toothpick. Repeat with the remaining lasagna and filling. Place in a lightly oiled glass baking dish so that a ruffled edge is up. Bake in a 375° oven for 25 minutes.

Serve with marinara or white sauce.
MAKES 6 SERVINGS.

Lattice Inn Bed & Breakfast

❧

1414 South Hull Street
Montgomery, Alabama 36104-5522
(334) 832-9931

Built in 1906 and situated in Montgomery's historic garden district, this B&B has been lovingly restored to provide a serene retreat for today's traveler. Guests can enjoy the view from the shady front porch or lounge in front of the fireplace. A pool and multilevel decks offer further opportunities for relaxation. All bedrooms are furnished with antiques and include a private bath. A separate cottage provides its own kitchen and all the comforts of home.

Lattice Inn

Easy Sour Cream Coffeecake Muffins

2 cups butter blend
2 cups sugar
1 ounce almond extract
8 eggs
1 cup sour cream
4 cups all-purpose flour
1 teaspoon baking powder
1 teaspoon baking soda
½ teaspoon salt
½ teaspoon ground ginger
½ teaspoon cinnamon
½ teaspoon ground cloves
½ teaspoon ground mace

In a large bowl blend the butter, sugar, and almond extract with an electric mixer on low until blended. Add eggs slowly, one at a time. Continue mixing and add the sour cream. In a separate bowl combine the flour, baking powder, soda, salt, and spices. Add the egg mixture all at once and stir just until moistened. The batter should be lumpy. Pour into greased muffin cups. Bake in a 350° oven for 25 minutes or until done. Cool in the pans for 10 minutes, and then turn out and completely cool.
MAKES ABOUT 36 MUFFINS.

Lattice Inn Reuben Casserole

10 slices rye bread, cut into ¾-inch
   cubes
1½ pounds cooked corned beef
2½ cups shredded Swiss cheese
6 eggs, slightly beaten
3 cups milk
  Salt and pepper to taste

Grease a 9 x 13-inch dish. Arrange the bread cubes on bottom. Layer the corned beef over this. Sprinkle Swiss cheese over this layer. In a medium bowl beat the eggs, milk, and seasonings until blended well. Pour this mixture over all. Cover with foil and refrigerate overnight.

Bake covered in a 350° oven for 45 minutes. Uncover and bake another 10 minutes, until bubbly and puffed.
MAKES 8 SERVINGS.

Crab Meat Breakfast Pie

8 large eggs
1 large red bell pepper, chopped
6 ounces crab meat
2 cups half and half
1 teaspoon salt
1 cup fresh breadcrumbs
1 bunch green onions, chopped
1 cup grated Swiss cheese
1 cup grated Cheddar cheese
½ teaspoon pepper
  Touch grated nutmeg

Butter a 10-inch quiche pan. In a large bowl beat the eggs. In a separate bowl mix all remaining ingredients together. And the mixture to the eggs. Pour into the prepared dish. Bake in a 350° oven until set, about 35 to 45 minutes. Cut into wedges and serve hot.
MAKES 6 TO 8 SERVINGS.

Michael's Wonderful Oatmeal Cookies

2 cups all-purpose flour
½ teaspoon salt
1 teaspoon baking powder
½ teaspoon baking soda
2½ to 3 teaspoons ground cinnamon
1⅓ cups butter
1¼ cups sugar
¾ cup firmly packed brown sugar
2 large eggs
1 plus teaspoon vanilla extract, or
  more
2 tablespoons water or orange juice
1¼ cups raisins
1 cup nuts
2½ cups uncooked oats (regular)

In a large bowl mix together the flour, salt, baking powder, soda, and cinnamon. Set aside.

In a separate bowl cream the butter with the sugars. Beat in the eggs, one at a time.

Add the vanilla and juice or water, and mix until blended well. To the dry ingredients, add the raisins, nuts, and oatmeal, and pour all into the liquid mixture. Blend together for about 4 minutes. Drop by spoonful onto ungreased cookie sheets. Bake in a 350° oven for 10 to 14 minutes or until light brown.

MAKES 5 TO 7 DOZEN COOKIES.

551 Clay Street, P. O. Box 1026
Montgomery, Alabama 36104
(334)264-0056

Red Bluff Cottage is a raised cottage situated high above the Alabama River in the historic Cottage Hill District. The guest rooms are on the ground floor, and the living, dining, music, and sitting rooms are upstairs. The deep porch overlooks downtown, the state capitol, and the river plain. The four guests rooms all have private baths.

Wild Rice Waffles

½	cup all-purpose flour
½	cup whole wheat flour
1¾	cups cooked wild rice, well-drained
⅓	cup dried cherries
2	tablespoons sugar
2	tablespoons baking powder
½	teaspoon baking soda
¼	teaspoon salt
1¼	cups buttermilk
2	large eggs
¼	cup unsalted butter, melted
	Fresh Alabama peaches, sliced
	Maple syrup

In a large bowl combine the flours, wild rice, cherries, sugar, baking powder, soda, and salt. Mix until combined. In a separate bowl combine the buttermilk, eggs, and melted butter. Whisk until combined well. Add the buttermilk mixture to the dry ingredients. Stir well. This may be made several hours ahead and refrigerated.

Heat a waffle iron. Ladle batter onto the waffle iron. Cook the waffles until browned and slightly crisp. Baked waffles may be kept warm in a 200° oven while the rest are cooked. Serve hot with fresh Alabama peaches and warm maple syrup.

MAKES 4 WAFFLES.

Eggs Red Bluff

1	tablespoon olive oil
¼	cup finely chopped green onions
¼	cup sliced mushrooms
¼	cup diced green bell peppers
6	eggs, beaten and seasoned with Jane's Krazy Mixed-up Salt to taste
¼	cup canned diced tomatoes, drained
1	tablespoon Parmesan cheese, grated
	Grated Cheddar cheese
	Fresh basil

Heat the oil in a 10-inch nonstick pan and add the onions, mushrooms, and bell peppers for about 1 minute until the vegetables are softened slightly, about 1 minute.

Pour the seasoned eggs over the vegetables and scramble, making certain the eggs remain moist. Gently stir in the drained tomatoes just to heat through. Remove to a serving dish and sprinkle with Parmesan cheese, then top lightly with grated Cheddar cheese. Garnish with slivered fresh basil.

MAKES 4 SERVINGS.

ALASKA

Glacier Bear

4814 Malibu Road
Anchorage, Alaska 99517
(907)243-8818

First-class accommodations characterize this contemporary B&B. A prime location near the world's largest seaplane base and the Anchorage airport promise an enjoyable Alaska experience without the hassle. Downtown shopping and fine dining are also nearby. Guests can enjoy biking and hiking around the area.

Cheese Baked Eggs

> 1 teaspoon butter
> 1 tablespoon heavy cream
> 1 large egg
>   Salt and pepper to taste
>   Grated Havarti cheese
>   Croissant

Butter a 3½-ounce ramekin or custard dish. Add the cream. Gently crack a large egg into the ramekin. Season with salt and pepper to taste. Sprinkle Havarti cheese on top. Baked in a 425° oven for 10 minutes or until the white is firm and the center is still soft. Serve with a croissant.
MAKES 1 SERVING.

Breakfast Casserole

> 7 slices white bread
> 2 cups shredded Cheddar cheese
>   Fried and crumbled bacon, browned sausage or ham (optional)
> 6 eggs
> 3 cups milk
> ½ teaspoon salt
> 1 teaspoon dry mustard
> ¼ teaspoon pepper

In a large bowl crumble the bread and add the Cheddar cheese. Add the bacon, if desired. Spread in the bottom of a greased 7 ½ x 12-inch baking dish. In a separate bowl beat the eggs and milk together and stir in the seasonings. Pour this over the bread-cheese mixture. Cover. Refrigerate overnight.

The next morning remove the cover. Bake uncovered in a 350° oven for 50 to 55 minutes.

Remove from the oven and serve just after the guests sit down, otherwise it may tend to fall. Tastes just as good but doesn't look as glamorous.
MAKES 6 TO 8 SERVINGS.

Pull-apart Rolls

> 1 package Rhodes frozen dinner rolls
> ½ cup chopped nuts
> ½ cup raisins
> 1 3-ounce package regular butterscotch pudding (not instant)
> ½ cup firmly packed brown sugar
> 1 teaspoon ground cinnamon
> 3 tablespoons milk
> ½ cup butter, melted

Grease a large bundt pan or angel food cake pan. Stack the frozen dinner rolls in the pan. Sprinkle nuts and raisins over the dough. In a small bowl mix together the powdered pudding, sugar, cinnamon, milk, and melted butter. Pour over the top of the frozen dinner rolls. Cover and refrigerate overnight.

Bake in a 350° oven for 40 minutes. Cool for 5 minutes and then turn upside-down on a plate. Pull apart and enjoy.
MAKES 6 TO 8 SERVINGS.

Birch Trails

22719 Robinson Road
Chugiak, Alaska 99567
(907)688-5713

Positioned only about thirty minutes north of Anchorage by car or bus, Birch Trails provides a great centrally located jumping-off place for exploring the "Great Land." Magnificent stands of birch are an attraction here. So are the sweeping mountain views. Guests can enjoy a *thrilling ride on a sled pulled by stout huskies, some of them veterans of Alaska's famed midwinter Iditarod race. Accommodations include queen beds, a private entrance, and all the amenities of home.*

Birch Trails

Smoked Salmon Breakfast Quiche

    3 eggs, beaten
    1 cup light cream
    1 teaspoon onion powder
    ½ teaspoon garlic powder
    1 unbaked 9-inch pie crust
    ⅔ cup smoked salmon
    ⅔ cup shredded Cheddar cheese

In a medium bowl mix the eggs, cream, onion and garlic powders, and salmon. Pour into the pie crust. Sprinkle Cheddar cheese on top. Bake in a 325° oven for 45 minutes.
MAKES 6 SERVINGS.

Old-fashioned Gingerbread

    1½ cups all-purpose flour
    1   egg
    ½   cup shortening
    ½   cup molasses
    ¼   cup sugar
    1   teaspoon baking soda
    ¾   teaspoon ground ginger
    ½   teaspoon salt
    ½   teaspoon ground cinnamon
    1   cup boiling water
        Butterscotch Sauce (recipe follows)

Grease a 9-inch square cake pan. In a large bowl combine all ingredients and beat with an electric mixer at low speed until mixed well, scraping the bowl with a rubber spatula. Beat at medium speed for 2 minutes, occasionally scraping the bowl. Pour the batter into the pan. Bake in a 350° oven for 35 minutes. Cool in the pan on a wire rack. Serve warm with Butterscotch Sauce, if desired.
MAKES 12 SERVINGS.

Butterscotch Sauce

    ¾ cup firmly packed brown sugar
    2 tablespoons all-purpose flour
    1 cup hot water
    1 tablespoon butter
    1 teaspoon vanilla extract

In a saucepan combine the sugar and flour. Add the hot water. Cook over high heat until the mixture begins to thicken. Turn the heat off and stir for 5 minutes. Add the butter and vanilla.

Pour over the gingerbread while the sauce is hot.
MAKES ABOUT 1½ CUPS.

Banana Crêpes à la Birch Trails

    2 eggs
    2 tablespoons sugar
    1 cup all-purpose flour
    1 cup milk
    3 bananas, cut up crosswise
    ¼ cup butter
    ½ cup firmly packed brown sugar
    ½ teaspoon banana extract (optional)

In a small bowl combine the eggs, sugar, flour, and milk, and blend to the consistency of eggnog.

In a saucepan combine the bananas, butter, brown sugar, and extract. Simmer over low heat until it becomes a thick sauce with somewhat recognizable banana bits.

In an 8-inch skillet melt a small amount of butter and cook the crêpes until lightly browned on both sides. Keep them warm in the oven with foil in between. Drizzled the sauce in the center, and roll the crêpe around. Crêpes can also be sprinkled with confectioners' sugar, sugar, or cinnamon-sugar.

Note: These measurements are approximate as I prepare according to sight, taste, and consistency.
MAKES 5 SERVINGS.

HC 64 Box 50, Milepost 52, Sterling Hwy.
Cooper Landing, Alaska 99572
(907)595-1266

One of Alaska's few remaining traditional log roadhouse lodges, Gwin's has been a landmark on the scenic Kenai Peninsula for nearly half a century. Visitors enjoy a variety of activities including fishing, hiking, clam digging, flightseeing, and scenic river rafting. Each of the rustic cabins comes with two double beds and a private bath. A Deluxe cabin also includes a loft bed and fully equipped kitchen.

Alaska-style Salmon-stuffed Halibut

    2   tablespoons butter
    ¼   cup chopped onion
    ¼   cup chopped celery
    ½   pound cooked salmon, flaked
    ¼   cup dry breadcrumbs
    1   teaspoon grated lemon zest
    ¼   teaspoon salt
        Dash pepper

    1½ pounds halibut fillets (halved)
    ⅛   teaspoon paprika
    2   tablespoons butter
    1½ tablespoons all-purpose flour
    ¼   teaspoon salt
        Dash pepper
        Dash paprika
    ¾   cup half and half
    ¼   cup white wine

In a small pan melt the butter and sauté the onion and celery. Stir in the cooked salmon, breadcrumbs, lemon zest, ¼ teaspoon of salt, and a dash of pepper. Remove the pan from the heat.

Place 1 of the halved halibut fillets in a buttered baking dish. Sprinkle it with paprika, and then spread the salmon stuffing evenly over the top of the base fillet. Place the remaining halibut fillet on top of the salmon stuffing. Cover the dish. Bake in a 425° oven for 20 to 25 minutes.

In a small pan melt 2 tablespoons of butter. Stir in the flour, ¼ teaspoon of salt, a dash of pepper, a dash of paprika, half and half, and white wine. Stir until thickened.

Remove the baked salmon-stuffed halibut from the oven and portion. Ladle sauce over each serving.

MAKES 4 SERVINGS.

Alaska-style Clam Chowder

 6   **cups milk**
 2   **cups water**
 2   **slices bacon**
 1   **large carrot, shredded**
1½   **stalks celery, finely chopped**
 1   **large boiling potato**
 1   **medium onion, finely chopped**
 ¼   **cup butter**
 ¼   **cup all-purpose flour**
 ¼   **teaspoon ground black pepper**
 ⅛   **teaspoon salt**
 ¼   **teaspoon clam base**
12   **ounces chopped clams**

In a medium saucepan heat the milk and water over low heat.

In a large skillet fry the bacon until crisp. Remove the bacon to paper towels to drain. Reserve the bacon drippings. In the same skillet sauté the carrots and celery in some of the bacon drippings until almost tender. Add the potato and cook until tender. Crumble the bacon and add it to the potato mixture.

Gwin's Lodge

In a separate skillet sauté the onion in some of the bacon drippings. Add the onion to the potato mixture.

In the same skillet melt the butter. Blend in the flour. Add the pepper, salt, clam base, and chopped clams, stirring until smooth. Pour the clam mixture into the scalded milk, stirring constantly. Add the potato mixture, stirring constantly. Heat through.

MAKES 4 SERVINGS.

Alaska-style Cheesecake

 ¾   **cup coarsely ground walnuts**
 ¾   **cup finely crushed graham cracker crumbs**
 ¼   **cup melted butter**

....

 4   **8-ounce packages cream cheese, softened**
 4   **large eggs**
1¼   **cups sugar**
 1   **tablespoon lemon juice**
 2   **teaspoons vanilla extract**

....

     Fruit pie filling
     Whipped Cream
     Crushed walnuts

Lightly butter a 9- or 10-inch springform pie pan. In a medium bowl combine the walnuts, graham cracker crumbs, and melted butter. Stir the crust mixture thoroughly, and place in pie pan. Press firmly onto the bottom of the pan.

In a separate bowl beat the cream cheese with an electric mixer until smooth. Add the eggs, sugar, lemon juice, and vanilla and beat until thoroughly mixed and smooth. Spoon the mixture over the crust. Bake in a 350° oven for 1 hour. Remove and allow to cool. Refrigerate.

Although ready to serve once it is cool, curing the cheesecake for approximately 24 hours in the refrigerator will further enhance its flavor. To serve, ladle desired pie filling (cherry, blueberry, raspberry, etc.) on top of the cake. Add a dollop of whipped cream and top with a sprinkle of crushed walnuts.

MAKES 8 SERVINGS.

North Face Lodge
❧

P. O. Box 67
Denali National Park, Alaska 99755
(907) 683-2290

Founded in 1951, Camp Denali is Alaska's original vacation lodge and nature center. Individual cabins, each with wood-burning stoves, patchwork quilts, and country charm, offer spectacular views of Mount McKinley. A dining room, living room, and rest room/shower buildings are centrally located nearby. North Face Lodge, a 12 x 18-foot log cabin, sits in Moose Creek Valley a mile away from Camp Denali. Its fifteen guest rooms with private baths are connected by a covered porch to the dining and living room.

Sourdough Starter

 1   **package active dry yeast**
 ½   **cup lukewarm water (105 to 115°)**
 ¾   **cup unbleached flour**

In a large jar or crock with a cover combine the yeast, water, and flour. Stir the ingredients to form a thick batter. Cover, leaving the lid loose in order to allow for expansion and let the batter rise overnight or longer in a warm (80 to 90°) place. The mixture should be warm but not hot. When ready, the starter "sponge" will be bubbly and have a pleasantly sour smell.

Sourdough Pancakes

1 cup sourdough starter (above)
2 cups lukewarm water (105 to 115°)
2 cups unbleached flour
½ cup whole wheat flour
3 egg yolks
2 tablespoons honey
2 teaspoons oil
¼ teaspoon salt
¼ cup nonfat powdered milk (or powdered buttermilk)
3 stiffly beaten egg whites
1 teaspoon baking soda

In a large bowl mix together the starter, water, and flours. Cover and set in a warm (80° to 90°) place overnight.

In the morning remove 1 cup of starter for future use and refrigerate it.

To the remaining batter add the egg yolks, honey, oil, salt, and powdered milk.

Let this mixture stand and lighten for 15 to 20 minutes. Fold in the egg whites. Stir in the soda lightly. Fry hotcakes on a lightly oiled griddle.

MAKES 6 TO 8 SERVINGS.

Sourdough French Bread

1 cup sourdough starter
¾ cup lukewarm water (105 to 115°)
¼ cup sugar
1 tablespoon active dry yeast
4 cups unbleached flour
½ cup whole wheat flour
¼ cup nonfat powdered milk
2 tablespoons oil
2 teaspoons salt

In a large bowl mix together the starter, water, and sugar. Add the yeast. When the mixture is foamy, add 2 cups of unbleached flour, the whole wheat flour, powdered milk, oil, and salt. Stir vigorously, about 200 strokes. Gradually stir in 1½ to 2 cups of unbleached flour until a kneadable dough develops.

Knead until the dough is smooth and elastic. Place in an oiled bowl, cover, and let rise until doubled in bulk.

Punch down and divide the dough in half. Allow to rest for 10 minutes.

Shape, rise, and bake as for French bread, 400° for 15 minutes or 350° for 30 minutes

MAKES 2 LONG LOAVES.

The Blue Goose
❧

4466 Dartmouth
Fairbanks, Alaska 99709
(907) 479-6973

---

*S*ituated in the university district about five miles from the Fairbanks city center, the Blue Goose offers a warm, family atmosphere to Alaska travelers looking for a little home-style comfort. A trilevel contemporary house with antique furnishings, it has three guest rooms, one with a private bath. Breakfast includes their blue-ribbon Alaska Rhubarb Pie. Sightseeing includes the museum, the riverboat Discovery, and the historic Pump House Restaurant.

Cream Cheese "Wreath" Christmas Cookies

2½ cups margarine
1 8-ounce package cream cheese
1 tablespoon vanilla extract
1¼ cups sugar
5 cups all-purpose flour
Red and/or green colored sugar
Red hots

In a large bowl combine the margarine, cream cheese, vanilla, sugar, and flour. Use a cookie press with a star tip to form little wreaths. Sprinkle with red and/or green sugar, and place a red hot candy in the center of each. Bake in a 375° oven for 12 minutes.

MAKES ABOUT 3 DOZEN.

Plum Cake

½ cup butter
½ cup sugar
1 egg
¼ cup milk
1½ cups all-purpose flour
¼ teaspoon salt
1 teaspoon baking powder
2 plums, sliced
½ cup sugar
1 teaspoon cinnamon

Grease a 9-inch round or square pan. In a large bowl cream the butter and sugar. Add the egg and mix well. Blend in the milk.

In a separate small bowl combine the flour, salt, and baking powder. Add the dry ingredients to the creamed mixture. Pour the batter into the prepared pan. Arrange the plum slices skin-side down on top of the batter.

In a small bowl combine ½ cup of sugar and the cinnamon. Sprinkle the cinnamon-sugar mixture over the batter and plums. Bake in a 350° oven for 35 minutes.

MAKES 6 TO 8 SERVINGS.

Oat Bran Muffins

½ cups oat bran
½ cup all-purpose flour
3 tablespoons firmly packed brown sugar
2 teaspoons baking powder
½ teaspoon salt
1 teaspoon cinnamon
1 egg
2 tablespoons oil
½ cup juice (apple or orange)
2 tablespoons honey
½ cup chopped nuts
½ cup berries
Cinnamon-sugar

In a medium bowl combine the oat bran, flour, brown sugar, baking powder, salt, and cinnamon.

In a large bowl mix the egg, oil, juice and honey. Add the dry ingredients, mixing just until moistened. Fold in the nuts and berries. Spoon into muffin cups. Sprinkle with cinnamon-sugar. Bake in a 375° oven for 20 minutes.

MAKES 12 MUFFINS.

The Blue Goose

Blueberry Buckle

2   cups all-purpose flour
½   cup sugar
1½   teaspoon baking powder
¾   teaspoon salt
¼   cup shortening
1   egg
¾   cup milk
1   cup blueberries
....

½   cup sugar
⅓   cup all-purpose flour
½   teaspoon cinnamon
¼   cup butter

In a large bowl combine 2 cups of flour, ½ cup of sugar, baking powder, and salt. Cut in the shortening. In a separate bowl beat the egg with the milk. Add the liquid ingredients to the flour mixture and blend. Pour half the batter into a 9-inch round or square pan. Sprinkle ½ cup of blueberries over the batter. Press the berries in a little. Carefully spread the remaining batter on top and sprinkle with the other ½ cup of berries. Press in gently.

In a small bowl mix ½ cup of sugar, ⅓ cup of flour, the cinnamon, and butter with a pastry blender. Sprinkle the topping evenly over the batter. Bake in a 375 ° oven for 45 to 50 minutes.
MAKES 6 TO 8 SERVINGS.

Pumpkin Muffins

1   cup mashed pumpkin (fresh-frozen)
½   cup oil
¼   cup water
2   eggs
1   cup sugar
1½   cup all-purpose flour
½   teaspoon salt
1   teaspoon baking soda
¼   teaspoon grated nutmeg
¼   teaspoon cinnamon
¼   teaspoon ground allspice
½   cup berries
½   cup chopped nuts
   Cinnamon-sugar

In a large bowl combine the pumpkin, oil, water, and eggs. In a separate bowl combine the sugar, flour, salt, baking soda, nutmeg, cinnamon, and allspice. Add the dry ingredients to the pumpkin mixture, stirring just until moistened. Add the berries and chopped nuts. Spoon into muffin cups. Sprinkle fairly heavily with cinnamon sugar. Bake in a 350° oven for 25 minutes.

Note: To freeze pumpkin, cut the pumpkin in pieces and bake in a 350° oven until a fork goes in easily. Cut away the skin and puree the pumpkin in the food processor with a steel blade. Pour 1-cup portions into small plastic bags and freeze. This is one of Glacier Bear's most asked for recipes, and the thing that makes it good is the fresh-frozen pumpkin.
MAKES 12 MUFFINS.

Alaska Rhubarb Pie

⅓   cup lard, cut up
1   cup all-purpose flour, cold
2-3   tablespoons ice-cold water
....

4   cups rhubarb, cut small
1¼   cups sugar
⅓   cup all-purpose flour
....

½   cup cold butter, cut up
1   cup all-purpose flour, cold
½   cup firmly packed brown sugar

In a food processor mix ⅓ cup of lard and 1 cup of flour. Add the water gradually, pulsing until a ball is formed. Roll out and place in a 9-inch pie pan, trimming to fit.

In a large bowl mix the rhubarb, sugar, and ⅓ cup of flour. Place in the pie pan. In a food processor mix the butter, 1 cup of flour, and brown sugar. Sprinkle over the rhubarb. Bake in a 400° oven for 1 hour. The pie is done when the filling is just starting to bubble.
MAKES 6 TO 8 SERVINGS.

7 Gables Inn
❧

P.O. Box 80488
Fairbanks, Alaska 99708
(907) 479-0751

This spacious Tudor-style home features a large floral solarium and garden and excellent views of the

Northern Lights. For those with a touch of Alaska chill in their bones, the private Jacuzzis will be especially welcome. Situated not far from the scenic Chena River, the inn offers convenient access to the university and airport. Canoes and bicycles are available for those interested in exploring.

The Gables Frittata

½   pound sausage
2   cups shredded zucchini
2   green onions, chopped
½   teaspoon dried oregano
½   teaspoon dried basil
1   tablespoon packaged dry Italian
   salad dressing mix
6   eggs
½   cup heavy cream
4   ounces cream cheese
1   cup shredded Cheddar cheese
1   cup shredded mozzarella cheese

In a skillet brown the sausage. Drain on a paper towel. Place the sausage in an 8-inch quiche pan or pie plate. Spread the zucchini and onions over the sausage, and sprinkle with seasonings and dressing mix.

In a separate bowl beat the eggs with the heavy cream and pour over zucchini and sausage. Cut the cream cheese into cubes and sprinkle evenly over the top. Cover with the mozzarella and Cheddar cheeses. Bake in a 325° oven for 45 minutes or until set.
MAKES 6 SERVINGS.

Alaskan Crab Soufflé

2   cups crab meat, cooked
12   eggs, beaten
2   cups small curd cottage cheese
1½   cups heavy cream
¼   cup cooking sherry

In a large bowl combine all ingredients. Pour into a greased 9 x 12-inch baking dish. Bake in a 350° oven for 1 hour.

Cut into 12 pieces and serve immediately.
MAKES 6 SERVINGS.

Salmon Broccoli Quiche

1   8-inch unbaked pie crust
1   cup shredded Swiss cheese
1½ cups broccoli pieces
1   cup cooked salmon
4   green onions
5   eggs
1½ cups heavy cream
    Lemon pepper

Cover the bottom of the crust with ½ cup of Swiss cheese. Add the broccoli, salmon, and onions. In a large bowl beat the eggs and add the heavy cream. Season with lemon pepper to taste. Pour the mixture into the crust. Sprinkle the remaining cheese over the top. Bake in a 375° oven for 15 minutes. Reduce the oven temperature to 350° and continue baking for 45 minutes. Cool before slicing.
MAKES 6 SERVINGS.

Evergreen Lodge at Lake Louise

❧

HC 01 Box 1709
Glennallen, Alaska 99588
(907) 822-3250

About three hours from Anchorage on the scenic Glenn Highway, the rooms here provide a breathtaking-view of beautiful Lake Louise. For guests who want to see even more, the lodge offers flights over the Wrangall and Chugach mountain ranges. They even offer video safaris to capture the experience on tape. Fishing in remote lakes and a dinner cruise promise further enjoyment, while the truly adventurous can be dropped at the wilderness cabin on the shore of Clarence Lake.

Lemon Pancake

½ cup all-purpose flour
½ cup milk
2   eggs, lightly beaten
    Grated nutmeg
½ cup butter
    Juice of ½ lemon
1   teaspoon confectioners' sugar

In a medium bowl stir the flour, milk, eggs, and nutmeg together. The mixture may be lumpy. In a copper crêpe pan melt the butter. Add the pancake mixture. Bake in a 350° oven for 10 to 12 minutes. When done, sprinkle with the lemon juice and sugar. Place back in the oven for 1 minute.
MAKES ABOUT 2 SERVINGS.

Rhubarb Butter

    Rhubarb, cut into pieces
1   tablespoon cinnamon
½ teaspoon ground allspice
1   teaspoon ground cloves
1   package Sure-Jel
5½ cups sugar

In a large saucepan barely cover the rhubarb with water and boil until cooked down to a very stringy pulp. Measure 4 cups of pulp. In a separate pan combine the pulp, cinnamon, allspice, cloves, and Sure-Jel. Bring to a hard boil. Add the sugar and boil for 2 minutes. Stir to prevent sticking. Serve over pancakes or pour into jars.
MAKES ABOUT 4 HALF-PINTS.

Good River Bed and Breakfast

❧

Box 37
Gustavus, Alaska 99826
(907) 697-2241

An ideal spot for those who want to experience Alaska's spectacular Glacier Bay National Park, the Good

River B&B is a lovely and rustic log home. In addition to four comfortable guest rooms, there is a secluded guest cabin with electricity but no running water. The innkeepers will book sightseeing and whale-watching tours for guests. Bicycles, fishing poles, boots, and rain gear are provided.

Good River

Orange-scented Scones

½ cup cold unsalted butter
1¾ cups all-purpose flour
1½ teaspoons baking powder
1   tablespoon sugar
    Grated zest of 1 orange
¾ cup buttermilk

In a large bowl cut the butter into the flour, leaving the butter in pieces about the size of small peas. Add the baking powder, sugar, and orange zest. Barely mix in the buttermilk. Do not overmix.

Place the dough on a board and shape into a 7-inch circle. Cut into 8 wedges. Place on a greased baking sheet. Bake in a 400° oven for 18 to 20 minutes.

Variation: Brush tops with buttermilk and sprinkle with sugar before baking.
MAKES 8 SCONES.

Barbecued Halibut with Sweet and Sour Berry Sauce

½ cup olive oil
2   tablespoons lemon juice
½ onion, finely minced
    Parsley to taste

Thyme to taste
Salt and pepper
Paprika
4 *large halibut fillets*

....

2 *cups berries (see note, below)*
½ *cup water*
½ *cup rice wine vinegar*
¼ *cup olive oil or butter*
All-purpose flour
Fresh herbs (see note, below)
Lemon wedges and fresh berries for
 garnish

....

¼ *cup olive oil*
All-purpose flour
Lemon wedges

In a glass dish combine ½ cup of olive oil, the lemon juice, onion, parsley, thyme, and seasonings to taste. Marinate the halibut. Turn occasionally to expose all surfaces to the marinade. Prepare a grill.

In a saucepan simmer the berries in the water and wine vinegar (or other mild vinegar) until they just become translucent and give up their juice. It is important to avoid overcooking, which spoils the flavor. Strain to remove the seeds. Set aside.

In a skillet heat ¼ cup of olive oil or butter and add enough flour to thicken. Set aside.

Grill the halibut fillets for, about 5 minutes per side, depending on the coals as well as the thickness of the fish.

To finish the sauce, add 1½ cups of the berry juice, to the roux. Add fresh herbs if desired. Heat but do not boil. Arrange the fish on a heated platter, pour sauce around, and garnish with lemon wedges and a few berries on top.

Note: Use any piquant berry such as nagoonberry, raspberry, blueberry, gooseberry, red currant, salmonberry, or Russian currant. It is best not to use strawberry on thimbleberry as the flavor is too delicate. Fresh herbs such as fennel, oregano, tarragon, or cilantro may be added.

Tartar Sauce

On a large butcher block place equal quantities of onion, sweet pickle and celery. Take 2 stout knives with straight blades (French knives are best for this) and chop, using a motion similar to playing a drum, alternating knives. Play some rhythmic music for this operation. Heap ingredients into a pile when they tend to spread and keep a-choppin'. It's messy but fun. Scoop into a bowl and add enough mayonnaise and yogurt in equal quantities to form the right texture. Store in refrigerator.

Variations: Add pimiento and parsley for a bit of color. Try some capers. If using all yogurt, add some mustard.

Gustavus Inn at Glacier Bay

❧

P.O. Box 60
Gustavus, Alaska 99826
(907) 697-2254

Built in 1928 as a homestead by a hardy couple with nine children, the original house was converted into a snug country inn more than thirty years ago. Among the attractions here are the scenic wonders of nearby Glacier Bay, kayaking, whale watching, and some of the best salmon and halibut fishing on the planet. Rooms offer expansive views of Icy Strait, mountains, and virgin rain forest. Guests share a cozy hearth room, naturalist's library, and family-style dining room.

Gustavus Inn

Mom's Pie Crust

½ *cup boiling water*
1 *cup lard*
3 *cups all-purpose flour*
½ *teaspoon baking powder*
1 *teaspoon salt*

In a large bowl pour boiling water over the room-temperature lard. (No substitute shortening will work.) Mix it with a fork until it resembles mushy ice cream, making sure all the lard is melted. In a separate bowl sift together the flour, baking powder, and salt. Mix quickly and thoroughly into the water and lard mixture. The dough will be very soft and very greasy looking. Form it into 2 balls, wrap them up in plastic wrap, and chill for several hours or until firm.

These crusts keep well in a refrigerator (just remember to take them out of the refrigerator before using to let them soften). Roll the dough out on a floured board. In order to make a nice firm high-fluted edge, roll the dough so it will be about 1 inch wider than the pie plate. Flute the edge as usual with fingertips to form a firm, fluted edge. If making a prebaked pie shell, prick it all over with a fork so big bubbles of air won't form underneath. Bake in a 350° oven for 12 minutes or until it looks dry and is faintly golden brown.

Note: This never-fail pie crust must be made in private. No one would believe such an icky looking mess would produce such a marvelous crust.

MAKES PASTRY FOR 2 9-INCH PIES.

Rhubarb Pie

2 *eggs*
1 *cup sugar*
¼ *cup all-purpose flour*
8 *cups chopped rhubarb*
1 *10-inch unbaked double pie crust*
 Cinnamon-sugar

In a medium bowl beat together eggs and sugar. Mix in the flour. Place the rhubarb in a large bowl. Add the sugar mixture and toss. Place in the pie shell. Cover with the top crust. Sprinkle with cinnamon-sugar. Bake in a 350° oven for at least 1 hour.

The pie should be nice and bubbly before taking it out of oven.

MAKES 8 SERVINGS.

Halibut Caddy Ganty

2 pounds halibut, fresh or thawed
White wine to cover
Sourdough breadcrumbs

....

2 cups sour cream
1 cup mayonnaise
1 cup finely chopped onions
Paprika

Cut the filleted halibut into pieces approximately 1-inch thick and 3-inches square. Place into a bowl salting lightly, and pour the wine over each layer until the fish is covered. Cover and set in a cool place to marinate for 2 hours.

Drain the fillets and pat dry with paper towel or cloth, then roll in dry breadcrumbs. Place the crumbed fillets in a single layer in a lightly greased baking dish which can be brought to the table.

In a small bowl mix the sour cream, mayonnaise, and chopped onions, and spread thickly on top of the fillets in the baking dish, smoothing it out to the edges so the fish is covered completely. Sprinkle the top with paprika. Bake in a 350° oven for 20 to 30 minutes or until light brown and bubbly and an instant-reading thermometer reads 125° in the thickest part. Serve at once.

MAKES 4 TO 6 SERVINGS.

Barbecued Salmon or Halibut

⅔   cup firmly packed brown sugar
    Juice of 1 lemon
¼   cup soy sauce
1   cup butter or margarine
3½   pounds king or coho salmon or halibut, filleted or steaked
    Lemon wedges

In a saucepan heat the brown sugar, lemon juice, soy sauce, and butter until dissolved and blended. Set aside some of this sauce to serve with the fish. Place the fish on a grill over hot coals, cover, and baste with sauce 2 or 3 times during cooking. When barbecuing filleted salmon, cook with skin on, skin-side down, and do not turn. Steaks may need to be turned. Grill until done, about 10 to 15 minutes. To test for doneness, place an instant-reading thermometer in the thickest part of the flesh: 120° is done. Or, flake apart, and

when the flesh has lost transparency, it is done. Serve with additional barbecue sauce and lemon wedges.

Note: Leftovers are great in sandwiches, or blended with sour cream, mayonnaise, and dill as a cracker dip. Add to the hot coals some alder chips soaked in water a few minutes before grilling. This gives the fish a smokier flavor.

MAKES 6 TO 8 SERVINGS.

The
Summer Inn

❧

P.O. Box 1198
Haines, Alaska 99827
(907) 766-2970

A five-bedroom historical home only a short walk from the heart of Haines, the Summer Inn provides access to the scenic Chilkat Valley. Visitors can enjoy mountains, glaciers, fjords, fresh and saltwater fishing, and the largest gathering of bald eagles in the world. Haines is a frequent stop for ferry passengers traveling Alaska's Inland Passage waterway. The house was built early in the twentieth century by Tim Vogal, a member of the famed Soapy Smith Gang.

The Summer Inn

Smoked Salmon Strata

1½   cups bread pieces
1   cup chopped smoked salmon
2   cups shredded Cheddar cheese

....

2   cups milk
6   eggs
¼   teaspoon dry mustard
¼   teaspoon cayenne pepper
¼   teaspoon paprika
¼   teaspoon pepper
    Parsley

In the bottom of a greased 9-inch square pan arrange the bread pieces. Layer smoked salmon and Cheddar cheese over the bread. Refrigerate overnight.

In a medium bowl beat the milk, eggs, and spices, and pour over the refrigerated layers. Top with parsley. Bake in a 375° oven for 40 to 45 minutes.

MAKES 6 SERVINGS.

Alaska
Wolf House

❧

1900 Wickersham Avenue, P.O. Box 21321
Juneau, Alaska 99802
(907) 586-2422

A four-thousand-square-foot western red cedar log home, this B&B inn stands on the side of Mount Juneau. Guests love the views of northern sunrises and sunsets and of the Gastineau Channel. There is plenty of sightseeing, shopping, and fun available in nearby Juneau, Alaska's capital city. However, the big attractions here are the spruce and hemlock setting, black bears, eagles, and other wildlife, and of course, the extraordinary views. Quilted beds, private decks, or a fireplace are some of the special touches provided here. Several of the suites include kitchens.

Brandied Peaches in Caramel Sauce

½   cup butter
¾   cup sugar
¼   cup apricot or peach brandy
4   sliced fresh peaches
    Caramel sauce
    Whipped cream

In a saucepan melt the butter over medium heat. Add the sugar, stirring constantly. Add the apricot or peach brandy, continuing to stir. When the sauce is smooth add the peaches. Turn over several times, allowing the peaches to warm. Serve hot in a glass dish with plenty of caramel sauce. Pass a bowl of whipped cream if desired.

Note: Fresh peaches are best but canned sliced peaches could be used in an emergency.

MAKES 6 SERVINGS.

Alaska Wolf House Bran Muffins

2   cups boiling water
4   cups All-Bran cereal
2   cups crushed shredded-wheat cereal

1   cup shortening
3   cups sugar
4   eggs
1   quart buttermilk
5   cups all-purpose flour
1   teaspoon salt
5   teaspoons baking soda
1   cup raisins

In a large bowl pour boiling water over the cereals. Allow to cool.

In a mixing bowl beat together the shortening, sugar, and eggs one at a time. Blend in the buttermilk. Add the flour, salt, soda, and raisins. Mix in the cereal. Spoon into greased muffin cups. Bake in a 400° oven for 25 to 30 minutes.

Note: The batter can be stored covered in the refrigerator for up to a month. Use as needed.

MAKES 2 DOZEN MUFFINS.

Glacier Bay Lodge

❧

520 Pike Street, Suite 1400
Seattle, Washington 98101
1(800)451-5952

---

*A*lthough the address for information and reservations is in Seattle, the inn itself is in the midst of a rain forest in southwestern Alaska. The lodge supplies the only available accommodations inside Glacier Bay National Park, so if you want to see this unmatched natural wonder up close, this is the place to stay. Park naturalists lead daily hikes beginning at the lodge and also conduct educational programs there each evening. Bay cruises aboard the Spirit of Adventure or the Wilderness Explorer take guests to the very heart of the bay where enormous blocks of glacial ice break off into the ocean. Since there are few roads in this part of Alaska, access to the area is by boat or air.

Halibut Alyeska

½   cup mayonnaise
½   cup sour cream
½   cup diced onion
16   ounces halibut fillets (sliced in half)
4   1-ounce slices Cheddar cheese
1   tablespoon breadcrumbs
⅛   teaspoon white pepper

In a small bowl combine the mayonnaise, sour cream, and onion to make a sauce.

In a 1½-quart casserole dish layer the bottom with half of the halibut fillets, cover with half of the cheese and top with half of the sauce. Add another layer of halibut, cheese, and the remaining sauce. Sprinkle with breadcrumbs and pepper. Bake in a 350° oven for 30 minutes.

MAKES 2 SERVINGS.

Glacier Bay Carrot Cake

3   eggs
¾   cup oil
¾   cup buttermilk
2   cups sugar
2   teaspoon vanilla extract

2   cups all-purpose flour
2   teaspoons baking soda
2   teaspoons ground cinnamon
½   teaspoon salt

2   cups grated carrots
½   cup crushed pineapple, drained
1   cup chopped nuts
3½   ounces coconut
    Buttermilk Frosting (recipe follows)

In a large bowl combine the eggs, oil, buttermilk, sugar, and vanilla. In a separate bowl combine the flour, soda, cinnamon, and salt. Add the dry ingredients to the liquid mixture. Add the remaining ingredients, mixing just until blended. Pour into a greased and floured 9 x 13-inch cake pan. Bake in a 350° oven for about 40 minutes.

MAKES 8 SERVINGS.

Buttermilk Frosting

1   cup sugar
½   teaspoon salt
½   cup buttermilk
¼   cup butter
1   tablespoons corn syrup
1   teaspoon vanilla extract

In a saucepan combine all of the ingredients except the vanilla and boil for 5 minutes. Add the vanilla. Pour onto hot carrot cake.

MAKES ABOUT 1¾ CUPS.

Mount Juneau Inn

1801 Old Glacier Highway
Juneau, Alaska 99801
(907) 463-5855

Surrounded by gardens, wetlands, and totem poles, the inn is a showcase of the region's natural wonders and native culture. Sitting at the foot of Mount Juneau, it is also only a short walk from the heart of the state's capital city. The inn offers seven country-style rooms and comfortably finished cottage. Guests will want to do some hiking, fishing, sightseeing, kayaking, or whale watching or pan for gold at historic Gold Creek Basin. The innkeepers are happy to help out with outdoor gear, day packs, fishing tackle, and so on.

Phil's Favorite Muffins

    2   cups all-purpose flour
   ½   cup sugar
  1½   teaspoons cinnamon
  1½   teaspoons ground allspice
    2   teaspoons baking soda
   ¼   teaspoon salt
  1½   cups shredded carrots
    1   15-ounce jar applesauce
    1   cup raisins
    1   cup walnut pieces
    3   eggs, beaten
   ½   cup oil
   ½   teaspoon vanilla extract

In a large bowl combine the flour, sugar, cinnamon, allspice, soda, and salt. Mix in the carrots, applesauce, raisins, and nuts. Stir in the eggs, oil, and vanilla just until blended the. Fill greased muffin cups. Bake in a 375° oven for 20 minutes.
MAKES 18 MUFFINS.

Karen's Cinnamon Nut Granola

  1½   cups honey (homemade fireweed honey if possible)
   ¾   cup oil
    3   tablespoons water
  1½   tablespoons vanilla extract
    2   cups wheat germ
    1   cup raw sunflower seeds
   ½   cup dry milk
    1   cup walnuts
    1   cup unsweetened coconut (flaked or shredded)
    7   cups rolled oats
    1   cup in-husk sesame seeds
    2   tablespoons cinnamon
    1   cup bran
    1   cup almonds
    1   cup raisins
    1   teaspoon ground allspice

In a saucepan combine the honey, oil, water, and vanilla and stir over low heat until blended. In a large bowl combine the dry ingredients. Add the honey mixture and mix well. Pour into a greased baking pan. Bake in a 250° oven for 1 hour and 30 minutes.
MAKES 18 CUPS.

Mt. Juneau Inn Cranberry Cake

  1½   cups sugar
    2   large eggs
   ¾   cup butter, melted and cooled
    3   tablespoons Trani Orgeat (almond) Syrup (or other Italian syrup)
  1½   cups all-purpose flour
    2   cups frozen cranberries
    1   cup coarsely chopped pecans

Butter a cake pan (a decorative bundt pan works nicely). In a large bowl beat the sugar and eggs until slightly thickened. Add the butter and almond syrup. Add the flour and stir until blended well. Stir in the cranberries and pecans. Pour the batter into the prepared pan (batter will be stiff). Bake in a 350° oven for about 1 hour. Transfer to a rack and cool completely.
MAKES 8 TO 12 SERVINGS.

Pearson's Pond

Pearson's Pond Luxury Inn

4541 Sawa Circle
Juneau, Alaska 99801
(907) 789-3772

Pearson's Pond Luxury Inn is convenient to Juneau, Alaska's compact capital and business hub of the southeastern panhandle. Spacious rooms feature living and dining areas, private kitchens, robes, slippers, and all the amenities, not to mention million-dollar views. The inn is adjacent to lovely Pearson's Pond, which was created by nearby Mendenhall Glacier. Visitors will enjoy the view from the hot tub.

Coconut Cookies

    1   cup butter
    1   cup firmly packed brown sugar
    1   cup sugar
    1   egg
        Pinch baking soda
    1   to 2 teaspoon vanilla extract
    2   to 3 cups all-purpose flour
    1   to 2 cups shredded coconut
    1   cup oatmeal
    1   12-ounce package semisweet chocolate chips

In a large bowl mix the butter with the sugars, egg, soda, and vanilla. Add flour to make a moderately dry consistency. Add the coconut and oatmeal, and mix. Add the chocolate chips. Drop by teaspoonful onto a greased cookie sheet. Bake in a 350° oven for approximately 10 to 12 minutes.

Note: The innkeeper's philosophy is that a person cannot undercook cookies. Place the cookies on an absorbent sheet (use old newspaper for something to read while eating a cookie). Sometimes improvise: use peanut butter instead of butter, etc.

MAKES ABOUT 4 DOZEN COOKIES.

Pearson's Pond Ham Bread

2 cups warm water (105 to 115°)
1 tablespoon sugar
2 tablespoons dry yeast
2 teaspoons salt
4½ cups all-purpose flour or high-gluten flour

....

1 to 2 pounds cooked ham, finely ground

....

Cornmeal

....

1 egg
1 tablespoon water

Warm a large mixing bowl. In the warmed bowl combine the water, sugar, and yeast. After the yeast has softened, stir in the salt. Beat in the flour, 1 cup at a time. Add more flour if needed. Turn the dough onto a lightly floured surface. Knead firmly and thoroughly until smooth and dimpled. Form into a ball and place in a clean, warm bowl. Cover with damp towel. Let rise until doubled in bulk.

Punch the dough down lightly and divide into 4 roughly equal parts. Let rest 10 minutes

Roll each portion on a lightly floured surface to a 10 x 18-inch rectangle.

Begin rolling the rectangle of dough from the wide side, sealing (by pressing) the roll against the rectangle with each half roll. After the first full roll, sprinkle a few tablespoon of ground ham along the sealed edge. After another half roll gently, but firmly seal the roll against the rectangle. Again, sprinkle a few tablespoon of ground ham along the sealed edge, roll over and seal again. Repeat until the entire rectangle has been rolled. Seal the edges and the final edge well. Place seam-

side down on a lightly greased long baking sheet that has been sprinkled with cornmeal.

Repeat with the remaining dough portions. Shallowly slash the tops diagonally in several places. In a small bowl beat the egg with 1 tablespoon of water. Brush the loaves with the mixture. Let rise until doubled in bulk.

Bake in a 365° oven for 20 minutes. Paint with the remaining egg mixture. Bake for 15 to 20 minutes. Cool on racks. Store in refrigerator.

MAKES 4 LOAVES.

Timberlings Bed and Breakfast ❧

P.O. Box 732
Palmer, Alaska 99645
(907) 745-4445

A log house on a mostly wild 150-acre property, the Timberlings appeals to travelers with a taste for the wilds and for the unique. Maintained by artists who work daily in a studio on the property, Timberlings is the perfect place to return to after a day of wandering through old gold mines, flying over Mount McKinley, river rafting, or shopping in nearby Anchorage. Visitors won't feel crowded here, as there is only one guest room.

Puff Pancakes

1 cup milk
⅔ cup all-purpose flour
2 tablespoons sugar
½ teaspoon salt
2 eggs
½ teaspoon grated nutmeg or cardamom
2½ tablespoons butter
Freshly squeezed lemon juice
Confectioners' sugar
Fresh berries or berry sauce

In a blender mix the milk, flour, sugar, salt, eggs, and nutmeg. In bottom of 2 8-inch pie pans melt 2½ tablespoons of butter. Pour half of the batter in each pan and bake for about 30 minutes. The edges will puff up and lightly brown. The center will be soft. Serve immediately.

Top with freshly squeezed lemon juice and confectioners' sugar, fresh berries, or berry sauces.

MAKES 2 PANCAKES.

Poor Man's Lobster (Boiled Halibut)

Cut halibut into 1-inch cubes. Drop into a pot of boiling water. When they float to the top they are done. Skim off and drain the fish. Serve immediately with melted butter and lemon for dipping, or a shrimp-style cocktail sauce.

In a small bowl combine catsup, horseradish, sugar, and lemon and lime juice to make a sauce.

Melon, Jicama, and Avocado Salad

2 tablespoons fresh lime juice
5 tablespoons olive oil
¼ teaspoon or more chili powder
Salt and pepper to taste

....

Assorted red and green lettuce, torn in pieces
½ cantaloupe
⅔ cup jicama (or substitute sliced water chestnuts)
1 avocado, sliced

In a small bowl whisk together the lime juice, olive oil, chili powder, salt, and pepper to taste. Add enough chili to be spicy, but not too hot. Set aside.

In a salad bowl combine the lettuces. Cut the cantaloupe into 4 or 5 wedges. Peel and slice crosswise into bite-sized pieces. Peel and cut the jicama into similar pieces. Add the cantaloupe, jimaca, and avocado to the lettuce. Whisk the dressing and pour it over the top. Gently toss.

MAKES 4 TO 6 SERVINGS.

Yukon Don's B&B Inn

1830 East Parks Avenue #386
2221 Yukon Circle
Wasilla, Alaska 99645
(907) 376-7472

Rick Swenson, five-time winner of the Iditarod, calls this "the best place to stay in Alaska." Located in the Mat-Su Valley, this B&B provides a 360-degree-view of some of the most unforgettable views in Alaska. Each room is decorated in authentic Alaskan decor and sleeps four. Suites include a private bath. The inn makes an ideal base for the independent traveler, explorer, or those on their first Alaskan adventure.

Salmon Stroganoff

¼ cup butter
2 tablespoons oil
½ pound fresh mushrooms, sliced
Salt and white pepper to taste
½ cup white wine
1 cup thinly sliced onion
1 teaspoon curry powder
2 cups heavy cream

¼ cup butter
1 tablespoon chopped fresh dill (or 1 teaspoon dried)
1 pound fresh egg fettuccine

1 pound salmon, boiled and skinned
¼ cup chopped parsley

In a 12-inch skillet or sauté pan melt 2 tablespoons of butter with the oil. Sauté the mushrooms in butter and oil over medium heat for about 5 minutes, stirring. Season to taste with salt and pepper. With a slotted spoon remove the mushrooms to a small bowl. Deglaze the pan with white wine and boil rapidly, about 1 minute. Add 2 tablespoons of butter and sliced onion. Cook over medium heat until soft, about 5 minutes, stirring. Remove the onion from the pan and set aside on a small plate. Add curry powder to the skillet and cook over low heat for about 30 seconds. Pour in the cream and bring to a gentle boil. Cook for 20 minutes, until reduced.

In large kettle bring 4 quarts of water to a boil. Lightly salt the water and cook the noodles. In a large saucepan melt the butter over low heat. Add the dill.

Drain the noodles in a colander and toss in the dilled butter. Turn onto a serving platter.

Slice the salmon into ½-inch strips and set aside. When the cream is reduced, add the salmon strips and poach until tender, about 5 minutes. Add the mushrooms, onions, and parsley, and serve immediately over fettiuccine.

MAKES 4 TO 6 SERVINGS.

Honey-glazed Grilled King Salmon

King salmon
¼ cup butter, melted
⅓ cup honey, softened
⅓ cup firmly packed brown sugar

On a grill cook the king salmon. In a small bowl blend the butter, honey, and brown sugar together. Baste the king salmon. Turning the salmon and baste the other side.

Absolutely mouth-watering honey-glazed king salmon. Excellent served with fresh garden vegetables.

MAKES HONEY BASTING SAUCE FOR 4 TO 6 SERVINGS.

ARIZONA

Ramsey Canyon Inn

31 Ramsey Canyon Road
Hereford, Arizona 85615
(520) 378-3010

Hummingbirds flock to this south-
eastern Arizona haven—fourteen
species are attracted to the inn's
feeders from March through Sep-
tember. Human visitors will also
find the inn highly attractive. Situ-
ated eighty miles east of Tucson, it
sits beside a rushing stream in the
Huachuca Mountains. Sycamore,
juniper, maple, and pine tower over
a B&B-style inn and a pair of creek-
side cottages with their own kitchen

Ramsey Canyon Inn

facilities. The adjacent Coronado
National Forest and a large Nature
Conservancy preserve offer plenty
of natural pleasures.

Lemon-Rhubarb Waffles

> 2   **cups all-purpose flour**
> ½   **teaspoon baking soda**
> ½   **teaspoon salt**
> 1   **teaspoon baking powder**
> ¼   **cup sugar**
> 2   **large eggs**
> 1   **cup lemon yogurt**
> ⅓   **cup lemon juice**
> ¼   **cup oil**
> 1   **cup buttermilk**
> 1   **cup diced rhubarb**
> ....
> 3   **cups sliced rhubarb**
> 1   **cup sugar**
> ½   **cup butter**

In a medium bowl combine the flour, soda,
salt, baking powder, and ¼ cup of sugar. In a
separate bowl beat the eggs. Add the yogurt,
lemon juice, oil, and buttermilk, and mix
together lightly. Add the dry ingredients and
mix with a wire whisk until smooth. Add 1
cup of diced rhubarb. Pour the batter onto a
preheated Belgian waffle iron. Bake until
done.

   In a saucepan combine 3 cups of rhubarb,
1 cup of sugar and the butter. Cook over
medium heat until the rhubarb is done and
the sauce thickens, about 20 minutes.
MAKES 4 SERVINGS.

Pumpkin Pancakes

> 2   **cups all-purpose flour**
> 3   **teaspoons baking powder**
> 1   **teaspoon salt**
> 2   **teaspoons ground cinnamon**
> 1   **teaspoon ground ginger**
> ½   **teaspoon ground cloves**
> 2   **tablespoons firmly packed brown**
>   **sugar**
> ½   **cup canned pumpkin**
> 1½ **cups evaporated milk**
> 2   **eggs**
> 2   **tablespoons oil**
> 1   **teaspoon vanilla extract**
> ½   **cup chopped walnuts**
> 1   **cup diced apples**

In a large mixing bowl combine all dry ingredients. Add the pumpkin, evaporated milk,
eggs, oil, and vanilla, and mix well. Fold in
the nuts and apples. Bake on a hot griddle.
MAKES 16 SERVINGS.

Stuffed French Toast with Cranberry-Maple Sauce

> 1   **8-ounce package cream cheese**
> 2   **tablespoons sugar**
> 1   **teaspoon vanilla extract**
> ½   **cup finely chopped walnuts**
> 16 **slices good quality French bread**
> ....
> 8   **eggs**
> 1½ **cups half and half**
> ¼   **cup sugar**
> 1   **teaspoon vanilla extract**
> 1   **teaspoon grated nutmeg**
>   **Melted butter**
> ....

2 cups fresh or frozen cranberries
1 cup sugar
1 cup maple syrup
1 teaspoon maple extract

In a medium bowl mix together the cream cheese, 2 tablespoons of sugar, 1 teaspoon of vanilla, and nuts. Spread the mixture on 8 slices of French bread. Top with the remaining 8 slices of French bread.

In a blender mix the eggs, half and half, ¼ cup of sugar, 1 teaspoon vanilla, and nutmeg. Pour half of the egg mixture into a buttered 9 x 13-inch glass dish. Place the French bread on top of the egg mixture and pour the remaining egg mixture on top of the French bread. Cover and refrigerate overnight.

The next morning brush the tops with melted butter. Bake in a 350° oven for 30 minutes. Turn the broiler on to brown the top.

While the French toast is baking, in a heavy saucepan combine the cranberries, 1 cup of sugar, maple syrup, and maple flavoring. Bring the mixture to a boil over high heat. Reduce the heat to medium and cook, stirring occasionally, until the cranberries pop, about 20 minutes. Serve the French toast topped with cranberry-maple sauce.
MAKES 8 SERVINGS.

Apple Pumpkin Muffins

3 large apples, peeled and diced
½ cup sugar
2 teaspoons ground cinnamon
¼ cup water
....
¼ cup all-purpose flour
⅓ cup sugar
1 teaspoon ground cinnamon
¼ cup finely chopped walnuts
3 tablespoons butter
....
3½ cups all-purpose flour
2½ cups sugar
2 teaspoons ground cinnamon
1 teaspoon ground ginger
½ teaspoon ground cloves
½ teaspoon salt
2 teaspoons baking soda
2 cups canned pumpkin
3 eggs
¾ cup oil
1 cup chopped walnuts

In a microwave-safe bowl combine the apples with ½ cup of sugar, 2 teaspoons of cinnamon, and water, and toss lightly. Cover and microwave for 5 minutes or until the apples are tender. Let cool.

In a small bowl mix together ¼ cup of flour, ⅓ cup of sugar, 1 teaspoon of cinnamon, and ¼ cup of walnuts. Cut in the butter.

In a large mixing bowl combine the flour, sugar, spices, salt, and soda. In a separate bowl combine the pumpkin, eggs, and oil. Add the liquid mixture to the dry ingredients and stir just until moistened. Stir in the cooked apples and 1 cup of nuts. Spoon the batter into greased muffins cups, filling three-fourths. Top with streusel topping. Bake in a 350° oven for 30 to 35 minutes or until done.
MAKES 36 MUFFINS.

Maricopa Manor

Maricopa Manor
❧

*15 West Pasadena Avenue
Phoenix, Arizona 85013
(602) 274-6302*

Built in 1928 as a showpiece of Spanish-style architecture, the Maricopa provides easy access to the Phoenix Convention Center, capital complex, museums, and other city attractions. Guest rooms are sumptuously furnished and decorated, each with its own special touch, such as a private entrance, a quaint setting room, or a sunroom. The spacious gathering room with outside deck, formal living, dining,

and music rooms, patio, and gazebo spa are available to guests for special events.

Peach Cheese Soufflé

1 20-ounce can peach halves, drained
½ cup butter, softened
8 ounces Velveeta cheese (room temperature), grated
¾ cup all-purpose flour
¾ cup sugar

Place 1 peach half in each of 8 small Pyrex cups. In a medium bowl combine the butter, Velveeta cheese, flour, and sugar until smooth. Spread the topping over the peach halves. Bake in a 325° oven for 30 to 45 minutes.
MAKES 8 SERVINGS.

Breakfast Cookies

⅔ cup butter
⅔ cup sugar
1 egg
1 teaspoon vanilla extract
¾ cup all-purpose flour
½ teaspoon baking soda
½ teaspoon salt
1¼ cups old-fashioned oats
1 cup grated Cheddar cheese
½ cup wheat germ
6 slices bacon, cooked crispy and crumbled

In a large bowl beat together butter, sugar, egg, and vanilla. Add the flour, soda, and salt and mix. Stir in the oats, Cheddar cheese, and wheat germ. Fold in the bacon. Drop by teaspoon onto a greased cookie sheet. Bake in a 350° oven for 12 to 14 minutes.
MAKES 3 DOZEN.

Baked Fruit

1 16-ounce can apricot halves
1 16-ounce can peaches
1 15¼-ounce can pineapple chunks
....
6 tablespoons butter
¾ cup firmly packed brown sugar
1 tablespoon curry powder

In a 9 x 13-inch baking dish combine the apricot halves, peaches, and pineapple chunks. Bake in a 350° oven for 15 minutes.

In a saucepan melt the butter. Add the brown sugar and curry powder. Add to the fruit and bake another 15 to 20 minutes.

MAKES 8 SERVINGS.

Inn at the Citadel

❧

8700 East Pinnacle Peak Road
Scottsdale, Arizona 85255
(602)585-6133

Rising from the midst of the color-ful Sonoran desert, this Scottsdale inn is one of a kind. It offers eleven spacious suites, each one individu-ally decorated. Three different restaurants provide a choice of fire-side or outdoor patio dining. A courtyard, art gallery, and bou-tiques make the inn a complete experience in itself. Those seeking additional entertainment will find nearby opportunities for golfing and Old West and Native American attractions.

Lemon Pepper Swordfish with Potato Walnut Cake

    Swordfish, cut in 3-ounce medal-
       lions
  ½ *teaspoon lemon pepper*
  3 *sprigs cilantro, chopped*
  ½ *teaspoon canola oil*
  1 *tablespoon white wine*

 10 *white potatoes*
  1 *large red onion*
     Olive oil
  ¼ *cup chopped walnuts*

     Pinch salt
  1 *teaspoon chopped fresh cilantro*
  1 *teaspoon fresh oregano*
  1 *teaspoon canola oil*

Sprinkle the fish with lemon pepper and cilantro on both sides. In a hot ovenproof sauté pan heat the canola oil. Add the fish. Add the wine next and turn the fish over. Remove the pan from the heat. Cook in a 350° oven until done.

Prick the potatoes. Bake in a 350° oven until soft in the center. Remove the potatoes from the oven. Cut in half and take out the insides of the potatoes. Dice the onion. In a skillet heat a small amount of olive oil and sauté the onion. Add the potato and cook until the potatoes are very smooth. Add the walnuts, and season with salt and fresh herbs. Spread the mixture ¼-inch thick on a cookie sheet. Cut into 2-inch circles with a cookie cutter. In a skillet heat 1 teaspoon of canola oil and pan-sear the walnut cakes until golden brown.

MAKES 4 TO 6 SERVINGS.

Sugar-roasted Walleye Pike

  2 *tablespoons firmly packed brown*
     sugar
  ¼ *teaspoon cayenne pepper*
  ¼ *teaspoon paprika*
  ¼ *teaspoon cumin*
  ¼ *teaspoon salt*
  1 *8-ounce fillet walleye pike*
  2 *teaspoons canola oil*
  1 *cup or 4 ounces Soba noodles*
  ¼ *teaspoon chopped fresh cilantro*
  ¼ *teaspoon chopped fresh mint*
  ¼ *teaspoon chopped shallots*

In a small bowl mix together the brown sugar, cayenne, paprika, cumin, and salt. Rub the mixture on both sides of the fish. In a skillet heat the canola oil and pan-sear the fish until done. Remove from the pan and keep warm.

In a saucepan cook the pasta in boiling water until tender. Using the skillet, sauté the pasta with the fresh cilantro, mint, and shal-lots, tossing together. Serve walleye pike on the bed of noodles.

MAKES 1 SERVING.

Blue Corn Muffins

  1 *cup sugar*
  1 *cup butter*
  1 *cup eggs*
  4 *cups all-purpose bread flour*
 1½ *cups blue cornmeal*
  1 *teaspoon salt*
  3 *tablespoons baking powder*
  1 *cup milk*

In a large bowl cream sugar and butter. Add the eggs one at a time. Add the flour, corn-meal, salt, and baking powder. Mix thor-oughly, scraping the bowl. Add the milk, mix well, scrape the bowl, and mix briefly. Spoon the batter into 36 muffin cups. Bake in a 420° oven until the muffins have risen. Reduce the heat to 400° until done.

MAKES 36 MUFFINS.

Pumpkin Soup

 10 *pounds banana squash, chopped*
  6 *tablespoons chopped white onions*
  2 *cloves garlic, minced*
  ¼ *cup sugar*
  3 *tablespoons chopped green onions*
  2 *ounces cilantro, chopped*
  1 *tablespoon cayenne pepper*
  ½ *teaspoon cumin*
  ½ *teaspoon paprika*
     Pinch black pepper
     Pinch salt
  ½ *teaspoon ground cinnamon*
  3 *gallons chicken stock*

In a 4-gallon pot sauté the squash, white onion, and garlic. Add the sugar, green onions, and cilantro. Cook until the white onions are transparent. Add the dry ingredi-ents to the squash and cook for 8 minutes. Add the chicken stock and bring to a simmer. When the squash is soft pour the soup into a blender and purée.

MAKES 21 8-OUNCE SERVINGS.

Bed and Breakfast at Saddle Rock Ranch

P.O. Box 10095
Sedona, Arizona 86339
(520) 282-7640

A country estate surrounded by breathtaking rock vistas, this historic homestead has native stone and adobe walls, massive beamed ceilings, and flagstone floors. It occupies three acres of hillside overlooking the town of Sedona. All suites are decorated in romantic western themes and feature their own rock fireplaces. A courtyard garden, deck, and pool area take advantage of the remarkable view. Many western movies have been filmed on the ranch itself or in the desert nearby. Just five minutes from Tlaquepaque, restaurants, shops, and art galleries.

Saddle Rock Ranch Super Easy Basic Salsa

- 1   **cup chopped cilantro**
- 1   **cup coarsely chopped tomato**
- ½   **to 1 16-ounce jar salsa**

In a medium bowl mix the tomato and cilantro. Add the salsa (mild, medium, or hot, depending on taste). Pulse 2 times in a food processor or stir if doing by hand.

Variation #1: Pineapple Salsa. To the basic salsa recipe, add one-third to one-half can drained crushed pineapple.

Variation #2: Mango Salsa. To the basic salsa recipe, add 1 fresh ripe mango, peeled and diced.

Variation #3: Peach Salsa. To the basic salsa recipe, add 1 fresh ripe peach, peeled and diced. All of these salsa variations are very good with chips or breakfast dishes, especially the Southwest Frittatas.

Saddle Rock Ranch French Toast

- 6   **eggs, room temperature**
- ½   **cup milk**
- 1   **cup Irish crème-flavored milk substitute, such as Mocha Mix**
- 1   **loaf whole wheat or cinnamon bread, cut in 1-inch slices**
- 2   **tablespoons butter**
     Cinnamon
     Raw sugar

In a blender beat the eggs for at least 1 minute. Add the milk and Irish crème-flavored creamer. Blend.

Grease a large pan with butter, or spray with cooking spray. Dip the bread in the egg the mixture. Do not soak. Place the bread in the prepared pan. Allow at least 2 pieces per person. Pour the excess egg mixture evenly over the bread. Sprinkle lightly with cinnamon and raw sugar.

Cover with plastic wrap and refrigerate overnight. Bake in a 350° oven for approximately 20 minutes or until lightly browned.

Serve 1 piece of French toast in the center of each plate with half a slice of turkey ham on either side of the toast. (Extra pieces can be served as seconds.)

Serve with butter and warmed maple syrup; blueberry topping and warmed blueberry syrup; fresh peach topping and pecans; or honey, sliced strawberries, and drained crushed pineapple mixed together.

MAKES 4 TO 6 SERVINGS.

Fergie and Diana's Favourite Dog Biscuits

- 3   **tablespoons peanut butter**
- 1½   **cups water**
- ½   **cup canola oil**
- 2   **medium eggs**
- 2   **teaspoons vanilla extract**

- ½   **cup cornmeal**
- 1½   **cups whole wheat flour**
- 1½   **cups unbleached flour**
- ½   **cup rolled oats**

In a large bowl combine the peanut butter, water, canola oil, eggs, and vanilla and blend well. In a separate bowl combine the cornmeal, whole wheat flour, unbleached flour, and rolled oats. Add the dry ingredients to the liquid mixture and blend well until a ball of dough forms.

Roll the dough out on a lightly floured board to a thickness of ¼ inch. Use a favorite cookie cutter and place cut biscuits on a lightly sprayed cookie sheet. Bake in a 400° oven for 20 minutes. Turn the oven off but do not remove the cookie sheet until the oven is cool.

MAKES ABOUT 4 DOZEN.

Emma Bruno's Easter Noodle Bake (Kugel)

- 1   **8-ounce package medium noodles, cooked**
- 1   **pound ricotta or low-fat cottage cheese**
- 1   **pound light sour cream**
- 4   **eggs, well beaten**
- ⅓   **cup sugar**
- ½   **cup softened butter**
- 1   **14-ounce can crushed pineapple, drained**
- 1   **tablespoon vanilla extract**
     Crushed corn flakes

In a large bowl mix all ingredients together except the corn flakes. Cover and refrigerate overnight.

Spray 10 to 12 individual casserole dishes with cooking spray. Pour equal amounts of noodle mixture into each dish. Top the dishes with sprinklings of corn flakes. Bake in a 350° oven for about 45 minutes.

Serve with toasted bagels and cream cheese, with sliced fruit garnish on the plate.

MAKES 10 TO 12 SERVINGS.

Boots & Saddles

2900 Hopi Drive
Sedona, Arizona 86336
(520) 282-1944

Boots and Saddles suggests the days of six-guns, lariats, and roundups, but the gourmet breakfast is better than anything one could have gotten from a chuck wagon. So is the coffee. The many-colored scenery of Arizona is the same, however, and it is all around for guests to enjoy.

Old West Sweet Bread

- ½ cup butter, softened
- 1 cup sugar
- 2 eggs
- 2 cups all-purpose flour
- 1 teaspoon baking soda
- 1 teaspoon baking powder
- ½ teaspoon salt
- 1 cup sour cream
- ⅓ cup sugar
- 2 teaspoons ground cinnamon

Spray a 5 x 9-inch loaf pan with cooking spray. In a large bowl combine the butter, sugar, and eggs, mixing well. In a separate bowl combine the flour, soda, baking powder, and salt. Add the dry ingredients to the butter mixture. Blend in the sour cream. Pour one-third of the batter in the prepared pan. Sprinkle the cinnamon-sugar over the batter. Top with another portion of the batter and sprinkle with the cinnamon-sugar. Repeat with the remaining batter and cinnamon-sugar. Bake in a 350° oven for 1 hour or until a toothpick inserted in the center comes out clean. Turn out onto rack to cook.

MAKES 1 LOAF.

Boots and Saddles Potato Omelet

- 8 eggs
- ¼ cup milk
- ½ teaspoon salt
  Pepper to taste
- 1 4-ounce can diced green chilies
- 2 tablespoons oil
- 1 cup chopped onion
- 2 medium potatoes, cooked and cubed
- 2 cups grated Monterey Jack cheese
  ....
  Sour cream
  Salsa

In a large bowl beat the eggs with the milk. Add the salt, pepper, and green chilies.

In a large skillet heat the oil and cook the onion and potatoes until the potatoes are crispy and onion is tender. Reduce the heat. Pour the egg mixture over the potatoes and sprinkle with Monterey Jack cheese. Cook until the eggs are set and the cheese is melted. Cut into 6 to 8 wedges and top each serving with sour cream and salsa.

Serve with sausage and biscuits with butter and honey.

MAKES 6 TO 8 SERVINGS.

Cowpoke Breakfast Fruit Salad

- 1 egg, beaten
- ⅔ cup sugar
- 3 tablespoons all-purpose flour
  Juice of 1 lemon
- 3 large ripe bananas
- 1 cup frozen blueberries, rinsed, but not thawed
- 1 20-ounce can tidbit pineapple chunks and juice
- 4 slices American cheese, stacked and cubed
  Strawberries for garnish

In a saucepan combine the beaten egg, sugar, and flour. Mix well. Add the lemon juice and pineapple juice and cook over medium heat until the sauce thickens. Remove the pan from the heat and set aside to cool.

When the sauce is completely cool, stir in the sliced bananas, blueberries, pineapple tidbits, and cheese. Cover and refrigerate until serving time.

Serve in small glass dishes and garnish with strawberries.

MAKES 4 TO 6 SERVINGS.

The Graham

The Graham

150 Canyon Circle Drive
Sedona, Arizona 86351
(520) 284-1425

Designed and built by the owners, the Graham Inn offers a near perfect view from every room, not to mention a heated pool, spa, expansive deck, and many other amenities. The innkeepers will tell you what you will see from each of the three rooms and two suites. For instance, the Champagne Suite affords an excellent view of Bell Rock and Courthouse Butte, two of Sedona's best known landmarks. The rooms feature marble baths and showers. Among the inn's most frequent guests are the desert song-birds that flock to the birdhouses and feeders on the decks.

Artichoke Frittata

- 1 8-ounce can artichoke hearts
- 2 tablespoons butter
- ½ cup grated Parmesan cheese

12 eggs
¾ cup half and half
1½ cups grated Monterey Jack cheese

Drain the artichoke hearts and cut into quarters. In a skillet melt the butter. Add the artichokes and sauté until coated with butter and heated through. Distribute the artichokes evenly in the bottom of an 8-inch square baking dish. Sprinkle with ¼ cup of the grated Parmesan, reserving the remaining ¼ cup of cheese for final topping.

In a small mixing bowl beat the eggs together with the half and half. Pour over the artichokes. Sprinkle the Monterey Jack cheese over the entire mixture. Stand the dish in a pan of water. Bake in a 350° oven for 30 minutes. Remove from the oven and sprinkle the reserved Parmesan over the frittata. Return to the oven for an additional 5 minutes. Serve hot with corn bread.
MAKES 8 TO 10 SERVINGS.

Blue Corn Waffles

2 eggs, separated
1½ cups milk
½ cup oil
1 teaspoon vanilla extract
1⅓ cups blue cornmeal
½ cup all-purpose flour
2 tablespoons sugar
1 tablespoon baking powder
½ teaspoon salt
 Prickly pear syrup or cinnamon
  apples for garnish

In a medium bowl beat egg whites until stiff, and set them aside. In a large bowl mix the egg yolks, milk, oil, and vanilla. In a separate bowl sift together the blue cornmeal, flour, sugar, baking powder, and salt. Stir the dry ingredients into the egg mixture. Fold in the beaten egg whites. Let the waffle batter stand for 20 minutes.

Pour onto a hot, greased waffle iron. Bake for 2 minutes. Serve with prickly pear syrup or cinnamon apples.
MAKES 4 SERVINGS.

Oatmeal Pancakes

1 cup rolled oats
1 cup plus 2 tablespoons milk
2 tablespoons canola oil or applesauce

2 beaten eggs
½ cup whole wheat flour
¼ cup firmly packed brown sugar
1 teaspoon baking powder
¼ teaspoon salt
 Apple butter, cottage cheese, maple
  syrup for garnish

In a mixing bowl combine the rolled oats and milk and let stand for 5 minutes.

Add the oil and beaten eggs to the oatmeal mixture. In a separate bowl stir together the whole wheat flour, brown sugar, baking powder, and salt. Add the dry ingredients to the liquid mixture and mix thoroughly. Let the batter stand for 5 minutes.

Cook on a hot griddle. Serve with apple butter and cottage cheese or maple syrup.
MAKES 4 SERVINGS.

The Lodge at Sedona

125 Kallof Place
Sedona, Arizona 86336
(800) 619-4467

Guests catch the scent of pine as they arrive at The Lodge. This modern, thoroughly western-style inn takes full advantage of its setting—tall red buttes and hardy, dark green pinon. The thirteen rooms and suites have private decks, brick fireplaces, and views of the mountains or woods. The elegant common rooms include fireside parlors, a library, and a morning porch, all accented with rough-hewn timbers and native red sandstone.

The Lodge at Sedona

Michelle's Cranberry Pears

2 whole allspice
2 whole cloves
3 small cinnamon sticks
3 cups cranberry juice
½ cup port wine
1 orange, sliced
½ cup sugar
2 tablespoons firmly packed brown
  sugar

....

8 pears, peeled

....

 Whipped cream
 Fresh mint
 Orange slices for garnish

In a large pot combine all ingredients, except the pears. Simmer for 10 minutes. Place the pears in the pot and poach gently for 1 hour, turning to be certain the pears are equally "cranberry" colored.

After the pears have cooled, cut in half and core them. Place on a cookie sheet, cover well with plastic wrap, and chill overnight. Reserve the pear liquid.

Prior to serving, in a saucepan reduce the pear liquid until thickened to a syrup consistency. Slice each pear half into a fan shape and arrange next to another pear half on each plate. Drizzle reduced pear syrup over the top. Add a dollop of whipped cream, a mint leaf, and orange slices for garnish.
MAKES 8 SERVINGS.

Bacon, Onion, and Monterey Jack Cheese Custard

¾ pounds bacon, diced
1 small onion, diced
4 slices white bread (trim crusts and
  cut each slice into 6 pieces)
2 cups shredded Monterey Jack cheese
9 eggs, beaten
¼ cup milk
1 cup half and half
¾ teaspoons salt
¼ teaspoon pepper
¼ teaspoon grated nutmeg
 Paprika

In a skillet cook the bacon until slightly brown. Add the onion and cook until translucent. Drain off the fat. Spray a 10-inch round pan with cooking spray. Add bread to the dish and top with shredded Monterey Jack cheese.

In a large bowl whip the eggs with the milk and half and half. Add the salt, pepper, and nutmeg. Pour the egg mixture over the bacon-onion mixture. Make sure the bread soaks up the egg mixture. Sprinkle lightly with paprika. Bake in a 350° oven for 45 minutes to 1 hour.

MAKES 6 TO 8 SERVINGS.

Territorial House

Territorial House

❧

65 Piki Drive
Sedona, Arizona 86336
(520) 204-2737

With its beamed ceilings and stone fireplaces, this B&B harkens back to the territorial era before Arizona became a state. Furnished and decorated with those earlier times in mind, the guest rooms allow you to glimpse Sedona's past, but you can also enjoy the here and now with a dip in the jacuzzi or an evening by a crackling fireplace.

Peaches and Cream French Toast

8   slices French or Italian bread, cut diagonally ¾-inch thick
3   eggs
1   cup light cream
2   tablespoons peach preserves
½   teaspoon grated nutmeg

3   tablespoons butter
3   cups fresh peeled, sliced peaches
    Confectioners' sugar

In a 9-inch square baking pan arrange the bread in a single layer. In a medium bowl beat the eggs, cream, preserves, and nutmeg until smooth. Pour over the bread. Turn once. Cover and refrigerate overnight.

On a hot grill melt the butter and sauté the bread until golden brown, about 5 minutes each side. Top with fresh peaches and sprinkle with confectioners' sugar.

MAKES 8 SERVINGS.

Fresh Vegetable Fritatta

1   large red bell pepper, chopped
1   cup sliced mushrooms
1½ cups shredded Swiss cheese, divided
¼   pound asparagus, cut into 1-inch pieces
7   large eggs, lightly beaten
½   cup mayonnaise
½   teaspoon salt
2   tablespoons chopped fresh basil

In a lightly greased 9½-inch deep-dish pie plate layer the pepper, mushrooms, and half of the cheese. Top with asparagus and the remaining cheese. In a large bowl combine the eggs with the mayonnaise and salt. Pour evenly over the cheese. Top with fresh basil. Bake in a 375° oven for 35 minutes or until a knife inserted in the center comes out clean. Let stand 5 minutes.

Serve hot or at room temperature.

MAKES 6 TO 8 SERVINGS.

Casa Alegre Bed and Breakfast

❧

316 East Speedway Boulevard
Tucson, Arizona 85705
(520) 628-1800

A sprawling 1915 Craftsman bungalow, each individually decorated room at this B&B reflects Tucson's rich past. Situated near the center of Arizona's bustling university city, the Casa Alegre is comfortable and friendly. Its location places guests within easy reach of the Tucson Convention Center, airport, and city center, as well as the University of Arizona, Arizona-Sonora Desert Museum, Mission San Xavier, and Sabino Canyon. Serene gardens, a pool and hot tub, a fireplace, and breathtaking sunsets promise a memorable stay.

Sausage and Green Chili Strata

1   pound pork sausage
6   slices white bread, cubed
1   cup diced green chilies
3   cups grated Cheddar cheese, grated
4   eggs
2   cups milk
¾   teaspoon salt
¾   teaspoon chili powder
¾   teaspoon pepper

In a skillet brown the sausage. Drain. Oil an oblong baking dish. Layer half the bread on the bottom of the dish. Spread half the chilies on top of the bread. Spread half the Cheddar cheese on top of the chilies. Distribute all of the sausage over the cheese. Repeat the layers of bread, chilies and cheese.

In a medium bowl mix together the remaining ingredients and pour over the layered casserole. Cover and refrigerate overnight.

Bake 350° oven for 30 minutes or until puffed and browned.

MAKES 8 TO 10 SERVINGS.

Cream Cheese Pound Cake

1½ cups softened butter
1   8-ounce package cream cheese, softened

3 cups sugar
6 eggs
3 cups sifted all-purpose flour
   Dash salt
1½ teaspoons vanilla extract
1 cup chopped pecans

Grease and flour a 10-inch tube pan and set aside. In a large bowl cream the butter and cream cheese. Gradually add the sugar, beating until light and fluffy. Add the eggs one at a time, beating well after each. Add the flour and salt, stirring until it combines. Stir in the vanilla and pecans. Pour into the prepared pan.

Bake in a 325° oven for 1 hour and 30 minutes or until a wooden pick inserted in the center of the cake comes out clean. Cool in the pan for 10 minutes, and remove to cook on a rack.

MAKES 8 SERVINGS.

Baked Upside-down French Toast

2 tablespoons light corn syrup
1 cup firmly packed brown sugar
5 tablespoons butter
1 16-ounce can pineapple or peaches, drained and chopped
1 loaf firm bread, cubed
1 3-ounce package cream cheese

....

10 eggs
1½ cups half and half
¼ cup maple syrup
½ cup melted butter
   Sour cream or fruit preserves for topping

Grease a 9 x 13-inch pan. Set aside. In a saucepan bring the corn syrup, brown sugar, and butter to a full boil. Pour into the prepared pan. Spread the chopped fruit over the syrup. Layer half of the cubed bread over fruit. Cut the cream cheese into small pieces and scatter across the bread. Cover with the remaining bread cubes. In a large bowl mix the eggs, half and half, syrup, and melted butter together. Pour the egg mixture over the bread cubes. Press the bread down to absorb the egg mixture. Cover and refrigerate overnight.

Bake in a 350° oven for 40 to 50 minutes. Top each serving with a dollop of sour cream or fruit preserves, if desired.

MAKES 6 TO 8 SERVINGS.

Catalina Park Inn

309 East 1st Street
Tucson, Arizona 85705
(520) 792-4541

The architecture of this mansion, built in 1927, testifies to the quality and craftsmanship of an earlier time. Cheerful, spacious rooms and a charming cottage showcase the park and mountain views. Relax by the fire in the expansive living room. Curl up with a book or puzzle in the study. Wander into the butler's pantry for a cup of tea. Or visit Tucson's West University historic district and the eclectic shops and restaurants of Fourth Avenue.

Biscotti

1½ cups all-purpose flour
1½ cups yellow cornmeal
¾ cup firmly packed light brown sugar
1½ tablespoons finely grated lemon zest
2 teaspoons baking powder
½ teaspoon salt
½ cup water
2 large eggs, lightly beaten
1 teaspoon vanilla extract
¼ pound whole shelled hazelnuts (about ¾ cups)
½ cup golden raisins

Lightly oil and flour a large baking sheet or line it with parchment paper.

In a large bowl whisk together the flour, cornmeal, sugar, lemon zest, baking powder, and salt until blended well.

In a small bowl whisk together the water, eggs, and vanilla and stir into the dry ingredients; the dough will be sticky. Stir in the hazelnuts and raisins.

Divide the dough into 3 equal portions. On a heavily floured work surface shape each portion into a log about 2 x 13-inches. Place the logs 2 inches apart on the prepared baking sheet. Bake in a 325° oven until logs are firm and golden brown on the bottom, about 45 minutes. Remove the logs from the baking sheet and cool on a wire rack for at least 30 minutes. With a clean serrated knife, cut each log into ½-inch thick diagonal slices. Place the slices in a single layer on a clean baking sheet (this will probably require 2 baking sheets). Bake in a 325° oven until the tops of the biscotti are golden brown, about 15 minutes. Turn the biscotti over and bake until golden brown and very dry, about 15 minutes more. Cool the biscotti completely on a wire rack before serving. Store in an airtight container for up to 1 month.

MAKES ABOUT 7 DOZEN.

Shortbread

2 cups butter, softened
½ cup sugar
½ cup confectioners' sugar
½ teaspoon vanilla extract
½ teaspoon ground cinnamon
½ teaspoon baking powder
½ teaspoon salt
   Zest of 1 lemon, finely minced
4 cups all-purpose flour
   Confectioners' sugar for dusting

In a food processor blend the butter and both sugars. Add the remaining ingredients except the flour. Mix again. Add the flour a cup at a time until incorporated. Divide the dough between 2 9-inch glass pie plates and spread evenly. Bake in a 350° oven for 20 to 25 minutes or until light golden brown. Remove from the oven and slice into desired number of wedges while it is still hot. Cool completely before removing from the plates. Dust with confectioners' sugar, if desired.

MAKES ABOUT 16 WEDGES.

Pear and Cranberry Crisp

  2 *tablespoons lemon juice*
  6 *to 8 pears, peel or leave natural,*
        core, and cut in ¼-inch slices
  ⅓ *cup dried cranberries*
  ¾ *cup firmly packed light brown sugar*
  ½ *cup unsalted butter*
  ¾ *cup all-purpose flour*
  ½ *cup regular oats*
  1 *teaspoon ground cinnamon*
  ½ *teaspoon ground ginger*
  ¼ *teaspoon ground nutmeg*
      Zest of 1 lemon, finely minced
      Vanilla yogurt or whipped cream for
        topping

Add the lemon juice to a bowl of cold water. Dip the sliced pears in the lemon water to prevent them from discoloring. Drain. Place in a buttered 9 x 13-inch ovenproof casserole. Sprinkle the cranberries over the pears. If you don't have dried cranberries, don't worry, it's going to taste great anyway.

In a medium bowl blend the sugar, butter, flour, oats, cinnamon, ginger, nutmeg, and lemon zest with an electric mixer at slow speed until crumbly. Scatter evenly on top of pears. Bake in a 350° oven for about 1 hour or until the topping is nicely browned and crisp. Serve warm with a dollop of vanilla yogurt or whipped cream, if desired.

MAKES 8 SERVINGS.

Papaya and Lime Scones

 2½ *cups all-purpose flour*
  2 *tablespoons firmly packed light*
      brown sugar
  1 *tablespoon baking powder*
  1 *teaspoon salt*
  ¼ *cup canola oil*
  ½ *cup low-fat milk*
  1 *large egg*
  ½ *teaspoons finely grated lime zest*
 1½ *teaspoons finely grated lemon zest*
  ½ *cup dried papaya, coarsely chopped*
      Fruit preserves or honey for garnish

In a large bowl stir together the flour, sugar, baking powder, and salt. Quickly stir in the canola oil with a fork until pea-size crumbs form. In a small bowl combine the milk, egg, lime and lemon zest, and papaya. Add the liquids to the flour mixture and stir with a fork until blended. Gather the dough into a ball and knead lightly for about 15 seconds. The dough should hold together without crumbling. Transfer the dough to an ungreased baking sheet and pat into a circle about 8½ inches in diameter and ¾ inch thick. Cut into 12 wedges. For mini scones, divide dough in half and form 2 discs about 5 inches in diameter and cut into 8 wedges each. Bake in a 425° oven until golden brown, 20 to 25 minutes.

Serve warm with fruit preserves or honey.

MAKES 8 LARGE OR 16 SMALL SCONES.

The Lodge on the Desert

❧

306 North Alvernon
Tucson, Arizona 85711
(602) 325-3366

One of the few remaining owner-operated resorts in the country, the lodge has treated guests to quiet, seclusion, and Old World charm for more than half a century. Most of the rooms are on the ground floor; many have mesquite log-burning fireplaces, and one room boasts its own heated indoor pool. Beamed ceilings, handpainted Mexican tile, and authentic Monterey furnishings accent the Spanish flavor of the lodge. While a tradition of fine dining made Duncan Hines a frequent visitor here, theaters, museums, shopping, and the many attractions of Tucson are convenient when desired.

Banana Chantilly

  3 *egg whites*
  ¾ *cup sugar*
  ½ *teaspoon vanilla extract*
  ½ *teaspoon vinegar*

  1 *cup banana pulp*
  ¼ *teaspoon salt*
 1½ *tablespoons lemon juice*
  ¼ *cup confectioners' sugar*
  1 *cup heavy cream, whipped*

Beat the egg whites nearly stiff. Gradually sugar, beating constantly. Add the vanilla and vinegar. Beat until blended well. Divide the meringue in 2 parts, and place each part, shaped to fit a refrigerator tray, on a buttered baking sheet. Bake in a 275° oven for 40 to 45 minutes or until delicately browned. Remove the meringues from the oven and cool.

In a medium bowl combine the banana pulp, salt, and lemon juice. In a small bowl combine the confectioners' sugar and whipped cream. Fold the whipped cream mixture into the banana mixture. Place 1 baked meringue in a refrigerator tray. Cover with filling and add the second meringue. Freeze about 3 hours.

MAKES 6 TO 8 SERVINGS.

Fire and Ice Tomatoes

  6 *large ripe firm tomatoes, skinned*
      and quartered
  1 *large green bell pepper, cut into*
      strips
  1 *large red onion, sliced into rings*
  1 *cucumber, peeled and diced*

  ¾ *cup vinegar*
 1½ *teaspoons celery salt*
 1½ *teaspoons mustard seed*
  ½ *teaspoon salt*
 4½ *teaspoons sugar*
  ⅛ *teaspoon ground red pepper*
  ⅛ *teaspoon black pepper*
  ¼ *cup cold water*

In a large bowl combine all of the vegetables. In a saucepan mix the remaining ingredients. Place over heat and bring to a boil, then boil furiously for 1 minute. While still hot, pour over the vegetables. Do this just before serving.

MAKES 4 TO 6 SERVINGS.

Peppertrees Bed and Breakfast Inn
❧

724 East University Boulevard
Tucson, Arizona 85719
(520) 622-7167

This inn takes its name from two very large California peppertrees that were planted out front just after the house was built in 1905. Spacious guest rooms and a pair of guest cottages in the back are furnished in antiques that reflect the home's nearly century-long history. Hidden behind the house is an attractive flower-filled patio with a fountain and sprawling shade trees. The inn is within walking distance of the University of Arizona campus and museums.

Chilaquiles

- 4 **corn tortillas**
- 3 **tablespoons oil**
- 1 **onion, chopped**
- 1 **ounce can green chilies**
- 2 **garlic cloves, chopped**
- ½ **cup chopped cooked chicken**
- 1 **large tomato, chopped**
- 1 **teaspoon chopped cilantro**
- 1 **teaspoon chili powder**
  Salt and pepper
- 2 **cups grated Monterey Jack cheese**
- 3 **eggs**
- ½ **cup chicken broth**
  Chili powder
  Salsa

Cut the corn tortillas into strips (they are best a day or two old) and fry in the hot oil until crisp and golden. Drain and place in the bottom of a 1½-quart casserole. In a skillet heat the oil and brown the onion. Add the chilies, garlic, chicken, tomato, and seasonings and cook gently for a few minutes. Put the onion mixture on the tortillas. Cover with cheese. Beat the eggs and broth together. Pour over the casserole, and sprinkle with chili powder. Bake in a 350° oven for about 30 minutes. Serve hot with salsa.
MAKES 4 SERVINGS.

Chilaquiles (Version II)

- 12 **corn tortillas**
- 2 **cups oil for frying**
- 2 **cups shredded cooked chicken or turkey**
- 1½ **cups shredded mozzarella or white cheese**
- 1 **large tomato, chopped**
- 1 **small onion, chopped very fine**
- 2 **cups sour cream**
- 1 **½ cups fresh salsa**
  Bunch fresh cilantro

Cut the tortillas into strips. In a skillet heat the oil and fry the strips until they are just crisp. Drain on paper towels until ready to use. In a large bowl toss the fried tortillas, chicken, cheese, tomato, and onion. Place the mixture in a 9 x 13-inch baking dish. Cover with sour cream. Bake in a 350° oven for 25 minutes. Serve with salsa and garnish with cilantro.
MAKES 4 TO 6 SERVINGS.

Peppertrees Pie

- 1 **pound ground turkey**
- 2 **tablespoons chorizo powder**
- 1 **4-ounce can green chilies**
- ½ **cups canola oil**
- 1 **cup yellow cornmeal**
- 1 **teaspoon salt**
- ½ **teaspoon baking soda**
- 1½ **cups milk**
- 1 **12-ounce can cream-style corn**
- 2 **eggs, well beaten**
- 1 **large onion, chopped**
- 1 **red bell pepper, chopped**
- 1 **green bell pepper, chopped**
- 1½ **cups shredded Jack cheese**
  Tomato
  Fresh sweet basil

In a skillet cook the turkey sprinkled with chorizo powder. Add the green chilies. Set aside.

In a large iron skillet that can go into the oven heat the oil over low heat. In a large bowl mix the cornmeal, salt, and soda, and add the milk and corn. Add the eggs and mix well. Stir in the hot oil from the pan and mix thoroughly. Pour half the batter back into the pan, crumble the chorizo over it, layer the onion, red and green peppers, and Jack cheese over the chorizo. Finish with the remaining cornmeal batter. Bake in a 350° oven for 45 minutes until the top is golden brown. Cut into wedges and serve with fresh sliced tomato and sweet basil for garnish.
MAKES 8 SERVINGS.

Cream Scones (Plain)

- 4 **cups all-purpose flour**
- ½ **cup sugar**
- 8 **teaspoons baking powder**
- ½ **teaspoon salt**
- 2 **eggs, beaten**
- 1 **cup milk**
- 1 **cup heavy cream**
  Extra sugar and milk

In a bowl sift all the dry ingredients together. In a separate bowl beat the eggs until frothy. Add the milk and heavy cream, and mix until incorporated. Pat out on a well-floured surface and cut in to rounds about ¾ inch thick. Place on an ungreased cookie sheet 1 inch apart. (For soft-sided scones place close together.) Brush the tops with milk and sprinkle with sugar. Bake in a 425° oven for about 15 minutes, until golden brown.
MAKES 24 SCONES.

Peppertrees

Oat Scones

1½ cups all-purpose flour
2 cups oats, preferably rolled
¼ cup sugar
4 teaspoons baking powder
½ teaspoon salt
½ cup currants
1 egg
½ cup melted butter or margarine
½ cup milk
   Butter and preserves

In a large bowl mix the flour, oats, sugar, baking powder, salt, and currants. Beat the egg until frothy. Add the melted butter and milk and pour into a well in the center of the dry ingredients. Stir to make a soft dough. Pat on a floured board, divide into 2 rounds, and place on a greased baking sheet. Score each round into wedges. Bake in a 425° oven for 15 minutes until risen and golden brown. Split and serve with butter and preserves.

MAKES ABOUT 16 SCONES.

Welsh Tea Cakes

2 cups all-purpose flour
½ cup sugar
2 teaspoons baking powder
½ teaspoon salt
¼ teaspoon ground cinnamon
¼ teaspoon grated nutmeg
½ cup butter
½ cup currants
¼ cup mixed citrus zest
1 egg
⅓ cup milk

These are very like scones only they are cooked on the griddle or a large cast-iron frying pan will work just as well.

In the bowl of a food processor combine all dry ingredients. Add the butter and process for 1 minute until combined and crumbly. Add the fruit.

In a small bowl beat the egg and milk together and work a little into the dry ingredients until it is just combined and holds together. Pat or roll out on a floured surface to ½-inch thickness. Cut into rounds with a cookie cutter. Cook on a griddle over medium heat for a few minutes on each side until nicely risen and browned. Serve with butter and preserves or cinnamon-sugar.

Note: They cook best when the griddle is not greased. Wonderful for breakfast or afternoon tea. They can be cooked in the oven on a cookie sheet, but they turn out like a soft breakfast cookie, also wonderful. Try them both ways.

MAKES 12 TO 15 TEA CAKES.

Angel Biscuits

2 teaspoons active dry yeast
¼ cup warm water (105 to 115°)
5 cups all-purpose flour
3 tablespoons sugar
3 tablespoons baking powder
1 teaspoon baking soda
1 teaspoon salt
2 cups butter
2 cups buttermilk

In a small bowl dissolve the yeast in warm water and set aside for 10 minutes. Measure all the dry ingredients into a large bowl and cut in the butter until it is all crumbly. (I find it easiest to do in the food processor). Combine the buttermilk and the yeast mixture and work softly into the dry ingredients. Knead the dough just enough to assist in holding it together. Roll it out on a floured board about ¾ inch thick and cut into rounds. Place the biscuits ungreased cookie sheet or a baking stone. Bake in a 400° oven for 15 minutes until nicely risen and beginning to brown.

MAKES ABOUT 3 DOZEN.

Buttermilk Biscuits

2 cups all-purpose flour
2 tablespoons sugar
2 teaspoons baking powder
½ teaspoon baking soda
½ teaspoon cream of tartar
½ cup butter
1 cup buttermilk (or soured milk)

In a large bowl sift all the dry ingredients together and cut in the butter. Stir in the buttermilk and combine until the mixture holds together in a ball. Turn out onto a floured surface and pat or roll out to ½ to ¾ inch thick, and cut into rounds. Place on a greased cookie sheet, close together for soft sides or 1 inch apart for more crusty sides.

Bake in a 450° oven for 12 or 15 minutes, until nicely golden brown.

Variations: Either of the above recipes can be made more exciting by adding one of the following to the dough as it is being mixed: Cheese: ½ cup sharp grated Cheddar cheese, or crumbled feta cheese; Chili: ¼-ounce can chopped green chilies, drained; Garlic: ½ teaspoon garlic powder; Parsley & Onion: ½ cup each of chopped spring onions, chives, and parsley; Pesto & Pine Nut: 2 tablespoons of fresh pesto and ½ cup pine nuts; Salsa: ¼ cup hot salsa; Sausage: ½ cup finely chopped summer sausage.

MAKES ABOUT 2 DOZEN.

Rim Rock West

3450 North Drake Place
Tucson, Arizona 85749
(520) 749-8774

This hacienda-style B&B features a gracious courtyard with a large sparkling fountain and lovely mountain views. Guest rooms are in the main hacienda, but a separate adobe guest cottage with a sunken living room, kitchen, and private walled patio is available. On chilly mornings breakfast is served by a crackling fire. Ski Mount Lemmon, hike some of the finest trails in the southwest, or shop in Tucson's finest.

Mexican Corn, Cheese, and Chili Soufflé

4 eggs, beaten
1 16-ounce can cream-style corn
1 4-ounce can chopped green chilies
⅔ cup milk
⅓ cup oil
1 cup cornmeal

1   cup biscuit mix
½   teaspoon salt
½   teaspoon baking soda
⅓   teaspoon chili powder
⅓   teaspoon pepper
1   cup grated cheese
    Asparagus tips, steamed

In a large bowl mix all ingredients except the cheese. Pour half of the batter in a 9-inch square pan. Sprinkle with cheese. Pour the remaining batter over the cheese. Bake in a at 375° oven for 45 minutes. Cut into squares. Serve on dinner plate with 3 or 4 asparagus tips. Good with or without maple syrup.

MAKES 9 SERVINGS.

Very Good Cheese Pie

1   12-ounce jar marinated artichokes
1   small onion, diced
1   clove garlic, minced
4   eggs
½   cup dry breadcrumbs or Bisquick
¼   teaspoon salt
⅛   teaspoon each pepper, oregano, and
    chili powder
½   pound sharp Cheddar cheese, grated
2   tablespoons parsley

Drain the artichokes. Place the liquid in a frying pan. Chop the artichokes and set them aside. Add the onion and garlic to the frying pan. Sauté. In a medium bowl beat the eggs. Add all remaining ingredients. Turn into a greased 9-inch pie pan. Bake in a 325° oven for 30 minutes.

MAKES 8 SERVINGS.

ARKANSAS

Arsenic & Old Lace

60 Hillside Avenue
Eureka Springs, Arkansas 72632
(501) 253-5454

Guests bask in Victorian-style luxury at this resort community inn where everything is all done up in antiques, imported wallpapers, fresh flowers, original artwork, and plenty of lace. Broad verandas provide views of the heavily wooded grounds and stone-terraced hillside.

Like the inn itself, the town of Eureka Springs is richly Victorian in spirit and appearance. Art galleries, antique shops, and small cafés lure visitors into the town known to some as Arkansas's "Little Switzerland." Since parking is limited, the trolley is the wisest and most enjoyable way to get around.

Arsenic and Old Lace Potato-Cheese Strata

- ½ cup green onions, chopped (optional)
- 2 tablespoons butter
- 1½ pounds frozen hash brown or O'Brien potatoes, thawed
- ⅔ cup cream of mushroom soup
- ⅔ cup milk
- 1½ cups sour cream
- 4 cups shredded Monterey Jack-Colby cheese
- 8 eggs
- ½ teaspoon Tabasco sauce
- ¼ teaspoon salt
- 15 slices bacon, cooked and crumbled
  Fresh fruit for garnish
  Fruit muffins

Microwave or sauté the chopped green onions in butter until tender. Bake the potatoes in a 250° oven for 1 hour. In a large bowl combine all ingredients except the bacon and mix well. Turn into a 3-quart glass baking dish sprayed with cooking spray. Bake in a 350° oven for 60 to 65 minutes. Sprinkle crumbled bacon over the casserole 10 minutes before the casserole is done. Let stand 5 minutes and cut into rectangles.

May be prepared in advance and refrigerated, covered. If placed in the oven directly from refrigerator, uncover and bake for 70 to 75 minutes.

Serve with fresh fruit garnish and fruit muffins.

Notes: Substitute cubed ham for the bacon; instead of onions, use ½ teaspoon onion powder in egg mixture. This is a big "stick to the ribs" favorite at this inn.
MAKES 6 TO 8 SERVINGS.

Arsenic and Old Lace Pecan Baked Pancake

- 1½ cups pancake batter
- 2 tablespoons butter, melted
- 1 cup peeled, cored, and sliced Granny Smith apples
- ½ teaspoon ground cinnamon
- ⅓ cup chopped pecans
- 3 tablespoons maple syrup

Prepare the pancake mix according to the package directions and set aside. Pour melted butter in 9-inch pie plate. Place apple slices in the bottom of the pie plate. Sprinkle with cinnamon and pecans, and drizzle syrup over the apples. Carefully pour the batter on top. Bake at 350° oven for 30 to 35 minutes or until the top springs back when touched.

Loosen the edges and invert onto a serving plate. Cut in wedges and serve with warm maple syrup and/or fresh apple butter, and sausage links.
MAKES 4 TO 6 SERVINGS.

Arsenic & Old Lace

Bridgeford House

263 Spring Street
Eureka Springs, Arkansas 72632
(501) 253-7853

This Queen Anne/Eastlake-style Victorian house sits in the heart of Eureka Springs's historic residential district. Guests can select from a two-room suite or any of three bedroom-and-bath combinations, all furnished in tasteful antiques. Shady porches invite relaxation in comfortable wicker chairs. Although far enough from the center of this resort community to provide plenty of peace and quiet, the Bridgeford House is only a short trolley ride from all the town's attractions.

Buried Treasure Muffins

 1 cup all-purpose flour
 ½ cup oatmeal
 ¼ cup sugar
 2 teaspoons baking powder
 ½ teaspoon salt
 1 egg
 ¾ cup milk
 ¼ cup oil
 ¾ cup strawberry jam

Line 12 muffin cups with paper liners. In a large bowl mix the flour, oatmeal, sugar, baking powder, and salt. Make a well in the middle. In another bowl break the egg and mix it with the milk and oil. Pour the liquid mixture into the well in the dry ingredients. Stir just until mixed. The batter will be lumpy. Fill the muffin cups halfway. Place a teaspoon of jam in the center, leaving an edge of batter all around. Completely cover the jam with a tablespoon of batter. Bake the muffins in a 400° oven for approximately 18 minutes or until golden brown.
MAKES 12 MUFFINS.

Bridgeford Eggs

 1 10 ½-ounce can cream of chicken soup
 1 10 ½-ounce can cream of mushroom soup
 1 cup Miracle Whip salad dressing
 ¼ cup sherry
 ¼ cup milk
 12 hard-boiled eggs, peeled
      Hot cooked rice

In a medium bowl combine the soups, salad dressing, sherry, and milk. Cover the bottom of 9 x 13-inch casserole dish with one-third of the sauce. Shred the eggs and sprinkle them into casserole. Cover with the remaining sauce. Bake in a 350° oven for 20 minutes. Serve over rice.
MAKES 10 TO 12 SERVINGS.

Fruit-stuffed French Toast with Strawberry Nut Sauce

 2 3-ounce packages cream cheese, softened
 12 slices raisin bread
 6 teaspoons strawberry jam
 3 eggs
 ¼ cup milk
 1 teaspoon vanilla extract
 2 teaspoons sugar
      Strawberry Nut Sauce (recipe follows)

Spread cream cheese on 6 slices of raisin bread. Spread strawberry jam on 6 slices of raisin bread. Place the bread slices together cream cheese-side to strawberry jam-side, and set aside.
    In a shallow bowl mix eggs, milk, vanilla, and sugar. Dip the sandwiches in the egg mixture, then grill on both sides. Cut diagonally and spoon Strawberry Nut Sauce over wedges before serving.
MAKES 6 SERVINGS.

Strawberry Nut Sauce

 2 teaspoons cornstarch
 ⅔ cup cold water
 1 cup strawberry jam
 2 teaspoons lemon juice
 ¼ cup chopped walnuts

Bridgeford House

In a small bowl mix the cornstarch and water, and set aside. In a saucepan heat the jam to a boil and add the water-cornstarch mixture. Bring to a boil, stirring constantly, then simmer 3 minutes. Add the lemon juice, then the chopped walnuts. Spoon approximately 1 tablespoon of sauce over each serving of 2 wedges of French toast.
MAKES 6 SERVING.

Dairy Hollow House

515 Spring Street
Eureka Springs, Arkansas
(501) 253-7444

Actually two homes on either side of a wooded valley, the Dairy Hollow House has received the highest of praises from numerous travel-conscious publications. The beautifully appointed suites of the late-1940s bungalow-style Main House present an air of unpretentious luxury, while a definite out-in-the-country feel reigns in the old-fashioned rooms of the 1880s Farmhouse. Sunny nooks, private porches, flower-filled gardens, and the elegant Restaurant at Dairy Hollow provide all a guest could need. Both homes offer easy access to the relaxed pleasures of Eureka Springs.

Pumpkin and Tomato Bisque

- 3 to 4 tablespoons butter or mild oil (such as corn or peanut)
- 1 large onion, chopped
- 3 to 4 cups well-flavored chicken or vegetable stock
- 1 28-ounce can whole tomatoes, with their juices
- 1 tablespoon maple syrup or honey
- 4 cups freshly made pumpkin or butternut squash purée or canned pumpkin purée
  Salt to taste
  Red pepper purée (optional)

In a 10-inch skillet melt the butter or heat the oil over medium-low heat. Add the onion and sauté slowly, stirring often, until limp but not brown, 6 to 7 minutes. Stir in 3 cups of the stock and let simmer, partially covered, about 15 minutes.

Pour the tomatoes with their juice into a food processor. Add the maple syrup or honey and purée. Add the pumpkin, and buzz again. Strain the stock and add the strained-out onions to the processor. Buzz again and if an extra-smooth soup is desired, put through a power strainer.

Add the tomato-pumpkin purée to the stock. Season with the salt. Reheat, and serve very hot. Garnish with the red pepper purée, if using.
MAKES 8 TO 10 SERVINGS.

Feather Bed Eggs

- 1 recipe Skillet-Sizzled Buttermilk Cornbread (recipe follows) crumbled into large chunks and left to dry overnight
  Salt and fresh ground black pepper to taste
- 1 ½ cups shredded sharp Cheddar or Swiss cheese
- 8 large eggs
- 2 cups milk (or combination of milk and heavy cream, half and half, sour cream, or evaporated skim milk)
  Dash Pickapeppa or Worcestershire sauce
  Tiny pinch dried dill
  Tiny pinch dried basil

Spray a 14 x 11-inch shallow baking dish with cooking spray. Spread the cornbread in an even layer in the prepared dish. Sprinkle lightly with salt and pepper. Pat the cheese over the top. In a large bowl whisk the eggs, milk, and seasonings together until blended; then pour this mixture over the cornbread. Bake in a 350° oven until the eggs are set and the top is lightly browned and slightly puffed, about 30 minutes. Do not overbake.

Note: This can also be baked in individual ramekins. Bake about 20 minutes.

Variation: Sprinkle ¾ cup diced ham over the cornbread and cheese before pouring on the egg mixture.
MAKES 6 TO 8 SERVINGS.

Skillet-sizzled Buttermilk Corn Bread

- 1 cup stone-ground yellow cornmeal
- 1 cup unbleached flour
- 1 tablespoon baking powder
- ¼ teaspoon salt
- ¼ teaspoon baking soda
- 1¼ cups buttermilk
- 1 large egg
- 2 to 4 tablespoons sugar
- ¼ cup mild oil (such as corn or peanut)
- 2 to 4 tablespoons butter

In a large bowl combine the cornmeal, flour, baking powder, and salt. In a small bowl stir the soda into the buttermilk. In a separate bowl whisk together the egg, sugar to taste, and the oil. Whisk in the buttermilk.

Spray an 8- or 9-inch cast-iron skillet with cooking spray. Place the skillet over medium-high heat, add the butter, and heat until the butter melts and is just starting to sizzle. Tilt the pan to coat the bottom and sides. Add the wet ingredients to the dry, and quickly stir together, using only as many strokes as needed to combine. Scrape the batter into the hot, buttery skillet. Immediately place the skillet into a 375° oven and bake until golden brown, about 25 minutes. Cut into wedges to serve.
MAKES AN 8 TO 9-INCH CORNBREAD.

Browned Butter Pecan Pie

- ½ cup butter
- ¾ cup light corn syrup
- ¼ cup honey
- 1 cup sugar
- 3 large eggs
- 1 teaspoon vanilla extract
- ⅛ teaspoon salt
- 1 cup chopped pecans
- 1 9-inch unbaked pie shell
  Real whipped cream

In a saucepan cook the butter over low to medium heat, watching closely but not stirring, until golden brown, about 5 to 8 minutes. Do not burn. Pour the browned butter into a small bowl and set aside.

In a food processor blend the corn syrup, honey, sugar, eggs, vanilla, and salt until smooth. Add the browned butter, and blend again. Add the pecans and process with just a few quick on-off pulses.

Pour the mixture into the pie shell. Bake in a 435° oven for 10 minutes. Lower the heat to 325° and bake another 40 minutes.

Note: The center of the pie will seem a bit liquid when removed from the oven. It sets up further as it cools. Let cool completely. Serve with a generous puff of real whipped cream.
MAKES 8 SERVINGS.

Mexican Corn Bread

1 cup cornmeal
2 eggs, beaten
1 cup milk
½ teaspoon baking soda
¾ teaspoon salt
1 16-ounce can cream-style corn
½ cup bacon fat
2 cups grated Cheddar cheese
½ pound ground beef, browned and
    crumbled
1 onion, finely chopped
4 hot peppers, chopped

In a large bowl combine the cornmeal, eggs, milk, soda, salt, corn, and bacon fat. Pour half of batter in a greased cast-iron skillet. Sprinkle with Cheddar cheese, browned meat, onion and hot peppers, in that order. Pour the remaining batter on top. Bake in a 350° oven for 45 to 50 minutes.

MAKES 6 TO 8 SERVINGS.

Herb Bubble Loaf

3 cups all-purpose flour
2 tablespoons sugar
1½ teaspoons salt
1 package active dry yeast
1¼ cups milk
2 tablespoons oil
1 egg
⅓ cup margarine, melted
2 tablespoons Parmesan cheese
1 tablespoon sesame seeds
1 tablespoon garlic salt
½ teaspoon paprika
½ teaspoon dried parsley
½ teaspoon dried rosemary
½ teaspoon dried thyme

In a large bowl mix 1 cup of flour, sugar, salt, and yeast. In a saucepan heat the milk and oil until very warm. Add the egg and milk mixture to the dry ingredients and beat with an electric mixer for 30 seconds on low, 3 minutes on medium. Stir in the remaining flour. Turn the dough onto a floured board, and knead until smooth, 1 to 2 minutes. Place in a warm greased bowl. Turn to grease the top. Cover and let rise in a warm place until doubled in bulk, 45 to 60 minutes.

Punch the dough down. Lightly grease 2 quart casserole bowl.

Pinch off walnut-sized balls of dough and dip in melted margarine. Place in the prepared casserole in a single layer. In a small bowl mix the Parmesan cheese, spices, and herbs. Sprinkle half over the first layer. Make a second layer of dough balls. Pour the remaining margarine over. Sprinkle with the remaining spices. Cover and let rise until it reaches the top of the dish, 30 to 45 minutes. Bake in a 400° oven for 25 to 30 minutes.

MAKES 1 LOAF.

Apple Crisp

4 cups sliced peeled apples
¼ cup water
¾ cup all-purpose flour
1 cup sugar
1 teaspoon ground cinnamon
½ teaspoon salt
½ cup butter

Place the apples and water in a 10 x 6-inch pan. In a large bowl sift the dry ingredients. Cut in the butter until the mixture resembles coarse crumbs. Sprinkle over the apples. Bake in a 350° for 40 minutes. Delicious!

MAKES 4 TO 6 SERVINGS.

Lemon Icebox Pie

1 14-ounce can sweetened condensed
    milk
1 6-ounce can frozen lemonade con-
    centrate, thawed
1 9-ounce container Cool Whip,
    thawed
1 9-inch graham cracker crust

In a large bowl combine the milk, lemonade, and Cool Whip. Spread the mixture evenly in the crust. Refrigerate until ready to serve.

MAKES 6 TO 8 SERVINGS.

The Heartstone Inn

"A.B.C." Bake (Apple, Bacon, Cheddar Bake)

2 cups sliced, peeled Granny Smith
    apples
2 tablespoons sugar
2 cups grated Cheddar cheese
⅓ cup bacon bits
2 cups milk
6 eggs
2 cups biscuit mix
    Maple syrup

Layer the apples, sugar, cheese, and bacon bits in this order in a greased 9 x 13-inch baking dish.

In a blender combine the milk, eggs, and biscuit mix beat just until mixed well. Pour the batter over the apples and cheese. Bake in preheated 375° oven for 40 minutes or until firm to the touch and lightly browned. Serve with maple syrup.

Variation: Try adding ½ cup of chopped pecans to the apple-cheese layers.
MAKES 8 TO 10 SERVINGS.

Crustless Potato Artichoke Quiche

- 12 eggs, beaten
- ½ teaspoon Lawry's seasoned salt
- ¼ teaspoon pepper
- 2 cups grated Cheddar cheese
- 4 large green onions, sliced
- 1 cup cottage cheese
- ⅓ cup bacon bits
- ½ cup salsa (medium-hot)
- 1 14-ounce can artichoke hearts, drained and chopped
- 1 24-ounce package unthawed, shredded hash brown potatoes
- Salsa for garnish
- Parsley

In a large bowl beat together the eggs, salt, and pepper. Add the Cheddar cheese, onions, cottage cheese, bacon bits, salsa, and artichoke hearts, blending well. Stir in the potatoes. Spoon into a greased 9 x 13-inch baking dish. Do not cover. Bake in a 350° oven for 55 to 60 minutes, until lightly browned and set. Let stand for 5 minutes before cutting.

Garnish with additional salsa and parsley sprig.
MAKES 8 TO 10 SERVINGS.

Olde Stonehouse Bed and Breakfast Inn

511 Main Street
Hardy, Arkansas 72542
(501) 856-2983

Recapture the romance of times past at this 1930s native-stone home on Main Street. Mere steps from Old Town Hardy's quaint shops, guests can relax amid period antiques, quilts, and old lace. Each room comes with a private bath, ceiling fan, and queen-size bed. Porches generously furnished with rockers and wicker are great for fresh-air reading and people watching. Three blocks up the hill, the 1905 Shaver Cottage provides several suites perfect for romantic interludes.

Vo's Strawberry Pie

- 2 pints strawberries, cleaned, hulled, and halved
- 2 cups sugar
- 1 3-ounce package strawberry gelatin
- 6 tablespoon cornstarch
- 2 cups boiling water
- 2 8-inch baked and cooled pie shells
- Whipped topping (optional)
- Whole strawberries for garnish

In a large bowl mix the strawberries and sugar. In a medium saucepan combine the gelatin, cornstarch, and water. Bring to a boil and cook for 1 minute. Refrigerate until thick, about 30 minutes.

Stir in the fruit and pour into the pie shells. Chill well.

Top with whipped topping and decorate with a few whole strawberries.

Variations: Use a graham cracker, cookie, or vanilla wafer crust. Fat-free version: Spoon into serving cups and top with frozen nonfat yogurt.
MAKES 12 SERVINGS.

Sour Cream Banana Bread

- ½ cup butter
- 1 cup sugar
- 2 eggs
- 1 teaspoon vanilla extract
- 1½ cups all-purpose flour
- 1 teaspoon baking soda
- ½ teaspoon salt
- 1 cup mashed bananas
- ½ cup sour cream
- ½ cup nuts, chopped

In a large bowl cream the butter and sugar. Add the eggs and vanilla. In a small bowl mix the dry ingredients together. Add the dry ingredients to the creamed mixture. Mix well. Add the mashed bananas and sour cream. Stir in the nuts. Pour into 2 8 x 4-inch greased loaf pans. Bake in a 350° oven for 1 hour.
MAKES 2 LOAVES

Broccoli-Corn Bread Casserole

- 2 10-ounce packages yellow corn bread mix
- 4 eggs
- 2 cups small curd cottage cheese
- ¾ cup margarine, melted
- 1 cup chopped smoked link sausage
- 2 10-ounce packages frozen chopped broccoli, thawed and drained
- 1 cup chopped onions
- 1 cup chopped celery
- 1 cup grated cheese

In a large bowl combine all ingredients. Pour into a well-greased 9 x 13-inch baking pan. Bake in a 350° oven for 35 to 45 minutes. Let set before slicing.
MAKES 8 SERVINGS.

Hash Brown Quiche

- 2 cups shredded hash brown potatoes
- ¼ cup chopped green onion, shredded
- ¼ cup all-purpose flour
- Salt and pepper to taste
- 3 eggs
- 1 cup diced cooked ham
- ½ cup grated Jack cheese
- ½ cup grated hot pepper cheese
- 1 cup grated Cheddar cheese
- ½ cup milk or cream
- ¼ teaspoon seasoned salt
- Pepper to taste

In a medium bowl mix the potatoes, onion, flour, salt, pepper, and 1 egg. Spray a 9-inch pie pan with cooking spray. Gently press the potato mixture into the bottom and sides. Bake in a 425° oven until browned.

Alternate layers of ham and cheeses in the crust. In a small bowl mix the milk, 2 eggs, seasoned salt, and pepper, and pour over the ham and cheese. Bake in a 350° oven for 30 to 40 minutes until knife inserted at the edge comes out clean.
MAKES 4 TO 6 SERVINGS.

Oak Tree Inn and River Cottages

1802 West Main Street
Heber Springs, Arkansas 72543
(800) 959-3857

Positioned on ten acres right beside the trout-filled Little Red River, this inn makes room for guests to stretch their arms and legs. All four second-floor guest rooms of the main residence feature fireplaces and whirlpool baths. The nearby river cottages are supplied with microwave, dishwasher, washer and dryer, and everything necessary for day-to-day living. Hammocks, grills, and canoes allow visitors to savor the woods and river.

Hot Fudge

> 2 **cups instant dry milk**
> 1⅓ **cups sugar**
> ¾ **cup unsweetened cocoa**
> 2 **teaspoons vanilla extract**
> 1 **cup water**
> ½ **cup margarine**

In a blender combine the dry milk, sugar, cocoa, and vanilla. In a large glass measuring cup combine the water and butter. Microwave the butter and water for 3 minutes. Pour the contents of the measuring cup into the blender and blend on the highest speed. Pour the contents of the blender into an 8- or 9-inch square pan and let cool. The fudge will thicken as it cools.

This may be heated in the microwave for about 1 minute before serving. Stir between microwaving and serving.

Variations: Buy some coconut and nut ready-to-spread frosting and add half of the contents into a batch of hot fudge. Or add 1 8-ounce block of cream cheese to the recipe.

MAKES ABOUT 1 DOZEN SQUARES.

English Muffins

> 3 **cups all-purpose flour**
> 1 **package active dry yeast**
> 1 **tablespoon sugar**
> ½ **teaspoon salt**
> ¼ **cup cornmeal**
> 1¼ **cups warm water (105 to 115°)**
> ·······························
> **Chive Sauce (recipe follows)**

In a large bowl combine the dry ingredients and mix with a wooden spoon. Add the water and stir. Knead into a smooth ball. Place in greased bowl, cover and let rise until doubled in bulk, about 1 hour.

Spray 2 clean coffee cans with cooking spray. Punch down the dough and shape into 2 balls. Place a ball of dough in each coffee can. Let rise again until doubled in bulk. Bake in a 375° oven for about 30 minutes. When cool, slice into muffins. Serve with Chive Sauce.

MAKES ABOUT 12 SERVINGS.

Chive Sauce

> 1 **8-ounce package cream cheese**
> ⅓ **cup milk**
> 2 **tablespoons margarine**
> ⅓ **cup white wine**
> 2 **tablespoons chopped chives**
> **Salt and pepper to taste**
> ½ **teaspoon dry mustard**

In glass bowl combine all ingredients. Microwave for 2 minutes. Beat well. Microwave another 2 minutes. Beat again.

Note: This is the Oak Tree Inn's version of Eggs Benedict. Toast the muffin in the toaster or butter and place under the broiler. Put 2 pieces of cooked bacon on muffin, place a poached egg on bacon, and top with Chive Sauce.

MAKES ABOUT 2 CUPS.

Cinnamon Waffles

> 2½ **cups all-purpose flour**
> 1 **tablespoon baking powder**
> ½ **teaspoon salt**
> 1½ **to 2 tablespoons ground cinnamon**
> 2 **tablespoons sugar**
> 2 **cups milk**
> ⅓ **cup oil**
> 4 **egg yolks**

> 4 **egg whites, beaten stiff**
> **Cinnamon Apples (recipe follows)**

In a large bowl combine all ingredients except the egg whites. Fold in the egg whites.

Spoon onto a hot greased waffle iron. Bake until done. The batter is best more thin than thick, so if it's too thick add a little more milk.

Serve with Cinnamon Apples, if desired.

MAKES 8 WAFFLES, 8 INCHES IN DIAMETER.

Cinnamon Apples

> 4 **Granny Smith apples, sliced or quartered**
> ¼ **to ½ cup firmly packed brown sugar**
> **Cinnamon**

Place the apples in a glass baking dish. Sprinkle with sugar and cinnamon. Microwave on high for 7 to 10 minutes until the apples are crisp or tender to taste.

Serve the apples over the waffles or on the side. Together with sausage, it makes a great breakfast.

MAKES ABOUT 3 CUPS.

Vintage Comfort Bed and Breakfast

303 Quapaw Avenue
Hot Springs National Park, Arkansas 71901
(501) 623-3258

A carefully restored Queen Anne-style house built in 1907, the Vintage Comfort sits on a tree-lined street a short walk from Hot Springs's historic Bathhouse Row. When they are not enjoying the town's art galleries, restaurants, and shops, guests can relax on the veranda in the shade of ancient magnolias. Four spacious rooms are available, each with private baths, ceiling fans, and period furnishings.

Orange Pecan Muffins

1   small orange, well scrubbed and wiped dry
½   cup pecans
½   cup butter, softened
1   cup plus 1 tablespoon sugar
2   large eggs
⅓   cup orange juice
1   teaspoon baking soda
2   cups all-purpose flour
1   cup plain yogurt

....

Orange juice for dipping
Sugar for dipping

Grease 12 muffin cups or line with paper or foil liners. Finely grate the orange peel and squeeze the orange for juice. Finely chop the pecans. In a large bowl cream the butter with electric mixer until pale and creamy. Beat in the sugar. Add the eggs one at a time. Blend in the orange juice. Stir in the soda and grated peel. Fold in half of the flour, then half of the yogurt. Repeat, then fold in the pecans. Scoop the batter into the muffin cups. Bake in a 375° oven for 20 to 25 minutes or until browned. When cool enough to touch, dip the muffins in orange juice and sprinkle with sugar.

MAKES 12 MUFFINS.

Vintage Comfort

Baked Mushroom Delight

2   tablespoons butter
½   pound fresh mushrooms, sliced
8   strips bacon, fried crisp, drained, and crumbled
3   cups shredded Monterey Jack cheese
8   eggs, beaten

Pepper to taste
¼   teaspoon ground or fresh thyme
¼   teaspoon ground or fresh rosemary

In a skillet melt the butter and sauté mushrooms until tender. Place the mushrooms in the bottom of a well-greased 8-inch square baking dish. Top with bacon and then Monterey Jack cheese.

In a medium bowl combine the eggs, pepper, thyme, and rosemary. Pour over the layered ingredients. Bake in a 275 ° oven for 45 minutes to 1 hour or until center is set and the top is golden.

MAKES 4 TO 6 SERVINGS

Fools Cove Ranch

❧

*P.O. Box 101
Kingston, Arkansas 72742
(501) 665-2986*

A 130-acre farm well up in the Boston Mountain Range of the Ozarks, the ranch is as good a place as any to taste the rural life. The farm has a private pond teeming with catfish and bass. The mountain views are beautiful; there are lots of trails and back roads to explore, and nearby Buffalo River is perfect for canoeing and swimming. A large suite with private bath and three guest rooms are available. Branson, Missouri is only a short drive away.

Bran Muffins

1   cup shortening (or 1 cup oil)
2   cups firmly packed brown sugar
1   cup white sugar
4   eggs
5   cups all-purpose flour
5   teaspoons baking soda

2   teaspoons salt
4   cups buttermilk
1   13-ounce box bran cereal
1   cup wheat germ
¼   cup honey
1   cup raisins
1   cup chopped dates
1   cup chopped prunes
4   medium or 3 large bananas, mashed (or 3 or 4 carrots, shredded or 1 large zucchini, shredded)

In a large bowl mix all ingredients. Pour into greased muffin cups. Bake in a 400° oven for 20 to 25 minutes or until a toothpick inserted in a center muffin comes out clean.

MAKES 3 DOZEN MUFFINS.

Creamed Spinach

½   cup margarine
1½   cups all-purpose flour
2   cups milk
2   cups water
2   10-ounce boxes frozen spinach, thawed, drained, and finely chopped
1   large onion, finely chopped
1   tablespoon seasoned salt
  Pepper to taste

In a large saucepan melt the margarine. Blend in the flour completely. Gradually add the milk and water, and simmer until thickened and creamy. Add the spinach and onion, seasoned salt, and pepper to taste. Cook, stirring often, for about 10 minutes.

MAKES ABOUT 6 SERVINGS.

Hotze House

❧

*1619 Louisiana Street, P.O. Box 164087
Little Rock, Arkansas 72216
(501) 376-6563*

When built in 1900, the Hotze House mansion was considered the finest house in Arkansas. Found in the Governor's Mansion district, the house is a Little Rock landmark and is listed on the National Register of Historic Places. Carefully restored to its former elegance, each of the inn's five bedrooms is individually appointed with an attractive and comfortable mixture of antiques and traditional furnishings. Four of the rooms have fireplaces. Business-people and others looking for a lot of room will find it here, as the mansion has four thousand square feet available for meetings, parties, receptions, or weddings.

Hotze House

"Hot Damn!" Baked Pears

4   **pears**
¼   **cup golden raisins**
3   **tablespoons finely chopped pecans**
3   **tablespoons white corn syrup**
1   **tablespoon lemon juice**
2   **tablespoons honey**
1   **tablespoon light corn syrup**
3   **tablespoons "Hot Damn!" (DeKuyper's hot cinnamon schnapps liqueur)**
2   **tablespoons hot water**
    Cinnamon

Peel the pears, leaving the stems on. Core the pears on the blossom end (the bottom). In a small bowl combine the raisins, pecans, 3 tablespoons syrup, and lemon juice and mix well. This mixture should be of a stiff consistency. Fill the cavity of each pear, dividing the filling equally. Place the pears upright in a deep baking dish, preferably with a cover.

Mix together the honey, syrup, liqueur, and hot water. This should make about ½ cup of liquid. If it does not, add a little more water. Pour over the pears into the baking dish. Sprinkle the pears with cinnamon. Cover the dish with its lid (or foil). Bake in a 350° oven for 1 hour and 15 minutes.

Serve warm or cold with some of the syrup spooned over each pear.

MAKES 4 SERVINGS.

Berry-Cherry-Apple Crisp

1   **cup quick or old-fashioned oatmeal, uncooked**
½   **cup firmly packed brown sugar**
⅓   **cup margarine or butter, melted**
2   **tablespoons all-purpose flour**

4   **cups peeled and thinly sliced Granny Smith apples, about 4 medium**
1   **cup fresh or frozen blueberries**
1   **cup frozen sweet dark cherries**
¼   **cup firmly packed brown sugar**
¼   **cup frozen orange juice concentrate, thawed**
3   **tablespoons all-purpose flour**
1   **teaspoon cinnamon**

In a medium bowl combine the oats, brown sugar, margarine, and flour. Set aside.

In a large bowl combine the fruit and remaining ingredients. Stir until the fruit is evenly coated. Spoon the filling into an 8-inch square glass baking dish. Sprinkle the topping evenly over fruit. Bake in a 350° oven for 30 to 35 minutes, until the apples are tender and the topping is golden brown. Serve warm with yogurt if desired.

Any that is left keeps well. It is delicious rewarmed by microwaving.

MAKES 4 TO 6 SERVINGS.

Sweet Potato Biscuits

2½   **cups biscuit mix**
⅓   **cup softened margarine or butter**
1   **cup sweet potatoes, cooked and mashed (canned may be used)**
½   **cup milk**

In a medium bowl combine all ingredients in the order given and mix until soft dough forms. Turn onto a surface dusted with flour or baking mix. Roll in the flour to coat. Shape the dough into a ball. Knead 3 or 4 times and roll to ½-inch thickness. Cut with a 2-inch cutter dipped in flour. Place the biscuits with their edges touching on an ungreased cookie sheet. Bake in a 450° oven for 10 to 12 minutes or until golden brown.

MAKES 18 TO 20 BISCUITS.

Margland Inns Bed & Breakfast

703 West 2nd Avenue
Pine Bluff, Arkansas 71601
(501)536-6000

The trio of vintage houses that comprise this people-friendly B&B sit side by side in an old-fashioned community of tree-lined streets, lovely old churches, and small museums of local lore. A Colonial Revival clapboard home dating to 1903, the oldest of the three is the Margland II. Featuring double parlors, a formal dining room, and Aubusson-patterned rugs, it is also the most elegant. The salt-box-style Margland III, built in 1896, offers a more casual feel, while the Margland IV, another Colonial Revival, is strictly Victorian. All three houses are connected by a brick-lined courtyard and terrace.

Ed's Omelet

2   **eggs**
    Pinch salt
⅛   **teaspoon pepper**
1   **tablespoon water**
1   **tablespoon butter**

¼   **cup sausage**
2   **chopped green onions**
½   **cup sliced fresh mushrooms**
½   **cup finely chopped ham**
½   **cup chopped green bell peppers**
2   **strips diced bacon**
1   **tomato, chopped**
½   **cup shredded Cheddar cheese**

Into a medium bowl break the eggs. Add the salt, pepper, and water, and beat lightly with a fork until the whites and yolks are thoroughly incorporated. Place an omelet pan on moderate heat until hot, then add the butter. It should sizzle but not brown. Pour in the egg mixture and stir rapidly with a fork until the outside of the omelet begins to set.

Lift the edges of the omelet carefully, and tilt the pan to let the uncooked eggs run under the set part. When the omelet is set, but not dry, sprinkle the half of the omelet that is on the side opposite the handle of the pan with sausage, onions, mushrooms, ham, green peppers, bacon, tomato, and Cheddar cheese. Tilt the pan away and slide a spatula under the unfilled side, carefully turning it over the filled side. Hold a warmed plate up to the pan and invert the pan over the plate so that the omelet will slide easily onto the plate. **MAKES 1 SERVING.**

Fried Pie Pastry

  1   *13-ounce can evaporated milk*
  1   *egg, beaten*
  5   *cups all-purpose flour*
  1   *tablespoon salt*
  1   *tablespoon sugar*
  1   *cup plus 1 teaspoon shortening*

    Fruit filling or pie filling
    Shortening for frying

In a small bowl mix the milk and egg, and set aside. In a separate bowl sift the flour, salt, and sugar to blend. Cut the shortening into the dry ingredients with a pastry blender. Add the egg-milk mixture and toss lightly to just moisten the dry ingredients. Roll the pastry in waxed paper and chill.

When needed, roll the pastry out on a floured board into 6-inch circles. Fill with fruit, fry in hot shortening, and serve. Fried pies may also be frozen.

Note: This pastry absorbs very little grease while frying.

CALIFORNIA

Garratt Mansion

900 Union Street
Alameda, California 94501
(510) 521-4779

W. T. Garratt, a turn-of-the-century industrialist, built this Colonial Revival residence in 1893. An outstanding example of Victorian era design and construction, it is found in the quiet island community of Alameda, about twelve miles from San Francisco. Guest rooms are decorated with period furnishings. The mansion makes an exceptional setting for weddings, receptions, and small meetings.

Frittata with Potatoes and Leeks

 3 **leeks, sliced**
 ½ **tablespoon butter**
 3 **potatoes, medium, sliced**
 1 **cup milk**
 6 **eggs, beaten**
    Pinch salt and pepper
 1½ **tablespoons butter**

In a skillet sauté the leeks in ½ tablespoon of butter. In a saucepan simmer the potatoes in the milk. When the potatoes are cooked, mash them into the milk. Add the sautéed leeks. Blend in the eggs. Season with salt and pepper.

In the same skillet heat 1½ tablespoons butter. When the butter is melted, add the egg mixture and stir occasionally until the desired texture.
MAKES 4 TO 6 SERVINGS.

Quick Cobbler

 ½ **cup butter**
 1 **cup sugar**
 1 **cup self-rising flour**
 1 **cup buttermilk or sour milk**
 1 **tablespoon vanilla extract**
 2 **to 4 cups of fresh fruit (sweetened**
      slightly if necessary)
    Dash cinnamon

In a 10-inch pie pan or 8 x 10-inch glass dish melt the butter. In a medium bowl mix the sugar, flour, buttermilk, and vanilla. Pour into the center of the melted butter. Add the fruit, carefully spreading the fruit to the sides of the batter. Sprinkle cinnamon over the fruit. Bake in a 350° oven for 35 to 45 minutes. The crust will be light brown and the fruit will bubble.

Great side dish for eggs or a great dessert!
MAKES 4 TO 6 SERVINGS.

Albion River Inn

P.O. Box 100
Albion, California 95410
(707) 937-1919

Just down the coast from Medocino, the inn's twenty clifftop rooms afford a sweeping view of the ocean and Albion Cove. Spacious yet cozy, each room is individually decorated and furnished, with its own private garden entrance, fireplace, and private bath—some with Jacuzzis. Guests are encouraged to enjoy the coastal wilderness through hiking, scenic drives, and whale watching. For those wanting a more continental entertainment, the clifftop restaurant and bar offers piano music on the weekends.

Thai Shrimp Cakes

 8 **ounces rock shrimp, peeled and**
      cleaned
 2 **tablespoons cream**
 1 **egg white**
 2 **tablespoons oyster sauce**
 2 **green onions, sliced**
 2 **ounces water chestnuts**

2 tablespoons chopped cilantro
1 tablespoon fresh ginger
2 cups Panko chips (Japanese breadcrumbs)
6 tablespoons peanut oil

....

Tossed greens
Coconut Curry Sauce (recipe fol-
 lows)
Lime wedges

In a food processor combine the shrimp, cream, egg white, oyster sauce, onions, water chestnuts, cilantro, and ginger. Process until smooth. Refrigerate the mixture for 1 hour.

Form into 12 equal-size pieces. Roll the pieces in Panko, one at a time, until they are all fully coated. Flatten lightly with hands into "cakes." In large skillet heat the peanut oil until almost smoking. Add the cakes and cook until golden brown on both sides. Place on a cookie sheet. Bake in a 350° oven for 5 minutes. Serve over tossed greens with a little Coconut Curry Sauce and lime wedges.

MAKES 4 TO 6 SERVINGS.

Coconut Curry Sauce

¼ cup sweetened coconut cream
½ cup mayonnaise
2 tablespoons lime juice
2 tablespoons chopped cilantro
1 tablespoon red curry paste
1 tablespoon green curry paste
1 tablespoon oyster sauce
1 tablespoon curry powder
2 tablespoons seasoned rice wine
 vinegar
 Salt and pepper

In a food processor combine all ingredients and process until blended. Adjust the seasonings.

MAKES ABOUT 1 CUP OF SAUCE.

Roasted Garlic, Whole-Grain Mustard, and Honey Glaze for Grilled Rack of Lamb

2 bulbs fresh garlic
2 tablespoons olive oil
2 tablespoons butter
2 large shallots, minced
3 ounces Madeira or sherry

1 cup veal stock or beef stock (bouillon)
2 tablespoons whole-grain mustard
¼ cup balsamic vinegar
 Honey
 Salt and pepper to taste

....

2 whole racks lamb, grilled and sliced
 into double chops

Sprinkle the garlic with olive oil and cover with aluminum foil. Bake in a 350° oven for 35 minutes. Remove from the oven and let cool. Squeeze gently to extract the garlic and set it aside.

In a sauté pan heat butter until browned. Add the shallots and garlic, reduce the heat to medium, and toss for approximately 2 minutes. Add the Madeira and reduce until almost dry. Add the beef or veal stock, mustard, and vinegar. Reduce by half and remove from the heat. Add the honey and salt and pepper to taste.

Served on grilled or broiled lamb chops or any other cut of lamb.

MAKES 4 SERVINGS.

Lime and Ginger Grilled Prawns with Cilantro-Garlic Butter

½ cup soy sauce
¼ cup lime juice
½ cup olive oil
2 tablespoons minced garlic
1 tablespoon horseradish
2 tablespoons minced ginger
2 tablespoons chopped cilantro
 Fresh cracked black pepper to taste

....

3 to 4 pounds prawns

....

1 tablespoon minced garlic
1 tablespoon minced shallots
½ tablespoon peanut oil

....

2 tablespoons white wine
2 tablespoons pineapple juice
2 tablespoons lime juice
2 tablespoons heavy cream
2 tablespoons butter
1 tablespoon chopped cilantro

In a food processor combine the soy sauce, lime juice, olive oil, 2 tablespoons of minced garlic, horseradish, ginger, 2 tablespoons of

cilantro, and pepper to taste. Blend until smooth. Marinate the prawns in the mixture for up to 2 hours.

In a small skillet lightly brown the garlic and shallots in peanut oil. Add the white wine, pineapple juice, and lime juice, and reduce slightly. Add the cream, and reduce until almost dry. Add the butter and cilantro, and turn off the heat.

MAKES 6 TO 8 SERVINGS.

Wild Berry Rhubarb Cobbler

3 cups whole berries, frozen or fresh
1 cup chopped rhubarb
1½ cups sugar
1 teaspoon vanilla extract
1 tablespoon lemon extract
 Zest and juice of 2 lemons
1 teaspoon ground cinnamon
4 heaping tablespoons cornstarch,
 with a little water added

....

1 cup unsalted butter
2 cups all-purpose flour
¼ cup firmly packed dark brown sugar
¼ cup sugar

....

 Whipped cream or ice cream

In a saucepan mix the berries, rhubarb, 1½ cups of sugar, extracts, zest and juice, and cinnamon. Bring to simmer. Add the cornstarch solution and simmer for 1 minute. Remove and cool.

In a large bowl mix the butter, flour, brown sugar, and ¼ cup of sugar and combine until crumbs are formed. Place the fruit mixture in a 9 x 13-inch ovenproof dish. Sprinkle the topping over the fruit. Bake in a 500° oven for about 10 minutes, until golden brown. Scoop out portions and top with whipped cream or ice cream.

MAKES 6 TO 8 SERVINGS.

Fensalden Inn

Fensalden Inn

P.O. Box 99
Albion, California 95410
(707) 937-4042

*T*his inn affords a panoramic ocean view enhanced by towering cypress trees and wandering deer. For nighttime comfort and contemplation, most rooms come with fireplaces. Sitting on twenty acres of the Mendocino coast, Fensalden Inn has a large main house with five spacious rooms, a bungalow, and a separate house, built around an 1890s water tower, with an additional room and suite. All rooms have a private bath.

Pear Pecan Bread

        3   eggs
        1   cup oil
    1½   cups sugar
        1   teaspoon vanilla extract
        ½   teaspoon fresh grated lemon peel
        3   cups all-purpose flour
        1   teaspoon salt
    1¼   teaspoons baking powder
        ¼   teaspoon baking soda
    1½   teaspoons cinnamon
             Pinch grated nutmeg
        3   fresh ripe pears, peeled and diced
        1   cup toasted chopped pecans

In a large bowl combine the eggs and oil. Add the sugar and mix well. Add the vanilla and lemon peel. In a separate bowl mix the dry ingredients. Add the egg mixture and mix well. The batter will be somewhat stiff. Fold in the diced pears and pecans. Pour into 2 greased 5 x 9-inch bread pans. Bake in a 325° oven for 50 to 55 minutes.
MAKES 2 LOAVES.

Arroyo Village Inn

407 El Camino Real
Arroyo Grande, California 93420
(805) 489-5926

*T*he inn offers a delightful blend of yesterday's charm and today's conveniences. Built in 1984, the inn is styled after an old English country-Victorian and offers the warmth and hospitality of a turn-of-the-century inn. Each of the seven spacious guest rooms is uniquely furnished with its own private bath, queen bed, and an abundance of candles for romantic ambiance. Beautiful antiques, window seats, balconies, and skylights are but a few of the inn's amenities. Nearby attractions include Hearst Castle and the Danish community of Solvang.

Spinach Quiche

        ½   cup butter
        1   garlic clove, crushed
        3   10-ounce boxes frozen spinach,
             squeezed dry
    ⋯⋯⋯⋯⋯⋯
    10   eggs
        3   cups cottage cheese
        1   cup Monterey Jack cheese, grated
        ¼   cup breadcrumbs

In a medium skillet melt the butter with garlic, and fry the spinach. Set aside to cool. In a large bowl combine the remaining ingredients. Add the cooled spinach and transfer to a large greased glass baking dish. Bake in a 350° oven for 30 to 45 minutes.
MAKES 12 SERVINGS.

Mexican Quiche

    10   eggs, beaten
        ½   cup all-purpose flour
        1   tablespoon baking powder
        ½   teaspoon salt
        7   green chilies, diced
        2   cups cottage cheese
        1   pound Monterey Jack cheese, grated
        ½   cup melted butter

Grease a 3-quart glass baking dish. In a large bowl mix all ingredients in the order given, adding the butter just before baking. Pour into the prepared dish. Bake in a 400° oven for 15 minutes. Reduce the heat to 350° and bake for 20 minutes until golden brown.
MAKES 12 SERVINGS.

Zucchini Frittata

        2   tablespoons oil
        6   medium zucchini, sliced
        ½   onion, chopped
        8   eggs, beaten
             Grated Romano cheese to taste
             Salt and pepper to taste

In a large skillet heat the oil and fry the zucchini and onion until tender. Add the beaten eggs and Romano cheese. Continue cooking until the eggs set, turning often. Season to taste with salt and pepper.
MAKES 6 TO 8 SERVINGS.

Italian Biscotti

        4   cups all-purpose flour
        2   cups sugar, dissolved in a little
             water
        4   eggs, beaten
        2   cups raisins
        2   cups chopped walnuts
        1   tablespoon oil
        2   teaspoons baking powder
        1   teaspoon vanilla extract
             Grated peel of 1 orange
             Grated peel of 1 lemon

In a large bowl mix all ingredients. Divide the dough in half and roll each half into a long roll about 1½ inches in diameter. Place on an ungreased baking sheet. Bake in a 350° oven for 15 minutes. Remove from the oven and slice crosswise ¾ inches thick. Lay cut-side-down and bake for additional 15 minutes.
MAKES ABOUT 3 DOZEN BISCOTTI.

Baywood Bed and Breakfast Inn

1370 2nd Street
Baywood Park, California 93402
(805) 528-8888

*W*ith a panoramic view of both the Pacific and the California coastal mountains, the inn is part of the quiet community of Baywood Park, a tiny peninsula projecting into Morro Bay. Each of the eleven suites and four rooms is individually decorated and has a sweeping view of the bay. Private entrances and fireplaces make them especially cozy. Shops, restaurants, golf courses, and boating facilities are nearby. The Hearst Castle and Montano de Oro State Park are only minutes away by car.

Quiche Lorraine

    1   9-inch unbaked pie shell
    6   slices bacon
    1   medium onion, chopped
    2   cups shredded Swiss cheese
    4   eggs
    2   cups milk
    1   teaspoon salt
    ¼   teaspoon grated nutmeg
    ⅛   teaspoon pepper

Bake the pie shell in a 425° oven for 5 minutes. Remove to a wire rack and cool slightly. Increase the oven temperature to 450°.

In a skillet fry the bacon until crisp. Drain all but 1 tablespoon of fat. Crumble the bacon. Sauté the onion in bacon fat until soft. Sprinkle the Swiss cheese evenly in the partly baked pie shell. Add the bacon and onion.

In a large bowl beat the eggs slightly. Slowly beat in the milk, salt, nutmeg, and pepper. Pour into the pie shell. Bake in a 450° oven for 15 minutes. Lower the heat

350° for 15 minutes or until the center is soft but almost set. Do not overbake. The custard will set as it cools. Let stand 15 minutes before serving. Cut into wedges.
MAKES 6 SERVINGS.

Granola

    7   cups old-fashioned oats
    2   cups coarsely chopped nuts
    1   tablespoon ground cinnamon
    ½   teaspoon salt
    ¼   cup wheat germ
    ¼   cup sesame seeds
    ½   cup bran
    ⅔   cup oil
    ⅔   cup honey
    1   cup raisins or dried fruit
    ½   cup hulled sunflower seeds

In a large bowl combine all ingredients except the oil, honey, dried fruit, and sunflower seeds.

In a small saucepan heat the oil. Add the honey, then mix well into the granola mixture. Spread onto 2 large baking sheets. Bake in a 350° oven for 25 to 30 minutes, turning after 10 minutes, then every 5 minutes. Cool and add the dried fruit and sunflower seeds.
MAKES 3 QUARTS.

Foothill House

3037 Foothill Boulevard
Calistoga, California 94515
(707) 942-6933

*S*ituated in the mountain foothills above California's famed Napa Valley, this inn affords a lovely view of Mount St. Helena. Quail, hummingbirds, hawks, and other wildlife abound in the surrounding woodland. The rooms pamper guests with four-poster beds, handmade quilts, fireplaces, and country antiques. The daily "wine appreciation hour" in the sunroom helps guests unwind

before evening. For sightseeing, visitors may visit Calistoga's shops, galleries, and wineries.

Foothill House

Foothill House Torte

    2   8-ounce packages cream cheese, softened
    ½   cup butter
    2   teaspoons minced garlic
    ½   pound thinly sliced Provolone cheese
    ½   to 1 cup pesto
    ½   cup oil-packed sun-dried tomatoes
    ¼   cup pine nuts
        Baguettes

In a food processor mix the cream cheese, butter, and minced garlic. Line a square or rectangular mold with plastic wrap. Line the mold with Provolone cheese (this serves to encase the mixture). Layer first with one-third of the garlic-cream cheese mixture. Next, layer with half of the pesto, a layer of Provolone cheese, then the sun-dried tomatoes. Sprinkle with the pine nuts.

Add another layer of the garlic-cream cheese mixture, the remaining pesto, and the remaining cream cheese mixture. Fold the sides of the cheese over the mixture to encase it. Refrigerate for several hours.

Before serving invert the mold onto the plate and remove the plastic wrap. Serve with baguettes.
MAKES 6 TO 8 SERVINGS.

Hungarian Casserole

    1½ pounds Jimmy Dean bulk pork sausage
    3   large tomatoes, cored and peeled
    3   large boiled potatoes, peeled
    5   hard-boiled eggs, peeled and sliced
    1   pint ranch dressing
    ¾   pound mozzarella cheese, sliced
        Hungarian paprika

Make 8 sausage patties and cook them. Place the patties in the bottom of individual ramekin dishes. Cut the tomatoes into slices the same thickness as the meat; place them on the meat patties. Peel the potatoes and slice them the same thickness as the meat and make another layer. Slice the eggs and arrange them to cover potatoes. Spread the ranch dressing over all ingredients and top with a slice of cheese. Sprinkle generously with paprika. Bake in a 350° oven for 30 minutes.

MAKES 8 SERVINGS.

Foothill House Gold Rush Brunch Breakfast

1   24-ounce package frozen hash browns (8 patties), thawed
1   10½-ounce can potato soup (undiluted)
2   cups sour cream
1   bunch green onions (including green tops), chopped
10   slices Canadian bacon, chopped
4   hard-boiled eggs, sliced
12   ounces shredded sharp Cheddar cheese

In a large bowl combine the thawed hash browns with the potato soup, sour cream, and green onions. Lightly grease a 9 x 13-inch baking dish or small ramekins. Layer the potato mixture first, followed by Canadian bacon and hard-boiled eggs. Top with Cheddar cheese. Bake in a 350° oven for 45 minutes.

MAKES 8 SERVINGS.

Silver Rose Inn

351 Rosedale Road
Calistoga, California 94515
(707) 942-9581

Calistoga is, perhaps, best known for its hot springs frequented by Indians for hundreds of years and by tourists since the 1860s. The Sil-

ver Rose takes advantage of the steamy mineral waters with its own spa. Each spacious room has a private bath and is tastefully decorated and carefully designed around a special theme, such as teddy bears, garden elegance, safari, western, and oriental mystique. Many rooms offer fireplaces, whirlpool tubs, and private balconies.

Sally's Hawaiian Bread

1   cup oil
2   cups sugar
3   eggs
....
2½   cups all-purpose flour
1   teaspoon baking soda
1   teaspoon ground cinnamon
2   teaspoons vanilla extract
1   cup crushed canned pineapple, drained
1   cup shredded coconut
2   cups grated carrots

In a large bowl cream the oil, sugar, and eggs until light. In a separate bowl sift together the flour, soda, and cinnamon. Add the dry ingredients to the creamed mixture.

Gently fold in the vanilla, pineapple, coconut, and carrots. Divide the batter in 2 well-greased 5 x 9-inch loaf pans. Let the batter rest for 20 to 30 minutes.

Bake in oven at 350° oven for 60 minutes.

MAKES 2 LOAVES.

Sally's Zucchini Bread

3   eggs
1   cup oil
1¾   cups sugar
3   tablespoons vanilla extract
3   cup all-purpose flour
1   teaspoon baking soda
1   teaspoon baking powder
2   teaspoons ground cinnamon
1   teaspoon grated nutmeg
2   cups coarsely grated zucchini
1   cup chopped walnuts (optional)

In a large bowl mix together the eggs, oil, sugar, and vanilla. Add the flour, soda, baking powder, cinnamon, and nutmeg. Fold in the zucchini and walnuts last. Pour into 3

greased 5 x 9-inch loaf pans. Bake in a 350° oven for 1 hour, or until a toothpick inserted in the center comes out clean.

MAKES 3 LOAVES.

The J. Patrick House

2990 Burton Drive
Cambria, California 93428
(805) 927-3812

An authentic log cabin bed and breakfast inn, the J. Patrick House is graced by a passion vine-covered arbor and garden. The house itself has only one guest room, while seven others are located in the nearby Carriage House. All rooms are spacious and individually furnished with antiques. Hand-stitched quilts, feather-filled duvets, and fireplaces add comfort to the charm. The Hearst Castle as well as many delightful antique shops, art galleries, and restaurants are nearby.

Irish Soda Bread

1   cup butter or margarine
6   tablespoons sugar
4   cups all-purpose flour
1½   teaspoon baking soda
1   teaspoon salt
2   cups sour cream
1   cup raisins
2   tablespoons caraway seeds
   Milk

The J. Patrick House

In a mixing bowl cream the butter and sugar. In a separate bowl sift the flour, soda, and salt. Add the dry ingredients to the creamed mixture and beat with an electric mixer on low until it crumbles. Mix in the sour cream, raisins, and seeds until a dough forms. Turn out onto a floured board and lightly knead. Divide the dough in half and place on a baking sheet. Pat each into a smooth flat round, and brush with an small amount of milk to create a shiny crust. Bake in a 350° oven for 50 to 60 minutes.

MAKES 2 LOAVES, 14 SERVINGS.

J. Patrick House Vegetarian Pâté

  1   *tablespoon margarine*
  1   *tablespoon oil*
  1   *medium onion, chopped*
  1   *8-ounce can petite point peas*
  3   *hard-boiled eggs*
      Salt and pepper to taste
  1   *garlic clove*
  1   *tablespoon water*
  1   *cup ground pecans*

In a small skillet, melt the margarine and add the oil. Sauté the onion until translucent. Drain the peas. In a food processor combine the peas, eggs, onion, salt and pepper to taste, garlic, water, and pecans, and mix well. Transfer the mixture to a serving dish and refrigerate until chilled.

MAKES 6 TO 8 SERVINGS.

Cold Spiced Eggplant

  2   *medium eggplants*
  3   *tablespoons light soy sauce*
  2   *tablespoons red wine vinegar*
  2   *tablespoons sugar*
 ¼   *teaspoon salt*
1½   *teaspoons dry sherry*
  1   *tablespoon sesame oil*
      ....
  1   *tablespoon peanut or corn oil*
  1   *tablespoon chopped garlic*
  1   *tablespoon chopped fresh ginger*
  1   *tablespoon sesame seeds, toasted*

In the top of a steamer place the eggplants. Steam for 30 minutes, until tender to the cores and in a collapsed condition. Let cool.

In a small bowl combine the soy sauce, vinegar, sugar, salt, sherry, and sesame oil.

Set aside. In a saucepan heat the peanut or corn oil with garlic and ginger for about 10 seconds. Add the soy mixture to the saucepan. Bring just to a boil. Remove from heat, then cool. Toast the sesame seeds in a saucepan until pale brown with a nutty aroma. Do not burn. Cut or pull the eggplants into pieces, discarding peel. Pour cool sauce over the eggplant and sprinkle with toasted sesame seeds.

MAKES 8 SERVINGS.

Cobblestone Inn

❧

P.O. Box 3185
Carmel, California 93921
(800) 833-8836

*C*obblestone is an English country inn in a quiet corner of Carmel-by-the-Sea—a charming village noted for its fine restaurants, flower gardens, art galleries, and antique stores. A large inn with twenty-four rooms, it features a slate courtyard and English gardens to complement the quaint atmosphere of the town. Each room has a stone fireplace.

Chocolate Meringue Cookies

  3   *large egg whites*
 ¾   *cup sugar*
  6   *ounces bittersweet chocolate, melted*
      and cooled
1½   *teaspoons vanilla extract*
 ½   *cup chopped walnuts, pecans or*
      toasted almonds

In a large bowl beat egg whites to soft peaks. Gradually add the sugar, beating until stiff and glossy. Fold in the melted chocolate, then the vanilla and chopped nuts. Drop by teaspoonfuls onto a cookie sheet lined with parchment paper. Bake in a 350° oven for 10 to 20 min-

utes. Let the cookies cool completely on the trays before removing them.

MAKES 4 DOZEN.

Fudge Mound Cookies

  2   *cups all-purpose flour*
  1   *teaspoon baking powder*
  2   *teaspoons ground cinnamon*
 ½   *teaspoon nutmeg*
  1   *teaspoon salt*
  1   *teaspoon baking soda*
  6   *tablespoons unsweetened cocoa*
 ½   *cup shortening*
 ¾   *cup sugar*
 ¾   *cup brown sugar*
  1   *teaspoon vanilla extract*
  1   *cup mashed potatoes*
  1   *egg*
 ½   *cup milk*
      ....
  2   *cups confectioners' sugar*
  3   *to 4 teaspoons sweetened cocoa*
  3   *to 4 tablespoons hot coffee*
 ½   *teaspoon vanilla extract*

In a medium bowl mix together the flour, baking powder, cinnamon, nutmeg, salt, soda, and unsweetened cocoa. In a large bowl cream together the shortening, sugars, 1 teaspoon of vanilla, mashed potatoes, and egg. Add the dry ingredients to the creamed mixture, alternately with the milk. Allow the dough to stand for 10 minutes before baking. Drop by the tablespoonfuls onto a greased cookie sheet. Bake in a 350° oven for 15 minutes.

In a medium bowl mix together confectioners sugar, sweetened cocoa, hot coffee, and ½ teaspoon of vanilla. This is a light frosting. Let the cookies cool, then frost.

MAKES 3 DOZEN.

White Sulphur Springs Ranch

White Sulphur Springs Ranch

❧

P.O. Box 136 (Highway 89)
Clio, California 96106
(916) 836-2387, (800) 854-1797

Built in the 1850s, the inn was a family-run ranch and hotel for the Truckee-Quincy stagecoach. Much of the original furnishings remain. There are six guest rooms furnished in handcrafted antiques. Also available are a pair of charming guest cottages. The ranch features an Olympic-sized pool filled with warm mineral waters.

Chocolate Cheesecake Muffins

    1   3-ounce package cream cheese (or
        more)
    2   tablespoons sugar
    1   cup all-purpose flour
    ½   cup sugar
    3   tablespoons unsweetened cocoa
    2   tablespoons baking powder
    ½   teaspoon salt
    1   beaten egg
    ¾   cup milk
    ⅓   cup oil
        ....
        Confectioners' sugar (optional)

In a small bowl blend the cream cheese and 2 tablespoons of sugar until fluffy. Set aside. In a large bowl stir together the flour, ½ cup sugar, cocoa, baking powder, and salt. Make a well in the center of the dry ingredients. In a small bowl combine the egg, milk, and oil. Add all at once to the dry ingredients, stirring until moistened. The batter should be lumpy. Spoon about 1 tablespoon of chocolate batter into each greased muffin cup. Drop 1 teaspoon of cream cheese mixture on top and then more chocolate batter. Bake in a 375° oven for 20 minutes. Dust with confectioners' sugar, if desired.

MAKES 1 DOZEN.

Cranberry-Stuffed Apples

    2   cups fresh or dried cranberries
    ½   cup firmly packed brown sugar
    ½   cup water
    2   tablespoons lemon juice
    ⅛   teaspoon ground cinnamon
    4   McIntosh or Granny Smith apples,
        pared
        Mint sprigs for garnish

In a large skillet combine all ingredients except the apples. Mix well. Heat over medium heat to simmering. Reduce the heat to low.

Cut the apples lengthwise into halves and core them. Place cut-side-up in the skillet. Cover and simmer until the apples are firm-tender, about 7 minutes. Remove the apples from the skillet and top with the cranberry mixture. Garnish with a sprig of mint.

MAKES 4 SERVINGS.

Blueberry Rice Hot Cakes

    1   cup all-purpose flour
    ¼   cup sugar
    ½   teaspoon salt
    ½   teaspoon baking soda
    1½ cups buttermilk
    1   cup cooked long grain rice, cold
    2   large eggs, separated
    2   tablespoons butter, melted
    1   teaspoon vanilla extract
    ¾   cup blueberries
    2   tablespoons oil
        Walnut Honey Butter (recipe
        follows)

In a large bowl mix the flour, sugar, salt, and soda. In a separate bowl mix the buttermilk, rice, egg yolks, butter, and vanilla. Add the buttermilk mixture to the flour mixture and stir to mix. In a small bowl beat the egg whites until stiff but not dry. Fold into the batter. Fold in the blueberries. In a 12-inch skillet heat the oil over medium heat until hot. Using ¼ cup batter for each pancake, cook over medium heat until light brown, 2 to 3 minutes per side. Serve with Walnut Honey Butter.

MAKES 6 TO 8 SERVINGS.

Walnut Honey Butter

    ½   cup butter, room temperature
    ½   cup honey

    ¼   cup finely chopped walnuts
    ¼   teaspoon vanilla extract

In small mixer bowl combine all ingredients. Beat until light and fluffy.

MAKES 1¼ CUPS.

Blue Lantern Inn

❧

34343 Street of the Blue Lantern
Dana Point, California 92629
(800) 950-1236 for reservations

A panoramic view of the Pacific Ocean from the guest rooms and dining room will add to the enjoyment of staying at Blue Lantern Inn. A closer view can be gotten by riding along the shore on bicycles provided by the inn. Near Laguna Beach, this luxury inn is less than an hour's drive from major attractions such as Disneyland, San Diego, and Newport Beach.

Egg Rolls

    2   pounds ground pork
    1   pound cooked shrimp, chopped
    ½   pound cooked crab meat, shredded
    2   tablespoons sugar
    4   medium carrots, shredded
    1   bunch green onions, chopped
    2   small packages Chinese rice noodles
        Salt and pepper to taste
    24 egg roll wrappers
    1   egg, beaten
        Oil for deep frying

In a skillet sauté the pork. Remove the pan from the heat and add the shrimp, crab meat, sugar, carrots, and green onions. Toss in the Chinese rice noodles and season with salt and pepper to taste. Mix well. Place 2 tablespoons of filling in each wrapper. Brush with beaten egg. Deep fry in very hot oil until golden brown.

MAKES 2 DOZEN.

Pasta Salad

4 cups tri-color rotelli pasta, cooked
  and cooled
1 red bell pepper, chopped
1 green bell pepper, chopped
2 cups broccoli, chopped
½ bunch green onions, chopped
½ bunch parsley, chopped
1 tablespoon dried basil
1 6-ounce can black olives, sliced
½ tablespoon sugar
¼ cup olive oil
3 tablespoons white vinegar

In a large salad bowl mix together all ingredients and season to taste. Serve cold.
MAKES 12 SERVINGS.

Elk Cove Inn

6300 South Highway 1, P.O. Box 367
Elk, California 95432
(800) 275-2967

The scenic village of Elk was known as Greenwood during its days as a lively lumber town. In 1883 the inn's main house was built by a lumber company as an executive guest house. It was destined to become one the first B&Bs in California. The ocean views are extraordinary, and the accommodations include such personal touches as feather beds, down comforters, terry robes, and fresh flowers. Shops and restaurants are within easy walking distance, while historic Mendocino, Anderson Valley wineries, and redwood forests are only a short drive away.

Stuffed French Toast

5 to 6 slices raisin bread, cubed
2 8-ounce packages cream cheese
5 to 6 slices sourdough bread, cubed
  (remove crusts if desired)

12 eggs
2 cups milk
½ cup maple or pancake syrup (or a
  combination)
  Vanilla extract to taste
  Dash salt
  Berry Topping (recipe follows)

Spray a 9 x 13-inch baking dish with cooking spray. Place a thick layer of raisin bread cubes on the bottom. Slice the cream cheese and place on top of the bread. Add cubed sourdough on top of the cream cheese.

In a large bowl mix the remaining ingredients and pour over the bread. Cover and refrigerate overnight.

Bake uncovered in a 350° oven for about 45 to 50 minutes or until done. Top with Berry Topping.
MAKES 6 TO 8 SERVINGS.

Berry Topping

In a saucepan heat any combination of frozen berries, such as blackberries, blueberries, and strawberries. Add a little blackberry juice or water and sugar to taste. Spoon over squares of French toast. Top with sour cream and a "snowfall" of confectioners' sugar.

Looks especially good on a black or red plate.
MAKES 6 TO 8 SERVINGS.

Southern Spoon Bread (Corn Pudding)

½ cup butter
1 egg
1 cup sour cream
1 8½-ounce box corn bread mix
1 cup cream-style corn
1 cup whole kernel corn, drained

Melt the butter in a 1½-quart casserole dish. Mix in the egg and then all remaining ingredients. Bake in a 350° oven for approximately 1 hour.

Note: This is a great side dish to serve with chicken or pork, or served with egg soufflés and salsa.
MAKES 8 SERVINGS.

The Gingerbread Mansion Inn

400 Berding Street, P.O. Box 40
Ferndale, California 95536
(707) 786-4000

Ferndale is famous for its Victorian mansions, little changed since the 1800s. The Gingerbread, built in 1899, is one of the more appealing of the fanciful old mansions found along Main Street and is among the most photographed buildings in Northern California. The rooms are appointed with period antiques. Some feature fireplaces, claw-foot tubs, and stained-glass windows. Nearby are rivers, redwoods, fishing, beaches, and country backroads.

Baked Polenta

½ clove garlic
2 cups chicken broth
½ cup polenta
2 tablespoons butter
¼ cup greted Cheddar cheese

The Gingerbread Mansion

¼ cup grated Parmesan cheese

....

Melted butter
Parmesan cheese for topping

In a large saucepan combine the garlic and the chicken broth. Bring to a boil on high heat. Gradually add the polenta while stirring the broth. Reduce the heat and boil gently, stirring constantly, until the polenta becomes thick and pulls away from the sides of the pan, about 20 to 30 minutes. When thick, add 2 tablespoons butter and the Cheddar and Parmesan cheeses. Stir well to combine. Pour the mixture into a greased 5 x 9-inch loaf pan. When cool, cover and refrigerate overnight.

To serve, remove from the pan and slice ¾-inch thick and place overlapping slices in greased shallow casserole. Pour melted butter over the top and sprinkle with Parmesan cheese. Bake uncovered in a 350° oven for 30 minutes. Serve hot.

An excellent side dish for breakfast or dinner.

MAKES 4 SERVINGS.

Eggs Florentine with Creamy Cheese Sauce

12   *eggs*
1   *pint cottage cheese*
2   *cups grated Swiss cheese*
2   *cups cubed feta cheese*
¼   *cup butter, softened*
2   *10-ounce boxes frozen chopped spinach, thawed and drained*
1   *teaspoon grated nutmeg*
    Creamy Cheese Sauce (recipe follows)

In a large bowl beat eggs slightly. Add the cheeses and butter, and mix well. Stir in the spinach and nutmeg. Pour the mixture into 12 greased 8-ounce ramekins. Bake in a 350° oven for 30 to 45 minutes or until a toothpick inserted in the center comes out clean. Serve with Creamy Cheese Sauce.

MAKES 12 SERVINGS.

Creamy Cheese Sauce

2   *tablespoons butter*
3   *tablespoons all-purpose flour*
2   *cups milk*
2   *cups grated Jack cheese*

½   *teaspoon salt*
¼   *teaspoon dry mustard*
¼   *teaspoon cayenne pepper*

In a saucepan melt the butter. Stir in the flour and cook, stirring constantly for several minutes. Add the milk, stirring constantly, until the sauce begins to thicken and bubble. Stir in the Jack cheese and seasonings, and cook until the cheese is melted.

MAKES ABOUT 4 CUPS.

Eggs Benedict

1   *package English muffins*
2   *cups grated Swiss cheese*
12   *slices Canadian bacon*
12   *eggs*
2   *cups milk*
    Cayenne pepper to taste
    Black pepper to taste

....

    Creamy Hollandaise Sauce (recipe follows)

Grease 12 8-ounce ramekins and set aside. Cube the English muffins and place enough in each ramekin to fill halfway. Sprinkle the muffins with a small handful of Swiss cheese. Place a slice of Canadian bacon on the cheese and top with more cheese. In a large bowl beat the eggs slightly. Add the milk and peppers to taste. Divide among the ramekins. Cover and refrigerate overnight.

Bake uncovered in a 350° oven for 30 minutes. Spoon Creamy Hollandaise Sauce on top and sprinkle with paprika before serving.

MAKES 12 SERVINGS.

Creamy Hollandaise Sauce

½   *cup butter*
1   *tablespoon lemon juice*
3   *dashes cayenne pepper*
3   *egg yolks*
1   *tablespoon sherry*

In a saucepan melt the butter to a low boiling point. In a blender combine the remaining ingredients and blend at low speed until mixed. Slowly pour in the melted butter and blend 10 seconds or until thick and creamy.

MAKES ABOUT ¾ CUP.

The Grey Whale Inn

615 North Main Street
Fort Bragg, California 95437
(707) 964-0640, (800) 382-7244

A romantic bed and breakfast within walking distance of art galleries, fine restaurants, antique shops, and beaches, the Whale Inn is located in Fort Bragg on California's winding, twisting, and extraordinarily scenic Highway 1. Guest rooms are named and decorated to suit a variety of tastes. Penthouse rooms feature private decks and expansive views of the Pacific. The inn is within strolling distance of fine restaurants, art galleries, antique and gift shops, the famous Skunk Train, and beaches.

Chicken with Artichokes

4   *whole chicken breasts*
    Paprika
    Salt and pepper
¼   *cup butter or margarine*
2   *14-ounce cans artichoke hearts (packed in water)*
1   *pound mushrooms, sliced*
    Generous pinch dried tarragon
3   *tablespoon all-purpose flour*
⅓   *cup dry sherry*
1½   *cups chicken broth*

Split and debone the breasts. Season with paprika, salt, and pepper. In a skillet melt 2 tablespoons of the butter and sauté the chicken until browned. Place the chicken in a greased 2-quart casserole and add the artichokes.

In a skillet melt the remaining butter and brown the mushrooms. Season with tarragon. Add the flour to the mushrooms, blending well. Add the sherry and broth. Simmer a few minutes. Pour the sauce over the chicken. Cover. Bake in a 375° oven for 45 minutes.

Note: I usually prepare this casserole the day before serving: In a large bowl mix 1 box of Uncle Ben's wild rice mix plus 1 cup plain rice and 2 cups water. Place in 3-quart greased casserole dish, place the prepared chicken-mushroom-artichoke mixture on top, and refrigerate overnight. This permits flavors to blend. Bake in a 350° oven for 1 hour.

MAKES 4 TO 6 SERVINGS.

Carrot Bread

- 2 **cups date crystals**
- 1 **20-ounce can crushed pineapple with juice**

- 6 **cups presifted all-purpose flour**
- 2 **teaspoons ground cinnamon**
- 2 **teaspoons baking soda**
- 2 **teaspoons salt**
- 2 **cups lightly toasted walnuts, coarsely chopped**

- 2 **cups oil**
- 4 **cups sugar**
- 1 **tablespoon vanilla extract**
- 6 **eggs, room temperature**

- 4 **cups coarsely grated carrots**

In a medium bowl combine the date crystals and crushed pineapple. Set the mixture aside.

In a food processor combine the flour, cinnamon, soda, and salt. Process for 1 minute. Transfer the mixture to a large bowl. Add the walnuts.

In the food processor combine the oil, sugar, and vanilla. Add the eggs and pulse to combine. Pour the mixture into the dry ingredients, mixing just until blended. Fold in the carrots, and the dates and pineapple. Pour the batter into 2 greased and floured 12-cup tube pans. Bake in a 350° oven for 1 hour and 30 minutes or until a toothpick inserted in a cake comes out clean.

Cool for 15 minutes in the pans on a wire rack. Gently remove to wire racks to cool.

Note: Date crystals available from Shields Date Garden, 80-225 Highway 111, Indio, California 92201. Phone: 619-347-0996.

MAKES ABOUT 24 SERVINGS.

Southern Pecan Pie

- 3 **large eggs**
- 2/3 **cup sugar**
  Dash salt
- 1 **cup dark corn syrup**
- 1/3 **cup melted butter or margarine**
- 1 **cup pecan halves**
- 1 **9-inch unbaked pie shell**

In a medium bowl beat the eggs thoroughly with sugar, salt, corn syrup, and melted butter. Add the pecans. Pour into the unbaked pie shell. Bake in a 350° oven for 50 minutes or until a knife inserted halfway between the outside and center of the filling comes out clean.

MAKES 6 TO 8 SERVINGS.

Benbow Inn

❧

445 Lake Benbow Drive
Garberville, California 95542
(707) 923-2126

---

*T*he Benbow Inn first opened its doors to the public in 1926 and has played host to the likes of Herbert Hoover, Eleanor Roosevelt, and Charles Laughton. Over the years, the inn has been handsomely restored to provide more comfort for guests and to take advantage of its status as a historic landmark. Many rooms now feature fireplaces, Jacuzzis, and country decor. Antiques, paintings, and other art objects carry on the inn's long tradition of elegance. Complimentary hors d'oeuvres are served from 5 to 6:30 P.M. There is a basket of mysteries in every room.

Pumpkin Hazelnut Soup

- 2 **tablespoons olive oil**
- 1 **cup chopped yellow onion**
- 1 **cup chopped celery**
- 1/2 **cup dry white wine**
- 3 **cups pumpkin purée**
- 8 **cups water or chicken broth**
- 2 1/2 **tablespoons hazelnuts, toasted and ground**
- 1 **bay leaf**
  Salt and pepper to taste
- 1/2 **cup maple syrup**
- 2 **cups heavy cream**

In a large soup pot heat the olive oil and cook the onions and celery over low heat until onions are translucent but not brown.

Add the wine, pumpkin, water, 2 tablespoons of hazelnuts, and bay leaf, and bring to a boil. Reduce the heat and simmer for 1 hour.

Add the salt, pepper, and maple syrup, and continue to cook for 45 to 60 minutes. If the soup appears too thick, adjust with more water. In a blender or food processor purée the soup. Return to the pot and add the cream. Cook for 30 minutes. Remove the bay leaf, adjust the seasonings, and garnish with reserved hazelnuts.

MAKES 6 TO 8 SERVINGS.

Benbow Inn

Scones

- 1 3/4 **cups all-purpose flour**
- 1/4 **cup sugar**
- 1 **teaspoon salt**
- 2 **teaspoons baking powder**
- 1/2 **teaspoon baking soda**
- 5 **tablespoons unsalted butter**
  Approximately 1/2 cup heavy cream
- 1/4 **cup orange juice**
- 1/4 **cup grated orange zest**
- 1/2 **cup currants**
  Egg white, beaten

In a large bowl combine the flour, sugar, salt, baking powder, and soda, and mix well. Cut in the butter until the mixture resembles coarse crumbs. Add just enough cream and orange juice to form a soft dough. Add the orange zest and currants, and mix until combined. Turn out onto a floured board and roll out to 1-inch thickness. Cut into hearts and place on an ungreased baking sheet. Brush lightly with beaten egg white. Bake in a 350° oven for 15 to 20 minutes or until golden brown.

MAKES ABOUT 2 DOZEN.

Oatcakes

    2   quarts very hot tap water
    2   cups firmly packed brown sugar
    1   cup melted butter
    3   cups quick oats
    1   cup wheat germ
....
    1   tablespoon vanilla extract
    ¼   cup ground cinnamon
    1   teaspoon ground nutmeg
    2   teaspoons salt
    8   eggs, beaten
....
    4½ cups Krusteaz pancake flour
....
    3   Granny Smith apples, diced
    3   tablespoons baking powder

In a mixing bowl combine the water, brown sugar, butter, oats, and wheat germ. Mix thoroughly but gently. Allow to stand 5 minutes. Add the vanilla, cinnamon, nutmeg, salt, and eggs, and mix gently. Add the pancake flour and blend until the mixture resembles thick pancake batter. Add the apples and baking powder, and blend. Cook on a medium-hot griddle until brown on each side.

MAKES 3 GALLONS OF BATTER.

Campbell Ranch Inn

Campbell Ranch Inn

❧

1475 Canyon Road
Geyserville, California 95441
(707) 857-3476

***T**he spectacular view from the Campbell Ranch Inn is undoubtedly the highlight of this 35-acre ranch in the heart of the Sonoma County wine country with rolling vineyards and abundant flower gardens. A professional tennis court, hot tub spa, bicycles, horseshoes, and Ping-Pong table provide plenty of alternative ways to relax. The inn has four spacious rooms in the main house and a separate guest cottage. The inn has its own cookbook called* The Campbell Ranch Inn Cookbook *available for sale at the inn.*

Raspberry Cream Cheese Coffee Cake

    2½ cups all-purpose flour
    ¾   cup sugar
    ¾   cup butter
    ½   teaspoon baking powder
    ½   teaspoon baking soda
    ¼   teaspoon salt
    ¾   cup dairy sour cream
    1   egg
    1   teaspoon almond extract
....
    1   8-ounce package cream cheese
    ¼   cup sugar
    1   egg
    ½   cup raspberry jam
....
    ½   cup sliced almonds

In a large bowl combine the flour and ¾ cup of sugar. Cut in the butter with a pastry blender until the mixture resembles coarse crumbs. Remove 1 cup of crumbs for topping. To the remaining crumb mixture add the baking powder, soda, salt, sour cream, egg, and almond extract. Blend well. Spread over the bottom and 2 inches up the sides of a greased and floured 9-inch springform pan. Batter should be ¼ inch thick on the sides.

In a small bowl combine the cream cheese, ¼ cup of sugar, and egg. Blend well. Pour over the batter in the pan. Spoon jam evenly over the cheese filling.

In a small bowl combine the reserved crumbs and almonds. Sprinkle over the top. Bake in a 350° oven for 60 to 65 minutes or until the cream cheese is set and the crust is a deep golden brown. Cool for 15 minutes. Remove the sides and cool completely. Serve warm, room temperature, or cold.

MAKES 6 TO 8 SERVINGS.

Chocolate-covered Macadamia Nut Caramels

    1   cup butter
    1   pound light brown sugar
    1   cup light corn syrup
    1   cup sweetened condensed milk
    1   teaspoon vanilla extract
    1   7-ounce jar macadamia nuts

In a saucepan melt the butter and dissolve the brown sugar over low heat. Add the corn syrup, condensed milk, and vanilla. Cook slowly, stirring frequently, until the candy reaches 234°. Continue boiling for a few minutes, then add the macadamia nuts. Pour into an 8-inch square pan. Chill for several hours, but let it stand at room temperature for at least an hour before cutting into squares.

For plain caramels, wrap in waxed paper. These will keep several months in the refrigerator or freezer.

To coat them in chocolate, in the top of a double boiler melt the chocolate chips and paraffin. Using a spoon, dip each caramel square into the chocolate and place on waxed paper to cool and harden. Store in an airtight container in the refrigerator or freezer.

MAKES ABOUT 64 CANDIES.

Pavlova

    3   large egg whites
    ¾   cup sugar
    1   cup whipped cream
....
    1   to 2 pints fresh strawberries
        Confectioners' sugar (optional)

Lightly oil a grease-proof paper or shopping bag. Place the egg whites in a large clean bowl and have the sugar measured and ready to use. Whisk the egg whites until they form soft peaks and you can turn the bowl upside down without them sliding out. It's important not to overbeat the eggs because they will start to collapse. Add sugar 2 tablespoons at a time.

Spoon the meringue onto the greased sheet, forming an 8-inch circle. Make a round depression in the center. Bake the meringue in a 275° oven for 1 hour.

Turn the heat off and leave the Pavlova inside the oven until the oven is cold. Bake the night before and leave in the oven all night if you wish.

Just before serving, spread the whipped cream on top of the meringue and arrange the berries on top of that. Dust with confectioners' sugar if desired. Raspberries may also be substituted. The person who gave me this recipe used raspberries. She assembled it ahead and froze it, then removed it from the freezer 4 hours before she served it.

MAKES 4 TO 6 SERVINGS.

Peach-glazed Cheesecake

  1 **inner package graham crackers**
  ½ **cup margarine, melted**
  ¼ **cup sugar**
  3 **8-ounce packages cream cheese**
  4 **extra large eggs**
  2 **teaspoons vanilla extract**
  1 **cup sugar**
  2 **cups sour cream**
  1 **teaspoon vanilla extract**
  ¼ **cup sugar**

  1 **package Townhouse Peach Glaze**

In a medium bowl crush the graham crackers and mix well with the margarine and ¼ cup of sugar. Press into the bottom of a 10-inch springform pan.

In a large bowl beat together the cream cheese, eggs, 2 teaspoons vanilla, and 1 cup sugar until very smooth. Pour the batter over the crust and bake in a 375° oven for 30 minutes. Remove and cool slightly.

In a medium bowl beat together the last 3 ingredients. Pour over the cheesecake. Bake in a 475° oven for 10 minutes.

Remove the cheesecake from the oven and cool before refrigerating. Cover and store in the refrigerator before serving or wrap tightly and freeze.

Before serving, mix up Townhouse Peach Glaze according to the package directions. Slice fresh peaches into the glaze and toss to coat the peaches. Carefully remove the sides of the pan from the cheesecake. Arrange the peaches overlapping all around the outer edge of the cheesecake. Make a second layer coming in about an inch toward center. Continue until the entire cheesecake is covered. It will look like a beautiful dahlia. Remove from the refrigerator about 30 minutes before serving.

MAKES 8 SERVINGS.

Hope-Bosworth House and Hope-Merrill House

❧

21238 & 21253 Geyserville Avenue , P.O. Box 42 Geyserville, California 95441 (707) 857-3356

F or those who love Victorian architecture and sensibilities, the historic town of Geyserville,

Hope-Merrill House

California, offers a special treat: a pair of carefully restored inns facing one another across Geyserville Avenue. Their furnishings, wallpapers, and hospitality are perfectly true to the period. Built in 1904 of heart redwood, following a Queen Anne pattern-book design, the Hope-Bosworth House offers four immaculately appointed guest rooms. The neighboring Hope-Merrill House is an Eastlake Stick-style Victorian dating to the 1880s, and offers eight rooms as well as a swimming pool, lattice gazebo, and grape arbor in the back.

Blueberry Sausage Breakfast Bake

  2 **cups all-purpose flour**
  1 **teaspoon baking powder**
  ½ **teaspoon baking soda**
  ½ **cup butter**
  ¾ **cup sugar**
  ¼ **cup brown sugar**
  1 **egg**
  1 **8-ounce carton sour cream**
  1 **pound bulk pork sausage, cooked and well-drained**
  1 **cup blueberries**
  ½ **cup chopped pecans**

  ½ **cup sugar**
  2 **tablespoons cornstarch**
  ½ **cup water**
  2 **cups frozen blueberries**
  ½ **teaspoon lemon juice**

In a medium bowl stir together the flour, baking powder, and soda, and set aside. In a large bowl beat the butter with an electric mixer until fluffy. Add ¾ cup of sugar and the brown sugar, and beat until combined. Add the eggs and beat for an additional minute. Alternately add the dry ingredients and sour cream to the batter, beating after each addition just until combined. Fold in the sausage and berries. Pour the batter into a greased 9 x 13-inch baking pan. Spread the batter evenly in the pan. Sprinkle the pecans on top. Cover, and refrigerate overnight.

Bake in a 350° oven for 35 to 40 minutes. Cool on a wire rack.

In a medium saucepan combine ½ cup of sugar and the cornstarch. Add the water and 2 cups of blueberries. Cook, stirring constantly, over medium heat until thickened and bubbly. Cook for an addional 2 minutes. Stir in the lemon juice. Cool slightly.

MAKES 8 SERVINGS.

Artichoke Rice Salad

1 **package chicken-flavored rice mix**
4 **green onions, thinly sliced**
½ **green pepper, chopped**
11 **pimiento-stuffed olives, sliced**
2 **6-ounce jars marinated artichoke hearts**
⅓ **cup mayonnaise**
¾ **teaspoon curry powder**

In a saucepan cook the rice according to the package directions, omitting butter. Transfer to a large bowl and allow to cool.

Add the green onions, pepper, and olives. Drain the artichoke hearts, reserving the marinade. Cut the artichoke hearts in half, and add to the rice mixture. In a small bowl combine the reserved marinade, mayonnaise, and curry powder. Add the dressing to the salad, and toss to combine. Chill.

MAKES 4 TO 6 SERVINGS.

Gaige House Inn

13540 Arnold Drive
Glen Ellen, California 95442
(707) 935-0237

T he Gaige House is a wonderful home base for touring the Sonoma County wine country, celebrated as the "Valley of the Moon" in the writings of Jack London. All nine rooms of this nineteenth-century Victorian-style inn are immaculately appointed. Oversized towels, fluffy robes, and Ralph Lauren fabrics typify the English-style hospitality. Some rooms have bay windows or claw-foot tubs.

Sunrise Scrambled Eggs with Balsamic Tomatoes

3 **tablespoons plus 2 teaspoons butter, divided**
1 **medium onion, sliced**
½ **cup cottage cheese**
½ **cup sour cream**
1 **sheet packaged puff pastry dough, thawed as per package directions**
8 **eggs**
2 **tablespoon chives, chopped**
4 **medium tomatoes, sliced ¼ to ½ inch thick**
   Balsamic vinegar
   Salt and pepper to taste
4 **slices smoked salmon**

In a skillet melt 1 tablespoon of butter and sauté the onion until limp but do not brown, approximately 5 minutes. Set aside.

In a food processor purée the cottage cheese and sour cream until smooth. Set aside.

Roll the pastry into a 16 x 16-inch square and cut into 4 equal squares. Leaving a ½-inch border, use a fork and prick the pastry at ¼-inch intervals. Place on a cookie sheet and refrigerate for 15 minutes.

Remove the pastry from the refrigerator. Leaving a ½-inch border, spread 2 tablespoons of the cheese mixture onto the center of each pastry square. Reserve the remaining cheese mixture. Divide the onions evenly between the 4 pastry squares. Bake in a 400° oven for 12 to 15 minutes, until golden brown.

In a small bowl beat the eggs. Whisk in chives, mixing lightly. Heat a medium skillet and melt 2 teaspoons of butter. Add the eggs to the skillet and cook until the eggs are softly scrambled.

Heat a medium skillet, and melt 2 tablespoons of butter. When sizzling, add the tomatoes. Drizzle each tomato slice with balsamic vinegar, and sauté for 30 seconds on each side. Season with salt and pepper to taste.

Place each puff pastry square on a serving plate. Put 1 slice of smoked salmon on each square over the cheese and onion mixture. Spoon scrambled eggs on top of the salmon

Gaige House Inn

and place a dollop of the remaining cheese mixture on the eggs. Place 2 slices of tomato beside the pastry and garnish with the chives.

MAKES 4 SERVINGS.

House Cured Pork Chops

½ **gallon water**
⅓ **cup sugar**
⅓ **cup kosher salt (must be kosher, regular salt is too salty)**
1 **onion, sliced**
1 **lemon, sliced**
1 **orange, sliced**
1½ **cups orange juice**
3 **or 4 cloves**
6 **thick-cut pork chops**

In a large pot, combine the water, sugar, and salt, and stir until dissolved. Add the remaining ingredients including the pork chops, cover, and refrigerate overnight.

Remove the pork chops from the brine and pat dry. Discard the brine.

Prepare a barbecue grill. Grill each pork chop 5 minutes on each side. Serve with Apple Compote and Johnny Cakes (recipes follow).

MAKES 6 SERVINGS.

Apple Compote

3 **Gala apples**
3 **Granny Smith apples**
½ **cup dried cranberries**
2 **cinnamon sticks**
   Apple juice to cover apples
   Lemon juice (optional)
   Light brown sugar (optional)

Peel the apples and remove the seeds. Cut each into eighths. Place in a saucepan with the dried cranberries and cinnamon sticks. Add apple juice to cover. Cook until the apples "give" when pressed with a finger. Taste, if too sweet add the lemon juice. If tart, add brown sugar to taste. Serve over pork chops.

MAKES 6 SERVINGS.

Johnny Cakes

1½ cups water
1 cup cornmeal
½ teaspoon kosher salt
4½ tablespoons unsalted butter
1 cup milk
½ cup half and half

In a heavy sauce pan bring the water to a boil. Add the cornmeal and salt and cook for 2 to 3 minutes, stirring constantly. Add the butter and stir until melted and combined. In a separate bowl mix the milk and half and half and add slowly to the cornmeal mixture. Stirring constantly for 6 to 7 minutes. The batter will be thick. Spoon approximately 2 tablespoons of the mixture at a time on a hot greased griddle. Cook on each side until crispy brown. Serve with apple compote.

MAKES 6 SERVINGS.

Applewood Inn

❦

13555 Highway 116
Guerneville, California 95446
(707) 869-9093

*E*ncircled by apple orchards and redwoods, the inn consists of two Mediterranean-style villas with a total of sixteen guest rooms, all individually decorated. Comforters, pressed linens, and European styling enhance the Continental atmosphere. A daily wine and hors d'oeuvres hour at sunset reflects Sonoma County's reputation for fine food and drink. Sundays at Applewood feature a champagne brunch with romantic guitar music.

Poached Eggs and Tomatoes on Bacon and Potato Pancakes with Basil Hollandaise

½ cup chopped onion
1½ cups coarsely grated, peeled russet potatoes (about 1½ large potatoes)
½ teaspoon salt
¼ teaspoon fresh ground pepper
2 slices of bacon, cooked and crumbled
4 slices vine-ripened tomatoes, ¼ inch thick
4 large eggs, poached
1 cup Basil Hollandaise (recipe follows)
4 basil sprigs for garnish

In a medium bowl combine the onion, potatoes, salt, pepper, and bacon. For each pancake, spread ½ cup of mixture on an oiled grill or skillet, keeping the pancakes 2 inches apart. Cook over moderately low heat, undisturbed, for 20 minutes. Increase the heat to moderate and cook the pancakes for 5 to 10 minutes more or until the undersides are browned. Turn the pancakes and cook them for 10 minutes more. The pancakes may be kept warm in a preheated 250° oven for up to 30 minutes, while you poach the eggs.

Arrange the pancakes on heated breakfast plates, top each with a tomato slice and then top each tomato with a hot poached egg. Spoon some of the hollandaise over the eggs. Garnish with the basil sprigs and serve.

MAKES 4 SERVINGS.

Basil Hollandaise

½ cup unsalted butter
2 large egg yolks
4 teaspoons fresh lemon juice
2 teaspoons Dijon mustard
1 cup packed basil leaves
Salt and freshly ground pepper to taste

In a saucepan melt the butter over moderate heat and keep it warm. In a blender or food processor blend the egg yolks, lemon juice, mustard, and basil leaves for 5 seconds. With the motor running add the melted butter in a slow stream. Process until smooth. Pour the

mixture into the top of a double boiler and cook over simmering water constantly, until the sauce is thick. Season with salt and pepper. Serve immediately.

MAKES ABOUT 1¼ CUPS.

Chicken with Riesling and Apples

2 tablespoons unsalted butter
4 Gravenstein apples, peeled and thinly sliced
1 tablespoon sugar
1 tablespoon candied ginger, sliced
3 tablespoons Calvados or applejack
¼ cup Alexander Valley Vineyards Johannisberg Riesling
8 whole boned, skinned chicken breasts
Salt and fresh ground pepper to taste
3 tablespoons unsalted butter
1 tablespoon oil
2 shallots, diced
½ cup rich chicken stock
1 pint heavy cream
Roasted potatoes

In a large skillet melt 2 tablespoons of butter over medium-low heat. Add the apples in a single layer, sprinkle with sugar and add the candied ginger. Sauté, turning, until slightly browned, 3 to 4 minutes.

In a small saucepan warm the Calvados over low heat. Carefully pour it over the apples and ignite, shaking the pan until the flames subside.

Add the Riesling and cook until the apples are tender, about 3 minutes. Set aside. Season the chicken breasts with salt and pepper. In a large skillet melt 3 tablespoons of butter with the oil over medium heat. Add the chicken and brown it on both sides. Remove from the skillet and set aside.

Let the skillet cool to medium. Add the shallots and sauté for 2 minutes. Return the chicken to the skillet, cover partially, and cook until just done, about 5 minutes. Set aside and keep warm.

Discard the fat in the skillet and add the broth. Cook over medium-high heat, scraping up the brown bits from the bottom of the skillet. Add the cream and reduce the heat to low. Gently simmer the broth and cream until thickened, about 5 minutes. Add the chicken and apples, and heat through. Serve with roasted potatoes.

MAKES 4 TO 6 SERVINGS.

Applewood's Mediterranean Orzo Salad

- ¾ *pound orzo*
- ½ *cup plus 1 tablespoon olive oil*
- 2 *teaspoons fresh lemon juice*
- 3 *tablespoons champagne vinegar*
  Pinch thyme
- ½ *teaspoon dried oregano*
- ¼ *teaspoon ground cumin*
  Salt and pepper to taste
- 1 *teaspoon Dijon mustard*
- ½ *cup pitted kalamata olives*
- ½ *sweet red bell pepper, chopped*
- ½ *yellow bell pepper, chopped*
- ¼ *cup minced green scallion*
- 2 *teaspoons capers*
- 2 *ounces herbed feta cheese, crumbled*
- 1 *bunch spinach, washed*
- 3 *tablespoons toasted pine nuts*

In a saucepan cook the orzo according to package instructions to al dente, drain, and place in an ice-water bath to stop cooking. Drain thoroughly and toss with 2 tablespoons of the olive oil. In a small bowl combine the remaining olive oil with lemon juice, vinegar, herbs, spices, and mustard. Whisk until smooth and set aside.

Place the orzo in a large bowl and add the olives, red and yellow peppers, scallions, and capers. When ready to serve add the feta cheese and dressing. Toss well.

Arrange the spinach leaves attractively on a serving platter or individual salad plates. Mound the orzo mixture on top of the spinach, allowing the spinach to peek out from under the salad. Garnish with pine nuts and serve.

Note: Regular feta cheese may be substituted if herbed feta is unavailable. Adding pieces of roasted chicken to the salad would make it a wonderful meal in itself when combined with crusty French bread and a bottle of excellent Sonoma County Chardonnay.

MAKES 6 TO 8 SERVINGS.

Torta Di Riso (Rice Torte)

- 4 *cups water*
- 1⅓ *cups rice*
- 2 *tablespoons olive oil*
- 1 *teaspoon salt*
- 1 *chicken bouillon cube*
- 3 *tablespoons finely minced onion*
- 3 *tablespoons finely chopped Italian parsley*
- 2 *cloves garlic, minced*
  Pinch fresh thyme
  Pinch fresh oregano
- ¾ *cup freshly grated Parmesan cheese*
- 4 *eggs, slightly beaten (beat and reserve 1 egg separately)*
- 2 *tablespoons olive oil*
- ½ *cup milk*
  Fresh breadcrumbs
- 2 *tablespoons olive oil*

In a saucepan bring the water to a boil. Add the rice, 2 tablespoon of olive oil, salt, and bouillon cube, and cook for 15 minutes. Cool.

Add the chopped onion, parsley, garlic, thyme, oregano, all but 3 tablespoons of the Parmesan cheese, 3 beaten eggs, milk, and 2 tablespoons of olive oil. Stir well.

Oil the bottom and sides of a 9 x 13-inch baking dish. Dust with breadcrumbs. Pour in the rice mixture. In a small bowl beat the remaining egg with the remaining 2 tablespoons of olive oil and spread over the top of the rice mixture. Sprinkle the reserved 3 tablespoons of Parmesan cheese over all. Bake in a 375° oven for 30 to 40 minutes. Cut into 1½-inch squares and serve warm or cold.

MAKES ABOUT 48 SQUARES.

Thai Coconut Cream Tart with Macadamia Nut Crust

- ⅔ *cup roasted, unsalted macadamia nuts*
- 1½ *cups unbleached flour*
- ¼ *cup sugar*
- ½ *teaspoon salt*
- ½ *cup chilled unsalted butter, cut into pieces*
- 2 *egg yolks*

....

- 1½ *teaspoons unflavored gelatin*
- 2 *tablespoons dark rum*
- 8 *egg yolks*
- 10 *tablespoons sugar*
  Pinch salt
- 2 *cups canned Thai coconut milk*
- 1 *cup chilled heavy cream, whipped into soft peaks*

....

- ¾ *cup sweetened shredded coconut, toasted*
- ¾ *cup coarsely chopped, unsalted macadamia nuts, toasted*

In a food processor finely chop the nuts using on/off pulses. Add the flour, ¼ cup of sugar, salt, and butter. Process until the mixture resembles coarse meal. Mix in the 2 yolks. Press the dough over the bottom and up the sides of an 11-inch tart pan with a removable bottom. Cover and place in the freezer for 30 minutes.

Bake in a 375° oven for about 30 minutes until golden brown. Cool completely on a rack.

In a small bowl sprinkle the gelatin over the rum. In a medium bowl whisk together the 8 yolks, 10 tablespoons of sugar, and salt. In a heavy saucepan bring the coconut milk to a boil. Gradually whisk some of the coconut milk into the yolk mixture. Return the mixture to the saucepan and stir over medium-low heat until the custard thickens and coats the back of a spoon. Do not boil. Pour into a bowl. Add the gelatin mixture and stir until dissolved. Refrigerate until thickened but not set, stirring frequently.

Fold the heavy cream into the coconut filling. Pour into the crust. Refrigerate until set, at least 2 and up to 6 hours.

Sprinkle toasted coconut and macadamia nuts over the tart. Cut into wedges and serve.

MAKES 8 TO 10 SERVINGS.

Blackberry Clafouti

- 1½ *cups all-purpose flour*
- ½ *cup unsalted butter, chilled and cut into small pieces*
- ¼ *teaspoon salt*
- ¼ *cup cold water*

....

- 3 *cups fresh blackberries, plus extras for garnish*

....

- 4 *large eggs*
- 1½ *cups sugar*
- ¾ *cup unsalted butter, melted and cooled*
- ¼ *cup all-purpose flour*
- 1 *teaspoon vanilla extract*

....

  Whipped cream, crème fraîche, or ice cream
  Confectioners' sugar for garnish
  Fresh berries for garnish

Grease an 11-inch tart pan with removable bottom. In a medium bowl combine 1½ cups of flour, ½ cup of butter, and salt. Cut the butter into the flour until it resembles coarse meal. Add the water and mix until the dough comes away from the sides of the bowl. Wrap in plastic wrap and refrigerate for 30 minutes.

Roll the pastry into a 12-inch circle and place in the prepared tart pan. Trim the edges, fill with the berries and set aside.

In a medium bowl mix together the eggs, sugar, ¾ cup of butter, ¼ cup of flour, and vanilla. Pour over the berries. Bake in a 350° oven for 1 hour. Serve warm or cooled with whipped cream, crème fraîche, or ice cream. Garnish with confectioners' sugar and fresh berries.

MAKES 8 SERVINGS.

Old Thyme Inn

❧

779 Main Street
Half Moon Bay, California 94019
(415) 726-1616

A Queen Anne Victorian built in 1899, it's seven guest rooms are named for herbs such as rosemary, mint, lavender, and so forth. The fragrant English herb garden has over 50 varieties of herbs and flowers, and is a tranquil setting for guests. Several rooms provide extra warmth with fireplaces and whirlpool baths. Only a short walk away are the beaches, shops, galleries, and cafés of historic Half Moon Bay.

Old Thyme Inn
Glazed Apple Bread

½ cup canola oil
1 cup sugar
1 teaspoon vanilla extract

Old Thyme Inn

2 large eggs
2 cups sifted unbleached flour
½ teaspoon ground cinnamon
½ teaspoon salt
2 teaspoons baking powder
2 tablespoons milk
½ cup raisins
2 large baking apples, chopped and unpeeled
½ cup chopped walnuts
½ cup confectioners' sugar, sifted
1 tablespoon water
2 tablespoons melted butter

In a large bowl combine the oil, sugar, and vanilla. Cream until light and fluffy. Add the eggs and beat well. In a small bowl sift together the flour, cinnamon, salt, and baking powder. Add the milk, raisins, apples, and nuts. Add the dry ingredients and stir only until just moistened. Pour the batter into a well-greased 5 x 9-inch loaf pan. Bake in a 350° oven for 50 to 60 minutes. Cool. Remove the bread from the pan.

In a small bowl combine the remaining ingredients. Mix well and pour over the loaf. Let the glaze set before the wrapping loaf tightly. Best if made a day prior to serving.

MAKES 1 LOAF.

George's Best
Blueberry Muffins

2 cups all-purpose flour
½ cup sugar
1 tablespoon baking powder
1 teaspoon baking soda
¾ teaspoon salt
2 large eggs
¾ cup buttermilk
6 tablespoons melted butter
2 teaspoons grated lemon zest

2 teaspoons vanilla extract
1½ cups blueberries
2 tablespoons sugar
½ teaspoon ground cinnamon

Grease and flour 12 muffin cups with cooking spray. In a large bowl sift together the flour, sugar, baking powder, soda, and salt. In a separate bowl combine the eggs, buttermilk, butter, lemon zest, and vanilla. Stir the liquid mixture into the dry ingredients just until moistened. Fold in the fruit, mixing just enough to combine. Fill the muffin cups three-fourths full. In a small bowl combine 2 tablespoons of sugar and the cinnamon. Top each muffin with a sprinkling of cinnamon-sugar. Bake in a 400° oven for 20 to 25 minutes or until golden brown. Best served piping hot!

MAKES 1 DOZEN.

Cranberry Orange Muffins

2½ cups all-purpose flour
⅔ cup sugar
1 teaspoon baking powder
1 teaspoon baking soda
½ teaspoon salt
2 eggs
½ cup canola oil
1 teaspoon vanilla extract
1 cup buttermilk
1 cup cranberries (fresh or frozen)
 Grated zest of 1 orange
 Cinnamon-sugar

In a medium bowl combine the dry ingredients. In a large bowl combine the cranberries and orange zest. In a 2-cup measure combine the eggs, oil, and vanilla, then fill to the 2-cup level with buttermilk. Add the liquid mixture to the cranberries. Add the dry ingredients to the liquid mixture. Fill 12 greased muffin cups. Sprinkle the tops with cinnamon sugar. Bake in a 400° oven for approximately 20 minutes. The tops should be firm, brown, and crunchy. Enjoy!

MAKES 1 DOZEN.

356 Main Street
Half Moon Bay, California 94019
(415) 726-3425

O*riginally called the Mosconi Hotel, this Half Moon Bay landmark was completed in 1905. Painstakingly restored, it operates today as a bed and breakfast inn. The twelve guest rooms are decorated with period antiques that bespeak the building's historic status. Victorian fixtures and stained glass enhance the overall feeling of elegance. The downstairs restaurant gives the sense of a French country inn.*

San Benito House Whole Wheat Bread

    2   cups warm water (105 to 115°)
 1½   tablespoons active dry yeast
 1½   tablespoons firmly packed brown
         sugar
....
    1   tablespoon salt
  ¾   cup dark molasses
  ¾   cup oil
    5   cups all-purpose flour
    2   cups whole wheat flour

In a large bowl combine the warm water, yeast, and brown sugar. Stir gently. Let the mixture rest for 20 minutes in a warm place, until bubbles form on the surface. Add the salt, molasses, and oil. Add the flours and mix until a dough forms. Turn the sticky dough onto a counter and knead for 2 to 3 minutes, adding up to 1 cup of all-purpose flour. The dough is finished when it is smooth and elastic and doesn't stick to your hands. Place in an oiled bowl, cover with plastic, and place in a warm place until it has doubled in bulk.

Shape the dough into 2 long loaves and place on a large baking tray. Let the loaves rise until doubled in bulk.

Bake in a 300° oven for 1 hour and 15 minutes.

MAKES 2 LARGE LOAVES.

211 North Street
Healdsburg, California 95448
(800) 727-8182

T*he Camellia Inn was originally built in 1869, and subsequently owned by a doctor who used the home for his residence, offices, and the town's first hospital. Conveniently situated two blocks from the tree-shaded town plaza of Healdsburg, the inn provides ready access to the Russian River and a notable array of recreational opportunities, such as hiking, fishing, canoeing, swimming, bicycling, golf, tennis, and ballooning. In the evening, guests often gather in the double parlors near the marble fireplaces.*

Spicy Macaroni and Spinach

    3   pounds fresh spinach
    4   serrano chilies chopped
    3   tablespoons butter
    3   tablespoons all-purpose flour
    2   cups hot milk
    1   cup heavy cream
         Salt and pepper to taste
    3   tablespoons butter or oil
  ½   cup chopped red bell pepper
  ½   cup chopped onion
    1   cup sliced mushrooms
 1½   pounds macaroni, uncooked
    1   cup grated Parmesan or Asiago
         cheese

Wash the spinach. In a saucepan cook the spinach with the water that clings to its leaves and the chilies until wilted.

In a small skillet melt 3 tablespoons of butter. Add the flour and cook for about 1 minute. Add the hot milk and stir until thickened. Add the cream and heat, then set aside. Season with salt and pepper.

In a food processor or blender purée the spinach and chilies. Add the purée to the white sauce.

In a skillet heat 3 tablespoons of butter or oil. Sauté the red pepper, onion, and mushrooms until tender.

In a large pot cook the macaroni in boiling water until just tender. Drain.

In a 3-quart casserole layer the macaroni, sautéed vegetables, and spinach sauce. Top with Parmesan or Asiago cheese. Bake in a 350° oven for 20 minutes.

MAKES 8 SERVINGS.

French Apple Quiche

    2   tablespoons dried currants soaked
  ¼   cup brandy
         Pastry for 1 9-inch pie
    2   cups sliced and peeled tart cooking
         apples
  /2   teaspoon ground cinnamon
    3   eggs
    1   cup heavy cream

In a small bowl soak the currants in the brandy until plumped. Drain.

Roll the pastry out to fit a 9-inch tart pan. Place the pastry in the pan. Bake in a 425° oven for 7 minutes. Arrange the sliced apples in the partially baked pie shell. Sprinkle with the currants and cinnamon. In a medium bowl beat the eggs lightly. Blend in the cream. Pour the egg mixture over the apple mixture. Bake in a 325° oven for 40 to 50 minutes or until set. Cool before serving.

Note: This is a wonderful breakfast served with ham or sausages. It is equally good as a dessert. Recipe can be doubled.

MAKES 8 TO 10 SERVINGS.

Rhubarb Tort

 1½   cups all-purpose flour
  ¼   cup confectioners' sugar
  ¾   cup butter, cut in pieces
    5   large stalks rhubarb
 2¼   cups sugar

4 eggs
1 tablespoon vanilla extract
¼ teaspoon salt
¼ cup all-purpose flour

Grease an 11 x 15-inch baking pan. In a food processor combine 1½ cups of the flour, the confectioners' sugar, and butter, processing until the mixture starts to come together, approximately 1 minute. Press into the bottom of a 9-inch square pan. Bake in a 350° oven for 20 minutes.

Slice the rhubarb coarsely and spread in the partially baked crust. In the food processor blend the sugar, eggs, vanilla, and salt until thick. Add ¼ cup of flour and process about 10 seconds. Cover the rhubarb with the batter mixture. Bake in a 350° oven for about 35 minutes, until the top is brown and firm. Cool completely before serving. Cut into squares.

MAKES 24 SQUARES.

Madrona Manor

*1001 Westside Road, P.O. Box 818
Healdsburg, California 95448
(707) 433-4231*

An amazing 1881 three-story Victorian, the Madrona is a nineteenth-century palace set in the heart of Sonoma County's wine country. The main house offers nine guest rooms, all with fireplaces and all lavishly decorated. Additional rooms and suites are located in the carriage house, garden cottage, and other manor buildings. The food, which emphasizes excellence in preparation and, of course, in wine pairings, is like the manor itself, nothing short of extraordinary.

Corn Cakes with Shrimp Salsa, Sour Cream, and Caviar

4 ears corn, scraped
1 tablespoon roasted green bell pepper, sliced
1 egg
  Salt and pepper to taste
1 teaspoon baking powder
½ cup masa flour
....
  *Rock Shrimp Salsa (recipe follows)
  Sour cream and caviar for garnish*

Grind the corn kernels or chop coarsely in a food processor. Strain off some of the liquid or "milk." Add the bell pepper, egg, salt, pepper, baking powder, and masa flour, and mix thoroughly. In a skillet heat a small amount of oil over moderate heat. Drop the batter by heaping tablespoons into the hot oil. Turn over after a few minutes and the cakes are a nice brown color. Serve with Rock Shrimp Salsa. Garnish with a dollop of sour cream and caviar.

MAKES 8 CAKES.

Rock Shrimp Salsa

½ cup rock shrimp, cooked and chopped
½ cup fresh corn kernels, blanched
1 tablespoon chopped cilantro
¼ red tomato, chopped
¼ yellow tomato, chopped
¼ orange tomato, chopped
  Juice of ½ lime or lemon
  Salt to taste
  Few strands saffron
¾ cup extra virgin olive oil

In a serving bowl combine all of the ingredients, and mix thoroughly.

MAKES ABOUT 2½ CUPS.

Madrona Manor

California Seafood Cocktail

2 cups fish broth or clam juice
¼ cup catsup
  Hot sauce to taste
4 calimari, cleaned and poached
4 scallops, cut in half and poached
3 ounces salmon, cut into ¼-inch cubes and poached
6 prawns, cleaned, poached
2 tablespoon diced red onions
1 tablespoon diced red bell pepper
¼ avocado, diced
1 tablespoon chopped cilantro
  Corn chips
  Lemon wedges

In a small bowl combine the fish broth, catsup, and hot sauce. Mix well.

Place the seafood in a margarita glass. Add the vegetables and cilantro. Pour the cocktail base over the seafood and vegetables. Garnish the plate with corn chips and lemon wedges.

MAKES 1 TO 2 SERVINGS.

Sonoma County Rack of Lamb with Honey-glazed Root Vegetables, Potato Gateau, and Currant-Marjoram Sauce

2 tablespoons olive oil
1 tablespoon red wine
1 teaspoon chopped garlic
1 tablespoon chopped mixed fresh herbs
  Salt and pepper to taste
1 rack of lamb
....
12 potatoes, peeled and sliced very thin
1 tablespoon chopped fresh herbs
  Salt and pepper to taste
3 tablespoons clarified butter
2 turnips, peeled, cut into wedges
2 rutabagas, peeled, cut into wedges
1 carrot, peeled, cut in half and then into wedges
2 parsnips, peeled and cut into wedges
2 tablespoons butter
2 teaspoons chopped mixed fresh herbs
1 tablespoon honey
  Salt and pepper to taste
....
1 cup reduced lamb stock

2 cups red wine
1 teaspoon marjoram, chopped
2 tablespoons currants

In a shallow bowl combine the olive oil, red wine, garlic, 1 tablespoon of mixed herbs, and salt and pepper to taste. Marinate the lamb in a glass dish for 3 hours in the mixture.

Grill the lamb to the desired temperature.

Line a 12 x 3 x 2½-inch terrine mold with plastic wrap. Toss the potatoes with 1 tablespoon of fresh herbs, salt, and pepper to taste. Layer the potatoes in the mold. Pour the butter over the potatoes. Cover with a lid or aluminum foil. Bake in a 350° oven for 1 hour and 15 minutes. Remove the potato gâteau from the oven and weigh down. Refrigerate overnight. To serve, unmold, slice down the middle, and cut into 16 pieces. Heat in a 350° oven for 15 minutes.

In a saucepan blanch the turnips, rutabagas, carrot, and parsnips. In a sauté pan heat 2 tablespoons of butter. Add the blanched vegetables, 2 teaspoons of fresh herbs, honey, and salt and pepper to taste. Sauté a few minutes to get a light golden color. Serve hot.

In a saucepan combine the lamb stock, red wine, marjoram, and currants. Bring the mixture to a boil. Reduce the heat and simmer until the sauce is reduced to the desired consistency. Transfer to a serving dish.

On serving plates arrange servings of lamb, potato gâteau, and the honey-glazed root vegetables. Serve the currant-marjoram sauce on the side.

MAKES 8 SERVINGS.

P.O. Box 1818
Idyllwild, California 92549
(909) 659-3202

The cedar-shingled exterior of this rambling large home in the San Jacinto Mountains blends in quietly with the surrounding pines and

oaks. Guests may enjoy full breakfast in the glassed-in porch. Decks and hammocks draw guests outside during the day, while on cool mountain evenings they may gather around the living room fireplace.

Strawberry Creek Inn

German French Toast with Bratwurst (Arme Ritter-Poor Knights)

4 eggs, separated
Grated zest of 1 lemon
2½ cups milk
1 to 2 cups unseasoned breadcrumbs
8 slices stale French bread, 1 inch thick
3 large Granny Smith apples, sliced
2 tablespoons lemon juice
4 links smoked bratwurst, sliced thin
¼ small onion, chopped
Cinnamon-sugar mixture
Maple syrup

In a shallow bowl combine the egg yolks, lemon zest, and milk and mix well. In a separate bowl beat the egg whites until smooth (not whipped). Place the breadcrumbs in a third bowl. Lightly grease a cookie sheet. Soak the bread in the egg-milk mixture, then the egg whites. Dip the bread into the breadcrumbs and place on the cookie sheet. Bake in a 435° oven for 15 minutes, turn and bake for another 10 minutes.

Meanwhile place the apple slices and lemon juice in a saucepan with water and bring to a boil. In a skillet sauté the smoked bratwurst until browned. Place 2 slices of toast on 4 plates, sprinkle with cinnamon-sugar, and add the apples. Place the sliced bratwurst with the toast and serve with maple syrup.

MAKES 4 SERVINGS.

Baked Sour Cream Omelet

½ loaf French bread, sliced
4 ounces Gruyère cheese, shredded
4 ounces Monterey Jack cheese, shredded
12 slices bacon, cooked and crumbled
2 scallions, chopped
8 medium eggs
1⅓ cups milk
⅓ cup white wine
1 teaspoon Dijon mustard
¾ cup sour cream
¼ teaspoon black pepper
⅛ teaspoon cayenne pepper
½ cup grated Parmesan cheese
Paprika

Spray a 9 x 13-inch baking dish with cooking spray. Cover the bottom with bread slices and sprinkle cheeses, bacon, and scallions over the bread. In a mixing bowl beat together the eggs, milk, wine, mustard, sour cream, and peppers until foamy. Pour the egg mixture evenly over the cheese and bread. Cover tightly with foil. Bake in a 325° oven for 45 minutes or until set. Remove the foil and sprinkle the omelet with Parmesan cheese and paprika. Return uncovered to the oven and bake until lightly browned, about 10 minutes.

May be made the night before, covered tightly with foil, and refrigerated. In the morning remove from the refrigerator and let stand at room temperature for 30 minutes, still covered tightly.

Ten Inverness Way Bed and Breakfast

10 Inverness Way, P.O. Box 63
Inverness, California 94937
(415) 669-1648

Only about an hour's drive from Napa, Sonoma, and San Francisco, Ten Inverness Way B&B is a great place for a quick escape. The adjacent *Point Reyes National Seashore is perfect for hikers, with lots of ocean birds and other wildlife and one of the most scenic lighthouses in the United States. Guest rooms have queen-size beds, private baths, and spectacular views of either Tomales Bay or Inverness Ridge. There's also a suite with a private patio and its own kitchen.*

Banana Buttermilk Buckwheat Pancakes

⅓ cup unbleached flour
⅓ cup whole wheat flour
⅓ cup buckwheat flour
1 tablespoon sugar
2 teaspoons baking powder
½ teaspoon baking soda
¼ teaspoon salt
1 egg
2 tablespoons oil
1 cup buttermilk
1 very ripe mashed banana
   Maple syrup

In a medium bowl combine the flours, sugar, baking powder, soda, and salt. In a large bowl combine the remaining ingredients except the maple syrup. Stir the dry ingredients into the liquid mixture. Drop by ¼ cupfuls on a hot griddle. Cook until lightly browned, turn and cook the other side.

Serve with maple syrup.

MAKES 2 TO 3 SERVINGS.

Ten Inverness Way No-fat Granola

8 cups rolled oats
1½ cups wheat germ
1 cup flaked coconut
1 cup firmly packed dark brown sugar
½ cup water
1½ teaspoons vanilla extract

In a large bowl combine the rolled oats, wheat germ, and flaked coconut. In a separate bowl combine the brown sugar, water, and vanilla. Add the mixture to the dry ingredients and mix all thoroughly. Spread in a 11 x 17-inch pan. Bake in a 300° oven for about 1 hour. Stir often or it will burn. Cool in the

pan before storing in an airtight container in the refrigerator.

MAKES 11 CUPS.

Barbara's Butterscotch Cookies

½ cup oil
2 cups firmly packed light brown sugar
2 eggs
2 teaspoons vanilla extract
1½ cups all-purpose flour
2 teaspoons baking powder
1 teaspoon salt
1 cup coarsely chopped walnuts

In a large bowl combine the oil, light brown sugar, eggs, and vanilla. In a large bowl mix the flour, baking powder, and salt. Mix the dry ingredients into the liquid mixture. Stir in the walnuts. Divide the dough and create logs by heaping spoonfuls onto sheets of plastic wrap. Wrap and freeze for use at any time.

Place semifrozen hunks of dough on an ungreased cookie sheet. Bake in a 350° oven for about 8 minutes. Do not overbake. The cookies firm up when cooled.

Note: Don't be dismayed that there's no butter in these cookies. The flavor and consistency is most definitely butterscotch. Best results are achieved when batter is made by hand.

MAKES 2 TO 3 DOZEN.

*214 Shakeley Lane
Ione, California 95640
(209) 274-4468*

*T*he Heirloom *dates to 1863 and was home to one of Ione Valley's earliest families. Nowadays it serves as an elegant and historic hideaway for those who want to enjoy the natural beauty, fine wines, and outdoor sports available here in the heart of the California Gold*

Country. Guest rooms are named for the seasons and decorated to match. The French country breakfast is served in one's room, on the veranda, or in the fireside dining room.

The Heirloom

Polenta Benedict

1 recipe polenta
12 thin slices ham or prosciutto
12 eggs
....
¼ cup butter or margarine
1 28-ounce can crushed tomatoes
½ teaspoon basil
½ teaspoon salt
¼ teaspoon pepper
   Chopped parsley for garnish

Prepare the polenta in a 9 x 13-inch pan as directed on the package or according to a favorite recipe. Cool in the pan.

Cut the cooled polenta into 3-inch squares. Top each square with a thin slice of ham or prosciutto. Bake in a 350° oven for 5 minutes, just before serving.

In a saucepan combine the butter, tomatoes, basil, salt, and pepper. Simmer until heated through.

Soft-poach the eggs in an egg cooker. Place an egg on top of each serving of heated polenta. Top with tomato sauce. Garnish with chopped parsley.

MAKES 12 SERVINGS.

Spinach Soufflé: Heart Healthy

2 tablespoons butter
1 tablespoon all-purpose flour
¼ teaspoon salt

¼ teaspoon pepper
  Dash nutmeg
1 cube chicken bouillon
1 green onion, chopped
1 cup milk
½ cup Swiss cheese
1 10-ounce box frozen spinach,
    chopped, cooked, and squeezed dry
4 egg whites

In a saucepan melt the butter. Add the flour and seasonings and blend. Add the bouillon and onion and sauté until tender. Blend in the milk and cook until slightly thickened. Add the cheese and stir until melted. Add the spinach and remove the pan from the stove.

In a medium bowl beat the egg whites just until peaks form. Fold the whites into the mixture. Spoon into a 1-quart soufflé dish or 2 smaller dishes. Place in a pan of water. Bake in a 375° oven for 30 minutes.
MAKES 4 SERVINGS.

Orange Breakfast Rolls

1 package active dry yeast
¼ cup warm water (105 to 115°)
1 cup sour cream
1 teaspoon salt
3 tablespoons sugar
⅛ teaspoon baking soda
1 egg
2 tablespoons melted butter
3 cup all-purpose flour

⅔ cups sugar
1 cup shredded coconut
2 tablespoons shredded orange zest

1 cup confectioners' sugar
3 to 4 teaspoons orange juice

In a cup dissolve the yeast in the warm water. Set aside. In a saucepan heat the sour cream to lukewarm. In a large bowl blend salt, sugar, soda, egg, melted butter, sour cream, and yeast mixture. Add the flour and beat well. Knead the dough on a floured board. Shape into a ball and let rest 5 minutes. Roll into a 6 x 24-inch rectangle.

Brush the dough with melted butter. In a small bowl combine the sugar, coconut, and orange zest. Sprinkle over the dough. Starting with a long side, roll the dough as for jelly roll. Cut into 1½-inch slices and place in greased muffin tins. Bake in a 350° oven for 12 minutes.

In a small bowl blend the confectioners' sugar and orange juice and drizzle on hot rolls.
MAKES 18 ROLLS.

11941 Narcissus Road
Jackson, California 95642
(209) 296-4300

The Wedgewood Inn offers six lovely guest rooms, while the grounds include richly landscaped English country-style gardens, a rose arbor, and Victorian gazebo. This Gold Country inn is a delightful Victorian replica with lots of stained glass and lace lampshades. Rooms are warmly furnished with American and European antiques. Besides playing croquet or horseshoes, or visiting Henry, the inn's Model T Ford, visitors will want to explore historic Amador County with its wineries, museums, and theatrical productions.

Baked Apple

1 large Golden Delicious apple (green)
  Ground cinnamon
1 tablespoon firmly packed light
    brown sugar
12 to 16 raisins
1 tablespoon chopped walnuts
  French vanilla ice cream

Cut the apple in half. Remove the core and stem. Place in a glass dish with the cut-side facing up. Sprinkle with cinnamon to taste. Spread with light brown sugar. Dot with raisins, spaced around fairly evenly. Sprinkle chopped walnuts on top. Cover the dish. Bake on the top rack in a 350° oven for about 40

The Wedgewood Inn

minutes, until the apples "explode." Allow to cool until just warm. Serve with a scoop of French vanilla ice cream.
MAKES 2 SERVINGS.

Almond Poppy Seed Cake

½ cup shortening
1 cup butter
3 cups sugar
5 eggs
3 cups all-purpose flour
½ teaspoon baking powder
1 cup milk
1 teaspoon vanilla extract
1½ to 2 teaspoons almond extract
2 teaspoons poppy seeds

  Confectioners' sugar
  Half and half
  Slivered almonds

In a large bowl cream the shortening, butter, and sugar until light and fluffy. Add the eggs one at a time. Add the dry ingredients alternately with the milk. Add extracts and poppy seeds. Pour into a greased and floured 10-inch tube pan. Place the pan in a cold oven. Turn the oven to 325° and bake for 1 hour and 30 minutes or longer.

In a small bowl make a glaze with confectioners' sugar and half and half. Top with slivered almonds.
MAKES 8 SERVINGS.

Crêpes

2 cups milk
6 eggs
3 tablespoons sugar
1 cup all-purpose flour
½ teaspoon salt
1 teaspoon vanilla extract
3 tablespoons butter, melted

Cinnamon for sprinkling
Fruit for topping

In a medium bowl combine all of the ingredients except the cinnamon and fruit, mixing until blended. Spray a medium frying pan with cooking spray (or cover the bottom with a light coat of melted butter) and place on low heat. Place ⅓ cup of batter in the pan. The pan is hot enough when a slight "sizzle" is heard. Immediately "swirl" the pan to coat the entire bottom with batter. Sprinkle with cinnamon. Pancake should be very thin. When the edges start showing light brown, turn the pancake over and cook for another minute or so. To get the pancake out of the pan, turn the pan over. It is not necessary to use additional cooking spray for each pancake. Roll and top with bananas, cooked apples, or fresh strawberries or peaches.

Variation: Fill with cheese blintz mixture. (recipe follows)

MAKES 12 TO 16 CRÊPES.

Cheese Blintzes

8   *ounces ricotta cheese*
4   *ounces cream cheese*
1   *tablespoon sugar*
1   *teaspoon vanilla extract*

12   *to 16 9-inch Crêpes (recipe precedes)*
     Fruit
     Sour cream
     Pecan halves

In a medium bowl combine the ricotta, cream cheese, sugar, and vanilla, and beat until smooth. Fill the crêpes, and top with fruit. Garnish with sour cream and pecan halves.

MAKES 6 SERVINGS.

Cranberry Orange Muffins

2   *cups all-purpose flour*
1   *cup sugar*
1   *12-ounce can Ocean Spray cran-*
     berry-orange flavor Cran-Fruit,
     drained
½   *teaspoon salt*
½   *cup butter, softened*
2½   *teaspoons baking powder*
2   *eggs*
½   *cup chopped pecans*
½   *cup orange juice*

½   *cup sugar*
½   *cup all-purpose flour*
2   *teaspoons ground cinnamon*
2   *tablespoons melted butter*

In a large bowl combine 2 cups of flour, 1 cup of sugar, the cranberry-orange "Cran-Fruit," salt, butter, baking powder, eggs, pecans, and orange juice. Spoon into greased muffin cups until about three-fourths full.

In a small bowl combine the remaining ingredients with a pastry blender. Sprinkle the top of the batter in each cup with topping mix. Bake in a 350° oven for 15 to 20 minutes or until light golden brown.

Note: If the Ocean Spray cranberry-orange mixture is not available, chop 1 whole orange (including zest) in a food processor. Add 1 can of whole berry cranberry sauce. Use 1½ cups of this mixture for the muffins, and freeze the remainder.

MAKES 1 DOZEN.

Artichoke Frittata (Vegetarian)

1   *12-ounce jar marinated artichoke*
     hearts, chopped
1   *bunch green onions, chopped*
2   *garlic cloves, minced*
10   *to 12 medium fresh mushrooms,*
     sliced
½   *teaspoon dried oregano*
2   *tablespoons minced fresh parsley*
24   *Carr's Croissant crackers, crushed*
16   *eggs, beaten*
6   *cups grated Cheddar cheese*
     Salsa (optional)

Drain the artichoke hearts, reserving ¼ cup of the liquid. In a skillet heat the liquid and sauté the onions, garlic, and mushrooms for 2 minutes. Add the oregano and parsley. Let cool.

In a large bowl mix the crackers into the beaten eggs. Gently add the grated cheese, then the artichoke and onion mixture. Pour into a buttered 9 x 13-inch pan. Bake in a 325° oven for 35 to 45 minutes or until firm. Serve with salsa, if desired.

MAKES 8 TO 10 SERVINGS.

The Jamestown Hotel

18153 Main Street, P.O. Box 539
Jamestown, California 95642
(209) 984-3902

*I*n 1848, the discovery of gold at nearby Wood's Crossing brought an avalanche of prospectors to Jamestown. Nowadays the area attracts visitors looking for a different sort of treasure: spectacular scenery and an array of refreshing outdoor activities such as skiing, horseback riding, fishing, and steam railroad excursions. In the center of this historic gold-mining community is the Jamestown Hotel, dating to the mid-1800s. Its eight rooms are furnished with antiques and brass showers recalling the days of the great California gold rush.

Salmon Candied in Ginger Syrup

¾   *cup sugar*
2   *to 3 tablespoons sake*
1   *teaspoon lemon juice*
½   *ounce fresh ginger, cut julienne*
2   *7-ounce cuts salmon fillet, salted*

½   *cup soy sauce*
2   *tablespoons lemon juice*
1   *teaspoon fresh ginger cut julienne*

1 *tablespoon cornstarch*
1 *tablespoon sake*

....

5 *ounces Soba noodles, boiled and*
    then chilled under running water
1 *tablespoon sesame oil*
    Toasted sesame seeds to sprinkle for
    finish

In saucepan combine the sugar, 2 table-spoons sake, 1 teaspoon lemon juice, and ½ ounce of ginger. Bring to a boil over high heat. When the liquid evaporates and the syrup reaches soft-ball stage, add salted salmon, nice side down. In a minute or so the sugar will start to brown. Swirl the pan to keep the color uniform. Turn the salmon over and place in a 375° oven for 3 to 5 minutes or until the sugar is dark brown and the fish is cooked. This is the crucial part. The ratio of sugar temperature to salmon thickness has to be right or the syrup will not burn and the fish will not be cooked or the fish will be overcooked and the syrup not brown enough.

In a saucepan boil the soy sauce, 2 table-spoons of lemon juice, and 1 teaspoon of ginger. Then add the cornstarch mixed with 1 tablespoon of sake.

Reheat the noodles by placing in a hot pan or wok with 1 teaspoon of sesame oil. Do this when taking the fish out of the oven. Let the salmon rest a bit as the syrup is very, very hot. Place the noodles in the middle of each serving plate. Carefully remove salmon from the pan with tongs or a slotted spatula and place across the noodles. Sprinkle with sesame seeds and then drizzle sauce around and over. Steamed vegetables such as asparagus or broccoli are good accompaniments.
MAKES 2 SERVINGS.

Sopaipillas

1 *envelope active dry yeast*
¼ *cup warm water (105 to 115°)*
1¾ *cups milk*
2 *tablespoons unsalted butter*
1¼ *cups sugar*
1 *egg, room temperature*
1 *teaspoon salt*
3 *all-purpose flour*
    Oil for deep frying
    Honey

In the bowl of a heavy-duty electric mixer sprinkle the yeast over the warm water and let dissolve. Stir to blend. Let stand 5 minutes.

In a saucepan scald the milk with the unsalted butter. Cool to 105°.

Mix the milk, sugar, egg, and salt into the yeast. Gradually add the flour and beat at low speed for about 4 minutes until the dough pulls away from sides of the bowl. Transfer the dough to a greased bowl, turning to coat the entire surface. Cover with a towel and let rise in a warm draft-free area until double in volume, about 45 minutes.

Roll the dough out to a thickness of ¼ inch on a lightly floured board. Cut into 4-inch triangles. In a deep fryer or large saucepan heat the oil to 375°. Add the sopaipillas in batches (do not crowd) and turn immediately. Cook until golden brown, about 30 seconds per side. Drain on a paper towel. Serve with honey.
MAKES 6 TO 8 SERVINGS.

National Hotel
❧

77 Main Street, P.O. Box 502
Jamestown, California 95327
(209) 984-3446

——————————

Situated in the center of Jamestown, the National Hotel has played host to travelers for over 130 years. Each room is charmingly authentic and individually appointed, and includes most of the original furnishings, as well as patchwork quilts and lace curtains. The Columbia State Park, Angels Camp, Calaveras big trees, and Bear Valley ski resorts are all nearby.

Eggs Blackstone

¼ *cup butter*
¼ *cup all-purpose flour*
1 *cup half and half*
3 *ounces grated Parmesan cheese*
¼ *teaspoon cayenne pepper*

....

2 *English muffins*
4 *strips bacon*
1 *medium tomato, cut into 4 slices*

4 *eggs, soft-poached*

In a saucepan melt the butter. Blend in the flour and mix until smooth. Gradually blend in the half and half, mixing until smooth. Add the Parmesan cheese and cayenne, and heat through.

Place a toasted English muffin half on each plate with a slice of tomato on each one, a piece of bacon on each tomato, and a soft-poached egg on top. Pour Mornay sauce over all. Serve with any breakfast potato or fresh fruit.
MAKES 4 SERVINGS.

Brandy Apple Pork

¼ *cup brandy*
1 *red apple, cored and diced*
1 *teaspoon fresh tarragon*
1 *teaspoon chopped shallots or red*
    onion
⅓ *cup firmly packed brown sugar*
10 *ounces boneless pork loin, sliced*
    and lightly pounded
¾ *cup all-purpose flour*
2 *tablespoons olive oil*
¾ *cup Knorr's demiglaze sauce*

In a shallow bowl combine the brandy, apples, tarragon, shallots, and brown sugar. Add the pork and marinate for 1 hour.

Lightly flour the pork. In a hot sauté pan heat the oil and brown the pork. Add the marinade and demiglaze. Simmer for 3 to 4 minutes. Serve immediately.
MAKES 2 SERVINGS.

Chicken Patrice

¼ *cup cream*
2 *tablespoons apricot brandy*
2 *6-ounce boneless chicken breasts,*
    pounded lightly

....

3 *ounces chopped spinach*

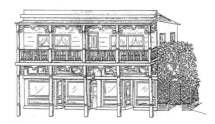

National Hotel

2　ounces bay shrimp, chopped
¼　teaspoon grated nutmeg
3　to 4 chopped canned apricots
¼　cup apricot brandy
½　cup chicken stock

In a shallow bowl mix the cream and 2 tablespoons of apricot brandy. Add the chicken and marinate for 1 hour.

In a large bowl mix the spinach, shrimp, nutmeg, apricots, and ¼ cup of brandy.

Stuff the chicken breasts with the filling. Place in a baking dish with the chicken stock and cover. Bake in a 400° oven for 20 to 25 minutes. Remove from the oven.

Pour the liquid from baking dish into a medium saucepan and add 2 tablespoons of apricot brandy cream. Cook over medium heat until the desired consistency. Pour the sauce over chicken.

MAKES 2 SERVINGS.

The Carriage House

1322 Catalina Street
Laguna Beach, California 92651
(714) 494-8945

A charming old New Orleans-style B&B only a few houses from the Pacific, the Carriage House is a Laguna Beach landmark. Guest rooms open onto a secluded brick courtyard with tropical plants and tiered fountain, a great place for reading or napping. Suites include a separate sitting room and bedroom, and some have their own kitchens. Individually decorated and furnished with antiques, each room has its own theme such as French country, tropical, or palms and wicker.

The Carriage House

Sleep-Tight Cinnamon Buns

1　package (18 to 20) frozen dough rolls
1　cup firmly packed dark brown sugar
⅓　cup instant vanilla pudding mix (or lemon or butterscotch)
1　to 2 teaspoons ground cinnamon
¾　cup raisins or nuts (or both)
½　cup melted margarine or butter

Grease a 10-inch fluted tube pan. Add the rolls, and sprinkle with the sugar, pudding, cinnamon, raisins, or nuts. Pour melted margarine over all. Cover the rolls with a damp cloth and leave out at room temperature overnight.

Bake in a 350° oven for 25 minutes. Let stand 5 minutes, then turn out onto a serving platter.

MAKES 12 TO 18 SERVINGS.

Apple-Cranberry Hot Fruit

8　to 10 good cooking apples, peeled, cored, and sliced
　　Sugar as needed
　　Water as needed
1　16-ounce can whole berry cranberry sauce
　　Spices as desired

In a saucepan cook the apples to make applesauce, adding sugar and water as needed. When done add the cranberry sauce. Add spices as desired.

Really good and pretty, too. Serve hot or cold.

MAKES 4 TO 6 SERVINGS.

Chateau du Lac

911 Hospital Road, P.O. Box 1098
Lake Arrowhead, California 92352
(800) 601-8722

The Chateau du Lac sits on a bluff overlooking Lake Arrowhead in the San Bernadino Mountains. Fireplaces and Jacuzzis make this woodsy lakeside inn an especially cozy spot for weekend getaways. Outdoor activities are plentiful and depending on the season, include swimming, boating, skiing, fishing, horseback riding, and ice skating. However, many guests prefer to relax, take in the view, and enjoy the shops and restaurants in the nearby village.

Party Rice

2　to 3 cups white and wild rice, such as Country Inns brand, cooked
3　tablespoons butter
1　onion, chopped very fine (use food processor)
1　cup currants
¾　cup toasted pine nuts or sliced almonds
　　Garlic powder

Cook the rice according to the package directions until moist and not dry.

While the rice is cooking, in a medium skillet melt the butter and cook the onion until transparent. Add a little more butter if needed.

Add the currants and nuts and a little garlic powder if desired, and cook a little longer. Add the cooked rice and stir until nicely mixed. Correct the seasonings to taste. Transfer to a casserole dish and keep warm until the main course is ready.

Note: This recipe will work with any entréc and is perfect for a vegetarian menu.

MAKES 6 TO 8 SERVINGS.

Chateau du Lac

Huevos California

½ cup butter
10 eggs
½ cup all-purpose flour
1 teaspoon baking powder
1 7-ounce can chopped chilies
1 16-ounce carton cottage cheese
2 cups grated Monterey Jack cheese

In a large bowl melt the butter. Pour half into a 9 x 13-inch pan or baking dish. In a large bowl combine the remaining ingredients with the remaining melted butter and pour into the buttered baking dish. Bake in a 400° oven for 15 minutes. Reduce the heat to 350° and bake for 35 minutes.

Remove and let sit for several minutes. Cut into rectangular serving portions.

Note: Serve with a prepared salsa as a condiment.

MAKES 12 SERVINGS.

Chocolate Decadence

2 cups all-purpose flour
2 cups sugar
1 teaspoon baking soda
½ cup margarine
3½ tablespoons unsweetened cocoa
1 cup water
½ cup buttermilk
2 eggs
2 teaspoons vanilla extract

In a large bowl mix the flour, sugar, and soda. In a saucepan mix the margarine, cocoa, and water. Bring just to a boil. Pour over the dry ingredients. Add the buttermilk, eggs, and vanilla, and mix well. Grease and flour an 11 x 14-inch pan. Pour the batter into the pan. Bake in a 400° oven for 20 minutes.

Note: When cut in thirds, this makes a wonderful torte, stacked on top of each other with filling or frosting in between. When mak-

ing a frosting for this cake, use cream cheese, confectioners' sugar, cocoa, coffee granules, vanilla, and a little almond flavoring, and of course milk or cream. Pipe some of the icing through a pastry tube to make edges and designs, if desired.

MAKES 6 TO 8 SERVINGS.

Windermere Manor

∾

P.O. Box 2177
Lake Arrowhead, California 92352
(909) 336-3292

The innkeepers have achieved a touch of England in the Mountains of California. The names of the well-appointed guest rooms reflect the mood: Lady Ashley, Kensington, Canterbury, Secret Garden, and of course, Windermere. Thoughtful touches add much to the comfortable atmosphere: Crabtree & Evelyn lotions, fluffy towels and robes, overflowing candy dishes, and gourmet coffees and teas.

Windermere Cheese Blintz Casserole

½ cup all-purpose flour
1 tablespoon sugar
½ teaspoon baking powder
   Pinch salt
1 large egg
½ cup milk
2 tablespoons unsalted butter
1 cup cottage cheese
¼ cup ricotta cheese
2 tablespoons sugar
½ teaspoon grated lemon zest
½ teaspoon grated orange zest
½ teaspoon vanilla extract

8 eggs
1 teaspoon vanilla extract
3 teaspoons sugar (superfine is best)
1 pint sour cream

½ cup butter, room temperature

**Blueberry Grand Marnier Sauce
   (recipe follows)
Sour cream**

In a large bowl stir together the flour, 1 tablespoon of sugar, baking powder and salt. In a separate bowl stir together the egg and milk. With a fork quickly stir the egg mixture into the dry mixture.

In a 5-inch crêpe pan melt 2 tablespoons of butter. Pour it into the batter, stirring well. Heat the crêpe pan over moderate heat and ladle in only enough batter to cover the bottom of the pan, swirling the pan to coat it quickly. Cook the crêpe until the edges turn golden. Remove it quickly from the pan cooked side up on a kitchen towel. Repeat this process until all of batter is used.

In a medium bowl combine the cottage cheese, ricotta, 2 tablespoons of sugar, lemon zest, orange zest, and vanilla, and mix together. Place a crêpes cooked-side-up on a work surface, and spoon about 1 tablespoon of filling in the center. Fold opposite sides over to enclose the filling. Repeat with the remaining crêpes and batter. The blintzes may be frozen at this point or proceed with the blintz casserole recipe.

In a blender combine 8 eggs, 1 teaspoon of vanilla, 3 teaspoons of sugar, sour cream, and ½ cup of butter. Blend well. Arrange the blintzes in a 3-quart casserole dish. Pour the sauce over the blintzes. Bake in a 350° oven for 1 hour or until a toothpick inserted in the center comes out clean.

Serve hot with Blueberry Grand Marnier Sauce and sour cream.

MAKES 6 TO 8 SERVINGS.

Blueberry Grand Marnier Fruit Sauce

1 cup confectioners' sugar
2 tablespoons cornstarch
½ cup butter
⅓ cup Grand Marnier
3 cups blueberries, frozen or fresh,
   finely chopped

In a saucepan combine the sugar and cornstarch. Add the butter, stirring until smooth. Add the Grand Marnier and cook over medium heat, stirring constantly until the mixture comes to a boil. Cook for 1 minute, add the blueberries, and cook 1 minute more.

Serve over Windermere Cheese Blintz Casserole.

MAKES ABOUT 4 CUPS OF SAUCE.

Windermere Carrot and Cranberry Mini Bundt Muffins

¾ cup honey
1¼ cups all-purpose flour
2 eggs
1 teaspoon baking powder
1½ cups shredded carrots
½ teaspoon salt
¼ cup dried cranberries
¼ cup water
¼ cup oil
1 teaspoon ground cinnamon
¼ cup chopped pecans

....

Half and half
1 cup confectioners' sugar
½ teaspoon vanilla extract

Grease and flour 12 mini bundt pans or 24 muffin cups. In a large bowl mix the first 11 ingredients together. Pour the mixture into the pans. Bake in a 350° oven for 20 minutes or until a toothpick inserted in the center comes out clean.

Cool on wire racks for 10 minutes. Remove the muffins from the pans and completely cool. Then frost and serve.

In a small bowl mix a small amount of half and half into the confectioners' sugar. Add the vanilla. Add only a small amount of liquid at a time and stir with a wire whisk, until smooth and the desired consistency.

MAKES 12 MINI BUNDT OR 24 REGULAR MUFFINS.

Little River Inn

Little River Inn

Drawer B
Little River, California 95456
(707) 937-5942

Only two miles south of historic Mendocino, the Little River Inn is a mecca for golf and tennis enthusiasts. A challenging nine-hole golf course, driving range, and two lighted tennis courts are only a few steps from the room. Some guest rooms include fireplaces and Jacuzzis.

Ole's Swedish Hotcakes

1 cup all-purpose flour
1 teaspoon sugar
¼ teaspoon salt
1 teaspoon baking powder
1½ cups milk
½ cup half and half
3 eggs
2 tablespoons melted butter

In a large bowl combine the flour, sugar, salt, and baking powder. In a separate bowl ombine the milk and half and half. Add the liquid mixture to the dry ingredients.

Separate the whites from the yolks. In a large bowl beat the whites until stiff. In a separate bowl beat the yolks. Add the yolks to the batter. Then fold in the whites. Add the melted butter. Bake on a hot greased griddle.

MAKES 4 SERVINGS.

Yucatan Chicken and Lime Soup

Corn tortillas for garnish (store-bought tortilla chips can be substituted)
Oil for deep frying
Clarified butter
½ cup chopped onions
1 teaspoon chopped garlic
½ cup chopped celery

---

4 medium tomatoes, diced
4 tomatillos, diced
Salt and pepper to taste
2 pounds chicken breast meat, cooked and diced
¼ cup fresh lime juice
3 cups chicken stock
½ bunch cilantro, chopped

Cut the corn tortillas diagonally to create 2 x ¼-inch strips. Deep fry in oil, drain on paper towels, and set aside.

In a skillet melt the butter and sauté the onions, garlic, and celery until the onions are transparent. Add the tomatoes and tomatillos. Season with salt and pepper. Add the cooked chicken, lime juice, and chicken stock. Bring to a boil. Adjust the flavor with lime juice, salt, and pepper. Just before serving, add the cilantro.

Serve in warmed bowls. Float tortilla chips on the soup for a garnish.

MAKES 6 SERVINGS.

Grilled Margarita Swordfish

1 medium shallot
2 garlic cloves
10 to 12 tomatillos
2 pasilla peppers, seeded
½ bunch cilantro
2 tablespoons lime juice
¼ cup tequila
½ cup olive oil

....

2 pounds swordfish, cut and trimmed into 4 pieces

....

Olive oil
1 red bell pepper, julienned
1 bell pepper, julienned
1 red onion, julienned
Fresh basil (optional)
White wine to taste
Salt and pepper to taste
½ cup bay shrimp, cooked

In a food processor chop the first 6 ingredients. Stir in the tequila and olive oil. In a shallow dish marinate the swordfish in the mixture for 8 hours or overnight.

Place the swordfish on a hot grill.

Meanwhile, in a skillet heat a small amount of olive oil and sauté the peppers, onions, and basil, if desired, until the onions are transparent. Add the white wine and season with salt and pepper to taste. Add the shrimp at the last moment so as not to over cook them.

Spread the ragout onto a warmed plate and place the swordfish on top.

Variation: Place rice in the center of warmed plates. Place the swordfish on top of the rice and surround with ragout.

MAKES 4 SERVINGS.

Los Olivos Grand Hotel

❧

2860 Grand Avenue
Los Olivos, California 93441
(800) 446-2455 for reservations

─────────────

Situated in the heart of Santa Barbara wine country, this resort-style inn features oversized guest rooms, each individually decorated and having a fireplace. Its elegant wine cellar has earned the Wine Spectator Award of Excellence. *Guests may enjoy golf, tennis, and private tours of wineries throughout the Santa Ynez Valley, all available by reservation through the inn staff.*

Hot Artichoke Dip

  3   **14-ounce cans artichoke hearts (not marinated), drained and cut coarsely**
1½   **cups mayonnaise**
  1   **cup grated Swiss cheese**
 ½   **cup grated Parmesan cheese**
  1   **clove garlic**

In a serving dish or a fondue dish combine all of the ingredients. Bake in a 350° oven until heated through. Keep warm when serving. Accompany with crusty French bread.

MAKES 8 CUPS.

Dishpan Cookies

  1   *cup sugar*
  1   *cup firmly packed dark brown sugar*
  1   *cup canola oil*
  2   *eggs*
  1   *teaspoon vanilla extract*
  2   *cups all-purpose flour*
  1   *teaspoon baking soda*
 ½   *teaspoon salt*
 ½   *cup shredded coconut*
 ½   *cup raisins*
 ½   *cup chopped nuts*
  2   *cups Puffed Rice cereal*

In a large bowl mix together the sugars, oil, eggs, and vanilla. Add the flour, soda, and salt, mixing well. Fold in the coconut, raisins, chopped nuts, and Puffed Rice. Drop by teaspoonfuls onto a cookie sheet. Bake in a 350° oven for 7 to 10 minutes.

MAKES 5 DOZEN.

Agate Cove Inn

❧

P.O. Box 1150
Mendocino, California 95460
(707) 937-0551

─────────────

Perched on a bluff overlooking the Pacific, this Mendocino inn is famous for its view. At its heart is a rambling farmhouse built during the 1860s by the town's first brewer. The exterior looks much as it did at the turn-of-the-century, while the interiors are elegant and comfortable. The dining room offers a front row seat to the drama of nature: pounding surf, seabirds, and even migrating whales.

Baked Apples

  5   *cooking apples (such as Granny Smith, Pippin, or McIntosh)*
 ½   *cup walnuts*
 ½   *cup cranberries*
 ½   *cup firmly packed brown sugar*
 ½   *cup granola*
  1   *teaspoon ground cinnamon*
     Zest of 1 lemon
  5   *tablespoons unsalted butter*
     Low-fat vanilla yogurt for topping

Wash and core the apples, then remove ½ inch from the bottom of each so they sit flat in a baking pan.

In a small bowl combine nuts, cranberries, sugar, granola, cinnamon, lemon zest, and butter. Stuff the apples with the filling, generously mounding on top. Bake in a 375° oven for approximately 25 minutes, until filling is cooked and bubbly.

Serve hot or cold, offering low-fat vanilla yogurt.

MAKES 5 SERVINGS.

Cheese Frittata

  5   *eggs*
 ¼   *cup all-purpose flour*
 ½   *teaspoon baking powder*
  1   *8-ounce carton small curd cottage cheese*
  2   *cups grated Jack cheese*
  1   *4-ounce can chopped green chilies, drained*
     Sour cream
     Salsa

In a large bowl combine the eggs, flour, and baking powder. Stir in the cheeses and green chilies. Pour into a well-greased 9- or 10-inch quiche pan. Bake in a 400° oven for 10 minutes.

Reduce the temperature to 350° and bake for an additional 20 minutes.

Serve with sour cream and salsa.

MAKES 5 TO 6 SERVINGS.

Baked Pears

  5   *ripe pears*
 ½   *cup firmly packed dark brown sugar*
 ½   *cup orange juice*
  3   *tablespoons butter*
     Ground cinnamon
     Grated nutmeg
     Ground cloves
     ·····························
     Low-fat vanilla yogurt

Slice the pears in half, remove the core and stem. Line the bottom of a glass baking dish with brown sugar. Place the pears cut-side-down on the brown sugar. Pour orange juice over the pears and dot each with butter. Sprinkle generously with cinnamon and nutmeg, and add a pinch of cloves. Bake in a 350° oven for 30 minutes or until the pears are tender.

Place each pear in a bowl. Pour some of the sauce on the pear. Serve with low-fat vanilla yogurt.

MAKES 5 SERVINGS.

The Headlands Inn

The Headlands Inn
❧

P.O. Box 132
Mendocino, California 95460
(707) 937-1400

Built in 1868 as a barber shop on Mendocino's Main Street, the building was later enlarged to provide a home for the barber's family. Later in the nineteenth century it was moved to its present location on the corner of Howard and Albion streets—horses pulled the house over logs used as rollers. Nowadays

it is a delightful inn with six individually decorated rooms. The shops, galleries, theaters, and restaurants of Mendocino are only steps away. Hiking, golf, horseback riding, whale watching, and a host of other outdoor activities are available.

Florentine Ham Rolls

2   **10-ounce boxes frozen, chopped spinach**
2   **cups packaged cornbread stuffing**
2   **cups sour cream**
24 **thin slices of boiled ham, preferable rectangular**
½   **cup butter**
½   **cup all-purpose flour**
4   **cups milk**
1   **cup sharp Cheddar cheese, grated**
     Grated Parmesan cheese
     Paprika

In a saucepan cook the spinach until just thawed, then drain well. In a bowl combine the spinach, stuffing, and sour cream. Spread a generous spoonful on each ham slice. Roll up and place seam-side-down in individual au gratin dishes or in a large casserole dish.

In a large saucepan melt the butter. Add the flour and blend well. Add the milk and continue stirring over medium-high heat until thick. Add Cheddar cheese and remove from the heat. Stir until all of the cheese is melted. Pour evenly over the ham rolls. Sprinkle with Parmesan cheese and paprika. Cover loosely with foil. Bake in a 350° oven for 20 minutes.

Remove the foil and continue baking another 10 minutes.

Note: Cream sauce can be prepared ahead and refrigerated.

MAKES 2 DOZEN.

Eggs Gruyère with Savory Garnish

2   **cups grated Gruyère cheese**
¼   **cup butter**
½   **teaspoon salt**
     Generous dash white pepper
1½ **teaspoons dry mustard**
1   **cup heavy cream**
12 **large eggs, slightly beaten**
2   **small tomatoes**

⅓   **cup butter**
¾   **cup seasoned breadcrumbs**
½   **cup unsalted sunflower seeds**
     Several sprigs parsley or several edible flowers for garnish

Spray a 9 x 13-inch glass baking dish with cooking spray. Spread the cheese evenly over the bottom of dish and dot with ¼ cup butter. In a bowl mix the seasonings with the cream and drizzle half of the mixture over the cheese. Slowly pour the eggs over the cheese and drizzle with the remaining cream mixture. Bake in a 325° oven for approximately 35 minutes or until the eggs are just set.

While the eggs bake, slice 6½-inch rounds of tomatoes and place on a foil-lined baking sheet. In a saucepan melt ⅓ cup of butter. Add the crumbs and sunflower seeds, remove from the heat, and mix well. During the last 20 minutes of baking, place the tomatoes in the oven on the bottom shelf. After 10 minutes, remove the tomatoes and top with crumb mixture. Return the tomatoes to the oven. When the eggs are set, remove from oven and divide into 6 portions. Serve in au gratin dishes and top with a tomato slice garnished with a sprig of parsley or an edible flower.

MAKES 6 TO 8 SERVINGS.

Joshua Grindle Inn
❧

44800 Little Lake Road, P.O. Box 647
Mendocino, California 95460
(707) 937-4143

Joshua Grindle, a Mendocino banker, built this house in 1879. The inn offers a view of the village, the bay, and the ocean. The town's businesses, art center, shops, galleries, and restaurants are only a short walk from the front steps. At the same time, the inn offers all the relaxed quiet atmosphere of a New England country retreat. The parlor has a cozy fireplace and pump *organ. There are five rooms in the Main House, two in the cottage, and three in the Water Tower.*

Joshua Grindle Inn

Raspberry Muffins

 1   *12-ounce package frozen raspberries*
 5   *cups all-purpose flour*
 ½   *cup sugar*
 ½   *cup firmly packed brown sugar*
 2   *tablespoons plus 2 teaspoons baking
       powder*
 1   *teaspoon ground cinnamon*
 4   *eggs, lightly beaten*
 2   *cups milk*
 1   *cup butter or margarine, melted*
 ....
 2   *cups chopped nuts*
 2   *cups firmly packed brown sugar*
 1   *cup all-purpose flour*
 2   *tablespoons grated orange zest*
 1   *tablespoon ground cinnamon*

In a medium bowl combine the raspberries and ½ cup of flour. In a large bowl combine 4½ cups of flour, ½ cup of sugar, ½ cup of brown sugar, baking powder, and cinnamon. In a separate bowl combine the eggs, milk, and melted butter. Add the liquid mixture to the dry ingredients. Stir just until blended, being careful not to overmix. Gently fold in the raspberries. Spoon into greased muffin cups.

For topping, in a medium bowl combine the remaining ingredients. Top each muffin with 1 teaspoon of topping mix. Bake in a 350° oven for 20 to 25 minutes.

MAKES 30 SERVINGS.

Thanksgiving Egg Delights

 1   *cup biscuit mix*
 3   *eggs*
 1   *cup sautéed onions*

 ¾   *cup milk*
       Mrs. Dash to taste
 ....
 4   *8-ounce packages cream cheese*
 1   *tablespoon minced garlic*
 2   *cups sautéed sliced mushrooms*
 ¾   *cup sun-dried tomatoes in oil*
 ½   *cup each sliced broccoli, crookneck
       squash, zucchini, and green
       onions*
 4   *eggs*
 2   *cups low-fat cottage cheese*
 2   *cups mozzarella cheese*
       Grated Parmesan cheese

Spray a 10 x 15-inch pan or 10 large ramekins with cooking spray. In a medium bowl combine the biscuit mix, eggs, sautéed onions, milk, and Mrs. Dash to taste. Spread in the prepared pan. Dot with grape-sized pieces of cream cheese.

In a skillet sauté the garlic, mushrooms, and sun-dried tomatoes for about 5 minutes. Add the remaining vegetables and sauté until tender. Remove from the heat and set aside.

In a large bowl beat the eggs. Add the cottage and mozzarella cheeses and stir in the vegetable mixture. Spoon the mixture over the crust and top with Parmesan cheese. Bake in a 350° oven for 50 to 60 minutes, until raised somewhat and lightly browned.

MAKES 10 TO 12 SERVINGS.

Potato Asparagus Quiche

 1   *pound 10 ounces frozen shredded
       potatoes*
       Mrs. Dash to taste
 ....
 1   *or 2 tablespoons oil*
 1   *cup chopped asparagus (save top 2
       inches)*
 2   *cups shredded Pepper Jack cheese (or
       Monterey Jack)*
       Oil
 ¾   *pound sliced mushrooms*
 1   *cup chopped green onions*
 ....
 3½ *cups low-fat milk*
 10 *eggs*
 1   *tablespoon grated nutmeg*
       Salt and pepper to taste

Spray 2 9-inch glass pie plates with cooking spray. Divide frozen potatoes evenly into each and toss with Mrs. Dash. Bake in a 350° oven for 10 minutes. When softened, spread the

potatoes evenly over bottoms and sides of the pans as for pie shells.

Place the cheese on the bottom of the pie shells. In a skillet heat a small amount of oil and sauté the mushrooms and onions, and distribute over the cheese. Place the chopped asparagus over the mushrooms and onions.

In a large bowl combine the milk, eggs, nutmeg, salt, and pepper to taste and pour into the shells. Place tops of asparagus on top in a decorative manner. Bake in a 350° oven for about 45 to 60 minutes or until custard is set and the top is puffed and brown. Serve hot, warm, or at room temperature.

MAKES 20 SERVINGS.

Spinach Mushroom Pesto Quiche

 3   *cups water*
 1   *cup polenta*
 ⅓   *cup grated Parmesan cheese*
 1   *teaspoon salt*
 ....
 2   *heaping tablespoons fresh or frozen
       pesto*
 2   *cups shredded mozzarella cheese*
 1   *to 2 tablespoons oil*
 2   *cups thinly sliced mushrooms*
 5   *garlic cloves, minced*
 ½   *cup chopped sun-dried tomatoes*
 6   *eggs, beaten*
 2½ *cups milk*
 1   *cup cottage cheese*
 1   *10-ounce box frozen spinach,
       thawed, with liquid squeezed out*
 ½   *cup grated Parmesan cheese*
 2   *to 3 Roma tomatoes, sliced thinly*

Spray 2 9-inch pie plates with cooking spray. In a saucepan bring the water to a boil. Gradually stir in the polenta until it begins to thicken. Remove the pan from the heat and stir in ⅓ cup of Parmesan and the salt. Spread evenly over the bottom of the prepared pie plates.

Divide the pesto into 2 equal portions and spread evenly over the bottoms of the crusts. Sprinkle each with 1 cup of mozzarella. In a skillet with a small amount of oil sauté the mushrooms, garlic, and sun-dried tomatoes. In a bowl beat together the eggs, milk, and cottage cheese. Add the sautéed mushroom mixture and spinach. Mix and pour evenly into the pie crusts. Top with ½ cup of grated Parmesan

and the Roma tomatoes. Bake in a 350° oven for 45 minutes, until the center is set.
MAKES 12 TO 16 SERVINGS.

Potato Pudding with Sun-dried Tomatoes

    4   large onions, diced
    8   cups diced potatoes
    8   eggs
    2   cups all-purpose flour
    2   teaspoons baking powder
    ½   cup diced sun-dried tomatoes
    1   cup butter
        Sour cream

In a food processor combine the onion and potatoes and blend until it is a fine texture. Add the eggs and blend well. Add the flour and baking powder, and blend until smooth. Fold in the sun-dried tomatoes.

Pour the mixture into greased 9 x 13-inch baking pan. Cut the butter into squares and evenly distribute over top. Bake in a 350° oven for 50 minutes. Remove from the oven and slice into 24 portions. Serve with sour cream.
MAKES 24 SERVINGS.

Chocolate Zucchini Cake

    ¾   cup butter
    2   cups sugar
    3   eggs
    2   teaspoons vanilla extract
    1   tablespoon orange zest
    2   cups grated raw zucchini
    2¾ cups all-purpose flour
    ½   cup unsweetened cocoa
    2½ teaspoons baking powder
    1½ teaspoons baking soda
    1   teaspoon salt
    1   teaspoon ground cinnamon
    ½   cup milk
    1   cup chopped walnuts
    ....
    1   tablespoon vanilla extract
    1   cup confectioners' sugar
        Grated orange zest
        Lemon juice

Grease and flour a bundt pan. In a bowl cream butter and slowly add the sugar, beating until smooth. In a small bowl beat the eggs and mix thoroughly. Stir in the 2 teaspoons of vanilla, orange zest, and grated

zucchini and blend well. In a separate bowl stir together the flour, cocoa, baking powder, salt, soda, and cinnamon. Add the dry ingredients to the zucchini mixture along with the milk, and beat until thoroughly mixed. Stir in the walnuts. Pour the batter into the pan. Bake in a 350° oven for about 1 hour or until a toothpick inserted in the center comes out clean. Cool for about 15 minutes.

To make a glaze, in a small bowl stir in 1 tablespoon of vanilla into the confectioners' sugar until a runny paste is formed. Stir in the zest and enough juice to make the glaze pourable and drizzle over the cake.
MAKES 8 SERVINGS.

Chocolate Biscotti Crunch Cookies

    1   cup butter
    1¾ cups sugar
    1   cup cottage cheese
    1   teaspoon vanilla extract
    2   eggs
    2½ cups all-purpose flour
    ½   cup unsweetened cocoa
    1   teaspoon baking soda
    1   teaspoon baking powder
    ½   teaspoon salt
    2   cups ground biscotti

In a large bowl cream the butter and sugar until fluffy. Add the cottage cheese and vanilla, and beat well. Add the eggs, one at a time, beating well after each addition. In a bowl mix together the flour, cocoa, soda, baking powder, and salt. Gradually add the dry ingredients to the creamed mixture. Fold in the biscotti crumbs. Drop by rounded teaspoonfuls onto a ungreased cookie sheet. Bake in a 350° oven for 15 minutes. Let stand a few minutes before removing from the cookie sheet.
MAKES ABOUT 3 TO 4 DOZEN.

Whitegate Inn

Whitegate Inn

P.O. Box 150
Mendocino, California 95460
(707) 937-4892

*I*n the heart of Mendocino village with its galleries, antique shops, boutiques, and performing arts center, this B&B offers a combination of European and Victorian elegance. Built during the 1880s, it is furnished with richly upholstered period antiques. Fresh floral bouquets are everywhere. Some guest rooms have fireplaces and claw-foot tubs.

Caramel Apple French Toast

    1   cup firmly packed brown sugar
    ½   cup butter
    2   tablespoons light corn syrup
    1   cup chopped pecans
    12   slices French bread
    8   thinly sliced green apples, cored
    6   eggs
    1½   cups milk
    1   teaspoon vanilla extract
         Ground cinnamon
         Grated nutmeg

In a saucepan combine the brown sugar, butter, and corn syrup. Cook over medium heat until thickened, stirring constantly. Spray a 9 x 13-inch glass baking dish with cooking spray. Pour the syrup mixture into the prepared pan. Sprinkle with chopped pecans. Place 1 layer of sliced French bread on the syrup and pecans. Top with green apples.

In a blender combine the eggs, milk, and vanilla. Pour half of the mixture over the apples. Place a second layer of sliced French bread on top of the apples and cover with the remaining egg mixture. Cover with plastic wrap and refrigerate overnight.

Sprinkle with cinnamon and nutmeg. Remove the plastic wrap. Bake in a 350° oven for 50 to 60 minutes.

Each person is served 1 double-layer serving. It can also be served with whipped cream.
MAKES 6 SERVINGS.

Whitegate Inn Classic Pizzelles

  6 eggs
1½ cups sugar
  1 cup margarine, melted and cooled
  2 tablespoons vanilla extract (or anise)
3½ cups all-purpose flour
  4 teaspoons baking powder
    Confectioners' sugar

In a large bowl beat the eggs, adding the sugar gradually. Beat until smooth. Add the margarine and vanilla or anise.

In a separate bowl sift the flour and baking powder. Blend the dry ingredients into the egg mixture until smooth. The dough will be sticky. Bake in a Pizzelle baker according to the manufacturer's instructions. To serve sprinkle with confectioners' sugar.

Note: It makes a beautiful presentation to serve these on a fluted glass cake stand with violets.

Variations: Add finely chopped nuts or melted chocolate.
MAKES ABOUT 6 SERVINGS.

Jabberwock

*598 Laine Street
Monterey, California 93940
(408) 372-4777*

*O*nce a convent, this Victorian-style B&B puts its guests within earshot of barking seals and pounding waves and within walking distance of Monterey's famed Cannery Row district and the Monterey Bay Aquarium. Goose down pillows and comforters on the huge Victorian beds enhance the Through the Look-

ing Glass *atmosphere of the rooms. The lush secluded garden in the back is a great place to relax.*

Jabberwock

Bacon and Stuff

  4 8-ounce packages cream cheese, softened
  1 cup mayonnaise
⅓ cup chopped fresh dill
1½ bunches green onions, chopped
  2 pounds bacon, chopped and fried crisp
    Crackers for serving

In a large bowl whip the cream cheese. Add the mayonnaise. Fold in the remaining ingredients and refrigerate. Serve with crackers.
MAKES 12 SERVINGS.

Caramel Peanut Apple Dip

  2 8-ounce packages cream cheese, softened
¾ cup firmly packed brown sugar
½ cup creamy peanut butter
½ cup sour cream
  2 tablespoons vanilla extract
    Sliced apples for dipping

In a medium bowl beat the cream cheese with an electric mixer. Add the remaining ingredients. Serve with sliced apples.
MAKES 6 TO 8 SERVINGS.

Downey House

*517 West Broad Street
Nevada City, California 95959
(916) 265-2815*

*H*istoric Downey House, built in 1869, provides a taste of California in its early boom days. Just a block from Nevada City's historic district, the inn features a curved veranda, winding hallways, and a beautiful garden. Guests can enjoy a leisurely stroll through this old town, where fine restaurants, shops, art galleries, and theaters abound.

Baked Eggs

  1 teaspoon butter
  1 teaspoon half and half
  1 egg
    Salt and pepper to taste
  2 tablespoons grated Havarti cheese

In an individual ramekin melt the butter. Add the half and half. Break the egg into the ramekin, and season with salt and pepper to taste. Sprinkle with Havarti cheese. Bake in a 375° oven for 10 minutes. The white should be baked firm and the yolk should remain liquid.
MAKES 1 SERVING.

Downey House Egg Dish

12 eggs, beaten
  1 pint cottage cheese
  1 pound grated cheese (Jack, Cheddar or Swiss, or a combination of all)
½ cup melted butter
½ cup all-purpose flour
  1 teaspoon baking powder
  1 medium zucchini, grated
  1 medium red potato, grated
  1 12-ounce can cream-style corn

In a large bowl combine all ingredients. Pour into a greased 9 x 13-inch pan. Bake in a 350° oven for 30 minutes.
MAKES 12 SERVINGS.

Orange Bran Muffins

5 cups all-purpose flour
3 cups sugar
5 teaspoons baking soda
1 cup raisins
1 15-ounce package All-Bran cereal

4 eggs, beaten lightly
1 quart buttermilk
½ cup oil
1 teaspoon grated orange zest
1 teaspoon orange extract
½ cup butter, melted

In a large bowl combine the flour, sugar, baking soda, raisins, and cereal, and mix well.

In a separate large bowl combine the eggs, buttermilk, oil, orange zest, and orange extract. Add the melted butter slowly. Fold in the dry ingredients, mixing just until blended. Spoon into greased muffin cups. Bake in a 375° oven for 20 to 30 minutes.

MAKES 30 REGULAR-SIZED MUFFINS.

The Inn at Occidental

≈

3657 Church Street, P.O. Box 857
Occidental, California 95465
(707) 874-1047

Occidental was a historical stopping point on the railroad between San Francisco and the Northwest. The Inn at Occidental, built in 1877, continues this historic tradition by offering luxury accommodations in a turn-of-the-century setting. Noted for its antiques, original art, fir floors, wainscoted hallways, and covered porches, this inn is conveniently positioned an hour's drive north of San Francisco. Nearby attractions include hiking, canoeing, golfing, and whale watching at Bodega Bay.

Orange Pancakes from the Inn at Occidental

2 cups all-purpose flour
1 teaspoon salt
2 teaspoon baking soda
¼ cup sugar
2 eggs, beaten
1¾ cups orange juice
¼ cup butter

½ cup butter melted
3 tablespoons cornstarch
1 pint orange juice
⅔ cup sugar
1 ounce julienne of orange zest
Maple syrup

In a large bowl mix the flour, salt, baking soda, and ¼ cup of sugar. Add the eggs, 1¾ cup of orange juice, and 14 cup of butter. On a greased griddle cook the pancakes until lightly browned.

In a saucepan melt ½ cup of butter. Blend in the cornstarch and cook for 1 minute. Cool. In a separate saucepan heat 1 pint of orange juice. Add the orange juice to the roux and cook, stirring constantly, until thickened. Add ⅔ cups of sugar and the orange zest, and bring the mixture to a boil. Reduce the heat and simmer for 5 minutes.

Serve the pancakes with orange butter and maple syrup.

MAKES 4 SERVINGS.

Gosby House Inn

≈

643 Lighthouse Avenue
Pacific Grove, California 93950
(800) 527-8828

This beautiful inn, with its English decor and period antiques, has been a guest house for more than one hundred years. It has a wide selection of rooms—from the luxurious to the charming and cozy, which

are less expensive. Situated in the heart of the Monterey Peninsula, it is convenient to the aquarium, a shoreline walking trail, and the famous Seventeen-Mile Drive along the Pacific coast.

Banana-Pear Muffins

1¼ cups all-purpose flour
2 teaspoons baking powder
¼ teaspoon baking soda
¼ cup sugar
½ cup chopped walnuts or granola
½ cup mashed ripe banana
½ cup mashed ripe pear
1 egg
2 tablespoons milk
¼ teaspoon vanilla extract
½ cup oil

In a large bowl stir together the flour, baking powder, soda, sugar and walnuts or granola. Add the remaining ingredients and stir until just moistened. Fill greased muffin cups three-fourths full. Bake in a 400° oven for 20 minutes.

MAKES 10 MUFFINS.

Cobblestone Hobo Breakfast

5 large, new red potatoes
2 tablespoons butter, divided
1 large onion, chopped
1 tablespoon oil
Paprika for browning agent
Salt and pepper to taste
3 tablespoons chopped parsley

8 eggs poached
1 tablespoon white vinegar

¼ cup butter
¼ cup all-purpose flour
1 cup half-and-half
1 tablespoon lemon juice
¼ cup crumbled bacon
Salt and pepper to taste

1 cup grated Cheddar cheese
Sour cream for garnish
Parsley sprigs for garnish

In a stock pot boil the potatoes in salted water until just tender, 20 to 30 minutes. Drain, cool, and cut into cubes. In a skillet melt 1 tablespoon butter and sauté the onion until tender, then set aside.

In a separate pan melt 1 tablespoon of butter with the oil and add the potatoes, paprika, salt, and pepper to taste. Fry, stirring as little as possible, until brown and crisp. Stir in the parsley and onions.

Fill a sauté pan half full of water and add 1 tablespoon white vinegar bring to a boil. Crack 8 eggs gently into the boiling water and poach for about 3 minutes. Remove carefully with a slotted spoon.

In a small saucepan melt ¼ cup of butter. Blend in the flour and cook over medium heat, stirring constantly, for 2 to 3 minutes. Add the half-and-half and cook until thickened, adding more half and half if necessary. Add the lemon juice and bacon bits. Season with salt and pepper.

Place a layer of the potatoes in a quiche pan and reheat in the oven. Add a layer of grated Cheddar cheese and return to the oven to melt. Gently place the poached eggs on top of the hot mixture. Top with dollops of cream sauce and a small piece of parsley. Serve hot.

MAKES 8 SERVINGS.

Green Gables Inn

&ve;

104 Fifth Street
Pacific Grove, California 93950
(800) 722-1774 for reservations

L*ocated on the edge of Monterey Bay, this inn offers a striking view of the Pacific shoreline from almost every guest room. Built in 1888, it is furnished with English antiques. Many guests enjoy riding along the shore on bicycles provided by the inn. Steinbeck's Cannery Row, with its fine shops and restaurants, and the Monterey Bay Aquarium are only a five-minute walk away.*

Coffee Pecan Muffins

    ½   cup melted butter
    2   cups firmly packed brown sugar
    ¾   cup milk
    1   teaspoon vanilla extract
    1   egg
    2   tablespoons instant coffee
   1¾   cups all-purpose flour
    1   tablespoon baking powder
    ¼   teaspoon salt
    ½   cup coarsely chopped pecans
   ....
    1   tablespoon sugar
    2   tablespoons finely chopped pecans

In a medium bowl cream the butter and brown sugar. Add the milk, vanilla, egg, and coffee, and mix well. In a separate bowl stir together flour, baking powder, salt, and chopped pecans. Add the liquid mixture and stir until just mixed, being careful not to overbeat. Fill greased muffin cups three-fourths full. In a small bowl combine the sugar and pecans. Before baking, sprinkle a little of the sugar-pecan topping on each muffin. Bake in a 350° oven for 15 to 20 minutes.

MAKES 10 MUFFINS.

Biscotti

    ⅔   cup sugar
    ½   cup oil
    1   tablespoon grated orange zest
   1½   teaspoons vanilla extract
    2   eggs
   2½   cups all-purpose flour
    1   teaspoon baking powder
    ¼   teaspoon baking soda
    ½   cup slivered almonds
    4   ounces semisweet chocolate, melted

In a large bowl mix the sugar, oil, orange zest, vanilla, and eggs. Stir in the flour, baking powder, soda, and almonds. Knead the dough on a lightly floured surface until smooth.

Shape the dough into 2 10 x 3-inch rectangles on an ungreased cookie sheet. Bake in a 350° oven for 25 to 30 minutes, or until a toothpick inserted in the center comes out clean. Cool on a cookie sheet for 15 minutes. Cut crosswise into ½-inch slices. Place slices, cut-side down, on the cookie sheet. Bake about 15 minutes, turning once, until crisp and light brown. Remove from the cookie sheet and cool completely. Once cooled, dip

one end of the biscotte into melted chocolate and set on cooling rack to dry.

MAKES 40 BISCOTTI.

8550 Highway 128, P.O. Box 166
Philo, CA. 95466
(707) 895-3069

B*uilt entirely of redwood, the inn was once a stagecoach stop on the old road to the North Coast. There is plenty to see in this part of California: giant redwoods, apple farms, wineries, and the spectacular Mendocino coast (about thirty minutes away). Back at the inn, five rooms furnished with antiques and made cozy with quilts, comforters, and lots of pillows await guests. The overall decor keeps the tradition of a turn-of-the-century farmhouse.*

Upside-Down Apple French Toast

    5   tablespoons butter
    6   large baking apples, peeled, cored,
        and sliced
   1¼   cups firmly packed brown sugar
    3   tablespoons dark corn syrup
    1   teaspoon ground cinnamon
    ½   cup raisins

The Philo Pottery Inn

½ cup chopped pecans
6 large eggs
2½ cups milk
1 teaspoon vanilla extract
1½ baguettes (approximately) cut into slices about ½-inch thick

In a large skillet melt the butter. Add the apple slices and sauté until tender. Add the brown sugar, corn syrup, and cinnamon. Continue to cook, stirring constantly, until the sugar dissolves.

Butter an 11 x 17-inch glass baking dish. Sprinkle the raisins and pecans evenly in the dish. Pour in the apple mixture and spread evenly.

In a large bowl beat the eggs until blended. Add the milk and vanilla, and beat until well mixed. Dip the bread slices in the egg mixture and make 2 layers over the apple mixture. Pour any extra egg mixture evenly over the bread layers. Cover the plastic wrap and refrigerate overnight.

Bake in a 350° oven for approximately 1 hour. After the first 15 minutes, cover loosely with aluminum foil to keep the top from getting too crisp. When done, remove from the oven and let the French toast sit for about 10 minutes. Loosen the edges with a knife and cover the dish with a larger cookie sheet or shallow baking dish. Invert the glass dish carefully onto a cookie sheet so that the apple layer is now on top. Cover loosely with foil and keep warm in a 200° oven.

Serve with additional maple syrup, if desired.

MAKES 10 SERVINGS.

Whole Wheat Buttermilk Pancakes

1 egg
1 cup buttermilk
2 tablespoons oil
½ cup whole wheat flour
½ cup unbleached flour
1 teaspoon baking powder
½ teaspoon salt
    Confectioners' sugar for dusting
    Berry Sauce or Cranberry Maple
        Syrup (see below)

In a bowl combine the egg, buttermilk, and oil. In a separate bowl combine the dry ingredients. Mix the dry ingredients into the buttermilk mixture just until moistened. Spoon batter onto a lightly oiled skillet and cook on both sides until browned.

Dust with confectioners' sugar and serve with warm Berry Sauce or Cranberry Maple Syrup.

Berry Sauce: In a saucepan combine sweetened blueberry sauce and unsweetened blueberry juice to taste in a sauce pan. Add frozen blueberries and pitted Bing cherries. Heat until the sauce bubbles. Thicken with cornstarch and water mixed to a thin paste. Serve warm with pancakes. Blueberry sauce is available in grocery stores (i.e. Smuckers) and blueberry juice is available in health food stores. Mixed berry juice can be used as a substitute.

Cranberry Maple Syrup: Add whole cranberries to maple syrup and heat until the cranberries are soft.

MAKES 2 SERVINGS.

Muesli

9 large shredded wheat biscuits, crumbled
3 cups rolled oats
1 cup wheat bran
1 cup wheat germ
¼ cup firmly packed brown sugar (to taste)
¾ cup raisins
¾ cup dried apricots, diced
½ cup sliced almonds

In a large bowl combine all ingredients. Toss and mix well. Store in an airtight container.

Serve with lots of fresh fruit and milk or yogurt.

Variation: Substitute any dried fruit, such as cranberries or cherries.

MAKES 4 TO 6 SERVINGS.

Apple-Oatmeal Pudding

2 cups milk
3 tablespoons brown sugar
1 tablespoon butter
¼ teaspoon salt
¼ teaspoon ground cinnamon
1 cup rolled oats
1 cup diced, peeled apple
½ cup raisins
    Cream, milk, or yogurt for garnish

In a saucepan combine the milk, brown sugar, butter, salt, and cinnamon, and heat just to boiling. Stir in the oats, apple, and raisins, and heat until bubbles appear at the edge of the pan. Turn into a buttered 1½-quart casserole (or individual ramekins) and cover. Bake in a 350° oven for 30 minutes. Cover loosely with foil and keep warm in a low oven (200°) until ready to serve.

Serve hot with cream, milk, or yogurt.

MAKES 4 SERVINGS.

The Pillar Point Inn

380 Capistrano Road
Princeton by-the-Sea, California 94018
(800) 400-8281

*T*he only harbor between San Francisco and Santa Cruz is Pillar Point Harbor and this is the only country inn and B&B there. European-style feather beds and fireplaces make it an especially warm and comfortable waterside hideaway. The sumptuous breakfast and afternoon tea, served fireside in the living room, add to the charm. Local attractions include the fisherman's wharf, marina, beaches, and giant elephant seals in the harbor.

Pecan Delight

1 cup sugar
½ cup butter
1 cup water
1 cup raisins
1 teaspoon ground cinnamon
½ teaspoon ground allspice
2 cups all-purpose flour

1   teaspoon baking soda
½   cup chopped pecans

....

½   cup butter
⅔   cup firmly packed brown sugar
3   teaspoons condensed milk
1   tablespoon all-purpose flour
½   cup shredded coconut
1   cup pecans

In a saucepan combine the sugar, ½ cup of butter, water, raisins, cinnamon, and allspice, and cook for at least 5 minutes, or until the sugar has dissolved.

In a large bowl combine 2 cups of flour, the soda, and ½ cup chopped pecans. Add the dry ingredients to the liquid mixture, mixing well. Pour the batter into a 9 x 13-inch pan. Bake in a 350° oven for 20 minutes.

In a saucepan heat the remaining ingredients together. Spread the icing on the cake. Bake in a 350° oven for 20 minutes more.

MAKES 8 SERVINGS.

Carolyn's Potato Pie

½   cup all-purpose flour
½   teaspoon baking powder
½   teaspoon salt
6   eggs, beaten until frothy
½   cup milk
¼   cup melted butter
2   tablespoons canola oil
1   cup small curd cottage cheese
2   cups shredded Monterey Jack cheese
2   cups shredded Colby cheese
     Dash red hot chili pepper (optional)
12   ounces frozen, shredded potatoes, thawed (use potatoes with mild-peppers and chilies or plain)

....

     California sun-dried tomato salsa

Spray 2 9-inch round glass pie pans with cooking spray.

In a medium bowl combine the flour, baking powder, and salt. In a separate bowl combine the eggs, milk, butter, and oil. Blend in the dry ingredients. Add the cheeses, chili pepper, then slightly more than half of the potatoes. Mix well. Pour into the prepared pie pans and spread the rest of the potatoes over the tops. Bake in a 350° oven for 35 minutes or more. Check midway through and move the pans around, if needed, to bake evenly.

Cut into wedges and serve with a small spoonful of salsa or similar topping.

MAKES 12 SERVINGS.

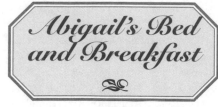

Abigail's Bed and Breakfast

❧

*2120 G Street
Sacramento, California 95816
(916) 441-5007, (800) 858-1568*

*A*bigail's is a 1912 Colonial Revival mansion situated on a street lined with old elms, near the heart of Sacramento. The inn is minutes away from the Convention Center and the capitol. There are fine restaurants, theaters, and museums within a short walk or drive. The five large guest rooms have private baths, sitting areas, and beautiful antiques. Thick terrycloth robes, magazines, radios, and beverages are provided for guests.

Abigail's Zucchini Walnut Sour Cream Waffles

3   cups all-purpose flour
2   teaspoons baking powder
1½   teaspoons baking soda
1½   teaspoons salt
½   cup chopped nuts
4   eggs, lightly beaten
2   cups sour cream
1   cup milk
½   cup oil
1   cup shredded zucchini
      Butter
      Maple Syrup

In a large bowl mix the flour with the baking powder, soda, and salt. Add the chopped nuts. In a medium bowl mix the eggs, sour cream, milk, oil, and zucchini. Blend well and pour all at once into the flour mixture. Stir the batter until smooth. Bake in pre-heated greased waffle iron according to the manufacturer's directions. Top with butter and maple syrup.

MAKES 10 TO 11 4-INCH WAFFLES.

Abigail's Granola

10   cups old-fashioned oats
2   cups wheat germ
1   cup oat bran
½   cup sesame seeds
1   cup chopped hazelnuts
½   cup slivered almonds
3   teaspoons ground cinnamon
1   teaspoon grated nutmeg
¼   teaspoon ground cloves
1½   cups Just Apples
½   cup Just Persimmons (or 2 cups raisins or other dried fruit)

....

½   cup canola oil
½   cup maple syrup
⅓   cup honey (Rewarewa from New Zealand is great)
1   tablespoon vanilla extract

In a large bowl mix the dry ingredients together.

In saucepan mix the remaining ingredients and heat until blended. Pour the syrup mixture over the dry ingredients, mixing well. Spread on greased cookie sheets. Bake in a 375° oven for 20 minutes.

Store in airtight containers.

MAKES ABOUT 18 CUPS.

Nicole's Low-Fat Lemon Yogurt Cake

1   cup margarine
2½   cups sugar
1¼   cups egg substitute
1   tablespoon vanilla extract
2¾   cups all-purpose flour
½   teaspoon salt
½   teaspoon baking soda
1   8-ounce carton vanilla or lemon nonfat yogurt
¼   cup lemon juice
      Grated zest of 1 medium lemon

....

½   cup lemon juice
¾   cup confectioners' sugar

In a large bowl cream together the margarine and sugar. Add the egg substitute ¼ cup at a time, beating well after each addition. Add the vanilla.

In a small bowl combine the dry ingredients. Slowly mix the dry ingredients into the wet mixture, alternating with the yogurt. Add ¼ cup of lemon juice and the zest and mix well. Pour into a greased bundt pan. Bake in a 350° oven for 45 minutes to 1 hour.

In a small bowl mix together the remaining ingredients until smooth. Pour over the cake while still warm.

MAKES 8 SERVINGS.

Abigail's

Diane's Broiled Grapefruit with Crunch Topping

1 cup old-fashioned oats
¼ cup firmly packed sugar
1 teaspoon almond extract
2 tablespoons finely chopped nuts
    (optional)
1 teaspoon ground cinnamon
8 teaspoons maple syrup

4 grapefruits, halved

In a small bowl combine the first 5 ingredients. Place 1 teaspoon of maple syrup on each grapefruit half. Cover with 1 to 2 tablespoons of topping. Broil for several minutes until slightly browned. Store remaining topping in an airtight container.

MAKES 8 SERVINGS.

Abigail's Nutmeg Coffeecake

3½ cups all-purpose flour
2 cups sugar
1 tablespoon baking powder
1 tablespoon nutmeg
1½ teaspoons salt
1 cup sweet butter
1¼ cups milk

¼ cup rum
2 teaspoons vanilla extract
3 eggs
¼ cup poppy seeds
1 cup golden raisins

Grease a 10-inch tube or bundt pan. In a large bowl combine all ingredients except the raisins. (If using a food processor, combine the first 5 ingredients and pulse several times, then add the remaining ingredients.) Mix for 3 minutes.

Pour the batter into the prepared pan. Sprinkle the raisins evenly over the top and stir them into the batter. Bake in a 350° oven for 1 hour and 15 minutes.

Let the cake cool for 15 minutes before removing from the pan.

MAKES 8 SERVINGS.

Cinnamon Bear

❧

1407 Kearney Street
St. Helena, CA 94574
(707) 963-4653

A classic Craftsman Bungalow with a spacious front porch and gabled dormer, this charming house was built in 1904 and remains today in near-mint condition. The owners have filled it with antiques, elegant, old-fashioned light fixtures, and oriental carpets. Guest may find a teddy bear or two in their rooms. In the heart of the Napa Valley wine

Cinnamon Bear

country, this B&B is only two blocks from St. Helena's Main Street shops and restaurants.

Cinnamon-Almond French Toast

3 eggs
1 cup half and half
1 tablespoon ground cinnamon
1 teaspoon grated nutmeg
2 tablespoons Torani (Orgeat) Almond Syrup or 1 teaspoon almond extract
12 pieces "Texas toast" bread
    Confectioners' sugar or cinnamon sugar
    Toasted almnds or fresh berries

In a large glass bowl whip the eggs. Add the half and half, nutmeg, and almond syrup and mix until light and frothy. Dip pieces of bread in the mixture and cook on a hot griddle until lightly browned. Dust with confectioners' sugar or cinnamon-sugar, adding toasted sliced almonds or fresh berries.

MAKES 12 SERVINGS.

Cinnamon Apple Crisp

1½ cups butter
10 Granny Smith apples
1½ cups firmly packed brown sugar
1½ tablespoons ground cinnamon
2 cups all-purpose flour
1 cup granola

Butter the bottom of a 2-quart glass baking dish with ¼ cup of butter. Peel, core, and finely slice the apples and spread them out evenly in the dish. Dot with ¼ cup of butter.

In a large saucepan melt 1 cup of butter over low heat. Add the brown sugar and milk, and simmer until a thick paste. Remove the pan from the heat. Add the cinnamon and flour, and mix very well. Add the granola. Sprinkle over the top of the apples. Bake in a 350° oven for 1 hour.

MAKES 6 TO 8 SERVINGS.

Meadowood, Napa Valley

Meadowood, Napa Valley
❧

900 Meadowood Lane
St. Helena, California 94574
(707) 963-3646

Sequestered on 250 wooded acres, this upscale resort is the home of the widely recognized Meadowood Wine School. Wine industry leaders hold conferences here, so food and wine connoisseurs are likely to feel right at home. The decor is modern and in immaculate taste. Rooms are washed in light and offer private decks opening onto the surrounding woods. The property includes its own hiking trails as well as a golf course and croquet lawns.

Roast Baby Pheasant with Apricot, Lemongrass, Cinnamon, and Cloves

  4 *baby pheasants*
 ½ *cup butter*
  2 *ounces ginger, peeled and sliced*
  1 *cinnamon stick*
  4 *sprigs lemongrass (2 sliced for sauce, 2 finely chopped for apricots)*
 12 *whole cloves*
  2 *cups white wine*
  1 *liter veal stock*
 ¼ *cup sugar*

 10 *ounces dried apricots, cut in quarters*
 ¼ *cup black currants*
    Grated zest of 2 limes
  2 *tablespoons olive oil*
    Chervil (optional)

Remove the breast and legs from each pheasant. Place in the refrigerator.

Chop the carcass of each pheasant into 4 pieces. Place in a saucepan with 1 tablespoon of butter. Cook until golden brown. Add the ginger, cinnamon, 2 slices of lemongrass, and cloves. Deglaze with white wine, and reduce until almost dry. Add the veal stock, and reduce by three-fourths. Strain and bring the sauce back to a boil. Add 2 tablespoons of butter. Mix thoroughly. Keep the sauce warm.

In a saucepan combine the remaining butter, sugar, apricots, black currants, lime zest, and 1 tablespoon of chopped lemongrass. Cook over low heat until well incorporated. Keep the mixture warm.

In a sauté pan heat 2 tablespoons olive oil over medium heat. Place the pheasant skin-side-down, browning for approximately 3 minutes each side. Remove the breasts. Transfer to a baking dish. Bake in a 425° oven for an additional 2 minutes.

In the center of each plate arrange a circle of 5 tablespoons of apricot mixture. Place the pheasant breasts and legs on top of apricot mixture. Pour approximately 5 tablespoons of boiling sauce over each plate. Garnish with chervil (optional). Serve immediately.
MAKES 4 SERVINGS.

Mille-Feuille of Caramelized Bananas, Black Currants, and Chocolate Chips with a Caramel Sauce

 1¼ *cups butter*
   6 *phyllo sheets (for layers)*
  ¾ *cup sugar*
   3 *ounces water (for sauce)*
  ¼ *cup cream (for sauce)*
   4 *bananas, sliced*
   2 *tablespoons dried currants*
   2 *tablespoons chocolate chips*
  ½ *teaspoon ground cinnamon*

In small saucepan bring ¾ cup of butter to a boil. Turn down the heat and continue to cook, skimming the foam off the top until the butter is clear yellow, approximately 20 minutes.

Brush each layer of phyllo thoroughly with clarified butter and sprinkle sugar (¼ cup total) evenly atop each layer, stacking one on top of another. Continue this process until all layers are completed. Cut into 3-inch squares. Lay the phyllo between 2 pieces of parchment paper and place on a baking sheet. Lay another baking sheet on top. Bake in a 375° oven until golden brown. Remove from the oven. Let cool. Remove from the baking sheet and set aside.

In a small saucepan combine 6 tablespoons of sugar and the water and whisk until dissolved. Bring to a boil, and cook until golden brown. Remove the pan from the heat. Let cool for 5 minutes. Add the cream and ¼ cup of butter and whisk constantly until well incorporated. Set aside and keep warm.

Melt ¼ cup of whole butter in a nonstick pan over medium heat. Add the bananas, currants, and 2 tablespoons of sugar, and cook until golden brown, approximately 2 minutes. At the last moment, add the chocolate chips. Remove the pan from the stove. Keep the bananas warm.

On each serving plate sprinkle cinnamon around the border. Place 2 tablespoons of banana mixture in the center of each plate. Place phyllo layer on top. Place another 2 tablespoons of bananas on top of phyllo and finish with another layer of phyllo. Pour 3 tablespoons of caramel sauce around each Mille-Feuille. Serve immediately.
MAKES 4 SERVINGS.

Petite Auberge
❧

863 Bush Street
San Francisco, California 94108
(800) 365-3004

Downtown San Francisco and the Petite Auberge just seem to go together because of this inn's charming French country decor. Its guest-pleasing features include delicate lace curtains, handcrafted armoires, terra cotta tiles, and a huge mural of a country market scene in the dining room. The inn is conveniently positioned just four blocks from San Francisco's Union Square and only two blocks from the Powell Street cable car.

Raspberry Pastry Bars

1½ cups sweet butter
1 cup sugar
½ cup brown sugar
1 teaspoon vanilla extract
2 eggs
3¾ cups all-purpose flour
1 12-ounce jar raspberry preserves
1 cup walnuts, chopped

In a large bowl cream together the butter and sugars until fluffy. Beat in the eggs and vanilla. Add 3½ cups of flour and mix to form a thick dough. Spread three-fourths of the batter on an 11 x 17-inch jelly roll pan. Spread the preserves evenly over the top and sprinkle with chopped nuts. Blend the remaining flour and dough and crumble on the top. Bake in a 350° oven for 35 minutes. Cool before cutting into bars.

MAKES 4 DOZEN BARS.

Italian Pine Nut Cookies

1½ cups slivered, blanched almonds
3½ cups pine nuts
1½ cups plus 6 tablespoons sugar
3 egg whites, room temperature
¼ teaspoon cream of tartar
¼ teaspoon almond extract

In a food processor with a metal blade grind the almonds, pine nuts, and 6 tablespoons of sugar to a fine powder. Set aside.

In a large bowl beat the egg whites and cream of tartar until soft peaks form. Add ½ cup of sugar and beat until shiny soft peaks form. Gently add the almond extract, ground almonds, and pine nuts. Drop by teaspoonfuls onto greased cookie sheets. Bake in a 375° oven for 15 to 18 minutes, or until golden brown.

MAKES 3 DOZEN COOKIES.

The Sherman House

2160 Green Street
San Francisco, California 94123
(415) 563-3600

Built in 1876 in the grandest Victorian style, this Mansard-roofed San Francisco landmark was for fifty years home of Leander Sherman, a renowned patron of music and the arts. Today the French-Italianate mansion is a small luxury hotel, but with its lovely formal decor it remains a fitting memorial to Sherman. Rooms feature canopy beds and fireplaces. Some offer views of the bay and Golden Gate Bridge; others overlook English gardens.

Lemon-Cornmeal and Buttermilk Pancakes

2 cups all-purpose flour
1 cup cornmeal
1 teaspoon vanilla extract
½ cup sugar
1 tablespoon baking powder
1 teaspoon salt
2 pounds fresh peaches, peeled, sliced thin (about 5 cups)
Juice and grated zest of 1 lemon
2 eggs
2 cups buttermilk
....
Caramel-Orange Syrup (recipe follows)

In a medium bowl combine the dry ingredients and stir until blended. Add the remaining ingredients and mix well. Preheat a nonstick skillet and coat with cooking spray. For each pancake use approximately 1½ ounces of batter. Cook until golden brown, and then flip to cook the other side.

Serve with Caramel-Orange Syrup.

MAKES ABOUT 8 SERVINGS.

Caramel-Orange Syrup

2 cups sugar
¼ cup water
½ cup soft butter
½ cup heavy cream
Juice and grated zest of 2 oranges

In a saucepan melt sugar and water together until it turns a light golden brown (do not stir). When it gets to the proper color plunge the pot into ice water to stop cooking. Add the butter, cream, orange zest, and orange juice. Whisk until well blended. (Be very careful when adding cool ingredients to the hot sugar mixture. Because of temperature difference there is a tendency for the mixture to foam up and over the sides of the pot.) Serve with pancakes.

MAKES ABOUT 3 CUPS OF SYRUP.

Lavender Sour Cream Waffles with Pistachio Praline Cream

¼ cup fresh lavender
½ cup hard-wheat flour
½ cup all-purpose flour
2 teaspoons baking powder
¼ teaspoon baking soda
3 tablespoons sugar
¼ teaspoon salt
3 eggs, separated
¾ cup milk
¾ cup sour cream
½ teaspoon vanilla extract
3 tablespoons melted, unsalted butter
Pistachio Praline Cream (recipe follows)

In a large bowl combine all of the dry ingredients and mix well. In a separate bowl combine the yolks, milk, sour cream, vanilla, and melted butter. Make a well in the dry ingredients and add the liquid mixture. Stir until just combined, being careful not to overmix. In a clean dry bowl beat the egg whites until soft peaks form. Fold the whites gently into the batter. Bake the waffles in a preheated waffle iron, according to the manufacturer's directions, until golden brown.

Serve with Pistachio Praline Cream.

MAKES 4 TO 6 SERVINGS.

Pistachio Praline Cream

- 2/3 cup firmly packed light brown sugar
- 2 tablespoons milk
- 2 teaspoons unsalted butter
- 1/2 cup shelled, unsalted pistachio nuts, skins removed

....

- 1/4 cup sugar
- 1/2 vanilla bean, split lengthwise and scraped
- 4 ounces cream cheese, softened
- 1/2 cup heavy cream
- 1/2 cup crème fraîche

Lightly oil an 8-inch square baking pan. In a saucepan combine sugar, milk, and butter, and cook on medium heat stirring often, until the mixture starts to foam up. Lower the heat until large bubbles slow and the praline turns medium to dark brown in color (300° or hard-crack stage). Add the pistachios. Pour the praline mixture onto an oiled pan and spread evenly. When the praline is cool transfer it to a food processor and pulse until it is in a semi-smooth state.

In a small bowl cream together the sugar, scraped vanilla bean, and cream cheese. Slowly add the cream and crème fraîche. Whisk until light and fluffy.

Fold together praline and cream mixture gently until combined.

MAKES ABOUT 2½ CUPS.

Local Organic Mesclun Greens with Warm Herbed Montrachet Tossed in Rosemary Honey and Mustard Vinaigrette

- 6 8-inch sprigs rosemary, chopped fine
- 1 medium shallot, diced fine
- 2 garlic cloves, crushed with 1/4 teaspoon salt
- 1/2 cup Dijon mustard
- 1/2 cup red wine vinegar
- 1/4 cup wildflower honey
  Salt and pepper to taste
- 1/2 cup olive oil
- 1/2 cup oil

....

- 4 sprigs thyme, stripped and chopped
- 1 sprigs rosemary, stripped and chopped

- 1/8 bunch parsley, chopped
- 4 leaves sage, diced fine (dice to avoid browning)
- 1 2/3 bunches chives, diced
- 3 sprigs oregano, stripped and diced fine
  Freshly ground black pepper
- 1 2-pound log Montrachet cheese (if unavailable substitute goat cheese)
  Mesclun greens

In a food processor combine the rosemary, shallot, garlic, mustard, vinegar, honey, and salt and pepper to taste. Add the oils slowly and whip together until emulsified.

In a shallow bowl combine all of the chopped herbs. Grind fresh pepper onto the log of cheese. Roll the log cheese in fresh herbs, applying light pressure. Wrap in plastic tightly to set herbs. Chill with the wrap intact.

To warm the cheese, leave in wrap and cut into ½-inch wheels. Remove the plastic wrap. Place the wheels on waxed paper. Bake in a 375° oven for 3 minutes.

While the cheese is warming, season the greens and add vinaigrette, then toss lightly to coat the greens. Place the greens on the center of a plate. Put warmed cheese on the center of the greens.

MAKES 8 SERVINGS.

Victorian Inn on the Park

301 Lyon Street
San Francisco, California 94117
(415) 931-1830, (800) 435-1967

———————————

A registered historic landmark, the inn was built in 1897 and has been restored to its original nineteenth century elegance. Every room is unique, and each of them has comforters and down pillows to ease guests off to sleep. Guests are invited to relax in the sitting room, parlor, or library. As its name implies, the inn looks across into

Victorian Inn on the Park

Golden Gate Park. Its central location places guests within minutes of the Civic Center, the University of San Francisco, museums, and countless other city attractions.

Zucchini Muffins

- 3 cups all-purpose flour
- 2 cups shredded, unpeeled zucchini
- 1½ cups sugar
- 1 teaspoon salt
- 1 teaspoon baking powder
- 3/4 teaspoon baking soda
- 1 cup raisins
- 1/2 teaspoon ground ginger
- 1 teaspoon ground cloves
- 1 teaspoon grated nutmeg
- 1 tablespoon ground cinnamon
- 3 eggs
- 1 cup oil

In a large bowl mix all ingredients except the eggs and oil. In a separate bowl mix the eggs and oil. Pour the liquid mixture over the dry ingredients. Stir until mixed well. Spoon into greased muffin cups. Bake in a 350° oven for 25 minutes.

MAKES ABOUT 24 MUFFINS.

Cranberry Bread

- 1/4 cup unsalted butter
- 2 cups sugar
- 2 eggs
- 4 cups cake flour
- 3 teaspoons baking powder

1   teaspoon salt
1   teaspoon baking soda
1   cup orange juice
1½ cups hot water
    Grated zest of ½ lemon
    Grated zest of ½ orange
2   cups walnuts
4   cups cranberries

In a large bowl cream the butter and the sugar. Blend in the eggs. In a separate bowl sift together the dry ingredients. Add the dry mixture to the butter mixture alternately with the liquids. Fold in the orange and lemon zests, walnuts, and cranberries. Pour the batter into 2 greased 5 x 9-inch pans. Bake in a 375° oven for about 50 minutes.

MAKES 2 LOAVES

White Swan Inn

845 Bush Street
San Francisco, California 94108
(800) 999-9570

Situated in downtown San Francisco, this inn has the flavor and atmosphere of a small London hotel, with distinctive poster beds, floral wallpaper, and wool mattress covers. Afternoon tea is served daily in the parlor. Another special touch is the well-stocked library, where guests may relax and browse in its quiet, unhurried atmosphere.

Roasted Garlic

2   whole heads garlic
½   cup crumbled blue cheese
1   tablespoon fresh rosemary leaves

Cut the tops off the heads of garlic. Place the garlic in a garlic roaster. Bake in a 375° oven for 45 minutes.

Remove from the oven and sprinkle with crumbled blue cheese and rosemary. Bake uncovered for another 15 minutes.

MAKES 4 SERVINGS.

Lemon-Orange Crunches

1   cup packed light brown sugar
½   cup shortening
1   tablespoon grated lemon zest
1   tablespoon grated orange zest
1   egg
1½ cups all-purpose flour
½   teaspoon baking soda
½   teaspoon cream of tartar
2   tablespoons sugar

In a large bowl mix the brown sugar, shortening, lemon and orange zests, and egg. Mix in the flour, soda, and cream of tartar. Stir until a thick dough forms. Shape the dough into 1-inch balls, and dip the tops in sugar. Place on an ungreased cookie sheet. Bake in a 350° oven for 10 to 12 minutes or until almost no indentation remains when touched.

MAKES 4 DOZEN COOKIES.

Bath Street Inn

1720 Bath Street
Santa Barbara, California 93101
(805) 682-9680

More than a century old, this Queen Anne home welcomes guest with an old-fashioned grace. Comfortable chairs, a warm fire, and a friendly golden retriever await them. The eight guest rooms in the main house are fitted into the nooks and crannies typical of Victorian-era construction. Two additional rooms in the adjacent Summer House offer extra space and privacy.

Bath Street Inn Scones

¼   cup sugar
3   tablespoons baking powder
1   teaspoon salt
½   teaspoon baking soda
4   cups all-purpose flour
....
¾   cup butter
1   cup buttermilk
1   cup currants or raisins
4   eggs

In a bowl mix together sugar, baking powder, salt, soda, and flour. Cut in the butter until the mixture resembles coarse crumbs. Blend in the buttermilk, currants, and eggs. Handle the dough gently, kneading a little. Form the dough into 4 balls and press into 6-inch rounds that are ¾-inch thick. Place the rounds on ungreased cookie sheets. Cut each round into a pinwheel. Bake in a 425° oven for 10 to 12 minutes.

MAKES 32 SCONES.

Bath Street Inn Granola

10 cups uncooked oatmeal
1   cup shredded coconut
2   cups sunflower seeds
2   cups sliced almonds (raw, unsalted)
1   cup wheat germ
1   tablespoon ground cinnamon
2   cups sesame seeds (raw)
....
1   cup oil
¼   cup water
1½ cup honey
3   teaspoons vanilla extract

In a large bowl combine the oatmeal, coconut, sunflower seeds, almonds, wheat germ, cinnamon, and sesame seeds. Divide the mixture equally among 2 large lasagna pans.

In a saucepan heat together slightly the oil, water, honey, and vanilla. Pour the mixture over the dry ingredients and mix well. Bake in a 350° oven for 30 minutes stirring every 10 minutes.

Cool and store in airtight containers.

Note: For a wonderful gift idea, make up a batch and place it in beautiful jars.

MAKES ABOUT 18 CUPS.

Glenborough Inn

1327 Bath Street
Santa Barbara, California 93101
(805) 966-0589

The inn consists of three houses: the Craftsman Bungalow Main House built in 1906, the White Farm House, dating to 1912, and the Victorian Cottage, which has stood here since 1886. Each has its own personality, and together, they offer accommodations to suit a wide variety of tastes. The emphasis, of course, is on the old-fashioned. The Main House features cross-cut oak beams, an Edison Victrola in the parlor, and a hot tub in the garden.

Mayan Maise Soufflé

- 2   8-inch flour tortillas
- 2   15-ounce cans baby corn, drained (reserve 1 cup liquid)
- 1   tablespoon fresh basil
- 2   cloves garlic, finely diced
- 1   4-ounce can jalapeño chilies, diced
- 1   small onion, finely diced
- 1   14-ounce can pimentos, drained and diced
- 1/3   cup shredded Jalapeño Jack cheese
- 1   2-ounce can sliced black olives
- 4   large eggs
- 1   teaspoon ground cumin
- 1   tablespoon lime juice
- 1/4   cup all-purpose flour
- 1   teaspoon pepper
- 1   teaspoon garlic powder
- 1/4   cup milk

Grease a 9-inch pie plate. Place 1 tortilla in the bottom of the pie plate. Layer baby corn in a spoke fashion, with points toward the center, and sprinkle with basil leaves, diced garlic, and green chilies.

Layer a second flour tortilla on top and add another layer of baby corn in the same fashion as the first. Sprinkle with diced onion

and pimentos to cover. Cover the layers with shredded jalepeño cheese and top with black olives.

In a blender combine 1 cup of liquid reserved from the baby corn, the eggs, cumin, lime juice, flour, pepper, garlic powder, and milk. Blend for 2 minutes. Pour the egg mixture over the layers, making sure to leave the top third of the dish free to allow the mixture to rise while cooking. Refrigerate for 2 hours or overnight.

Bake in a 350° oven bakc for 45 minutes to 1 hour, until firm, golden brown, and set in the middle.

Cool 15 minutes before cutting.

MAKES 6 SERVINGS.

Chili Relleno Soufflé

- 12   corn tortillas, cut into 1/4-inch strips
- 1   tablespoon oregano
- 1   16-ounce can Anaheim chili peppers, seeded and sliced
- 2   garlic cloves, finely diced
- 1   teaspoon lemon pepper
- 1   large onion, finely diced
- 1   teaspoon garlic salt
- 1 1/2   cups shredded sharp Cheddar cheese
- 1 1/2   cups shredded Monterey Jack cheese
- 1 1/2   cups water
- 1/2   cup nonfat dry milk
- 1   teaspoon cayenne pepper
- 1   teaspoon coriander powder
- 1   teaspoon cumin
- 1   large tomato, cut in quarters
- 1   bunch fresh cilantro, washed

Glenborough Inn

- 1   cup all-purpose flour
- 8   large eggs
- 1   large red bell pepper, finely diced

Layer enough tortilla strips to cover the bottom of a greased 9 x 13-inch pan. Sprinkle the oregano over the strips and then layer some of the Anaheim chili slices over the strips. Sprinkle garlic and lemon pepper over the chilies and then cover with another layer of tortilla strips. Layer Ahaheim chili slices over the strips and then sprinkle onion and garlic salt over the chilies. Place the remaining tortilla strips on top and cover with a mix of both cheeses.

In a blender blend the water, nonfat milk, cayenne, coriander, cumin, tomato pieces, cilantro (10 sprigs), flour, and eggs for 2 minutes. Pour egg mixture over the layers and top with red pepper. Refrigerate for 2 hours or overnight.

When ready to cook, preheat the oven to 350° and then reduce the heat to 300°. Bake in a 300° oven for 45 minutes. Increase the oven temperature to 350° and continue to bake for 15 minutes, until the center is set.

Remove from the oven and cool for 15 minutes before cutting.

Top with sour cream, salsa, and a few springs of cilantro.

Note: Watch not to burn the edges. If the edges or sides get too brown before the middle is set, reduce the heat to 300° and bake longer. To reduce the fat content of this recipe, reduce or eliminate the cheeses.

MAKES 8 SERVINGS.

Persimmon Cookies

- 1   cup shortening
- 2   cups sugar
- 2   cups chopped nuts
- 2   cups raisins
- 4   cups all-purpose flour
- 1/2   teaspoon ground cloves
- 1/2   teaspoon ground cinnamon
- 1/2   teaspoon grated nutmeg
- 2   teaspoons baking soda, dissolved in persimmon pulp
- 2   cups persimmon pulp
- 2   eggs, beaten

In a large bowl cream together the shortening and sugar. In a separate bowl combine the nuts, raisins, flour, cloves, cinnamon, and nutmeg. Add the dry ingredients to the creamed mixture. In a medium bowl blend the baking soda into the persimmon pulp. Blend in the eggs. Add the persimmon mixture to the creamed ingredients, mixing well. Drop by spoonful onto a greased cookie sheet. Bake in a 350° oven for 12 to 15 minutes.

MAKES ABOUT 4 DOZEN.

Simpson House Inn

121 East Arrellaga Street
Santa Barbara, California 93101
(805) 963-7067

An Eastlake-style Victorian mansion, the Simpson House is as grand a home for a B&B as one is likely to find in California. Built in 1874, it dates to a time when one could only reach Santa Barbara from the sea or by a thirty-six hour stagecoach ride from San Francisco. The six guest rooms in the main house are furnished and decorated in high-Victorian style. In what was once the estate's barn, four additional rooms take a completely different approach with rustic pine floors covered by oriental carpets. Three charming garden cottages are also available.

Artichoke Dip

- 1 5-pound 8-ounce can artichokes in water (drain in colander)
- 1 pound grated mozzarella cheese
- 1 pound grated Parmesan cheese
- 3 cups mayonnaise
- 3 garlic cloves, minced (or 1½ teaspoons chopped garlic)

In a food processor lightly process the artichokes. In a large bowl stir together the artichokes and remaining ingredients. Transfer the desired amount to a baking dish. Bake in a 350° oven for about 20 minutes, until bubbling, and serve on toasted pieces of sourdough bread. Refrigerate the unused portion.

MAKES ABOUT 18 CUPS.

Simpson House Banana Muffins

- 1 cup butter
- 1 cup sugar
- 2 eggs
- 2 cups mashed ripe bananas
- 2 teaspoons baking soda, dissolved in 2 tablespoons hot water
- 3 cups all-purpose flour
- ½ teaspoon salt
- 2 teaspoons nutmeg
- 1 cup chopped walnuts

Spray 24 muffin tins with cooking spray. In large bowl cream together butter and sugar. Add eggs, bananas, and dissolved soda, mixing well. Stir in the flour, salt, nutmeg, and walnuts, blending well. Pour the batter into the prepared muffin tins. Bake in a 375° oven for 20 minutes or until done.

MAKES 2 DOZEN.

Pesto

- 3 cups basil leaves
- ⅔ cup olive oil
- 5 ounces Parmesan cheese, grated
- 2 cups pine nuts
- 8 garlic clove

In a food processor combine all ingredients and process until smooth.

MAKES 3 CUPS.

Boursin

- 4 8-ounce packages cream cheese
- ¼ cup crushed garlic
- ¼ cup caraway seeds
- ¼ cup basil
- ¼ cup dill

In a large mixing bowl soften the cream cheese. Add the garlic, caraway seeds, basil, and dill. Mix together well.

Divide into 4 to 5 equal portions on plastic wrap and shape into 1-inch thick circles. Wrap tightly with plastic. Freeze. Thaw as needed. Serve with bread or crackers.

MAKES 5 CUPS.

Simpson House's Best Stolen Chocolate Chip Recipe

- 2 cups butter
- 2 cups sugar
- 2 cups firmly packed brown sugar
- 4 eggs
- 2 teaspoons vanilla extract
- 4 cups all-purpose flour
- 2 teaspoons baking powder
- 2 teaspoons salt
- 2 teaspoons baking soda
- 2 cups white chocolate chips (Ghirardelli are best)
- 2 cups chocolate chips
- 2 cups raisins
- 3 cups nuts
- 2 cups old-fashioned oats
- 3 cups granola (homemade is great, otherwise use an orange/almond mix)

In a large bowl blend the butter, sugar, and brown sugar, until creamy. Add eggs and vanilla. In a separate bowl sift the flour, baking powder, salt, and soda. Add to the butter mixture and beat well. Stir in the remaining ingredients

Mix well and shape into golf ball sized balls. Place on an ungreased cookie sheet. Bake in a 375° oven for 8 to 10 minutes. Baking longer will produce a crunchier cookie.

MAKES ABOUT 5 DOZEN.

Simpson House Corn Blueberry Muffins

- 1 cup buttermilk
- 6 tablespoons butter, melted
- 1 egg, beaten
- 1 cup cornmeal
- ⅓ cup sugar
- 1 cup all-purpose flour
- 2½ teaspoons baking powder
- ¼ teaspoon salt
- 1½ cups blueberries

In a large bowl combine the buttermilk, butter, and egg. In a separate bowl sift the dry ingredients together. Add the dry ingredients to the liquid mixture stirring just until moistened. Fold in the blueberries. Pour into greased muffin cups. Bake in a 400° oven for 20 to 25 minutes.

MAKES 12 MUFFINS.

Simpson House Roasted Garlic

¼ cup olive oil
8 whole heads elephant garlic

Coat the bottom of a shallow baking dish with oil. Cut the heads of garlic in half horizontally, leaving the skins on for roasting. Place cut-side-down in the oil. Cover with foil and bake slowly in a 325° oven for 40 to 50 minutes until the garlic is tender and spreadable.

May be baked in a 400° oven for 20 minutes.

Serve spread on homemade crostini or baguette slices.

MAKES ABOUT 16 TO 30 SERVINGS.

Simpson House Marinated Mushrooms

5 pounds mushrooms
9½ cups olive oil
3¼ cups balsamic or red wine vinegar
1 teaspoon crushed fresh rosemary
1½ teaspoons crushed oregano
1 teaspoon crushed basil
2 tablespoons garlic powder
2 tablespoons crushed fresh garlic
2½ teaspoons black pepper
½ cup firmly packed brown sugar
2½ teaspoons Tabasco sauce
¼ cup Worcestershire sauce

Wash and trim the stems from the mushrooms. In a large bowl mix together remaining ingredients very well. Put the mushrooms and liquid in large containers. Store in the refrigerator overnight. Stir or shake full containers once or twice during storage time to marinate all mushrooms.

MAKES 10 TO 15 SERVINGS.

Simpson House Pear Chutney

6 or more cups peeled and cubed green ripe pears
   Salt to taste
6 cups firmly packed dark brown sugar
1½ cups cider vinegar
2 large yellow onions, peeled and diced
1 large garlic head, peeled and minced
2½ cups seedless raisins
½ cup gingerroot, peeled, cut, and minced
2 tablespoons canned jalapeño pepper
2½ teaspoons ground allspice
1½ teaspoons ground cloves
1½ teaspoons grated nutmeg
1 teaspoon ground ginger

Sprinkle the pears with salt and allow to stand overnight in a colander. Rinse and drain thoroughly.

In a saucepan boil the sugar, vinegar, half of the pears, and remaining ingredients for 30 minutes. Add the remaining fruit and cook until thick and dark. This can sometimes take as much as 2 hours.

Sterilize 8 half-pint jars. Pour the hot chutney into sterilized jars. Seal and process in a water bath for 5 minutes. Check the seals.

Serving suggestions: Serve on whole meal bread with cream cheese and cucumber slices for tea sandwiches or pour over a shaped round of cream cheese for hors d'oeuvres.

MAKES 8 HALF PINTS.

Simpson House Savory Eggs

¼ cup butter
¼ cup all-purpose flour
¼ teaspoon thyme
¼ teaspoon dried marjoram
¼ teaspoon dried basil
1 cup whole milk
1 cup heavy cream
16 ounces grated white Cheddar cheese
¼ cup chopped parsley
18 hard-boiled eggs, peeled and sliced thinly
   Bacon bits

In a saucepan melt the butter and blend in the flour to make a roux. Add the herbs except for the parsley. Add the milk and cream slowly, stirring continuously, until boiling and thickened. Add the cheese, stirring until melted. Add parsley, and then set the sauce aside.

Place the sliced eggs in a 9 x 13-inch baking dish or individual-sized baking dishes, layering with sauce. Bake in a 350° oven for 20 or 25 minutes.

Top with bacon bits. Serve hot.

MAKES 8 SERVINGS.

Sun-dried Tomato Pesto

1 cup sun-dried tomatoes
2 cups fresh basil or spinach
6 cloves garlic
¼ cup lemon juice
½ cup plus 2 tablespoons olive oil
½ cup pine nuts
¾ cup grated Parmesan cheese

In a medium bowl soak the tomatoes in hot water to soften. Drain. In a food processor combine the tomatoes and remaining ingredients and process until blended well.

MAKES ABOUT 4 CUPS.

Blue Cheese Tapenade

32 ounces drained pitted black olives
4 large cloves garlic or 2 teaspoons minced garlic (without oil)
¾ cup pine nuts
⅔ cup olive oil
1 pound blue cheese, crumbled
1 8-ounce package cream cheese

In a food processor combine all ingredients and process until well blended.

MAKES ABOUT 8 CUPS.

Kalamata Tapenade

2 cloves garlic, peeled
1 cup kalamata olives, pitted
1 tablespoon capers
1½ tablespoons lemon juice
1½ tablespoons olive oil (unless olives are in oil, then decrease to ¾ tablespoon)
   Ground black pepper to taste

In a food processor combine all ingredients and process until blended well.

Note: We serve tapenade with homemade herbed crostini or fresh sourdough bread for hors d'oeuvres. It's also delicious served with endive spears. It is a perfect complement to any Mediterranean menu.

MAKES ABOUT 1 CUP.

The Darling House

≈

314 West Cliff Drive
Santa Cruz, California 95060
(408) 458-1958

Set among towering palms and a citrus orchard, the Darling House was designed by the famous architect William Weeks and built in 1910. It takes full advantage of its seaside location. Beveled glass, Tiffany lamps, and open hearths recall its early days as a splendid coastal mansion.

Chile-Egg Puff

    10 eggs
    ½ cup all-purpose flour
    1 teaspoon baking powder
    ½ teaspoon salt
    1 pint small curd cottage cheese
    4 cups shredded Monterey Jack cheese
    ½ cup margarine
    2 4-ounce cans diced green chilies

In a large bowl beat the eggs until light and lemon colored. Add the flour, baking powder, salt, cheeses, and margarine and blend well. Stir in the chilies. Pour the mixture into a well-greased 9 x 13-inch pan. Bake in a 350° oven for 35 minutes or until the center is firm and the top is brown. Serve hot.
MAKES 10 TO 12 SERVINGS.

Master Matthew's Gingerbread Mix

    8 cups all-purpose flour
    2¼ cups sugar
    2½ teaspoons baking soda
    2 tablespoons baking powder
    3 tablespoons ground ginger
    3 tablespoons ground cinnamon

    1 teaspoon ground cloves
    1 tablespoon salt
    2¼ cups shortening

In a large bowl sift together twice all ingredients except the shortening. Cut the shortening into the dry ingredients until the mixture resembles cornmeal. Transfer to a tightly covered jar and refrigerate. Keeps for 3 months.
MAKES 6 8-INCH SQUARE PANS.

Gingerbread

    3 cups gingerbread mix
    1 beaten egg
    ½ cup dark molasses
    ½ cup boiling water

In a large bowl combine all ingredients and blend until smooth. Pour into a greased 8-inch square pan. Bake in a 350° oven for 35 minutes.
MAKES 6 TO 8 SERVINGS.

Channel Road Inn

≈

219 West Channel Road
Santa Monica, California 90402
(310) 459-1920

Guests enter the inn through massive doors and step into a living room that evokes images of a Santa Monica home in the early 1920s. A shingle-clad Colonial Revival home built in 1910, it originally stood on Santa Monica's Second Street but was moved to it present location in 1962. The inn's light, airy rooms are individually decorated and furnished. Some feature pine four-posters, while others emphasize white wicker. The J. Paul Getty Museum, Santa Monica Municipal Pier, and Will Rogers Park are nearby.

Blueberry Bread

    ½ cup butter, softened
    1 cup sugar
    2 eggs
    ½ teaspoon vanilla extract
    1 cup sour cream
    2 cups all-purpose flour
    1 teaspoon baking powder
    1 teaspoon baking soda
    1 cup fresh or frozen blueberries

In a large bowl cream the butter and sugar with an electric mixer. Beat in the eggs, vanilla, and sour cream. Mix in the flour, baking powder, and baking soda. Slowly fold in the blueberries. Pour the batter into a greased 5 x 9-inch loaf pan. Bake in a 350° oven for 1 hour or until a toothpick inserted in the center comes out clean.
MAKES 1 LOAF.

Channel Road Inn

Vanilla Streusel Coffee Cake

    3 cups all-purpose flour
    1½ teaspoons baking powder
    1½ teaspoons baking soda
    ¼ teaspoon salt
    1½ cups butter, softened
    1½ cups sugar
    3 eggs
    1½ cups sour cream
    1½ teaspoon vanilla, extract
    ¾ cup firmly packed brown sugar
    ¾ cup chopped nuts
    1½ teaspoons ground cinnamon
    2 tablespoons vanilla extract mixed with 2 tablespoons water

Butter a 10-inch tube pan.

In a medium bowl sift together flour, baking powder, soda, and salt and set aside. In large bowl combine the butter and sugar and beat until fluffy. Add the eggs one at a time, beating well after each addition. Blend in the sour cream and vanilla. Gradually add the sifted dry ingredients and beat well. In a separate bowl combine the brown sugar, nuts, and cinnamon. Turn one-third of the batter into the tube pan and sprinkle with half of the nut mixture. Repeat. Add the remaining batter. Spoon diluted vanilla over top. Bake in a 325° oven for 60 to 70 minutes.

Cool completely before removing from the pan.

MAKES 10 TO 12 SERVINGS.

The Gables Inn

4257 Petaluma Hill Road
Santa Rosa, California 95404
(707) 585-7777

Completed in 1876, the Gables is a near-perfect example of the high-Victorian Gothic Revival style. Its twelve-foot ceilings, marble fireplaces, and spectacular mahogany staircase make an emphatic architectural statement. Fifteen gables crown a series of unusual keyhole-shaped windows. Visitors will appreciate the care with which it has been preserved and the attention to even the smallest details. In their rooms, freshly cut flowers and cozy down comforters offer guests an almost irresistible invitation to settle in for the evening.

Amaretto Cream Topping

- 1 **cup sour cream**
- 2 **tablespoons confectioners' sugar**
- 2 **tablespoons Amaretto**
- ½ **teaspoon ground cinnamon**
- 1 **cup heavy cream, whipped**

The Gables Inn

In a medium bowl stir together all ingredients except the whipped cream. Then fold into the whipped cream. Serve a generous dollop on fresh tropical fruits such as pineapple chunks, papaya and mango slices, banana slices, strawberry halves, and kiwi slices. At the Gables, we serve this combination of fruit in crystal goblets topped with the Amaretto cream, then sprinkled with toasted coconut.

MAKES ABOUT 6 TO 8 SERVINGS.

The Gables' Popovers

- 2 **cups milk**
- 2 **teaspoons sugar**
- ½ **teaspoon salt**
- 4 **eggs**
- 2 **cups all-purpose flour**

In a blender combine all ingredients except the flour. Blend for a few seconds, then add the flour. Blend until smooth, but don't overmix. Pour into 6 greased giant or Texas-size muffin cups (6-ounce capacity). Put into a cold oven, set the oven at 425°, and bake for 30 minutes.

Reduce the oven temperature to 400° and bake 30 more minutes.

A great popover should be crisp on the outside, tender and moist on the inside. You may need to adjust the oven time and temperature to achieve perfect results, but our guests think they are spectacular and worth the effort! Popovers should be well-browned and 2 or more inches above the tops of muffin cups. Serve immediately with butter and jam.

MAKES 6 POPOVERS.

Melitta Station Inn

5850 Melita Road
Santa Rosa, California 95409
(707) 538-7712

In its long career, this hard-working inn has served as a stagecoach stop and railway freight station, as a home for the workers who hauled the stones that paved San Francisco's streets, and as a general store and post office. Now more than a century old, it's a delightful inn catering to visitors to California's famed wine country and the Valley of the Moon. Rooms are furnished with antiques and country collectibles.

Strata

- 12 **slices bread, remove crusts removed and cut into cubes**
- 2 **cups Cheddar cheese, shredded**
- 1½ **cups diced ham (I use turkey ham)**
- 1 **pound fresh asparagus, or canned, cut into 1- to 2-inch pieces (If using fresh, boil them for 4 minutes only)**
- 7 **eggs**
- 2 **tablespoons minced instant onion**
- 1 **teaspoon salt**
- 2 **teaspoons dry mustard**
- 3 **cups milk**

Butter a 9 x 13-inch glass pan and place the bread in 2 layers on the bottom. Sprinkle a little cheese on the bread. Then add the diced ham, the asparagus, then the cheese. In a medium bowl mix the eggs, instant onion, salt, dry mustard, and milk, and pour the egg mixture over the casserole. Cover with plastic wrap and refrigerate overnight.

Bake in a 350° oven for about 50 minutes. Easy and delicious.

MAKES 8 SERVINGS.

Apple Omelet

1 tablespoon butter or margarine
1 large tart apple, cored and sliced
2 teaspoons raisins
2 teaspoons slivered almonds
1½ teaspoons firmly packed brown
    sugar
½ teaspoon vanilla extract
1 tablespoon lemon juice (or lime)
2 tablespoons butter
4 eggs
    Confectioners' sugar and 1 table-
    spoon sour cream for garnish

In a small skillet melt 1 tablespoon of butter. Add the apple, raisins, almonds, brown sugar, vanilla, and lemon juice, and sauté until the apples are tender.

In a separate skillet melt 2 tablespoons of butter and make a 4-egg omelet. Place the apple mixture in the middle of the omelet and cook until the bottom is crusty. Turn into the skillet in which the apple mixture was prepared. Slide to a warm platter and sprinkle with confectioners' sugar. Garnish with sour cream.

MAKES 2 SERVINGS.

Apple Pancake

6 tablespoons butter
2 large tart apples, peeled, cored, and
    sliced
3 tablespoons lemon juice
¼ teaspoon ground cinnamon
5 tablespoons confectioners' sugar
3 eggs
½ cup all-purpose flour
½ cup milk
    Confectioners' sugar for dusting

In a 10-inch skillet or shallow pan melt the butter and remove the pan from the heat. If the handle of the skillet is not ovenproof,

Melitta Station Inn

wrap with several layers of foil. Remove 2 tablespoons of the melted butter and set it aside in a small bowl. Place the apple slices in a large bowl with the lemon juice. Stir the cinnamon into the sugar and sprinkle the sugar mixture over the apple slices. Toss to mix. Put the skillet back on the burner and turn the heat to medium. Add the apples and cook, stirring often, for about 3 or 4 minutes, or until tender.

In a separate bowl beat the eggs. Add the flour and milk, a little at time, and beat until smooth. Add the reserved 2 tablespoons of butter. Spread the apples evenly over the bottom of the skillet and pour the batter on top. Bake in a 425° oven for about 20 minutes, or until golden and puffy. Turn immediately onto a warm platter. Dust with confectioners' sugar. Serve at once.

MAKES 3 TO 4 SERVINGS.

Vintners Inn

❧

4350 Barnes Road
Santa Rosa, California 95403
(707) 575-7350

An Old World atmosphere prevails here. Inn buildings are arranged around a central plaza with a large fountain and tile walkways bordered by flowers. Each of the forty-five rooms is individually decorated on a French country theme with antique European pine furnishings. The morning sun slanting down through orderly rows of grapes around Vintners Inn helps create the ambiance of a small European country inn, yet its setting is the exact "crossroads" of the Sonoma County wine country, just 60 miles north of San Francisco.

Scott and Marge Noll's Espresso Coffee Cake

2 cups sifted all-purpose flour
½ teaspoon baking soda
1 teaspoon baking powder
¼ teaspoon salt
¾ cup unsalted butter, softened
1 cup sugar
2 large eggs
2 teaspoons vanilla extract
1 cup sour cream
2 tablespoons instant espresso pow-
    der, dissolved in 1 tablespoon hot
    water
....
2 to 3 tablespoons strong brewed cof-
    fee
1½ teaspoons instant espresso powder
¾ cup confectioners' sugar

In a medium bowl sift the flour, soda, baking powder, and salt. In a large bowl cream the butter and add the sugar gradually, beating until light and fluffy. Add the eggs, one at a time, beating well after each addition. Beat in the vanilla. Add the flour mixture alternately with the sour cream, beginning and ending with the flour mixture, and blending well after each addition.

In a cup dissolve 2 tablespoons of espresso powder in the hot water. Transfer about one-third of the batter to a small bowl and stir in the espresso mixture, stirring until well combined. Spoon half of the plain batter into a well-buttered 8-inch bundt pan and spread evenly. Spoon the coffee batter over the plain batter, and spread evenly. Top with the remaining plain batter, spreading evenly. Bake in a 350° oven for 55 to 60 minutes or until golden and toothpick inserted into the center comes out clean.

Let the cake cool in the pan for 30 minutes. Invert onto a rack and cool thoroughly.

In a small bowl stir together 2 tablespoons of the brewed coffee and 1½ teaspoons of espresso powder, stirring until the powder is dissolved. Sift the confectioner's sugar, and blend it into the coffee. (If necessary, add more coffee to obtain a pouring consistency.) Pour the glaze over the cooled coffee cake and let it stand for 10 minutes or until the glaze is set.

MAKES 8 SERVINGS.

Ham and Cheese Bread Pudding

4   eggs
6   egg yolks
1   quart cream
1   quart half and half
2½ cups grated Cheddar cheese
2½ cups grated smoked Gouda cheese
1   small onion, diced
4   cups ground smoked ham
¼   cup Dijon mustard
⅓   cup sugar
2   tablespoons fresh oregano
1   loaf cubed brioche bread (remove crusts)

In a large bowl beat the eggs, egg yolks, cream, and half and half together. Add the remaining ingredients except the cubed bread. Mix well. Add the cubed brioche bread and let it soak for 1 hour.

Pour into a 9 x 14-inch pan and place the pan in a water bath. Bake in a 375° oven until firm.

MAKES 8 SERVINGS.

2520 Lillie Avenue
Summerland, California 93067
(805) 969-9998

A bit of old New England-style hospitality can be found on the sunny coast of Southern California at the Inn on Summer Hill. Rooms feature

Inn on Summer Hill

canopied beds, down comforters, and their own libraries. Some also have jacuzzis and spectacular views of the Pacific. Summerland is only a few miles from Santa Barbara with its famous pier, miles of white sandy beach, and hundreds of interesting shops and restaurants.

Blueberry Cream Cheese Crunch

1½ cups all-purpose flour
1   cup graham cracker crumbs
2   tablespoons baking powder
¼   cup sugar
¼   cup slivered almonds
½   cup melted butter
....
3   8-ounce packages cream cheese
¾   cup sugar
4   large eggs
2   tablespoons all-purpose flour
1   teaspoon vanilla extract
1½ cups fresh or frozen blueberries
1½ cups muesli cereal or granola
    Vanilla ice crema or whipped cream for garnish

In a medium bowl sift together 1½ cups of flour, cracker crumbs, baking powder, and sugar. Add the slivered almonds. Blend in the melted butter and spread evenly on the bottom of a 9 x 13-inch pan. Bake in a 350° oven for 20 minutes.

In a food processor blend the cream cheese, sugar, eggs, 2 tablespoons of flour, and vanilla, or blend with a hand blender. Spread the cream cheese filling over the baked crust. Sprinkle the blueberries over the filling and then sprinkle the muesli or granola over the top. Bake in a 350° oven for 45 minutes.

This can be served hot or cold. Serve with vanilla ice cream or whipped cream.

MAKES 12 SERVINGS.

"Huevos Especial" Summer Hill-Style

10 slices light bread with crusts cut off
10 ounces grated Jalepeño Jack cheese
1   tablespoon white pepper
1   tablespoon oregano
1   large tomato, diced
2   medium red bell peppers, diced
1   bunch fresh cilantro, chopped
1   bunch green onion, chopped
12 eggs
2   cups half and half (or any milk product)
⅓   cup seasoned breadcrumbs
8   tablespoons cream cheese
    Salsa

Place the bread in the bottom of a greased 9-inch round cake pan. Layer the cheese over the bread. Sprinkle with some of the white pepper and oregano. Next layer the tomato, bell peppers, cilantro, onion, and spices.

In a large bowl beat the eggs and whisk in the half and half or milk. Slowly pour the mixture over the bread, cheese, and vegetable layers. Sprinkle with the breadcrumbs. Place 8 dots of cream cheese evenly around the edge of the pan. Let sit for at least 2 hours or the bread will float to the top.

Bake in a 350° oven for 45 to 50 minutes or until the egg is fully cooked. Serve immediately with salsa.

MAKES 8 SERVINGS.

Mimosa Truffles

10 ounces bittersweet chocolate, melted
2   egg yolks, beaten
1   cup confectioners' sugar
½   cup heavy cream
¼   cup butter
1   ounce Grand Marnier
2   ounces champagne
    Cocoa powder

In a double boiler over simmering water or in the microwave melt the chocolate. Set aside.

In a small bowl beat the egg yolks with ½ cup of the sugar.

In a saucepan or double boiler bring the cream, ½ cup of sugar, and butter to a boil, stirring constantly. Cool slightly.

Whisk the cream mixture into the cooled egg yolks and then gradually add the melted chocolate, Grand Marnier, and champagne until blended well. Allow the mixture to cool and "set" in the refrigerator.

When the mixture is set, roll into 1-inch balls and roll in the cocoa powder.

MAKES APPROXIMATELY 40 TRUFFLES.

The Foxes

The Foxes
∾

77 Main Street, P.O. Box 159
Sutter Creek, California 95685
(209) 267-5882

---

*T*he gold rush began here along
Sutter Creek during the late
1840s, and the house now known
as the Foxes was built not long
afterwards, in 1857. For those who
want to see the California Gold
Country, the Foxes would be a good
choice for a base. The seven guest
rooms will appeal to a variety of
tastes and temperaments. Most
have fireplaces.

Zucchini Eggs

½ *onion, finely chopped*
2 *tablespoons oil, butter, or*
   margarine
5 *small zucchini, thinly sliced*
3 *eggs, slightly beaten*
   Salt, pepper, and garlic salt
   Freshly grated Romano cheese

In a skillet sauté onion in oil, butter, or margarine until transparent. Add the zucchini and
cook until tender. Pour the eggs over and season to taste with salt, pepper, and garlic salt.
Cook until the eggs are done. Top with freshly
grated Romano cheese and serve.
MAKES 2 SERVINGS.

Marmalade French Toast

2 *eggs (or 4 egg whites)*
½ *cup orange juice*
1 *tablespoon firmly packed brown*
   sugar
6 *slices sourdough French bread sliced*
   ⅞-inch thick
1 *to 2 tablespoons oil or margarine*
   Orange marmalade

In a small bowl combine the eggs, orange
juice, and brown sugar, beating with a fork
until mixed well. Pour into a pie plate, then
dip the bread in the egg mixture for 10 seconds on each side. In a frying pan heat the oil
or margarine over medium heat. Cook the
bread for 3 to 4 minutes on each side or until
golden brown. Pass the marmalade.
MAKES 6 SERVINGS.

Mashed Potato Waffles

3 *eggs*
2 *cups mashed potatoes, cooled*
1 *tablespoon oil*
1 *teaspoon salt*
1 *cup milk*
1 *cup all-purpose flour*
2 *teaspoons baking powder*

In a food processor combine all ingredients
and blend until mixed well. Bake immediately
on a hot waffle iron.
MAKES 6 SERVINGS.

The Lost
Whale Inn
∾

3452 Patrick's Point Drive
Trinidad, California 95570
(707) 677-3425

---

*R*ooms at the Lost Whale offer
spectacular ocean views, and the
food is wonderful. The Lost Whale is
one of the only inns on the West
Coast that can boast of a scenic
wooded trail leading to a secluded
and primitive cove of jutting rocks,

tidepools, and abundant marine
life. Not far away is an entire
canyon of ferns and rhododendron.
Only a few miles to the north are
the tallest trees in the world in Red-
wood National Park. Also nearby is
Patrick's Point State Park with a
beach where one can find agate and
jade tossing about in the surf. Just
to the south, the village of Trinadad
offers some of thefreshest and tasti-
est seafood in all of California.

Cream Cheese Coffee Cake

2¼ *cups all-purpose flour*
 1 *cup turbinado sugar*
⅔ *cup butter, softened*
 1 *teaspoon ground cinnamon*
½ *teaspoon baking powder*
½ *teaspoon baking soda*
¾ *cup sour cream*
 2 *eggs*
 1 *teaspoon almond extract*
12 *ounces soft cream cheese*
 1 *cup blackberry jam*
½ *cup chopped or sliced almonds*

Butter and flour a 10-inch springform pan. In
a large bowl combine the flour, ¾ cup of
sugar, and butter. Mix until crumbly. Set aside
1 cup of this crumb mixture. To the rest of
the crumb mix, add the cinnamon, baking
powder, soda, sour cream, 1 egg, and extract.
Blend well and spread on the bottom and
sides of the pan. The batter will be a little
lumpy. Mix the cream cheese, ¼ cup of sugar,
and 1 egg. Spread carefully in the pan on top
of the batter. Then, spoon the jam smoothly
over the cream cheese mixture. Finally, sprinkle the reserved crumbs and almonds on top.
Bake in a 350° oven for 1 hour. Cool for 15
minutes before removing the ring. Serve.
MAKES 10 SERVINGS.

Peach Streusel Coffee Cake

2½   cups all-purpose flour
½   cup turbinado sugar
3   teaspoons baking powder
½   teaspoon salt
½   cup melted butter
1   cup milk
2   eggs
1   teaspoon almond extract
2   pounds fresh peaches, peeled, sliced thin (about 5 cups)

⅔   cup all-purpose flour
½   cup butter, softened
½   cup loosely packed light brown sugar
½   teaspoon ground cinnamon

Butter and flour a 9-inch springform pan. In a medium bowl combine 2½ cups of flour, the sugar, baking powder, and salt. In a large bowl combine the butter, milk, eggs, and almond extract. Fold the dry ingredients into the liquid mixture, stirring just until moistened. Spread the mixture in the prepared pan. Arrange the peach slices, overlapping, to cover the batter. In a medium bowl combine the remaining ingredients and sprinkle over the peaches. Bake in a 400° oven for 40 to 45 minutes.

Cool for 10 minutes before removing the ring. Slice and serve warm.

MAKES 8 SERVINGS.

Apple Cake with Hot Buttered Rum

2   cups turbinado sugar
½   cup melted butter
2   eggs
2   cups all-purpose flour
1   teaspoon baking powder
1   teaspoon baking soda
½   teaspoon salt
½   teaspoon grated nutmeg
½   teaspoon ground cinnamon
4   cups peeled and diced apples
1½   cups chopped walnuts

1   cup sugar
¼   cup dark rum
½   cup half and half
2   tablespoons butter

Grease and flour a 10-inch tube or bundt pan. In a large bowl combine the turbinado sugar, melted butter, and eggs. Add the flour, baking powder, soda, salt, nutmeg, and cinnamon. Mix gently. Fold in the apples and walnuts. Pour into the prepared baking pan. Bake in a 350° oven for 50 to 60 minutes, until done.

Cool for 10 minutes, remove from the pan and place on a platter. In a heavy saucepan stir the sugar and rum together over medium heat. When the sugar is dissolved, add the half and half and stir until thickened. Turn off the heat and add the butter, blending until smooth. Pour hot rum over the cake and serve.

MAKES 8 SERVINGS.

Corn Frittata

¼   cup butter
13   eggs
1   17-ounce can cream-style corn
1   7-ounce can chopped green chilies
3   cups grated Cheddar cheese
2   teaspoons garlic powder
1   teaspoon pepper
½   teaspoon red chili pepper flakes
2   teaspoons Worcestershire sauce
  Chopped chives or scallions for garnish
  Salsa

In a 9 x 13-inch glass baking dish melt the butter in a 375° oven. Remove from the oven when butter has melted.

In a large bowl beat the remaining ingredients with a whisk. Pour into the glass pan. Bake in a 375° oven for 50 to 60 minutes, until the eggs are set and the top is lightly browned.

Remove from the oven and slice into 15 squares. Place on a platter and garnish with chopped chives or scallions. Serve warm, accompanied with salsa.

Note: For a stronger, spicier variation, use sharp Cheddar cheese instead of mild and add another ½ teaspoon of red chili pepper.

MAKES 15 SQUARES.

Crab Cakes

¼   cup butter
2   small yellow onions, chopped
⅔   pound cooked crab meat
1   cup dry breadcrumbs
½   cup chopped green onion
½   cup chopped celery
2   eggs
½   cup milk
¼   teaspoon dried sage
¼   teaspoon dried red chili peppers
  Pepper to taste
  Lemon wedges for garnish

In a skillet melt the butter and sauté the onions until brown. In a mixing bowl combine all ingredients, including the sautéed onions. Shape into patties. In a griddle or frying pan cook the crab cakes in butter or oil over medium heat for 4 minutes on each side.

Serve hot with lemon wedges.

MAKES ABOUT 4 SERVINGS.

Oak Hill Ranch

18550 Connally Lane, P.O. Box 307
Tuolumne, California 95379
(209) 928-4717

A *Victorian-style ranch home set on fifty-five acres, this B&B looks out toward the lofty Sierras from an elevation of over 3,000 feet. The ranch was part of an 1850s homestead near the old lumber town of Tuolumne. The home itself was built in 1980, but its design, wall-*

paper, and antiques recall the earliest days of the homestead.

Crustless Swiss Quiche

- 2 tablespoons oil
- 1 green bell pepper, thinly sliced and chopped
- 6 or 7 stems of scallion, chopped
- 7 or 8 fresh mushrooms, sliced
  Dash oregano
  Salt and pepper to taste
- 2 drops Tabasco sauce
  Garlic salt to taste
- ¼ cup bacon bits (or minced ham)
- 2 cups coarsely grated Swiss cheese
- 1½ cups milk
- 4 eggs
- ½ cup biscuit mix
  Pinch salt and pepper
  Sour cream
  Dash paprika
  Parsley sprigs

In a frying pan heat the oil and sauté the bell pepper, scallions, mushrooms, oregano, salt, pepper, Tabasco sauce, and garlic salt until the bell pepper is tender. Add the cooked bacon bits if desired. Spread this mixture in the bottom of a quiche plate. Sprinkle a liberal amount of grated Swiss cheese over it.

In a blender mix the milk, eggs, and Bisquick with a dash of salt and pepper. Pour this into the quiche plate to nearly the top. Place on bottom shelf of oven. Bake in a 400° oven for 35 minutes. When done the crust should be brown. Let the quiche stand for about 5 minutes before cutting.

Cut into 4 pieces. Sprinkle more Swiss cheese over each piece. Add a dollop of sour cream. Sprinkle with paprika and add a sprig of parsley.

MAKES 4 SERVINGS.

Sandy's Scrumptious Spuds

- ¼ cup butter
- 2 tablespoons oil
- 2 tablespoons onion flakes
- 1 tablespoon parsley flakes
- 1 stem scallion, chopped
  Dash garlic salt
  Pepper to taste
- 2 garlic cloves, squeezed in garlic press

- 2 medium baking potatoes, sliced ⅜-inch thickness (scrub well but leave skins on)

In a cast-iron, skillet with a cover melt the butter. Add the oil, onion flakes, parsley flakes, scallions, garlic salt, pepper and squeezed garlic cloves. Stir and distribute evenly in the skillet. Arrange the sliced potatoes over the sautéed mixture without overlapping if possible. Cover and cook over low heat for about 20 minutes. After the potatoes are slightly brown, turn and cook for another 20 minutes.

Note: This dish goes well with omelets and quiches. Garnish with fresh parsley.

MAKES 4 SERVINGS.

Crêpes Normandie

- ½ cup raisins
- 2 tablespoons brandy

....

- 1 egg
  Dash salt
- ⅔ cup all-purpose flour
- 1 teaspoon oil
- ¾ cup milk
- 1 cup Mott's chunky applesauce
  Dash ground cinnamon
  Dash ground cardamom
- 1 cup chopped walnuts
- ¼ cup sour cream
- 1 tablespoon firmly packed brown sugar
- 1 cup blueberries, blackberries, or raspberries

In a small bowl soak the raisins in the brandy for 30 minutes.

In a medium bowl combine the egg, salt, flour, oil, and milk. Beat to a thin consistency. Set aside.

In a separate bowl mix the applesauce, raisins, cinnamon, cardamom, and ¼ cup of the walnuts. Set the filling aside.

In a small bowl mix the sour cream and brown sugar. Set the dressing aside.

In a crêpe pan cook the crêpes on medium heat until barely brown. Fill each crêpe with 2 tablespoons of filling and roll up. Place in a baking pan. Bake in a 350 °oven for 15 minutes.

After baking, top with dressing and sprinkle with the berries and remaining nuts.

Serve hot with a garnish of fresh fruit, with sausages, bacon, or ham. A sprig of fresh mint will enhance the presentation.

MAKES ABOUT 4 SERVINGS.

2605 Vichy Springs Road
Ukiah, California 95482
(707) 462-9515

---

*N*amed after the world-famous springs discovered by Julius Caesar in France, the waters of Vichy Springs are said to taste just like those of its European predecessor. The resort dates to 1854 and has attracted notables such as Mark Twain, Jack London, and Teddy Roosevelt. Now fully restored, it offers twelve modern guest rooms and two separate cottages with their own kitchens.

Easy Clam Chowder

- 1 cup water
- 1 8-ounce can minced clams, undrained
- 2 cups diced potatoes
- 2 cups thinly sliced carrots
- 1 chicken bouillon cube
- 1½ cups minced onions
- 1 tablespoon chopped parsley
- 1 10¾-ounce can cream of celery soup
- 2 cups milk
- 2 cups grated Monterey Jack cheese
- 2½ teaspoons seasoned salt

Pour the water and the juice from the drained clams into saucepan. Add the potatoes, carrots, bouillon, onions, and parsley. Simmer until the vegetables are tender. Add the cream of celery soup, clams, milk, cheese, and seasoned salt, and mix thoroughly. Heat gently but do not boil.

MAKES 7 SERVINGS.

No Yeast Apple Coffee Cake

¼ cup butter
1 cup sugar
3 eggs, beaten
1 teaspoon vanilla extract
2½ cups all-purpose flour
3 teaspoons baking powder
1 teaspoon salt
1 teaspoon vanilla extract
1 cup milk
5 apples, peeled and grated
Sugar
Cinnamon
2 tablespoons margarine or butter
½ cup sugar
½ cup all-purpose flour
1¼ cups confectioners' sugar
2 tablespoons milk

Grease a 10 x 15-inch pan. In a large bowl cream ¼ cup of butter with 1 cup of sugar until light. Add the eggs and vanilla, and blend well. In a separate bowl sift 2½ cups of flour with the baking powder and salt. Add the dry ingredients to the creamed mixture alternately with the milk. Spread the dough in the prepared pan. Sprinkle the apples over the dough. Sprinkle with sugar and cinnamon.

In a small bowl combine 2 tablespoons of butter with ½ cup of sugar and ½ cup of flour. Sprinkle the crumb mixture over the apples. Bake in a 350° oven for 40 minutes.

In a small bowl blend the confectioners' sugar with 2 tablespoons of milk until smooth. Ice the coffee cake.

MAKES 8 SERVINGS.

The Venice Beach House

The Venice Beach House

❧

#15 30th Avenue
Venice, California 90291
(310) 823-1966

The Venice Beach House recalls the turn of the century when Abbot Kinney built an "American Venice" in the marshes north of Los Angeles. The nine guest rooms and suites combine modern conveniences with hand-detailed antique furnishings. Guests can borrow bicycles from the innkeepers to explore Venice and its famous pier. The Los Angeles International Airport is nearby.

Willi's Buttercup Eggs

Sliced sourdough or whole wheat bread
Dried rosemary
6 large eggs
Grated Swiss cheese
Diced tomatoes (optional)
Salt and pepper to taste

Grease 6 2-to 3-inch deep muffin pans. Press a piece of the bread (holding it by the crust) into each cup. Sprinkle with rosemary and break 1 egg into each cup. Sprinkle grated Swiss cheese over the top of each egg. Bake in a 250° oven for 30 minutes.

Pull the cups out of the tin and serve on a plates. They will look like buttercups.

MAKES 6 SERVINGS.

Linne's Wild Blackberry Creamy Coffee Cake

1 cup butter, softened
2 cups sugar
4 large eggs
2 teaspoons vanilla extract
4 cups all-purpose flour
3 teaspoons baking powder
2 teaspoons baking soda
2 teaspoon salt
2 cup sour cream
....
1 pound wild blackberries
1 cup chopped pecans
1 teaspoon firmly packed brown sugar
4 teaspoons ground cinnamon

In a large bowl mix butter, sugar, eggs, and vanilla by hand until creamy. In a separate bowl mix the flour, baking powder, soda, and salt. Add the dry ingredients to the butter mixture alternately with the sour cream. In a small bowl combine the pecans, brown sugar, and cinnamon. Divide half of the batter among 2 greased bundt pans. Reserve the remaining batter. Sprinkle each with wild blackberries and half of the pecan filling. Pour in the rest of the batter and top the cakes with the remaining filling. Bake in a 375° oven for 45 minutes in the middle of the oven, covering them with foil at 20 minutes to keep from burning.

Remove the cakes and let the cool for about 10 minutes. Remove from the pans and serve warm.

MAKES 16 SERVINGS.

Maison Fleurie

❧

6529 Yount Street
Yountville, California 94599
(800) 788-0369

In the heart of Napa Valley wine country, Maison Fleurie welcomes guests with its French country atmosphere in a serene and peaceful setting. Its thirteen rooms are housed in three rustic, vine-covered brick buildings with terra cotta tiles and paned windows. Exploring the Napa Valley on bicycles provided by the inn is a favorite activity of guests. Maison Fleurie is one hour's drive from San Francisco.

Savory Cauliflower Tart

2½ cups packed grated raw potato
½ teaspoon salt
1 egg, beaten
1 large yellow onion, finely chopped

⋯⋯⋯⋯⋯⋯⋯⋯⋯⋯⋯⋯⋯⋯⋯

3 cloves garlic, minced
2 tablespoons olive oil
1 medium head of cauliflower, broken
    or chopped into very small florets
½ teaspoon thyme
½ teaspoon basil
½ teaspoon salt
2 eggs
½ cup 1% milk
1 cup packed grated sharp Cheddar
    cheese
    Pepper to taste

Oil a 9-inch pie pan. Grate the potato and sprinkle with salt. Let stand in a colander for 15 minutes, then squeeze out the excess liquid. Mix in 1 egg and ¼ cup of onion. Pat the mixture into the pie pan. Bake in a 375° oven for 30 minutes, then brush with oil and bake for 15 minutes more. When done reduce the oven to 375°.

While the crust is cooking, prepare the filling. In a skillet sauté the rest of the onion and the garlic in olive oil until soft. Add the cauliflower and herbs, cover, and simmer for 10 minutes.

In a small bowl beat 2 eggs with the milk. To build the pie sprinkle ½ cup of cheese over the crust, then the vegetables, then the second half of the cheese. Pour the egg and milk over the top. Bake in a 400° oven for 30 to 40 minutes.

MAKES ABOUT 6 SERVINGS.

Linguine Frittata

½ pound linguine
¾ cup grated Gouda
¼ cup grated Parmesan
1 tablespoon olive oil
¼ cup unsalted butter, melted
6 eggs, beaten
2 green onions, chopped
½ cup red bell pepper, finely diced

In a large pot of boiling water cook pasta to al dente and drain. Rinse in cold water.

In a large bowl combine the cheeses, olive oil, and 2 tablespoons of butter. Add the eggs and stir. Toss with the linguine. In a 12-inch skillet melt the remaining butter and sauté the onions and peppers for 2 minutes. Add pasta mixture and spread evenly in the pan. Cook for 4 minutes. Position the front half of the pan over the flame and cook until brown at the edges. Shift to the back of the pan and repeat. Turn the frittata onto a large platter. Slide back into the pan browned-side up and repeat the previous browning instructions. Cut into 8 to 10 pieces and serve warm or at room temperature.

MAKES 8 TO 10 SERVINGS.

COLORADO

Cottonwood Inn Bed and Breakfast

123 San Juan Avenue
Alamosa, Colorado 81101
(719) 589-3882, (800) 955-2623

The inn offers five guest rooms warmly decorated with antiques and artwork by area artists. This B&B is a good choice for those seeking to explore the San Luis Valley, a truly extraordinary high desert basin bounded by the 14,000-foot Sangre de Cristo Mountains to the east and the San Juans to the west. Many choose to see the valley and mountain scenery by way of the Cumbres and Toltec Scenic Railroad, a narrow-gauge steam line left over from the days of the Colorado gold and silver rushes.

Pumpkin Pancakes

> 1 cup unbleached all-purpose flour
> 1 cup whole wheat flour
> 4 teaspoons baking powder
> 1/2 teaspoon salt
> 1 teaspoon ground cinnamon
> 1/2 teaspoon grated nutmeg
> 4 eggs, separated
> 1 1/2 cups milk
> 1 16-ounce can pumpkin
> 1/4 cup butter, melted

In a medium bowl combine the flours, baking powder, salt, cinnamon, and nutmeg. In a large bowl combine the remaining ingredients. Add the dry ingredients to the liquid mixture, mixing just until blended. Do not overmix. In a separate bowl beat the egg whites until peaks form. Gently fold the egg whites into the batter. Pour small amount onto a hot griddle and cook until golden brown on both sides.

Serve these with warm maple syrup and homemade sausages.

MAKES 4 TO 6 SERVINGS.

Cottonwood Inn

Melted Chocolate for Dipping

> 1 pound semisweet chocolate
> 2 tablespoons water
> 3 tablespoons brandy, or kahlua, or Triple Sec

In a glass bowl combine the chocolate, water, and brandy. Melt on high for 45 seconds in microwave. Stir, melt again for 45 seconds, and stir. Continue until the chocolate is creamy.

Set out in a bowl with dipping things, i.e. bananas, apples, oranges, sugar cookies, pecans, graham crackers, pound cake.

MAKES ABOUT 2 CUPS.

Allenspark Lodge

184 Main Street, P.O. Box 247
Allenspark, Colorado 80510
(303) 747-2552

Constructed of native stone and ponderosa pine in 1933, the lodge is perfectly suited to its Rocky Mountain setting, some 8,451 feet above sea level. A massive stone fireplace welcomes guests to the spacious Great Room, while well-appointed rooms with mountain views await them upstairs. The Hideaway Room has a brass bed and bear-claw-footed tub. Separate cabins are also available.

Beef Burgundy Vegetable Medley Soup

    2   tablespoons olive oil
   10   slices bacon, cut into 1-inch lengths
    2   pounds beef stew meat, cut into 1-inch lengths
        Freshly ground black pepper to taste
   10   small leeks, with 2 inches of green left on
    6   carrots, peeled, cut into 3-inch lengths
    6   medium parsnips, peeled, cut into 3-inch lengths
    2   tablespoons sugar
    4   13¾-ounce cans beef broth
    3   cups burgundy wine
   ¼   cup unsalted butter
   ¼   cup red currant jelly
    4   teaspoons fresh thyme
    8   small red new potatoes, cut in half
    6   garlic cloves, peeled, minced
    6   ripe plum tomatoes, coarsely chopped
   ½   cup chopped Italian parsley
        Parsley sprigs for garnish

In a large skillet heat the olive oil. Add the bacon and cook until the fat is rendered. Remove the bacon to a heavy casserole safe for the stovetop. Brown the beef stew meat in skillet in small batches, sprinkling with pepper. Remove to a casserole with bacon. In the same skillet quickly sauté the leeks, carrots, and parsnips, sprinkling with sugar to caramelize slightly. Remove from the skillet and reserve. Add the beef broth and wine to the skillet and bring to a boil, scraping up the brown bits. Reduce the heat, swirl in the butter, red currant jelly, and thyme and cook for a minute more.

Pour the mixture over the beef in the casserole. Add the potatoes and garlic to the casserole and bring to a boil. Cover. Bake in a 350° oven for 45 minutes.

Remove the casserole from the oven. Add the reserved leeks, carrots, and parsnips, plus the plum tomatoes and parsley. Stir gently. Adjust the seasonings, and bake uncov-

ered for an additional 45 minutes or until the beef is tender. Garnish with parsley.
MAKES 10 SERVINGS.

Peanut Butter Bread

   ⅔   cup peanut butter
   ¼   cup sugar
    1   egg, well beaten
    2   cups all-purpose flour
    1   teaspoon salt
    4   teaspoons baking powder
    1   cup milk
   ....
    2   tablespoons peanut butter
    2   tablespoons milk
   ¾   cup confectioners' sugar

In a large bowl cream the ⅔ cup of peanut butter and sugar. Add the egg and beat until smooth. In a separate bowl sift together the flour, salt, and baking powder. Add the dry ingredients to the peanut butter mixture alternately with the milk. Beat well and pour into a greased loaf pan. Bake in a 350° oven for 50 minutes.

In a small bowl combine the remaining ingredients. Add milk if needed to make a glaze. Drizzle or spread over the Peanut Butter Bread.
MAKES 1 LOAF.

Shenandoah Inn
❧

*0600 Frying Pan Road, P.O. Box 578
Basalt, Colorado 81621
(303) 927-4991*

Situated beside Frying Pan Creek just off the road from Glenwood Springs to Aspen, this inn and B&B is a recently restored home filled with the woodsy aromas and ambiance of the Colorado Rockies. Guests are treated to full gourmet breakfasts. Each bedroom has an unobstructed view of the river with its gold medal trout waters. The

living and dining rooms share a sixteen-foot-high rock fireplace. Within walking distance of the fine restaurants and shops of Basalt, centrally situated 20 minutes from the ski slope and cultural events of Aspen, and 25 minutes from the Glenwood Hot Springs Pool.

Shenandoah Apple Walnut Crêpes

    3   eggs
   ¾   cup milk
   ⅓   teaspoon salt
   ¾   cup all-purpose flour
   ⅓   cup water
   ....
    6   Granny Smith apples, peeled and sliced semi-thin and tossed with 2 tablespoons lemon juice
   ⅓   cup raisins
   ½   cup chopped walnuts
    3   tablespoons firmly packed brown sugar
    3   teaspoons ground cinnamon
        Pinch cloves
    6   tablespoons butter for sautéing
   ⅓   cup light cream
   ½   cup Calvados, dark rum, or apple juice
        Lightly sweetened whipped cream for garnish
        Finely chopped nuts for garnish
        Confectioners' sugar for garnish

In a medium bowl whisk together the eggs, milk, salt, flour, and water until smooth. Lightly spray an 8-inch skillet with cooking spray. Heat the skillet and pour in a small amount of batter, just enough to thinly coat the bottom of skillet. Cook over medium-high heat, turning once, just until golden brown. Gently remove the crêpes from the pan onto a cloth towel to cool slightly, and repeat until all crêpes are prepared.

Makes 12 8-inch crêpes.

In a separate bowl combine the apples, raisins, walnuts, brown sugar, cinnamon, and cloves. In large sauté pan heat the butter and sauté the apple mixture over medium heat for 2 minutes, stirring constantly. Add the cream and Calvados. Continue to cook for another minute or 2 until bubbling. Do not overcook. The apples should stay firm.

Arrange the crêpes on warm plates, 2 per plate. Using a slotted spoon, fill with apple filling and a dollop of whipped cream and fold the tops in toward the center. Drizzle the folded crêpes with syrup from the pan and dust with finely chopped nuts and confectioners' sugar.

MAKES 6 SERVINGS.

Frying Pan River Champagne Mustard

½   cup dry mustard
½   cider vinegar
....
1   beaten egg
½   cup sugar
    Dash salt
1   teaspoon cornstarch
1   cup mayonnaise

In a small bowl combine the dry mustard and vinegar until smooth. Refrigerate overnight. The next day bring to room temperature. In a saucepan combine the mustard mixture, egg, sugar, salt, and cornstarch. Cook slowly until thickened, 10 to 15 minutes. Cool.

Add the mayonnaise. Stir well and refrigerate.

Note: This is served at our annual Christmas Eve buffet, with chilled and thinly sliced rare tenderloin of beef. Also a terrific garnish for Quiche Lorraine, or in coleslaw dressing.

MAKES 2 CUPS.

Irie Banana Salsa

1   large, firm banana, slightly under ripe, peeled and diced
½   cup seeded and diced red bell pepper
½   cup seeded and diced green bell pepper
½   cup seeded and diced yellow bell pepper
3   tablespoon chopped fresh cilantro
2   scallions, chopped
2   tablespoons fresh lime juice
1   tablespoon firmly packed brown sugar
2   teaspoons minced ginger
2   teaspoons olive oil
1   teaspoon minced Scotch bonnet (aka habañero) pepper, seeded (or to taste, or 2 teaspoons minced jalapeño)

In a medium bowl combine all of the ingredients, taste, and adjust the seasonings. Serve within 1 hour. This is HOT! Better keep some milk nearby.

Note: Irie is the rasta word for cool, positive vibrations, in the flow of things.

MAKES ABOUT 2 CUPS.

Berthoud Bed and Breakfast

❧

444 First Street
Berthoud, Colorado 80513
(303) 532-4566

---

*T*his 105-year-old Victorian home is in a small country town in the shadow of the towering Colorado Front Range. Each guest room has been decorated to reflect a different theme. For instance, the Egyptian Room has marble floors, ancient Egyptian art, and Egyptian linens; the Madame Pompadour Room is a Louis XV-style room in the upper turret with a twenty-foot spire ceiling and a seven-foot round bed; and the Frontier Room brings to mind Wyatt Earp and Sitting Bull. Those who have caught a chill in the high Rockies may appreciate the Tropical Room.

Herb Baked Eggs

3   eggs
¼   cup yogurt
1   teaspoon Dijon mustard
¾   cup shredded Cheddar cheese
1   teaspoon minced chives
1   teaspoon minced parsley
1   teaspoon minced tarragon

In a medium bowl mix together all ingredients.

Grease 2 ramekin dishes. Pour the mixture into the ramekins. Bake in a 375° oven for 20 minutes, until brown.

MAKES 2 SERVINGS.

The Boulder Victoria Historic Inn

The Boulder Victoria Historic Inn

❧

1305 Pine Street
Boulder, Colorado 80302
(303) 938-1300

---

*T*his grand old mansion that dates to the 1870s has been restored in award-winning fashion. Rooms are furnished with period antiques, and beds feature down comforters and pillows. The innkeepers dry their own flowers and create lush floral arrangements. The inn provides easy access to downtown Boulder with its Pearl Street pedestrian mall. Also close by are the University of Colorado and the Rockies.

Blueberry-Lemon Bread

1½   cups all-purpose flour
1   teaspoon baking powder
¼   teaspoon salt
6   tablespoons unsalted butter, room temperature
1   cup sugar
2   large eggs
2   teaspoons grated lemon zest
½   cup milk

1½ cups fresh blueberries, or frozen,
 thawed, and drained
 All-purpose flour
⅓ cup sugar
3 tablespoons fresh lemon juice

Butter, flour, and sugar an 8½ x 4½-inch loaf pan. In a small bowl combine the flour, baking powder, and salt. In a large bowl, cream the butter with 1 cup of sugar with an electric mixer until light and fluffy. Add the eggs one at a time, beating well after each addition. Add the lemon zest. Mix in the dry ingredients alternately with the milk, beginning and ending with the dry ingredients. In a separate bowl lightly coat blueberries with flour. Fold the blueberries into the batter. Spoon the batter into the prepared loaf pan. Bake in a 325° oven for about 1 hour and 15 minutes until golden brown and a toothpick inserted in the center comes out clean.

Meanwhile, in a small saucepan bring the remaining ⅓ cup of sugar and lemon juice to a boil, stirring until sugar dissolves.

Pierce the top of the hot loaf several times with a toothpick. Pour the hot lemon mixture over the loaf in the pan. Cool for 30 minutes in the pan on a rack.

Turn the bread out of the pan and cool completely on a rack.

MAKES 1 LOAF.

Kim's Chewy Gingersnap Cookies

¾ cup shortening
1 cup firmly packed brown sugar
1 egg
¼ cup molasses
1¾ cups all-purpose flour
2 teaspoons baking soda
½ teaspoon salt
1 teaspoon ground cinnamon
1 teaspoon ground ginger
1 teaspoon ground cloves
 Sugar

In a medium bowl combine the shortening, brown sugar, egg, and molasses and mix together until creamy. In a separate bowl sift together the flour, soda, salt, cinnamon, ginger, and cloves. Add the dry ingredients to the molasses mixture and stir well. Form the dough into quarter-sized balls and roll in

sugar. Place on a greased cookie sheet. Bake in a 350° oven for 8 to 10 minutes.

MAKES ABOUT 2 TO 3 DOZEN.

The Boulder Victoria's Lemon Curd

¾ cup butter
½ cup fresh lemon juice
4 teaspoons grated lemon zest (or ½
 teaspoon lemon extract)
1½ cups sugar
5 large eggs

In a heavy medium saucepan melt the butter with the lemon juice and lemon zest over medium-high heat, stirring occasionally. Bring to a boil. Remove the pan from the heat. In separate bowl stir the sugar and eggs together until blended. Whisk in the hot lemon mixture. Return the mixture to the saucepan. Whisk over medium heat until the mixture thickens, about 6 minutes (watch the clock, and remove from heat if you are interrupted). Do not boil. Pour into a bowl. Press plastic wrap on the surface of the curd to keep skin from forming. Chill overnight.

MAKES ABOUT 3 CUPS.

Briar Rose Bed and Breakfast ❧

2151 Arapahoe Avenue
Boulder, Colorado 80302
(303) 442-3007

A 1890s era brick home, the Briar Rose became Boulder's first B&B in 1981. Each of the nine guest rooms has its own distinct character. Period antiques, original artwork and fresh flowers decorate the rooms. The carefully groomed gardens offer an ideal setting for personal reflection, quiet conversation,

or simple enjoyment of the many plants, flowers, trees, and shrubs. The Briar Rose is near the University of Colorado campus and the Pearl Street pedestrian mall.

Shortbread Cookies

2 cups butter
1 cup confectioners' sugar
1 cups all-purpose flour
 Pinch salt
 Jam or nuts for filling (optional)

In a large bowl cream the butter and sugar together. Add the flour and salt. Mix well. Shape into balls a bit smaller than a golf ball. Place on ungreased cookie sheets. Press down with 3 fingers. Fill the centers with jam or nuts or leave plain. Bake in a 350° oven for 8 to 10 minutes or until the edges are golden brown.

MAKES ABOUT 2 DOZEN.

Whole Wheat Crêpes

¼ cup all-purpose flour
½ cup whole wheat flour
 Pinch salt
1¼ cups milk
1 egg plus 1 egg yolk
1 tablespoon melted butter or oil

In a blender combine all of the ingredients and run at high speed for 10 to 15 seconds. The batter may be used immediately.

MAKES 12 CRÊPES.

Briar Rose

B&B Banana Filling for Crêpes

 2 *tablespoons butter*
⅓ *cup firmly packed brown sugar*
 2 *tablespoons tart orange or lemon*
    marmalade
 4 *to 6 ripe but firm bananas (1*
    banana per serving)
¼ *teaspoon almond extract*
¼ *teaspoon vanilla extract*
1½ *ounces B&B liqueur*
¼ *teaspoon ground cinnamon*
    Warm crêpes

In a skillet or chafing dish melt the butter over medium heat. Add the brown sugar and marmalade and allow them to melt completely. Cut the bananas in half lengthwise and across. Cook the bananas in the marmalade mixture for 2 to 4 minutes, turning gently until they are just soft. Add the extracts, B&B liquor, and sprinkle cinnamon over the entire mixture. Fold the mixture very gently and remove from the heat. Spoon the banana mixture into warm crêpes and fold or roll as desired.

MAKES FILLING FOR 12 CRÊPES.

B&B Melba Sauce

 1 *12-ounce package frozen raspber-*
    ries, thawed
 3 *tablespoons sugar*
    Juice of ½ lemon or 1 tablespoon
    lemon juice
 1 *ounce B&B liqueur*
 1 *teaspoon cornstarch dissolved in 1*
    tablespoon cold water

In a blender combine the raspberries, sugar, lemon juice, and liqueur. Purée at high speed for 10 to 15 seconds. Strain the liquid through a fine sieve to remove the seeds, and pour into a saucepan. Bring the liquid just to a boil and add the cornstarch-water mixture. Stir a few minutes, until thickened. May be made ahead and cooled, or served warm.

Cover the center of a 10- or 12-inch plate with a thin layer of melba sauce. Arrange 1 or 2 filled crêpes on the plate, and pour additional melba sauce over the crêpes. Garnish with lemon peel curls or small rosettes of whipped cream.

MAKES ABOUT 1½ CUPS.

Ridge Street Inn
❧

212 North Ridge Street, P.O. Box 2854
Breckenridge, Colorado 80424
(970) 453-4680

Built prior to 1890 by a local merchant, this Victorian-style bed and breakfast is in the heart of the Breckenridge Historic District, within easy walking distance to shops, restaurants, the bike path, and town shuttle. It offers five comfortably furnished rooms plus the Parlor Suite. The Summit Stage stops nearby and offers free shuttle service among the Copper Mountain, Keystone, Arapahoe Basin, and Breckenridge ski areas. Other winter activities include ice skating, snowmobile rides, sleigh rides, dog sled rides, and many miles of cross country trails. Summer activities include nearby fishing, hiking, biking, rafting, golfing, and the Alpine Slide.

Ridge Street Inn

Whole Wheat Bread

 2 *packages active dry yeast*
½ *cup warm water (105 to 115°)*
 3 *tablespoons butter*
1½ *cups milk*
¼ *cup honey*
1½ *cups cold water*
 2 *cups whole wheat flour*
 7 *cups bread flour*
 1 *teaspoon salt*

In a small bowl sprinkle the yeast over the warm water and stir to dissolve. In a saucepan drop the butter into the milk and scald. Add the honey and mix together. In a large mixing bowl combine the scalded milk mixture and cold water. Stir in the yeast. Add the whole wheat flour and 2 cups of bread flour. Add salt. Mix together with an electric mixer at high speed for about 10 minutes. Put the remaining 5 cups flour on kneading counter. Turn the dough out onto a floured counter and knead for about 10 minutes, using most of the flour.

Place the dough in a large greased bowl, cover, and let rise until doubled in bulk.

Punch down and turn onto a lightly floured board. Knead lightly for 1 minute. Divide the dough into 3 parts and form into 3 loaves. Place in greased bread pans and allow to rise until nearly double in bulk. Bake in a 350° oven for approximately 45 minutes. Remove the loaves from the pans and butter the crusts. Cool completely and slice for toast. Freeze.

MAKES 3 LOAVES.

Bread Pudding with Nutmeg Sauce

 6 *cups cubed bread*
 4 *cups milk, scalded with ½ cup of*
    butter
 1 *cup sugar*
 4 *eggs, slightly beaten*
½ *teaspoon salt*
 2 *teaspoons ground cinnamon*
 1 *teaspoon grated nutmeg*
 1 *cup raisins*

 1 *cup sugar*
 2 *tablespoons cornstarch*
 2 *cups water*
¼ *cup butter*
 2 *teaspoons grated nutmeg*

Place the bread cubes in a 3-quart baking dish. In a medium bowl combine the milk, 1 cup of sugar, eggs, salt, cinnamon, 1 teaspoon of nutmeg, and raisins. Place the baking dish in a pan of hot water (1 inch deep). Bake in a 350° oven for 40 to 45 minutes or until a knife inserted 1 inch from the edge comes out clean.

In a saucepan mix 1 cup of sugar and the cornstarch. Gradually stir in the water. Boil for 1 minute, stirring constantly. Stir in the butter and 2 teaspoon, of nutmeg. Pour nutmeg sauce over the bread pudding and serve warm.

MAKES 8 TO 12 SERVINGS.

Bailey's Irish Cream Cake

¼ cup sliced almonds
1 angel food cake
3 cups heavy cream
1 teaspoon vanilla extract
½ cup confectioners' sugar
⅔ cup Bailey's Irish Cream

Toast the almonds in the oven. Set aside to cool.

Slice off the top 1¼-inch of an angel food cake. Remove cake center leaving 1-inch walls inside.

Whip the cream until stiff. Add the vanilla and confectioners' sugar. Slowly fold in the Bailey's Irish Cream. Fill the cake with two-thirds of the whipped cream mixture. Set the top in place and frost with the remaining cream mixture. Sprinkle toasted almonds on top. Store in the freezer. When the cream is firm, cover tightly. Set out 10 minutes before serving in slices.

MAKES 6 TO 8 SERVINGS.

Williams House and Victorian Cottage

❧

303 Main Street, P.O. Box 2454
Breckenridge, Colorado 80424
(970) 453-2975, (800) 795-2975

*T*hese *two historic Breckenridge homes have been converted into a unique high Rocky Mountain B&B. Both date to the early 1900s and have been furnished with fine antiques. A large deck and outdoor*

hot tub afford one of the most spectacular mountain views to be seen anywhere. Several top ski areas are nearby.

Raspberry-Lemon Yogurt Muffins

2 cups all-purpose flour
½ cup sugar
2 teaspoons baking powder (1 teaspoon for high altitude)
½ teaspoon baking soda (¼ teaspoon for high altitude)
½ teaspoon salt
1 8-ounce carton lemon yogurt
¼ cup oil
1½ teaspoons grated lemon zest
2 eggs
1 cup fresh or frozen raspberries, unthawed
½ cup chopped pecans
....
⅓ cup sugar
¼ cup all-purpose flour
2 tablespoons butter

In large bowl combine 2 cups of flour, ½ cup of sugar, baking powder, soda, and salt. In a small bowl combine the yogurt, oil, lemon zest, and eggs. Mix well. Add the liquid mixture to the dry ingredients and stir until just moistened. Gently fold in the raspberries and pecans. Fill muffin cups three-fourths full. In a small bowl combine the remaining ingredients with a fork until crumbly. Sprinkle the topping over the batter.

Bake in a 400° oven for 20 to 25 minutes.

MAKES 16 MUFFINS.

Noodle Kugel

1 8-ounce package cream cheese
½ cup butter
½ cup sugar
1 cup milk
4 eggs
1 8-ounce package broad noodles, boiled and rinsed
¾ teaspoon vanilla extract
1 tart apple, peeled and chopped
Cinnamon-sugar
Low-fat granola cereal

In a large bowl combine the cream cheese, butter, sugar, and milk, mixing well. Blend in the eggs, 1 at a time. Add the noodles. Stir in the vanilla and apple. Pour the mixture into a buttered 2-quart casserole dish.

Sprinkle with cinnamon-sugar. Top with low-fat granola cereal. Bake in a 375° oven for 1 hour.

Note: This is served for breakfast with fresh bagels and cream cheese or sometimes with fried turkey pastrami.

MAKES 6 SERVINGS.

Spring Skiing Casserole

½ cup butter
½ cup all-purpose flour
6 large eggs
1 cup milk
1 pound Monterey Jack cheese, cubed
1 3-ounce package cream cheese, softened
2 cups cottage cheese
1 teaspoon baking powder (½ teaspoon baking powder for high altitude)
½ teaspoon salt
1 teaspoon sugar
⅛ teaspoon cream of tartar
2 chopped green onions
Parsley sprig for garnish

In a saucepan melt the butter. Add the flour and cook until smooth. In a large bowl beat the eggs. Add the milk, cheeses, baking powder, salt, sugar, cream of tartar, onions, and butter-flour mixture. Stir until blended. Pour into a well-greased 9 x 13-inch pan. Bake uncovered in a 350° oven for 30 to 40 minutes.

Looks pretty garnished with a sprig fresh of fresh parsley.

MAKES 8 SERVINGS.

Williams House and Victorian Cottage

Ambiance Inn Bed and Breakfast

❧

66 North Second Street
Carbondale, Colorado 81623
(800) 350-1515

*A*mbiance Inn is a contemporary chalet-style home offering one suite and three rooms. Its rooms are decorated to reflect a variety of themes—Santa Fe, New Orleans, and Kauai Island—and are exceptionally spacious. The Ambiance Inn is conveniently within walking distance of the community's quaint shops and restaurants. The inn and the town of Carbondale are right on the road to Aspen with its world-class ski areas.

Banana Chocolate Chip Cake

2¼   cups sifted cake flour
1   teaspoon baking powder
¾   teaspoon baking soda
1   teaspoon salt
⅔   cup shortening
1½   cups sugar
2   eggs, beaten
1   teaspoon vanilla extract
1   cup mashed banana
½   cup buttermilk
1   cup chocolate chips

In a medium bowl sift the dry ingredients. In a large bowl cream the shortening with the sugar. Add the beaten eggs and vanilla. Add the dry ingredients alternately with the banana and buttermilk. Stir in chocolate chips. Pour the batter into a 5 x 9-inch loaf pan. Bake in a 350° oven for 50 minutes.
MAKES 4 TO 6 SERVINGS.

Chocolate Carrot Cake

2   cups all-purpose flour
1½   cups sugar
1   cup oil
½   cup orange juice
¼   cup unsweetened cocoa
2   teaspoons baking soda
1   teaspoon salt
1   teaspoon ground cinnamon
1   teaspoon vanilla extract
4   eggs
2   cups shredded carrots
1   4-ounce package coconut
  Confectioners' sugar glaze or icing

In a large bowl combine the flour, sugar, oil, orange juice, cocoa, soda, salt, cinnamon, vanilla, and eggs until blended, scraping often. Increase the speed to high and mix for 2 minutes. Stir in the carrots and coconut. Spoon into a greased and floured bundt pan. Bake in a 350° oven for 50 to 55 minutes or until a toothpick inserted in the cake comes out clean.

Cool on wire rack for 10 minutes. Remove the cake from the pan. Pour a glaze over or ice it.
MAKES 8 SERVINGS.

Pumpkin Nut Bread

1   cup raisins
⅔   cup hot water
2   teaspoons baking soda
2⅓   cups sugar
⅔   cup shortening
4   beaten eggs
2   cups pumpkin
3⅓   cups all-purpose flour
1   teaspoon ground cinnamon
1   teaspoon salt
1   teaspoon baking powder
¼   teaspoon ground cloves
⅔   cup chopped nuts
1   cup semisweet chocolate chips
  Chopped nuts for topping

In a large bowl combine raisins, hot water, and soda. In a separate bowl cream the sugar and shortening. Add the eggs, pumpkin, flour, cinnamon, salt, baking powder, and cloves. Add the raisin mixture, ⅔ cup of chopped nuts, and chocolate chips. Pour into 2 greased 5 x 9-inch loaf pans. Sprinkle chopped nuts on top of mixture. Bake in a 325° oven for 1 hour. Let cool for 15 minutes, then remove from pans.
MAKES 2 LOAVES.

Holden House 1902 Bed & Breakfast

Holden House 1902 Bed & Breakfast

❧

1102 West Pikes Peak Avenue
Colorado Springs, Colorado 80904
(710) 471-3980

*T*he Holden House is a Colonial Revival filled with antiques and family heirlooms. The period wallpapers and antiques that decorate the inn throughout are true to its early-twentieth-century origins. Guest rooms are named for famous Colorado mining town such as Aspen, Leadville, and Cripple Creek. Fine restaurants, unique gift shops, and area attractions all nearby, some within walking distance.

Southwestern Eggs Fiesta

24   eggs
6   snack-size flour tortillas
12   ounces Cheddar cheese
  Bacon bits or crumbled cooked turkey bacon
  Chopped cilantro (fresh if available)
  Sour cream for topping
  Mild picante sauce for topping
  Parsley for garnish

Grease 12 individual soufflé dishes with cooking spray and break 2 eggs into each dish. Slice the tortillas in half and place in dishes with flat edge down outside the eggs, to form a U-shape around the outer edge of the dish. Top with a 1-ounce slice of Cheddar and bacon bits, and sprinkle with a dash of cilantro. Bake in a 375° oven for 30 minutes or until the eggs are done, the cheese is melted, and the tortilla is slightly brown. Top with a dab of sour cream and 1 teaspoon of picante sauce. Sprinkle of cilantro on top and serve on a plate. Garnish with parsley if desired.

MAKES 12 SERVINGS.

Chocolate Chunk-White Chocolate Chip Cookies

- ¾ cup firmly packed brown sugar
- ¾ cup butter or margarine
- 2 eggs
- 1 teaspoon vanilla
- 2½ cups all-purpose flour
- 1 teaspoon baking soda
- 1 cup chocolate chunks
- 1 10-ounce package vanilla chips
- ¼ cup chopped walnuts

In a large bowl soften the brown sugar and butter in the microwave for 1 minute on high. Add the eggs and vanilla, and mix well. Add the flour and baking soda and mix well. Fold in the chocolate chunks, vanilla chips, and walnuts. Drop by well-rounded teaspoonfuls onto an ungreased insulated cookie sheet. Bake in a 375° oven for 10 to 12 minutes or until slightly brown on top.

MAKES APPROXIMATELY 2 DOZEN.

Ruffled Crêpes Isabel

- 1¼ cups all-purpose flour
- 2 tablespoons sugar
    Pinch salt
- 3 eggs
- 1½ cups milk
- 2 tablespoons melted butter
- 1 teaspoon lemon extract (optional)
    ....
- 1½ cups milk
- ½ teaspoon salt
- ¼ teaspoon pepper
- 1 tablespoon all-purpose flour
- 6 slices cooked turkey bacon, crumbled
    Sharp Cheddar cheese
    Sour cream for garnish
    Fresh dill, parsley, or tarragon for garnish

In a medium bowl combine 1¼ cups of flour, sugar, salt, eggs, 1½ cups of milk, melted butter, and lemon extract. Blend well. Let the batter rest for approximately 5 minutes. Make 5-inch crêpes using either a well-greased skillet or crêpe maker. Extra crêpes may be stored in refrigerator for later use.

In a separate bowl combine 1½ cups of milk, ½ teaspoon of salt, pepper, and 1 tablespoon of flour.

Generously grease 24 muffin cups with cooking spray. Press the crêpes into the cups, lightly ruffling the edges but being careful not to tear the crêpes. Place a small square of cheese in the bottom of each crêpe and pour the egg mixture carefully into each crêpe, filling just to below the top of the rim. Top with crumbled bacon (vegetarian bacon bits may be substituted). Bake in a 375° oven for 15 to 20 minutes, or until the mixture is firm and the crêpes are just lightly brown.

Cool slightly, and carefully loosen crêpe cups from the muffin pan with a fork or knife, taking care not to break the crêpe edges. Remove from the pan with a spoon, place 2 on each plate, and top with a small dab of sour cream and chopped fresh dill, parsley, or tarragon.

MAKES 12 SERVINGS.

Baked Islander French Toast

- 2 loaves sliced French bread (24 medium slices)
- 7 eggs
- 3 cups milk
- ½ teaspoon pineapple extract
- ½ teaspoon coconut extract
- ½ teaspoon banana extract
- 1½ cups firmly packed light brown sugar
- 1 cup butter
- 2 tablespoons corn syrup
- ½ cup flaked coconut
- ½ cup slivered almonds
- 2 medium bananas, sliced into rounds
    Whipped cream for garnish
- 12 rings canned pineapple for garnish
    Mint leaves
    Grated coconut
    Dash grated nutmeg for garnish

Grease 12 1-ounce soufflé dishes and place 2 bread slices, cut into halves, in the bottom of each dish. In a large bowl whip the eggs, milk, and flavorings together. Pour the egg mixture over the slices of bread. In an oven-proof bowl melt the brown sugar, butter, and corn syrup in the microwave, and mix well. Ladle the sugar mixture evenly over the bread slices. Top with coconut, almonds, and banana slices. Cover and refrigerate overnight.

Bake in a 400° oven for 20 to 30 minutes. When serving, top with a dollop of whipped cream. Garnish additionally with a ring of pineapple, a few mint leaves, and sprinkle a little coconut and nutmeg over the top.

MAKES 12 SERVINGS.

1572 Race Street
Denver, Colorado 80206
(303) 331-0621

***O**ne of Denver's grandest mansions in the historic Capitol Hill district, the Castle-Marne was built in 1889. Designed by William Lange, who also designed the "Unsinkable" Molly Brown's nearby house, it glows with polished wood, ornate fireplaces, and stained glass. Furnished with period antiques, family heirlooms, and carefully chosen reproductions, the guest rooms are quite luxurious. Nearby are Denver City Park, Art Museum, and Botanic Gardens.*

Castle-Marne

Raspberry Truffles

1 cup semisweet chocolate chips
2 1-ounce squares unsweetened chocolate, chopped
1½ cups confectioners' sugar
½ cup butter, softened
2 tablespoons raspberry liqueur
  Chocolate sprinkles
  Cocoa
  Chopped nuts
  Cookie crumbs

In a small heavy saucepan melt the chocolate chips and unsweetened chocolate over low heat, stirring constantly. Set aside

In a medium bowl combine the confectioners' sugar, butter, and liqueur. Beat with an electric mixer until blended. Beat in the cooled chocolate until smooth. Refrigerate for about 30 minutes or until the mixture is fudgy and can be shaped into balls.

Shape the mixture into 1-inch balls by rolling in the palms of hands. Then roll the truffles in chocolate sprinkles, cocoa, chopped nuts, or cookie crumbs to add flavor and prevent the truffles from melting so easily.

MAKES ABOUT 48 TRUFFLES.

The Denver Dry Goods Tea Room Chicken á la King

1 cup butter or margarine
1½ cups all-purpose flour
8 cups chicken broth, or more as needed
1 cup half and half
1 pound cooked, skinned chicken breasts, diced
1 large red bell pepper, cut into ¼-inch strips
1 large green bell pepper, cut into ¼-inch strips
½ pound sliced mushrooms, sautéed in butter
  Salt and white pepper to taste
  Baked puff pastry shells or phyllo dough cups

In a large saucepan melt butter. Whisk in the flour, cooking over moderate heat for a few minutes. Gradually add the chicken broth,

whisking and cooking until thickened. Whisk in the half and half. Simmer over low heat for about 20 minutes. Add more chicken broth if needed for the desired consistency. Add the chicken, bell peppers, mushrooms, salt, and pepper. Cook over low heat until heated through. Serve in pastry shells or phyllo cups.

MAKES 6 TO 8 SERVINGS.

Maple Walnut Muffins

2 cups whole wheat flour
2 cups all-purpose flour
5 teaspoons baking powder
1 teaspoon salt
½ cup butter, softened
1 cup maple syrup
½ cup sour cream
2 eggs
1 cup water
1 tablespoon vanilla extract
1 cup chopped walnuts
  Raw sugar for sprinkling

In a medium bowl mix the dry ingredients together and set aside. In a large bowl beat the butter and maple syrup until smooth. Stir in the sour cream, eggs, water, and vanilla. Fold in the dry ingredients, and add the walnuts. Fill greased muffin cups almost full and sprinkle the tops with raw sugar. Bake in a 400° oven for 20 to 25 minutes or until the tops are browned and set. Serve warm.

MAKES 2 DOZEN.

Marne Beer Bread

½ cup butter
3 cups self-rising flour
1 tablespoon sugar (optional)
12 ounces beer
  Caraway seed
  Dill seed
  Poppy seed or any favorite

Coat 6 small loaf pans with cooking spray, and pour in enough butter to just cover the bottom. In a large bowl mix the flour, sugar, and beer together until the dry ingredients are just moistened. Portion the dough and place in the pans. Pour the remaining butter on top and sprinkle with seeds, if desired. Bake in a 350° oven for 50 to 60 minutes or until bread is golden brown and crusty.

Remove the loaves from the pans and let stand a few minutes. Tell your guests to just tear off chunks of the crust. Serve with jam, marmalade, or honey butter.

Note: Use smaller baking containers, which will serve 2 or 3 persons. International Coffee-type cans are about the right size. Different types and brands of beer will each impart their special flavor to the bread. Add other flavorings to the dough, and sprinkle on top caraway seed, dill seed, poppy seed, or try any favorite. Home-brewed beer makes exceptionally flavorful bread.

MAKES 6 SMALL LOAVES.

Pumpkin Bisque Soup

½ cup butter
1 large onion, diced
2½ pounds diced pumpkin (or 3 cups pumpkin purée, homemade or canned)
6 cups chicken stock
½ teaspoon salt
3 tablespoons all-purpose flour
¼ cup chopped parsley
  Croutons for topping

In a large saucepan melt the butter Add the diced onion and sauté until golden. Add the pumpkin, chicken stock and salt. Cook over medium heat for 10 minutes.

Take out 1 cup of liquid and blend add the flour into it. Stir with a whisk until all lumps are gone. Add the flour mixture to the soup and stir with a whisk. Cook 5 minutes whisking occasionally, to cook the flour. Adjust the seasonings and add the parsley. Serve with croutons.

MAKES 8 SERVINGS.

The Queen Anne

The Queen Anne

2147 Tremont Place
Denver, Colorado 80205
(303) 296-6666

Denver's oldest urban B&B, the inn consists of two side-by-side homes dating to 1879 and 1886, and both built in the Queen Anne Victorian style. Located in the Clements historic district, the inn is only three blocks from downtown Denver. Gallery suites are decorated with art reproductions celebrating the work of Alexander Calder, Frederic Remington, Norman Rockwell, and John James Audubon. Guest rooms are double-sized and furnished with period antiques.

Spinach Mushroom Quiche

5 large eggs
1½ cups heavy cream
Pinch salt
Pinch white pepper
⅛ teaspoon grated nutmeg
¼ teaspoon paprika

8 ounces frozen spinach
1 9-inch pie shell, baked
1 4-ounce can sliced or chopped mushrooms

In a medium bowl blend together the eggs, cream, salt, pepper, nutmeg, and paprika.

Thaw the spinach and let it drain. Squeeze out as much moisture as possible. Place the drained spinach on the bottom of pie shell. Drain the mushrooms and spread a layer over the spinach. Pour the custard over all, filling the shell to the top edge. Bake in a 350° oven for 20 to 22 minutes, or until the filling is well set. Freeze immediately if not to be served at once.

MAKES 6 GENEROUS SERVINGS.

Crunchy and Sweet Pecans

3 cups water
1 cup pecan halves
3 tablespoons brown sugar
Peanut oil

In a saucepan bring the water to boil and add the nuts. Return to a boil for 1 minute. Drain the nuts and rinse with warm water. Mix with brown sugar. In a skillet heat enough peanut oil to cover the bottom of the pan. Add the nuts to the peanut oil and stir until the nuts are lightly browned. Pour onto waxed paper until cool. Keeps up to 2 weeks.

MAKES 4 TO 6 SERVINGS.

Crunchy and Savory Almonds

2 tablespoons olive oil
2 teaspoons curry powder
½ teaspoon garlic powder
¼ teaspoon onion powder
⅛ teaspoon cayenne pepper
1 cup almonds

In a saucepan combine the olive oil, curry powder, garlic powder, onion powder, and cayenne. Mix well and heat through. Add the almonds and stir until coated. Bake the nuts on a foil-covered cookie sheet in a 300° oven for about 10 minutes, until lightly browned. Stir twice while baking. Keeps up to 2 weeks.

Note: There is a bottomless nut jar out all the time for guests as opposed to a bottomless cookie jar. These are 2 of the nut recipes that are popular with the guests.

MAKES 4 TO 6 SERVINGS.

Leland House

Leland House and Rochester Hotel

721 East Second Avenue
Durango, Colorado 81301
(970) 385-1920

The recently renovated Rochester Hotel offers fifteen large rooms with high ceilings and decorated in an Old West motif. The Victorian-style Leland House, in a residential neighborhood, offers B&B suites with western theme decorations and furnishings. Both place guests within easy reach of Durango's and southern Colorado's many attractions, including the ancient Mesa Verde ruins and the Durango & Silverton Narrow Gauge Railroad.

Black Bean Breakfast Quesadilla

½ cup black beans, cooked
½ cup corn
¼ cup chopped green onion
1 tablespoon chopped cilantro
8 eggs
¼ cup heavy cream
½ cup salsa
½ cup Jack cheese, grated
4 flour tortillas
Salsa and sour cream for garnish

In a medium bowl mix the black beans, corn, green onion, and cilantro. Set aside. In a separate bowl whisk the eggs, cream, and salsa together. Set aside. Warm the tortillas. In a skillet cook the eggs until scrambled. Place cheese on each tortilla to melt. Add a portion of the cooked egg mixture and then the black bean mixture. Fold over and garnish with salsa or sour cream.

MAKES 4 SERVINGS.

Diane's Garden Turkey Sausage

- 2 pounds ground turkey
- ¼ cup chopped celery
- ¼ cup chopped carrots
- ¼ cup chopped green onion
- ¼ cup chopped broccoli
- ¼ cup chopped parsley
- ½ teaspoon dried basil
- ½ teaspoon dried thyme
- ½ teaspoon ground allspice
- 1 teaspoon black pepper
- 1 egg
- ½ cup apple juice
- Butter for sautéing

In a large bowl combine the turkey, celery, carrots, onions, and broccoli. Add the herbs and spices, egg, and apple juice, and work with hands to combine. Mold and roll into a log. Wrap in plastic wrap and foil. Refrigerate overnight.

Form into patties and sauté in butter until done.

MAKES ABOUT 8 SERVINGS.

Salsa Diane

- 20 Italian plum tomatoes
- 1 white onion
- 2 jalapeño chilies
- 1 bunch cilantro
- 1 bunch green onions
- Juice of 1 of 2 limes
- Salt to taste
- Pinch cumin

Clean and chop the ends off of the tomatoes. Place the tomatoes in a food processor and pulse until chopped and a bit soupy. Place in a mixing bowl. Next, place the onion, chilies, cilantro, green onions, and lime juice in the food processor and pulse until chopped well. Mix with the tomatoes and add salt and cumin to taste.

Fresh salsa does not have a long shelf life so make it the morning it is to be served.

MAKES 4 CUPS.

Lightner Creek Inn

Lightner Creek Inn

❧

999 C.R. 207
Durango, Colorado 81301
(970) 259-1226

Resembling a French manor house, the inn sits on twenty pristine acres at the edge of the San Juan Mountains and has its own duck pond and trout stream. A carefully renovated 1903 country home, it has eight guest rooms, each displaying it own style of Victorian charm. The rooms are light and airy and keep guests in close touch with flower gardens, fields, and woodlands just outside and the wilderness beyond.

Rhonda's Rummy Starter

- 1½ cups sour cream
- 2 tablespoons confectioners' sugar
- 2 tablespoons firmly packed brown sugar
- 1 tablespoon rum
- 1 teaspoon finely shredded orange zest
- ½ teaspoon ground cinnamon
- ¼ teaspoon grated nutmeg
....
- Toasted pecans (finely chopped)
- 4 bananas
- 4 peaches
- Unsalted butter
- Brown sugar
- Ground cinnamon
- Lemon juice
- Dash rum

- Canned whipped cream
- Brown sugar for sprinkling

In a small bowl stir together the sour cream, confectioners' sugar, brown sugar, rum, orange zest, cinnamon, and nutmeg until combined. Cover and refrigerate the Romanoff Sauce for up to 24 hours to let flavors blend.

Toast the chopped pecans in the oven. Set aside. Slice the bananas lengthwise and the peaches thinly. In a non-stick pan melt a dab of unsalted butter over medium heat. Lightly sauté the peaches and bananas. Sprinkle with brown sugar and cinnamon. Turn the fruit over and sprinkle again with brown sugar and cinnamon, and a little lemon juice. Watch carefully to avoid overcooking. When slightly golden, add dashes of rum to the pan and swirl the pan around until the rum evaporates. Place the fruit slices on a plate in a fan, and drizzle with Romanoff Sauce. Spray dollop of whipped cream, sprinkle with toasted pecans, and sprinkle with brown sugar. Serve warm.

MAKES 4 SERVINGS.

Nutty Chocolateers

- 3½ cups sifted all-purpose flour
- ½ teaspoon baking soda
- 2 cups softened sweet cream butter
- 3 teaspoons vanilla extract
- 1½ cups sugar
- 1½ cups firmly packed dark brown sugar
- 2 eggs
- 1 cup unsweetened cocoa
- ¼ cup heavy cream
- 1 cup macadamia nuts
- 1 cup semisweet chocolate chips
- 1 cup white chocolate chips

In a medium bowl combine the flour and soda, and set aside. In a large bowl cream the butter, vanilla, and sugars until light and fluffy. Beat in the eggs. Add the cocoa and heavy cream, mixing until creamy and fluffy. Mix in the flour and baking soda just until blended. Stir in the nuts and chocolate chips. Drop by rounded teaspoonfuls onto foil-lined baking sheets. Bake in a 350° oven for 15 to 20 minutes.

Remove from the oven and cool slightly before removing from the baking sheets.

MAKES 6 DOZEN.

Frozen Oranges with Raspberry Sauce

6 large oranges
Frozen vanilla yogurt
Sugar
1 cup fresh or frozen raspberries
1 tablespoon honey
½ teaspoon vanilla extract
1 teaspoon cornstarch
2 tablespoons water
Pinch salt
Heavy cream
Firmly packed brown sugar

Cut the oranges in half. Cut the center core out. Scoop out the sections. In a blender combine the orange sections and frozen yogurt, and blend until creamy. Freeze overnight. Roll the orange shell halves in sugar and freeze overnight.

Once frozen, scoop the creamy mixture into orange shell.

In a saucepan, combine the raspberries, honey and vanilla. Stir over low heat until just boiling. In a cup mix the cornstarch with the water and salt, and add the mixture to the raspberries. Cook over low heat until thickened. Pour the sauce mixture over the frozen oranges, and top with whipped cream and a pinch of brown sugar.

MAKES 12 SERVINGS.

35060 U.S. Highway 550 North
Durango, Colorado 81301
(970) 259-4396

Logwood Bed and Breakfast is just twelve miles north of Durango and thirteen miles south of Purgatory Ski Resort on the banks of the Animas River. Maroon-shaded mountains soar skyward on every side. The Durango-Silverton Narrow Gauge Railroad passes close enough for guests to catch the scent of locomotive smoke. All of the guest rooms have private baths and large picture windows, and all are attractively furnished with colorful home-stitched quilts to match the inn's colorful robust surroundings. The two-story vaulted living room with its river rock fireplace is a great place for mingling with other guests and making new friends.

Chocolate Sour Cream Pound Cake

1 cup butter
2 cups sugar
1 cup firmly packed brown sugar
6 large eggs
2½ cups all-purpose flour
¼ teaspoon baking soda
½ cup cocoa
1 8-ounce carton sour cream
2 teaspoon vanilla extract
Confectioners' sugar (optional)

In a large bowl beat the butter with electric mixer at medium speed for about 2 minutes until soft and creamy. Gradually add the sugars and blend for 5 minutes. Add the eggs one at a time until the yellow disappears.

In a separate bowl combine the flour, baking soda, and cocoa. Add the dry ingredients to the creamed mixture alternately with the sour cream. Mix at the lowest speed just until blended after each addition. Stir in the vanilla. Spoon the batter into a greased and floured 10-inch tube pan. Bake in a 325° for 1 hour and 20 minutes until a toothpick comes clean.

Cool in the pan on a wire rack for 10 to 15 minutes.

Remove and cool on a wire rack. Sprinkle with confectioners' sugar, if desired.

MAKES 8 SERVINGS.

Logwood

Logwood Popovers

2⅓ tablespoons oil
1 cup milk
1 cup all-purpose flour
2 large eggs
¼ teaspoon salt

Pour ½ teaspoon of oil into each of 8 muffin cups. Place the tin in a 450° oven. In a food processor or blender mix the milk, flour, eggs, salt, and the rest of the oil. Blend at high for about 20 seconds, or until the batter is smooth. Turn off the blender and, with a rubber spatula, scrape off the sides of the container. Blend for a little longer. Remove the muffin tin from the oven. Pour the batter into the hot cups, filling them halfway. Bake in a 450° oven for 30 minutes or until the popovers are puffed and browned. Do not open the door while baking.

MAKES 4 SERVINGS (8 POPOVERS).

Mad Creek Bed and Breakfast
✎

167 Park Avenue, P.O. Box 404
Empire, Colorado 80438
(303) 569-2003

A Victorian cottage built in 1881, this B&B provides a rustic, old, mountain atmosphere with antiques, original artwork, and nineteenth-century artifacts. It places its guests in the midst of Colorado's gold and silver mining bonanza country. Empire was among the best known of the strike-it-rich mining camps along with Georgetown, Silverplume, Idaho Springs, and Central City, all nearby.

Mad Creek Crunch

- 6 cups old-fashioned oats
- 1 cup oat bran
- 1 cup coconut
- 1 cup sesame seeds
- 1 cup sunflower seeds
- 1 cup walnuts or almonds
- 1 cup firmly packed brown sugar
- 1 tablespoon ground cinnamon
- ½ cup oil
- ½ cup hot water

....

- 1 cup chopped dates, dried cranberries, or apricots

In a large bowl combine the oats, oat bran, coconut, sesame seeds, sunflower seeds, walnuts, brown sugar, and cinnamon. In a separate bowl combine the oil and water. Pour the liquid mixture over the dry ingredients, mixing well. Spread the granola on a greased cookie sheet. Bake in a 350° oven for 30 to 40 minutes. Mix occasionally during baking.

Add the dates, after it has cooled.

MAKES ABOUT 13 CUPS.

Cranberry Oat Crunch Muffins

- 2½ cups all-purpose flour
- ½ cup sugar
- 1 tablespoon baking powder
- 1 teaspoon salt
- 1 teaspoon ground cinnamon
- 1 cup dried cranberries
- 2 eggs
- ¼ cup oil
- 1 cup milk
- ¼ cup butter
- ⅓ cup all-purpose flour
- ⅓ cup firmly packed brown sugar

In a large bowl combine the 2½ cups of flour, the sugar, baking powder, salt, cinnamon, and cranberries. In a separate bowl mix the eggs, oil, and milk. Add the liquid mixture to the dry ingredients, and mix well. Pour into greased muffin cups. In a small bowl combine the butter, ⅓ cup all-purpose flour, and brown sugar. Sprinkle the mixture over the batter. Bake in a 350° oven for 30 to 40 minutes.

MAKES 1 DOZEN.

Black Dog Inn

Black Dog Inn

❧

650 South St. Vrain Avenue, P.O. Box 4659
Estes Park, Colorado 80517
(970) 586-0374

***B**uilt in 1910, the inn was one of the earliest homes in the high-mountain village of Estes Park. The inn and its four guest rooms are decorated with history in mind. A gateway to the Rocky Mountain National Park, Estes Park is a popular travel destination. A footpath running in front of the inn leads to delightful shops and restaurants as well as the fairgrounds, theater, golf course, and public pool. But most visitors come here to go even higher in the mountains on llama treks, cross-country skiing expeditions, or sightseeing trips. In May, don't miss the duck races.*

Apricot-Walnut Wheat-Free Scones

- 1¼ cups oat flour
- 1 teaspoon baking powder
- ½ teaspoon baking soda
- ¼ teaspoon salt (optional)
- ¼ cup sugar

....

- ¼ cup butter
- ¼ cup shortening

....

- 1 cup rolled oats
- ⅓ cup chopped dried apricots
- ⅓ cup chopped walnuts (process these
   together and the apricots won't
   stick together)
- ¼ cup currants (can add some orange
   zest)
- ⅓ to ½ cup buttermilk

In a large mixing bowl combine the oat flour, baking powder, soda, salt, and sugar.

Cut the butter and shortening into the dry ingredients with a fork or pastry blender until the mixture just starts to adhere (this is a moist mixture).

Add the oats, apricots, walnuts, and currants. Add the buttermilk and mix until moistened.

With floured hands gather the dough and knead a few turns on a floured board. Press the dough into a 9-inch round pie plate and score into 8 wedges, or roll dough into a 7-inch circle and cut with a biscuit cutter. Bake in a 375° oven for 12 to 15 minutes.

Note: These scones are a nice accompaniment to eggs, served with jam or honey. I think they are tastier when served warmed the next day.

MAKES 8 WEDGES OR 10 ROUNDS.

High Country Hash Browns

- ¼ cup oil
- 5 large pre-cooked baking potatoes,
   cubed (covered and refrigerated
   overnight)
- 1 medium onion, cut in chunks
- ½ green bell pepper, cut in chunks
- ½ sweet red pepper, cut in chunks
- 1 large tomato, chopped
- ½ pound bacon, cooked and crumbled
- ½ cup shredded medium Cheddar
   cheese
- ½ cup shredded Monterey Jack cheese
   Salsa Cruda (recipe follows) or
   prepared salsa
   Sour cream

In a large skillet heat about ¼ cup of oil and brown the potatoes on both sides, turning once. While browning the potatoes, in a separate skillet sauté the onion and peppers until tender. Add the tomatoes and heat until warm. Spray a 9-inch square baking dish with cooking spray and add the potatoes. Cover with the hot vegetables, sprinkle with bacon. Top with the cheeses. Cover with foil to melt the cheese, and keep warm until ready to serve.

Cut the potatoes into 4 squares, place on serving plates, and top with Salsa Cruda and sour cream.

MAKES 4 SERVINGS.

Salsa Cruda

- 1 large tomato, peeled and chopped
- 2 serrano chilies, seeded and chopped
- 2 jalapeño peppers, seeded and chopped
- 5 green onions, chopped
- 1 teaspoon fresh lime juice
- 1 teaspoon fresh cilantro, minced
- 1 teaspoon cumin
- 1 teaspoon sugar
- ½ teaspoon freshly ground black pepper

In a large bowl combine all of the ingredients and mix together.

Note: Best if prepared ahead so the flavor can mix overnight.

MAKES 6 SERVINGS.

Apple Spice Bars

- ⅔ cup light firmly packed brown sugar
- ½ cup unsweetened applesauce
- ¼ cup margarine
- 1 cup finely chopped apple (such as McIntosh), skin left on
- 1 cup all-purpose flour
- 1 cup bran flakes, crushed
- ¾ teaspoon baking soda
- ¼ teaspoon ground cinnamon
- ¼ teaspoon grated nutmeg
- ¼ teaspoon ground allspice
- 1 egg white
- ⅔ teaspoon lemon juice
- ½ cup confectioners' sugar

In a saucepan combine the brown sugar, applesauce, and margarine. Heat gently until the margarine melts. Stir in the apple. In a large bowl combine the flour, bran flakes, soda, and spices. Stir into the apple mixture. Stir in the egg white and blend. Pour the batter into a greased 8 x 11-inch baking dish. Bake in a 350° oven for 20 minutes.

In a small bowl mix the lemon juice and confectioners' sugar. Frost the bars. Cut into squares and serve.

MAKES 8 SERVINGS.

*Eagle Cliff
Bed &
Breakfast*

❧

P.O. Box 4312
Estes Park, Colorado 80517
(970) 586-5425

Eagle Cliff House is a warm and friendly bed and breakfast set among ponderosa pines at the base of Eagle Cliff Mountain in Estes Park. The earth-toned southwestern decor invites relaxation, as do the sun-drenched deck and the down comforters on the beds. To the advantage of those with outdoor adventure and natural grandeur in mind, the Eagle Cliff is so close to Rocky Mountain National Park guests can walk to it.

Eagle Cliff

Fruit Smoothies

- 2 or 3 bananas (ripe, overly ripe, or frozen)
- 1 16-ounce can peaches, pears, fruit cocktail (or any extra ripe fruit)
- 1 cup orange juice
- 1 cup pineapple juice
  Sugar or honey to taste
- 1 10-ounce box frozen strawberries or raspberries
- 1 scoop frozen vanilla yogurt per serving

In a blender blend the bananas, canned fruit, orange juice, pineapple juice, and sugar on high. Add the frozen strawberries or raspberries and continue to blend until the desired consistency.

Place a scoop of frozen yogurt in a glass and pour the smoothie mixture on top.

MAKES ABOUT 5 CUPS OF SMOOTHIE MIXTURE.

Eagle Cliff Granola

- 2 cups raw cashews
- 3 cups chopped walnuts
- 4 cups pecans, chopped or whole
- 2 cups wheat bran
- 2 cups dried bananas
- 1 cup chopped dried apricots
- 1 cup chopped dates
- 15 cups rolled oats
- 3 cups raw sunflower seeds
- 2 cups sliced almonds
- 2 cups coconut
- 2 cups chopped dried apples
- 1 cup dried pineapple pieces
- 3 tablespoons ground cinnamon
- 1 teaspoon ground ginger
- 1 teaspoon grated nutmeg
- 1 teaspoon ground cloves
- 1 cup wheat germ
- 4 cups canola oil
- 1 cup apple juice or orange juice
- 2 cups honey
- 1 cup pineapple juice
- 1 teaspoon salt

In a large bowl mix all of the ingredients well. Spread ¾ inch thick on a cookie sheet. Bake in a 300° oven for 30 to 45 minutes. Stir frequently. Turn off the oven and open the door. Let the granola stand for at least 1 hour.

MAKES ABOUT 40 CUPS.

Mexican Eggs

- ½   cup finely chopped onion (or more)
- ½   cup chopped green bell pepper
- 1   10-ounce can Pillsbury Grands biscuits
- 3   strips browned and crumbled bacon
- ½   cup sliced turkey
- ½   cup grated Cheddar or mozzarella cheese
- ½   cup grated Parmesan cheese
- 5   eggs, beaten
     Garlic, cumin, oregano

In a glass dish combine the onion and bell pepper, and microwave for 5 minutes. Spread the biscuits in an oiled 9 x 13-inch pan. Press down until the biscuits touch. Add the bacon, turkey, and vegetables. Add the cheeses. Sprinkle the spices over the vegetables. Pour the eggs over entire combination. Bake in a 350° oven for 45 minutes.

If the crust is moist, place in the microwave a few minutes to finish. Do not overbake.

MAKES 8 SERVINGS.

Emerald Manor

441 Chiquita Lane, P.O. Box 3592
Estes Park, Colorado 80517
(970) 586-8058

*E*arly Estes Park settler Frank Bond built this handsome Tudor home in 1917. Today, with its tasteful furnishings, antiques, and stained glass, it remains true to his original gracious vision of it. Meals are

Emerald Manor

served in the formal dining room on Bavarian china and cut crystal. All three of the guest rooms offer spectacular views of the Rockies.

Asparagus Cheese Toast

-     Butter
- 4   slices Texas toast
     Parmesan cheese
- 12 slices cooked bacon
- 1   15-ounce can asparagus, drained
- 4   slices white cheese (Muenster, Havarti, etc.)

Butter the Texas toast, sprinkle with Parmesan cheese and toast. Flip the bread over and place cooked bacon on the bread, then add some asparagus and finally cover with cheese. When ready to serve, grill until the cheese is melted and the sides are brown.

Note: This recipe has no official name but is delicious for brunch, for breakfast, or as a snack. It is simple, elegant, and fun. Serve it with fresh fruit and a warm coffee cake.

MAKES 4 SERVINGS.

Brown Bread

- 4   cups all-purpose flour
- 3   cups whole wheat flour
- 6   tablespoons wheat germ
     About ¼ cup All Bran
- 2   heaping teaspoons baking soda
- 1   teaspoon salt
- ¼   cup margarine
- 2   cups buttermilk
- 1   egg

In a large bowl combine the dry ingredients. Cut in the margarine with a pastry blender. Add the buttermilk and egg and form into a soft ball. Place on a greased baking sheet, mold into a round shape, and make a cross on top. This allows one to cut into quarters when cooked. These are known in Ireland as farrels. Bake in a 325° oven for 15 minutes. Reduce the oven to 325° and bake for 50 minutes longer.

Serve warm with butter and fresh preserves.

MAKES 1 LOAF.

RiverSong

RiverSong Bed and Breakfast Inn

P.O. Box 1910
Estes Park, Colorado 80517
(970) 586-4666

A small country inn at the foot of giant Track Mountain, the River Song sits on twenty-seven wooded acres. Gentle hiking trails provide access to breathtaking mountain views and, occasionally, elk, deer, eagles, and raccoons. The nine well-appointed guest rooms are named after Rocky Mountain wildflowers, such as chiming bells and Indian paintbrush, and are decorated in the same colorful spirit.

John Wayne Casserole

- 2   large onions, chopped
- 2   green chilies (anaheims are good), chopped
- 1   large red bell pepper, chopped
- 2   cloves garlic
- 1   jalapeño pepper, minced
- 3   tablespoons butter
- 12 eggs, separated
- ¾   cup milk
- ¾   cup all-purpose flour
- 2   tablespoons ground black pepper
- 4   cups sour cream
- 3   cup shredded cheese
- ¾   cup crumbled blue corn tortilla chips
- 2   teaspoons Dijon mustard

2 tablespoons sugar
Sour cream, chopped chives and
chopped tomatoes for garnish

In a large frying pan combine the onions, green chilies, and red pepper. Add the garlic, jalapeño, and butter. Sauté lightly and remove from the heat.

In a large bowl beat together the egg yolks, milk, flour, and black pepper. Add the sour cream, cheese, tortilla chips, Dijon mustard, and sugar, and the now cooled sauté. Mix all together. Beat the egg whites until they are stiff. Fold the egg whites into the mixture. Pour the mixture into 2 greased 9 x 13-inch baking dishes. Bake in a 350° oven for approximately 1 hour. The casserole is done when the top is a little crusty and starts to crack.

Serve a little sour cream on the side, sprinkled with chopped chives and tomatoes.
MAKES 18 SERVINGS.

Grape Nuts Puff

½ cup butter
¼ cup sugar
2 teaspoons grated fresh lemon zest
¼ cup honey
4 egg yolks
5 tablespoons lemon juice
2 cups milk
¼ cup all-purpose flour
½ cup Grape Nuts cereal
4 egg whites
Whipped cream, blackberries or raspberries, and fresh mint for garnish

Spray 6 ramekins with cooking spray. In a large bowl cream the butter with the sugar, lemon zest, and honey. Add the egg yolks and beat until fluffy. Blend in the lemon juice, milk, flour, and Grape Nuts. The mixture will look curdled but the appearance will not affect the final dish. In a separate bowl beat the egg whites until they are stiff. Fold them into the mixture. Pour the mixture into the prepared ramekins. Place the ramekins in a water bath. Bake in a 325° oven for 1 hour, or until the tops spring back when touched. Garnish with a little whipped cream and place a raspberry or blackberry on top with a sprig of mint.
MAKES 6 SERVINGS.

Cherry Almond Coffee Cake

1 cup sugar
½ cup unsalted butter, room temperature
2 large eggs
1 teaspoon vanilla extract
½ teaspoon almond extract
2 cups all-purpose flour
1 teaspoon baking powder
1 teaspoon baking soda
½ teaspoon salt
1 cup sour cream
½ 21-ounce can cherry pie filling
½ cup thinly sliced almonds

Butter a 10-inch diameter springform pan. In a large bowl beat sugar and butter until light and fluffy. Add the eggs, the vanilla, and almond extracts. Beat well. In a medium bowl sift the flour, baking powder, soda, and salt. Mix half of the dry ingredients into the butter mixture. Mix in the sour cream, then the remaining dry ingredients. Pour two-thirds of the batter into the prepared pan. Drop the pie filling by tablespoons evenly over the batter. Drop the remaining batter by spoonfuls over pie the filling. Using the back of the spoon, carefully spread the batter over the filling. Sprinkle with almonds. Bake in a 350° oven until a toothpick inserted in the center of the cake comes out clean, about 1 hour and 5 minutes.

Cool in the pan on a rack. Run a knife around the sides of the pan and remove pan.
MAKES 8 SERVINGS.

Elizabeth Street Guest House

Elizabeth Street Guest House

❦

202 East Elizabeth Street
Fort Collins, Colorado 80524
(970) 493-2337

A *beautifully restored American four-square brick home, the Guest House has been nicely finished with family antiques, old quilts, and plants. The names of the guest rooms speak for the individuality of their decor: Kansas, Colorado, Alaska, and Barbados. The Fort Collins historic district and Colorado State University are nearby.*

Salmon Party Ball

1 8-ounce can salmon
1 8-ounce package cream cheese
1 tablespoon lemon juice
2 teaspoons grated onion
1 teaspoon horseradish
1 teaspoon liquid smoke
¼ teaspoon salt
½ cup finely chopped pecans
2 tablespoons chopped parsley
Assorted crackers

Drain and flake the salmon remove the bones, if desired. In a small bowl combine the cream cheese, lemon juice, onion, horseradish, liquid smoke, salt, and salmon. Mix well. Chill for several hours. Shape into a ball. Roll in nuts and parsley. Serve with assorted crackers.
MAKES 6 SERVINGS.

Popover Muffins

1 cup all-purpose flour
Dash salt
2 eggs
1 cup milk

Spray a 12-cup muffin tin (preferable heavy tin-like cast iron or aluminum) with cooking spray. Place in the freezer. Do not preheat the oven.

In a small bowl mix all of the ingredients with a fork until just moistened. The batter will be lumpy. Do not overmix. Remove the muffin tin from the freezer and fill the muffin cups one-half to two-thirds full. Place the tin in a cold oven. Turn on the oven to 450° and bake for 20 minutes. Do not peek.

Check and bake 1 to 2 minutes longer if needed, until lightly brown.

MAKES 12 MUFFINS.

Chile Egg Puff

5 eggs
½ teaspoon baking powder
¼ cup all-purpose flour
½ teaspoon salt
2 tablespoons olive oil
1 cup creamed small curd cottage cheese
2 cups grated Monterey Jack cheese
1 7-ounce can diced green chilies (hot or mild)
1 9-inch unbaked pie shell
Salsa and sour cream for garnish

In a medium bowl beat the eggs until light with a wire whisk. Add the baking powder, flour, salt, and olive oil, and beat well. Blend in the cottage cheese and Monterey Jack cheese. Add the chilies. Mix well and pour into the unbaked pie shell. Bake in 350° oven 45-55 minutes until brown and knife inserted comes out clean.

Serve with salsa and dollop of sour cream.

MAKES 6 TO 8 SERVINGS.

Outlook Lodge

Outlook Lodge Bed & Breakfast
❧

6975 Howard Street, P.O. Box 5
Green Mountain Falls, Colorado 80819
(719) 684-2303

---

*O*riginally a church parsonage, the lodge dates to 1889, when this part of Colorado was still a frontier. The four guest rooms are individually decorated, and breakfast is served in a large, sunny dining room. Nearby attractions include the incomparable Garden of the Gods rock formations, Pikes Peak, the charming mountain village of Manitou Springs, and the U.S. Air Force Academy.

Ham Strata

12 slices white bread
¾ pound Old English cheese slices (or shredded Cheddar)
1 10-ounce package frozen broccoli, thawed
2 cups cooked ham slices
6 eggs
2½ cups milk
2 tablespoons instant onion
½ teaspoon salt
¼ teaspoon dry mustard
Shredded Cheddar cheese

Cut 12 round shapes from the bread with a cookie cutter or top of a drinking glass. Place the remaining bread scraps in the bottom of a 9x13-inch pan. Arrange the cheese slices on the scraps. Add a layer of broccoli, then the ham. Place the bread circles on top. In a medium bowl combine the remaining ingredients except the Cheddar, pour over the casserole and cover for 6 to 8 hours or overnight.

Bake uncovered in a 325° oven for 65 minutes. Sprinkle with shredded cheese and bake until melted.

Let stand 5 minutes before cutting.
MAKES 8 SERVINGS.

Strawberry Bread

3 cups all-purpose flour
1 teaspoon baking soda
1 teaspoon salt
1 tablespoon ground cinnamon
2 cups sugar
4 eggs, beaten
2 cups strawberries (fresh or frozen, thawed)
1½ cups oil
1¼ cups chopped pecans or walnuts

In a medium bowl sift the dry ingredients together. In a large bowl combine the eggs, strawberries, and oil. Add the dry ingredients and mix until blended. Fold in the pecans or walnuts. Spoon into a greased 5 x 9-inch loaf pan. Bake in a 325° oven for about 1 hour.

MAKES 1 LOAF.

Waunita Hot Springs Ranch
❧

8007 County Road 887
Gunnison, Colorado 81230
(970) 641-1266

---

*S*ituated ten miles west of the Continental Divide at an elevation of just under nine-thousand feet, the Waunita Hot Springs Ranch is literally at the end of the road—"about as far as the snowplow dares to go in winter," say its owners. A year-round American Plan guest ranch, it places visitors in the heart of the Colorado wilds and near the Crested Butte ski area and Monarch winter sports area. Guest rooms combine modern comfort and old-fashioned charm.

Foccacia

2 cups lukewarm water
1 tablespoon sugar
1 tablespoon active dry yeast
1½ tablespoons olive oil
1 tablespoon salt
4 cups all-purpose flour, or as needed
....
1 tablespoon dried basil
1 tablespoon dried oregano
4 cloves garlic, minced
2 16-ounce cans chopped tomatoes,
     well drained
½ cup Parmesan cheese

In a large bowl combine the water, sugar, and yeast. Set aside for 5 minutes.

Add the oil, salt, and flour. Turn onto a lightly floured surface and knead until soft and silky, adding more flour if needed. Place in a greased bowl, cover, and set aside in a warm place to rise until doubled in bulk, about 2 hours.

In a small bowl combine the remaining ingredients. Roll out the dough into 2 equal rounds about ½ inch thick. Place the rounds on an oiled baking sheet. Spread the topping over the rounds, pressing lightly into the dough. Let the dough rise for about 20 minutes.

Bake in a 450° oven for 20 to 30 minutes or until nicely browned. Serve hot.
MAKES 2 LOAVES.

Crispy Oven-fried Chicken

⅓ cup buttermilk
4 chicken breast halves
¼ cup dry seasoned breadcrumbs
¼ cup yellow cornmeal
¾ teaspoon salt
¾ teaspoon chili powder
¾ teaspoon dried cilantro
½ teaspoon cumin
½ teaspoon pepper

Spray a baking sheet lightly with cooking spray. Pour the buttermilk into a shallow dish. Rinse the chicken under cold water and pat dry. Dip in buttermilk, turning to coat. Set aside. In a separate shallow dish combine the remaining ingredients. Dip the chicken in the crumb mixture, coating well. Place on the prepared baking sheet and spray with cooking spray. Bake in a 425° oven for 20 minutes (or less for boneless chicken). Remove the

pan from the oven and spray the chicken again. Bake for an additional 10 minutes or until the juices run clear when the chicken is pierced.

Variation: Substitute for the breadcrumbs and seasonings ⅓ cup of biscuit mix, ¼ cup of finely chopped pecans, ½ teaspoon of paprika, and ½ teaspoon of salt.

Beef Brisket

1 4- to 5-pound brisket
1½ teaspoons salt
½ cup catsup
¼ cup vinegar
½ cup finely chopped onion
1 tablespoon Worcestershire sauce
1½ teaspoons liquid smoke
1 bay leaf, crumbled
¼ teaspoon pepper

Rub the meat with salt. Place the brisket in a large pan. In a small bowl combine the remaining ingredients, and mix well. Pour over the meat. Cover tightly. Bake in a 275° oven for 3 hours.
MAKES 4 TO 6 SERVINGS.

Mock Toffee Bars

   Waverly or Club crackers
1 cup butter (not margarine)
1 cup light brown sugar
1 12-ounce package chocolate chips
1 cup chopped nuts

Line a 15 x 10-inch jelly roll pan with foil. Cover the bottom of the pan with a layer of crackers, breaking the crackers to fit the ends and sides of the pan. In a saucepan combine the butter and brown sugar, and heat until boiling. Boil for 3 minutes, stirring constantly. Pour the mixture over the crackers. Bake in a 350° oven for 5 to 6 minutes. Remove the pan from the oven and immediately sprinkle with chocolate chips. Spread the melted chocolate over the bars like frosting. Top with nuts. Refrigerate until chilled.

Peel the foil from the bars and break into pieces. Store in a cool place.
MAKES 6 TO 8 SERVINGS.

The Lovelander Bed and Breakfast Inn
❧

217 West Fourth Street
Loveland, Colorado 80537
(907) 669-0798

Originally a private residence, the inn was the home of a country doctor and later served as a boarding house. Guest rooms combine Victorian styling with contemporary emphasis on comfort and convenience. The Lovelander offers eleven spacious and inviting guest rooms, all with private baths. Set against the foothills of the Rockies, the town of Loveland is a thriving artists' colony.

Hawaiian French Toast with Rum Sauce

16 croissants
4 eggs
½ cup milk
1 teaspoon vanilla extract
1 teaspoon rum extract
¼ teaspoon grated nutmeg
¼ teaspoon salt
1⅓ cups firmly packed brown sugar
1 cup reserved pineapple juice
½ cup butter
¼ cup plus 2 tablespoons fresh lemon
     juice
4 teaspoons rum flavoring
....
6 to 8 ripe bananas
1 cup crushed pineapple, well-
     drained, reserve juice
1 cup lightly toasted flaked coconut
1 ripe mango, chopped
   Confectioners' sugar
   Toasted chopped macadamia nuts

Split the croissants along the curved edge, being careful not to slice them all the way through. Tear out a little of the inside top of the croissant to make room for the stuffing. This can be done the night before if croissants are stored in an airtight bag.

In a medium bowl beat the eggs and blend in the milk, vanilla, rum extract, nutmeg, and salt. Set aside.

In a saucepan combine the brown sugar, pineapple juice, butter, and lemon juice over low heat (or microwave in a glass container on low). Stir to reduce, cooking the sauce until it reaches a thin caramel-like state. Add 4 teaspoons of rum flavor and cook slightly longer, until the alcohol aroma is gone. (Do not overcook.) At this point, it should be the consistency of maple syrup. This can be made ahead and stored in the refrigerator or freezer.

Heat a griddle to 375°. Slice the bananas thin, on the bias, and place in a bowl. Have the pineapple, coconut, and mango assembled and ready to use. Place a few slices of banana in the croissant and add some pineapple, coconut, and mango. Brush the griddle surface with butter (or spray with cooking spray) and, using a slotted spatula, dip the croissant top in the custard. Turn it along the seam that is uncut and finish by dipping the bottom in and turning the croissant, cut–side-down, to allow the excess to drip back into the bowl. Place croissant, top down on the griddle, pressing gently to increase the surface exposed to the heat. Cook for 3 to 4 minutes, until golden. Turn and finish cooking until done.

Pour the warm rum sauce into a squeeze bottle with a small hole. Paint a prewarmed plate with sauce in an artsy, freeform design or zig zags. Dust the plate with confectioners' sugar and sprinkle with toasted macadamias. Arrange the croissants in the center of the plate and top with more macadamias and a

The Lovelander

little more of the coconut. Serve with warm maple syrup or more of the rum sauce.

MAKES 16 CROISSANTS.

Pumpkin Apple Waffles with Caramel Pecan Sauce

- 1   cup all-purpose flour
- 2   teaspoons baking powder
- 2   tablespoons sugar
- ½   teaspoon salt
- ½   teaspoon grated nutmeg
- ¼   teaspoon ground ginger
- ½   cup canned pumpkin
- 1½ cups milk
- 3   eggs, beaten
- 2   cups chopped, unpeeled tart apple
....
- 1   cup unsalted butter
- 2½ cups firmly packed brown sugar
- ¼   teaspoon salt
- ¼   cup light corn syrup
- 1½ cups chopped toasted pecans
- 1   cup heavy cream
      Confectioners' sugar
      Cinnamon

In a medium bowl sift together the dry ingredients and set aside. In a large bowl combine the pumpkin, milk, and eggs. Add the dry ingredients to the liquid, stirring just until the mixture is combined. Stir in 1 cup of the chopped apple. (This can be stored in the refrigerator overnight.)

In a saucepan over low heat (or in the microwave) melt the butter. Add the brown sugar and salt, and cook over low heat until melted and smooth. Stir in the syrup and pecans. Cook over low heat for 5 to 10 minutes. Stir in the cream and cook for 5 more minutes. (Cook very slowly or the sauce will turn sugary.) The sauce can be made ahead and refrigerated or frozen. It can also be thinned with half and half or more cream for a milkier sauce. Preheat a waffle iron and brush with oil or spray with cooking spray. Spoon the batter onto the prepared waffle iron and cook according to the manufacturer's directions to the desired crispness. Warm the sauce.

To serve, dust prewarmed plates with confectioners' sugar. Sprinkle a few pinches of cinnamon around the edge of the platter. Center 2 waffles on the plate and top with some of the chopped apple. Drizzle with

caramel pecan sauce and serve. Waffles can be held in a 200° oven directly on the oven rack, uncovered.

Note: These are especially wonderful with peeled fresh peaches in place of the apples. Also, the addition of raisins (or sweetened dried cranberries) with either of these fruits is pretty and provides a nice taste contrast.

MAKES 4 SERVINGS.

Glazed Smoked Sausages with Apples and Walnuts

- 2   pounds fully cooked smoked sausage
- ¼   cup butter
- 2   tablespoons fresh lemon juice
- 1   teaspoon fresh grated ginger root
- 6   Jonathan apples, cored and sliced to ¼-inch pieces
- ¾   cup firmly packed brown sugar
- 1   cup toasted walnut pieces
- 1   tablespoon lemon zest

Slice the sausage on the diagonal to ½-inch thickness. Sauté in a skillet to draw out the extra fat. Remove and hold in a warm oven. Drain the fat.

In the same skillet melt the butter, add the lemon juice and ginger, and heat through. Add the apple slices and cook until tender-crisp. Do not overcook.

In a baking pan combine the apples and sausages and sprinkle with brown sugar, walnuts, and lemon zest. Bake in a 350° oven, stirring gently to distribute the sugar, until the sausages are well-browned, apples are tender, and the syrup has cooked to a glaze.

Serve warm as a breakfast side dish or on top of waffles or buttered grits.

MAKES 6 TO 8 SERVINGS.

Cheese and Pepper Grits and Zesty Tomato Sauce

- 1½ cups instant grits
- 3   cups boiling water
- 2   garlic cloves
- 1   poblano chili pepper, seeded and sectioned
- 1   red bell pepper, seeded and sectioned
- ½   green bell pepper, seeded and sectioned
- ¾   cup chopped scallions
- ¾   teaspoon salt

¼ teaspoon fresh ground pepper
¾ teaspoon Tabasco sauce
¼ cup plus 2 tablespoons butter,
    melted
2 eggs, beaten
1½ cups shredded sharp Cheddar cheese
¾ cup fresh grated Parmesan cheese
3 cups chunky salsa
    Fresh cilantro
3 Roma tomatoes, seeded and chopped

In a pan cook the grits in boiling water to the consistency of Cream of Wheat. Set aside and allow to cool slightly. In the bowl of a food processor combine garlic and all peppers and pulse to a fine mince. In a large mixing bowl stir together the grits and the minced vegetables. Add the scallions, seasonings, butter, and eggs and mix well. Stir in the cheeses.

Spray individual ramekins, or muffin cups with cooking spray. Spoon the grits mixture into the ramekins packing tightly. Place the ramekins on a baking sheet or place the muffin cups in the oven. Bake in a 350° oven for 30 minutes or until golden on top and completely set in the middle. (Baking times will vary depending on the container you use and the oven. If using a convection oven, cover with foil to avoid drying out the grits.)

While the grits are baking, prepare the tomato sauce. In a blender or food processor purée the salsa until smooth. Pour the purée through a fine strainer to remove any remaining chunks. Pour into a saucepan and cook over medium heat to reduce, (or microwave on HIGH for several minutes to evaporate enough liquid that the sauce is not watery. Cool and pour into a squeeze bottle.

To serve, paint plates with zesty tomato sauce. Coarsely chop some of the cilantro and sprinkle randomly on the plate. Unmold the grits from the ramekins or muffins cups and place on serving plate. Top with a little of the chopped tomato and garnish with a sprig of fresh cilantro.

MAKES 8 SERVINGS.

Garden Sunflower Potatoes

2 tablespoons butter
1 small carrot, sliced thin on the diagonal
½ red onion, chopped
1 medium zucchini, sliced thin
8 scallions, chopped, including tops
1 medium summer squash, sliced thin
¼ cup chopped parsley
½ cup milk
¼ cup half and half
½ cup sour cream
1 teaspoon dillweed
6 medium red potatoes, boiled tender, peeled, and thinly sliced
    Salt and pepper to taste
1 cup shredded Monterey Jack cheese
1 cup sunflower seeds, toasted

In a skillet melt the butter and sauté the carrots just until the rawness leaves. Add the red onion and cook until the onion begins to soften and the carrots are crisp tender. Add the zucchini, scallions, summer squash, and parsley, and cook all just until the squash are crisp tender.

In a large bowl, combine the milk, half and half, sour cream, and dill. Add the potatoes and vegetables to the bowl and toss gently to combine so that all vegetables are coated. Season with salt and pepper to taste. Pour half of the potato mixture into a greased shallow baking dish. Sprinkle with half of the cheese and half of the sunflower seeds. Top with the remaining potatoes and finish with the remaining cheese and sunflower seeds. Bake in a 350° oven for 35 to 45 minutes, until the sauce is bubbly and the top is slightly browned.

MAKES 6 SERVINGS.

Savory Strudel of Wild Mushrooms, Piñon Nuts, Goat Cheese and Watercress

4 ounces dried mixed wild mushrooms
¼ cup unsalted butter

....

    Cream sherry

....

1 pound domestic mushrooms, sliced
¼ cup sweet red onion, chopped
    Fresh ground pepper, to taste
2 teaspoons fresh oregano
2 tablespoons sherry, or to taste
1 cup toasted piñon nuts plus extra for garnish
2 bunches watercress or arugula
6 to 8 ounces fresh goat cheese, crumbled
6 to 8 ounces fresh goat cheese, crumbled
    Puff pastry sheets
1 egg, beaten
    Paprika

Rinse and clean the wild mushrooms well to remove all grit. Pat dry and place in a shallow bowl, pouring sherry over to nearly cover. Let stand 30 minutes or until the mushrooms are rehydrated, checking occasionally to push the dried mushrooms on top down into the sherry. Remove from the bowl and squeeze dry, reserving the liquid for other uses. Trim off the woody stem ends and chop the mushrooms.

In a skillet melt the butter and sauté the wild and domestic mushrooms to extract the liquor. Mix in the onion, pepper, oregano, sherry, and piñon nuts and continue cooking until the mushrooms are browned and well-seasoned. Drain well and cool.

If using frozen commercial puff pastry sheets, thaw completely and allow to come close to room temperature so the pastry will not crack when handled. Unfold 1 pastry sheet and roll or pat out into a rectangle about 10 inches long and about 8 inches wide. Arrange half of the watercress in a single layer, overlapping the ends to cover the pastry completely to within ½ inch of the edges. Sprinkle with goat cheese. Sprinkle half of the mushroom mixture over that layer and press the filling slightly into the pastry to keep it in place when rolling the dough. Roll up from short end to short for larger servings and long end to long for smaller. Pinch the seam, and tuck the ends to seal the dough, and place seam-side down on an ungreased baking sheet. Brush the dough with egg and sprinkle with paprika. Repeat with the remaining pastry and filling. Bake in a 400° oven for 25 to 30 minutes or until puffed and golden. Allow to sit for 20 minutes before slicing. Arrange on a bed of watercress and scatter extra piñon nuts around the platter.

MAKES ABOUT 6 TO 8 SERVINGS.

Western Slope Trifle

2 cups heavy cream
7 egg yolks
¼ cup sugar
2 teaspoons cornstarch
1 teaspoon vanilla extract

6 cups day-old pound cake, cut in 1 ½-
    inch cubes
    Seedless raspberry jam
½ to ¾ cup sherry
¾ cup fresh blackberries or raspberries
1 cup fresh dark sweet cherry halves
1 cup fresh peaches, sliced and sprin-
    kled with lemon juice
1 cup heavy cream
½ teaspoon vanilla extract
1 tablespoon confectioners' sugar
½ cup slivered almonds, toasted

In a heavy saucepan gently heat the cream but do not boil. While the cream is heating, in a small bowl whisk together the yolks, sugar, and cornstarch. Pour a little of the hot cream into the yolk mixture, whisking constantly to warm it. Return all of this mixture back into the rest of the cream. Cook the custard over low heat until thick. Add 1 teaspoon of vanilla. Allow to cool.

Spread the cubes of cake with raspberry jam and place in a large glass trifle bowl. Sprinkle sherry over the cake pieces. Top with fruit and toss gently. Cover with cooled custard. Cover with plastic wrap and refrigerate at least 4 hours or up to 2 days. Before serving, whip the cream with ½ teaspoon of vanilla and confectioners' sugar and spread over the trifle. Sprinkle with slivered almonds and serve.

MAKES 10 TO 12 SERVINGS.

Victorian Vinegar Cookies

½ cup butter
½ cup margarine
¾ cup sugar
1 tablespoon white vinegar
1¾ cups all-purpose flour
½ teaspoon baking soda
1 cup finely chopped walnuts

In a large bowl cream the butter and margarine until light. Add the sugar and vinegar and beat until fluffy. In a separate bowl mix the flour with the soda. Stir the dry ingredients into the butter mixture until evenly blended, but do not overwork the dough. Stir in the nuts. Drop by teaspoons onto a greased baking sheet. Bake in a 300° oven for 20 to 30 minutes until lightly golden. Cool on parchment paper to absorb excess oil and keep cookies light.

MAKES 6 DOZEN.

Two Sisters Inn

❧

Ten Otoe place
Manitou Springs, Colorado 80829
(719) 685-9684

***B**uilt in 1919 by a pair of enterprising sisters, this rose-colored Victorian provides lodgings only one block from the center of historic Manitou Springs. The four Victorian-style bedrooms feature original bedsteads, hand-pressed linens, and fresh flowers. Some have claw-foot tubs and skylights.*

Mango Melon Soup

1 small melon, peeled and cubed
1 ripe banana, peeled
1 mango, peeled and cubed (divided)
1 tablespoon lemon juice
1 tablespoon honey
    Dash vanilla
6 mint leaves for garnish
6 raspberries for garnish

In a blender combine the melon cubes and process until smooth. Add the banana, ¼ cup of mango cubes, lemon juice, honey, and vanilla and blend until smooth. Chill the mixture for several hours or overnight. Also chill the remaining mango cubes.

Two Sisters Inn

When ready to serve, divide the mango cubes among 6 parfait cups. Stir the chilled mixture and pour equally over the fruit. Garnish with the raspberries and mint leaves.
MAKES 6 SERVINGS.

Fresh Ginger Muffins

1 to 2 ounce piece gingerroot
1 cup sugar, divided
2 tablespoons chopped lemon zest
½ cup butter
1 cup buttermilk
2 eggs
2 cups all-purpose flour
½ teaspoon salt
¾ teaspoon baking soda

Grease a 12 muffin tin.

Chop the unpeeled ginger into fine pieces (approximately ¼ cup). In a small pot combine the ginger and ¼ cup of sugar and cook over medium heat until the sugar has melted. Remove from the heat and let cool.

Combine the lemon zest with ¼ cup of sugar and add to cooled ginger mixture. Set aside.

In a medium bowl cream the butter with the remaining ½ cup of sugar. Add the eggs and beat well. Add the buttermilk and mix. Add the flour, salt, and baking soda, and beat until smooth. Add the ginger-lemon mixture and combine.

Spoon the batter into the prepared muffin tins. Bake in a 375° oven for 15 to 20 minutes.
MAKES 1 DOZEN.

Two Sisters' Gems (Cherry Diamonds)

1 5-ounce package dried cherries
⅓ cup butter
¼ cup Grand Marnier (or frozen
    orange juice concentrate)
½ cup butter or margarine
1/4 cup sugar
1⅓ cups flour
2 eggs
1 cup firmly packed brown sugar
½ teaspoon vanilla
½ teaspoon baking powder
¼ teaspoon salt
½ cup chopped nuts
½ cup shredded coconut (preferably
    unsweetened)

In a small saucepan combine the cherries, water, and Grand Marnier. Simmer gently for 10 minutes. Remove from the heat and cool in the pan. Carefully check for pits, then chop and set aside.

In a medium bowl blend together the butter, sugar, and 1 cup of flour until crumbly. Pat into the bottom a greased 8- or 9-inch square pan. Bake in a 350° oven for about 15 minutes or until golden brown.

In a medium bowl beat the eggs, brown sugar, and vanilla until creamy.In a separate bowl sift the remaining flour with the baking powder and salt, then blend into the the egg mixture. Stir in the cherries, nuts, and coconut. Spread over the baked layer and bake for approximately 30 minutes longer. Cool, then cut into diamonds.

MAKES 16 SERVINGS.

Meadow Creek Bed and Breakfast Inn

13438 U.S. Highway 285
Pine, Colorado 80470
(303) 838-4167

Built in 1929 by a European nobleman, the inn was once part of the sprawling Douglass Ranch. It sits in a secluded meadow walled in by tall pines and aspens and crossed by a spring-fed stream. Only an hour's drive from Denver, it makes a splendid getaway.

Hot Cheese Bread

    1   egg
    ¼   cup milk
    1½ cups baking mix
    1   cup shredded Cheddar cheese
    1   tablespoon poppy seeds
    3   tablespoons Jalapeño cheese mix
        (optional) found in deli section
    2   tablespoons margarine or butter,
        melted

Grease an 8-inch round pan or pie plate.

In a large bowl blend the egg, milk, and baking mix with a fork to form a soft dough. Stir in the Jalapeño cheese mix and half of the shredded cheese mix and half of the shredded Cheddar cheese. Spread the dough in the prepared pan. Sprinkle the remaining cheese and poppy seeds over the top. Drizzle with the margarine. Bake in a 400° oven for 20 to 25 minutes or until a toothpick inserted into the center comes out clean. Cut into wedges and serve immediately.

MAKES 6 SERVINGS.

Ham Quiche Biscuit Cups

    1   8-ounce package cream cheese, soft-
        ened
    2   tablespoons milk
    2   eggs
    ½   cup shredded Swiss cheese
    2   tablespoons chopped green onions
    1   10-ounce can refrigerated flaky
        biscuits
    ½   cup finely chopped ham

Grease 10 muffin cups.

In a medium bowl combine the cream cheese, milk, and eggs until smooth. Stir in the Swiss cheese and green onion. Separate the dough into 10 biscuits. Place one biscuit in each muffin tin and firmly press in the bottom and up the sides forming a ¼-inch rim. Place half of the chopped ham in the bottoms of the dough cups. Spoon about 2 tablespoons of the cheese mixture over the ham in each cup. Top with the remaining ham. Bake in a 375° oven for about 25 minutes until the filling is set and the edges of the biscuits are golden brown. Remove from the pan and serve immediately.

MAKES 10 SERVINGS.

Meadow Creek

Sausage Apple French Toast Pie

    1   tablespoon butter
    1   apple, peeled and sliced thin
    5   eggs
    2   cups milk
    ⅓   cup pure maple syrup
    ½   teaspoon nutmeg
    ½   large loaf French bread cut into 1/2-
        inch pieces
    ½   pound bulk country sausage, cooked
        and drained well

In a skillet melt the butter and cook the apples for about 3 minutes.

In a medium bowl combine the eggs, milk, maple syrup, and nutmeg.

Place about three-fourths of the bread slices in a buttered 10-inch pie plate. Top with sausage, apples, and remaining bread. Pour the milk mixture evenly over the top. Cover and refrigerate overnight.

Bake in a 350° oven for 55 to 60 minutes until set and golden. Serve immediately with additional maple syrup.

MAKES 6 TO 8 SERVINGS.

New Sheridan Hotel

P.O. Box 980
Telluride, Colorado 81435
(800) 200-1891

The New Sheridan Hotel and its' elegant restaurant have been welcoming guests to Telluride since 1895. Each of its 38 rooms and suites is immaculately restored to reflect the Victorian elegance of the period, combined with the relaxed comfort of an alpine lodge. Enjoy a hearty country breakfast each morning before heading out to enjoy the surrounding wilderness. In the afternoon, wine and *hors d'oeuvres will welcome guests back to the comfortable lobby of the inn.*

Chocolate Cake Supreme

- ¾ cup sugar
- ¼ cup water
- 8 ounces semisweet chocolate
- 2 ounces unsweetened chocolate
- 1 cup unsalted butter
- 5 eggs
- ¼ cup sugar
- 1 teaspoon vanilla extract
  Whipped cream (optional)
  Raspberry purée (optional)

Grease a 9-inch springform pan. In a heavy saucepan, bring ¾ cup of sugar and ¼ cup of water to a boil. Cook for 1 to 2 minutes. Stir in the chocolate and butter, and stir until melted. Remove the pan from the heat. In a separate bowl beat the eggs with the ¼ cup of sugar until doubled. Pour into the chocolate mixture and blend well. Pour the batter into the prepared pan, and place the pan inside a larger baking pan, and fill with 1 inch of water. Bake in a 350° oven for 35 to 40 minutes, or until set. Cool in the pan, then refrigerate at least 3 hours before serving. Serve with whipped cream or raspberry purée.

MAKES 8 SERVINGS.

Brie and Pesto in Puff Pastry

- ¼ cup fresh spinach
- 1 cup fresh basil
- ½ cup grated Parmesan cheese
- ¼ cup walnuts or pine nuts
- 5½ tablespoons olive oil
  Salt and pepper to taste

....

- 1 16-ounce wheel Brie cheese
  Puff pastry, homemade or store bought, 12 x 12-inch sheet

....

- 1 egg white, beaten

In a food processor mix the spinach, basil, Parmesan cheese, walnuts, olive oil, and salt and pepper to form a paste.

Spread a thick layer of pesto over the top of the wheel of Brie. Place pesto-side down on the pastry and fold the dough over firmly to secure. Extra pastry can be used to decorate the top. Brush with the egg white. Bake in a 350° oven until golden brown. Cool for at least of 30 minutes before serving.

MAKES 8 SERVINGS.

CONNECTICUT

Inn at Chester

318 West Main Street
Chester, Connecticut 06412
(860) 526-9541

With its ferry, arching oaks, Old Meeting House, and quaint shops, Chester is one of the most charming towns in New England. A quiet dignity prevails throughout the inn, built around an old farm homestead dating to 1778. It offers forty-two rooms and one suite, all furnished with hand-made colonial reproductions. Meals are served in a converted barn, which houses the inn's excellent Post and Beam dining room.

Roast Rack of Lamb

    1   dozen Brussels sprouts, cleaned
    ....
    1   dozen pearl onions, peeled
    1   dozen baby carrots, peeled
    ¼   pound green beans or haricots verts
    ¼   pound asparagus
    2   full racks lamb (ask butcher to
          French them)
    1   dozen cloves garlic
    ½   cup Chardonnay
    ¼   cup tomato juice

    ½   cup demiglace (Swiss Knorr will suf-
          fice)
    1   sprig rosemary, chopped
    4   sprigs thyme, chopped
        Salt and pepper to taste
        Olive oil
        Chopped chives for garnish
    1   tomato, quartered

Clean and peel the vegetables as appropriate. In a saucepan blanche them separately for 3 to 5 minutes. Cool in an ice bath.

In an iron skillet sear the lamb on all sides. Add the garlic cloves and sauté until light brown. Add the wine and reduce by half. Add the tomato juice and demiglace, and simmer for 15 minutes. Add the herbs, and salt and pepper to taste.

Finish cooking the lamb racks in a 400° oven for 8 to 10 minutes. Let the racks rest for 5 minutes while heating up the vegetables in olive oil, salt, and pepper. Slice the racks along the bone. Ladle sauce on half of each plate and shingle the lamb on top. Arrange the vegetables on the other half of each plate. Garnish with chopped chives and tomato quarters.

MAKES 4 SERVINGS.

Thai Shrimp with Pineapple Mango Chutney

    28 to 30 ounces shrimp (jumbo, 3 to 4
          shrimp per portion)
    ....
    ½   cup peanut oil
    1½ teaspoons chili powder
    1   teaspoon coriander
    2   tablespoons finely ground peanuts

    1   teaspoon sugar
        Pinch cayenne pepper
    ....
    1   pineapple, finely diced or 1½ cups
          black beans
    1   ripe mango, finely diced
    1   red bell pepper, finely diced
    1   red onion, finely diced
    1   bunch scallions, chopped
    ....
        Juice and zest of 1 lime
    3   tablespoons sesame oil
    ¼   cup coarsely chopped cilantro
    ½   teaspoon chili powder
    1   teaspoon paprika
    1   teaspoon cumin
        Salt and pepper to taste
        Lime and lemon slices for garnish
        Several sprigs of cilantro

Peel and devein the shrimp. In a large shallow dish combine the peanut oil, chili powder, coriander, peanuts, sugar, and cayenne. Add the shrimp and toss to coat. Set aside to marinate.

In a medium bowl combine the pineapple, mango, bell pepper, onion, and scallions.

In a small bowl combine the lime juice and zest, sesame oil, cilantro, chili powder, paprika, cumin, and salt and pepper to taste. Sprinkle the mixture over the diced ingredients, tossing until evenly coated.

Just before serving, cook the shrimp on high heat either on a grill, under a broiler, or in a 450° oven for 3 to 4 minutes. Place 3 or 4 shrimp on each plate with a spoonful of salsa. Garnish with lime and lemon slices and a sprig of cilantro.

MAKES 4 TO 6 SERVINGS.

Captain Dibbell House

Captain Dibbell House

21 Commerce Street
Clinton, Connecticut 06413
(860) 669-1646

*A*n 1866 Victorian built by Captain Edwin A. Dibbell, this small inn has only four rooms, and that is part of its charm. Another is that it has always been a private residence for hardy New Englanders—it did not have indoor plumbing or central heating until the 1960s. Yet another is its proximity to the Connecticut shore with its sunny summer days and world-class sailing. Hamonassett State Beach and the popular Mystic Seaport Museum are only minutes away.

Captain's Baked Eggs

  5   *eggs*
  ¼   *cup all-purpose flour*
  ½   *teaspoon baking powder*
  ¾   *cup cottage cheese*
  2   *cups shredded Monterey Jack cheese*
  ½   *cup sliced fresh mushrooms*
  ½   *cup broccoli florets*

In a medium bowl beat the eggs with a whisk. Add the flour and baking powder, and mix well. Stir in the remaining ingredients. Spray an 8-inch square baking dish with cooking spray. Pour the mixture into the pan. Bake in a 375° oven for 20 to 25 minutes, until set.

Variations: ½ pound bulk sausage, cooked and crumbled, may be added to the ingredients or serve sausage links on the side. Summer vegetable variations: In the place of broccoli use chopped zucchini or green peppers. Cheddar cheese is good with these vegetables. Sprinkle the baked eggs with chopped fresh tomatoes after removing from the oven.

MAKES 4 TO 6 SERVINGS.

Breakfast Apple Pie

  7   *cups apples, pared, cored, and thinly sliced*
  ½   *to ¾ cup firmly packed light brown sugar*
 1½   *teaspoons cornstarch*
  ¾   *teaspoon ground cinnamon*
  1   *teaspoon apple pie spice*

  ¾   *cup unbleached all-purpose flour*
  ¼   *cup packed firmly packed light brown sugar*
  ¼   *cup quick or old-fashioned uncooked oats*
  ¼   *cup butter, melted and cooled*

In a large bowl place the apples. Set aside. In a separate bowl mix ½ cup of brown sugar, cornstarch, cinnamon, and apple pie spice together, adjusting according to the tartness of the apples, and stir gently into the apples. Layer the apple mixture into a greased 2-quart casserole.

In a small bowl mix the flour, ¼ cup of brown sugar, and oats. Add the melted butter and mix gently with floured fingers to make moist crumbs. Sprinkle the mixture on top of the apples. Bake in a 375° oven until the top is golden brown and the apples are fork-tender.

MAKES 6 SERVINGS.

Maple Hill Farm

Maple Hill Farm

365 Goose Lane
Coventry, Connecticut 06238
(800) 742-0635

*T*hose who want a glimpse of early colonial New England should consider a stay at this B&B, a chestnut, oak, and stone farmhouse dating to 1731. Its four guest rooms are large, quiet, and furnished with antiques. Area attractions include the Nathan Hale Homestead, Strong House Museum, and Mark Twain House in nearby Hartford.

Minted Berries

  ¼   *cup fresh lemon juice*
  ¼   *cup chopped or snipped fresh mint*
  2   *tablespoons sugar or to taste*
  4   *cups berries (blue or blackberries are best!)*

In a large bowl combine the first 3 ingredients and gently toss in the berries. Chill overnight to allow the flavors to blend.

Wonderfully easy, and guests love it!

MAKES 6 TO 8 SERVINGS.

Applesauce Granola Bake

  2   *cups applesauce*
  ½   *teaspoon ground cinnamon*
  ⅛   *teaspoon grated nutmeg*
  2   *tablespoons firmly packed brown sugar*
  ⅓   *cups raisins*
  1   *cup granola*
  1   *tablespoon wheat germ*
     Vanilla yogurt

In a baking dish mix the applesauce, cinnamon, nutmeg, brown sugar, and raisins. Cover with granola and wheat germ. Bake in a 350° oven for 20 minutes. Top with vanilla yogurt.

MAKES 4 TO 5 SERVINGS.

Mock Apple Crisp

5   cups peeled, sliced zucchini
1   teaspoon ground cinnamon
¾   cup water
½   cup sugar
¼   cup lemon juice
....
6   tablespoons butter
½   cup firmly packed brown sugar
½   teaspoon salt
1   cup all-purpose flour
1   teaspoon baking powder

In a saucepan combine the zucchini, cinnamon, water, sugar, and lemon juice and cook for 30 to 45 minutes. Place in a 9 x 13-inch pan.

In a medium bowl mix the remaining ingredients and crumble on top. Bake in a 350° oven for 30 minutes.

This is what to do when the garden produces too many zucchini.

MAKES 8 SERVINGS.

Bishopsgate Inn

❧

*Goodspeed Landing, P.O. Box 290
East Haddam, Connecticut 06423
(860) 873-1677*

Horace Hayden, who built tall ships for a living, also built this exceptional Colonial home in 1818. Today it offers six guest rooms, four with open fireplaces, and a suite complete with sauna. Travelers who stay here may want to take in a show at Goodspeed Opera House or visit the nearby Gillette Castle and Devil's Hopyard. In summer, a popular scenic steam railway connects the nearby steamboat landing with the Connecticut coast.

Peach Coffee Cake

½   cup butter
1   cup sugar
2   eggs
1   cup all-purpose flour
    Pinch salt
1   29-ounce can sliced peaches, drained
1   teaspoon sugar
1   tablespoon lemon juice
    Ground cinnamon

In a medium bowl cream the butter and sugar. Add the eggs, flour, and a pinch of salt, and mix thoroughly. Pour into a greased and lightly floured 9-inch cake pan. Cover the entire surface with peach slices. Sprinkle the top with 1 teaspoon of sugar, the lemon juice and lightly sprinkle with cinnamon. Bake in a 350° oven for 1 hour.

MAKES 8 SERVINGS.

Lisa's Baked Breakfast

6   slices white bread
¼   cup softened butter
6   slices Gouda cheese
2   eggs
1   cup milk
    Salt and pepper to taste

Butter an 8-inch square glass baking dish. Remove the crusts from the bread and butter each slice on one side. Arrange the bread in the baking dish butter-side up. Overlap the slices if necessary. Cover the bread with the sliced Gouda cheese. In a medium bowl beat the eggs with the milk and season with salt and pepper to taste. Pour the mixture over the bread and cheese. Bake in a 350° oven for 30 to 40 minutes or until golden brown.

MAKES 4 SERVINGS.

Brunch Soufflé

16 slices of white bread
6   eggs
3   cups milk
½   teaspoon onion salt
½   teaspoon dry mustard
12 ounces sliced Swiss cheese
12 ounces sliced Cheddar cheese
16 ounces sliced ham (thinly sliced)
3   cups crushed Kellogg's corn flakes
½   cup melted butter

Grease a 9 x 13-inch baking dish. Remove the crusts from the sliced bread and cut each slice in half. In a mixing bowl beat the eggs, milk, onion salt, and dry mustard until smooth.

Layer the bottom of the dish with half of the bread. Cover the bread with half of the Swiss cheese and half of the Cheddar. Cover the cheese layer with half of the ham. Top with the remaining bread, cheeses, and ham, repeating the layering. Pour the egg-milk mixture over the layers of bread, cheese, and ham. Refrigerate overnight.

Remove from the refrigerator and sprinkle corn flakes over the casserole. Drizzle with melted butter. Bake in a 375° oven for 40 minutes.

MAKES 12 SERVINGS.

Bishopsgate Inn

Quiche

1   tablespoon butter
1   tablespoon oil
1   large onion, chopped
¾   cup sliced mushrooms
1   10-ounce box frozen chopped spinach, thawed
5   eggs
¾   pound Muenster cheese, finely grated
    Salt and pepper to taste

Butter a 9-inch pie plate. Heat the butter and oil in a skillet to medium-high heat. Add the onion and mushrooms and sauté until the onion is translucent.

Drain the thawed chopped spinach and squeeze until as dry as possible. Add the spinach to the onion and mushrooms and sauté until the excess moisture is boiled off. Remove the spinach, onion, and mushrooms from the heat and allow to cool.

In a mixing bowl beat the eggs. Fold the Muenster cheese into the eggs until thoroughly mixed. Stir the cheese-egg mixture into the spinach, onion, and mushrooms until thoroughly combined. Season with salt and pepper to taste. Pour the quiche mixture into the pie plate. Bake in a 350° oven for 40 to 45 minutes, until the top is lightly browned and a toothpick inserted into the center comes out clean.

MAKES 6 TO 8 SERVINGS.

Farmington Inn

827 Farmington Avenue
Farmington, Connecticut 06032
(860) 677-2821

Historic memorabilia, fresh flowers, antique furnishings, and original paintings by local artists provide the ambiance at this seventy-two-room inn at Farmington just to the southwest of Hartford. Guests can dine beside the scenic Farmington River. Among the many area attractions are the Wadsworth Atheneum, Hillstead Museum, and Mark Twain House.

Health Cinnamon Apple Pecan Pancakes

½ cup whole wheat flour
½ cup all-purpose flour
¼ cup old-fashioned oats
¼ cup chopped pecans
⅛ teaspoon nutmeg
⅛ teaspoon cinnamon
1 teaspoon baking soda
¼ cup cornmeal
1½ cup 2% milk
2 eggs, lightly beaten
1 cup buttermilk
¼ cup melted butter
1 tablespoon oil
¼ cup honey
1½ Granny Smith apples, cored and sliced into rings

In a large bowl combine all dry ingredients until blended well. Add the milk, eggs, buttermilk, butter, oil, and honey, and mix together. The batter should be thin to pour easily. Ladle butter onto a hot griddle. Spray the inner rim of pancake molds with cooking spray and set on the griddle. Place an apple ring in each mold. Slowly pour the batter over the apple to fill the molds. Cook the pancakes until they look dry on top. Then remove the molds and turn the pancakes with wide spatula. Cook until lightly golden. Serve hot with any favorite topping.

MAKES 20 PANCAKES

The Inn on Lake Waramaug

107 North Shore Road
New Preston, Connecticut 06777
(860) 868-0563

With its own private beach and boathouse, the inn takes full advantage of its setting on Lake Waramaug in the scenic Litchfield Hills of Connecticut. Guests may enjoy canoeing, sailing, or just warming themselves on the sandy beach. A year-round resort, the inn also offers a heated pool, sauna, game room, and tennis courts. Anchored by a white colonial mansion, it has been in operation since 1880. Its restaurant has an excellent wine cellar and has won awards for its food.

Halibut Concasse

12 ounces halibut, cut into portions for two
1 whole tomato, diced
1 red onion, small, diced
1 jalapeño pepper, diced

The Inn on Lake Waramaug

¼ bunch cilantro, chopped fine
1 tablespoon capers
½ cup extra virgin olive oil
Salt and pepper to taste
Cooked risotto

In a sauté pan toss the diced tomatoes in 2 tablespoons of the oil. Place the pan in the oven. Roast the tomatoes until they get dark in color, approximately 15 to 20 minutes.

While the tomatoes are roasting, mix the onion, diced pepper, cilantro, and capers with the remaining oil. When the tomatoes are cool then mix them together with the pepper mixture and season with salt and pepper to taste.

In a hot skillet sauté the halibut about 3 minutes on each side. While the halibut is cooking, heat the tomato mixture.

When the halibut is cooked, place on a plate and top with the tomato mixture.

Serve with risotto.

MAKES 2 SERVINGS.

Absolutely Peppar Penne

½ pound penne pasta
1 teaspoon garlic chopped
3 tablespoons extra virgin olive oil
1 medium roasted red pepper, julienned
2 tablespoons capers
1 14-ounce can artichoke hearts, grilled
4 ounces Absolut Peppar Vodka
½ bunch fresh basil, chopped
3 cups heavy cream
¼ cup Reggiano Parmesan cheese, grated

In a large pot bring several quarts of water to a boil. Cook the pasta al dente. Drain.

Meanwhile, in a deep skillet over medium heat brown the garlic in the olive oil. Add the pepper, artichokes, and capers, and sauté for

2 minutes. Add the vodka slowly and reduce for 3 minutes (be careful when adding vodka with a gas stove as it may flame).

Add the basil and cream, then bring to a boil. Reduce the heat and simmer for about 5 minutes.

Add the cooked penne pasta. Divide among pasta bowls, top with Parmesan, and serve.

MAKES 4 TO 6 SERVINGS.

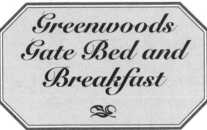

Greenwoods Gate Bed and Breakfast

❧

*105 Greenwoods Road East
Norfolk, Connecticut 06058
(860) 542-5439*

The Federal-era Greenwoods Gate is in Norfolk, home of the Yale Music and Arts Festival held each summer. Furnishings consist of fine antiques, period pieces, and collections that provide a relaxed, New England country atmosphere. Suites are spacious and quite luxurious. Freshly cut flowers, robes, and ironed linens add to guests' enjoyment.

Baked Eggs in Crêpe Cups with Assorted Filling

  1 **cup all-purpose flour**
     Pinch salt
  2 **eggs**
1¼ **cups milk**
  1 **tablespoon butter, melted**

12 **eggs**
¾ **cup heavy cream**

In a medium bowl sift the flour and salt. Make a well in the center and add 2 eggs and a little bit of milk. Beat well with a wooden spoon, working in all the flour. Gradually beat in the remaining milk until bubbles form on top of the batter. Stir in butter.

Add a small amount of oil to a 7-inch crêpe pan—enough to barely cover the base—and place over high heat. Pour in 2 to 3 tablespoons of batter and quickly tilt the pan so that the batter covers the base thinly and evenly. Cook for about 1 minute over high heat until lightly browned underneath. Turn the crêpe with a metal spatula and cook the other side for about 30 seconds. Continue until all of the batter is used.

Generously grease a standard-size muffin pan and line each cup with the crêpe. (They will have a fluted appearance). Fill each crêpe cup half full with the chosen filling combination (below). Break an egg into each filled crêpe cup and drizzle each with 1 tablespoon of heavy cream. Bake in a 400° oven for 15 to 20 minutes or until the desired doneness is reached. Carefully remove from the pan and serve immediately.

Suggested crêpe cup fillings and accompaniments: 1. Smoked salmon, minced onion, and cream cheese. Garnish the top of the egg cups with a dollop of sour cream and a sprig of fresh dill. Serve with fresh warm bagels and Baked Tomatoes (recipe follows). 2. Asparagus tips, thinly sliced grated Swiss cheese, and minced onions. Garnish with a dollop of sour cream and slivers of blanched asparagus tips. Serve with home-fried new potatoes and croissants. 3. Prepared salsa of desired strength, scallions, and grated Pepper Jack cheese. Garnish with sour cream, and chopped black olives, a small slice of tomato, and a sprig of fresh parsley. Serve with toasted cornbread wedges. A slice of ripe avocado squeezed with fresh lemon juice is a nice addition to this southwestern-style dish.

MAKES 8 TO 12 CRÊPES, OR 4 TO 6 SERVINGS.

Baked Tomatoes with Seasoned Corn Flake Topping

  1 **tablespoon butter**
¼ **teaspoon seasoned salt**
½ **teaspoon garlic powder**
½ **teaspoon dill**
¾ **cup corn flake crumbs**
  4 **medium tomatoes, cut in half**

In a small bowl combine all ingredients except the tomatoes. Spread the mixture over the cut side of the tomatoes and place in a shallow dish. Refrigerate overnight.

Bake in a 400° oven for 15 minutes.

MAKES 4 SERVINGS.

Individual Oven-puffed Pancakes

½ **cup unsalted butter**
  4 **eggs**
  1 **cup low-fat milk**
  1 **cup unbleached flour**
  1 **teaspoon almond extract (optional)**
  2 **teaspoons grated lemon zest (optional)**

½ **cup low-fat cottage cheese**
¼ **cup frozen orange juice concentrate, thawed and undiluted**
  2 **tablespoons confectioners' sugar**
  1 **pint strawberries, hulled and sliced**
    Confectioners' sugar for dusting

Place 2 tablespoons of butter into each of 4 4-inch ovenproof baking dishes or ramekins. Heat in the oven until the butter has melted. In a medium bowl beat the eggs with a wire whisk until light and bright yellow. Gradually beat in the milk, then the flour, until smooth. Stir in the almond extract and lemon zest. Divide the batter among the 4 ramekins of hot butter. Bake in a 475° oven for about 12 minutes until puffed and golden.

In a blender combine the cottage cheese, orange juice concentrate, and confectioners' sugar, and blend until smooth. Top each baked pancake with the orange crème filling, adorn with sliced strawberries, and a dusting of confectioners' sugar. Serve at once.

MAKES 4 SERVINGS

Apple Kuchen

- ¾ cup sugar
- ⅓ cup solid shortening
- 1 egg
- 1½ cups all-purpose flour
- 2 teaspoons baking powder
- ½ teaspoon salt
- ¼ teaspoon fresh grated nutmeg
- ½ cup half and half
- 4 to 5 medium cooking apples, peeled, cored and thinly sliced (Golden Delicious, Jonathan, or Rome Beauty)
- 1½ cups cranberries (or blueberries)
- 1 tablespoon sugar mixed with ½ teaspoon ground cinnamon
   Heavy cream

In a medium bowl cream together the sugar, shortening, and egg with an electric mixer or by hand until fluffy and lemon colored. In a separate bowl combine the flour, baking powder, salt, and nutmeg. Add the dry ingredients and the half and half alternately to the sugar-shortening mixture, stirring until just mixed. The batter will be stiff.

Spoon the batter into a lightly greased 9-inch pie or cake pan. Press the apple slices ¼ inch apart, core-side-down, into the batter in a circular pattern around the outside edge. Press the berries into the center of the batter. Sprinkle with the cinnamon-sugar. Bake in a 350° oven for 45 minutes, or until a cake tester inserted in the center comes out clean.

Slice, drizzle with a bit of heavy cream, and serve.

MAKES 8 SERVINGS.

Chocolate French Toast with Raspberry Sauce

- 4 petite croissants (found in freezer section, Sara Lee brand)
- 4 ounces semisweet chocolate or sweet German chocolate, grated
- ½ cup whipped cream cheese
- 2 large eggs
- ½ cup half and half
- 2 heaping tablespoons confectioners' sugar
- ¼ teaspoon vanilla extract
- ¼ teaspoon ground cinnamon
- 1 10-ounce package frozen raspberries, defrosted
- ¼ cup red currant jelly
- 1 tablespoon orange juice
- 3 to 4 tablespoons sweet butter
   Fresh raspberries and mint sprigs for garnish

On the inside edge of each croissant cut a pocket from end to end, being careful not to cut all the way through.

In a small bowl mix together the chocolate and whipped cream cheese to make a paste. Add extra chocolate if desired. Squeeze the croissants gently to open the pocket and fill with a generous amount of filling, about 1 heaping tablespoon.

Whisk together the eggs, half and half, confectioners' sugar, vanilla, and cinnamon. Pour into a large shallow dish. Place the filled croissants in the egg mixture and set aside to soak.

In a saucepan combine the raspberries, red currant jelly, and orange juice, and cook over moderate heat. Stir until the jelly is melted and the mixture is hot. Pour through a strainer, rubbing the pulp against the sieve to extract all the juice. Discard the seeds.

In a large skillet heat the butter and cook the croissants. Turn to cook evenly on each side and then very carefully stand on the end that is not open to complete the cooking.

Place on plates and serve with warm raspberry sauce. Garnish with fresh raspberries and a sprig of mint.

MAKES 4 SERVINGS.

Bacon Curls

- ½ pound thick-sliced bacon

Cut the bacon strips in half. Roll into circle and secure with toothpicks. Place on a broiler rack. Bake in a 450° oven for 10 to 15 minutes or until crisp and cooked. Remove the toothpicks and serve.

MAKES 4 SERVINGS.

Manor House

Manor House

69 Maple Avenue, P.O. Box 447
Norfolk, Connecticut 06058
(860) 542-5690

*T*he Manor House was built in 1898 by Charles Spofford, designer of the London subway system. Today it retains its original polished-panel, Victorian Tudor elegance. Each guest room has its own distinct, old-fashioned character; for instance, the Lincoln Room features a hefty sleigh bed, while in the Spofford Room guests sleep in a draped canopy bed. Norfolk is a great place for music lovers as it puts them within easy reach of the Tanglewood, Music Mountain, and Yale Music festivals.

Orange Waffles

- 1 cup all-purpose flour
- 1 tablespoon sugar
- ¼ teaspoon salt
- 1½ teaspoons baking powder
- ⅛ teaspoon grated nutmeg
- 2 eggs
- ½ cup milk
   Grated zest of 1 orange
- 2 tablespoons melted butter

In a medium bowl mix the dry ingredients. In a separate bowl mix the eggs, milk, and orange zest. Let the mixture sit separately at room temperature for 30 minutes. Add the dry ingredients to the liquid ingredients and beat until the batter is smooth. Add the melted butter to the batter and mix until fully combined. Follow manufacturer's instructions for waffle iron operation. Pour or spoon ½ to ¾ cup of batter onto the preheated waffle iron sections. Bake at a high heat until the waffles turn golden brown.

Caution: Do not overbake. The timing on many waffle irons will overcook the waffle when cooked at high heat. Experiment!

MAKES ABOUT 4 SERVINGS.

A to Z Bread

3 cups all-purpose flour
1 teaspoon salt
1 teaspoon baking soda
3 teaspoons ground cinnamon
½ teaspoon baking powder
3 eggs
1 cup oil
2 cups sugar
2 cups A to Z mix (see below)
3 teaspoons vanilla extract
1 cup chopped nuts

In a medium bowl sift the dry ingredients and set aside. In a large bowl beat the eggs. Add the oil and sugar and cream well. Add A to Z mix and vanilla to the mixture. Add the sifted dry ingredients and mix well. Stir in the chopped nuts. Spoon into 2 well-greased 5 x 9-inch loaf pans. Bake in a 325° oven for 1 hour.

A to Z mix: Use 1 or a combination to equal 2 cups except as indicated: grated apples, applesauce, chopped apricots, mashed bananas, grated carrots, pitted and chopped cherries, fresh grated coconut, pitted and chopped dates, ground eggplant, finely chopped figs, seedless grapes, honey (omit sugar), ½ cup lemon juice, marmalade (omit 1 cup sugar), mincemeat, chopped oranges, chopped fresh or canned peaches, chopped pears, drained crushed pineapple, 1 cup chopped pitted prunes, canned pumpkin, raisins, raspberries, chopped rhubarb, fresh or frozen (drained) strawberries, cooked tapioca, grated sweet potatoes, tomatoes (add an extra ½ cup sugar), cooked and mashed yams, plain or flavored yogurt, and grated zucchini.

MAKES 2 LOAVES.

Cinnamon Raisin Bread

1 tablespoon dry active yeast
1 cup oatmeal
3 cups bread flour
1 tablespoon sugar
1 teaspoon salt
1 tablespoon butter, softened
12½ ounces hot water
1 cup raisins
2 to 4 tablespoons ground cinnamon

In an automatic bread machine, add the yeast, oatmeal, flour, sugar, salt, butter, and water. Follow the manufacturer's instructions for adding ingredients and baking. When there are 3 minutes left in the second kneading process, add the raisins. When the kneading cycle completes, remove the dough from the machine. On a floured surface shape the bread by hand into a circle and cover with cinnamon to taste. Roll the dough to about ½-inch thickness and then fold it. Place the bread dough back in the machine so that the folded end is down and continue the baking process.

MAKES 1 LOAF.

Route 272
Norfolk, Connecticut 06058
(860) 542-6991

***T**his nineteenth-century Victorian country inn is in northwest Connecticut in the foothills of the Berkshire Mountains. Built in 1875, it fits in perfectly with the rest of Norfolk, a village with a sprawling green, soaring bell towers, and picture-postcard attractiveness. The seven guest rooms are furnished with antiques. The dining room and garden porch are available for receptions.*

Sweet Basil Chicken and Bowties

1 tablespoon butter or butter blend
1 pound sliced boneless skinless chicken breasts
½ cup sliced fresh mushrooms
½ cup heavy cream
3 tablespoons grated Parmesan cheese

Mountain View Inn

1 tablespoon hot sauce
¼ cup quartered cherry tomatoes
2 tablespoons roasted red peppers
1 pound precooked bowtie pasta or similar
Salt and pepper to taste
¼ cup thinly sliced scallions

In a heavy skillet melt the butter, and sauté the chicken slices until lightly browned. Add the mushrooms and sauté lightly. Add the heavy cream, Parmesan cheese, and hot sauce and cook for 5 to 8 minutes over medium heat until thickened and reduced. Add the tomatoes, roasted red peppers, and the precooked bowtie pasta. Reduce the heat and simmer for 5 minutes, until fully warmed. Season with salt and pepper. Add the scallions just prior to serving.

MAKES 4 TO 6 SERVINGS.

Roast Pork with Port Wine and Rosemary

1 tablespoon fresh minced garlic
1 tablespoon fresh rosemary
1 teaspoon fresh ground pepper
½ teaspoon seasoned salt
2 tablespoons Dijon mustard
1 6- to 7-pound boneless pork loin
½ cup port wine mixed with ½ cup water

In a mixing bowl blend the garlic, rosemary, pepper, salt, and mustard. Trim the pork and place it in a roasting pan. Spread the flavoring mixture thoroughly along the top side of pork. Refrigerate for at least of 1 hour.

Add the port wine-water mixture blend to the bottom of the pan. Cover the roasting pan with aluminum foil. Bake in a 400° oven for 45 minutes.

Remove the foil and roast in a 450° oven for 15 minutes. The internal temperature should be 160°. Slice and serve immediately.

MAKES 6 TO 8 SERVINGS.

85 Lyme Street
Old Lyme, Connecticut 06371
(800) 434-5352

*B*uilt during the 1850s, the inn remained a working farm for more than one-hundred years. Carefully restored, it now offers thirteen well-appointed rooms to those who want to enjoy its nineteenth-century rural grace. The original ornate iron fence, tree-shaded lawn, and bannistered front porch greet arriving guests. Today the very old village of Old Lyme, founded during the 1600s, is an artists' colony.

Old Lyme Inn Clam Chowder

- ½ cup butter
- 2 ounces smoked bacon, diced
- 1 cup diced onion
- 1 cup diced boiling potato
- 1 cup sliced carrot
- 1 cup sliced celery
- 1 cup all-purpose flour
- 1 quart clam broth
- 2 cups cream
- 2 bay leaves
- 1 tablespoon dried thyme
- 2 tablespoons chipotle peppers in adobo, puréed
- 1 quart chopped clams
- 1 cup kernel corn
  Salt and pepper to taste

In a stockpot melt the butter and sauté the diced bacon for 5 minutes. Add the onion, potato, carrot, and celery. Cover and cook for 15 minutes on low heat. Blend in the flour and cook uncovered for 5 to 10 minutes.

Reduce the heat to low. Add the clam broth and cream, mixing well. Bring to a slow boil, and add the bay, thyme, and chipotle. Reduce to the desired thickness. Add the

clams, corn, salt, and pepper. Discard the bay leaves.
MAKES 6 SERVINGS.

Roast Rack of Venison with Cranberry Walnut Sauce

- 1 9-rib rack of venison or loin, seasoned with salt, pepper, thyme, and rosemary
- 2 tablespoons clarified butter

··

- 1 tablespoon walnut oil
- 1 cup chopped walnuts
- ½ cup game stock or strong chicken stock
- ½ cup maple syrup
- 1 tablespoon Dijon mustard
- ¼ cup cranberry juice
- 1 cup fresh cranberries

In a pan large enough to fit the venison, brown the meat on high heat on all sides with the butter. When brown, roast in a 400° oven for 12 minutes per pound. It should be cooked medium rare.

In a skillet heat the walnut oil and sauté the walnuts until lightly browned. Add the remaining ingredients and bring to a boil. Reduce the heat to a simmer, and reduce the sauce by half.

Slice the venison and serve with the Cranberry Walnut Sauce.
MAKES 6 SERVINGS.

Crab Cakes

- 1 pound flaked Blue or Jonah crab body meat
- ¾ pound crab leg meat
- 1 egg
- ⅓ cups mayonnaise
- 2 tablespoons chopped parsley
- 1 tablespoon Worcestershire sauce
- ½ tablespoon Dijon mustard
- ½ teaspoon salt
- ½ teaspoon white pepper
- ½ cup breadcrumbs
- 2 tablespoons minced celery
- ¼ cup finely sliced scallion
  Oil
  Caper Tarter Sauce (recipe follows)

In a large bowl blend all ingredients. Chill for 2 hours.

Form into about 12 3-ounce patties and coat with additional breadcrumbs. Chill for 1 hour.

In a large skillet heat a small amount of oil and pan-fry the patties until golden on both sides. Serve with Caper Tarter Sauce.
MAKES 4 SERVINGS.

Caper Tarter Sauce

- 1½ cups mayonnaise
- ¼ cup capers
- ¼ cup relish
- 1½ teaspoons dry mustard
- 1½ teaspoons Worcestershire sauce
- 1½ teaspoons lemon juice
- ¼ teaspoon hot sauce

In a medium bowl blend all ingredients. Serve with crab cakes.
MAKES ABOUT 2 CUPS.

Veal Bradiole Old Lyme Inn

- ½ cup butter, softened
- 4 ounces Gorgonzola cheese, room temperature
- 2 tablespoons butter
- 1 ounce pine nuts
- 1 tablespoon minced garlic
- 10 ounces stemmed spinach, rinsed and dried
- ½ teaspoon salt
- ½ teaspoon black pepper
- ¾ cup red pepper purée
- ¾ cup yellow pepper purée
- ¼ cup butter
- 4 6-ounce veal top round cutlets, pounded ⅛-inch thick
- 2 ounces (8 paper thin slices) prosciutto di parma
- ¼ cup clarified butter

In a blender or food processor mix ½ cup of softened butter and the Gorgonzola cheese. Set aside.

In a 12-inch pan, melt 2 tablespoons of butter and sauté the pine nuts and minced garlic. Add the stemmed spinach and sauté for 2 minutes, until collapsed. Season with salt and pepper.

In separate saucepans reduce the red and yellow pepper purées by one-third. Add 2 tablespoons of butter to each when reduced. Set aside and keep warm.

Lay out the veal cutlets on a work surface. Cover each cutlet with 2 slices of prosciutto and spread one-fourth of the butter-Gorgonzola mixture on each cutlet. Place a fourth of the spinach mixture in the center of each cutlet. Roll the veal around the spinach stuffing and secure with a toothpick. In a hot pan heat the clarified butter and sauté the veal rolls on all sides. Remove to a sizzle platter and roast in a 425° oven for 8 to 10 minutes.

Place 1 ounce each of red and yellow pepper sauce side by side on a plate. Slice the veal rolls into 4 to 6 slices each, and arrange over the pepper sauces and serve.

MAKES 4 SERVINGS.

Under Mountain Inn

422 Undermountain Road
Salisbury, Connecticut 06068
(860) 435-0242

Built in the early 1700s, the Under Mountain Inn offers an array of intimate parlors and dining rooms, each with a fireplace. There is always a comfortable corner for playing checkers, reading a good book, savoring a quiet conversation, or relaxing under shade trees that predate George III. The seven charming rooms, all with private baths, are delightfully distinctive. Breakfast is of the full-English variety and is served in a dining room with colonial furnishings and a fireplace.

Sour Cream Coffee Cake

- ½ cup butter
- 1 cup firmly packed brown sugar
- 1 cup sour cream
- 1 teaspoon almond extract
- 2 eggs
- 2 cups all-purpose flour
- ¼ teaspoon salt
- 1 teaspoon baking powder
- 1¼ teaspoon baking soda
- 1½ teaspoon ground cinnamon
- 1 cup dried cranberries
- ½ cup firmly packed dark brown sugar

In a large bowl mix the butter and 1 cup of brown sugar. Add the sour cream and almond extract. Beat in the eggs 1 at a time. Add the remaining ingredients except ½ cup of brown sugar, and mix together. Pour the batter into a 9-inch greased tube pan and sprinkle ½ cup of brown sugar on top. Bake in a 350° oven for 40 minutes or until toothpick comes out clean.

MAKES 8 SERVINGS.

Tarragon Scramble

- 2 eggs
- ¼ cup heavy cream
- ½ teaspoon fresh tarragon (or ¼ teaspoon dried)
- Dash pepper
- 1 tablespoon butter

In a small bowl mix the eggs, cream, tarragon, and pepper. In a skillet melt the butter and cook the eggs until done to taste.

Serve with English muffins and Canadian bacon.

MAKES 1 SERVING.

Tolland Inn

63 Tolland Green
Tolland, Connecticut 06084
(860) 872-0800

Settled in 1715 on the old post road linking New York and Boston, Tolland has been a travelers' town for almost three centuries. It remains so today with its delightfully eclectic architecture, museums, Homestead Country Store, and

Tolland Inn. Fronting on the village green, the inn offers six rooms and a suite with kitchen.

Apple Tarts

- ½ cup sugar
- ½ cup butter, softened
- 2 large eggs
- Grated zest of 1 lemon
- 2 cups all-purpose flour
- Pinch salt

....

- 2 Granny Smith apples, peeled, cored, and chopped
- Juice of 1 lemon
- 2 tablespoons sugar
- ½ cup currants

In a mixer or food processor beat ½ cup of sugar, the butter, eggs, and lemon zest. In a large bowl combine this with the flour and salt. Refrigerate to firm the dough, 2 hours or more.

In a medium bowl combine the apples, lemon juice, 2 tablespoons of sugar, and currants.

Remove the dough from the refrigerator and let stand until warmed enough to work. Roll out three-fourths of the dough on a well-floured board to ½-inch thickness. Cut 3 ½-inch rounds and fit them into foil baking cups that have been flared open. Set these on a baking sheet or tart pan. Bake in a 350° oven until lightly browned.

Cool the tart shells. Roll the remaining dough to the same thickness and slice into ½ x 3-inch strips. Fill the tart shells with apple mixture and lay 2 or 3 strips over the filling in an X pattern. Bake tarts in a 350° oven for 15 minutes or until the dough strips are lightly browned.

MAKES 3 TARTS.

Tolland Inn

Steve's Secret Recipe Cookies

2 cups margarine
1 cup chunky peanut butter
1½ cups firmly packed brown sugar
1 cup sugar or honey
3 large eggs
5 cups rolled oats
3 cups all-purpose flour
2 teaspoons baking soda
1 teaspoon salt
2 teaspoons ground cinnamon
2 cups chocolate chips

In a medium bowl beat the margarine, peanut butter, brown sugar, and sugar until fluffy. Beat in the eggs. In a large bowl combine the remaining ingredients and mix well. Add the peanut butter mixture to the dry ingredients and mix well by hand. Spoon small balls of dough onto a cookie sheet. These don't spread a lot, so place them fairly close together. Bake in a 350° oven for 8 to 10 minutes, or until light brown.

This recipe makes a whole mess of cookies, which is necessary due to their addictive nature.

MAKES ABOUT 6 DOZEN COOKIES.

Orange Roll-Ups

Grated zest of 1 large orange
¾ cup sugar

·······························

2 cups sifted all-purpose flour
2 tablespoons sugar
3 teaspoons baking powder
½ teaspoon salt
⅓ cup unsalted butter, softened

·······························

1 large egg
¾ cup milk

In a small bowl combine the orange zest and ¾ cup of sugar. Set aside. In a large bowl combine the flour, 2 tablespoons of sugar, baking powder, and salt. Cut in the butter.

In a smaller bowl combine the egg and milk and beat well. With a large rubber spatula mix the liquid ingredients into the dry ingredients. Mix just until combined, adding more milk if needed to make a soft dough. Turn out onto a floured board. Flatten by hand into a 14 x 8-inch rectangle. Spread the orange zest mixture evenly over the dough. Roll tightly into a 14-inch roll. Cut the roll in 1-inch slices and lay them on a cookie sheet. Bake at 350° oven for 15 minutes or until lightly browned.

MAKES 14 COOKIES.

DELAWARE

Savannah Inn

330 Savannah Road
Lewes, Delaware 19958
(302) 645-5592

*T*he town of Lewes is known for its lighthouses and its rich history. It was here that a small militia force withstood a fierce, day-long bombardment from an entire British fleet and won one of the American victories in the War of 1812. The Savannah Inn puts visitors near the history, the lighthouses, and the ferry to Cape May.

Savannah Inn

Oatmeal Muffins

1 cup quick (not instant) oatmeal
1 cup buttermilk
1 egg
½ cup firmly packed brown sugar
⅓ cup butter
1 cup all-purpose flour
½ teaspoon salt
1 teaspoon baking powder
½ teaspoon baking soda

In a container with a cover soak the oatmeal in buttermilk overnight in the refrigerator.

In a food processor combine the oatmeal mixture, egg, firmly packed brown sugar, and butter. Pour into a large bowl.

Combine the flour, salt, baking powder, and baking soda, and sift the dry ingredients into the liquid mixture. Stir gently to combine. Spray 10 to 12 muffin cups with cooking spray. Pour the batter into the prepared muffin cups. Bake in a 400° oven for 15 to 20 minutes.

Cool slightly before removing. These muffins are very tender and fragile.

MAKES 10 TO 12 MUFFINS.

Many Bean Chili

1 pound packages of as many kinds of beans as can be found (i.e. lentils, split peas, black beans, red beans, etc.)
2½ cups mixed beans
5 cups water
1 large onion, chopped
2 cloves garlic, pressed
1 16-ounce can tomato sauce
1 30-ounce can chopped tomatoes
4 teaspoons Creole seasoning
1 teaspoon chili powder
1 teaspoon garlic powder
½ teaspoon ground sage

In a large pot soak the beans in lots of water for 8 to 12 hours. Drain and rinse.

In a large pot combine the water, onion, garlic, tomato sauce, chopped tomatoes, Creole seasoning, chili powder, garlic powder, sage. Bring the mixture to a boil. Skim off the foam. Reduce the heat to a simmer, cover, and simmer for 5 hours. Stir occasionally. Add water if necessary.

Note: The gourmet boxed many-bean chili mixes are great, but the high price is not. This recipe is a close approximation. This chili is spicy, but not terribly hot. Add more chili powder (or cayenne, etc.) if desired. This is also very low in fat and high in fiber, with 330 calories per serving.

MAKES 8 SERVINGS.

Cantwell House Bed and Breakfast

107 High Street
Odessa, Delaware 19730
(302) 378-4179

*N*amed for the Russian Black Sea resort city, Odessa was a principal commercial port on the Delaware River until the 1890s, when it was eclipsed by other, more industrial-

ized trading centers. The Cantwell House, a narrow, sea-green Victorian built about 1840, is the only bed and breakfast in town. The furnishings and decor of the rooms faithfully reflect early Victorian times. The film Dead Poets Society *was filmed at the nearby St. Andrews prep school.*

Fruit Cobbler with Oatmeal Biscuits

- *⅓ cup chopped dried apricots*
- *¼ cup raisins*
- *¾ cup apple cider, apricot or white grape juice*
- *2 Golden Delicious apples, peeled, cored, and thinly sliced*
- *2 ripe Bartlett or Bosc pears, peeled, cored, and thinly sliced*
- *2 teaspoons lemon juice*
- *¼ cup water*
- *½ cup coarsely chopped walnuts*

....

- *½ cup all-purpose flour*
- *½ cup old-fashioned rolled oats*
- *2 tablespoons sugar*
- *1 teaspoon baking powder*
- *½ teaspoon baking soda*
- *½ teaspoon salt*
- *¼ cup unsalted butter, chilled and cut into bits*
- *½ cup yogurt, buttermilk, or milk*

In a medium saucepan mix the apricots, raisins, and cider and let stand 30 minutes at room temperature.

Add the apples, pears, lemon juice, and water to the saucepan and bring to a boil over moderate heat. Cover, reduce the heat to moderate low, and simmer until the fruit is tender, about 10 or 20 minutes. If the mixture starts to boil dry, add more fruit juice or water.

Divide the mixture into 6 individual 8-ounce ramekins or custard cups.

In a medium bowl combine the flour, oats, sugar, baking powder, soda, and salt. With a pastry blender or 2 knives cut in the butter until the mixture resembles coarse meal. Add the yogurt (if using milk omit soda and increase baking powder to 1½ teaspoons). Stir just until blended.

Place the dough on a lightly floured surface. With floured hands, pat out to ½-inch thickness. Cut out six 2-inch circles.

Arrange the biscuits on top of each individual ramekin. Bake in a 450° oven for 20 minutes or until the biscuits are golden brown.

MAKES 6 SERVINGS.

Broiled Citrus Cocktail

- *2 pink grapefruit, halved and sectioned*
- *1 white grapefruit, halved and sectioned*
- *3 oranges, skinned and pith removed, sectioned*
- *1 lime, skinned and pith removed, sectioned*
- *1 tablespoon plus 1 teaspoon sweet sherry*
- *2 tablespoons plus 2 teaspoons firmly packed light brown sugar*
- *1 tablespoon plus 1 teaspoon butter Sprigs of lemon balm for garnish*

In a large bowl mix the grapefruit, orange, and lime sections. Reserve any juices. Arrange the fruit sections in 4 grapefruit shells. Sprinkle each with 1 teaspoon of sherry and 1 teaspoon of brown sugar. Top each with 1 teaspoon of butter.

Broil until the brown sugar melts. Top with reserved juices and garnish with lemon balm sprigs.

MAKES 4 SERVINGS.

Honeydew Melon with Pear Sauce

Purée a ripe pear.

Arrange a wedge of honeydew on a plate and top with puréed pear. Sprinkle with tiny slivers of fried apricot and grated lemon zest. Add sprigs of mint for garnish.

MAKES 1 SERVING.

Poached Pears with Pistachio Nuts, Stuffed with Mascarpone

- *1 cup water*
- *2 tablespoons sugar Juice 1 lemon*
- *4 pears, peeled, left whole with stems*
- *6 ounces mascarpone (cream cheese), softened*
- *1 cup of chopped pistachios*

In a microwave-safe dish mix the water, sugar, and lemon juice. Cut the pears evenly on the bottoms, allowing them to stand erect. Place in the dish. Cover with plastic wrap. Microwave for 8 minutes or until tender. Spoon the syrup over the pears so they will not discolor. Refrigerate until cold. Halve the pears, remove the cores of pear with a melon ball scoop, and stuff the cavities with cream cheese. Roll each pear in pistachios. Add a mint sprig at the stem for garnish.

MAKES 8 SERVINGS.

Tomato Peach Preserves

- *4 cups tomatoes, skinned and seeded*
- *3 cups sugar*
- *9 yellow peaches, peeled and sliced*
- *1 tablespoon vanilla extract*

In a large pan cook the tomatoes and sugar for 1 hour. Add the peaches and cook an additional 1 hour or until thick. Add the vanilla and pour into sterilized jars.

MAKES ABOUT 6 PINTS.

Corner Cupboard Inn

*50 Park Avenue
Rehoboth Beach, Delaware 19971
(302) 227-8553*

A tradition in some families for generations, the Corner Cupboard has welcomed Rehoboth Beach vacationers for over sixty years. The shops and boutiques of bustling downtown Rehoboth are only a block away. The Atlantic is close enough to allow guests to hear the constant roar of the surf. Visitors to this often balmy resort community are glad for the air conditioning available in all eighteen rooms. The inn is well-known for its delicious seafood.

Crab Dip

> 3 *8-ounce packages cream cheese*
> 1 *pound fresh crab meat (or 2 cans crab meat)*
> ½ *cup mayonnaise*
> 2 *tablespoons prepared mustard*
> 1 *tablespoon horseradish*
> 1 *teaspoon onion juice*
> *Salt and pepper to taste*
> ½ *cup sherry*

In the top of a double boiler over simmering water combine all ingredients except the sherry and heat until creamy. Add sherry to taste (half a cup is not too much, depending on whether it is to be served from a chafing dish or as a dip, when the mixture should be slightly thicker). Serve with crackers.

MAKES ABOUT 5½ CUPS.

Crab Cakes

> 5 *pounds crab meat (picked over)*
> 10 *eggs*
> 6 *teaspoons Worcestershire Sauce*
> 1¼ *cups mayonnaise*
> 5 *teaspoons Old Bay seasoning*
> 6 *teaspoons baking powder*
> *Pinch salt and pepper*
> 12 *pieces bread, crumbled*

In a large bowl mix together all ingredients except the crumbs. Shape into patties. Roll lightly in breadcrumbs and fry.

MAKES 12 SERVINGS.

Crab Imperial

> 1 *pound crab meat (picked over)*
> ¼ *cup finely chopped green bell pepper*
> ½ *cup chopped onion*
> 2 *slices white bread*
> 2 *eggs*

> *Mayonnaise*
> *Dash Worcestershire*
> ⅛ *teaspoon dry mustard*
> *Juice of ½ lemon*
> 1 *tablespoon mustard*
> *Pinch paprika*

In a medium bowl mix the crab meat, green pepper, and chopped onion. Remove and discard the crusts from the white bread. Crumble the bread into the crab mixture and then add the eggs, mayonnaise as needed, Worcestershire, dry mustard, lemon juice, and mustard. Mix gently.

Spoon into a baking dish and top with mayonnaise and a pinch of paprika. Bake in a 350° oven until lightly browned. Serve at once.

MAKES ABOUT 4 SERVINGS.

Scallops in Garlic and Tomatoes

> *Scallops*
> *All-purpose flour*
> ....
> *Equal amounts butter and olive oil*
> 1 *good scoop diced tomatoes, dusted lightly with garlic powder*
> *Parsley flakes*

Lightly dust scallops in all-purpose flour. In a skillet heat the olive oil and butter and sauté the scallops until they just start to brown, being careful not to turn too many times. Add the tomatoes and parsley, and continue cooking until the tomatoes and parsley are well mixed and the scallops are tender.

Delaware Soft Top Rolls

> ½ *cup shortening*
> 1 *cup hot mashed potatoes*
> 2 *teaspoons salt*
> ⅔ *cups sugar*
> 1 *package active dry yeast*
> 2 *cups milk*
> 2 *eggs plus 1 yolk*
> 6 *cups (about) all-purpose flour*

In a medium bowl mix the shortening with the potatoes, salt, and sugar.

In a small bowl dissolve the yeast in milk. Add the yeast to the potato mixture.

In a large bowl beat the eggs and yolk. Pour in the potato mixture and stir well with

a spoon. Add enough flour to make a soft dough. Turn onto a floured surface and knead. Rub the surface with melted fat. Leave in a warm place to double in bulk, about 3 hours.

Use hands to form rolls, pinching off pieces the size of pullet eggs. Place in large muffin pans. Let rise again until doubled.

Bake in a 450° oven for about 10 minutes.

MAKES 5 DOZEN.

Pecan Pie

> 1 *heaping cup nuts*
> 3 *eggs, beaten*
> 1 *cup light firmly packed brown sugar*
> 1 *cup light corn syrup*
> 1 *tablespoon butter*
> 1 *tablespoon vanilla extract*

Place the nuts in the crust. In a medium bowl mix together the remaining ingredients in the order given, and pour over the nuts. Bake in a 350° oven for 45 minutes or until the custard has cooked through.

MAKES 6 TO 8 SERVINGS.

The
Boulevard Bed and Breakfast
❧

1909 Baynard Boulevard
Wilmington, Delaware 19802
(302) 656-9700

---

*I*n *one of Wilmington's tree-lined historic residential districts, the Boulevard is a beautifully restored old city mansion. Built in 1913, it is listed on the National Register of Historic Places. Furnishings blend traditional antiques with family heirlooms. From the foyer, a magnificent staircase leads to a landing with fluted columns and leaded glass windows.*

The Boulevard

Charlie's Fluffy Three-Cheese Omelet

2   *eggs*
1   *teaspoon water*
3   *drops Tabasco sauce*
    Grated Vermont sharp Cheddar
      cheese
    Grated Havarti cheese
    Grated Muenster cheese

In a small bowl beat the eggs with the water and Tabasco sauce. Heat a lightly buttered 8-inch frying pan and add the egg mixture to the pan. When partially cooked, sprinkle with the three grated cheeses. Fold the omelet over when partially melted and finish cooking.

MAKES 1 OR 2 SERVINGS.

Chunky Apple Pancakes

1   *cup unbleached all-purpose flour*
1   *cup whole wheat flour*
3   *teaspoons baking powder*
½   *teaspoon salt*
1   *tablespoon firmly packed brown*
      sugar
2   *medium-sized apples*
2   *eggs*
1⅔ *cups milk*
3   *tablespoons oil*

In a large bowl mix the dry ingredients together. Peel, core, and cut apples into thin slices. Then cut the slices into ½-inch pieces. In a separate bowl beat the eggs and milk, and add with the oil to the dry mixture. Blend well. Fold in the apple pieces.

Bake on a preheated oiled griddle until browned on both sides. The apples will remain crisp. Serve hot, perhaps with maple syrup.

MAKES ABOUT 24 THREE-INCH PANCAKES.

The Best Blueberry Muffins

½   *cup butter or margarine, at room*
      temperature
1   *cup sugar (or slightly less depending*
      on sweetness of blueberries)
2   *large eggs*
1   *teaspoon vanilla extract*
2   *teaspoons baking powder*
¼   *teaspoon salt*
2½ *cups fresh blueberries or 1 12-ounce*
      bag frozen blueberries (no sugar
      added), not thawed
2   *cups all-purpose flour*
½   *cup milk*
....
1   *tablespoon sugar mixed with ¼ tea-*
      spoon grated nutmeg

Grease 18 regular-size muffin cups (12 for large muffins) or line with paper or foil baking cups. In a medium bowl beat the butter with a wooden spoon or electric mixer until creamy. Add the sugar and beat until pale and fluffy. Add the eggs one at a time, beating after each addition. Beat in the vanilla, baking powder, and salt. If using fresh blueberries, mash ½ cup and stir into the batter.

With a rubber spatula, fold half the flour, then half the milk into the batter. Repeat with remaining flour and milk. Fold in the remaining fresh blueberries or all of the frozen. Spoon the batter into the muffin cups. In a small bowl combine 1 tablespoon of sugar with the nutmeg. Sprinkle with topping. Bake in a 375° oven for 25 to 30 minutes, until golden brown and the top feels springy to the touch when pressed.

MAKES 18 REGULAR OR 12 LARGE MUFFINS.

Featherlight Yogurt Pancakes

2   *cups all-purpose flour*
2   *teaspoons baking powder*
1   *teaspoon baking soda*
1   *tablespoon sugar*
1   *teaspoon salt*
1   *cup plain yogurt*
1   *cup milk*
2   *eggs, slightly beaten*
¼   *cup melted butter or margarine*

In a large bowl sift together the flour, baking powder, soda, sugar and salt. In a separate bowl combine the yogurt, milk, and eggs. Stir in the butter. Pour the liquids into the dry ingredients, mixing just until dampened. Pour ¼ cup of batter on a hot greased griddle for each pancake. Cook until lightly golden on each side.

MAKES 16 PANCAKES, 4½-INCHES IN DIAMETER.

FLORIDA

The Fairbanks House

227 South Seventh Street
Amelia Island, Florida 32034
(904) 277-0500

*A*n air of refined elegance hangs
over the Fairbanks House, an 1885
mansion designed by famed architect Robert Schuyler. Intricately
carved moldings and ten stately
fireplaces attest to the home's formal Victorian origins, and each of
the eight guest rooms are furnished
with suitable antiques. A pair of
English country-style guest cottages
are also available. A "Gourmet Getaway" package is available
including champagne and

The Fairbanks House

chocolate-dipped strawberries waiting for guests in their room.

Peach Upside-Down French Toast

½ cup margarine
1¼ cups firmly packed brown sugar
1 tablespoon water
1 29-ounce can sliced peaches
1 loaf French bread, unsliced
6 eggs, beaten
1½ cups milk
1 tablespoon vanilla extract
Liquid from canned peaches
2 tablespoons cornstarch
⅓ cup orange juice (or 1 teaspoon lemon extract)

In a small saucepan melt the margarine. Stir
in the brown sugar and water and cook, stirring constantly, until the mixture has thickened. Pour into a well-greased 10 x 15-inch
or 9 x 13-inch baking dish.

Drain the peaches and reserve the liquid.
Place the peaches on top of the cooled sugar
mixture. Slice the French bread into 1-inch-
thick slices. Place the bread on top of the
peaches, filling in all the gaps.

In a medium bowl mix the eggs, milk, and
vanilla. Pour the mixture over the bread.
Cover and refrigerate overnight.

In the morning, uncover and bake in a
350° oven for 40 minutes. Cool for 5 minutes. Place a serving tray over the baking pan
and invert.

In a saucepan mix the reserved peach liquid with the cornstarch. Stir over low heat
until thickened. Stir in the orange juice or
lemon extract. Serve warm.

MAKES 8 TO 12 SERVINGS.

Cheese Omelet Oven-style

6 slices bacon
1½ cups shredded sharp Cheddar cheese
½ cup shredded Swiss cheese
2 to 3 tablespoons all-purpose flour
2 to 3 tablespoons diced pimento, drained
3 to 4 sprigs parsley, leaves only
8 eggs, beaten
1 cup milk

In a skillet fry the bacon until crisp. Drain.

Butter a 1½-quart casserole. In a medium
bowl toss cheeses and flour together. Place in
the casserole dish. Crumble the bacon and
sprinkle over the cheese mixture. Dot the
cheese with pieces of pimento and parsley
leaves.

In a separate bowl beat the eggs and milk
together. Pour over the ingredients in the
casserole. Bake in a 350° oven for 25 to 30
minutes, until puffed and starting to brown.

MAKES 6 SERVINGS.

Island Hotel

P.O. Box 460
Cedar Key, Florida 32625
(904) 543-5111

Built in 1859 of sea shell tabby with oak supports, the walls of the Island Hotel have withstood hurricanes for almost 150 years. There are no telephones or televisions in any of the ten rooms, just a lot of romantic ambiance provided, in part, by featherbeds, claw-foot tubs, and hand-cut wooden walls and floors. All rooms have access to the balcony.

Island Hotel
Original Palm Salad

    Lettuce
½ cup fresh palm cabbage
½ cup fresh fruit (e.g. bananas,
     berries, melon, kiwi, pineapple,
     etc.)
1 teaspoon chopped dates

1 pint vanilla ice cream
1 pint lime sherbet
¼ cup crunchy peanut butter
¼ cup mayonnaise

In a shallow salad dish arrange the lettuce. Cover the base with a layer of palm cabbage. Decorate with fruit to taste. Sprinkle with chopped dates.

In a large bowl blend the remaining ingredients until smooth. Freeze to ice cream consistency. Place 1 large scoop in the center of the salad base to serve.
MAKES 4 SERVINGS.

Fish Island Hotel-style

¼ cup butter
¼ cup white wine
1 6-to 8-ounce grouper fillet (or other
    firm white fish)
2 teaspoons Spike
2 tablespoons sesame seeds
    Lemon wedges for garnish
    Herbed pasta

In a baking dish place the butter and white wine. Coat both sides of the fish in the wine and butter mixture. Sprinkle Spike over the fish and top with sesame seeds. Bake in a 350° oven for about 15 minutes per inch thickness of fish. Serve with lemon wedges and herbed pasta.
MAKES 1 SERVING.

Fish in Paper

1 piece parchment paper
1 teaspoon olive oil
1 6- to 8-ounce fillet grouper, pom-
    pano, or other firm fish
½ teaspoons fennel seed
½ teaspoons dried thyme
½ teaspoons white pepper
¼ teaspoon Spike or salt/pepper mix
1 tablespoon chopped parsley
2 slices lemon
    Lemon wedges for garnish
    Herbed brown rice

Cut the parchment paper to size, and cover with olive oil. Place the fillet on the paper, coating both sides with oil. Sprinkle the herbs and spices evenly over the fish. Place the lemon slices on top. Fold the parchment over the fish and fold the edges to seal. Place on a baking sheet. Bake in a 350° oven for 10 minutes per inch thickness of fish. Serve with lemon wedges and herbed brown rice.
MAKES 1 SERVING.

1844 Cherry Street
Jacksonville, Florida 3220
(904) 384-1999

Antiques and collectables furnish the guest rooms of this small inn overlooking the St. John River. In a older home in the historic Riverside community, it is less than ten minutes from downtown Jacksonville. With its beaches, cosmopolitan atmosphere, military bases, and of course, the Gator Bowl, the burgeoning city of Jacksonville is enjoying growing popularity as a travel destination.

Healthy Yogurt
Muesli Muffins

1½ cups packaged biscuit mix
1 cup muesli
¼ cup firmly packed brown sugar
2 eggs, beaten
1 8-ounce carton strawberry-banana
    yogurt
3 tablespoons oil

Grease 12 muffin cups or line with paper baking cups.

In a large bowl combine the biscuit mix, muesli, and brown sugar. Make a well in the center. In a small bowl stir together the eggs, yogurt, and oil. Add the egg mixture all at once to the muesli mixture. Stir just until moistened. The batter should be lumpy. Fill the prepared muffin cups two-thirds full. Bake in a 400° oven for 16 to 18 minutes or until golden. Remove from the pans and serve warm.
MAKES 1 DOZEN.

600 Fleming Street
Key West, Florida 33040
(305) 292-1919

A twenty-seven room luxury inn in Key West's Historic District, the Marquesa is listed on the National Register of Historic Places. The property includes the original Key West landmark Marquesa Hotel and two nearby houses dating to the 1880s. All have been lavishly refurbished, furnished, and decorated in a dignified early twentieth century style. The lush central garden with its three-tiered brick waterfall and pool are a key attraction here. The attractions of Key West itself are legendary, and waiting for Marquesa guests to enjoy.

Pan-seared Snapper Fingerlings with Mushroom and Leek Ragout

> ¼   **cup butter**
> 4   **ounces mushrooms (oysters and shiitake), stemmed and sliced**
> 4   **ounces leeks, cleaned and sliced ⅛-inch thick**
> ¼   **cup fish stock**
> 6   **tablespoons heavy cream**
>   **Thyme to taste, snipped**
>   **Salt and white pepper to taste**
> 12   **ounces snapper fillets, cut in 1-ounce portions**
>   **All-purpose flour**
> ½   **cup oil**
> 2   **ounces tomato concassée**
>   **Frizzled leeks (1 leek each, cleaned, julienned and deep-fried) for garnish**

In a medium sauté pan melt the butter over medium high heat and sauté the mushrooms and leeks for 10 minutes, tossing frequently. Deglaze the pan with fish stock and simmer for 3 to 4 minutes. Add the heavy cream and simmer for 5 minutes or until slightly thickened. Season with thyme, salt, and pepper.

Season the snapper with salt and white pepper. Dredge the snapper in flour and shake off the excess. In a large sauté pan heat the oil over high heat until smoking begins. Sauté the snapper until golden. Turn the fish, lower the heat and cook until the fish is just done and flakes easily, 1 to 2 minutes.

Mound the ragout in the center of a plate, allowing the cream to cover a small portion of the plate. Lay the fish upon the ragout, sprinkle tomato concassée around, and top with frizzled leeks.

MAKES 2 SERVINGS.

Potato-Wild Rice Fritter

> 1½   **cups butter**
> 1   **tablespoon minced garlic**
> 5   **pounds new potatoes, cooked until tender**
> ½   **pound wild rice, cooked**
> 2   **teaspoons salt**
> 1   **red bell pepper, diced**
> 1   **yellow bell pepper, diced**
> 1   **green bell pepper, diced**
> 1   **cup basil, chopped**
>   **Salt and white pepper to taste**
>   **Nutmeg to taste**

In a saucepan melt the butter and sauté the garlic.

In a large bowl whip the cooked potatoes (can leave skins on) with a paddle. Add the remaining ingredients while the potatoes are warm, mixing well. Shape the potato mixture into a log shape. Bread with flour. Deep fry in 350° oil.

MAKES 6 SERVINGS.

Chalet Suzanne

Chalet Suzanne

3800 Chalet Suzanne Drive
Lake Wales, Florida 33853
(941) 676-1814

Owned and operated by a single (Hinshaw) family for more than sixty years, the Chalet Suzanne offers the sort of unforced elegance made possible by decades of innkeeping experience. Situated on a quiet, seventy-acre estate, the Chalet has its own airstrip and offers such comforts as private entrances, private baths, air conditioning, telephone, and televisions. The thirty rooms and amenities are distinctive and appeal to refined tastes.

Chalet Suzanne's Veal Chops

> ¾   **cup or more butter**
> 2   **medium onions, sliced**
> 2   **cups sliced fresh mushrooms**
> ½   **teaspoon celery salt**
> ½   **cup dry vermouth**
>   **Salt and pepper to taste**
> 4   **6- to 8-ounce veal chops**
>   **Flour for dusting**
> 2   **cups chicken broth (homemade or commercial)**
> 1   **cup or more sour cream**
> 8   **ounces pasta, cooked and seasoned**
> 2   **or more bananas, sliced**
>   **Brown sugar to taste**

In an ovenproof skillet melt 2 to 3 tablespoons of the butter and sauté the onions until tender. Set the onions aside. Add 3 to 4 tablespoons of butter to the skillet and sauté the mushrooms until barely tender. Sprinkle them with celery salt and set aside with the onions. Deglaze the skillet with a little vermouth, then pour the remaining vermouth over the onions and mushrooms.

Season the veal with salt and pepper, and lightly dust with flour. In the same skillet melt

4 tablespoons of butter and brown the veal on both sides.

Add the chicken broth to the veal, and cover. Bake in a 300° oven for about 40 minutes.

Add the mushrooms, onions, and sour cream, and bake until heated through. Serve over seasoned pasta.

In a separate skillet melt 2 or more tablespoons of butter and quickly sauté the banana slices, sprinkling with brown sugar, until brown. Arrange on plates with the veal and pasta.

MAKES 4 SERVINGS.

Gâteau Christina

> 4 egg whites
> 1½ cups sugar
> ⅓ cup blanched ground almonds
> ....
> 2 egg whites
> ½ cup sugar
> 2 tablespoons sweetened cocoa
> 1 cup butter, softened
> 4 ounces semisweet chocolate, melted

Cut aluminum foil into 4 8-inch circles and grease each lightly. In a large bowl whip 4 egg whites until stiff, gradually adding 1½ cups of sugar and the almonds as the eggs begin to stiffen. Place the foil rounds on a large baking sheet and spread each evenly with meringue. Bake in a 250° oven for 15 minutes or until the meringue is dry. Carefully turn the meringues over and bake 5 minutes longer.

For filling, in the top of a double boiler over hot (not boiling) water beat 2 egg whites until foamy. Gradually add ½ cup of sugar, the cocoa, butter, and chocolate, beating until thick and creamy. Remove the pan from the heat and cool.

Place the best meringue layer on the bottom and spread with chocolate. Top with another meringue, pressing down lightly to make the layers fit together. Spread with chocolate. Repeat until all of the meringues are used and the top is liberally coated with chocolate. Cover and refrigerate for at least 24 hours.

Note: These may be stored in tin boxes for gifts.

MAKES 1 4-LAYER GÂTEAU.

Royal Spinach

> 1 cup water
> 2 pounds fresh spinach, washed well (or 2 10-ounce boxes frozen chopped)
> 6 tablespoons butter
> 2 teaspoons Worcestershire sauce
> 2 teaspoons lime or lemon juice
> 1 cup sour cream
>   Salt and fresh ground pepper to taste
> 1 pound fresh mushrooms, slice
> 1 tablespoon dry sherry or chicken broth

In a saucepan bring the water to a boil. Add the spinach, cover and cook over low heat until tender. Remove and drain well, then finely chop.

Put the chopped spinach in the saucepan with 3 tablespoons of the butter. Add the Worcestershire sauce, lime or lemon juice, sour cream, salt, and pepper to taste. Stir well.

In a separate saucepan melt the remaining 3 tablespoons of butter and lightly sauté the sliced mushrooms. Add the mushrooms to the spinach mixture. Then add the dry sherry or chicken broth. Mix together then serve warm.

To serve with pasta, simply add ½ cup more sour or heavy cream to the spinach mixture, then season with the salt and pepper to taste.

MAKES 6 SERVINGS.

Chicken Paprika

> 4 boneless, skinless chicken breasts, cut into strips
>   Salt to taste
> 10 tablespoons butter
> ½ cup chopped red onion
> 1 tablespoon paprika
> 1 teaspoon tarragon vinegar
> ¼ cup chicken broth
> ¼ cup dry sherry (or ¼ cup additional chicken broth)
> ½ cup sour cream
> ½ cup toasted, sliced almonds
>   Wild rice and broccoli

Sprinkle the chicken strips with salt and set aside. In a heavy skillet melt butter and sauté the onions until tender, but not brown. Remove the onions. Add the chicken, shaking the pan to prevent burning. As soon as the chicken is lightly sautéed, though not brown, add the paprika, tarragon vinegar, chicken broth, and dry sherry (or additional chicken broth). Cover and gently simmer 5 to 10 minutes. Stir in the sour cream.

Before serving, sprinkle the chicken with almonds. Serve with wild rice and broccoli.

MAKES 4 SERVINGS.

The Herlong Mansion

P.O. Box 667
Micanopy, Florida 32667
(352) 466-3322

---

*T*he architecturally extraordinary Herlong Mansion was built in a mid-Victorian design in 1845. In 1910, the original structure was encased in a Classic Revival brick shell and fitted with the fluted columns typical of the Southern Colonial style. Visitors who stay in one of the mansion's dozen antique-filled guest rooms can enjoy its delightfully split personality. In-room fireplaces and elegant breakfasts add to the pleasure of a stay at this Old South B&B.

The Herlong Mansion

Herlong Decadent Bread

1 loaf French bread, unsliced
2 eggs
¾ cup sugar
3 cups 2% milk
1 cup half and half cream
½ cup melted butter
1 tablespoon vanilla extract
  Grated nutmeg
  Ground cinnamon
  Walnuts for syrup for topping

Slice the French bread 1½-inch thick and place in individual ramekins. In a large bowl combine the eggs, sugar, milk, half and half, butter, vanilla, nutmeg, and cinnamon, and pour over the bread. Allow 5 minutes to soak. Then turn the bread over and refill to three-fourths level. Bake in a 350° oven for 45 minutes. Garnish with fresh fruit. Serve with walnuts, syrup, and sausage on the side.
MAKES 6 SERVINGS.

Herlong Refrigerated Bran Muffins

1 20-ounce box Raisin Bran cereal
3 cups sugar
5 cups all-purpose flour
5 teaspoons baking soda
2 teaspoons salt
1 cup walnut pieces
4 cups buttermilk
1 20-ounce can crushed pineapple
4 eggs
1 cup oil

Pour the Raisin Bran into a large bowl. Add the sugar and stir. Sift the flour, soda, and salt into the cereal and sugar. Add the walnuts and stir.

In a separate large bowl combine the buttermilk, pineapple, eggs, and oil. Stir until completely mixed. Then pour the liquid mixture into the dry ingredients and completely stir. Transfer the batter to a container with a top. The mixture can be refrigerated for up to 6 weeks.

Pour into greased mini muffin cups. Bake in a 350° oven for 17 minutes.
MAKES ABOUT 7 DOZEN MINI MUFFINS.

Five Oaks Inn
❧

1102 Riverside Drive
Palmetto, Florida 34221
(941) 723-1236

The original owners of the fine, early twentieth century home known today as the Five Oaks Inn literally bought the house right out the Sears and Roebuck Catalog. The company shipped the home to Palmetto where it was constructed on the site of an old log schoolhouse. Its unusual past does nothing to diminish the inn's elegance, however, and certainly adds to the fun of staying here. Rooms are well appointed and comfortable. The airy, air-conditioned solarium is a wonderful place to relax with a book or newspaper.

Cajun Toast

4 well-ripened bananas, mashed
2 cups milk
2 eggs
1 tablespoon firmly packed brown
  sugar
½ teaspoons vanilla extract
¼ teaspoon ground cinnamon
¼ cup dark rum (optional)
2 pats butter
8 thick slices Italian bread
  Confectioners' sugar

In a blender or with an electric mixer mix the bananas, milk, eggs, brown sugar, vanilla, cinnamon, and rum. In a frying pan or griddle melt some of the butter. Dip the bread in liquid mixture and cook until browned. Flip the bread. When done, place on a serving plate and sprinkle with confectioners' sugar. Repeat with the remaining butter and bread.
MAKES 4 SERVINGS.

Ten-Minute Chocolate Seven Layer Cake

1 frozen pound cake (i.e. Sara Lee)
1 can ready-made chocolate frosting
  (i.e. Betty Crocker)

On a cutting board, slice the frozen pound cake lengthwise into 7 ¼-inch-thick layers. Stack each piece upside down on top of each other. With a knife or spatula frost the bottom slice of cake. Add another piece, frost that, and so on, until the top piece is in place. Cover the whole cake with frosting. Refrigerate.

To serve, slice the cake in very thin pieces.
MAKES 10 SERVINGS.

German Cheese Pie

1¼ cups all-purpose flour
¾ teaspoon baking powder
¼ teaspoon salt
¼ cup sugar
½ cup butter
1 beaten egg
....
2 8-ounce packages cream cheese
1½ teaspoons all-purpose flour
1 cup sugar
2 beaten eggs
1½ cups milk
1 teaspoon vanilla extract
  Cinnamon

In a medium bowl sift 1¼ cups of flour, the baking powder, and salt together. Add ¼ cup of sugar. With fingers mix in the butter. Add the egg and mix well. Add a little flour if the mixture is too sticky. Pat the crust into the sides and bottom of a 9-inch pie plate and flute the edges.

In a medium bowl or blender mix the cream cheese, 1½ teaspoons of flour, and 1 cup of sugar together. Beat in the eggs. Slowly add the milk and vanilla. Mix well. The mixture will be very liquid. Pour the filling into the crust. Sprinkle with cinnamon. Bake in a 350° oven for 45 minutes.
MAKES 6 TO 8 SERVINGS.

Casa De Solana

Casa De Solana

❧

21 Aviles Street
St. Augustine, Florida 32084-4441
(904) 824-3555

---

*N*ow a small bed and breakfast inn
with four guest suites, this brick-
tiled home dates to 1763 and the
Spanish Colonial era. Painstakingly
renovated and beautifully landscaped, it is perfectly suited to
Florida's old Spanish capital. Suites
are full-sized and offer views of
either the garden or Matanzas Bay.

Easy One-Dish Ham Bake

- 1 16-ounce package frozen broccoli
  cuts, rinsed and drained
- 1 10¾-ounce can cream of mushroom
  soup
- 1 10¾-ounce can Cheddar cheese soup
- 1 cup milk
- 3 cups cut-up cooked ham, chicken,
  turkey, or beef
- ½ teaspoon onion powder
- 2 cups original or reduced-fat baking
  mix
- 1½ cups milk
  Chopped parsley (optional)

In an ungreased 9 x 13-inch baking dish mix
the broccoli, soups, 1 cup of milk, the ham,
and onion powder. In a medium bowl mix the
baking mix and 1½ cups of milk. Pour evenly
over the soup mixture. Sprinkle with parsley

if desired. Bake in a 450° oven for 27 to 30
minutes or until light golden brown. Let stand
at least 5 minutes.
MAKES 8 SERVINGS.

Lemon Tea Bread

- 1 8-ounce package cream cheese, softened
- ½ cup butter or margarine, softened
- 1¼ cups sugar
- 2 eggs
- 2¼ cups all-purpose flour
- 1 tablespoon baking powder
- ½ teaspoons salt
- ¾ cup milk
- 1 tablespoon grated lemon zest,
  divided
- ⅔ cup finely chopped blanched
  almonds, toasted
- ⅔ cup sifted confectioners' sugar
- 2 tablespoons lemon juice

In a large bowl beat the cream cheese and
butter with an electric mixer at high speed
until light and fluffy. Gradually add the sugar,
beating well. Add the eggs 1 at a time, beating
well after each addition.

In a separate bowl combine the flour, baking powder, and salt. Add the dry ingredients
to the creamed mixture alternately with the
milk, beginning and ending with the flour
mixture. Mix after each addition. Stir in 2
teaspoons of lemon zest and the almonds.
Pour the batter into 2 greased and floured
8½ x 4½-inch loaf pans. Bake in a 350° oven
for 45 to 50 minutes, or until a wooden pick
inserted in the center comes out clean.

In a small bowl combine the confectioners' sugar and lemon juice, stirring until
smooth. Stir in the remaining 1 teaspoon of
lemon zest. Spoon the glaze over the warm
loaves. Cool in the pans for 10 minutes.
Remove the loaves from the pans, and cool
completely on a wire rack.

Variation: Instead of blanched almonds,
use poppy seeds. Instead of lemon glaze,
sprinkle poppy seeds on top of each loaf
before baking.
MAKES 2 LOAVES.

Lost Bread

- 2 slices French bread (1½ to 2 inches
  thick)
  Strawberry preserves
- 2 large eggs
- 2 tablespoons half and half
  Splash vanilla extract
  Confectioners' sugar

Cut the crust off the bottom sides of the bread
and then cut a pocket in the bottom. Fill the
pocket with a heaping tablespoon of strawberry preserves and press the pocket closed.
In a large bowl beat the eggs, half and half,
and vanilla. Soak the bread in egg mixture for
a minute or so. In a deep skillet (we use a
Chinese wok) heat oil to completely cover the
slice of bread so that when you lay the filled
slice of bread in it, the bread will brown
quickly. As soon as it is brown on 1 side, turn
over and brown on the other. Drain on a
paper towel and sprinkle with confectioners'
sugar.

Note: If preparing for a large number,
keep warm in the oven and sprinkle with
sugar just before serving.
MAKES 1 SERVING.

Castle Garden Bed and Breakfast

❧

15 Shenandoah Street
St. Augustine, Florida 32084
(904) 829-3839

A recently renovated Moorish
Revival inn dating to the 1860s, the
Castle Garden is tucked away on a
quiet historic street near the old
fort. After more than 135 years, its
original coquina stone exterior
remains in near perfect condition.
All six rooms are furnished with
period antiques. Bridal suites at

Castle Garden

this old, romantic inn come with sunken bedrooms, Jacuzzis, and cathedral ceilings.

Spirulina Muffins

    1   level teaspoon Spirulina
    2   cups Quaker Oat-Bran cereal
    2   teaspoons baking powder
    1   cup skim milk
    2   eggs, or whites for healthier muffins
    ½   cup honey or molasses
    2   tablespoons oil
    ½   teaspoons salt (optional)

Line 12 muffin cups with paper liners or spray the bottoms only with cooking spray. In a large bowl combine the Spirulina, cereal, baking powder, and salt. In a separate bowl combine the milk, eggs or egg whites, honey, and oil. Add the liquid mixture to the dry ingredients, mixing until moistened. Fill the prepared muffin cups almost full. Bake in a 425° oven for 15 to 17 minutes or until golden brown.

Store the muffins in the freezer. To reheat, microwave at high about 30 seconds.

Variations: Fold in ½ cup of fresh or frozen blueberries, or 1 medium mashed ripe banana, or ½ cup raisins.

MAKES 1 DOZEN.

Castle Garden Soufflé

    6   slices white bread
    6   eggs
    2   cups milk
    1   cup cooked meat (crumbled bacon, or cut-up sausage links, or diced ham)
    1   cup grated Cheddar cheese

Remove the crusts from the bread and cut the bread into cubes. In a medium bowl beat the eggs and add the milk. Stir, then add the cubes of bread. Let soak. Beat with an electric mixer then refrigerate overnight.

The next morning, pour half of the mixture into the top of a double boiler over simmering water. Add all of the meat and ¾ cups of grated Cheddar cheese. Pour in the rest of the egg mixture and sprinkle the rest of the grated cheese on top. Transfer to a 1-quart casserole dish. Bake in a 325° oven 1 hour, or until golden brown.

Variations: Add cooked broccoli or cauliflower or any kind of cooked vegetable.

MAKES 4 TO 6 SERVINGS.

Potato Pancakes

    6   medium potatoes, grated
    ½   medium onion, grated
    3   tablespoons all-purpose flour
    2   tablespoons milk
    1   egg
        Garlic salt
        Salt and pepper to taste
        Oil for frying

In a medium bowl combine the potatoes, onion, flour, milk, egg, and garlic salt. Season with salt and pepper to taste. Mix well. In a skillet heat a small amount of oil for frying. Shape the potato mixture into patties and fry in the hot oil until browned lightly on each side.

MAKES 4 TO 6 SERVINGS.

Cow Patties

    2   cups sugar
    3   tablespoons cocoa
    ½   cup butter or margarine
    ½   cup milk
    ....
    1   teaspoon vanilla extract
    ½   cup peanut butter
    3   cups instant oatmeal

In a saucepan bring the sugar, cocoa, butter, and milk to a boil. Boil for 1 minute. Remove the pan from the heat and add the remaining ingredients. Stir and drop by spoonfuls onto waxed paper. Cool. Refrigerate before serving.

MAKES ABOUT 2 TO 3 DOZEN.

Bayboro House

*1719 Beach Drive Southeast
St. Petersburg, Florida 33701
(813) 823-4955*

An early twentieth century Victorian, Bayboro House was built by Charles Harvey, a St. Petersburg civic leader and owner of the town's first Cadillac. Beautiful wallpapers and antiques accent the guest rooms. A quiet veranda with swing, rockers, chaise and wicker chairs invites relaxation with the complimentary morning newspaper. Wine is served in the parlor each evening.

Best Banana Bread

    1¾ cups all-purpose flour
    1½ cups sugar
    1   teaspoon baking soda
    2   eggs
    1   cup mashed very ripe bananas
    ½   cup oil
    ¼   cup buttermilk (or milk and 1 teaspoon vinegar)
    1   teaspoon vanilla extract
        Lots of nuts

In a large bowl combine all of the ingredients. Pour into a greased and floured 5 x 9-inch loaf pan. Bake in a 325° oven for 1 hour or until a toothpick inserted in the center comes out clean.

Note: This recipe may be doubled, as 1 loaf is never enough.

MAKES 1 LOAF.

Bayboro House

Tampa Bay Roll Ups

1 10-ounce can crescent rolls
   Sausage, cooked (optional)

Cut each piece of crescent rolls in half. Place a small piece of sausage on the dough piece and roll up. Place on a cookie sheet. Bake in a 375° oven for about 10 minutes or until golden brown.

Variation: Use puff pastry, and cut it into small triangles. Place a bit of ham and a small amount of cheese in each piece, and roll up. Bake in a 375° oven until golden brown. There aren't usually any leftovers.

MAKES 4 TO 6 SERVINGS.

Wakulla Springs Lodge

Wakulla Springs Lodge
❧

1 Spring Drive
Wakulla Springs, Florida 32305
(904) 224-5950

*P*once de Leon believed he had found the fountain of youth when he came upon Wakulla Spring, so clear that pebbles could be seen 185 feet below the surface. The spring is now protected in a state park, and if visitors like, they can sample the

waters to test the Spaniard's hypothesis. If the result is disappointing, the nearby white-washed, mission-style Wakulla Springs Lodge will at least make one feel younger. A menagerie of wrought iron ibis, heron, egret, and other creatures, the lodge is an Old South wonder with marble floors and banisters, high ceilings, and twenty-seven light, airy rooms.

Navy Bean Soup

1 pound dried Great Northern Beans
4 cups water
2 14 ½-ounce cans chicken broth
2 14 ½-ounce cans beef broth
2 tablespoons butter
2 onions, chopped
1¾ pounds Russet potatoes, peeled, and diced
3 cups chopped carrots
3 bay leaves
2 cups diced ham (about 12 ounces)
   Salt and pepper to taste

Place the beans in a large bowl. Add enough water to cover by 3 inches. Soak the beans overnight. Drain.

In a large pot combine the beans, 4 cups of water, and broths. Cover and simmer for about 1 hour and 15 minutes, until the beans are almost tender.

In a large heavy skillet melt the butter. Add the onions and sauté until tender, about 10 minutes. Add the onions, potatoes, carrots, bay leaves, and ham to the beans. Cover and simmer until the vegetables are tender, about 30 minutes. Season with salt and pepper to taste. Discard the bay leaves. Serve hot.

MAKES 6 TO 8 SERVINGS.

Wakulla Shrimp Supreme

1 pound medium shrimp (21 to 25 count), shelled and deveined
8 strips bacon, each cut into 3 pieces (1 slice bacon for 3 shrimp)
   Paprika
   Softened butter

Hush puppies
Whole Broiled Tomatoes

Wrap each shrimp in bacon and fasten with a toothpick. Sprinkle lightly with paprika and dot with a little butter. Broil in a shallow pan with small a amount of water to prevent sticking. Turn once when the bacon begins to crisp. When cooked on both sides, about 5 minutes, remove the toothpicks and serve with hushpuppies and Whole Broiled Tomatoes (recipe follows).

MAKES 3 SERVINGS.

Whole Broiled Tomatoes

3 tomatoes
   Breadcrumbs
   Salt and pepper to taste
   Parmesan cheese
   Butter

Remove the stem from the tomatoes and cut out the pulp about a third of the way in. Fill with breadcrumbs and seasoning to taste. Sprinkle with Parmesan cheese and dot with butter. Place in a pan with a little water to prevent sticking. Bake in a 350° oven for 15 to 20 minutes.

MAKES 3 SERVINGS.

Blueberry Sour Cream Pie

1 cup sugar
½ teaspoons salt
¼ cup all-purpose flour
2 eggs
2 cups sour cream
¾ teaspoon vanilla extract
1 9-inch graham cracker pie shell, unbaked
1 21-ounce can blueberry pie filling
1 cup whipped cream

In a mixing bowl combine the sugar, salt, flour, eggs, sour cream, and vanilla and mix well. Pour the filling into the pie shell. Bake in a 350° oven for 30 minutes or until the center is set. Top the hot pie with blueberry filling. Chill several hours. When ready to serve, top with whipped cream.

MAKES 6 TO 8 SERVINGS.

Stuffed Cornish Hens Supreme with Wild Rice

4   1½ -pound Cornish hens
1¼   cups chopped scallions
1   cup chopped mushrooms
2   tablespoons butter
2   cups soft breadcrumbs
1   hard-boiled egg, chopped
¼   cup sour cream
¼   teaspoon garlic salt
⅛   teaspoon pepper
¾   cup milk
½   cup water
1   ⅞-ounce envelope chicken gravy mix
2   dashes grated nutmeg
1   4-ounce package wild rice, cooked

Rinse the hens and pat them dry. In a skillet cook 1 cup of the scallions and ½ cup of the mushrooms in butter until tender and the liquid evaporates. Remove the pan from the heat and add the breadcrumbs, egg, sour cream, garlic salt, and pepper. Lightly stuff the hens with this mixture. Truss the hens and place breast-side up, in a large shallow baking pan.

Cover with foil and roast in a 350° oven for 1 hour. Uncover and baste with drippings. Return the hens to the oven and roast 30 to 40 minutes or until tender and browned.

In a small saucepan sauté the remaining onions and mushrooms in the reserved drippings. Stir in the milk, water, gravy mix, and nutmeg. Bring to a boil, stirring constantly. Simmer for 1 minute. Serve the hens on a bed of wild rice with sauce.

MAKES 4 SERVINGS.

GEORGIA

Bellaire House

1234 Bellaire Drive
Atlanta, Georgia 30319
(404) 262-1173

In the upscale Buckhead section, the Bellaire replaces the flashing lights and hurried waiters of city hotels with a sound night's sleep in a comfortable bed, followed by a hardy breakfast. The Bellaire is located near Atlanta's famous Lenox Square shopping center and is convenient to the MARTA commuter rail line.

Bellaire House "Sock It To Me" Coffee Cake

    1   18-ounce box yellow cake mix
    1   cup sour cream
    4   eggs
    ½   cup sugar
    ⅔   cup oil
    1   teaspoon vanilla extract
    1   cup pecan pieces
    ....
    ¼   cup firmly packed brown sugar
    2   tablespoons ground cinnamon
    ....

    ½   cup milk
    ¼   cup confectioners' sugar
    1   tablespoon vanilla extract

Grease and flour a bundt pan. In a large bowl mix the cake mix, sour cream, eggs, sugar, oil, 1 teaspoon of vanilla, and pecans. In a separate bowl, mix the brown sugar and cinnamon, and set aside. In a small bowl, mix the milk, confectioners' sugar, and the 1 tablespoon of vanilla, and set aside.

Pour half of the cake batter into the bundt pan and sprinkle the brown sugar-cinnamon mixture over the batter, avoiding the edges of bundt pan. Add the remaining batter. Bake in a 350° oven for 40 to 45 minutes.

After cooling, turn the cake onto a cake plate and top with the glaze.

MAKES 8 SERVINGS.

Shellmont Bed and Breakfast Lodge

821 Piedmont Avenue Northeast
Atlanta, Georgia 30308
(404) 872-9290

A classic Victorian home in mid-town Atlanta, the Shellmont is graced with Tiffany windows, magnificent woodwork, and authentic period furnishings. There is more than 100 years of tradition to appreciate here, and complimentary beverages, chocolates, and a delicious breakfast add to the enjoyment of each spacious suite. The Shellmont places travelers near the center of Atlanta, one of the most exciting cities not just in the South or the nation, but the world.

Peach Chutney

    5   cups peaches, nearly ripe
    3   cups apples, peeled, and cored
    1   lemon, chopped
    1   cup golden raisins, ground
    2   cups vinegar
    ¾   cup candied ginger
    1   tablespoon salt
    ¼   teaspoon cayenne pepper
    2½   cups firmly packed brown sugar
    ½   cup walnuts, chopped

Shellmont

Peel the peaches and remove the pits. In a large saucepan mix all ingredients except the nuts and simmer for 1 hour and 30 minutes. During the last 20 minutes add the chopped walnuts. Spoon into sterilized jars and seal.

MAKES 3 QUARTS.

Graham Cracker Cake

1½   cups butter
2   cups sugar
5   eggs
1   tablespoon baking powder
1   cup milk
1   16-ounce box graham crackers, crushed
1   cup coconut
1   cup pecans, chopped

....

1   16-ounce box confectioners' sugar
½   cup butter
1   20-ounce can crushed pineapple, well-drained
1   cup coconut

In a bowl cream the butter and sugar. Add the eggs, 1 at a time. In a separate bowl mix the baking powder and crackers. Add the cracker mixture to the creamed mixture alternately with the milk. Stir in the coconut and pecans. Pour into 2 well-greased and floured 8-inch round cake pans. Bake in a 350° oven for 30 minutes.

In a saucepan melt the butter. Add the confectioners' sugar and stir until dissolved. Remove the pan from the heat and add the pineapple and coconut. Frost the cooled cake.

MAKES 8 SERVINGS.

Shellmont's Chicken with Mashed Potatoes

6   chicken breasts with skin left on
    Salt and pepper to taste
6   tablespoons Italian dressing
    Mashed Potatoes (recipe follows)
6   slices bacon

Place the washed and dried chicken breast, skin-side down in a 9 x 13-inch pan. Season with salt and pepper. Drizzle 1 tablespoon of Italian dressing on each chicken breast. Place a heaping portion of mashed potatoes on each chicken breast. Place 1 folded slice of bacon over the potatoes on each chicken

breast. Bake in a 350° oven for 1 hour. Occasionally baste with pan juices. The potatoes should be golden brown when done.

MAKES 6 SERVINGS.

Mashed Potatoes

6   to 8 boiling potatoes, boiled until tender
½   cup butter
    Salt and pepper to taste

In a bowl mash the potatoes with the butter. Season with salt and pepper to taste. Do not add milk or cream.

MAKES 6 SERVINGS.

Brunswick Manor

Brunswick Manor

❧

825 Egmont Street
Brunswick, Georgia 31520
(912) 265-6889

The antique furnishings, stained glass windows, high ceilings, beveled glass mirrors, bric-a-brac mantles, and carved oak staircase are all pure Victorian, as is the Manor itself, which was built in 1886. Guest rooms and amenities match the architecture. Situated in Old Town Brunswick just across from Halifax Square, the Manor places its guests only a few miles from the white beaches of Jekyll and St. Simon's islands.

Peanut Butter Surprises

1   pound white chocolate, cut into chunks
18   ounces chunky peanut butter
2   cups mini marshmallows
1   12-ounce package butterscotch bits
12   ounces dry-roasted peanuts
2   cups Rice Krispies

In a large baking dish assemble the white chocolate, peanut butter, marshmallows, and butterscotch bits. Bake in a 300° oven until the ingredients are soft. Remove from the oven and mix in the peanuts and Rice Krispies. Drop the mixture by spoonfuls onto waxed paper on cookie sheets. Refrigerate until set. Store in a plastic container in the refrigerator until ready to serve.

MAKES 2 TO 3 DOZEN.

Carrot Bars

4   eggs
2   cups sugar
2   cups sifted all-purpose flour
2   teaspoons baking soda
2   teaspoons ground cinnamon
1   teaspoon salt
1½   cups oil
3   cups grated carrots
1½   cups chopped walnuts
1½   cups shredded coconut

....

4   ounces cream cheese
3   tablespoons milk
2½   cups confectioners' sugar

In a large bowl beat the eggs. Beat in the sugar. In a separate bowl sift the flour with the soda, cinnamon, and salt. Alternately add the oil and dry ingredients to the liquid mixture. Mix well. In a separate bowl mix the carrots, nuts, and coconut. Add the carrot mixture to the batter and mix well. Grease 2 9 x 13-inch pans. Spread half of the mixture in each pan. Bake in a 350° oven for 25 to 30 minutes. Cool on a rack.

In a small bowl mix the softened cream cheese with 1 tablespoon of milk or cream. Add the confectioners' sugar and 3 tablespoons of milk and beat until smooth. Spread the frosting onto the bars when cooled. May be baked, cooled, and frozen. Add the frosting just before serving or omit the frosting and dust with confectioners' sugar.

MAKES 8 TO 10 SERVINGS.

Glen-Ella Springs Inn

Glen-Ella Springs Inn

❧

*Bear Gap Road
Route 3, Box 3304
Clarkesville, Georgia 30523
(706) 754-7295*

This 100-year-old inn listed on The National Register of Historic Places has been restored to a degree of luxury and comfort not found at the turn of the century when guests came for the summer to enjoy the cool mountain breezes. The inn's sixteen guest rooms and suites have been individually furnished with locally crafted antiques. The grounds stretch across seventeen acres of mountain woodland bounded by a sparkling creek and provide plenty of room for guests to stretch their legs. Dahlonega, Tallulah Falls, and the half-timbered Swiss village of Helen are all less than an hour's drive away. Incongruously, metropolitan Atlanta itself is less than two hours away.

Fresh Strawberry Sherbet

2½ quarts fresh strawberries
3½ cups sugar
5 tablespoons fresh lemon juice
2 cups plain nonfat yogurt

Wash, stem, and slice the strawberries. In a bowl mix the strawberries with sugar and lemon juice and set aside for 1 hour or more.

In a food processor combine the yogurt and the strawberry mixture, and process until smooth. Freeze in a 1-gallon ice cream churn according to the manufacturers' directions.

Note: This is such an easy and flavorful dessert, and with no fat. The amount of sugar can be reduced by ½ to 1 cup if the strawberries are very ripe and sweet.

MAKES 16 SERVINGS.

Mountain Top Lodge at Dahlonega

❧

*Route 7, Box 150
Dahlonega, Georgia 30533
(706) 864-5257*

At the end of the drive that curves across rolling pastures and then climbs to the top of the wooded mountain stands a rustic cedar lodge flanked with spacious porches and large decks. The scenery here is spectacular at all times of the year, and the lodge, with its expansive vistas, is the perfect place to enjoy it. This rustic cedar lodge with thirteen, antique-filled guest rooms, makes guests feel they are part of the mountain environment.

Rose's Torte

1 8-ounce package cotto salami
1 8-ounce package cream cheese, softened
  Garlic powder
  Onion powder
  Fresh black pepper
  Salt
  Dry mustard
  Worcestershire sauce

Tabasco sauce
1 2.12-ounce bottle poppy seeds

Separate the salami slices and place on paper towels to absorb the excess fat. In a medium bowl combine the cream cheese, garlic powder, onion powder, pepper, salt, dry mustard, Worcestershire sauce, and Tabasco sauce to taste, approximately 2 to 3 "shakes" of dry ingredients and 2 to 3 drops of liquid. Blend well.

Place 1 slice of salami on waxed paper and with a knife spread the cream cheese mixture (like icing a cake), then another slice of salami, cream cheese, etc. When all the salami has been layered, spread the entire torte with cream cheese. Sprinkle poppy seeds evenly over the cream cheese mixture. Wrap and refrigerate for several hours or overnight.

Before serving, cut the torte in half and then in half again (not like a pie). Cut each "quarter" into cracker-sized slices, place on crackers, and serve.

MAKES 6 TO 8 SERVINGS.

Kathy's Mushroom Rolls

¼ cup butter
½ pound white mushrooms, finely chopped
1 bunch scallions, with green tops, chopped
3 tablespoons all-purpose flour
¾ teaspoon salt
1 cup sour cream
1 teaspoon lemon juice
1 ½-pound loaf cracked wheat bread
½ cup butter, melted
  Dried dill

In a skillet melt the butter and sauté the mushrooms and scallions. Blend in the flour and salt. Cook for 2 minutes. Add the sour cream, and cook until thick. Add the lemon juice. Cool.

Remove the crusts from the bread. Place the slices on damp towels. Spread with mushroom filling and roll up. Brush with melted butter and sprinkle with dillweed. Slice in half. Bake in a 400° oven for 7 to 10 minutes, until golden brown.

This is a great "do ahead" appetizer. They freeze well.

MAKES 46 PIECES.

Green Eggs and Grits

½ cup quick-cooking grits
1   tablespoon butter or margarine
12 large eggs
    Dash Tabasco sauce
    Salt and pepper to taste
4   ounces frozen spinach, defrosted but
    not cooked
1   3-ounce package cream cheese, cut
    into ½-inch cubes

Prepare the grits according into the package directions. Grease an 8-inch pan. Pour the grits into the prepared pan and cool to room temperature. Cover the pan tightly and refrigerate overnight.

About 30 minutes before serving, remove the grits from the pan and cut into 1-inch cubes. In a large skillet melt 1 tablespoon of butter or margarine over medium heat. Add the grits "cubes" and sauté, stirring gently until golden brown. While the grits are browning prepare the egg mixture.

In a medium bowl combine the eggs, Tabasco, salt, and pepper, and beat lightly. Drain the spinach and remove as much moisture as possible. Add the spinach to the egg mixture. Pour the spinach mixture over the grits. Add the cream cheese. As the eggs begin to set, lift the edge of the eggs to allow the uncooked egg mixture to flow to the bottom. Cook until the eggs are just set.

Note: At Mountain Top Lodge this dish is served with ham and the title is borrowed from Dr. Seuss.

MAKES 6 SERVINGS.

The Stovall House

The Stovall House

1526 Highway 255 North
Sautee, Georgia 30571
(706) 878-3355

*T*he innkeepers describe their Stovall House as "a place of quiet and simple pleasures," and that it is. An unpretentious country inn with a sweeping view of the Sautee Valley and the North Georgia mountains, it's a perfect hideaway from the rush and roar of Atlanta or the jingle-jangle of the nearby tourist village of Helen. The Stovall has won several awards for its food and service.

Pork and Chinese Vegetable Phyllo

1   pound pork roast, diced
1   to 2 tablespoons oil
2   tablespoons soy sauce
2   tablespoons sherry
½   teaspoon granulated garlic
½   cup chopped carrots (diagonal cut)
1½   cups chopped celery (diagonal cut)
½   small head white cabbage, finely
     sliced
1   medium onion, finely sliced
16   sheets phyllo pastry
     Melted butter for brushing
½   teaspoon butter
1   tablespoon cornstarch
1   cup water
¼   cup apple cider vinegar
½   cup firmly packed brown sugar
½   teaspoon ground ginger

In a skillet heat the oil and sauté the meat until lightly brown. Add the soy sauce, sherry, and garlic, mixing well. Add the vegetables and cook, covered, about 5 minutes.

Brush the top of each sheet of phyllo pastry with melted butter. Layer 2 sheets of pastry for each roll. Put ½ cup of filling in the center of each sheet about 1 inch from the bot-

tom edge. Fold over the left side, the right side, then roll up.

Place the phyllo rolls on a greased pan loose-end down, and brush the top with melted butter. Bake in a 350° oven for 10 to 15 minutes, until lightly brown on top.

In a saucepan combine the remaining ingredients and simmer for 15 minutes.

Serve with the sauce in a side dish.

MAKES 8 SERVINGS.

Vegetable Casserole

1   to 2 tablespoons butter
1   pound thinly sliced zucchini, yellow
     squash, or broccoli
½   cup chopped onion

3   eggs
1   16-ounce carton ricotta cheese
2   cups grated sharp Cheddar cheese
3   tablespoons all-purpose flour
     Dash grated nutmeg
     Grated Parmesan cheese

In a skillet melt the butter and lightly sauté the vegetable and onion.

In a large bowl mix the remaining ingredients except the Parmesan. Add to the vegetable mixture and place in a 1½-quart baking dish. Sprinkle with Parmesan. Bake in a 375° oven for 35 to 40 minutes.

MAKES 6 SERVINGS.

Culpepper House

35 Broad Street
Senoia, Georgia 30276
(770) 599-8182

*W*hen Dr. John Addy returned from the Civil war, he re-established his life and practice in Senoia and built this house in 1871. Later it was substantially renovated by another Senoia physician, Dr. Wilbur Culpepper, who lived here for more than five decades. The home has *been fully restored to showcase unique architecture that suggests the Steamboat Gothic style. The heart pine floors, twelve-foot ceilings, stained glass windows, and period antiques give the home a turn-of-the-century feeling. Guests can enjoy this fine house as well as the old-time Georgia town of Senoia and still be only an hour's drive from Atlanta.*

Culpepper House

Asparagus Bisque

¼ cup butter
¼ cup all-purpose flour
2 13¾-ounce cans chicken broth
2 14½-ounce cans asparagus cuts
2 celery stalks
¼ cup milk
    Paprika

In a large pan combine the butter and flour to make a roux. Add the chicken broth and cook over medium heat. In a blender liquify both cans of the asparagus (including liquid) and the celery stalks. Add the asparagus mixture to the broth and bring to a boil. Add the milk, and heat through. Garnish with paprika.

MAKES 2 QUARTS.

Breakfast Fruit Salad

1 to 2 small Granny Smith apples, cubed
2 bananas, sliced
2 tablespoons lemon juice
¼ cup frozen or fresh blueberries
¼ cup sliced strawberries
3 tablespoons brown sugar
3 tablespoons Triple Sec
½ cup lowfat strawberry/banana yogurt
½ cup orange juice

In a large bowl combine the apples, bananas, and lemon juice. Add the remaining ingredients. Cover and chill. Serve in wine glasses with a dollop of whip cream and sprinkle with cinnamon.

MAKES 4 TO 6 SERVINGS.

HAWAII

Merryman's Bed and Breakfast

P.O. Box 474
Kealakekua, Hawaii 96750
(800) 545-4390
(808) 323-2276

This is Hawaii, after all, so complimentary snorkel gear and beach supplies are provided to all guests at this small Kona Coast B&B. Set on a breezy hillside in coffee growing country about twelve miles south of the bustling little village of Kailua-Kona, Merryman's offers four spacious rooms and an abundance of Hawaiian style hospitality. Cushioned wicker furnishings, a huge deck, and a steaming Jacuzzi set a distinctly relaxed mood. The ocean view is a breath-taking bonus.

Tea Time Hawaiian Chocolate Banana Cake

- 2 cups sugar
- 1 cup shortening or butter
- 2 eggs
- 2 large bananas, mashed (about 1 cup)
- 2 squares unsweetened chocolate, melted
- 1 teaspoon vanilla extract
- 2½ cups all-purpose flour
- 2 teaspoons baking soda
- ½ teaspoon salt
- 1 teaspoon baking powder
- ½ cup buttermilk
- 1 cup boiling water

....

- 1 cup firmly packed dark brown sugar
- ½ cup butter
- 6 tablespoons evaporated milk
- 2 cups confectioners' sugar
- ½ teaspoon vanilla extract

In a large bowl cream together the sugar and shortening. Add the eggs 1 at a time. Add the bananas, chocolate, and vanilla. Mix in the dry ingredients alternately with the buttermilk. Add 1 cup of hot water and mix well. Pour into a greased 10-inch tube pan. Bake in a 350° oven for 45 minutes. Cool.

In a saucepan cook the brown sugar and butter for 3 minutes. Then add the remaining ingredients and heat until smooth. It will thicken as it cools. Frost the cake.

MAKES 8 SERVINGS.

Sour Cream Pancakes

- ½ cup all-purpose flour
- 1 teaspoon salt
- 1 tablespoon sugar
- ¼ teaspoon baking soda
- 4 eggs
- 1 cup sour cream
  Fresh fruit and maple syrup for topping

In a medium bowl combine the flour, salt, sugar, and soda. In a separate bowl whisk the eggs and sour cream. Add the sour cream mixture to the dry ingredients. Bake on a greased griddle. Serve topped with fresh fruit and maple syrup.

These pancakes are very light.

MAKES ABOUT 2 SERVINGS.

My Favorite Overnight Pancakes

- 1 package active dry yeast
- ¼ cup warm water (105 to 115°)
- 4 cups all-purpose flour
- 2 tablespoons baking powder
- 2 teaspoons baking soda
- 1 teaspoon salt
- 2 teaspoons sugar
- 6 eggs
- 4 cups buttermilk
- ¼ cup oil

In a cup combine the yeast and water. Let stand for 5 minutes. In a bowl combine the dry ingredients. In a separate bowl combine the eggs, buttermilk, and oil. Add the liquid mixture to the dry ingredients. Stir in the yeast mixture. Cover and refrigerate overnight or up to 1 week. Remove from the refrigerator and stir well. Cook on a greased griddle.

MAKES 6 TO 8 SERVINGS.

Kalani Oceanside Eco-Resort

RR2, Box 4500
Kehena Beach, Hawaii 96778
(908) 965-7828
(800) 800-6886

*T*he Kalani resort sits inside Hawaii's largest conservation area, a tropical Eden with beaches frequented by dolphins and forests filled with colorful birds. But far from rustic, this wilderness resort provides comfortable accommodations, deliciously healthful cuisine, a sauna, Jacuzzi, and Olympic-size swimming pool. Nearby are thermal springs, steam vents, rainbow-colored tidal pools, and Volcanoes National Park.

Cheese Enchiladas with Cauliflower

2 *cups finely chopped cauliflower*
1 *7-ounce can mild green chilies, chopped*
2 *cups soy cheese (tofu)*
½ *cup minced yellow onion*
1 *tablespoon Spike*

1½ *teaspoons ground cumin*
½ *cup creamed tofu*
1 *10-ounce can enchilada sauce*
12 *corn tortillas*
½ *cup sliced black olives*
   Chopped cilantro for garnish

In a bowl combine the cauliflower, chilies, soy cheese, onion, Spike, cumin, and tofu.

Pour one-third of the enchilada sauce a 10 x 13-inch pan to cover the bottom. Pour the remainder of the sauce in a pie plate and dip 12 tortillas, 1 at a time, into the sauce. Fill the tortillas with filling, roll up, and place seam-side down in a baking dish. Sprinkle with olives. Drizzle the remaining enchilada sauce over the tortillas. Cover with foil. Bake in a 350° oven for 30 minutes.

MAKES 6 SERVINGS.

Penne Pasta with Nuts and Mild Chilies

1 *tablespoon olive oil*
½ *cup whole or chopped macadamia nuts (or cashews)*
5 *cloves garlic, finely minced*
1 *cup sliced mild green chilies*
1 *tomato, chopped*
½ *cup chopped sun dried tomatoes, rehydrated*
½ *cup diced canned tomatoes*
8 *cups penne pasta, cooked, coated with a little olive oil*
2 *tablespoons chopped fresh oregano (or 1 tablespoon dried)*
   Grated Parmesan cheese for garnish

In a sauté pan heat the oil on medium-high heat and cook the nuts until browned. Remove the nuts from the pan. In a sauté pan combine the garlic, chilies, and all tomatoes, and sauté for 3 minutes. Immediately toss with the pasta, nuts, and oregano. Sprinkle with Parmesan cheese and serve hot.

MAKES 4 SERVINGS.

Victoria Place

P.O. Box 930
Lawai, Kauai, Hawaii 96765-0930
(808) 332-9300

*P*erched high in the lush hills of southern Kauai Island, this B&B overlooks sprawling cane fields and jungle, as well as the deep blue Pacific. But there is more to enjoy here than just the view. Three of the guest rooms open onto a pool walled in by bougainvillaea, hibiscus, and ginger. A private path leads to a secluded studio suite with its own kitchen. Breakfast features hot, homemade breads and muffins, and lots of tropical fruits and Hawaiian coffee.

Pineapple Bread Pudding

1 *quart milk*
4 *cups Hawaiian sweet bread cubes (or egg bread)*
6 *eggs*
1½ *cups sugar*
2 *tablespoons vanilla extract*
1 *cup golden raisins*
1 *cup crushed pineapple, drained*

In a large bowl pour the milk over the bread cubes. Let the mixture stand 1 hour.

Butter a 9 x 13-inch pan. In a large bowl beat the eggs, sugar, and vanilla together. Pour over the bread mixture. Stir in the raisins and pineapple. Pour into the greased pan. Bake in a 325° oven for about 1 hour or until a knife inserted in the center of the pudding comes out clean.

Delicious served with French vanilla or Amaretto cream.

MAKES 8 SERVINGS.

IDAHO

Cricket on the Hearth

1521 Lakeside Avenue
Coeur d'Alene, Idaho 83814
(208) 664-6926

The symbolic cricket, for which this bed and breakfast is named, is the first clue that hospitality underscores an enjoyable stay. The guest rooms, furnished with warmth, reflect the theatrical background of the hosts: Cats, Carousel, Kabuki, and Molly Brown recall a variety of moments on the stage. Live theater, music, and dance are also available year-round in cities within an hour's drive from the inn. Guests may choose to shop at the nearby

Cricket on the Hearth

Silver Lake Mall or factory outlets. More athletic pursuits include water sports, hiking, biking, snow skiiing, and golfing at the world's only floating green. Lake Coeur d'Alene is only seven blocks away.

Quick No-fail Hollandaise Sauce for Eggs Benedict

- ¾ cup light mayonnaise
- 1 egg yolk
- 1 tablespoon butter or margarine
- 1 tablespoon lemon juice
- 2 or 3 tablespoons milk
  Dash hot pepper sauce

In a small saucepan mix the mayonnaise, egg yolk, butter, and lemon juice. Add milk to the desired consistency. Add hot pepper sauce. Cook over low heat until mixture is hot and slightly thickened, stirring occasionally. Do not boil. Serve with Eggs Benedict or over hot vegetables.

MAKES 1 CUP.

Impossible Quiche

- 12 slices bacon (about ½ pound), crisply fried and crumbled
- ½ cup shredded Swiss cheese
- ½ cup shredded mozzarella cheese
- ½ cup finely chopped onion
- 1 to 2 cups milk
- ½ cup baking mix
- 4 eggs

Salt and pepper to taste
Grated nutmeg

Lightly grease an 8- or 9-inch square baking dish. Sprinkle the bacon, cheeses, and onion evenly over the bottom of dish. In a blender combine remaining ingredients. Blend on high speed for 1 minute. Pour over the bacon and cheese mixture. Bake in a 350° oven for 30 minutes or until brown.

MAKES 6 SERVINGS.

Three Rivers Resort

HC 75, Box 61
Kooskia at Lowell, Idaho 83539
(208) 926-4430

Local, wild huckleberries have been a source of food for Native Americans, early settlers, and local black bears and grizzlies. At Three Rivers, guests may enjoy delicious huckleberry sundaes and take home jelly and toppings for later enjoyment. A resort in the midst of the Idaho wilderness, Three Rivers includes of a motel, restaurant, campground, and bed and breakfast cabins set beside the clean and clear Lochsa River. Also available is a seventy-year-old former forest ranger's lodging on a hill high above the river. Farther up the mountain is the open-beamed "Loft" with a full kitchen, indoor Jacuzzi, and antique brass bed.

Mike's Moose Mince Meat with Brandy

4 *pounds cooked ground moose meat (trim fat first)*
2 *pounds raisins*
2 *pounds currants*
5 *quarts Idaho-grown tart apples, chopped*
1 *pound ground suet*
1 *cup molasses*
½ *pound candied citron, chopped*
6 *cups sweet apple cider*
1 *tablespoon salt*
1 *teaspoon cinnamon*
1 *teaspoon ground cloves*
4 *pounds sugar*
1 *cup good-quality brandy*

In a big kettle mix everything except the brandy. Cook slowly for 5 hours. Add the brandy. Place in a crock and store in a cool place, or refrigerate for several weeks. Stir every few days and add more brandy to taste. Use immediately or freeze in freezer containers. Use for Moose Mince Meat Pie.

MAKES 10 QUARTS.

Three Rivers Resort Huckleberry Topping

4 *cups fresh or frozen huckleberries*
2 *tablespoons lemon juice*
1 *tablespoon powdered pectin*
2 *cups sugar*

In a saucepan heat the huckleberries until warm. Mash them slightly. Add the lemon juice and pectin, and bring to a boil. Add the sugar and boil gently for 5 minutes. Seal in sterilized jars or freeze.

Use for milk shakes, sundaes, on homemade ice cream, or on cheesecake.

MAKES ABOUT 6 HALF-PINTS.

ILLINOIS

Brierwreath Manor Bed and Breakfast

216 North Bench Street
Galena, Illinois 61036
(815) 777-0608

*T*his Queen Anne Victorian, dating to 1884, is one short block from Galena's historic Main Street. In the dining room, an antique wardrobe filled with heirloom cut crystal and pressed glass covers an entire wall. One guest room and a pair of spacious suites, featuring antique oak and walnut furnishings, provide the accommodations. Special arrange-

Brierwreath Manor

ments may be made for a weekend "Breakfast with General Grant" or a Christmas Dinner package.

Date Nut Bread

1 cup dates, chopped
2 cups boiling water
2 teaspoons baking soda
4 cups all-purpose flour
1 teaspoon salt
2 tablespoons butter
2 cups sugar
2 eggs
2 teaspoons vanilla extract
1 cup nuts

In a saucepan combine the dates, boiling water, and baking soda. Be careful, this mixture sometimes boils over. Cool.

In a medium bowl sift the flour and salt. In a separate bowl cream the butter and sugar. Add the eggs, 1 at a time, and beat well. Add the dry ingredients alternately with the date mixture, and beat until smooth. Stir in the vanilla and nuts. Grease the sides and bottom of 4 20-ounce cans (remove the labels and wash fruit or vegetable cans thoroughly). Fill two-thirds full. Bake in a 350° oven for about 1 hour.

MAKES 4 LOAVES.

Brierwreath's Apple-Blueberry-Walnut Pancake

3 cups biscuit mix
½ cup sugar
1½ teaspoons ground cinnamon
1½ cups milk
3 eggs
¾ cup chopped walnuts
¾ cup blueberries, fresh or frozen
1½ cups chopped apple

1 cup sugar
3 teaspoons biscuit mix
¼ teaspoon cinnamon
2 cups apple cider
¼ cup butter

In a large bowl mix 3 cups of biscuit mix, ½ cup of sugar, 1½ teaspoons of cinnamon, milk, and eggs thoroughly. Add the walnuts, blueberries, and apple. Pour into a greased 9 x 13-inch pan. Bake in a 400° oven for 30 minutes.

In a saucepan combine 1 cup of sugar, 3 teaspoons of biscuit mix, ¼ teaspoon of cinnamon, the apple cider, and butter, and heat until thick. Serve the warm pancakes with the apple cider sauce.

MAKES 8 SERVINGS.

The
Herrington
Inn

15 South River Lane
Geneva, Illinois 60134
(708) 208-7433

*T**ucked away in the picturesque town of Geneva, the Herrington blends the intimacy of a French country inn with the amenities of a big city hotel. Rooms are spacious and include whirlpool, fireplace, and a terrace with a view of the Fox River. Originally the Geneva Rock Springs Creamery, the inn's forty guest rooms have been transformed into a landmark of luxury.*

Four-colored Shellfish Canneloni with Lobster Sauce and Anise Oil

10 ounces shrimp, peeled and deveined
10 ounces scallops
10 ounces lump crab meat
 1 ounce brunoise red bell pepper
 1 ounce brunoise yellow bell pepper
 1 ounce brunoise green bell pepper
 1 ounce minced shallots
 1 ounce marsala wine
 ¼ ounce chopped basil
 ¼ ounce chopped tarragon
 2 ounces egg white
   Salt and pepper to taste
12 5-inch square pieces 4-color sheet pasta
....
 6 cups lobster bisque
36 rosemary sprigs
....
 1 cup chopped fennel bulb
 2 cups virgin olive oil
 ½ cup oil
 1 teaspoon salt
   Chopped fresh fennel sprigs
....
   Goat cheese for garnish

Asparagus spears for garnish
Lobster roe for garnish

In a food processor blend the shrimp and scallops. Stir in the crab meat and brunoise of peppers. In a sauté pan sweat the shallots for 1 minute. Add the marsala wine and reduce until dry. Remove from the stove and let cool before adding to the shellfish mixture. Finish the mixture with chopped herbs, egg white, and seasonings.

Place 3 ounces of filling in a 5-inch square piece of sheet pasta and roll like a cannelloni. Repeat with the remaining filling and pasta. Poach in a sauté pan.

In a large saucepan combine the bisque and rosemary, and reduce by half. Strain.

In a separate saucepan combine the fennel, olive oil, oil, and 1 teaspoon of salt. Bring to a boil and cook for 5 minutes. Reduce to a simmer for 15 to 20 minutes. Let cool and strain. Finish the oil with chopped fresh fennel sprigs.

In a 4-inch circle in the middle of each serving plate spread 2 ounces of lobster sauce. Cut the canneloni on a heavy bias and stack on top of each other. Drizzle anise oil around the canneloni. Garnish with 2 pieces of goat cheese with asparagus spears and lobster roe.

MAKES 12 SERVINGS.

Apple Tea Smoked Breast of Moullard with Wild Mushroom Flan

 1 cup apple wood chips
 ½ cup Earl Grey tea
 1 cup apple cider
 1 cup white wine (chardonnay)
 ½ cup water
 2 cinnamon sticks
 8 ounces Moullard breast
   Salt and pepper to taste
 ½ teaspoon fresh thyme
 ½ teaspoon fresh basil
....
 8 cups portabella mushrooms
 4 cups shiitake mushrooms
 4 cups white mushrooms
 ½ cup garlic
   Oil
 1 cup sherry
 1 cup red bell pepper, minced
 1 cup green bell pepper, minced

 1 cup green onions, minced
 5 eggs
 2½ cups heavy cream
   Salt and pepper to taste
....
   Butternut Squash, Beet, and Potato Rissoto (recipe follows)
   Pinot Noir Broth (recipe follows)

In a shallow dish combine the tea, cider, white wine, water, and cinnamon. Soak the apple chips in the mixture overnight.

Prepare the grill. When the charcoal briquettes are smoldering, cover with the wood chip mixture. Season the moullard with salt and pepper, and sprinkle with thyme and basil. Place the moullard on the rack and smoke until medium-rare. (Re-wet chips as needed when coals are too hot.)

In a food processor mince all of the mushrooms and garlic. In a hot rondeau heat a small amount of oil and sauté the mushrooms and garlic together for 10 to 15 minutes. Deglaze with sherry and reduce until dry. When dry add the peppers and green onions, and let cool.

In a medium bowl combine the eggs and cream, and fold into the mushroom mixture. Season and place into a greased timbale mold. Cover and place in a water bath. Bake in a 350° oven for 45 minutes. Makes 2 ounces.

In the center of the plate, unmold the flan and place right-side-up. Slice the Moullard on a heavy bias and shingle around the flan. Sprinkle risotto around the base of plate and finish dish by drizzling 1 to 2 ounces of pinot noir broth on the risotto. Garnish with crispy fried beef chiffonade.

MAKES 1 SERVING.

Butternut Squash, Beet, and Potato Risotto

 1 ounce butternut squash, very finely diced
 1 ounce beet, very finely diced
 1 ounce Yukon Gold potato, very finely diced
 1 tablespoon chicken stock
 2 tablespoons demiglace
   Pinch rosemary, chopped
   Pinch thyme, chopped
   Salt to taste
   Fresh crushed black pepper to taste

In a hot sauté pan, sauté the squash, beet, and potato until just lightly browned. When colored, add ½ tablespoon of stock and the herbs. Reduce until dry. Finish with the remaining stock and season the salt to taste.

MAKES 1 SERVING.

Pinot Noir Broth

     2   *shallots, minced*
     3   *cloves garlic, minced*
     2   *cinnamon sticks*
     2   *ounces dried cherries*
     4   *fresh thyme sprigs*
     2   *ounces firmly packed brown sugar*
     2   *cups pinot noir*
    1½   *quarts demiglace*
         Pinch salt and pepper

In a saucepot, sweat the shallots, garlic, cinnamon sticks, cherries, and fresh thyme for 5 to 7 minutes. Add the brown sugar, and deglaze with pinot noir. Reduce until dry and add the demiglace, lightly season, and reduce to 1 quart. Strain and adjust the seasonings.

MAKES 1 QUART.

Oscar Swan Country Inn

❦

1800 West State Street
Geneva, Illinois 60134
(708) 232-0173

*A*n eight-acre private estate converted into a B&B-style country inn, the Oscar Swan offers seven master guest suites. The house dates to the turn of the century, and the furnishings and decor reflect that period. Nearby attractions include the Sandwich Antique Market, the Fox River with its scenic hiking and biking paths, and the interesting shops and restaurants of Geneva. Special holiday dinners are available, including a Colonial*

Williamsburg Christmas Dinner in early December.

Roasted Little Red Potatoes

Start with new fresh little red potatoes, and scrub them clean. Split into halves or quarters. In a large bowl toss the potatoes with extra virgin olive oil.

Crush dried rosemary leaves between olive oil-coated hands. Season wit salt and pepper, and toss all together. Spread on a jelly roll pan. Bake in a 450° oven for 45 minutes, depending on potato size and oven. A convection oven is faster, bake at 400° for 30 minutes.

Other seasonings and herbs may be substituted. Bake until golden brown and tender.

Inn on the Square

Inn on the Square

❦

3 Montgomery Street
Oakland, Illinois 61943
(217) 346-2289

*T*here is plenty to do here, but one of the favorite activities of guests at this B&B is plain, old, fashioned "sittin' and rockin'." The country pleasures emphasized by the inn are enhanced by the comfortable furnishings of the upstairs guest rooms and the opportunity to relax with a*

jigsaw puzzle in the library. For most small towns, the square is the center of community life, and that is true for Oakland. For this reason, guests can walk out the inn's front door to local landmarks or take a short drive to Walnut Point—a beautiful conservation park, Lincoln Log Cabin State Park, or a nearby Amish community.

Buttermilk Pecan Pie

    ½   *cup butter or margarine*
     2   *cups sugar*
     5   *eggs*
     2   *tablespoons all-purpose flour*
     2   *tablespoons lemon juice*
     1   *teaspoon vanilla extract*
     1   *cup buttermilk*
     1   *cup chopped pecans*
     1   *unbaked 10-inch pastry shell*

In a medium bowl cream the butter and sugar. Add the eggs 1 at a time, beating well. Blend in the flour, lemon juice, and vanilla.

Stir in the buttermilk and pecans. Pour the filling into the pie shell. Bake in a 325° oven for 55 minutes or until set. Cool. Store in the refrigerator.

MAKES 8 SERVINGS.

Shaker Lemon Pie

     2   *large lemons*
     2   *cups sugar*
     4   *eggs, well-beaten*
         Pastry for 2-crust 9-inch pie
         Milk
         Sugar for sprinkling

Slice the lemons as thin as paper. In a large bowl combine the lemons and sugar. Let stand 2 hours or longer, stirring occasionally.

Add the beaten eggs. Turn into a 9-inch pie shell, arranging the lemon slices evenly. Cover with the top crust. Cut slits near the center. Brush the top crust with milk and sugar. Bake in a 450° oven for 15 minutes. Reduce the heat to 375° and bake for 20 minutes, or until a silver knife inserted in the pie comes out clean. Cool.

Variation: For the top crust cut strips of pie dough and alternate layers across the top of the pie. Brush the top crust with milk and sugar.
MAKES 6 TO 8 SERVINGS.

Baked Chicken Salad Pie

- 1 **unbaked 9-inch pie crust**
- 2 **eggs**
- 2 **cups diced cooked chicken meat**
- ½ **cup shredded Cheddar cheese**
- ¼ **cup water chestnuts, sliced**
- ½ **cup chopped celery**
- ¼ **cup onion, diced**
- ½ **cup cream of chicken soup**
- ½ **cup sour cream**
- ½ **cup mayonnaise**
- 2 **tablespoons all-purpose flour**

Prick the crust lightly and partially bake in a 350° oven for 7 to 10 minutes. In a medium bowl beat 2 eggs slightly. Add the remaining ingredients and mix well. Fill the crust with chicken mixture. Bake in a 350° oven for 45 to 50 minutes until slightly browned.
MAKES 4 TO 6 SERVINGS.

Country Salmon Pie

- 6 **sheets puff pastry**
  Grated Parmesan cheese
  ....
- 2 **tablespoons butter**
- 1 **large onion, diced**
- 1 **clove garlic, finely chopped**
- 2 **cups sour cream**
- 4 **eggs**
- 1 **16-ounce can salmon, cleaned and broken into pieces**
- 1 **cup finely chopped, sautéed mushrooms**
- 1½ **cups shredded Swiss cheese**
- 1 **teaspoon dill**
- ¼ **teaspoon salt**

Press the pastry into a 9-inch springform pan and make 2-inch sides up from the bottom of the pan. Sprinkle with Parmesan cheese. Set aside.

In a skillet melt the butter and sauté the onion and garlic until soft. In a large bowl beat together the sour cream and eggs until blended. Stir in the salmon, mushrooms, sautéed onion and garlic, 1 cup of Swiss cheese, dill, and salt. Pour the mixture into the pastry-lined pan. Top with the remaining ½ cup of cheese. Turn the sides of the dough in to form an edge. Bake in a 375° oven for 40 to 50 minutes until set.
MAKES 8 TO 10 SERVINGS.

Pasta Twists with Chicken and Garlic Pepper Cream

- 1 **cup chicken broth**
- 6 **medium carrots, julienned**
- 6 **cloves garlic, peeled**
- 2 **8-ounces packages cream cheese**
- ¼ **cup grated Parmesan cheese**
- 1 **teaspoon pepper**
- 1 **teaspoon salt**
- ¼ **cup milk**
- 4 **cups pasta spirals, cooked**
- 3 **cups cooked cubed chicken**
- 1 **bunch green onions**
  Grated Parmesan cheese for garnish
  Parsley for garnish

In a medium saucepan bring the chicken broth to a boil. Add the carrots and garlic and cook until tender. Drain, reserving the broth.

In a food processor blend the garlic, cream cheese, Parmesan cheese, pepper, salt, and chicken broth. Add the milk and process until smooth.

Toss the pasta with the cream cheese mixture, carrots, chicken, and green onions. This mixture can also be served over the pasta instead of mixing it into the pasta. Sprinkle with Parmesan cheese and parsley to serve.
MAKES 8 SERVINGS.

Yesterday's Memories

303 East Peru
Princeton, Illinois 61356
(815) 872-7753

---

*S*urveyor, author, and world traveler Nehemiah Matson built this twenty-one-room Greek Revival home during the 1850s. Now a B&B

with three pleasant guest rooms, the house is filled with collections: dolls, dollhouses, old toy trains, and all sorts of youthful treasures. The collectibles can be found even in the kitchen where an assortment of century-old culinary tools forms an interesting display. The latticed screened porch provides a perfect place for breakfast in the summer.

Yesterday's Memories

Pumpkin Pancakes

- 2 **cups all-purpose baking mix**
- 2 **tablespoons sugar**
- 1 **teaspoon pumpkin pie spice**
- 1 **cup milk**
- 2 **eggs**
- 1 **cup canned pumpkin**
- ¼ **cup oil**
  Hot Pecan Syrup (recipe follows)

In a large bowl mix all ingredients just until smooth. Pour ½ cup of batter at a time onto a hot greased griddle. When bubbles form, turn and bake the other side.

Serve with Hot Pecan Syrup.
MAKES 4 TO 6 SERVINGS

Hot Pecan Syrup

- 1 **cup maple syrup**
- ¼ **cup chopped pecans**

In a microwave-safe bowl combine the syrup and pecans. Microwave for 90 seconds on high.
MAKES 1¼ CUPS.

Coyla's Baked Oatmeal

3 cups quick-cooking oatmeal
1 cup firmly packed brown sugar
2 teaspoons baking powder
1 teaspoon ground cinnamon
1 teaspoon salt
1 cup milk
½ cup melted margarine or butter
2 eggs, beaten
½ cup nuts, chopped
½ cup raisins (optional)
   Extra milk for garnish

In a large bowl combine all ingredients. Spoon into a greased 9-inch pan. Bake in a 350° oven for 35 to 45 minutes. Serve warm with additional milk.

MAKES 6 SERVINGS.

My Grandma's Kolacky (European Fruit Pastries)

1 cup butter
1 8-ounce package cream cheese
2 cups all-purpose flour
2 teaspoons baking powder
1 cup confectioners' sugar
   Fruit jam, any flavor (apricot, strawberry, or peach is excellent)
   Confectioners' sugar for sprinkling

In a medium bowl blend the butter and cream cheese together. In a separate bowl sift the dry ingredients together. Blend the dry ingredients into the butter and cheese with a pastry fork. Chill.

Roll the dough on a floured surface to ¼-inch thickness and cut out circles with a cookie cutter. Place on a lightly greased cookie sheet, 1 inch apart. Make a depression in the center of each pastry with a spoon and fill with 1 tablespoon of jam. Bake in a 350° oven for 15 minutes. Sprinkle the tops with additional confectioners' sugar.

MAKES ABOUT 1 DOZEN.

Potter House

Potter House Bed and Breakfast
❧

1906 Seventh Avenue
Rock Island, Illinois 61201
(309) 788-1906

---

*T*he Potter House is a restored Colonial Revival built by a Rock Island newspaper publisher in 1907. The stained glass, leather wall coverings, six fireplaces, and mahogany-paneled dining room provide ample evidence of the home's early-century beginnings, as do the antiques in the guest rooms. Visitors especially enjoy the player piano in the parlor. The numerous area attractions include jazz, blues, and Mozart festivals, a plethora of antique shops, and the Quad Cities riverboat casinos.

Christmas Cocoa Mix

2 cups nonfat dry milk
1 cup sugar
¾ cup nondairy creamer (Coffee-Mate Lite with no tropical oils for less cholesterol)
⅔ cup unsweetened cocoa
¼ teaspoon salt

In a large resealable bag mix all ingredients. When completely mixed, place in a plastic container with a tight-fitting lid.

To serve, use 3 heaping teaspoons per mug. Add boiling water and stir well. Add vanilla ice cream for a creamier drink.

MAKES ABOUT 32 SERVINGS.

Country Apple-Sausage Ring

2 pounds sage-flavored bulk sausage
2 eggs, slightly beaten
½ cup milk
1½ cups herbed or Italian breadcrumbs
¼ cup minced onion
1 cup finely chopped apple

In a large bowl combine all ingredients and mix thoroughly. Press lightly into a greased 6-cup ring mold. Bake in a 350° oven for 1 hour. Drain.

MAKES 6 TO 8 SERVINGS.

Wheaton Inn
❧

301 West Roosevelt Road
Wheaton, Illinois 60187
(708) 690-2600

---

*T*he inn's sixteen guest rooms are furnished and decorated in the tradition of Colonial Williamsburg, and each has a distinct personality. The same can be said for the inn as a whole with its chandeliers, fireplaces, and warm wood tones. Nearby are the Morton Arboretum, Cantigny war museum, McCormick Museum, and the Billy Graham Center at Wheaton College.

Green Chili Quiche

5 eggs
¼ cup all-purpose flour
½ teaspoon baking powder
¼ teaspoon salt
¼ teaspoon pepper
½ teaspoon minced garlic
1 cup small curd creamed cottage cheese
¼ cup melted butter
2 cups shredded Monterey Jack cheese
1 4-ounce can chopped green chilies, drained

In a large bowl beat the eggs until light and fluffy. Add the flour, baking powder, salt, pepper, and garlic. Stir together, then add the cottage cheese and melted butter. Beat with an electric mixer until combined. Add the shredded Monterey Jack cheese, then the green chilies. Pour into a greased 10-inch quiche pan. Bake in a 350° oven for 35 minutes or until the center is firm.

MAKES 8 SERVINGS.

Grand Marnier French Toast

6   *eggs*
⅔   *cup orange juice*
⅓   *cup Grand Marnier*
⅓   *cup milk*
3   *tablespoons sugar*
¼   *teaspoon vanilla extract*
¼   *teaspoon salt*
    Finely grated zest of 1 orange
8   *¾-inch-thick slices French bread*
    Orange slices for garnish
    Confectioners' sugar

In a large bowl beat the eggs. Add the orange juice, Grand Marnier, milk, sugar, vanilla, salt, and orange zest. Mix well.

Layer the bread slices in a 9 x 13-inch pan. Pour the egg mixture over all. Turn several times. Refrigerate overnight.

Melt the butter in a jelly roll pan. Place the bread slices on the baking sheet. Bake in a 400° oven for 8 minutes. Turn and continue baking until brown. Arrange on a plate with orange slices. Top with confectioners' sugar. Serve with warm syrup.

MAKES 4 SERVINGS.

INDIANA

Wisteria Manor

Wisteria Manor Cinnamon Cakes

- ¾ cup sugar
- 2 teaspoons baking powder
- 2 cups all-purpose flour
- 1 tablespoon butter
- 1 cup milk
  Flour extra brown sugar, cinnamon, and butter for topping

In a medium bowl combine all of the dry ingredients. Cut in 1 tablespoon of butter. Add the milk and stir until blended well.

Divide the batter between 2 well-greased 9-inch pie plates. Sprinkle the tops with flour, brown sugar, and cinnamon. Push chunks of butter into the dough. Bake in a 350° oven for 25 to 30 minutes.

MAKES 12 TO 16 SERVINGS.

Sugar Cream Pie

- ¼ cup sugar
- ¾ cup firmly packed brown sugar
- ⅓ cup all-purpose flour
- 1 unbaked 9-inch pie crust
- 2 cups heavy cream
- 2 teaspoons vanilla extract
- ¼ cup butter, cut into chunks
  Cinnamon

Mix the sugars and flour lightly in the pie shell with a finger, taking care not to break the crust. In a medium bowl mix the cream, vanilla, and butter. Pour over the dry ingredients in the crust. Sprinkle with cinnamon.

Bake in a 350° oven for 35 to 45 minutes. At about 20 minutes stir carefully to blend the butter.

MAKES 6 TO 8 SERVINGS.

Indiana Mile High Biscuits

- 3 cups all-purpose flour
- 2 tablespoons sugar
- 1 tablespoon plus 1½ teaspoons baking powder
- ¾ teaspoon cream of tartar
- ½ teaspoon salt
- ¾ cup shortening
- 1 egg
- 1 cup milk

In a large bowl blend all of the dry ingredients. Cut in the shortening until the mixture is dime-size chunks. Add the egg and milk, and mix just until moistened. Don't handle the mixture too much or the biscuits will be tough. Pat into a rectangle on a baking sheet and cut into about 12 pieces. Bake in a 375° oven for about 10 to 12 minutes.

MAKES ABOUT 1 DOZEN.

Peanut Brittle

- 2 cups sugar
- 1½ cups water
- 1 cup light corn syrup
- ¼ teaspoon salt
- 1 pound raw peanuts
- ½ cup butter
- 2 teaspoons baking soda

In a heavy saucepan mix the sugar, water, syrup, and salt. Boil to 236°. Add the raw peanuts and boil to 300° or the hard-crack stage. Remove the pan from heat and add the butter and soda. Stir until the mixture foams. Pour onto a buttered cookie sheet or a marble slab. When the mixture hardens, break the brittle into pieces.

MAKES ABOUT 3½ POUNDS OF BRITTLE.

Apple Pie

- ¾ cup all-purpose flour
- ¼ cup sugar
- 1 tablespoon ground cinnamon
- ½ teaspoon salt
- ½ cup plus 2 tablespoons butter
- ¼ cup cider or water

....

- 8 to 10 McIntosh apples, peeled and sliced
- 1⅔ cups sour cream
- 1 cup sugar
- ½ cup all-purpose flour
- 1 egg
- 2 teaspoons vanilla extract

....

- 1 cup chopped walnuts
- ½ cup all-purpose flour
- ½ cup firmly packed brown sugar
- 1 tablespoon cinnamon
  Dash salt
- ½ cup butter

In a medium bowl combine ¾ cup of flour, ¼ cup of sugar, 1 tablespoon of cinnamon, ½ teaspoon of salt, ½ cup plus 2 tablespoons of butter, and the cider. Mix well. Roll out and ease into a 10-inch deep dish pie plate.

In a large bowl combine the apples, sour cream, 1 cup of sugar, ½ cup of flour, 1 egg, and vanilla. Spoon the filling into the crust. Bake in a 450° oven for 10 minutes. Reduce the heat to 350° and bake for 40 minutes.

In a medium bowl combine the remaining ingredients and mix until crumbly. Sprinkle the top of the pie and bake for 15 minutes more.

MAKES 8 SERVINGS.

Gray Goose Inn

❧

350 Indian Boundary Road
Chesterton, Indiana 46304
(219) 926-5781

An English country house set under century-old oaks, the Gray Goose is decorated in traditional English style. There are always plenty of fresh flowers around. The inn looks out onto Lake Palomara, and the dining room takes advantage of the view. Area attractions include Oz Days in Chesterton, Dunes State Park and National Lakeshore, Lighthouse Plaza's factory outlets, Bailly Homestead, and Mount Baldy.

Surprise Cupcakes

- 1 cup butter
- ½ cup confectioners' sugar
- 1¾ cups sifted all-purpose flour
- 1 tablespoon cornstarch
  Preserves of choice

....

- 1 egg, beaten
- ½ cup sugar
- 1 cup coconut

In a medium bowl cream the butter and confectioners' sugar. In a separate bowl sift the flour and cornstarch. Add the dry ingredients to the creamed mixture, and mix by hand. Form the mixture into small balls and press into the bottom and sides of greased 1-inch muffin cups. Place ½ teaspoon of preserves in each pastry.

In a small bowl mix the remaining ingredients. Top each cupcake with 1 teaspoon of topping. Bake in a 350° oven for 30 minutes.

Note: The topping can be varied by substituting 1 cup of firmly packed brown sugar, 1 well-beaten egg, and ¼ cup finely chopped pecans.

MAKES ABOUT 2 DOZEN.

Christmas Bubbles

- 2 packages active dry yeast
- ¼ cup warm water (105 to 115°)
- 2 cups butter
- 1 cup sugar
- 1 egg
- 4½ cups all-purpose flour
  Colored sugar

In a cup dissolve the yeast in the warm water. In a large bowl cream the butter. Add the sugar and beat until light and fluffy. Beat in the egg. Blend in yeast and then the flour. Mix well. Shape into small balls and dip into colored sugar. Place on a greased cookie sheet. Bake in a 375° oven for 10 to 12 minutes.

MAKES ABOUT 3 DOZEN.

Ice Cream Kolacky

- 4 cups all-purpose flour
- 2 tablespoons sugar
- 2 cups butter
- 1 pint vanilla ice cream, partially softened
  Filling such as nuts, apricot, date, prune, etc.

In a large bowl measure the flour and blend it with the sugar. Cut in the butter until the mixture resembles cornmeal. Add the ice cream and blend. Refrigerate the dough for about 1 hour for easier handling.

Roll the dough out and cut it into squares or rounds. Fill with any desired filling. Fold the dough partly over the filling. Place the pastries on baking sheets. Bake in a 375° oven until light brown. Buttery, light, and wonderful.

MAKES ABOUT 4 DOZEN.

Easy and Quick Corn Bread Pudding

- 2 15-ounce cans whole kernel corn, drained
- 2 15-ounce cans cream-style corn
- 2 8½-ounce boxes Jiffy Corn Bread Mix
- ½ cup butter, melted

In a large bowl combine all ingredients and blend well. Pour into a greased 9 x 13-inch pan. Bake in a 350° oven for 1 hour.

MAKES 10 SERVINGS.

East Buttery Pound Cake

1   cup butter
1   8-ounce package cream cheese
1½   cups sugar
4   eggs
1½   teaspoons vanilla extract
1¾   cups sifted all-purpose flour
1½   teaspoons baking powder

In a large bowl combine the butter and cream cheese, and beat until creamy. Add the sugar and beat for 5 minutes. Add the eggs 1 at a time, beating well after each addition. Blend in the vanilla. Mix in the flour and baking powder. Pour the batter into a greased and floured bundt pan. Bake in a 350° oven for 1 hour.

MAKES 8 SERVINGS.

Cragwood Inn Bed and Breakfast

❧

303 North Second Street
Decatur, Indiana 46733
(219) 728-2000

Built at the turn of the century, this Queen Anne Victorian B&B offers spacious guest rooms furnished with tasteful antiques. Decatur is close enough to Fort Wayne for a convenient drive into the city, but the town itself has plenty to offer the traveler, including lovely paths along the St. Marys River. Innovative weekend seminars throughout the year focus on various needleworking skills. The largest and most complete museum in the world dedicated to Abraham Lincoln is a short drive away.

Quiche Florentine

1   egg
½   teaspoon garlic powder
¼   cup grated Parmesan cheese
1   cup orzo, cooked and drained
....
5   eggs (or egg substitute, recipe follows)
½   cup skim milk
¼   teaspoon garlic powder
1   teaspoon Italian seasoning
1   10-ounce package frozen spinach, thawed, drained, and pressed
1   2-ounce can sliced mushrooms

In a medium bowl beat together 1 egg, ½ teaspoon of garlic powder, and the Parmesan cheese. Stir in the orzo until blended. Spray a 9-inch deep-dish pie plate with cooking spray. Spread the orzo mixture over the bottom and up the sides of the pie plate. In a separate bowl beat together 5 eggs, the milk, ¼ teaspoon of garlic powder, and the Italian seasoning until blended well. Stir in the chopped spinach and mushrooms. Pour into the orzo crust. Bake in a 375° oven for 30 to 40 minutes. Let stand 5 minutes before slicing.

MAKES 6 SERVINGS.

Raspberry Almond Scones

2   cups all-purpose flour
½   teaspoon baking soda
¼   teaspoon salt
2   teaspoons baking powder
¼   cup sugar
3   tablespoons cold margarine, cut into small pieces
1   8-ounce carton nonfat yogurt
¼   cup raspberry spread
2   tablespoons chopped almonds

In a large bowl combine the flour, soda, salt, baking powder and sugar. Cut in the margarine until the mixture resembles coarse meal. Add the yogurt and stir until just moistened. The dough will be sticky. Turn onto a floured surface. Knead 4 or 5 times. Pat into an 8-inch circle. Place on a greased baking sheet. Score 12 wedges on the dough. Make a slit in each wedge. Place 1 teaspoon of raspberry spread in each slit. Sprinkle with almonds. Bake in a 400° oven for 13 minutes. Serve warm.

MAKES 12 SCONES.

Pineapple French Toast

1   15¼-ounce can pineapple chunks in juice
1   cup halved strawberries
¼   cup toasted coconut
4   tablespoons sugar, divided
1   loaf French bread, unsliced
3   eggs (or egg substitute, recipe follows)
1½   cups 2% milk
1   teaspoon vanilla, extra
¼   teaspoon salt
1   tablespoon butter
   Ambrosia

Drain the pineapple, reserving ¾ cup of juice and the pineapple pieces separately. In a small bowl combine the strawberries, coconut, reserved pineapple pieces, and 2 tablespoons sugar. Set aside.

Cut the bread in ¾-inch slices. Arrange them in a single layer in a 10 x 15-inch jelly roll pan. Set aside. In a large bowl beat together the eggs, milk, vanilla, salt, 2 tablespoon of sugar, and the reserved pineapple juice. Pour the egg mixture over the bread, turning to coat completely. Cover and refrigerate overnight.

Spray a large skillet with cooking spray. Melt the butter over medium heat. Add the bread slices a few at a time, and cook until browned on both sides, turning once. Serve with ambrosia.

MAKES 6 SERVINGS.

Blueberry Cheese Strata

6   slices firm bread, cubed
2   cups frozen blueberries
⅓   cup sugar
1   cup shredded low-fat Swiss cheese
4   eggs (or egg substitute, recipe follows)
2   cups low-fat milk
1   teaspoon vanilla extract
¼   teaspoon salt
½   teaspoon ground cinnamon
   Low-fat vanilla yogurt for topping

In an 8-inch square baking dish layer half the bread cubes. Layer the berries, sugar, Swiss cheese, and the rest of the bread cubes in it. In a large bowl combine the eggs, milk, vanilla, and salt. Mix well. Pour over the bread mixture. Sprinkle with cinnamon. Cover and refrigerate overnight.

Cragwood Inn

Remove the cover. Bake in a 325° oven for 55 minutes. Let the strata stand for 10 minutes. Top with low-fat vanilla yogurt.

MAKES 6 SERVINGS.

Egg Substitute

6   egg whites
¼   cup dry milk
1   tablespoon oil

In a container with a cover combine all ingredients and blend until smooth. Cover and refrigerate. Keeps 1 week.

MAKES ¾ CUP. ¼ CUP=1 EGG.

Rhubarb Dumplings

1½   cups sugar
1   tablespoon all-purpose flour
¼   teaspoon ground cinnamon
¼   teaspoon salt
1½   cups water
⅓   cup butter
1   teaspoon vanilla extract
   Red food coloring

....

2   cups all-purpose flour
2   tablespoons sugar
2   teaspoons baking powder
¼   teaspoon salt
2½   tablespoons cold butter
⅔   cup milk

....

2   tablespoons butter, softened
2   cups finely chopped rhubarb
½   cup sugar
   Ground cinnamon
   Cream for topping (optional)

In a small pan combine 1½ cups of sugar, 1 tablespoon flour, cinnamon, and salt. Gradually add the water and ⅓ cup of butter and mix well. Bring the mixture to a boil and cook for 1 minute. Add the vanilla and red coloring to make the mixture a light pink. Let cool.

In a medium bowl combine 2 cups of flour, 2 tablespoons of sugar, the baking powder, and ¼ teaspoon of salt. Cut in 2½ tablespoons of cold butter until the mixture resembles coarse meal. Add the milk and mix quickly. Gather into a ball and roll out on a floured board into a 10 x 12-inch rectangle. Spread the dough with 2 tablespoons of softened butter and arrange the rhubarb on top. Sprinkle ½ cup of sugar over it and sprinkle liberally with cinnamon. Roll up from the long side and put on a cutting board seamside-down. Cut the roll into 12 slices. Arrange cut-side up in a greased baking dish. Pour the cooled sauce over the slices. Bake in a 350° oven for 35 minutes or until golden brown. Serve with cream, if desired.

MAKES 12 SERVINGS.

Prize-winning Orange Pecan Muffins

2   11-ounce cans mandarin orange segments
1   3-ounce package cream cheese
1   cup sugar
2   teaspoons vanilla extract
1   jumbo egg
2   cups all-purpose flour
1   teaspoon salt
1   teaspoon baking soda
½   cup sour cream
1   tablespoon grated orange zest
½   cup chopped pecans

....

3   tablespoons margarine
2   cups confectioners' sugar
3   tablespoons orange juice
2   tablespoons grated orange zest
   Pecan pieces for garnish

Drain the orange segments and cut them into thirds. In a large bowl beat the cream cheese, sugar, and vanilla with an electric mixer until smooth. Add the egg and beat for 1 to 2 minutes more. In a separate bowl combine the flour, salt, and soda. Add the dry ingredients and sour cream alternately to the cream cheese mixture, blending on low speed. Fold in the orange segments, 1 tablespoon of zest, and pecans. Pour into 12 lined muffin cups. Bake in a 350° oven for 25 minutes.

In a medium bowl combine the remaining ingredients and beat with an electric mixer on high speed until smooth. Frost the cooled muffins. Garnish with pecan pieces.

MAKES 1 DOZEN.

Cherry Banana Nut Muffins

1   cup sugar
½   cup margarine, softened
1   teaspoon vanilla extract
2   jumbo eggs
2   cups all-purpose flour
1   teaspoon baking soda
   Dash salt
2   tablespoons cherry juice
3   large bananas, mashed
1   10-ounce jar maraschino cherries, quartered
1   cup chopped walnuts

....

2   tablespoons sugar
2   tablespoons firmly packed brown sugar
2   tablespoons chopped walnuts

In a large bowl beat 1 cup of sugar, the margarine, vanilla, and eggs with an electric mixer at high speed until smooth. In a separate bowl blend together the flour, soda, and salt. Stir the dry ingredients into the egg mixture. Add the cherry juice, stirring only to blend. Fold in the mashed bananas, cherries, and 1 cup of walnuts. Spoon into foil-lined muffin cups.

In a small bowl combine 2 tablespoons of sugar, the brown sugar, and walnuts. Sprinkle the topping mixture over the batter. Bake in a 350° oven for 25 minutes.

MAKES 1 DOZEN.

Checkerberry Inn

64644 CR 37
Goshen, Indiana 46526
(219) 642-4445

Fourteen individually decorated rooms with views of unspoiled countryside await travelers at the Checkerberry. This is the Amish corner of Indiana, and visitors see plenty of horses and buggies. The food, too, is typical of the areas and emphasizes fresh ingredients, herbs, and local produce. The inn is on a 100-acre tract including a remarkable twenty-acre stand of virgin woods.

Carpaccio of Michigan Venison with Roasted Shallot and Chive Vinaigrette

1¼ pounds venison loin (preferable 1 whole piece)
    Salt and pepper
6   tablespoons oil
¼   pound shallots (6 medium shallots)
3   tablespoons balsamic vinegar
2   tablespoons extra virgin olive oil
1   bunch chives, chopped
1   large yellow squash
1   large zucchini
1   large carrot
    Edible flowers or chive blossoms for garnish

Trim any excess fat or silver from the loin. Heat a cast-iron or any heavy pan until smoking hot. Season the venison with salt and pepper and drizzle with oil to coat. Brown the meat quickly on all sides, remove, and refrigerate.

Cut the shallots in half, leaving the skins on. Place in a shallow pan and season with salt and pepper. Drizzle with 1 tablespoon of oil. Roast in a 400° oven for 20 minutes or until brown and somewhat shriveled. Let cool. Remove the roasted shallots from the skins and place in a blender. Add 2 tablespoons of vinegar and blend. Slowly add 3 tablespoons of oil and 2 tablespoons of extra virgin olive oil. Season with salt and pepper. Transfer to a bowl and add the chopped chives.

Cut the squash and zucchini in 2-inch intervals to make so you have little log-shaped pieces. Using a mandolin or box shredder, shred the zucchini and squash, making sure to only shred the top layer, discarding the seeds. Peel the carrot and shred in the same manner, using the whole carrot. Put the vegetables in a nonreactive bowl and drizzle with 1 tablespoon of oil plus 1 tablespoon of balsamic vinegar. Season with salt and pepper, mix well, and refrigerate.

At the top of a cold plate place a couple of tablespoons of marinated vegetables. Repeat with the remaining vegetables on the other 5 plates. Slice the venison as thin as possible. Place a serving on each plate, fanning the meat out. Drizzle the plates with the vinaigrette and garnish with edible flowers or chive blossoms.
MAKES 6 SERVINGS.

Purviance House Bed & Breakfast

326 South Jefferson Street
Huntington, Indiana 46750
(219) 356-4218

The Italianate-Greek Revival Purviance House was built in 1859 and is listed on the National Register of Historic Places. The winding cherry staircase, original interior shutters, ornate ceilings, parquet floors, and tile fireplaces give the house its unique character. The five guest rooms contain period furnishings. The Huntington Reservoir provides facilities for summer and winter sports, and the beautiful Sunken Gardens are a special highlight in December.

Swiss Pleaser

1   8-ounce can crescent rolls
1½ cups grated Swiss cheese (or Cheddar)
3   eggs
¾   cup milk
1   tablespoon instant minced onion
4   slices crisp bacon (or chopped ham)
1   tablespoon chopped parsley

Unroll the crescent rolls and press into a greased 9 x 13-inch pan, sealing the perforations. Layer the cheese over the rolls. In a medium bowl beat the eggs, and add the milk and onion. Pour over the cheese. Sprinkle bacon or ham and parsley over the top. Bake in a 425° oven for 15 to 18 minutes or until set.
MAKES 8 SERVINGS.

Brunch Fruit Cup

1   3-ounce package lemon gelatin
2   cups boiling water
1   6-ounce can frozen orange juice concentrate
1   20-ounce can pineapple chunks
1   11-ounce can mandarin oranges
1   banana, sliced

In a large bowl dissolve the gelatin in the boiling water. Stir in the orange juice. Add the undrained canned fruit and refrigerate for several hours or overnight. Add the banana just before serving.

Variation: Green or red grapes, pears, or other fresh fruits may be added or substituted.
MAKES 10 SERVINGS.

Breakfast Casserole Surprise

4   *English muffins*
1   *pound pork sausage*
8   *eggs*
½   *cup grated Cheddar cheese*
1   *3-ounce can chopped lemon or chili peppers*

Butter the English muffins and place buttered-side-down in 9 x 13-inch pan.

In a skillet brown the sausage. Sprinkle over the muffins. In a medium bowl beat the eggs. Add the Cheddar cheese and chopped lemon or chili peppers, and pour the mixture over the casserole. (The amount of peppers may be adjusted to taste.) Cover and refrigerate overnight. Bake in a 350° oven for 35 to 40 minutes.

MAKES 8 TO 10 SERVINGS.

Thorpe House Country Inn

🌿

P.O. Box 36, 19049 Clayborne Street
Metamora, Indiana 47030
(317) 647-5425

The decorative transoms and fancy cast hinges of the Thorpe House date all the way back to its beginnings in the 1840s. This century-and-half-old traditional American home has been meticulously renovated and now serves as a bed and breakfast inn. Guests arriving on the scenic Whitewater Valley Rail-

Thorpe House

road can be met by horse-drawn carriage, if they like. Period antiques and country accessories in the rooms complete the old-time feeling.

Crock Pot Rice Pilaf

4   *cups water (or 2 cups water plus 2 cups chicken or beef stock)*
1½ *cups long grain brown rice*
1   *teaspoon sea salt*
¾   *cup chopped onion*
2   *tablespoons margarine or olive oil*
¼   *teaspoon dried rosemary*
¼   *teaspoon dried marjoram*
¼   *teaspoon dried thyme*
1   *teaspoon coriander*
2   *tablespoons parsley*
1   *clove garlic, minced*
1   *pound fresh mushrooms, sliced*

In a crock pot combine all of ingredients. Turn to low setting and cook for 6 hours.

Variation: On the stove top, cook over medium heat for about 45 minutes.

MAKES 6 SERVINGS.

French Salad Dressing

1   *cup oil*
⅓   *cup catsup*
¼   *cup vinegar*
1   *small onion, diced*
2   *teaspoons sea salt*
2   *teaspoons paprika*
⅔   *cup sugar*

In a blender combine all ingredients Mix thoroughly. Pour into a container with a tight-fitting lid. Cover and refrigerate.

MAKES ABOUT 2½ CUPS.

Frozen Fruit Fantasy Cups

5   *ounces unsweetened frozen strawberries, thawed*
6   *tablespoons unsweetened frozen orange juice concentrate, thawed*
1   *cup unsweetened crushed pineapple*
5   *ounces mandarin oranges*
2   *tablespoons lemon juice*
2   *bananas, diced*

Do not drain the fruits. In a large bowl combine all ingredients. Spoon into serving dishes or paper cups. Freeze until firm.

Note: Individual servings can be easily stored in plastic bags in the freezer. These make a wonderful snack, light dessert, and get rave reviews at the breakfast table.

MAKES ABOUT 6 SERVINGS.

Victorian Guest House

Victorian Guest House

🌿

302 East Market Street
Nappanee, Indiana 46550
(219) 773-4383

It took five years for Frank Coppes, noted kitchen cabinet maker, to build this house, which was completed in 1887. The effort proved worthwhile, however, as the grand old home has stood the test of time and looks much today as it did a century ago. Now listed on the National Register of Historic Landmarks, the Victorian Guest House offers five rooms and a suite each, providing a taste of life in a quieter era. Enhancing the quiet is the Amish farmland that attracts visitors to the area. The Notre Dame campus is only forty-five minutes away.

Chocolate Chip Cheesecake

    2 tablespoons margarine, melted
 2½   cups chocolate cookie crumbs
....
    4 8-ounce packages cream cheese, soft-
        ened
    1 cup sugar
    4 eggs
    1 teaspoon all-purpose flour
    1 teaspoon vanilla extract
    1 cup sour cream
    1 cup miniature chocolate chips
....
  ¾ cup chocolate chips
  ¼ cup margarine

Grease a 10-inch springform pan. In a small bowl combine the melted margarine and cookie crumbs. Press the mixture into the bottom and up the sides of the prepared pan.

In a large bowl combine the cream cheese, sugar, eggs, and flour. Mix until smooth. Add the vanilla and sour cream, and mix just until blended. Stir in the miniature chocolate chips. Pour into the crust. Bake in a 325° oven for 1 hour. Turn the oven off and open the door. Leave the cheesecake in the oven for an additional 30 minutes.

In a small pan melt together ¾ cup of chocolate chips and ¼ cup of margarine, stirring until smooth. Spread the mixture onto the cheesecake. Store in the refrigerator.
MAKES 8 SERVINGS.

English Muffin Bread

    5 cups all-purpose flour, divided
    2 packages active dry yeast
    1 tablespoon sugar
    2 teaspoons salt
  ¼ teaspoon baking soda
    2 cups warm milk (120 to 130°)
  ½ cup warm water (120 to 130°)
        Cornmeal

In a large mixing bowl combine 2 cups of flour, the yeast, sugar, salt, and soda. Add the milk and water and beat with an electric mixer on low speed for 30 seconds, scraping the bowl occasionally. Beat on high for 3 minutes. Stir in the remaining flour (the batter will be stiff). Do not knead.

Grease 2 standard loaf pans. Sprinkle the pans with cornmeal. Spoon the batter into the pans and sprinkle cornmeal on top. Cover and let rise in a warm place until doubled in bulk, about 45 minutes. Bake in a 375° oven for 35 minutes, or until golden brown. Remove from the pans immediately and cool on wire racks.

This bread is wonderful to toast and make egg and ham or egg and bacon sandwiches.
MAKES 2 LOAVES.

Apple-Raisin Quiche

  ¾ cup cubed ham or browned sausage
    1 unbaked 9-inch pie shell
    1 Granny Smith apple, peeled and
        sliced
  ½ cup raisins
  ¼ cup firmly packed brown sugar
    2 tablespoons all-purpose flour
    1 teaspoon ground cinnamon
    2 eggs
    1 12-ounce can evaporated milk
  ½ teaspoon salt
    1 cup grated Cheddar or Colby-Jack
        cheese
        Parsley

Place the ham or sausage in an unbaked pie shell. Spread the sliced apple over the meat. Sprinkle the raisins, brown sugar, flour, and cinnamon on top. In a medium bowl whisk together the eggs, evaporated milk, and salt. Pour into the pie crust. Spread the cheese on top. Bake in a 350° oven for 45 minutes or until set. Sprinkle parsley on top before to serving.

Note: This quiche may be baked immediately or prepared the night before and placed in the refrigerator until ready to bake.
MAKES 6 TO 8 SERVINGS.

Braxtan House Inn

Braxtan House Inn and Tea Room

210 North Gospel Street
Paoli, Indiana 47454
(800) 627-2982

A prominent Quaker businessman named Thomas Braxtan built this Queen Anne Victorian in 1893, incorporating parts of an earlier house that had stood here since the 1830s. The home has been carefully restored and now offers six guest rooms highlighted by stained-glass windows and oak, cherry, and maple woodwork. The house is listed on the National Register of Historic Places. Paoli, a winter resort area, is nearby, as are Amish farms, Spring Mill State Park's pioneer village, former Celtic Larry Bird's home, and a memorial museum for astronaut Gus Grissom.

Breakfast Mini Muffins

  ⅓ cup shortening
  ½ cup sugar
    1 egg
 1½   cups all-purpose flour
 1½   teaspoons baking powder
  ½ teaspoon salt
  ¼ teaspoon nutmeg
  ½ cup milk
  ½ cup butter, melted
  ½ cup sugar mixed with ½ teaspoon
        ground cinnamon

In a large bowl cream the shortening, sugar, and egg. In a separate bowl stir together the flour, baking powder, salt, and nutmeg. Add the dry ingredients to the creamed mixture alternately with the milk. Fill greased mini muffin cups two-thirds full. Bake in a 350°

oven for 20 to 25 minutes. Remove the muffins from the oven and immediately roll in melted butter, and then in the cinnamon-sugar.

Note: Guests at the inn love these. They say they taste more like cake! Make them "mini" because people feel too guilty eating a full-size muffin this decadent!

MAKES ABOUT 2 DOZEN.

Double Chocolate Chip Cookies

  2¼ cups all-purpose flour
    1 teaspoon baking soda
  ¼   teaspoon salt
    1 cup butter, softened
  ¾   cup sugar
  ¾   cup packed firmly packed brown
       sugar
    1 teaspoon vanilla extract
    2 eggs
    1 cup chocolate chips
    1 cup white chocolate chips

In a small bowl combine the flour, soda, and salt. In a large bowl beat the butter, sugar, brown sugar, and vanilla until creamy. Beat in the eggs. Gradually beat in the dry ingredients. Stir in the chocolate chips. Drop by spoonfuls onto ungreased baking sheets. Bake in a 350° oven for 12 minutes or so. Let the cookies stay on the baking sheets for about 5 minutes, otherwise, they will be too soft. Then remove to cooling racks.

MAKES ABOUT 5 DOZEN.

Ginger Cinnamon Chocolate Chip Cookies

    1 cup butter
  1½ cups firmly packed brown sugar
    1 egg
    2 cups all-purpose flour
    1 teaspoon baking soda
  ½   teaspoon salt
    1 teaspoon ground cinnamon
    1 teaspoon ground ginger
    2 cups chocolate chips
    1 teaspoon vanilla extract

In a large bowl cream the butter. Add the brown sugar and egg, and beat well. In a separate bowl mix together the flour, soda, salt,

cinnamon, and ginger, and blend well. Combine with the butter mixture. Stir in the chocolate chips and vanilla. Drop by spoonfuls onto greased baking sheets. Bake in a 375° oven for 10 minutes. Let the cookies stay on the baking sheets for about 5 minutes, then remove to cooling racks.

MAKES ABOUT 6 DOZEN.

Chocolate Truffles

  ⅓   cup Bailey's Irish Cream (or other
       Irish Cream)
    2 tablespoons coffee liqueur
  ½   cup heavy cream
    2 teaspoons instant coffee crystals
    2 cups chocolate chips
  ¼   cup butter, chopped into pieces
       Unsweetened cocoa (use a fine dark
       cocoa)

In a small bowl mix together the liqueurs and heavy cream, then stir in the coffee crystals. Set aside. In a saucepan melt the chocolate and butter over low heat, stirring constantly to avoid scorching the chocolate. Remove the pan from the heat. Re-stir the liqueur mixture (the coffee crystals settle to the bottom), then stir the liqueur mixture into the melted chocolate until blended well. Transfer the mixture from the saucepan to a bowl with a tight lid. Chill in the refrigerator for about 2 hours. Stir the mixture about every 30 to 45 minutes (set a timer), otherwise, the mixture will set up too firm.

When the mixture is firm (about the consistency of cold cookie dough), form the truffles by placing about a tablespoon onto a baking sheet lined with waxed paper. (The truffles will not be perfect shapes at this time.) Refrigerate the truffles (on the baking sheet) for about 1 hour.

Quickly roll each piece in your hands to make a nicely shaped candy. This step is kind of messy—t helps to work quickly and also to rub palms of hands with ice cubes before rolling. Chill a little longer.

Roll in cocoa (use a fine dark cocoa rather than the grocery-type baking cocoa. It tastes better). As an alternative to rolling in cocoa, the truffles can be dipped in melted (tempered) chocolate, or confectionery coating.

Variations: For Amaretto truffles, substitute Amaretto liqueur for all of the Irish and coffee liqueurs and omit the coffee crystals.

For hazelnut truffles, substitute hazelnut liqueur (Frangelico) for all of the Irish cream and leave in the coffee liqueur and coffee crystals.

MAKES 25 TO 45 TRUFFLES, DEPENDING ON THE SIZE.

Bourbon Balls

  2½ cups finely crushed vanilla wafers
    1 cup confectioners' sugar
    2 tablespoons baking cocoa
    1 cup crushed walnuts
    3 tablespoons light corn syrup
  ¼   cup bourbon
       Confectioners' sugar

In a medium bowl mix the vanilla wafers, confectioners' sugar, cocoa, and walnuts well. Add the syrup and bourbon and mix well. Roll into 1-inch balls, then roll in confectioners' sugar. Chill in the refrigerator.

The best way to eat these bourbon balls is to keep them small enough to pop in the mouth all at once, rather than nibbling on them. This gives the most intense flavor, especially the bourbon.

Variation: Substitute 1 cup of coconut for the walnuts. Also, 3 tablespoons of molasses can be substituted for the corn syrup. All variations are good! Another variation developed at Braxtan House is as follows: Substitute 1 cup of crushed hazelnuts for the walnuts, and ¼ cup of hazelnut liqueur (Frangelico) instead of the bourbon. Increase the cocoa to 3 tablespoons. This variation lacks the intense flavor from the bourbon, but has a rich and interesting flavor of its own. A good choice for those who dislike the taste of bourbon.

Chicken Stir-Fry

    4 boneless, skinless chicken breasts
    1 teaspoon granulated garlic (or
       minced fresh garlic)
    1 tablespoon olive or peanut oil
    1 cup sweet & sour sauce
  ¼   cup soy sauce or gourmet sauce
    2 tablespoons cornstarch
  ½   cup water
    4 cups frozen stir-fry vegetables
       White rice, cooked

Cut the chicken into bite-sized pieces and sprinkle with garlic. In a large skillet heat the oil and sauté the chicken over medium heat until lightly brown. Add the sweet-and-sour sauce and soy sauce to the chicken. Bring the sauce to the bubbling point, stirring constantly. In a cup blend the cornstarch with the water. Thicken the sauce with the cornstarch mixture to the desired consistency. Add the frozen vegetables and cook stirring constantly until thawed and hot. Serve over a bed of white rice.

MAKES 4 TO 6 SERVINGS.

Rice with Chicken and Peppers

        2 **tablespoons olive oil**
        4 **boneless, skinless chicken breasts,
            cut into small pieces**
    1½ **teaspoons ground cumin**
        2 **cups brown rice, cooked with 4 cups
            chicken broth**
        1 **red bell pepper, seeded and diced**
        1 **green bell pepper, seeded and diced**
        4 **green onions, chopped (tops and all)**
        3 **tablespoons lemon juice**
        1 **teaspoon salt**
            Pepper to taste

In a large skillet heat the oil and cook the chicken over medium heat, stirring frequently, until browned and tender. Stir in the cumin and cook for about 1 minute longer.

In a large bowl toss together the cooked chicken, rice, red and green bell peppers, onions, lemon juice, salt, and pepper until well mixed.

Note: This is a delicious, low-fat dinner entrée that is easy to make. It is also good with couscous substituted for the rice.

MAKES 4 TO 6 SERVINGS.

Crunchy Salad

        2 **cups chopped celery**
        1 **cup chopped green onions (tops and
            all)**
        1 **head cauliflower, broken up**
        1 **bunch broccoli, broken up**
        2 **cups frozen peas**

        1 **cup sour cream**
        1 **cup mayonnaise**
        2 **tablespoons vinegar**
        1 **tablespoon sugar**
    ½ **teaspoon salt**
        1 **teaspoon dillweed**
        1 **teaspoon celery seed**
    ½ **teaspoon garlic powder**

In a large bowl combine the vegetables. In a separate bowl combine the remaining ingredients for the dressing. Mix the dressing into the vegetables. Refrigerate for several hours or overnight.

This recipe can also be halved for a smaller group.

MAKES 8 TO 12 SERVINGS.

Rosewood Mansion Inn
❧

54 North Hood Street
Peru, Indiana 46970
(317) 472-7051

A nineteen-room Victorian home located near downtown Peru, the Rosewood Mansion dates to 1872. Among its nineteenth-century splendors are lovely stained-glass windows, an oak-paneled library, and a spectacular three-story staircase. The Rosewood offers eight well-furnished guest rooms or suites. Points of interest include the International Circus Hall of Fame, recreation at Mississinerva Reservoir, and Cole Porter's birthplace, home, and burial site.

Sausage Strudel

        3 **pounds bulk sage sausage**
        2 **onions, chopped**
        3 **pounds mushrooms, sliced**
    1½ **cups cream cheese**
            Phyllo dough
    ½ **cup butter**

In a large skillet fry the sausage. Transfer the sausage to a large bowl. In the same skillet fry the onions and mushrooms until just dry. Add the sautéed mixture to the large bowl. Blend in the cream cheese.

Spread 5 phyllo leaves with butter and stack them. Spoon on about 2 cups of filling and roll the dough around it. Repeat until the filling is used. Brush with butter before baking. Bake in a 400° oven for 25 minutes.

MAKES 5 STRUDELS OF 4 SERVINGS EACH.

Apple Crisp

        5 **to 6 McIntosh, Jonathan, or Granny
            Smith apples**
            Ground cinnamon
        1 **cup all-purpose flour**
        1 **cup sugar**
        1 **teaspoon baking powder**
    ½ **teaspoon salt**
    ⅓ **cup butter, melted and cooled**
        1 **egg**

Peel and slice the apples into an ungreased 8-inch square pan. Sprinkle with cinnamon.

In a medium bowl combine the flour, sugar, baking powder, and salt. Add the melted butter and egg. Stir together and crumble over the apples. Bake in a 350° oven for 40 to 60 minutes.

Note: The recipe can be doubled and baked in a 9 x 13-inch pan.

MAKES 6 SERVINGS.

Rosewood Mansion Inn

IOWA

Chestnut Charm Bed and Breakfast

1409 Chestnut Street
Atlantic, Iowa 50022
(712) 243-5652

*C*hestnut Charm is only a short drive away from the area made famous in The Bridges of Madison County. *The 1898 Victorian with turret, sunroom, fountained patio, and natural hardwood floors, returns guests to the turn of the century. It is also a comfortable place to stay with five elegant guest rooms each with its own theme and furnishings that recall the past. Golfing enthusiasts will enjoy the*

Chestnut Charm

two championship golf courses nearby. Gourmet dinners are served by reservation only.

Breakfast Fruit Puffs

2 cups bread flour
1 envelope fast-rising active dry yeast
¾ cup water
½ teaspoon salt
2 tablespoons sugar
¼ cup oil
1 egg
   Fresh or frozen fruit, sweetened, or canned pie filling
   Margarine or butter, melted
   Confectioners' sugar

In a large bowl combine 1 cup of flour and the yeast and heat with an electric mixer. In a saucepan, combine the water, salt, sugar, and oil. Warm to about 95°. Add the warm liquid to the flour and yeast mixture and mix well. Add the egg and continue mixing. Start adding just enough flour to make a ball, using a wooden spoon. The dough should be smooth, not sticky. Turn onto a floured surface and keep adding just enough flour while kneading until it feels smooth, elastic, and the dough makes bubbles.

Place the dough in a greased bowl. Place the bowl in a warm oven with a pot of boiling water. Let rise until doubled in bulk. Cut into the 12 equal balls.

In a separate bowl sweeten the fruit with additional sugar or artificial sweetener (or use pie filling instead). Flatten each dough

ball to make a small bowl, then put about a tablespoon of fruit in the middle of each ball. Enclose the fruit with the dough by pinching closed. Place each filled dough ball in a greased muffin cup, seam-side down. Let rise in a warm moist oven until almost doubled.

Bake in a 350° oven for about 20 minutes. Remove the pan from the oven. Let cool for a short while.

Dip in melted margarine or butter, then into confectioners' sugar. Serve and enjoy!
MAKES 1 DOZEN.

Florentine Benedict

4 medium potatoes, washed, pierced several times with fork
   Oil for frying
....
1 tablespoon butter or margarine
1½ to 2 tablespoons all-purpose flour
¼ teaspoon dry mustard
⅛ teaspoon white pepper
1 tablespoon chives
1¼ cups skim milk
½ cup shredded Cheddar cheese (2 ounces)
....
1 pound fresh young spinach leaves, washed and torn into small pieces
8 slices bacon, cooked, drained, and crumbled
¼ pound mushrooms, cleaned, trimmed, and sliced
4 thin red onion slices
8 eggs, poached
4 pieces bread, toasted

Bake the unpeeled potatoes for about 15 minutes in the microwave. Set aside to cool slightly. Dice in medium cubes, then fry in oil until browned. Remove from the pan and drain on paper towels. Keep warm.

In a sauté pan melt the butter over very low heat. Stir in the flour, mustard, pepper, and chives, and mix until smooth. Add the milk gradually, stirring constantly. Add the Cheddar cheese and continue to stir until the mixture is thick. If the mixture is too thick, add more milk. If the mixture is not thick enough, carefully add more flour paste (flour mixed with milk) and stir well. Keep warm.

Divide the browned potatoes into 4 equal portions and place on dinner plates. Place the spinach on top of the hot potatoes. Sprinkle on bacon, mushrooms, and red onion slices. Place 2 poached eggs on each plate. Add the sauce and serve immediately.

Serve toast as a side attraction to this very healthy dish.

MAKES 4 SERVINGS.

Chicken Almond Puff Appetizers

- ½ cup butter or margarine
- ¼ teaspoon salt
- 1 cup chicken stock and 1 teaspoon chicken bouillon
- 1 cup all-purpose flour
- 4 eggs
- ¾ cup finely diced, cooked chicken
- 3 tablespoons sliced, toasted almonds
- ⅛ teaspoon paprika

In a medium saucepan combine the butter, salt, chicken stock, and bouillon. Heat over low heat until butter is melted. Add the flour all at once and stir vigorously over low heat until the mixture forms a ball and leaves the sides of the pan. Remove from heat and cool to room temperature. Add the eggs, 1 at a time, beating thoroughly after each addition. Continue beating until a thick dough is formed. Stir in the chicken, almonds, and paprika. Mix well. Drop by small teaspoons onto a greased baking sheet. Bake in a 450° oven for 10 minutes.

Reduce the heat to 350° and bake for about 5 to 10 minutes longer or until golden brown.

MAKES 4 TO 5 DOZEN.

Spicy Apple Punch

- 2 cups of applesauce
- 1 cup apple juice
- 2 tablespoons firmly packed brown sugar
- 1 teaspoon ground ginger

....

- 2 quarts apple juice or apple cider, chilled
- 3 cups presweetened lemonade, chilled
- 1 quart lemon/lime soda, such as 7-Up or Sprite, chilled
- 1 Granny Smith apple, cored and sliced into rings for garnish

In a large pot combine the applesauce, apple juice, brown sugar, and ginger. Bring to a boil, stirring constantly. Cover, reduce the heat, and simmer for 10 minutes. Remove the pan from the heat, cool, and refrigerate the apple concentrate until cold.

When ready to serve, add the chilled apple juice or cider, lemonade, and soda to the apple concentrate. Garnish with apple slices.

Note: The concentrate can be cooked and refrigerated up to 2 days ahead or frozen until needed.

MAKES ABOUT 3 QUARTS.

The Abbey Hotel

❧

1401 Central Avenue
Bettendorf, Iowa 52722
(319) 355-0291

———————

The Abbey is an imposing Romanesque structure on a bluff overlooking the Mississippi River. Constructed in 1914-1917, it first served as a cloistered monastery for Carmelite Sisters and later as a retreat house maintained by the Franciscan Brothers. The current hotel reflects luxury unknown to the first inhabitants, and the magnificent Gothic chapel now serves as a romantic setting for many weddings. The Quad Cities area offers guests distractions, including riverboat casinos, theater, a harness race track, and a PGA championship golf course.

Chef James Shrimp Gumbo Recipe

- 5 tablespoons olive oil
- 10 cloves garlic, diced
- 1 celery stalk, diced
- 1 bunch green onions, diced
- 1 red onion, diced
- 1 white onion, diced
- 2 green bell peppers, diced
- 2 red bell peppers, diced
- 1 serrano pepper, diced
- ½ pound andouille sausage
- 2 cups white rice, uncooked
- 1½ gallons chicken stock
- 1 cup okra, diced
- 6 tomatoes, diced
- 2 pounds 16- to 20-count shrimp, shelled and deveined
- 1 bunch cilantro
- 1 tablespoon Tabasco sauce
- 1 tablespoon Worcestershire sauce
- ½ teaspoon black pepper
- ½ teaspoon parsley flakes
- ½ teaspoon filé powder
- ½ teaspoon cayenne pepper
- ½ teaspoon paprika
- ½ teaspoon salt

In a large stock pot heat the oil and sauté the garlic, celery, onions, and peppers until caramelized. Add the sausage and rice and cook for 1 minute. Add stock. Bring to a boil. Cook until the rice is just cooked through. Add the okra, tomatoes, shrimp, and the remaining ingredients and cook until the shrimp is done. Serve heated.

MAKES ABOUT 6 SERVINGS.

Chef James Caesar Dressing Recipe

- 8 large cloves garlic
- 1 2-ounce tin anchovy fillets in oil
- 3 egg yolks or pasteurized egg yolk product
- 3 tablespoons stone-ground mustard
- 1 tablespoon sherry vinegar

1   *teaspoon Worcestershire sauce*
½   *teaspoon Tabasco sauce*
5   *ounces grated Parmesan cheese*
1½   *cups olive oil*
     Juice of 1 lemon
     Salt to taste
     Fresh ground black pepper, to taste

In a food processor combine all ingredients except the olive oil, lemon juice, salt, and pepper. Mix well. Drizzle in the olive oil very slowly until the mixture forms the consistency of mayonnaise. Transfer the mixture to a medium bowl. Whisk in the lemon juice, salt, and pepper. Refrigerate for 24 hours.

MAKES ABOUT 3 CUPS.

Caramelized Onion and Prosciutto Tartlet

1⅓   *cups all-purpose flour*
½   *cup cold unsalted butter*
½   *teaspoon salt*
2½   *tablespoons ice water (approximately)*

1   *onion, julienned*
1   *clove garlic, minced*
½   *teaspoon sugar*
5   *eggs*
1   *pint heavy cream*
     Salt to taste
     Pepper to taste
2   *sprigs rosemary*
     Pinch freshly grated nutmeg
6   *ounces smoked Gouda cheese, grated*
24   *paper-thin slices prociutto ham (dry cured)*

     Grilled Asparagus (recipe follows)

In a food processor combine the flour, butter, and salt. Blend the mixture into a coarse meal. Slowly add water until the mixture forms a ball. Refrigerate for at least 1 hour.

Roll out and cut into 12 pieces. Place in individual tart molds. Bake in a 350° oven for about 10 minutes or until lightly browned.

In a dry sauté pan sauté the onion and garlic until the onion is slightly caramelized (adding sugar will help the process). In a small bowl whisk the eggs, cream, salt, pepper, rosemary, and nutmeg together. Place some of the onion mixture and Gouda cheese in each tart shells. Pour the egg mixture into each shell. Bake in a 350° oven for 10 to 12 minutes. Place 2 slices of proscuitto on top of each tart. Place on top of Grilled Asparagus and serve immediately.

MAKES 12 SERVINGS.

Grilled Asparagus

¼   *cup olive oil*
½   *teaspoon dried oregano*
1   *clove garlic, minced*
1   *tablespoon balsamic vinegar*
     Salt and pepper to taste
     Juice of ½ lemon
48   *small asparagus, peeled and blanched*

In a shallow bowl mix together all ingredients except the asparagus to form a vinaigrette. Marinate the asparagus in vinaigrette for about 10 minutes. Grill until heated through and serve on heated plates.

MAKES 12 SERVINGS.

Roasted Iowa Pork Tenderloin

2   *pork tenderloins*
¼   *cup olive oil*
1   *teaspoon fresh thyme*
1   *teaspoon fresh rosemary*
     Freshly ground pepper to taste
     Salt to taste

1   *teaspoon olive oil*
½   *red onion*
1   *stalk celery*
1   *cup dried cherries*
½   *cup dried figs*
¼   *cup honey*
1   *cup crumbled corn bread*
½   *teaspoon fresh ground pepper*
     Salt to taste
1   *teaspoon fresh thyme*

½   *cup dried cherries*
¼   *cup Kirschwasser or cherry brandy*
¼   *cup white vinegar*
¼   *cup sugar*
2   *tablespoons arrowroot*
2   *tablespoons water*

Make an incision in the center of the tenderloins with a knife, approximately ¾-inch wide through the entire length of the tenderloin. In a shallow pan mix the next 5 ingredients together. Place the pork in a pan and marinate for at least 2 hours.

In a skillet heat the olive oil and sauté the onion and celery over medium-high heat until the onions become translucent. Add 1 cup of cherries and the figs. Cook for about 1 minute, and add the honey. Remove the pan from the heat. Stir in the crumbled corn bread. Mix well and add the seasoning. Place the mixture in a pastry bag with a round tip and stuff the pork. Place the tenderloins on a roasting rack. Bake in a 350° oven for about 45 minutes, or until a meat thermometer reads 130°.

In a small bowl soak ½ cup of cherries in brandy for 30 minutes. In a saucepan bring the vinegar and sugar to a boil. Add the cherries and brandy, and flambé off the alcohol. In a small bowl combine the arrowroot and cold water. Add to the sauce and whisk thoroughly to prevent lumping. Cook for 5 minutes to thicken. Serve over sliced pork.

MAKES 2 SERVINGS.

Calmar Guesthouse and Bed and Breakfast

❧

103 West North Street
Calmar, Iowa 52132
(319) 562-3851

Prominent lawyer and poet John B. Kaye built this home in 1890 following a design that utilized solid wood for ceilings, walls, and floors. The living room features a stained-glass window depicting a wild rose, Iowa's state flower. There are five guest rooms all tastefully furnished. In addition to recreation provided by the Upper Iowa River and local lakes, the Laura Ingalls Wilder Museum is nearby in Burr Oak.

Apple Caramel Dip

    1 8-ounce package cream cheese
    ¾ cup firmly packed dark brown sugar
    2 teaspoons vanilla extract

In a small bowl cream all ingredients and
serve. Good with apple slices or other fruit.
Nuts may be added.
MAKES ABOUT 2 CUPS.

Dill Dip

    1 cup sour cream
    1 cup mayonnaise
    1 teaspoon chives
    ½ teaspoon Jane's Crazy Mixed-Up Salt
    ¼ cup dillweed
    ⅛ teaspoon Beau Monde spices

In a medium bowl mix all ingredients
together. Best if made 24 to 48 hours ahead.
    Serve with carrots, cauliflower, celery,
broccoli, or any fresh vegetables.
MAKES ABOUT 2 CUPS.

Cheese Potato Soup

    6 cups cubed potatoes
    1 cup diced carrots
    1 cup chopped celery
    1   onion or green bell pepper, chopped
       Green pepper or onion
    ½ teaspoon parsley
    2 chicken bouillon cubes
    2 cups water (or more)
    ¼ cup all-purpose flour
    3 cups milk
    1 pound Velveeta cheese, cut into
       chunks
       Dash pepper

In a pot cook the potatoes, carrots, celery,
onion or green pepper, parsley, and chicken
bouillon cubes in the water for 20 minutes.
In a cup mix the flour into the milk and add
to the potato mixture and cook, stirring constantly until thickened. Add the cheese in
chunks, and stir until melted. Season. After
the vegetables are cooked, transfer the soup
to a crock pot so that milk and cheese don't
scorch on the bottom. It improves the flavor
to simmer a bit more in the crock pot.
MAKES ABOUT 8 SERVINGS.

Juniper Hill Farm

❧

15325 Budd Road
Dubuque, Iowa 52002
(800) 572-1449

*E*ight miles northwest of downtown Dubuque and adjacent to
Sundown Ski Area, Juniper Hill
Farm is surrounded by hills, woods,
and nature trails. Built in 1940 as a
Scottish cottage, it was recently
expanded and remodeled in a country motif. The proximity of the non-
working farm to year-round
outdoor activities has earned the
home recognition as "An Inn for All
Seasons." The fresh produce grown
on the farm is often used for breakfast selections and late afternoon
refreshments. The three guest
suites offer views of the woods,
valley, or garden.

Juniper Hill Farm
Sour Cream Pancakes

    4 eggs
    6 heaping tablespoons all-purpose
       flour
    2 tablespoons sugar
    1 teaspoon baking soda
    ½ teaspoon salt
    1 pint sour cream
    ....

    2 cups fresh blueberries
    ½ cup light corn syrup
    2 teaspoons cornstarch
    1 tablespoon water
    ¼ teaspoon pumpkin pie spice
    1 tablespoon lemon juice

In a large bowl beat the eggs. Add the flour,
sugar, soda, salt, and sour cream, beat well.
Bake on a lightly greased griddle at 325°
using a scant ¼ cup per pancake.

In a medium saucepan combine the blueberries and light corn syrup. In a small bowl
combine the cornstarch, water, and pumpkin
pie spice. Stir into the blueberry mixture.
Bring to a boil over medium heat, stirring
gently and constantly. Remove from the heat
and stir in the lemon juice. Serve warm with
pancakes or waffles.
MAKES 24 SMALL PANCAKES.

Garden Delight Dip

    2 cups grated Cheddar cheese
    2 cups grated mozzarella cheese
    1 large tomato, seeded and diced
    1 medium green bell pepper, seeded
       and finely diced
    1 medium onion, finely diced
   10 shakes hot pepper sauce
       Ranch dressing to moisten
       Assorted crackers

In a large bowl combine the cheeses, fresh
vegetables, and hot pepper sauce. Moisten to
the desired consistency with ranch dressing.
    Make 1 to 2 hours prior to serving to
allow the flavors to blend. Serve with assorted
crackers.
MAKES 6 CUPS.

Peach Kuchen

    1 18-ounce box white cake mix
    1 cup flaked coconut
    ½ cup butter
    3 cups fresh sliced peaches, peeled
    2 tablespoons sugar
    ½ teaspoon ground cinnamon
    1 cup sour cream
    1 lightly beaten egg

In a large bowl combine the cake mix,
coconut, and butter until crumbly. Press
lightly into the bottom and up ½ inch on the
side of a 9 x 13-inch pan. Bake in a 350°
oven for 10 to 15 minutes. Cool. (This may
be done the night before.)
    Arrange peach slices over the crust. In a
small bowl combine the sugar and cinnamon
and sprinkle over the peaches. In a separate
bowl combine the sour cream and egg and
spread over all. Bake in a 350° oven for 25
minutes. Cool to room temperature before
serving.
MAKES 8 SERVINGS.

Hot Spiced Cider

- 4 cups apple cider
- 4 cups Cranapple juice
- 3 sticks cinnamon
- 2 teaspoons mulling spices
  Rum or Schnapps (optional)

In a kettle combine the cider, Cranapple juice, cinnamon sticks, and mulling spices. Bring to boil. Cover and simmer for 20 minutes.

Stir in the rum or Schnapps. Serve warm.

MAKES 8 SERVINGS.

Skiers Warm Beer Dip

- 1 8-ounce package cream cheese, softened
- 8 ounces Cheddar cheese with jalapeño pepper, cubed
- ½ cup beer
- 1 15-ounce can black beans, drained and rinsed
- ½ cup green onions, finely sliced
- ½ cup seeded and chopped tomato
  Tortilla or pretzel chips

In a medium saucepan heat the cream cheese, Cheddar cheese, and beer over low heat until melted and smooth. Stir in the beans, green onions, and tomato and heat through. Serve warm with tortilla or pretzel chips.

MAKES 8 SERVINGS.

The Mandolin Inn

199 Loras Boulevard
Dubuque, Iowa 52001
(319) 556-0069

N. J. Schrup, a leading Dubuque financier, built this extraordinary mansion in 1908. With its glazed-tile roof, turret, mosaic floors, and colorful windows, this Edwardian mansion was home for Schrup, who served two terms as state senator and received a knighthood from Belgium following World War I. Today it is a sumptuous inn with eight guest rooms decorated with period antiques. The inn takes its name from a leading painted glass window depicting Saint Cecelia, patron of musicians.

Cranberry Cake with Vanilla Sauce

- 2 cups all-purpose flour
- 1 cup sugar
- 2 teaspoons baking powder
- ½ teaspoon salt

....

- 3 tablespoons butter
- 1 cup evaporated milk
- 1 12-ounce package cranberries

....

- ½ cup butter
- 1 cup sugar
- ¾ cup half and half
- 2 teaspoon vanilla extract

In a medium bowl sift together flour, 1 cup of sugar, baking powder, and salt. In a large bowl combine 3 tablespoons of butter and the milk. Add the liquid to the dry ingredients and mix well. Add cranberries. Pour into a 5 x 9-inch loaf pan. Bake in a 350° oven for 1 hour.

In the top of a double boiler over simmering water melt ½ cup of butter. Add 1 cup sugar. Add the half and half and vanilla, and reduce the heat. Bring to a boil and simmer for 15 to 20 minutes until thickened slightly. Ladle the sauce on dessert plates and place slices of cake on the sauce.

MAKES 6 TO 8 SERVINGS.

The Mandolin Inn

Wild Rice Quiche

- 1 cup cooked wild rice (cooked with finely chopped carrots, onions, and celery)
- 1 cup shredded Monterey Jack cheese
- 8 eggs
- ½ cup half and half
- ½ teaspoon salt
- ½ teaspoon dried tarragon

Spray a 9-inch deep-dish pie plate with cooking spray. Place the rice and then the cheese in the bottom of the pie plate. In a medium bowl beat the eggs. Add the half and half, salt, and tarragon. Pour over the cheese and rice. Bake in a 350° oven for 1 hour or until the center is set.

MAKES 6 TO 8 SERVINGS.

The Richards House

1492 Locust Street
Dubuque, Iowa 52001-4714
(319) 557-1492

High Victorian architecture makes this bed and breakfast inn one of the finest and most original in Dubuque. A four-story, stick-style house, it features seven types of woodwork, eight ornate fireplaces, and nearly ninety stained glass windows. The inn places its guests within easy reach of Dubuque's most popular attractions including the Riverboat Museum, Cable Car Square, National Rivers Hall of Fame, and the Dubuque Dogtrack.

Apricot Coffee Cake

- 2 cups all-purpose flour
- 1 cup sugar
- 2 teaspoons baking powder
- ½ cup margarine
- 1 egg

The Richards House

About 1 cup of milk
1½ cans apricot pie filling

....

1 cup sugar
1 cup all-purpose flour
½ cup margarine

In a large bowl mix 2 cups of flour, 1 cup of sugar, baking powder, and ½ cup of margarine. In a 1-cup measure break the egg and fill with milk. Add the egg mixture to the batter. Spread in a 9 x 13-inch baking pan. Cover with the apricot pie filling.

In a medium bowl mix 1 cup of sugar, 1 cup of flour, and ½ cup of margarine. Mix until crumbly. Sprinkle the topping over the pie filling. Bake in a 350° oven for 45 minutes.

MAKES 8 SERVINGS.

Scalloped Pineapple

3 beaten eggs
1¼ cups sugar
8 slices bread, cubed
½ cup butter or margarine, melted
1 20-ounce can pineapple chunks

In a large bowl mix the eggs and sugar together. Add the bread cubes and butter. Add the pineapple and mix well. Pour into a 2-quart greased casserole dish. Bake in a 350° oven for 30 minutes, or until the top is golden brown.

MAKES 6 TO 8 SERVINGS.

Pumpkin Roll

3 eggs, beaten
1 cup sugar
⅔ cup pumpkin
1 teaspoon lemon juice

¾ cup all-purpose flour
1 teaspoon baking powder
½ teaspoon salt
½ teaspoon grated nutmeg
1½ teaspoons ground cinnamon
Confectioners' sugar

....

1 8-ounce package cream cheese, softened
¼ cup margarine
1 cup confectioners' sugar
½ teaspoon vanilla extract

In a large bowl combine the eggs, sugar, pumpkin, and lemon juice, and blend well. In a separate bowl combine the flour, baking powder, salt, nutmeg, and cinnamon. Add the dry ingredients to the pumpkin mixture, and blend well. Pour into a 10½ x 15-inch waxed-paper-lined pan. Bake in a 375° oven for 12 to 15 minutes..

Sprinkle a linen towel with confectioners' sugar. After baking, turn the cake onto the towel. Remove the waxed paper, and roll up jelly roll style. Cool for 30 to 40 minutes, rolled. Prepare the filling while the roll cools.

In a medium bowl combine the remaining ingredients. Unroll the cake, spread with the filling, and reroll.

MAKES ABOUT 6 SERVINGS.

Mason House Inn of Bentonsport

❧

Route 2, Box 237
Keosauqua, Iowa 52565
(319) 592-3133

Steamboat passengers traveling from St. Louis to Des Moines used to stay at the Mason House Inn, which was built in 1846 by Mormon craftsmen. Original appointments include coat hooks on the walls instead of closets and the only copper-lined, fold-out tub in Iowa. Breakfasts are served in the Keeping Room beside an 1880 Buck's cook

stove. There are plenty of outdoor activities nearby, including canoeing, hiking, golfing, swimming, cross country skiing, picnicking, and much more. The innkeepers will pack a lunch for daily outings into the countryside.

Mason House Inn

Pecan Sandies

2 cups margarine, softened
1 cup confectioners' sugar
2 teaspoons vanilla extract
4½ cups all-purpose flour
2 cups chopped pecans
Extra confectioners' sugar

In a large bowl combine all ingredients in the order given. Roll into 1-inch balls. Place on a parchment lined cookie sheet, about an inch apart. Bake in a 350° oven for 20 minutes. Don't brown. When cool, roll in extra confectioners' sugar.

Note: Unbaked dough can be frozen. They also keep well after baking.

MAKES 6 DOZEN.

Blueberry Buckle

1½ cups sugar
1½ cups margarine
3 eggs
6 cups all-purpose flour
1½ teaspoons salt
2 teaspoons baking powder
1½ cups milk
4 cups blueberries

....

1 cup sugar
½ cup margarine
⅔ cup all-purpose flour
½ cup old-fashioned oats
1 teaspoon ground cinnamon

Spray a 10 x 15-inch jelly roll pan with cooking spray, or line with parchment paper. In a large bowl cream 1½ cups of sugar and 1½ cups of margarine. Add the eggs, and beat well. In a separate bowl sift together 6 cups of flour, salt, and baking powder. Add the milk to the creamed mixture alternately with the dry ingredients. Spread two-thirds of the batter in the pan and sprinkle berries on top. Drop the remaining batter over the berries.

In a medium bowl mix the remaining ingredients and sprinkle it evenly over all. Bake in 350° oven for 40 to 50 minutes, or until a toothpick inserted in the center comes out clean.

MAKES 12 SERVINGS.

PB Monster Cookies

  1 cup margarine, softened
  1 18-ounce jar chunky peanut butter
  1 1-pound box brown sugar
  2 cups sugar
1½ teaspoons corn syrup
  6 eggs
  2 teaspoon vanilla extract
  9 cups quick oats
  4 teaspoons baking soda
  ½ teaspoon salt
  1 12-ounce package chocolate chips

In a large bowl combine the ingredients in the order given. Drop by tablespoons onto parchment-lined cookie sheets. Bake in a 350° oven for 12 minutes. Don't brown too much. They will be soft, but they firm up after cooking.

Note: The dough can be rolled and frozen, then sliced before baking. They also freeze well after baking.

MAKES ABOUT 6 DOZEN.

La Corsette Maison Inn

La Corsette Maison Inn

❧

629 First Avenue East
Newton, Iowa 50208
(515) 792-6833

This opulent, Mission-style mansion was built in 1909 by Iowa state senator August Bergman. The oak original woodwork, brass light fixtures, and art nouveau stained-glass windows give the inn its charm. The guest rooms reflect the French country decor with down-filled pillows and comforters. La Corsette menus often include seasonal herbs and vegetables from the backyard garden and the hostess's famous French bread.

Sausage Quiche

  3 eggs, beaten
  1 cup sausage, cooked and crumbled
    (Jimmy Dean Regular)
  2 tablespoons Dijon mustard
  ¼ cup diced onion
  1 cup light cream
  ½ cup grated Swiss cheese
  ¼ teaspoon salt
  ⅛ teaspoon pepper
  1 unbaked 9-inch pie shell

In a large bowl combine the eggs, sausage, mustard, onion, cream, Swiss cheese, salt, and pepper. Pour the filling into the shell. Bake in a 375° oven for 35 to 40 minutes, or until a knife inserted in the center comes out clean.

MAKES 6 TO 8 SERVINGS.

Broccoli Quiche

  1 bunch green onions, chopped
    (including green tops)
  1 10-ounce package chopped broccoli,
    cooked and drained
  6 eggs
  1 cup evaporated milk (or cream)
  ½ teaspoon cayenne pepper
  ½ teaspoon salt
  3 cups grated Swiss cheese
    Paprika

Grease an 8-inch quiche pan. Sprinkle chopped onions over the bottom of the pan. Add the broccoli.

In a large bowl beat together eggs, milk, cayenne, and salt. Pour over the broccoli mixture. Sprinkle Swiss cheese over the top. Bake in a 350° oven for 1 hour.

Sprinkle paprika over the top.

MAKES 6 TO 8 SERVINGS.

Almond Cream

  ½ cup sugar
  1 envelope unflavored gelatin
  ½ cup water
  1 cup heavy cream
  1 cup sour cream
  1 teaspoon almond extract
    Strawberries, blueberries, grapes, or
    sliced fruits such as peaches, melons, or pears

In a small saucepan blend the sugar, gelatin, and water. Let stand for 5 minutes. Bring the gelatin mixture to a rolling boil. In a large bowl whip the cream until soft peaks form. Add the sour cream, gelatin mixture, and almond extract. Turn into a 4- or 6-cup mold and chill until set.

Unmold onto a platter and surround with fruit.

Variation: Almond Cream and fruit may be may spread on thin sugar cookies and topped with fruit as desired.

MAKES ABOUT 4 SERVINGS.

The Woodlands

The Woodlands Bed and Breakfast

Box 127
Princeton, Iowa 52768
(800) 257-3177

*T*he Woodlands is a retreat in the midst of Iowa's rolling farm country. Outdoor activities include boating, golfing, fishing, hiking, and cross country skiing. Guests may also enjoy the privacy and solitude of the surrounding woods. A short drive away Iowa's Quad City metropolitan area, with its art galleries, theaters, shopping, and sporting events. An elegant breakfast is served by the swimming pool or a cozy fireplace.

Soup from the Woodlands

- 5 strips bacon, cut into ½-inch pieces
- 1 medium onion, coarsely chopped
- 2 large carrots
- 2 stalks celery
- 1 teaspoon dried marjoram
- 8 cups water
- 8 chicken bouillon cubes
- 2 large potatoes, peeled and cut into ½-inch cubes
- 1 teaspoon margarine
- 1 8-ounce package cream cheese

In a stockpot brown the bacon. Drain the fat. Add the onion, carrots, celery, and marjoram, and cook over medium heat for 15 minutes.

In a separate pot bring 8 cups of water to a boil. Add the bouillon cubes and boil until dissolved.

To the sautéed vegetables add the potatoes, margarine, and chicken broth. Bring the soup to a boil. Reduce the heat and simmer for 50 minutes.

Add the cream cheese and stir until blended.

Variations: Start with onions, a ham hock, and chunks of ham, sour cream or heavy cream, and a small amount of garlic just to spice it up a little. Add as much or as little of anything to fit your liking.

MAKES 6 TO 8 SERVINGS.

Babi's Bed and Breakfast

2788 Highway #6 Trail
South Amana, Iowa 52334
(319) 662-4381

*P*erfect for those who come to tour the Amana Colonies, this B&B is located on ten, tree-lined acres between the charming towns of South Amana and Homestead. It offers six rooms, a suite, and a "hayloft" with its own kitchen, living room, skylights, and sun deck. The inn gets its name from the old world term for "Grandma," and awakens guests to memories of home.

Prune Bread

- 1 cup sugar
- ⅔ cup shortening
- 3 eggs
- 2 cups all-purpose flour
- ½ teaspoon baking powder
- ½ teaspoon grated nutmeg
- ½ teaspoon ground allspice
- ½ teaspoon ground cinnamon
- 1 teaspoon salt
- 1 cup prunes, chopped
- 1 teaspoon baking soda
- ¾ cup prune juice
   Hot Caramel Sauce (recipe follows)

In a large bowl mix the sugar, shortening, and eggs together well. In a separate bowl sift the dry ingredients. Add the prunes. In a cup dissolve the soda in the juice. Add to the sugar mixture alternately with the dry ingredients, and mix well. Pour into a greased 4 x 8-inch loaf pan. Bake in a 350° oven for 30 minutes or until done. Serve with Hot Caramel Sauce.

MAKES 1 LOAF.

Hot Caramel Sauce

- 1 cup sugar
- 2 tablespoons butter
- ½ cup water
- ¼ cup light corn syrup
- ½ teaspoon baking soda
- ½ teaspoon vanilla extract

In a saucepan combine all ingredients and bring to a boil over medium heat. Cook until the color is golden. Skim off the foam.

MAKES ABOUT 2½ CUPS.

Cherry Pork Chops

- 2 cups cherry pie filling
- 2 teaspoons lemon juice
- ½ teaspoon chicken bouillon granules
- ⅛ teaspoon snipped parsley
- 6 pork chops, browned and seasoned with salt and pepper

In a crock pot combine the cherry pie filling, lemon juice, bouillon, and parsley, and stir to combine. Add the pork chops. Cook on low for 4 to 5 hours.

MAKES 6 SERVINGS.

KANSAS

*T*he Chenault Mansion was built as a home for the Edwin R. Chenault family in 1887. Furnished throughout with antiques, it features ornate woodwork of cherry, ash, and oak; curved glass windows; leaded glass; and beautiful fireplaces. Its Victorian parlor reflects the graciousness and hospitality of a bygone era. Attractions in Fort Scott include a restored military fort from the 1840s, and art, craft, and antique shopping in the downtown historic district.

Confetti Dip

3 eggs
3 tablespoons sugar
3 tablespoons vinegar
....
1 teaspoon butter
   Dash Tabasco sauce
⅓ to ½ cup salad dressing
1 small onion, chopped
*   Salt and pepper to taste*
1 8-ounce package cream cheese
½ cup chopped pimento-stuffed olives
1 green bell pepper, chopped

In the top of a double boiler over simmering water combine the eggs, sugar, and vinegar, and cook until thickened, stirring constantly.

Remove the pan from the simmering water and add the butter, Tabasco, salad dressing, onion, salt, pepper, cream cheese, olives, and green pepper. Blend well. Transfer to a serving dish.

This is very good with vegetables or chips.
MAKES ABOUT 2 CUPS.

Baked Lasagna

2 eggs
1 16-ounce carton ricotta cheese
¼ cup oil
1 onion, chopped
1 clove garlic, chopped
¼ cup chopped parsley
1 pound ground meat (½ beef and
   ½ pork)
1 16-ounce can tomato purée
1½ cups water
1 teaspoon salt
½ teaspoon pepper
1 teaspoon basil
1 16-ounce package lasagna noodles
4 cups grated mozzarella cheese
¼ cup grated Parmesan cheese

In a medium bowl beat together the eggs and ricotta. Set aside. In a large skillet heat the oil and sauté the onion, garlic, and parsley. Add the meat and brown. Add the tomato purée, water, salt, pepper, and basil, and simmer for 45 minutes. Grease a baking dish and cover the bottom with a thin layer of meat sauce. Layer half of the lasagna noodles on the meat sauce and cover with more meat sauce, half of the mozzarella, ricotta mixture, and sprinkle with Parmesan cheese. Repeat with the remaining noodles, meat sauce, and cheeses. Bake in a 350° oven for 30 minutes.
MAKES 8 SERVINGS.

Brownie Bombs

4 ounces unsweetened chocolate
½ cup butter
1⅓ cups sugar
½ teaspoon vanilla extract
3 eggs
¾ cup all-purpose flour
⅓ cup sugar
1 8-ounce package cream cheese
4 teaspoons all-purpose flour
1 egg
¼ teaspoon vanilla extract
½ cup semisweet chocolate pieces

In a saucepan melt the unsweetened chocolate and butter over low heat. Remove the pan from the heat and stir in 1⅓ cups of sugar and ½ teaspoon of vanilla. Cool for 15 minutes.

Beat in 3 eggs and ¾ cup of flour.

In a separate bowl mix together the remaining ⅓ cup of sugar, cream cheese, 4 teaspoons of flour, 1 egg, and ¼ teaspoon of vanilla. Spray an 8-inch square baking pan with cooking spray. Spread two-thirds of the chocolate batter in the pan. Spoon the cream cheese layer over the batter. Spoon the remaining chocolate batter over the cream cheese layer. Bake in a 350° oven for 20 minutes.

Sprinkle with chocolate pieces and bake for 12 minutes. Cool.

Cover and store in the refrigerator. Let stand at room temperature for 30 minutes to serve. Very rich.

MAKES 16 SERVINGS.

Cashew Cookies

- ½ cup butter
- 1 cup firmly packed light brown sugar
- 1 egg
- ½ teaspoon vanilla extract
- 2 cups sifted all-purpose flour
- ¾ teaspoon baking powder
- ¾ teaspoon baking soda
- ¼ teaspoon salt
- ⅓ cup sour cream
- 1¾ cups cashews, cut in pieces

....

- ½ cup butter, browned
- 2 cups confectioners' sugar
- 3 tablespoons heavy cream
- ½ teaspoon vanilla extract
  Cashew halves for garnish

In a large bowl cream ½ cup of butter and the brown sugar. Add the egg and beat thoroughly. Add the vanilla. In a medium bowl sift the flour, measure 2 cups, and add the baking powder, soda, and salt. Sift again. Add the dry ingredients to the creamed mixture. Stir in the sour cream and the cashews.

Drop from a teaspoon onto a greased cookie sheet. Bake in a 375° oven for 10 minutes.

In a medium bowl combine the remaining ingredients. Spread the icing on the cookies. Top each cookie with a cashew half.

MAKES 65 TO 75 COOKIES.

Peaceful Acres

Peaceful Acres Bed and Breakfast

❧

Route 5, Box 153
Great Bend, Kansas 67530
(316) 793-7527

A comfortable, sprawling old farm house, Peaceful Acres will remind visitors of lazy days spent at their grandparents' farms. Besides a working windmill, there are chickens, guineas, dogs, cats, and ten acres for roaming around. Breakfast is farm-style, complete with fresh eggs and homemade hot breads. A zoo, tennis courts, and museum are five miles away in Great Bend.

Caramel Pecan Rolls

- 1 package active dry yeast
- 1 cup warm water (105 to 115°)
- ¼ cup sugar
- 1 teaspoon salt
- 2 tablespoons margarine, melted
- 1 egg
- 3¼ to 3½ cups all purpose flour
- ½ cup sugar
- 2 teaspoons ground cinnamon
- 1 tablespoon corn syrup
- ⅓ cup margarine, melted
- ½ cup firmly packed brown sugar
- ⅔ cup pecan halves

In a mixing bowl dissolve the yeast in warm water. Stir in ¼ cup of sugar, the salt, 2 tablespoons of margarine, egg, and 2 cups of flour. Beat until smooth. With spoon or hand work in enough remaining flour until the dough is easy to handle. Place in a greased bowl, turn to coat, and cover tightly. The dough may be refrigerated overnight or up to 4 days or make into rolls and then refrigerate overnight.

Roll the dough into a rectangle and sprinkle with ½ cup of sugar and the cinnamon, roll up lengthwise, and cut in 1-inch pieces. In a bowl mix the syrup, ⅓ cup of margarine, brown sugar, and pecans. Pour the syrup into the bottom of a 9 x 12-inch pan. Place the rolls in the syrup. Bake in a 350° oven until lightly browned. Turn out onto a tray upside-down, so the sticky part is on top.

MAKES ABOUT 1 DOZEN.

Oatmeal Waffles

- 1½ cups all-purpose flour
- 1 cup quick-cooking oats
- ½ teaspoon ground cinnamon
- ¼ teaspoon salt
- 2 tablespoons firmly packed dark brown sugar
- 2 eggs, slightly beaten
- 1½ cups milk
- 6 tablespoons butter, melted

In a medium bowl mix the dry ingredients. In a large bowl mix the remaining ingredients. Add the dry ingredients to the liquid mixture, stirring to blend. Bake in a hot waffle iron.

MAKES 6 SERVINGS.

Thistle Hill Bed and Breakfast

❧

Route 1, Box 93
Wakeeney, Kansas 67672
(913) 743-2644

---

*T*histle Hill is often described by guests as an "oasis on the prairie." A 320-acre farm with sixty acres set aside for wildflowers, this is just the place to watch sunsets or stare up into a big black bowl of stars overhead. The three guest rooms in the cedar farm house are comfortable and unpretentious. Guests will have

a hearty breakfast by the brick fire-place while enjoying the view of an old fashioned English-style wild-flower and herb garden.

Almond Tea

    4 cups water
    ½ to ⅔ cup freshly squeezed lemon
         juice
    1½ cups sugar
    7 cups boiling water
    2 family-sized tea bags
    1½ teaspoons vanilla extract
    1½ teaspoons almond extract

In a saucepan boil the water, lemon juice, and sugar together for 5 minutes.

In another 3 cups of boiling water, steep the tea bags for 5 to 10 minutes. Mix the tea with the sugar syrup, and add the vanilla and almond extract. Add 4 more cups of boiling water. Serve steaming hot. May be cooled, refrigerated, and reheated as needed.

MAKES ABOUT 12 SERVINGS.

Warm Fruit Compote

    2 apples
    1 cup apple juice
    ½ cup orange juice
    2 tablespoons firmly packed brown
         sugar
    ¼ teaspoon ground cinnamon
    ⅛ teaspoon grated nutmeg
    ⅛ teaspoon ground cloves
    1 tablespoon cornstarch
    ¼ cup raisins

Core and cut each apple into 8 wedges. Cut each wedge in half. In a microwave-safe bowl stir together the apples, juices, sugar, and spices. Cover loosely and microwave on high for 8 to 10 minutes or until the fruit is tender-crisp, stirring after 4 minutes. Remove 1 tablespoon of juice to a small dish. Stir in the cornstarch until dissolved. Stir the cornstarch mixture back into the fruit mixture. Microwave uncovered on high for 2 to 3 minutes, stirring every minute until the mixture begins to thicken. Stir in the raisins.

MAKES 4 SERVINGS.

Featherweight Whole Wheat Pancakes

    2 cups whole wheat flour
    1 teaspoon baking soda
    3 tablespoons sugar
    ½ teaspoon salt
    2 eggs, well beaten
    ¼ cup white vinegar
    1¾ cups milk
    ¼ cup oil

In a medium bowl sift the flour, soda, sugar, and salt together. In a large bowl combine the eggs, vinegar, milk, and oil and mix well. Add the dry ingredients to the liquid mixture and stir only until smooth. Pour the batter from the tip of a large spoon onto a heated large frying pan or griddle. When the underside is browned and before the bubbles burst on top, turn, and brown the second side.

MAKES 6 SERVINGS.

Wakefield's Country Bed and Breakfast

❧

197 Sunflower Road
Wakefield, Kansas 67487
(913) 461-5533

A touch of country living awaits at this lovingly restored home. Guests will experience Kansas rural life in this farm setting. The innkeepers are the third generation to make a living on this diversified grain and livestock farm. The spacious bedrooms offer queen beds. The sunrises and sunsets are beautiful, and there is plenty of space for peaceful walks.

Overnight Crunch Coffee Cake

    2 cups all-purpose flour
    1 teaspoon baking powder
    1 teaspoon baking soda
    1 teaspoon ground cinnamon
    ½ teaspoon salt
    ⅔ cup butter
    1 cup sugar
    ½ cup firmly packed brown sugar
    2 eggs
    1 cup buttermilk
    ....
    ½ cup firmly packed brown sugar
    ½ cup walnuts
    ½ teaspoon ground cinnamon
    ¼ teaspoon grated nutmeg

In a medium bowl sift together the flour, baking powder, soda, 1 teaspoon of cinnamon, and salt. In a large bowl cream the butter, sugar, and ½ cup of brown sugar. Add the eggs one at a time, beating well after each addition. Add the dry ingredients alternately with the buttermilk, beating well after each addition. Spread in a greased and floured 9 x 13-inch pan.

In a bowl mix together the remaining ingredients. Sprinkle the topping over the batter. Refrigerate overnight.

Bake in a 350° oven for 45 minutes.

Variation: Divide the batter between 2 8-inch cake pans and make 1 without the nuts.

MAKES 8 SERVINGS.

Cranberry-Banana Frappé

    2 cups cranapple juice
    1 cup orange juice
    ¼ cup heavy cream or milk
    1 tablespoon lemon juice
    2 bananas, peeled
    ¾ cup crushed ice
         Fresh mint leaves for garnish

In a blender combine all ingredients. Blend on high for 1 minute. Serve in frosted glasses. Garnish with fresh mint leaves.

MAKES 2 SERVINGS.

Wakefield's

KENTUCKY

Jailer's Inn

111 West Stephen Foster
Bardstown, Kentucky 40004
(502) 348-5551

If you've picked out the card that says "Go directly to jail, and do not pass go," here is a choice spot to serve out your time. This place was a lockup from 1819 until as recently as 1987. Now it's unlocked—or, at least, they'll give you the key—and operates as a unique B&B inn in the heart of charming old Bardstown, where Stephen Foster wrote many of his songs.

Cheese Strata

    12 slices bread, cubed
     2 cups grated Cheddar cheese
     8 eggs
    ¼ cup butter, melted
     2 cups milk
        Dash Worcestershire sauce
    ½ to ¾ cup chopped ham

Spray a 9 x 13-inch baking pan with cooking spray. Layer the bread and Cheddar cheese in the pan.

In a large bowl mix the eggs, butter, milk, and Worcestershire sauce and pour over the bread and cheese. Top with the chopped ham. Cover and refrigerate overnight.

Bake in a 350° oven for 45 minutes.

MAKES 8 TO 10 SERVINGS.

Cheese-stuffed Toast

    10 slices French bread, 2 inches thick
    10 tablespoons strawberry preserves
     6 ounces cream cheese, cubed into 10
        pieces
     5 eggs
     1 cup milk
    ½ cup butter, melted
    ¼ cup maple syrup
        Dash grated nutmeg
        Maple syrup or melted strawberry
        preserves for topping

Cut a pocket in each slice of bread. Fill the pockets with 1 tablespoon preserves and 1 cube of cream cheese. Press together lightly. Place in a greased 9 x 13-inch baking dish.

In a bowl blend the eggs, milk, butter, maple syrup, and nutmeg. Pour over the bread slices and refrigerate overnight.

Bake in a 350° oven for 40 minutes or until golden brown.

Serve with maple syrup or melted preserves.

MAKES 8 TO 10 SERVINGS.

Baker House

Baker House Bed and Breakfast

406 Highland Avenue
Carrollton, Kentucky 41008
(502) 732-4210

With its ornate woodwork, hand-carved cherry staircase, massive walnut doors, seven hand-painted fireplaces, and original oil lamp chandeliers, the Baker House is a Victorian treasure. Built in 1882, by lumber mill owner Paschal Todd

Baker, the house remained in the family until 1946. After a 1979 restoration, the home has earned a spot on the National Register of Historic Places. Operated as a B&B with four elegant guest rooms, it is only a short walk from the broad Ohio River and Carrollton's Old Stone Jailhouse, or a few minutes drive from General Butler State Park.

Blueberry Yogurt Pancakes

1 cup all-purpose flour
1 tablespoon sugar
1 teaspoon baking powder
½ teaspoon baking soda
¼ teaspoon salt
⅛ teaspoon grated nutmeg
1 egg
½ cup plain yogurt
½ cup milk
2 tablespoons oil
¾ cup fresh or unsweetened frozen blueberries
Butter and syrup for topping

In a medium bowl stir together the flour, sugar, baking powder, soda, salt, and nutmeg. In a large bowl beat the egg with the yogurt and milk. Beat in the oil; then add the flour mixture, and stir just until moistened. The batter can be a little lumpy.

Grease a seasoned pancake griddle if necessary, and place over medium heat until a few drops of water dance on the hot griddle. For each pancake, pour a scant ¼ cup of batter onto the hot griddle. Sprinkle each pancake with several blueberries.

Cook the pancakes on one side until they are puffed, full of bubbles, and look dry at the edges. Turn and cook until the other side is golden brown. Serve at once with butter and syrup.

MAKES ABOUT 1 DOZEN 4-INCH PANCAKES.

Fresh Fruit with Vanilla Yogurt Sauce

1 3-ounce package light cream cheese
⅓ cup firmly packed light brown sugar
½ teaspoon vanilla extract
1 cup plain nonfat yogurt
8 cups assorted fresh fruit, cut into pieces
Chopped nuts (optional)
Shredded coconut (optional)

In a small bowl combine the cream cheese, brown sugar, and vanilla. Beat with an electric mixer on medium speed until fluffy. Add the yogurt and beat until smooth. Spoon the sauce over assorted fresh fruit. If desired, top with nuts or coconut.

MAKES 8 SERVINGS.

Gingerbread Pancakes

1⅓ cups all-purpose flour
1 teaspoon baking powder
¼ teaspoon baking soda
¼ teaspoon salt
½ teaspoon ground ginger
1 teaspoon ground cinnamon
1 egg
1¼ cups milk
¼ cup molasses
3 tablespoons oil
Lemon Sauce (recipe follows)

In a medium bowl stir together the flour, baking powder, soda, salt, ginger, and cinnamon. In a large bowl beat the egg with the milk. Beat in the molasses, then the oil. Add the flour mixture and stir just until moistened. The batter can be a little lumpy.

Grease a seasoned pancake griddle, if necessary, and place over medium heat until a few drops of water dance on the hot griddle. Pour a scant ¼ cup of batter onto a hot griddle. Cook the pancakes on one side until they are puffed, full of bubbles, and look dry at the edges. Then turn and cook until the other side is browned. Serve with hot Lemon Sauce.

MAKES ABOUT EIGHTEEN 3½-INCH PANCAKES.

Lemon Sauce

½ cup sugar
1 tablespoon cornstarch
Pinch grated nutmeg
1 cup hot water
2 tablespoons butter or margarine
½ teaspoon grated lemon zest
2 tablespoons lemon juice

In a medium saucepan mix the sugar, cornstarch, and nutmeg. Gradually mix in the hot water. Cook over medium heat, stirring constantly, until the mixture is thick and clear.

Add the butter, lemon zest, and lemon juice, stirring until the butter melts. Serve hot.

MAKES ABOUT 1½ CUPS.

Almond Biscotti

½ cup sugar
¼ cup margarine, softened
2 eggs
1 teaspoon almond extract
¼ teaspoon anise extract
1¾ cups all-purpose flour, divided
½ cup ground almonds
¼ teaspoon salt
1 teaspoon baking powder

In a large bowl combine the sugar, margarine, eggs, almond extract, and anise extract. Beat with an electric mixer at medium speed until blended well.

In a separate bowl combine 1½ cups of flour, the almonds, salt, and baking powder. Add the dry ingredients to the egg mixture, beating well. Stir in the remaining ¼ cup of flour to make a soft dough. Cover and chill the dough at least 2 hours.

Coat 2 sheets of heavy-duty plastic wrap with cooking spray. Divide the dough in half. Shape each half into a 12-inch log on the prepared plastic wrap. Transfer the logs to a cookie sheet coated with cooking spray. Remove the plastic. Flatten the logs to ¾-inch thickness. Bake in a 350° oven for 20 minutes. Transfer logs to a wire rack and let cool.

Slice the logs diagonally into ¼-inch slices. Place on cookie sheets, cut-side down. Bake in a 300° oven for 15 minutes. Turn the cookies over and bake an additional 15 minutes or until dry. Cool on wire racks.

MAKES 4 DOZEN COOKIES.

Sesame Waffles

1 cup all-purpose flour
1½ teaspoons baking powder
⅛ teaspoon salt
1 tablespoon sesame seeds
2 eggs, separated
¾ cup milk
½ teaspoon vanilla extract
¼ cup butter or margarine, melted and cooled
Butter and syrup for topping

In a medium bowl stir together the flour, baking powder, salt, and sesame seeds.

In a large bowl beat the egg yolks with the milk. Blend in the vanilla and melted butter. Add the dry ingredients and stir just until moistened.

In a separate bowl beat the egg whites until stiff but not dry. Fold the egg whites into the batter. Spoon the batter into the center of a heated waffle iron, using about a fourth of the batter for each waffle. Bake until the steaming stops, about 5 minutes. Remove the waffles carefully and serve at once with butter and syrup.

MAKES 4 WAFFLES.

The Ridge Runner

The Ridge Runner Bed and Breakfast

208 Arthur Heights
Middlesboro, Kentucky 40965
(606) 248-4299

Middlesboro is located near the point where Kentucky, Virginia, and Tennessee come together. Not far from here, Daniel Boone and other settlers pushed westward through the Cumberland Gap during the eighteenth century. The Ridge Runner doesn't go back quite that far, but it is a genuine Victorian mansion built during the 1890s, and visitors will find a lot of history to appreciate. They will also like the relaxed atmosphere, comfortable guest rooms, and delicious family-style breakfasts.

Apricot-stuffed French Toast

1   8-ounce package cream cheese, softened
1½   teaspoons vanilla extract
½   cup finely chopped walnuts
1   1½-pound loaf French bread
4   eggs
1   cup heavy cream
½   teaspoon grated nutmeg
1   jar apricot preserves
½   cup orange juice

In a mixing bowl beat the cream cheese and 1 teaspoon of vanilla until fluffy. Stir in the nuts. Set aside. Cut the bread into 1½-inch slices. Cut a pocket in each slice. Fill each pocket with 2 tablespoons of the cream cheese mixture. In a separate bowl beat the eggs, cream, nutmeg, and remaining ½ teaspoon of vanilla. Dip both sides of the bread into the egg mixture. Cook on a lightly greased griddle until golden brown on both sides. Place on an ungreased baking sheet. Bake in a 300° oven for 20 minutes.

In a small saucepan combine the preserves and orange juice and heat through. Drizzle over hot French toast.

MAKES 8 SERVINGS.

Baked Oatmeal

⅓   cup oil
½   cup sugar
1   large egg
2   cups quick-cooking oats
½   teaspoon baking powder
½   teaspoon salt
¾   cup milk

In a large bowl combine the oil, sugar, and egg. In a separate bowl, combine the oats, baking powder, salt, and milk. Add the dry ingredients to the liquid mixture. Pour into a greased 8-inch square pan. Bake in a 350° oven for 25 to 30 minutes.

Variations: Add raisins or other dried fruit before baking. Top the oatmeal with spiced apple rings before baking, so the apples are heated and the red juice adds a nice color.

MAKES 2 SERVINGS.

Diuguid House Bed and Breakfast

603 Main Street
Murray, Kentucky 42071
(502) 753-5470

With only three guest rooms and 5,000 feet of floor space, the Diuguid House offers distinctly personal service. Rooms are quite spacious, and the front parlor is a fine place to relax, play the piano, or meet with friends. Built by Kentucky pioneer and merchant Edwin S. Diuguid, the home is listed on the National Register of Historic Places. Another key attraction in the area is the Land Between the Lakes, an extraordinary fifty-mile-long peninsula created by a pair of TVA lakes, where visitors may explore The Homeplace, a living history farm depicting life as it was in 1850.

Eggs Florentine

6   large eggs
1   16-ounce carton creamed cottage cheese
½   pound feta cheese, cubed
2   cups grated Swiss cheese (or mozzarella)
½   cup butter or margarine
1   10-ounce package frozen chopped spinach
   Fresh grated nutmeg
   Hot pepper sauce

In a large bowl beat the eggs lightly. Add the cheeses and butter, and mix well. In a saucepan cook the spinach. Drain well, squeezing the excess moisture out in a towel. Add the spinach to the egg-cheese mixture.

Add the nutmeg and a few dashes of hot pepper sauce. Pour into a 3-quart baking dish. Bake in a 350° oven for 1 hour.

Cut into squares and serve. May be prepared the night before and kept in the refrigerator overnight or frozen and baked when needed. Split into 2 pans, keeping a frozen one in reserve.

MAKES 10 SERVINGS.

Breakfast Baked Apples

    2 large baking apples (about 8
          ounces)
    ½ pound ground pork
    1 cup chopped onions
    ½ teaspoon grated orange zest
          Scant ½ teaspoon freshly ground
          pepper
    ¼ teaspoon salt substitute
    ⅛ teaspoon fennel seed
    ⅛ teaspoon ground cinnamon
    1 cup sliced fresh mushrooms
    2 tablespoon water
    8 tablespoon reduced-calorie maple
          syrup (optional)

Cut the apples in half horizontally, core, and scoop out leaving about a ¼-inch thick shell. Chop the removed apple pieces.

In a skillet brown the pork with the onions, orange zest, pepper, salt substitute, fennel seeds, and cinnamon. Stir in the chopped apple and mushrooms, and cook until the mushrooms are tender. Drain off any excess fat. Spoon the mixture into the apples shells and arrange in a shallow baking dish. Add 2 tablespoons of water to the dish. Bake in a 375° oven for 40 minutes or until the apple shells are tender. If desired, drizzle each apple half with 2 teaspoons of reduced-calorie maple syrup.

MAKES 4 SERVINGS.

Diuguid House

Banana French Toast

    4 large eggs
    ¼ cup milk
    1 teaspoon vanilla extract
    ⅛ teaspoon ground cinnamon
    1 3-ounce package cream cheese (or
          more), softened
   12 slices raisin bread, crusts removed
    3 tablespoons butter
    3 tablespoons oil
    2 ripe bananas
          Orange Fruit Sauce (recipe follows)
          Sour cream

In a large bowl beat the eggs, milk, vanilla, and cinnamon until blended well. Gently spread the cream cheese on one side of 6 slices of bread. In a large skillet melt the butter with the oil. Zest and slice the bananas and place on top of the cream cheese. Dip these carefully in the egg mixture and place on the hot grill (300° is about right). Dip both sides of the remaining bread and place each slice over the banana slices. Cook on each side until golden brown. Serve with Orange Fruit Sauce and sour cream.

MAKES 6 SERVINGS.

Orange Fruit Sauce

    ½ cup sugar
    ¼ cup orange juice
    2 tablespoon lemon juice
    ½ teaspoon vanilla extract
    1 tablespoon orange liqueur (Triple
          Sec)

In a heavy saucepan combine the sugar, orange juice, and lemon juice, and heat until the sugar melts. Add the vanilla, and simmer until thickens (it is deceptive, it doesn't always look thick when it is). Remove the pan from the heat, stir in the orange liqueur.

The sauce may be stored in the refrigerator for future use, since this makes more than enough for 1 recipe.

MAKES ABOUT ¾ CUP.

French Breakfast Puffs

    ⅓ cup shortening
    ½ cup sugar
    1 egg
   1½ cups sifted all-purpose flour

   1½ teaspoons baking powder
    ½ teaspoon grated nutmeg
    ½ cup milk
          Melted butter
          Cinnamon-sugar
          Fruit jam (optional)

In a large bowl mix the shortening, sugar, and egg thoroughly. In a separate bowl sift together the dry ingredients. Add the dry ingredients alternately with the milk to the shortening mixture beginning and ending with the flour. Fill greased muffin cups three-fourths full. Bake in a 350° oven for 20 minutes or until golden brown. Brush the tops with melted butter and sprinkle with cinnamon-sugar.

Serve warm with a little jam, if desired.

MAKES 1 DOZEN.

Sills Inn

270 Montgomery Avenue
Versailles, Kentucky 40383
(800) 526-9801

---

*T*hose who love lush green pastures, whitewashed rail fences, and, above all, horses, should strongly consider a visit to Versailles and a stay at the Sills Inn. A restored Victorian Inn dating to 1911, the Sills places its guests right in the middle of the Kentucky Bluegrass horse country. The Kentucky Horse Park, Keeneland Race Course, and dozens of major breeding and training farms are nearby. A short drive away, Pleasant Hill (Shakertown) provides an interesting look at the simple life and distinctive furniture of the unusual religious commmunity. Pioneer life is recreated at the old fort at Harrodsburg.*

Cheesecake

1 16-ounce package graham crackers, crushed
⅓ cup butter, melted
¼ cup sugar
   Dash grated nutmeg
·······························
3 egg whites
·······························
1 8-ounce package cream cheese, softened
¾ tablespoon salt
1 tablespoon vanilla extract
½ cup sugar
3 egg yolks
·······························
1 cup sour cream
¼ cup sugar
¾ teaspoon vanilla extract
¼ cup graham cracker crumbs

In a medium bowl mix the graham crackers, butter, sugar, and nutmeg. Reserve ¼ cup for topping. Press the mixture into a 10-inch pie pan.

In a small bowl beat the egg whites. In a separate bowl mix the cream cheese, salt, 1 tablespoon of vanilla, ½ cup of sugar, and egg yolks. Fold in the egg whites. Pour the filling into the crust. Bake in a 325° oven for 30 minutes. Let rest 10 minutes.

In a medium bowl mix the sour cream, /4 cup of sugar, and ¾ teaspoon of vanilla. Spread on top of the baked pie and top with

¼ cup of graham cracker crumbs. Bake in a 325° oven for additional 10 minutes.
MAKES 6 TO 8 SERVINGS.

Baked Cheese Grits

3 cups water
¾ cup quick grits
1 egg, beaten
1 cup shredded Cheddar cheese
2 tablespoons margarine
⅛ teaspoon garlic powder
⅛ teaspoon hot sauce

In a microwave-proof dish microwave the water and grits. Stir in the egg. Add the Cheddar cheese, margarine, garlic powder, and hot sauce. Cook over low heat for 1 minute or until the cheese has melted. Spray a 9-inch pie plate with cooking spray. Pour the grits mixture into the prepared pie plate. Bake in a 350° oven for 30 to 40 minutes. Let stand 5 minutes before serving. Cut into wedges.
MAKES 6 TO 8 SERVINGS.

Spinach Soufflé

1 10-ounce package frozen chopped spinach, cooked, drained, and squeezed dry
2 eggs
1 8-ounce package cream cheese, softened
2 garlic cloves, minced
1 teaspoon salt
8 dashes Tabasco sauce
   Dash pepper
2 cups grated, Monterey Jack cheese
8 tomato slices

In a large bowl mix the spinach, eggs, cream cheese, garlic, salt, Tabasco, and pepper. Mix well with an electric mixer. Add the Monterey Jack cheese.

Spray 8 individual 4-inch ramekins with cooking spray. Divide evenly among the prepared ramekins. Bake in a 375° oven for 30 minutes.

Top with tomato slices 5 minutes before removing from the oven. Serve immediately.
MAKES 8 SERVINGS.

LOUISIANA

La Maison de Campagne, Lafayette

825 Kidder Road
Carencro, Louisiana 70520
(318) 896-6529

The French influence appears throughout La Maison de Campagne. Filled with quilts, canopied beds, and the scent of Cajun cooking, it is located in the heart of Acadiana within minutes of Vermillionville, with its museums and music, and Lafayette, with its world-renowned restaurants. Settled beneath the spreading limbs of pecan trees, the main house was once the home of a prosperous sugar cane plantation family. The balcony is the right place to enjoy a steaming cup of Louisiana coffee.

Grand Prize
Sweet Potato Cake Roll

- 3 eggs
- 1 cup sugar
- 2/3 cup cooked, mashed sweet potatoes or yams
- 1 tablespoon lemon juice
- 3/4 cup all-purpose flour
- 1 teaspoon baking powder
- 1 teaspoon ground cinnamon
- 1/2 teaspoon ground ginger
- 1/4 teaspoon grated nutmeg
- 1/2 teaspoon salt
- 3/4 cup chopped pecans
  Confectioners' sugar

....

- 1 8-ounces package cream cheese, softened
- 1/4 cup margarine, softened
- 1 cup confectioners' sugar
- 2 teaspoons concentrated orange juice (or 1 teaspoon orange juice concentrate and 1 teaspoon lemon juice)
- 1/2 teaspoon grated orange zest (or dried orange zest, or lemon zest)

Line a 10 x 15-inch jelly roll pan with waxed paper. Grease and flour the paper. In a mixer bowl beat the eggs with an electric mixer at high speed for 5 minutes. Add the sugar gradually. Stir in the yams and lemon juice. In a separate bowl stir the flour, baking powder, spices, and salt together. Fold the dry ingredients into the yam mixture. Pour the batter into the prepared jelly roll pan. Sprinkle nuts on the top. Bake in a 375° oven for 15 minutes.

Turn out onto a dish towel sprinkled with confectioners' sugar. Roll together with the towel and waxed paper. Cool. Unroll and peel off the paper. While the cake roll cools prepare the filling.

In a medium bowl whip the cream cheese and margarine together until fluffy. Add the confectioners' sugar and orange juice, and beat until smooth. Unroll the cake and spread with the filling. Roll up the cake with the filling. Wrap in waxed paper. Chill for 2 to 4 hours before serving.

Sprinkle with confectioners' sugar before serving. Freezes well for 2 to 4 weeks.
MAKES 12 SERVINGS.

Divine Day-old
Doughnut Pudding

- 4 cups scalded milk, cooled slightly
- 2/3 cup sugar
- 2 tablespoons butter, melted
- 2 tablespoons vanilla extract
- 4 eggs, beaten
- 1/2 teaspoon salt
- 6 to 8 day-old doughnuts, each cut into about 8 pieces each
  Orange Sauce (recipe follows)

In a large bowl beat together the milk, sugar, butter, vanilla, eggs, and salt. Add the doughnut pieces and pour into a greased baking dish. Place the baking dish in a larger pan. Fill the larger pan with water to about halfway up the sides of the baking dish. Bake in a 350° oven until set. Serve with Orange Sauce.
MAKES 6 TO 8 SERVINGS.

Orange Sauce

2   teaspoons cornstarch
¾   cup water
½   cup sugar
1½ cups orange juice
1   teaspoon fresh grated orange zest

In a saucepan make a paste of the cornstarch and 2 tablespoons of water. Set on low heat, add the sugar, then the remaining water and the juice. Cook until slightly thickened. Add the zest. Serve under and over each serving of Divine Day-old Doughnut Pudding.

Note: If the sauce becomes too thick, add 1 teaspoon of margarine and a little water.

MAKES ABOUT 2½ CUPS OF SAUCE.

Pralines Acadienne

2   cups firmly packed dark brown sugar
1   cup sugar
1   cup heavy cream
¼   cup butter
2   tablespoons light corn syrup
¼   teaspoon vanilla extract
2   cups pecan, halves

In a heavy saucepan combine all ingredients except the vanilla and pecans and cook until the temperature reaches 236° on a candy thermometer. Remove from the heat and let stand for 5 minutes. Add the vanilla and pecans. Beat with a wooden spoon until the candy looses its gloss. Drop onto waxed paper by spoonful.

MAKES ABOUT 48 PRALINES.

Walnut Grove Plantation

Bayou Boeuf Road #1488
Cheneyville, Louisiana 71325
(318) 279-2203

A plantation home of historic distinction, Walnut Grove dates to 1830. It has been meticulously restored with great care taken to preserve unique architectural details, including the Tudor-like beams of the ceiling and the classic room arrangements. Huge glass bowls of fresh-cut flowers, enormous urns of potpourri, and harpsichord music add to the ambiance of gracious hospitality. Local attractions include the Trinity Episcopal Church, sites of cotton gins, grain elevators, and antique shops.

Banana Fritters

1   cup sifted all-purpose flour
1¼ teaspoons baking powder
¼   teaspoon salt
1   egg, beaten
⅓   cup milk
2   teaspoons oil
3   bananas, chopped into quarters
    Oil for frying

In a medium bowl combine the dry ingredients. In a large bowl beat the egg with the milk and 2 teaspoons of oil. Stir in the dry ingredients. Dip the bananas into the batter and fry in a large skillet of oil at 375° until golden. Drain and serve hot.

Note: Good with confectioners' sugar or a dollop of raspberry jam.

MAKES ABOUT 4 SERVINGS.

Plantation Ham Creme

6   tablespoons butter
3   tablespoons all-purpose flour
2   cups milk
1   cup grated Swiss cheese
2   cups diced ham
    Pimentos and parsley for garnish
    Salt and pepper

In a saucepan melt the butter and blend in the flour. Gradually add the milk and stir into a smooth sauce. Cook, stirring constantly, until thickened. Add the Swiss cheese and diced ham. Garnish with pimentos and parsley, and season with salt and pepper to taste.

Note: Great over toast points or English muffins. For a lunch menu, serve in pastry shells with fresh asparagus and fruit.

MAKES ABOUT 8 SERVINGS.

The Acadian Cottage

Arabella near Prytania
Box 52257
New Orleans, Louisiana 70152
(800) 729-4640

This is the sort of quiet hideaway many New Orleans visitors hope to find. A quaint center-hall cottage built in 1902, the Acadian offers a casual charm enhanced by period antiques and crystal. At the same time, it is very near Magazine Street with all its eclectic shops, galleries, and cafes. Also close by is the St. Charles Avenue streetcar line-which takes guests past mansions to the French Quarter and the Uptown Riverbend district.

Apricot Nut Bread

2½ cups all-purpose flour
1   cup sugar
3½ teaspoons baking powder
1   teaspoon salt
1   cup finely chopped walnuts
1   cup finely chopped dried apricots
4   teaspoons fresh grated orange peel
1   cup orange juice
½   cup milk
3   tablespoons oil
1   large egg

Grease and flour 2 8½ x 4½-inch loaf pans. In a large bowl combine all ingredients. Beat with an electric mixer for about 30 seconds on high speed, scraping the sides constantly. When well blended, pour into the prepared pans. Bake in a 350° oven for 50 to 60 minutes or until a toothpick inserted in the center comes out clean. Place on wire racks to cool.

MAKES 2 LOAVES.

Chimes Bed and Breakfast

Constantinople and Coliseum
Box 52257
New Orleans, Louisiana 70152
(800) 729-4640

*T*he stained- and leaded-glass windows, French doors, cypress staircases, and brick courtyard at the Chimes are eloquent reminders of New Orleans' special charm. The relaxed atmosphere of the home and gracious hospitality of the hosts make the perfect accompaniment for the gourmet continental breakfast. Nearby, you can take the St. Charles streetcar into the city for an evening of world-class dining and excellent jazz.

New Orleans French Bread Pudding

  3   **large eggs**
1½   **teaspoons ground cinnamon**
1½   **teaspoons grated nutmeg**
1¾   **teaspoons vanilla extract**
 ¾   **cup sugar**
 ½   **cup warm, melted butter**
1½   **cups low-fat milk**
 ½   **cup raisins**
 ½   **cup chopped walnuts**
  6   **cups stale French bread, with crust (or stale bread or dinner rolls)**
      Bread Pudding Sauce (recipe follows)

In a mixer bowl beat the eggs with an electric mixer until small bubbles appear, approximately 3 minutes. Add the cinnamon, nutmeg, vanilla, sugar, and butter, and beat until mixed well. Slowly add the milk. Gently stir in the raisins and walnuts.

In a large mixing bowl, combine the stale French bread and the egg mixture and mix together. Let stand for 15 minutes, then push the bread down into the mixture to soak. Let stand for another 15 minutes, then push the bread down. Repeat.

Spray a 9 x 13-inch glass dish with cooking spray. Pour the mixture into the dish. Bake in a 300° oven for 45 minutes. Increase the heat to 400° and continue to bake for 20 minutes to brown. Serve with Bread Pudding Sauce.

MAKES 8 SERVINGS.

Bread Pudding Sauce

  3   **eggs**
  1   **cup warm, melted butter**
 ½   **cup sugar**
  2   **teaspoons brandy, bourbon, or rum**

In a blender whip the eggs until soft peaks form. Slowly, add butter while continuing to gently beat. Slowly, add the sugar while beating gently. Beat until cool. Add the liquor. Spoon the sauce over warm French Bread Pudding.

Note: Sauce may be served at room temperature or heated in a saucepan very slowly over low heat.

MAKES ABOUT 2 CUPS.

Barrow House Inn

9779 Royal Street
P.O. Box 700
St. Francisville, Louisiana 70775
(504) 635-4971

*C*onsisting of a pair of guesthouses, one dating to 1809 and the other to the late 1700s, the inn is located right in the middle of the historic district in one of Louisiana's most charming small towns. Rooms and suites are furnished with canopied beds, armoires, clawfoot tubs, and other antiques as much as 150 years old. The Mississippi River can be seen from the gazebo in the garden. An Arnold Palmer golf course is within 15 minutes as are eight area plantations for touring.

Barrow House Inn

Ricotta Cheese Pie for Breakfast

1½   **cups all-purpose flour**
 ½   **cup sugar**
 ½   **cup butter or margarine**
  1   **teaspoon ground cinnamon**

 ¾   **cup butter or margarine**
 ¾   **cup sugar**
  6   **extra large to jumbo eggs**
  1   **teaspoon orange extract**
  1   **teaspoon vanilla extract**
  1   **16-ounce carton ricotta cheese**
  2   **9-inch pie crusts**
  1   **egg white, beaten**

In a food processor mix the flour, ½ cup of sugar, ½ cup of butter, and cinnamon. Set aside to use, as a pie topping.

In a large bowl cream the butter and sugar with an electric mixer. Add the eggs, one at a time, and beat after each addition. Mix in the orange extract and vanilla. Add the ricotta and mix well again.

Brush the pie crusts with the beaten egg white, and then pour the filling into them. Sprinkle on the topping. Bake in a 375° oven for 1 hour. Let the pies cool for at least 10 minutes before serving.

MAKES 12 TO 16 SERVINGS.

Praline Parfait

 ¾   **cup butter or margarine**
  1   **cup sugar**
  2   **cups firmly packed light brown sugar**

½ cup heavy cream
1 cup milk
2½ cups chopped pecans
1 teaspoon vanilla extract

....

Vanilla ice cream
Whipped cream
Chopped pecans

In a large pot melt the butter or margarine. Add the sugars and cream and cook for 1 minute, stirring constantly. Add the milk and half of the pecans, then cook for 4 minutes, stirring occasionally. Reduce the heat to medium and cook another 5 minutes.

Add the remaining pecans and vanilla and to cook for another 15 to 20 minutes. Cool and refrigerate until needed, or use at once.

Reheat the praline sauce. Place 1 scoop of vanilla ice cream in a footed glass. Pour 2 tablespoons of hot praline sauce on top. Decorate with a spoonful of whipped cream and chopped pecans.

MAKES 25 SERVINGS.

Muffaletta Bread

1 large or regular loaf of French bread
½ cup margarine, softened
1 cup grated mozzarella cheese
½ cup grated Parmesan cheese
¼ cup chopped pimento-stuffed green olives
2 green onions, chopped
2 cloves garlic, finely chopped
¼ cup finely chopped salami or summer sausage
½ teaspoon dried oregano
½ cup mayonnaise

Slice the bread lengthwise, but not all the way through (like a po-boy bun is sliced).

In a medium bowl mix the other ingredients and spread on the bread thickly. Slice the bread, and then wrap the loaf in aluminum foil. Heat in a 350° oven for 20 to 25 minutes.

MAKES 8 TO 10 SERVINGS.

Creole Mustard Shrimp

3 tablespoons butter or margarine
2 dozen jumbo shrimp (or 3 dozen frozen large shrimp) peeled
⅓ cup dry sherry
1 cup butter or margarine
2 chopped green onions
1 teaspoon dried tarragon
2 tablespoons all-purpose flour
1 cup light cream or milk
1 teaspoon chicken broth granules
4 teaspoons Creole or Dijon mustard
2 tablespoons chopped green chives or green onion tops
Salt and white pepper to taste

In a large sauté pan melt 3 tablespoons butter over high heat. When hot, stir-fry half of the shrimp for 2 to 3 minutes. Remove from the pan and repeat with the remaining shrimp. Deglaze the pan with sherry until the liquid has evaporated.

Add ¼ cup of butter, then sauté the onions and tarragon for about 2 minutes. Add the flour and cook for 3 minutes. Add the cream and chicken broth granules, then cook for about 4 minutes or until the mixture thickens.

Whisk in the remaining butter, 2 tablespoons at a time. Add the mustard, chives, and salt and pepper to taste. If the sauce separates, re-whisk it briskly. Add the shrimp and heat.

MAKES 4 SERVINGS.

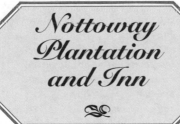

Nottoway Plantation and Inn

❧

P.O. Box 160
White Castle, Louisiana 70788
(504) 545-2730

*T*he Nottoway is a Greek Revival and Italianate mansion offering thirteen guest rooms. The biggest attraction of the inn, however, is the food of Johnny "Jambalaya" Percle, one of the Cajun Country's best known chefs. This cooking embodies the "good, straight forward, unpretentious cuisine" that he considers the soul of Louisiana food.

Nottoway's Oyster-Artichoke Soup

1 cup butter
½ cup chopped onion
½ cup chopped celery
2 cups chicken stock
1 cup quartered artichoke hearts
1 quart fresh oysters, chopped
4 cups heavy cream
2 cups half and half

In a large saucepan melt the butter and sauté the onions and celery for 5 minutes. Add the chicken stock and cook on low heat for 15 minutes. Add the artichokes and oysters, and simmer for 10 minutes longer.

Finally, add the cream and half and half. Heat thoroughly for 15 minutes on low heat.

MAKES 12 SERVINGS.

Nottoway's Sweet Potato Cinnamon Muffins

¾ cup cooked, mashed sweet potatoes
¼ cup melted butter
⅔ cup milk
¼ teaspoon vanilla extract
1¼ cups all-purpose flour
4 teaspoons baking powder
2 tablespoons sugar
1 teaspoon salt
1 teaspoon ground cinnamon

In a bowl beat the mashed sweet potatoes together with the melted butter. Mix in the milk and vanilla. Add the remaining ingredients and stir to blend. Do not overmix.

Spoon the dough into muffin cups lined with paper liners. Bake in a 450° oven for 15 minutes.

MAKES 1 DOZEN.

MAINE

Black Friar Inn

10 Summer Street
Bar Harbor, Maine 04609-1424
(207) 288-5091

*T*he Black Friar takes its name
from an English monastic order
noted for their generosity to travel-
ers. Operated in the spirit of the
hospitable friars, the inn offers six
tastefully furnished guest rooms
and a restful atmosphere. Wallpa-
pers are Waverly prints or Laura
Ashley, and the beds are dressed in
fine linens. The house dates to 1903,
and was one of the few mansions
that survived the 1947 fire storm
that destroyed much of
Bar Harbor. The finest
natural attractions of Acadia
National Park are only
minutes away.

Black Friar's Breakfast Juice

> *Orange juice (the kind with pulp is best)*
> *Cranberry juice*

Fill a juice glass about three-fourths full with chilled orange juice. Carefully fill the rest of the way with chilled cranberry juice. (The resulting juice will not combine, but remain separate, resembling a "tequila sunrise.") The exact look depends on the pulp in the orange juice-less pulp, less separation.
MAKES 1 SERVING.

Jim's Baked Apples

> 6   *Granny Smith apples*
> 1   *cup firmly packed dark brown sugar*
> ¼   *cup raisins*
> ¼   *cup walnuts (optional)*
> 6   *teaspoons butter or margarine*
>   *Cinnamon and nutmeg to taste*
>   *Ground cloves to taste*
> 1   *cup apple cider*
>   *Half and half or cream (optional)*

Black Friar Inn

Remove the core from the apples and peel away the top third of the skin. Place in a 9 x 13-inch baking dish. In a bowl mix the sugar, raisins, and nuts, and stuff the apples with this mixture. Place a teaspoon of butter on each apple and sprinkle with cinnamon and nutmeg, and dust lightly with clove. Pour the cider into the dish. Bake in a 350° oven for 50 to 60 minutes (don't cook them until the skin cracks, or the result will be apple-sauce), basting every 20 minutes.

Cool about 20 minutes before serving, or they will be very hot. Can be served with half and half or cream.
MAKES 6 SERVINGS.

Grandma Wilkin's Baked Eggs

> 3   *slices bacon*
> 2   *large eggs*

Precook the bacon partially, enough to cook away most of the fat, but leave the slices flexible. (If using the microwaveable kind, don't crisp them either.) Line 2 standard muffin cups with the bacon (depending on the bacon, this may take 1½ slices of bacon). Drop about 5 drops of bacon fat in the bottom of each cup, to prevent sticking (or lightly spray them with cooking spray). Crack one egg into each cup. Bake in a 350° oven for 20 minutes. Check the eggs by inserting a knife between the yolk and white to immediately tell if they're done, because the appearance can be deceiving.
MAKES 1 SERVING.

Graycote Inn

40 Holland Avenue
Bar Harbor, Maine 04609
(207) 288-3044

*T*he parlor here has a cheery fire-place where guests enjoy leisurely evenings and quiet conversation. The warmth and elegance of the parlor extend throughout the inn. Guest rooms blend traditional decor and furnishings with the comfort of modern amenities. Graycote Inn is within easy access to the pristine Acadia National Park and Cadillac Mountain. Breakfast is served on a sunny porch.

Apricot Hazelnut Biscotti

    1/3   cup butter or margarine
    2/3   cup sugar
    2   teaspoons baking powder
    1/2   teaspoon cardamom (or ground cin-
          namon)
    2   eggs
    1   teaspoon vanilla extract
    2   cups all-purpose flour
    3/4   cup toasted chopped hazelnuts
    3/4   cup finely snipped dried apricots
    1   egg yolk (optional)
    1   tablespoon water (optional)

In a large mixing bowl beat the butter with an electric mixer on medium for 30 seconds or until softened. Add the sugar, baking powder, and cardamom, and beat until combined. Beat in the eggs and vanilla. Beat in as much flour as possible. By hand, stir in any remain-

ing flour, as well as the nuts, and apricots.

Divide the dough in half. If necessary, cover and chill for 1 to 2 hours or until easy to handle. Shape each portion into a 9-inch-long log. Place the logs 4 inches apart on a lightly greased cookie sheet. Flatten slightly until about 2 inches wide. For a shiny sur-face, in a bowl stir together the egg yolk and water and brush onto the logs.

Bake in a 375° oven for 25 to 30 minutes or until a toothpick inserted near the center comes out clean. Cool on the cookie sheet on a wire rack for 1 hour. With a serrated knife, cut each log diagonally into 1/2-inch-thick slices. Lay the slices cut-side down on an ungreased cookie sheet. Lower the oven temperature to 325° and bake for 8 minutes. Turn the slices over and bake for 8 to 10 minutes more or until dry and crisp. Do not underbake. Cool on a wire rack. Store in an airtight container at room temperature for up to 2 days, or freeze in a freezer container for up to 6 months.

Variations: Leave out the nuts and apri-cots and substitute 1 tablespoon of orange zest and 1 cup of mini chocolate chips.
MAKES 32 SLICES.

Sour Cream-Apple Coffee Cake

    3   cups all-purpose flour
    3/4   teaspoon baking soda
    1   tablespoon baking powder
    1/2   teaspoon salt
    3/4   cup butter or margarine, softened
    1   cup sugar
    1/2   cup firmly packed brown sugar
    1   teaspoon vanilla extract
    3   eggs
    1 1/2 cups sour cream
    ....
    1/2   cup sugar
    1 1/2 teaspoons ground cinnamon
    1/2   cup finely chopped walnuts
    2   medium apples, peel, cored, and
          shredded
    1/2   cup golden raisins
    2   tablespoons cold butter, cut in
          pieces
    ....
    1/2   cup confectioners' sugar
    1   teaspoon soft butter or margarine
    1   tablespoon warm water
    1/2   to 1 teaspoon lemon juice

In a large bowl stir together the flour, soda, baking powder, and salt. In a large mixer

bowl cream 3/4 cup of butter with the sugars until light and fluffy. Blend in the vanilla. Add the eggs one at a time, beating well after each addition. Add the dry ingredients to the creamed mixture alternately with the sour cream, mixing to blend after each addition. In a medium bowl combine 1/2 cup of sugar, the cinnamon, and walnuts. Reserve 1/4 cup of the mixture. To the rest of the filling add the apples and raisins. Spoon the reserved 1/4 cup of filling over the bottom of a well-greased, lightly floured, 10-inch kugelhopf, bundt, or other tube pan with a capacity of 10 to 12 cups. Spoon in a third of the batter. Sprinkle evenly with half of the apple filling. Dot with 1 tablespoon of cold butter. Add another third of the batter, the remaining apple filling, and the last tablespoon of butter. Cover with the remaining third of the batter. Bake in a 350° oven for 55 minutes to 1 hour and 10 min-utes, until a long skewer is inserted in the thickest part comes out clean. Let the pan stand on a wire rack for about 10 minutes, then invert and remove the pan.

In a small bowl mix the remaining ingredi-ents until smooth and creamy. Drizzle on the cake.
MAKES 8 TO 10 SERVINGS.

Plum Cake

    1   16-ounce can purple plums packed
          in syrup
    1   cup unsalted butter
    3/4   cup sugar
    3/4   cup firmly packed dark brown sugar
    2   large eggs
    1   teaspoon vanilla extract
    2 1/2 cups all-purpose flour
    2   teaspoons baking powder
    1   teaspoon baking soda
    1/2   teaspoon salt
    2   teaspoons ground cinnamon
          Confectioners' sugar

Drain the plums, reserving the syrup. Pit and chop the plums.

In a large bowl beat the butter until creamy and light. Gradually add the sugars, beating until creamy and smooth. Beat in the eggs, then the vanilla. In a separate bowl sift the flour, baking powder, soda, salt, and cin-namon together. Sift the dry ingredients into the butter mixture, alternating with 1/2 cup of reserved syrup, beginning and ending with the dry ingredients. Stir in the plums. Pour the batter into a buttered 9 x 13-inch pan. Bake in a 400° oven for 25 to 30 minutes. Turn out on a rack and allow to cool. Dust with confectioners' sugar.

MAKES 12 TO 15 SERVINGS.

Eggs Dijon

6 hard-boiled eggs
½ cup mayonnaise or salad dressing
2 teaspoons pure maple syrup
2 teaspoons Dijon mustard
4 English muffins, split
8 thin slices ham
½ cup grated Cheddar cheese
Freshly ground black pepper
Chopped chives

In a medium bowl chop the hard-boiled eggs into rough chunks. In a large bowl combine the mayonnaise, maple syrup, and mustard, and blend well. Add the eggs. Toast the muffins very lightly, then top each muffin half with ham, then ¼ cup of the egg mixture. Sprinkle Cheddar cheese on top.

Place on a baking sheet. Bake in a 400° oven for 5 to 7 minutes or until thoroughly heated and the cheese is melted.

Before serving, sprinkle with a touch of fresh ground pepper and chives.

MAKES 4 SERVINGS.

Country Scramble

5 to 6 medium potatoes
2 tablespoons butter
1 large onion, chopped
15 eggs
½ to ¾ cup cold water
Salt and pepper to taste
1 tablespoon parsley
¾ cup sour cream
1 cup shredded Cheddar cheese

Peel and boil the potatoes until cooked. Chop into small pieces and let cool. In a skillet melt the butter and lightly sauté the onion. Add the potatoes and cook for about 20 minutes, stirring occasionally, on medium heat until cooked through and hot. In a bowl lightly beat the eggs, water, salt, pepper, and parsley. Add to the onion-potato mixture and scramble until almost set. Fold in the sour cream and Cheddar cheese. Cook until set.

MAKES 10 SERVINGS.

The Blue Hill Inn

❧

Union Street, P.O. Box 403
Blue Hill, Maine 04614
(207) 374-2844

This is an old-fashioned harbor village inn, which has been receiving guests since the 1840s. There are eleven guest rooms, some with fireplaces and separate sitting areas, and all have been furnished with period antiques. The decor is quietly and unpretentiously historic. Perhaps the biggest attraction of the inn is Blue Hill itself, a coastal village largely undiscovered by tourists. Guests will enjoy exploring Acadia National Park and the Maine coast.

Apple Breakfast Tarts

1 sheet frozen puff pastry
1 egg, beaten
1 tablespoon water
½ cup blanched almonds or hazelnuts, chopped finely
½ cup loosely packed light brown sugar
¼ cup raisins
2 medium Granny Smith or McIntosh apples

Line a cookie sheet with parchment paper. Allow the puff pastry to sit at room temperature for 5 minutes.

Cut 6 circles 2½-inches in diameter from the pastry. Place the circles on the cookie sheet. Mix the egg with the water, and brush onto the pastry.

Sprinkle each circle with nuts, sugar, and raisins, reserving 1½ tablespoons each of nuts and sugar. Pare and core the apples. Cut into ¼-inch slices. Using one-third of an apple per circle, overlap the slices and arrange into crescent shapes. Sprinkle with the reserved sugar and nuts. Bake in a 375°

The Blue Hill Inn

oven for 10 to 15 minutes, or until the pastry is golden brown.

Place on warm plates, dust with confectioners' sugar, and serve.

MAKES 6 SERVINGS.

Omelet with Smoked Salmon and Avocado

3 eggs
1 teaspoon cold water
Butter
3 slices avocado
1 ounce sliced smoked salmon
Whole-grain toast

In a small bowl beat the eggs with 1 teaspoon of cold water with a fork to blend the yolks and whites.

In an 8-inch nonstick skillet melt 1½ teaspoons of butter over high heat. When the butter melts pour the eggs into the pan. Vigorously move the pan back and forth until the eggs are set but the top is still moist.

Turn off the heat, place the salmon and avocado on half of the omelet, and flip the other half over. Place on a warmed plate and serve with whole-grain toast.

MAKES 1 SERVINGS.

Lillian Nold's Sticky Buns

2 packages active yeast
½ cup tepid water
1 teaspoon sugar
2 cups milk
½ cup sugar
2 eggs, beaten
½ cup shortening
2 teaspoons salt
5 to 6 cups all-purpose flour

½ to 1 cup butter
3 tablespoons ground cinnamon

1½   **cups firmly packed brown sugar**
2   **cups chopped walnuts**
2   **cups raisins**

....

½   **cup butter**

In a small bowl sprinkle the yeast over the tepid water. Add 1 teaspoon of sugar to the yeast and water and let the mixture stand. In a saucepan bring the milk to a boil and scald. Let the milk stand until tepid.

In a large bowl combine ½ cup of sugar, the eggs, shortening, salt, and milk, and mix well. Add the yeast, and stir in 2 cups of flour to make a soft sponge. Beat with an electric mixer at medium-high speed for 2 minutes. Stir in the remaining flour as needed until the dough does not stick to the sides of the bowl.

Turn the dough out onto a lightly floured surface and knead until elastic and smooth. Roll the dough into a rectangle approximately ¼ inch thick. Spread ½ to 1 cup butter thickly over the entire surface. Sprinkle the surface with cinnamon, brown sugar, chopped walnuts, and raisins until generously covered. Roll the dough lengthwise, jelly roll fashion, stretching the dough out towards the ends while rolling.

Cut into 1-inch slices. Cover the bottoms of two 9-inch square baking pans with the remaining butter and brown sugar. Place the slices in the pans, cover with a clean linen towel, and let rise until doubled in bulk. Bake in a 375° oven for 15 minutes or until done. When done, remove the rolls immediately by turning the pan upside down. Serve warm with butter.

MAKES ABOUT 1 DOZEN.

Lobster in Fragrant Ginger Broth

6   **1½ -pound lobsters**
3   **ounces ginger root, sliced into coins**
2   **medium fennel bulbs, chopped**
1   **dried star anise**
1   **cup Fino sherry**
2   **tablespoons Pernod**
    Extra gingerroot
    Extra sherry
3   **medium cucumbers, peeled, seeded, and sliced into ⅜-inch slices**
2   **tablespoons chopped cilantro**

In a pot steam the lobsters in 2 inches of boiling seawater or tap water salted with sea salt. Turn off the heat and drain just after they turn red. When cool, remove the tail and take out the tail meat. Remove the claws and reserve for another recipe.

Chop the lobster bodies into 2 or 3 pieces with a cleaver. In a large non-reactive stockpot combine the lobster bodies, ginger, fennel, anise, sherry, and Pernod. Add cold water to cover. Bring to a boil and simmer gently for 1 hour and 30 minutes, skimming the foam frequently from the surface.

Turn off the heat, and let the pot sit for 30 minutes. Strain through a coarse and then very fine sieve. Return the broth to the pot, cover, and set aside for 30 minutes. Skim off any foam and any pink or tan liquid that rises to the surface. Strain again, discarding any sediment from the bottom of the pot. Reduce over high heat with additional ginger and sherry.

In each of 6 serving bowls place 3 to 4 slices of lobster tail over a handful of cucumber slices. Cover each with 6 to 8 ounces of hot broth and sprinkle with cilantro.

MAKES 6 SERVINGS.

Soufflé Grand Marnier

2   **seedless oranges**
2   **tablespoons Grand Marnier**
2   **tablespoons sugar**
1   **tablespoon all-purpose flour**
4   **egg yolks**
1   **cup milk**
¼   **cup Grand Marnier**
5   **egg whites**
    Confectioners' sugar

Peel the zest from 1 orange and slice it into very fine julienne. Squeeze the juice from the orange. Zest the other orange and separate the segments, removing any white strands. In an ovenproof dish combine the juice, zest, segments, and 2 tablespoons of Grand Marnier. Bake in a 350° oven for about 1 hour or until the juice is very thick. Cool and cut the segments into 3 pieces each. (Increase the oven temperature to 400° if baking the soufflés immediately.)

Butter and sugar 4 8-ounce soufflé cups. In a heavy bottom saucepan blend the sugar, flour, and egg yolk. Gradually add the milk and cook over low heat until the sauce has the consistency of very thick cream, stirring constantly. Stir in ¼ cup of Grand Marnier and let the mixture cool. (This can all be done several hours before serving.)

About 20 minutes before serving, in a bowl beat the egg whites until stiff but not dry. Gently fold one-third of the whites into the custard until blended, then fold in the remaining whites, filling each cup about half full. Place one-fourth of the orange segments and zest on each cup and cover with more of the soufflé mixture, until each cup is almost full. Bake in a 400° oven for 12 to 15 minutes, or until fully puffed and brown on top. Remove from the oven, sprinkle with confectioners' sugar, and serve immediately.

MAKES 4 SERVINGS.

Kenniston Hill Inn

Kenniston Hill Inn

P.O. Box 125
Boothbay, Maine 04537
(207) 633-2159

*T*his country inn, first owned by a shipbuilder, claims a history that reaches back to 1786, before the U.S. Constitution was signed. Guest rooms are tastefully decorated, and acres of wild flowers, gardens, and shady maples invite visitors to explore the natural beauty of Boothbay. In addition to golfing and antique shopping, guest may plan an excursion to see puffins, seals, and whales.

Philadelphia-style Chicken Soup

    1   cup butter
    1   small onion, peeled and finely diced
    ½   carrot, peeled and finely diced
    3   stalks celery, finely diced
   20   medium mushrooms, sliced
    ¾   cup all-purpose flour
   1½   quarts chicken stock
    1   to 2 pounds cooked boned chicken
        meat, cubed
    1   cup sour cream
    1   teaspoon curry powder
        Dash salt and pepper

In a large thick-bottomed pot melt the butter and sauté the onion, carrot, celery, and mushrooms over medium heat, stirring constantly until the onions are translucent. Lower the heat and add the flour. Stir the flour until a roux forms. Simmer over low heat for about 2 minutes, stirring occasionally so it doesn't stick. Add the chicken stock and stir until the roux and stock are completely mixed. Add the chicken meat, sour cream, curry powder, and salt and pepper to taste. Simmer for about 30 minutes, stirring occasionally.

MAKES 10 SERVINGS.

Chicken Dijon

    4   boneless and skinless roaster
        chicken breasts, 6 to 8 ounces
        each
        Dijon mustard
        Salt and freshly ground pepper to
        taste
    ⅓   cup dry vermouth
    ½   teaspoon fresh lemon juice
    ¾   cup heavy cream or crème fraîche
    1   teaspoon dried tarragon
    2   tablespoons butter

Coat the chicken breasts with mustard and cover with plastic wrap to marinate for 2 hours. Arrange the chicken in a baking dish. Season with salt and pepper to taste and pour the vermouth over the chicken. Set the dish on the center rack of oven. Bake uncovered in a 350° oven for approximately 25 minutes or until done.

Scrape the mustard off the chicken and back into the cooking liquid in the baking dish. Transfer chicken to separate dish and cover with foil to keep warm. Pour and scrape the liquids into a sauté pan, add the

lemon juice, and bring to a boil. Reduce slightly. Whisk in the cream and tarragon. Turn the heat down to medium-high and continue to whisk the sauce until thickened, about 5 to 10 minutes. Whisk in the butter. Season with salt and pepper to taste. Slice the chicken lengthwise and fan out on serving plates. Spoon the sauce over the chicken slices.

MAKES 4 SERVINGS.

Ham and Swiss in Puff Pastry

    4   5 x 5-inch puff pastry squares
    1   tablespoon butter
    2   tablespoons finely chopped onion
    1   beaten egg
    1   cup shredded Swiss cheese (or three
        cheese mix-Swiss, Monterey Jack,
        and Cheddar)
    ⅔   cup coarsely chopped cooked ham
    1   tablespoon snipped fresh parsley
    1   teaspoon dried dillweed (or 1 table-
        spoon snipped fresh)
        Dash garlic powder
        Dash fresh ground pepper
    1   egg yolk
    2   tablespoons water

If using frozen puff pastry, let the pastry come to room temperature.

In a small saucepan melt the butter and sauté the onion until tender but not browned. In a medium mixing bowl combine the egg, cheese, ham, parsley, dillweed, garlic powder, and pepper. Stir in the sautéed onions.

Place 2 to 3 tablespoons of the filling just off center on each pastry square. Moisten the edges of the pastry with water and fold in half diagonally. Seal the edges by pressing with fingers or the tines of a fork. Place the pastry on an ungreased baking sheet. In a small bowl beat the egg yolk with the water. Coat the pastry with egg wash. Place in a 400° oven, immediately reduce the temperature to 350° and cook for 20 to 25 minutes, until browned nicely.

MAKES 4 SERVINGS.

Three-Cheese Pie with Tomato and Sweet Basil

   3½   cups coarsely grated mixed Cheddar,
        Monterey Jack, and Swiss cheese
    1   tablespoon all-purpose flour
    6   eggs, beaten
    ½   cup half and half
    1   medium tomato, diced
        Dried sweet basil
    3   to 6 strips of cooked bacon (well-
        drained), crumbled

Spray an 8-inch quiche dish with cooking spray. In a bowl toss 1 cup of cheese with 1 tablespoon of flour. Place in the bottom of the quiche dish. Spread the remaining cheese mixture on top. In a large bowl lightly whisk 6 eggs together. Add the half and half to the eggs and whisk until frothy. Pour over the cheese mixture. Spread diced tomato evenly on top of the cheese. Sprinkle with basil. Top with crumbled bacon. Bake in a 350° oven for 35 to 40 minutes, until the center is domed and nicely browned.

Let stand out of the oven for 20 to 30 minutes to allow the cheese to set up.

MAKES 6 SERVINGS.

Anchor Watch

A flashing lighthouse, lobster boats, fir trees, and beautiful sunsets provide the backdrop for the Anchor Watch. This oceanside B&B offers four delightful guest rooms, three of them with ocean views. The lawn slopes to a private pier. It is only a short walk to Boothbay's shops and the Monhegan Island Ferry.

"Cin" Pops

    1 egg
    ½ cup all-purpose flour
    ½ cup milk
       Melted butter
       Cinnamon-sugar

In a medium bowl whisk together the egg, flour, and milk until smooth. Pour into a mini-muffin pan sprayed with cooking spray. Bake in a 400° oven for about 15 minutes. While warm roll or brush with butter and sprinkle with cinnamon-sugar.

Variation: Place a piece of fruit in the center of each before baking.

MAKES 1 DOZEN.

Maine Muffins

    ½   cup oil
    1¼ cups buttermilk
    1   egg
    1   cup firmly packed brown sugar
    1   teaspoon vanilla extract
    2½ cups all-purpose flour
    1   teaspoon baking powder
    1   teaspoon baking soda
    ¼   teaspoon grated nutmeg
    2   cups small Maine blueberries
    ½   cup chopped cranberries
    ½   cup chopped pecans or walnuts
        Sugar for sprinkling

In a large bowl mix all ingredients except the fruit and nuts. Stir gently just until the flour is absorbed. Fold in the Maine blueberries and cranberries. Spray the muffin cups with cooking spray. Pour the batter into the prepared muffin cups. Do not use paper liners. Sprinkle with nuts and a little sugar. Bake in a 350 to 375° for 18 to 20 minutes. Adjust the time according to the oven. For the best taste these should be just a little crisp on the outside.

MAKES 1 DOZEN.

Blue Harbor House

❧

67 Elm Street
Camden, Maine 04843
(800) 248-3196

A restored 1810 New England cape, the Blue Harbor House offers ten guest rooms and carriage house suites. Some have canopied beds, and all are furnished with antiques and quilts. Nearby Camden harbor and village offer guests pleasant shops and restaurants, as well as a place for a quiet, evening stroll. Breakfast specialties include lobster quiche, cheese soufflé, and blueberry pancakes.

Blue Harbor House

Chocolate Brownie Soufflé

    ¼ cup sugar
    1 tablespoon unsalted butter, melted
    1 cup Bavarian Cream (recipe follows)
    ¼ cup unsweetened cocoa powder
    2 ounces semisweet chocolate
    2 egg yolks
    ¼ cup walnuts (optional)
    6 egg whites
    ....
    ½ cup heavy cream
    2 teaspoons rum
    1 tablespoon sugar
       Strawberries for garnish

Using a pastry brush, coat 8 4-ounce ramekin dishes with melted butter. Then line with half of the sugar. Refrigerate until needed.

In the top of a double boiler over simmering water melt the butter and chocolate. In a large bowl mix the Bavarian Cream, cocoa powder, the remaining sugar, melted butter, and chocolate. When the mixture becomes smooth and creamy, mix in the egg yolks one at a time. If the mixture appears too thick, add a small amount of milk until the mixture becomes light and creamy. Fold in the walnuts.

In a large bowl whip the egg whites until stiff. Fold into the chocolate mixture and spoon into ramekin dishes until they are three-fourths full. Bake in a 450° oven for 8 to 12 minutes on a wire oven rack. While they are cooking, make the whipped cream topping.

In a medium bowl combine the cream, rum, and 1 tablespoon sugar. Beat until stiff. When the soufflés are finished baking they should puff up and look like a small chocolate cake. Remove from the oven and serve immediately with whipped cream topping and a strawberry for garnish. Enjoy.

MAKES 8 SERVINGS.

Bavarian Cream

    6 tablespoons sugar
    2 whole eggs
    2 egg yolks
    2 tablespoons cornstarch
    2 cups milk
    1 tablespoon vanilla extract (adjust
       to taste)
    2 tablespoons unsalted butter, cut
       into ½-teaspoon pieces

In a medium bowl mix 3 tablespoons of sugar, the eggs and egg yolks, and cornstarch. In a saucepan scald the milk, 3 tablespoons of sugar, and the vanilla. Slowly stir the scalded milk into the egg mixture. Return to the saucepan. Cook slowly until the desired thickness. Remove the pan from the heat and pour the mixture into a mixing bowl. Place the mixing bowl in a larger bowl with ice and beat until cool, adding butter a little at a time. Add more cornstarch to thicken if needed. The cream will hold for some time in the refrigerator.

MAKES ABOUT 2 CUPS.

Maine Fiddlehead Cheese Soufflé

¼ cup butter or margarine
¼ cup sifted all-purpose flour
   Salt to taste
   Dash cayenne pepper
1 cup milk
2 cups grated sharp Cheddar cheese
3 egg yolks
4 to 6 ounces fresh fiddlehead ferns
½ teaspoon butter
2 ounces diced mushrooms
1 ounce diced onion
....
6 egg whites
   Confectioners' sugar

In a saucepan melt the butter and blend in the flour, salt, and cayenne. Add the milk all at once. Cook over medium heat until the mixture thickens and bubbles. Remove the pan from the heat, add the cheese, and stir until the cheese melts. In a separate bowl beat egg yolks until thick and lemon colored. Slowly add the egg yolks to the cheese mixture, stirring constantly. Cover the roux and keep it warm.

In a pot steam the fiddleheads. In a skillet melt ½ teaspoon of butter and sauté the fiddleheads, mushrooms, and onion. Reserve.

In a bowl beat the egg whites into stiff peaks. In a mixing bowl add the roux to the fiddleheads and fold in the egg whites. Pour the mixture into an ungreased soufflé dish or individual ramekins. Bake in a 400° oven for 15 to 20 minutes in a hot water bath until the top hat is lightly browned. Sprinkle with confectioners' sugar and serve immediately.

MAKES 6 4-OUNCES SOUFFLÉS.

Lobster Quiche

   Meat from 2¼ pounds lobsters
1 medium onion, chopped
   Dash dried tarragon
¼ cup grated Cheddar or Jack cheese
¼ cup chopped scallions
1 tablespoon all-purpose flour
¼ cup chopped fresh vegetables (peas, broccoli, etc.)
1 unbaked 9-inch pie shell
1 4-egg package egg substitute
1 cup half and half
½ cup chopped almonds

In a skillet sauté the lobster, onion, and tarragon until done. In a large bowl mix the lobster, cheese, scallions, flour, and vegetables. Form the pie shell into a quiche dish, and add lobster mixture. In a medium bowl combine the egg substitute, and half and half. Pour the mixture over the lobster mixture. Sprinkle with almonds. Bake in a 325° oven for 1 hour.

MAKES 5 SERVINGS.

Lobster Stew

2 lobsters (about 2 cups meat)
2 quarts salted water
....
4 medium red potatoes
2 cups water
....
6 teaspoons butter
½ cup chopped onion
½ cup chopped celery
½ cup grated carrots
¼ cup chopped scallions
¼ cup chopped leeks
¼ cup chopped red bell pepper
¼ cup chopped green bell pepper
1 cup evaporated milk
2 cups whole milk
1 cup sherry
1 teaspoon sesame seed
   Salt and pepper to taste
   Fresh parsley sprigs for garnish

In a large stockpot or lobster pot boil the lobsters in 2 quarts of salted water until done, about 20 minutes. Discard the water. Allow the lobsters to cool.

Remove the meat and tamali (the green stuff) from shells. Save the tail and claw shells.

In a pot boil the potatoes in 2 cups of water until completely cooked and very soft. Drain and reserve the water. Cut the potatoes into quarters.

In a large non-reactive stock pot melt 4 teaspoons of butter, and sauté the onion, celery, carrots, scallions, leeks, and green bell peppers. Add the evaporated and whole milk, sherry, potatoes, and potato water to the pot. Lower the heat to a simmer.

Cut the lobster meat into pieces. In a skillet melt 2 teaspoon of butter and sauté the lobster meat and tomalley and 1 teaspoon of sesame seed for 5 minutes. Add to the stew. In the same skillet sauté the shells for 5 minutes, and add them to the stew. The shells will give the stew a roasted flavor. Cook over low heat for 1 hour and 30 minutes. Season with salt and pepper to taste. Remove the lobster shells and serve in large soup bowls. Garnish with a sprig of fresh parsley.

MAKES 4 SERVINGS.

Fat-free Stuffed French Toast

6 ounces fat-free cream cheese
6 ounces fat-free yogurt
3 ounces fat-free sour cream
....
2 8-ounce packages egg substitute
1 cup skim milk
1 teaspoon vanilla extract
....
12 slices whole wheat bread, crusts removed
1 cup fresh Maine blueberries
½ cup frozen raspberries, crushed
....
   Confectioners' sugar
   Maine maple syrup

In a medium bowl mix the cream cheese, yogurt, and sour cream.

In a separate bowl mix together the egg substitute, milk, and vanilla. Coat 6 slices of whole wheat bread with stuffing and place stuffing-side-up in a large pan. Sprinkle fruit generously on top of the stuffing. Coat the remaining 6 slices with stuffing and place stuffing-side down on top of the fruit, making a sandwich. Pour the batter over the sandwiches and soak for 30 minutes. Cook on a grill at medium heat until golden brown, turning several times. Slice diagonally, place on a large plate, and serve hot with confectioners' sugar and Maine maple syrup.

MAKES 4 SERVINGS.

Edgecombe-Coles House

Edgecombe-Coles House

HC60, Box 3010
Camden, Maine 04843
(207) 236-2336

One wing of this delightfully rambling house dates to the beginning of the 19th century, while the rest of the inn is not nearly so old—only one century—as it was built in 1891. The inn sits well back from the road behind a high stone wall and hedge. The porch has a swing, wicker chairs, and breakfast tables for nice weather. Guest rooms feature country antiques, oriental rugs, and original art. Camden's harbor and business district are within an easy walk.

Peach Schnapps French Toast

    2   cups sliced peaches (fresh or
            canned)
    1   cup Peach Schnapps
    1   cup cream
    1   teaspoon ground cinnamon
    ¼   cup firmly packed light brown sugar
    36 slices French bread
            Confectioners' sugar or crushed
            cornflakes (optional)

In a blender combine the peaches, Schnapps, cream, cinnamon, and sugar and process on high until fully liquefied. Pour the mixture into flat pans and soak the bread slices in it overnight.

In the morning cook the bread on a lightly oiled nonstick griddle over medium-high heat. The bread may be dipped in crushed cornflakes before cooking. If not, sprinkle with confectioners' sugar before serving.
MAKES 12 SERVINGS.

Scrambled Eggs Edgecombe-Coles

    24 large eggs
    6   tablespoons Worcestershire sauce
            Fresh ground pepper
    2   tablespoons butter
    8   ounces sharp Cheddar cheese, cut
            into 1-inch chunks
    1   pound bacon, cooked crisp, drained,
            and crumbled

In a large bowl mix the eggs, sauce, and pepper thoroughly with a wire whisk. In a large nonstick pan or wok melt the butter over medium to high heat. Pour the egg mixture into the pan with the cheese and bacon. Stir constantly with wooden spoon until the eggs are moist but not runny. Serve with waffles or pancakes

Variation: Substitute egg whites for the eggs, ½ cup of imitation bacon bits for the bacon, 4 ounces of grated Parmesan for the Cheddar, and olive oil for the butter. Add 2 cups of stir-fried asparagus chunks to this version.
MAKES 12 SERVINGS.

The Elms

The Elms

84 Elm Street
Camden, Maine 04843
(204) 236-6250

Seafarer Captain Calvin Curtis built this handsome Colonial house in 1806. Furnishings are appropriate to the period, and a relaxed and friendly feeling prevails. On cool evenings, guests enjoy warming themselves beside the Franklin stove. The hosts share their collection of art, books, and nautical mementos, especially those items that reveal their interest in lighthouses. Breakfast may feature blueberry-cornmeal pancakes, plum-tomato and fresh basil quiche, or French toast with peaches.

Apple Yogurt Kuchen

    ½   cup margarine or butter, softened
    ¼   cup sugar
    1   teaspoon vanilla extract
    1   egg
    1   cup all-purpose flour
    ½   teaspoon baking powder
    ¼   teaspoon salt

    ½   cup fat-free vanilla yogurt
    1   egg
    1½ thinly sliced, peeled apples
    1   teaspoon ground cinnamon
    3   tablespoons sugar

Grease a 9-inch springform pan.

In a large bowl, cream the margarine and ¼ cup of sugar until light and fluffy. Add the vanilla and egg, and beat well. In a separate bowl combine the flour, baking powder, and salt. Gradually add the dry ingredients to the margarine mixture, mixing well. Spread the dough over the bottom and 1-inch up the sides of the pan.

In a small bowl combine the yogurt and egg. Spread over the dough. Arrange the sliced apples over the filling. Sprinkle with cinnamon and 3 tablespoons of sugar. Bake in a 350° oven for 35 to 45 minutes or until golden brown. Cool for 10 minutes. Remove the sides of the pan. Store in the refrigerator.
MAKES 6 TO 8 SERVINGS.

Apple and Cheese Baked Pancake

    ¼   cup margarine or butter
    1   cup all-purpose flour
    1   cup milk
    ¼   teaspoon salt
    4   eggs

1 cup shredded Swiss cheese (or white
    Cheddar or Monterey Jack cheese)
½ lemon
2 medium tart apples (or pears),
    thinly sliced
    Confectioners' sugar

In a 9 x 13-inch pan heat the margarine in a 425° oven until hot and bubbly.

In a medium bowl beat together the flour, milk, salt, and eggs until blended well. Pour the batter into the pan with the hot melted butter.

Bake in a 425° oven for 20 to 25 minutes until the sides of the pancake are puffed and deep golden brown. Remove the pan from the oven and sprinkle with cheese. Squeeze the juice from the lemon half over the apple slices to keep from getting brown. Arrange the apple slices in the center of the pancake. Sprinkle with confectioners' sugar.

MAKES 4 SERVINGS.

Poached Pears with Raspberry Sauce

4 medium ripe pears (such as Anjou or
    Bosc)
    Lemon juice
½ cup sugar
1 teaspoon grated lemon zest
3 whole cloves
1 cinnamon stick
4 cups water
1 10-ounce package frozen raspberries
    in syrup (or plain frozen raspber-
    ries with sugar to taste)

Peel the pears. Remove the core from the bottom and leave the stems attached. Brush the pears with lemon juice.

In a large kettle combine the sugar, lemon peel, cloves, cinnamon stick, and water, and bring the mixture to a boil. Add the pears in an upright position. Reduce the heat, cover, and simmer for 20 to 25 minutes or until the pears are tender. Chill the pears in the poaching liquid.

Meanwhile, force the raspberries through a sieve to remove the seeds. Chill.

To serve, place the pears upright in individual dessert dishes. Spoon sauce over each pear.

MAKES 4 SERVINGS.

Hawthorn Inn

❧

9 High Street
Camden, Maine 04843
(207) 236-8842

A stately Victorian house built in 1894 by a prosperous coal merchant, the Hawthorn takes advantage of the harbor and the hills. The home has retained many original features, including two parlors, original stained glass windows, and period antique furnishings. Guests may choose from six rooms in the main house or four large luxury rooms in the carriage house, with views of the harbor or Camden Hills. Adventurous guests may sign up for sea kayaking or day sails on Penobscot Bay.

Sour Cream Apricot Coffee Cake

1 cup all-purpose flour
1 tablespoon baking powder
½ teaspoon salt
¾ cup plus 1 tablespoon finely chopped
    dried apricots
¾ cup firmly packed light brown sugar
½ cup butter, softened
¾ cup almond paste
1⅓ cups light sour cream
2 large eggs
½ cup apricot preserves
½ cup confectioners' sugar
¼ cup apricot preserves
¼ teaspoon water
    Sliced natural almonds

Grease and lightly flour a 10-inch bundt pan or other decorative tube pan. In a medium bowl sift together the flour, baking powder, and salt. Stir in ¾ cup of chopped apricots until lightly coated with the flour mixture. Set aside.

Hawthorn Inn

In a large bowl beat the sugar and butter with an electric mixer on medium speed until light and fluffy. Crumble in the almond paste and beat until blended. Add the sour cream and eggs and beat until blended. Stir in ½ cup of apricot preserves.

With an electric mixer on very low speed add the flour mixture to the sour cream mixture and beat just until blended. Do not overmix. Spoon the batter into the prepared pan. Bake in a 350° oven for 50 to 60 minutes or until a cake tester inserted in the center comes out clean.

Cool the cake in the pan on a wire rack for 10 minutes. Turn the cake out onto a serving plate and cool completely. Meanwhile, prepare the apricot glaze. In a small bowl stir together ½ cup of confectioners' sugar, ¼ cup of apricot preserves, and ¼ teaspoon of water until the sugar dissolves.

Just before serving, decorate the cake. Stir 1 teaspoon of apricot glaze into the remaining tablespoon of chopped apricots and set aside. Spread the remaining glaze over the top of the cake, allowing it to run down the sides. Make "flowers" on top of the cake by clustering sliced almonds and placing a glazed chopped apricot in the center of each flower.

MAKES 8 SERVINGS.

Lezlee's Exotic Eggs

10 tablespoons butter
6 tablespoons all-purpose flour
1½ teaspoons salt
4 cups milk
3 cups shredded Cheddar cheese
¼ cup dried onions (or ½ cup fresh,
    chopped fine)
2 cups thinly sliced fresh mushrooms
24 eggs, beaten
3 tablespoons chopped fresh herbs
2 cups fresh breadcrumbs

In a saucepan melt 4 tablespoons of butter. Blend in the flour and salt and make a roux by stirring for 3 to 5 minutes over medium heat. Gradually stir in the milk. Cook over medium heat until the mixture just comes to a boil and thickens. Add the Cheddar cheese, cover, and set aside.

In a large skillet melt 4 more tablespoons of butter and sauté the onions and mushrooms until tender and the liquid has evaporated. Add the eggs and herbs, and continue cooking and stirring until the mixture is just set. Stir the cheese sauce into the eggs. Spoon the mixture into a 9 x 13-inch glass dish. In a saucepan melt the remaining 2 tablespoons of butter. Toss with the breadcrumbs. Sprinkle over the egg and sauce mixture. Cover and refrigerate overnight.

Bake uncovered in a 350° oven for 25 to 30 minutes or until heated through.

MAKES 12 TO 14 SERVINGS.

Swan House

Swan House

49 Mountain Street
Camden, Maine 04843
(207) 236-8275

The Swan House is named, not for the stately water birds, but for the hardy family of Mainers who lived here for generations. With a touch of whimsy, however, the innkeepers have named the six guest rooms of this B&B after different varieties of feathered swans. This charming Old Victorian home at the foot of Mt. Battie is only a short walk from the village, which is home to the Windjammer fleet, the Camden Shakespeare Company, and the Camden Opera House. The Farnsworth Art Museum in Rockland holds a

collection of Wyeths works and sculpture by Louise Nevelson. Breakfast is served on the sunporch.

Creamed Eggs á la Asparagus

½ **pound fresh asparagus**
3 **tablespoons butter**
3 **tablespoons all-purpose flour**
½ **teaspoon salt**
¼ **teaspoon ground white pepper**
2 **cups milk**
½ **cup shredded Cheddar cheese**
6 **hard-boiled eggs, sliced**
   Paprika

In a pan steam the fresh asparagus until tender. Chop the asparagus and set it aside. In a saucepan melt the butter. Blend in the flour, salt, and pepper. Gradually add the milk and cook over medium heat, stirring constantly, until thickened. Stir in the cheese. Fold in the egg slices. Serve over toast. Arrange the asparagus on top. Sprinkle with paprika.

Serve immediately.

MAKES 4 SERVINGS.

Caramel Crunch Apple Pie

1 **cup all-purpose flour**
¼ **teaspoon baking powder**
½ **cup solid shortening**
¼ **teaspoon salt**
¼ **cup cold water**

....

28 **vanilla Kraft caramels**
2 **tablespoons water**
4 **cups peeled, sliced baking apples**
¾ **cup all-purpose flour**
⅓ **cup sugar**
½ **teaspoon ground cinnamon**
⅓ **cup butter**
½ **cup chopped walnuts**

In a medium bowl mix 1 cup of flour, the baking powder, shortening, and salt. Add water and let the mixture stand for 10 minutes. The dough will be quite moist but is easily handled after standing. Turn the dough onto a floured surface and roll out to fit a 9-inch pie plate. Place the dough in the pie plate, and trim the edges.

In the top of a double boiler over simmering water melt the caramels with 2 table-

spoon of water, stirring until the mixture is smooth.

Layer the sliced apples in the unbaked pie shell. Pour the melted caramels evenly over the apples. In a medium bowl combine the flour, sugar, and cinnamon. Cut in the butter until the mixture is crumbly. Stir in the walnuts. Crumble the mixture over the apples. Bake in a 375° oven for 55 minutes. Halfway through baking, cover the edges of the pie crust with aluminum foil to prevent overbrowning.

MAKES 8 SERVINGS.

Windward House

6 High Street
Camden, Maine 04843
(207) 236-9656

A Greek Revival house built in 1854, this B&B sits at the base of Mount Battie in the heart of Camden's historic district. Eight rooms reflect the charm of period furnishings. Guests can walk to the shops downtown and to the harbor with its windjammers. Camden is nearly

Windward House

unique on the east coast in that it offers both mountain and ocean scenery. Its centuries old maritime tradition is a traveler's bonus. Guests begin each day with a hearty breakfast that may include frittatas, quiches, waffles, or French toast.

Blueberry-Lemon Streusel Coffee Cake

- ¾ cup firmly packed brown sugar
- ½ cup all-purpose flour
- 1 teaspoon ground cinnamon
- ¼ cup butter

....

- ½ cup butter, softened
- 1 cup sugar
- 2 eggs
- 1 teaspoon vanilla extract
- 2 cups all-purpose flour
- 1 teaspoon baking powder
- ½ teaspoon baking soda
- ½ teaspoon salt
- 1 cup sour cream
- 1 tablespoon grated lemon zest
- 2 cups blueberries

In a medium bowl stir together the brown sugar, ½ cup of flour, and cinnamon. Cut in ¼ cup of butter until crumbly. Set aside.

In a large mixing bowl cream ½ cup of butter with an electric mixer. Add the sugar and beat until light and fluffy. Beat in the eggs, one at a time. Blend in the vanilla.

In a bowl stir together 2 cups of flour, the baking powder, soda, and salt. Using a wooden spoon, stir the dry ingredients into the creamed mixture alternately with the sour cream. Stir in the lemon zest. Spread half of the batter in a greased and floured 9-inch springform pan. Sprinkle with half of the streusel and half of the blueberries. Spread the remaining batter over the top. Sprinkle with the remaining blueberries, then the remaining streusel. Bake in a 350° oven for about 1 hour and 15 minutes or until a tester inserted in the center comes out clean. Cool in the pan for 10 minutes. Remove the side of the pan and serve warm.

MAKES 8 TO 10 SERVINGS.

Baked Pears with Lemon Sauce

- 5 cups sliced, peeled Bosc pears
- 1 tablespoon sugar
- ½ teaspoon finely shredded lemon zest
- ⅔ cup regular rolled oats
- ⅓ cup firmly packed brown sugar
- ⅓ cup all-purpose flour
- ¼ teaspoon cardamom
- ¼ cup butter
- ⅓ cup sliced almonds
  Lemon Sauce (recipe follows)

In a 2-quart square baking dish toss the pears with 1 tablespoon of sugar and half of the shredded lemon zest.

In a medium bowl combine the oats, brown sugar, flour, cardamom, and the remaining lemon zest.. Cut in the butter until the mixture resembles coarse crumbs. Stir in the almonds. Sprinkle the topping over the fruit.

Bake in a 375° oven for 30 to 35 minutes or until the fruit is tender and the topping begins to brown. Serve warm with Lemon Sauce.

MAKES 6 SERVINGS.

Lemon Sauce

- ¼ cup sugar
- 2 teaspoons cornstarch
- ½ cup water
- 1 beaten egg yolk
- 1 tablespoon butter
- ¼ teaspoon finely shredded lemon zest
- 1 tablespoon lemon juice (fresh)

In a 1-quart saucepan stir together the sugar and cornstarch. Add the water and stir until combined. Cook and stir over medium heat until thickened and bubbly. Cook and stir for 2 minutes more. Remove the saucepan from the heat. Stir a little of the hot mixture into the beaten egg yolk. Return all of the mixture to the saucepan. Cook and stir over low heat until nearly bubbly. Cook and stir for 1 minute more. Remove the pan from the heat. Stir in the butter, shredded lemon zest, and lemon juice. Serve the sauce warm.

MAKES ABOUT ⅔ CUP.

Herb Baked Eggs

- 8 slices ham
- 12 eggs
- 4 teaspoons prepared mustard
- 1 cup plain yogurt
- 3 cups shredded Cheddar cheese
- 8 teaspoons chives or parsley
  Salt and pepper to taste

Grease 8 au gratin dishes or spray them with cooking spray. Line each with a ham slice. In a bowl beat the eggs with the mustard and yogurt. Stir in one-fourth of the grated Cheddar cheese. Stir in half of the parsley or chives. Pour or spoon the egg mixture into the dishes. Sprinkle with the remaining cheese and herbs. Bake in a 375° oven for 15 to 20 minutes.

MAKES 8 SERVINGS.

Inn By the Sea
❧

*40 Bowery Beach Road
Cape Elizabeth, Maine 04107
(207) 767-0888*

*T*his luxury hotel overlooks the Atlantic from Cape Elizabeth's headlands. Most of its 43 guest suites offer striking ocean views, as does the inn's Audubon Dining Room. The decor and amenities are striking. For instance, Chippendale cherry furnishes the guest rooms in the main building, and Audubon etchings and other artwork can be found throughout the inn.

Maine Crab Cakes

- 2 onions, finely chopped
- 1 bunch celery, finely chopped
- ¼ cup finely chopped jalapeños, strained
- 4 red bell peppers, finely chopped
- 3 cups mayonnaise
- 4 pounds fresh Maine crab meat

2   tablespoons Old Bay seasoning
2   teaspoons salt
2   teaspoons pepper
2   tablespoons fresh chopped tarragon
4   teaspoons Worcestershire sauce
12 eggs
    Fresh breadcrumbs (3 to 5 cups)
    Cornmeal
2   tablespoons clarified butter
    Lemon slices for garnish
    Greens for garnish
    Jalapeño Aioli (recipe follows)

In a large mixing bowl combine the onions, celery, jalapeños, red peppers, mayonnaise, crab meat, seasonings, tarragon, Worcestershire sauce, and eggs, and incorporate thoroughly. Add the breadcrumbs slowly until the mixture is fairly tight and not too wet. Once the mixture is set, form into 1 ½-ounce portions. Dust a sheet pan with cornmeal. Form the crab cakes into round patties. Let chill slightly in the refrigerator for about 1 hour and 30 minutes to 2 hours.

In a sauté pan heat the clarified butter on medium-high heat, and place the crab cakes in the pan. Let the crab cake get golden brown, then turn over and finish in a 350° oven for about 5 to 8 minutes. Serve accompanied with lemon slices, greens, and Jalapeño Aioli.

MAKES ABOUT 1 DOZEN.

Jalapeño Aioli

⅓   cup strained jalapeños
1   red bell pepper, minced
2   cups mayonnaise
2   cups sour cream
1   teaspoon salt
½   teaspoon lemon juice
1½ teaspoons Montreal Steak Seasoning
¼   cup minced shallots

In a medium bowl combine all ingredients and mix thoroughly. Serve chilled with Maine Crab Cakes.

MAKES ABOUT 4½ CUPS.

Cucumber Dill Concassée

4   cucumbers, peeled and seeded
2   cups mayonnaise
2   cups sour cream
1   teaspoon Worcestershire sauce
2   tablespoons fresh chopped dill
    Pinch salt and pepper

2   teaspoons lemon juice
¼   teaspoon lemon pepper

Finely chop the cucumbers. In a large bowl combine the cucumbers and remaining ingredients. Refrigerate until chilled. Serve with crab cakes or as a dip for vegetable crudité.

MAKES 6 TO 8 SERVINGS.

Baked Stuffed Maine Lobster

1   1½-pound Maine lobster
2   large scallops
2   peeled and deveined shrimp
1   2-ounce baked croissant
¾   cup heavy cream
¼   cup clarified butter
1   teaspoon fresh chopped tarragon
1½ cups white wine
    Lemon slices and melted butter for garnish

On a cutting board place the lobster backsides down and split lengthwise. Remove the brain sac and sand vein from the tail. Place the scallops in the body cavity and the shrimp in the tail section of the lobster. Place the lobster in a shallow baking pan.

Chop the croissant into ¼-inch cubes and place on top of the tail and body sections. Pour the heavy cream, butter, and tarragon over the croissant. Pour the wine in the bottom of the pan. Bake in a 350° oven for about 18 to 25 minutes or until the scallops are cooked. Serve with lemon slices and melted butter.

MAKES 1 SERVING.

Mustard Garlic-crusted Rack of Lamb

2   13- to 16-pound racks of baby New Zealand lamb
1   cup Dijon mustard
¼   teaspoon fresh chopped rosemary
1¼ teaspoons chopped garlic
¼   teaspoon chopped parsley
    Pinch salt
    Pinch pepper
1½ cups fresh breadcrumbs
    Melted butter
1   teaspoon chopped shallot
1   cup Fresh Mint Sauce (recipe follows)

In a medium bowl combine the mustard, rosemary, garlic, parsley, salt, and pepper. Add 2 tablespoons of breadcrumbs to the mixture and mix well. In a sauté pan sear the racks of lamb loin-side-down for 4 to 6 minutes. Turn the lamb over and spread the mustard mixture on the lamb. Sprinkle breadcrumbs over the mustard, drizzle melted butter over the breadcrumbs, and sprinkle shallot over the top. Bake the lamb in a 400° oven for about 20 to 25 minutes, until done to taste. Serve with Fresh Mint Sauce and a potato and vegetable of choice.

MAKES 8 SERVINGS

Fresh Mint Sauce

2   tablespoons fresh chopped mint
2   cups sugar
1   cup water

In a saucepan combine the fresh chopped mint, sugar, and water, and simmer over medium-high heat for 8 to 10 minutes. Reduce until slightly thick. Serve with lamb, or as a dip for fruit.

MAKES ABOUT 2 CUPS.

Smoked Grapefruit Sorbet

24 pink grapefruits
12 cups simple syrup
¼   teaspoon grated nutmeg
    Pinch ground Indian mace
    Pinch ground ginger
    Fresh mint and champagne for garnish

Cut the grapefruits in half and place in a smoker for 45 minutes. Using hickory chips will give the best flavor. Add more smoking chips and smoke for another 45 minutes. Remove the grapefruits and place on a sheet pan to cool for about 30 minutes. Remove the juice from the grapefruits using a juicer. This works best if they are still warm. Chill the juice and save for later. There should be about 16 cups.

Make a simple syrup by combining 12 cups of sugar and 6 cups of water. Reduce slowly over medium heat until slightly thick. Let cool. In an ice cream freezer, place the grapefruit juice, 12 cups of syrup, the nutmeg, mace, and ginger, and freeze according to the manufacturer's directions, or mix in a shallow pan and freezer overnight. Remove from the freezer and purée until smooth. Return to the freezer. Freeze overnight.

Serve with a garnish of fresh mint and a drizzle of champagne.

MAKES ABOUT 1 GALLON.

Lemon and White Chocolate Cheesecake with Ginger Shortbread Crust

1   cup all-purpose flour
½   cup confectioners' sugar
1   teaspoon ground ginger
½   cup unsalted butter, cold, cut into small pieces
....
4   8-ounce packages cream cheese, room temperature
½   cup sour cream
⅓   cup sugar
4   eggs
1   egg yolk
¼   cup lightly salted butter, melted
16   ounces good-quality white chocolate, melted
     Juice of 2 lemons
1   tablespoon vanilla extract
     Fresh raspberries or strawberries for garnish
     Whipped cream

Spray the sides and bottom of a 10-inch springform pan with cooking spray and dust with flour. In a food processor process the flour, confectioners' sugar, and ginger. Add the cold butter and pulse until the mixture resembles coarse meal. Press the shortbread crumbs into the bottom of the pan. Chill for 15 minutes.

Bake in a 350° oven for 10 minutes or until the crust is golden brown. Set aside. Reduce the oven temperature to 300°. In a mixer bowl beat the cream cheese until light and fluffy. Beat in the sour cream and sugar until smooth. Beat in the eggs one at a time, and then add the egg yolk. Scrape the sides down. Add the melted butter and white chocolate, and mix well. Blend in the lemon juice and vanilla. Carefully pour the filling into the shortbread crust, and smooth the top. Place the pan in a large pan partially filled with water.

Bake in a 350° oven for 1 hour and 30 minutes. The cheesecake should be a light golden brown, and just set.

Cool completely, then refrigerate until firm, preferably overnight. Cut with a wet, hot knife, wiping the knife clean with each slice. Serve with fresh raspberries or strawberries and whipped cream.

MAKES 16 TO 20 SERVINGS.

Main Street, P.O. Box 41
Castine, Maine 04421
(207) 326-4365

The Castine Inn, built in 1898, is a perfect place to enjoy a relaxing vacation and an ideal base from which to explore the maritime scenery of Penobscot Bay. A visit to the coastal town reveals bowers of elms, saved from blight by the unified effort of residents, the town council, and the Marine Maritime Academy. The inn offers guest rooms with harbor views, public rooms resplendent with paintings of seascapes, and New England-style menus.

Corned Beef Hash with a Poached Egg

3   medium baking or Russet potatoes (not peeled)
10   ounces cooked corned beef (use leftovers)
2   tablespoons unsalted butter
1   medium Spanish onion, diced
     Black pepper to taste
6   large eggs, poached

In a pan place the potatoes in heavily salted cold water. Simmer for about 20 minutes, until the potatoes just slowly slip off the blade of a paring knife plunged halfway into them. Drain and refrigerate uncovered overnight. (If the potatoes don't cool thoroughly, the result will be a gooey, starchy mess rather

than light, separate shreds.) Shred the potatoes on a coarse hand grater.

Slice the corned beef against the grain into ⅛-inch-thick slices and chop into rough pieces. In a skillet melt the butter and sauté the onion until limp.

In a large bowl combine the potatoes, onions, and corned beef. Toss together lightly but never squeeze or crush with a spoon. Season to taste with black pepper.

In a large, lightly oiled iron skillet cook the hash mixture over medium-high heat until brown and crisp on both sides. Serve with a poached egg on top of each serving.

MAKES 6 SERVINGS.

Blueberry Pie

3   tablespoons cornstarch
⅛   teaspoon salt
1   scant cup sugar
½   teaspoon ground cinnamon
4   cups blueberries (1 quart)
1   cup water
1   tablespoon butter
     Grated zest of ½ lemon
1   prebaked 9-inch pie shell
     Whipped cream

In a heavy-bottomed non-reactive saucepan mix all of the dry ingredients together well. Add 1 cup of blueberries and the water. Cook over medium heat, stirring constantly, until the cornstarch is cooked and the mixture turns clear and thick. Add the butter, lemon zest, and the remaining 3 cups of blueberries. Remove the pan from the heat. Pour the filling into the pie shell. Refrigerate until chilled. Serve with whipped cream.

MAKES 8 SERVINGS.

Mussel and Corn Chowder

2   pounds mussels, in their shells
½   cup white wine
4   slices bacon, diced
1   medium onion, finely chopped
2   cups heavy cream (not ultra-pasteurized)
2   10-ounce boxes frozen corn, thawed (or the shaved kernels of 6 ears fresh corn)
     Salt and pepper to taste
3   green onions, chopped

Scrub the mussels under cold running water and remove the beards. Discard any mussels that have cracked or broken shells or that do not close when handled. Pour the wine into a non-reactive saucepan, add the mussels and steam them until they open, about 4 to 5 minutes. Transfer the mussels and the liquid to a bowl and let cool. Discard any mussels that have not opened.

In the same saucepan sauté the bacon until crisp. Remove the bacon from the pan and pour out all but 4 tablespoons of fat. Add the diced onion and stew gently for 10 minutes. Remove the mussel meats from the shells and check again for cleanliness. Strain the liquid through several layers of cheesecloth into the saucepan. Add the cream, bacon, and mussel meats. Add the corn to the pot and simmer very gently for 20 minutes. Taste and adjust the salt and pepper, and garnish with the chopped green onions.

MAKES 6 SERVINGS.

Craignair Inn

533 Clark Island Road
Clark Island, Maine 04859
(207) 594-7644

S*et on a granite ledge above the sea and surrounded by flower gardens, the Craignair was built in 1928 to house workers at the nearby limestone quarries. Clark Island was once and remains to this day a hard-working community. The union hall still stands, as does the old general store and post office.*

Craignair Inn

Bedrooms at the inn are furnished simply but comfortably with quilts, colorful wall coverings, and hooked rugs. Guests can explore the miles of coastline or sit in the garden and watch the activities of shorebirds, clammers, and lobstermen.

Baked Stuffed Potatoes

- 4 **baked Russet potatoes**
- ½ **cup butter**
  Salt and pepper to taste
- 4 **slices finely chopped bacon**
- ½ **cup shredded Cheddar cheese**
  Cream, enough to hold the mashed potato together
- 1 **egg**

Hollow the baked potatoes. In a large bowl mash the potatoes. Add the remaining ingredients and mix well. Transfer the mixture to a pastry bag and pipe into the hollow potatoes. Place in a baking pan or on a baking sheet. Bake in a 400° oven for 15 minutes.

MAKES 4 SERVINGS.

Bouillabaisse

- 1 **tablespoon olive oil**
- ½ **cup medium diced onion**
- 4 **julienne leeks, white part only**
- 5 **cloves garlic, finely chopped**
- 1 **28-ounce can whole tomatoes, with liquid**
- ¼ **cup fresh orange juice**
- 3 **tablespoons tomato paste**
- 2 **bay leaves, crushed**
- ½ **teaspoon celery seed**
  Pinch saffron/several threads (substitute turmeric for less cost, and a slightly different flavor)
- ⅓ **cup finely chopped parsley**
  Salt and pepper to taste

- 4 **pounds (2 bags) Great Eastern Mussels, rinsed and debearded**
- 4 **pounds (about 40) littleneck or Manila clams**
- 2 **or 3 1¼-pound lobsters, tails quartered, claws chopped (or similar amount of whole crab or shrimp)**
  Garlic bread

In a large stockpot heat the oil and sauté the onions, leeks, garlic, and tomatoes until onions are translucent. Add the orange juice, tomato paste, bay leaves, celery seed, saffron, and parsley. Simmer for 10 minutes.

Add all of the seafood and cover with warm water (about 4 cups). Simmer for 15 to 20 minutes, until the mussels and clam shells open.

Serve with garlic bread.

MAKES 6 SERVINGS.

Pilgrim's Inn

Pilgrim's Inn

Deer Isle, Maine 04627
(207) 348-6615

T*he inn's glowing hearths, antique furnishings, and pumpkin pine floors, worn smooth with time, evoke the feeling of a bygone era. All guest rooms are decorated in soft Colonial colors and contain unique, handmade furnishings. The common room features an eight-foot-wide fireplace and beehive oven that serve as a backdrop for afternoon hors d'oeuvres. The gardens and lawn lead down to the waters of Mill Pond. Guests may sail on Penobscot Bay, visit Acadia National Park, or engage in a lecture or two of the Haystack School, a renowned school of arts and crafts.*

Risotto with Maine Lobster and Chanterelle Mushrooms

2 1½-pound lobsters

....

2 tablespoons olive oil
1 small onion, diced
1 stalk celery, diced
1 carrot, peeled and diced
1 garlic clove (left whole)
2 tablespoons chopped fresh parsley
1 tablespoon chopped fresh thyme
1 tablespoon chopped fresh chervil
1 bay leaf
1 cup white wine
6 cups water
1 tablespoon lemon juice

....

¼ cup butter
2 cups cleaned and sliced chanterelle
     mushrooms
   Salt and pepper to taste
2 tablespoons olive oil
2 tablespoons finely diced shallots
1 tablespoon finely diced garlic
1 leek, white part only, cleaned and
     finely diced
1 cup arborio rice
1 cup dry white wine
1 tomato, peeled, seeded, and chopped
1 tablespoon chopped fresh parsley
1 tablespoon chopped fresh chervil

In a pot steam the lobster for 8 minutes. Remove from the heat and let cool. Remove the lobster meat from the tail and claw sections, dice the meat and set aside for the risotto. Reserve all of the lobster shell for the stock.

Split the body section of the lobster in half and discard the green tomalley, the sand sac behind the eyes, and the gill tissues. Rinse the body section under cold water. Chop along with the tail and claw shells into small pieces.

In a 6-quart stockpot heat 2 tablespoons of olive oil over medium heat. Add the onion, celery, carrot, and garlic, and sauté the vegetables for 3 minutes, stirring occasionally. Add the chopped lobster shells, parsley, thyme, chervil, bay leaf, 1 cup of wine, water, and lemon juice. Reduce the heat and simmer for 30 minutes. Remove the stock from the heat and strain through a cheesecloth or a fine mesh strainer. Return 4 cups of the stock to the stockpot and set aside until needed.

In a sauté pan heat 2 tablespoons of butter over medium heat. Add the mushrooms, season with salt and pepper, and cook for 3 to 4 minutes. Set aside.

Heat the lobster stock to a simmer and maintain a slow simmer while the risotto is being prepared. In a large heavy saucepan heat 2 tablespoons of olive oil and 2 tablespoons of butter. Add the shallots, garlic, and leek, and cook for 2 minutes, stirring often. Add the rice and stir to coat the rice with the liquid. Cook for 1 minute. Add 1 cup of wine and cook until nearly evaporated. Add enough stock to just barely cover the rice. Adjust the heat to maintain a gentle simmer. As the rice absorbs the stock, add more stock to keep the level just above the rice, stirring often. After 15 minutes, add the mushrooms and cook for 2 minutes. Add the lobster meat, tomato, and herbs, and season with salt and pepper. Cook for 1 minute. Remove from the heat and serve immediately.

MAKES 4 SERVINGS.

Spinach, Wild Mushroom, and Arugula Tart

1¼ cups all-purpose flour
    Pinch salt
6   tablespoons chilled butter
4   to 5 tablespoons cold water
8   cups spinach, washed, stems
      removed
2   tablespoons olive oil
1   clove garlic, minced
1   small onion, finely diced
1   cup chopped fresh wild mushrooms
2   tablespoons pine nuts, toasted
1   cup chopped arugula
    Pinch grated nutmeg
    Black pepper
1   3-ounce package cream cheese, soft-
      ened
⅔ cup sour cream
3   eggs
⅓ cup grated Parmesan cheese

In a bowl combine the flour and salt. Cut in the butter until pieces are the size of small peas. Slowly add the water and mix with a fork until the dough is moist and can be formed into a ball of dough (use hands if needed). Let the dough rest for 1 hour.

Roll the dough out on a lightly floured surface to a 13-inch circle. Transfer to an 11-inch tart pan with removable bottom. Trim

the dough even with side of the pan. Line the tart shell with a double thickness of foil and fill with pie weights or beans. Bake in a 400° oven for 15 minutes. Remove the foil and weights, and bake 10 minutes longer.

In a pan steam the spinach for 3 minutes or until wilted. Drain well and squeeze out the excess liquid. Finely chop the spinach and set aside. In a large skillet heat the olive oil over medium-high heat. Add the garlic and cook until it just starts to brown. Add the onion and mushrooms, and cook for 5 minutes. Stir in the pine nuts, spinach, arugula, and nutmeg, and season with salt and pepper. Remove from heat and set aside.

In a mixing bowl beat the cream cheese and sour cream with an electric mixer on low speed until smooth. Add the eggs at a time and mix until just combined. Stir in the spinach mixture and the Parmesan cheese. Pour into the tart shell. Bake in a 400° oven for 20 to 25 minutes or until a knife inserted near the center comes out clean.

MAKE 8 TO 10 SERVINGS.

Sesame Ginger Mussels

½   cup soy sauce
½   cup peanut oil
¼   teaspoon sesame oil
1   teaspoon rice wine vinegar
½   teaspoon sugar
1   teaspoon Dijon mustard
2   teaspoons chopped fresh ginger
2   tablespoons chopped fresh cilantro
2   tablespoons chopped fresh parsley
1   red onion, peeled and finely diced

....

24 mussels, debearded and cleaned
½   cup white wine
1   teaspoon chopped fresh ginger
1   teaspoon chopped garlic

....

2   ounces pickled ginger, sliced

In a stainless steel bowl combine the first 10 ingredients and whisk until blended. Set aside.

In a large heavy saucepan, combine the mussels, wine, 1 teaspoon fresh ginger, and garlic, cover, and cook over medium-high heat until the mussels have opened, about 6 to 8 minutes. Remove from the heat and allow to cool. Remove the mussels from the shells and add them to the marinade. Reserve the shells. Cover the mussels and allow to marinate at room temperature for 1 hour.

Place 1 mussel in each shell along with a little of the marinade. Top each mussel with a slice of pickled ginger and serve.

MAKES 4 SERVINGS.

The Bagley House

1290 Royalsborough Road
Durham, Maine 04222
(207) 865-6566

*J**ust ten minutes from Freeport, with its dozens of manufacturer's outlets, the Bagley House is a quiet and welcome retreat from a busy day of bargain hunting. Built in 1772 by Captain O. Israel Bagley, a store owner, the house has five guest rooms furnished with antiques and hand-sewn quilts. Like many very old New England houses, it is a comfortable home. The large country kitchen has wide pine floors, hand-hewn beams, a beehive oven, and an enormous brick fireplace. Special lobster weekends are available for a minimum of five people.*

Zucchini and Apple Chutney

> 4 *pounds zucchini, peeled and chopped into small pieces*
> 2 *pounds cooking apples, peeled and chopped*
> 3 *onions, finely chopped*
> 1 *tablespoon salt*
> 4 *cups sugar*
> 1 *teaspoon chopped chilies*
> 1 *tablespoon chopped fresh ginger*
> 1 *tablespoon black peppercorns*
> 1 *tablespoon whole allspice, bruised*
> 6¾ *cups vinegar*

Arrange the prepared zucchini in a bowl, sprinkling salt on each layer. Leave for 24 hours.

Drain the zucchini and rinse well.

In a large saucepan combine all ingredients. Bring to a boil, and simmer until the chutney thickens. Spoon it into sterilized jars, seal, and store for at least 4 weeks before opening.

This is a mild chutney that goes well with pork, chicken, egg, or rice dishes.

MAKES ABOUT 12 HALF-PINTS.

Scones for Aspiring Anglophiles

> 2 *cups all-purpose flour*
> ¼ *cup sugar*
> 1 *tablespoon baking powder*
> ½ *teaspoon salt*
>
> 5 *tablespoons chilled butter, cut in pieces*
> 1 *egg*
> 1 *egg, separated*
> ⅓ *cup milk*
> ⅓ *cup plain or vanilla low-fat yogurt*
>   *Sugar for sprinkling*

In a large bowl combine the dry ingredients. Cut in the butter until the mixture resembles coarse cornmeal. For variations, add the additional dry ingredients (see below). Mix well.

In a separate bowl beat the egg plus additional yolk with the milk and yogurt. For variations add the liquid flavorings. Add the liquid mixture to the flour mixture. Mix rapidly with a fork until the mixture pulls away from the bowl. Turn the dough onto a lightly floured board and knead gently until smooth. Pat out to 1-inch thickness. Cut into 3-inch rounds with a glass or cookie cutter. Place the rounds on an ungreased baking sheet. Brush the tops with beaten egg white. Sprinkle with sugar. Bake in a 400° oven for 18 to 20 minutes.

Serve warm or at room temperature with butter or honey or jam.

Variations: For Orange Scones, add ⅓ cup of dried currants and 1 teaspoon of grated orange zest or ½ teaspoon of orange essence. For Cranberry Scones, add ⅓ cup of dried cranberries, 1 teaspoon of grated orange zest or ½ teaspoon of orange essence. For Blueberry Scones, add ⅓ cup of fresh or frozen blueberries, and 1 teaspoon of grated lemon zest or ½ teaspoon of lemon essence. For Almond Scones, add 1 teaspoon of almond essence and sprinkle slivered almonds on top. For Ginger Scones, add 1 teaspoon of ground ginger and sprinkle crystallized ginger on top. For Cheese Scones, reduce the sugar to 2 tablespoons and add 1 cup of extra-sharp Cheddar cheese and 1 teaspoon of red pepper, and use plain yogurt only.

MAKES ABOUT 10 3-INCH SCONES.

Route 101
Eliot, Maine 03903
(207) 439-0590

*M**erchant shipbuilder Elliot Frost built this Colonial house in 1736. The original exposed beams, wide floor boards, and wood panelling can still be seen in many of the rooms. High Meadows is only a few minutes from historic Portsmouth, New Hampshire, and Kittery, Maine. Shopping enthusiasts will enjoy the*

High Meadows

nearby malls, and those who love the sea will be tempted by whale watching, harbor cruising, and beachcombing.

Sausage Ring

2 **pounds bulk sausage**
1 **apple, chopped**
2 **eggs**
½ **cup milk**
1½ **cups crushed crackers or herb stuffing (Pepperidge Farm is good)**
¼ **cup minced onion**

8 **eggs, scrambled**

In a large bowl combine all ingredients except the scrambled eggs. Press into a lightly greased 6-cup jelly round mold. Bake in a 350° oven for 1 hour. The ring can be baked for 30 minutes, refrigerated overnight, and baked for 30 minutes just before serving. After cooking, place on a round glass serving dish and fill the middle with 8 scrambled eggs.

MAKES 8 SERVINGS.

Conch Fritters

1¾ **pounds chopped conch**
1 **large green bell pepper, chopped**
2 **medium onions, chopped**
1½ **cups all-purpose flour**
1½ **teaspoons baking powder**
1 **egg**
1½ **cups milk**
1 **teaspoon thyme**
1 **teaspoon parsley**

In a large bowl mix all the ingredients together. In a skillet fry in bacon fat or oil by the spoonful until golden on both sides.

MAKES ABOUT 6 SERVINGS.

Admiral Peary House

Admiral Peary House

9 Elm Street
Fryeburg, Maine 04037
(207) 935-3365

Once the home of the famed explorer Admiral Robert E. Peary, this historic B&B is just the place for guests to have a hearty breakfast before discovering the beautiful vistas of surrounding mountains and lakes. Bicycling, hiking, and canoeing are all popular here, and a red clay tennis court is right out back. Midwinter also provides perfect weather for the the downhill or cross-country ski enthusiast.

Carrot Spice Cake

1 **cup chopped walnuts**
4 **medium carrots, grated (2 cups)**
3 **eggs**
2 **cups sugar**
1 **cup canola oil**
2 **teaspoons vanilla extract**
2 **cups all-purpose flour**
2 **teaspoons baking soda**
1 **teaspoon baking powder**
½ **teaspoon salt**
1 **tablespoon ground cinnamon**
1 **cup raisins**
  Confectioners' sugar to sprinkle for decoration

Process the eggs and sugar using the steel blade for 1 minute. While the machine is running, add the oil and vanilla through the feed tube and process about 45 seconds longer. Add the carrots and process for 10 seconds. In a separate mixing bowl mix all of the dry ingredients. Add the carrot mixture all at once to the dry ingredients. Mix until blended, about 45 seconds. Stir in the nuts and raisins. Pour the batter into a greased and floured 9 x 13-inch baking pan. Bake in a 350° oven for 55 to 60 minutes. Cool completely. Dust each individual serving with con-

fectioners' sugar. This treatment looks especially great on a dark-colored plate!

Note: This can also be baked in a 12-cup bundt pan. Cool for 15 minutes before removing from the pan. A small vase of flowers can then be placed in the center after dusting the entire cake with confectioners' sugar. This looks spectacular on a buffet table.

MAKES 12 TO 15 SERVINGS.

Penguin Pie

½ **cup butter or margarine, melted**
1½ **cups milk**
¼ **teaspoon salt**
⅛ **teaspoon pepper**
1 **teaspoon dried chives (or 2 teaspoons fresh)**
¼ **teaspoon baking mix**

½ **to ¾ cup chopped cooked smoked sausage or ham ("penguin")**
1 **cup grated Swiss cheese**
3 **eggs, beaten**

In a blender mix butter, milk, salt, pepper, chives, paprika, and baking mix for 1 to 2 minutes on blend. Spray a 10-inch pie plate with cooking spray. Pour the blended ingredients into the pie plate. Sprinkle the batter with sausage and push down into the batter. Sprinkle grated Swiss cheese over the top. Pour beaten eggs over all. Bake in a 375° oven for 30 to 40 minutes.

Cool somewhat before cutting and serving. Plan on serving seconds!

MAKES 6 TO 8 SERVINGS.

Crocker House Country Inn

Hancock Point Road
Hancock, Maine 04640
(207) 422-6806

The Crocker House Country Inn, tucked away on the peninsula of Hancock Point, was built in 1884, and carefully restored in 1986. Its quiet, out of the way location, fine cuisine, and individually appointed guest rooms each with a private bath, combine to make the Crocker House a refreshing and memorable experience.

Crocker House

Port Wine and Stilton Vinaigrette

1 egg
¼ cup sugar
1 tablespoon Dijon mustard
⅓ cup red wine vinegar
⅓ cup port wine
12 teaspoon salt
3 tablespoons chopped onion
2 cups corn-olive blend oil
2 ounces Stilton cheese

In a food processor combine all ingredients except the oil and Stilton. Process for 1 to 2 minutes. Slowly dribble in the oil and add 1 ½ ounces of the Stilton. When all of the oil is used, check the taste, and add the remaining Stilton if desired. The more slowly the oil is processed, the creamier the dressing becomes.

MAKES 1 QUART.

White Chocolate and Chambord Cheesecake

1¾ cups vanilla wafer cookies, processed finely
⅓ cup butter, melted
....
3 8-ounce packages cream cheese, softened
1¼ cups sugar
6 ounces white chocolate, melted
2 tablespoons all-purpose flour

1 teaspoon vanilla extract
¼ cup Chambord
4 eggs
Fresh raspberries for garnish

In a medium bowl combine the cookies and butter and press into an oiled 9-inch springform pan. Chill.

In a large bowl cream the cheese and sugar. Blend in the melted white chocolate, flour, vanilla, and Chambord. Add the eggs one at a time, combining well without overbeating. Pour into the prepared pan. Bake in a 350° oven for 45 to 50 minutes.

Chill overnight. Serve with fresh raspberries.

MAKES 8 SERVINGS.

The Keeper's House
❧

P.O. Box 26
Isle au Haut, Maine 04645
(207) 367-2261

Here is a truly unique B&B experience that allows venturesome travelers to taste the solitary life of the men and women who once kept America's coastal lights burning. A restored light station on remote Isle au Haut is now operated as a summertime B&B, and guests who don't mind spending a day or two far from the nearest telephone, power cable, automobile, or fellow tourist will love it. Four guest rooms in the keeper's house and another in the old oil house provide simple, though comfortable accommodations. An extension of Acadia National Park, it takes up about half of the island, which must be reached by mail boat from Stonington. The tiny but active fishing village of Isle au Haut is nearby.

Lemon or Orange Pancakes

6 eggs, separated
1 cup unbleached all-purpose flour
1½ cups cottage cheese
¼ cup butter, melted
¼ cup sugar
½ teaspoon salt
2 tablespoons grated lemon or orange zest

In a large bowl stir together the egg yolks, flour, cottage cheese, butter, sugar, salt, and lemon or orange zest until mixed well. In a separate bowl whip the egg whites until they are stiff. Fold the egg whites into the yolk mixture. Spoon onto a greased griddle and bake.

Delicious with plain yogurt and maple syrup or fresh blueberries or raspberries.

MAKES 4 SERVINGS.

Keeper's House Famous Yummy Bars

½ cup butter or margarine
½ cup sugar
1½ teaspoons vanilla extract, divided
1 cup all-purpose flour
¼ teaspoon baking powder
1 teaspoon salt, divided
1 cup firmly packed dark brown sugar
2 eggs
1 cup chopped walnuts
1 cup chocolate bits

In a large bowl cream the butter, sugar, and ½ teaspoon of vanilla until light and fluffy. In a separate bowl combine the flour, baking powder, and ¼ teaspoon of salt. Blend the dry ingredients into the creamed mixture. Spread into a greased 9 x 13-inch pan. Bake

The Keeper's House

in a 350° oven for 15 minutes. Cool for 5 minutes.

In a medium bowl combine the brown sugar, eggs, 1 teaspoon of vanilla, and ¾ teaspoon of salt and beat until thick. Stir in the nuts and chocolate bits. Spread over the baked layer. Bake in a 350° oven for 25 minutes.

MAKES 8 SERVINGS.

Captain Lord Mansion

P.O. Box 800
Kennebunkport, Maine 04046
(207) 967-3141

The guest rooms at this inn have been decorated with period reproduction wallpaper, antique beds, and fine linens. The absence of telephones and televisions adds to the relaxed atmosphere. A sixteen-room, true country inn, the Captain Lord Mansion overlooks the Kennebunk River. The quiet, residential neighborhood is only a few blocks from the shops and restaurants of the Port's Dock Square area. In addition to participating in seasonal sports, guests may visit the Rachel Carson Wildlife Refugee, Seashore Trolley Museum, and historical Knott House.

Artichoke Squares

> 4 eggs, beaten
> 1 tablespoon chopped parsley
> 1 teaspoon salt
> ¼ teaspoon pepper
> 6 soda crackers, crushed
> 2 cups grated Cheddar cheese
> ¼ cup milk
> ....
> 2 14-ounce jars marinated artichoke hearts, chopped
> 1 clove garlic, chopped
> 1 bunch green onions, chopped

In a large bowl mix the eggs, parsley, salt, pepper, crackers, Cheddar cheese, and milk.

In a skillet heat the oil from 1 jar of artichokes and sauté the artichokes, garlic, and onions. Add the sautéed mixture to the cheese mixture and stir. Pour into a 9-inch square dish. Bake in a 325° oven for 20 to 30 minutes.

MAKES 20 TO 25 SERVINGS.

Pineapple Nut Upside-Down Muffins

> ¼ cup firmly packed dark brown sugar
> 2 tablespoons melted butter (margarine)
> 12 walnut halves
> ....
> 1½ cups 40% bran flakes
> 1 8-ounce can crushed pineapple, with juice
> ¼ cup milk
> ....
> 1 egg
> ¼ cup oil
> ½ cup chopped nuts
> ....
> 1¼ cups all-purpose flour
> 3½ teaspoons baking powder
> 1 teaspoon salt
> ⅓ cup sugar

In a small bowl combine the brown sugar and melted butter. Place a scant teaspoon of the mixture in the bottom of 12 muffin cups. Place half a walnut in each.

In a large mixing bowl combine the bran flakes, pineapple, and milk and let stand for 2 minutes. Add the egg and stir vigorously. Add the oil and nuts. Stir well.

In a separate bowl sift together the flour, baking powder, salt, and sugar. Pour the dry

ingredients into the wet and stir until just blended. The batter will be thick. Portion evenly into greased muffin cups. Bake in a 375° oven for 20 minutes. Turn the muffins upside down immediately onto a serving plate.

MAKES 1 DOZEN.

Tex Mex

> 3 soft avocados
> 1 tablespoon lemon juice
> 1 package taco seasoning mix
> 1 cup sour cream
> 2 cans jalapeño bean dip
> 1 7¼-ounce can black olives, pitted and chopped
> 1 bunch green onions, chopped
> 12 large tomatoes, chopped
> 2 cups grated Cheddar cheese
> Tortilla chips for dipping

In a medium bowl mash the avocados. Add the lemon juice and mix well. In a separate bowl mix the taco seasoning with the sour cream.

On a large cake or meat plate layer in order the bean dip, (about ¼-inch thick), avocado mixture, taco-sour cream mixture, chopped black olives, chopped onions, chopped tomatoes, and grated Cheddar cheese. Spread the cheese like frosting on the top and sides. Serve with tortilla chips. Take a chip and scoop a little of each layer and enjoy!

MAKES 8 SERVINGS.

English-style Porridge

> 4 cup water
> 1 teaspoon salt
> ....
> 2 cups 1-minute oats (quick-cooking kind)
> ....
> 5 tablespoons butter
> ¼ teaspoon ground cinnamon
> ¼ teaspoon grated nutmeg
> 2 tablespoons firmly packed brown sugar
> 2 ounces maple syrup
> ⅔ of a 5-ounce can evaporated milk

In a large saucepan bring the water and salt to a boil. Add the oats and cook for 1 minute, stirring constantly. Remove the pan from the heat and add the butter, cinnamon, nutmeg, brown sugar, syrup, and evaporated milk.

Stir the mixture well and serve.

MAKES 6 SERVINGS.

Kennebunkport Inn

1 Dock Square
Kennebunkport, Maine 04046
(207) 967-2621

Dock *Square is at the center of the famous coastal village of Kennebunkport with all its shops, galleries, restaurants, and summertime bustle. A 19th-century mansion and attached annex dating to the 1930s offer thirty-four rooms, all individually decorated and furnished with period antiques. The dining room features Maine lobster and other native seafood served by candlelight in relaxed elegance.*

Kennebunkport Inn

English Trifle

18   **egg yolks**
¾   **cup sugar**
2¼ **cups milk, scalded**
1¼ **cups heavy cream, scalded**
¼   **cup cornstarch dissolved in 6 tablespoons milk**
1   **teaspoon vanilla extract**
¼   **teaspoon fresh grated nutmeg**

....

1   **12-ounce pound cake, cut into cubes**
⅔   **cup cream sherry**

....

36 **1½-inch macaroons**
½   **cup Amaretto liqueur**

1   **12-ounce jar strawberry jam**

....

6   **pints fresh strawberries (or 4 10-ounce packages frozen berries, thawed and drained)**
2   **cups heavy cream**
2   **tablespoons sugar**
½   **teaspoon vanilla extract**
¼   **cup toasted almonds, crushed**

In a large bowl beat the egg yolks and sugar until thick and lemon colored. Blend in the milk, 1¼ cups of heavy cream, and the cornstarch mixture. Pour into the top of a double boiler and whisk constantly over simmering water until the mixture thickens. Do not allow the mixture to boil. Remove the pan from the heat. Add the vanilla and nutmeg, cover with waxed paper, and allow to cool.

In a large bowl soak the pound cake cubes in the sherry.

Brush the flat sides of 15 macaroons with liqueur. Arrange the flat sides around the sides of a 12-cup glass or trifle bowl, then line the bottom, flat-sides up. Cover with some of the strawberry jam, 1¼ cups of custard, and a layer of pound cake soaked in sherry. Then cover the pound cake with more of the jam, half the strawberries, and another 1¼ cups of custard. Repeat layering with pound cake, jam, berries, and custard.

Arrange the remaining macaroons flat-side down over the top and brush with sherry. Plastic wrap can be placed over the top at this point and kept up to 2 days.

Before serving, whip 2 cups of cream with 2 tablespoons of sugar and ½ teaspoon of vanilla until stiff. Decorate the top of the trifle with whipped cream. A final garnish of almonds may be sprinkled over the top.

Variation: Other fruit can be used in place of strawberries (raspberries, bananas, kiwis, etc.).

MAKES 8 SERVINGS.

Lobster Quiche with Mascarpone Cheese

2½ **cups heavy cream**
4   **eggs**
1   **cup mascarpone cheese**
¼   **teaspoon salt**
4   **twist of pepper mill**
1   **tablespoon dry sherry**
8   **ounces fresh picked lobster meat, cut into bite-sized pieces**

1   **unbaked 11-inch pie crust**
2   **teaspoons garlic chives, snipped**

In a large bowl whisk together the cream, eggs, cheese, salt, pepper, and sherry. Spread the lobster meat evenly on the bottom of the pie shell and sprinkle with the chives. Slowly pour the cream mixture into the pie shell. Bake in a 400° oven for 15 minutes. Reduce the oven temperature to 325° and continue to bake for 35 minutes or until a knife inserted in the center comes out clean. Remove from the oven and allow to sit for at least 10 minutes before serving.

MAKES 8 SERVINGS.

Maine Stay Inn

Maine Stay Inn and Cottages

34 Maine Street, P.O. Box 500A
Kennebunkport, Maine 04046
(207) 967-2117

Built *as a private home around 1860, the Maine Stay has served as an inn for more than fifty years. Features of Queen Anne style architecture were introduced to the original square-block Italianate design during the early 1900s when the house was given its remarkable suspended spiral staircase, starburst crystal windows, and ornately carved mantels and moldings. Warmth and hospitality accompany the elegant breakfast. The inn offers seventeen rooms, including several located in separate cottages. In all* *seasons, the Maine Stay is a perfect setting for a romantic getaway or family retreat.*

Mrs. Milld's Oatmeal Cookies

- 2 cups sugar
- 2 cups all-purpose flour
- 2 cups margarine
- 4 cups old-fashioned oatmeal
- 2 teaspoons baking soda

In a large bowl mix all ingredients together. Form into 1-inch balls. Place on greased cookie sheets and flatten each cookie with the bottom of a glass. Bake in a 350° oven for 10 to 15 minutes.

MAKES ABOUT 3 DOZEN.

Julie's Family Sugar Cookies

- 1 cup butter (not margarine), softened
- 1 cup sugar
- 2 large eggs
- 1 teaspoon vanilla extract
- 3¾ cups all-purpose flour
- 2 teaspoons baking powder
  Decorative sprinkles, colored sugar, or icing, if desired
- ¼ cup heavy cream

In a large bowl beat the butter and sugar with an electric mixer until pale and fluffy. Beat in the eggs and vanilla until blended. With the mixer on low gradually beat in the flour, baking powder, and cream until blended well.

Press the dough into a ball, then divide it in half. Wrap each half and chill 3 hours or until firm enough to roll.

Spray cookie sheets with cooking spray. On a lightly floured surface, roll 1 piece of dough at a time. Keep the rest refrigerated. Roll to ¼-inch thickness. With cookie cutters cut into the desired shapes. Decorate with sprinkles or colored sugars, if desired. Bake in a 350° oven for 14 minutes or just until the bottoms and edges are brown. Cool completely on a wire rack. Repeat with the remaining dough.

If preferred, decorate with icings. Store in an airtight container up to 2 weeks or freeze in single layers.

MAKES ABOUT 3 DOZEN.

Applesauce Bread Pudding

- 8 slices cinnamon raisin bread, toasted
- ⅓ cup margarine, melted
- 2 cups applesauce
- 1 cup granola
- ¼ cup firmly packed brown sugar
- ½ teaspoon ground cinnamon
- ½ teaspoon grated nutmeg
- ½ teaspoon salt
- 1 teaspoon lemon zest
- 2 tablespoons lemon juice
- 3 eggs
- ¼ cup sugar
- 1½ cups milk

Arrange 4 slices of toast to cover the bottom of a 9-inch square baking pan. Brush the bread with half of the melted margarine. In a medium bowl mix the applesauce, granola, brown sugar, spices, salt, and lemon zest together. Spread the mixture on the cinnamon bread over the butter. Top with 4 more slices of toast and brush the top with melted margarine. In a separate bowl beat the lemon juice, eggs, sugar, and milk together. Pour the mixture over the toast. Cover the pan with foil. (May be refrigerated overnight). Set the baking pan in a 9 x 13-inch pan filled with 1 inch of water. Bake in a 350° oven for 45 to 60 minutes. Uncover the pan for the last 15 minutes of baking time. Cut into 8 pieces and serve warm.

MAKES 8 SERVINGS.

Apricot Scones

- 4 ounces dried apricots
- ¼ cup water
- 1 tablespoon lemon juice
- 2 tablespoons honey
- ....
- 1 cup margarine
- ¼ cup sugar
- 3 large eggs
- 1 teaspoon vanilla extract
- 3 cups all-purpose flour
- 1 tablespoon baking powder
- ¼ teaspoon salt
- ⅔ cup plain yogurt

In a food processor combine the apricots, water, lemon juice, and honey and finely chop until the consistency of a thick purée. Set aside.

In a food processor or electric mixer beat the margarine until creamy. Add the sugar, eggs, and vanilla, and beat until fluffy. In a medium bowl mix the flour, baking powder, and salt. Add the dry ingredients to the butter mixture and beat until blended well. Scrape the sides. Add the yogurt and mix until blended well. Fold the apricot purée into the batter with a rubber spatula just until the purée is swirled through.

Using an ice cream scooper, scoop the dough onto an ungreased cookie sheet, placing the mounds about 2 inches apart. Loosely cover with plastic wrap and freeze overnight. When the individual scones are hard, remove to a freezer bag or airtight container and freeze for up to 6 weeks.

Place the scones on cookie sheets. Bake in a 350° oven for 15 minutes. Reduce the temperature to 325° and bake 10 minutes longer, until a golden brown. Cool, uncovered, on a wire rack.

MAKES 12 TO 14 SCONES.

Apple Spice Pancakes

- 2 cups all-purpose flour
- 3 tablespoons sugar
- 3 teaspoons baking powder
- ¾ teaspoon salt
- 1 teaspoon ground cinnamon
- ¼ teaspoon ground allspice
- 1 cup milk
- 2 large eggs
- 2 tablespoons oil
- 1 teaspoon vanilla extract
- 1 cup applesauce
  Maple syrup

In a large bowl combine the flour, sugar, baking powder, salt, cinnamon, and allspice. In a separate bowl whisk together the milk, eggs, oil, and vanilla. Stir in the applesauce. Pour the liquid mixture into the dry ingredients and stir with a wooden spoon until moistened well. Set the batter aside. Warm a griddle to medium-high heat (about 375° on an electric griddle). Brush the griddle with oil. When the griddle is ready, stir the batter, adding more milk if necessary until the batter is the consistency of thick heavy cream. Pour ¼ cup of batter for each pancake onto the griddle.

Cook the pancakes until bubbles that have formed around the edge are broken. Turn the pancakes over and cook the other side. Stir additional milk into the batter as needed to maintain a pourable consistency. Serve the pancakes with lots of warm Maine maple syrup.

MAKES 4 TO 6 SERVINGS.

P.O. Box 406
Northeast Harbor, Maine 04662
(207) 267-3344

For 130 years, the Asticuo has operated continuously in highly scenic Northeast Harbor where, in summer, yachts and sailboats can be seen regularly. Tucked away in a quiet corner of Mount Desert Island, home of Acadia National Park, the original inn was built by Augustas Chase Savage, a schooner captain and entrepreneur. The Asticou, with its oriental rugs and cheerful fireplaces, retains the quiet elegance of its history. Birds, seals, and whales make regular appearances, and guests are surrounded by breathtaking scenery.

Maine Crab Cakes

- 1 **pound Maine crab meat (leg meat)**
- 1 **tablespoon fresh lemon juice**
- 1 **tablespoon finely minced red bell pepper**
- 1 **tablespoon finely minced yellow bell pepper**
- 1 **tablespoon finely minced green bell pepper**
- 1 **tablespoon finely minced shallot**
- 1 **egg, beaten**
  Dash Worcestershire sauce
  Dash Tabasco sauce
  Salt and pepper to taste
  Old Bay seasoning to taste
- 1 **tablespoon fresh chopped chervil**

- 1 **tablespoon mayonnaise**
- 1 **teaspoon Dijon mustard**
- 1 **cup fresh seasoned breadcrumbs**
  Butter for sautéing

In a medium bowl mix all ingredients except the breadcrumbs until moistened. Place the breadcrumbs in a pie plate. Gently form the crab mixture into patties and coat well with the breadcrumbs. Place on a waxed paper-lined pan, wrap, and chill for several hours.

Sauté in butter for about 5 minutes each side until golden brown.

MAKES 4 SERVINGS.

Roasted Game Hens with Raspberry Hazelnut Dressing and Sauce Forestier

- ½ **cup butter, melted in a sauté pan**
- 1 **stalk celery, diced**
- 1 **leek, white and pale green parts, chopped**
- 1 **shallot, chopped**
- 2 **cups chicken stock**
- 1 **teaspoon chopped fresh thyme**
- 1 **teaspoon chopped fresh parsley**
- 1 **teaspoon chopped fresh sage**
- 2½ **cups cornbread dressing crumbs**
  Salt and pepper to taste
- ½ **cup roasted hazelnuts, chopped**
- ¼ **cup hazelnut liqueur (optional)**
- ½ **pint fresh raspberries**
- 6 **12- to 16-ounce game hens, cavities rinsed**
  Butter for basting
- 1 **cup white wine, or to taste**
....
- 3 **strips bacon, diced**
- 1 **shallot, chopped**
- ¼ **cup butter**
- 2 **cups sliced portabella mushrooms**
- 2 **cups Merlot or other robust red wine**
- 1 **tablespoon fresh tarragon**
....
  Fresh raspberries for garnish

In a saucepan melt the butter and sauté the celery, leek, and shallot until limp and just browning. Add the chicken stock and reduce to 1½ cups. Add the fresh herbs and pour over the cornbread in a bowl. Stir to moisten well. Let cool. Add the salt and pepper, the hazelnuts, and the liqueur, and mix well. Gently stir in the fresh berries. Taste and adjust the seasonings if needed.

Pat the hens dry. Salt and pepper the cavities and stuff with the dressing. Truss the legs together with twine. Place the hens on a rack in a roasting pan. Coat them with a little butter. Add some white wine to the pan, about a cup. Bake in a 350° oven for 1 hour and 30 minutes until crisp and plump, basting often. In the meantime, make the sauce.

In a hot sauté pan add the diced bacon and brown until crisp and the fat is rendered. Stir in the shallot and butter. Add the mushrooms and sauté until browned and the moisture is released. Add the red wine, bring to a boil, and reduce until the sauce is thickened and glossy. Stir in the tarragon and keep warm.

Remove the twine from the hens and place on serving plates. Nap with sauce, and sprinkle with a few fresh raspberries. This is an excellent dish for a company dinner.

MAKES 6 SERVINGS.

Chocolate Blackberry Chambord Cake with Buttercream

- 2 **cups unsifted cake flour**
- ⅔ **cup premium unsweetened cocoa**
- 3 **tablespoons Ghirardelli ground chocolate**
- 1¼ **teaspoons baking soda**
- ¼ **teaspoon baking powder**
- 5 **eggs**
- 1⅓ **cups sugar**
- 1 **teaspoon vanilla extract**
- ¼ **cup Chambord**
- 1 **cup 2% milk**
- 1 **cup real mayonnaise**
....
- 1 **12-ounce jar pure blackberry fruit spread**
- 1 **16-ounce can blackberries, drained**
- ¼ **cup Chambord**
....
- ¾ **cup butter**
- 1 **16-ounce box confectioners' sugar**
- 3 **tablespoons Ghirardelli ground chocolate**
- ¼ **cup espresso or strong coffee**
  Fresh blackberries and chocolate curls for garnish

Grease and flour 2 9-inch cake pans. In a medium bowl combine the flour, 3 tablespoons of cocoa, chocolate, soda, and baking powder. In a large bowl beat the eggs with the sugar until doubled in volume and pale in color. Add the vanilla and Chambord. Alternately fold in one-third of the flour mixture, and half of the milk blending well. Repeat the additions, ending with the flour. Lastly, fold the mayonnaise into the cake batter. Divide evenly between the pans. Bake in a 350° oven for 30 to 35 minutes, or until the centers spring back upon touch. Cool for 10 minutes. Remove the cakes from the pans and cool on racks for 1 hour.

In a saucepan melt the fruit spread. Add the berries and Chambord and cook for 5 minutes until thickened. Set the filling aside to cool.

In a large bowl beat the butter until fluffy. Add the confectioners' sugar, and slowly add the chocolate and espresso until creamy.

Split the cake layers in half. Spread the bottom layer with half of the filling. Place the next layer on and top with one-fourth of the frosting. Add the third layer and top with the remaining fruit filling. Add the last cake layer. Frost the sides, then the top with the frosting. Decorate the top with fresh berries and chocolate curls if desired.

MAKES 12 SERVINGS.

Inn on Carleton

❧

46 Carleton Street
Portland, Maine 04102
(207) 775-1910

---

*T*his restored 1869 Victorian townhouse places its guests in a quiet residential corner of Portland, but still very near the center of things. The Portland Museum of Art, Maine Medical Center, Performing Arts Center, and central business district are all a short walk from its front steps. Arched double doors welcome visitors to the front hall where a curving staircase leads to seven guest rooms on the second and third floors. Original artwork and

an amazing collection of old and new clocks highlight the decor.

Blueberry Coffee Cake

 2 **cups baking mix**
 1 **cup all-purpose flour**
 1 **cup sugar**
 ¼ **teaspoon grated nutmeg**
 1 **teaspoon ground cinnamon**
 3 **eggs, beaten**
 ¼ **cup oil**
 1 **teaspoon vanilla extract**
 ¾ **cup milk**
 2 **cups blueberries**

 ¼ **cup firmly packed brown sugar**
 ¼ **cup all-purpose flour**
 ¼ **cup pecans**
 2 **tablespoons melted butter**

Grease a 13 x 9-inch pan. In a large bowl mix together the dry ingredients. In a separate bowl mix together the eggs, oil, vanilla and milk. Pour the liquid mixture into the dry mixture and blend well. Fold in the blueberries.

Pour the butter into the prepared pan.

In a medium bowl combine the remaining ingredients. Sprinkle the topping over cake batter. Bake in a 350° oven for 30 to 40 minutes.

MAKES 10 TO 12 SERVINGS.

Spice Muffins

 1½ **cups all-purpose flour**
 2 **teaspoons baking powder**
 ½ **cup sugar**
 1 **teaspoon ground cinnamon**
 ½ **teaspoon pumpkin pie spice**
 ½ **teaspoon salt**

 2 **eggs**
 ⅓ **cup oil**
 ½ **cup milk**
 1 **teaspoon vanilla extract**
 1½ **teaspoons butter**
  Cinnamon-sugar

In a large bowl sift together the dry ingredients. In a separate bowl beat the eggs with a fork until frothy. Add the oil, milk, and vanilla. Add the liquid mixture ingredients to the dry mixture very quickly. Do not overmix. Fill greased muffin cups full. Top each muffin with ¼ teaspoon of butter and sprinkle with

cinnamon-sugar. Bake in a 400° oven for approximately 20 minutes.

MAKES 6 MUFFINS.

Black Point Inn

Black Point Inn

❧

510 Black Point Road
Scarborough, Maine 04074
(207) 883-4126

---

*M*ost of the eighty-five rooms in this resort inn offer spectacular views of the Atlantic. At night guest can hear waves breaking against the rocky cliffs. Artist Winslow Homer's studio is near the inn, and it was this stretch of the rugged Maine coast that he depicted in many of his most famous oil paintings. The largest collection of Homer's paintings is on display at the Portland Museum of Art. There is plenty to do here bedsides enjoy the view. The inn has its own private yacht and right next door is a PGA golf course and fourteen clay and all-weather tennis courts.

Pecan French Toast with Maine Blueberry Syrup

 2 **cups canola oil**
 2 **cups dry white breadcrumbs**
 2 **cups crushed pecans**
 3 **eggs**
 ½ **teaspoon vanilla extract**
 1 **teaspoon ground cinnamon**
 6 **slices thick white bread (Texas toast)**

Confectioners' sugar

....

3 cups Maine blueberries
1 cup maple syrup

In a cast-iron skillet heat the oil over medium heat. In a shallow dish combine the bread-crumbs and pecans. In a bowl whisk together the eggs, vanilla, and cinnamon. Dip the Texas toast in the egg mixture, coating both sides. Roll in the breadcrumb and pecan mixture, covering both sides. In a skillet brown the bread on each side (approximately 2 minutes on each side) until golden. Remove from the skillet and place on a paper towel to remove excess oil. Cut the pieces diagonally and serve 3 per serving. Dust with confectioners' sugar.

In a non-reactive saucepan combine the blueberries and syrup. Bring the syrup to a boil. Reduce the heat to simmer and skim. Reduce the liquid to half. Remove from the heat and keep syrup warm. Serve the blueberry syrup on the side.

MAKES 4 SERVINGS.

Fresh Haddock Topped with Maine Crab Meat

4 ounces Maine crab meat, picked and cleaned (also known as peeky toe crab)
1 tablespoon seeded and minced red bell pepper
1 tablespoon seeded and minced green bell pepper
1 tablespoon seeded and minced yellow bell peppers
2 teaspoons peeled and minced red onion
1 shallot, peeled and minced
1 teaspoon chopped parsley
1 teaspoon lemon juice
½ teaspoon Dijon mustard
1 tablespoon mayonnaise
Dash Tabasco sauce
Dash Worcestershire sauce
1½ cups dry white breadcrumbs
1 egg
Salt and white pepper to taste

....

20 ounces haddock fillet, cut into 4- to 5-ounce portions

In a bowl combine the crab meat, peppers, onion, shallot, parsley, lemon juice, mustard, mayonnaise, Tabasco, and Worcestershire sauce, and mix thoroughly. Add the bread-crumbs and egg and mix. Season with salt and white pepper, and let sit 5 minutes to absorb moisture.

Spray a baking sheet or shallow roasting pan with cooking spray. Place the haddock portions in the pan and top with 1½ to 2 ounces of the crab mixture, spreading it evenly over the surface of the fish. Sprinkle the fish with a small amount of water. Bake in a 375° oven for 15 to 18 minutes. The fish should be firm but not dry.

MAKES 4 SERVINGS.

141 Lookout Point Road
South Harpswell, Maine 04079
(800) 843-5509

————————————

T he colonial-style Harpswell Inn dates to 1761 and is so gracious in appearance that it is almost impossible to believe it was once the cookhouse of a shipyard. Stout schooners and other sailing ships were built here during the Civil War era. The old bell on top of the inn dates to that period when it was used to summon hungry shipwrights to their dinner. From its vantage point on the finger-like peninsula, the inn overlooks a snug harbor filled with bobbing lobster boats. Excellent summer theatre productions, art galleries, and the Maine Maritime Museum are a short 15 to 20 minute drive from Harpswell Inn.

Harpswell Inn Casserole

4 cups herbed croutons
2 cups shredded sharp cheese
2 pounds crumbled, cooked sausage
12 eggs
1 teaspoon dry mustard
1 10½-ounce can cream of mushroom soup
4 cups milk
1 2½-ounce can mushrooms, drained

In a 9 x 13-inch buttered baking dish place the croutons, cheese, and sausage.

In a separate large bowl beat together the eggs, dry mustard, and mushroom soup. Add the milk and beat again. Add the mushrooms, if desired. Pour the liquid over the croutons, cheese, and sausage in the pan, cover, and refrigerate overnight.

Bake in a 325° oven for 1 hour.

MAKES 8 SERVINGS.

Quiche Elaine

2 cups half-and-half
6 eggs
1 cup shredded Swiss cheese
1 teaspoon onion powder
Pinch grated nutmeg
8 slices bacon, cooked and crumbled
½ cup chopped green onions
1 9-inch unbaked pie shell

In a blender combine the half and half, eggs, Swiss cheese, onion powder, and nutmeg. Sprinkle the bacon and green onions in the bottom of the pie shell. Pour the egg mixture over this. Bake in a 375° oven for 30 to 35 minutes.

MAKES 6 TO 8 SERVINGS.

60 Clark Point Road
Southwest Harbor, Maine 04679
(207) 244-9828

————————————

A stately Maine house built in 1857, the inn offers a warm fireplace, wicker-filled sun porch, and sparkling harbor views. The charming coastal village of Southwest Harbor is on what some call "the quiet side" of Mount Desert Island, which bustles with droves of summer visitors who come to see Acadia National Park. Antique shops, art galleries, and the Oceanarium are within walking distance.

The Lambs Ear Inn

Misty Morning Crisp

3 ripe bananas, sliced in ½-inch
    rounds (approximately 2 cups)
1 20-ounce can pineapple chunks,
    drained (reserve ¼ cup juice)
2 tablespoons apricot preserves
....
½ cup old-fashioned oats
½ cup firmly packed light brown sugar
¼ cup all-purpose flour
¼ cup shredded coconut
¼ cup butter, cut into small pieces

In a shallow 1½-quart baking dish gently mix the bananas and pineapple. Stir the preserves into the reserved pineapple juice. Pour over the fruit mixture.

In medium bowl mix the oats, sugar, flour, and coconut. Cut in the butter with a pastry blender until the mixture resembles crumbs. Sprinkle the topping over the fruit. Bake in a 400° oven for 15 to 20 minutes, until the topping is lightly browned and juices bubble.
MAKES 2 SERVINGS.

Fresh Spinach Pie

6 eggs
2 cups heavy cream
½ cup fresh breadcrumbs
½ teaspoon salt
¼ teaspoon grated nutmeg
2 tablespoons frozen orange juice
    concentrate
1 cup chopped fresh spinach (frozen
    may be used)
1 unbaked 9-inch pastry shell

In a bowl beat the eggs and heavy cream together, and stir in the breadcrumbs. Add the salt, nutmeg, orange juice, and spinach. Blend together. Pour into the pastry shell and bake in a 375° oven for 15 minutes. Reduce the oven temperature to 350° and bake for an additional 25 minutes. It's ready when a knife inserted in the center comes out clean.
MAKES 6 SERVINGS.

Broad Bay Inn and Gallery

❧

*1014 Main Street
Waldoboro, Maine 04572
(207) 832-6668*

T his lovingly restored 1830 inn is handsomely appointed with Victorian furnishings. There is an art gallery in the barn. Tea and sherry are served in the afternoon. The river, tennis, theater, and antique shops are within walking distance, and it is a short drive to the lighthouse, Audubon sanctuary, and fishing villages.

Broad Bay Inn

Plum Torte (Or Apple-Cranberry Torte)

¾ cup sugar
½ cup unsalted butter
1 cup unbleached flour, sifted
1 teaspoon baking powder
    Pinch salt (optional)
2 eggs
24 halves pitted purple plums
    Sugar, lemon juice, and cinnamon
      for topping
    Whipped cream (optional)

In a medium bowl cream the sugar and butter. Add the flour, baking powder, salt, and eggs, and beat well.

Spoon the batter into an 8-, 9-, or 10-inch springform pan. Place the plum halves skin-side up on top of the batter. Sprinkle lightly with sugar and lemon juice, depending on the sweetness of the fruit. Sprinkle with about 1 teaspoon of ground cinnamon, or to taste. Bake in a 350° oven for 1 hour. Remove and cool. Refrigerate or freeze, if desired. Or cool to lukewarm and serve plain or with whipped cream.

To serve a torte that was frozen, defrost and reheat it briefly in a 300° oven.

Variation: To make an apple-cranberry torte, follow the directions for plum torte but peel, seed, quarter, and slice 2 or 3 large tart baking apples. Arrange ½ cup of raw cranberries over the batter and top with the apple slices. Sprinkle generously with cinnamon, squeeze ½ to 1 tablespoon of lemon juice over the apples. Sprinkle with sugar and bake as above.
MAKES 8 SERVINGS.

Scrambled Eggs in Tulip Croustades

12 slices soft white bread, crusts
    removed
    Oil for brushing the croustades
8 large eggs
¼ cup minced fresh tarragon (or 1
    tablespoon crumbled dried)
½ cup minced scallion, including the
    greens
¼ cup milk
    Salt and pepper
3 tablespoons unsalted butter
    Tarragon sprigs for garnish

Roll each slice of bread flat with a rolling pin and brush both sides of each slice with some of the oil. Fit each slice gently into a ½ cup muffin cup. Bake the croustades in a 350° oven for 20 minutes, or until the edges are golden.

In a bowl whisk together the eggs, minced tarragon, scallion, milk, salt, and pepper to taste. In a heavy saucepan melt the butter over moderate heat until it is foamy, add the egg mixture, and reduce the heat to moderately low. Cook the egg mixture, stirring it with a whisk, for 3 to 5 minutes, or until it is just set. The scrambled eggs should have small curds and appear very creamy. Divide the eggs among the croustades and garnish them with the tarragon sprigs.

Variation: Sprinkle with bacon bits; red, yellow and green bell peppers; onion, diced; a dollop of yogurt on top; and some chopped parsley. Leave out the tarragon. Serve with Canadian bacon, Chinese pea pods, and fresh fruit. Looks and tastes delicious.

MAKES 4 TO 6 SERVINGS.

Blueberry Buckle

¾ cup sugar
¼ cup butter
1 egg
½ cup milk
2 cups sifted all-purpose flour
2 teaspoons baking powder
½ teaspoon salt
2 cups fresh blueberries
....
½ cup sugar
⅓ cup sifted all-purpose flour
½ teaspoon ground cinnamon
¼ cup butter, softened

In a large bowl mix thoroughly ¾ cup of sugar, ¼-cup of butter, and the egg. Stir in the milk. In a separate bowl sift together the sifted flour, baking powder, and salt. Add the dry ingredients to the batter, stirring well. Toss the fresh blueberries in a little flour, then add them. Spread the batter in a greased and floured 9-inch square pan.

In a small bowl combine the remaining ingredients. Sprinkle the mixture over the batter. Bake in a 375° oven for 45 to 50 minutes.

MAKES 6 TO 8 SERVINGS.

Cheesy Broccoli-Sausage Delight

6 small baked pastry shells
1 pound browned sausage, crumbled
1½ cups cooked chopped broccoli
6 eggs, scrambled
½ cup grated Cheddar cheese
1 cup prepared cheese soup from a can
Grated Parmesan cheese
Chopped chives for garnish

Fill the pastry shells with a layer of each of sausage, broccoli, and eggs. Sprinkle Cheddar cheese over each. Bake in a 350° oven for 10 minutes.

Prepare the cheese soup as directed on the can. Serve the pastries with the cheese soup ladled over them and a garnish of Parmesan cheese. Garnish with chopped chives.

MAKES 6 SERVINGS.

The Roaring Lion Bed and Breakfast

❦

995 Main Street, P.O. Box 756
Waldoboro, Maine 04572
(207) 832-4038

---

*B*uilt in 1905, the Roaring Lion features classic woodwork, tin ceilings, two large fireplaces, and a big screened porch. Located just off Highway 1 in the village of Waldoboro, it is near the coastal mountains and the sea and within a short drive to Augusta, the state capital. The popular Boothbay area, rugged Pemaquid Point, and Camden are all only a short drive from Waldoboro. Full breakfasts are varied and include the hosts' special "Lion Eggs" and sourdough pancakes.

The Roaring Lion

Roaring Lion Total Muffins

1⅓ cups milk
1 scant cup crushed Total flakes (any of the Total cereals can be used)
1½ cups unbleached flour
1 tablespoon baking powder
½ teaspoon salt
½ cup sugar
1 egg
¼ cup oil
½ cup pecan meal or chopped nuts (optional)

In a medium bowl add the milk to the crushed cereal and let sit for up to 10 minutes to let the flakes absorb the milk.

In a large bowl thoroughly mix the dry ingredients together. Add the egg and oil to the cereal mixture and mix well. Add the dry ingredients and mix until just moistened. Pour into greased muffin cups, filling each cup about three-fourths full. Bake in a 400° oven for 20 minutes.

MAKES 1 DOZEN.

Mully's Coffee Cake

3 scant cups unbleached all-purpose flour
1 cup firmly packed brown sugar
1 cup sugar
1 teaspoon ground cinnamon
1 teaspoon grated nutmeg
1 teaspoon salt
1 scant cup oil
....
1 teaspoon baking soda
1 egg
1 cup buttermilk

In a large bowl mix the flour, brown sugar, sugar, cinnamon, nutmeg, salt, and oil. Reserve 1 cup of the mixture. To the rest add the soda, egg, and buttermilk. Mix the batter well. Pour into a well-greased 9 x 13-inch pan. Sprinkle the reserved dry mixture on top. Bake in a 375° oven for 25 to 35 minutes.

MAKES 8 SERVINGS.

Potato, Sauerkraut, and Cheese Casserole

     2   to 3 tablespoons oil
   1½   pounds sauerkraut, chopped
     1   cup chopped onion
     3   tablespoons sesame seeds
   2½   cups mashed potatoes
     ½   teaspoon caraway seeds
          Salt and pepper to taste
     2   teaspoons firmly packed brown
          sugar
     1   cup sour cream
   1½   cups grated Cheddar cheese
          Black olives, red pepper strips, and
          green chili strips for garnish

In a skillet heat the oil and sauté the sauerkraut and onion until tender. Then add the sesame seeds, potato, seasonings, sugar, and sour cream. Place in a well-greased 1½-quart casserole. Sprinkle with the Cheddar cheese. Bake in a 350° oven until the cheese has melted and bubbles. Garnish and serve.

MAKES 6 TO 8 SERVINGS.

The Squire Tarbox Inn

RR 2, Box 620
Wiscasset, Maine 04578
(207) 882-7693

*B*uilt in 1763, the Squire Tarbox predates the American Revolution. The name is taken from Squire Samuel Tarbox who remodeled and expanded the house in 1825. Original floors, carvings, beams, moldings, and fireplaces have been

The Squire Tarbox Inn

preserved. Guests will enjoy the quiet pastoral setting. Nearby Wiscasset offers a community of local craftsmen and artists and the Musical Wonder House with one of the world's finest antique music box collections. Before dinner, guests may savor a fresh soft herbed chèvre from the inn's own dairy herd and cheese-making enterprise.

Leek and Goat Cheese Pizza

     ¼   cup butter
     1   tablespoon olive oil
     2   cups finely diced leeks (white part
          only, about 6 medium leeks)
     1   cup finely chopped onion
     2   large pinches saffron threads
          Salt to taste
          Cornmeal
     ½   recipe basic pizza dough
     6   ounces goat cheese, crumbled
     6   halves sun-dried tomatoes in oil,
          drained, and cut in julienne slivers (or pitted Italian black olives,
          coarsely chopped)

In a skillet heat the butter and oil and sauté the leeks and onion over low heat, covered, until very tender but not brown. Stir from time to time as they cook. Crumble the saffron into the skillet, add the salt and mix. Cover and continue to cook 10 minutes, stirring a few times.

Dust a large baking sheet with cornmeal. Divide the dough into 4 equal portions. Shape each into a circle about 6 inches in diameter with a rim of about ½ inch and place on a baking sheet. Spread each circle of dough with the saffron-flavored leek mixture.

Sprinkle crumbled goat cheese evenly over each pizza. Then arrange the strips of sundried tomatoes like the spokes of a wheel over the cheese. If using olives, sprinkle the pieces in a circular pattern on each pizza. Bake on the bottom level of the oven until lightly browned and the cheese has melted, about 20 minutes. Serve at once.

MAKES 4 6-INCH PIZZAS.

Fettuccine with Goat Cheese and Walnut Sauce

     2   cups heavy cream
          Salt to taste, if desired
          Fresh ground pepper to taste
     ¼   teaspoon fresh grated nutmeg
     1   cup toasted walnuts, coarsely
          chopped
     1   16-ounce package fettuccine
     8   ounces goat cheese, coarsely chopped
     3   tablespoons butter
          Fresh grated Parmesan cheese
     2   tablespoons cognac

In a saucepan bring 1 cup of cream to a simmer. Add salt and pepper, and cook for about 5 minutes. Add the nutmeg. Add the remaining cream and the walnuts and bring to a boil.

In a large pot cook the fettuccine to the desired degree of doneness. Drain and add it to the walnut sauce. Place the saucepan over low heat. Immediately add the goat cheese and butter, and toss until the butter is melted and the cheese is thoroughly hot. Sprinkle with additional pepper and ½ cup freshly grated Parmesan cheese. Sprinkle with cognac, toss briefly, and serve immediately with extra Parmesan cheese on the side.

MAKES 4 TO 6 SERVINGS.

The Stacked Arms Bed and Breakfast

R.F.D. 2, Box 146
Birch Point Road
Wiscasset, Maine 04578
(207) 882-5436

*F*lower beds and fruit trees surround this inn which has a fine view of the lovely village of Wiscasset. Its three guest rooms are nicely appointed and decorated in a variety of country styles. Nearby Wiscasset and the town of Bath provide plenty to see and do. Bath is home to an active shipyard and the Maine Maritime Museum. Freeport, home of L. L. Bean, Inc., is only 45 minutes away. In every direction, guests may delight in the natural beauty of the rocky Maine countryside and seasoast.

Homestead Inn

The Stacked Arms Scallops

    1   to 2 tablespoons oil
    1   cup bay scallops (scallops cut into
        quarters)
    1   cup shrimp, peeled and deveined
    ½   cup chopped onions
    5   eggs
    2   cups evaporated milk
    ¾   teaspoon salt
        Dash nutmeg
        Dash cayenne pepper
        Dash black pepper
    1   10-inch unbaked pie shell
    1   cup grated Swiss cheese

In a skillet heat the oil and sauté the scallops, shrimp, and onions until the shrimp and scallops are opaque, a short time. In a bowl beat the eggs, milk, and seasonings together. Place the seafood into pie shell, sprinkle the cheese, and pour the egg mixture over all. Bake in a 450° oven for 10 to 15 minutes. Reduce the heat to 300° and continue baking for 25 to 30 minutes or until puffed and brown. Allow 15 minutes for cooling.

MAKES 8 SERVINGS.

Homestead Inn

8 South Main Street
York Beach, Maine 03910
(207) 363-8952

*T*he innkeepers take the "home away from home" approach at this B&B, a beach-lover's delight. A restored turn-of-the-century boarding house, it offers four charming guest rooms with views of the Atlantic, the shore hills, and Mount Agamenticus. A secluded sun deck in the back and a big fireplace in the living room add to guests' pleasures. Within a short distance are Nabble Lighthouse, Historic York Village, and factory outlets.

Rhubarb Coffee Cake

    1   cup finely chopped rhubarb

    1½ cups all-purpose flour
    2   teaspoons baking powder
    ½   teaspoon salt
    ½   teaspoon baking soda
    ¼   teaspoon grated nutmeg
    ⅔   cup sugar
    ⅓   cup butter
    2   eggs

Soften the rhubarb by pan-boiling or placing in the microwave.

In a medium bowl combine the flour, baking powder, salt, soda, and nutmeg. In a separate bowl cream the sugar and butter. Beat in the eggs. Fold in the rhubarb. Add the dry ingredients. Pour the batter into a 9 x 13-inch pan. Bake in a 350° oven for 45 to 50 minutes

MAKES 8 SERVINGS.

MARYLAND

Betsy's

1428 Park Avenue
Baltimore, Maryland 21217
(410) 383-1274

***T**his four story "petite estate," overlooks a quiet, tree-shaded street lined with row houses in the architecturally significant Bolton Hill community near downtown Baltimore. Built just after the Civil War, the house features ceiling medallions, carved marble mantels, and a*

center staircase rising to a skylight. Family heirloom quilts, coverlets, and brass rubbings decorate the expansive walls. Baltimore offers many world class attractions such as the Inner Harbor, National Aquarium, Pimlico Race Course, the B&O Railroad Museum, and the H.L. Menken House.

Sourdough Cinnamon Waffles

- 1 **envelope active dry yeast (2 teaspoons)**
- 2 **cups lukewarm water (105 to 115°)**
- 2 **cups presifted all-purpose flour (such as Wondra)**
- 1 **teaspoon sugar**
  ....
- 1 **teaspoon baking soda**
- 1 **teaspoon salt**
- 3 **tablespoons sugar**
- 3 **eggs**
- 3 **tablespoons melted butter**
- 1 **teaspoon vanilla extract**
- 1 **teaspoon ground cinnamon**

In a bowl mix the yeast, water, flour, and 1 teaspoon of sugar. Cover and let stand in a warm place overnight. Heat the waffle iron. To the flour mixture add the soda, salt, 3 tablespoons of sugar, eggs, butter, vanilla, and cinnamon.

After mixing all the ingredients, let the batter stand for 5 minutes.

Bake the waffles. Cool on a rack if using as dessert. Serve immediately if using for breakfast. Use any syrup or topping for breakfast. For dessert, garnish with raspberries, blueberries, or heavy cream.
MAKES 4 SERVINGS.

Corn Fritters

- 2 **cups cooked corn**
- ½ **cup milk**
- 1½ **cups all-purpose flour**
- 1 **teaspoon salt**
- 2 **teaspoons baking powder**
- 1 **tablespoon melted shortening (or oil)**
- 2 **eggs**

In a bowl mix all ingredients together. In a skillet heat a small amount of oil. Cook the batter like pancakes.
MAKES 4 TO 6 SERVINGS.

Twin Mountain Muffins

- ¼ **cup butter or margarine**
- ¼ **cup sugar**
- 1 **egg, well-beaten**
- 2 **cups all-purpose flour**
- 5 **teaspoons baking powder**
- ½ **teaspoon salt**
- 1 **cup milk**

In a large bowl cream the butter. Add the sugar and egg, mixing well. Add the flour with the baking powder and salt alternately with the milk. Pour into greased muffin cups. Bake in a 425° oven for 20 minutes.
MAKES 15 MEDIUM OR 12 LARGE MUFFINS.

Apple Topping for Pancakes

- ½ cup water
- 4 medium to large tart apples, peeled and thinly sliced
- ⅓ cup firmly packed brown sugar
- 1 tablespoon lemon juice
- ¼ teaspoon ground cinnamon
- 2 tablespoons cornstarch
- 2 tablespoons cold water
- Raisins or currants (optional)

In a saucepan bring the water and sliced apples to a boil. Cook for 5 to 8 minutes. Add the sugar, lemon juice, and cinnamon.

In a cup mix together the cornstarch and water. Use as much as needed to thicken the apple mixture. Add raisins or currants, if desired. Serve warm on freshly cooked pancakes.

MAKES ABOUT 3 CUPS.

Breakfast Baked Potatoes

- 4 baking potatoes, thinly sliced
- 1 small onion, thinly sliced
- Salt and pepper to taste
- Parmesan cheese

Spray a 1-quart pan generously with cooking spray. Arrange the potatoes in the pan. Arrange the onion slices on top. Sprinkle with salt and pepper. Re-spray with additional cooking spray. Bake in a 425° oven for 15 to 20 minutes. Remove from the oven and sprinkle with Parmesan cheese. Serve immediately.

MAKES 4 SERVINGS.

Sautéed Nectarines

- 1 nectarine (or peach)
- 1 tablespoon butter, melted
- 1 teaspoon firmly packed dark brown sugar
- Ground cinnamon and grated nutmeg to taste
- Fresh cream

Slice the nectarine. In a skillet melt the butter and sauté the nectarine slices for 10 minutes. Add the sugar and spices, and sauté until tender. Serve warm with fresh cream.

MAKES 1 SERVING.

Celie's Waterfront Bed and Breakfast

1714 Thames Street
Baltimore, Maryland 21231
(410) 522-2323

*W*ith skylights and an abundance of windows, the seven rooms of this B&B in the Fell's Point waterfront district are light and airy. Guests will enjoy the antiques and collectibles that recall Baltimore's past as a city of seafarers. Shipyards near here built the famous Baltimore Clippers. The old Navy frigate **Constellation** *is on display at nearby Harborplace.*

Baked Apples

- 12 apples (Cortlands preferably, otherwise McIntosh)
- ¼ cup lemon juice
- 1 cup apple cider
- ¾ to 1 cup firmly packed dark brown sugar
- ⅓ cup currants
- Ground cinnamon
- Cardamom

Core the apples with a melon baller. Slice the skin around each apple to allow for expansion. Place in a glass bowl. Sprinkle lemon juice and apple cider in and around the apples. Sprinkle brown sugar and currants in and around the apples. Sprinkle with spices to taste. Bake uncovered in a 350° oven for 30 minutes or until soft.

Note: Add more or less liquid to sugar for a thicker or thinner sauce. If the apples are done before the sauce, remove the apples and simmer the sauce on the stove for a few minutes until thick. Also add chopped hazelnuts for an unusual flavor.

MAKES 12 SERVINGS.

Dried Fruit Compote

- 4 cups fruit juice (pure cranberry, peach, apple, or combination)
- ¼ cup lemon juice
- 2 cinnamon sticks
- Whole cloves
- 3 tablespoon grated fresh ginger
- 1 teaspoon cardamom
- 1 2-inch piece vanilla bean
- 1 pound dried apricots
- ¼ pound dried apples
- ¼ pound dried pears
- ¼ pound dried peaches
- ¼ pound dried prunes
- ⅓ cup dried cranberries
- ⅓ cup dried cherries
- ⅓ cup dried currants

In a saucepan simmer the juice and spices for approximately 10 minutes until mulled well. Remove the cinnamon, cloves, and ginger. Slice open the vanilla bean and remove the seeds into the mixture; discard bean. Add the fruit and cover. Let stand overnight so the fruit absorbs the juice.

Note: In winter try the cranberry juice (using 2 cups pure cranberry with 2 cups water) or a mixture of cranberry and apple cider as the weather turns toward spring, but if the weather is still cool try using something like Dole Peach juice.

MAKES 6 SERVINGS.

Celie's Waterfront

Brampton Inn

25227 Chestertown Road
Chestertown, Maryland 21620
(410) 778-1860

Built in 1860, Brampton is listed on the National Register of Historic Places and stands today as it was originally constructed. The tall, many-paned windows, columned porch, wide-board floors, and carved fireplaces leave little doubt of its historical and architectural significance. Century-old trees grace the surrounding thirty-five-acre estate. Those who wish to enjoy this 19th-century elegance may choose from seven guest rooms, each of them decorated with period antiques or custom reproductions. Migrating ducks, swans, and Canadian geese are in abundance during the winter.

Ginger Lemon Muffins

- ½ cup butter, softened
- 1 cup sugar
- 2 large eggs, room temperature
- 2 tablespoons grated or chopped fresh ginger
- 2 to 3 lemons, scrubbed and zested
- 1 teaspoon baking soda
- 1 cup buttermilk
- 2 cups unbleached all-purpose flour
- ½ cup freshly squeezed lemon juice
- ½ cup sugar

Have all ingredients ready at room temperature.

In a large bowl beat the butter and 1 cup of sugar with an electric mixer until pale and fluffy. Add the eggs one at a time. Beat vigorously after each egg. Add the ginger and lemon zest.

In a separate bowl stir the baking soda into the buttermilk. It will begin to bubble.

Fold the flour into the ginger mixture alternately with the buttermilk mixture. Do not overmix. Spoon into buttered muffin cups. Bake in a 375° oven for 20 to 30 minutes, depending on the size of the muffins, until springy to the touch. Let the muffins cool for 5 minutes before taking out of the pans.

While the muffins are baking, in a sauce pan mix the lemon juice and ½ cup sugar and bring to a quick boil just until the sugar is dissolved. Turn off the heat and let cool. Dip the top of the still-warm muffins into the lemon syrup. They taste the best when still warm.

MAKES 12 NORMAL OR 6 GIANT MUFFINS.

Puffed Pancakes with Poached Pears

- 1 cup 1% or 2% milk
- 1 cup unbleached all-purpose flour
- 4 large eggs
- 9 tablespoons butter
- 3 ripe but firm pears
- ½ orange, juiced
- ¼ cup maple syrup
  Dash grated nutmeg

In a medium bowl mix the milk, flour, and eggs with an electric mixer. It should be fluffy and foamy.

In the bottom of 6 individual ramekin dishes, melt 1½ tablespoons of butter in each, making sure the butter is well-distributed. Measure ⅓ cup of batter into each buttered dish. Bake in a 500° oven for 10 to 12 minutes until nicely puffed and golden brown.

While the pancakes are baking, peel and core the pears. Cut each pear into 12 slices and layer in a large saucepan. In a bowl mix the orange juice and maple syrup. Pour over pears and cook until barely soft. Season with dash of nutmeg.

To serve, place each puffed pancake onto a dinner plate. Carefully arrange 6 slices of the pears on each pancake and pour 1 to 2 tablespoons of juice on top. Serve immediately.

MAKES 6 INDIVIDUAL PANCAKES.

Lemon Cheesecake Brampton

- 10 graham crackers
- ¾ cup sugar
- ½ cup sweet ground chocolate
- ½ cup melted butter, cooled

....

- 4 8-ounce packages cream cheese, softened
- 1½ cups sugar
- 4 large eggs, room temperature
- ¼ cup all-purpose flour
- 2 lemons, scrubbed and zested
- ½ cup fresh squeezed lemon juice
- ½ teaspoon salt
- 1 bunch of mint

Butter a 12-inch springform pan. In a food processor combine the crackers, ¾ cup of sugar, and chocolate, and chop until it looks like coarse cornmeal. Add the melted butter and mix.

Press the dough into the bottom of the prepared pan and cool for 10 minutes in the refrigerator. It is important to have all the ingredients at room temperature.

In a mixer bowl mix the cream cheese and 1½ cups of sugar at medium speed. Add the eggs one at a time, mixing well after each addition. Scrape the sides of the bowl and add the flour, lemon zest, lemon juice, and salt. Mix until very smooth. Pour into the springform. Bake in a 325° oven for 1 hour or until just set. Do not overcook or the cake top will crack. Cool for at least 4 hours in the refrigerator. Carefully remove the sides and lift onto a cake platter. It helps to use a good-sized spatula. Garnish with sprigs of mint.

MAKES 12 GENEROUS SLICES.

The Inn at Mitchell House

8796 Maryland Parkway
Chestertown, Maryland 21620
(410) 778-6500

*T*his historic manor house built in 1743 overlooks Stoneybrook Pond. Its atmosphere is simultaneously old-world gracious, relaxed, and close to nature. Songbirds, migrating geese, white-tailed deer, and the occasional red fox can be seen on the grounds. It is said that during the War of 1812 a wounded British officer was treated here following the battle of Caulk's Field. The unfortunate man died, and his body was transported back to England preserved in a barrel of rum.

Blueberry Surprise French Toast

    6   slices fresh Italian or French bread
    6   teaspoons blueberry all-fruit jam
    2   eggs
    ½   cup milk
    ¼   cup heavy cream
    1   teaspoon vanilla extract
    1   tablespoon cinnamon-sugar mix
        Butter for frying
        Confectioners' sugar
        Maple syrup and fresh blueberries
          for garnish

Cut a slit in each slice of bread to form a pocket. Spread a teaspoon of jam in each pocket. In a bowl mix the eggs, milk, cream, vanilla, and cinnamon-sugar. Dip the bread in the mixture and place in a 9 x 13-inch baking pan. Pour the remaining egg mixture over the slices. In a skillet heat the butter and fry the slices until golden on each side. Sprinkle with confectioners' sugar, garnish with fresh blueberries, and serve with maple syrup.
MAKES 6 TO 8 SERVINGS.

Mitchell House Home Fries

    3   medium sweet potatoes
    3   medium white potatoes
    4   red potatoes
    ¼   to ⅓ cup bacon fat

    ½   cup chopped scallions, greens
          included
    1   to 2 tablespoons lemon pepper

Wash, but do not skin the potatoes. Chop into cubes. In a skillet heat the bacon fat and fry the potatoes until golden. Add the scallions and lemon pepper. Fry a couple more minutes. Serve immediately.
MAKES 4 SERVINGS.

Chestertown Crab Quiche

    ½   cup milk
    ½   cup mayonnaise
    2   eggs
    3   tablespoons all-purpose flour
    1   tablespoon Old Bay seasoning
    1   large shallot, chopped
    1   tablespoon chopped parsley
    1   teaspoon dry mustard
    2   tablespoons dry sherry
         Dash cayenne pepper
    1½   cups Swiss cheese, shredded
    1   pound fresh crab meat, (or canned)
    1   unbaked 9-inch pie shell

In a large bowl mix the milk, mayonnaise, eggs, and flour. Stir in the remaining ingredients except the pie crust, being careful not to break up the crab meat too much. Pour into the pie shell. Bake in a 350° oven for 50 to 60 minutes. Serve warm.
MAKES 6 TO 8 SERVINGS.

*Turning
Point Inn*

❧

*3406 Urbana Pike
Frederick, Maryland 21704
(301) 874-2421*

*T*ravelers could hardly find a more historic area than this. Near New Market, Harpers Ferry, and Antietam, it is less than an hour's drive from Gettysburg, Washington, D.C., Baltimore, and the Virginia horse country. Built in 1910 by a local doctor, the Turning Point is

decorated and furnished to reflect that era. It offers five lovely guest rooms and a pair of charming cottages.

Turning Point Inn

Rosemary Pepper Biscuits

    8   cups cake flour
    ⅓   cup baking powder
    2   to 3 tablespoons blanched, chopped
          fresh rosemary
    1   tablespoon coarse-cracked black
          pepper
    1   tablespoon salt
    ¼   cup sugar
    1   cup diced butter
    4   cups heavy cream
    ....
    1   egg
    1   tablespoon water

In a bowl combine all of the dry ingredients together with the butter and crumble by hand to incorporate the butter evenly. Add the cream and mix by hand just until moistened.

Knead the dough only to bind together and roll out ¾-inch thick.

Cut into biscuits and place on a lined tray. Beat the egg with the water. Brush with egg wash and refrigerate until needed for service.

Bake in a 350° oven for approximately 10 minutes or until golden.
MAKES 40 BISCUITS.

Chesapeake Eggs Benedict

    8   slices Canadian bacon, warmed
    4   English muffins, split and toasted
    4   ounces lump crab meat, picked over
          well
    8   eggs, poached
    4   egg yolks
         Pinch salt and white pepper
    2   teaspoons lemon juice
    1¾   cups melted butter
    2   teaspoon fresh chives, chopped

Place the bacon on English muffins and top each with ½ ounce of crab. Place 1 egg on each, on top of the crab. Place all on baking sheet and warm in a 325° oven for 5 to 7 minutes.

In the top of a double boiler over simmering water beat the yolks until smooth. When they turn creamy, add salt, pepper, and lemon juice. Remove from the heat and slowly incorporate the butter until slightly thickened.

Top with Hollandaise sauce immediately before serving and sprinkle with fresh chives.

MAKES 4 SERVINGS.

Pork Loin with Wild Rice Walnut Stuffing

¼ cup butter
⅔ cup grated carrots
½ cup chopped walnuts
6 scallions, sliced
1 green apple, peeled, cored and finely diced
2 tablespoons lime juice
1 cup cooked wild rice
¼ teaspoon salt
Pepper to taste
¼ teaspoon grated nutmeg
1 3- to 4-pound boneless pork loin, pocket cut in side
¼ cup dry white wine
2 tablespoons raspberry preserves
Pinch dried whole thyme

In a skillet melt the butter and sauté the carrots, walnuts, scallions, and apple in butter and lime juice for 3 to 4 minutes. Remove the pan from the heat and stir in the rice, salt, pepper, and nutmeg. Set aside to cool.

Spoon half of the mixture in the pocket of the pork. Tie the loins at 2- to 3-inch intervals. Place fat-side down on a rack in a roasting pan.

In a saucepan combine the wine, preserves, and thyme. Pour over the roast. Spoon the remaining stuffing into a greased shallow casserole. Bake the pork loin in a 325° oven for 1 hour and 45 minutes. Remove and let stand 10 minutes before carving.

Cover and bake the reserved stuffing at 325° oven for 25 to 30 minutes.

MAKES 6 TO 8 SERVINGS.

Vandiver Inn

301 South Union Avenue
Havre de Grace, Maryland 21078
(410) 939-5200

A restored three-story mansion built in 1886, the inn is surrounded by historic sites, museums, and antique shops. The Chesapeake Bay and a full-service marina are nearby. Most of the eight guest rooms have fireplaces, and all are furnished with antiques appropriate to the mansion's past. Havre de Grace was named by the Revolutionary General Lafayette, and most of the city was burned by the British during the War of 1812.

Roasted Tomato Vinaigrette

5 very ripe Roma tomatoes
¾ cup olive oil
Kosher salt
Ground pepper
¼ cup balsamic vinegar
5 cloves garlic
2 tablespoons fresh basil
2 tablespoons fresh parsley

Cut the tomatoes in half and toss in a small amount of olive oil. Season with salt and pepper. Place on a hot grill skin-side-down or broil skin side up until the skin has become blistered and slightly charred. Set aside and cool. In a food processor combine the tomatoes, vinegar, garlic, and herbs and purée. On slow speed add the olive oil in a steady stream. Season with salt and pepper.

Serve on a salad of mixed greens or on chicken, fish, or beef.

MAKES 2 CUPS.

Holiday Sweet Potato Casserole

3 cups cooled mashed sweet potatoes
½ cup sugar
½ cup butter, softened
1 tablespoon vanilla extract
2 eggs
....
½ cup firmly packed brown sugar
½ cup all-purpose flour
⅓ cup butter
1 cup nuts

In a large bowl beat the mashed potatoes, sugar, softened butter, vanilla, and eggs. Place in a greased 1½-quart casserole.

In a small bowl combine the brown sugar, flour, ⅓ cup of butter, and nuts. Mix the topping with fingers and sprinkle over the potatoes. Bake in a 350° oven for 1 hour.

MAKES ABOUT 6 SERVINGS.

9 West Main Street, P.O. Box 299
New Market, Maryland 21774
(301) 865-5055

The completely restored National Pike Inn has five beautifully furnished guest rooms—each decorated to celebrate a different period from the past. Travelers will find plenty of antiques at the inn and even more in New Market, which boasts more than forty shops. Guests enjoy the private courtyard surrounded by azaleas. A carriage house and smoke house, both dating to the 1830s are the only ones remaining in town in useable condition. Historic sites, tennis, golf, and wineries are nearby.

Banana Butterscotch Bread

½ cup butter or margarine, softened
¾ cup sugar
1 egg
3 ripe bananas, mashed
2 cups all-purpose flour
1 teaspoon baking powder
½ teaspoon baking soda
½ teaspoon salt
⅛ teaspoon grated nutmeg
½ teaspoon ground cinnamon
¾ cup butterscotch morsels
½ cup chopped English walnuts
   (optional)

In a large bowl cream the butter, sugar, and egg. Add the mashed bananas. Blend in the flour, baking powder, soda, salt, nutmeg, and cinnamon. When blended, add the morsels and nuts if desired. Grease 2 5 x 9-inch loaf pans. Divide the batter evenly among the pans. Bake in a 350° oven for 25 to 30 minutes or until a toothpick inserted in the center of 1 loaf comes out clean. Cool in the pan for 15 minutes. Remove.

Variation: For Chocolate Chip Banana Bread substitute mini chocolate chips for the butterscotch morsels.

MAKES 2 LOAVES.

Shoo-Fly Crumb Cake

4 cups all-purpose flour
2 cups sugar
1 teaspoon salt
1 cup shortening
....
2 cups warm water
1 cup molasses
1 tablespoon baking soda
....
½ cup all-purpose flour
½ cup sugar
¼ cup margarine
1 teaspoon ground cinnamon

In a large bowl mix 4 cups of flour, 2 cups of sugar, salt, and shortening together. Reserve 1 cup of the mixture for crumb topping.

In a separate bowl mix together the water, molasses, and soda. Add the dry ingredients,

mixing well. Pour into a greased and floured 10 x 13-inch baking pan.

In a small bowl blend ½ cup of flour, ½ cup of sugar, margarine, and cinnamon. Add the reserved cup of crumbs. Blend again. Sprinkle the crumbs over the cake. Bake in a 350° oven for 50 to 60 minutes until a toothpick inserted in the center comes out clean.

MAKES ABOUT 12 SERVINGS.

Granny Duvall's 1-2-3-4 Pound Cake

1 cup milk
2 cups sugar
1 cup butter or margarine, softened
3 cups all-purpose flour
4 eggs
2 teaspoons vanilla extract
2 teaspoons baking powder
½ teaspoon salt

In a large bowl combine all ingredients. Grease and line a large loaf pan with waxed paper. Spoon in the batter. Bake in a 350° oven for 1 hour.

MAKES 6 SERVINGS.

Granny Duvall's Gingerbread

2 eggs, beaten
¾ cup firmly packed brown sugar
¾ cup molasses
¾ cup shortening, melted
2¼ cups all-purpose flour
2½ teaspoons baking powder
¾ teaspoon ground ginger
1½ teaspoons ground cinnamon
½ teaspoon ground cloves
½ teaspoon ground nutmeg
1 cup boiling water

In a large bowl combine the eggs, sugar, molasses, and shortening. In a separate bowl sift the dry ingredients. Add the dry ingredients to the egg mixture. Blend, add the hot water, and blend again. Pour into a greased 9 x 13-inch pan. Bake in a 350° oven for 40 minutes.

MAKES 12 SERVINGS.

Strawberry Inn

❧

*17 West Main Street
New Market, Maryland 21774
(301) 865-3318*

An 1837 restored Maryland farmhouse, the inn offers five guest rooms, all furnished with antiques. New Market is about thirty-five miles north of Washington, D.C., and is more than two centuries old and so steeped in history that the town itself has been placed on the National Register of Historic Places. With more than 40 shops in town, New Market is know as the "Antiques Capital of Maryland."

Baked Tomato French Toast

16 slices firm white bread, crusts
    removed
2 tablespoons melted butter
12 slices Canadian bacon
2 cups shredded Cheddar cheese
8 eggs
3 cups half and half
1 teaspoon salt
¼ teaspoon pepper
3 large tomatoes, cored and sliced

In a 10 x 15-inch baking pan place the bread in a single layer. Brush lightly with butter and turn the bread butter-side down. Arrange the Canadian bacon over the bread. Sprinkle with 1¾ cups of cheese.

In a large bowl, lightly beat the eggs with the half and half, salt, and pepper until blended. Slowly pour the mixture over the bread and cheese. Bake uncovered in a 350° oven until nearly firm, about 15 minutes. Arrange the tomatoes over the top and bake for about 8 more minutes. Sprinkle with the remaining ¼ cup of cheese. Cut into squares and serve.

MAKES 12 SERVINGS.

Strawberry Inn

Easy Banana Muffins

- ½ cup butter
- 1 cup sugar
- 2 eggs, beaten
- 1½ cups all-purpose flour
- 1 teaspoon ground cinnamon
- 1 teaspoon baking soda
- 3 to 4 ripe bananas, mashed

In a large bowl cream the butter and then add the sugar. Blend thoroughly. Beat in the eggs.

In a separate bowl combine the flour, cinnamon, and soda. Add the flour mixture to the creamed butter mixture alternately with the bananas. Pour into greased muffin cups. Bake in a 375° oven for 30 minutes.

MAKES 1 DOZEN.

Applesauce Oatmeal Muffins

- 1 cup all-purpose flour
- 2 teaspoons baking powder
- ¼ teaspoon salt
- ½ cup quick-cooking oats
- 6 tablespoons firmly packed dark brown sugar
- ½ teaspoon ground cinnamon
- ½ cup skim milk
- ¼ cup unsweetened applesauce
- 1 tablespoon oil
- 2 egg whites

In a medium bowl combine the dry ingredients. Make a well in the center of the mixture. In a separate bowl combine the milk, applesauce, oil, and egg whites. Add the mixture to the dry ingredients, stirring just until the dry ingredients are moistened.

Spoon the batter into greased cups, filling each three-fourths full. Bake in a 400° oven for 18 to 20 minutes or until golden. Remove from the pan immediately.

MAKES 8 TO 10 MUFFINS.

Strawberry Butter

- ½ cup butter, softened
- ½ cup confectioners' sugar
- 2 tablespoons dry milk
- ⅓ cup strawberry preserves

In a medium bowl combine all ingredients and mix thoroughly. Keep refrigerated for up to 1 week.

MAKES ABOUT 1 CUP.

Mike's Harvest Cut

- 3 apples, sliced or cubed
- 1 banana, sliced
  Handful grapes, cut in half
- ½ cup chopped walnuts
  Strawberry yogurt

In a bowl mix together the apples, banana, grapes, and walnuts. Spoon into fruit cups. Top with yogurt.

MAKES ABOUT 6 SERVINGS.

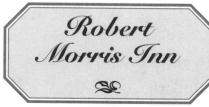

Robert Morris Inn

❧

314 North Morris Street
Oxford, Maryland 21654
(410) 226-5111

---

*N*amed for an English trading agent who lived in the house in 1730, the inn's hallmarks are simple comfort, quiet hospitality, and seafood from the Chesapeake Bay. Robert Morris, Jr., the agent's son, was a signer of the Declaration of Independence, the Articles of Confederation, and the United States Constitution. The waterbound village of Oxford was once Maryland's largest port of call. It is now a protected harbor for watermen who harvest the Bay's bounty.

Spicy Crab and Shrimp Soup

- 2 tablespoons butter
- ½ cup chopped onions
- ½ cup chopped celery
- 8 cups tomato juice
- ¼ teaspoon baking powder
- ¼ teaspoon crab base
- 1 teaspoon Old Bay seasoning
- 1 teaspoon Worcestershire sauce
- ¼ teaspoon dried oregano
- 1 teaspoon dry sherry
- ¼ teaspoon black pepper
- 2 cups diced tomatoes
  Dash Tabasco sauce
- 1 bay leaf
- ¼ teaspoon ground cayenne pepper
- 1 cup cooked barley
- 1 pound small shrimp, cooked
- ½ pound Maryland Backfin crab meat

In a 3-quart saucepan melt the butter and sauté the onions and celery until tender. Add the tomato juice and simmer for 5 minutes, stirring occasionally. Add the baking powder, crab base, Old Bay seasoning, Worcestershire, oregano, sherry, pepper, tomatoes, Tabasco, bay leaf, and cayenne. Bring to a simmer. Add the cooked barley, shrimp, and Maryland crab meat, and heat through. Remove the bay leaf before serving.

MAKES 7 SERVINGS.

Oyster Casserole

- ½ cup dry breadcrumbs
- ½ cup coarse cracker crumbs
- 5 tablespoons melted butter
- 1 pint oysters
- ½ teaspoon salt
- ⅛ teaspoon pepper
- ⅛ teaspoon grated nutmeg
- 2 tablespoons chopped parsley
- 1 10½-ounce can condensed cream of mushroom soup

In a large bowl combine the breadcrumbs, cracker crumbs, and butter. Place half of the mixture in a greased 1-quart casserole. Arrange the oysters in layers, sprinkling each layer with seasonings. Pour the mushroom soup over the oysters. Top with the remaining crumbs. Bake in a 350° degrees oven for 1 hour.

MAKES 4 SERVINGS.

Inn at Perry Cabin

*308 Watkins Lane
St. Michaels, Maryland 21663
(800) 722-2949*

A long, low pearly-white Colonial mansion, the inn stands amid expanses of dark green lawn. Beyond the grass is water in nearly every direction, as the inn and the town of St. Michaels became a part of the Chesapeake Bay. This inn was the first of a series established by Bernard Ashley, co-founder of the Laura Ashley Company. Here English and American antiques serve to produce a graciously blended and immaculately tasteful decor. Chesapeake specialties and international fare highlight the inn's excellent cuisine.

Crab Spring Roll with Pink Grapefruit, Avocado, and Toasted Almonds

¼ **head bok choy**
½ **bunch scallions**
2 **slices Japanese pickled ginger**
½ **teaspoon chopped fresh cilantro**
   Juice from 1 lime
   Salt and fresh ground black pepper
4 **ounces jumbo lump crab meat**
4 **sheets spring roll casing**
1 **egg, beaten**
1 **teaspoon sugar**
   Juice from 2 pink grapefruit, squeezed
   Juice from 1 lime
½ **cup oil**
½ **cup olive oil**
   Salt and pepper
2 **ounces mesclun salad**
1 **avocado**
1 **pink grapefruit**
2 **ounces toasted sliced almonds**
2 **tomatoes, blanched and skinned**

1 **small bunch chives**
   Pickled chervil or cilantro for garnish

Shred the bok choy and blanch or steam in a saucepan in boiling salted water. Slice the scallions and blanch, squeezing out most of the water. Add the sliced ginger, cilantro, and lime juice, salt, and pepper. Add the crab meat. Wrap in the spring roll casing, and brush with egg to help seal.

In a saucepan melt the sugar and add the pink grapefruit juice. Reduce by half, then add the lime juice, oil, and olive oil. Lightly season. Mix the mesclun salad with the dressing.

Quarter, peel, and slice the avocado. Arrange the slices in the bottom of 4 salad plates. Garnish around the outside with 3 grapefruit segments per plate, sliced toasted almonds, diced tomato, and chopped chives. Place the mixed salad on top. Deep fry the spring rolls, cut in half on the slant and arrange on the salads. Garnish with picked chervil or cilantro and a spoonful of dressing around the outside of the plate.
MAKES 4 SERVINGS.

Poached Oysters in Champagne with a Julienne of Vegetables and Leaf Spinach

20 **oysters (plus juice)**
1 **carrot**
1 **leek**
2 **ounces snow peas**
8 **ounces fresh leaf spinach**
3 **shallots, sliced**
1 **glass white wine**
2 **tablespoons cream**
½ **cup butter, cut into small cubes**
   Salt and pepper to taste
½ **cup heavy cream**
2 **ounces champagne**
1 **clove garlic**
   Salt and fresh ground pepper

Shuck the oysters, wash the shells, and rinse the oysters. Reserve the oyster juice. Cut the vegetables into strips. Pick over and blanch the spinach. Peel and cut the shallots into

small dice. Place in a saucepan and reduce with the white wine until only 1 tablespoon remains. Add the 2 tablespoons of cream and reduce for 30 seconds, then whisk in the butter. Season with salt and pepper. Heat a sauté pan and add the spinach, ½ cup of the cream, the oysters, champagne, and garlic, and gently poach for 2 to 3 minutes. Remove the pan from the heat and add the butter sauce.

Spoon the spinach into the oyster shells. Then top with the oysters and place a small pile of vegetables on each oyster. Serve on a bed of blanched seaweed or on a bed of mixed peppercorns.
MAKES 4 SERVINGS.

Back Creek Inn

*Alexander and Calvert Streets, P.O. Box 520
Solomons, Maryland 20688
(410) 326-2022*

For more than a century, this former home of a hard-working waterman has stood on the banks of Back Creek, one of Maryland's many scenic waterways opening onto the Chesapeake Bay. Handmade quilts, antiques, and fresh floral bouquets help make a stay at this B&B especially pleasant. There are seven guest rooms, some with fireplace and water view. Bountiful fishing and crabbing, exploring the tranquil countryside by bicycle, and engaging in various water sports keep guests entertained.

Simple Sweet Lemon Scones

2½ **cups all-purpose flour**
1 **tablespoon baking powder**
½ **teaspoon salt**
1 **tablespoon fresh grated lemon zest**

½ cup cold unsalted butter, cut up
¼ cup sugar (use ⅓ cup for slightly
    sweeter scones)
⅔ cup milk
....
2 teaspoons fresh lemon juice
2 tablespoons sugar

In a large bowl combine the flour, baking powder, and salt, stirring to mix well. Add the grated lemon zest to the flour mixture. Add the butter and cut in with a pastry blender or rub in with fingers until the mixture looks like fine granules. Add the sugar and toss to mix. Add the milk and stir with a fork until a soft dough forms. Form the dough into a ball, turn onto a lightly floured board, and knead 10 to 12 times.

Cut the dough in half. Knead each half lightly into a ball and turn smooth-side-up. Pat or roll into a 6-inch circle. Cut each circle into 6 or 8 wedges. Place the wedges on an ungreased cookie sheet, slightly apart for crisp sides, touching for soft sides.

In a small bowl mix 2 teaspoons of fresh lemon juice with 2 tablespoons of sugar, top each scone with ¼ teaspoon of the mixture before baking. Bake in a 425° oven for about 12 minutes or until medium brown on top. Put on a linen or cotton dish towel on a wire rack. Transfer the scones to the cloth-covered rack. Cover loosely with the cloth and cool completely before serving.
MAKES 12 TO 16 SCONES.

Curry Chicken Salad

6 cups mayonnaise
½ cup lemon juice
6 tablespoons soy sauce
3 heaping tablespoons curry powder
½ cup chopped green onions
9 cups bite-sized cooked chicken or
    turkey
3 8-ounce cans sliced water chestnuts
6 cups grapes (green or red)
6 16-ounce cans pineapple chunks,
    well drained
  Toasted almonds for topping

In a large bowl mix the mayonnaise, lemon juice, soy sauce, and curry powder. Fold in the remaining ingredients. Refrigerate several hours before serving. Top with toasted almonds.
MAKES 12 SERVINGS.

Cozy Country Inn

*103 Frederick Road
Thurmont, Maryland 21788
(301) 271-4301*

Cozy Country Inn offers lodging, dining, and shopping in the beautiful Catoctin Mountains. One of the rooms here is dedicated to President Jimmy Carter who frequented nearby Camp David. Other rooms and cottages celebrate the lives, accomplishments, and personalities of Franklin Roosevelt, John Kennedy, Ronald Reagan, Richard Nixon, Lyndon Johnson, Dwight Eisenhower, and Winston Churchill. In this way and others, the Cozy is an absolutely unique country inn. National and international news reporters often stay and eat here during presidential retreats.

Cozy Restaurant's Mexican Wedding Cake

2 cups cake flour
2 cups sugar
2 teaspoons baking soda
½ teaspoon salt
2 medium eggs
2½ cups crushed pineapple
2 teaspoons vanilla extract
1 cup chopped pecans
  Cream Cheese Frosting (recipe follows)
3 or 4 whole pineapple slices for garnish
  Cherries for garnish

In a large bowl mix together the flour, sugar, soda, and salt. Add the eggs and crushed pineapple and mix until combined well. Add the vanilla and mix about 30 seconds. Fold in the pecans. Pour into a greased 9 x 12-inch

pan. Bake in a 325° oven for 30 to 35 minutes or pour into a greased bundt cake pan and bake for about 60 minutes, until a toothpick inserted in the center comes out clean. Frost cake with Cream Cheese Frosting and garnish with pineapple slices and cherries.
MAKES 12 SERVINGS.

Cozy Country Inn

Cream Cheese Frosting

1 8-ounce package cream cheese, softened
½ cup margarine or butter, softened
2 cups confectioners' sugar, sifted
1 teaspoon vanilla extract

In a medium bowl mix the ingredients in the order given.
MAKES ABOUT 2 CUPS.

Cozy Restaurant's Turkey Corn Soup

7 cups turkey broth, homemade or
    commercial
1 cup chopped celery
1 16-ounce can whole kernel corn
2 tablespoons butter
¼ teaspoon pepper
1 tablespoon plus 2 teaspoons sugar
¼ teaspoon dried thyme
1½ teaspoons dried parsley
1½ teaspoons chicken bouillon granules
1½ teaspoons Accent or monosodium
    glutamate (optional)
1 to 2 drops yellow food coloring
    (optional)
6 tablespoons all-purpose flour
1 egg yolk

In a large soup pot combine the turkey broth and all ingredients except the flour and egg yolk. Cook for 45 minutes, stirring often.

Mix the flour with the egg yolk and crumble on top of the soup. Stir and cook for 10 minutes more.
MAKES 6 SERVINGS.

MASSACHUSETTS

Ashley Manor

3660 Main Street, Box 856
Barnstable, Massachusetts 02630
(508) 362-8044

Built in 1699, this Cape Cod
manor house has evolved gracefully
over the centuries. Nearly 300 years
worth of additions and remodelings
have done little to alter its original
gracious character. Wide board
flooring, huge open-hearth fireplaces, a beehive oven, and hand
glazed wainscotting mark it as an
architectural treasure. In keeping
with the inn's historic nature, the
guest rooms feature canopied beds,
New England shuttered windows,
and colorful spackled floors.

Ashley Manor

Crêpes

- ½ cup all-purpose flour
- ½ cup whole wheat flour
- 3   eggs, well-beaten
- ¾ cup milk
- ¼ cup water
- 1 tablespoon vanilla extract
- 2 tablespoons sugar
     Pinch salt
     Butter

....

- 12 ounces farmer cheese
- ½ cup plus 2 tablespoons sugar
- 4½ teaspoons vanilla extract
- 4 ounces egg substitute

....

- 1 quart hulled fresh strawberries (or
     frozen berries)
- 3 ounces 50/50 simple sugar syrup

In a medium bowl blend the flours, eggs,
milk, water, vanilla, sugar, and salt. Refrigerate for 30 minutes.

Heat a 6- to 8-inch omelet pan over high
heat until very hot. Grease the pan with a light
coating of butter and while holding the pan
off the heat slowly ladle enough batter to
lightly coat the pan. Pour the excess back into
the batter. (Gradual pouring and a deft wrist
are important to get a light but full coat over
the bottom of the pan.) If the batter blisters
on pouring into the pan, the pan is too hot. In
that case, hold the pan off the heat for about
a minute. Place the pan back on the heat, cut
and remove the "tail," and cook until the
edge of the crêpe shows brown and the center bubbles slightly. While cooking, gently run
a dull knife around the edge of the crêpe to
lift the edges. When done invert the pan over

a plate and tap the pan to the plate to free the
crêpe. Re-butter the pan and pour more batter for the next crêpe. There should be
enough batter for at least 18 crêpes.

In a medium bowl combine the farmer
cheese, sugar, vanilla, and egg substitute.

In a blender purée the berries with the
simple syrup.

Place 1 tablespoon of cheese filling on the
top side of each crêpe and fold in half twice
to make a triangle with a rounded side. Place
3 filled crêpes on each plate as a serving,
pour 2 to 3 tablespoons of strawberry syrup
in the spaces between the filled crêpes, and
serve.

MAKES 6 SERVINGS.

Ashley Manor's Waffles

- 2 eggs, separated
- 1¾ cups milk
- 1¾ cups sifted all-purpose flour
- ¾ cup sifted whole wheat flour
- 1 tablespoon baking powder
- ½ cup sugar
- 2 tablespoons maple extract
- 3 tablespoons vanilla extract
- ½ cup chopped walnuts
- 6 dried peaches, diced
     Pinch salt
- ½ cup melted butter

In a bowl beat egg yolks with milk. Add the
sifted flour and remaining ingredients, except
the butter and egg whites. Stir the butter in
slowly. In a bowl beat the egg whites until stiff
and "cut" the beaten whites into the mixture
with a rubber spatula. The batter should have
a slow pouring consistency, but if too thick,

stir in more milk until the desired consistency is achieved. Bake on a greased waffle iron.

MAKES 6 SERVINGS.

Captain Freeman Inn

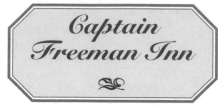

15 Breakwater Road
Brewster, Massachusetts 02631
(508) 896-7481

During the late 1800s, Brewster was home to more deepwater sea captains than any town in America. Built in the 1860s, the inn was the home of William Freeman, a wealthy clipper ship captain. A picture of Captain Freeman's ship, the Kingfisher, hangs in the entrance. The ornate plaster moldings, commanding central staircase, marble fireplace, and windows that reach to the floor all date to its earliest days. The house is sizable, big enough for a dozen spacious guest rooms and suites all furnished with antiques and brightened with freshly cut flowers. Brewster provides a convenient central location for those who want to explore Cape Cod's many beaches and attractions.

Captain Freeman Inn

Best Blueberry Pancakes

- 1 **cup unbleached flour**
- 1 **tablespoon baking powder**
- ½ **teaspoon salt**
- 2 **egg whites**
- 1 **tablespoon fresh grated orange peel**
- ½ **cup plain nonfat yogurt**
- ½ **cup skim milk**
- 1 **cup fresh or frozen blueberries**
   Real Maple Syrup for topping

In a medium bowl mix all the ingredients except the blueberries until very smooth.

Heat a griddle or large iron skillet until very hot and then spray with cooking spray. Pour ¼ cup of batter onto the griddle for each pancake and immediately sprinkle with 10 to 12 blueberries. If the blueberries are frozen, they will cook perfectly in the pancakes. Turn the pancakes when bubbles appear on the surface and cook until the sides are dry and the center is slightly puffed. Serve immediately with real maple syrup.

MAKES 2 SERVINGS.

Chewy Maple Sugar Cookies

- 2 **cups sugar**
- 1½ **cups unsalted butter**
- 2 **eggs**
- ½ **cup maple syrup**
- 1½ **teaspoons ground cinnamon**
- 1½ **teaspoons ground cloves**
- ½ **teaspoon grated nutmeg**
- 1 **teaspoon salt**
- 3½ **teaspoons baking soda**
- 4½ **cups all-purpose flour**
   Sugar for rolling cookies

In a large bowl cream the sugar, butter, and eggs. Add the maple syrup and beat until fluffy. Add the dry ingredients and mix thoroughly. Shape into walnut-sizes balls of dough and roll in sugar. Place on an ungreased cookie sheet. Bake in a 350° oven for 12 minutes.

Cookie dough can be made ahead and refrigerated for up to 1 week.

MAKES 4 DOZEN COOKIES.

Hot Mulled Cider

- ½ **gallon fresh apple cider**
- ½ **cup rum**
- 10 **whole peppercorns**
- 8 **whole cloves**
- 1 **orange, washed and sliced with the peel on**
- 8 **cinnamon sticks or extra rum**

In a large saucepan or Dutch oven heat all the ingredients until just simmering. Do not boil. Serve with cinnamon sticks or an extra shot of rum.

MAKES ABOUT 8 SERVINGS.

Chatham Town House Inn

11 Library Lane
Chatham, Massachusetts 02633
(508) 945-2180

When this house was built in 1881, parts of a much earlier home dating to the 1820s were incorporated in the structure. Much of the old woodwork depicting harpoon and oar motifs was retained and still exists today, along with the original hemlock flooring. The inn consists of the old Chatham House and four nearby additions that offer a total of twenty-six guest rooms. Some rooms have canopied beds, balconies, or decks. Guests can walk to all of the town beaches, antique shops, fashionable stores, and restaurants.

Lemon Bread with Lemon Glaze

1 cup butter
2 cups sugar
4 eggs
½ teaspoon salt
½ teaspoon baking soda
3 cups all-purpose flour
1 cup buttermilk
1 cup chopped nuts
Zest of 1 lemon, grated

....

Juice of 3 lemons
1 cup sugar

In a large bowl cream the butter and 2 cups of sugar. Add the eggs one at a time, beating well after each addition. In a separate bowl sift the dry ingredients. Add the dry ingredients to the batter alternately with the buttermilk, beginning and ending with the dry ingredients. Fold in the nuts and lemon zest. Grease and flour 2 loaf pans. Pour in the batter. Bake in a 350° oven for 1 hour.

In a saucepan combine the lemon juice and 1 cup of sugar. Stir until the sugar is dissolved. When the bread is baked, remove from the pan and place on foil. Spoon the juice over the hot loaves. Let cool, then wrap lightly in foil. Freezes very well.

MAKES 2 LOAVES.

H'lands Pankaka

1½ cups water
½ cup farina
½ teaspoon salt

....

1 cup milk
½ cup all-purpose flour
½ cup sugar
1½ cups milk
¼ cup melted butter
3 eggs, slightly beaten
3 teaspoons cardamom
Speck grated nutmeg and ground cinnamon

In a saucepan mix the water, farina, and salt. Boil slowly for 10 minutes. Add 1 cup of milk. In a small bowl mix the flour in a little milk or water and add to the farina mixture. Add the sugar, 1½ cups of milk, melted butter, eggs, and spices. Pour into a cast-iron skillet. Bake in a 400° oven for 45 minutes.

MAKES 4 SERVINGS.

Anderson-Wheeler Homestead

❧

154 Fitchburg Turnpike, Route 117
Concord, Massachusetts 01742
(508) 369-3756

A *stagecoach stop and tavern once stood on the property now known as the Anderson-Wheeler Homestead. During the 1890s, it was known as as the Frank Wheeler Farm, named after the men who developed a rust-free variety of asparagus. The Homestead has a lovely wrap-around veranda and offers five guest rooms furnished with antiques and accented with window seats. Historis Concord Center, Walden Pond, and the Audubon Center are only three miles away.*

Sour Cream Cheesecake (New York-style)

2 8-ounce packages cream cheese
1 16-ounce carton Ricotta cheese
1½ cups sugar
4 eggs
3 tablespoons all-purpose flour
3 tablespoons cornstarch
2 teaspoons vanilla extract
¼ cup melted butter, cooled
1 pint sour cream
Canned fruit topping

In a large bowl mix the cream cheese and ricotta with an electric mixer. Add the sugar gradually. Add the eggs, one at a time. Add the dry ingredients and mix well. Add the vanilla and butter and mix in. Fold in the sour cream. Pour the mixture into an ungreased 10-inch springform pan. Bake in a 325° oven on the middle rack for 1 hour.

Turn off the heat and leave the cheesecake in the oven for 2 more hours. When ready to serve, top with canned fruit topping.

MAKES 8 SERVINGS.

Whipped Cream Frosting

2 tablespoons all-purpose flour
½ cup milk
¼ cup butter
¼ cup shortening (or all butter)
½ cup sugar
1 teaspoon vanilla extract

In a saucepan mix the flour and milk, and cook over low heat until thick. Cool.

In a mixer bowl cream the butter and shortening with an electric mixer for 4 minutes. Add the sugar gradually and beat again for 4 minutes. Add the cooled mixture. Beat. Add the vanilla and blend.

MAKES FROSTING FOR A 2-LAYER CAKE.

Rhubarb Custard Pie

2 cups sugar
¼ cup all-purpose flour
¾ teaspoon grated nutmeg
3 eggs
2 tablespoons plus 2 teaspoons milk
4 cups cut up rhubarb
Pastry for 1 9-inch 2-crust pie (recipe follows)
1 tablespoon butter

In a large bowl mix the sugar, flour, and nutmeg. Beat in the eggs and milk. Add the rhubarb. Pour into the unbaked pie shell and dot with 1 tablespoon of butter.

Weave strips of pie crust on top for a nice presentation. Bake in a 400° oven for 30 minutes.

MAKES 6 TO 8 SERVINGS.

Pie Crust

4 teaspoons hard butter
1 cup lard
4 cups all-purpose flour
1½ teaspoons salt
4 teaspoons sugar
2 eggs
2 tablespoons cold water

In a large bowl cut the butter and lard into the flour until combined well. Add the remaining ingredients and knead until a ball is formed. Chill for 1 hour. Makes enough to freeze extra.

MAKES PASTRY FOR 2 2-CRUST PIES.

Spinach Casserole

- 2 **10-ounce packages frozen chopped spinach**
- ¼ **cup butter**
- 2 **tablespoons all-purpose flour**
- 2 **tablespoons chopped onion**
- ½ **cup evaporated milk**
- ½ **cup liquid reserved from spinach**
- ½ **teaspoon black pepper**
- ¼ **teaspoon celery salt**
  Cayenne pepper to taste (about ⅛ teaspoon)
- ¼ **teaspoon garlic salt**
- ½ **teaspoon salt**
- 6 **ounces Jalapeño Jack cheese (cut into small pieces)**
- 1 **teaspoon Worcestershire sauce Buttered unseasoned breadcrumbs (optional)**

In a saucepan cook the spinach according to the package directions. Drain and reserve the liquid. In a pan melt the butter over low heat. Add the flour, stirring until blended and smooth, but not brown. Add the onion and cook until soft, but not brown. Add the milk and spinach liquid slowly, stirring constantly. Cook until smooth and thick. Add the seasonings and cheese, stirring until melted. Add the Worcestershire sauce. Fold in the spinach.

Bake immediately or top with buttered crumbs and refrigerate. The flavor is improved if refrigerated overnight. Bake in a 350° oven for 30 minutes. Freezes well.

MAKES 4 SERVINGS.

Hawthorne Inn

Hawthorne Inn

462 Lexington Road
Concord, Massachusetts 01742
(508) 369-5610

The town of Concord and the Hawthorne Inn are replete with history. The inn's property once belonged to Ralph Waldo Emerson, Nathanial Hawthorne, and the Alcott family, and nearby Sleepy Hollow Cemetery serves as the final resting place for members of all three families. The inn's guest rooms are also reminiscent of the past, and are beautifully appointed with wood floors, period antiques, rag rugs, and quilts. Following a breakfast that includes home-baked breads and seasonal fruit, guests may visit nearby Walden Pond, memorialized by Thoreau.

Transcendental Chicken

- 1 **quart virgin cold-pressed olive oil**
- 1 **small bulb garlic**

....

- 3 **pounds concord grapes**
- 1 **pound catawba grapes**

....

- 2 **cups orange juice**
- ⅓ **cup Rose's lime juice**
- ½ **teaspoon whole clove**
- 1 **2-inch stick cinnamon Fresh grated ginger to taste Sugar**

....

- **Grated zest of 2 oranges**
- 8 **chicken halves**
- 8 **large whole plums Mint leaves for garnish**

Prepare the garlic olive oil in advance. Peel the paper off the garlic cloves and cut off both tips. Drop the garlic in the oil and seal the container. Store for at least 1 week. Do

---

not refrigerate. (Small bubbles form as the juices are drawn from the garlic.)

Remove the stems from the grapes and place them in a large pot. Add the orange juice, lime juice, cloves, cinnamon, and ginger. Cook until the grapes separate from their skins. Mash and allow to sit for 1 hour. Strain or mash through a jelly bag. Add ⅓ to ½ cup of sugar for each cup of grape juice. Cook until thickened.

Coat the bottom of a roasting pan with garlic olive oil. Sprinkle the bottom of the pan with the zest of 1 orange. Rub the chicken pieces with garlic olive oil and sprinkle with a layer of orange zest.

Nestle the plums among the chicken. (Do not pit the plums.) The plum skin must not be pierced. Ladle the sauce onto the chicken and plums until half covered. If more liquid is needed, add orange juice. Bake in a 375° oven for 35 minutes. Turn the chicken over and bake for 10 to 15 minutes.

Gently lift the whole cooked plums to individual bowls. Spoon the broth into the bowls. Serve each chicken half garnished with a single mint leaf.

MAKES 8 SERVINGS.

Morning Breakfast Cake

- 2 **cups butter**
- 6 **eggs**
- 1 **cup milk**
- 1 **heaping tablespoon baking powder**
- 2 **cups sugar**
- 1 **teaspoon vanilla extract**
- 3 **to 4 mashed bananas**
- ¾ **cup shredded coconut**
- ¾ **cup slivered almonds**
- 4 **cups all-purpose flour Fresh whipped cream Flavored yogurt Fruit jam**

In a food processor mix all ingredients except the flour the well. Pour into a bowl and add the flour.

Pour into 1 large and 1 small buttered and floured bundt pan. Bake in a 350° oven in for 1 hour and 25 minutes or until done.

Serve with a topping of equal parts fresh whipped cream folded gently with flavored yogurt and add a few teaspoons of jam just for a bit of color.

Variations: Instead of the bananas, coconut, and almonds, add 3 puréed apples,

¾ cup walnuts, ½ cup raisins, and ¾ cup chocolate (for an afternoon tea dessert); or the juice of 1 lemon or orange, 2 tablespoons grated lemon zest or orange zest, and 1½ cups blueberries, raspberries, or blackberries; or substitute 1 cup buttermilk for regular milk and add ¾ cup blueberries, and ¾ cup halved, pitted fresh cherries; or substitute 1 cup buttermilk for regular milk and add 1½ cups poppy seeds mixed with ¼ cup sugar.

MAKES 16 SERVINGS.

Salty Dog Bed and Breakfast Inn

❧

451 Main Street
Cotuit, Massachusetts 02635-3114
(508) 428-5228

---

*O*riginally owned by a sea captain, the Salty Dog dates to the 1850s. it served for many years as the home of a cranberry farmer. Today it is a small gracious inn offering five well-appointed rooms and access to the many scenic pleasures of Cape Cod. The main street of the seaside village of Cotuit has been described as "one of the most beautiful in America."

Orange Breeze

- ½ **cup water**
- ½ **cup milk**
- 1 **6 ounce can frozen orange juice concentrate**
- ½ **cup sugar**
- ½ **teaspoon vanilla extract**
- 14 **ice cubes**

In a blender combine all ingredients and blend until smooth. Serve immediately.

MAKES 6 SERVINGS.

Fruit Smoothie

- 1 **banana, peeled and frozen**
- 1 **cup apple juice**
- ½ **cup chopped fresh fruit (not citrus fruit)**
- 1 **tablespoon chopped nuts**

In a blender combine all ingredients and mix well. Pour into glasses and serve.

MAKES ABOUT 2½ CUPS.

Strawberry Shake

- ½ **cup (or 1 cup) strawberries**
- 2 **tablespoons honey**
- 1 **cup cold milk**
- 1 **cup vanilla yogurt**
  Large whole strawberries for garnish

In a blender purée the strawberries and honey. Add the milk and yogurt and blend until smooth. Pour into stemmed glasses and garnish each with a whole strawberry.

MAKES ABOUT 2 CUPS.

New England Johnny Cakes

- 2 **cups yellow stone-ground cornmeal**
- 1 **cup all-purpose flour**
- ¾ **cup sugar**
- 1 **tablespoon baking powder**
- ¾ **teaspoon salt**
- ½ **cup chilled butter, diced**
- 1½ **cups milk**
- 3 **large eggs**
- 2 **cups frozen blueberries, unthawed**
  Warm maple syrup

Grease the bottom of a 9 x 13-inch pan. In a medium bowl mix the cornmeal, flour, sugar, baking powder, and salt with an electric mixer. Add the butter and mix until the mixture resembles coarse meal. In a large bowl beat the milk and eggs until blended. Stir in the cornmeal mixture. Mix in the blueberries. Pour the batter into the prepared pan. Bake in a 400° oven for 25 minutes or until a toothpick inserted in the center of the corn bread comes out clean.

Cut into large squares and serve warm with maple syrup.

MAKES 8 TO 12 SERVINGS.

Salty Dog

Ice Cream Scones

- 2 **cups all-purpose flour**
- 2 **tablespoons sugar**
- 3 **teaspoons baking powder**
- ½ **teaspoon salt**
- ¼ **cup melted butter**
- ¾ **cup milk**
- ¼ **cup melted vanilla ice cream**
- ½ **cup raisins**
  Butter and jam for garnish

In a large bowl mix the ingredients together in the order given. Drop by heaping teaspoon onto a greased cookie sheet. Bake in a 450° oven for 10 minutes or until golden brown. Serve with butter and jam.

MAKES 12 SCONES.

Cumworth Farm

❧

472 West Cummington Road
Cummington, Massachusetts 01026
(413) 634-5529

---

*T*raffic weary urbanites who want an escape to country life should try the Cumworth. A real working sheep farm, it also produces maple syrup and berries in season. There are six comfortably furnished rooms in the 200-year-old farm. A hot tub is available.

Irish Soda Bread

- 3 **cups all-purpose flour**
- 2 **cups whole wheat flour**
- 1 **tablespoon baking powder**

2 teaspoons baking soda
2 tablespoons firmly packed brown
    sugar
2½ cups buttermilk

In a large bowl mix all ingredients together
and form into 2 round loaves. Place on a
lightly greased cookie sheet. Bake in a 350°
oven for 45 minutes.

MAKES 2 LOAVES.

Kiev-to-Cumworth Farm Strudel

1 egg
½ cup lukewarm water
¼ cup orange juice
1 teaspoon baking powder
    Pinch salt
5 tablespoons sugar
3 cups all-purpose sifted flour
¼ cup oil (or more, as needed)

2 cups walnuts or pecans, ground
2 cups corn flakes, crumbled
1 cup sugar
    Cinnamon to taste

1 8-ounce jar cherry or berry preserves
1 8-ounce jar orange marmalade
1 16-ounce box raisins

In a large bowl combine the egg, water,
orange juice, baking powder, salt, sugar,
flour, and oil, until a dough forms. Turn the
dough onto a floured surface and knead several times. Form into 2 balls, wrap in plastic
wrap, and refrigerate for 30 minutes. Refrigerate for 30 minutes.

In a medium bowl mix together the walnuts, corn flakes, 1 cup of sugar, and cinnamon to taste until crumbly. In a separate bowl
combine the preserves and marmalade. In a
small bowl place the raisins.

Dip each ball of dough in flour and roll
out separately on a floured board into a pie-
shape. Sprinkle the dough lightly with oil.
Sprinkle half of the corn flake mixture all
over the dough. Spread the preserve mixture
on one end of the dough. Sprinkle raisins all
over the dough. Roll tight, making sure there
are no holes in the dough while rolling. Place
the strudel rolls on a lightly greased cookie
sheet. Bake in a 250° oven for 25 minutes.
Increase the oven temperature to 325° and
bake for another 20 minutes.

While cooking, mark the dough with a
knife so the strudel roll can be cut into pieces
when cooled.

MAKES 24 TO 30 SERVINGS.

Isaiah Hall Bed and Breakfast Inn

152 Whig Street, P.O. Box 1007
Dennis, Massachusetts 02638
(508) 385-9928, (800) 736-0160

---

*T*ucked away on a quiet street in
the Cape Cod village of Dennis, this
1857 farmhouse was originally the
home of Isaiah Hall, a barrel maker.
Isaiah's brother, Henry Hall, cultivated America's first cranberry bogs
a short distance behind the inn. The
barrels were used to transport the
cranberries. The inn has eleven
rooms where guests can sleep on
antique iron and brass beds
warmed by handmade quilts. A
breakfast with hearty homebaked
breads and muffins is served on a
twelve-foot cherry table in the spacious dining room.

Isaiah Hall

Old-Fashioned Oatmeal Cookies

1 cup shortening
1½ cups firmly packed brown sugar
2 eggs
½ cup buttermilk
1¾ cups sifted all-purpose flour
1 teaspoon baking powder
1 teaspoon baking soda
1 teaspoon salt
1 teaspoon grated nutmeg
1 teaspoon ground cinnamon
3 cups quick cooking rolled oats
½ cup chopped nuts
½ cup raisins

In a large bowl cream together the shortening, sugar, and eggs until light and fluffy. Add
the buttermilk. In a separate bowl sift
together the flour, baking powder, soda, salt,
and spices. Add to the creamed mixture and
mix well. Stir in the oats, nuts, and raisins,
and mix well. Drop the mixture from a teaspoon onto a greased cookie sheet. Bake in a
400° oven for 8 to 10 minutes.

Cool for a minute before removing from
the sheet to cooling racks.

MAKES ABOUT 4 DOZEN.

Peanut Butter Cookies

1 cup shortening
1 cup firmly packed dark brown sugar
1 cup sugar
1 cup peanut butter
2 eggs
1 teaspoon vanilla extract
2½ cups all-purpose flour
2 teaspoons baking soda
½ teaspoon salt

In a large bowl cream shortening, sugars,
and peanut butter. Add eggs and vanilla. Beat
well. In a separate bowl sift the flour, soda,
and salt. Add the sifted dry ingredients to the
creamed mixture, and mix well. Roll into
small balls. Place on an ungreased cookie
sheet. Press down with the tines of a fork.
Bake in a 375° oven for 8 to 10 minutes.

Cool for a minute before removing to cooling racks.

MAKES ABOUT 3 DOZEN.

Nauset House Inn

143 Beach Road, Box 774
East Orleans, Massachusetts 02643
(508) 255-2195

Cape Cod visitors may count themselves lucky to discover this secluded retreat. It offers access to one the world's great ocean beaches, while placing its guests near the galleries, antique shops, and sophisticated restaurants for which the Cape is famous. The inn features a turn-of-the-century conservatory filled with flowers and wicker.

Nina's Fruit Torte

1 cup butter
2 cups sugar
4 eggs, beaten

....

2 cups all-purpose flour
½ teaspoon salt
2 teaspoons baking powder

....

Sugared blueberries
Sliced Italian plums
Lemon juice

....

2 teaspoons all-purpose flour
¼ cup sugar
Cinnamon to taste

In a large bowl cream the butter and 2 cups of sugar together with an electric mixer. Add the eggs.

In a separate bowl mix together 2 cups of flour, the salt, and baking powder. Add the dry ingredients to the creamed mixture, blending well.

Grease a 12-inch springform pan and press the dough into it. Cover with sugared blueberries and sliced Italian plums. Sprinkle the top with lemon juice.

In a bowl mix 2 teaspoons of flour, ¼ cup of sugar, and the cinnamon. Sprinkle over the fruit. Bake in a 350° oven for 1 hour and 15 minutes or until firm.

MAKES ABOUT 10 SERVINGS.

Herb Cheese

3 cloves garlic
2 8-ounce packages cream cheese
1 teaspoon caraway seeds
1 teaspoon dried basil
1 teaspoon dill
1 teaspoon fresh chives
1 teaspoon fresh parsley

In a food processor mince the garlic. Add the remaining ingredients and process until blended. Transfer to a dish and refrigerate overnight.

MAKES 2 CUPS.

The Captain Dexter House of Edgartown

Box 2798
Edgartown, Massachusetts 02539
(508) 627-7289

A sea captain's house in Edgartown on the twenty mile-long island of Martha's Vineyard, this historic inn dates to the 1840s. Victorian and Edwardian antiques seen throughout the house are reminiscent of the grace and dignity of the past. The skills of long-ago craftsmen appear in the original, wide floorboards, graceful mouldings, and Court Rumford fireplaces. Guests are within a short walk to the beach, excellent shops, and restaurants.

Lemon Bread

½ cup margarine
⅔ cup sugar
2 eggs
1½ cups all-purpose flour
1 teaspoon baking powder
½ teaspoon salt
½ cup milk
3 tablespoons fresh lemon juice
1½ tablespoons grated lemon zest

....

¼ cup sugar
¼ cup lemon juice

Grease a 5 x 9-inch loaf pan. In a large bowl cream the margarine and ⅔ cup of sugar together in a large bowl. Beat in the eggs one at a time.

In a separate bowl sift together the flour, baking powder, and salt. Add the dry ingredients to the creamed mixture alternately with the milk. Mix well. Stir in 3 tablespoons of lemon juice and zest. Bake in a 325° oven for 1 hour to 1 hour and 10 minutes until the loaf is light golden brown and springs back to the touch.

In a small bowl mix ¼ cup of sugar and ¼ cup of lemon juice, and pour onto the warm bread.

MAKES 1 LOAF.

Scones

2 cups all-purpose flour
2 tablespoons sugar
1 teaspoon baking powder
½ teaspoon salt
¼ teaspoon baking soda
6 tablespoons butter or margarine
½ cup dried currants (or raisins, or cranberries, or chocolate chips)
½ cup buttermilk
2 eggs

In a large bowl combine the flour, sugar, baking powder, salt, and soda. Cut in the butter with a pastry blender or two knives, until the mixture resembles course crumbs.

Stir in the currants. In a small bowl combine the buttermilk and eggs. Add this to the dry ingredients and stir to form a soft dough. With floured hands, knead gently and briefly to combine. Divide the dough in half. On an ungreased cookie sheet pat each piece of dough into a 6-inch round. Cut each round into 6 pieces but do not separate. Bake in a 425° oven for 12 to 15 minutes, until golden brown.

Separate the wedges and serve warm.

MAKES 12 SCONES.

The Grafton Inn

The Grafton Inn

❧

*261 Grand Avenue, South
Falmouth, Massachusetts 02540
(508) 540-8688*

An exploration of the miles of Falmouth beaches can start outside the front door of this renovated Victorian inn. Glorious ocean views can be enjoyed from the guest rooms and the enclosed porch. Rooms come with extra pillows, French-milled soaps, homemade chocolates, and plenty of fresh flowers. Take advantage of a cruise to the islands or go deep-sea fishing out of the harbor before returning for a relaxing evening at the Grafton Inn.

Molasses Cookies

    1   cup shortening (part butter)
    1   cup firmly packed dark brown sugar
    1   egg, beaten
    1   cup molasses
    ½   cup hot water
    3½ cups all-purpose flour
    2   teaspoons baking soda
    1   teaspoon salt
    ⅛   teaspoon ground cloves
    1   teaspoon ground ginger
    1   teaspoon ground cinnamon
    1   teaspoon grated nutmeg
    ½   cup raisins (chopped fine), if desired
        Sugar for sprinkling
        Walnut or pecan halves

In a large bowl blend the shortening and sugar. Add the egg, then the molasses, and hot water to which the soda has been added. In a separate bowl sift the flour, salt, cloves, ginger, cinnamon, and nutmeg. Add the dry ingredients to the batter, then the raisins. Drop from a spoon 2- inches apart on a baking sheet, sprinkle with sugar, and place 1 nut on top of each. Bake in a 400° oven for 10 to 12 minutes. Cookies will drop slightly after baking.

MAKES ABOUT 3 DOZEN.

Mostly Hall Bed and Breakfast

❧

*27 Main Street
Falmouth, Massachusetts 02540
(508) 548-3768, (800) 682-0565*

This plantation-style home, built in 1849, is the only house of its kind on Cape Cod. Secluded from the road on more than an acre of beautiful gardens and lawn, the inn is across from Falmouth's historic district. Shops, restaurants, theaters, galleries, beaches, and island ferries are nearby. Six spacious corner bedrooms with private baths feature queen-size four poster canopy beds, shuttered windows with garden views, ceiling fans, reading chairs, and a combination of antiques and traditional furnishings.

Cheese Blintz Muffins

    1   16-ounce carton part-skim ricotta
        cheese
    3   eggs
    2   tablespoons sour cream (or yogurt)
    ¼   cup butter or margarine, melted
    ½   cup reduced-fat baking mix
    ⅓   cup sugar

    1   tablespoon cornstarch
    ⅓   cup warm water (105 to 115°)
    ⅓   cup sugar
    2   tablespoons lemon juice
    2   cups fresh or frozen blueberries
        Sour cream for garnish

In a large bowl combine the ricotta, eggs, sour cream, and butter. Blend in the biscuit mix and ⅓ cup of sugar, and mix just until moistened. Spoon into greased muffin cups. Bake in a 350° oven for 30 minutes or until lightly browned.

In a saucepan combine the cornstarch with the warm water, and dissolve the lumps. Add ⅓ cup of sugar, lemon juice, and blueberries. Cook over medium heat, stirring until the mixture is thickened.

Place 2 muffins on each plate and spoon warm blueberry sauce over them. Top each with a dollop of sour cream.

MAKES 1 DOZEN.

Frittata Italiano

    2   tablespoons oil
    1   small onion, chopped
    2   small zucchini, chopped
    1   cup cooked pasta of choice
    2   medium tomatoes, chopped
    ½   pound turkey kielbasa, cubed
    8   eggs
    1   teaspoon Italian seasoning
    1   cup shredded Swiss cheese
        Paprika

In a 10- to 12-inch skillet heat the oil and sauté the onion until soft. Add the zucchini and tomatoes, and cook until tender. Add the pasta and kielbasa. In a medium bowl beat the eggs with Italian seasoning and pour over the mixture. Cover and cook on top of the stove without stirring until set, but the top is still moist. Cover with shredded Swiss cheese and place under a broiler until the top is lightly browned. Sprinkle with paprika and cut into wedges.

MAKES 6 TO 8 SERVINGS.

Cranberry Swirl Coffee Cake

    ½   cup butter or margarine, softened
    1   cup sugar
    2   eggs
    2   cups all-purpose flour

1 teaspoon baking powder
1 teaspoon baking soda
½ teaspoon salt
1 cup nonfat plain yogurt
2 teaspoons vanilla extract
1 17-ounce can whole cranberry sauce
⅓ cup chopped nuts

In a mixer bowl cream the butter and sugar. Add the unbeaten eggs, mixing at medium speed. Add the dry ingredients, yogurt, and vanilla, mixing until combined.

Grease an 8- to 9-inch tube pan. Pour a layer of batter in the pan. Swirl half of the cranberry sauce on the batter. Add the remaining batter and swirl the remaining cranberry sauce on top. Sprinkle with nuts. Bake in a 350° oven for 55 minutes. Cool the cake in the pan before removing.

MAKES 8 SERVINGS.

The Palmer House Inn

81 Palmer Avenue
Falmouth, Massachusetts 02540
(508) 584-1230

Palmer House on the Falmouth village green, clearly shows its Victorian era beginnings with stained glass windows, polished hardwood floors, carved woodwork, and antique furnishings. The romantic feeling is enhanced with lace, silk flowers, and scented linens. The inn provides an excellent central location for exploring Cape Cod or tak-

The Palmer House Inn

ing day trips to Nantucket or Martha's Vineyard.

Grand Marnier Truffles

8 ounces white chocolate
¼ cup Grand Marnier
½ cup sweet butter, softened
¾ cup pulverized vanilla wafers
2 cups finely chopped walnuts or pecans

In a saucepan melt chocolate with the Grand Marnier over low heat, stirring constantly. Whisk in the butter, a little at a time, until the mixture is smooth and the butter is melted. Beat in the pulverized cookies. Chill the mixture in the refrigerator for about 2 hours until firm. With a small scoop, gather up some of the mixture and roll between palms of hands, like making small meatballs. Roll the balls in finely chopped walnuts or pecans. Keep covered in the refrigerator until serving time. Serve in frilled paper cups.

MAKES ABOUT 2 DOZEN.

Cranapple Frappe

2 cups cranberry juice
2 cups apple juice
1 small ripe banana, peeled
¼ cup heavy cream
1 tablespoon lemon juice
Sugar to taste
4 cubes ice

Thoroughly chill all ingredients before beginning.

In a blender combine the juices, banana, cream, lemon juice, and sugar, and process on high speed for 30 seconds. Add the ice cubes and continue blending until smooth. Pour into a frosted pitcher and serve immediately.

MAKES 4 SERVINGS.

Cranberry Scones

3 cups all-purpose flour
2 tablespoons baking powder
½ teaspoon baking soda
1½ tablespoons sugar
1 cup ice-cold butter, cut into small chunks

1 cup chopped fresh or frozen cranberries, sweetened to taste, and drained thoroughly
2 cups buttermilk (approximately)
Sugar for sprinkling
Orange marmalade
Devonshire cream

In a large bowl combine the flour, baking powder, soda, and sugar and mix thoroughly. Cut the butter into the dry mixture with a pastry blender until the mixture resembles course meal. Chill for 10 minutes.

Add the cranberries and mix until the cranberries are coated with flour mixture. Add the buttermilk a little at a time, mixing until all ingredients are moistened and a dough forms. Gather into a ball. Turn onto a floured surface and knead about 15 times. Roll out dough to a 1-inch thickness. Cut out the scones with a floured, heart-shaped 2-inch biscuit cutter. Place on an ungreased baking sheet close together, but not touching. Brush the tops with buttermilk and sprinkle with sugar. Bake in a 400° oven for 20 minutes or until golden brown. Serve hot with orange marmalade and Devonshire cream.

MAKES 12 SCONES.

Victorian Porridge

3 cups water
½ teaspoon salt (optional)
1⅓ cups quick-cooking oats
½ cup granola
¼ cup raisins
1 tablespoon firmly packed brown sugar
2 tablespoons chopped walnuts or sliced almonds
Dash cinnamon
Milk for topping
Cinnamon-sugar or light brown sugar for sprinkling

In a 3-quart pot combine the water and salt, and bring to a boil. Add the remaining ingredients and stir to combine. Lower the heat and simmer for 3 to 5 minutes, stirring occasionally. Cover the pan and remove from the heat. Let stand for 5 minutes. Stir and serve with milk and a sprinkling of cinnamon-sugar or brown sugar.

MAKES 4 SERVINGS.

Finnish Pancake with Strawberry Soup

1 tablespoon margarine or butter
4 eggs
⅓ cup sugar
½ teaspoon salt
1 teaspoon vanilla extract
2½ cups milk
½ cup all-purpose flour
   Strawberry Soup (recipe follows)

Set the oven temperature to 425° and place a 10-inch glass pie plate in the oven to heat for 10 minutes. Take out and place the pan on a kitchen towel. Melt the margarine in the pan, coating the bottom and sides.

Meanwhile, in a large bowl beat together the eggs, sugar, salt, vanilla, and milk until combined well. Stir in the flour. Pour slowly into the hot pie plate. Bake in a 425° oven for 25 minutes or until puffed and lightly browned.

Let sit for 10 minutes before serving. Serve with Strawberry Soup.

MAKES 4 TO 6 SERVINGS.

Strawberry Soup

¼ cup water
1 pint frozen strawberries, defrosted
2 tablespoons cornstarch
   Sugar to taste

In a heatproof bowl mix the cornstarch and water and stir until smooth. Add the strawberries and sugar and stir. Microwave on high for 3 to 6 minutes, until thick and clear. Stir halfway through. Let cool slightly, then purée in a blender until smooth.

MAKES ABOUT 2 CUPS.

Windflower Inn

❧

684 South Egremont Road
Great Barrington, Massachusetts 01230
(413) 528-2720

A Federal-style country inn built during the late 1800s, the Windflower sits on a ten-acre estate in the midst of the Berkshire Mountains. A challenging 18-hole golf course is a short distance from the inn. Summer visitors can enjoy the nearby Jabob's Pillow Dance Festival, Berkshire Theatre Festival, and Tanglewood Music Festival.

Vegetarian Mexican Lasagna

1 19-ounce can black beans
2 15-ounce cans chick peas
1 15-ounce can red kidney beans
1 6-ounce can black olives
1 28-ounce can chunked peeled Italian tomatoes
¼ cup chili powder
½ cup medium salsa
12 corn tortillas
4 cups grated mozzarella cheese

Drain the beans and olives and cut the olives into thirds. In a deep skillet over medium heat combine the beans, olives, tomatoes, chili powder, and salsa. Bring to a slow simmer, and cook for about 20 minutes to reduce the liquid. Place a layer of tortillas in the bottom of a greased 11 x 7½-inch glass pan. Add almost half of the bean mixture and then almost half of the cheese. Repeat, ending with just a little bit of the remaining bean and liquid mixture and the remaining cheese. Bake in a 350° oven for about 30 minutes.

Note: For convenience refrigerate before baking and then bring to room temperature, and bake about 45 minutes to heat through.

MAKES ABOUT 6 SERVINGS.

Boursin Crab Cakes

2 teaspoons butter or olive oil
1 bunch scallions, sliced into small rounds
1 medium white boiling potato, peeled, boiled, mashed
2 6-ounce cans crab meat
1½ tablespoons chopped Italian parsley
1 teaspoon fresh dill
1 5.2-ounce package Herb Boursin (or any herb cheese), softened
2 teaspoons Pommerey mustard
   Pinch salt and fresh pepper
1 egg, beaten
   Seasoned breadcrumbs
   Olive oil

....

3 plum tomatoes, peeled, seeded, and coarsely chopped
1 teaspoon chopped fresh basil

In a skillet melt the butter and sauté the scallions until limp. Finely mash the boiled potato (or put it through a small strainer to make sure there are no lumps). Drain the excess liquid from the crab meat. Place the drained crab meat in a bowl and break up the large pieces. Add the scallions, parsley, and dill. Mix half of the boursin and the mustard, then the potato. Add a pinch of salt and pepper, and mix in the beaten egg. (This can be made the day before and refrigerated).

Form the mixture it into patties about 2⅔ inches in diameter. Coat in the breadcrumbs on all sides. Make all the cakes, then, cook them immediately or refrigerate if desired.

In a sauté pan heat the olive oil and cook a few crab cakes at a time on both sides until golden brown. Drain on paper towels. They can be reheated in a hot oven.

In a medium bowl combine the tomatoes, basil, and remaining boursin. Serve with tomato herb boursin sauce on the side.

MAKES 4 SERVINGS.

Peach Brandy Chicken

2 tablespoons butter
4 boneless chicken breasts, with or without skin
2 tablespoons all-purpose flour with pinch salt and pepper
⅓ cup chicken stock
4 small to medium peaches, peeled and sliced
3 ounces peach brandy
1 pinch dried tarragon or sprig fresh tarragon
2 tablespoons heavy cream

In a 12-inch nonstick sauté pan heat the butter. Dip the chicken in flour and sauté skin-side down over medium to high heat until brown, about 4 to 5 minutes. Turn the breasts and cook another 4 to 5 minutes. Remove the chicken from the pan and deglaze the pan with chicken stock. Add the peaches, brandy, and tarragon. Reduce the heat and cook approximately 2 minutes. Return the chicken, along with any accumulated juices, to the pan. Add the heavy cream and cook until the chicken is hot and cooked through. Place the chicken on a platter or plates and top with peaches and sauce. If the sauce is not quite thick enough after removing chicken and peaches reduce quickly on high heat before pouring over the chicken.

MAKES 4 SERVINGS.

Mill House Inn

Route 43, P.O. Box 1079
Hancock, Massachusetts 01237
(413) 738-5348

---

*T*he rough-sawn paneling and beams add to the feeling of country-style friendliness at the Mill House. Each of the twelve rooms is individually decorated with antiques. When weather permits, breakfast is served on the garden deck.

Stone-Ground Wheat Cakes

- ½ cup stone-ground wheat flour
- 1 cup all-purpose flour
- ½ teaspoon salt
- 3⅓ teaspoons baking powder
- 2 tablespoons sugar
- 1 egg
- 2 cups milk
- 2 tablespoons oil
- Butter

In a large bowl combine the flours, salt, baking powder, and sugar. In a small bowl mix together the egg, milk, and oil. Pour the wet ingredients into the dry and stir gently until they are mixed thoroughly. Do not overmix. Heat a griddle and butter it well. Spoon the batter onto the hot griddle. Cook until bubbles appear, then flip and brown other side of each pancake.

MAKES 4 SERVINGS.

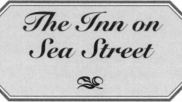

355 Sea Street
Hyannis, Massachusetts 02601
(508) 775-8030

---

*O*nly a short walk from the beach or downtown Hyannis, the inn consists of a pair of Victorian houses dating to the mid 1800s. These feature country antiques, lacy fabrics, and breakfasts served on china, silver, and crystal. In addition to the nine light and airy guest rooms, the inn also offers a small, all white cottage with peaked ceiling and its own kitchen.

Irish Brown Cake

- 1½ cups raisins
- 2½ cups water
- 2½ cups all-purpose flour
- 1 cup firmly packed dark brown sugar
- 2 tablespoons oil
- 1 teaspoon salt
- 2 teaspoons baking powder
- ½ teaspoon baking soda
- 1 egg, slightly beaten

In a saucepan cover the raisins with the water and bring to a boil. Drain, reserving 1½ cups of the water for the batter.

In a large bowl combine all ingredients including the raisins and reserved water. Pour into a greased and floured 5 x 9-inch loaf pan. Bake in a 325° oven for 1 hour and 15 minutes.

MAKES 1 LOAF.

Crab Scramble

- 9 eggs
- ½ cup milk
- 1 8-ounce package cream cheese, cubed
- 1 6-ounce can crab meat
- ½ teaspoon salt
- ¼ teaspoon pepper
- ½ cup butter
- 1 tablespoon chopped fresh baby dill

In a large bowl beat the eggs and milk. Add the cream cheese, crab meat, salt, and pepper. In a 7 x 12-inch pan melt the butter. Pour the egg mixture into the pan. Sprinkle with chopped dill. Bake in a 350° oven for 30 minutes.

MAKES 6 SERVINGS.

Pear Coffee Cake with Ginger Pecan Crunch Topping

- 2½ cups all-purpose flour
- ¾ cup sugar
- 1 cup firmly packed dark brown sugar
- 1 teaspoon salt
- 1 teaspoon grated nutmeg
- ¾ cup oil
- 2 cups chopped ripe pear
  ....
- 1 slightly beaten egg
- 1 cup buttermilk
- 1 teaspoon baking soda
- 1 teaspoon baking powder
  ....
- ½ teaspoon ground ginger
- 1 cup chopped pecans

In a large bowl combine the flour, sugar, brown sugar, salt, nutmeg, and oil. Set aside 1 cup of the mixture for topping. Add the chopped pear to the remaining mixture. Add the egg, buttermilk, soda, and baking powder. Spread the batter into a greased jelly roll pan. In a small bowl combine the reserved mixture, ginger, and pecans. Sprinkle the topping over the batter. Bake in a 350° oven for 40 minutes or until a knife inserted in the center comes out clean.

MAKES 8 SERVINGS.

Mocha-Chocolate Chip Coffee Cake

2 cups all-purpose flour
2 teaspoons baking powder
½ teaspoon salt
½ teaspoon baking soda
¾ cup sugar
2 eggs, beaten
Dash vanilla extract
¼ cup butter, melted
⅓ cup coffee made stronger by adding 4 teaspoons freeze-dried coffee powder
1 cup sour cream

....

3 tablespoons all-purpose flour
½ cup firmly packed dark brown sugar
2 tablespoons butter, softened
1 cup semisweet chocolate chips
¾ cup chopped walnuts
¼ cup sliced almonds

In a large bowl mix 2 cups of flour, baking powder, salt, soda, and sugar. In a separate bowl combine the eggs, vanilla, butter, coffee, and sour cream. Stir the liquid mixture into the dry ingredients, but do not beat. In a separate bowl cut 3 tablespoons of flour and the brown sugar into the soft butter until crumbly. Add the chocolate chips and nuts. Pour the batter into greased 9 x 14-inch baking pan. Sprinkle the topping over the top and press into the batter slightly with a spatula. Bake in a 350° oven for 30 to 35 minutes.

MAKES 8 SERVINGS.

Whole Wheat Bread

9 cups whole wheat flour
1 tablespoon salt
1 quart plus ¼ cup regular milk
3 tablespoons honey
1 package active dry yeast
Milk for topping

In a large bowl combine half of the flour with the salt. In a saucepan heat the milk to warm. In a separate small bowl combine ⅓ cup of warm milk with the honey and yeast. Let stand 10 minutes.

Add the yeast mixture and milk to the dry ingredients alternately with the remaining flour. The dough will be sticky. Divide the dough in half and place in 2 greased 5 x 9-inch loaf pans. Cover with a towel and let rise in a warm place until doubled in bulk. Bake in a 375° oven for 30 minutes. Brush the tops with milk.

MAKES 2 LOAVES.

Rhubarb Coffee Cake with Vanilla Sauce

1 cup sugar
1 egg
2 tablespoons melted margarine
1 cup buttermilk

....

2 cups all-purpose flour
1 teaspoon baking powder
½ teaspoon baking soda
½ teaspoon salt
1½ cups chopped rhubarb

....

2 tablespoons margarine, melted
½ cup sugar

....

¾ cup sugar
½ cup margarine
½ cup evaporated milk
1 teaspoon vanilla extract

In a large bowl combine 1 cup of sugar, the egg, 2 tablespoons of melted margarine, and buttermilk and blend with a whisk. Add the flour, baking powder, soda and salt, and mix well. Stir in the rhubarb. Pour the batter into a 9 x 13-inch pan. In a small bowl combine 2 tablespoons of melted margarine and ½ cup of sugar. Sprinkle the mixture over the batter. Bake in a 350° oven for 1 hour.

In a saucepan mix ¾ cup of sugar, ½ cup of margarine, and evaporated milk. Bring to rolling boil. Cook for 1 minute, stirring constantly. Remove from the heat and add the vanilla. Pour Vanilla Sauce over each serving.

MAKES 8 SERVINGS.

The Inn on Sea Street

JB's Victorian Delight

½ loaf French bread, cubed
½ pound loose hot sausage, cooked and crumbled

....

2 tablespoons all-purpose flour
1 tablespoon dry mustard
⅛ teaspoon black pepper
Pinch cayenne pepper
¼ teaspoon dried basil
½ teaspoon salt
2 cups milk
7 eggs, beaten slightly
1 cup grated Cheddar cheese
Grated mozzarella cheese

Grease a 7 x 11-inch pan and line the bottom with French bread. Distribute the crumbled sausage over the top evenly. In a small bowl combine the flour, dry mustard, black pepper, cayenne, basil, and salt. Sprinkle the mixture over the sausage. In a medium bowl mix the milk and eggs and pour over the top. Sprinkle grated cheese over all. Cover with foil and refrigerate overnight.

Bake covered in a 350° oven for 1 hour.

MAKES 6 SERVINGS.

Apple-Tree Inn

334 West Street
Lenox, Massachusetts 01240
(413) 637-1477

On twenty-two hilltop acres directly across the road from the Tanglewood Festival, Apple Tree Inn boasts stunning views of the Berkshires in western Massachusetts. The splendid Victorian atmosphere of the century-old house is enhanced by four-posters, brass beds, and old-fashioned wallpapers. The oak-beamed tavern is just the place to relax after a day of exploring the mountains.

Chef's Sour Cream Coffee Cake

½ cup finely chopped walnuts
½ cup sugar
1 teaspoon ground cinnamon
....

1 cup sugar
½ cup butter
2 cups all-purpose flour
1 cup sour cream
2 eggs
1 teaspoon baking powder
1 teaspoon baking soda
1 teaspoon vanilla extract

In a large bowl combine the nuts, ½ cup of sugar, and cinnamon.

In a large bowl beat 1 cup of sugar and the butter with an electric mixer until fluffy. Add the remaining ingredients and beat for 3 minutes at medium speed. Spread half of the batter in a greased 9-inch tube pan. Sprinkle with half of the nut mixture. Repeat the layers. Bake in a 350° oven for 60 to 65 minutes. Cool in the pan for a few minutes. Remove from the pan and cool completely.

MAKES 8 SERVINGS.

Birchwood Inn

7 Hubbard Street
Lenox, Massachusetts 01240
(413) 637-2600

Few country inns are as elegant as the Birchwood, built in 1767. Guests may look out from a hill overlooking the historic Berkshire Village of Lenox and enjoy cool breezes that drift across the porch. The theme for decorations and furnishings is 18th century, and the library and parlor invite guests to relax in front of a fire. Guest rooms are immaculate and have the charm of a bygone era.

Birchwood Inn

Gingerbread Pancakes

2 cups biscuit mix
1 tablespoon ground ginger
1 teaspoon ground allspice
½ teaspoon ground cloves
¼ teaspoon ground cardamom
2 eggs
⅓ cup unsulphured dark molasses
⅔ cup milk

In a large bowl mix the dry ingredients together until blended and the lumps are reduced to a minimum. Add the eggs, molasses, and milk, and blend until the batter is smooth. Be careful not to overmix.

Hints: Mixing is a bit easier if you blend the milk and molasses separately before adding to the batter. Cooking the pancakes can be a bit tricky—if the batter is too thin, the pancakes can be difficult to turn because it takes longer for them to set up than a normal pancake. If the batter is too thick, the pancakes become very dark before they are fully cooked.

MAKES 4 SERVINGS.

Ginger-Lemon Sauce

1½ cups sugar
⅔ cup lemon juice
2½ tablespoons cornstarch
Finely minced zest of 1 lemon
2 tablespoons fresh ginger, finely minced

In a large saucepan mix all ingredients and bring slowly to a boil, stirring frequently. Simmer for about 15 minutes, taking care not to allow it to boil over. (It expands exponentially once it starts to boil and makes a bloody awful mess of the stove.) Strain through a fine mesh strainer and serve with pancakes.

Hint: Serve the syrup warm with a dollop

of lightly salted butter melted in it at the last minute. The syrup will store indefinitely, unrefrigerated, in a bottle with a good seal.

MAKES ABOUT 2 CUPS.

Tarte D'Alsace

4 large Spanish onions
¼ cup unsalted butter
¼ cup sugar
Dash Liquid Smoke (optional)
6 eggs, beaten
2 cups sour cream
Salt and pepper to taste
2 unbaked 9-inch pie shells
2 ounces bacon bits (or substitute)

Peel and slice the onions, across the rings, in slices about ½ inch wide, and then cut again at 90 degrees into pieces roughly ½ inch wide by 1½ inch long. In a large, heavy skillet or heavy Dutch oven melt the butter until bubbling. Add all of the onions and sauté on high heat. When the onions turn slightly brown, add the sugar and a dash of Liquid Smoke and continue to brown the onions. Continue stirring the mixture, cooking until the onions are a rich chocolate brown in color. This may take up to 30 minutes but is the key to the full flavor of the authentic tarte.

Set the onions aside to cool. In a medium bowl beat the eggs. Blend in the sour cream, salt, and pepper. When the pan used to cook the onions is cool enough to touch, add the egg mixture. Whisk together well, picking up all the browned coating on the pan.

Distribute the combined eggs, cream and onions equally among the pie shells. Sprinkle the bacon bits on top. Bake in a 400° oven for 1 hour or until the top of the pie is a rich golden brown and the crust is crisp. Serve immediately.

Excellent as a main course for lunch or brunch or as a starter for formal dinners.

Hints: Onions may be sautéed a day in advance and the final preparation begun just before to baking. Prebaked pie crusts are not recommended since the long cooking time for the quiche mixture might cause the exposed crusts to burn.

Note: The Liquid Smoke provides a very authentic flavor to the tarte since the Alsatians normally bake this quiche in wood ovens.

MAKES 12 SERVINGS.

Huevos Rancheros

- ¼ cup olive oil
- 1 large Spanish onion, coarsely diced
- 4 cloves garlic, minced
- 1 green bell pepper, coarsely diced
- 1 red bell pepper, coarsely diced
- 1 tablespoon chili powder
- ½ teaspoon dried oregano
  Cracked red pepper to taste
- 1 8-ounce can tomato paste
- 1 28-ounce can crushed tomatoes
- ½ cup red wine
- 12 small corn tortillas
- 3 cups shredded sharp Cheddar cheese
- 12 eggs
  Grated Parmesan cheese
  Cayenne pepper

In a deep, iron skillet or Dutch oven heat the olive oil and sauté the onion until soft and translucent. Add the garlic and continue to sauté over medium-high heat until the onion is lightly brown. Add the bell peppers, and cook until they are softened. Add the seasonings and tomato paste and combine thoroughly with the onion, garlic, and peppers, allowing the mixture to coat the bottom of the pan and brown slightly. Add the crushed tomatoes and wine and fully blend all ingredients. Cover and simmer over low heat for at least 1 hour. The consistency should be fairly thick. Cook the mixture down, uncovered, if it is at all watery. The base may be refrigerated overnight or frozen for future use.

In 6 individual oven proof serving dishes, place 2 tortillas on the bottom and then cover with the tomato mixture to a depth of ½ inch. Cover with a generous layer of Cheddar cheese. Break 2 eggs over the cheese, keeping the yolks whole. Cover with Parmesan and sprinkle cayenne pepper on top. Bake in a 400° oven for about 15 minutes until firm. Serve with corn bread.

MAKES 6 SERVINGS.

The Village Inn

16 Church Street, P.O. Box 1810
Lenox, Massachusetts 01240
(413) 637-0020

The Village Inn is situated on a quiet street in the village of Lenox, once the chosen retreat of America's most wealthy and fashionable families. A town of quaint shops, working craftsmen, galleries, antique stores, historic buildings, old churches, and wooded parks, Lenox still plays host to thousands of summer visitors who come here for the cool mountain breezes or the nearby Tanglewood music festival. Dating to 1771, the inn is Colonial in appearance and spirit. Some of its thirty-two guest rooms have fireplaces, all are furnished with country antiques.

Pecan-breaded Breast of Chicken

- 8 ounces boneless, skinless chicken breast
  Salt and white pepper to taste
  Flour
- ¼ cup coarsely chopped pecans
  Clarified butter for sautéing

- 1 tablespoon chopped shallots
- 2 tablespoons white wine
- 1 tablespoon Dijon mustard
- ¼ cup heavy cream
- 1 tablespoon butter
  Juice from ½ small lemon
  Salt and white pepper to taste

Season the chicken breast with salt and pepper and lightly coat with flour. Allow to sit at room temperature for 1 minute until the flour

becomes sticky on the surface of the chicken. Dredge in coarsely chopped pecans. Barely cover the bottom of a small sauté pan with clarified butter and place over heat. When very hot, add the chicken and sauté on each side until the pecans begin to brown. Bake in a 375° oven briefly to finish cooking.

When the chicken is done, remove to a holding pan. In the same sauté pan add the shallots, white wine, and mustard, and allow to cook briefly. Add the heavy cream and bring to a boil. Swirl in the butter and finish with lemon juice, salt, and white pepper. Place the chicken on a service plate and cover with the sauce.

MAKES 1 SERVING.

Orange Blossom Muffins

- 1 egg, slightly beaten
- ¼ cup sugar
- ½ cup orange juice
- 2 tablespoons oil
- 2 cups biscuit mix
- ½ cup orange marmalade
- ½ cup chopped pecans

- ¼ cup sugar
- 1½ tablespoons all-purpose flour
- ½ teaspoon ground cinnamon
- ¼ teaspoon grated nutmeg
- 1 tablespoon butter or margarine

In a large bowl combine the egg, ¼ cup of sugar, orange juice, and oil. Add the biscuit mix and beat vigorously for 30 seconds. Stir in the marmalade and pecans. Grease 12 muffin cups or line with paper liners. Fill each cup two-thirds full.

In a small bowl combine ¼ cup of sugar, 1½ tablespoons of flour, cinnamon, and nutmeg. Cut in the butter until crumbly. Sprinkle over the batter. Bake in a 400° oven for 20 to 25 minutes.

MAKES 1 DOZEN.

The Farmhouse at Nauset Beach

The Farmhouse at Nauset Beach

❧

163 Beach Road
Orleans, Massachusetts 02653
(508) 255-6654

This old farmhouse provides a quiet, pastoral setting for a stay on Cape Cod. Guests have easy access to all the Cape's attractions, but without having to bother with the crowds and traffic. The Academy Playhouse is nearby, and Cape Cod Bay makes charter fishing a convenient diversion.

Cape Cod Juice

- 1 12-ounce can frozen orange juice
- ½ cantaloupe, cut in large cubes
- ½ cup fresh strawberries, cleaned and hulled
- 4½ cups water
- 6 strawberries for garnish

In a blender combine the frozen orange juice, cantaloupe, strawberries, and water, and blend until smooth. Pour into serving glasses and garnish with whole strawberries.
MAKES 6 SERVINGS.

Cranberry Nut Conserve

- 1 16-ounce can whole berry cranberry sauce
- 1 16-ounce can pear halves, drained and coarsely chopped
- ¼ cup seedless raisins
- ¼ to ½ cup chopped walnuts
- 1 teaspoon minced, peeled ginger (or 1 teaspoon ground)

In a medium bowl combine all of the ingredients. Chill several hours before serving.
MAKES 6 TO 8 SERVINGS.

Baked Oatmeal

- 3 cups quick-cooking oats
- 1 cup firmly packed light brown sugar
- 2 teaspoons baking powder
- 1 teaspoon ground cinnamon
- 1 teaspoon salt
- 1 cup milk
- ½ cup butter/margarine, melted
- 2 eggs, beaten
  Milk for topping

In a large bowl mix all ingredients together. Spoon the batter into a greased 9-inch square pan. Bake in a 350° oven for 40 to 45 minutes. Serve warm with milk drizzled on top.
MAKES 9 SERVINGS.

Pumpkin Butter

- 1 16-ounce can solid pack pumpkin
- ⅔ cup firmly packed brown sugar
- ¼ cup honey
- 1 tablespoon lemon juice
- ¼ teaspoon ground cinnamon
- ⅛ teaspoon ground cloves

In a medium saucepan combine all ingredients and mix well. Bring to a boil over medium-high heat, stirring frequently. Reduce the heat and simmer for 20 minutes or until thickened, stirring frequently.
MAKES ABOUT 3 CUPS.

West End Inn

❧

44 Commercial Street
Provincetown, Massachusetts 02657
(800) 559-1220

A Greek Revival inn at Provincetown, the West End is only about a mile from the tip of Cape Cod. Closer to the beach than to town, the inn is just across the street from the spot where the Cape's first settlers landed.

Yvon's Magic Muffins

- 6 tablespoons butter
- 1 teaspoon lemon juice
- ⅓ cup sugar
- 3 ripe bananas
- 1⅓ cups all-purpose flour
- 1 teaspoon baking soda
- 1 teaspoon baking powder
  Pinch salt
- 1 teaspoon vanilla extract
- ½ cup walnuts
- 1 cup cranberries

In a food processor combine the butter, lemon juice, and sugar. Mix in the bananas. Then mix in the remaining ingredients. Fill muffin cups about three-fourths full. Bake in a 350° oven for 25 minutes or until golden.
MAKES ABOUT 14 MUFFINS.

West End Inn Chicken

- 1 pound mushrooms, sliced
- 4 whole boneless, skinless chicken breasts
- ¾ cup Rose wine
- ¼ cup water
- ¼ cup soy sauce
- 2 tablespoons olive oil
- 2 tablespoons firmly packed brown sugar
- 2 tablespoons cornstarch
- 2 cloves garlic, pressed
- ½ teaspoon dried oregano

In the bottom of a 9 x 13-inch baking pan spread the mushrooms. On top of that place the chicken breasts. In a small bowl mix the remaining ingredients to produce a thin sauce. Pour over the chicken and mushrooms. Bake in a 325° oven for 1 hour and 15 minutes, basting occasionally.
  Note: Serve with rice or linguine.
MAKES 4 SERVINGS.

Eden Pines Inn

Eden Pines Inn

48 Eden Road
Rockport, Massachusetts 01966
(508) 546-2505

Eden Pines rests on a rocky ledge overlooking the Atlantic toward two of the oldest lighthouses in America and is within walking distance of sandy beaches. It takes advantage of its setting with a wicker-filled open porch and a large brick deck affording excellent views of the ocean scenery. All but one of the six guest rooms have their own sitting areas and decks facing the ocean. Breakfast is served in the sunroom where guests may view the ocean in three directions.

Carrot Cake

    2   cups all-purpose flour
    2   teaspoons baking powder
    1½ teaspoons baking soda
    ¼   teaspoon salt
    1   teaspoon ground cinnamon
    1   cup sugar
    ½   cup oil
    4   eggs
    2   cups finely grated carrots
    1   20-ounce can crushed pineapple,
          well-drained
    ½   cup chopped nuts
          Confectioners' sugar

In a medium bowl sift together the flour, baking powder, soda, salt, and cinnamon. In a separate bowl mix the sugar, oil, and eggs. Add the dry ingredients, and then the carrots, pineapple, and nuts. Pour into a 9 x 13-inch baking pan. Bake in a 350° oven for 35 to 40 minutes. Cut into squares.

Freezes well. Take from the freezer to the microwave and it tastes like it was just baked. Serve this warm with confectioners' sugar sprinkled on top instead of the traditional cream cheese frosting.

MAKES 12 SERVINGS.

Apple Cake

    1   cup sugar
    3   cups all-purpose flour
    1   teaspoon baking powder
    2   teaspoons baking soda
    1   cup butter
    1   cup milk, divided
    2   eggs
    4   cups finely chopped tart apples
    ⋯⋯⋯⋯⋯⋯⋯⋯⋯⋯⋯⋯
    ½   cup sugar
    4   teaspoons ground cinnamon
    1   cup chopped nuts

In a large bowl sift 1 cup of sugar, the flour, baking powder, and soda. Add the butter and ½ cup of milk and beat with an electric mixer at low speed for 2 minutes. Add the eggs and beat for 1 minute. Add the remaining milk and beat for 1 minute more. Fold in the chopped apples. Spread in a lightly greased 9 x 13-inch pan. In a small bowl combine ½ cup of sugar, the cinnamon and nuts. Sprinkle the topping over the batter. Bake in a 350° oven for 40 minutes or until done. This is a moist cake.

MAKES 12 SERVINGS.

The Inn on Cove Hill

The Inn on Cove Hill

37 Mt. Pleasant Street
Rockport, Massachusetts 01966
(508) 546-2701

More than two centuries old, the inn was built in 1791 with the proceeds of pirate gold unearthed at nearby Gully Point. Many of the Federal style architectural and decorative features of this authentic Colonial home have been carefully preserved or restored. They can be seen in its clapboard walls and shutters or spiral staircase, and enjoyed in any one of the inn's eleven guest rooms. Rockport is located on Cape Ann, which with its coves, beaches, and villages, is great bicycling country.

Orange Buttermilk Muffins

    6   tablespoons shortening
    ½   cup sugar
    1   egg
    ½   orange
    1   cup buttermilk
    2   cups all-purpose flour
    1   teaspoon baking powder
    1   teaspoon baking soda
    ¼   teaspoon salt

In a bowl cream the shortening and sugar together. Beat in the egg.

In a blender whack up half of an orange, including the peel, with 1 cup of buttermilk. Add the orange mixture to the creamed mixture. Mix all of the dry ingredients into the liquid mixture. Mix only until all ingredients are just moistened. Pour into greased muffin cups. Bake in a 400° oven for 20 to 25 minutes.

MAKES 1 DOZEN.

Moist Bran Muffins

- 1 **cup buttermilk**
- ¼ **fresh lemon, peel and all**
- ⅓ **cup oil**
- ½ **teaspoon vanilla extract**
- 1 **egg**
- 1 **cup bran**
- ½ **cup old-fashioned oats**
- ⅔ **cup firmly packed brown sugar**
- ½ **cup raisins (or dates)**

In a blender mix the buttermilk and lemon. Add the oil and egg, and blend well. Pour into a large bowl. In a separate bowl mix the dry ingredients. Add the dry ingredients to the liquid mixture and mix just until moistened. Pour into greased muffin cups. Bake in a 400° oven for 20 to 25 minutes.

MAKES 1 DOZEN.

Apple Muffins

- 1 **egg**
- ½ **cup milk**
- ¼ **cup melted shortening**
- 1 **cup chopped unpeeled tart apples**
- 1½ **cups all-purpose flour**
- ½ **cup sugar**
- 2 **teaspoons baking powder**
- ½ **teaspoon salt**
- ½ **teaspoon ground cinnamon**

In a large bowl mix the egg, milk, shortening, and apples. In a separate bowl mix the dry ingredients. Add the dry ingredients to the liquid mixture and mix just until moistened. Pour into greased muffin cups. Bake in a 400° oven for 20 to 25 minutes.

MAKES 1 DOZEN.

Berry Muffins

- 1¾ **cups all-purpose flour**
- ¼ **cup sugar**
- 1 **teaspoon baking powder**
- ¼ **teaspoon baking soda**
- ¼ **teaspoon salt**
- 1 **beaten egg**
- ¾ **cup or buttermilk (or sour milk)**
- ⅓ **cup oil**
- 1 **cup berries (blackberries, blueberries, cranberries)**

In a medium bowl mix the dry ingredients. In a separate bowl mix the egg, milk, and oil. Add the dry ingredients to the liquid ingredients and mix just until moistened. Bake in a 400° oven for 20 to 25 minutes.

MAKES 1 DOZEN.

Yankee Clipper Inn

96 Granite Street
Rockport, Massachusetts 01966
(508) 546-3407

Consisting of four separate buildings, the Yankee Clipper is on the Massachusetts North Shore in the picturesque village of Rockport. It offers twenty-nine rooms, most with sweeping views of the Atlantic. Some rooms feature canopied beds, period antiques, sun decks, and glass-enclosed porches.

Cioppino Verde

- 2 **tablespoons olive oil**
- 2 **teaspoons chopped shallots**
- 2 **links sweet sausage**
- 1 **teaspoon minced garlic**
- 2 **jumbo shrimp, shelled and deveined**
- 12 **New Zealand green lip mussels (or regular New England black mussels)**
- 2 **lobster claws, cracked but not separated**
- 2 **2- to 3- ounce fillets ocean-water catfish (or monkfish or cusk)**
- 6 **ounce scallops (use scallops in shell for an extra-special appearance)**
- 2 **red-skin potatoes, cut into quarters**
- 2 **cups white wine**
- 6 **tablespoons pesto sauce**
   Chopped parsley
   Garlic bread

In a large sauté pan heat the olive oil and sauté the shallots, sausage, and garlic, until browned. Add the seafood and potatoes and continue to cook and toss a bit in the pan. Be careful not to break the fish.

Add white wine, cover, and cook until the mussels open and all fish is cooked through.

Add the pesto and heat through.

Serve in a bowl with fresh parsley garnish and garlic bread or serve over pasta

MAKES 2 SERVINGS.

Cranberry Cream Cheese Muffins

- ¼ **cup plus 3 tablespoons butter**
- ½ **cup sugar**
- 2 **eggs**

- 2 **cups all-purpose flour**
- ½ **teaspoon salt**
- 4 **teaspoons baking powder**
- 1 **cup milk**

- 1 **cup chopped cranberries**
- ¼ **cup cream cheese**
   Cinnamon-sugar for topping

In a large bowl cream together the butter, sugar, and eggs. Add the flour, salt, baking powder, and milk and mix until smooth. Fold in the cranberries and cream cheese. Spoon into muffin cups. Sprinkle with cinnamon-sugar. Bake in a 350° oven for 25 minutes or until puffed and golden brown, and a toothpick inserted in the center comes out clean.

MAKES 12 MUFFINS.

Captain Ezra Nye House

152 Main Street
Sandwich, Massachusetts 02563
(800) 388-2278

The pineapple was long recognized as a symbol of hospitality by New England seamen such as Captain Ezra Nye, who built this Federal-style house in 1829. That is why the innkeepers of this B&B have chosen the pineapple as a decorative theme throughout the Captain Nye House. Located in the village of Sandwich, the B&B is within walking distance of many of Cape Cod's most popular attractions including the Scenic Railroad, Heritage Plantation, Doll and Glass Museum, and Hoxie House.

Morning Glory Muffins

- 2   cups all-purpose flour
- 2   teaspoons baking soda
- 1   cup sugar
- 2   teaspoons ground cinnamon
- 3   eggs
- 1   tablespoon vanilla extract
- 1   cup oil
- 1   Granny Smith apple, grated
- ½   cup walnuts
- 2   cups grated carrots

In a medium bowl sift together the dry ingredients. In a separate bowl beat the eggs, vanilla, and oil. Add the dry ingredients. Stir in the apple, walnuts, and carrots. Spray muffin cups with cooking spray. Pour the batter into the prepared muffin cups. Bake in a 350° oven for 25 minutes.

MAKES 1 DOZEN.

Cherry Puffs

- 12   puff pastry shells
- 1   21-ounce can cherry pie filling
- 1   teaspoon almond extract
- ¾   cup heavy cream
-     Sugar

Bake the frozen puff pastries in a 400° oven for 20 minutes. Remove from the oven and pull off the top part. Ladle pie filling in the center of the bottom part, and put the top on this. Return to the oven for 10 minutes. Serve immediately. While the pastries are baking, whip the cream until stiff peaks form, adding the almond extract and sugar to taste. Pass the whipped cream.

MAKES 12 SERVINGS.

Captain Ezra Nye House

The Summer House
❧

158 Main Street
Sandwich, Massachusetts 02563
(508) 888-4991

A*n excellent Cape Cod example of Greek Revival architecture, the Summer House dates to 1835. It was once owned by glassmakers who worked nearby for the well-known Boston and Sandwich Glass Company. Bedrooms are decorated and appointed to evoke the spirit of the 19th century. One of the special attractions of this B&B is the complimentary afternoon tea brewed in antique silver pots and served with frosted tea cakes and English bisquits. Attractions in Sandwich Village include the Quaker Meeting House, area museums, and Heritage Plantation.*

Fruit Cobbler

- 1½   cups orange juice
- ¼   cup sugar
- 1   tablespoon cornstarch
- 4   cups any kind of fruit, cut into bite-sized pieces
- 1   cup all-purpose flour
- 2   tablespoons sugar
- 1½   teaspoons salt
- ¼   cup butter, melted (or margarine or oil olive or canola oil)
- ½   cup nonfat buttermilk
- 1   tablespoon sugar with dash ground cinnamon mixed in

In a heavy saucepan stir the orange juice, ¼ cup or more sugar, and cornstarch until blended. Heat until bubbly. Add the fruit and simmer until just cooked. (This can be done the night before, if necessary.) Remove from the heat and set aside.

Spray a 9 x 13-inch baking dish with cooking spray. Pour the fruit mixture into the baking dish.

In a medium bowl combine the flour, 2 tablespoons sugar, and salt and whisk until blended. Add the oil and fold in with a rubber spatula until the mixture looks crumbly. Add the buttermilk and stir in just until a light fluffy dough forms. Spoon dollops of dough onto the fruit, leaving some fruit to show through. Sprinkle with cinnamon-sugar.

Bake in a 375° oven on the low rack of the oven for about 8 minutes or until the fruit begins to bubble. Do not overbake. If the dough has not turned a bit golden on top, set on the high rack of the oven and broil for about 30 seconds to brown the top. Serve immediately.

Variation: Serve warm with ice cream on top as a dessert instead of breakfast fare.

MAKES 8 SERVINGS.

The Summer House

Avocado and Bacon Frittata

- 1   tablespoon olive oil
- 1   medium potato, boiled, cooled, and peeled
- 1   small onion, chopped finely
-     Mrs. Dash seasoning
- 1   ripe avocado, cubed
- 3   strips bacon, fried crisp and crumbled
- 1   small tomato, chopped and drained on paper towel
- 3   large eggs
- 1   teaspoon water
- ¼   cup shredded Swiss cheese
- 1   tablespoon pine nuts
-     Snipped chives

In a 10-inch ovenproof nonstick skillet heat the olive oil. Cut the potato into bite-sized pieces. Add the potato and onion to the skillet, and season with Mrs. Dash to taste. Stir occasionally over high heat until the potato begins to brown. Lower the heat. To the skillet add the avocado, bacon, and tomato. In a small bowl whisk the eggs with the water and pour evenly over the vegetables in the skillet. Sprinkle with cheese, pine nuts, and chives. Cook over medium heat until set around the edge. Place the pan on the top rack of the oven and broil for about 1 minute or until the center is set. Cut in half with a wooden spatula and gently slide onto plates.

MAKES 2 SERVINGS.

Currant and Cheese Pancakes

- ½ cups all-purpose flour
- 1 tablespoon sugar
- 1 teaspoon baking powder
- ¼ teaspoon ground cinnamon
- 2 large eggs
- ½ cup cream-style cottage cheese
- 2 tablespoons milk
- 1 tablespoon olive oil
- 1 teaspoon vanilla extract
- 2 tablespoons currants
  Butter or margarine for topping
  Maple syrup

In a large bowl combine the flour, sugar, baking powder, and cinnamon. In a separate bowl beat together the eggs, cottage cheese, milk, oil, and vanilla. Add the liquid mixture to the dry ingredients, and stir until blended but still slightly lumpy. Stir in the currants. For each pancake pour 1 rounded tablespoon of batter onto a hot, lightly greased nonstick griddle. Cook until golden, turning to cook the other side when the pancakes have a bubbly surface. Serve with butter or margarine and maple syrup.

MAKES 12 PANCAKES.

Feta, Phyllo, and Spinach Croustade

- 8 sheets frozen phyllo dough (17 x 12-inch rectangles)
- 3 tablespoons margarine or butter
- ½ cup finely chopped onion
- 1 10-ounce box frozen chopped spinach, thawed and squeezed dry
- 3 tablespoons all-purpose flour
- ⅛ teaspoon pepper
- ½ teaspoon dried tarragon, crushed

- 1 cup milk
- 2 eggs
- 1 cup cream-style cottage cheese
- ½ cup crumbled feta cheese
- 2 tablespoons melted butter or margarine

Remove the phyllo dough from the freezer the night before and place in the refrigerator to thaw.

In a large nonstick skillet melt 3 tablespoons of butter and sauté the onion until tender. Add the squeezed spinach, breaking up with a plastic fork. Stir in the flour, pepper, and tarragon, and add the milk. Cook and stir over low heat until thick and bubbly. In a small bowl lightly beat 2 eggs and add to the skillet in a folding motion. When the eggs have set fold in the cottage cheese and feta cheese. Turn to lowest heat and assemble the phyllo as follows.

Place a large nonstick pizza pan in the middle of the counter. Carefully remove the phyllo dough from the carton and unfold. Fold 1 sheet in thirds lengthwise. Place 1 end of the folded sheet in the center of the pizza pan, extending the other end out over the side of the pan. Repeat with 7 more sheets arranging them in spoke fashion evenly around pan. (The inner ends of each sheet should overlap in center of pan and should be about 3 inches apart at the outer ends of each spoke.) Spread the filling in an 8-inch circle in the center of the phyllo dough. Lift end of 1 phyllo strip and gently "bunch together" and place on top of the filling. Repeat with the other 7 strips, trying to leave a 3-inch circle of filling in the center exposed. Drizzle with 2 tablespoons of melted butter. Bake in a 350° oven on the middle rack for about 15 minutes or until the dough is golden brown. Use a plastic knife to cut into 8 wedges and serve immediately.

MAKES 8 SERVINGS.

Eggs on Pastry Shells

- 1 10-ounce package frozen pastry shells
- ¼ cup butter or margarine
- 1 cup cooked ham, julienned
- ½ cup chopped green bell pepper
- ¼ cup sliced green onions
- 2 tablespoons all-purpose flour
- 2 cups milk
- 4 hard-boiled eggs, sliced

- 1½ cups cooked asparagus, cut into 1-inch pieces

Prepare the pastry shells according to the package directions. In a saucepan melt the butter and brown the ham. Add the green pepper and green onions and cook for several minutes, stirring frequently, until the vegetables are tender.

Add the flour and cook, stirring constantly, until bubbling and smooth. Remove from the heat and gradually stir in the milk. Heat, stirring constantly, until thickened and smooth.

Add the eggs and asparagus and heat through. Spoon into hot pastry shells.

MAKES 6 SERVINGS.

Route 23
South Egremont, Massachusetts 01258
(413) 528-9580

The Weathervane is in the Berkshire village of South Egremont in the far southwestern corner of Massachusetts, about halfway between New York City and Boston. A farmhouse built in 1785, it still has its original beehive oven, wideboard floors and unique hand-carved moldings. The ten guest rooms are filled with antiques, and each has it own individual character. The inn is listed on the National register of Historic Places. The Norman Rockwell Museum is a special area attraction.

Heart Warmin' Chili

- 1 tablespoon oil
- 1 clove garlic, finely chopped
- 2 pounds round steak, chopped
- 3 large onions, chopped
- 2 large green bell peppers, chopped
- 1½ pounds canned tomatoes

2 16-ounce cans kidney beans
1 6-ounce can tomato paste
2 tablespoons chili powder
2 whole cloves
   Salt and pepper to taste
1 teaspoon ground cumin
1 bay leaf
   Rice or corn chips

In a large skillet heat the oil and sauté the garlic until golden. Crumble the meat into the garlic and oil and cook until the meat is not red anymore. Add the onions and peppers and sauté until soft. Add the remaining ingredients and simmer 1 hour. Remove the bay leaf before serving.

Serve over rice or corn chips.

MAKES 6 TO 8 SERVINGS.

Black Bean Soup

1 pound dried black beans, picked
   over and rinsed thoroughly
6 slices bacon, chopped
2 large onions, chopped
1 large carrot, peeled and diced
3 cloves garlic, crushed
1 medium green bell pepper, seeded
   and diced
1 tablespoon chili powder
1 to 2 teaspoons dried oregano
1 teaspoon cumin
1 bay leaf
   Salt and ground pepper to taste
9 to 10 cups hot chicken broth or
   water
   Juice of 1 lemon
½ cup dry sherry
   Sour cream
   Minced onions

Wash the beans and soak them in water overnight, or place the beans in a 3-quart microwave-safe casserole with 6 cups of hot water and microwave for 18 minutes on high. Let stand, covered, for 1 hour.

In heavy-bottomed pot sauté the bacon until crisp. Add the onions, carrot, garlic, and green pepper, stirring until everything is limp. Drain the beans and add them to the vegetable mixture. Stir in the chili powder, oregano, cumin, bay leaf, salt, and pepper. Add the liquid (water or chicken broth) and simmer for 2 hours or until the beans are tender. Remove the bay leaf.

In a food processor purée the soup in batches if necessary. Return to the pot. Stir in the lemon juice and sherry.

Serve with a dollop of sour cream and minced onions on top.

MAKES 8 SERVINGS.

Gingersnaps

½ cup butter or margarine
½ cup firmly packed light brown sugar
⅓ cup molasses
2 cups all-purpose flour
2 teaspoons baking soda
¼ teaspoon salt
½ teaspoon ground cloves
1 teaspoon ground cinnamon
1½ teaspoon ground ginger
1 large egg
¼ cup sugar

In a saucepan melt the butter. Stir in the brown sugar and molasses. Set aside to cool to room temperature.

Lightly grease 2 baking sheets with cooking spray or shortening. Into a large bowl measure the flour, soda, salt, cloves, cinnamon, and ginger. Stir the egg into cooled molasses mixture. Stir the molasses mixture into the dry ingredients until mixed well. If the mixture is too soft to handle, place in the freezer for a few minutes. Shape into 1-inch balls. Roll the balls in sugar and place 2 inches apart on prepared baking sheets. Do not flatten. Bake in a 350° oven for about 10 to 12 minutes or until the until cookies have flattened and are crinkly and firm on top. Remove to a cooling rack and cool completely. Store in an airtight container.

MAKES 3 DOZEN.

Publick House

Publick House Historic Inn
❧

On the Common, Route 131, P. O. Box 187
Sturbridge, Massachusetts 01566

*T*he Publick House Historic Inn offers four unique lodging facilities. The Publick House Inn maintains 18th century ambiance while providing 20th century comforts, and offers seventeen rooms with private baths and charming period furnishings. The Chamberlain house features four gracious suites and one guest room, all with the style and warmth of the Publick House. The Colonel Ebenezer Crafts Inn is an eight-room federalist farmhouse built in 1786, offering tastefully appointed guest rooms with private baths, afternoon tea, and a private outdoor swimming pool. The Country Motor Lodge features country-style guest rooms, overlooks the Public House, and is connected via a private walkway and road to the Inn.

Salmon En Croûte

1 ounce fresh spinach, cleaned
1 cup feta cheese
1 egg
4 scallions, chopped
1 tablespoon butter
¼ cup cottage cheese
   Salt and pepper to taste
   Pastry (for 1 2-crust 9-inch pie)
8 ounces salmon fillet

In a large bowl mix all ingredients but the salmon and pastry. On as floured board roll out the pastry into a large rectangle. Place the salmon on the center of the pastry. Place the stuffing on top of the salmon fillet and wrap in the pastry. Bake in a 400° oven for 20 minutes.

MAKES 6 SERVINGS.

Tourtière

- 2 *pounds lean ground pork*
- 2 *pounds lean ground beef*
- 1 *medium onion, diced fine*
- 1 *teaspoon ground cinnamon*
- ½ *teaspoon ground cloves*
- 2 *cups Brown Gravy (recipe follows)*
- 1 *cup finely ground breadcrumbs*
- 1 *cup diced cooked potatoes*
   Salt and pepper to taste
   Pastry for 1 2-crust 9-inch pie
- 1 *egg*
- 1 *teaspoon water*

In a skillet sauté the pork, beef, and onion until browned. Add the cinnamon, cloves, and gravy, and simmer for 5 minutes. Add the breadcrumbs and diced potatoes. Season to taste. Stir well and remove from the heat. Spread the filling in the pie shell and cover with pastry crust. Beat the egg with the water. Brush the pastry with the egg wash. Bake in a 375° oven for 45 minutes or until browned.

MAKES 6 SERVINGS.

Brown Gravy

- 1 *stalk celery, chopped*
- ½ *medium onion, chopped*
- 1 *carrot, chopped*
- 2 *quarts rich beef stock*
- ½ *cup butter or margarine*
- 1 *cup all-purpose flour*
   Salt and pepper to taste

In a saucepan add the chopped vegetables to the beef stock and boil for 15 minutes. In a small skillet melt the butter. Blend in the flour. Add the roux to the stock and whip until dissolved. Simmer for 30 minutes. Strain through a fine strainer. Add salt and pepper to taste.

MAKES GRAVY FOR 2 TOURTIÈRES.

The Captain Dexter House

The Captain Dexter House of Vineyard Haven

Box 2457
Vineyard Haven, MA 02568
(508) 693-6564

One of two Captain Dexter Houses on the charming island of Martha's Vineyard—the other is at Edgartown—this inn at Vineyard Haven places its guests in the middle of town with beaches, shops, and restaurants only a short walk from your room. The ferry slip is just one block away. Breakfast may be served in the elegant dining room or in the flower-filled garden.

Carrot Cake Muffins

- 1¾ *cups all-purpose flour*
- ⅔ *cup firmly packed brown sugar*
- 1 *teaspoon baking powder*
- ½ *teaspoon baking soda*
- ½ *teaspoon salt*
- 1 *teaspoon ground cinnamon*
- ½ *cup crushed pineapple, in juice*
- ½ *cup oil*
- 1 *egg, lightly beaten*
- 1½ *teaspoons vanilla extract*
- 2 *cups shredded carrots*
- ½ *cup raisins*

Grease 12 muffin cups. In a large bowl stir together the flour, brown sugar, baking powder, baking soda, salt, and cinnamon. In a separate bowl stir together the pineapple, oil, egg, and vanilla until blended. Make a well in the center of dry ingredients. Add the pineapple mixture and stir just to combine. Stir in the carrots and raisins.

Spoon the batter into the prepared muffin cups. Bake in a 400° oven for 15 to 20 minutes. Cool 5 minutes before removing the muffins from the cups.

MAKES 12 MUFFINS.

Sunny Pines (Claddagh) Inn

77 Main Street, P.O. Box 667
West Harwich, Massachusetts 02671
(800) 356-9628

Definitely Irish in spirit, the inn features a pub called the Claddagh—a Gaelic work meaning "friendship, love, and loyalty." Accommodations include six guest rooms in the main house and two others in a cottage set back in a pine grove. All are furnished with antiques and decorated with lace curtains and oriental rugs. Day trips may be made to Nantucket, Martha's Vineyard, and Plymouth.

Gaelic Steak-Claddagh

- 2 *tablespoons butter or oil*
- 1 *8- to 12-ounce sirloin strip*
- ¼ *cup Irish whiskey*
- ¼ *cup heavy cream*
- ½ *cup sliced fresh mushrooms*

In a skillet heat the butter and cook the steak to the desired doneness. Remove the steak.

Brown the juices over medium-high heat. Add the whiskey. This will flame. Once the flame ceases, add the cream, and reduce to half. Add the mushrooms. Pour the juices over the steak.

Note: Serve with mashed potatoes and green vegetables.

MAKES 1 SERVING.

Claddagh Schrod

- *6 to 8 ounces cod fish*
- *½ cup cooked spinach*
- *½ cup cooked mushrooms*
- *¼ cup white wine*
- *2 ounces sliced mild cheese*

In an individual microwaveable dish place the ingredients, except the cheese, in the order given. Microwave in 2-minute increments, waiting 30 seconds in between, until the fish is opaque (white). Be careful not to overcook. Place the fish on a broiling pan. Top with cheese and place the under broiler until the cheese is golden and bubbly.

Note: Serve with rice and vegetable medley of choice.

MAKES 1 SERVING.

Cranberry Conserve

- *1 16-ounce can whole cranberry sauce*
- *½ cup walnuts*
- *½ cup honey*
- *½ cup raisins*

In a saucepan combine all ingredients. Simmer for 5 minutes. Cool. Refrigerate for up to 3 weeks.

Use on Irish oatmeal or put between French bread slices with cream cheese. Proceed to make French toast.

Variation: For a wonderful chutney add 1 teaspoon of powdered mustard, 2 teaspoon of vinegar, and 1 teaspoon of curry powder.

For Salsa, add chopped tomato, onion, ½ green bell pepper or red bell pepper, lime juice, and Tabasco sauce to taste.

Grilled Riley (Irish Reuben)

- *4 ounces shaved corned beef*
- *2 ounces Swiss or Irish cheese*
- *2 tablespoons coleslaw*
- *2 pieces rye bread or marble*
  Oil or butter

Place the corned beef, cheese, and coleslaw on 1 slice of bread. Top with the other slice.

In a skillet grill the sandwich in oil or butter until heated and the bread is crispy.

MAKES 1 SERVING.

The Williamsville Inn

The
Williamsville
Inn

❧

Route 41
West Stockbridge, Massachusetts 01266
(413) 274-6118

---

*T*he inn sits at the foot of Tom Ball *Mountain, which is named for a Native American who once owned much of the land. A Revolutionary War soldier named Christopher French built a farm house here in 1797. This large plank house still stands and is now home to the Williamsville Inn. The sixteen guest rooms are spacious and comfortable. The inn has its own cozy tavern and sheep and goats graze on the surrounding acreage. The summer brings performing arts to nearby Tanglewood.*

Spinach Cakes with Shiitake Mushrooms and Roasted Red Pepper Sauce

- *1 tablespoon butter*
- *1 tablespoon sesame oil*
- *½ pound shiitake mushrooms, stemmed and sliced*
- *3 cloves garlic, minced*
  Salt and pepper to taste
- *8 cups spinach*
- *2 sliced scallions*
- *2 eggs*
- *¼ teaspoon cream of tartar*
- *¼ cup milk*
- *½ cup all-purpose flour*
- *1 teaspoon baking powder*
- *¼ cup (2 ounces) chevre cheese*
- *1 cup ricotta cheese*

- *2 red bell peppers*
- *¼ cup extra virgin olive oil*
  Salt and pepper to taste

In a pot melt the butter and sesame oil and sauté the shiitake mushrooms, and garlic. Season with salt and pepper.

Wash and stem the spinach. In a sauté pan sauté the spinach using only the water that clings to the leaves. Drain, cool, and squeeze all liquid from the spinach. Rough-chop the spinach and add to the mushrooms along with the scallions.

Separate 2 eggs, placing the whites in a mixing bowl with the cream of tartar.

In a separate bowl whisk together the yolks, milk, flour, baking powder, chevre cheese, and ricotta cheese. To this mixture add the spinach and mushrooms.

Whip the egg whites into stiff peaks and fold them into the spinach mixture. Form cakes by dropping rounded soup spoonfuls into a hot lightly greased pan and sauté. Flip over and finish on a baking sheet in the oven until lightly browned.

Roast the red peppers in a 375° oven until the outside skin is charred black, about 20 to 30 minutes. Peel and seed them. In a blender purée the pepper with the olive oil. Season to taste with salt and pepper. Serve the cakes with the sauce.

MAKES 10 TO 12 3-INCH CAKES.

Braised Short Ribs of Beef with Roasted Carrots

6 cups red wine
1 tablespoon chopped garlic
1 bay leaf
1 tablespoon crumbled dried rosemary
1 tablespoon dried thyme
1 tablespoon black peppercorns
4 pounds beef short ribs
....
2 tablespoons olive oil
1 large onion, diced
1 rib celery, diced
1 carrot, diced
2 tablespoons all-purpose flour
4 cups beef broth
....
¼ cup butter
2 tablespoons firmly packed brown sugar
4 large carrots, peeled and cut into ½-inch rounds

In a saucepan combine the red wine, garlic, bay leaf, rosemary, thyme, and peppercorns. Bring the mixture to a boil. Reduce the heat and simmer for 10 minutes. Cool

In a shallow dish pour the marinade over the ribs and marinate for 24 hours.

Drain the marinade into a saucepan, and cook over medium heat until reduced by half. Remove the bay leaf.

In a stockpot heat the olive oil and sauté the onion, celery, and carrot until soft and partially cooked. Blend in the flour. Add the beef broth and the reduced marinade. Bring to a simmer, add the ribs and return to a simmer. Cover the pot and braise in a 325° oven for 3 hours or until the meat is very tender.

In a sauté pan melt the butter. Add the brown sugar, stirring to blend. Add the carrots and stir to coat. Transfer to a 1-quart baking dish. Roast in a 325° oven for about 30 minutes or until tender.

Serve braised short ribs and roasted carrots over mashed potatoes with horseradish blended into the potatoes to taste.

MAKES 6 SERVINGS.

The Marlborough

320 Woods Hole Road
Woods Hole, Massachusetts 02543-0238
(508) 548-6218

A faithful reproduction of a an old Cape Cod home, the Marlborough offers six comfortable guest rooms, each decorated with handmade quilts, needlework, collectibles, and fresh flowers, regardless of the season. Woods Hole is home to an acquarium, and ferries to Nantucket and Martha's Vineyard are minutes away.

Broccoli Bisque

1¼ to 1½ pounds fresh broccoli (or 2 10-ounce packages frozen broccoli)
2 13¾-ounce cans chicken broth
1 medium onion, quartered
2 tablespoons butter
    Salt to taste
1 teaspoon curry powder
    Dash pepper
2 tablespoons lime juice
    Lemon slices for garnish
    Sour cream for garnish

In a saucepan cook the broccoli, broth, onion, butter, salt, curry, and pepper at a simmer for about 8 to 12 minutes or until the broccoli is just tender. In a blender purée the broccoli mixture. Add the lime juice.

Pour into serving bowls. Garnish with lemon slices and sour cream to serve.

MAKES 4 TO 6 SERVINGS.

Feta and Spinach Pie

½ package phyllo pastry dough
½ pound fresh spinach
6 ounces feta cheese
....
3 eggs, beaten
    Pepper to taste
1 cup butter, melted
    Broiled Basil Tomato (recipe follows)

Follow the package directions for thawing and handling of phyllo pastry dough.

Remove the stem and spine of the spinach, wash, and drain well. Break the cheese into small pieces. In a small bowl mix the spinach, feta cheese, and eggs. Season with pepper to taste.

In a quiche dish or pie pan place a sheet of phyllo on the bottom, letting it overlap the edges. Brush with butter. Repeat 4 times for 5 layers total. Spread the spinach and cheese mixture on the pastry. Add 5 more sheets of phyllo, brushing each layer with butter before layering.

Fold the excess pastry over and onto the top of the pie. Brush with the remaining butter. Cut into serving-sized pieces before baking. Bake in a 350° oven for 30 minutes or until golden brown. Serve warm with Broiled Basil Tomato.

MAKES 6 SERVINGS.

Broiled Basil Tomato

4½ tablespoons chopped fresh basil
3 large, firm tomatoes, cut in half
4½ tablespoons olive oil
3 tablespoons feta cheese
    Salt and pepper to taste

Arrange basil on each tomato half. Sprinkle with oil, feta cheese, salt, and pepper. Place the tomatoes in a baking pan. Place under the broiler until warm and slightly brown. Serve on a bed of large basil leaves while still hot.

MAKES 6 SERVINGS.

The Marlborough

77 Route 6A
Yarmouth Port, Massachusetts 02675
(508) 362-3976

*T*his fine sea captain's home, built in 1825, retains all its early 18th century charm. Nearby are dozens of buildings and historic sites dating to Cape Cod's earliest settlements. There are five traditionally appointed rooms, each with its own personality. The hosts offer help in arranging for theater tickets at the famous Cape Playhouse, whale watching excursions, or tee time at any one of a dozen local golf courses

Liberty Inn

Shrimp Supreme Baked Eggs

  2 **tablespoons butter**
12 **fresh mushrooms, chopped**
  1 **10 ½-ounce can shrimp soup**
 ½ **cup milk**
16 **eggs**
  8 **slices toast**

Grease 8 ramekins. In a skillet melt the butter and sauté the chopped mushrooms. Add the shrimp soup and mix in the milk, stirring constantly. Simmer for 3 minutes. Divide the sauce evenly amount the 8 ramekins. Break 2 eggs on top of the sauce in each ramekin. Bake in a 400° oven for 15 minutes. Serve with toast.

MAKES 8 SERVINGS.

Puffy Omelet with Shallots and Peppers

  1 **tablespoon butter**
  3 **shallots, peeled and thinly sliced**
 ½ **large green bell pepper, thinly sliced**
 ½ **large red bell pepper, thinly sliced**
  4 **eggs, separated**
  1 **tablespoon water**
 ⅛ **teaspoon ground red pepper**
  1 **tablespoon butter**
 ½ **cup shredded Monterey Jack cheese**

In a skillet melt 1 tablespoon of butter and cook the sliced shallots medium-low heat for 2 minutes, stirring occasionally. Add the green and red pepper strips, and cook 3 minutes more. Cover and keep warm while preparing the omelet.

In a medium bowl beat the eggs whites and the water with an electric mixer until stiff but not dry. In a separate bowl beat the egg yolks and red pepper on high speed for about 5 minutes, until the yolks are thick and lemon colored. Fold the yolks into egg whites just until blended. Do not overblend.

In a 10-inch ovenproof skillet or omelet pan melt 1 tablespoon of butter. Pour the egg mixture into the skillet, smoothing the top with a spatula. Cook over medium heat, uncovered, for about 5 minutes or until the bottom is golden brown. Bake in a 350° oven for about 8 minutes or until a knife inserted in the center comes out clean.

With a spatula, make an indentation down the center of the omelet where the fold should be. Loosen the underside of the top half of the omelet with a spatula. Spoon warm filling over the bottom half of the omelet. Tilt the skillet and fold the top half of the omelet over the filling. Slide the omelet onto a heat-proof platter. Sprinkle cheese over the omelet. Return to the oven just until the cheese is melted. Serve at once.

MAKES 2 OR 3 SERVINGS.

MICHIGAN

The Urban Retreat Bed and Breakfast

*2759 Canterbury Road
Ann Arbor, Michigan 48104
(313) 971-8110*

A contemporary home centrally located in Washtenaw County, this B&B is only minutes from downtown Ann Arbor and Ypsilanti. The neighborhood's quiet tree-lined streets invite evening strollers while a nearby farm road leads to jogging trails. The Ann Arbor area is alive with seasonal festivals and events, including an annual summer festival and arts fair and a major flower show.

Cherry-Stuffed French Toast

    4   1½-inch slices challah (or other egg
          bread)
    4   ounces cream cheese, softened
    ½   cup tart cherries (drained, if
          canned), chopped
    1   teaspoon sugar
    ⅛   teaspoon almond extract
    2   eggs, beaten
    ¼   cup half and half
    ½   teaspoon ground cinnamon
          Butter
          Confectioners' sugar
          Maple syrup

Cut a pocket in each slice of bread to within ¼ inch of the bottom. Trim the crusts.

In a small bowl combine the cream cheese, cherries, sugar, and almond extract. Divide among the bread, spreading the filling evenly in the pockets.

In a separate bowl combine the eggs, half and half, and cinnamon. Dip each slice in the egg mixture to coat all sides. In a skillet melt enough butter to coat the bottom and sauté the toast until golden. Gently cut each slice into triangles. Dust with confectioners' sugar and serve with maple syrup.

MAKES 2 SERVINGS.

Strawberries with Crème Anglaise

    1   quart perfectly ripe strawberries
    1   cup milk
    1   tablespoon cornstarch
    1   egg
    ¼   cup sugar
    ½   teaspoon vanilla extract

Leaving the stems intact, wash the strawberries and dry on paper towels. Reserve 2 whole berries. Remove the caps and slice into quarters. Set aside.

In a 1-quart glass bowl combine the milk and cornstarch and stir well. Microwave uncovered on high for 3 minutes, stirring with a whisk after each minute.

In a small bowl combine the egg and sugar. Gradually add about one-fourth of the hot milk mixture to the egg mix, stirring well to prevent the egg from curdling. Add the mixture carefully to the remaining hot milk, stirring well. Reduce the microwave to medium and cook for 2 to 4 minutes, until thickened and bubbly, stirring with a whisk after every 45 seconds. Stir in the vanilla.

To serve, line individual fruit dishes with crème Anglaise, top with berries, and garnish with a whole berry (stem attached). Serve warm or chilled.

MAKES 2 SERVINGS.

Chicago Street Inn

*219 Chicago Street
Brooklyn, Michigan 49230
(517) 592-3888*

The entry and adjacent dining and sitting rooms of this B&B have hand-wrought moldings, fretwork, stained glass windows, and old-fashioned electric chandeliers. These details set a romantic

Victorian tone which is continued in the guest rooms with their period antiques and decorations. The peaceful community of Brooklyn is less than an hour from Detroit, Kalamazoo, and Lansing.

Chicago Street Inn

Sour Cream Muffins

- ½   **cup butter or margarine**
- 1½   **cups sugar**
- ½   **teaspoon salt**
- 4   **eggs**
- 1   **teaspoon baking soda**
- ⅛   **teaspoon grated nutmeg**
- 1½   **cups sour cream**
- 2¾   **cups cake flour**
- 1   **to 2 cups fresh or frozen "dry pack" blueberries (optional)**

....
- ½   **cup all-purpose flour**
- ½   **cup firmly packed brown sugar**
- ¼   **cup butter**

In a large bowl cream the butter, sugar, and salt until light and fluffy. Add the eggs, soda, nutmeg, sour cream, and flour, beating well after each addition. Gently stir in the blueberries (can use any berries). Fill greased or paper-lined muffin cups three-fourths full. In a small bowl combine the remaining ingredients. Sprinkle with the streusel topping. Bake in a 450° oven for 15 minutes.

Variation: Substitute low-fat sour cream or part plain yogurt for sour cream, unbleached flour for cake flour, or raspberries for blueberries.

MAKES 1 DOZEN.

Strawberry Rhubarb Muffins

- 1¾   **cups all-purpose flour**
- ½   **cup sugar**
- 2½   **teaspoons baking powder**
- ¾   **teaspoon salt**
- 1   **egg, slightly beaten**
- ¾   **cup milk**
- ⅓   **cup canola oil**
- ½   **cup sliced fresh strawberries**
- ¾   **cup diced fresh rhubarb**
- 6   **strawberries, halved**
     Sugar

In a large bowl combine the flour, sugar, baking powder, and salt. In a small bowl combine the egg, milk, and oil. Stir the liquid mixture into the flour mixture with a fork until just moistened. Fold the sliced strawberries and rhubarb into the batter.

Fill greased or paper-lined muffin cups two-thirds full with batter. Press a strawberry half gently into top of each muffin. Sprinkle the tops generously with sugar. Bake in a 400° oven for 20 to 25 minutes or until golden.

MAKES 1 DOZEN.

Kingsley House

626 West Main Street
Fennville, Michigan 49408
(616) 561-6425

Built in 1886 by the prominent Kingsley family, the house reflects the Queen Anne architecture the Kingsleys first saw when it was introduced to the U.S. at the Centennial Exposition in 1876. Inside, antique furnishings match the fancifulness and grace of the exterior. Canopied beds and lush, flower-print wallpapers help make this B&B a highly Victorian experience. The scenic rolling countryside sur-

rounding Fennville contains many fruit orchards, some of which were once owned by the Kingsleys.

Cauliflower Quiche

- ¼   **loaf French bread (day old)**
- 1   **cup fresh cauliflower florets**
- 3   **eggs**
- 1   **cup milk**
- 1½   **cups shredded Cheddar cheese**
- ¾   **cup shredded Swiss cheese**
- 1½   **teaspoons chopped parsley**

Break the bread into 1-inch pieces. Cover the bottom of an ungreased pie plate or quiche dish with the bread pieces. Add the cauliflower florets. In a medium bowl whisk together the eggs and milk, and gently pour over the bread and cauliflower. Top with the Cheddar and then the Swiss cheeses. Sprinkle with parsley. Bake in a 350° oven for 40 minutes or until a knife inserted in the center comes out clean. Allow to cool for 10 minutes before slicing.

MAKES 6 TO 8 SERVINGS.

Honey-Glazed Pecan French Toast

- 1   **loaf French bread (day old)**
- 3   **eggs**
- 1½   **teaspoons honey**
- 1½   **teaspoons ground cinnamon**
- 1   **cup milk**
- 1   **teaspoon vanilla extract**

....
- 2   **tablespoons melted butter**
- ½   **cup firmly packed light brown sugar**
- ½   **cup chopped pecans**
- 2   **tablespoons honey**
     Maple syrup (optional)

Kingsley House

Grease 2 9 x 13-inch glass pans. Slice the French bread diagonally into 1-inch-thick pieces. In a large bowl whisk together the eggs, 1½ teaspoons of honey, and cinnamon. When thoroughly mixed stir in the milk and vanilla. Dip the bread pieces in the mixture, coating both sides. Arrange in the greased pans, cover, and refrigerate overnight.

In the morning remove the pans from the refrigerator 30 minutes before baking and uncover. Drizzle the melted butter over the bread slices, followed with a sprinkling of the brown sugar and pecan pieces. Top with a drizzling of honey. Bake in a 350° oven for 20 minutes. Serve with warm maple syrup, if desired.

MAKES ABOUT 12 SERVINGS.

Bed and Breakfast at the Pines

❧

327 Ardussi Street
Frankenmuth, Michigan 48734
(517) 652-9019

---

*B*ed and Breakfast at the Pines is a friendly ranch-style home with a casual atmosphere in a quiet residential neighborhood. Guest rooms feature heirloom quilts, ceiling fans, cotton sheets, and fresh flowers. Excellent restaurants and tourist areas can be reached with a leisurely walk.

The Pines Granola

      4   *cups old-fashioned oats*
     ⅓   *cup honey*
     ¼   *cup oil*
      1   *teaspoon vanilla extract*
      1   *teaspoon almond extract*
      1   *cup chopped nuts (pecans are good)*
     ¾   *cup bran cereal*
      1   *cup flaked coconut*
      1   *teaspoon cinnamon*
      1   *teaspoon nutmeg*

      1   *cup raisins*
      1   *cup chopped dates*

In a 9 x 12-inch roasting pan spread the oats over the bottom. Bake in a 350° oven for 5 minutes, until heated. Remove from the oven, stir, and heat 5 minutes more.

In a small saucepan heat together the honey and oil. Remove the pan from the heat and add the vanilla and almond extracts.

In a medium bowl combine the nuts, bran cereal, and coconut. Add the mixture to the oats and mix thoroughly. Pour the honey mixture over the oat mixture. Mix thoroughly. Add the cinnamon and nutmeg, tossing to combine. Bake in a 350° oven for 20 to 25 minutes, until evenly browned.

Remove the pan from the oven and add the raisins and dates. Mix thoroughly. Cool, and store in an airtight container.

MAKES ABOUT 8 CUPS.

Caraway-Rye Bread

      3   *tablespoons sugar*
      1   *tablespoon salt*
      2   *tablespoons brown sugar*
    2½   *cups lukewarm water (105 to 115°)*
      2   *tablespoons molasses*
      2   *cakes compressed yeast or 2 package*
          active dry
      2   *tablespoons soft shortening or oil*
      2   *tablespoons caraway seeds*
      1   *cup rye flour*
      6   *to 6½ cups all-purpose flour*

In a large bowl mix the sugar, salt, and brown sugar together. Add the water and molasses. Add the yeast and stir until dissolved. Add the shortening, caraway seeds, and rye flour, and stir until mixed.

Add the flour in 2 additions, using the amount necessary to handle easily. Turn onto a floured board and knead until smooth and elastic. Place in a greased bowl, turning once to grease the top. Cover and let rise in a warm place, until doubled in bulk. Punch the dough down, cover, and let rise again.

Punch the dough down and divide to form 2 loaves. Place the loaves in greased 5 x 9-inch loaf pans. Cover and let rise in a warm place until doubled in bulk.

Bake in a 350° to 375° oven for 30 to 40 minutes, depending on the oven and the color or crust preferred.

MAKES 2 LOAVES.

Dutch Colonial Inn

❧

560 Central Avenue
Holland, Michigan 49423
(616) 396-3664

---

*T*his small inn with five individually decorated guest rooms, features spacious common areas with fireplace, TV and VCR, many family heirloom antiques, a cozy sunporch, and a formal dining room with furnishings from the 1930s. The open porch with white rockers offers a relaxing place to spend part of a summer afternoon.

Steeple Chase

     ½   *cup fresh mushrooms*
      1   *cup cubed yellow onions*
    1½   *pounds mild bulk sausage*
     12   *slices of wheat bread*
      5   *eggs*
      1   *cup grated Cheddar cheese*
      2   *cups milk*
      1   *tablespoon Dijon mustard*
      1   *teaspoon mustard*
     ⅛   *teaspoon pepper*
      2   *tablespoons parsley*

In a glass dish cook the mushrooms and onions in the microwave. In a skillet brown the sausage well. Drain. In a 9 x 13-inch dish layer half of the bread, half of the mushrooms and onions, half of the sausage, and half of the cheese. Repeat the layers. In a medium bowl, mix the remaining ingredients except the parsley. Pour over the casserole and refrigerate overnight.

Sprinkle with parsley. Bake in a 325° oven for 1 hour.

MAKES 8 SERVINGS.

Stuffed French Toast

          Cubed white bread (use a thick,
          sturdy bread)
     15   *ounces ricotta cheese*

Dutch Colonial Inn

Vanilla yogurt
½ to ¾ cup firmly packed brown sugar
12 eggs
⅓ cup maple syrup
2 cups milk
Ground cinnamon

Spray a 9 x 13-inch glass dish with cooking spray. Fill the dish half full with cubed bread. In a bowl mix together the ricotta cheese and enough vanilla yogurt to thin it. Spread the ricotta mixture on the cubed bread. Sprinkle with brown sugar. Place more cubed bread over the brown sugar, filling the dish to the top. In a large bowl beat the eggs, syrup, and milk. Pour over the bread. Sprinkle with cinnamon. Cover and refrigerate overnight.

Bake in a 325° oven for 45 minutes. Let set 10 minutes before serving.
MAKES 8 SERVINGS.

The Munro House

202 Maumee
Jonesville, Michigan 49250
(800) 320-3792

Among the oldest houses in Michigan, this American Greek Revival home was built in 1834 by George C. Munro, who was a brigadier general during the Civil War. The Munro family lived here for more than a century. With its sweeping staircase, twelve-foot ceilings, ten fireplaces, and many chandeliers, the Munro House offers B&B guests a taste of a bygone era.

Munro House French Toast

1   loaf unsliced bread, ends removed
6   eggs
¾   cup orange juice
¾   cup half and half or evaporated milk
2   tablespoons vanilla extract
¼   cup sugar

....

2   cups orange marmalade
2   cups apricot preserves
¼   cup sugar
¼   cup orange juice

Slice the bread in 8 thick slices. In a large bowl mix the eggs, ¾ cup of orange juice, half and half, vanilla, and ¼ cup of sugar. Dip each slice of the bread in the mixture, then place in a shallow baking pan. Pour any remaining egg mixture over the bread slices. Cover and refrigerate overnight. The next morning grill slowly (250° on an electric griddle) until golden brown on both sides.

May be held in a 150° oven for 2 hours in a foil-covered pan with corners turned up to allow the steam to escape.

In a saucepan combine the marmalade, preserves, ¼ cup of sugar, and ¼ cup of juice, and cook over low until heated. Serve the toast with warmed orange apricot syrup.
MAKES 4 SERVINGS.

Black Russian Cake

1   18½-ounce package devil's food cake mix
1   4.6-ounce package instant chocolate pudding
4   eggs, well beaten
1¼ cups cold extra-strong coffee
½   cup Amaretto
½   cup Crème de Cacao
½   cup oil

....

½   cup butter, at room temperature
1   8-ounce package cream cheese, softened
1   cup sugar

In a large bowl combine the devil's food cake mix, chocolate pudding, eggs, coffee, Amaretto, Crème de Cacao, and oil, mixing well. Pour the batter evenly into 2 9-inch cake pans that have been coated with cooking spray. Bake in a 350° oven for 30 to 35 minutes.

In a medium bowl combine the butter, cream cheese, and sugar, and beat until creamy. Frost the cooled cake. Store the cake in the refrigerator.
MAKES 8 SERVINGS.

Oven Baked Stew

1   to 2 pounds stew meat
1   cup chopped celery
1   cup chopped onion
1   cup chopped carrots
1   cup chopped potatoes
1   cup tomato juice
1   cup beef bouillon
2   tablespoons sugar
4   tablespoons tapioca
2   teaspoon salt

In a heavy pot or casserole combine the stew meat, celery, onion, carrots, and potatoes.

In a medium bowl or large glass combine the tomato juice, bouillon, sugar, and tapioca and stir well. Pour the mixture over the stew and stir well. Cover tightly. Bake in a 225 to 250° oven all day. No peeking!
MAKES 4 TO 6 SERVINGS.

Sweet and Sour Dressing

1   cup sugar
2   teaspoons paprika
2   teaspoons salt
2   teaspoons celery seed
2   teaspoons dry mustard
2   cups oil
½   cup vinegar

In a medium bowl mix all of the dry ingredients. Add approximately one-third of the oil and mix very well. Add approximately one-third of the vinegar and mix very well. Repeat twice. To prevent separation, the dressing needs to be mixed very well after each addition. Store in a container with a tight-fitting lid.

This dressing is especially good on spinach salad.
MAKES ABOUT 3 CUPS.

The Munro House

*Leelanau
Country Inn*

❧

149 East Harbor Highway
Maple City, Michigan 49664
(616) 228-6192

*This inn on Little Traverse Lake in
the Upper Peninsula of Michigan is
noted for its fine dining, particularly fresh seafood from the ocean
and the surrounding lakes. Its
signature Swiss onionsoup has been
featured in* Gourmet *magazine. The
inn was built in 1894 as a private
home, and it has undergone
several additions and renovations
over the years.*

Crab Stuffed Mushrooms

20 *large button mushrooms*
½ *cup Herbal Breading (recipe fol-
      lows)*
½ *cup grated sharp Cheddar cheese*
½ *cup sour cream*
½ *cup Crab Meat Stuffing (recipe fol-
      lows)*
2 *tablespoons green onions, chopped*
1 *egg*
1 *tablespoon light soy sauce*
2 *tablespoons margarine, melted*

Remove and reserve the mushroom stems.
With a spoon, hollow out the center of the
caps. Wash the caps and drain well, patting
dry. (Thoroughly drying the mushroom caps
is essential to the integrity of the dish. Excess
moisture will cause the mushrooms to fall
apart when baked.)

Finely chop ¼ cup of the mushroom stems.
In a large bowl combine the Herbal Breading,
Cheddar cheese, sour cream, Crab Meat Stuffing, green onions, egg, and soy sauce, and
mix well. Brush the rounded end of the caps
with melted margarine and stuff the cap with
the mixture, rounding the top. Place stuffed-
side-up in a baking dish or casserole. Bake in
a 350° oven for 20 minutes.
MAKES 20 STUFFED MUSHROOMS.

Crab Meat Stuffing

2 *tablespoons butter*
3 *tablespoons all-purpose flour*
2 *cups milk*

....

¾ *cup butter*
2 *cups crab meat, cartilage removed*
½ *cup finely chopped onions*
¾ *cup plain breadcrumbs*

In a saucepan melt 2 tablespoons of butter.
Add the flour, stirring constantly. Cook for
about 5 minutes, nearly boiling the roux,
carefully stirring to prevent scorching. At the
same time, bring the milk to a scald. Mix the
hot milk and the roux together, stirring
vigorously. Allow the white sauce to cool.

In a small saucepan or skillet melt ¾ cup
of butter. Allow the solids to settle and carefully pour off the liquid. Measure ½ cup of
the liquid. This liquid is drawn butter and
may be cooled and stored for later use or
used immediately.

In a sauté pan heat the drawn butter and
sauté the onions until tender. Set aside to
cool. (It is very important that hot and cold
items are not mixed together as this can
cause the stuffing to sour.) Add 1½ cups of
cooled cream sauce, cooled onions, crab
meat, and breadcrumbs, and mix well.
Refrigerate and allow to set up, approximately 1 hour.

Notes: Have the milk and roux very hot
prior to mixing. This will bring the sauce to a
smooth, medium-thick consistency quickly,
with less stirring. Use Cape Cod Jonah Stone
Crab for this recipe. It is a sweet crab and the
flakes make an excellent stuffing. King Crab,
Blue Crab or another favorite may be used as
well, but avoid imitation crab!
MAKES ABOUT 3½ CUPS OF STUFFING.

Herbal Breading

2¾ *cups very fine dried breadcrumbs*
¼ *pound Romano cheese, grated*
1 *tablespoon dried thyme*
1 *tablespoon dried basil*
1 *tablespoon dried oregano*
1 *tablespoon garlic purée*
2 *tablespoons fresh parsley chopped*

In a medium bowl thoroughly mix all ingredients.

May be stored in the refrigerator for 1 to 2
months. Useful breading for shrimp, chicken,
steaks, and chops, for either baking or frying.

Note: This breading requires very fine
breadcrumbs. If Japanese-style, i.e. coarse
crumbs, are available, process for 1 or 2
minutes in a food processor to reduce the
size of the crumb.
MAKES 3 CUPS.

Stewed Tomatoes

5 *large ripe tomatoes*
3 *tablespoons canola oil*
1 *cup thinly sliced onion*
1 *teaspoon garlic purée*
½ *teaspoon dried basil*
½ *teaspoon dried oregano*

Place the tomatoes in a pot and cover with
water. Bring to a boil and cook until the
tomato skins begin to split. Remove the tomatoes from the hot water, and plunge into cold
water. Peel the skins from the tomatoes and
set the tomatoes aside.

In a blender purée 1 tomato.

In a sauté pan heat the oil and add the
sliced onion, garlic purée, basil, and
oregano, and sauté until very tender but not
browned, then add the tomato purée. Place
the skinned tomatoes in a serving casserole
dish, top with sautéed onion mixture, and
cover. Bake in a 350° oven for 15 to 20 minutes.
MAKES 4 SERVINGS.

Pan-fried Lake Perch

24 *fillets lake perch, fresh or frozen*
2 *cups milk*
¼ *cup butter*
½ *cup all-purpose flour*
½ *teaspoon paprika*
¼ *cup dry sherry*
3 *tablespoons lemon juice*
6 *tablespoons butter, cubed*
2 *tablespoons chopped fresh parsley*

If frozen fillets are used, thaw. Be sure the fillets are free from scales and bones. In a
small resealable container place the milk and
layer the fillets in the milk so all are covered.
Seal and refrigerate for at least 24 hours.

Drain the milk and discard, leaving the fillets moist. In a sauté pan melt ¼ cup of butter and get very hot, without burning. In a

shallow dish combine the flour and paprika. Lightly dredge the fillets in flour. Do not thickly coat with flour. Place the fillets in the sauté pan skin-side-up, immediately add sherry around but not over the fillets, and cook until golden brown, turning the fillets to brown on each side.

In a saucepan bring the lemon juice to a boil. Remove the pan from the heat and add the cubed butter. Stir vigorously until melted. Top each 6-fillet serving with 2 tablespoons of the lemon butter sauce and sprinkle with fresh parsley.

MAKES 4 SERVINGS.

Wild Rice Salad

- 2 6-ounce packages long grain and wild rice mix
- 1 15-ounce can sliced water chestnuts, drained
- 2 6-ounce jars marinated artichoke heart halves, drained
- 1 cup diced celery
- 2 cups frozen peas, thawed
- 2 cups sliced fresh mushrooms
- 1½ cups Greek Dressing (recipe follows)

Prepare the rice according to package directions. Refrigerate for 1 hour.

In a large bowl combine the chilled rice, water chestnuts, artichoke heart halves, celery, peas, mushrooms, and Greek Dressing. Mix well and chill before serving.

MAKES 12 CUPS.

Greek Dressing

- 2 cups canola oil
- ¾ cup apple cider vinegar
- 1½ teaspoons sugar
- 1½ teaspoons salt
- ¼ teaspoon dried basil
- ⅛ teaspoon white pepper
- 1½ teaspoons dried whole oregano
- ¾ tablespoon garlic purée

In a container with a tight-fitting lid mix all ingredients well.

May be refrigerated for up to 1 month. It's always best to make dressings at least a day ahead of use, to allow the flavor to marry. In addition to a lettuce or pasta salad dressing, this makes a great meat and poultry marinade.

MAKES ABOUT 3 CUPS.

Peanut Butter Pie

- 1 cup graham cracker crumbs
- ¼ cup sugar
- ¼ cup butter, softened

....

- 1 8-ounce package cream cheese, softened
- 2 tablespoons butter, softened

....

- 1 cup creamy peanut butter
- 1 cup confectioners' sugar
- ½ cup heavy cream
- 2 tablespoons confectioners' sugar
- 1 tablespoon vanilla extract

....

- ½ cup heavy cream
- 1 cup semisweet chocolate morsels

In a medium bowl combine the graham cracker crumbs, sugar, and ¼ cup of softened butter. Mix together and press into a buttered 9-inch pie pan, forming a shell. Refrigerate for 1 hour.

In a large bowl beat together the softened cream cheese, 2 tablespoons of softened butter, and peanut butter with an electric mixer. Add 1 cup of confectioners' sugar and beat until fluffy. In a separate bowl beat ½ cup of heavy cream until a peak forms. Gradually add 2 tablespoons of confectioners' sugar and the vanilla, and beat to a stiff peak. Fold the beaten cream into the peanut butter mixture, mixing well. Place the filling in the shell and refrigerate until firm, 2 to 3 hours.

In a small saucepan bring ½ cup of heavy cream to a simmer over low heat. Add the chocolate and stir until melted and smooth. Cool to lukewarm. After the filling has firmed for 2 to 3 hours, spread the topping over the pie. Refrigerate again until the topping is firm, about 3 hours. Cut into 8 pieces and serve.

MAKES 8 SERVINGS.

The Pentwater Inn

The Pentwater Inn

180 East Lowell, P.O. Box 98
Pentwater, Michigan 49449
(616) 869-5909

The Pentwater Inn is a good choice for those who want to explore nearby Mears State Park, with its rolling dunes, or rummage through the area's many quaint shops. Built in 1886, the inn is Victorian, but the hospitality and food are European in flavor. Guests may want to make use of the inn's hot tub or relax on one of several porches.

Oatmeal Currant Scones

- 4 cups all-purpose flour
- ⅓ cup sugar
- 1 tablespoon baking powder
- 1 teaspoon baking soda
- 1 teaspoon salt

....

- 1 cup butter, chilled
- 3 cups rolled oats
- 1 cup currants or raisins
- 2 cups buttermilk
   Jam and butter for garnish

In a large bowl mix the flour, sugar, baking powder, soda, and salt. Cut in the cold butter until the mixture resembles coarse crumbs. Add the oats and currants, tossing with a fork to distribute. Add the buttermilk and stir with a fork until the dough can be gathered into a rough ball.

Turn onto a floured a board and knead 6 or 7 times, working lightly. Divide the dough into 3 equal balls. Pat each ball into a ½-inch-thick circle on the floured board. Cut each circle into 8 or 10 wedges. Place the wedges on an ungreased baking sheet about ½-inch apart. Bake in a 375° oven for 20 to 25 minutes, until lightly browned.

May be frozen and thawed as needed. After they are thawed, warm in the microwave for 35 seconds. Serve with jam and butter.

MAKES 24 TO 30 SCONES.

Chocolate Truffles

¼ cup butter (do not use margarine)
1 teaspoon vanilla extract (or any favorite liqueur)
2 cups real semisweet chocolate chips
1 cup heavy cream
    Powdered cocoa or finely chopped nuts

In a blender combine the butter, vanilla, and chocolate chips. In a saucepan heat the heavy cream until it is hot but not boiling. Pour the hot cream over the ingredients in the blender and blend until all of the chocolate is melted and smooth. Pour into a buttered dish, cover with plastic wrap, and freeze until firm.

Scoop out a teaspoon of the truffle mixture and roll into a ball. Roll in powdered cocoa or finely chopped nuts. Put into plastic containers with tight-fitting lids and freeze. Thaw slightly before serving.

MAKES ABOUT 1 DOZEN.

Tart Cherry Crêpes

4 eggs
1½ cups milk
2 tablespoons butter, melted
1 cup all-purpose flour
1 teaspoon sugar
....
2 cups tart cherries, drained
1 cup sugar
2 tablespoons cornstarch
1 tablespoon butter
    Red food coloring (optional)
    Confectioners' sugar

In a blender combine the eggs, milk, melted butter, flour, and 1 teaspoon of sugar and blend for 1 minute. Set aside for 10 minutes and make the cherry sauce.

In a small saucepan combine the cherries, 1 cup of sugar, and cornstarch. Cook over medium heat until thickened. Add 1 tablespoon of butter and a few drops of red food coloring, if desired. If the sauce is too thick add a few tablespoons of the cherry juice. It should be more like a syrup.

In a 9-inch frying pan seasoned with a little oil, on medium-high heat pour about ¼ cup of batter in the pan and tip the pan to distribute the batter over the bottom. When the top is dry and the bottom of the crêpe is golden, flip and cook for 30 seconds.

Crêpes will keep well in a warm oven covered with a damp dishtowel until ready to assemble. Fold crêpes in half twice, pour on cherry sauce, and dust with confectioners' sugar.

MAKES 6 SERVINGS.

Terrace Inn

Terrace Inn

216 Fairview, P.O. Box 266
Petoskey, Michigan 49770
(616) 347-2410

*T*he three-story Terrace Inn was built in 1910 and supplied with Albert Pick oak furnishings. Today's guests will find that little has changed here since then. The inn, with it's forty-four well-appointed guest rooms, solid wood-paneled lobby, and spacious porch, remains distinctly Victorian. The surrounding community of Bay View began as a summer resort in 1875. Many of the summer cottages belong to the same families that built them more than a century ago.

Terrace Inn Cherry Crisp

2 pounds frozen pitted cherries
1 18½-ounce box yellow cake mix
2 cups whole pecans or pieces
1 cup butter
    French vanilla ice cream (optional)

Cover the bottom of an ungreased 12 x 18-inch cookie sheet with cherries 1 layer thick. Shake the yellow cake mix evenly over the cherries. Do not stir into the cherries. Spread

the pecans over the cake mix at random. In a saucepan melt the butter and pour evenly over the pecans and cake mix. Do not stir at any time.

Bake in a 375° oven for 15 to 20 minutes or until golden brown. Ovens may vary so check periodically. Remove from the oven and allow to cool slightly. Can be served plain or topped with French vanilla ice cream.

MAKES 8 SERVINGS.

Chicken Hemingway

1 cup all-purpose flour
1 teaspoon salt
2 teaspoons pepper
2 to 3 tablespoons olive oil
4 6-ounce skinless, boneless chicken breasts
1 cup chicken stock
2 tablespoons chopped fresh basil leaves
¼ cup white wine
¼ cup heavy cream
    Dried red cherries
    Cooked pasta

In a shallow dish mix the flour, salt, and pepper to make breading. Coat the chicken breasts in the breading. In a skillet heat the olive oil and sauté the chicken for 3 to 4 minutes each side. Add the chicken stock, basil, and wine. Simmer to reduce by half.

Add ¼ cup heavy cream and simmer over low heat to the desired thickness. Add the dried cherries. Serve over pasta.

MAKES 2 SERVINGS.

Maplewood Hotel

428 Butler Street
Saugatuck, Michigan 49453
(616) 857-1771

*T*he Maplewood was built during the 1860s in an unmistakable Greek Revival style, and it has served as a luxury resort hotel through most of its 135 year-history. It offers fifteen

Maplewood Hotel

guest rooms, each uniquely deco-
rated and furnished. A wooden
wraparound deck, full-sized heated
pool, and garden gazebo invite
guests to spend time outdoors. The
Mitchell Lounge, Butler Library,
Burr Tillstrom Dining Room, and
other common areas are spacious
and elegantly furnished.

Spiced French Toast with Broiled Grapefruit

- 4 *eggs*
- 1 *cup milk*
- 1 *teaspoon vanilla extract*
- ½ *teaspoon ground cinnamon*
- ½ *teaspoon grated nutmeg*
- ½ *teaspoon orange zest*
- ½ *teaspoon sugar*
- 8 *slices Brioche bread*
  Canola oil
- 2 *grapefruit*
- ⅓ *cup brown sugar*

In a large bowl mix the eggs, milk, vanilla, cinnamon, nutmeg, orange zest, and sugar. Set aside. Slice bread into ½-inch-thick slices and soak in egg mixture until just saturated. In a hot skillet coated with canola oil brown the bread on both sides.

Cut the grapefruit in half and section out into an ovenproof dish. Sprinkle brown sugar over the fruit. Broil until hot and bubbly, about 5 minutes.

MAKES 4 SERVINGS.

Berry Muffins

- 2 *cups sifted all-purpose flour*
- 1 *teaspoon baking soda*
- 1½ *teaspoons baking powder*
- ¼ *teaspoon salt*
- ½ *cup butter, softened*
- 1 *cup sugar*
- 2 *eggs, unbeaten*
- 1½ *teaspoons vanilla extract*
- 1 *cup buttermilk*
- ½ *cup fresh strawberries*
- ½ *cup fresh blueberries*
- ½ *cup fresh raspberries*
  Confectioners' sugar

Grease or line with paper liners 24 muffin cups. In a medium bowl sift the flour, soda, baking powder, and salt together. Set aside.

In a large bowl cream the butter, sugar, eggs, and vanilla until light and fluffy. Begin adding one-fourth of the flour, mixing well. Add one-fourth of the buttermilk, mixing well. Repeat until all ingredients are used. Cover the bottom of the muffin cups with a tablespoon of the batter. Add 2 of each kind of berry into the muffin cups. Cover the berries with more batter filling each cup two-thirds full.

Bake in a 375° oven for 20 to 25 minutes or until golden brown. Remove the muffins to a wire rack to cool slightly. Serve warm, sprinkled with confectioners' sugar.

MAKES 2 DOZEN.

Wickwood
Inn

❧

510 Butler Street
Saugatuck, Michigan 49453
(616) 857-1097

S*augatuck was founded in 1824*
and with its tall shade trees, sail-
boats, and quaint homes, reminds
one of a small New England coastal
village. Filled with overstuffed
chairs, French and English antiques,
oriental rugs, and old flower vases,
the Victorian Wickwood is well
suited to the village. Rooms feature
featherbeds with down comforters,
a unique decorating scheme,
antique linens, robes, and plenty of
plants. The host is a long-time resi-

dent of Saugatuck, who knows
almost everyone and every nook
and cranny. The hostess founded
The Silver Palate gourmet food
shop, and is the author of four
best-selling cookbooks.

Hawaiian Fruit Salad

- 1 *large cantaloupe, peeled, seeded, and cut into chunks*
- 1 *large papaya, peeled and cut into chunks (about 2 cups)*
- 1 *14-ounce can mandarin oranges, plus juice*
- 1 *tablespoon chopped macadamia nuts (optional)*

Place all ingredients in a salad bowl and toss to combine. Serve immediately or cover and refrigerate until ready to serve.

Note: Lace these pale yellow and orange fruits with a pinch of mint, crystallized ginger, cinnamon, or vanilla extract.

MAKES 4 SERVINGS.

Very Berry Muffins

- 2 *cups sugar*
- ¼ *cup canola oil*
- 1 *teaspoon minced lemon zest*
- 1 *large egg*
- 1 *egg white, lightly beaten*
- ½ *cup unsweetened applesauce*
- 1 *cup Nonfat Blend (recipe follows)*
- 1½ *teaspoons vanilla extract*
- 2 *teaspoons fresh lemon juice*
- 2 *cups all-purpose flour*
- 1 *tablespoon baking powder*
- 1 *teaspoon baking soda*
- 1 *pint fresh raspberries, blueberries or a mixture of berries*

Lightly spray standard-sized muffin cups with cooking spray. In a large bowl combine the sugar, oil, and lemon zest. Add the egg and egg white and mix well. Add the applesauce and Nonfat Blend and stir well. Add the vanilla and lemon juice and stir. Add the flour, baking powder, and soda, stirring gently until completely blended. When the batter is smooth, gently fold in the berries, taking care not to overmix or break the berries. Fill the muffin cups three-fourths full. Bake in a 400° oven for 5 minutes. Reduce the temperature to 350° and bake for about 20 minutes or until a toothpick inserted in the center of a muffin comes out clean.

Allow to cool in the pan for 1 minute before turning the muffins out onto a wire rack to cool. Serve warm or at room temperature. Store in an airtight container as they can become sticky the next day—if there are any left.

MAKES 1 DOZEN.

Pecan Bundt Coffee Cake

½ cup coarsely chopped pecans
¼ cup firmly packed light brown sugar
1½ teaspoons ground cinnamon
2 cups sugar
¼ cup canola oil
2 tablespoons finely minced lemon zest
1 large egg, lightly beaten
2 large egg whites, lightly beaten
1 cup Nonfat Blend (recipe follows)
2½ teaspoons vanilla extract
4 teaspoons lemon juice
2 cups all-purpose flour
1 tablespoon baking powder

Lightly spray a 10-inch bundt pan with cooking spray and lightly dust with flour. Tap out any excess flour.

In a small bowl combine the pecans, brown sugar, and cinnamon and stir to mix. Set aside.

In a large bowl beat the sugar, oil, and lemon zest with an electric mixer on medium-high speed until evenly moistened. Add the egg and egg whites and mix for about 1 minute. Add the Nonfat Blend and mix until blended. Add the vanilla and lemon juice and mix until blended.

In a separate bowl whisk together the flour and baking powder. Slowly add the dry ingredients to the batter, stirring until completely blended. Pour two-thirds of the batter into the pan.

Sprinkle the nut mixture evenly over the batter and then gently pour in the remaining batter, smoothing into place with a spatula. Bake in a 350° oven for 50 to 55 minutes or until a toothpick inserted near the center of the cake comes out clean. Cool in the pan for 4 to 5 minutes and then invert on a wire rack and release by gently tapping the pan. Cool completely on the wire rack.

MAKES 24 SERVINGS.

Nonfat Blend

1 cup nonfat plain yogurt
1 cup nonfat cottage cheese

In a blender combine the yogurt and cottage cheese and blend until smooth. The mixture can also be blended by hand. A food processor will not give the proper consistency.

Note: Stash it in a plastic container in the refrigerator to use by the cup or spoonful in a myriad of ways such as in mousses and sauces, muffins and dips, and as a replacement for sour cream, mayonnaise, or heavy cream.

MAKES 2 CUPS.

Spicy Sausage Strata

1 cup cleaned, stemmed, and quartered mushrooms
4 slices white bread, crusts removed and reserved
1 cup nonfat cottage cheese
1 large egg
3 large egg whites
1½ teaspoons dry mustard
1 cup skim milk
2 tablespoons heavy cream
½ cup spicy ground turkey, browned
1 teaspoon finely minced fresh sage
2 ounces Brie cheese, rind on
Dash Tabasco sauce
Pinch crushed red pepper flakes
¼ cup chopped scallions, green tops only
Fresh ground black pepper to taste
3 tablespoons Parmesan cheese shards

In a nonstick skillet lightly sprayed with olive oil spray sauté the mushrooms over medium heat for 4 to 5 minutes, until softened and they begin to release their liquid. Set aside.

Lightly spray an 8-inch pan with olive oil spray. Spread the bread crusts over the bottom of the pan and arrange the bread slices on top.

In a blender blend the cottage cheese until smooth. Transfer to a bowl, add the egg, egg whites, mustard, milk, and cream, and blend well. Pour over the bread, cover, and refrigerate overnight.

In the morning, sprinkle the turkey, sage, and mushrooms over the bread mixture and dot with pieces of Brie cheese. Add Tabasco, red pepper flakes, and scallions, and season to taste with pepper. (So that ingredients

don't float to the surface, tuck some under the bread slices, if necessary.) Sprinkle with Parmesan cheese. Bake in a 350° oven for 45 to 50 minutes, until golden. Serve immediately.

MAKES 6 SERVINGS.

Spicy Carrot Muffins

2½ cups all-purpose flour
1½ cups firmly packed light brown sugar
2 teaspoons baking powder
1 teaspoon baking soda
1 teaspoon salt
2 teaspoons ground cinnamon
1 teaspoon ground ginger
½ teaspoon ground cloves
¼ cup canola oil
½ cup unsweetened applesauce
1 egg
¼ cup buttermilk
2 teaspoons vanilla extract
2 2.5-ounce jars baby food strained carrots
1 tablespoon minced orange zest
4 ounces unsweetened crushed pineapple, with juice
¾ cup loosely packed shredded coconut
3 tablespoons confectioners' sugar (optional)

Lightly spray 18 standard-sized muffin cups with cooking spray. In a large bowl combine the flour, brown sugar, baking powder, soda, salt, cinnamon, ginger, and cloves. Add the oil, applesauce, egg, buttermilk, vanilla, strained carrots, orange zest, and crushed pineapple with juice. Mix well. Stir in the coconut. Fill muffin cups two-thirds full. Bake in a 400° oven for 5 minutes, then reduce the temperature to 350° and bake for about 20 minutes longer or until a toothpick inserted in the center of a muffin comes out clean. Turn the muffins out onto a wire rack. Serve

Wickwood Inn

warm or cooled. Sprinkle lightly with confectioners' sugar, if desired. Store in an airtight container.

MAKES 18 MUFFINS.

Summer Roasted Red Pepper Tart

    3   medium red bell peppers
    1   tablespoon lemon juice
 1½   tablespoons sugar, to taste
   ⅛   teaspoon cayenne pepper
    1   clove garlic
 1½   teaspoons olive oil
    2   sheets puff pastry, defrosted
 1½   cups shredded mozzarella cheese
  10   Roma tomatoes, ripened and sliced
        into ¼-inch slices
 1½   cups shredded Parmesan cheese
   ¼   cup finely minced fresh basil
    1   cup Parmesan cheese shards

Preheat the broiler. Wash the peppers and slice in half. Remove the stem, membrane, and seeds. Cut ¼-inch vertical slits, 1 inch apart around the bottom of the pepper half and flatten with your hand. Broil the halves skin-side-up about 4 inches from the heat source until completely blackened. Place the peppers in a large brown paper (or plastic) bag and close tightly. Allow them to steam for 15 to 20 minutes. Cool and zest off the skin.

In a blender or food processor purée the peppers. Add the lemon juice, sugar, cayenne, garlic, and olive oil, and blend until smooth. The sugar should be added at tablespoon at a time, to taste, as some peppers are sweeter than others and will require less sugar. Pesto will keep for 1 week, tightly covered and refrigerated.

Roll out 2 9-inch square pieces of puff pastry to fill a 16½ x 12 x 1-inch baking sheet. Cut and piece together, seaming with water, if necessary. Make certain the tart crust sides are even with or higher than the sides of the baking sheet.

Evenly spread ½ cup of red pepper pesto on the puff pastry. Sprinkle mozzarella evenly over the pesto, then place tomato slices in rows over the mozzarella. Then sprinkle with the shredded Parmesan cheese and the basil. Top with Parmesan shards. Bake in a 375° oven for 45 minutes, until the cheese and tart crust have become golden. Serve immediately.

MAKES 12 SERVINGS.

Silver Dollar Corn Cakes

 1½   cups pure maple syrup
    2   cups fresh or frozen corn kernels
   ½   cup cornmeal
    2   tablespoons all-purpose flour
   ½   teaspoon baking soda
   ¼   teaspoon salt
 1½   teaspoons canola oil
   ¾   cup buttermilk
    1   large egg, lightly beaten

In a small saucepan heat the maple syrup and 1 cup of the corn kernels over low heat for 10 to 15 minutes, until the corn is tender and the mixture heated through.

In a bowl combine the cornmeal, flour, soda, and salt. Stir in the oil, buttermilk, and egg until just combined. Gently fold in the remaining corn kernels.

Lightly spray a nonstick skillet with cooking spray and heat over medium heat until a few drops of water scattered on the pan evaporate quickly. Drop 1 tablespoon of batter for each cake onto the skillet and cook for 1 minute each side or until lightly golden. Spoon the warm maple syrup and corn over the cakes and serve.

MAKES 8 SERVINGS.

Lime French Toast

   ¼   cup unsalted butter
   ½   cup firmly packed light brown sugar
   ¼   cup light corn syrup
        Finely minced zest of 3 limes
   ¼   cup frozen limeade concentrate
    2   eggs
    3   egg whites
 1½   cups skim milk
    1   tablespoon vanilla extract
    1   loaf French bread, cut into ¾-inch
        slices

Spray a 9 x 13-inch baking dish with cooking spray. In a medium saucepan over low heat combine the butter, brown sugar, corn syrup, zest, and limeade, and cook for 3 to 5 minutes, until the butter and sugar have melted. Pour into the baking dish.

In a small bowl mix the eggs, egg whites, milk, and vanilla and blend well. Arrange the bread slices 1 layer over the syrup mixture and pour the egg mixture over the bread. Cover and refrigerate overnight.

Remove the French toast from the refrigerator 30 minutes before baking and allow to

return to room temperature. Bake in a 350° oven, uncovered, for 30 minutes, until golden brown. Serve immediately.

MAKES 12 SERVINGS.

Cool and Green Fruit Salad

   ½   honeydew melon, zested, seeded,
        and cut into chunks
 1⅓   cups whole seedless green grapes
    2   kiwi, zested and sliced
   ⅓   cup blackberries, raspberries, or a
        mixture of both
    2   tablespoons frozen limeade concentrate
    4   teaspoons minced fresh mint

In a large bowl gently toss all ingredients together. Serve slightly chilled.

MAKES 4 SERVINGS.

Great Granola

    3   cups uncooked rolled oats (not
        instant)
    3   cups crisp rice cereal (like Rice
        Krispies)
    1   cup multi-grain cereal
    1   very ripe banana
   ¼   cup honey
   ½   cup unsweetened applesauce
   ⅓   cup frozen apple juice concentrate
    1   tablespoon ground cinnamon
    1   tablespoon vanilla extract
   ½   cup blanched almonds, toasted
    1   cup golden raisins or dried cherries

In a large bowl combine the oats and both cereals and toss well.

In a small bowl mash the banana. Add the honey, applesauce, apple juice concentrate, cinnamon, and vanilla, and mix well. Pour over the oat mixture and toss by hand. Do not break the clumps apart. Pour onto a baking sheet, spreading evenly. Bake in a 300° oven for 45 to 50 minutes, tossing gently occasionally.

Add the almonds and raisins, mix well, and set the baking sheet on a wire rack to cool completely. Store in an airtight container.

MAKES 6 CUPS.

Chocolate Banana Muffins

1¼ cups cake flour (not self-rising)
 1   cup unsweetened cocoa powder
 1   teaspoon baking soda
 ¼   teaspoon salt
 2   very ripe bananas, mashed
 ½   cup nonfat sour cream
 ¼   cup unsalted butter, softened
 ¼   cup canola oil
 1   cup sugar
 ½   cup firmly packed light brown sugar
 1   egg
 2   egg whites
 1   tablespoon coffee
 1   teaspoon vanilla extract

Lightly spray 18 standard-sized muffin cups with cooking spray. In a large bowl sift together the flour, cocoa powder, soda, and salt. In a small bowl stir together the bananas and sour cream. In a separate large bowl with an electric mixer beat together the butter, oil, and sugars until light and fluffy. Beat in the egg and whites, one at a time. Beat in the coffee and vanilla. Beat in the dry ingredients in batches alternately with the banana mixture, until the batter is just combined.

Spoon into muffin cups, filling two-thirds full. Bake in a 350° oven for 15 minutes, until a toothpick inserted in the center comes out clean, and they pull away from the sides of the cups. Cool in cups for 10 minutes, then invert on a wire rack to cool completely. Store in an airtight container.

MAKES 18 MUFFINS.

The Water Street Inn

140 East Water Street
Sault Sainte Marie, Michigan 49783
(906) 632-1900

A restored turn-of-the-century Queen Anne Victorian home, the Water Street Inn is situated little more than a block from the famed Sault locks. In keeping with the setting, the four individually decorated guest rooms are known as Flag Ship, Captain's Quarters, Stateroom, and Bridge. The inn is graced with Victorian trimmings, such as stained glass windows, carved woodwork, and Italian marble fireplaces.

The Water Street Inn

Oatmeal Pancakes with Poached Apples

 2   cups old-fashioned oats
 2   cups buttermilk
 2   eggs, slightly beaten
 ¼   cup butter, melted
 ½   cup all-purpose flour
 2   tablespoons sugar
 1   teaspoon baking powder
 1   teaspoon baking soda
 ½   teaspoon ground cinnamon
 ¼   teaspoon salt
....
 2   to 3 tablespoons butter
 3   to 4 tablespoons sugar
 1   teaspoon ground cinnamon
 2   cups frozen apple slices or fresh
     apples
....
     Sour cream
     Butter
     Maple syrup

In a bowl combine the oatmeal and buttermilk. Blend, cover, and refrigerate overnight.

In the morning, add the eggs, melted butter, flour, 2 tablespoons of sugar, baking powder, soda, cinnamon, and salt to the oatmeal mixture, mixing until blended.

Preheat a griddle. Glaze the hot griddle with grease and spoon ½ cup of batter for each pancake onto the griddle. Cook over medium heat until they appear dry (peek under an edge and look for golden color), turn and cook the other side. Serve with poached apples, sour cream, butter, and maple syrup.

In a sauté pan melt the butter. Add the sugar and cinnamon. Add the apples and cook over low heat until the apples are soft. Spoon over each serving.

MAKES 18 PANCAKES.

Wild Rice Pancakes

 3   eggs
1¼ cups low-fat buttermilk
 ½   teaspoon baking soda
1¼ cups all-purpose flour
 1   teaspoon baking powder
 ½   teaspoon salt
 1   teaspoon sugar
 2   tablespoons melted butter
 1   cup cooked wild rice
....
 2   cups frozen or fresh blueberries
 ¼   to ½ cup sugar
     Butter
     Maple syrup
     Blueberries for garnish

In a large bowl beat the eggs, buttermilk, and soda. In a separate bowl mix the flour, baking powder, salt, and sugar. Add the dry ingredients to the egg mixture. Stir in the melted butter and wild rice. Cook the pancakes on a hot, greased griddle until golden on both sides.

In small saucepan combine the blueberries and sugar, and cook slowly until hot. Use ½ cup per serving over 4 pancakes as they are served. Serve with butter, maple syrup and blueberries.

MAKES 8 SERVINGS OF 4 SMALL PANCAKES EACH.

Power Muffins

8½ cups raisin bran flakes
 5   cups all-purpose flour
 3   cups sugar
 1   tablespoon plus 2 teaspoons baking
     soda
 2   teaspoons salt
 4   eggs, beaten
 1   quart low-fat buttermilk
 1   cup oil
 1   16-ounce box raisins
 1   cup shredded coconut
1½ cups grated carrots
1½ cups grated zucchini
 2   cups chopped nuts
 1   cup dried cranberries

In a large bowl combine the first 5 ingredients. Mix well and add the eggs, buttermilk, and oil. Add the raisins and remaining ingredients. Cover and refrigerate. This will keep 6 weeks. Use as needed.

Bake in a 400° oven for 15 to 20 minutes.
MAKES 6 DOZEN.

Wake-Up Juice

1   **12-ounce can frozen orange juice concentrate**
1   **banana**
1½   **cups pineapple juice**
½   **cup mango juice (when available)**
    Bits of fruit (apples, pears, berries, kiwi, peaches, nectarines, plums, etc.)

In a blender combine all ingredients and blend at high speed. Serve ice cold.

Note: This may be prepared in advance and refrigerated overnight.
MAKES 8 SERVINGS.

Ross House

Ross House
Bed and
Breakfast

❧

229 Michigan Avenue
South Haven, Michigan 49090
(616) 637-2256

The Ross House, built in 1886, provides a delightful atmosphere with a country flavor. The lounge, with its television and comfortable chairs, offers a place to relax after a busy day at the beach or sightseeing.

The guest rooms are uniquely furnished with all the comforts of home.

Orange Knots

1   **package active dry yeast**
¼   **cup warm water (110 to 115° degrees)**
1   **cup warm milk (110 to 115° degrees)**
⅓   **cup sugar**
½   **cup butter or margarine, softened**
1   **teaspoon salt**
2   **eggs**
¼   **cup orange juice**
2   **tablespoons grated orange zest**
5¼   **to 5¾ cups all-purpose flour**
....
1   **cup confectioners' sugar**
2   **tablespoons orange juice**
1   **teaspoon grated orange zest**

In a mixing bowl dissolve the yeast in the water. Add the milk, sugar, butter, salt, eggs, orange juice, orange zest, and 3 cups of flour. Beat until smooth. Add enough remaining flour to form a soft dough. Turn onto a floured board and knead until smooth and elastic, about 6 to 8 minutes. Place in a greased bowl, turning once to grease the top. Cover and let rise in a warm place until doubled, about 2 hours.

Punch the dough down and roll into a 16 x 10-inch rectangle, about ½-inch thick. Cut into 10 x ¾-inch strips, roll lightly, and tie into a knot. Place on greased baking sheets, and tuck the ends under. Cover and let rise until doubled, about 30 minutes.

Bake in a 400° oven for 10 to 12 minutes or until golden brown. Cool on wire racks. In a small bowl combine the confectioners' sugar, 2 tablespoons of orange juice, and 1 teaspoon of orange zest, blending until smooth. Drizzle over the rolls.
MAKES 18 SERVINGS.

Yelton Manor

Yelton Manor

❧

140 North Shore Drive
South Haven, Michigan 49090
(616) 637-5220

A*djacent to five miles of pristine Lake Michigan shoreline, this Victorian inn is located in the small home-style resort town of South Haven. Dating to 1890, the manor overlooks the lake and is near many lovely parks and fine restaurants. The grounds include award-winning perennial and rose gardens.*

Endive and Walnut Salad

6   **tablespoons olive oil**
2   **tablespoons minced green onions**
2   **teaspoons Dijon mustard**
1½   **teaspoons sugar**
1   **Granny Smith apple, peeled and cubed**
6   **large Belgian endives**
2   **to 3 tablespoons coarsely chopped walnuts**
2   **to 3 tablespoons finely cubed Roquefort cheese**
    Fresh ground pepper to taste

In a salad bowl combine the oil, onions, mustard, sugar, and apple and whisk thoroughly until blended.

Endive should be wiped not washed; water makes it bitter. Core the endive and lay the leaves in the bowl on the dressing. Sprinkle on the walnuts, cheese, and pepper.

Just before serving, toss the salad and then arrange on individual plates.
MAKES 4 SERVINGS.

Quiche Elaine

1   **unbaked 9-inch pie shell**
½   **cup (4 ounces) diced chicken breast**
3   **tablespoons slivered almonds**
⅔   **cup chopped broccoli**
⅓   **cup chopped carrot**
1½   **cup grated Gruyère or Swiss cheese**
3   **eggs, slightly beaten**

1½   cups milk
½   teaspoon salt
    Pepper to taste
3   tablespoons grated Parmesan cheese

In the bottom of the pie shell place the chicken, almonds, broccoli, and carrots. Sprinkle with Gruyère cheese. In a medium bowl combine the eggs, milk, salt, and pepper. Pour the egg mixture slowly over the cheese. Sprinkle the top with Parmesan cheese. Bake in a 375° oven for 30 to 35 minutes.

Allow to stand 10 minutes before serving to set up.

Note: It helps to put a cookie sheet underneath to catch overflow.

MAKES 4 SERVINGS.

Cream of Acorn Squash Soup

½   cup butter
4   leeks, thinly sliced
2   large acorn squash, zested, seeded, and cut into small pieces
6   cups chicken stock
2   cups unsweetened apple cider
1   cup heavy cream
    Salt and pepper to taste
    Dash curry powder (optional)
    Fresh parsley (never dried)

In a large heavy saucepan melt the butter. Add the leeks and cook, stirring constantly, until lightly browned, about 5 minutes. Add the squash, stock, and cider. Simmer until the squash is tender, about 20 minutes.

Let cool slightly. In a blender purée the squash mixture. Leave the soup with a few squash "lumps" for texture if desired.

Stir in the cream to the desired thickness and heat through but do not boil. Add the salt, pepper, and perhaps a dash of curry powder. Garnish with parsley in the center of each bowl.

MAKES 12 SERVINGS.

Cider House

Cider House Bed and Breakfast

❧

5515 Barney Road
Traverse City, Michigan 49684
(616) 947-2833

---

*T*he emphasis is on country living and country fare at the Cider House, appropriately situated in an apple orchard less than three miles from Traverse City. Visitors are invited to enjoy cider and Scottish shortbread on the porch. The five guest rooms are named Ida Red, Cortland, McIntosh, Rome Beauty, and Red Delicious.

Soufflé Apple Pancake

6   eggs, separated
½   cup sugar
¾   cup buttermilk baking mix
½   cup milk
1   teaspoon vanilla extract
2   tablespoons lemon juice
3   cups chopped pared tart apples
¼   cup butter
1   tablespoon sugar
¼   teaspoon ground cinnamon
    Maple syrup

In a large bowl beat the egg whites until foamy. Add ½ cup of sugar and beat until stiff. Beat the egg yolks in a small bowl until light. Add the baking mix, milk, and vanilla. Sprinkle lemon juice over the apples, and stir the apples into the egg yolk mixture. Fold the egg whites into the egg yolk mixture.

In a 9 x 13-inch pan melt the butter. Pour the batter into the pan. Mix 1 tablespoon of sugar and the cinnamon. Sprinkle over the batter. Bake in a 350° oven for 30 minutes. Serve with maple syrup.

MAKES 6 SERVINGS.

Sausage with Peaches

2   pounds fully cooked kielbasa, cut into 1-inch slices
1   29-ounce can sliced peaches, drained

In a 12-inch skillet cook the sausage over medium high heat, turning occasionally until brown, about 10 minutes. Add the peaches. Cover and heat over low heat.

MAKES 4 SERVINGS.

The Inn at Union Pier

❧

9708 Berren, P.O. Box 222
Union Pier, Michigan 49129
(616) 469-4700

---

*O*riginally built as a summer resort in the 1920s and now totally refurbished, the Inn at Union Pier offers 16 spacious guest rooms decorated in a mix of Scandinavian country and lakeside cottage styles. In cool weather guests can enjoy the warmth of a kakelugn, a Swedish-style ceramic fireplace. However, all types of weather in every season can be enjoyable here. The inn is only a few hundred feet from a fine Lake Michigan beach. A sauna and hot tub are available. Inn decor is a combination of Scandinavian Country and Lakeside Cottage styles.

Crocodile Johnny's Famous Oatmeal Cookies

1   cup shortening
1   cup firmly packed dark brown sugar
¾   cup sugar
....
2   eggs
1   cup all-purpose flour

½ teaspoon baking soda
1 teaspoon salt
3 cups old-fashioned oats
1 teaspoon vanilla extract
1 teaspoon ground cinnamon

In a large bowl cream the shortening, brown sugar, and sugar. Add the eggs, flour, soda, and salt, and mix well. Beat in the oatmeal, vanilla, and cinnamon. Drop by spoonful onto a greased cookie sheet. Bake in a 350° oven for 8 to 10 minutes.

Hint: Johnny says "slam the pan after 5 to 6 minutes."

MAKES 3 DOZEN.

Prosciutto and Parmesan Pinwheels

Nances's Mustard to cover pastry
*   sheet*
1 sheet Pepperidge Farm puffed pastry
4 to 5 thin slices proscuitto (less than
*   ¼ pound)*
½ cup (approximately) fresh grated
*   Parmesan cheese*
1 egg beaten with 1 teaspoon water

Spread the mustard on the pastry sheet. Cover the entire sheet with sliced proscuitto. Sprinkle with Parmesan cheese. Press flat with rolling pin. Roll up the sheet from both sides, meeting in the center, like a scroll. Slice into about 15 pieces and place on a cookie sheet covered with parchment paper. Brush with egg wash. Bake in a 375° oven for 20 to 25 minutes or until golden.

MAKES ABOUT 15 PINWEELS.

Country Fruit Crisp

6 cups fresh fruit, peeled and sliced
*   (pears, peaches, apples)*
⅓ cup sugar
1½ teaspoons lemon juice
½ teaspoon lemon zest, finely grated
1 cup quick-cooking oats
⅓ cup firmly packed brown sugar
2 tablespoons all-purpose flour
½ teaspoon ground cinnamon
½ teaspoon ground ginger
¼ cup butter

In a large bowl toss the fruit with the sugar, lemon juice, and lemon zest. Place 1 cup of fruit in each of 6 lightly greased ceramic boats.

In a medium bowl combine the oats, brown sugar, flour, cinnamon, and ginger. Cut in the butter with a fork or pastry blender until the mixture is crumbly. Sprinkle over the fruit. Bake in a 400° oven for 25 to 30 minutes or until the fruit is bubbling and the topping is crisp. Keep warm in a 175° oven, covered with foil.

MAKES 6 SERVINGS.

Chocolate Chip Cookies

2 cups butter
2 cups sugar
2 cups firmly packed brown sugar
4 eggs
2 teaspoons vanilla extract
5 cups all-purpose flour
4 cups old-fashioned oats (blended to
*   a powder)*
1 teaspoon salt
2 teaspoons baking powder
2 teaspoons baking soda
32 ounces chocolate chips
3 cups chopped nuts

In a large bowl cream together the butter and sugars. Beat in the eggs and vanilla. In a separate bowl mix together the remaining ingredients. Add the dry ingredients to the creamed mixture. Bake in a 375° oven for 8 to 10 minutes.

MAKES 6 DOZEN.

The Inn at Union Pier

MINNESOTA

Mrs. B's Historic Lanesboro Inn

101 Parkway
Lanesboro, Minnesota 55949
(507) 467-2154

Surrounded by 400,000 acres of hardwood forest, Lanesboro—population 900—is definitely one of those communities where the trees outnumber the people. Mrs. B's is a circa 1870 limestone building right in the middle of town. The ten guest rooms are furnished with comfortable reading chairs and interesting locally made furniture, such as sleigh and cupboard-style beds. Some rooms feature fireplaces, and all are decorated in a Victorian Country motif. Bicyclers will love the thirty-five-mile recreation trail that loops out from town.

Chocolate Truffle Cake

1   cup butter
8   ounces bittersweet or semisweet
    chocolate

6   eggs, separated
2   tablespoons all-purpose flour
¼   cup sugar
¼   cup orange liqueur

....

Confectioners' sugar
Fresh raspberries
Whipped cream

In a saucepan melt the butter over low heat. Remove the pan from the stove. Cut up the chocolate and stir it into the butter. Stir occasionally until melted completely. Stir in the egg yolks one at a time. Add the flour, sugar, and liqueur. In a large bowl whip the whites until stiff. Gently fold the egg whites into the chocolate mixture. Pour into a greased 12-inch springform pan. Bake in a 350° oven for 25 minutes or until the center is set.

Cool completely. Dust with confectioners' sugar and serve with fresh raspberries and whipped cream.

MAKES 8 TO 12 SERVINGS.

Mrs. B's Historic Lanesboro Inn

Lindgren's Bed and Breakfast

County Road 35, P.O. Box 56
Lutsen, Minnesota 55612-0056
(218) 663-7450

Those who want to experience the rugged North Shore region of Lake Superior should consider a stay at this secluded B&B. Approximately two hours northeast of Duluth, it has almost five-hundred feet of lake frontage, not to mention access to nearby hiking and cross country ski trails. A rustic, 1920s era log home, it has been extensively remodeled to take even more advantage of its spectacular location. The living room features an eighteen-foot beamed ceiling and a huge stone fireplace. Rooms offer views of the lake and surrounding woods. Some have fireplaces.

Wild Blueberry-Banana Bread

⅔　cup sugar
1½　cups all-purpose flour
¼　teaspoon salt
2　teaspoons baking powder
¾　cup quick-cooking oats
⅓　cup oil
2　eggs, slightly beaten
2　large bananas, mashed
¾　cup wild blueberries (fresh or
　　frozen)

In a large bowl sift together the sugar, flour, salt, and baking powder. Stir in the oats. Add the oil, eggs, bananas, and blueberries and stir just until moistened. Pour into a greased and floured 5 x 9-inch loaf pan. Bake in a 350° oven for 60 to 65 minutes.

Cool in the pan for 10 minutes, remove from the pan and cool on a wire rack. Wrap and store in the refrigerator several hours before slicing.

Variation: Substitute ¾ cup of wild raspberries or strawberries for blueberries.
MAKES 1 LOAF.

Lindgren's Caramel Torte

6　egg yolks
1½　cups sugar
1　teaspoon baking powder
2　teaspoons vanilla extract
6　egg whites, beaten stiff
2　cups finely crushed graham cracker
　　crumbs
1¼　cups chopped pecans
1　pint heavy cream, whipped
　　Caramel Sauce (recipe follows)

In a large bowl beat the egg yolks well. Add the sugar, baking powder, and vanilla, and mix well. Fold the beaten egg whites into the egg yolk mixture. Fold in the graham cracker crumbs and nuts, and blend well. Line 2 9-

Lindgren's

inch round cake pans with waxed paper. Pour in the batter. Bake in a 325° oven for 35 minutes. Cool on wire racks.

Cut each layer in half to make 4 layers. Spread each layer with whipped cream, stack, and spread the top with whipped cream. Drizzle the entire cake with Caramel Sauce.
MAKES 10 SERVINGS.

Lindgren's Caramel Sauce

1¼　cups lightly packed brown sugar
1　tablespoon all-purpose flour
¼　cup butter
¼　cup orange juice
¼　cup water
1　beaten egg
1　teaspoon vanilla extract

In the top of a double boiler combine the sugar, flour, butter, orange juice, water, and egg. Cook uncovered over simmering water, stirring until boiling and thickened. Add the vanilla. Cool and drizzle over the cake.
MAKES ABOUT 1½ CUPS.

Nippy Cheese Baked Eggs in Toast Cups

12　thin slices fresh bread
9　tablespoons melted butter
12　eggs
　　Nippy Cheese Sauce (recipe follows)

Trim the crusts from the bread and brush both sides of each slice with melted butter. Press gently into 3-inch muffin tins. Bake in a 350° oven for 10 to 15 minutes, until lightly browned. Break an egg into each toast cup. Bake in a 350° oven for 15 to 20 minutes, until the eggs are set. Serve with Nippy Cheese Sauce.
MAKES 1 DOZEN.

Nippy Cheese Sauce

3　tablespoons butter
3　tablespoons all-purpose flour
2　cups whole milk
2　teaspoons Worcestershire sauce
　　Dash hot pepper sauce
　　Dash cayenne pepper
½　teaspoon salt
⅛　teaspoon pepper
2　cups shredded Cheddar cheese

In the top of a double boiler over simmering water melt the butter. Add the flour and blend together. It will save time to heat half of the milk. Add the cold milk first and blend, then stir in the hot milk, sauces, and cayenne. Cook until thick and smooth, stirring constantly. (The simmering water shouldn't touch the bottom of the top pan.) Add the salt and pepper. Cover and cook for 5 to 8 minutes. Turn off the heat, add the cheese, and let stand until the cheese is melted. Stir enough to blend.
MAKES 12 SERVINGS.

Jailhouse Historic Inn

🌿

P.O. Box 422
109 Houston Street
Preston, Minnesota 55965
(507) 765-2181

*T*his unique and comfortable inn is in the old Filmore County Jail built in 1869 in an Italianate style. Since its days as a lockup, the decor has been completely redone, of course, and reflects Victorian times. The town of Preston and the surrounding country have much to offer in the way of attractions, including parks, trails, a large Amish community, plenty of antique shops and art galleries, and an excellent selection of restaurants.

Fresh Fruit Pizza

1　cup all-purpose flour
¼　cup sifted confectioners' sugar
½　cup butter
1　20-ounce can pineapple chunks in
　　juice
½　cup sugar
5　teaspoons cornstarch
1　teaspoon lemon juice
1　8-ounce package cream cheese

⅓ cup sugar
1 teaspoon vanilla extract
2 to 3 cups assorted fresh fruit (such as blueberries, cut-up strawberries, sliced banana, and/or sliced kiwi fruit)

In a medium bowl combine the flour and confectioners' sugar. Cut in the butter until the mixture resembles fine crumbs and starts to cling together. Form into a ball and knead until smooth. Between 2 sheets of waxed paper, roll out the crust into a 10-inch circle about ¼ inch thick. Transfer the crust and waxed paper to a baking sheet. Remove the waxed paper from the crust top. Flute or crimp the edge, if desired. Bake (on waxed paper) in a 325° oven for 15 minutes or until the crust is light brown. Let the crust cool on the baking sheet.

Drain the pineapple, reserving the liquid. Set the pineapple chunks aside. Measure 1 of cup pineapple juice. Add water, if necessary, to equal 1 cup.

In small saucepan combine ½ cup of sugar and the cornstarch. Stir in the pineapple juice and lemon juice. Cook, stirring constantly until thickened and bubbly. Cook and stir mixture 2 minutes more. Remove the pan from the heat. Cover the surface of the mixture with plastic wrap. Cool slightly.

In small bowl combine the cream cheese, ⅓ cup of sugar, and vanilla. Beat with an electric mixer until well combined.

To assemble the tart, carefully remove the waxed paper and place the crust on a serving platter. Spread the cream cheese mixture over the cooled crust. Arrange the reserved pineapple and other fresh fruits on top of the cream cheese mixture. Carefully spoon the cooled glaze over the fruit. Chill the tart for up to 3 hours before serving.
MAKES 10 SERVINGS.

Chicken Crêpes with Mornay Sauce

1 cup milk
3 eggs
¾ cup all-purpose flour
1 tablespoon oil
5 tablespoons butter
¼ cup chopped onion
4 teaspoons all-purpose flour
¼ teaspoon salt
⅓ cup chicken broth

¼ cup half and half or light cream
½ teaspoon snipped fresh rosemary
1 cup chopped cooked chicken
1 cup cooked asparagus pieces
1 cup sliced shiitake mushrooms
2 tablespoons all-purpose flour
½ teaspoon chicken bouillon granules
1½ cups milk
½ cup shredded Swiss cheese
¼ cup grated Parmesan cheese

In blender combine 1 cup of milk, the eggs, ¾ cup of flour, and oil. Blend until smooth. Let the batter stand for 1 hour. Heat a lightly greased 6-inch skillet. Remove the pan from the heat. Spoon in 2 tablespoons of the batter, stirring between each use. Lift and tilt the skillet to spread the batter. Return to the heat and brown on one side only. Invert the pan over paper towels, and remove the crêpe. Repeat with the remaining batter, greasing the skillet occasionally. Reserve 10 crêpes. (Stack any unused crêpes between 2 layers of waxed paper, wrap, and refrigerate up to 1 week or freeze up to 3 weeks.)

In a medium saucepan melt 3 tablespoons of butter. Add the onion and cook until just tender. Stir in 4 teaspoons of flour and the salt. Add the broth and half and half. Cook and stir until thickened and bubbly. Stir in the rosemary, chicken, asparagus pieces, and mushrooms, and heat through. Cover and keep warm.

In a separate saucepan melt the remaining 2 tablespoons of butter. Stir in 2 tablespoons of flour and the bouillon granules. Add the 1½ cups of milk and cook, stirring constantly, until thickened and bubbly. Cook and stir 1 minute more. Add the cheeses and stir until melted.

Spoon a scant ¼ cup of filling down the center of each crêpe. Roll up. Place 2 filled crêpes on each plate. Spoon sauce atop crêpes. Garnish with asparagus tips, if desired.
MAKES 5 SERVINGS.

Spicer Castle Bed and Breakfast Inn

11600 Indian Beach Road
Spicer, Minnesota 56288
(320) 796-5870

K*nown for its murder mystery participatory dinner theater presentations, the Spicer Castle is the perfect setting for this sort of "dark and stormy night" fun. Guest rooms each have their own quite interesting personalities and the castle has its own boat, the Spicer Belle, for tours of Green Lake.*

Hawaiian Banana Bread

3 cups all-purpose flour
2 cups sugar
1 teaspoon baking soda
½ teaspoon salt
1 teaspoon ground cinnamon
1 cup nuts (optional)
3 eggs
1½ cups oil
2 mashed bananas
1 8-ounce can crushed pineapple, well-drained
2 teaspoons vanilla extract

In a large bowl combine the dry ingredients. In a separate bowl combine the remaining ingredients. Add the liquid mixture to the dry ingredients and mix just until blended. Pour into a greased 5 x 9-inch loaf pan. Bake in a 350° oven for 1 hour and 5 minutes or until a toothpick inserted in the center comes out clean. Cool on a rack.
MAKES 1 LOAF.

Peaches-N-Cream Muffins

2 cups sugar
4 cups all-purpose flour
½ teaspoon salt

2 teaspoons baking powder
3 eggs
¾ cup oil
2 cups milk
2 cups drained and diced canned peaches (reserve 1 tablespoon liquid for filling)

....

1 8-ounce package cream cheese, softened
¾ cup sugar
1 teaspoon almond extract
Cinnamon-sugar for topping

In a large bowl mix 2 cups of sugar, flour, salt, baking powder, eggs, oil, and milk. Stir in the peaches. In a separate bowl mix the cream cheese, ¾ cup of sugar, almond extract, and reserved peach syrup. Fill muffin cups three-fourths full of batter, drop in 1 teaspoon of filling, and swirl. Sprinkle with cinnamon-sugar. Bake in a 350° oven for 20 minutes.

These muffins have a cake-like texture.

MAKES 2 DOZEN.

Baked Peaches

6 fresh peach halves
½ cup sugar
3 almond macaroon cookies, crumbled
4 egg yolks
Spiced rum

Scoop 1 teaspoon of pulp out of each peach half. In a small bowl mash the pulp with the sugar, cookies, and egg yolks. Place the peaches close together in a glass baking dish. Spoon the pulp mixture into the center of each peach. Drizzle each peach half with 1 teaspoon of spiced rum. Bake in a 325° oven for 30 minutes.

MAKES 6 SERVINGS.

Spicer Castle

Lemon Bon Bon Cookies

1 cup butter, softened
½ cup confectioners' sugar
¾ cup cornstarch
1 cup all-purpose flour

....

2 tablespoons butter, melted
1 cup confectioners' sugar
1 teaspoon lemon juice
½ teaspoon grated lemon zest

In a medium bowl cream 1 cup of butter. Add ½ cup of confectioners' sugar, cornstarch, and flour, and blend well. Roll into balls and place on an ungreased baking sheet. Bake on a 350° oven for 15 minutes or until set. Cool.

In a small bowl combine the remaining ingredients. Frost the cooled cookies.

MAKES 2 DOZEN.

Log House and Homestead

P.O. Box 130
Vergas, Minnesota 56587
(218) 342-2318

These two hospitable homes are situated in the heart of central Minnesota's still-rustic pioneer country. The Log House, built by the innkeeper's great-grandfather, stands on a knoll overlooking Spirit Lake. Set on 4,000 feet of private lakeshore, it is part of a 115-acre property that includes open fields, hills, and woodlands covered in maples. Furnished throughout with antiques, wicker, and primitive pieces, it suggests a much earlier and quieter time. The nearby Homestead is much bigger but no less old-fashioned. All bedrooms have fireplaces.

Spirited Baked Apples

4 Granny Smith apples, cored
Brown sugar
Butter
Currants and fine-ground nuts
Watkins Apple Bake Spice or combo of cinnamon and allspice
⅓ cup water
⅓ cup Bourbon
Heavy cream or whipped cream

Remove a strip of peel around each apple and place in an 8- or 9-inch glass baking dish. Fill each hole with brown sugar and press down to pack. Add a teaspoon of butter and press down. Add a few currants and fine-ground nuts. Add brown sugar to cover the opening and sprinkle with spice. Add to dish ¼ to ⅓ cup of firmly packed brown sugar (or to taste) and 3 tablespoons of butter. Pour in the water and Bourbon. Bake in a 375° oven for 1 hour or until the apples are soft when pierced with a toothpick. Baste every 15 minutes.

Serve the apples warm in footed dishes with some of the sauce. Pass a cream pitcher or whipped cream, as desired.

MAKES 4 SERVINGS.

Puff Pancake with Strawberry Almond Butter

3 eggs
¼ teaspoon almond extract
¾ cup milk
¾ cup sifted all-purpose flour
¼ cup butter

....

½ cup butter
2 cups confectioners' sugar
2 cups hulled strawberries
½ cup almonds

In a medium bowl beat the eggs and almond extract until foamy. Alternately add the milk and flour until very smooth. In an ovenproof 12-inch skillet, melt the ¼ cup of butter until hot and bubbly. Pour the batter into the prepared skillet. Bake in a 425° oven until puffed and brown. Cut in half and place on 2 plates.

In a food processor cream together ½ cup of butter and confectioners' sugar. Add the hulled strawberries and almonds, and pulse until just blended. Serve the butter mixture and sweetened strawberries each in pretty footed bowls.

MAKES 2 SERVINGS.

Sour Cream Soufflé

6 *egg yolks*
½ *cup sour cream*
¼ *teaspoon salt*
6 *egg whites, stiffly beaten*
3 *tablespoons butter*
½ *cup sour cream, sweetened*
   Fresh berries

In a large bowl beat the egg yolks until thick and lemon colored, about 5 minutes. Beat in ½ cup of the sour cream and salt. Fold in the egg whites. Melt the butter in a heavy 10-inch ovenproof skillet. Pour in the egg mixture, leveling gently. Cook over very low heat for 10 minutes. Carefully move to a 325° oven and bake for 15 minutes, until golden and puffed.

Cut into 4 wedges and serve with a dollop of the sweetened sour cream and top with berries.

MAKES 4 SERVINGS.

Log House and Homestead

MISSISSIPPI

Cedar Grove Mansion Inn

2200 Oak Street
Vicksburg, Mississippi 39180
(800) 862-1300

*T*his impressive fifty-room mansion was built by John Alexander Klein in 1840 for his bride Elizabeth, who was William T. Sherman's cousin. Years later, General Sherman and would use the mansion as a military hospital during the siege of Vicksburg. A Union cannonball is still embedded in the parlor wall. Carefully restored, the mansion has thirty large guest rooms, a restaurant and piano bar, and several other grand public areas. Rooms are lavishly decorated and furnished with period antiques that recall the antebellum South. The grounds are covered in formal gardens with gazebos, fountains, and courtyards. There are also tennis courts, a swimming pool, and croquet lawn.

Grilled Rack of Lamb with Honey-Mustard Sauce

2 2-pound racks of lamb
¼ teaspoon salt
¼ teaspoon pepper
¼ tablespoon finely chopped fresh sage
¼ cup fresh cut rosemary
¼ cup fresh cut thyme
2 tablespoon cut fresh parsley
⅓ cup lemon juice

....

Honey-Mustard Sauce (recipe follows)

Trim the fat from the top of the rib roast. Them trim and scrape the top and sides of each rib so ½ inches of each bone is completely exposed. Sprinkle the roast with salt and pepper.

In a small bowl combine the sage, rosemary, thyme and parsley. If desired, reserve 2 tablespoons for garnish. Sprinkle the herbs on the roasts, patting the mixture until well coated. Grill the meat over medium fire (to test for medium fire, you should be able to hold your hand over the grill for 5 seconds). Place the roast meaty-side up on the grill. Insert a meat thermometer, cover, and grill for 1 hour or until it registers 150°, basting occasionally with lemon juice.

To serve, cut the roasts between the rib bones into chops. Spoon the Honey-Mustard Sauce onto each warm plate and arrange 3 chops in a fanned position on top of the sauce. If desired, sprinkle with reserved herbs.

MAKES ABOUT 4 SERVINGS.

Honey-Mustard Sauce

1 cup dry white wine
4 shallots, chopped
3 cloves garlic, minced
½ cup firmly packed brown sugar
1 cup olive oil
1 cup vinegar
3 tablespoons Dijon mustard
2 tablespoon honey

In a 10-inch skillet stir together the wine, shallots, garlic, brown sugar, olive oil, and vinegar. Cook uncovered over high heat for 15 minutes. Reduce the heat and gently boil uncovered for 10 minutes or until the mixture is thickened and reduced to 2 cups. Cool slightly.

In a blender combine the Dijon mustard, honey, and wine mixture, and blend until smooth. Strain.

MAKES ABOUT 2¼ CUPS.

Cedar Grove Mansion Inn

Brandy Bread Pudding with Brandy Sauce

8   cups crumbled fresh bread
3   pints hazelnut cream
8   eggs
2   14-ounce cans sweetened condensed milk
3   tablespoons vanilla extract
2   cups butter, softened
1   tablespoon ground cinnamon
2   tablespoons grated nutmeg
....
2   cups butter, softened
½   cup brandy
4   cups confectioners' sugar
2   tablespoons vanilla extract
3   cups heavy cream

In a large casserole dish layer the bread crumbs. In a large bowl combine the cream, eggs, milk, 2 cups of butter, 3 tablespoons of vanilla extract, cinnamon, and nutmeg. Pour the mixture over the bread. Cover. Bake in a 350° oven for 45 minutes. Uncover and bake at 375° for 15 minutes.

In a medium bowl combine 2 cups of butter, the confectioners' sugar, 2 tablespoons of vanilla extract, and heavy cream, and mix well. Add the brandy and blend well. Pour the brandy sauce over each serving of bread pudding.

MAKES 6 TO 8 SERVINGS.

Cedar Grove Orange-glazed Southern Hen

2   Cornish game hens
¼   cup butter, melted
¼   teaspoon salt
1   6-ounce package long grain and wild rice mixture
1   4-ounce can chopped mushrooms
¼   cup julienned orange zest
½   cup water
3½ tablespoons firmly packed light brown sugar
2¼ tablespoons cornstarch
⅔   cup orange juice
1½ tablespoons brandy

Rinse the hens and pat dry. Brush with butter and salt. Bake in a 350° oven for 1 hour, brushing with more butter halfway through cooking.

While the hens are cooking, cook the rice according to the package directions. When the rice is cooked, stir in the mushrooms. Keep warm.

In a small saucepan combine the orange peel and water, and simmer for 15 minutes. Drain well, reserving the water and orange peel separately.

In a medium saucepan combine the brown sugar and cornstarch. Blend in the water and orange juice. Cook and stir over low heat until thickened, 2 to 3 minutes. Remove the pan from the heat and stir in the orange peel and brandy.

Arrange the hens on a platter and cover with sauce. Serve with rice.

MAKES 2 SERVINGS.

André Jambalaya

2   pounds chicken pieces
½   teaspoon cayenne pepper
1   tablespoon olive oil
8   ounces smoked sausage (andouille or kielbasa), cut in ¼-inch slices
1   medium onion, chopped
1   medium bell pepper, seeded and chopped
1   stalk celery, sliced
3   cloves garlic, minced
1   teaspoon dried thyme
1   cup long grain rice
1   16-ounce can whole tomatoes in juice
1   cup fish stock or bottled clam juice
½   to 1 cup water
1   bay leaf
½   pound medium shrimp, shelled and deveined
4   green onions, sliced thin
½   teaspoon Tabasco sauce, or to taste

In a large pan heat the olive oil. Pat the chicken dry. Sprinkle on all sides with cayenne. Add the chicken to the pan and cook for 4 minutes on each side until browned, in batches if necessary.

Add the sausage and cook, stirring occasionally, for about 3 minutes, until it begins to brown.

Remove the chicken and sausage, leaving any liquid in the pan. Add the onion, bell peppers, celery and garlic to same pan and cook for 3 to 4 minutes, stirring frequently, until the vegetable begin to soften.

Add the thyme and rice, stirring until the rice is coated with oil. Add the tomatoes with juice, breaking them up with a spoon. Stir in the fish stock, ½ cup of water, and bay leaf. Return the chicken and sausage to the pan, and bring to a simmer over medium heat. Reduce the heat to low, cover, and cook for 15 minutes.

Place the shrimp on top of the rice and press lightly. Cover, and cook for 15 minutes more or until the shrimp and chicken are cooked and the rice is tender. If the rice has absorbed all of the liquid, add up to ½ cup of water and cook for a few minutes longer.

Remove the pan from the heat. Stir in the green onions and season with hot pepper sauce to taste.

MAKES 6 SERVINGS.

MISSOURI

Garth Wood-side Mansion

Route #1, Box 304
Hannibal, Missouri 63401
(573) 221-2789

*T*o those who love literature, this
house is truly historic as it was the
home of two of the closest friends of
Samuel Clemens, also known as
Mark Twain. Clemens visited the
Garths here often, and it is easy to
imagine him relaxing in the parlor.
Built in 1871, the house was known
to the Garths as Woodside. Today it
remains much the same Victorian
manor house it was more than century ago. Furnishings and decor are
entirely in keeping with its past.
Guests will enjoy charming touches
such as nightshirts provided for
their nineteenth century-style
sleeping comfort.

Poached Pears with Caramel Sauce

¼ cup margarine
½ cup firmly packed brown sugar
1 tablespoon water
¼ cup sour cream
4 large pears, cut in half
   Sprigs fresh mint for garnish

In a saucepan melt the margarine over
medium heat. Add the brown sugar and stir
until melted. Add the water and continue
heating until bubbles form and the mixture
becomes foamy. Be careful not to burn the
sauce. Add the sour cream and stir until
melted and smooth. Reduce the heat to
warm.

In a pot of water place the pears and boil
until tender. Remove, core, and stem. Place
on individual plates. Spoon 1 or 2 tablespoons of sauce over each pear. Garnish with
a sprig of fresh mint.

Variations: Other options might include
sprinkles of cinnamon, shredded coconut, or
chopped nuts.

MAKES 8 SERVINGS.

Eggs Picante

12 eggs
1 cup sour cream
½ pound sausage
¼ cup chopped onion
½ cup salsa or picante sauce
4 ounces sliced mushrooms
2 cups shredded Cheddar cheese
2 cups shredded mozzarella or Jack
   cheese

In a blender combine the eggs and sour
cream, and blend well. Pour into a greased 9
x 13-inch baking dish. Bake in a 350° oven
for about 15 minutes, until set. Cool slightly.

In a skillet sauté the sausage and onion.
Drizzle with ¼ cup of salsa. Spoon the
sausage-onion mixture and mushrooms over
the salsa and eggs. Mix the cheeses together
and sprinkle over the sausage. Bake in a 350°
oven for 25 to 30 minutes or until bubbly.

Drizzle with the remaining salsa.

MAKES 8 TO 10 SERVINGS.

Our Own Cream Sauce

1 cup sour cream
½ cup confectioners' sugar
¼ cup lemon juice

In a small bowl stir together the sour cream,
confectioners' sugar, and lemon juice. Cover
and refrigerate.

This can be mixed with fresh raspberries
or any other fruit or with strawberry or any
other jelly. When the basic recipe is changed,

Garth Woodside Mansion

adjust lemon juice (thick or thin consistency) or adjust sugar for sweetness to taste.

Variations: Add raisins, chopped nuts, shredded coconut, or orange extract.

MAKES 1¾ CUPS.

Good Morning Plum Cake

2   cups sifted all-purpose flour
1   cup sugar
½   teaspoon baking soda
½   teaspoon baking powder
½   teaspoon salt
1   teaspoon ground cinnamon
½   teaspoon ground cloves (optional)
3   eggs
2   4¾-ounce jars strained plums
....

1   cup confectioners' sugar
1   tablespoon lemon juice

In a large bowl combine the flour, sugar, soda, baking powder, salt, cinnamon, cloves, eggs, and plums, and blend with an electric mixer until the eggs are well blended. Pour into a greased tube pan. Bake in a 300° oven for 1 hour and 10 minutes.

In a small bowl combine the confectioners' sugar and lemon juice, mixing until blended. Frost the hot cake with the frosting.

MAKES 8 SERVINGS.

Fluted Quiche Cups

½   pound bulk sausage
¼   cup chopped onion
½   cup milk
3   eggs
½   cup mayonnaise
2   cups shredded Cheddar cheese
....

12   to 14 Crêpes (recipe follows)

In a skillet brown the sausage with the onion. Drain. In a large bowl combine the sausage and remaining ingredients. Line greased muffin cups with crêpes. Fill each crêpe three-fourths full of sausage mixture. Bake in a 350° oven for 15 minutes. Cover loosely with foil bake and for 15 additional minutes or until set.

MAKES 12 TO 14 SERVINGS.

Crêpes

4   eggs
¼   teaspoon salt
2   cups all-purpose flour
2¼   cups milk
¼   cup butter, melted
     Oil or butter

In a blender combine all of the ingredients except the oil and blend for 1 minute. Scrape down the sides and blend for another 15 seconds or until smooth. Refrigerate the batter 1 hour or longer.

In a small skillet heat a small amount of oil and cook the crêpes until the bottom is browned. Carefully turn with a spatula. Brown the other side for a few seconds. Remove from the pan with a spatula, and stack on a plate or tray. Freeze in muffin cups, then remove and store in plastic bags.

MAKES 32 TO 36 CRÊPES.

The Captain Wohlt Inn

❧

123 East Third Street
Hermann, Missouri 65041
(573) 486-3357

___

Built in 1886 by a riverboat captain, the inn is as stately and solid as the grand steamers its original owner once operated. The five bedrooms and three suites are furnished with heirloom antiques and reproductions. The inn is in the Hermann historic district only a few blocks from the Missouri River.

Sunday Morning Waffles

2½   cups all-purpose flour
1   tablespoon sugar
½   teaspoon nutmeg
2   tablespoons active dry yeast
½   teaspoon salt
½   teaspoon ground cinnamon

4   egg yolks
1   teaspoon vanilla extract
2   cups lukewarm milk
½   cup butter, melted
4   egg whites

In a large bowl sift together all of the dry ingredients. In a separate bowl beat the egg yolks and vanilla in ½ cup of the milk. Add the remaining milk and mix well. Add the liquid mixture to the dry mixture. Add the melted butter and mix thoroughly.

In a medium bowl beat the egg whites until dry and stiff. Fold into the batter carefully. Let the batter stand in a warm place for at least 30 minutes.

Bake in a waffle iron according to the manufacturers' instructions. (Use a medium setting and bake for about 3 minutes.)

Waffles may be kept warm and crisp on the open oven racks with the oven setting on warm.

Variation: This recipe may also be used for Belgian waffles. Just add 2 tablespoons malted milk powder to the dry ingredients.

Mixed Fresh Fruit and Dressing

1   cup sour cream or plain yogurt
1   tablespoon fresh squeezed orange
     juice
2   tablespoons honey
1   teaspoon fresh grated orange zest
....

Fresh fruits

In a small bowl combine the sour cream, orange juice, honey, and orange zest.

Note: Use any combination of fresh fruits in amounts suitable for the number to be served. Mix together the evening before. In the morning ladle fruit into individual serving dishes. Add a teaspoon of fruit dressing to each serving. Garnish with maraschino cherry.

MAKES 1 CUP OF DRESSING.

Rice Pudding

4   eggs, beaten
1   cup heavy cream
1   cup sugar
1   cup milk or half and half
....

1   teaspoon lemon juice
1½   teaspoons vanilla extract
    Dash ground cinnamon
    Dash grated nutmeg
½   cup cooked white rice
½   cup golden raisins (optional)

In a large bowl combine the eggs, heavy cream, sugar, and milk, and whisk until blended well. Fold in the remaining ingredients.

Grease a 2-quart soufflé dish thoroughly. Pour in the egg mixture.

Pour boiling water into a large pan. Set the soufflé dish in the pan of hot water. Bake in a 350° oven for 1 hour. Remove from the water and cool on a wire rack. The center will be slightly loose but will set as it cools. Serve with fresh or frozen fruit, maple syrup, etc.

MAKES 10 TO 12 SERVINGS.

Angelic Bananas

6   large bananas
¾   cup brown sugar
½   cup melted butter
1   cup sour cream

Peel the bananas and cut into ½-inch slices. Arrange the banana slices in a shallow baking dish. Sprinkle brown sugar evenly over the top. Pour melted butter over the top. Bake in a 375° oven for 20 to 30 minutes. Gently stir with a wooden spoon after 10 minutes.

Remove from the oven and spread the sour cream on the top. Serve warm.

MAKES 6 TO 8 SERVINGS.

Down to Earth Lifestyles

12500 N.W. Crooked Road
Parkville, Missouri 64152
(816) 891-1018

Situated on eighty-six acres of peaceful woodland, this B&B is described as "an earth-integrated home." Rooms are private, cozy, and quiet, while common areas invite relaxing and mingling with other guests. The surrounding woods and pastures are filled with cattle, horses, geese, and wildlife.

Sausage Pie

1   pound sausage
1   cup finely rolled cracker crumbs
½   cup chopped green pepper
¼   cup chopped onion
1   10½-ounce can condensed tomato
    soup
1   unbaked 10-inch pie shell
3   cups cooked white rice
1   cup grated Cheddar cheese

In a large skillet brown the sausage. Drain. In a large bowl combine the sausage, cracker crumbs, green pepper, onion, and ½ can of soup. Mix well and pat into the pie shell. In a small bowl combine the remaining soup with the rice and Cheddar cheese. Pour over the sausage. Bake in a 350° oven for 40 minutes.

MAKES 8 SERVINGS.

Chocolate Cherry Bars

1   10½-ounce package fudge cake mix
1   21-ounce can cherry pie filling
1   teaspoon almond extract
2   eggs, beaten

....

1   cup sugar
5   tablespoon butter
⅓   cup milk
1   6-ounce package semisweet chocolate chips

Grease and flour a 9 x 13-inch or 10 x 15-inch pan. In a large bowl combine the cake mix, cherry pie filling, almond extract, and eggs, and stir until mixed well. Pour into the prepared pan. Bake in a 350° oven for 20 to 30 minutes.

In a small pan combine the sugar, butter, and milk and bring to a boil, stirring constantly. Boil for 1 minute. Remove the pan from the heat and add the chocolate chips, stirring until smooth. Pour over the bars.

MAKES ABOUT 3 DOZEN.

Cameron's Crag

P.O. Box 526
Point Lookout, Missouri 65726
(417) 335-8134, (800) 933-8529

Perched on a bluff overlooking Lake Taneycomo, Cameron's Crag places its guests only three miles from Branson with all its country music attractions. The three very large guest suites with decks have extraordinary views of the lake and the colorful Branson skyline. One of the suites is in a detached guest house with its own spa.

Sweetheart Casserole

2   large russet potatoes
8   eggs
¾   cup cottage cheese
¼   cup sour cream
⅛   teaspoon black pepper
    Sausage, cooked and drained
    (optional)
8   slices lean ham or Canadian bacon
½   cup shredded Swiss or Cheddar
    cheese
    Salsa
    Green bell pepper, sautéed
    Mushrooms

Scrub the potatoes and wrap in paper towels. Microwave at high power for 7 to 8 minutes. Peel and cube the potatoes. In a large dish combine the potatoes, eggs, cottage cheese, sour cream, and pepper. Spray a heart-shaped baking dish with cooking spray. In one half of the dish place the well-drained sausage, and Canadian bacon in the other half. Spread the egg mixture over the meat. Bake in a 350° oven for about 50 minutes.

Sprinkle with the cheese and return to the oven to melt. Serve with salsa, sautéed green bell peppers, and mushrooms.

MAKES 6 SERVINGS.

Cameron's Crag

Banana Split Supreme

2 bananas, sliced lengthwise
1 8-ounce container strawberry yogurt
1 cup sliced strawberries
½ cup granola
Canned whipped cream (optional)
Sliced kiwi (optional)

Place the bananas in banana boats. In a small bowl combine the yogurt and strawberries. Spoon ½ cup of yogurt mixture on each of the banana slices. Top with granola, whipped cream, and kiwi, if desired.

MAKES 4 SERVINGS.

Inn St. Gemme Beauvais

78 North Main Street
Ste. Genevieve, Missouri 63670
(573) 883-5744

The inn is in a grand brick home built in 1848. It has operated as an inn for nearly fifty years, and was completely renovated following the floods of 1993. A central walk leads guests to the semi-circular brick stairway, and the main portal features etched glass in romantic designs. The high ceilings and elaborate woodwork are reminders of the building's long history.

Marinated Carrots

2 to 3 pounds carrots, peeled and cut on the diagonal
1 teaspoon salt

¾ cup vinegar
1 cup tomato soup
1 tablespoon Worcestershire sauce
⅔ cup sugar
½ cup oil
1 tablespoon Dijon mustard
½ teaspoon salt
1 medium onion, very thinly sliced
1 green bell pepper, very thinly sliced

In a large pot of boiling water cook the carrots with 1 teaspoon of salt until tender-crisp, about 10 minutes. Drain and transfer the carrots to a serving dish.

In a medium bowl mix together the vinegar, tomato soup, Worcestershire sauce, sugar, oil, Dijon mustard, and ½ teaspoon of salt.

Arrange the onion and bell pepper slices over the drained carrots. Pour the vinegar mixture over the sliced carrots. The sauce should cover the carrots. Refrigerate overnight. Serve cold.

Carrots will keep up to 4 weeks in the refrigerator.

MAKES 4 TO 6 SERVINGS.

Peach St. Gemme

2 peaches, halved
4 teaspoons mincemeat

Arrange the peach halves in a baking dish with the center up. Fill each hole with 1 teaspoon of mincemeat. Bake in a 350° oven for about 15 minutes, until heated through. Serve hot with a sprig of mint on the side.

Very tasty and also a very pretty fruit dish. Pear halves may be done the same way.

MAKES 4 SERVINGS.

Peach Trifle

1 18½-ounce package yellow cake mix
½ cup butter, melted
2 cups shredded coconut

1 29-ounce can sliced peaches, syrup reserved
2 teaspoons sugar

1 teaspoon ground cinnamon
1 teaspoon grated nutmeg
2 eggs
1 cup sour cream

Red food coloring
Sugar to taste
Cinnamon to taste
Nutmeg to taste
1 tablespoon cornstarch

1 pint heavy cream
1 teaspoon rum
2 tablespoons confectioners' sugar

In a large bowl combine the cake mix, butter, and coconut, and mix until crumbly. Press evenly in the bottom of a greased cookie sheet. Bake in a 350° oven for about 30 minutes, until it starts to brown.

Arrange the peach slices over the cake mixture. In a small bowl combine 2 teaspoons of sugar, 1 teaspoon of cinnamon, and 1 teaspoon of nutmeg. Sprinkle the mixture over the peaches, reserving some for the top.

In a small bowl beat together the eggs and sour cream. Spread the mixture over the peaches, making sure to cover all of the peaches. Sprinkle with the remaining sugar mixture. Bake in a 300° oven until the sour cream is set or doesn't stick to a finger.

In a saucepan combine the peach syrup, add a few drops of red food coloring, some sugar, cinnamon, and nutmeg. Add the cornstarch and cook until thickened. Pour into a jar.

In a medium bowl whip the cream with the rum and confectioners' sugar.

To serve, break up the cake into pieces and put into serving dishes. Add a little peach sauce just before time to serve. Top with whipped cream.

MAKES 15 SERVINGS.

Inn
St. Gemme Beauvais

Walnut Street Inn

Walnut Street Inn

❧

900 East Walnut
Springfield, MO 65806
(417) 864-6346

Walnut Street is a nationally registered historic district with fine
examples of Victorian architecture.
Among these is the Walnut Street
Inn, built in 1894. The inn's
Corinthian columns frame a wide
veranda with a wicker porch swing
and rockers. A beveled-glass door
opens to welcome guests inside

where they will find period decor
and antique furnishings. Guest
rooms provide bath robes and other
comforts. Some feature Jacuzzis.

Crêpes Florentine

12   slices ham
1   pound Swiss cheese, cut into chunks
1   16-ounce carton ricotta cheese
¼   cup Dijon mustard
1   24-ounce box frozen spinach,
      thawed
12   prepared plain crêpes

....

3   tablespoon butter
3   tablespoons all-purpose flour
½   teaspoon crushed tarragon
1   teaspoon seasoned salt
¼   teaspoon pepper
½   carton half and half
½   cup grated Parmesan cheese
1   teaspoon fresh parsley, chopped

In a food processor combine the ham, Swiss
and ricotta cheeses, Dijon mustard, and
spinach, and process until thoroughly mixed.
Place a spoonful in each crêpe and fold the
ends together. Place the crêpes seam-side
down in a greased baking dish. Bake in a
375° oven for about 10 to 15 minutes, until
lightly browned on top.

In a medium saucepan melt the butter.
Blend in the flour, tarragon, seasoned salt,
and pepper. Gradually add the half and half,
stirring constantly over medium heat until the
mixture thickens and bubbles. Stir in the
Parmesan and parsley. Lower the heat to simmer and continue cooking for 1 to 2 minutes.
Spoon over the cooked crêpes.

Note: Serve with banana nut bread and
slices of oranges and apples. This makes an
impressive brunch or breakfast.

MAKES 4 TO 6 SERVINGS.

Ozark Lemon Feathercakes

3   eggs, separated
1¼   cups all-purpose flour
¾   cup cottage cheese
¼   cup butter, melted and cooled
2   tablespoons sugar
¼   teaspoon salt
1   tablespoon grated lemon zest

In a large bowl beat the egg whites until they
hold stiff peaks. In a separate bowl stir
together the yolks, flour, cottage cheese, butter, sugar, salt, and lemon zest until mixed, or
use a blender. Fold the egg whites into the
yolk mixture. Heat a griddle over medium
heat. Cook the pancakes slowly for about 1 to
2 minutes, then turn.

MAKES ABOUT 4 SERVINGS.

O'Duachain Country Inn

675 Ferndale Drive
Bigfork, Montana 59911
(406) 837-6851

A three-level log home set on five acres, the inn is between Flathead Lake and Swan Lake about five miles from Bigfork Village, Montana. Giant conifers surround the inn, and the grounds feature a pond, waterfowl, exotic birds, wild flowers, horses, and even a miniature donkey. The interior, with its two rock fireplaces, has the feel of a woodland lodge.

Huevos Rancheros de Margot

- Butter
- 3 *flour tortillas*
- 3 *tablespoons green enchilada sauce*
- 1 *16-ounce can refried beans*
- 3 *eggs*
- ¼ *cup grated Cheddar cheese*
- 1 *tomato, chopped*
- ¼ *cup chopped black olives (for garnish)*
- ¼ *cup chopped green onions (for garnish)*
- *Fresh or commercial salsa*
- 2 *tablespoons lemon juice*

Brush large muffin cups (3-inch diameter) with melted butter. Soften the tortillas in a microwave on medium power for 30 seconds. Line the muffin cups with the tortillas. Brush the tortillas with butter, especially the edges.

In a medium bowl mix the green enchilada sauce into the beans. Divide the bean mixture among the tortilla cups. Crack an egg into each muffin on top of the beans. Bake in a 350° oven for about 30 minutes or until the eggs are poached well. Sprinkle about 2 teaspoons of lemon juice on each before garnishing.

Garnish with Cheddar cheese, tomato, olives, and green onions. Serve with salsa. These will lift easily out of the tin once cooked.

MAKES 3 SERVINGS.

Molly Barrett Eggs

- 1 *pound Jimmy Dean sausage (regular)*
- ½ to ¾ *large onion, chopped*
- 2 *10-ounce boxes frozen spinach, thawed and squeezed*
- ¾ *cup dry shiitake mushrooms, cooked according to package directions, drained, and chopped*
- 1 *cup sour cream*
- 1 *cup grated mozzarella cheese*
- 10 *eggs*
- *Fresh grated Parmesan cheese*
- *Paprika*

In a skillet fry the sausage until it loses the pink color. Drain on paper towels. In the same skillet fry the onion until soft in the sausage grease. Drain. In a large bowl mix the spinach, mushrooms, sour cream, mozzarella cheese, sausage, and onion. Spray a 9 x 13-inch pan with cooking spray. Spread the mixture in the pan. Make 10 depressions in the spinach with the back of a ladle or other round object, pressing into the spinach to make a well. Crack the eggs one at a time into the wells. Sprinkle with Parmesan cheese, then with paprika. Bake in a 350° oven for 30 to 40 minutes, until the eggs are poached well.

Before serving, let the casserole cool at room temperature for 5 to 10 minutes, so it will cut and serve easily.

MAKES 8 SERVINGS.

Lone Mountain Ranch

P.O. Box 160069
Big Sky, Montana 59716
(800) 514-4644

Lone Mountain is Yellowstone without the crowds. The guest ranch is within the Yellowstone natural system, and while there are no geysers nearby, most of the plants and wildlife in the nation's popular national park are also present here. The park, with its famed lakes and thermal features is only a short drive down the scenic Gallatin River. Fly fishing is a big attraction here. So is hiking, horseback riding, white-water rafting, and cross-country skiing.

Lone Mountain Ranch

Lone Mountain Ranch Trout Florentine

    1   cup olive oil
    1   pound fresh spinach
    1   cup milk
    6   ounces Brie cheese, cut into small
            pieces
        Pinch grated nutmeg
        Salt and pepper to taste
    ½   cup crushed pine nuts
    1   cup all-purpose flour
    2   8- to 10-ounce trout
    1   cup white wine
        Lemon juice

In a saucepan heat a little of the olive oil and braise the spinach until tender. Add half of the milk and all of the Brie. Cook until it becomes creamy. Season with nutmeg, pepper, and salt. Set aside to cool.

In a medium bowl mix the pine nuts with the flour for the dredge.

Fill the trout with the spinach Florentine. Season the trout with salt and pepper. Dip the trout in the remaining milk and roll in the pine nut-flour dredge.

In a sauté pan heat the rest of the olive oil and cook the trout until golden brown, about 6 to 7 minutes, on each side. Take the trout out and keep warm. Turn down the heat and add the wine to the oil in the sauté pan with some lemon juice. Place the trout on the plates and spoon the wine and olive oil sauce over the trout.

MAKES 2 SERVINGS.

Halibut with Tomato Dressing

    1   tablespoon balsamic vinegar
    2   tablespoons olive oil
    ¼   cup tomato juice
    1   clove garlic, crushed
        Juice of ½ lemon
    2   large ripe tomatoes
    1   shallot, diced
    2   8-ounce halibut fillets
    4   fresh basil leaves, cut julienne
        Fresh ground pepper and sea salt to
            taste

In a small bowl combine the vinegar, oil, tomato juice, garlic, and lemon juice, blend together well. Cut the tomatoes into ¼-inch pieces.

In a sauté pan heat a little oil and sauté the diced shallot until transparent. Then add the oil-and-vinegar mixture. Bring quickly to a boil and take off the stove. Add the tomatoes.

Grill the halibut fillets to the desired temperature.

Spread the warm tomato dressing onto 2 large plates. Sprinkle with basil and place the halibut fillets in the middle on top of the dressing. Season with pepper and salt.

MAKES 2 SERVINGS.

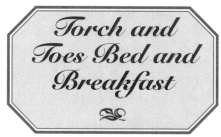

Torch and Toes Bed and Breakfast

❧

309 South Third Avenue
Bozeman, Montana 59715
(406) 586-7285

From the street, the tall brick and frame Colonial revival house still looks much as it did in 1906 when its first owner, mining company executive Wilbur Williams, moved in. Lace curtains, leaded glass, and period antiques help keep its past alive. Especially delightful are the collections of gargoyles, mouse

traps, and old postcards, and the old Victrola with early Frank Sinatra records. Located in the historic Bon Ton district of Bozeman, the Torch and Toes offers three nostalgia-filled guest rooms and a spacious carriage house suite with loft.

Fried Apples

    4   tart cooking apples, peeled and
            sliced
    3   tablespoons lemon juice
    ¼   cup firmly packed brown sugar
    ½   teaspoon ground cinnamon
    ¼   cup granola
    2   tablespoons butter

In a large bowl toss the apples in lemon juice. In a separate bowl combine the sugar, cinnamon, and granola. In a large skillet melt the butter and cook the apples over medium heat for about 5 minutes, turning frequently. Sprinkle with sugar mixture during the last 30 seconds of cooking.

MAKES 4 SERVINGS.

Banana Pecan Pancakes

    1   cup all-purpose flour
    ½   teaspoon baking soda
    ¼   teaspoon salt
    ½   cup cornmeal
    ¼   cup oat bran
    1   ripe banana
    1   egg, beaten
    1½   cups buttermilk
    2   tablespoons melted margarine
    2   teaspoons honey
    ¼   cup chopped toasted pecans

Torch and Toes

In a large bowl stir together the flour, soda, and salt. Add the cornmeal and oat bran. In a separate bowl mash the banana. Add the egg, buttermilk, margarine, and honey. Add the liquid mixture to the dry ingredients until just moistened. Fold in the pecans. In a greased griddle pour in ¼ cup of batter for each pancake. Cook until lightly browned on each side.

MAKES ABOUT 4 SERVINGS.

Herbed Brie Scrambled Eggs

     1   tablespoon butter
     6   eggs
     ¼   cup milk
     3   tablespoons chopped green onions
     ¼   teaspoon salt
     2   ounces herbed Brie cheese, cut up
     4   English muffins, split and toasted

In a skillet melt the butter over medium heat. In a medium bowl beat the eggs. Add the milk, green onions, and salt. Mix together. Pour into the skillet all at once. With a spatula, draw the eggs to the center of the pan until cooked but still very moist. Remove the pan from the heat. Quickly stir in the Brie. Serve on toasted English muffins.

MAKES 4 SERVINGS.

Maple Pecan Scones

     3½   cups all-purpose flour
     1   cup finely chopped pecans
     4   teaspoons baking powder
     1   teaspoon salt
     ⅔   cup shortening
     1   cup milk
     ½   cup maple syrup
     ½   teaspoon maple extract

In a large bowl combine the flour, pecans, baking powder, and salt. Cut in the shortening with a pastry blender until the mixture resembles coarse crumbs. Add the milk, ⅓ cup of maple syrup, and maple extract, and mix lightly with a fork until a soft dough forms. Turn out onto a lightly floured surface and knead 5 to 6 times. Divide the dough in half and pat each portion into a 7-inch round. Cut in 6 wedges. Place the scones 1 inch apart on a greased baking sheet. Pierce the tops with a fork. Brush the tops with the remaining

maple syrup. Bake in a 425° oven for 15 to 18 minutes until golden brown.

MAKES 1 DOZEN.

Voss Inn

319 South Willson
Bozeman, Montana 59715
(416) 587-0982

In 1883 mining engineer and journalist Matt Anderson built this home for his lovely bride Martha for $5,000, a handsome sum at the time. The house has been restored to its original elegance, and the guest rooms maintain the old-fashioned charm. The inn and Bozeman are close enough to Yellowstone National Park to allow for day trips.

Eggs Florentine Voss Inn

     2   10-ounce packages fresh spinach, washed and trimmed
     12   ounces cream cheese (room temperature)
     ½   teaspoon grated nutmeg
     ¾   teaspoon salt
     ¼   teaspoon black pepper
          Cheese-and-garlic-flavored croutons
     10   slices bacon, cooked until crisp and crumbled
     10   eggs
     3⅓   cups White Cheese Sauce (recipe follows)
     10   tablespoons sliced almonds

Shake off the excess water from the spinach. In a large pot cook the spinach with no added moisture until just cooked but still bright green. Drain and dry the spinach on paper towels to remove excess moisture, and coarsely chop. In a bowl combine the softened cream cheese, nutmeg, salt, and pepper with the chopped spinach and mix well.

Spray 10 8-ounce ramekins with cooking spray. Sprinkle a layer of croutons in the bottom of each ramekin. (Voss Inn uses Mrs.

Wright's Cheese and Garlic Croutons, but any seasoned crouton will work). Divide the spinach mixture evenly between the ramekins, making a small well in the center. Sprinkle bacon bits evenly over the spinach layer. Crack an egg in each well on top of the bacon. Top each ramekin with ⅓ cup of cheese sauce and sprinkle each portion with 1 tablespoon of sliced almonds. Place the ramekins on a cookie sheet. Bake in a 350° oven for 25 to 30 minutes, until browned and bubbly.

MAKES 10 SERVINGS.

White Cheese Sauce

     1   cup butter
     1   cup all-purpose flour
     1½   teaspoons salt
     ½   teaspoon pepper
     1½   teaspoons dry mustard powder
     6   cups milk
     4   cups grated Fontina cheese
     4   cups grated Swiss cheese

In a large saucepan melt the butter over medium high heat. Don't let it brown! Add the flour and stir vigorously. Add the salt, pepper, and dry mustard and stir continuously for approximately 2 minutes.

Slowly add 2 cups of the milk and mix until smooth, adding more milk as needed to keep from thickening. Add the cheeses to the mixture and reduce the heat to medium. Let the cheeses melt, stirring constantly, and add as much of the rest of the milk as needed to make a thick sauce.

The cheese sauce can be made ahead and stored in the refrigerator for a few days or can be saved in the freezer for up to a month.

MAKES ABOUT 12 CUPS.

Egg with Salsa

     2   tablespoons oil
     ½   corn tortilla, cut into 1½-inch pieces
     2   slices Canadian bacon, cut into bite-sized pieces
     2   tablespoons Homemade Salsa (recipe follows, or use La Victoria Salsa Suprema)
     2   tablespoons sour cream
     1   egg
     3   to 4 tablespoons grated Cheddar cheese (sharp or medium)

Spray an 8-ounce ramekin with cooking spray. In a skillet heat the oil and fry the corn tortilla until soft and slightly golden. Arrange a layer of Canadian bacon in the bottom of the ramekin and top it with the tortilla. Spoon the salsa on top of the tortilla and sour cream on top of the salsa, making a slight well in the center. Break an egg into the well in the sour cream. Top with the Cheddar cheese. Bake in a 350° oven for 20 to 25 minutes or until the egg is set and the cheese is bubbly. (Timing depends a lot on altitude, the oven, and how many ramekins are in the oven at one time.)

MAKES 1 SERVING.

Homemade Salsa

    6 to 9 jalapeño peppers
    1 clove garlic, peeled
    1 small yellow onion, chopped
    1 32-ounce can plum tomatoes
    1 bunch cilantro
    3 limes

In a small microwave bowl cook the jalapeños on high with water to cover halfway for 1 minute and 30 seconds. Let stand for approximately 2 minutes. Wearing rubber gloves, remove the stems and seeds of the jalapeños.

In a food processor with the blade running, drop in the garlic. Once it is finely minced, add the jalapeños and their cooking liquid and chop finely, but do not purée. Add the chopped onion and the canned tomatoes and pulse twice.

Wash and dry the cilantro and discard the stems. Add the cilantro leaves and the juice of 3 limes to the salsa in the food processor. Pulse twice to mix. The salsa should be chunky with definite red and green colors. It will keep in the refrigerator for up to 1 week.

Note: Inasmuch as jalapeños differ in size and intensity of flavor, it is helpful to remove the chopped jalapeño mixture from the processor and add it back in little by little after mixing the onion and tomatoes, just to make sure that the salsa won't take anyone's head off. The finished product can be hot when eaten with chips, but quite mild when cooked in the egg dish.

MAKES ABOUT 5 CUPS.

Pineapple Macadamia Nut Upside-down Muffins

    ½ cup butter
    1 cup firmly packed dark brown sugar
    48 fresh pineapple pieces
    1¼ cups coarsely chopped macadamia
        nuts

    ....

    1½ cups unbleached all-purpose flour
    ½ cup firmly packed dark brown sugar
    2 teaspoons baking powder
    1½ teaspoons grated orange zest
    1 teaspoon ground cinnamon
    ¼ teaspoon salt
    2 eggs
    ½ cup butter, melted and cooled
        slightly
    ½ cup milk

Grease a 12-cup muffin pan with cooking spray. In a small saucepan or in a microwave melt the butter until bubbly. Add 1 cup of brown sugar and cook until the sugar and butter are combined well. Divide the mixture evenly between the muffin cups. Place 4 pineapple pieces in each muffin cup and sprinkle 1 tablespoon of coarsely chopped macadamia nuts over the pineapple.

In a large mixing bowl combine the flour, ½ cup of brown sugar, baking powder, orange zest, cinnamon, and salt. In a separate bowl beat the eggs with the melted butter, and milk. Add the dry ingredients and mix until just combined. Divide the batter evenly between the muffin cups on top of the pineapple and macadamia nuts. Bake in a 375° oven for 25 minutes or until a tester inserted in the center comes out clean. Immediately invert onto a warming rack, removing the muffin tin carefully. (If some of the pineapple pieces stay in the tin, remove them and place them on top of the muffins again.) Allow the muffins to cool for 5 minutes before serving. Serve upside-down.

Variations: For Pineapple Macadamia Nut Muffins, omit the topping from the Upside-Down Muffins. Using the same batter mix in 1½ cups of pineapple pieces and 1 cup of chopped macadamia nuts. Spoon the batter into 12 muffin cups, top with more chopped nuts, and bake in a 375° oven for 25 minutes or until a toothpick inserted in the center comes out clean.

MAKES 1 DOZEN.

Izaak Walton Inn

*P.O. Box 653
Essex, Montana 59916
(406) 888-5700*

The Izaak Walton was built in 1939 to provide lodging for train crews who served the Great Northern Railway. The nearby working rail yard remains one of its attractions, but there are many more. Located at the southwestern edge of Glacier National Park, among America's most beautiful natural areas, it provides views of forests, streams, and towering, snowcapped mountains. Cross-country ski packages are available.

House Dressing (Sweet and Creamy Onion)

    1 cup sugar
    1 cup vinegar
    2 cups chopped onion
    2 teaspoons salt
    2 teaspoons dry mustard
    1 teaspoon celery seed
    2 cups oil

In a blender combine the sugar, vinegar, onion, salt, dry mustard, and celery seed, and blend well. Slowly add the oil.

Note: It will take 3 batches to fill a gallon container.

MAKES ABOUT 6 CUPS.

Rhubarb Custard Pie

    5   cups fresh rhubarb, cut into ½-inch
        pieces
    1   unbaked 10-inch pie shell (recipe
        follows)
  1½   cups sugar
    2   tablespoons all-purpose flour
   ¼   teaspoon grated nutmeg
    4   eggs, slightly beaten

Place the rhubarb in the pastry shell. In a medium bowl combine the sugar, flour, and nutmeg. Add the eggs and beat well. Pour the egg mixture into the pastry shell. To prevent overbrowning, cover the edge with foil. Bake in a 375° oven for 25 minutes. Remove the foil and bake 20 minutes more or until pie is nearly set (pie appears soft in the center but sets when cooling). Cover and store in the refrigerator.

MAKES 8 SERVINGS.

Never-Fail Pie Crust

    3   cups all-purpose flour
    1   teaspoon salt
  1¼   cups shortening
    1   egg, beaten
   ⅓   cup water
    1   tablespoon vinegar

In a large bowl combine the flour and salt. Cut in the shortening with a pastry blender until the mixture resembles coarse crumbs. In a separate bowl combine the egg, water, and vinegar. Add the liquid mixture to the dry ingredients, mixing until a dough forms.

Use as needed. Refrigerate or freeze unused portions.

MAKES 2 DOUBLE-CRUST SHELLS OR 3 10-INCH SINGLE CRUSTS.

Huckleberry Chicken

    1   cup water
    1   cup huckleberries
   ¾   cup sugar
    1   tablespoon cornstarch
   ⅛   teaspoon salt
    1   teaspoon lemon juice
    ....
    1   cup butter
    2   cups all-purpose flour
    4   cups milk
   ⅛   teaspoon granulated garlic

    1   quart heavy cream
    1   cup white wine
    ....
    2   12-ounce packages fettucine, cooked
    8   5-ounce boneless chicken breasts,
        grilled

In a saucepan boil the water. Add the huckleberries. In a small bowl combine the sugar, cornstarch, and salt. Stir the mixture into the berries and cook until thickened. Add the lemon juice.

In a saucepan melt the butter. Blend in the flour to form a roux. Add the milk and blend until smooth and thickened. Add the garlic, heavy cream, and wine. Blend and cook until the correct consistency. Add the fettucine and toss to combine.

Divide the fettucine among 8 serving plates. Top each serving with a grilled chicken breast. Pour about 2 tablespoons (1 ounce) of huckleberry sauce over each portion of chicken

Note: Serve with a side dish of fresh vegetables.

MAKES 8 SERVINGS.

Sportsman's High Bed and Breakfast

❧

750 Deer Street
West Yellowstone, Montana 59758
(406) 646-7865

---

*T*his spacious home with its wraparound porch combines Colonial, farmhouse, and rustic styles. Located in three acres of aspen and pine forest, it places guests within eight miles of the western entrance of Yellowstone Park. Rooms are individually decorated and furnished with antiques.

Sportsman's Benedict

   10   croissants, frozen
   10   large eggs
    2   tablespoons olive oil
    2   medium onions, sliced
    1   large green bell pepper, sliced
    1   large red pepper, sliced
    4   cups half and half
   ¼   cup cornstarch
    8   tablespoons butter
    1   pound Velveeta cheese, cubed
   30   thin slices ham
    3   teaspoons dried parsley dried
    2   teaspoons paprika
    ....
    1   pound mushrooms

Following package directions the night before, place the 10 frozen croissants on a cookie sheet to rise overnight. Bake the following morning according to package directions.

After baking, cool for 30 minutes, slice the croissants in half, and place each on the center of a prepared plate.

In a large pot of cold water, add the eggs and bring to a boil. Boil uncovered for 10 minutes. Remove the pan from the heat, cover, and let stand for 10 minutes.

Drain and shell the eggs. Slice each egg with an egg slicer and set aside, keeping eggs separate.

In a skillet heat 1 tablespoon olive oil and sauté the sliced onions and peppers. Set aside. In the same skillet heat another 1 tablespoon olive oil and sauté the mushrooms. Set aside.

In a large glass bowl pour 4 cups of half and half. Add ¼ cup of cornstarch and mix until smooth. Microwave on high power for about 6 minutes, stirring frequently. Add 8 tablespoons of butter and heat an additional 4 to 6 minutes, until the mixture is thickened, stirring frequently. Add the Velveeta cheese. Stir and heat in the microwave for 1 to 2 minutes, until melted. Stir well. Ladle 2 ounces of cheese sauce over the top of each croissant, then layer in the following order the remaining ingredients: ½ slice ham, ½ sliced hard-boiled egg, 1 slice ham, ½ sliced hard-boiled egg, onions, 1 slice green pepper, 1 slice red pepper, and mushrooms.

Reheat the cheese sauce in the microwave for about 45 seconds, until hot. Ladle the cheese sauce over the croissants. Sprinkle with paprika and parsley. Serve immediately.

MAKES 10 SERVINGS.

Sportsman's High

No-Crust Breakfast Quiche

8   ounces bacon, cut in pieces
¼   large green bell pepper
¼   large red bell pepper
    Oil
½   pound sliced mushrooms
8   large eggs
½   cup half and half
¾   cup shredded Cheddar cheese
1   medium tomato

In a hot skillet fry the bacon until brown. Drain and set aside.

Finely chop the green and red peppers. Set aside.

In a nonstick skillet heat a small amount of oil and sauté the mushrooms. Set aside.

In a large bowl add the eggs and beat in the half and half. Add the Cheddar cheese, bacon, peppers, and mushrooms, and stir. Pour into a 12-inch round nonstick baking pan. Bake in a 325° oven for 35 to 40 minutes or until done.

Slice the tomato in rings, cut each slice halfway to the center, and twist. Set aside.

Cut the quiche into 6 equal slices and serve individually with a tomato slice on top.

MAKES 6 SERVINGS.

Almond French Toast

1   pound blackberries, frozen
6   large eggs
1   cup half and half
3   tablespoons sugar
¼   cup canola oil
2   teaspoons almond extract
½   teaspoon ground allspice
16 slices French bread
⅓   cup slivered almonds
1   tablespoon butter
¼   cup confectioners' sugar
    Canned whipped topping

Thaw the blackberries overnight in the refrigerator. Drain and set aside.

In a large bowl combine the eggs, half and half, and sugar. Whip until blended well. Add ¼ cup of oil, the almond extract, and allspice. Mix well. Dip each slice of bread into the egg mixture, making sure it is soaked well. Place on a hot griddle and cook for 5 minutes, until brown. Turn over and cook for another 5 minutes or until done.

While the toast is browning, in a skillet sauté the almonds in butter. Set aside. To serve, dust the toast with confectioners' sugar. Spoon on top the thawed blackberries and the almonds. Top each serving off with canned whipped topping.

MAKES 8 SERVINGS.

Sportsman's High Celebration Delight

6   cups whole milk
1   6-ounce can orange juice concentrate
¼   cup sugar
1   tablespoon vanilla extract
1½ teaspoons almond extract
12 ice cubes

In a blender combine all ingredients and blend on high speed until smooth and all of the ice is gone. Serve immediately in wine glasses or goblets.

Note: This is served for special events such as birthdays, anniversaries, or honeymoons.

MAKES 6 SERVINGS.

Duck Inn

Duck Inn

1305 Columbia Avenue
Whitefish, Montana 59937
(406) 862-3825

***O**n the Whitefish River, the Duck Inn offers ten well-appointed rooms with fireplaces and deep-soak tubs. The inn also has an inviting Jacuzzi. Whitefish is within easy driving distance of scenic Flathead Lake and Glacier National Park.*

Citron Muffins

5½ cups all-purpose flour
3   teaspoons baking powder
3   teaspoons baking soda
2   teaspoons salt
2⅔ cups sour cream
2⅔ cups sugar
4   teaspoons vanilla extract
1⅓ cups butter
8   large eggs
1   16-ounce carton candied citron
·························
    Brown sugar
    Butter
    Cinnamon

In a large bowl combine the flour, baking powder, soda, and salt. In a separate large bowl combine the sour cream, sugar, vanilla, butter, and eggs. Beat with an electric mixer until blended. Fold in the citron. Add the dry ingredients and mix just until moistened. Spoon into greased muffin cups.

In a small bowl mix together a small amount of brown sugar, butter, and cinnamon. Sprinkle the mixture over the batter. Bake in a 350° oven for 22 minutes.

This mixture can be stored up to 2 weeks in the refrigerator before baking.

MAKES ABOUT 3 DOZEN.

NEBRASKA

Pine Cone Lodge

Route 2, Box 156C
Broken Bow, Nebraska 68822
(308) 872-6407

In the sandhills area of southeastern Nebraska, the lodge is surrounded by pine, spruce, and locust
trees. The emphasis here is on
country fare and lifestyles. The
lodge offers three comfortable
rooms. Breakfast is served beside a
large bay window offering views of
sunrises and outdoor life.

Rhubarb Sour Cream Coffee Cake

- ½ cup sugar
- ½ cup chopped walnuts
- 1 tablespoon margarine
- 1 teaspoon ground cinnamon
- ½ cup shortening
- 1½ cups firmly packed brown sugar
- 1 egg
- 2 cups all-purpose flour
- 1 teaspoon baking powder
- ¼ teaspoon salt
- 1½ cups chopped rhubarb
- 1 cup sour cream

In a small bowl mix the sugar, walnuts, margarine, and cinnamon until crumbly. Set
aside.

In a large bowl cream the shortening,
brown sugar, and egg. Stir in the flour, baking
powder, and salt. Fold in the rhubarb and
sour cream. Spread into a 9 x 13-inch pan.
Sprinkle the crumbly mixture on top. Bake in
a 350° oven for 45 minutes.

MAKES 8 SERVINGS.

Apple Pecan Pancakes

- 1 cup all-purpose flour
- 2 tablespoons firmly packed brown sugar
- 2 teaspoons baking powder
- ½ teaspoon salt
- ½ teaspoon ground cinnamon
- 2 egg yolks
- ¾ cup plus 2 tablespoons milk
- 1 teaspoon vanilla extract
- ½ cup finely chopped peeled tart apples
- ½ cup finely chopped pecans
- 2 egg whites
   Apple Spice Syrup (recipe follows)

In a large bowl combine the flour, brown
sugar, baking powder, salt, and cinnamon.
Stir in the egg yolks, milk, and vanilla. Add
the apples and pecans. In a separate bowl
beat the egg whites until stiff. Fold the egg
whites into the batter. Pour ¼ cup of batter at
a time onto a hot greased griddle, turning
when cooked on 1 side. Serve with Apple
Spice Syrup.

MAKES ABOUT 4 SERVINGS.

Apple Spice Syrup

- ¼ cup firmly packed brown sugar
- 2 tablespoons cornstarch
- ¼ teaspoon ground allspice
- ⅛ teaspoon grated nutmeg
- 1¾ cups apple juice or cider

In a saucepan combine all ingredients and
bring to a boil over medium heat until slightly
thick. Serve hot.

MAKES ABOUT 1¾ CUPS SYRUP.

Pine Cone Lodge

Peach Breakfast Parfait

- 4 fresh peaches, peeled and pitted
- 1 tablespoon lemon juice
- 1½ cups nonfat plain yogurt
- 1 8-ounce can crushed pineapple, drained
- 1½ tablespoons honey
- 1 cup low-fat granola
   Mint leaves (optional)

In a blender or food processor purée 2
peaches with the lemon juice. Add the yogurt,
pineapple, and honey. Slice the remaining
peaches. In 4 parfait glasses, layer the sliced
peaches with the yogurt mixture and granola,
ending with peach slices. Serve chilled. Garnish with mint leaves, if desired.

MAKES 4 SERVINGS.

Kirschke House Bed and Breakfast

1124 West Third Street
Grand Island, Nebraska 68801
(308) 381-6851

*F**ounded by railroad companies during the 1860s, the town of Grand Island takes its name from a forty-mile-long island created by the forked channels of the Platte River. Otto Kirschke, one of the town's earliest settlers, built this two-story brick house. Victorian through and through, it features a windowed cupola, turret, open oak staircase, and stained glass windows. Guest rooms mirror the spirit of the architecture with lace, period furnishings, and antique accessories. There is a hot tub in the lantern-lit brick wash house.*

Breakfast Pasta

4   *ounces spaghetti*
1   *egg*
2   *teaspoons butter*
¼   *cup grated cheese of your choice*
    Pepperoni, ham, or crumbled bacon
    (optional)

In a stock pot cook the pasta in boiling water until tender. Drain and return to the pan. In a small bowl beat the egg and pour over the hot pasta along with the butter and most of the cheese. Place over low heat and stir until the egg is set on the pasta and the cheese is melted.

Pepperoni, ham, or crumbled bacon may be added, if desired.

Top each serving with more grated cheese.
MAKES 2 SERVINGS.

French Onion Bread

1   *package active dry yeast*
¼   *cup warm water (105 to 110°)*
1   *envelope onion soup mix*
2   *cups water*
2   *tablespoons sugar*
1   *teaspoon salt*
2   *tablespoons grated Parmesan cheese*
2   *tablespoons shortening (or oil)*
6   *to 6½ cups sifted all-purpose flour*
    Cornmeal
1   *egg white*
1   *tablespoon water*

In a cup soften the dry yeast in ¼ cup of warm water (or compressed yeast in lukewarm water). In a saucepan combine the soup mix and 2 cups of water and bring to a boil. Cover, reduce the heat, and simmer for 10 minutes. Add the sugar, salt, cheese, and shortening and stir. Cool to lukewarm. Stir in 2 cups of the flour and beat well. Stir in the yeast mixture. Add enough of the remaining flour to make a moderately stiff dough. Turn out onto a lightly floured surface. Cover and let rest for 10 minutes. Knead until smooth and elastic, 8 to 10 minutes. Place in a lightly greased bowl, turning once to grease the surface. Cover and let rise in a warm place for 1 hour and 15 minutes to 1 hour and 30 minutes.

Punch down and divide in half. Cover and let rest for 10 minutes. Shape in 2 long loaves, tapering the ends. Place on a greased baking sheet sprinkled with cornmeal. Gash the tops diagonally, ⅛- to ¼-inch deep. Cover and let rise until almost doubled, about 1 hour. Bake in a 375° oven for 20 minutes.

In a small bowl beat the egg white with 1 tablespoon of water. Brush the mixture on the bread. Bake 10 to 15 minutes longer or until done.
MAKES 2 LOAVES.

Kirschke House

Sowbelly Bed and Breakfast Hide-a-way

407 Sowbelly Road
Harrison, Nebraska 69346
(308) 668-2537

*T**his B&B offers an unusual and educational experience in that it is partially earth-sheltered for energy efficiency. A huge glass-door wall opens the home to a cascade of light, while a sunny patio invites enjoyment of the outdoors.*

Mother's Coffeetime Doughnuts

1   *cup sugar*
4   *cups all-purpose flour*
5   *teaspoons baking powder*
1   *teaspoon salt*
½   *teaspoon grated nutmeg (optional)*
3   *eggs*
1   *cup milk*
1   *teaspoon vanilla extract*
3   *tablespoons butter melted*
    Oil for deep-frying

In a large bowl sift the dry ingredients together. In a separate bowl beat the eggs well. Add the milk and vanilla. Add the liquid mixture to the dry ingredients. Add the melted butter and mix. Roll out on a floured surface, cut, and deep-fry in 375 to 400° oil.
MAKES ABOUT 30 DOUGHNUTS.

Delicious Sowbelly Pancakes

    2   cups all-purpose flour
    1   teaspoon baking soda
    ¼   cup sugar
    1   teaspoon salt
    1   teaspoon baking powder
    2   cups buttermilk
    2   eggs
    2   or 3 tablespoons thick cream (or
        melted butter)

In a large bowl combine all ingredients together except the cream and beat just until moistened. Do not overbeat. Fold in the cream. Fry on a hot griddle.

MAKES 6 TO 8 SERVINGS.

Biscuits in Minutes

    8   cups all-purpose flour
    1   cup instant nonfat dry milk
    ¼   cup baking powder
    4   teaspoons salt
    1⅓ cups shortening (or lard)

In a large container combine all ingredients and mix thoroughly. Cover with a tight-fitting lid and store in the refrigerator.

In a large bowl combine 3 cups biscuit mix and ⅔ to ¾ cup of water. Mix until a dough forms. Turn onto a floured surface and knead 10 times. Roll to ½ inch or more thickness. Cut with a biscuit cutter and place on a greased baking sheet. Bake in a 400° oven for 15 minutes.

MAKES 15 BISCUITS.

Special Barbecue Sauce from Sowbelly

    1¼ cups firmly packed brown sugar
    1¾ cups catsup
    1   tablespoon dry mustard
    2   tablespoons Worcestershire sauce
    2   tablespoons vinegar
    2   cups strong brewed coffee
    ½   cup finely chopped onions
    1   teaspoon salt
    ¼   teaspoon pepper
        Dash Tabasco sauce

In a saucepan combine all ingredients. Bring to a boil and cook for 10 minutes, stirring often, as it scorches easily. Reduce the heat and simmer 30 minutes more, stirring occasionally. Simmer longer to thicken more. It gets better the longer it cooks.

Recipe for 1 gallon: 5 cups of firmly packed brown sugar, 52 ounces of catsup, ¼ cup of dry mustard, ½ cup of Worcestershire sauce, ½ cup of vinegar, 8 cups of strong brewed coffee, 2 cups of diced onion, 4 teaspoons of salt, ½ teaspoon of pepper, and a shake or 2 of Tabasco sauce. Proceed as if cooking a quart.

MAKES 1 QUART.

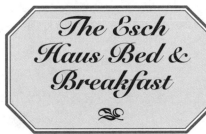

The Esch Haus Bed & Breakfast

≈

Route 1, Box 140
Spalding, Nebraska 68665
(308) 497-2628

A modern home with five comfortable guest rooms, this B&B benefits from its A-frame construction that allows for a very large loft consisting of three bedrooms and a large living area. Guest rooms on this level offer beautiful views. An inviting deck for lounging and enjoying the sun wraps around the house. The Esch Haus is about one hour from Burwell where the Nebraska Rodeo is held each year.

Ham and Cheese Custard Pie

    1   cup all-purpose flour
    ¼   cup rye flour
    ¼   teaspoon salt
    ¼   cup cold butter or margarine
    2   tablespoons lard or soft shortening

    1   egg yolk
    2   tablespoons cold water
    ··································
    2   tablespoons butter
    ½   pound thinly sliced baked or boiled
        ham, cut in thin strips
    ¼   cup grated Parmesan cheese
    5   eggs
    1   cup sour cream
    ½   teaspoon salt
        Pinch ground nutmeg
        Pinch white pepper

In a medium bowl combine the flours and salt. Cut in the butter and lard with a pastry blender or 2 knives until the mixture resembles coarse crumbs. Add the egg yolk and water and stir with a fork until the dough forms a ball. Roll out and place in a 9-inch pie plate.

In a large frying pan melt the butter over medium heat and cook the ham, stirring occasionally, until lightly browned. Spoon evenly into the rye pastry shell. Sprinkle with cheese.

In a medium bowl beat the eggs well with the sour cream, salt, nutmeg, and white pepper. Pour over the ham and cheese. Bake in a 450° oven for 10 minutes. Reduce the heat to 350° and continue baking until the crust is nicely browned and the filling is just set in the center, 20 to 25 minutes. Let stand about 3 minutes before cutting in wedges to serve.

MAKES 6 SERVINGS.

Blue Cheese Quiche

    ½   cup crumbled blue-veined cheese
    1   cup grated Swiss cheese
    1   unbaked 9-inch pie shell
    2   tablespoons butter
    2   shallots, finely chopped (or ¼ cup
        finely chopped mild onion)
    4   eggs
    1   cup half and half
    1   teaspoon Dijon mustard
    ½   teaspoon salt
    ¼   teaspoon each paprika and ground
        nutmeg
        Pinch white pepper

Distribute the cheeses evenly in the pie shell. In a small frying pan over medium heat melt the butter and cook the shallots until soft and golden. Sprinkle the mixture over the cheese.

In a medium bowl beat the eggs with the half and half, mustard, salt, paprika, nutmeg, and white pepper. Pour over the cheese. Bake in a 450° oven for 10 minutes. Reduce the heat to 350° and bake for 20 to 25 minutes, until the quiche is nicely browned and just set in the center.

Let stand about 3 minutes before cutting in wedges to serve.

MAKES 6 SERVINGS.

Fresh Salmon Quiche

- ½ **pound salmon fillet**
- 2 **tablespoons butter**
- 4 **green onions, thinly sliced**
- ½ **teaspoon dried dillweed**
- 1 **9-inch unbaked pie shell**
- 1 **cup grated Swiss cheese**
- 3 **eggs**
- 1 **cup half and half**
- ¾ **teaspoon salt**
- ½ **teaspoon dry mustard**
   Pinch white pepper

In a medium frying pan place the salmon on a rack over about ½ inch of water. Bring the water to a boil. Cover, reduce the heat, and steam until the salmon flakes when tested with a fork, 6 to 8 minutes. Remove and discard the skin, and flake the salmon gently.

In a medium frying pan over moderate heat melt the butter and cook the green onions until limp and bright green, about 3 minutes. Remove the pan from the heat. Mix in the salmon and dillweed. Distribute the salmon mixture evenly in the pie pastry. Sprinkle with cheese.

In a medium bowl beat the eggs with the half and half, salt, dry mustard, and white pepper. Pour the egg mixture over the cheese. Bake in a 450° oven for 10 minutes. Reduce the heat to 350° and bake for 20 to 25 minutes until the crust is nicely browned and the filling is just set in the center.

Let stand about 3 minutes before cutting in wedges to serve.

MAKES 6 SERVINGS.

NEVADA

Deer Run Ranch Bed and Breakfast

5440 Eastlake Boulevard
Carson City, Nevada 89704
(702) 882-3643

*T*his casual, contemporary ranch
house uses a passive-solar design to
stay warm in winter and cool in the
high-desert summer. At the same
time, it clearly reflects its southwestern heritage. The views of the
desert and Sierras from the guest
rooms are extraordinary. Legend
has it that spring-watered gardens
here produced food for the miners
working the Comstock lode
during the late 1800s.

Deer Run Ranch

Pears with Gorgonzola Cream

½ **cup water**
½ **cup Marsala wine**
½ **cup sugar**
1 **small piece lemon zest (yellow zest only)**
3 **large hard-ripe Bartlett or Anjou pears, halved, peeled and cored**
....
½ **cup grated or broken-up Gorgonzola cheese**
½ **cup cream cheese**
¼ **cup sugar**
½ **cup heavy cream**
....
½ **cup slivered almonds**

In a saucepan combine the water, wine, ½
cup of sugar, and lemon zest, and bring to
boil. Reduce the heat to barely simmering.
Carefully place the pears in the hot liquid and
simmer until just tender. Do not overcook.
Chill pears in the poaching liquid for several
hours or overnight.

Soften the cheeses together in the
microwave or a warm spot in the kitchen. In
a small bowl cream the cheeses together. Add
¼ cup of sugar and the cream, and whip until
smooth. Chill.

Toast the almonds lightly. Set aside. In 6
pretty serving glasses or bowl place a pear
half. Place a dollop of cheese topping on
each pear and sprinkle with the toasted
almonds.
MAKES 6 SERVINGS.

Coffee Custard

3 **cups milk**
½ **cup ground coffee**
4 **eggs**
½ **cup sugar**
Pinch salt

In the top of a double boiler over simmering
water scald the milk with the coffee. Steep for
30 minutes. Strain through several layers of
fine cloth or cheesecloth.

In a separate bowl beat the eggs. Add the
sugar and a pinch of salt.

Add the egg mixture to the milk mixture
with a whisk.

Butter 6 individual custard cups. Pour the
milk mixture into the prepared cups and
place the cups in a large flat pan that has a
double layer of paper towels in the bottom.
Add boiling water until it is about three-
fourths of the way up the sides of the cups.
Bake in a 350° oven for about 40 minutes,
until firm and a knife inserted in the center
comes out clean. Serve warm or cold.
MAKES 6 SERVINGS.

Winter Creek Inn

1201 Highway 395 North
Carson City, Nevada 89704
(702) 849-3500

The inn provides delightful views of Nevada's pine and fir-forested mountains. In scenic Washoe Valley, the inn places its guest within easy reach of Reno and the popular Lake Tahoe area. Weddings, receptions, and banquets are welcome.

Super Natural Bran Muffins

1   *cup whole bran cereal (not flakes)*
1   *cup boiling water*
½   *cup oil*
1¼   *cups firmly packed brown sugar*
¼   *cup honey*
2   *eggs*
2   *cups buttermilk*
2½   *cups whole wheat flour*
2½   *teaspoons baking soda*
1   *teaspoon salt*
2   *cups granola*
  Raisins or nuts (optional)

In a large bowl combine the bran and water, and let stand for 10 minutes.

Add the oil, sugar, and honey, and mix well. Beat in the eggs. Add the buttermilk and then the remaining ingredients. Cover and refrigerate for several hours or overnight. The batter can be frozen or kept in the refrigerator for up to 4 weeks. (Though they always are eaten before!)

Spoon into greased muffin cups as needed. Bake in a 400° oven for 22 to 25 minutes. These are fairly healthy and hearty muffins, freshly baked without having to make up a new batter daily!

MAKES 3 TO 4 DOZEN.

Strawberry-Nut Bread

3   *cups all-purpose flour*
1   *teaspoon baking soda*
1   *teaspoon salt*
1   *tablespoon ground cinnamon*
2   *cups sugar*

1¼   *cups oil*
2   *cups thawed or fresh strawberries*
1¼   *cups chopped nuts*

In a large bowl sift together the flour, baking soda, salt, cinnamon, and sugar. In a separate bowl combine the remaining ingredients. Add the liquid mixture to the dry ingredients, mixing just until moistened. Pour into 2 oiled and floured 5 x 9-inch loaf pans. Bake in a 350° oven for 55 to 60 minutes (or less in smaller pans). Cool for 5 minutes, then remove from the pans.

This is a moist, sweet bread that is wonderful for strawberry lovers.

MAKES 2 LOAVES.

Haus Bavaria

Haus Bavaria

593 North Dyer Circle
Incline Village, Nevada 89450
(702) 831-6122(800) 731-6222

Rustic wood paneling and a delightful collection of German bric-a-brac fills this B&B with Alpine charm. Each of the five upstairs guest rooms offer breathtaking views. The emerald shores of Lake Tahoe are only a short walk away. Summer guests will want to take advantage of the private beach and swimming pool.

Grandmother Alice's Cormeal Pancakes

3   *cups buttermilk*
1½   *teaspoons salt*
1½   *teaspoons baking soda*
1½   *cups all-purpose flour*
1½   *cups cornmeal*
3   *teaspoons baking powder*
3   *eggs*
4   *to 5 tablespoons bacon fat*

In a large bowl combine the buttermilk, salt, and baking soda, and stir until the mixture forms bubbles around the edges. Mix in the remaining ingredients. Laddle the batter onto a hot, greased griddle grill. Turn when bubbles appear and the edges are set.

MAKES ABOUT 8 SERVINGS.

NEW HAMPSHIRE

Adair
Country Inn

80 Guider Lane
Bethlehem, New Hampshire 03574
(603) 444-2600

T*he Adair has played host to presidents, Supreme Court justices, and a host of other notables, and it is not hard to see why. The inn, built during the "Roaring" 1920s, is elegant and the surrounding country magnificent. Mt. Washington, with its famous cog railroad, is nearby, as is Franconia Notch, with its rushing streams. The village of Bethlehem has its own attractions—plenty of fresh air and a dozen quaint little shops.*

New Cumberland Baked Pears

8   ripe Bosc pears
½   cup currants
⅓   cup finely chopped pecans
⅓   cup firmly packed brown sugar
2   tablespoons lemon juice
¼   cup water
¼   cup corn syrup

Peel the pears, leaving the stems on. Core the pears from the bottom. In a small bowl combine the currants, nuts, brown sugar, and lemon juice. Fill the cavity of each pear with mix. In a separate bowl combine the water and corn syrup. Place the pears upright in custard cups and pour 1 tablespoon of syrup on each. Cover with foil. Bake in a 350° oven for about 1 hour and 30 minutes, until easily pierced with a fork. The time will vary depending on the ripeness of the pears.
MAKES 8 SERVINGS.

Baked Egg Blossoms

24   7-inch squares phyllo (6 per custard cup)
¼   cup melted butter, approximately
1   cup shredded Cheddar cheese
4   eggs
⅓   cup cream
1   teaspoon dry mustard
¼   teaspoon salt
    Dash cayenne pepper (or Tabasco sauce)

Grease 4 standard custard cups. For each "blossom" assemble 6 phyllo squares in layers, buttering each layer and rotating to form a star. Create the "blossom" by pressing the layered phyllo squares gently into each cus-

Adair Country Inn

tard cup. Place the cheese gently on the bottom. Break each egg over the cheese and stir gently to break the yolk. In a bowl mix the cream and spices together. Pour 1½ tablespoons of cream mixture over each egg, stirring gently. Place the custard cups on a baking sheet. Bake in a 350° oven for 20 minutes, until golden brown. Remove from the cup and serve immediately (eggs will fall if not served right away).

Variations: Mix in a little chopped spinach, scallions, and/or mushrooms with cheese. Can be made and served in greased ramekins if phyllo is not available.

Note: It is very important to work with phyllo quickly, otherwise it will dry and become brittle. Half a package of phyllo (14 x 18 inches) will make 10 "blossoms."
MAKES 4 SERVINGS.

Red Hill Inn

RFD #1, Box 99M
Center Harbor, New Hampshire 03226
(603) 279-7001

O*ld-fashioned comfort and charm are the rules at the Red Hill Inn, located on sixty heavily wooded acres near Squam Lake. The majestic White Mountains form the horizon to the north, while Lake*

Winnipesaukee is only five miles south. The twenty-three guest rooms vary in size and appointments. Most have fireplaces, and some offer private balconies. An 1850s era farmhouse and a number of separate cottages are also available.

Cranberry Muffins

- 2 **cups all-purpose flour**
- 1 **cup sugar**
- ½ **teaspoon salt**
- ½ **cup oil**
- 2 **eggs**
- 1 **cup milk (or half and half)**
- 1 **teaspoon almond extract**
- 1 **cup cranberries**

In a large bowl mix the flour, sugar, and salt. Add the oil, eggs, milk, and almond extract, and mix well. Fold in the cranberries stirring carefully as to not break the cranberries. Fill muffin cups lined with paper liners three-quarters full. Bake in a 375° oven for 30 minutes.

MAKES 1 DOZEN.

Cranberry Pepper Glaze

- 2 **12-ounce packages cranberries**
- 2 **large green bell peppers**
- 2 **cups sugar**
-   **Dash salt**
- 2 **cups water**

Chop the cranberries and green peppers into small pieces. In a saucepan combine the cranberries, peppers, sugar, salt, and water and bring to a low boil, stirring constantly. Reduce the heat and simmer for 5 to 10 minutes, until the cranberries and peppers are soft. Serve with chicken, duck or turkey as a glaze.

Note: The unused portion can be cooled, refrigerated, and used as a relish on sandwiches.

MAKES ABOUT 8 CUPS.

MapleHedge

MapleHedge B & B Inn

Main Street
Charlestown, New Hampshire 03603
(603) 826-5237

Almost two-and-one-half centuries old, the MapleHedge has history on its side. This impressive home has commanded strategic Great Road— now Route 12—since Charlestown was a remote Colonial frontier outpost. In many ways, its attractions are much the same as they were then: comfort, the nearby lakes, the fresh mountain berries, the sugar maples, and the solid wood furnishings—known now as antiques. Each of the five guest rooms has its own theme. For instance, the Cobalt Room features a collection of cobalt blue glass.

Dutch Babies

- 1 **egg**
- ¼ **cup all-purpose flour**
- ¼ **cup milk**
- 1 **tablespoon butter or margarine**
-   **Confectioners' sugar**
-   **Lemon wedges**

In a blender combine the egg, flour, and milk. In a ramekin melt the butter or margarine. Pour the batter into the ramekin. Bake in a 450° oven for 12 minutes or until

the sides have puffed up and browned. Quickly remove from the oven and sprinkle with confectioners' sugar. Serve with lemon wedges and encourage guests to squeeze lemon on top.

Variation: Fill with fresh berries.

MAKES 1 SERVING.

California Scramble

-   **Butter**
- 3 **eggs, beaten**
- ⅓ **cup mixed vegetables (scallions, green bell peppers, broccoli, grated carrots, mushrooms or anything on hand), finely chopped**
- ¼ **cup diced cheese (Cheddar, Jack, or Swiss)**
-   **Sour cream for garnish**

In a hot buttered pan scramble the eggs with the vegetables until the eggs are almost set. Add the diced cheese and stir until it starts to melt. Place on a plate and garnish with a dollop of sour cream.

MAKES 1 SERVING.

Darby Field Inn

Bald Hill Road, P.O. Box D
Conway, New Hampshire 03818

At the end of a road atop of a mountain stands Darby Field Inn, a unique haven best described as "a rambling mountain retreat." Surrounded by the beautiful White Mountains, it offers an array of guest rooms, each distinctively

Darby Field Inn

decorated. Guests enjoy the field-stone fireplace in the living room, the large pool, and the beautiful gardens. Nearby activities include mountain climbing, skiing, canoeing, biking, sledding, shopping, and riding a scenic train.

Chicken Marquis

- 1 **pound boneless, skinless breast of chicken**
- 1 **tablespoon all-purpose flour**
- 1 **tablespoon clarified butter or olive oil**
- 2 **cloves garlic, sliced**
- 4 **cups thinly sliced mushrooms**
- 3 **tablespoons Tamari soy sauce**
- ¼ **cup dry white wine**
- 3 **tablespoons fresh lemon juice**
- 3 **tablespoons chicken stock or water**
- 1½ **cup fresh tomatoes, cubed**
- ¼ **cup sliced scallions**

Lightly flatten the chicken with the side of a meat mallet or heavy cleaver and slice into bite-sized pieces. Assemble all other ingredients, as this dish is very quick to cook.

Dredge the chicken in flour and lightly shake off the excess. In a large frying pan or cast-iron skillet heat the clarified butter or oil and the garlic, and sauté the chicken over medium heat until the chicken is browned on 1 side. Flip the chicken and add the mushrooms, stirring with a wooden spoon until the mushrooms begin to darken. Then add the liquid ingredients and stir for about 2 minutes while the pan sauce thickens. Add the tomatoes and scallions, stir briefly, and serve.
MAKES 4 SERVINGS.

Curried Apple and Zucchini Soup

- 2 **tablespoons margarine or butter**
- 1 **large onion, chopped**
- 1 **apple, peeled, cored and chopped**
- 1 **to 2 teaspoons curry powder**
- 4 **cups chicken stock**
- ¼ **cup uncooked rice**
- 2 **cups diced, unpeeled zucchini (½ pound)**
- ½ **teaspoon salt**
- 1 **cup milk**

In a large saucepan melt the butter and sauté the onion and apple until soft. Sprinkle with curry powder and cook, stirring constantly, for a few seconds. Pour in the chicken stock and bring to a boil. Add the rice, zucchini, and salt. Cover and cook for about 3 minutes until the rice and zucchini are tender. Pour into a blender and blend until smooth and return to the pan. Add the milk and heat through. Serve hot.
MAKES 8 SERVINGS.

Spinach Pie with Almonds

- 3 **tablespoons butter**
- ¼ **cup all-purpose flour**
- 1 **cup milk**
- ¼ **cup heavy cream**
  - **Dash salt**
  - **Dash white pepper**
  - **Dash nutmeg**
- 2 **bags fresh spinach, washed, stemmed, and blanched (or 1 12-ounce box frozen)**
- ⅓ **cup almonds, sliced or slivered, and toasted**
- 1 **cup grated Swiss cheese**
- 6 **5-inch squares puff pastry, thawed**
- 1 **egg, beaten**

Prepare the Béchamel sauce. In a small saucepan over medium heat melt the butter. Add the flour and stir with a spoon or whisk for a couple of minutes without browning the mixture. Add the milk and whisk constantly, until the mixture thickens. Add the cream, salt, pepper, and nutmeg. The mixture should be a thick consistency. Cool.

Chop the cooked spinach and make sure it is drained thoroughly. In a mixing bowl combine the cooled Béchamel sauce and the spinach. Add the almonds and Swiss cheese, and mix together. Taste for seasoning and adjust. If the mixture is too loose to hold its shape, add some fresh white breadcrumbs to thicken. Place about ¼ cup of spinach mixture in the center of each puff pastry square and, with a pastry brush, brush the outside edges of each square with the beaten egg. Fold each corner into the middle, overlapping and sealing with fingers. Turn each pie over so the seam is on the bottom and place on a lightly greased baking sheet. Brush the top of each pie with egg wash. Bake in a 425°

oven for 10 to 12 minutes or until golden brown. Serve immediately.
MAKES 6 SERVINGS.

Eaton Center, New Hampshire 03832
(603) 447-2880

Amidst 450 acres of fields, woods, ponds, and mountains, its horses, cows, pigs, geese, llamas, peacocks, chickens, and kittens, the Rockhouse offers the unique combination of vacation atmosphere and actual working farm. The delicious food here can best be described as "American." Special activities include Saturday night steak roast on the back lawns, weekly hayride for kids, and Swift River cookout and swim.

Walnut Coffee Cake

- ⅓ **cup ground walnuts**
- 3 **tablespoons firmly packed brown sugar**
- 2 **cups sifted all-purpose flour**
- 1¾ **cups sugar**
- 1 **teaspoon baking powder**
- 1 **teaspoon baking soda**
- ½ **teaspoon salt**

....

- 1 **egg, beaten**
- 1 **cup buttermilk**
- ⅔ **cup melted butter, cooled**
- 1 **teaspoon vanilla extract**

Butter a 2½-quart tube pan, and coat it with ground walnuts and brown sugar. In a medium bowl sift the sifted flour, sugar, baking powder, soda, and salt. In a separate bowl combine the egg, buttermilk, melted butter and vanilla. Quickly add the dry ingredients to the liquid mixture, beating until the batter is smooth. Pour into the prepared pan. Bake in a 350° oven for 1 hour, until a tester inserted in the cake comes out clean. Let the cake cool completely and then turn it out on a rack.

Note: Sometimes the cake may drop in the middle. Don't worry, it still cuts well, and tastes the same. It freezes well.

MAKES 8 SERVINGS.

Light Coffee Cake

½   cup butter or margarine
1   cup sugar
2   egg yolks, beaten
2   cups all-purpose flour
2   teaspoons baking powder
½   teaspoon salt
    Grated zest of 1 lemon
⅔   cup raisins
2   egg whites
    Cinnamon-confectioners' sugar mixture
    Melted butter

In a large bowl cream together the butter and sugar. Add the beaten egg yolks and mix well. In a small bowl sift together the flour, baking powder, and salt. Add the dry ingredients to the batter, folding in gently. Fold in the grated lemon zest and raisins. In a bowl beat the egg whites until stiff. Fold into the batter carefully, avoiding over-beating. Pour into 2 greased 8-inch round cake tins. Sprinkle the top with a mixture of cinnamon and confectioners' sugar. Dot with melted butter. Bake in a 325° oven for about 20 minutes, or until a cake tester inserted in the center comes out clean.

MAKES 8 TO 12 SERVINGS.

Salmon Casserole

2   cups herb-seasoned croutettes
1   16-ounce can salmon, drained and flaked
2   cups grated Cheddar cheese
4   eggs, beaten
2   cups milk
    Salt and pepper to taste
    Medium white sauce

In a 1-quart casserole alternate the croutettes, salmon, and Cheddar cheese in layers. In a medium bowl combine the eggs and milk and season to taste. Pour the liquid over the salmon. Bake in a 350° oven for

about 1 hour, until a knife inserted in the center comes out clean.

Serve with a medium white sauce with hard-boiled egg added, seasoned with Worcestershire, mustard, and salt.

MAKES 4 SERVINGS.

Blanche's

Blanche's Bed and Breakfast
❧

*351 Easton Valley Road
Franconia, New Hampshire 03580
(603) 823-7061*

The guest rooms here are named after wildflowers—Pansy, Lilac, Periwinkle, Wild Rose, and Sunflower—and the decor is colorfully matched to those themes. For instance, guests in the Lilac room will find these flowers forever abloom on the glazed walls. The house looks out on Kinsman Ridge, which is traversed by the Appalachian Trail.

Honey Nut Rolls

1   loaf frozen bread dough, defrosted
¼   cup firmly packed dark brown sugar
¼   cup honey
½   teaspoon ground cinnamon
½   cup chopped walnuts or pecans
2   tablespoons butter, melted

Roll out the dough to a 12 x 18-inch rectangle. Sprinkle the sugar over dough. Roll up like a jelly roll beginning with the long side.

Slice into 1½-inch pieces. Spread the honey in a 9-inch pie plate. Sprinkle cinnamon and nuts over the honey. Arrange the dough pieces in a pie plate evenly spaced. Cover with a dish towel and leave in a warm place to rise overnight.

In the morning brush the risen dough with melted butter. Bake in a 325° oven for 25 minutes. Invert onto a plate and serve hot.

MAKES 1 DOZEN.

Raised Waffles

1   package active dry yeast
½   cup warm water (105 to 110°)
2   cups milk, warmed
½   cup butter, melted
1   teaspoon salt
1   teaspoon sugar
2   cups all-purpose flour
2   eggs
¼   teaspoon baking soda
    Maple syrup

In a large bowl sprinkle the yeast over the water. Dissolve for 5 minutes.

Add the milk, butter, salt, sugar, and flour, and beat with a wire whisk until smooth. Cover the bowl with plastic wrap and let stand overnight at room temperature.

Just before cooking the waffles, beat in the eggs. Add the soda and stir until well blended. The batter will be very thin. Pour about ½ cup into a very hot waffle iron. Bake until golden and crisp.

Serve with pure maple syrup. The batter keeps well for several days in the refrigerator.

MAKES ABOUT 8 SERVINGS.

Pumpkin Ginger Muffins

1   15-ounce can unsweetened pumpkin
2   cups firmly packed dark brown sugar
1   cup butter, melted
4   large eggs
½   cup apple cider
3½   cups unbleached flour
2   teaspoons baking soda
2   teaspoons baking powder
4   teaspoons ground cinnamon
5   teaspoons ground ginger
1   teaspoon grated nutmeg
½   teaspoon ground cloves
1   cup crystallized ginger, finely chopped

Grease 28 muffin cups. In a large bowl combine the pumpkin, brown sugar, and butter, and stir until blended. Add the eggs and mix until smooth. Add the cider. In a separate bowl sift the flour, soda, baking powder, cinnamon, ginger, nutmeg, and cloves. Gradually stir the dry ingredients into the pumpkin mixture. Mix until thoroughly combined. Fold in the ginger. Fill the prepared muffin cups two-thirds full. Bake in a 350° oven for 20 to 25 minutes.

MAKES 28 MUFFINS.

Maple Yogurt

- 2 **cups plain low-fat yogurt**
- 2 **tablespoons maple syrup**
- 2 **teaspoons vanilla extract**

In a serving bowl mix all ingredients together until smooth. Serve as an accompaniment to fresh fruit. Small bits of toasted coconut, ground nuts, and/or granola can also be sprinkled on as garnishes.

MAKES 2 CUPS.

Cornmeal Rye Pancakes

- 1 **cup yellow cornmeal**
- ½ **cup rye flour**
- 1 **teaspoon salt**
- ½ **teaspoon baking soda**
- 3 **tablespoons melted butter (optional)**
- 2 **cups Almond Milk (recipe follows)** **Maple syrup**

In a large mixing bowl mix the cornmeal, rye flour, salt, and soda together. Stir in the butter and Almond Milk, and mix until blended. Heat a griddle to medium hot and film with grease. Spoon on about 2 tablespoons batter for each pancake. Cook until a few bubbles form on top, turn the pancakes over, and cook until the bottoms are lightly browned. Serve hot with pure maple syrup.

MAKES ABOUT 6 TO 8 SERVINGS.

Almond Milk

- ½ **cup shelled raw almonds**
- 1 **tablespoon maple syrup**
- 2 **cups water**

In a blender grind the almonds to a fine powder. Add the maple syrup and 1 cup of water. Blend for 1 to 2 minutes. With the blender running on high, add the remaining cup of water. Blend for 2 minutes. This will keep in the refrigerator for 4 to 5 days.

MAKES 2 CUPS.

Bungay Jar

❧

P.O. Box 15, Easton Valley Road
Franconia, New Hampshire 03580
(603) 823-7775

---

*I*n his poetry, Robert Frost described lonely roads and other tranquil scenes in New Hampshire's Easton Valley. The Bungay Jar started out as an 1800s English-style barn, but Yankee ingenuity and a lot of hard work has made it over into a truly unique B&B. With its decks, balconies, massive hand-hewn beams, and two-story common room, it has character to spare. A collection of antique toys adds to the fun. A stone terrace leads by a lily pond to a hidden river in the woods.

Oatmeal Pancakes

- 2 **cups old-fashioned oats (not instant)**
- 2 **cups milk**
- 2 **eggs**
- ½ **cup all-purpose flour**
- 1 **teaspoon baking powder**
- ½ **teaspoon baking soda**
- 2 **to 4 tablespoons melted butter**

In a large bowl combine the oats and milk. Cover and leave on the counter overnight.

In the morning add the remaining ingredients. Cook on a hot griddle.

Note: Serve with sautéed apples, raisins, maple syrup, and ham.

MAKES 4 TO 5 SERVINGS.

Crustless Veggie Quiche

- 4 **eggs**
- ¾ **cup biscuit mix**
- ½ **cup shredded Gruyère or Swiss cheese**
- ¼ **cup shredded Cheddar cheese**
- 1 **cup shredded carrots**
- 1 **zucchini, chopped**
- 1 **red bell pepper, chopped** **Dill** **Thyme** **Basil**

Mix together and pour into a buttered 9-inch pie pan. Bake in a 350° oven for 30 minutes.

MAKES 4 SERVINGS.

Lovett's Inn

❧

Route 18, Profile Road
Franconia, New Hampshire 03580
(800) 356-3802

---

*T*he inn, dating to 1794, is listed on the National Register of Historic Places. Close by is Franconia Notch State park, a wonderland of narrow passages cut through solid stone by rushing mountain streams. An early example of the central chimney Cape Cod style, the house has stood on Lafayette Brook for more than 200 years. Guest rooms and cottages are decorated and furnished in Colonial fashion.

Lovett's Inn

Cold Bisque of Fresh Spinach Soup

1   **tablespoon butter**
1   **shallot, chopped**
1   **pound fresh spinach, washed**
1½   **quarts cream of chicken soup (diluted)**
1   **cup light cream**
1   **cup Noilly Prat dry vermouth**
    Sour cream

In a saucepan melt the butter and sauté the shallot until tender. Add the spinach, cover, and cook only until tender. Remove the pan from the heat. Add the chicken soup and cream, and refrigerate until chilled.

Add the vermouth. Serve in chilled cups with a spoonful of sour cream on each.

Note: This soup may be served hot as well, but only ½ cup vermouth should be used. Otherwise it is far too strong.

MAKES 4 SERVINGS.

Stillmeadow Bed and Breakfast

❧

545 Main Street, P.O. Box 565
Hampstead, New Hampshire 03841
(603) 329-8381

*F*or those with a taste for the formal graces of nineteenth-century living, the Stillmeadow is an excellent choice. The living and dining areas are meticulously furnished and decorated, while guest rooms are comfortable and romantically old fashioned. Just across the meadow are the grass courts of the Hampstead Croquet Association.

Stillmeadow Fruit Sundae

    Melon balls
    Sliced strawberries
    Mandarin oranges
    Kiwi fruit, sliced
    Sliced grapes
    Sliced bananas
    Grape Nuts cereal
    Star fruit or cherries or red grapes

In individual glass compote dishes arrange the melon balls, strawberries, oranges, kiwi, and grapes until almost filled. Circle around edge with bananas, and sprinkle with Grape Nuts. Garnish with star fruit, cherries, or red grapes.

Stillmeadow Stuffed French Toast

1   **loaf cinnamon bread (Pepperidge Farm is best)**
   Cream cheese, softened
   Cinnamon-sugar
6   **eggs**
½   **cup maple syrup**
¾   **cup milk**
   Apple Compote (recipe follows)

Remove the crusts from as many slices of bread needed to fit in the bottom of a greased 9 x 13-inch casserole dish. Spread with cream cheese, and sprinkle with cinnamon-sugar. Top with matching slices of crustless bread.

In a medium bowl beat the eggs, syrup, and milk until frothy. Pour over the bread. Don't worry if it floats! Refrigerate overnight.

Bake in a 350° oven for about 35 minutes, until puffed and golden. Top with Apple Compote and serve with extra syrup.

MAKES 6 SERVINGS.

Apple Compote for French Toast

4   **to 5 tart apples**
2   **tablespoons butter**
¼   **cup firmly packed brown sugar**
¼   **teaspoon cinnamon**

Stillmeadow

¼   **teaspoon ginger**
¼   **cup apple juice**

Cut the apples into wedges and peel. In a skillet brown the butter with the brown sugar, cinnamon, and ginger. Sauté the fruit, adding apple juice to moisten.

Serve over French toast or on the side.

Variation: Add nuts, raisins, or cranberries.

MAKES 4 SERVINGS.

Hancock Inn

Hancock Inn

❧

33 Main Street
Hancock, New Hampshire 03449
(603) 525-3318
(800) 525-1789

*T*he Hancock has operated as an inn since 1798, the same year the U.S. Constitution was written and approved and only six years after the end of the Revolutionary War. President Franklin Pierce was a frequent guest here. The inn has been restored and remains true to its origins. The eleven guest rooms have four-poster beds, antique appointments, custom-made quilts, and plenty of individual personality. The inn is not the only old structure hereabouts. Every building on Hancock's Main Street has earned a listing on the National Register of Historic Places.

Liver Pâté

- 3   pounds chicken livers
- ½   cup stick of butter
- ½   teaspoon cayenne pepper
- ½   teaspoon nutmeg
- ½   cup crushed fresh pineapple
     Chopped red onions for garnish

In a stock pot boil the chicken livers in simmering water. Don't overcook. In a food processor combine the livers and remaining ingredients. Chill and serve with a garnish of chopped red onions.

MAKES 6 TO 8 SERVINGS.

New England Baked Beans

- 2   pounds dried pea or navy beans
- 4   teaspoons dry mustard
- 1   cup firmly packed brown sugar
- ¼   cup pure maple syrup
- ¾   cup molasses
- ½   teaspoon salt
- 1   medium yellow onion, diced
- 2   tablespoons cider vinegar
- 9   ounces thickly sliced bacon (fatty end or lean salt pork)

In a large pot soak the beans overnight in enough cold water to cover the beans by 2 inches.

Drain the beans. Add fresh water to cover and bring to a boil. Cover the pot, reduce the heat, and simmer for 45 minutes, or until tender. Preheat the oven to 325 degrees.

Drain the beans when tender and the skins have just barely started to break. Reserve the liquid. In a medium bowl combine the mustard, sugar, maple syrup, molasses, salt, onion, and vinegar. Mix in the beans.

Cut the bacon into ½-inch cubes. In the bottom of a 3-quart bean pot place half of the bacon. Add the beans to the pot. Pour the reserved cooking liquid over the beans, covering the beans by ½ inch. Top with the remaining bacon and salt pork. Cover the pot tightly. Bake in a 325° oven for 5 to 6 hours, until the beans are tender but not mushy. Check the beans every hour and add bean liquid a little at a time to the keep beans moist. If the bean liquid runs out, use tap water.

MAKES 6 TO 8 SERVINGS.

Hancock Creamy Caesar Dressing

- 4   eggs
- 3   cups oil
- ½   cup white vinegar
- 1   teaspoon salt
- 1   teaspoon white pepper
- ½   teaspoon garlic powder
- ½   teaspoon oregano
     Juice of 1 lemon
- ½   cup grated Parmesan cheese
- 2   ounces anchovies, chopped finely

In a large bowl whip the eggs with an electric mixer or hand blender until light and frothy. Slowly add the oil and mix well. Slowly add the remaining ingredients.

MAKES ABOUT 4 CUPS.

Colby Hill Inn

≈

The Oaks
P.O. Box 778
Henniker, New Hampshire 03242
(603) 428-3281

Centerpiece of the inn is a rambling 1795 farmhouse surrounded by six acres of fields and gardens. With its weathered barns, restored carriage house, and winter skating rink, the property looks very much as it did during the late eighteenth century. Each of the sixteen guest rooms has its own personality, some have fireplaces. Guests are

Colby Hill Inn

welcome to stroll the grounds, pause on the gazebo, or gather around a fire in the parlor.

Pork Medallions with Glazed Apples and Cider Sauce

- 2   cups cider
     Pinch cinnamon
     Pinch cloves
     Pinch nutmeg
     Pinch ginger
- ½   teaspoon Dijon mustard
- 2   ounces low-salt chicken broth
     Cornstarch
- 1   tablespoon water
- 1   tablespoon firmly packed brown sugar
- 1   Red Delicious apple, sliced
- 2   6-ounces pork tenderloin medallions
     Salt and pepper
     Flour
- 1   tablespoon butter
- 1½   ounces applejack brandy
- ¼   cup glazed apples

In a saucepan combine the cider, spices, and mustard. Bring to a simmer and reduce to 1 ½ cups. Add the chicken broth. Thicken slightly with cornstarch and water.

In a skillet heat the water and brown sugar. Add the apple slices and let sit for 2 to 3 minutes.

Trim the excess fat and tissue from the tenderloin. Slice on the bias into ¼-inch pieces. Pound lightly between plastic wrap. Season with salt and pepper. Lightly dust and flour.

In a sauté pan melt the butter. Add the pork and brown 1 minute on each side. Remove the pan from the heat and add the applejack brandy. Add the cider sauce and add the glazed apples.

MAKES 2 SERVINGS.

Poached Salmon with a Mustard Cream Sauce

- 2   7 ounce salmon fillets
     Salt and pepper
- 3   ounces dry white wine
- 1   tablespoon dry vermouth
- 1   teaspoon chopped shallots

4   teaspoons Dijon mustard
¼   cup heavy cream
    Chopped chives, for garnish

Season the salmon fillet with salt and pepper. In a 9-inch sauté pan combine the white wine, vermouth, shallots, mustard, and cream, and bring the mixture to a simmer. Add the fillets, cover, and cook for 10 to 15 minutes.

Remove the fillets. Reduce the sauce and add the chives, salt, and pepper to taste.

Spoon over the salmon filets.

MAKES 2 SERVINGS.

Tomato Basil Vinaigrette

⅛   cup Dijon mustard
2   ounces balsamic vinegar
1   clove garlic, minced
1   teaspoon shallots
3   ounces olive oil
3   ounces oil
¼   cup canned whole peeled tomatoes, seeded, chopped, juice reserved
1   tablespoon fresh basil, chopped
    Salt and fresh cracked black pepper to taste
1   tablespoon sugar

In a container with a tight-fitting lid whisk together the mustard, vinegar, garlic, and shallots. Slowly add the oils and then the tomatoes, basil, salt, pepper, and sugar. Add ⅛ cup of reserved tomato juice.

MAKES 2 CUPS.

Fudge Walnut Truffle Tort

1¾   cups finely chopped walnuts
⅔   cup sugar
¼   cup butter or margarine, melted
....
2   cups heavy cream
16   ounces good-quality semisweet chocolate, chopped
....
1   16-ounce box brown sugar
2   cups heavy cream
2   cups butter or margarine
2   teaspoons vanilla extract
....
    Fresh whipped cream

In a 10-inch tart pan with a removable bottom combine the walnuts, sugar, and melted butter, and press into the bottom and sides.

Bake in a 350° oven for about 15 minutes or until lightly browned. Cool.

In a saucepan over medium heat bring 2 cups of cream just to a full boil. Remove the pan from the heat and stir in the chocolate. Stir until completely melted. Pour into cooled crusts and refrigerate until set.

In a saucepan combine the brown sugar, 2 cups of cream, and 2 cups butter. Bring the mixture to a slow boil. Cook until all of the sugar is dissolved. Add the vanilla. Keep the caramel sauce warm.

Garnish each serving of tort with dollop of whipped cream and a drizzle of warm caramel sauce.

Note: This is The Colby Hill Inn's favorite sauce. It's unbeatable on ice cream with toasted pecans!

MAKES 6 TO 8 SERVINGS, ABOUT 1 PINT OF SAUCE.

The Inn on Golden Pond

The Inn on Golden Pond
❧

Route 3, P.O. Box 680
Holderness, New Hampshire 03245
(603) 968-7269

*T**he inn is a gracious country home built in 1879 amid some of New England's most picturesque countryside. It sits on fifty-five mostly wooded acres with plenty of trails for strolling and appreciating nature. Nearby Squam Lake was the setting for the well known film* On Golden Pond, *hence the name of the inn. There are seven spacious guest rooms and two extra large suites, all with private baths, furnished to provide maximum comfort.*

Rhubarb Muffins

1¼   cups firmly packed brown sugar
1   egg
½   cup oil
2   teaspoons vanilla extract
1   cup sour milk (milk with 1 tablespoon lemon juice)
1½   cups diced rhubarb
2½   cups all-purpose flour
1   teaspoon baking soda
1   teaspoon baking powder
½   teaspoon salt
1   tablespoon butter, melted
⅓   cup sugar
2   teaspoons cinnamon

In a large bowl combine the brown sugar, egg, oil, vanilla, and sour milk. Add the rhubarb. In a separate bowl stir together the flour, soda, baking powder, and salt. Add the dry ingredients to the batter, and stir until just blended. Fill greased muffin cups two-thirds full of batter. In a small bowl combine the butter, sugar, and cinnamon. Sprinkle the mixture over the batter. Bake in a 400° oven for 20 to 25 minutes.

MAKES 20 MUFFINS.

Puffed Apple Pancake

6   eggs
1½   cups milk
1   cup all-purpose flour
3   tablespoons sugar
1   teaspoon vanilla extract
½   teaspoon salt
½   teaspoon ground cinnamon
½   cup butter
3   large tart apples, peeled and sliced thin
¼   cup firmly packed brown sugar
    Maple syrup

In a medium mixing bowl mix the eggs, milk, flour, sugar, vanilla, salt, and cinnamon. In a 9 x 13-inch glass baking dish melt the butter. Add the sliced apples. Pour the batter over the apples and sprinkle with brown sugar. Bake in a 425° oven for 25 minutes. Serve hot with maple syrup.

MAKES 6 SERVINGS.

Ellis River House

Ellis River House

❧

Route 16, P.O. Box 656
Jackson, New Hampshire 03846
(603) 383-9339, (800) 233-8309

*T*he *Ellis River, originally a country farm, has almost 400 feet of river frontage. It offers twenty guest rooms, some with canopied beds or four-posters. Choose from rooms with fireplaces, whirlpool baths, and private balconies. All rooms have mountain views. Also available is a riverfront cottage with fireplace.*

Barry's Beer Bread

    3   cups all-purpose flour
    3   teaspoons baking powder
    1   cup sugar
    2   teaspoons salt
    ¼   cup oil
    1   12-ounce can beer (less 1 sip for
        baker)

In a large bowl mix together all ingredients until moistened. Pour the batter into a greased 5 x 9-inch loaf pan. Bake in a 400° oven for 1 hour.
MAKES 1 LOAF.

Mushroom Sauté

    ¼   cup butter
    1   shallot, chopped
    2   cups sweet vermouth
    8   ounces fresh mushrooms, sliced

In a sauté pan melt the butter and sauté the chopped shallot. Increase the heat and add the vermouth. Reduce the pan liquid to half. Add the mushrooms and sauté until tender.
MAKES 4 SERVINGS.

Blueberry Pancakes

    1½ cups all-purpose flour
    4   teaspoons baking powder
    ½   teaspoon salt
    2   eggs
    1   cup milk
    5   tablespoons shortening
    2   cups blueberries

In a large bowl mix the flour, baking powder, and salt. In a separate bowl mix the eggs, milk, and shortening. Add the dry ingredients to the liquid mixture, mixing with a whisk. Gently fold in the blueberries. Cook on a greased, hot and smoking griddle.
    Variation: Try raspberries or sliced bananas.
MAKES 4 SERVINGS.

The Benjamin Prescott Inn

❧

433 Turnpike Road
Jaffrey, New Hampshire 03452
(603) 532-6637

*S*urrounded *by the rolling hills and quiet country roads of southern New Hampshire, this Greek Revival inn lulls its guests with a feeling of timelessness. Built in 1853 by a pioneer family whose ancestors came here on foot, it has the solid feeling of permanence. Guests will enjoy the spacious rooms as well as the nooks and crannies of this old house. The Colonial village of Jaffrey's Corner is perfect for those who like to explore the past.*

Fresh Apple and Walnut Honey Cake

    3   eggs
    ½   cup oil
    ½   cup honey
    2   teaspoons vanilla extract
    2   cups all-purpose flour
    1½ cups sugar
    1   teaspoon baking powder
    1   teaspoon baking soda
    2   teaspoons ground cinnamon
    3   tart apples, peeled, cored, and thinly
        sliced
    2   cups coarsely chopped walnuts
        Confectioners' sugar
        Apple juice

In a large bowl combine the eggs, oil, honey, and vanilla, and beat well. In a separate bowl combine the flour, sugar, baking powder, soda, and cinnamon. Add the dry ingredients to the liquid mixture and mix just until blended. Do not overmix. Stir in the apples and walnuts. Pour the batter into a buttered 12-cup bundt pan. Bake in a 350° oven for about 60 to 65 minutes, or until a cake tester inserted in the center comes out clean. Allow to cool in the pan. When cool, drizzle the top with confectioners' sugar thinned with apple juice.
MAKES 24 SLICES.

Corn Flake Waffles

    1¼ cups all-purpose flour
    ½   cup crushed corn flakes
    ¼   cup crushed bran flakes
    1   tablespoon baking powder
    ¼   teaspoon salt
    2   beaten egg yolks
    1¾ cups milk
    ½   cup oil
    2   egg whites

In a large bowl combine the flour, corn flakes, bran flakes, baking powder, and salt. In a small bowl combine the egg yolks, milk, and oil. Stir into the flour mixture. In a medium bowl beat the egg whites until stiff peaks form. Fold the liquid mixture into the dry ingredients. Pour the batter onto a lightly greased waffle iron. Close the lid quickly and do not open during baking.
MAKES 6 WAFFLES.

Raspberry Butter

- 1   *cup unsweetened raspberries*
- 2   *tablespoons water*
- 1   *tablespoon sugar (or 1 envelope Sweet 'N Low)*
- ½   *cup butter, softened*
- 2   *tablespoons confectioners' sugar*
- 1   *teaspoon Chambord (blackberry liqueur)*
- ¼   *teaspoon lemon juice*

In a small saucepan combine the raspberries, water, and sugar. Bring the mixture to a boil and cook over medium heat until syrupy, stirring frequently, about 5 minutes. Strain through a sieve to remove the seeds. Cool. Process with the remaining ingredients until smooth and mixed well. Transfer to small ramekins. Cover and chill.

This can be prepared 1 day ahead. It will separate if kept too long. Bring to room temperature before serving.

MAKES 6 TO 8 SERVINGS.

Eggs in a Nest

- 1   *15-ounce can corned beef hash*
- 1   *cup French-fried thin potato sticks*
- 4   *large eggs*
      Ketchup

The night before cut the can of hash into 4 patties. For each patty, spread ¼ cup potato sticks onto a flat place or piece of waxed paper. Place the patty on top and press the sticks into the bottom and sides. With the back of a spoon, make a 2-inch wide and 1-inch deep indention on top. Lift the nests onto a greased cookie sheet. Bake in a 400° oven for 25 to 30 minutes, until slightly browned. Cool. Refrigerate overnight.

The next morning, warm in a 250° oven. Poach the eggs for 3½ minutes and place in warm nests. Serve with ketchup.

MAKES 4 SERVINGS.

The Benjamin Prescott Inn

The Jefferson Inn

Route 2
Jefferson, New Hampshire 03583
(603) 586-7998

An 1896 Victorian-style farmhouse, the Jefferson Inn sits at the foot of Mt. Starr King at the edge of New Hampshire's spectacular Presidential Range. Every window offers a lovely mountain view. The inn is named for Thomas Jefferson, and several of the guest rooms have names that remind visitors of the nation's third president. The Monticello Room features a turret and romantic four-poster bed. This area is a hiker's dream with mountains and forests on all sides.

Stuffed Orange Marney French Toast

- 8   *eggs*
- 4   *egg whites*
- 1   *cup sugar*
- ½   *teaspoon salt*
- 6   *cups milk*
- 2   *tablespoons Grand Marnier*
      Grated zest of 2 oranges
- 2   *loaves French bread*
- 12   *ounces cream cheese*
- 1½   *teaspoons vanilla extract*
- ¾   *cup finely chopped walnuts*
      Apricot or blueberry preserves
      Confectioners' sugar
      Fresh bananas or blueberries
      Grated nutmeg

In a large mixing bowl whisk together the eggs, egg whites, sugar, and salt. Add the milk, Grand Marnier, and orange zest. (This is a terrific late evening task because you can justify pouring yourself a small snifter of Grand Marnier to sip while you work. Just to insure it hasn't gone bad since the last time you used it, of course!) Whisk again and set

aside. Slice the bread into 1-inch-thick slices. Cut a slice in the middle for a pocket. The easiest way is to cut the end off. Make a cut about three-fourths of the way through the loaf about ½-inch from the end, then make the next cut all the way through the bread about 1-inch from the end. (Continue the same routine for both loaves.) In a small bowl beat the cream cheese and vanilla until light and creamy. Stir in the walnuts. Fill each bread pocket with about 2 teaspoons of the cream cheese mixture and 1 teaspoon of preserves. Dip each slice into the egg mixture until the bread is saturated, about 1 minute. Arrange on a baking sheet and refrigerate overnight.

In the morning, lightly oil a hot griddle (about 350°). Slowly brown both sides of the bread for about 2 to 3 minutes per side. Remove and place on a clean baking sheet that has been sprayed with cooking spray. Sprinkle with nutmeg, if desired. Bake in a 425° oven for 20 minutes. Arrange on a warm platter. Top with fresh banana slices or blueberries and sprinkle with confectioners' sugar.

MAKES 12 SERVINGS.

Easy Cranberry Pie

- 2   *cups fresh cranberries*
- 1   *unbaked 9-inch pie shell*
- ⅓   *cup sugar*
- ¼   *cup chopped walnuts*
- 1   *egg*
- 6   *tablespoons melted butter*
- ½   *cup sugar*
- ½   *cup all-purpose flour*
      Vanilla ice cream (optional)

Spread the cranberries over the bottom of the pie shell. Sprinkle with ⅓ cup of sugar and the nuts. Set aside. In a small bowl beat the egg well. Add the melted butter and ½ cup of sugar, and stir with a wooden spoon until thoroughly mixed. Add the flour and continue to stir until smooth. Pour the batter gently over the cranberries. Use a rubber spatula to carefully spread the topping smoothly out to the edge of the pie shell. Bake in a 350° oven for approximately 45 to 55 minutes, or until the crust is golden brown. Serve warm with real vanilla ice cream, or cool and serve later.

MAKES 8 SERVINGS.

Jefferson

Aebelskivers

3 **eggs, separated**
2 **teaspoons sugar**
½ **teaspoon salt**
2 **cups buttermilk**
2 **cups all-purpose flour**
1 **teaspoon baking soda**
1 **teaspoon baking powder**
   Butter
   Applesauce, preserves, or cooked berries
   Confectioners' sugar
   Maple syrup

In a large bowl beat the egg yolks until bright yellow. Add the sugar, salt, and buttermilk. In a separate bowl sift together the flour, soda, and baking powder. Stir the dry ingredients into the egg yolk mixture. In a medium bowl beat the egg whites until stiff. Fold the egg whites into the batter. Heat an aebelskiver pan over low heat. Drop about ½ teaspoon of butter into each cup. Fill the cups with batter. Spoon ½ teaspoon of applesauce or preserves or berries into center of each cup, then barely cover with a few drops of batter. (Use the back of the spoon to cover the filling.) Cook until bubbly. Turn carefully with a 6- to 8-inch wooden skewer. If they are hard to turn, they are either too ready or not ready enough. Keep rolling them around in the cup until they are evenly browned on all sides. Sprinkle with confectioners' sugar and serve with warm maple syrup.

Note: The most important part is to not get discouraged if they don't come out exactly right the first time. Get the feel for the temperature and the timing. Also, the center cup always cooks a little faster than the others, so try to turn it first.
MAKES ABOUT 21 "SKIVERS."

Orange Wreath Cake

¾ **cup sugar**
1 **tablespoon grated orange zest**

2 **8-ounce packages Pillsbury Orange Sweet Rolls (8 rolls per package)**
¼ **butter, melted**
¼ **cup shredded coconut**
¼ **cup chopped walnuts**

In a small bowl combine the sugar and orange zest. Open the sweet rolls, set aside the icing, and separate the rolls. Lightly grease a 10-inch glass pie plate. Dip each roll in melted butter, then roll in the sugar mixture. Arrange the rolls in a circle on the outer edge of the bottom of the pie plate, overlapping like fallen dominoes. Bake in a 425° oven for 20 minutes, or until golden brown and bubbly. Remove from the oven. Melt the icing in the microwave for 15 seconds. Drizzle melted icing over the hot wreath cake. Sprinkle with coconut and nuts. Serve hot.
MAKES 8 TO 9 SERVINGS.

Peep-Willow Farm
❧

51 Bixby Street
Marlborough, New Hampshire 03455
(603) 876-3807

Horse lovers will be right at home here. This is an eighteen-acre working farm where thoroughbreds are born, raised, and trained for competition. Guests are welcome to help with the chores as well as talk, pet, and feed the livestock. The colonial-style farmhouse has lots of wood accents and some antiques.

Apple, Cheese, and Walnut Salad

3 **tablespoons olive oil**
2 **tablespoons balsamic vinegar**
2 **teaspoons Dijon mustard**
1 **clove garlic, crushed**
   Freshly ground black pepper to taste
....
8 **cups torn mixed salad greens**

2 **medium Fuji apples, halved, cored, and sliced ⅛-inch thick**
⅓ **cup crumbled blue cheese**
¼ **cup coarsely chopped toasted walnuts**

In a small bowl whisk together the olive oil, vinegar, mustard, garlic, and pepper. In a small bowl combine the salad greens, apple slices, and vinaigrette. Toss to coat. Sprinkle the blue cheese and walnuts over the top.
MAKES 6 SERVINGS.

Peep-Willow Farm Linguine

Toss walnuts, black olives, green olives with pimentos on linguine which was simmered in garlic and oil. Add white wine, tamari, red pepper flakes, and parsley if desired. Sprinkle with Parmesan cheese. Quick and fabulous, a totally different pasta.

Shrimp with Bowtie Pasta

1 **16-ounce box bowtie pasta**
1½ **teaspoons butter**
2 **tablespoons olive oil**
3 **to 4 tomatoes, chopped**
3 **cloves garlic**
¾ **pound mushrooms, sliced or quartered**
1 **cup white wine**
½ **to 1 teaspoon basil**
½ **to 1 teaspoon oregano**
   Salt and black pepper to taste
   Few dashes red pepper, to taste
2 **pounds shrimp, cleaned**
2 **tablespoons all-purpose flour**
¼ **cup water**
¼ **cup chopped fresh parsley**
   Grated Parmesan cheese

Cook the pasta according to the package directions.

In large frying pan heat the butter and oil and sauté the tomatoes, garlic, and mushrooms until soft. Add the wine, basil, oregano, salt, peppers, and shrimp and sauté for about 10 minutes, until the shrimp is cooked enough. In a small bowl mix the flour and water. Stir into the sauce and simmer for about 5 minutes, until slightly thickened.

Add the parsley. Pour the shrimp mixture over the pasta. Serve with Parmesan cheese.
MAKES 4 TO 6 SERVINGS.

24 Maple Street
Milford, New Hampshire 03055
(603) 654-6440

The inn takes it unusual name from the Bible story in which Abraham finds a ram caught in a thicket to use as a substitute sacrifice for his son Isaac. This old Victorian mansion makes a very nice substitute indeed for more ordinary lodgings. Its carefully restored interior features crystal chandeliers, a hand-carved fireplace, and a dining room decorated with lovely blue delft tiles.

Parmesan Dill Bread

4   cups all-purpose flour
1   tablespoon baking powder
⅓   cup instant dried onions
2   teaspoons salt
½   cup sugar
½   cup shortening
1   egg
2   cups milk
     Grated Parmesan cheese
     Dill

In a large bowl combine the dry ingredients. Cut in the shortening until pea-sized crumbs form. In a measuring cup whisk the egg and add the milk. Stir into the dry ingredients until moistened. Pour into a greased 9 x 13-inch pan. Sprinkle with grated Parmesan cheese and dill. Bake in a 350° oven for about 1 hour, or until light golden and firm in the center.

Recipe can be halved for an 8-inch square pan.

MAKES 8 SERVINGS.

Dutch Spice Bread

2   eggs
2   cups sugar
½   cup firmly packed brown sugar
1   cup oil
2   teaspoons baking soda
2   cups sour milk (milk with 2 tablespoons lemon juice)
4   cups all-purpose flour
1   teaspoon grated nutmeg
3   teaspoons ground cinnamon
1   teaspoon ground cloves
1   teaspoon salt
1   teaspoon baking powder

In a large bowl combine the eggs, sugars, and oil with an electric mixer until blended. In a small bowl dissolve the soda in the sour milk. In a separate bowl combine the dry ingredients. Add the remaining dry ingredients to the liquid mixture alternately with the sour milk. Pour into 2 buttered and floured 5 x 9-inch loaf pans. Bake in a 350° oven for 1 hour or until a toothpick inserted in the center comes out clean.

Variations: Add 1 cup of floured raisins and/or 1 cup of chopped nuts or ½ cup of poppy seeds.

MAKES 2 LOAVES.

Sugar Shack Pork

2   cups maple syrup
½   cup vinegar
3   tablespoons Dijon mustard
1   tablespoon dry mustard
1   teaspoon pepper
....
1   cup light cream
1   tablespoon dry mustard
1   tablespoon all-purpose flour
½   cup maple syrup
½   teaspoon salt
2   egg yolks
¼   cup vinegar
1   tablespoon Dijon mustard

In a saucepan combine 2 cups of maple syrup, ½ cup of vinegar, 3 tablespoons of Dijon mustard, 1 tablespoon of dry mustard, and pepper. Simmer for about 20 minutes.

In a small pan mix the cream and 1 tablespoon of dry mustard. Whisk in the remain-

ing ingredients and bring to a boil. Boil gently and whisk for 1 minute.

Use the glaze for pork roast or individual pork tenderloins, basting every 15 to 20 minutes until done. Serve with mustard cream sauce.

The sauce is also excellent with scallops or chicken.

MAKES ABOUT 2½ CUPS OF GLAZE AND 2 CUPS OF SAUCE.

The Inn at New Ipswich

11 Porter Hill Road, P.O. Box 208
New Ipswich, New Hampshire 03071
(603) 878-3711

Built in 1790, this farmhouse is filled with early American charm. A classic red barn adjoins the house, and the grounds are bordered by stonewalls and gardens with fruit trees. The six guest rooms are comfortably furnished, and the screened porch has lots of wicker.

Breakfast Ambrosia Puff

16   slices white sandwich bread, crusts removed, bread cut in small cubes
1   20-ounce can crushed pineapple in its own juice, drained and juice reserved
2   11-ounce cans mandarin oranges, drained and juice discarded
     Orange juice
12   jumbo eggs
½   teaspoon almond extract
¼   teaspoon ground ginger
3   tablespoons sugar

1½ cups half and half
½ cup shredded coconut
¼ cup sliced almonds

Spread the bread cubes evenly in a greased 9 x 13-inch baking pan or dish. Distribute the drained crushed pineapple evenly over the bread. Cut the drained oranges into thirds and spread over the pineapple. In a 2-cup measure combine the pineapple juice and enough orange juice to equal 1½ cups of liquid. Set aside. In a large bowl whisk the eggs, almond extract, ginger, and sugar, blending well. Add the reserved pineapple/orange juice and the half and half, stirring well. Pour the egg and juice mixture slowly over the bread cubes, covering all of the bread. Cover the dish and refrigerate for 8 hours or overnight.

Before baking, let stand for 30 minutes at room temperature. Uncover and sprinkle with coconut and almonds. Bake in a 350° oven for 45 to 50 minutes or until puffed and the center is set. Allow 5 minutes before cutting.

Note: Good with brown-and-serve breakfast sausage.

MAKES 12 SERVINGS.

Cranberry-Walnut Brunch Cake

2 cups all-purpose flour
2 teaspoons baking powder
1 cup sugar
¼ teaspoon salt
1 teaspoon ground cinnamon
¼ teaspoon grated nutmeg
½ cup chopped walnuts

3 jumbo eggs
½ cup oil
1 16-ounce can whole berry cranberry sauce

¼ cup firmly packed brown sugar
¼ cup quick oats
¼ cup finely chopped walnuts

In a large bowl mix flour, baking powder, sugar, salt, cinnamon, nutmeg, and walnuts together. In a medium bowl beat the eggs and oil together. Stir the cranberry sauce until smooth and broken up and add it to the egg mixture. Mix well. Add the liquid mixture to the dry ingredients and mix with a spoon until smooth. Pour into a greased 9 x 13-inch

baking pan. In a small bowl mix the remaining ingredients and sprinkle over the batter. Bake in a 350° oven for 40 to 45 minutes. Serve warm.

MAKES 8 SERVINGS.

Blueberry Sauce

3 cups blueberries
2 tablespoons lemon juice
½ cup light corn syrup
¾ cup sugar
2 teaspoons cornstarch
   Dash salt
¼ teaspoon ground cinnamon
   Dash ground cloves

In a saucepan mix the blueberries, lemon juice, and corn syrup. Add the remaining ingredients. Cook and stir until the mixture boils. Simmer until thickened well, mashing the berries. Serve hot.

Serve with pancakes or waffles.

MAKES 4 CUPS.

Pleasant Lake Inn

125 Pleasant Street, P.O. Box 1030
New London, New Hampshire 03257
(603) 526-6271, (800) 626-4907

The Pleasant Lake Inn dates to 1790 when it was built as a Cape-style farmhouse. It was converted in 1787 for use as a summer resort. Located down a winding back road, it is tucked away in one of the Sunapee-Dartmouth region's most beautiful valleys. For those who like the outdoors, there is plenty to do here, for instance, swimming, boating, and fishing in the nearby lake, hiking and skiing on forest trails, and golfing and tennis in the excellent local facilities.

Leek Soup

6 cups sliced leeks (about 2 pounds)
2 cups peeled and cubed potatoes
   (about 4 medium)
1 large onion, chopped
2 stalks celery, chopped
1½ quarts chicken broth
½ teaspoon fresh ground pepper
   Salt to taste (about 2 teaspoons)
   Milk or cream

In a large pot combine the leeks, potatoes, onion, and celery. Add the chicken broth. Bring the broth to a boil. Cover and cook until the vegetables are tender. Remove the vegetables and place in a food processor. Process until pulp. Put through a food mill if necessary. Return to the broth and add the seasonings.

At this point the soup may be refrigerated or frozen. Before serving, add milk or cream to the desired thickness, reheating the soup in a double boiler.

MAKES 4 SERVINGS.

Poppy Seed Dressing

⅔ cup vinegar
3 tablespoons chopped onion
1 cup sugar
½ cup honey
2 teaspoons dry mustard
2 teaspoons salt
2 cups canola oil
3 tablespoons poppy seeds

In a blender purée the vinegar and onion. Add the sugar, honey, mustard, and salt, and blend well. With the blender running, add the oil slowly and continue blending until thick. If the oil does not blend in, remove to a bowl and whisk. Add the poppy seeds. Store in a covered container in the refrigerator.

MAKES ABOUT 3 CUPS.

Pleasant Lake Inn

Beef Tenderloin with Madeira Sauce

Madeira Sauce (recipe follows)

....

2   tablespoons clarified butter
2   tablespoons oil
8   6-ounce pieces beef tenderloin
1   teaspoon chopped garlic
1   teaspoon chopped shallots
¼   cup Madeira
¼   cup burgundy
1   pound fresh mushrooms, sliced

Prepare the Madeira Sauce and allow it to cool.

Heat a sauté pan until very hot, and add the butter and oil. Brown the steaks very well but still rare in the center. Place the steaks in 9 x 13-inch baking pan. Sauté the garlic and shallots in the same sauté pan, adding more butter and oil if needed. Add the wines, scraping the pan. Add the mushrooms and cook until lightly firm. Divide the mixture among the steaks.

Strain the Madeira Sauce and pour over the steaks. Bake in a 400° oven uncovered for 15 to 20 minutes for medium-rare. Spoon the sauce over steaks when serving.

MAKES 8 SERVINGS.

Madeira Sauce

3   tablespoons clarified butter
2   teaspoons chopped garlic
1   teaspoon chopped shallots
½   teaspoon cracked pepper
¼   cup burgundy
½   cup Madeira
4   cups beef gravy or brown sauce
2   teaspoons tomato paste
   Salt (optional)

In a skillet heat the butter and sauté the garlic, shallots, and pepper until lightly brown. Add the wines and cook until reduced by one-third. Add the remaining ingredients and simmer for 30 minutes. Add salt if needed.

MAKES 8 SERVINGS.

The Buttonwood Inn

The Buttonwood Inn

❧

Mt. Surprise Road, P.O. Box 1817
North Conway, New Hampshire 03860
(603) 356-2625, (800)258-2625

Situated about two miles from bustling North Conway, the inn is a quiet hideaway where guests enjoy the true New England countryside. The Mount Washington Valley, with its theaters, outlet shopping, and many other year-round activities, is only minutes away.

Mixed Grain and Wild Rice Cereal

2   cups water
½   cup wild rice (or brown rice)
6   cups water
½   cup pearl barley
½   cup steel-cut oats (or regular oats)
½   cup bulgur wheat
½   cup raisins
½   cup chopped pitted dates
¼   cup plus 2 tablespoons firmly
     packed dark brown sugar
3   tablespoons butter
¾   teaspoon salt
½   teaspoon ground cinnamon

In a saucepan bring 2 cups of water to a boil. Add the rice and simmer for 20 minutes. Drain.

Butter a 2½-quart ovenproof dish. In the prepared dish mix the rice with the remaining 6 cups of water. Stir in the remaining ingredients. Cover loosely with foil. Bake in a 375° oven until the grains are tender, water is absorbed, and cereal is creamy, stirring occasionally, about 1 hour and 30 minutes.

MAKES 4 TO 6 SERVINGS.

Chocolate Chip Sour Cream Coffee Cake

1   cup sugar
½   cup margarine
2   eggs, beaten
1   cup sour cream
2   tablespoons milk
2   cups all-purpose flour
1   teaspoon baking soda
1   teaspoon baking powder
1   6-ounce package chocolate chips
2   teaspoons ground cinnamon
½   cup sugar

Grease and flour a 9-inch tube pan. In a medium bowl cream together 1 cup of sugar and the margarine. Beat in the eggs until the mixture is light and fluffy. In a separate bowl combine the sour cream and milk and set aside. In a medium bowl sift together the flour, soda, and baking powder. Add the dry ingredients to the creamed mixture alternately with the sour cream until blended well. Fold in the chocolate chips. Spoon half of the batter into the prepared pan. In a cup combine the cinnamon and ½ cup of sugar. Sprinkle half of the mixture over the batter. Spoon in the remaining batter and sprinkle with the remaining cinnamon mixture. Bake in a 350° oven for 45 minutes. Cool on a wire rack.

MAKES 14 SERVINGS.

To-Die-For French Toast

1   cup firmly packed brown sugar
½   cup butter
2   tablespoons light corn syrup
2   tart apples, peeled and sliced
1   loaf French bread
5   eggs
1½   cups milk
1   teaspoon vanilla extract
   Spicy Apple Syrup (recipe follows)

In a saucepan cook the sugar, butter, and syrup until syrupy. Pour into a 9 x 13-inch baking dish. Spread the apple slices over this. Slice the bread into ¾-inch slices and place on top of the apple slices. In a medium bowl whisk together the eggs, milk, and vanilla. Pour over the bread. Cover and refrigerate overnight.

Bake in a 350° oven uncovered for 40 minutes. Serve with Spicy Apple Syrup.

MAKES 8 SERVINGS.

Spicy Apple Syrup

1   cup applesauce
1   10-ounce jar apple jelly
½   teaspoon ground cinnamon
⅛   teaspoon ground cloves
    Dash salt

In a small saucepan combine all ingredients. Cook over medium heat, stirring constantly, until the jelly melts and the syrup is hot.
MAKES ABOUT 2 CUPS.

Sunny Side Inn

Seavey Street, P.O. Box 557
North Conway, New Hampshire 03860
(603) 356-6239

From the inn it is only a five-minute walk to North Conway Village with its scenic railroad, golf course, skating rink, restaurants, and night clubs. The inn's nine guest rooms are each uniquely appointed with colorful quilts, coverlets, and wallpapers. The entrance to the peak-climbing Mt. Washington auto road is only about half an hour away.

Pear Cobbler

1½ tablespoons cornstarch
½   cup firmly packed brown sugar
½   cup water
4   cups sliced, peeled Bartlett pears
      (fresh and ripe)
1   tablespoon butter
....
1   cup sifted all-purpose flour
2   tablespoons sugar
1½ teaspoons baking powder
¼   teaspoon salt
½   to ¾ cup butter, softened
¼   cup milk
1   beaten egg
    Vanilla ice cream

In a saucepan combine the cornstarch, brown sugar, and water. Cook and stir until thickened. Add the pears and 1 tablespoon of butter and cook until the pears are hot, about 5 minutes. In a medium bowl sift the flour, sugar, baking powder, and salt. Cut in the butter until the mixture resembles coarse crumbs. In a cup combine the milk and egg. Add to the dry mixture and stir to moisten.

Pour the fruit filling into an 8-inch round baking dish. Spoon on biscuit topper in 6 mounds. Bake in a 400° oven for 20 to 25 minutes. Serve warm with ice cream.
MAKES 4 TO 6 SERVINGS.

Woodstock Inn

Woodstock Inn

135 Main Street
North Woodstock, New Hampshire 03262
(603) 745-3951

A century-old Victorian located in the heart of the White Mountains, the Woodstock Inn has nineteen individually appointed rooms, some with gas fireplace and Jacuzzis. The inn offers guests several dining options, including the candlelit Clement room, Woodstock Station—where Italian and other ethnic foods are featured—and the Woodstock Brewing company—a cozy pub and brewery.

New England Clam-stuffed Mushrooms

6   tablespoons melted butter
6   tablespoons finely diced sweet onion
2   stalks celery, finely diced
1   tablespoon fish base or bouillon
2   6-ounce cans chopped clams, well
      drained
½   cup cranberries, fresh or frozen
1½ tablespoons hot pepper relish
5   ounces Ritz cracker crumbs
2   ounces breadcrumbs
4   ounces Provolone cheese, sliced
30 medium mushrooms, stems removed

In a skillet melt the butter and sauté the onion and celery until soft. Add the fish base, clams, cranberries, and relish, and stir until just bubbling. Add the crackers and breadcrumbs, mixing until stiff. Stuff the mushrooms until full. Place the stuffed mushrooms in a baking dish. Lay Provolone cheese over the top. Bake in a 375° oven for 12 to 15 minutes or until tender.
MAKES 30 STUFFED MUSHROOMS.

Seafood-stuffed Mushroom Caps

1   stalk celery, finely diced
4   tablespoons finely chopped sweet
      onion
2   ounces finely diced shrimp
5   ounces diced scallops
1   6-ounce can chopped clams, drained
1½ teaspoons grated garlic
¼   cup sherry
    Dash lemon juice
2   tablespoons red pepper relish
2   8-ounce packages cream cheese
¼   teaspoon salt
30 medium mushrooms, stems removed

In a large pot steam the celery, onion, shrimp, scallops, clams, and garlic in sherry until reduced by one-half. Add the lemon juice, pepper relish, cream cheese, and salt. Let cool.

Fill the mushrooms. Place in a casserole dish. Bake in a 375° oven for 10 to 15 minutes until the stuffing is hot and the mushrooms are soft.
MAKES 30 STUFFED MUSHROOMS CAPS.

Spent Grain Bread

    2   tablespoons active dry yeast
    ¾   cup warm water (105 to 115°)
    ¼   cup butter
    ¾   cup milk
    1   cup apple juice
    ¼   cup molasses
    1   tablespoon salt
    ¼   cup sugar
    1½ cups spent grain, plus extra for top-
            ping
    1   cup wheat flour
        Cornmeal
    4   to 5 cups all-purpose flour
    ....
    1   egg
    1   tablespoon water

In a large mixing bowl sprinkle the yeast over the water and let dissolve. In a saucepan melt the butter with the milk. Remove the pan from the heat and add the apple juice, molasses, salt, and sugar. By now, the yeast has started to work, so add the milk mixture, then add the spent grain and wheat flour. Start to mix and add the all-purpose flour gradually until the dough is workable and is not sticky. Knead the dough for several minutes. Cover with a clean cloth and let rise until doubled in bulk.

Punch the dough down and divide into 2 loaves. Place on a baking sheet pan lined with parchment paper that is sprinkled with corn-meal. Cover and let rise until doubled in bulk.

In a small bowl beat the egg with 1 table-spoon of water. Brush the loaves with the egg wash and sprinkle with additional spent grain. Bake in a 325° oven for about 45 minutes.

Note: Spent grain would be available from local breweries or home brewers.

MAKES 2 LOAVES.

Woodbound Inn

Woodbound Inn

❧

62 Woodbound Road
Rindge, New Hampshire 03461
(603) 532-8341

O*n the shores of Lake Contoocook, the inn provides wonderful views of Mt. Monadnock. The inn complex includes the historic main building, an annex, and separate cabins. Golf on the inn's own 9-hole course, or play a few sets of tennis on the clay courts. It even has its own hiking trails.*

Toasted Sesame Chicken Dijon

    3   tablespoons toasted sesame seeds
            (see note, below)
    3   ounces crushed Rice Krispies
    6   6-ounce boneless, skinless chicken
            breasts
    ¼   cup mayonnaise
    ½   cup clover honey
    6   tablespoons Grey Poupon Dijon
            mustard

Mix 2 tablespoons of toasted sesame seeds with the crushed Rice Krispies to make the coating. Place 1 chicken breast at a time in a plastic bag, add the coating mix, and shake to coat thoroughly. Place the coated chicken breasts in a baking pan. Bake in a 350° convection oven.

In a small bowl mix the mayonnaise, honey, and mustard.

After about 5 minutes, generously spoon the honey mustard mixture onto the coated chicken. Continue to bake until the chicken is fully cooked and the sauce has turned golden and thickened. Garnish the top of the chicken breasts with reserved toasted sesame seeds.

Note: Toast the sesame seeds in a 350° oven until the seeds have turned golden brown. Honey Mustard Sauce ratio can be adjusted to taste. Most of our guests prefer a sauce with a little sweeter taste, thus the heavier emphasis on honey over mustard. The secret to the sauce is the mayonnaise; use a good quality.

MAKES 6 SERVINGS.

Woodbound's "Wicked Good" Baked Stuffed Mushrooms

    12 slices assorted dried breads and
            rolls (best to mix dark and light)
    36 to 48 large mushrooms (portabellas
            or extra large white button mush-
            rooms)
    1   large red onion, quartered
    4   stalks celery, with leaves
    1   pound sweet sausage
    1   teaspoon chopped garlic in oil
    ½   cup butter
    1   cup hot water
    1   tablespoon Minor's chicken base
    ¼   cup minced parsley
    ½   teaspoon pepper
    ½   teaspoon dried oregano
    ½   cup shredded Provolone cheese
        Marinara sauce (homemade or good-
            quality store-bought)
        Grated Parmesan cheese
        Red kale
        Chopped parsley

In a large bowl crush the bread into coarse crumbs and cubes. De-stem and scoop out the centers of the mushrooms, reserve. Place mushroom caps into a pan of simmering water for approximately 2 minutes. Immediately remove using a strainer, and chill under cold running water. Place the mushrooms upside-down in a pan to drain and refrigerate until chilled.

In a food processor coarsely chop the reserved mushroom centers, stems, red onion, celery, sausage, and garlic. In a large hot skillet melt the butter and sauté the mixture. In a measuring cup mix the hot water and chicken base. When the onions in the frying pan are opaque, add the chicken base mixture along with the chopped bread mixture, parsley, pepper, and oregano. Heat for 5 to 7 minutes and keep warm. The mixture should be fully cooked and moist. Stuff each mushroom with 2 to 3 pieces of shredded Provolone cheese. Using a small scoop add stuffing on top of the cheese, lightly packing it into each mushroom. Crown the stuffing with a generous scoop of homemade marinara. Bake in a 350° convection oven for approximately 7 minutes. Mushrooms will start to wilt and pucker at this time but still be firm. Finish by lightly dressing the mushrooms with fresh Parmesan cheese. Return them to the oven until the cheese is just melting, approximately 1 minute. Garnish with finely chopped red kale and parsley.

MAKES 3 TO 4 DOZEN.

Woodbound Inn's Herbed Homefries

    4   to 5 tablespoons butter or clarified
          butter
    4   to 6 russet potatoes, cut in wedges
    ¼   teaspoon granulated garlic
    ½   teaspoon onion powder
    1   teaspoon Lawry's Seasoning
    ¼   teaspoon fresh ground black pepper
    ½   teaspoon dried basil
    ½   teaspoon dried thyme

In a sauté pan over medium heat melt 3 to 4 tablespoons of butter or clarified butter, add the potatoes, and turn to coat with butter thoroughly. Add the granulated garlic, onion powder, and Lawry's Seasoning. Cook for 2 to 3 minutes to allow the potatoes to absorb the flavors, then add the black pepper, basil, and thyme. Cook over medium heat until lightly browned, continuing to add butter if necessary to keep moist. Finished potatoes should be lightly browned, not crispy.

Note: Adjust the seasonings to taste with an emphasis on the garlic and herbs.

MAKES 4 SERVINGS.

Woodbound's Maple Basil Candied Carrots

    2   pounds fresh carrots
    ¼   cup butter
    ½   teaspoon lemon juice
    ¼   cup firmly packed dark brown sugar
    ¼   cup maple syrup
    1   tablespoon dried basil

Peel and wash the carrots, and cut at 45 degree angles. Place in a pan of boiling water. Cover and simmer carrots for 10 minutes. Carrots should be tender but still firm. Drain the carrots and return to the pan. Over medium heat add the butter, lemon juice,

brown sugar, maple syrup, and basil. Turn carrots gently until all carrots are coated and heat approximately 5 minutes. The sauce will have thickened when finished.

MAKES 6 SERVINGS.

The Hilltop Inn

The Hilltop Inn

≈

Route 117
Sugar Hill, New Hampshire 03585
(603) 823-5695

Dating to 1895, the inn is situated in the village of Sugar Hill surrounded by the spectacular White Mountains. Guest rooms and common areas are furnished with solid but unusual antiques. Beds are covered with and-pieced quilts.

Deviled Egg Mold

    2   envelopes unflavored gelatin
    1   cup water
    ¼   cup lemon juice
    2   teaspoons salt
    2   teaspoons Worcestershire sauce
    ⅛   teaspoon cayenne pepper
    1½ cups mayonnaise
    8   hard-boiled eggs
    1   cup finely diced celery
    ½   cup finely diced green bell pepper
    ¼   cup chopped pimento
    ¼   cup grated onion

In a small saucepan sprinkle the gelatin over the water. Melt over low heat until the gelatin

is dissolved, stirring constantly. Remove from the heat. Stir in the lemon juice, salt, Worcestershire, and cayenne. Gently stir in the mayonnaise. Fold in the remaining ingredients. Pour into a 6-cup mold. Refrigerate until set, about 3 hours.

MAKES 12 SERVINGS.

Lobster-Stuffed Artichoke Bottoms

    1   tablespoon finely chopped shallots
          or scallions
    1   tablespoon chopped fresh tarragon
          (or 1 teaspoon dried tarragon)
    ¼   cup white wine
    4   egg yolks
    ½   teaspoon salt
          Dash Tabasco sauce
    1   tablespoon lemon juice
    ½   cup melted butter
    ....
    1   cup prepared bread stuffing
    ½   cup cut-up lobster meat
    1   7⅖-ounce can artichoke bottoms
          Sliced mozzarella cheese

In a skillet combine the shallots, tarragon, and wine, and sauté until tender. Cool.

In a blender combine the scallion mixture, egg yolks, salt, Tabasco, and lemon juice, and mix on high speed. While the blender is running, slowly add the melted butter, mixing until thickened. If the sauce should curdle while adding the butter pour 1 tablespoon of hot water into the sauce while the blender is running.

In a medium bowl combine the stuffing and lobster. Stuff the artichoke bottoms with the stuffing. Place mozzarella on each and top with Béarnaise sauce. Bake in a 350° oven for 10 to 15 minutes, or microwave for 3 minutes on high.

MAKES 3 TO 4 SERVINGS.

Curried Vidalia Mango Brandy Sauce

          Olive oil
    1   large Vidalia onion, chopped
    2   large mangos, peeled and chopped
          Mango chutney
          Curry powder
    ½   cup brandy

In a skillet heat the olive oil and sauté the onion until translucent. Add the mangos, chutney, curry powder, and brandy, and sauté for 5 more minutes on medium.

Great on duck, chicken, pork tenderloin, or whatever.

MAKES ABOUT 2 CUPS.

The Tamworth Inn

15 Cleveland Hill Road
Tamworth, New Hampshire 03886
(603) 323-7721

*T*he inn, with its back lawn bordering the Swift River, is the centerpiece of the village of Tamworth. The inn dates all the way back to 1833 when it was built to serve stage coach customers. The decor is distinctly Victorian. Tamworth's Barnstormers Summer Theatre is the oldest "actors equity" house in the United States.

Broccoli Cheddar Soup

2   tablespoons margarine
1   cup sliced celery
1   cup chopped onions
²⁄₃ cup all-purpose flour
4   cups chicken stock
    Salt and pepper to taste
2   cups chopped broccoli
2   to 3 cups milk
2   cups shredded Cheddar cheese

In a saucepan melt the margarine and cook the celery and onions until tender. Stir in the flour until smooth. Gradually add the chicken stock, salt, and pepper to taste, and the broccoli. Bring to a boil. Reduce the heat, cover, and simmer for 15 minutes. At that point, refrigerate (or freeze). When ready to serve, add the milk and Cheddar cheese, and heat until the cheese melts.

MAKES 6 SERVINGS.

The Tamworth Inn

Christmas Apple and Cranberry Cobbler

½   cup apple juice (or water)
½   cup sugar
1   tablespoon cornstarch
1½ cups fresh or frozen cranberries
2   Granny Smith apples, unpeeled, sliced
½   cup raisins (optional)
¾   cup all-purpose flour
½   cup sugar
⅓   cup butter or margarine
1   cup oats (quick or old-fashioned)
¼   cup applesauce

Grease a 9-inch baking dish. In a medium saucepan combine the apple juice, ½ cup of sugar, and cornstarch. Stir in the cranberries and bring to a boil. Reduce the heat and simmer for 5 minutes or until the cranberries pop. Stir in the apples and raisins and pour into a 9-inch square baking dish. In a medium bowl combine the flour and ½ cup of sugar. Cut in the butter until the mixture resembles coarse crumbs. Stir in the oats and applesauce, and mix well. Crumble evenly over the top of the fruit. Bake in a 400° oven for 30 to 35 minutes or until the top is golden brown.

MAKES 8 SERVINGS.

Raisin Bread French Toast

2   8-ounce packages cream cheese, softened
2   tablespoons sugar
½   teaspoon vanilla extract
½   cup sour cream or plain yogurt
1   teaspoon ground cinnamon
2   ripe bananas, mashed

24 slices raisin bread
1¼ cups milk
8   eggs
2   tablespoons confectioners' sugar
½   teaspoon vanilla extract
1   teaspoon ground cinnamon
    Additional confectioners' sugar, if desired
    Maple syrup for topping

Generously butter a 15 x 10-inch baking pan. In a small bowl combine the cream cheese, sugar, vanilla, sour cream, cinnamon, and bananas. Spread filling evenly over 1 side of half of the bread, and top with the remaining bread. In a bowl combine the remaining ingredients, beating until blended well. Pour into a large bowl. Dip the sandwiches in the milk mixture, turning to coat both sides evenly. Place in the prepared a baking pan. Bake in a 350° oven for 8 to 10 minutes. Turn the sandwiches over and continue baking another 8 minutes or until golden brown. Dust lightly with additional confectioners' sugar, if desired. Serve with warmed maple syrup.

Variations: Red raspberry preserves or strawberry preserves can be substituted for the bananas, or use fresh strawberries.

MAKES 12 SERVINGS.

Birchwood Inn

❧

Route 45
Temple, New Hampshire 03084
(603) 878-3285

---

*T*he inn is said to have been in operation as early as 1775, which means it is older than the U.S. itself. The present structure probably replaced an earlier building around 1800. Among its early guests was Henry David Thoreau.

Homemade Breakfast Sausage

3 *pounds fresh pork, ground*
½ *cup breadcrumbs*
2 *tablespoons salt*
1 *teaspoon black pepper*
½ *teaspoon sage*
1 *teaspoon ground coriander*
   Pinch grated nutmeg

In a large bowl combine the ingredients and mix thoroughly. Shape into a loaf. Wrap and refrigerate. Slice as needed, and cook as with any other sausage.

MAKES 3 POUNDS.

Maple-Butterscotch Sauce

½ *cup butter*
¼ *cup maple syrup*
1 *16-ounce box brown sugar*
2 *tablespoons cornstarch*
¼ *cup heavy cream*
1 *teaspoon vanilla extract*

In a saucepan melt the butter. Add the syrup and sugar, and cook over low heat until the sugar is melted. In a small bowl combine the cornstarch and cream. Stir into the syrup mixture. Cook over medium heat, stirring constantly, until thick and smooth. Remove from the heat and stir in the vanilla.

Serve on ice cream.

MAKES ABOUT 3 CUPS.

Spinach Casserole with Brown Rice

2 *tablespoons margarine*
½ *cup chopped onion*
1 *10-ounce box frozen spinach*
½ *cup water*
   Sautéed mushrooms
¾ *cup mayonnaise*
½ *teaspoon curry powder*
1 *10½-ounce can condensed cream of mushroom soup*
   Salt to taste
   Cooked brown rice, for 4 servings
   Grated cheese

In a skillet melt the margarine and sauté the onion. Add the spinach and water, and cook until the spinach separates. Add the mushrooms. In a medium bowl mix the mayonnaise, curry powder, and soup. Season. Blend the mayonnaise mixture into the spinach. Add the rice. Transfer the mixture to a 1½-quart casserole dish. Bake in a 350° oven for 25 to 30 minutes. Sprinkle the top with grated cheese.

MAKES 4 SERVINGS.

Chicken and Sausage Stir-fry

2 *whole chicken breasts, boned and sliced in strips*
   Flour
4 *links hot Italian sausage, sliced*
8 *strips red bell pepper*
8 *Tuscan peppers*
2 *tablespoons red wine vinegar*
2 *tablespoons red wine*
   Rice or spinach linguine for 4 servings, cooked

Lightly dredge the chicken strips in the flour. In a skillet stir-fry the sausage with the floured strips of chicken. Add the peppers, vinegar, and wine, and stir-fry for 5 minutes.

Serve over rice or spinach linguine.

MAKES 4 SERVINGS.

Birchwood Inn

NEW JERSEY

212 Centre Street
Beach Haven, New Jersey 08092
(609) 492-3553

*I*n the heart of Beach Haven's historic district, the Green Gables dates to 1880 and is listed on the National Register of Historic Places. Its six uniquely styled guest rooms place visitors within sight and sound of sea gulls and the rolling Atlantic, but the inn is known primarily for its food. Its five-course price-fixed dinners are the sort of experience that would have stars attached to them if they were eaten in Europe.

Cream of Toasted Garlic and Sherry Fino Soup

- ¼ cup cold pressed extra virgin olive oil
- 1 whole head garlic, cloves separated but not shelled (at least 10 cloves)
- Salt
- Pinch pepper
- 6 ounces dry sherry or Muy Fino (imported from Portugal)
- ½ cup water
- ¼ cup unsalted butter
- 1 cup all-purpose flour
- 3 to 4 cups heavy cream
- Pinch nutmeg
- 4 cups chicken stock (warm)

In a nonreactive pot (stainless steel, enamel) warm the oil and garlic cloves, unpeeled. Do not fry or brown. Add the salt, pepper, and sherry, cover and simmer until most of the sherry has evaporated and the garlic is very soft, about 45 minutes. Three-quarters of the way through cooking time, check the remaining liquid and add ½ cup of water, if needed.

In a separate nonreactive pot melt the butter and add the flour. Cook gently for a few minutes, stirring constantly. Add the heavy cream ½ cup at a time until this base is the desired consistency. Add salt, pepper, nutmeg, and check again. Strain whatever is leftover in the pot containing the garlic, oil, and sherry through a chinois or fine sieve. There should be 2 to 3 spoons of a creamy substance. Add to the base 1 spoonful of the creamed garlic and enough chicken stock until the thickness desired. Taste and keep adding the creamed garlic a teaspoon at a time until the desired flavor is reached.
MAKES 6 SERVINGS.

Warm Chicken Tenderloin Salad

- 24 nice Belgian endive leaves
- Salt and pepper
- 4 cups chicken stock, heated almost to boiling
- 1¼ pounds skinless, boneless chicken breasts, cut in 6 equal portions
- 2 medium carrots, cut julienne
- 1 zucchini, cut julienne
- 1 baked beet, peeled and diced
- Cold pressed extra-virgin olive oil

Arrange Belgian endive leaves in each of 6 warmed plates. In a pot add salt to the chicken stock (yes, it has to be highly salty) and cook the chicken without ever bringing the stock to a boil, 5 to 7 minutes. Reserve, and keep warm.

Cook the julienne carrots for 4 minutes and the julienne zucchini for 1 minute. Reserve, keep warm.

Slice each chicken portion into 4 strips (should be slightly pink inside). Return to the hot stove for 30 seconds. Arrange the chicken strips over the Belgian endive. Drizzle the julienned carrots, zucchini, and the beets over the chicken strips. Drizzle olive oil and pepper over the strips and vegetables.
MAKES 6 SERVINGS.

Angel Hair Pasta and "Fresh Caviar"

- ½ bunch fresh dill
- 6 tablespoons and cold pressed, extra virgin olive oil

¼ cup sweet butter

2 peeled cloves garlic, finely minced

6 very red, very plump, large plum
   tomatoes, peeled, seeded, diced
   small

8 ounces brand angel hair pasta

1 large or 2 medium fresh fish roe, any
   type, provided they are not more
   than a day old (should be fragrant
   and smell of seaweed)

2 tablespoons very finely minced Italian parsley (mince at last
   minute)

¼ teaspoon cracked black java pepper

In a large pot bring to a boil 1½ to 2 gallons of water and the dill, tied in a bunch. In a large skillet warm the oil, butter, and garlic. Do not brown. Add the diced tomatoes. Once the water boils remove the dill. Add enough salt and cook the angel hair for 4 to 5 minutes. Angel hair continues to cook even after it is drained, so drain it a little before reaching the al dente stage. Be sure to save 2 cups of the cooking water.

Rapidly add the drained angel hair to the warm oil, adding ½ cup of the cooking water at this time. Make sure the angel hair is not sticking and is well-oiled. Using a rotary strainer, strain the shad roe (or other roe) over the skillet containing the angel hair. The membrane will remain inside the strainer. With a spatula, rub the bottom of the strainer. Mix well. The heat will "cook" the microscopic eggs on contact but will not overcook them.

Add a little more cooking water, blend well, and add the parsley and cracked java pepper. Spoon onto warmed plates, and marvel.

MAKES 6 SERVINGS.

Bluefish en Papillote (Steamed Bluefish)

6 ounces extra virgin olive oil

2 cloves garlic, peeled and minced
   very finely

2 medium onions, peeled and finely
   diced

3 pounds bluefish fillets, skin, bones,
   and dark back muscles removed

¾ cup brandy

1 teaspoon ground thyme

½ teaspoon black pepper
   Salt to taste

½ cup breadcrumbs

½ pound mozzarella cheese, sliced in
   12 pieces

12 small basil leaves

2 large ripe tomatoes, peeled and
   finely diced

In a skillet heat 5 tablespoons of olive oil and cook the chopped garlic and onions over low fire. Chop about 1 pound of the bluefish and add to the oil before the garlic and onions brown, about 3 to 5 minutes. Sauté for 2 to 3 minutes or until the color changes. Add the brandy, and flambe. Wait until the flame goes out and add the thyme, black pepper, and salt. Cook until the liquid is almost gone. Add the breadcrumbs. Flip the skillet a few times until all ingredients are thoroughly mixed. Set aside to cool (there should be 15 to 20 tablespoons of the mixture).

Cut the remaining 2 pounds of bluefish in 12 pieces. Cut 12 rectangles of aluminum foil measuring 8 x 5-inches and brush 1 side with olive oil. Place 1 piece of bluefish in the center of the first foil rectangle. To understand how to fold the foil, pretend that you are looking north, with the longer side placed in the north/south direction and the shorter sides facing the east/west directions. Pound the bluefish with the heel of your hand or a meat cleaver until the fish broadly covers half the foil. Try to center it and place 1 piece of mozzarella and 1 basil leaf over each flattened piece of bluefish. Add 1 tablespoon of the breadcrumb mixture and roll the foil from south to north, then wrapping it tightly from the sides to make a tight wrapper (like saltwater taffy is wrapped). Repeat until all 12 papillotes (paupiettes) are done. Bake in a 375° oven for 20 minutes. Let cool for 10 minutes and unwrap delicately.

Heat the leftover mixture to very warm (almost browned) and add the diced tomatoes. Do not cook, just warm the mixture. When serving, spoon the mixture over the paupiettes on warmed plates.

MAKES 6 SERVINGS.

Albert Stevens Inn

≈

127 Myrtle Avenue
Cape May, New Jersey 08204
(609) 884-4717

Guests at this inn enjoy a brief respite from the complexities of modern life. The Albert Stevens Inn sits on a quiet, secluded one-way street-away from traffic noise. But the major attractions of Cape May—such as the beaches, the ferry, and fine shopping and dining—are just a few blocks away. Another nice feature of this inn is the adjoining garden, landscaped with hundreds of flowers and herbs.

Norwegian Fruit Pizza

½ cup confectioners' sugar

1½ cups all-purpose flour

¾ cup butter

1 8-ounce package cream cheese, softened

½ cup sugar

½ teaspoon vanilla extract or almond
   extract
   Peaches
   Bananas
   Kiwis
   Strawberries
   Blueberries

1 cup fruit juice

2 tablespoons cornstarch

1 tablespoon lemon juice

½ cup sugar

In a medium bowl combine the confectioners' sugar and flour. Cut in the butter with a pastry blender until crumb-like. Pat into a pizza pan. Bake in a 350° oven for about 13 minutes, until golden brown. Do not let the crust overbake.

In a small bowl mix the cream cheese, ½ cup of sugar, and vanilla. Spread over the cooled crust. Place the fresh and canned fruit on top.

In a saucepan combine the fruit juice, cornstarch, lemon juice, and ½ cup of sugar. Cook over medium heat until clear and thick, stirring constantly. Cool. Spread on top of the pizza over sliced fruit.

MAKES 12 SERVINGS.

Sweet Potato Bread

⅔ cup oil
2⅔ cups sugar
4 eggs
2 cups sweet potatoes, peeled, boiled until tender, and mashed
¼ cup crushed pineapple
⅔ cup water
3⅓ cups all-purpose flour
2 teaspoons baking soda
½ teaspoon baking powder
1½ teaspoons salt
1½ teaspoons ground cinnamon
1½ teaspoons ground cloves
⅔ cup raisins
⅔ cup chopped walnuts
1 teaspoon all-purpose flour

In a large bowl mix the oil and sugar. Add the eggs, sweet potatoes, pineapple, and water. In a separate bowl sift the flour soda, baking powder, salt, cinnamon, and cloves. Add the dry ingredients to the liquid mixture gradually until mixed well. In a small bowl mix in the raisins and nuts with 1 teaspoon of all-purpose flour, then fold into the batter. Spoon into a greased bundt pan. Bake in a 350° oven for 1 hour and 10 minutes.

MAKES 8 SERVINGS.

DeWitt Cornbread and Honey Butter

½ cup cornmeal
½ cup all-purpose flour
1 tablespoon baking powder
1½ teaspoons salt
1 teaspoon sugar
Milk
....
½ cup butter
½ cup honey

In a medium bowl mix the cornmeal, flour, baking powder, salt, and sugar. Add milk until the batter is a creamy texture. Pour into a small iron skillet or 8-inch square pan. Bake in a 375° oven for 20 minutes or until golden.

In a sauce pan heat and butter and honey, and drizzle over hot corn bread.

MAKES 4 TO 6 SERVINGS.

Whiskey-Raisin Cake

1 cup raisins
1 cup cold water
¾ cup sugar
½ cup butter
1 egg
1½ cups all-purpose flour
1 teaspoon baking powder
½ teaspoon salt
½ teaspoon ground cinnamon
½ teaspoon ground allspice
½ cup chopped walnuts
2 tablespoons good whiskey
....
¼ cup butter
2 cups confectioners' sugar
½ teaspoon vanilla extract
1 tablespoon whiskey

In a saucepan cook the raisins in water for 10 minutes. Drain the raisins, reserving ½ cup of water. In a large bowl cream the sugar and butter, and beat in the egg. In a small bowl sift the dry ingredients together. Add to the creamed mixture alternately with the reserved raisin water. Stir in the raisins and walnuts. Add the whiskey. Pour the batter into greased 8-inch round layer cake pans. Bake in a 350° oven for 25 minutes. Cool the layers.

In a small bowl combine ¼ cup of butter, the confectioners' sugar, and vanilla. Add the whiskey a little at a time. Frost the cooled cake.

MAKES 8 SERVINGS.

Alexander's Inn

Alexander's Inn

653 Washington Street
Cape May, New Jersey 08204
(609) 884-2555

Built as a private home in 1883, Alexander's Inn has been beautifully restored and is authentically furnished in elegant Victorian style. The service is elegant as well. Breakfast is brought to the room, and there is tea every afternoon, complete with baked treats. There are seven guest rooms with private baths.

Oysters with Vodka Gelée

2 tablespoons unflavored gelatin powder
1 cup water
1 cup vodka
1 cup dry white wine
½ cup lemon juice
24 large fresh oysters, shucked
Lemon wedges for garnish
Parsley sprigs

Place the gelatin powder in a 2-quart glass or ceramic bowl. In a saucepan heat the water to boiling and pour over the gelatin. Stir until moistened. Let set until softened. Add the remaining liquids, mix thoroughly, and chill about 2 hours to set.

To serve, "chip" pieces of gel and arrange about ½ inch deep on a glass plate. Place the oysters on top (6 per person) and present with lemon wedges and parsley sprigs.

Note: The gelée looks like cracked ice.

MAKES 4 SERVINGS.

Spiced Cashew Mayonnaise

¾ cup roasted cashew nuts, unsalted
2 cloves garlic
2 eggs

2 tablespoons apple cider vinegar
1 cup peanut oil
 Pinch dried basil
 Pinch cayenne pepper

In a food processor blend the cashews, garlic, eggs, and vinegar. With the motor running, slowly pour in the peanut oil to make a thick, smooth emulsion. Stir in the basil and pepper, and refrigerate for about 8 hours to allow the flavors to grow. This will keep several weeks.

Serve as a sandwich spread or dip for vegetables and fish.

MAKES 1½ CUPS.

Barnard
Good House
❧

238 Perry
Cape May, New Jersey 08208
(609) 884-5381

---

*W*ithin walking distance of the prime historic sites in a National Historic Landmark City, the Barnard Good House offers five well-appointed guest rooms. The inn is known for its four-course breakfasts. The main Cape May swimming beach is only two blocks away.

Pear and Sauterne Soup

1 vanilla bean, split
1 750-ml bottle Sauterne
2 4-inch strips lemon zest (yellow part only)
2 to 3 tablespoons sugar
3 large pears, peeled, cored, and coarsely chopped
....
5 ounces fresh raspberries or unsweetened frozen, thawed
2 to 3 teaspoons sugar
6 tablespoons sour cream
½ cup heavy cream, whipped to soft peaks
18 fresh raspberries or partially thawed

Scrape the vanilla seeds into a 4-quart heavy non-aluminum saucepan. Add the bean. Add wine, lemon zest, and 2 tablespoons of sugar. Boil for 10 to 15 minutes until reduced to 1 cup. Add the pears and simmer until soft, about 8 minutes. Add more sugar if desired. Remove the vanilla bean. In a food processor purée the pear mixture until smooth. Cool. Refrigerate until well chilled (can be prepared 10 hours ahead).

In a food processor purée 5 ounces of raspberries with sugar to taste. Strain. Refrigerate until chilled well (can be prepared 10 hours ahead).

Fold the sour cream, then whipped cream, into the pear soup. Let stand at room temperature for 10 minutes.

Ladle into 6 bowls. Spoon 2 teaspoons of raspberry purée into the center of each bowl. Using a teaspoon handle, swirl the raspberry purée through the soup, forming a pinwheel design. Place 3 berries in the center of each.

MAKES 6 SERVINGS.

Deep-dish Chili Cheese Pie

¼ cup oil
1 teaspoon minced fresh ginger
7 mild long green chiles, seeded, deveined, and chopped (see note)
1 large onion, chopped
1 large clove garlic, minced
1 15-ounce can garbanzo beans, rinsed and drained
1½ teaspoons cilantro
1 teaspoon dried oregano (or 2 teaspoons fresh)
¼ teaspoon cumin
¼ teaspoon cayenne pepper
1 cup pitted black olives, chopped
1 4-ounce jar or can pimentos, drained and chopped
 Salt and fresh ground pepper
½ pound fresh or frozen corn kernels
4 cups sharp Cheddar cheese, shredded
1½ cups milk
3 eggs
⅛ teaspoon fresh ground pepper
 Pinch cayenne pepper
 Pinch cilantro
....
1½ cups unbleached flour
⅔ cup yellow cornmeal
¼ cup cake flour
½ teaspoon salt

3 tablespoons minced chives or green onion tops
½ cup plus 2 tablespoons cold unsalted butter
½ cup (about) cold water

In a large skillet heat the oil over high heat. Add the ginger and stir-fry for 30 seconds. Add the chiles, onion, and garlic, and stir-fry for 2 to 3 minutes. Add the garbanzo beans, cilantro, oregano, cumin, and cayenne, and stir-fry another minute. Remove from the heat and add the olives, pimento, salt, and pepper. Cool slightly. Stir in the corn and set aside to cool completely. Drain if necessary, then stir in the shredded cheese.

Position a rack in the center of the oven. Butter a shallow 2½-quart baking dish. In a medium bowl combine the milk, eggs, salt, ⅛ teaspoon of pepper, cayenne, and cilantro, and beat well. Spoon the vegetable mixture into the dish and pour the custard over the top. In a large bowl combine the flour, cornmeal, cake flour, salt, and chives. Cut in the butter with a pastry blender until the mixture resembles coarse meal. Add the water and mix until a dough forms. Roll out the pastry on a floured surface to a thickness of about ⅛ inch. Roll out the dough and cut with fancy cookie cutters. Place them close together, leaving small spaces for steam. Bake in a 350° oven for about 1 hour to 1 hour and 30 minutes or until a knife inserted in the center comes out clean. Serve either hot or at room temperature.

Note: Always use caution when working with chiles as their oils can burn the skin. Be sure to wash your hands thoroughly after handling the peppers. For more of the chiles natural hotness to come through, do not seed or devein, just discard the stem and chop the entire pepper as fine as desired.

MAKES 10 TO 12 SERVINGS.

Torn Turkey Pie

5 phyllo sheets
....
2 eggs
3 cups chopped cooked turkey
1 cup cooked corn, drained well
1 cup chopped cooked spinach (squeezed dry)
1½ cups shredded mozzarella cheese
2 tablespoons grated Parmesan cheese
1 tablespoon chopped fresh parsley

Salt and pepper to taste
2 *turns cardamom seed*
3 *tablespoons butter or margarine, melted*

Unroll the phyllo sheets on a working surface. Cover them with a sheet of waxed paper, then with a damp cloth or towel to prevent drying. Cover the pile again while working with 1 sheet at a time.

In a large mixing bowl beat the eggs. Add the remaining ingredients, with seasoning to taste, and mix well. Set aside. Butter a 9-inch pie plate. Fold 1 phyllo sheet in half and line the pan with it. Let the dough hang over the edge of the pan. Brush with some of the melted butter or margarine. Place 3 more folded phyllo sheets in the pan 1 at a time, brushing each as before. Fill the pastry with the filling. Fold over the loose ends of the dough. Do not worry if it breaks. Tear the remaining sheet of dough into tattered pieces and cover the pie with them. Dot with remaining butter or margarine. Bake in a 375° oven for 35 to 40 minutes, until the top is puffed and crisp. Serve hot.

MAKES 6 SERVINGS.

Horse's Teeth Pie

Pasta Frolla Semplice (recipe follows)
1 *cup "horse's teeth" pasta, or any small pasta*
2 *eggs, lightly beaten*
1 *cup grated Parmesan cheese*
  Salt and pepper to taste
2 *pounds fresh asparagus, blanched and drained*
1 *tablespoon butter, plus butter for dotting*
1 *cup shredded smoked mozzarella cheese*
¼ *cup chopped prosciutto*

Butter a 10- to 11-inch pie pan. Divide the Pasta Frolla Semplice dough into 3 parts. Roll 1 part out to a round sheet as thin as possible, and line the prepared pan. Trim the excess dough. Chill the pie shell. Keep the remaining dough covered.

In a pot cook the pasta in salted boiling water just until al dente. Drain the pasta and pour into a mixing bowl. Reserve 2 tablespoons of the beaten egg in a cup. Stir the remaining eggs into the pasta. Add 2 to 3

tablespoons of Parmesan and salt and pepper to taste. Stir and set aside.

Cut the tender parts of the asparagus into ½-inch pieces. In a skillet melt 1 tablespoon of butter. Add the asparagus and cook very briefly, just to heat through. Set aside.

Pour half of the pasta mixture into the chilled shell. Scatter half of the asparagus pieces all over, then half of the mozzarella and prosciutto. Sprinkle with some of the Parmesan. Roll out another piece of dough into a thin round, and top the pasta mixture with it. Sprinkle with Parmesan and dot with butter. Pour in the remaining pasta, smooth the top, and add the remaining asparagus, mozzarella, proscuitto, and Parmesan as before.

Roll out the last piece of dough and top the pie with it. Trim the excess dough. Moisten the edges of the pie and pinch the dough all around in a decorative edge. Decorate the pie with scraps of dough. Pierce the top and brush with the reserved beaten egg. Bake in a 400° oven for 20 to 25 minutes. Cool for 10 minutes before slicing.

MAKES 6 SERVINGS.

Barnard Good House

Pasta Frolla Semplice

3 *cups all-purpose flour*
½ *cup instantized flour*
¼ *cup butter*
¼ *cup lard or shortening*
  Water
1 *egg*
1 *tablespoon sugar*
  Pinch salt
½ *cup milk*

Before starting, fit the steel blade in the food processor. In the bowl of the processor, combine both flours and both fats. Turn the machine on and off until the mixture resem-

bles coarse meal. Add the remaining ingredients, process until a ball of dough forms on the blades. If necessary, add a little water.

Wrap the dough in plastic wrap and chill until ready to use.

MAKES PASTA FOR 6 SERVINGS.

Tomato Flans

3 *cherry tomatoes, halved*
2 *tablespoons butter*
1 *tablespoon olive oil*
1 *cup minced onion*
1 *pound tomatoes, peeled, seeded, and chopped*
4 *eggs*
½ *cup heavy cream*
¼ *cup grated Parmesan cheese*
¼ *cup grated Gruyère cheese*
  Salt and fresh ground pepper to taste

Generously butter 6 ½-cup custard cups or ramekins. Place 1 cherry tomato half skin-side down in each cup.

In a large heavy skillet melt the butter with oil over medium-low heat. Add the onion and cook until translucent, stirring occasionally, about 10 minutes. Increase the heat to high. Add the chopped tomatoes and cook until all liquid evaporates, stirring frequently. Cool slightly.

In a medium bowl beat the eggs and cream to blend. Stir in the cheeses and tomato mixture. Season with salt and pepper. Carefully spoon the mixture into the prepared cups. Arrange the cups in a roasting pan. Pour enough water into the pan to come halfway up the sides of the cups. Bake in a 375° oven for 30 to 35 minutes until a tester inserted in the center of a flan comes out clean. Let stand for 10 minutes. Run a knife around the edge of the cups to loosen the flans. Invert onto plates and serve immediately.

MAKES 6 SERVINGS.

Potato Casserole

3 *large potatoes, peeled*
½ *cup milk*
2 *tablespoon butter*
2 *eggs*
1½ *teaspoons salt*
  Pepper to taste
1 *medium onion, chopped*
  Paprika

In a food processor shred the potatoes to measure 4 cups. Put the potatoes in cold water to keep from discoloring, and set aside. Remove ¼ cup of water from the potatoes and place in a saucepan with milk and 2 tablespoons of butter. Cook over medium heat just under boiling. Set aside.

Beat the eggs with salt and pepper. Continue beating and slowly pour the milk mixture over the eggs, blending well.

Drain the potatoes well in a colander. Combine the potatoes, onions, and egg mixture. Butter a 2-quart casserole dish and spoon the mixture into the dish. Sprinkle with paprika. Bake uncovered in a 375° oven for 50 minutes until the edges are crusty.

MAKES 6 SERVINGS.

Cabbage Patch Bread

- 1 **package active dry yeast**
- ⅓ **cup warm water (115 to 120°)**
- 1 **5-ounce can low-fat evaporated milk**
- ¼ **cup oil**
- 1 **egg or 2 egg whites**
- ¾ **cup coarsely chopped cabbage**
- 1 **carrot, cut up**
- ¼ **cup sliced celery**
- ¼ **cup snipped parsley**
- 1 **tablespoon honey**
- 1 **teaspoon salt**
- 3 **cups whole wheat flour**
- 1¼ **cups all-purpose flour**

In a large mixing bowl dissolve the yeast in warm water. In a blender container or food processor bowl combine the evaporated milk, oil, egg, cabbage, carrot, celery, parsley, honey, and salt. Cover and blend until smooth. Add to the yeast mixture. Using a spoon stir in the whole wheat flour and as much of the all-purpose flour as possible. Turn out onto a lightly floured surface. Knead in enough of the remaining all-purpose flour to make a moderately stiff dough that is smooth and elastic, 6 to 8 minutes. Shape into a ball. Place in a greased bowl, and turn once. Cover and let rise in a warm place until doubled, about 1 hour and 15 minutes.

Punch down and divide the dough in half. Cover and let rest for 10 minutes. Shape the dough into 2 round loaves. Place on a greased baking sheet. Cover and let rise until doubled, about 30 minutes. Bake in a 350° oven for 30 minutes or until done. If necessary, cover with foil the last 10 minutes to prevent overbrowning. Cool on a wire rack. Serve warm. Store the bread in the refrigerator.

MAKES 2 LOAVES.

Plum and Almond Tart

- 2 **cups sifted all-purpose flour**
- ¼ **cup sugar**
- ½ **cup well-chilled unsalted butter**
- 3 **egg yolks**
- ¾ **teaspoon grated lemon zest**
- 1½ **to 2 tablespoons sweet white wine or water**

....

- ½ **cup sugar**
- ½ **cup unblanched almonds**
- 2 **tablespoons all-purpose flour**
- ¾ **teaspoon cinnamon**
- 6 **egg whites, room temperature**
  Pinch cream of tartar
  Pinch salt
- 1½ **pounds slightly underripe red plums, quartered and pitted**

In a large bowl mix 2 cups of flour and ¼ cup of sugar. Cut in the butter until coarse meal forms. Make a well in the center of the dry ingredients. Add the yolks, lemon zest, and 1½ tablespoons of wine, and work into dry the ingredients, adding more wine if necessary to bind the dough. Gather into a ball and flatten into a disk. Wrap the dough and refrigerate for at least 30 minutes. (Can be prepared 2 days ahead).

Roll the dough out on lightly a floured surface to a ¼-inch-thick round. Transfer to a 9-inch springform pan and trim the edges. Refrigerate for 1 hour.

Line the crust with parchment and fill with dried beans or pie weights. Bake in a 375° oven for 10 minutes. Remove the beans and parchment and bake the crust until brown, about 15 minutes. Cool. Reduce the temperature to 350°.

In a food processor blend ½ cup of sugar, almonds, 2 tablespoons of flour, and cinnamon until the almonds are finely ground. In a large bowl beat the egg whites with cream of tartar and salt until stiff but not dry. Gently fold in the almond mixture, then the plums. Turn the filling into the crust. Bake in a 350° oven for 45 minutes, until the top is golden brown and a knife inserted in the center comes out clean. Cover the edges with foil if browning too quickly. Cool 15 minutes. Serve warm.

MAKES 6 TO 8 SERVINGS.

805 Stockton Avenue
Cape May, New Jersey 08204
(609) 884-4158

---

*T*he Bedford Inn has been welcoming guests since 1880 when it was built to serve vacationers in this quiet, seaside Victorian town. Its eleven guest rooms are furnished with authentic period antiques, and many have old-fashioned claw-foot tubs and showers. The inn is right in the middle of the Cape May's gaslight historic district and only one block from the beach.

Bedford Inn

Gourmet Brownies

- 3 **1-ounce squares unsweetened chocolate**
- ½ **cup shortening**
- 3 **eggs**
- 1½ **cups sugar**
- 1½ **teaspoons vanilla extract**
- ¼ **teaspoon salt**
- 1 **cup all-purpose flour**
- 1½ **cups chopped walnuts**
- ⅓ **cup raspberry jam**

....

- 1 **1-ounce square unsweetened chocolate**
- 2 **tablespoons butter**
- 2 **tablespoons light corn syrup**
- 2 **cups confectioners' sugar**
- 1 **tablespoon milk**
- 2 **teaspoons vanilla extract**

In a double boiler over simmering water melt 3 squares of chocolate with the shortening. Cool slightly. In a large bowl blend together the eggs, sugar, 1½ teaspoons of vanilla, and salt. Stir in the chocolate mixture, then the flour. Fold in the walnuts. Turn into a well-greased 8-inch square pan. Bake in a 325° oven for about 40 minutes. Spoon the jam over the hot brownies and spread carefully. Let cool.

In a saucepan over low heat melt 1 square of chocolate. Blend in the butter and light corn syrup. Stir in the confectioners' sugar, milk, and 2 teaspoon of vanilla, and mix well. Spread the Velvet Chocolate Glaze over the brownies.

MAKES 6 TO 8 SERVINGS.

Cozy Bread Eggs

        4   slices Canadian bacon
        2   large eggs
        1   cup mayonnaise
        1   tablespoon lemon juice
    1½   teaspoons dried parsley flakes
        1   teaspoon grated onion
       ½   teaspoon Dijon mustard
       ¼   teaspoon dried tarragon leaves,
            crushed
        2   tablespoons butter, softened
        4   large eggs
        2   English muffins
       ½   cup butter, melted
            Paprika

Place 1 slice of bacon in the bottom of each of 4 individual greased baking dishes. In a small saucepan beat 2 eggs. Stir in the mayonnaise, lemon juice, parsley, onion, mustard, and tarragon until blended well. Cook and stir over low heat for 5 minutes or until thickened. Do not boil. Remove the pan from the heat. Stir in the butter until melted. Spread ⅓ cup in each baking dish.

Break an egg into the center of each dish. Split the English muffins and spread with butter. Cut each half into 2 pieces. Stand 2 pieces at the sides of each baking dish. Sprinkle the eggs with paprika. Bake in a 375° oven for 15 to 18 minutes or the until eggs are set to the desired doneness.

MAKES 4 SERVINGS.

Creamed Chipped Beef

       ¼   cup butter
       ¼   cup all-purpose flour
            Fresh ground pepper to taste
        2   cups milk
       ½   teaspoon Worcestershire sauce
       ⅓   cup freshly grated Parmesan cheese
       ½   cup dry white wine
        8   ounces chipped beef
        1   cup sliced fresh mushrooms
       ⅔   cup sour cream

In a saucepan melt the butter. Add the flour and pepper and cook, stirring constantly for 1 to 2 minutes. Slowly add the milk and cook, stirring constantly, until thickened well. Add the Worcestershire sauce, Parmesan cheese, and wine. Stir and cook until fairly thick and just beginning to boil. Add the beef and mushrooms, and heat throughout. Add the sour cream and heat until just hot. Do not boil. Serve over waffles, toasted bread, or English muffins.

MAKES 6 SERVINGS.

Salsa Oven Omelet

       ¾   cup mild salsa
        1   cup chopped artichoke hearts
       ¼   cup grated Parmesan cheese
        1   cup shredded Monterey Jack cheese
        1   cup shredded sharp Cheddar cheese
        6   eggs
        1   8-ounce carton sour cream

Grease a quiche dish and spread salsa evenly over the bottom. Sprinkle chopped artichokes over the salsa, then sprinkle with Parmesan. Top with the Jack and Cheddar cheeses. In a blender combine the eggs with sour cream, and blend until smooth. Pour the egg mixture over the cheeses. Bake in a 350° oven for about 40 to 45 minutes. Cut into wedges.

MAKES 6 TO 8 SERVINGS.

The Mainstay Inn

The Mainstay Inn

635 Columbia Avenue
Cape May, New Jersey 08204
(609) 884-8690

A pair of lucky gamblers pooled their winnings and built this fine old Victorian inn as a clubhouse for gambling and other gentlemanly amusements. They gave it fourteen-foot ceilings, elaborate chandeliers, a sweeping veranda, and the finest walnut furnishings, all of which remain to this day. Nowadays the building is no longer a clubhouse but serves instead as an elegant inn offering sixteen guest rooms. Some rooms are located in the nearby Cottage or across the street in the Officers Quarters, an early twentieth century building once used for housing the families of naval officers.

Almond Coffee Cake

        1   3½-ounce package almond paste,
            cut up
       ½   cup confectioners' sugar
       ¼   cup margarine or butter
       ½   cup sliced almonds
....
    1½   cups sugar
       ¾   cup margarine or butter, softened
    1½   teaspoons vanilla extract
        3   eggs
        3   cups all-purpose flour
    1½   teaspoons baking powder
    1½   teaspoons baking soda
       ¾   teaspoon salt
    1½   cups sour cream
....
       ½   cup confectioners' sugar
       ¼   teaspoon vanilla extract
        1   to 2 teaspoons milk

In a saucepan heat the almond paste, $\frac{1}{2}$ cup of confectioners' sugar, and $\frac{1}{4}$ cup of margarine over medium heat, stirring constantly, until smooth. Stir in the almonds.

Grease a 10-inch tube pan. In a large bowl beat the sugar, margarine, $1\frac{1}{2}$ teaspoons of vanilla, and eggs with an electric mixer on medium speed for 2 minutes, scraping the bowl occasionally. In a separate bowl mix the flour, baking powder, soda, and salt. Add the flour mixture and sour cream alternately to the egg mixture, beating on low speed. Spread one-third of the batter into the pan. Sprinkle with one-third of the filling. Repeat twice. Bake in a 325° oven for about 50 minutes or until a toothpick inserted near the center comes out clean.

Cool for 20 minutes. Remove the cake from the pan.

In a small bowl combine the remaining ingredients. Drizzle the glaze over the cake.

MAKES 8 SERVINGS.

Buttermilk Orange Cupcakes

$\frac{1}{2}$ cup butter or margarine, softened
1 cup sugar
2 eggs
1 teaspoon baking soda
2 cups all-purpose flour
$\frac{1}{4}$ teaspoon salt
$\frac{2}{3}$ cup buttermilk
....
 Juice of 2 oranges
 Juice of 2 lemons
1 cup sugar

In a large bowl cream the butter and 1 cup of sugar. Add the eggs one at a time. Sift in the dry ingredients alternately with the buttermilk. Fill greased miniature muffin cups less than half full. Bake in a 375° oven for 12 minutes.

In a saucepan mix and cook the remaining ingredients until the sugar is dissolved. Spoon 1 teaspoon of orange sauce over each cake when removed from the oven but still in the pans. After adding the sauce, let the cupcakes cool in the pans, then remove. Serve warm or cold.

MAKES 60 MINIATURE CUPCAKES.

Banana-Pineapple Crisp

3 ripe bananas, sliced in $\frac{1}{2}$-inch
 rounds (about 2 cups)
1 20-ounce can pineapple chunks,
 drained (reserve $\frac{1}{4}$ cup juice)
2 tablespoons apricot preserves
....
$\frac{1}{2}$ cup old-fashioned oats
$\frac{1}{2}$ cup firmly packed light brown sugar
$\frac{1}{4}$ cup all-purpose flour
$\frac{1}{4}$ cup coconut
$\frac{1}{4}$ cup butter, cut in small pieces

In a shallow $1\frac{1}{2}$-quart baking dish gently mix the bananas and pineapple. Stir the preserves into the reserved pineapple juice and pour over the fruit mixture. In a medium bowl mix the oats, brown sugar, flour, and coconut. Add the butter and cut in with a pastry blender until the mixture resembles crumbs. Sprinkle over the fruit mixture. Bake in a 400° oven for 15 to 20 minutes, until the topping is lightly browned and the juices bubble.

MAKES 6 SERVINGS.

Gingerbread Date Muffins

2 cups all-purpose flour
$1\frac{1}{2}$ teaspoons baking powder
$\frac{1}{2}$ teaspoon baking soda
$1\frac{1}{2}$ teaspoons ground ginger
1 teaspoon ground cinnamon
$\frac{1}{2}$ teaspoon grated nutmeg
$\frac{1}{4}$ teaspoon ground cloves
$\frac{1}{4}$ teaspoon salt
1 large egg
$\frac{3}{4}$ cup milk
$\frac{1}{4}$ cup molasses
$\frac{1}{4}$ cup maple syrup
2 tablespoons sugar
$\frac{1}{2}$ cup chopped dates
$\frac{1}{4}$ cup butter, melted

Grease 12 muffin cups. In a large bowl combine the flour, baking powder, soda, spices, and salt, and stir to mix thoroughly. In a separate bowl beat the egg and add the milk, molasses, syrup, sugar, dates, and butter. Mix well and pour over the dry ingredients. Stir just until moistened. Pour the batter into the muffin cups. Bake in a 350° oven for 20 minutes.

MAKES 1 DOZEN.

Chocolate Streusel Bars

$1\frac{3}{4}$ cups all-purpose flour
$1\frac{1}{2}$ cups confectioners' sugar
$\frac{1}{2}$ cup unsweetened cocoa
1 cup cold butter
1 8-ounce package cream cheese, softened
1 14-ounce can sweetened condensed milk (not evaporated milk)
1 egg
2 teaspoons vanilla extract
$\frac{1}{2}$ cup chopped walnuts

In a large bowl combine the flour, sugar, and cocoa. Cut in the butter until crumbly (mixture will be dry). Reserve 2 cups of crumb mixture. Press the remainder on the bottom of a 9 x 13-inch baking pan. Bake in a 350° oven for 15 minutes.

In a large bowl beat the cream cheese until fluffy. Gradually beat in the milk until smooth. Add the egg and vanilla and mix well. Pour over the prepared crust.

Add the walnuts to the reserved crumb mixture. Sprinkle evenly over the cheese mixture. Bake 20 minutes more or until bubbly. Cool. Chill. Cut into bars. Store covered in the refrigerator.

MAKES 8 SERVINGS.

*Sea Holly
Bed and
Breakfast*
❧

*815 Stockton Avenue
Cape May, New Jersey 08204
(609) 884-6294*

An elegant three-story Gothic Cottage with Italianate detailing, the Sea Holly is located in the Cape May historic district. All rooms are furnished with authentic Renaissance Revival and Eastlake antique pieces. Only one block from the ocean, it places guests within walking distance of the Victorian Mall, shops, and restaurants.

Jam Crescents

⅓ cup any jam
2 tablespoons chopped walnuts
1 8-ounce package refrigerator crescent rolls

In a small bowl combine the jam and walnuts. Unroll the crescent rolls and cut along the perforations to make 8 pieces. Spread each with the jam and walnut mixture. Roll up as the package directs. Lightly grease a cookie sheet. Place the crescents 2 inches apart on the sheet. Bake in a 350° oven for 10 to 12 minutes, until golden brown.

Remove from the cookie sheet to a cooling rack. Cool and serve.

MAKES 8 SERVINGS.

Cherry Pockets

2 to 3 tablespoons ground cinnamon
¾ cup sugar

1 10-ounce can refrigerated biscuits
¼ cup margarine, melted
½ can cherry pie filling

In a small bowl mix the cinnamon and sugar together. Set aside. Unwrap the biscuits. Dip each in melted margarine, then roll in cinnamon-sugar. Pat each biscuit flat. Place 2 or 3 cherries in the center of each biscuit. Fold over to make a half-moon shape and seal the edges. Place on an ungreased pizza pan or baking sheet. Bake in a 350° oven for 12 to 15 minutes. Remove to a wire rack to cool. Serve as a breakfast treat or alongside ice cream for dessert.

MAKES 10 SERVINGS.

Sea Holly

Sausage-Potato Pie

1 5.25-ounce box au gratin potatoes
  Boiling water
16 eggs
½ cup sour cream
½ cup milk
2 tablespoons dried onion
2 teaspoons dill weed
6 to 8 cooked (2 ounces) sausages, sliced into 1-inch pieces
  Sliced tomatoes for garnish

Grease a 9 x 13-inch baking dish or pan. Place the potatoes (set cheese aside) in a medium bowl and cover with boiling water. Let stand until soft, about 20 minutes.

In a large bowl whip the eggs, sour cream, milk, onion, and dill until mixed. Arrange the sausage in the bottom of the baking dish. Drain the potatoes and mix in the cheese from the package. Lay the potatoes on top of the sausage. Pour the egg mixture over sausage and potatoes. Bake in a 350° oven for about 45 minutes or until a knife inserted in the center comes out clean. Plan to serve right out of the oven. Cut in squares and garnish with sliced tomatoes.

MAKES 8 TO 10 SERVINGS.

Lemon Blueberry Sour Cream Cake

3 cups all-purpose flour
¼ teaspoon baking soda
½ teaspoon salt
1 cup margarine
2 teaspoons lemon extract
3 cups sugar
6 eggs
1 cup sour cream
1½ cups blueberries

Grease and flour a 10-inch tube pan. In a medium bowl sift together the flour, soda, and salt. In large bowl cream the margarine with an electric mixer. Add the lemon extract and gradually add the sugar, and beat for 2 minutes. Beat in 2 eggs at a time, beating until thoroughly mixed after each addition and 2 to 3 minutes after the last addition. On the lowest speed, add half of the flour, beating only until blended. Add all of the sour cream, then the balance of the flour. Mix until smooth. Stir in the blueberries. Pour into the prepared pan. Bake in a 350° oven for 60 to

80 minutes. Cool in the pan for 20 minutes. Turn onto a cooling rack.

MAKES 14 SERVINGS.

Orange-Pineapple Cake

1 18½-ounce package orange cake mix
1 cup crushed pineapple, undrained
4 eggs
½ cup margarine
1 4.8-ounce package vanilla instant pudding mix

2 teaspoons grated orange zest
½ cup confectioners' sugar
  Enough milk to make thin icing (1 or 2 teaspoons)

In a large bowl combine the cake mix, pineapple, eggs, margarine, and pudding mix, and beat with an electric mixer on low speed until moistened, then on medium for 2 minutes.

Pour the batter into a greased and floured 10-cup bundt pan. Bake in a 350° oven for 40 to 50 minutes, until a toothpick inserted in the center comes out clean. Cool for 10 minutes.

Remove from the pan and finish cooling. In a small bowl combine the remaining ingredients and drizzle over the cake.

MAKES 16 SERVINGS.

Windward House
❧

24 Jackson Street
Cape May, New Jersey 08204
(609) 884-3368

***A** meticulously restored Edwardian Inn, the Windward House features a fine collection of stained and beveled glass. Accented by oak and chestnut doors and paneling, guest rooms contain museum quality antiques. The town of Cape May is a National Historic Landmark with many glorious old homes and build-*

ings from the Victorian period. It also offers inviting beaches, boating, fishing, bicycling, an annual tulip festival, and an impressive array of fine restaurants.

Windward House

Breakfast Pasta

 1 pound bacon
 1 medium onion, chopped
 ⅓ cup all-purpose flour
   Salt and pepper to taste
 4 cups milk
 2 cups grated Swiss cheese
 ½ cup grated Parmesan cheese
 12 lasagna noodles, cooked and
   drained
 1 dozen hard-boiled eggs, sliced
   Fresh parsley, chopped

In a skillet cook the bacon until crisp. Drain the bacon and set it aside. Sauté the onion in bacon drippings until opaque. Add the flour, salt, and pepper and cook until pasty. Slowly add the milk and cook until thickened. Add 1 cup of Swiss cheese and the Parmesan. Stir until melted and set aside. Grease a 9 x 13-inch baking pan and spoon a small amount of sauce into the bottom. Layer the noodles, crumbled bacon, eggs, sauce, and remaining Swiss cheese until completely used. Sprinkle with parsley. Bake in a 350° oven for 30 minutes. Cool slightly before cutting.

MAKES 8 SERVINGS.

Corn Pudding

 2 tablespoons cornstarch
 2 eggs
 ⅓ cup sugar
 1 5-ounce can evaporated milk
 1 15-ounce can cream-style corn
 2 tablespoons melted butter

In a large bowl mix the first 3 ingredients thoroughly. Add the milk and corn, and mix again. Pour into a greased 1-quart casserole dish. Pour melted butter on top. Bake in a 325° oven for 1 hour or until firm.

MAKES 4 SERVINGS.

Tomato Pie

 3 eggs
 ½ to 1 can mushroom soup
 ½ cup milk
 1¼ cups shredded Swiss cheese
 2 tomatoes, chopped and drained
 1 baked 9-inch pie shell
 6 to 10 slices bacon

In a medium bowl beat the eggs, soup, and milk. Place 1 cup of cheese and the tomatoes in the shell and sprinkle with bacon. Pour the milk mixture over the tomatoes. Top with cheese and bacon. Bake in a 350° oven for 40 to 50 minutes.

MAKES 6 TO 8 SERVINGS.

Cheese-filled Coffee Cake

 1 package active dry yeast
 ¼ cup lukewarm water (105 to 115°)
 1 teaspoon sugar
 1 egg, lightly beaten
 ¾ cup butter or margarine
 2 cups sifted all-purpose flour
 ¼ teaspoon salt
 2 8-ounce packages cream cheese,
   room temperature
 1 teaspoon fresh lemon juice
 1 cup sugar
   Confectioners' sugar

In a large bowl mix the yeast, water, and 1 teaspoon of sugar. Let stand for 10 minutes. Add the egg. In a separate bowl cut the butter into the flour and salt. Mix well. Add the yeast mixture. Roll the dough on waxed paper into a 12 x 15-inch rectangle. In a medium bowl combine the cream cheese, lemon juice, and 1 cup of sugar. Spread the filling on the dough to within 1 inch of the edges. Fold each long end toward the middle, making sure the edges overlap. Fold the ends up about 1½ inches. Flip onto a baking sheet so the folds are down. Bake in a 370° oven for about 30 minutes. Cool and sprinkle with confectioners' sugar.

MAKES 6 SERVINGS.

Crescent Date Honey Buns

 ½ cup butter or margarine
 ⅓ cup chopped pecans or walnuts
 2 tablespoons firmly packed brown
   sugar
 2 tablespoons honey
 1 8-ounce can crescent dinner rolls
 12 pitted dates

In a small bowl combine the butter, pecans, brown sugar, and honey. Pour into an ungreased 8- or 9-inch square baking pan and heat in the oven until the butter melts. Stir and set aside.

Separate the crescent dough into 8 triangles. Cut the dates in half. Place 1½ dates inside each triangle and roll up. Place on top of the butter mixture. Bake in a 400° oven for 15 to 18 minutes. Cool for 3 minutes. Invert the pan and serve warm.

MAKES 8 BUNS.

Jam Biscuits

 1 10-ounce can flaky refrigerated biscuits
 ¼ cup butter
 ½ cup sugar
 ½ teaspoon ground cinnamon
 ¼ cup preserves (apricot or
   strawberry)

Separate the biscuits and let them warm to room temperature. In a small dish melt the butter. In a separate dish combine the sugar and cinnamon.

Dip the biscuits in the butter, coating the top and bottom. Roll completely in the sugar mixture and place on an ungreased baking sheet with sides. Make an indention with thumb and fill each thumbprint with preserves. Bake in a 375° oven for 15 to 20 minutes, until golden brown.

MAKES 10 BISCUITS.

Raspberry Cream Cheese Coffee Cake

 2¼ cups all-purpose flour
 ¾ cup sugar
 ¾ cup margarine or butter
 ¾ teaspoon baking powder
 ½ teaspoon baking soda
 ¼ teaspoon salt
 ¾ cup sour cream

1 egg
1 teaspoon almond extract
1 8-ounce package cream cheese, softened
¼ cup sugar
1 egg
½ cup raspberry preserves (or ½ can pie filling)
½ cup sliced almonds

Grease and flour the bottom and sides of a 9- or 10-inch springform pan. In a large bowl combine the flour and ¾ cup of sugar. Cut in the margarine with a pastry blender or fork until the mixture resembles coarse crumbs. Reserve 1 cup of crumb mixture. To the remaining crumb mixture add the baking powder, soda, salt, sour cream, 1 egg, and almond extract. Blend well. Spread the batter over the bottom and 2 inches up sides the of the prepared pan. (Batter should be about ¼ inch thick on the sides.)

In a small bowl combine the cream cheese, ¼ cup of sugar, and 1 egg. Blend well. Pour over the batter in the pan. Carefully spoon preserves evenly over the cheese filling.

In a small bowl combine 1 cup of reserved crumb mixture and the sliced almonds. Sprinkle over the top. Bake in a 350° oven for 45 to 55 minutes or until the cream cheese filling is set and the crust is deep golden brown. Cool for 15 minutes.

Remove the sides of the pan. Serve warm or cool. Cut into wedges. Refrigerate leftovers.

MAKES 16 SERVINGS.

Poached Peaches

3 cups water
1½ cups sugar
⅓ cup lemon juice
1 tablespoon vanilla extract
6 medium peaches, halved, peeled and pits removed
....
½ cup part-skim ricotta cheese
¼ cup Neufchâtel cheese
3 tablespoons confectioners' sugar
1½ teaspoons lemon zest
½ teaspoon vanilla extract

In a large glass bowl microwave the water, sugar, lemon juice, and 1 tablespoon of vanilla on high for 10 minutes. Stir until the sugar dissolves. Add the peach halves to the

syrup. Microwave for 4 minutes. Cover and refrigerate.

In a medium bowl beat together the remaining ingredients. To serve, place a peach half in each serving plate, cut-side up, and scoop a dollop of mousse on top.

MAKES 12 SERVINGS.

The Cabbage Rose Inn

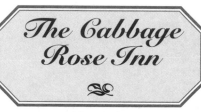

The Cabbage Rose Inn

❧

162 Main Street
Flemington, New Jersey 08822
(908) 788-0247

An enormous oak door and entry with a grand staircase and stained-glass window welcome guests to the Cabbage Rose. Inside, antique furnishings, hand-painted porcelain, a baby grand piano, and fanciful wallpapers continue the Victorian theme. Guest rooms are romantically decorated and luxurious. One has a fireplace. The cookie jar is always full of homemade goodies.

Chocolate Macaroon Muffins

2 eggs
¾ cup sugar
½ cup butter, melted
¾ cup milk
1½ cups flaked sweetened coconut
1½ cups sifted all-purpose flour
3 tablespoons unsweetened cocoa
½ cup chocolate chips

1½ teaspoons baking powder
½ teaspoon baking soda
¼ teaspoon salt

In a medium bowl combine the eggs, sugar, butter, milk, and coconut. In a separate bowl combine the remaining ingredients. Pour the dry ingredients into the wet and fold together gently just until mixed. Spoon into greased muffin cups. Bake in a 350° oven for 15 to 20 minutes.

MAKES 1 DOZEN.

Plum Coffee Cake

½ cup butter
1 cup sugar
2 cups sifted unbleached flour
1 teaspoon baking powder
Pinch salt
2 eggs
12 Italian or purple plums, halved
Sugar to taste
1 teaspoon ground cinnamon

In a large bowl cream together the butter and sugar. Add the flour, baking powder, salt, and eggs, and beat well. Spoon the batter into a 9-inch springform pan. Place the plum halves skin-side-up on top of the batter. Sprinkle lightly with sugar and cinnamon. Bake in a 350° oven for 1 hour. Cool to lukewarm and serve.

Variation: Substitute fresh peaches or nectarines or apples when plums are not in season.

MAKES 6 TO 8 SERVINGS.

Apple Cream Coffee Cake

½ cup chopped walnuts
2 teaspoons ground cinnamon
1½ cups sugar
½ cup butter or margarine
2 eggs
1 teaspoon vanilla extract
2 cups all-purpose flour
1 teaspoon baking soda
½ teaspoon salt
1 teaspoon baking powder
1 cup sour cream or yogurt
1 medium tart apple, sliced

In a small bowl mix the nuts, cinnamon, and ½ cup of sugar, and set aside. In a large bowl cream the butter and add the remaining sugar. Mix well. Beat in the eggs and vanilla.

In a separate bowl measure flour, soda, salt, and baking powder. Beat dry ingredients into creamed mixture, alternating with sour cream or yogurt. Spread half the batter into a greased 9-inch springform pan. Top with apple slices and half of the walnut mixture. Cover with the remaining batter. Sprinkle with the remaining nut mixture. Bake in a 375° oven for 40 minutes. Cool before serving.

MAKES 6 TO 8 SERVINGS.

Ashling Cottage

🙠

106 Sussex Avenue
Spring Lake, New Jersey 07762
9908) 449-3553

---

*G*eorge *Huelett, a prominent builder responsible for much of Spring Lake's remarkable architecture, built the Ashling Cottage in 1877 using lumber from the 1876 Philadelphia Exposition. Spring Lake is filled with antique shops, quaint boutiques, and nineteenth century charm. The lake area offers abundant opportunities for outdoor activities including golf, tennis, horseback riding, and canoeing.*

Pepper Buttermilk Biscuits

3¾ cups all-purpose flour
2 tablespoons baking powder
2 teaspoons ground pepper
1¼ teaspoons salt
6 tablespoons chilled butter, cut into pieces
⅓ cup chilled shortening, cut into pieces
1½ cups chilled buttermilk

In a large bowl mix together the flour, baking powder, pepper, and salt. Add the butter and shortening and rub this together with fingers until coarse crumbs form. Mix in the buttermilk. Turn the dough out onto a floured surface and knead gently until combined. Roll out the dough to about ½-inch thickness and cut into biscuits with a 2-inch biscuit cutter. Place on ungreased baking sheets. Bake in a 450° oven for approximately 15 minutes.

Note: These are nice served with whipped honey butter. Beat 2 cups of softened unsalted butter mixed with ¼ cup of honey until smooth and soft.

MAKES 2 DOZEN.

Lemon Pound Cake

1½ cups unsalted butter
1 8-ounce package cream cheese
3 cups sugar
¼ cup fresh lemon juice
1½ tablespoons vanilla extract
1 tablespoon grated lemon zest
6 eggs
3 cups all-purpose flour
¼ teaspoon salt
1¾ cups confectioners' sugar
3 tablespoons milk
1 tablespoon fresh lemon juice

Grease and flour a 10-inch angel food pan. In a large bowl cream together the butter and cream cheese. Gradually add the sugar, and beat until light and fluffy, 2 minutes. Add ¼ cup of lemon juice, the vanilla, and lemon zest. Add the eggs 2 at a time. Add the flour and salt, and beat just until the batter is smooth and creamy. Spoon into the prepared pan. Bake in a 350° oven for 1 hour and 30 minutes or until a toothpick inserted in the center comes out clean. Cool completely.

In a small bowl mix together the confectioners' sugar, milk, and 1 tablespoon of lemon juice until smooth. Spoon over the cake, allowing the glaze to drip down the sides. Let stand until the glaze sets, about 30 minutes.

MAKES 8 TO 10 SERVINGS.

Ashling Cottage

Bread Pudding with Whiskey Sauce

1 loaf stale French bread, crumbled (6 to 8 cups)
4 cups milk
2 cups sugar
½ cup melted butter
3 eggs
2 tablespoons vanilla extract
1 cup raisins
1 cup sweetened flaked coconut
1 cup chopped pecans
1 tablespoon ground cinnamon
1 tablespoon grated nutmeg

½ cup butter
1½ cups confectioners' sugar
2 egg yolks
½ cup bourbon, or to taste

In a large bowl combine the bread, milk, sugar, melted butter, eggs, vanilla, raisins, coconut, pecans, cinnamon, and nutmeg. Mix well. Pour into a buttered 9 x 13-inch baking dish. Place in a cold oven. Turn the oven to 350° and bake for 1 hour and 15 minutes or until the top is golden. Serve warm with Whiskey Sauce.

In a saucepan over medium heat whisk together ½ cup of butter and the confectioners' sugar. Remove the pan from the heat and blend in the egg yolks. Return to heat and simmer 5 minutes, stirring constantly until thickened. Pour in bourbon, stirring constantly.

MAKES 8 SERVINGS.

Normandy Inn

🙠

21 Tuttle Avenue
Spring Lake, New Jersey 07762
(908) 449-7172

---

*A*n *Italianate Villa with accented Queen Anne modifications, the Normandy Inn was built in 1888 as a private mansion. It has served as an inn for almost eighty years. The* *furnishings and decor are classic Victorian: Herter beds, woven Brussels carpets, an antique English case clock. There are eighteen guest rooms, each with its own personality and decorated with antiques.*

Normandy Inn

Anne Marie's Warm Fuzzy

¼ **cup butter**
½ **cup brown sugar (light or dark)**
 Apple Cider
 Cinnamon sticks

In a sauté pan melt ¼ cup of butter with ½ cup firmly packed brown sugar (light or dark, depending on preference) until combined well to make butterscotch. Set this aside to cool.

When it is cooled, warm some apple cider in a saucepan. Drop a teaspoon of the butterscotch into a mug and pour in some of the warm cider. Stir to melt the butterscotch, add a cinnamon stick, and serve.

Note: Though this variation is not served at the inn, substitute a shot of rum and boiling water for the cider, to have an excellent Hot Buttered Rum.

MAKES 8 TO 10 SERVINGS.

Nicki's Frittata

1 **tablespoon butter**
1 **cup total chopped red bell pepper, onion, tomato, mushrooms, and zucchini**
3 **beaten eggs**
2 **tablespoons total chopped fresh basil, chives, and parsley**
⅓ **cup good-quality Parmigiana cheese (or ½ cup sharp Cheddar, Swiss, or any favorite cheese, optional)**
 Sour cream
 Chives for garnish

In an ovenproof pan melt the butter and sauté the vegetables until tender-crisp. Pour off the excess liquid and add the eggs to the pan. Cook until the edges are done. Sprinkle fresh herbs over the top and place under the broiler to finish cooking. The frittata is done when the eggs are a golden brown. (If adding the cheese, scatter over the frittata halfway through cooking under the broiler.) Slide the frittata out of the pan onto a plate (do not flip over) and top with a dollop of sour cream and a dash of the chives.

MAKES 2 SERVINGS.

Pico de Gallo

1 **medium tomato, seeded and chopped**
1 **small onion, chopped**
¼ **cup chopped fresh cilantro**
 Juice of 1 lime
 Chopped jalapeño pepper to taste, optional
 Salt and pepper to taste

In a small bowl mix all ingredients and allow them to rest for at least 30 minutes to allow the flavors to blend.

MAKES ABOUT 1 CUP.

Susan's Classic Bread Pudding

1½ **pounds stale bread**
8 **eggs**
1 **quart half and half**
¼ **cup vanilla extract**
¾ **cup sugar**
1 **teaspoon ground cinnamon**
1 **cup raisins**
2 **apples, cored and chopped into bite-sized pieces (peeled or unpeeled)**
1 **cup chopped walnuts (optional)**

Spray a 12½ x 10½-inch baking dish with cooking spray. Shred the bread into pieces into the baking dish. In a large bowl combine the eggs, half and half, vanilla, sugar, and cinnamon, and beat until mixed well. Add the raisins, apples, and nuts. Pour this mixture over the shredded bread, making sure that all of the bread is moistened by the mixture. Refrigerate for 1 hour, so the bread might soak up the egg mixture. Bake in a 350° oven for 25 to 30 minutes or until the bread has puffed up like a soufflé (don't get excited, the

soufflé effect does not last) and is golden brown. Let cool slightly and serve warm.

Note: Normandy Inn changes seasonally what is served with this bread pudding. In the summer, lightly whipped cream and fresh blueberries. In the fall, a cooked cranberry purée or warm homemade applesauce.

MAKES 10 TO 12 DESSERT SERVINGS OR 12 TO 16 BREAKFAST SERVINGS.

Sea Crest by the Sea

19 Tuttle Avenue
Spring Lake, New Jersey 07762
(908) 449-9031

The Sea Crest is an elegant old-fashioned gem in a town known for its nineteenth-century wonders. The extensive collection of French, English, and heirloom antiques that furnish the inn were gathered as a labor of love by the innkeepers. There are twelve guest rooms, each with its own themed decor. Their names speak for themselves: Sleigh Ride, Flamingo Grove, Yankee Clipper, Mardi Gras, and Casablanca, to name a few. The Queen Victoria Suite is very stately indeed. Breakfast here begins at a civilized hour—nine o'clock—and for a constitutional afterwards, a quiet beach and boardwalk wait only half a block away.

Featherbed Eggs

14 **eggs**
1½ **cups milk**
1½ **cups half and half**
 Approximately 8 cups cubed or shredded bread, any heavy crusts removed
 Salt and pepper to taste
 Herbs of your choice to taste

Butter a 9 x 11-inch baking pan. In a large bowl beat the eggs until frothy. Add the milk and half and half and beat again until blended well. Place the bread cubes in the prepared dish (they should fill the dish approximately three-fourths full). Slowly pour the egg mixture over the bread. Season to taste. Cover and refrigerate for 6 to 8 hours or overnight. Bake in a 350° oven for about 1 hour to 1 hour and 30 minutes, until lightly browned and puffy like a featherbed.

Variations: Simply tuck the added ingredients into the mixture after it is assembled in the pan: Sautéed sliced mushrooms, fresh rosemary, thyme, and sage; shredded Cheddar, mozzarella, Swiss cheese, or any combination; dollops of salsa and sour cream, with fresh cilantro and shredded Monterey Jack cheese; parboiled broccoli flowerets and shredded Swiss cheese; diced ham, bacon, or sausage with any shredded cheese; slivered sun-dried tomatoes, fresh basil, and shredded mozzarella.

MAKES 8 SERVINGS.

Raspberry Chocolate Chip Muffins

2   *cups all-purpose flour*
¼   *to ½ cup sugar*
2½   *teaspoons baking powder*
½   *teaspoon salt*
¼   *teaspoon grated nutmeg*
½   *cup butter, melted and cooled*
1   *cup milk*
1   *egg, slightly beaten*
1   *cup raspberries*
¼   *cup mini chocolate chips*
    Confectioners' sugar

Grease 12 standard muffin cups. In a large bowl stir together the flour, sugar, baking powder, salt, and nutmeg. In a separate bowl combine the butter, milk, and egg. Make a well in the middle of the dry ingredients. Add the butter mixture and stir just until combined. Stir in the berries and chocolate chips with just a few additional strokes. Spoon into muffin cups. Bake in a 400° oven for 20 to 30 minutes or until a toothpick inserted in the center comes out clean. Cool 5 minutes and remove muffins to wire rack to finish cooling. For a nice touch, dust with confectioners' sugar before serving.

MAKES 1 DOZEN.

Sea Crest Buttermilk Scones

2   *cups all-purpose flour*
⅓   *cup sugar*
1½   *teaspoons baking powder*
½   *teaspoon baking soda*
¼   *teaspoon salt*
6   *tablespoons unsalted butter, chilled*
½   *cup buttermilk*
1   *large egg*
1½   *teaspoons vanilla extract*
⅔   *cup currants or raisins (optional)*

In a large bowl stir together the flour, sugar, baking powder, soda, and salt. Cut the butter into ½-inch cubes and distribute them over the flour mixture. With a pastry blender or 2 knives cut in the butter until the mixture resembles coarse crumbs. In a small bowl stir together the buttermilk, egg, and vanilla. Add the buttermilk mixture to the dry ingredients and stir to combine. Stir in the currants, if desired. With lightly floured hands, pat the dough into an 8-inch circle on an ungreased baking sheet. With a serrated knife, cut into 8 wedges. Bake in a 400° oven for 18 to 20 minutes or until the top is lightly browned and a toothpick inserted into the center of a scone comes out clean.

Remove the baking sheet to a wire rack and cool for 5 minutes. Using a spatula, transfer the scones to the wire rack to cool. Recut into wedges, if necessary. Serve warm or cool completely and store in an airtight container.

MAKES 8 SCONES.

Sea Crest by the Sea

Whistling Swan Inn

≈

110 Main Street
Stanhope, New Jersey 07847
(201) 347-6369

*T*he deep wraparound porch of this grand Victorian invites summertime lounging and rocking. The interior of the home with its lovely, old-fashioned furnishings is no less relaxing, conveying the sense that time is a very relative thing here. All rooms have private baths and are furnished in themes. Breakfast is served outside when the weather is warm, or by the fireplace on winter mornings.

Paula's Chunky Fruit Soup

4   *cups pineapple juice*
½   *cup tapioca*
4   *cups orange juice*
2   *cups tart diced apples*
1   *cup crushed or chunk pineapple*
1   *12-ounce can mandarin oranges, drained*
2   *cups green grape halves*
½   *to 1 cup sugar (optional)*
    Toasted coconut flakes for garnish (optional)

In a large saucepan combine the pineapple juice and tapioca. Let stand for 5 minutes.

Place the pan over low heat and cook, stirring constantly, until the tapioca becomes clear. Remove from the heat and add the orange juice. Cool.

Add the cut fruit. Taste and add sugar to the desired sweetness. Chill thoroughly.

Serve in small fruit bowls. Garnish with coconut.

MAKES 12 SERVINGS.

Baked Fruit Compote

1   20-ounce can cherry pie filling
1   cup water
¼   cup white wine
1   20-ounce can pineapple chunks, in
      juice
4   cups pitted prunes
1   12-ounce package dried apricots
⅓   cup slivered almonds
2   apples (green or red), cubed
½   cup cinnamon-maple sprinkle
1   11-ounce box golden raisins
2   16-ounce cans whole cranberries (or
      1 bag frozen)

In a large mixing bowl combine the pie filling, water, wine, and juice from the pineapple. Stir to blend. Add the remaining ingredients, including pineapple chunks, and stir. Place in a deep 9-inch casserole. Bake in a 350° oven for about 1 hour and 30 minutes, adding more water if necessary.

Can also be prepared by placing the mixed ingredients in a pot and cooking over low to medium heat, stirring occasionally. When the mixture comes to a full boil, reduce the heat to simmer and cook for 10 to 15 minutes, stirring almost constantly.

This casserole freezes and reheats beautifully. Can be served warm from a crock pot. It is also good on waffles or toast.

MAKES 6 TO 8 SERVINGS.

Lazy River Dill Bread

3   cups self-rising flour
2   heaping tablespoons sugar
2   teaspoons dillweed
1   teaspoon salt
1   12-ounce can beer, room tempera-
      ture
    Sesame seeds
2   tablespoons butter

In a large bowl mix the dry ingredients. Add the beer and mix until moistened. Place the mixture in a well-greased loaf pan. Sprinkle sesame seeds on top. Allow to rise in warm place for 15 minutes. Bake in a 350° oven for 55 minutes. Remove the loaf from the oven and dot with butter. Return to the oven and bake an additional 15 minutes.

MAKES 1 LOAF.

Whistling Swan Inn

Farmhouse Corn Cakes

2½   cups corn kernels, fresh or frozen
1½   cups all-purpose flour
½   cup yellow cornmeal
2   tablespoons sugar
2   teaspoons baking powder
2   teaspoons salt
3   eggs
¾   cup milk
¼   cup butter, melted

Before using the corn, thaw and precook the frozen corn or cook the fresh ears and cut from the cob. In a large bowl sift the dry ingredients together. In a separate bowl mix the eggs, milk, and butter. Add the liquid mixture to the dry ingredients, stirring gently. Add the corn and stir. Pour in 4-inch circles onto a well-buttered, heated skillet. Cook 3 to 4 minutes or until golden. Flip the cakes, and cook 3 minutes more.

MAKES 10 TO 12 CORN CAKES.

NEW MEXICO

Bottger Mansion Bed and Breakfast

110 San Felipe N.W.
Albuquerque, New Mexico 87104
(505) 243-3639

An early twentieth century style building, the Bottager Mansion stands in sharp contrast to the Pueblo style structures in Albuquerque's famed Old Town. With its shaded garden courtyard, it is sequestered by a wall that shuts out the bustle and noise of the historic district. Among the guests who have stayed here was the notorious gangster Machine-gun Kelly. While Kelly may have been interested in the city's banking establishments, mansion visitors today will want to stroll through Old Town, see the historic San Felipe Church, sample the fine southwestern art galleries near the plaza, and tour the nearby natural history museum that features fossil remains from the largest dinosaur ever found.

Wild Rice Pancakes with Raspberry Applesauce

    3   cups water
    1   cup wild rice
 1½   teaspoons salt
  ¾   cup sifted all-purpose flour
  ½   teaspoon baking powder
  ½   teaspoon baking soda
  ¼   teaspoon ground black pepper
  ½   cup buttermilk
    1   large egg
    1   tablespoon heavy cream
  ¼   cup chopped pecans, toasted
 1½   tablespoons chopped chives
    1   teaspoon or more olive oil
        Raspberry Applesauce (recipe follows)

In a medium saucepan mix the water, wild rice, and 1 teaspoon of salt and bring to a boil. Reduce the heat and simmer until the wild rice is tender, about 40 minutes. Drain well. Cool to room temperature. Can be prepared 1 day ahead; covered, and refrigerated. In a medium bowl mix the flour, baking powder, soda, ground black pepper, and remaining ½ teaspoon of salt. In a separate bowl whisk the buttermilk, egg, and heavy cream to blend. Add to the dry ingredients and stir until blended well. Mix in the cooked wild rice, chopped pecans, and chopped chives. In a large nonstick skillet heat the olive oil over medium-high heat. Pour the batter into the skillet, forming 5-inch diameter pancakes. Cook until golden brown, about 2 minutes per side.

Bottger Mansion

Repeat with the remaining batter, adding olive oil as needed. Serve with Raspberry Applesauce.
MAKES 6 SERVINGS.

Raspberry Applesauce

    8   medium apples, cored
    1   cup fresh or frozen raspberries
  ⅓   cup raspberry cider

In a blender combine the apples, raspberries, and raspberry cider. Purée to the consistency of applesauce. Must be prepared the same day.
MAKES 6 SERVINGS.

Chicken Quesadilla

  ¼   cup chopped onions
  ¼   cup chopped cilantro
  ½   cup chopped tomatoes
    2   flour tortillas
  ½   cup shredded Cheddar cheese
    1   chicken breast, cooked and shredded
    1   tablespoon butter or olive oil

In a medium bowl mix the onion, cilantro, and tomato. Set aside. Warm the flour tortillas and fold in half. Inside each folded tortilla add Cheddar cheese, shredded chicken, and tomato mixture.

In a skillet heat the butter or olive oil. Fry the filled tortillas until crispy on both sides. Remove from the pan and cut each into 4 pieces.

Variation: Garnish with guacamole or any favorite salsa.

MAKES 4 TO 6 SERVINGS.

Casa Del Granjero

Casa Del Granjero

❧

414 de Baca Lane N.W.
Albuquerque, New Mexico 87114
(505) 897-4144

Casa Del Granjero means "the farmer's house," and likely as not, that's just what it was. Like so many structures in New Mexico, it is difficult to say just how long this old territorial house has stood here in Albuquerque's far North Valley. Kiva fireplaces, handmade tiles, and carved Mexican furnishings give it a feeling of timelessness like that of the surrounding desert country. The Casa offers five suites and two rooms furnished and decorated in a manner that suggests old Spain.

Breakfast Swiss Soufflé

- 1   **small loaf sourdough French bread, broken into small pieces**
- ⅓   **pound Swiss cheese, grated**
- ¼   **pound Monterey Jack cheese, grated**
- 2   **cups milk**
- 10   **eggs, lightly beaten**
- ¼   **cup dry wine**
- 2   **scallions, minced**
- 2   **teaspoons prepared mustard**
      Salt to taste
- ¼   **teaspoon fresh ground pepper**
- 1   **cup sour cream**
- ½   **cup freshl grated Parmesan cheese**
- 1   **cup chunky salsa**

In a 9 x 13-inch buttered baking dish place the pieces of bread. Sprinkle the cheeses on top. In a large bowl combine the milk, eggs, wine, scallions, mustard, salt, and pepper. Beat the ingredients together well. Pour the mixture over the bread. Cover the baking dish with foil and refrigerate overnight.

Remove the baking dish from the refrigerator and let it come to room temperature. Bake in a 325° oven for 1 hour or until it is firmly set.

In a small bowl combine the sour cream and Parmesan cheese, and mix them together. Spread the mixture on top of the soufflé. Return the soufflé to the oven and bake it for 10 minutes more or until it is lightly browned. Remove the soufflé. Cut into servings and serve with salsa.

MAKES 8 SERVINGS.

Lemon Piñon Rice

- ½   **cup butter**
- ½   **cup piñon nuts (pine nuts)**
- ½   **cup seeded and finely chopped red bell peppers**
- ¼   **cup seeded and finely chopped green bell peppers**
- ¼   **cup seeded and finely chopped yellow bell peppers**
- 1   **tablespoon fresh garlic, minced**
- 4   **scallions, minced**
- 1½   **cups cooked white rice**
- ½   **cup lemon juice, fresh squeezed**
- ½   **cup minced fresh parsley**
- 1   **lemon, cut into wedges**
- 6   **fresh parsley sprigs**

In a large skillet melt the butter over medium heat until it is hot. Add the pinon nuts and

sauté for 3 minutes or until they are lightly browned.

Add the bell peppers, garlic, and scallions, and sauté for 5 minutes or until the vegetables are tender-crisp. Add the cooked rice and mix well. Add the lemon juice and minced parsley.

Garnish each serving with a lemon wedge and parsley sprig.

MAKES 6 SERVINGS.

Custard French Toast

- 12   **very thick slices dense French bread**
- 10   **eggs, lightly beaten**
- 3   **cups milk**
- ¾   **cup sugar**
- ½   **cup apricot nectar**
- 2   **tablespoons vanilla extract**
- 2   **tablespoons butter**
- 1   **tablespoon canola oil**

In a large buttered baking dish place the slices of bread in 1 layer. In a large bowl combine the eggs, milk, sugar, apricot nectar, and vanilla. Mix the ingredients together. Pour the mixture over the bread. Cover the dish with plastic wrap and refrigerate overnight.

In a large nonstick skillet combine the butter and canola oil and heat over medium heat until the butter is melted and hot. Add the bread slices and cook for 3 minutes on each side or until lightly browned.

MAKES 6 SERVINGS.

Sarabande

❧

5637 Rio Brande Boulevard N.W.
Albuquerque, New Mexico 87107
(505) 345-4923

The Sarabande is situated in Rio Rancho, on the west side of the Rio Grande and well away from the traffic and hubbub of Albuquerque's central business core. Visitors can enjoy its peaceful courtyard fountain and country kitchen as well as the city's fine museums, zoo, and historic Old Town.

Fruit Pancakes

> 5 tablespoons butter
> 2 apples, cored and sliced
>   Juice of ½ lemon
> 5 tablespoons confectioners' sugar
>   Dash ground cinnamon
> ¼ cup dried cranberries
> 3 eggs, room temperature
> ½ cup milk
> ½ cup all-purpose flour

In a skillet melt the butter and sauté the apples until tender. Add the lemon juice, confectioners' sugar, cinnamon, and cranberries. In a medium bowl beat the eggs. Add the milk and flour. Place the apple mixture in a buttered pie plate. Pour the egg mixture over the apples. Bake in a 425° oven for 15 to 20 minutes.

Serve immediately.

Note: This pancake will rise to 6 inches and fall almost immediately. We serve with vanilla yogurt.

MAKES 4 SERVINGS.

Sarabande Sausage

> 1 pound Jimmy Dean plain sausage
> 1 Granny Smith apple, peeled and
>   chopped finely
> 3 green onions, chopped finely
> ¼ teaspoon red pepper
> ¼ teaspoon white pepper
> ¼ teaspoon black pepper

In a large bowl mix all ingredients well. Shape into patties. Fry, covered, over low heat for 30 minutes. Turn once.

MAKES ABOUT 4 SERVINGS.

Hacienda Vargas

Hacienda Vargas

❧

P.O. Box 307
Algodones, New Mexico 87001
(505) 867-9115
(800) 261-0006

---

*N*orth of Albuquerque on the historic El Camino Real, the Hacienda Vargas has been both a stagecoach stop and Indian trading post. The furnishings and decor of the five suites and two guest rooms are in keeping with its past. The Hacienda features its own adobe chapel.

Cuban Black Beans

> 1½ pounds onions, chopped
> 1½ green bell peppers, chopped
> 2 4-ounce cans red pimentos
> 2 cups olive oil
> 2½ pounds black beans, cooked
>   Salt and pepper to taste
> 2 teaspoons sugar
> ⅓ cup white vinegar

In a skillet cook the onions and bell peppers until the liquid is evaporated. Add 1 can of pimentos and half of the olive oil. Fry all the above and add to the cooked beans. Season with salt, pepper, and sugar. Cook very slowly for approximately 3 hours, until the mixture thickens. During this time, add the remaining olive oil, vinegar, and the other can of red pimentos with juice.

MAKES 15 TO 20 SERVINGS.

Chorizo Roll

> 4 links Mexican chorizo
> 12 eggs
> 1½ cups milk
> 2 cups shredded Cheddar cheese
>   Salt and pepper to taste
> 2 cups cubed French bread
> 1 8-ounce package cream cheese, soft-
>   ened

> 1 tablespoon diced green chile
>   Salsa
>   Avocado slices for garnish

In a skillet fry the chorizo. Drain. In a large bowl beat the eggs. Add the milk, chorizo, Cheddar cheese, salt, pepper, and French bread, and mix well. In a separate bowl mix the cream cheese with the green chile. Set aside. Spray a jelly roll pan with cooking spray. Line the pan with foil, including the sides. Spray generously with cooking spray. Spread the bread mixture in the pan. Bake in a 350° oven for 45 minutes to 1 hour, until the eggs are firm.

Wait until it cools. Turn the egg out onto waxed paper. Carefully peel off the foil using waxed paper as a helper. Spread the cream cheese with green chile on the entire surface. Roll the egg mixture into a tight cylinder. Garnish with salsa and avocado.

MAKES 6 SERVINGS.

Sopaipillas De Vargas

> 4 cups all-purpose flour
> 2 teaspoons baking powder
> 1 teaspoon salt
> ¼ cup shortening
> 1½ cups warm water
>   Shortening
>   Honey

In a medium bowl combine the dry ingredients. Cut in the shortening. Make a well in the center of the dry ingredients. Add water to the dry ingredients and work into a dough. Knead the dough until smooth, cover, and set aside for 20 minutes.

In a heavy pan heat 2 inches of shortening at medium-high heat. Roll the dough to ⅛-inch thickness on a lightly floured board. Cut the dough into 4-inch squares and fry until golden on both sides, turning once. (If the shortening is sufficiently hot, the sopaipillas will puff and become hollow shortly after being placed in the shortening.) Drain the sopaipillas on paper towels. Serve with honey.

MAKES 48 SOPAIPILLAS.

Savory Potato Pancakes

> 3 large potatoes, peeled
> 2 tablespoons finely grated onion
> 2 eggs
> 1 teaspoon salt

Pepper to taste
Fresh grated nutmeg to taste
⅓ *cup all-purpose flour*
    Oil and butter for frying
    Applesauce
    Sour cream

In a food processor or by hand grate the potatoes, pressing out the excess moisture between 2 paper towels.

In a medium bowl combine the potatoes, onion, eggs, salt, pepper, nutmeg, and flour.

In a large heavy skillet heat a thin layer of oil and butter. Drop the potato mixture by heaping tablespoons into the fat, flattening each mound with a spatula. Fry the pancakes for about 4 minutes on each side, until uniformly crisp and golden brown. Drain on paper towels.

Serve hot with applesauce and sour cream.

MAKES 4 TO 6 SERVINGS.

Sierra Mesa Lodge

Fort Stanton Road, P.O. Box 463
Alto, New Mexico 88312
(505) 336-5415

Settled on a hillside overlooking the Capitan Mountains, the lodge is near Ruidoso with its shops, restaurants, and world famous quarter horse track. Also nearby is the Sierra Blanca "Apache" ski area. Rooms feature period antique furnishing as well as goose down pillows and comforters. Outdoor activities, such as hiking, horseback riding, hunting, and fishing, abound in this southern mountain region of New Mexico.

Sierra Mesa Lodge's Chocolate Chip Streusel Cake

½ *cup sugar*
⅓ *cup firmly packed brown sugar*
1   *teaspoon ground cinnamon*
1   *6-ounce package chocolate chips*
1   *cup chopped walnuts or pecans*

....

½ *cup butter*
1   *cup sugar*
2   *eggs*
1   *8-ounce carton sour cream*
1   *teaspoon baking soda*
1   *teaspoon baking powder*
1   *teaspoon salt*
2   *teaspoons vanilla extract*
2   *cups all-purpose flour, sifted*

In a medium bowl combine ½ cup of sugar, the brown sugar, cinnamon, chocolate chips, and walnuts. Set aside.

In a large bowl cream the butter and add the sugar, beating until smooth. Add the eggs, sour cream, soda, baking powder, salt, and vanilla. Add the flour and mix until smooth. Grease a tube pan. Sprinkle some topping mixture in the bottom, then spoon half of the batter over the mixture. Alternate layers, ending with the topping. Bake in a 325° oven for 45 to 60 minutes.

MAKES 15 TO 20 SERVINGS.

Make-Ahead Layered Mushrooms and Eggs

1   *10¾-ounce can condensed cream of mushroom soup*
3   *tablespoons dry sherry or milk*
1½ *cups shredded sharp Cheddar cheese*
1½ *cups shredded Monterey Jack cheese*
18 *eggs*
2   *tablespoons milk*
1   *teaspoon parsley flakes*
½ *teaspoon dillweed*
⅛ *teaspoon pepper*
¼ *cup butter or margarine*
¼ *pound mushrooms, sliced*
¼ *cup chopped green onion*
   Paprika

Sierra Mesa Lodge

In a pan over medium heat stir the soup and sherry until hot and smooth. Remove from the heat and set aside.

In a small bowl toss the cheeses lightly to mix. Set aside.

In a medium bowl beat together the eggs, milk, parsley, dillweed, and pepper. Set aside.

In a wide frying pan over medium-low heat melt the butter. Add the mushrooms and onion, and cook, stirring constantly, until the onion is limp. Add the egg mixture and cook, gently lifting the cooked portion to allow the uncooked portion to flow underneath, until the eggs are softly set. Remove from the heat. Spoon half the scrambled eggs into a 7 x 11-inch baking dish. Spoon half the soup mixture over the eggs, then sprinkle evenly with half the cheese mixture. Repeat layers; sprinkle top with paprika. If made ahead, cool, cover, and refrigerate.

Bake uncovered in a 300° oven for 30 to 50 minutes or until hot and bubbly. Let stand for 10 minutes. Cut into squares.

MAKES 8 TO 10 SERVINGS.

Monte Cristo Breakfast Sandwich

2   *slices white sandwich bread*
2   *or more pieces cold sliced turkey or chicken breast*
2   *or more pieces thinly sliced ham*
2   *or more pieces Jack or Swiss cheese*
2   *eggs, well-beaten*
1½ *tablespoons heavy cream*
   Dash salt
   Butter or margarine
   Strawberry jam

Assemble a sandwich of bread, turkey, ham, and cheese. Cut in half. In a medium bowl mix the eggs, cream, and salt. Dip the sandwiches in the mixture. In a skillet sauté in butter or margarine until golden brown on each side. Serve with strawberry jam.

MAKES 1 SERVING.

La Hacienda Grande

21 Baros Lane
Bernalillo, New Mexico 87004
(505) 867-1887

*O*ver 250 years old, this historic hacienda combines gracious decor and hospitality with its magnificent architecture dating to the Spanish Colonial era. The adobe walls, heavy beams, wooden ceilings, and brick floors make it a showcase of southwestern-style elegance. Situated in Bernalillo, one of the oldest European settlements in the country, the hacienda offers six spacious suites.

Breakfast Casserole

    6 cups bread pieces
    3 eggs
    2 cups milk
    2 teaspoons prepared mustard
    1 teaspoon salt
    1 cup shredded Cheddar cheese
    ....
    ⅔ cup sour cream (optional)
    ¼ cup salsa (optional)

Cover the bottom of a buttered 9 x 13-inch pan with plain crumbs or small bread pieces. In a small bowl beat the egg, milk, and, mustard, salt, and pour over the bread. Sprinkle with cheese. May be refrigerated overnight. Bake in a 325° oven for 45 minutes.

Mix the sour cream and salsa and put a dab on each serving piece, if desired.

Variation: Add 2 cups diced ham, turkey ham, or bacon on top of the crumbs.
MAKES 8 SERVINGS.

Amaretto French Toast

    6 eggs
    ⅓ cup Amaretto
    ⅓ cup half and half
    3 tablespoons maple syrup
    1 tablespoon grated orange zest (or ½ teaspoon dried)
    ⅓ cup orange juice
       Pinch salt
       French bread (⅓- to ½-inch slices)
       Butter
       Cinnamon
       Maple syrup

In a large bowl whisk together the eggs, Amaretto, half and half, maple syrup, orange zest, orange juice, and salt. Dip the bread slices in the egg mixture and let soak a minute or so on each side. Cook on a hot grill that has been thinly coated with butter or oil. Sprinkle with cinnamon and serve with butter and maple syrup.
MAKES 6 TO 8 SERVINGS.

Salad with Honey Mustard Dressing

    1 cup raw honey
    1 cup Dijon mustard
    1 cup apple cider vinegar
    ½ cup white wine
    ½ cup olive oil
    ....
    1 cup grated carrot
    1 cup grated jicama
    1 cup grated zucchini
    1 cup grated yellow squash
       Pine nuts, pumpkin seeds, or sesame seeds

In a blender combine the honey, mustard, vinegar, and wine, and blend for 1 minute. Dribble in the oil. Place in a covered jar and chill. Makes 1 quart.

In a serving bowl toss the vegetables with the dressing. Sprinkle with pine nuts, pumpkin seeds, or sesame seeds.
MAKES 4 TO 6 SERVINGS.

La Posada Chimayo

La Posada Chimayo

P.O. Box 463
Chimayo, New Mexico 87522
(505) 351-4605

A small inn located on a back road in the bucolic community of Chimayo, La Posada offers two large farmhouse rooms as well as two spacious suites in a separate guest house. Both houses are traditional adobe brick with viga ceilings and corner kiva-style fireplaces. Rooms are appointed with Mexican hand-loomed rugs, hand-woven spreads on high beds, and leather furniture. Santa Fe and Taos are both within easy reach, and six historic Pueblos are within half an hour's drive of Chimayo.

Chimayó Red Chile

    ½ pound pork (ground or chopped)
    1 to 2 cloves garlic
    2 cups water
    2 tablespoons lard
    2 tablespoons all-purpose flour
    1 heaping tablespoon ground red chile (chimayó chile is the best)

In a large pot stew the pork with the garlic in 2 cups of water.

In a heavy saucepan melt the lard. Blend in the flour and cook until bubbly. Add the red chile, and stir until you can smell it. Do not burn!

Slowly add the liquid from the pork, then the pork meat, and simmer. If too thin, add a little flour.

Red Chile is excellent served over eggs, beans or potatoes.
MAKES 4 TO 6 SERVINGS.

Bread Pudding

3   eggs
     Heaping ½ cup sugar
1½   teaspoons vanilla extract
     Dash salt
2   cups half and half
¼   cup melted butter or margarine
4   cups homemade-type bread, cut in 1-
     inch cubes
½   to ⅔ cup raisins
     Confectioners' sugar

In a medium bowl beat the eggs. Add the sugar, vanilla, salt, half and half, and most of the melted butter. Add the bread and raisins. Let it soak up the liquid for 5 minutes.

Pour into a well-buttered 9-inch square dish. Place in a larger pan of hot water. Drizzle top with the remaining melted butter before baking. Bake in a 350° oven for 45 to 60 minutes. Sprinkle with confectioners' sugar and serve hot.

MAKES 4 SERVINGS.

Carriage House Bed and Breakfast
❧

925 Sixth Street
Las Vegas, New Mexico 87701
(505) 454-1784

With over 900 buildings on the National Register of Historic Places, Las Vegas, New Mexico, might be considered a museum of nineteenth century architecture. One its finest old homes is the Carriage House, built in 1893 and renovated to its original Victorian elegance. This B&B offers six well appointed guest rooms to visitors who want to sample the past of one of the wildest towns in the old west.

Carriage House

Ginger Carrot Muffins

2   cups all-purpose flour
1   cup firmly packed brown sugar
1   teaspoon baking powder
1   teaspoon baking soda
¼   teaspoon ground ginger
¼   teaspoon salt
2   eggs, lightly beaten
½   cup sour cream
½   cup oil
2   cups grated carrots
2   tablespoons fresh grated ginger
½   cup golden raisins
¼   cup coarsely chopped walnuts

In a large bowl sift together the flour, brown sugar, baking powder, soda, ginger, and salt. In a separate bowl combine the eggs, sour cream, and oil. Pour onto the dry ingredients and mix gently. Add the carrots, ginger, raisins, and nuts. Do not overmix. Spoon into paper-lined muffin cups. Bake in a 425° oven for 15 to 20 minutes.

MAKES ABOUT 18 MUFFINS.

Crab and Cheddar Muffins

1   cup grated sharp Cheddar cheese
3   to 4 tablespoons mayonnaise
1   6½-ounce can crab meat
2   to 3 scallions, finely chopped
4   English muffins, halved
     Red pepper
     Parsley sprigs

In a medium bowl mix together the Cheddar cheese, mayonnaise, crab, and scallions. Spread on English muffin halves. Lightly sprinkle with red pepper. Place on a baking sheet. Bake in a 325° oven for approximately 10 minutes or until the cheese has melted. Cut in halves or quarters. Decorate with parsley sprigs and enjoy.

MAKES 4 SERVINGS.

Orange Shortbread

1   cup all-purpose flour
6   tablespoons cornstarch
½   cup butter
¼   cup fine sugar
     Grated zest of 1 orange
     Sugar for sprinkling

In a medium bowl sift the flour and cornstarch together. In a large bowl cream the butter. Add the sugar and beat until pale and creamy. Add the orange zest. Work in the dry ingredients, 1 tablespoon at a time. Lift the shortbread onto a large baking tray. Roll out to an 8-inch circle. Pinch the edges and prick the shortbread well with a fork. Cut through into 12 sections with the back of a knife and sprinkle with a little sugar. Chill in the refrigerator for 15 minutes.

Bake in a 325 to 350° oven for 35 minutes or until golden brown. Cool in the baking tray for a few minutes, and then lift onto a wire tray to finish cooling.

MAKES 12 SERVINGS.

Casa De Patron Bed and Breakfast Inn
❧

Highway 380 East, P.O. 27
Lincoln, New Mexico 88338
(505) 653-4676

Billy the Kid slept in this adobe house, although he likely would have preferred to be elsewhere. The notorious gunslinger was briefly imprisoned here before his escape and fatal encounter with Pat Garrett. Originally the home of the prominent Patron family, the house is now a B&B with seven delightful guest rooms. Local museums tell Billy's story and recount the history of the Lincoln County War.

Dutch Babies

¼ cup butter or margarine
6 eggs
1½ cups milk
1½ cups all-purpose flour

Spray the sides of a 10-inch pie pan with cooking spray. Place the butter or margarine in the pan, and melt in the oven (do not burn).

In a blender combine the eggs and milk, and whirl until beaten well. Add the flour to the blender and whip for 15 to 20 seconds at high speed. Pour the mixture into the hot melted butter and return to the oven. Bake in a 425° oven for 25 minutes, when it will become puffed and golden.

Note: Serve with squeezed fresh lemon and confectioners' sugar, any kind of preserves, syrup, or any kind, fresh fruit compote, yogurt, or sour cream.

MAKES 4 SERVINGS.

Calienti Tortilla Soup

2 tablespoons oil
1 small onion, chopped
2 jalapeño peppers, chopped
2 cloves garlic, crushed
2 pounds round steak, cut into bite-sized pieces
1 15-ounce can stewed tomatoes
1 13¾-ounce can beef bouillon
1 13¾-ounce can chicken broth
1 10½-ounce can tomato soup
1½ cups water
1 tablespoon beef base
1½ teaspoon ground cumin
1 teaspoon chili powder
1 teaspoon salt
Pepper to taste
2 teaspoons Worcestershire sauce
1 tablespoon Pickapeppa sauce
4 corn tortillas, in ¼-inch strips, fried
¼ cup shredded Monterey Jack cheese

In a skillet heat the oil and sauté the onion, peppers, garlic, and meat. Add the tomatoes, soups, water, and seasonings, and bring to a boil. Reduce the heat and simmer for 1 hour. Add the tortillas and Monterey Jack cheese for the last 10 minutes.

MAKES 6 SERVINGS.

Adobe Abode Bed and Breakfast Inn

❧

202 Chapelle
Santa Fe, New Mexico 87501
(505) 983-3133

Just as Santa Fe itself is an inspiring mix of Native American, Hispanic, and Anglo cultures, so too is the Adobe Abode. Antiques from France and England, mahogany chairs from the Philippines, handmade Aspen pole beds, folk art from Oaxaca, and Spanish Colonial furnishings are brought together in such a way that no two rooms here are alike. For those not accustomed to adobe-style architecture, that too is a wonder. The walls can be a foot or more thick and the interior temperature of the house is always comfortable. Three of the guest rooms are in the original adobe home, while three others open onto a walled courtyard behind the main house. The Adobe Abode is only a few blocks from the central Santa Fe Plaza and the old Governor's Palace with its Native American weavers, potters, and jewelers.

Adobe Abode

Artichoke, Peppers, and Black Olive Soufflé

½ cup all-purpose flour
1 teaspoon baking powder
10 eggs, lightly beaten
½ cup butter, melted in the microwave for 1½ minutes
4 cups grated Monterey Jack cheese
2 cups small curd cottage cheese
1 14-ounce can artichoke hearts, quartered or chopped
1 2-ounce jar chopped pimentos (or 1 jar roasted red peppers)
1 6-ounce can sliced black olives
Salt and pepper to taste

In a large mixing bowl measure the flour and baking powder, and mix with a whisk. Pour in the beaten eggs and melted butter mix thoroughly. Mix in the remaining ingredients. Pour into a greased 9 x 13-inch glass baking pan. Level the top with a rubber spatula. Bake in a 400° oven for 30 minutes or until the top is lightly browned.

Cut in as many servings as you like for breakfast or brunch (up to 12) or cut into very small squares and serve as appetizers. May be frozen and reheated in the microwave.

MAKES 10 TO 12 SERVINGS.

Crustless Spinach Quiche

1 tablespoon oil
1 large onion, chopped
1 10-ounce box frozen spinach, thawed and squeezed dry (or broccoli or any vegetable)
5 eggs
¾ pound Muenster cheese, chopped or grated
Salt and pepper to taste

In a skillet heat the oil over medium-high heat. Add the onion and sauté until wilted. Add the spinach and cook until the excess moisture is evaporated. Let cool.

In a bowl beat the eggs. Add the Muenster cheese. Stir into the onion-spinach mixture and season to taste with salt and pepper. Spread evenly into a buttered 9-inch pie plate. Bake in a 350° oven for 40 to 45 minutes, until the top is nicely browned and a toothpick inserted in the center comes out clean.

MAKES 6 TO 8 SERVINGS.

Ginger Lime Honeydew Compote

Zest of 1 lime, removed in strips with vegetable peeler
½ *cup fresh lime juice*
½ *cup sugar*
1 *tablespoon grated peeled fresh ginger*
⅓ *cup water*
1 *honeydew melon, scooped into balls*
1 *tablespoon fresh mint leaves*

In a small heavy saucepan combine the zest, lime juice, sugar, ginger, water. Bring to a boil, stirring until the sugar is dissolved. Boil for 5 minutes. Pour the syrup through fine a sieve into a bowl and let cool.

In a serving bowl toss the melon balls with the syrup and mint. Cover and refrigerate for at least 2 hours or overnight.

MAKES 4 SERVINGS.

Mock Margarita Punch

1 *cup orange juice*
¾ *cup unsweetened grapefruit juice*
1 *6-ounce can (⅔ cup) frozen limeade, thawed*
2 *cups Sprite*
Ice cubes
Orange, lemon, and/or line slices

In a pitcher stir together everything but the Sprite. Just before serving, add the Sprite. Add ice cubes and citrus slices.

MAKES 2 SERVINGS.

Marinated Zucchini and Mushrooms

8 *ounces small whole fresh mushrooms (3 cups)*
2 *small zucchini, bias-sliced into ½-inch-thick slices (2 cups)*
1 *small red bell pepper, cut into square pieces (½ cup)*
¼ *cup lemon juice*
2 *tablespoons olive oil or vegetable oil*
1 *tablespoon sugar*
¼ *teaspoon salt*
¼ *teaspoon dried tarragon or oregano, crushed*
¼ *teaspoon pepper*
1 *clove garlic, minced*

In a plastic bag combine the mushrooms, zucchini, and red pepper. Set in a deep bowl. In a small mixing bowl stir together the lemon juice, oil, sugar, salt, tarragon or oregano, pepper, and garlic. Mix well. Pour the marinade over the vegetables in the bag. Seal the bag. Refrigerate overnight, turning occasionally.

MAKES 8 SERVINGS.

Mustard-sauced Corn

1 *10-ounce package frozen whole kernel corn*
1 *medium green or red bell pepper, chopped (¾ cup)*
¼ *cup chopped onion*
1 *tablespoon water*
2 *teaspoons margarine*
2 *teaspoons prepared mustard or Dijon mustard*
Dash salt and pepper
Radicchio lettuce

In a 1-quart casserole combine the corn, green or red pepper, onion, and water. Cook in a microwave on high, covered, for 6 to 8 minutes, until the corn and onion are tender, stirring once. Stir in the margarine, mustard, salt, and pepper. Cook, covered, on high for 1 minute more. Stir to mix well. Serve in radicchio lettuce cups.

MAKES 4 SERVINGS.

Alexander's Inn

529 East Palace Avenue
Santa Fe, New Mexico 87501
(505) 986-1431

*J**ust a short walk from Santa Fe's central Plaza or Canyon Road with its dozens of art galleries, the Alexander Inn is a peaceful hideaway only steps from the city's most popular attractions. A 1903 craftsman-style home, it offers guests a country cottage feeling enhanced by dried flowers, family antiques, and hand-stenciled decorations. In the summer, roses, peonies, and masses of other garden blossoms fill the inn with flowery fragrance. In winter, guests may take their breakfast beside a big wood stove in the kitchen.*

Alexander's Inn

Apple Muffins

3 *cups finely chopped apples*
2 *cups sugar (half firmly packed brown and half white)*
1 *teaspoon baking soda*
1 *tablespoon ground cinnamon*
1 *cup oil*
3 *eggs*
2 *cups chopped nuts*
2 *teaspoons vanilla extract*
3½ *cups all-purpose flour*

In a large bowl thoroughly combine the apples and sugar. Add the soda and cinnamon. Mix well. Add the oil, eggs, nuts, and vanilla. Then mix in the flour just until moistened. The batter will be very thick and gooey. Fill greased muffin cups two-thirds full. Bake in a 350° oven for about 30 minutes. Can be frozen.

MAKES 2 DOZEN.

The Best Banana Bread (No Kidding)

1½ *cups melted butter*
1¾ *cups firmly packed brown sugar*
2½ *teaspoons vanilla extract*
½ *teaspoon almond extract*
Grated zest of 1 orange
4 *eggs*
4 *cups all-purpose flour*
1 *teaspoon salt*
½ *teaspoon baking soda*
3 *teaspoons baking powder*
½ *teaspoon grated nutmeg*
2 *teaspoons ground cinnamon*

2   *cups mashed ripe bananas soaked in*
    1 cup strong black coffee
1   *cup chopped walnuts*
1   *cup raisins*

In a large bowl beat together the melted butter, brown sugar, vanilla, almond extract, and orange zest. Add the eggs one at a time. Then add the flour, salt, soda, baking powder, nutmeg, and cinnamon alternately with the banana mixture to the butter mixture. Mix gently. Then add the nuts and raisins.

Grease 2 loaf pans. Pour in the batter. Bake in a 350° oven for 40 to 50 minutes.

MAKES 2 LOAVES.

512 Webber Street
Santa Fe, New Mexico 87501
(505) 982-2550

---

*C*ompleted in 1992, the Four Kachinas Inn is built around a lush private courtyard. It offers four guest rooms, each furnished with Southwestern art and handiwork including antique Navajo rugs, Hopi Kachina dolls, and handmade wooden furniture. The guest lounge, constructed with adobe blocks made on the property, resembles an old western trading post and features fine art and wares made by local Native American and other artists.

Old-fashioned Pan Rolls

2   *packages active dry yeast*
½   *cup warm water (about 110°)*
4½ *cups all-purpose flour*
¼   *cup sugar*
1   *teaspoon salt*
1   *cup butter, melted*
1   *egg*
1   *cup warm milk (about 110°)*

In a large bowl dissolve the yeast in water. Let stand until bubbly, about 15 minutes. In a bowl stir together 2 cups of the flour, the sugar, and salt until mixed well. Add 5 tablespoons of the melted butter along with the egg, yeast mixture, and milk. Beat for 5 minutes to blend well. Gradually beat in the remaining 2½ cups of flour. Cover the bowl and let the dough rise in a warm place until doubled, about 45 minutes.

Pour half of the remaining melted butter in a 9 x 13-inch baking pan, tilting the pan to coat the bottom. Beat down the batter and drop by the spoonful into the buttered pan, making 12 large rolls. Grandmother's old ice cream scoop (#12) works for this job; it makes 12 rolls exactly. Or use a ⅓ cup measuring cup.

Pour the remaining butter over the rolls. Cover lightly and let rise in a warm place until almost doubled in bulk (about 20 to 30 minutes). Bake in a 425° oven for 12 to 15 minutes or until browned. Serve hot.

MAKES 12 ROLLS.

Potato Cinnamon Buns

1   *large baking potato*
1   *cup milk*
¾   *cup butter, melted*
¼   *cup sugar*
½   *teaspoon salt*
1   *package active dry yeast*
1   *tablespoon sugar*
¼   *cup warm water (about 110°)*
4½ *to 5 cups all-purpose flour*
1   *egg*
1   *teaspoon vanilla extract*

....

½   *cup firmly packed brown sugar*
¼   *cup sugar*
1   *tablespoon ground cinnamon*

....

½   *cup raisins (optional)*
1   *cup confectioners' sugar*
⅛   *teaspoon ground cinnamon*
2   *tablespoons melted butter*
½   *teaspoon vanilla extract*
1   *to 2 tablespoons hot water*

Peel and dice the potato. Place the potato pieces in a large saucepan with plenty of water to cover. Bring the water to a boil and cook over medium heat until the potato is tender. Drain and mash. Gradually add milk to the mashed potato, blending well. Add 4 tablespoons of the melted butter, ¼ cup of

sugar, and salt. Warm over low heat, stirring constantly, until lukewarm (about 110°).

In a large bowl dissolve the yeast and 1 tablespoon of sugar in ¼ cup of warm water. Let stand until bubbly.

Add the potato mixture, 2 cups of the flour, egg, and vanilla; beat until smooth and blended well. Gradually stir in 2 cups more flour. Turn out on a heavily floured board and knead until smooth and elastic, 10 to 15 minutes. Add the remaining flour as needed to prevent sticking. Turn the dough over in a greased bowl, cover, and let rise in a warm place, for 1 hour to 1 hour and 15 minutes until doubled

In a small bowl combine the brown sugar, ¼ cup of sugar, and 1 tablespoon of cinnamon.

Punch the dough down. Knead just to expel air. Roll the dough out to a 15 x 18-inch rectangle. Brush with half of the remaining melted butter and sprinkle with cinnamon filling and raisins. Starting at the wide end, roll up, jelly roll fashion to end up with an 18-inch-long log. Cut crosswise into 12 equal pieces. Place the pieces, cut-side up, in a greased 9 x 13-inch baking pan. Pour the remaining melted butter over the tops of the rolls. Cover and let rise in a warm place until almost, but not quite, doubled, 35 to 45 minutes.

Bake in a 375° oven for 12 to 15 minutes or until richly browned. Remove from the oven and let set for 5 minutes.

In a small bowl combine the confectioners' sugar, ⅛ teaspoon of cinnamon, 2 tablespoons of butter, ½ teaspoon of vanilla, and hot water. Blend until smooth, adding water gradually until the glaze is a consistency to drizzle over the buns. Remove the buns from the pan and drizzle with glaze. When cool, they can be wrapped in foil and reheated as needed.

MAKES 12 BUNS.

Pumpkin Bread

1   *cup oil*
3   *eggs*
1   *16-ounce can pumpkin*
2½ *cups sugar*
3½ *cups all-purpose flour*
1   *teaspoon baking powder*
1   *teaspoon baking soda*
1   *teaspoon ground cinnamon*
1   *teaspoon grated nutmeg*

1   teaspoon ground allspice
1   teaspoon ground cloves
1   teaspoon ground ginger
1   cup raisins (plumped)
½   cup chopped nuts (optional)

In a large bowl mix the oil, eggs, and pumpkin. In a separate bowl combine the dry ingredients. Stir the raisins and nuts into the dry ingredients. Add the dry ingredients to the pumpkin mixture and blend well. Pour the batter into 5 greased and floured 3¼ x 6-inch loaf pans. Bake in a 325° oven for 35 to 45 minutes or until a toothpick inserted into a loaf comes out clean.

Remove from the oven and cool for 10 to 15 minutes in the pan. Remove from the pan and continue to cool on a rack.

MAKES 5 LOAVES.

Rich Baked Cheese Cake

1   cup all-purpose flour
¼   cup sugar
    Finely grated zest of 1 lemon
½   cup butter
1   egg yolk
1   teaspoon vanilla extract
2   teaspoons water

    ....

3   8-ounce packages cream cheese
1   cup sugar
1   teaspoon vanilla extract
½   cup sour cream
4   eggs
1   egg yolk

    ....

1½ cups sour cream
2   tablespoons sugar
½   teaspoon vanilla extract
    Pinch salt

In a medium bowl mix the first 3 ingredients, then cut in the butter until the mixtures resembles fine crumbs. In a separate bowl mix together one egg yolk, 1 teaspoon of vanilla, and water. Add it all at once to the flour mixture and stir lightly with a fork until a dough forms.

Roll out the dough on a floured board until it is about ⅜ inch thick. Place a 9-inch springform pan bottom on the rolled out dough. Trace a circle on the dough by running the tip of a knife around the edge of the pan. Cut out the round and place it on the bottom of the greased springform pan. Bake in a 350° oven for 8 to 10 minutes until it

turns a light gold. Watch it carefully after the first few minutes so it does not overbrown. Remove the pan from the oven and cool.

While the bottom crust is baking, take the left over bits of pastry and press them onto the sides of the springform pan right to the top. When the bottom is cooled, attach the sides of the pan to the bottom. Lock the pan. Press the dough on the sides of the pan gently down until it is sealed to the bottom crust.

In a large bowl soften the cream cheese thoroughly, stirring until it is free of lumps. Add 1 cup of sugar, 1 teaspoon of vanilla, ½ cup of sour cream, eggs, and yolk, and mix until smooth. Pour into the pastry-lined pan. Bake in a 350° oven for about 1 hour or until done. The filling will rise above the sides of the pan and turn a pale gold.

Remove the cheesecake from the oven and cool on a rack for about 30 minutes. As it cools, it will settle back down into the crust. A fissure may appear as it cools. Not to worry: the topping will fill it in and cover it.

In a medium bowl mix 1½ cup of sour cream, 2 tablespoons of sugar, ½ teaspoon vanilla, and pinch of salt until smooth. Pour over the filling. If necessary, coax it up to the sides with a spatula so it makes contact with the crust. Bake in a 475° oven until set, about 5 to 8 minutes. Remove from the oven and cool completely on a rack. This will take several hours.

When cool, loosen the crust from sides of the pan by dipping a thin knife into hot water, wiping it dry, and inserting it between the crust and the sides of the pan, and carefully running it around the pan. Reheat the knife as necessary. Unlock the pan and carefully remove the sides. Refrigerate the cake.

When the cake is thoroughly cold, remove the bottom of the pan. This may be easily done by putting the whole thing, cake and pan bottom, on a low flame and listening until the grease on the pan bottom begins to sizzle. Then run a long spatula under the cake to completely loosen it. Working quickly while the pan bottom is still hot (and slippery, which allows the cake to slide off), tilt the pan over a serving plate. Hold the edge of the cake in place over the plate. Remove the pan bottom.

MAKES 8 TO 12 SERVINGS.

Shortbread Cookies

1   cup butter, softened
½   cup confectioners' sugar
2   cups all-purpose flour
½   cup finely chopped walnuts
½   cup mini chocolate chips

Lightly grease a 9-inch square baking pan. In a large bowl cream together the butter and sugar until light and fluffy. Stir in the flour, nuts, and chocolate chips, and blend well. Press the dough evenly over the bottom of the prepared pan. Bake in a 325° oven for 40 to 50 minutes or until pale golden brown.

Transfer pan to a wire rack and cut into small squares while warm. Cool in the pan.

MAKES ABOUT 9 SERVINGS.

Toffee Bars

1   cup butter
1   cup firmly packed brown sugar
1   teaspoon vanilla extract
2   cups all-purpose flour
1   cup nuts
6   ounces mini chocolate chips (half of
    a 12-ounce bag)

In a large bowl cream together the butter, brown sugar, and vanilla until smooth and uniform. Add the flour, nuts, and chocolate chips and stir together until well mixed. Press the mixture into a greased 9 x 13-inch pan. Bake in a 325° oven on the middle rack for 20 to 25 minutes, until the bars just begin to get a darker brown around the edges. Remove from the oven and cool in the pan on a rack. Cut into squares while still warm. Finish cooling in the pan.

MAKES 48 PIECES.

Casa De Las Chimeneas

Casa De Las Chimeneas

405 Cordoba Road, Box 5303
Taos, New Mexico 87571
(505) 758-4777

In Spanish, Chimeneas means "chimneys," and every room of this Pueblo-style adobe inn has its own kiva fireplace. Little more than two blocks from Taos's historic central plaza, the inn is nonetheless a quiet retreat. Its seven-foot-high adobe walls block all awareness of the noise and bustle of the town. The garden breaks into a riot of color every spring.

Sopa (Indian Bread Pudding)

    4   cups water
  1½   cups firmly packed brown sugar
    5   tablespoons butter
    1   teaspoon ground cinnamon
    1   teaspoon grated nutmeg
    1   teaspoon ground allspice
    1   teaspoon vanilla extract
    1   cup raisins
        Half loaf white bread
    2   apples
    4   cups grated Cheddar cheese
        Whipped cream

In a saucepan make a syrup by heating the water with the brown sugar, butter, spices, and vanilla. Add the raisins.

Toast the bread slices on a cookie sheet in the oven. Break the toasted bread into small pieces and place in a greased ovenproof 9 x 13-inch pan. Slice the apples on top of the bread. Sprinkle grated cheese over the apples. Pour the warm syrup and raisins over the bread, apples, and cheese. Cover with foil. Bake in a 350° oven for 20 minutes. Serve warm or cold with whipped cream.
MAKES 8 SERVINGS.

Fruit Frappé

        Ice
        Papaya nectar
    1   6-ounce can pineapple juice
  ½   banana
    8   to 10 frozen blackberries
    2   tablespoons Coco Lopez

Fill a blender one-third full with ice. Add papaya nectar to the 2-cup mark. Add the remaining ingredients. Blend until smooth.
MAKES 2 SERVINGS.

Huevos Rancheros

        Butter
    4   blue or yellow corn tortillas
  1⅓   cups cooked pinto beans
    4   eggs, poached
  ¾   cup grated cheese
    1   cup Homemade Green Chile (recipe follows)
    4   strips well-done bacon, crumbled
        Sour cream for garnish

In a skillet with melted butter lightly cook the tortillas. Assemble in equal quantities on 4 warmed plates: tortilla on the bottom, beans spread on the tortilla, poached egg, grated cheese, green chile, and crumbled bacon. Top with a dollop of sour cream.
MAKES 4 SERVINGS.

Homemade Green Chile

    1   pound ground pork
    3   cloves garlic, crushed
    6   tablespoons all-purpose flour
    4   8-ounce containers frozen green chiles (3 mild, 1 hot) or 2 pounds freshly roasted and peeled mild green chiles
        Salt
        Water

In a skillet brown the ground pork. Drain the fat into large pot. Sauté the garlic in the fat. Add the flour and stir until brown. Add the green chiles, pork, and salt to taste. Add water to cover. Cook at least 30 minutes, until hot and bubbling. Great by itself as a stew or on top of most anything!
MAKES ABOUT 1 QUART.

Breakfast Burrito

        Butter or margarine
    1   clove garlic, crushed
  ¼   red onion, diced
  ½   cup diced ham
  ½   cup diced green bell pepper
    8   eggs, beaten
        Salt and pepper to taste
    4   flour tortillas, warmed
  ½   cup grated cheese
        Homemade Green Chile (see recipe)
        Sour cream

In a skillet heat a small amount of butter and lightly sauté the garlic, onion, ham, and bell pepper. Add the eggs, season, and scramble to the desired firmness. Place the warmed tortillas on plates. Spread eggs across the center of the tortillas and roll up to make "burritos." Top with red or green chile or warmed salsa. Sprinkle on grated cheese and top with a dollop of sour cream.
MAKES 4 SERVINGS.

Ice Box Gingerbread Muffins

    1   cup butter or margarine
    1   cup sugar
    4   eggs
    1   cup molasses
    4   cups all-purpose flour
    2   teaspoons ground ginger
  ¼   teaspoon ground cinnamon
  ¼   teaspoon ground allspice
    2   teaspoons baking soda
    1   cup sour milk or cream (or use sweet milk with 2 teaspoons vinegar and increase butter to 1½ cups)
  ½   cup raisins or dates
  ½   cup nuts

In a large bowl cream the butter, add sugar, eggs, and molasses. In a separate bowl sift the flour, ginger, cinnamon, and allspice together. Add the soda to the milk. Add the milk and dry ingredients alternately to the batter. Add the raisins and nuts dredged in flour. Cover and refrigerate for as long as a month.

Spoon into muffin cups. Bake in a 400° oven for 15 to 18 minutes.
MAKES 3 DOZEN.

Pecan Crusted Chicken in Orange Vodka Sauce

15   baby carrots, peeled
  2   chicken breasts, boned and skinned
  2   tablespoons butter
  2   tablespoons olive oil
 ⅓   cup all-purpose flour
 ⅓   cup pecans, ground or chopped
      finely
    Salt and pepper to taste
  1   cup chicken broth
    Small bunch snow peas
  1   tablespoon orange zest
    Juice from ½ orange
 ¼   cup Stolichnaya Ohranji Vodka
  2   cups boiled or steamed basmati rice
    Cilantro for garnish, lightly chopped

In a saucepan of boiling water cook the carrots for 8 minutes, then cover and leave in water to stay hot and finish cooking. Cut the chicken breast in half, then pound the thicker parts with a mallet until evenly thick. In a skillet melt the butter and add the olive oil. In a shallow bowl mix together the flour and ground pecans, and season with salt and pepper. Dredge the chicken in the pecan mixture and brown in the skillet over medium-high heat. (Reserve unused pecan mixture for thickening sauce later.) When the chicken is brown on both sides, transfer to a glass pan. Bake uncovered in a 350° oven to finish cooking.

Deglaze the skillet drippings with chicken broth and add the snow peas. While the peas are cooking, drain the carrots and return them to the warm saucepan. When the peas turn bright green, remove them from the skillet with a slotted spoon and add to the carrots to keep warm. Add 1 tablespoon of pecan mixture to the sauce in the skillet and whisk briskly to combine. Add the orange peel and juice, salt to taste, then vodka. Return the chicken and vegetables to the skillet to coat with sauce. Serve over rice with chopped cilantro as garnish.

MAKES 2 LARGE SERVINGS.

Box 5702
Taos, New Mexico 87571
(505) 751-1258

A luxurious European-style small hotel, the Neon Cactus stands in sharp contrast with the historically oriented inns and shops of old Taos. Art Deco decor is the rule here, and Hollywood is the theme. Guest rooms are furnished with antiques and collectibles from the 1930s through 1950s "golden Era" of the movies. Rooms are named after movie stars, and guests may select from the James Dean, Rita Hayworth, or Marilyn Monroe accommodations among others. The ambiance of Morocco prevails in the Casablanca Room.

Casa Blanca Breakfast Cake

 ¾   cup dark brown sugar
  3   tablespoons butter, softened
  3   tablespoons all-purpose flour
 ½   teaspoons cinnamon
 ½   cup chopped walnuts

 1½ cups sifted all-purpose flour
 2½ teaspoons baking powder

  1   egg
 ¾   cup sugar
 ⅓   cup butter, melted
 ½   cup milk
 1½ teaspoons vanilla extract

Grease a 9-inch bundt or angel food cake tube pan or 8-inch square cake pan.

In a small bowl combine the brown sugar, butter, 3 tablespoons of flour, cinnamon, and walnuts, and mix until crumbly. Set aside.

In a small bowl combine 1½ cups of flour and the baking powder. Set aside.

In a medium bowl beat the egg until frothy. Add the sugar, butter, milk, and vanilla, and mix well. Stir in the flour mixture with a wooden spoon until blended well. Spread half of the batter in the prepared pan. Spoon on half of the filling. Add the remaining batter in clumps, and the remaining filling by spoonfuls. Bake in a 375° oven for 25 to 30 minutes. Serve warm.

MAKES 8 SERVINGS.

The Willows Inn

NDCBU 6560
Taos, New Mexico 87571
(505) 758-2558

The Willows was once home to E. Martin Hennings, one of the notable artists who built Taos' reputation as an art colony during the 1920s. With its thick adobe walls and its two enormous willows—among the largest in North America—the atmosphere of the inn is restful and elegant. Upon arrival, guests may find fresh baked goods, flowers, or fruit waiting for them in their rooms.

Gooey Lemon Piñon Bars

  1   18½-ounce box lemon cake mix
 ½   cup butter or margarine, softened
  1   egg
  1   cup toasted piñon nuts (or chopped pecans)
  1   16-ounce box confectioners' sugar
  1   8-ounce package cream cheese, softened
  2   eggs
  2   teaspoons vanilla extract

In a large bowl mix the cake mix, butter, and one egg, and pat into a greased and floured 9 x 13-inch pan. Pat up the sides of the pan a little and make sure the corners are not too thick. Use the back of a wet spoon to smooth if needed. Sprinkle piñon nuts evenly over this. In a bowl mix together the confectioners' sugar, cream cheese, two eggs, and vanilla until very smooth. Pour this over the crust and nuts already in the pan. Bake in a 350° oven for about 30 to 45 minutes.

No icing needed, it's very rich. Bars will set upon cooling. Wait to cut until cool.

MAKES 24 SERVINGS.

Banana Piñon Muffins

1   cup all-purpose flour
1   cup wheat or oat bran
1   teaspoon baking soda
½   teaspoon salt
1   cup mashed ripe bananas (2 large
    bananas)
½   cup unsalted butter, softened
½   cup firmly packed brown sugar
1   egg
½   cup piñon nuts

In a medium bowl stir and toss together the flour, bran, soda, and salt. Set aside. In a separate medium bowl beat together the mashed banana and softened butter until mixed. Don't worry if the mixture looks lumpy and curdled. Add the brown sugar and egg, and beat until completely mixed. Add the dry ingredients slowly, beating until all is mixed. Mix in the piñons. Spoon into greased muffin cups, filling each cup about three-quarters full. Bake in a 375° oven for 15 to 20 minutes, until a toothpick inserted in the center of a muffin comes out clean. Cool in the tins for 5 minutes, then remove.

MAKES 1 DOZEN.

Chocolate Chip Piñon Brownies

2   ounces unsweetened chocolate
½   cup butter
1   cup sugar
2   eggs
1½   teaspoons vanilla extract
½   teaspoon ground cinnamon
½   cup all-purpose flour (add another 2
    tablespoons if at high altitude)
¼   teaspoon salt
1   cup piñon nuts
1   cup chocolate chips

Grease and flour 9 x 13-inch pan. In the top of a double boiler over simmering water, melt the chocolate and butter. Remove the pan from the heat. Cool to lukewarm.

Gradually blend in the sugar. Add the eggs, vanilla, and cinnamon. Add the sifted flour and salt a little at a time, mixing completely between additions. Add piñon nuts and chocolate chips. Spread into the prepared pan. Bake in a 350° oven for 25 to 35 minutes. May be frosted or dusted with confectioners' sugar, but is very rich as is. Cool completely before cutting.

MAKES 20 SERVINGS.

Doug's Refried Black Beans

1   16-ounce package dried black beans
1   whole yellow onion, diced
1   clove garlic, minced
4   slices bacon
    Salt and pepper to taste

Rinse and sort the dried black beans. Place in a large pan or crock pot with plenty of water. Add more water as necessary to keep the beans covered. Bring the beans to a boil, then reduce the heat to a simmer. Add the onion and garlic and continue to cook until done, stirring occasionally, 3 to 5 hours. Cool as time allows.

In a blender combine the beans and juice and purée until smooth. Cut the bacon strips into small chunks and cook in a large frying pan (cast-iron is best) until crisp. Leave the bacon and renderings in the frying pan and add the puréed bean mixture. Cook on low heat until the beans thicken to the desired consistency. Salt and pepper to taste.

MAKES 8 SERVINGS.

The Willows Inn

NEW YORK

Mansion Hill Inn

115 Philip Street
Albany, New York 12202
(518) 465-2038

A distinctly urban inn, the Mansion Hill is located in a residential neighborhood near the heart of Albany, New York. Situated just south of the Empire State Plaza, it is only a few minutes walking distance from the State Capitol. The inn consists of a cluster of Victorian-era buildings offering spacious rooms and suites with views of the Hudson River, the Berkshires, or the Helderberg Mountains. The main inn building is a mansion built in 1861 for an Albany brush manufacturer.

Stuffed New York Strip Steak

2 1¼-inch-thick New York strip steaks (boneless)
2 ounces chèvre, or other soft goat cheese
1 tablespoon unsalted butter

6 ounces fresh spinach, stems removed, washed, and spun dry
2 cloves garlic, minced
6 halves sun-dried tomatoes, cut julienne
   Salt and fresh ground pepper to taste

Cut a deep pocket in each strip steak. Sprinkle chèvre along the bottom. Set aside. In a skillet melt the butter and sauté the spinach, garlic, and tomatoes until the spinach is wilted but still bright green. Season with salt and pepper. Place the spinach filling inside each steak. Charbroil over hot coals for 5 to 6 minutes on each side for medium-rare.
MAKES 2 SERVINGS.

Wild Mushroom Salad

2 cup sliced fresh wild mushrooms, (shiitake, oyster, crimini)
1½ cups sliced button mushrooms
¼ cup sun-dried tomatoes, rehydrated in hot water, drained and cut julienne
¼ cup chopped roasted red bell pepper
½ cup very thinly sliced red onion
1 tablespoon minced fresh garlic
2 tablespoons fresh chopped basil
2 teaspoons dried oregano
¼ cup balsamic vinegar
½ to ¾ cup olive oil
   Salt and pepper to taste
6 cups torn mixed salad greens
   Basil leaves for garnish

In a large bowl combine all ingredients except the greens. Let stand at room temperature for 1 to 2 hours, stirring occasionally.

Warm the mixture in a saucepan before serving. Divide the greens among 6 salad plates and spoon mushrooms over the top. Garnish with fresh basil leaves.
MAKES 6 SERVINGS.

Mansion Hill Inn

Mansion Hill Inn Granola

4 cups rolled oats
1½ cups shredded sweetened coconut
1½ cups coarsely chopped pecans
½ cup unsalted butter
¼ cup firmly packed dark brown sugar
½ cup golden raisins
½ cup dried tart cherries

In a large bowl combine the oats, coconut and pecans. Set aside. In a heavy saucepan melt the butter and brown sugar, stirring constantly. Bring the mixture to a boil. Pour over the oat mixture and stir to coat the dry ingredients evenly. Spread the mixture on a shallow greased baking pan. Bake in a 325° oven for 30 to 40 minutes or until golden brown. Stir the mixture every 10 minutes to prevent the edges from burning. Remove the pan from the oven and stir in the raisins and cherries. Let the granola cool completely before storing in an airtight container.

MAKES ABOUT 2 QUARTS.

Route 22
Berlin, New York 12022
(518) 658-2334

Described in some travel publications as "the quintessential country inn," the Sedgewick sits on twelve wooded acres in the scenic Taconic Valley. The heart of the inn is a two-century-old Colonial-style at the foot of the Berkshire Mountains. The inn offers eleven guest rooms, each with its own distinct period setting. It also has its own gift shop in the old estate carriage house and antique shop, an 1834, tin-lined structure once used as a Civil War recruiting station.

Frozen Chocolate Mousse Pie

- ¾ cup unblanched almonds
- 12 Social Tea cookies
- 2 tablespoons butter, melted
- ½ gallon vanilla ice cream
- ⋯⋯⋯⋯⋯⋯⋯⋯⋯⋯⋯⋯
- 4 egg yolks, at room temperature
- 6 ounces semisweet chocolate
- ⋯⋯⋯⋯⋯⋯⋯⋯⋯⋯⋯⋯
- ½ cup water
- ⅓ cup sugar
- 1 cup heavy cream

Toast the almonds in a 350° oven for 10 minutes until lightly browned. In a food processor chop the warm almonds. Set aside.

In a food processor chop the cookies. Add two-thirds of the chopped almonds and the melted butter, and toss until thoroughly

mixed. Press into the bottom of a 9- or 10-inch springform pan. Freeze.

Remove from the freezer and fill with softened vanilla ice cream halfway up the springform. Return to the freezer.

In a medium bowl beat the yolks with an electric mixer at high speed for 10 minutes, until they have the consistency of mayonnaise.

In a double boiler melt the chocolate over hot water and keep warm while preparing the sugar syrup.

In a saucepan heat the water and sugar, stirring until the sugar is dissolved. Then cook without stirring until the syrup reaches 238° on a candy thermometer (soft-ball stage). Add syrup in a slow stream to the beaten egg yolks, beating with the electric mixer at low speed. Increase the speed and beat until the mixture has cooled.

In a medium bowl beat the cream until stiff. Slowly add the melted chocolate to the egg mixture and blend well. Fold in the whipped cream and mix carefully until blended.

When the ice cream is firm top with mousse, sprinkle with reserved almonds, and return to the freezer for at least 6 hours before serving.

MAKES 6 TO 8 SERVINGS.

Queen Victoria Soup

- 2 tablespoons butter
- 1 small onion, chopped
- 3 stalks celery, finely chopped
- ½ pound mushrooms, diced
- 4 cups chicken broth
- ½ cup diced cooked chicken
- ½ cup diced cooked ham
- 1 tablespoon quick-cooking tapioca
- 1 cup light cream
-    Salt and white pepper to taste

In a large saucepan heat the butter and sauté the onion until golden but not brown. Add the celery and mushrooms, and cook over low heat for 10 minutes, stirring frequently.

Add the chicken broth, chicken, ham, and tapioca, and cook for 20 minutes, until lightly thickened.

Before serving add the cream and bring back to serving temperature. Season.

MAKES 4 SERVINGS.

Sun-dried Tomato and Sweet Italian Sausage Soup

- 1½ cups sun-dried tomatoes
- 4 cups chicken broth
- ⅓ pound sweet Italian sausage
- 1 medium onion, chopped
- 3 cloves garlic, minced
- 1 28-ounce can whole tomatoes in juice
- ¼ cup grated Parmesan cheese, plus extra for topping
- 1 teaspoon basil
-    Salt and pepper to taste
-    Granulated garlic to taste

In a stockpot simmer the tomatoes in the chicken broth for 10 minutes. Dice fine, and return to the broth.

In a sauté pan cook the sausage meat, breaking it up as it browns. Add the onion and garlic, and cook until translucent.

Dice the canned tomatoes. Add to the broth with their juice, sausage mixture, and sun-dried tomatoes, and simmer for 15 minutes.

Add cheese, and basil and simmer for another 5 minutes. Season to taste with salt, pepper, granulated garlic, and additional Parmesan cheese.

MAKES 10 SERVINGS.

Baked Mussels with Oven Dried Tomatoes and Roasted Garlic

- 24 medium plum tomatoes
-    Salt and white pepper to taste
-    Olive oil
- 1 head garlic
- 2 medium onions, diced
- ¼ cup water
- 2 tablespoons grated Parmesan cheese
- 1 teaspoon dried basil
- 24 mussels on half shell (preferably New Zealand Greenlip, if available)

Cut the tomatoes in half lengthwise. Coat with olive oil and place skin-side-down on a cookie sheet. Sprinkle with salt and white pepper. Bake in a 275° oven for 4 to 5 hours, depending on size, until wrinkled but still soft. (Will keep in the refrigerator for week or so.)

Cut the top off the garlic and coat well with olive oil. Roast in a small dish in olive oil halfway up the garlic head in a 325° oven until soft, 30 minutes or more.

In a skillet sauté the diced onions in 3 tablespoons of olive oil until translucent. Squeeze the garlic flesh out of the cloves, coarsely chop the tomatoes, and add both to the onions with ¼ cup of water. Simmer. Add the Parmesan cheese and basil. Continue to simmer until thick.

In a baking dish top the mussels with tomato sauce. Bake in a 425° oven for 15 minutes.

MAKES ABOUT 4 SERVINGS.

The Portico

The Portico Bed and Breakfast ❧

3741 Lake Road
Brockport, New York 14420
(716) 637-0220

A unique example of Greek Revival architecture, this 1850s home has massive columns, three porches, painted glass foyer panels, ten-foot ceilings, a cupola, and loads of charm. Although it has been thoroughly remodeled to supply the comforts of modern life, its integrity as a historic building remains unencumbered. Attractions in the area include Hamlin Beach,

the Margaret Woodbury Strong Museum, and the unique Cobblestone Museum.

German Chocolate and Cinnamon Bundt Cake

2½ cups all-purpose flour
1½ cups sugar
 ½ cup butter, softened
 3 eggs
 ¾ cup sour cream
 1 teaspoon baking soda
 1 teaspoon vanilla extract
 ¼ cup sour cream
 1 teaspoon baking powder
 2 tablespoons ground cinnamon
 2 tablespoons sugar
 1 8-ounce package German sweet
     chocolate, chopped

Grease and flour a bundt cake pan. In a large bowl blend the flour, sugar, and butter. Gradually add the eggs and ¾ cup of sour cream, beating after each addition. Add the soda, vanilla, ¼ cup of sour cream, and baking powder. Beat well. Pour half of the batter into the bundt pan. Mix half of the cinnamon and 2 tablespoons of sugar in a small bowl. Sprinkle over the batter. Scatter chopped chocolate over the cinnamon and sugar. Sprinkle with the remaining cinnamon and sugar. Add the remaining batter. Bake in a 325° oven for about 50 minutes. Cool in the pan.

MAKES 8 SERVINGS.

Potica (Honey-Walnut-filled Bread)

 1 cake compressed yeast
 1 cup milk, scalded and cooled to
     lukewarm (95°)
 ¼ cup butter
 ½ cup sugar
 1 teaspoon salt
 2 eggs, well-beaten
4½ cups all-purpose flour
....
 ½ cup honey
 1 teaspoon ground cinnamon
 2 eggs, slightly beaten
 2 tablespoons melted butter
 1 teaspoon vanilla extract
 ¾ pound walnuts, ground very fine

In a small bowl dissolve the yeast in milk. In a large bowl cream the butter and sugar. Add the salt, eggs, and yeast mixture. Mix in the flour, stirring until smooth. Place in a greased bowl, and cover with a towel. Let rise in a warm place until doubled in bulk.

In a medium bowl combine the remaining ingredients. When the dough is ready, roll to a rectangle on floured surface. Spread on the filling. Roll up tightly like a jelly roll. Curl into a snail shape. Leave no openings. Place on a greased pizza pan. Let rise again.

Bake in a 350° oven for about 1 hour.

MAKES 6 SERVINGS.

Apple-Cabbage Slaw

     Juice of 1 orange
     Juice of ½ lemon
 2 medium red apples, cored and diced
 4 cups shredded cabbage
 ½ cup mayonnaise
 ¼ cup applesauce
 1 teaspoon prepared horseradish
 1 teaspoon prepared mustard
 2 tablespoons minced parsley
 2 tablespoons chopped nuts

In a large bowl pour the fruit juices over apples. Add the cabbage and mix lightly. In a separate bowl mix the mayonnaise, applesauce, horseradish, and mustard. Pour over the apples and cabbage and toss carefully. Sprinkle with parsley and nuts.

MAKES 6 SERVINGS.

Orange Pecan Bread

2¾ cups whole wheat flour
2½ teaspoons baking powder
 ½ teaspoon baking soda
 1 teaspoon salt
 2 tablespoons soft butter, softened
 1 cup honey
 1 egg
 2 tablespoons grated orange zest
 ¾ cup orange juice
 2 cups chopped pecans

Grease a 5 x 9-inch loaf pan. In a large bowl stir together the dry ingredients. Set aside. In a separate bowl beat the butter and honey until creamy. Add the egg and orange zest and mix well. Add to the dry ingredients alternately with the orange juice, and stir well. Stir in the nuts. Spoon into the prepared pan.

Bake in a 325° oven for 1 hour and 10 minutes or until done.

MAKES 1 LOAF.

Fruit Dip

1 16-ounce carton Ricotta cheese
¼ cup confectioners' sugar
2 tablespoons brandy
¼ teaspoon ground cinnamon
   Assorted plain cookies and fresh
      fruits

In a large bowl beat together the Ricotta cheese, sugar, brandy, and cinnamon with an electric mixer.

Cover and chill for several hours.

Serve as a dip for cookies and fruit.

MAKES 2 CUPS.

Gazpacho (Cold Summer Soup)

½ cup tomato juice (or V-8 juice)
¼ cup chopped onion
½ cup unpeeled chopped cucumber
½ cup unpeeled chopped tomato
½ cup chopped green bell pepper
1 tablespoon oil
2 tablespoons wine vinegar
½ teaspoon salt
   Tabasco or Worcestershire sauce to
      taste
   Sour cream for garnish

In a serving bowl combine all ingredients. Chill.

Serve with a dollop of sour cream on top of each serving.

MAKES 4 TO 6 APPETIZER SERVINGS.

Cucumber Tea Sandwiches

2 small cucumbers, peeled
¼ teaspoon salt
8 slices firm wheat bread, crusts
      removed
¼ cup mayonnaise
1 teaspoon vinegar
   Dash pepper
   Fresh herb sprigs (optional)

Cut cucumbers in half lengthwise and remove the seeds. Cut crosswise into paper-thin

slices. In a bowl toss the cucumbers with salt. Let stand 15 minutes.

Spread bread slices with mayonnaise. Drain the cucumbers and pat dry on paper towels. In a separate bowl toss the cucumbers with vinegar and pepper. Arrange on 4 slices of bread. Top with the remaining 4 slices of bread. Cut each sandwich into 4 squares or triangles. Place on a tray. Cover with slightly damp paper towels and plastic wrap. Refrigerate until serving time.

Top each with a fresh herb sprig, if desired.

MAKES 4 SERVINGS.

Salmon Manicotti

10 large manicotti shells
1 15½-ounce can of salmon
2 cups small curd cottage cheese
2 eggs, beaten-well
½ cup minced onion
¼ cup fresh chopped parsley
½ teaspoon dillweed

3 tablespoons butter
3 tablespoons all-purpose flour
¼ teaspoon salt
   Milk
2 cups shredded Monterey Jack cheese
¼ cup grated Parmesan cheese

In a pan cook the manicotti shells in boiling water. Drain.

Drain the salmon, reserving the liquid. In a large bowl flake the salmon with a fork. Combine the salmon, cottage cheese, eggs, onion, parsley, and dillweed. Gently stuff the cooked manicotti shells with the salmon mixture. Set aside.

In a saucepan melt the butter and stir in the flour and salt. To the reserved salmon liquid add enough milk to equal 1½ cups. Gradually stir into the dry ingredients. Cook and stir over medium heat until thickened. Add 1 cup of the Monterey Jack cheese and stir until melted. Pour half of the sauce into the bottom of a 3-quart baking dish. Arrange the filled manicotti shells on the sauce. Top with the remaining sauce. Sprinkle with the rest of the Monterey Jack cheese and the Parmesan cheese. Cover. Bake in a 450° oven for 10 minutes. Uncover and bake 10 minutes longer or until the sauce is bubbly and the cheese is golden brown.

MAKES 4 OR 5 SERVINGS.

Friends Lake Inn
≈

Friends Lake Road
Chestertown, New York 12817
(518) 494-4751

***T**he Friends Lake Inn places emphasis on fine dining complimented by the best wines. While the food and wine may be the highlight of a stay at this fourteen-room Adirondack region inn, there is also much to do hereabouts. Opportunities for outdoor activities are abundant, but the area is probably best known for its cross-country skiing. Most rooms have mountain or lake views and in-room Jacuzzis. Common rooms have large fireplaces, which are especially welcome after a long day on the ski trails.*

Grilled Duck Breast with Wild Mushrooms and Smoked Cherries

½ cup sun-dried cherries
1 cup Pinot Noir wine
½ cup chanterelle mushrooms
½ cup shiitake mushrooms, sliced
½ cup crimini mushrooms, sliced
¾ cup veal demiglace
½ teaspoon kosher salt
   Pinch white pepper
4 whole duck breasts, cut in half

In a sauce pan combine the cherries and wine and simmer for 20 minutes. Add the mushrooms and demiglace. Simmer over medium heat for 1 to 2 hours, until a viscous consistency is reached. Season with salt and pepper. Place the duck breast skin-side-down on a grill. Allow to flame up and char until most of the fat is rendered. Turn and cook until medium-rare. Slice the breast and fan. Top with mushrooms and cherries.

MAKES 4 SERVINGS.

Friends Lake Inn

Honey Oatmeal Bread

3 cups lukewarm water (105 to 115°)
¾ cup honey
2 envelopes active dry yeast
1 scant tablespoon salt
8 cups bread flour
2 cups quick oats
Cornmeal

Measure the warm water into the bowl of a heavy-duty electric mixer. Dissolve the honey in the water. Sprinkle the yeast over the water and stir. Let stand until foamy, about 5 minutes. Mix the salt into the yeast mixture. Add the bread flour and oats, and mix for 5 minutes with a dough hook attachment, until the dough is elastic.

Grease a large bowl with oil. Add the dough, turning to coat the entire surface. Cover with plastic wrap. Let rise in a warm draft-free area until tripled in volume, about 1 hour and 30 minutes. To test, press 2 fingers into the dough. If fully risen, the indentions will remain. If not, cover with plastic and let rise longer.

Grease 2 baking sheets and lightly dust with cornmeal. Turn the dough out onto a lightly floured work surface and punch down. Knead the dough until smooth, about 2 minutes. Divide the dough into 4 equal pieces. Roll 1 piece out on the work surface to a 14-inch-long rectangle, oiling the rolling pin if the dough sticks. Roll dough up jelly roll fashion, starting at a long side. Roll the ends between palms and work surface to taper slightly. Transfer to the prepared baking sheets, seam-side down. Repeat rolling and shaping with the remaining dough. Slash each with 3 long diagonal cuts about ⅓ inch deep. Let the loaves rise in a warm draft-free area until tripled in volume, about 45 minutes.

Preheat oven to 400°. Position 1 oven rack in the lowest position and the second rack in the center of the oven. Place a baking pan on the lowest shelf. Pour boiling water into the baking pan in the oven (water will steam). Close the oven for 2 minutes. Place the bread on the center rack. Bake in a 400° oven until golden brown and crisp, about 20 minutes. Cool the loaves on rack.
MAKES 4 LOAVES.

Granola Parfait

½ cup Granola (recipe follows)
¼ cup nonfat vanilla yogurt
½ cup sliced strawberries (or favorite fruit)

Place half of the granola in a parfait glass. Top with half of the yogurt. Arrange half of the strawberries over the yogurt. Top with the remaining granola, yogurt, and strawberries.
MAKES 1 SERVING.

Granola

5 cups mixed wheat, rye, and oat flakes
1 cup sunflower seeds
½ cup sesame seeds
1 cup chopped nuts
½ cup safflower oil
½ cup honey
2 teaspoons vanilla extract
5 cups wheat flakes
2 cups raisins

In a large bowl stir the mixed flakes, seeds, and nuts together. In a small bowl stir the oil, and honey (mixed with vanilla) together. Add the honey mixture to the granola, mixing well. Spread the granola thinly on greased cookie sheets. Bake in a 400° oven for 2 to 4 minutes, until lightly toasted. (Watch closely, as the flakes will brown quickly.) Stir in the remaining flakes and raisins to prevent the hot mixture from sticking together in lumps. Cool completely. Store in a covered container.
MAKES ABOUT 3 QUARTS.

Le Refuge Inn
❧

620 City Island
City Island, New York 10464
(718) 885-2478

A B&B operated by one of New York City's best known chefs, Le Refuge Inn is just the place to escape the flash and thunder of the big city and still be within easy reach of Manhattan. Situated among the shipyards, seafood restaurants, chandlers, and marine antique shops on City Island, the inn is a three-story Victorian home sequestered behind a high wooden fence. Exposed oak beams lend a rustic feeling to the interior. In the parlor stands a handcrafted grandfather clock, an heirloom of the owner's family. Nearby is Pelham Bay Park, New York City's largest, with its sandy beach, horseback riding trails, and two 18-hole golf courses. Before going out to enjoy the city or the park, take some time to savor the morning cappuccino and croissants.

Raspberry Délice

6 eggs, room temperature
1 cup plus 2 tablespoons sugar
½ teaspoon vanilla extract
1¼ cups sifted all-purpose flour
1 tablespoon oil
....
9 cups (6 half-pints) fresh raspberries (or 3 12-ounce packages frozen dry pack raspberries, thawed)
....
½ cup sugar
2 envelopes unflavored gelatin
½ cup cold water
2 cups heavy cream
....
¾ cup seedless red raspberry jam
2 tablespoons raspberry liqueur
Custard sauce (optional)

Generously butter and flour 2 jelly roll pans.

In a large mixer bowl beat the eggs, 1 cup plus 2 tablespoons of sugar, and vanilla with an electric mixer at high speed until the mixture triples in volume and runs off the beaters in thick ribbons, about 7 to 8 minutes. Add one-fourth of the flour at a time, sifting it evenly over the egg mixture and then folding it in with a large rubber spatula. Drizzle the oil over the top of the egg mixture and fold in. Gently spread the batter evenly in the pans. Bake in a 350° oven for 20 to 25 minutes, until the cake is golden brown and springs back when gently touched in the center. Cool the cake completely in pans set on racks.

In a food processor blend the berries in several batches, pulsing several times until the berries are liquefied. Do not overprocess or the seeds will be ground up and impossible to remove. Press the purée through a fine sieve a little at a time, until all juice is extracted. Discard the seeds. Measure 2 cups plus another separate 3 tablespoons of purée. Cover and refrigerate any remaining purée to use another time.

In a large bowl combine 2 cups of raspberry purée and ½ cup of sugar. Mix well to dissolve the sugar. Set aside.

In a small saucepan sprinkle the gelatin over the cold water. Let soften for 10 minutes. Add 3 tablespoons of raspberry purée. Stir over medium-low heat until the gelatin dissolves. Stir into the raspberry-sugar mixture.

In a large chilled mixer bowl beat the cream to soft peaks. Fold into the raspberry mixture. Set the raspberry Bavarian cream aside.

Butter and sugar 10 6-ounce ramekins or molds that measure about 3 inches in diameter and 1½ inches deep.

Using a cookie cutter, cut the cake into 20 rounds the same diameter as inside the rim of the ramekins (about 2¾-inch) . Remove the cake rounds from the pan with a small spatula. Place 1 cake round in the bottom of each ramekin. Reserve the remaining cake rounds. Spoon the Bavarian cream into the ramekins, filling almost to the top. Arrange the remaining cake rounds atop the Bavarian cream layer. Cover and refrigerate overnight.

In a small saucepan combine the raspberry jam and liqueur. Stir over medium heat until melted and smooth. Cool 5 to 10 minutes:

To serve, dip the molds briefly in hot water. Run a knife around the edge of the molds to loosen. Unmold and arrange topside-up on serving plates. Spoon warm raspberry glaze over the top cake rounds. Refrigerate for 15 minutes to set. If desired, serve with custard sauce.

Note: Pound cake cut in rounds ⅜-inch-thick may be substituted for the cake.
MAKES 10 SERVINGS.

Duckling with Star Fruit Sauce

- 2   4- to 4½-pound domestic ducklings
- 1   teaspoon dried thyme
- 1   teaspoon chopped fresh parsley
- 2   bay leaves
- 1   small onion, chopped
- 1   carrot, thinly sliced
- 1   small stalk celery, chopped
     Salt and pepper to taste

- 1   cup dry white wine
- 1   cup medium dry sherry or port
- ¼   cup rice vinegar
- 1   teaspoon tomato paste
- 1   7-ounce star fruit, pared, puréed and sieved (⅓ cup), plus additional for garnish

Remove the giblets and fat from the body cavities of the ducklings and reserve for another time. Rinse the ducklings inside and out with cold water. Pat dry with paper towels.

Stuff the ducklings with thyme, parsley, bay leaves, onion, carrot, celery, salt, and pepper to taste. Tie the legs together with string. Pierce the skin all over with the point of a small knife. Arrange the ducklings on a rack in a large shallow roasting pan. Roast in a 375° oven for 1 hour and 30 minutes to 2 hours until, a meat thermometer inserted between the leg and thigh registers 180°. Spoon off the fat from the roasting pan several times during baking. Remove the ducklings and rack from the pan, reserving the drippings in the pan. Keep the ducklings warm.

Skim the fat from the pan drippings in the roasting pan. Set the pan with drippings over 2 burners. Pour in the white wine. Cook over medium-high heat, scraping up the browned bits from the bottom of the pan. Stir in the sherry, rice vinegar, tomato paste, and puréed star fruit. Bring to boiling. Boil gently, stirring occasionally, until reduced by half. Strain. Bone duckling if desired. Serve with fruit sauce.

Cut whole star fruit crosswise in slices. Garnish each duck with star fruit slices.

Note: To purée star fruit, also known as carambola, cut the fruit in half crosswise.

Using a small sharp knife, carefully peel off the thin waxy skin by cutting down along both sides of each rib that forms the "star" points. Section the fruit like an orange, discarding the center membrane and seeds. Purée the fruit in a food processor. Sieve, reserving the smooth pulp.
MAKES 4 SERVINGS.

Vegetable Terrine

- 1¾   ounces dry shiitake mushrooms
- 6   to 7 large cabbage leaves (preferably savoy)
- 1   12-ounce bunch spinach, stemmed
- 12   ounces fresh asparagus, trimmed and peeled
- 2   8-ounce red bell peppers, cut in lengthwise strips
- 12   ounces carrots, cut lengthwise in julienne
- 1   14½-ounce can artichoke hearts, drained and quartered lengthwise

- 4   eggs
- ½   cup buttermilk
- 1   tablespoon chopped fresh parsley
- 1   teaspoon dried thyme
- 1   teaspoon dried tarragon
- 2   shallots, chopped
     Salt and pepper to taste

- 1   large tomato, peeled, seeded, and chopped (1 cup)
- ¼   cup buttermilk
- 1   tablespoon tomato paste
     Pinch cayenne pepper
- 1   clove garlic, chopped
     Salt and pepper to taste

In a small bowl combine the dry mushrooms and hot water to cover. Let stand 30 minutes. Drain

While the mushrooms are rehydrating, bring a large pot of water to boiling. Blanch the vegetables in separate batches in the boiling water. Blanch the cabbage leaves for 3 minutes, spinach leaves for 1 minute, asparagus and red pepper strips for 3 minutes, and carrots for 4 minutes. Plunge the vegetables into ice water after blanching. Drain.

Pat all blanched vegetables, mushrooms, and artichokes dry between 2 to 3 layers of paper towels, applying gentle pressure to squeeze out as much liquid as possible. (Spinach leaves should be opened out flat to assume the original shape.)

In a medium bowl combine the eggs, ½ cup of buttermilk, parsley, thyme, tarragon, shallots, salt, and pepper to taste. Whisk until blended. (This batter is highly seasoned because it will season all the vegetables in the terrine.)

Generously butter a 5 x 9-inch loaf pan. Using a triangular-shaped cut, remove 1 to 2 inches of hard white stem end from each cabbage leaf to make the leaves more flexible.

Line the sides, then the bottom of the pan with cabbage leaves, overlapping the leaves generously to form a leakproof "shell" and allowing the leaves to extend well over the rim of the pan. (The tops of the cabbage leaves will be folded over the top of the finished terrine.) Pour ½ cup of batter over the cabbage in the bottom of the pan. Arrange asparagus spears lengthwise in the pan, packing the spears tightly together. Add 2 layers of red pepper strips placed crosswise in the pan. Pour in a little more batter, pressing the peppers down gently. Layer the mushrooms over the peppers. Layer carrots lengthwise in the pan. Pour in a little more batter, pressing the carrots down gently. (Pressing down each layer will raise the level of the batter.) Layer half the spinach leaves over the carrots. Add a layer of artichoke hearts over the spinach, then add a little more batter. Gently press down the artichoke hearts. Top with a layer of remaining spinach leaves, adding the remaining batter and pressing down each layer. Fold the ends of the cabbage leaves over the top of the terrine.

Cover the loaf pan with buttered parchment paper cut to fit inside the edge of the pan. Place the loaf pan in a 9 x 13-inch baking pan. Pour hot water around the loaf pan to a depth of 1 inch. Bake in a 350° oven for 2 hours, until firm. Remove from the water bath. Cool on a rack (still covered with parchment paper) for 2 hours. Refrigerate, still covered, overnight.

In a blender combine the chopped tomato, ¼ cup of buttermilk, tomato paste, cayenne, garlic, salt, and pepper to taste. Blend until smooth.

Loosen the edges of the terrine with a knife. Invert on a serving platter. Cut the cold terrine in crosswise slices with a serrated knife. Spread a thin layer of tomato sauce on each serving plate. Arrange slices of terrine over the sauce.

MAKES 8 SERVINGS.

De Bruce Country Inn on the Willowemoc

R.D. 1, Box 286A
De Bruce, New York 12758
(914) 439-3900

This country inn is located high in the Catskills on its own forest and wildlife preserve. Surrounded by wooded trails and streams, it places guests as close to nature as they are likely to get without a tent. When not out hiking or taking in the wild scenery, guests may want to take advantage of the sauna, pool, and fitness center.

De Bruce Country Inn

Waughmaughkyll Chicken

4 cups chicken bouillon
2 cups rice
1 whole chicken breast, boned and skinned, cut into thin strips
5 tablespoons soy sauce
1 tablespoon sugar
5 to 10 cloves garlic, peeled and chopped
¼ teaspoon curry powder
2 tablespoons cornstarch
¼ cup oil
1 large onion, chopped
1 small zucchini, quartered lengthwise and cut into ¼-inch-thick pieces

2 stalks celery, cut into ¼-inch-thick slices
½ cup sliced mushrooms
1 tablespoon minced fresh ginger
1 8-ounce can pineapple chunks, with juice

In a large saucepan bring the bouillon to a boil. Stir in the rice, cover, and return to a boil. Reduce the heat and cook until the liquid is absorbed, about 20 minutes.

In a medium bowl combine the chicken strips, 1 tablespoon of the soy sauce, 1½ teaspoons of the sugar, and the chopped garlic. Sprinkle the curry powder over the chicken and mix well. Set aside. In a separate bowl mix the cornstarch with 2 tablespoons of the soy sauce and set aside. In a large skillet or wok heat 2 tablespoons of the oil over high heat. Sauté the chicken mixture. Add the onion after 2 minutes, and sauté until browned. Remove from the skillet. Heat the remaining 2 tablespoons oil of in the same skillet. Stir in the zucchini, celery, and mushrooms, and cook until lightly browned. Add the remaining 1½ teaspoons of sugar, the remaining soy sauce, the ginger, and the pineapple chunks and juice and stir well. Add the cornstarch mixture and stir. Return the chicken and onion to the skillet. Stir until the sauce thickens. Serve with the rice.

MAKES 4 TO 6 SERVINGS.

Debrosses Trout

1 teaspoon finely chopped celery
1 teaspoon finely chopped shallot
1½ teaspoons finely chopped mushrooms
½ teaspoon finely chopped onion
½ teaspoon butter
1 tablespoon white vermouth
½ teaspoon chopped fresh dill (or ¼ teaspoon dried)
½ teaspoon chopped fresh parsley
Salt and pepper to taste
....
1 whole dressed trout
....
5 white lettuce leaves (use loose-leaf lettuce), blanched
2 tablespoons butter, melted
....
¼ cup chopped shallots
⅓ cup dry white wine
1 teaspoon coriander
4 bay leaves
⅛ teaspoon sage

⅛ teaspoon paprika
⅛ teaspoon ground mace
   Several fresh sorrel leaves
¼ cup crushed, peeled tomatoes
⅛ teaspoon black pepper
2 cups boiling water
....
1 teaspoon cornstarch or arrowroot
1 tablespoon water
   Lemon wedges for garnish

In a medium bowl combine the celery, 1 tea-spoon shallot, mushrooms, onion, butter, ver-mouth, dill, parsley, salt, and pepper. Fill the fish cavity with the stuffing and sew up with a needle and thread, if necessary.

On the bottom of a fish poacher rack, arrange the blanched lettuce leaves so they overlap and completely cover the bottom. Brush both sides of the fish with melted but-ter. Place the fish on top of the leaves. Pull the leaves up to cover the fish completely. Add the ¼ cup shallots, wine, coriander, bay leaves, sage, paprika, mace, sorrel leaves, tomatoes, and ⅛ teaspoon pepper, and pour in the boil-ing water. Cover tightly. Bake in a 400° oven for 20 to 25 minutes.

Transfer the fish to a warmed platter. Remove sewing thread if used. Strain the liq-uid from the poacher through cheesecloth into a heavy saucepan. Boil until reduced to about 1 cup, then thicken with cornstarch or arrowroot dissolved in 1 tablespoon water. Spoon the sauce over the fish and garnish with lemon wedges.

MAKES 1 SERVING.

White Pillars Inn

82 Second Street
Deposit, New York 13754
(607) 467-4191

---

*A*n 1821 combination Federal and Greek Revival mansion, the White Pillars takes its name from its four impressive columns. Located in the historic village of Deposit in the foothills of the Catskills, the inn

White Pillars Inn

places its guests near a natural wonderland of pristine hiking trails and high mountain scenery. It also offers the sort of elegance that sup-posedly disappeared a century or more ago. Magnificent floral arrangements, museum quality antiques, Persian carpets, and hand-crafted beds provide a truly genteel atmosphere.

Baked Apple in Caramel Sauce

4 McIntosh apples, peeled and cored
4 5 x 5-inch puff pastry sheets
   Cinnamon-sugar
   Raisins (optional)
   Walnuts (optional)
....
1 cup sugar
¼ cup water
1 cup heavy cream

Place each apple on the center of a puff pas-try sheet. Sprinkle with cinnamon-sugar and stuff the core with raisins and walnuts. Bring 2 opposite corners together and press to seal. Repeat with the other corners. Place the pas-try-wrapped apples on a baking sheet. Bake in a 375° oven for 35 to 40 minutes until golden.

In a saucepan dissolve the sugar in water and heat until boiling. Allow the sugar to begin to toast. When it reaches a light amber to gold tone, turn down the heat and slowly drizzle in cream until fully incorporated. Drizzle warm caramel sauce over the apples.

Can be made ahead of time and refriger-ated until ready to use.

MAKES 4 SERVINGS.

Breakfast Burrito

2 flour tortillas
2 eggs, scrambled
1 tablespoon sour cream
¼ cup shredded Cheddar cheese
   Pinch cumin
   Chopped fresh cilantro
   Salsa

In a saucepan large enough to allow a tortilla to lay flat, place a tortilla on medium heat. Add the scrambled eggs, sour cream, Ched-dar cheese, cumin, cilantro, and salsa. Roll the tortilla and heat 2 minutes until cheese is melted. Repeat with the other tortilla. Serve with extra salsa and sour cream.

MAKES 2 SERVINGS.

Old Drovers Inn

Old Route 22
Dover Plains New York 12522
(914) 832-9311

---

*T*his inn is as authentically old-fashioned as they come. It has been welcoming guests for almost two and a half centuries, in fact, ever since it opened as the Clear Water Tavern in 1750. Visitors can still enjoy a crackling fire under the heavy wood-smoked beams of the original tap room. The inn is widely celebrated for its food, which emphasizes American country specialties.

Berry Cobbler

3 pints berries (whatever is fresh and
   in season)
1½ tablespoons all-purpose flour
⅓ cup strawberry jam
....
1½ cups all-purpose flour
½ teaspoon salt
1½ tablespoons sugar

   2¼ *teaspoons baking powder*
    6 *tablespoons butter, room temperature*
   ¾ *cup cream*

In a bowl mix the berries with 1½ tablespoons of flour and strawberry jam. Set aside. In a large bowl sift 1½ cups of flour, the salt, sugar, and baking powder together. Cut in the butter. Slowly add the cream. Roll out to about ½ inch thick. Use a water glass to cut circles. Fill an ovenproof soufflé mold with berries. Top with dough. Bake in a 450° oven for 8 minutes, or until golden brown and bubbly.

MAKES 8 SERVINGS.

Old Drovers Inn

Sautéed Red Snapper with Mediterranean Vegetables and Curry

   1 *carrot*
   1 *bell pepper, any color*
   2 *shallots*
   1 *tomato, finely chopped*
   ½ *cup finely chopped eggplant*
   ½ *cup finely chopped zucchini*
   1 *clove garlic, mashed*
   2 *tablespoons olive oil*
      Sea salt to taste
      White pepper to taste
   4 *red snapper fillets (leave skin on but remove bones)*
      Pinch saffron
   2 *teaspoons curry powder*
   1 *cup Hollandaise sauce*

Finely dice all vegetables. In a skillet heat the olive oil and sauté the vegetables. Season with salt and pepper.

Season the red snapper fillets with saffron, sea salt, and white pepper. In a skillet sauté the snapper in olive oil.

Mix the curry powder with the Hollandaise. Place a mound of vegetables in the center of each warm plate. Arrange the fillet on top. Spoon the sauce around.

MAKES 4 SERVINGS.

Old Drovers Inn Cheddar Cheese Soup

   ¼ *cup butter*
   1 *cup shredded carrot*
   ½ *cup chopped onion*
   ½ *cup chopped celery*
   1 *quart poultry stock*
   3 *tablespoons blond roux*
   4 *cups grated extra sharp Vermont Cheddar*
   1 *cup heavy cream*
      Sea salt to taste
      Hot pepper sauce to taste
      Worcestershire sauce to taste
      White pepper to taste

In a heavy-gauge soup pot heat the butter and sauté the vegetables until tender and translucent. Add the poultry stock and bring to a simmer. Whisk in the cold roux. Allow to simmer for 20 minutes to cook out any flour taste. Add the Cheddar cheese, then the cream. In a blender purée the soup. Season with sea salt, hot pepper sauce, Worcestershire sauce, and white pepper.

MAKES 6 SERVINGS.

Big Moose Lake
Eagle Bay, New York 13331
(315) 357-2042

*T**he Big Moose is a turn-of-the-century Adirondack inn offering sixteen comfortable rooms. As with all traditional inns in this region, a big part of its attraction is its setting amid pristine lakes, mountains, and forests. The inn's dining room features an extensive list of excellent wines.*

Maple-Apple Cake

  1½ *cups all-purpose flour*
   1 *teaspoon baking powder*
   ½ *teaspoon baking soda*
      Pinch ground cinnamon
   ½ *cup sugar*
   ¼ *teaspoon salt*
   1 *egg, beaten*
  1½ *cups chopped tart apples*
   ½ *cup maple syrup*
   ½ *cup raisins*
  1½ *teaspoons grated orange zest*
   ⅛ *teaspoon vanilla extract*
   ⅓ *cup applesauce*
   ⅓ *cup oil*

   ½ *cup heavy cream*
   ½ *cup sour cream*
   ½ *cup maple syrup*

In a medium bowl sift together the dry ingredients. Set aside. In a large bowl combine the egg and apples. Stir in ½ cup of syrup, the raisins, orange zest, vanilla, applesauce, and oil. Add the dry ingredients, stirring just until combined. Spread the batter into a greased and floured 8-inch square pan. Bake in a 350° oven for 40 to 45 minutes or until a toothpick inserted in the center comes out clean. Brush the warm cake with additional maple syrup.

In a bowl beat the heavy cream until stiff. In a separate bowl stir together the sour cream and ½ cup of maple syrup. Fold into the whipped cream. Serve immediately with the warm or room temperature cake.

MAKES 4 TO 6 SERVINGS.

Penne Alla Russe

   1 *pound penne pasta*
   1 *tablespoon butter*
   2 *ounces (¼ cup) vodka*
   2 *ripe tomatoes, peeled, seeded, chopped*
   2 *cups heavy cream*
   ¼ *cup grated Parmesan cheese*
      Salt and pepper to taste
   8 *fresh basil leaves, chopped*

In a pot of boiling water cook the pasta until al dente. In the meantime, in a large pan melt the butter. Add the vodka and flame until it evaporates. Add the tomatoes and cook for 2 minutes over medium heat. Add the cream, Parmesan cheese, salt, and pepper, and reduce to desired consistency, approximately

by half. Drain the pasta and mix with the sauce. Sprinkle with basil and serve.
MAKES 4 TO 6 SERVINGS.

Elegant Marinade for Broiled Pork Chops

    ½ cup firmly packed brown sugar
    ¼ cup cider vinegar
    3 teaspoons brown mustard
    1 teaspoon Worcestershire sauce
       Dash ground cloves (optional)
    ¼ teaspoon ground marjoram

In a shallow dish mix all ingredients. Marinate pork chops for at least 1 hour or as long as overnight. Broil.

Serve the pork on a bed of long grain and wild rice, and pour drippings over the rice and sprinkle fresh parsley over all.
MAKES ABOUT ¾ CUP OF MARINADE.

Roast Potatoes

    1 tablespoon olive oil
    1 clove garlic, crushed
    ¼ teaspoon salt
    ¼ teaspoon fresh ground black pepper
    1½ pounds small new red potatoes,
       scrubbed and quartered
    1 tablespoon chopped fresh parsley

In a 9-inch square baking pan mix the oil, garlic, salt, and pepper. Add the potatoes and toss to coat with oil. Bake in a 425° oven for 30 to 45 minutes or until tender and browned. Sprinkle with parsley.
MAKES 6 SERVINGS.

French Silk Pie

    1¼ cups graham cracker crumbs
    2 tablespoons sugar
    ¼ teaspoon ground cinnamon
    ¼ cup melted butter
    ....
    ½ cup butter, softened

Big Moose Inn

    ¾ cup sugar
    2 teaspoons vanilla extract
    2 squares unsweetened chocolate,
       melted
    2 eggs
    ....
       Sweetened whipped cream
       Chopped nuts
       Grated semisweet chocolate

In a medium bowl combine the cracker crumbs, sugar, cinnamon, and melted butter. Mix well and press into the bottom and sides of pie plate. Bake in a 400° oven for approximately 8 minutes. Chill.

In a medium bowl cream the ½ cup of butter, ¾ cup of sugar, vanilla, and melted chocolate. Add the eggs one at a time, beating for 5 minutes at high speed after each. The constant beating is the key. Pour into the crust and refrigerate for 4 hours or overnight.

Before serving, spread with whipped cream and sprinkle with nuts and chocolate.
MAKES 6 TO 8 SERVINGS.

Mill House Inn

*33 North Main Street
East Hampton, New York 11937
(516) 324-9766*

In New York's famed Hamptons near the far end of Long Island, the Mill House dates all the way back to 1790. It took on its present Dutch colonial style during a renovation in 1898 and has changed little since. People visit the Hamptons to enjoy the peace and quiet, the beaches, and outdoor activities such as sailing, fishing, horseback riding, bicycling, golf, and tennis. A few miles from East Hampton is Montauk Point and one the oldest and finest lighthouses in the United States.

Cranberry-Orange Pecan Scones

    2 cups unbleached all-purpose flour
    ⅓ cup sugar
    3 tablespoons wheat germ
    1 teaspoon baking soda
    1 teaspoon baking powder
    ½ teaspoon salt
    6 tablespoons cold unsalted butter,
       cut into ¼-inch pieces
    1 cup sour cream
    1 large egg
    1 teaspoon lemon extract
    ½ teaspoon vanilla extract
       Finely grated zest of 1 orange
    1½ cups fresh or dried cranberries
    ½ cup chopped fresh pecans

Lightly spray a large baking sheet with cooking spray. In a large bowl mix the flour, sugar, wheat germ, soda, baking powder, and salt. Add the butter and cut it in, using fingers or a pastry blender, until the mixture resembles cornmeal. In a separate bowl whisk together the sour cream, egg, extracts, and orange zest. Make a well in the dry ingredients, add the liquid, and quickly mix to blend. Gently fold in the cranberries and the pecans.

The dough will be sticky so form the scones using floured hands. Use a spoon to scoop enough dough into floured hands to form 1 scone. Round it gently by hand and place on the prepared cookie sheet. Repeat for the remaining scones, leaving some room between for spreading. If necessary use a second cookie sheet.

Bake in a 400° oven for 20 minutes, until golden brown and crusty. Cool for several minutes before serving.
MAKES 10 SCONES.

Poached Pears with Cranberry Maple Sauce

    1 10-ounce package fresh cranberries
    ½ cup sugar
    1 cup water
    10 ripe pears
    2 cups orange juice
    ½ cup pure maple syrup
    2 tablespoons butter, cut into bits
    ¼ cup chopped pecans
    10 orange slices, cut in half

Mill House Inn

In a medium saucepan combine the cranberries, sugar, and water. Bring to a boil, then simmer for about 15 minutes, until cranberries begin to pop and the sauce thickens. Remove the sauce from the heat and reserve.

Peel the pears, cut in half, and remove the core and stem. Place the pears in a baking pan large enough to hold the pears in 1 layer, cut-side-up (this will prevent the pears from turning brown during cooking). In a small bowl combine the orange juice and maple syrup. Pour the mixture over the pears, basting the pears so that each is fully moistened with cooking liquid. Dot with butter.

Bake in a 350° oven for approximately 30 minutes or until tender but not falling apart, basting 2 or 3 times during cooking. Cooking time will vary slightly depending on the ripeness of the pears. Remove from the oven. Measure out 1½ cups of the orange-maple cooking liquid. Add ½ cup of the liquid to the reserved cranberry sauce and return to a simmer for 5 minutes stirring to incorporate orange-maple mixture. Add more of the reserved liquid to the cranberry mixture if needed to create a medium-thick sauce.

For each serving, ladle 2 ounces of the cranberry-orange sauce onto a plate, spreading the sauce out into a pool on the plate. Place 2 pear halves per serving side by side on the sauce. Garnish with 1 teaspoon of chopped pecans and 2 half orange slices.

MAKES 10 SERVINGS.

Potato, Scallion, and Monterey Jack Cheese Frittata with Tomato-Green Chile Sauce

- 1 tablespoon olive oil
- ½ medium onion, chopped
- 1 28-ounce can crushed tomatoes
- 1 cup water
- 1 teaspoon sugar
- 1½ teaspoons ground coriander
- 1½ teaspoons ground cumin
- 1½ teaspoons chili powder
- Salt and pepper to taste
- ½ cup canned chopped mild green chile peppers

....

- 1 baking potato per 2 servings
- 1 tablespoon olive oil
- Salt and pepper to taste
- 2 tablespoons chopped scallions
- 6 eggs
- 6 tablespoons milk
- 6 tablespoons grated Monterey Jack cheese
- Chopped parsley (optional)
- Orange and strawberry slices

In a medium saucepan heat 1 tablespoon of olive oil and sauté the onion until softened. Add the crushed tomatoes, water, sugar, coriander, cumin, chili powder, salt, and black pepper, and green chili peppers. Stir to combine. Bring to a boil, then simmer for 20 to 30 minutes, until the sauce is thickened. Remove from the heat and reserve. Sauce can be made ahead of time reheated at serving time, thinned with water if necessary.

Peel the potato, then cut in half vertically and each half sliced thin horizontally to form half moon slices. In a skillet sauté the potato in 1 tablespoon of olive oil until cooked through and golden brown. Season with salt and pepper to taste. Add the scallions and stir to combine. Remove from the heat.

For each frittata: Lightly spray a nonstick omelet pan with cooking spray. Add half of the potato-scallion mixture and heat over medium heat. In a small bowl whisk together 3 eggs, 3 tablespoons of milk, and 3 tablespoons of grated Monterey Jack cheese. Pour the egg mixture into the omelet pan, distributing evenly over the potato mixture. Allow

eggs to cook for a minute or 2 to set the bottom. Then using a rubber spatula gently lift an edge of the eggs and tipping the pan, allow uncooked egg to run underneath, building up the height of the frittata. Continue this gentle cooking process until the eggs are nearly cooked through, about 5 minutes. Do not have the heat too high, as the bottom of the frittata may burn. To finish cooking the top of the frittata, slide pan under the broiler for a minute or 2. Repeat this procedure for the second frittata.

Slide the finished frittata out of the pan and onto a plate. May be garnished with chopped parsley or orange and strawberry slices. Reheat the tomato chile sauce and serve on the side.

MAKES 2 SERVINGS.

52 East Main Street
Fredonia, New York 14063
(716) 672-2103

Stately columns at the entrance suggest that this is a very traditional country inn, and so it is. With its twenty-three well-appointed rooms and suites, the inn has been serving visitors to the historic village of Fredonia for over half a century. As one might expect, special emphasis is placed on dining here, and the inn was a charter member of the original Duncan Hines "Family of Fine Restaurants."

The White Inn

Irish Tenderloin of Beef

- 4 to 5 ounces tenderloin steaks (filet mignon)
- 1 tablespoon cracked black peppercorns
- ⅓ cup olive oil
- 4 ounces dark beer
- 1 tablespoon chopped shallots
- ½ teaspoon chopped garlic
- 2 tablespoons julienne smoked ham
- 6 ounces demiglace
- 1½ teaspoons chopped parsley

Lightly coat the steaks with cracked black peppercorns. In a skillet heat the olive oil and sauté the steaks. Set aside. Deglaze the pan with dark beer. Add the shallots, garlic, ham, and demiglace. Reduce by one-third. Finish the sauce with parsley and serve with seared steaks.

MAKES 4 SERVINGS.

Breast of Chicken Tarragon

- 4 skinless chicken breasts
  Flour for dredging
- ⅓ cup oil
- 4 ounces sherry or Marsala wine
- 1½ teaspoons dried tarragon
- 6 ounces demiglace
- 1½ teaspoons chopped shallots
- ½ cup sliced mushrooms
- 1½ teaspoons butter (optional)
  Salt and pepper to taste

Dredge the chicken in flour. In a skillet heat the oil and sauté the chicken to 165°. Set aside. Deglaze the pan with wine. Add the tarragon, demiglace, shallots, and mushrooms. Reduce. Season to taste. Add the butter. Place the chicken fillets in the sauce. Heat and serve.

MAKES 4 SERVINGS.

Basic Pie Crust

- 2 cups all-purpose flour
- 1½ teaspoons salt
- ½ cup oil
- ¼ cup water

Into a medium bowl sift the flour and salt. Pour the oil and water over the top all at once without mixing. Stir these ingredients lightly until blended. Do not overwork. Form into a ball. Divide into 2 parts, flatten slightly, and roll out thin or to desired thickness. Patch any tears by sticking them together or by adding a small piece of dough. Place the dough in 9-inch pie pans and form.

MAKES 2 9-INCH CRUSTS.

Bourbon Pecan Pie

- 1½ cups sugar
- 4 or 5 eggs
  Pinch salt (small)
- 6 tablespoons melted butter
- ¾ cup light corn syrup
- ¾ cup dark corn syrup
- ¾ cup heavy cream
- ¼ cup bourbon
- 4 cups pecans
- 2 unbaked 9-inch pie shells

In a medium bowl blend all ingredients except the pecans. Divide the pecans among the pie shells. Pour the filling over the pecans. Bake in a 375° oven until the centers are set and the crusts are brown.

MAKES 2 PIES, 12 TO 16 SERVINGS.

Chocolate Mousse Cake

- 1½ pounds semisweet chocolate chips
- 8 eggs
- 1 cup heavy cream
- 1½ cups sugar
- 2 tablespoons rum
- 2 tablespoons brandy
- 2 tablespoons coffee

Place a rimmed cookie sheet in the oven and fill half full with water. Coat a 9-inch cake pan with butter. In the top of a double boiler over simmering water melt the chocolate. Place the uncracked eggs in a bowl of hot water to warm up.

In a medium bowl whip the cream to soft peaks. Set aside. In a large bowl whip the eggs and sugar until doubled in volume. In a large bowl combine the melted chocolate, rum, brandy, coffee, and whipped cream. Mix well with a wire whisk. Fold in one-third of the egg mixture, then gently add the remaining mixture. Pour into the prepared pan, taking care to fill the pan full. Place in the water bath. Bake in a 375° oven for approximately 45 minutes.

Let the cake rest with oven door open for 20 minutes. Chill well.

To remove from the pan, heat the pan on stove over low heat, then flip out onto a cardboard cake circle.

MAKES 1 9-INCH CAKE, 8 SERVINGS.

Saratoga Rose Inn

❧

4174 Rockwell Street
Hadley, New York 12835
(518) 696-2861

A Victorian mansion located in the southern Adirondacks, the Saratoga Rose is centrally situated within easy driving distance of Lake George, Glen Falls, and Saratoga. Built in the late 1800s, the mansion has been immaculately restored. Guest rooms are furnished with period antiques. Nearby, visitors can enjoy swimming, boating, fishing, white-water rafting, or just a quiet walk in the woods. The less athletically inclined might prefer antiquing, sunbathing, or testing their luck at the world famous Saratoga Race Track.

Harvest Chicken

- 1 cup apple cider
- 2 Granny Smith apples, peeled and diced
- ¼ cup raisins
- 2 slices white bread, diced
- 1 tablespoon firmly packed brown sugar
- 1 teaspoon ground cinnamon
- ½ teaspoon ground allspice
- 2 6-ounce boneless chicken breasts
  2 slices New York State Cheddar
  Flour, egg, and breadcrumbs for breading

1 cup olive oil
1 shot of pear Cognac or brandy
¼ cup maple syrup

In a small sauté pan over low heat combine ½ cup of cider, the apples, raisins, bread, brown sugar, cinnamon, and allspice. Cook slowly until thickened. Pound the breasts lightly. Put some of the apple mixture on each breast. Add the Cheddar cheese. Carefully roll the breasts, making sure all sides are closed. Dip in flour, egg, and breadcrumbs.

In a skillet heat the olive oil. Place the chicken in the heated olive oil and sauté until brown. Remove the chicken from the pan and drain on a paper towel to remove the excess oil. Place in a lightly buttered casserole dish. Add the remaining cider, Cognac, and maple syrup. Bake in a 350° oven for 12 to 15 minutes.

MAKES 2 SERVINGS.

Nancy's Chocolate Chocolate Chip Muffins

2 eggs
½ cup oil
1 cup milk
1 teaspoon vanilla extract
1¾ cups all-purpose flour
2 cups sugar
¼ cup unsweetened cocoa
1 tablespoon baking powder
1 cup chocolate chips

Grease 12 muffin cups or line with colorful paper muffin liners. In a large bowl combine the eggs, oil, milk, and vanilla. Mix well. In a smaller bowl mix the flour, sugar, cocoa, baking powder, and chocolate chips. Add the dry ingredients to the liquid mixture, stirring just to moisten. Spoon into the muffin cups. Bake in a 400° oven for 15 minutes.

MAKES 12 MEDIUM MUFFINS.

Saratoga Rose Inn

Saratoga Rose Shrimp

24 medium or large shrimp, peeled and deveined
Flour for dredging
¼ cup butter
1 small onion, chopped
¼ pound prosciutto
1 large roasted red bell pepper, sliced
1 medium tomato, chopped
Fresh basil
1 tablespoon garlic
¼ cup olive oil
¼ cup water
6 ounces crab meat
1 teaspoon paprika
Pepper to taste
1 pound linguine or angel hair pasta, cooked
⅓ cup grated Asiago cheese
Chopped parsley for garnish

Coat the shrimp with flour. Set aside.

In a large saucepan over medium heat melt half of the butter and sauté the onion, prosciutto, roasted pepper, tomato, basil, and garlic. Add the olive oil and water. Simmer for 1 minute.

In a skillet melt the remaining butter and sauté the shrimp and crab with the paprika and pepper until done. Add the onion mixture to the crab and shrimp. When done, pour over the cooked pasta. Mix lightly. Divide into 4 servings. Sprinkle Asiago cheese over the top and serve. Garnish with parsley.

MAKES 4 SERVINGS.

Sandy Creek Manor House

❧

*1960 Redman Road
Hamlin, New York 14464
(716) 964-7528*

The hospitality is European-style at this western New York inn located on six wooded acres. The Victorian Sandy Creek Manor House looks like a place where an intriguing mystery might unfold. In fact, the inn regularly hosts murder mystery

parties and offers special packages to participants. Guest rooms feature Amish quilts.

Manor House French Toast

1 loaf Italian or French bread, cut into 1½-inch slices
1½ cups eggnog
3 tablespoons Amaretto
2 tablespoons sugar
½ teaspoon grated nutmeg
½ to 1 cup slivered almonds
Maple syrup
Confectioners' sugar

Arrange the bread slices in a large baking dish. In a bowl combine the eggnog, Amaretto, sugar, and nutmeg. Pour over the bread and turn to coat all sides. Cover and refrigerate overnight.

Coat the bread with the slivered almonds. In a skillet fry the bread in butter over medium heat until golden brown on both sides. Serve with warm maple syrup. Sprinkle with confectioners' sugar.

Note: Eggnog can be frozen, so this breakfast treat can be enjoyed all year long. Freeze it in 1- or 2-cup plastic containers, which makes it easier to thaw and it is just the right amount.

MAKES 6 SERVINGS.

Apple Volcanoes

¾ cup all-purpose flour
¾ cup milk
4 eggs
1 teaspoon grated nutmeg
1 tart apple, peeled and cored
2 tablespoons lemon juice
½ teaspoon ground cinnamon
¼ cup sugar
1 tablespoon maple syrup, plus extra for topping
Confectioners' sugar

In a medium bowl mix together the flour, milk, eggs, and nutmeg until blended well. The mixture will be lumpy. Pour into 4 greased ramekins or soup bowls. Thinly slice the apple. In a bowl sprinkle the apples with lemon juice, cinnamon, sugar, and maple syrup. Mix well. Arrange the apple slices in a circular pattern around the top of the batter in each ramekin. Bake in a 375° oven for about 20 to 25 minutes. The volcanoes will puff up and out of the bowl. Lift out of the bowl, sprinkle with confectioners' sugar, and serve with warm maple syrup.

Variation: Bake additional apples with chopped nuts to serve with these.

MAKES 4 SERVINGS.

Chocolate Cherry Cream

- ½ cup thawed Cool Whip
- 1 tablespoon maraschino cherry juice
- 2 teaspoons cherry or berry jam
  Sliced fresh fruit
  Chocolate sauce

In a small bowl mix the Cool Whip, cherry juice, and jam and place a dollop over slices of fresh fruit. Garnish with grapes, berries, or other small pieces of fruit.

Drizzle fruit and cream with a thin line of chocolate sauce, creating a swirling or other type of fancy pattern.

MAKES ½ CUP.

*Country Life
Bed and
Breakfast*

237 *Cathedral Avenue
Hempstead, New York 11550
(516) 292-9219*

*T**his seventy-year-old Dutch Colonial house is situated in the middle of Long Island and within easy reach of beaches and the world's capital city. Each of the guest rooms has its own charm. One has a four-poster bed, while another features Queen Anne furnishings. Guest are welcome to tour the village of Hempstead in one of the inn's vintage 1929 Fords.*

Mexican Scramble

- 2 tablespoons butter or margarine
- 1 cup chopped onion
- 1 cup chopped green bell pepper
- 1 small jalapeño, chopped (optional)
- 1 cup drained diced tomatoes
- ¾ teaspoon salt
- ½ teaspoon paprika
  Dash pepper
- ¼ pound (1 cup) diced processed
  cheese
- 3 eggs, beaten (or egg substitute)
- 4 to 5 slices buttered toast, cut in half

In a skillet melt the butter and sauté the onion and peppers until tender but not brown. Add the tomatoes and simmer for 5 minutes. Add the seasonings and cheese, stirring to melt the cheese. Stir a small amount of the hot mixture into the eggs, and return all to the hot mixture. Cook until the consistency of scrambled eggs, but moist, stirring frequently. Serve over hot toast. Bacon, sausage, or orange slices make the plate look nice.

MAKES 4 TO 5 SERVINGS.

Fruit Cheese Toasties

- 1 16-ounce carton low-fat Ricotta
  cheese
- ½ cup apricot, strawberry, or peach
  preserves, depending on fruit
  selected
- 8 slices cinnamon-raisin bread
  Cinnamon
- 8 tablespoons honey
  Bananas, strawberries, kiwi, or
  peaches, sliced
  Wheat germ

In a medium bowl mix the ricotta cheese with preserves. Spread each slice of bread with the ricotta mixture. Place on a baking sheet. Sprinkle with cinnamon and drizzle each with 1 tablespoon of honey. Arrange fruit slices on top to cover. Sprinkle with wheat germ. Bake in a 350° oven for 10 minutes.

MAKES 4 SERVINGS.

Hanshaw House

*Hanshaw
House
Bed and
Breakfast Inn*

15 *Sapsucker Woods Road
Ithaca, New York 14850
(607) 257-1437*

*F**ramed by a white picket fence, this 1830s restored farmhouse overlooks ponds, gardens, and woodlands. Rooms are furnished with antiques and colorful chintzes in an English decor. Nearby are Ithaca's exquisite waterfalls and gorges as well as Cornell University.*

Sweet Potato Waffles

- 2 tablespoons sugar
- ½ cup canned or fresh (cooked) sweet
  potato
- 3 eggs
- 2 tablespoons butter, melted
- 1 cup whole wheat flour
- 2 teaspoons baking powder
- ½ teaspoon salt
- ⅛ teaspoon fresh grated nutmeg
- ½ teaspoon ground cinnamon
- ⅓ cup orange juice, with pulp
- ⅔ cup milk
  Maple syrup for topping

In a food processor blend all ingredients. Thin with more milk if necessary. Bake in a greased waffle iron. Serve with real maple syrup.

MAKES 5 TO 6 WAFFLES.

Sweet Potato and Apricot Purée with Pecan Streusel

- 6 ounces dried apricots
- 1 tablespoon sugar
- 3 large eggs
- 1 40-ounce can whole yams or sweet
  potatoes, drained (or 5 large fresh

*sweet potatoes, baked and
scooped out of skins)*
- ⅛ *teaspoon fresh grated nutmeg*
- ½ *teaspoon ground cinnamon*
- 1 *tablespoon all-purpose flour*
- ⅓ *cup firmly packed light brown sugar*
- 1 *tablespoon butter*
- ⅔ *cup chopped pecans*

In a saucepan simmer the apricots in 1 to 2 inches of water for 30 minutes. Reserve the liquid after cooking. In a food processor purée the apricots with the sugar, and 2 tablespoons of cooking liquid. Add the eggs and blend. Add the potatoes, nutmeg, and cinnamon to the apricot purée. Blend. Place the mixture in a buttered 2-quart shallow baking dish. In a small bowl blend the flour, brown sugar, butter, and pecans. Crumble over the purée. Bake in a 350° oven for about 15 minutes.

MAKES 8 TO 10 SERVINGS.

Chocolate Waffles with Raspberry Purée

- 1 *10-ounce package frozen raspberries, thawed and drained*
- 1 *cup sugar*
  Fresh lemon juice to taste
- ¾ *pound bittersweet chocolate*
- 1¼ *cups butter*
- 6 *eggs*
- ½ *cup milk*
- 1 *cup all-purpose flour*
- 2 *teaspoons baking powder*
- ¼ *teaspoon salt*
- ⅛ *to ¼ teaspoon fresh grated nutmeg*
- 1 *cup heavy cream*
- ½ *teaspoon vanilla extract*
- 1 *teaspoon confectioners' sugar*

In a blender purée the raspberries until smooth. Strain through a fine strainer to remove the seeds, pushing all pulp through with a wooden spoon. In a saucepan combine the purée, ½ cup of sugar, and the lemon juice, and cook over low heat until the sugar is dissolved. Set aside. In the top of a double boiler over simmering water melt the chocolate and butter. Cool.

In a medium bowl blend the eggs, ½ cup of sugar, milk, chocolate, flour, baking powder, salt, and nutmeg. If the mixture becomes too thick, thin with more milk. Pour into a hot greased waffle iron and bake. Whip the

cream with the vanilla and confectioners' sugar. Serve the waffles with raspberry purée and dollops of whipped cream.

MAKES APPROXIMATELY 6 TO 8 WAFFLES.

Peregrine House

Peregrine House

*140 College Avenue
Ithaca, New York 14850
(607) 272-0919*

Built in 1874, this brick Victorian home with slate mansard roof stands in the shade of big trees right in the heart of Ithaca. It is convenient to all the city's attractions, including the Cornell Performing Arts Center and the main university campus. Not far away are lakes, gorges, waterfalls, and fields of wildflowers. Guest rooms are furnished with plump down comforters, lace curtains, and Laura Ashley prints.

Sunday Morning Sunshine

- 2 *large yellow bell peppers*
- 1 *large sweet Vidalia onion*
- 2 *tablespoons butter*
- ¼ *cup extra virgin olive oil*
- 10 *to 12 sliced mushrooms*
- 1 *clove garlic, minced*
  Fresh basil leaves, finely chopped

- 12 *eggs*
- ⅓ *cup cream*
- ¼ *cup grated Parmesan cheese*
  Salt and coarse ground pepper to taste

Julienne the peppers and onion. In a skillet heat the butter and olive oil and sauté the vegetables until caramelized, 20 to 30 minutes. Add the mushrooms, garlic, and chopped basil. Meanwhile, in a large bowl beat eggs. Add the cream, Parmesan cheese, salt, and pepper. Pour the egg mixture over the vegetables and cook until set but still soft on top. Place under the broiler briefly to set.

This can be cut like a pie into wedges and served with hot cornbread and a basil leaf or 2.

MAKES 6 TO 8 SERVINGS.

Red Bananas and Strawberries with Cream

- 1 *ripe red banana*
- 2 *strawberries*
- 1 *tablespoon heavy cream*
  Toasted pecans

Into a serving bowl slice the ripe red banana on the diagonal. Slice a strawberry or 2 into this and pour a tablespoon of cream over it. Top with a sprinkle of toasted pecans.

MAKES 1 SERVING.

The Bark Eater Inn

*Alstead Mill Road, P.O. Box 139
Keene, New York 12942
(518) 576-2221*

A 150-year-old farmhouse, the Bark Eater stands beside the Adirondack's highest mountains. In all it offers nineteen antique-furnished guest rooms in the main house, a carriage house, and a log-hewn cottage deep in the nearby woods. It has served as a country inn since the nineteenth century when it catered to stagecoach passengers on their way to Lake Placid. The inn takes its name from the word Adirondack *which, loosely translated, means "they who eat trees." The term was an Indian insult applied to the local Algonquins by their Mohawk neighbors to the south.*

Granola

16 cups (1½ cartons) old-fashioned
      oats
 2 cups coconut
 1 cup wheat germ
1½ cups sunflower seeds
 ½ cup poppy seeds
1½ teaspoons salt
1½ cups cashews
1½ cups almonds
 ¼ cup ground cinnamon
....

 2 cups butter, melted
 1 cup honey
 1 cup firmly packed brown sugar
 ½ cup molasses
1½ cups peanut butter
 3 tablespoons vanilla extract

In a large bowl mix all of the grains, nuts, and seeds. Add the cinnamon. In a separate bowl mix the remaining ingredients. Combine the mixtures. Spread on cookie sheets. Bake in a 375° oven for 30 minutes. Turn after 15 minutes.
MAKES ABOUT 6 QUARTS.

The Bark Eater Inn

Carrot Wild Rice Soup

 1 tablespoon olive oil
 4 cloves garlic, chopped
 3 onions, chopped
12 carrots, peeled and sliced
 ¼ cup white wine
 1 gallon vegetable stock
 ¼ cup wild rice
 ½ cup white rice
 3 tablespoons fresh dill
     Cracked pepper to taste
     Salt to taste
     Chives to taste

In a skillet heat the oil and sauté the garlic and onions until brown. Add the carrots and simmer until soft. Add the wine and stock. Add the rices and cook until the rice is done. In a blender purée the soup and add the spices and seasonings. Garnish with fresh chopped chives.
MAKES ABOUT 1 GALLON.

Poached Salmon Fillets

 2 quarts water
 1 cup white wine
 2 tablespoons fresh chopped parsley
 1 lemon
 4 salmon fillets
     Cracked pepper and salt to taste

In a large pot combine the water, wine, and parsley. Bring to a simmer. Quarter the lemon and add to the pot. Cook salmon fillets in the liquid for approximately 10 minutes, until the salmon becomes firm. Sprinkle with pepper and salt to taste.
MAKES 4 SERVINGS.

Interlaken Inn

15 Interlaken Avenue
Lake Placid, New York 12946
(518) 523-3180

*T*he inn looks out over two lakes toward lofty Whiteface Mountain. Built in 1906, the Interlaken has been restored to its original Edwar-

dian-era splendor. Two separate winter Olympics have been held in Lake Placid. Not surprisingly, outdoor sports are the area's prime attraction. Hiking, fishing, biking, golf, and, of course, cross-country and downhill skiing are all available just minutes from the inn.

Sour Cream Cherry Coffee Cake

 ¾ cup butter, softened
 1 cup sugar
 2 eggs
 1 cup sour cream
 2 cups sifted all-purpose flour
 1 teaspoon baking powder
 1 teaspoon baking soda
 ½ teaspoon salt
 1 teaspoon grated nutmeg
 1 cup dried sour cherries
 ¾ cup firmly packed brown sugar
 ½ cup chopped walnuts
 1 teaspoon ground cinnamon

In a large bowl cream the butter and sugar until light and fluffy. Add the eggs and sour cream, and mix well. In a separate bowl combine the flour, baking powder, soda, salt, and nutmeg. Add the sour cherries and dry ingredients to liquid mixture and mix well. Pour into a greased and floured 9 x 13-inch baking pan. In a separate bowl mix together the brown sugar, walnuts, and cinnamon. Sprinkle over the batter. Cover and refrigerate overnight.

Bake in a 350° oven for 35 to 40 minutes.
MAKES 12 SERVINGS.

Scallops with a Maple Mustard Cream Sauce

 3 pounds fresh scallops
 1 pound bacon
....

 ¼ cup honey mustard
 ¼ cup Dijon mustard
 ¼ cup maple syrup
 1 cup heavy cream

Wrap each scallop with 1 strip of bacon, and secure with toothpick. Place the scallops on a baking sheet. Bake in a 350° oven for 20 minutes, or until the bacon is done.

In a medium sauté pan combine the honey mustard, Dijon mustard, and maple syrup. Heat thoroughly and add the cream. Reduce by one-third. Keep warm. Pour over the scallops and enjoy.

MAKES 6 SERVINGS.

Duck Breast au Poivre

    4 **fresh duck breasts**
       Cracked black peppercorns
       ....
    2 **tablespoons brandy**
    2 **tablespoons honey**
    ¼ **cup demiglace**
    ¼ **cup heavy cream**
       Salt and pepper to taste

Score the duck on the skin side and coat with peppercorns. In a greased skillet sauté skin-side down over medium-high heat for 4 to 5 minutes. Turn over and continue cooking the other side for 5 to 6 minutes over medium heat. When done, place on a serving platter and keep warm. Deglaze the sauté pan with brandy (with the pan off the heat). Add the honey, demiglace, and cream, and return to heat. Reduce by half. Season to taste. Pour over the duck breasts and serve.

MAKES 4 SERVINGS.

Eggs Sardou

    2 **egg yolks**
    2 **tablespoons very hot water**
    1 **cup butter, melted**
    2 **teaspoons lemon juice**
       Dash Tabasco sauce
       ....
       Water
    2 **teaspoons vinegar**
    8 **eggs**
    2 **12-ounce packages Stouffer's**
       Spinach Soufflé
    2 **8-ounce cans artichoke bottoms**
    16 **strips bacon, cooked**

In a blender drop in the egg yolks and blend on high speed. Add 2 tablespoons of hot water. Then very slowly, with the blender running, add the butter. The mixture will thicken. Then the add lemon juice and Tabasco. In a large poaching pan combine water and the vinegar. Heat until just boiling, and reduce the heat to simmer. Poach the eggs. Prepare

the spinach soufflé according to the package instructions. Heat the artichokes in a microwave-proof dish until just warm.

In a skillet cook the bacon until crisp. On 4 serving plates place spinach, then an artichoke heart. Place a poached egg in the artichoke heart, place bacon on top, and then the sauce.

MAKES 4 SERVINGS.

5170 Lewiston Road
Lewiston, New York 14092
(716) 285-4869

———————

*T*his modern home provides exactly what its name implies—a country club atmosphere. The deck overlooks the challenging Lewiston golf course. The three guest rooms are comfortably furnished. One features a four-poster while another has an in-the-room sauna.

Date and Nut Muffins

    1½ **cups all-purpose flour**
    1   **cup wheat bran**
    ½   **cup firmly packed brown sugar**
    1   **tablespoon baking powder**
    ½   **teaspoon salt**
    ¼   **teaspoon ground cinnamon**
    1   **cup chopped pitted dates**
    ½   **cup chopped walnuts or pecans**
    1   **egg**
    1½ **cups milk**
    ⅓   **cup butter, melted**
    3   **tablespoons molasses or honey**
    12 **walnut or pecan halves (optional)**

In a medium bowl combine the flour, bran, sugar, baking powder, salt, and cinnamon. Stir in the dates and ½ cup of chopped nuts. In a separate bowl whisk the egg with the milk, melted butter, and molasses. Stir the milk mixture into the flour just until combined. Spoon the batter into 12 greased or paper-lined muffin cups. Place a nut on each

muffin, if desired. Bake in a 400° oven for 20 to 25 minutes.

MAKES 1 DOZEN.

The Country Club Inn

Banana Cranberry Nut Bread

    ½   **cup butter or margarine**
    ¾   **cup sugar**
    2   **eggs**
    1½ **cups bananas, mashed (about 3**
        large)
    1   **teaspoon grated orange zest**
    ½   **teaspoon salt**
    4   **teaspoons baking powder**
    1⅔ **cups all-purpose flour**
    ½   **cup coarsely chopped cranberries**
    ⅓   **cup chopped walnuts**

In a large bowl beat together the butter and sugar until light and airy. Add the eggs, bananas, and orange zest. In a separate bowl combine the salt, baking powder, and flour. Add the dry ingredients to the butter mixture and mix well. Stir in the cranberries and walnuts. Pour into a greased 5 x 9-inch loaf pan. Bake in a 375° oven for 45 to 55 minutes or until a toothpick inserted in the center comes out clean.

Remove from the pan and cool on a wire rack.

MAKES 1 LOAF.

Glazed Blueberry Orange Muffins

    1½ **cups all-purpose flour**
    1   **cup whole wheat flour**
    1   **tablespoon baking powder**
    1   **teaspoon ground cinnamon**
    ½   **teaspoon salt**
    1   **egg**
    1¼ **cups milk**
    ⅓   **cup butter, melted**
    ⅓   **cup honey or maple syrup**
    1   **teaspoon grated orange zest**

1½ cups fresh or frozen (unthawed)
blueberries
....

½ cup confectioners' sugar
2 teaspoons orange juice
1 teaspoon grated orange zest

Grease 12 large muffin cups or line with paper baking cups. In a large bowl mix the flours, baking powder, cinnamon, and salt. In a separate bowl combine the egg, milk, butter, honey, and 1 teaspoon orange zest. Stir the liquid mixture into the dry ingredients, stirring just until moistened. Fold in the blueberries. Do not overmix. Spoon the mixture into muffin cups, filling each to the top. Bake in a 400° oven for about 20 minutes, or until the tops are firm to the touch. Cool in the pan for 5 minutes.

Remove the muffins to a rack. In a small bowl combine the remaining ingredients until smooth. Spoon over the tops of the muffins. Cool.

MAKES 12 LARGE MUFFINS.

Genesse Country Inn

❧

948 George Street
Mumford, New York 14511
(716) 538-2500

A grey stone cottage, the inn sits beside an old mill pond in a story-book setting that might have appealed to Hans Christian Anderson. Inside, the antique furnishings and sturdy reproductions continue the old-fashioned feeling. Fishing is available in the pond, and not far away is the Genesee Country Village Museum, Mumford Nature Center, and a myriad of opportunities for outdoor activities such as hiking, bicycling, and cross-country skiing.

Fruit Bread

5 cups all-purpose flour
¾ teaspoon baking powder
2¼ teaspoons salt
3 teaspoons ground cinnamon
4½ cups sugar
3 teaspoons baking soda
3 teaspoons ground cloves
1½ teaspoons grated nutmeg
1½ cups oil
6 eggs
1½ cups water
3 cups canned pumpkin, applesauce,
or mashed bananas
1½ cups chopped nuts

In a large bowl combine the dry ingredients. Stir in the oil, eggs, and water. Add the fruit and nuts, and stir until well blended. Pour into 5 greased 8 x 4-inch loaf pans. Bake in a 325° oven for about 1 hour or until done.

MAKES 5 LOAVES.

Vanilla Pancake Sauce

1 cup sugar
3 tablespoons all-purpose flour
½ teaspoon ground cinnamon
2 cups water
1 teaspoon vanilla extract
2 tablespoons butter

In a saucepan combine the sugar, flour, and cinnamon. Whisk in the water, and bring mixture to a boil. Cook until the sugar is dissolved. Let the mixture simmer for 2 minutes. Remove from the heat and whisk in the vanilla and butter until the butter is melted. Serve immediately over pancakes or pour into a tightly closed jar and refrigerate for up to a month.

MAKES ABOUT 3 CUPS.

Genesse Country Inn

Colonial Sugar Cookies

½ cup butter or margarine
1 egg, well-beaten
½ teaspoon vanilla extract
1 tablespoon milk
1 cup sugar
1½ cups all-purpose flour
1 teaspoon baking powder
¼ teaspoon salt
Colored sugar

In a large bowl cream the butter, egg, vanilla, milk, and sugar. In a separate bowl combine the flour, baking powder, and salt. Add the dry ingredients to the liquid mixture, mixing well. Roll small portions of dough in decorative sugar and press pn a greased cookie sheet with the bottom of a glass to make the cookies round. Bake in a 400° oven for 8 minutes.

MAKES ABOUT 3 DOZEN.

Park Place Bed and Breakfast

❧

740 Park Place
Niagara Falls, New York 14301
(716) 282-4626

---

*B*uilt in 1913 by James Marshall, a founder of the giant Union Carbide Corporation, the house stands on a tree-line street in a neighborhood of turn-of-the-century homes. Its half-timbered architecture shows the influence of the Prairie School and Craftsman movements. The five guest rooms are furnished and decorated in period fashion.

Park Place

Peanut Butter Super Cookies

1   cup butter or margarine
1   cup peanut butter
1   cup sugar
1   cup firmly packed brown sugar
2   eggs
2   cups all-purpose flour
1   teaspoon baking soda
1/2   cup chocolate chips
1/2   cup peanut butter chips

In a large bowl cream the butter and peanut butter. Add the sugars and cream together. Add the eggs one at a time and beat until smooth. In a separate bowl sift the dry ingredients. Add to the creamed mixture. Stir in the chips. Drop from a teaspoon onto greased baking sheets. Flatten the cookie dough slightly with the back of a spoon. Bake in a 325° oven for 15 minutes. Let cool before removing.

MAKES 6 DOZEN COOKIES.

Dartmouth House

❧

215 Dartmouth Street
Rochester, New York 14607
(716) 271-7872

*T*his spacious Edwardian-era Tudor dates back to 1905. In the heart of Rochester's thriving cultural district, it is only a mile from the city's downtown business cen-

ter. Furnished with antiques, it features leaded-glass windows, box-beamed ceilings, and a grand piano. Step out the front door and stroll to antique shops, quaint bookstores, boutiques, galleries, and many fine restaurants.

Vidalia Onion Spoonbread

1   large Vidalia or sweet white onion, sliced
1/4   cup butter, melted
1   8 1/2-ounce box Jiffy Corn Muffin Mix
1   egg
1/3   cup milk
1   cup cream-style corn
1   cup sour cream
1/2   teaspoon salt
1   cup shredded sharp Cheddar cheese

Separate the onion into rings. In a skillet melt the butter and cook the onion slowly until transparent. (In the microwave, covered, this takes about 5 minutes on high, stirring once or twice.) While the onions are cooking, in a bowl combine the muffin mix, egg, milk, and corn. Pour evenly into a buttered 8-inch square pan. To the cooked onion add the sour cream, salt, and 1/2 cup of the cheese. Mix well and spread evenly over the corn batter. Sprinkle with the remaining cheese. Bake in a 425° oven for 30 minutes. Serve hot.

MAKES 6 SERVINGS.

Corkscrew Bacon

8   slices bacon

Twist the of bacon into spirals. Arrange them in rows on the rack of a broiler pan and put skewers across the ends of the bacon rows so that the spirals will not untwist while cooking. Bake the spirals in a 350° oven for 20 minutes, or until they are crisp. Transfer them to paper towels to drain.

MAKES 4 SERVINGS.

Banana Orange Power Drink

1   egg
1/2   cup orange juice
1/2   ripe banana, sliced
1   tablespoon plain yogurt
1   teaspoon honey (optional)
    Nutmeg for dusting
    Mint sprigs for garnish

In a blender combine all ingredients until smooth. Serve in a stemmed glass dusted with nutmeg and garnished with mint leaves. For persons watching cholesterol, the egg may be omitted and 1 tablespoon of wheat germ substituted.

MAKES 1 SERVING.

Apple Tort from Jackie

1/2   cup butter (don't substitute)
1   cup sugar
2   eggs, room temperature
1 3/4   cups all-purpose flour
2   teaspoons baking powder
8   large tart apples, pared, cut in eighths, and cored
    Ground cinnamon to sprinkle
    Sugar to sprinkle

1/2   cup butter
1   cup sugar
2   eggs
    Whipped cream
    Nutmeg

In a large bowl melt 1/2 cup of butter. Add 1 cup of sugar gradually. Beat well. Add 2 eggs and mix thoroughly. Sift the flour and baking powder together and add gradually. Spread on the bottom of a buttered and floured 9-inch springform pan. Stand apples on end in the batter (which is rather stiff) and arrange them in a circular pattern. Sprinkle the tops

Dartmouth House

of the apples lightly with cinnamon and sugar. Bake in a 350° oven for 1 hour.

In a large bowl cream ½ cup of butter, 1 cup of sugar, and 2 eggs. Pour over the baked tort. Bake in a 325° oven another 20 to 25 minutes.

This freezes very well. Freeze it in the pan, and then pop it out of the pan and wrap in freezer paper.

Serve either warm or cold. It can be topped with whipped cream and some grated nutmeg.

MAKES 6 TO 8 SERVINGS.

Six Sisters Bed and Breakfast

❧

149 Union Avenue
Saratoga Springs, New York 12866
(518) 583-1173

A uniquely-styled 1880 Victorian, the house features an outstanding display of Tiger Oak and multi-colored stained glass. The spacious guest rooms are individually decorated. Visitors are attracted to Saratoga Springs by its famed mineral waters, its word-class race track, and its extraordinary scenery.

Mushroom and Egg Casserole

- 2 *tablespoons milk*
- 2 *tablespoons Marsala wine*
- 1 *10-ounce can condensed cream of mushroom soup*
- 18 *eggs*
- 1 *teaspoon parsley flakes*
- ½ *teaspoon dillweed*
- ⅛ *teaspoon pepper*
- ¼ *cup butter*
- ¼ *pound sliced mushrooms*
- ¼ *cup chopped onion*
- 1½ *cups shredded sharp Cheddar cheese*

- 1½ *cups shredded jalapeño cheese*
- ⅛ *teaspoon paprika*

In a saucepan stir the milk, wine, and soup over medium heat until smooth. Set aside. In a large bowl beat together the eggs, parsley flakes, dill, and pepper. Set aside.

In a skillet over medium heat melt the butter. Add the eggs, mushrooms, and onion. Cook until the mixture is softly set. Spoon half of the egg mixture into a greased 7 x 11-inch dish. Spoon half of soup mixture over the eggs and sprinkle half of the cheese.

Repeat the layers and sprinkle the top with paprika. Bake in a 300° oven for 30 to 35 minutes. Let stand for 10 minutes. Cut into squares.

MAKES 8 SERVINGS.

Six Sisters

Poppy Seed Muffins

- 1 *18½-ounce box yellow cake mix*
- 1 *3-ounce box vanilla instant pudding*
- ½ *cup poppy seeds*
- 4 *eggs*
- 1 *cup sour cream*
- ½ *cup cream sherry*
- ¼ *cup melted butter*

In a large bowl mix all ingredients completely. Fill 18 paper-lined small muffin cups. Bake in a 400° oven for 10 to 15 minutes.

MAKES 18 MUFFINS.

Lakehouse Inn

❧

Shelley Hill Road
Stanfordville, New York 12581
(914) 266-8093

---

*T*he inn glories in its setting on a private lake. Built to take advantage of its surroundings, it features museum quality antiques that fill its eight guest rooms. Some rooms have jacuzzis and fireplaces. Guests who can tear themselves away from the inn can explore the Hudson Valley with its antique shops, fairs, and old mansions.*

Granola

- 2 *pounds quick or regular rolled oats*
- 1 *pound wheat germ*
- 1 *pound Quaker mixed-grain hot cereal mix (optional)*
- ⅔ *cup assorted nuts, sliced almonds, chopped walnuts*
- 1½ *cups assorted seeds, i.e. sunflower, pumpkin (optional)*
- 1 *8 ounces shredded coconut*
- ⅔ *cups raisins*
- 2 *cups dried cranberries*
- 2 *cups dried apricots*
- 2 *tablespoons ground cinnamon*
- ¾ *cup sugar*
- 2 *to 3 cups honey*

Spread the oats, wheat germ, mixed grains, nuts, and seeds on separate baking sheets. Lightly toast in a 350° oven. Mix the toasted oats, wheat germ, mixed grains, nuts, and seeds together in a large bowl or bucket. While the grains are still warm, mix in the coconut and dried fruits. Mix in the cinnamon and sugar. Add the honey and mix together by hand, coating all of the grains.

Let cool thoroughly and store in plastic bags in the freezer. One bag can be kept out of the freezer if it is being used regularly.

Note: The portions given are just a guide. The granola should be primarily oats. Which and how much fruit and nuts to add depends on individual tastes and what is available.

MAKES ABOUT 4 QUARTS.

Apple Lasagna

- 16 *lasagna noodles*
- 3 *21-ounce cans Comstock apple pie filling*
- 3 *16-ounce cartons ricotta cheese*

Lakehouse Inn

4 eggs
¾ cup sugar
2 teaspoons vanilla extract
....
6 tablespoons butter or margarine
½ cup rolled oats
1 cup all-purpose flour
1 cup firmly packed brown sugar
1 teaspoon ground cinnamon
½ cup chopped nuts
....
⅔ cup nondairy hazelnut cream
⅓ cup sour cream

In a large pot of boiling, salted (2 teaspoons salt) water cook the lasagna noodles. Cook until slightly under done, about 12 minutes.

Drain and rinse with cold water. Return to the pot with a small amount of cold water. Spread two-thirds of a can of apple filling each on the bottoms of 2 9 x 12-inch pans. Layer 4 noodles in each pan across the apples, overlapping slightly. Trim the ends of the noodles if they are too long.

In a large bowl combine the ricotta cheese, eggs, sugar, and vanilla. Spread half of the ricotta mixture in each pan. Layer 4 noodles across the cheese in each pan. Spread two-thirds of a can of apple filling on top of the noodles in each pan.

In a medium bowl combine the butter, oats, flour, brown sugar, cinnamon, and nuts, and mix with hands to form a crumbly mixture. Spread on top of the apples. Wrap well with plastic and cover with foil if being frozen. Remove the night before use and let defrost.

Bake in a 350° oven for 45 minutes. Let set 20 minutes before serving.

Mix together the hazelnut cream and sour cream until smooth. Serve with the apple lasagna.

MAKES 12 TO 18 SERVINGS.

Pecan-stuffed French Toast

1 8-ounce package cream cheese, soft-ened
½ cup pecans, chopped
1 teaspoon vanilla extract
2 tablespoons sugar
1 loaf French bread
....
½ cup milk (or half and half)
2 eggs
½ teaspoon vanilla extract
2 tablespoons sugar
....
1 cup raspberry preserves
½ cup orange juice

In a medium bowl combine the cream cheese, pecans, vanilla, and 2 tablespoons of sugar by hand or with a paddle. Cut the French bread in 2-inch-wide slices. Cut a pocket in each slice about three-fourths of the way through. Spread about 1 tablespoon of the filling in the slit and press closed. Freeze or refrigerate the bread as needed. This will last in the refrigerator about 1 week and in the freezer 1 month. Serve 2 pieces per person. Defrost the number of pieces needed by putting in the refrigerator the night before use.

In a shallow bowl combine the milk, eggs, ½ teaspoon of vanilla, and 2 tablespoons of sugar. Dip the bread in the egg mixture. Bake in a 350° oven until light brown and warm all through or cook in a frying pan with a little butter.

In a saucepan combine the preserves and orange juice, and cook until hot and mixed well. Serve the hot raspberry drizzle with the French toast.

MAKES 6 TO 8 SERVINGS.

Three Village Inn

150 Main Street
Stony Brook, New York 11790
(516) 751-0555

A farmer named Richard Hallock built this house in 1751 using heavy beams and other sturdy materials that were meant to last for ages. His house remains as solid today as when he moved in almost 250 years ago, only now it serves as the heart of a landmark Long Island country inn. The historic Three Village Inn offers its guests excellent meals and an authentic colonial setting. The original pre-Revolutionary fireplace and beehive oven remain intact in the dining room. Nearby, the picturesque village of Stony Brook has more than thirty quaint shops and is perfect for strolling.

Long Island Corn Chowder with Peconic Bay Scallops

5 ounces Pancetta ham or bacon
3 medium onions, diced
1 red bell pepper, diced
2 green bell peppers, diced
1 bunch celery, diced
3 pounds potatoes, diced
15 ears corn (3 pounds), scraped
3 gallons clam broth
6 sprigs fresh thyme leaves
   Pinch cayenne pepper
   Pinch white pepper
2 tablespoons salt
3 pounds bay scallops
1 quart heavy cream

In a 5-gallon pot render the fat from the Pancetta. Cook for 3 minutes, then remove the ham. Add the onions, bell peppers, and celery, and cook until transparent. Add the potatoes and corn. Add the broth and bring to a boil. Add the thyme and peppers. Add the salt, and simmer until the potatoes are cooked.

Add the scallops and cream, and heat through. Serve and enjoy.

MAKES 4 GALLONS.

*2 Hudson Street
Warrensburg, New York 12885
(518) 623-2449*

***O**wned for more than a century by the family of a Revolutionary War veteran, the house's Greek Revival front was added during the 1850s. However, at its core is a much older structure built in 1812 and brought here from an old homestead several miles away. Fireplaces and nineteenth century country antiques make this an especially warm and homey inn. The antique shops and galleries of Warrensburg are within strolling distance.*

Anadama Bread

½ **cup cornmeal**
1 **cup water**
2 **tablespoons oil**
½ **cup molasses**
2 **cups warm water (105 to 110°)**
3 **packages active dry yeast**
3½ **cups all-purpose flour**
3½ **cups whole wheat flour**
3 **teaspoons salt**

Soak the cornmeal in 1 cup of water. Add the oil and molasses. In a large bowl dissolve the yeast in 2 cups of warm water. In a separate bowl mix together the flours and salt.

Add the cornmeal mixture to the yeast mixture, blending with an electric mixer, and gradually add the flour. The dough will start to pull away from the sides of the bowl. Turn the dough out onto a floured board and knead about 5 minutes. Place in a greased bowl and cover with a cloth. Let rise until doubled in volume.

Knead again and divide into 2 loaves. Place in greased bread pans, cover, and rise again.

Bake in a 350° oven for approximately 50 minutes.

Note: For a tasty open-faced sandwich, sauté sliced onions, mushrooms, and fresh spinach and place on top of a thick slice of Anadama bread, cover with Monterey Jack cheese, and place under a broiler to melt the cheese.

MAKES 2 LOAVES.

Merrill Magee House

Chicken Salad Veronique

3 **cups cubed cooked chicken**
1 **cup Thompson seedless grapes (green), cut in half**
½ **cup toasted slivered almonds**
½ **cup finely chopped celery**
½ **cup finely chopped onion**
½ **cup mayonnaise**
⅓ **cup lemon yogurt**
1 **tablespoon dry white wine**
½ **teaspoon Dijon mustard Leaf lettuce**

In a large bowl mix the chicken, grapes, almonds, celery, and onion. In a separate bowl mix the mayonnaise, yogurt, wine, and mustard. Fold the mayonnaise into the chicken mixture. Refrigerate.

To serve, spoon chicken salad onto lettuce leaves and garnish with a small cluster of grapes.

MAKES 6 SERVINGS.

How to Brew a Good Cup of Tea

Whatever the preference of blend of tea (for example orange pekoe and black tea) the method is the same.

First have a lovely china or silver teapot ready. Boil the water and pour a little boiling water into the pot and let it sit a minute. Drain the water and add 1 teaspoon of tea for each guest plus 1 for the pot. Fill the pot with boiling water. Just before serving stir the tea once and cover with a tea cosy to keep it hot. When serving, pour a little milk, not cream, into the cup. Add the tea and ask if the guest would like sugar. Lump sugar is most often used. Pass the tea to the guest along with a napkin.

*East Main Road, P.O. Box 505
Westfield, New York 14787
(716) 326-6262*

***T**he house dates to 1840 when it was built as a homestead. During the 1860s it was renovated in Gothic Revival style. In the past, the Westfield House has been used as a public tea room, editorial offices for an antique journal, and guest house. Today it offers seven individually decorated and named guest rooms.*

Lemon Sponge Pudding

1 **cup sugar**
¼ **cup all-purpose flour**
⅛ **teaspoon salt**
2 **tablespoons margarine**
5 **tablespoons lemon juice**
1 **teaspoon lemon zest**
2 **beaten egg yolks**
1 **cup scalded milk**
2 **egg whites, beaten until stiff**

In a large bowl combine the sugar, flour, salt, and margarine. Add the lemon juice, lemon zest, egg yolks, and milk. Fold the mixture into the egg whites. Pour into a greased 1½-quart shallow casserole. Place in a pan with 1 inch of hot water. Bake in a 325° oven for 1 hour.

MAKES 4 SERVINGS.

Westfield House Rolls

1 cup shortening
¾ cup sugar
1 cup boiling water
1 cup cold water
2 packages active dry yeast
6 cups all-purpose flour
1 teaspoon salt

In a large bowl cream the shortening and sugar. Pour the boiling water over the mixture to dissolve. Then add the cold water. Add the yeast. In a separate bowl combine the flour and salt. Add the dry ingredients to the shortening mixture. Let the dough rise in a warm place until doubled in bulk.

Shape into Parkerhouse or breakfast rolls. Let rise. This is a basic recipe that can be kept in the freezer or refrigerator for several days.

Bake in a 350° oven for about 25 minutes golden until brown.

MAKES ABOUT 3 DOZEN.

Poppy Seed Dressing

¼ cup honey
2 tablespoons frozen limeade concentrate, thawed
2 tablespoons oil
½ teaspoon orange zest
¼ teaspoon poppy seeds
⅛ teaspoon dry mustard

In a glass jar with a tight-fitting lid combine all ingredients. Cover and shake well.

MAKES ABOUT ½ CUP.

Woven Waters Street

Woven Waters Street

6624 Route 41
Willet, New York 13863
(607) 656-8672

This B&B features a high beamed ceiling, big stone fireplace, and a hostess who is also a master weaver. Guests enjoy a lovely lake view from the elevated porches. The four guest rooms feature antiques and collectibles. The lake features —occasionally—a blue heron.

Shortbread for Afternoon Tea

1 cup butter
½ cup confectioners' sugar
1 teaspoon vanilla extract
2 cups all-purpose flour

In a large bowl beat the butter. Add the confectioners' sugar and vanilla. Gradually add the flour and blend well. Divide the mixture in half. Chill for 30 minutes.

Roll the dough ¼ inch thick and cut into small heart shapes. Prick each with a fork and place on an ungreased cookie sheet. Bake in a 325° oven for 15 to 20 minutes. Do not brown.

MAKES ABOUT 24 SHORTBREADS.

Apple Custard Cake

½ cup margarine or butter
¼ cup sugar
1 teaspoon ground cinnamon
1 cup sifted all-purpose flour
1 egg
1 3-ounce package vanilla pudding mix (not instant)
1½ cups milk
1 tablespoon lemon juice

½ teaspoon grated lemon zest
1 21-ounce can apple pie filling

In a medium bowl beat the margarine and sugar well. Add the cinnamon and blend in the flour. Divide the dough in half. Press half into a buttered 8-inch square baking pan. Add the egg to the other half and mix well. Prepare the vanilla pudding according to the package directions, using 1½ cups of milk. Pour half over the dough in the pan. In a large bowl stir the lemon juice and zest into the apple pie filling. Spread over the vanilla pudding. Cover the apples with the remaining vanilla pudding. Sprinkle the reserved crumbly egg-flour mixture over the pudding. Bake in a 350° oven for 35 minutes, or until the top is lightly browned. Cool and cut into squares. Serve warm or cool.

MAKES 6 TO 8 SERVINGS.

Ham Vegetable Pie

1 cup chopped cooked ham
1 cup chopped broccoli
1 fresh tomato, chopped
½ cup chopped onion
¼ cup chopped green bell pepper
½ small can sliced mushrooms
½ cup packed grated sharp Cheddar cheese
....
1 cup milk
½ cup biscuit mix
2 eggs
½ teaspoon salt
½ teaspoon pepper

In a large bowl combine the ham, broccoli, tomato, onion, green pepper, and mushrooms. Sprinkle this mixture over the bottom of a buttered pie plate. Sprinkle the Cheddar cheese over the mixture in the pie plate.

In a blender combine the milk, biscuit mix, eggs, salt, and pepper for 15 seconds. Pour over the ingredients in the pie plate. Bake in a 400° oven for 35 minutes, or until a knife inserted in the center comes out clean.

Let stand 5 minutes before cutting.

MAKES 6 SERVINGS.

NORTH CAROLINA

Corner Oak Manor

Corner Oak Manor

53 Saint Dunstans Road
Asheville, North Carolina 28803
(704) 253-3525

This English Tudor home surrounded by oak, maple, and pine trees offers four guest rooms with private baths, flowers, and chocolates in each room. Oak antiques and other hand-made items are seen throughout as well as hand-stitched and woven arts. Guests will enjoy the outdoor jacuzzi available except during the winter months. There is a baby grand piano in the living room.

Mushroom-Brie Strata

> 1 *pound mushrooms, washed and sliced*
> 2 *tablespoons butter*
> 1 *loaf French bread, sliced 1 inch thick*
> 3 *tablespoons country-style or grainy Dijon mustard*
> 2½ *cups diced Brie cheese, about 12 ounces (remove and discard rind before dicing)*
> 9 *eggs*
> 3 *cups milk*
> 1 *tablespoon chopped fresh tarragon (or 2 teaspoons dried)*
> ½ *teaspoon salt*
> ¼ *teaspoon freshly ground pepper*

In a skillet sauté the mushrooms in butter until just tender. Spread the mushrooms evenly in a 9 x 13-inch pan that has been sprayed with cooking spray. Trim the crusts from the bread slices. Spread 1 side of the slices with Dijon mustard. Cut into 1-inch cubes. Place the bread cubes on top of mushrooms. Spread diced Brie evenly over the bread cubes.

In a large bowl, beat together the eggs, milk, tarragon, salt, and pepper. Pour this mixture over the bread and cheese cubes as evenly as possible. Cover with plastic wrap and chill overnight.

Bake uncovered in a 350° oven for 40 to 50 minutes or until a knife inserted in the center comes out clean. Let stand 10 minutes before serving.

Note: For best results be sure to use a good-quality French bread and make sure the cubes are at least 1-inch thick.

MAKES 8 TO 10 GENEROUS SERVINGS.

Orange Marmalade Croissants

> 6 *large croissants, split in half lengthwise*
> 1 *18-ounce jar orange marmalade*
> ¼ *cup orange juice*
> *Finely grated zest of 1 orange (avoid white pith)*
> 1 *teaspoon almond extract*
> 1 *cup half and half or cream*
> 5 *eggs*
> 3 *orange slices (halved)*
> 6 *strawberries*
> *Whipped cream*

Spray a 9 x 13-inch pan with cooking spray. Place the bottoms of the croissants in the pan. In a medium bowl thin the marmalade with the orange juice. Reserve ⅓ cup. Top each croissant bottom with the remaining marmalade, dividing evenly. Replace the tops. In a medium bowl beat together the zest, extract, cream, and eggs and pour over the croissants. Spoon of the reserved ⅓ cup of marmalade over the croissant tops to create a glaze. Cover with plastic wrap and chill overnight.

Bake uncovered in a 350° oven for 25 minutes, or until the egg is set and the tops are golden. Allow to set for 5 minutes before serving. Cut out around the croissants to lift out for service. Garnish each with an orange slice, a strawberry, and a dollop of whipped cream.

MAKES 6 SERVINGS.

Cranberry-Pistachio Biscotti

1⅓   cups (about ¼ pound) dried cran-
     berries
2½   cups unbleached all-purpose flour
1   cup sugar
½   teaspoon baking soda
½   teaspoon baking powder
½   teaspoon salt
3   large eggs
1   teaspoon vanilla extract
1   cup shelled natural pistachio nuts
1   large egg
1   teaspoon water

In a medium bowl soak the cranberries in enough hot water to cover for 5 minutes. Drain well and pat dry with paper towels. In a large bowl stir together the flour, sugar, soda, baking powder, and salt. Add 3 eggs and the vanilla, and beat with an electric mixer until a dough is formed. Stir in the cranberries and the pistachios.

Turn the dough out onto a lightly floured surface, knead it several times, and halve it. Working on a large buttered and floured baking sheet, with floured hands form each piece of dough into a flattish log 13 inches long and 2 inches wide. Arrange the logs at least 3 inches apart on the sheet. In a small bowl beat 1 egg with 1 teaspoon of water. Brush the logs with the egg wash. Bake the logs in the middle of a 325° oven for 30 minutes. Cool on the baking sheet on a rack for 10 minutes. On a cutting board cut the logs crosswise on the diagonal into ¾-inch-thick slices. Arrange the biscotti, cut-sides down, on the baking sheet. Bake in a 325° oven for 10 minutes on each side, or until they are pale golden. Transfer the biscotti to racks to cool. Store them in airtight containers. They can be frozen in resealable freezer bags.

MAKES ABOUT 36 BISCOTTI.

Whole Wheat Blueberry Bars

1⅓   cups plus 3 tablespoons whole wheat
     pastry flour (optional: use some
     all-purpose flour)
½   teaspoon baking powder
½   teaspoon baking soda
½   teaspoon salt
1   cup firmly packed dark brown sugar
2   tablespoons butter, softened

2   tablespoons oil
1   large egg
1   teaspoon vanilla extract
½   cup sugar
2   tablespoons all-purpose flour
1   teaspoon grated lemon zest
2   cups blueberries
1   tablespoon lemon juice
     Confectioners' sugar (optional)

Spray a 9 x 13-inch pan with cooking spray. In a medium bowl stir together 1⅓ cups of pastry flour, baking powder, soda, and salt. Set aside. In a large bowl beat the brown sugar, butter, oil, egg, and vanilla with an electric mixer until smooth. Add the dry ingredients and stir until blended well. The mixture will be firm. Reserve ½ cup for topping.

Place the remaining dough in the pan. Cover with plastic wrap and use it to press the dough into the bottom of the pan. Remove the plastic. Bake in a 350° oven for 15 minutes or until puffed and golden.

Using fingertips gradually mix 3 tablespoons of pastry flour into the reserved topping until it gets crumbly. Set aside.

In a small bowl combine ½ cup of sugar, 2 tablespoons of all-purpose flour, and the lemon zest. Set aside.

In a saucepan combine the berries and lemon juice. Cook over medium heat, stirring constantly until berries exude juice. Add the sugar mixture and stir until the filling simmers and thickens. Spread over the baked crust, pushing down the sides with a wooden spoon. Sprinkle with topping. Bake in a 350° oven for 15 to 20 minutes or until golden. Cool on a rack. Store at room temperature only lightly covered. Dust with confectioners' sugar, if desired.

MAKES 24 BARS.

Strawberry Jam Butter

½   cup butter, softened
2   tablespoons nonfat dry milk powder
½   cup strawberry jam
½   cup confectioners' sugar

In a food processor process the butter until smooth. Scrape down as necessary. Add 1 tablespoon of milk powder, the jam, and sugar. Process until blended well. Add the remaining milk powder and process until smooth, scraping as necessary. Store in the

refrigerator. Bring to room temperature before serving.

MAKES 1 CUP.

Orange-Honey Butter

½   cup butter, softened
1   teaspoon grated orange zest
¼   cup honey

In a food processor combine all ingredients, or with beaters, or by hand. Serve at room temperature.

MAKES ¾ CUP.

The Lion and the Rose

276 Montford Avenue
Asheville, North Carolina 28801
(704) 255-7673, (800) 546-6988

*B*uilt in 1898, this Queen Anne Georgian-style residence stands in the Montford Historic District, notable for its architecture as well as artistic and literary significance. The house has been faithfully restored to its original elegance typified by high embossed ceilings, golden oak, and classic leaded-glass windows. The grounds are graced by flower gardens and century-old sugar maples.

The Hall Family Irish Soda Bread

4   cups all-purpose flour
¼   cup sugar
½   teaspoon salt
2   rounded teaspoons cream of tartar
1½   teaspoons baking powder
2   tablespoons caraway seeds
1½   cups raisins
1   egg
1½   cups milk with 1½ teaspoons lemon
     juice

In a large bowl mix the flour, sugar, salt, cream of tartar, and baking powder.

Add the caraway seeds and raisins. Make a hole in the center and add the egg and milk (save 2 teaspoons of milk for later). Work either by hand or with dough hooks.

Grease and flour an 8-inch round cake tin. Place the round dough in the tin in a mound-like way. With a knife score the bread into quarters and pat with the remaining milk. Bake in a 325° oven for 1 hour, until slightly browned and a knife comes out clean. Cool on a rack and serve with butter.

MAKES 12 SERVINGS.

Southwestern Baked Omelet

- ½   cup salsa
- 2   cups shredded cheese
- 6   eggs
- ½   cup sour cream
- ½   cup cottage cheese
-     Chopped red and green bell peppers
-     Chopped tomato

Spray an 9-inch glass pie plate completely with cooking spray. Layer the salsa, then the cheese. In a medium bowl whisk the eggs, sour cream, and cottage cheese. Pour over the cheese. Bake in a 350° oven for 45 minutes. Let set, then quarter.

Garnish with chopped peppers and tomato.

MAKES 6 TO 8 SERVINGS.

The Lion and the Rose

Quick Little Chocolate Pastries

- 1   sheet puff pastry, cut in 3 x 3-inch squares
-     Pieces semi-sweet or sweet chocolate
- 1   egg mixed with 1 teaspoon cream

Set a piece (or pieces) of chocolate in the middle of the pastry and wrap, glazing with egg mixture. Place on a baking sheet. Bake in a 400° oven for 8 to 10 minutes. Serve warm or cooled.

MAKES ABOUT 12 PASTRIES.

High Hampton Inn & Country Club

≈

P.O. Box 338
Cashiers, North Carolina 28717-0338
(704) 743-2411

---

*T*his inn is unique in that it is both a country inn and a complete resort—offering attractions such as golf, tennis, fitness facilities, boating, nature trails, and a playground for children—on a fourteen-hundred acre estate. The inn section of the resort was built originally as a summer home for the Hamptons of South Carolina. It is about sixty-five miles west of Asheville.

Spanish Eggplant

- 2   large eggplants, pared, cubed and placed in salted water
- 1   tablespoon butter
- 1   cup chopped onions
- 1   cup chopped green bell pepper
- 2   14½-ounce cans stewed tomatoes
....
- ½   cup firmly packed brown sugar
-     Grated Parmesan cheese
-     Salt and white pepper to taste
- 1   teaspoon garlic powder, at least
-     Buttered breadcrumbs for topping

In a pot of boiling water parboil the eggplant and drain. Place in a large bowl. In a skillet melt the butter and sauté the onions and pepper. Drain the tomatoes well and add to the eggplant. Season with brown sugar, Parmesan cheese, salt, white pepper, and garlic powder. Add the sautéed onions and peppers to the eggplant and tomatoes. Transfer the mixture to a greased casserole. Sprinkle with buttered breadcrumbs and more Parmesan cheese. Bake in a 350° oven until brown.

MAKES 4 SERVINGS.

Black Bottom Pie

- 1½   cups crushed zwieback
- ¼   cup confectioners' sugar
- 6   tablespoons butter, melted
- 1   teaspoon ground cinnamon
....
- 1   tablespoon unflavored gelatin
- ½   cup cold water
- 2   cups whole milk
- 4   egg yolks, beaten lightly
- 1   cup sugar
- 4   teaspoons cornstarch
- 1½   ounces semisweet chocolate, melted
- ½   teaspoon vanilla extract
- 1   teaspoon almond extract
- 3   egg whites
- ¼   teaspoon salt
- ¼   teaspoon cream of tartar
- ¼   cup sugar
- 1   cup heavy cream
- 2   tablespoons confectioners' sugar

In a 9-inch pie pan mix the zwieback, ¼ cup of confectioners' sugar, melted butter, and cinnamon well and pat along the sides and bottom to make a crust. Bake in a 350° oven for 15 minutes.

In a cup soak the gelatin in cold water. In a saucepan scald the milk. In the top of a double boiler combine the egg yolks, 1 cup of sugar, and cornstarch. Gradually stir in the milk and cook over hot water until the custard will coat a spoon. Take out 1 cup of custard and add chocolate to it. Beat until blended well and cool. Add the vanilla and pour into the pie shell.

Dissolve the gelatin in the remaining custard. Cool, but do not permit it to stiffen. Stir in the almond flavoring.

In a medium bowl beat the egg whites and salt until blended. Add the cream of tartar and beat until stiff. Gradually add ¼ cup of sugar. Fold in the remaining custard and cover the chocolate custard with the almond-flavored custard. Chill and set.

In a small bowl whip the heavy cream. Add the confectioners' sugar, and spread over the pie. Enjoy!

MAKES 6 TO 8 SERVINGS.

Sunny Silver Pie

1½   *teaspoon unflavored gelatin powder*
⅓   *cup cold water*
4   *eggs, separated*
3   *tablespoons lemon juice*
  Grated zest of 1 lemon
1   *cup sugar, divided*
  Few grains salt
1   *9-inch baked pie shell*
1   *cup heavy cream*

In a cup soften the gelatin in cold water. In a rounded-bottom enamel bowl combine the 4 egg yolks, lemon juice, lemon zest, and ½ cup of sugar. Set the bowl in a larger pan of boiling water. Keep boiling. Whip the egg mixture until it becomes quite firm and creamy. When it reaches this stage, turn the heat down and fold in the gelatin. Add the salt. Turn off the stove. In a glass bowl beat the egg whites until very stiff and combine with the remaining ½ cup of sugar. Then fold this into the yolk mixture. Pour the filling into a baked pie shell and refrigerate for 2 hours.

In a bowl whip the cream until stiff and spread over the top of the pie just before serving.

Note: Served every Sunday evening since 1923.
MAKES 6 TO 8 SERVINGS.

Plum Duff

1   *cup firmly packed brown sugar*
½   *cup melted butter*
2   *cups prunes, cooked, pitted, and chopped finely*
2   *eggs*
1   *cup all-purpose flour*
⅛   *teaspoon salt*
1   *teaspoon soda dissolved in 1 tablespoon milk*

In a saucepan melt the brown sugar in the butter. Add the prunes and eggs. Stir in the flour and salt. Add the milk in which the soda has been dissolved. Steam in a greased coffee can with a lid or a loaf pan with a lid in a 400° oven for 1 hour and 30 minutes in a kettle of water.

Then reduce the heat to low and steam for 30 minutes. The water kettle should be covered, too.
MAKES 4 TO 6 SERVINGS.

Layer Cookies

½   *cup shortening*
1   *cup sugar*
2   *eggs, well-beaten*
½   *teaspoon salt*
1   *teaspoon vanilla extract*
1   *teaspoon baking powder*
1½   *cups all-purpose flour*
....
1   *cup brown sugar*
½   *teaspoon vanilla, extract*
2   *egg whites, beaten stiff*
¾   *cup chopped nuts*

In a bowl cream the shortening and sugar. Add the eggs, salt, and 1 teaspoon of vanilla. In a separate bowl sift the baking powder with the flour. Add the dry ingredients to the creamed mixture. Spread in a long shallow greased pan.

In a small bowl mix the brown sugar, ½ teaspoon of vanilla, egg whites, and nuts. Spread this mixture over the first layer. Bake in a 350° oven until lightly browned. Cut into squares when cool. They freeze well.
MAKES 8 TO 12 SERVINGS.

The Jarrett House

P.O. Box 219
Dillsboro, North Carolina 28725
(704-586-0265)

Back when it was known as the Mount Beulah Hotel, trains stopped here so their passengers could enjoy the food. Although they are unlikely to come by train, guests still come here today. The fried chicken, trout, and ham with red-eye gravy is just as good as it used to be in the old days. There are twenty-two guest rooms decorated to enhance the nostalgic feeling of the place. The mountains of North Carolina can be seen in all directions.

Jarrett House Vinegar Pie

½   *cup margarine, melted and cooled*
1½   *cups sugar*
2   *tablespoons all-purpose flour*
1   *tablespoon vanilla extract*
2   *tablespoons apple cider vinegar*
3   *eggs*
1   *unbaked 9-inch pie shell*

In a medium bowl combine the margarine, sugar, flour, vanilla, vinegar, and eggs. Pour into the unbaked pie shell. Bake in a 300° oven for 45 minutes.
MAKES 6 TO 8 SERVINGS.

Jarrett House Chicken 'n Dumplings

1   *cut-up chicken or baking hen*
  Salt and pepper to taste
  Crushed red pepper
  Parsley
  Chicken base or bouillon
  Butter or margarine
  Dough for biscuits

In a pot boil the chicken until done. Remove from the broth and debone. To the broth add salt, pepper, crushed red pepper, parsley, and chicken base or bouillon. Add a little butter or margarine.

Make a dough as for biscuits, using a little less shortening and milk instead of buttermilk. Roll out on a floured board and cut into small squares. Bring the broth to a rolling boil and drop the dough into the broth. Boil about 15 minutes or until the dough is done. Serve the dumplings with the chicken.
MAKES 4 TO 6 SERVINGS.

Arrowhead Inn

106 Mason Road
Durham, North Carolina 27712
(919) 477-8430

At about the time the American Revolution was breaking out, a North

Carolina planter built the old house known today as the Arrowhead Inn. Dating to 1774-1776, the inn offers its guests a look at an authentic eighteenth-century plantation home. There are five guest rooms in the main house and another two in the adjacent carriage house. The grounds are shaded by magnolias almost as old as the house itself.

Arrowhead Inn

Little Monkeys

- 16 to 20 whole pecans
- ½ cup chopped pecans
- ½ cup butter
- 1 cup firmly packed light brown sugar
- 2 tablespoons water
- 2 10-ounce cans refrigerator biscuits

Grease 8 custard cups. Place 2 or 3 whole pecans in each cup, and sprinkle half of the chopped pecans over them. In a saucepan melt the butter. Add the sugar, water, and the remaining chopped nuts. Cut the biscuits in half and roll into balls. Place 3 in each cup, then drizzle with sauce. Add 2 balls and drizzle with the remaining sauce. Bake in a 350° oven for 15 minutes.

MAKES 8 MONKEYS.

Gazpacho Soup

- 1 large can V-8 juice
- 1 8-ounce can chopped tomatoes
- ¼ cup white wine vinegar
- ⅓ green bell pepper, chopped
- ⅓ cucumber, chopped
- ½ teaspoon salt
- ½ teaspoon fresh ground pepper
  Dash Tabasco sauce
- ¼ cup olive oil
- 1 teaspoon grated onion

In a blender combine all ingredients and blend to purée.

Serve with small bowls of chopped cucumber, chopped fresh tomato, croutons, chopped chives or parsley, and sour cream.
MAKES 1½ QUARTS.

Skillet Potatoes

- 4 to 5 medium potatoes
- 5 to 6 tablespoons butter
  Salt and pepper
  Other seasonings (optional)

Generously butter the sides and bottom of a 6-inch heavy ovenproof skillet. Peel the potatoes and slice as thinly as possible. Arrange the potato slices in a spiral pattern around the bottom of the pan. After 2 layers, butter and season. Continue layering potatoes, buttering and seasoning every second layer. Spread any remaining butter on a piece of foil and cover the pan securely. Put an ovenproof plate on the top of the foil and press down to prevent steam from escaping during baking. Set the pan on moderate heat on top of the stove and cook for 15 minutes, or until the potatoes are browned on the bottom.

Transfer the pan to a 400° oven and bake for 30 minutes, or until the potatoes are tender. Remove from the oven and discard the foil. Place a serving plate on top of the skillet and invert. The potatoes should be a golden cake.

Although best right out of oven, the potatoes are tasty when reheated.
MAKES 4 SERVINGS.

Gougères

- 1 cup water
- 5 tablespoons butter
- 1 teaspoon salt
- ¼ teaspoon fresh ground pepper
- ¼ teaspoon grated nutmeg
- 1 cup all-purpose flour
- 1 cup grated Swiss or Gruyère cheese
- 5 large eggs, at room temperature
- 1½ teaspoon water

In a medium saucepan bring the water, butter, salt, pepper, and nutmeg to a boil. When the butter melts, remove the pan the heat. Add the flour to the liquid mixture and stir until the dough pulls away from the sides of the pan. Add the cheese and beat until incorporated. Mix in 4 eggs, one at a time. Beat until the mixture is shiny. Drop by teaspoon-

fuls onto a greased cookie sheet. In a small bowl beat the remaining egg with 1½ teaspoons of water. Brush the egg wash on the tops of Gougères. Bake in a 425° oven for 20 minutes or until golden and doubled in size. Best served right from oven.
MAKES 3 DOZEN.

771 Nutbush Road
Henderson, North Carolina 27536
(919) 438-2421

*O*riental rugs, antiques, and polished silver greet guests at the entryway and set the tone for their experience at the La Grange Plantation Inn. Meticulously restored to its grand, eighteenth-century condition, the plantation house is listed on the National Register of Historic Places. The glass-enclosed dining room looks out over rolling fields and an old cemetery. The nearby lake is a challenge to sailors and fishermen alike.

Pineapple Soufflé

- 1 16-ounce can crushed pineapple in its own juice, undrained
- 3 eggs, beaten lightly
- ¼ cup sugar
- 2 tablespoons all-purpose flour
- ¼ cup butter
- 3 slices white bread, crusts removed

La Grange Plantation Inn

In a medium bowl mix the pineapple, eggs, sugar, and flour. In a frying pan melt the butter. Cube the bread slices and fry in butter until light brown. Spread pineapple mixture in a lightly buttered 1-quart casserole dish. Top with bread cubes. Bake in a 350° oven for 30 minutes.

Note: Serve with country ham or a wedge of center-cut ham.

MAKES 4 TO 6 SERVINGS.

Sausage and Corn Casserole

- 1 **pound bulk sausage**
- 3 **tablespoons all-purpose flour**
- 1½ **cups skim milk**
- 1 **12-ounce can corn with peppers (Mexican-style)**
- ½ **teaspoon salt**
- ⅛ **teaspoon black pepper**
- 1 **cup cracker crumbs**
- 2 **tablespoons melted butter**

In a skillet fry and crumble the sausage until no longer pink. Remove from the pan and drain on paper towels. Remove all but 3 tablespoons of fat from the pan and over medium heat, stir in the flour. Gradually add the milk, stirring constantly, until the sauce is slightly thickened. Add the corn, salt, and pepper, and mix well.

Grease a 2-quart baking dish. Sprinkle ¾ cup of cracker crumbs evenly over the bottom. Pour in the corn mixture and top with sausage. Sprinkle the rest of the crumbs and drizzle with melted butter. Bake in a 350° oven for 25 to 30 minutes or until bubbly.

MAKES 4 GENEROUS SERVINGS.

Burgundy Bread

- 2 **cups raisins**
- 1 **cup butter or margarine**
- 1 **cup shortening**
- 2 **cups sugar**
- 3 **eggs**
- 4 **cups all-purpose flour**
- 4 **teaspoons unsweetened cocoa**
- 4 **teaspoons baking soda**
- 2 **teaspoons ground cinnamon**
- 1 **teaspoon ground allspice**
- 1 **teaspoon grated nutmeg**
- 2½ **cups Burgundy**
- 2 **cups chopped walnuts**

In a saucepan cover the raisins with cold water and bring to a boil. Drain in a sieve and set aside.

In a large bowl cream the butter and shortening together, then blend in the sugar thoroughly. Beat in the eggs one at a time, mixing well before each addition. In a separate bowl sift the flour, cocoa, soda, and spices together. Add the dry ingredients to the batter alternately with the wine. Add the raisins and walnuts. Divide into 6 greased and floured loaf pans. Bake in a 350° oven for approximately 1 hour and 45 minutes or until a toothpick i comes out clean.

MAKES 6 LOAVES.

41 South Main Street
P.O. Box 749
Mars Hill, North Carolina 28754
(704) 689-5722

The Baird House was built just after the turn of the century by a doctor who practiced medicine in this mountainous area for many years. Its 225-foot well is said to produce some of the "sweetest water in the world." Located near Mars Hill College and the center of this charming Appalachian Mountain community, the inn has five guest rooms all furnished with fine antiques. The wide porches are generously supplied with rocking chairs for North Carolina-style relaxation.

Granola

- 2 **cups corn flakes**
- 2 **cups wheat flakes**
- 2 **cups rice flakes**
- 2 **cups oat flakes**
- 2 **teaspoons grated nutmeg**
- ½ **cup butter, melted**
- 1 **cup honey**
- 2 **cups broken walnuts**

In a large bowl mix together the corn, wheat, rice, and oat flakes. In a medium bowl mix the nutmeg, butter and the honey with an electric mixer until blended. Blend with the cereal flakes.

Line a large roasting pan (or broiler pan) with foil. Spread the flakes on the pan. Toast in a 300° oven for about 10 minutes. Remove from the oven and mix with the broken walnuts. Store in plastic bags. These will keep almost indefinitely in the refrigerator.

MAKES ABOUT 2½ QUARTS.

Poppy Seed Bread

- 1½ **cups sugar**
- 3 **eggs, beaten**
- 1½ **teaspoons vanilla extract**
- 1 **teaspoon almond extract**
- 1½ **teaspoons butter flavoring**
- 1 **cup oil**
- 3 **cups all-purpose flour**
- 1 **teaspoon salt**
- 1½ **teaspoons baking powder**
- 1½ **cups milk**
- 1½ **tablespoons poppy seeds**

....

- ¼ **cup freshly squeezed orange juice**
- ¾ **cup confectioners' sugar**
- ½ **teaspoon vanilla extract**

In a large bowl combine the sugar and beaten eggs. Add the flavorings. Add the oil to the egg mixture. In a separate bowl mix the flour, salt, and baking powder. Add the milk and dry ingredients alternately to the egg mixture. Fold in the poppy seeds. Pour into 2 greased and floured 7-inch loaf pans. Bake in a 350° oven for 1 hour. In small bowl blend together the orange juice, confectioners sugar, and vanilla. Glaze the loaves with the mixture.

MAKES 2 LOAVES.

Grape Nut Pudding

- ½ **cup Grape Nuts cereal**
- 2½ **cups milk**
- ½ **cup firmly packed brown sugar**
- 3 **eggs, beaten**
- 1 **teaspoon vanilla extract**
  Pinch salt
  Butter

In a large bowl mix the Grape Nuts, milk, and sugar and let sit for about 15 minutes.

Add the beaten eggs, vanilla, and salt. Pour into a 1½-quart casserole. Place little dabs of butter on top. Set the casserole in a pan of hot water. Bake in a 350° oven for 15 minutes. Stir after the butter melts and continue baking for approximately 15 minutes.

MAKES 4 SERVINGS.

215 Pollock Street
New Bern, North Carolina 28560
(919) 636-3810

*L*isted on the National Register of Historic Places, the Harmony House dates to 1809. It began as a four-room Greek Revival structure but was enlarged and renovated several times. Today it can accommodate nine spacious guest rooms, some with fireplaces and canopied beds. Visitors interested in the past will appreciate the location, right in the middle of New Bern's historic district.

St. Timothy's Coffee Cake

        2   cups all-purpose flour
        1   teaspoon baking powder
       ¼   teaspoon salt
        1   teaspoon ground cinnamon
        1   cup chopped pecans
       ½   cup raisins
        1   cup margarine
        2   cups sugar
       ½   teaspoon vanilla extract
        2   eggs
        1   cup sour cream
            Cinnamon-sugar

In a bowl sift together the flour, baking powder, salt, and cinnamon. Add the pecans and raisins to the dry ingredients and stir to coat. In a separate bowl cream the margarine until light and fluffy. Add the sugar gradually and continue to cream. Blend in the vanilla. Add the eggs one at a time, beating well after each addition. Add the dry ingredients to the

Harmony House Inn

creamed mixture alternately with the sour cream. Blend well until the batter looks like whipped cream tinged with honey. Turn into a greased bundt pan. Bake in a 350° oven for 1 hour or until a toothpick inserted in coffee cake comes out clean. Remove from the oven and leave in the pan for 1 hour. Shake the pan to loosen, then turn out on a wire rack. Just before serving, sprinkle the top of the coffee cake with cinnamon-sugar.

MAKES 8 SERVINGS.

Apple, Bacon, and Cheese Quiche

        3   large tart apples
      1½   cups grated Cheddar cheese
        6   slices bacon
        4   eggs
      1½   cups milk
        1   cup baking mix
       ½   cup all-purpose flour

Butter an 8 x 12-inch glass baking dish. Peel and slice the apples and layer them in the bottom of the dish in a single layer. Sprinkle the grated cheese on top of the apples. In a skillet cook the bacon. Break it into bite-sized pieces. Sprinkle the bacon pieces on top of the cheese.

In a bowl beat the eggs. Add the milk and beat to blend. Add the baking mix and flour, and beat into a batter. The batter should be fairly thin, but not watery. Add either more milk or baking mix if necessary to bring the batter to the proper consistency. Pour the batter over the apples, bacon, and cheese. Bake in a 375° oven for about 45 minutes.

MAKES 8 SERVINGS.

709 Broad Street
New Bern, North Carolina 28560
(919) 636-2250

*C*entrally located in the old colonial town of New Berne, the inn is within easy walking distance of the Tyron Palace and numerous other historic sites. A Colonial Revival house set under massive magnolia, pecan, and camellia trees, its offers its guests a comfortable porch, a fine garden, and oversized hammocks. The seven guest rooms feature queen or king-size beds, private baths, and telephones. Two weekends each month are reserved for a who-done-it mystery package.

Made-This-Morning Bread

        4   cups self-rising flour
        1   teaspoon salt
        6   tablespoons butter or margarine,
              softened
      1⅓   cups milk
              Herbs of choice

In a large bowl stir together the flour and salt. Rub in the butter until the mixture resembles coarse crumbs. Mix in the milk. Turn out onto a lightly floured board and knead 10 times. If too stiff add more milk. Divide the dough in half and knead in the herbs, etc. Shape each into a round disk and flatten to a 7-inch diameter. Place on a sprayed baking sheet , smooth- side up. Bake in the middle of a 400° oven for 25 to 30 minutes, or until lightly brown. Remove from the baking sheet and cut into 4 wedges each.

Note: Made-This-Morning Bread is really a cross between a small loaf of bread and a giant biscuit. The addition of herbs, seeds, nuts, or dried fruit (1 to 2 teaspoons per

loaf) makes it very special. The recipe doubles or triples, reheats, and toasts beautifully.
MAKES 8 SERVINGS.

Onion Cake

   3 tablespoons butter or margarine
   2 medium onions, peeled, sliced, separated into rings
   1 10-ounce package refrigerated biscuits
   1 egg
   ½ teaspoon salt
   1 cup sour cream
   1 teaspoon poppy seeds

In a skillet melt the butter and sauté the onions slowly until soft. Separate the 10 biscuits and place in a single layer in an ungreased 8-inch layer cake pan, pressing together to cover the bottom completely. In a medium bowl beat the egg slightly and mix in the salt and sour cream. Spoon the onions over the biscuits. Spoon the sour cream mixture over the onions. Sprinkle with poppy seeds. Bake in a 375° oven for 25 to 30 minutes. Serve warm.
MAKES 8 SERVINGS.

Baked Ham

   ⅓ cup dry breadcrumbs
   1 tablespoon firmly packed brown sugar
   1 egg yolk, beaten
   1 teaspoon dry mustard
   1 teaspoon Worcestershire sauce
   1 2-pound slice ham
      Milk

In a small bowl make a paste of crumbs, sugar, yolk, mustard, and Worcestershire sauce. Place the ham in a shallow baking dish, and spread the crumb mixture over the ham. Add enough milk to half cover the ham. Bake in a 325° oven for 45 minutes.
MAKES 6 SERVINGS.

New Berne House Inn

Strata

   4 slices bread, cubed (any kind or combine several)
   ¼ cup diced onion
   ¼ cup diced celery
   ¼ cup diced green bell pepper
   ¾ cup grated cheese (Cheddar, Jack, and/or Swiss)
      Parsley, basil, oregano, garlic powder, and pepper to taste
   ¼ cup grated Parmesan cheese
      Sliced tomatoes
      Sliced olives
   3 eggs
   1 cup milk
   1 tablespoon Dijon mustard

In an 8-inch square pan layer the bread cubes, onion, celery, bell pepper, and cheese. Sprinkle with parsley, basil, oregano, garlic powder, and pepper to taste. Sprinkle with Parmesan cheese. Top with tomatoes and olives.

In a small bowl combine the eggs, milk, Dijon mustard. Pour over the strata. Press down with a large spoon to absorb all liquid. Refrigerate overnight.

Bake in a 350° oven for 50 to 60 minutes or until a toothpick inserted in the center comes out clean.
MAKES 4 TO 6 SERVINGS.

Tar Heel Inn

508 Church Street, P.O. Box 176
Oriental, North Carolina 28571
(919) 249-1078

*A*n *English country-style inn, the Tar Heel offers eight guest rooms individually decorated with Laura Ashley prints, hand stencilling, and fine antiques. Dating to the mid-1800s, the inn is located in the picturesque village of Oriental near the confluence of the Neuse River and Pamlico Sound on the Intercoastal Waterway. Guests returning from a long day of bicycling, fishing,*

sailing, or shopping will find cool refreshments and fresh baked sweets waiting for them at the inn.

Lindsay's Blue Ribbon Cookies

   1 cup sugar
   1 cup firmly packed dark brown sugar
   1 cup unsalted butter
   2 eggs
   2 tablespoons milk
   2 teaspoons vanilla extract
   2 cups all-purpose flour
   1 teaspoon baking powder
   1 teaspoon baking soda
   1 teaspoon salt
   2½ cups old-fashioned oats
   2 cups semisweet chocolate chips
   1½ cups chopped walnuts or pecans

In a large bowl cream the sugars and butter together with an electric mixer. Add the eggs, milk, and vanilla, mixing just until blended. Then add the flour, baking powder, soda, and salt. Mix until blended. Stir in the oats, chocolate chips, and nuts. Drop onto a greased cookie sheet by spoonfuls, about 1 ½ inches apart. Bake in a 350° oven for 10 to 15 minutes. Let stand for 1 minute, then remove to cooling racks.

Note: Cookies freeze well, as does the cookie dough, for fresh cookies anytime.
MAKES ABOUT 4 DOZEN.

Banana Pancakes with Cinnamon Syrup

   2 cups all-purpose flour
   2 tablespoons sugar
   ½ teaspoon salt
   1 teaspoon baking soda
   2 cups buttermilk
   2 eggs
   2 tablespoons oil
   2 mashed bananas
   ....
   2 cups sugar
   1 cup light corn syrup
   ½ cup water
   1 teaspoon ground cinnamon
   1 cup heavy cream

In a large bowl sift together the flour, sugar, salt, and soda. In a separate bowl mix together the buttermilk, eggs, and oil. Stir just until mixed. Add the bananas. Mix the liquid mixture with the dry ingredients. Preheat a griddle and pour the batter by ¼ cupfuls. Cook until dry around the edges, then flip and cook until browned. Serve with cinnamon syrup.

In a saucepan stir together 2 cups of sugar, syrup, water, and cinnamon. Stir constantly and bring to a boil over medium heat. Boil for 2 minutes. Remove from the heat and stir in the cream. Cool for 30 minutes. The syrup will thicken as it cools.

Note: Honey can be substituted for corn syrup. Cinnamon syrup keeps for months in the refrigerator.

MAKES 4 TO 6 SERVINGS.

Fearrington House Inn

2000 Fearrington Village Center
Pittsboro, North Carolina 27312
(919) 542-4000

*R*ooms and suites at the inn are decorated with English pine antiques and original art. The eighteenth-century village surrounding the inn grew up around the Fearrington family farm founded in 1786. Clustered around a romantic courtyard or overlooking a central park, the inn's twenty-four rooms and suites are luxuriously decorated with original art and antiques, and all have private baths. The inn is located about eight miles from Chapel Hill, home of the University of North Carolina.

Potato and Leek Soup

4   leeks, white portion, cleaned and sliced
2   cloves garlic, chopped
¾   cup unsalted butter
1   cup dry white wine
4   baking potatoes, peeled and cubed
1   gallon cold water
1   bouquet garni (celery stalk, parsley, thyme, and bay leaf)
1   cup heavy cream, hot
    Salt and white pepper to taste

In a large saucepan sweat the leeks and garlic in ¼ cup of butter over low heat until translucent. Add the white wine and reduce until almost dry. Add the potatoes and water and bring to a boil. Skim as necessary. Add the bouquet garni, reduce the heat and simmer for 30 minutes.

Remove from the heat and strain, reserving the liquid and pulp separately. Discard the bouquet garni. In a blender or food processor purée the potato and leek pulp until smooth. (Hint: add some of the reserved liquid while blending to get a more uniform texture.)

Combine the potato mixture and remaining reserved liquid, and bring back to a boil. Reduce the heat and simmer for 30 minutes.

Just prior to serving, add the cream and season to taste with salt and white pepper. Finish by whisking in the remaining butter.

MAKES 6 TO 8 SERVINGS.

Fruit Gazpacho

1   to 2 tablespoons olive oil
5   shallots, peeled, cleaned and chopped
1   clove garlic, peeled, cleaned, and chopped
1   leek, peeled, cleaned, and chopped
1   red bell pepper, cleaned and chopped
1   yellow bell pepper, cleaned and chopped
1   European cucumber, cleaned and chopped
2   scallions, cleaned and chopped
1   small onion, cleaned and chopped
1   cup diced cantaloupe
1   cup kiwi pulp
3   cups V-8 juice
    Juice of 1 lemon
    Juice of 1 lime

¼   cup white vinegar
2   tablespoons chopped fresh cilantro

In a saucepan heat the olive oil and sauté the shallots, garlic, and leek for 5 minutes, then remove from the heat to cool.

In a blender or food processor blend the remaining vegetables plus the cantaloupe and kiwi pulp, until completely puréed. Add the V-8 juice, the lemon and lime juices, and white vinegar. Season with salt and black pepper to taste and cilantro.

MAKES 4 TO 6 SERVINGS.

Smoked Trout

½   cup soy sauce
½   cup olive oil
1   tablespoon honey
    Trout fillets

In a glass bowl whisk together the soy sauce, olive oil, and honey. Soak the trout fillets for 20 minutes. Lay in a stove top smoker. Cook with 2 tablespoons of fruit wood chips for 10 to 15 minutes.

MAKES 1 CUP OF MARINADE.

Real Cornbread

1½   cups all-purpose flour
1½   cups cornmeal
1   tablespoon black pepper
1   tablespoon kosher salt
4½   teaspoons baking powder
4   eggs
1¾   cups milk
½   cup melted shortening
¼   cup honey
1   16-ounce can white (very sweet) corn
1   1-pound package smoked sausage, sliced into quarter-sized pieces
1½   cups shredded sharp Cheddar cheese
1   small minced onion
1   small diced apple

In a large bowl mix together the flour, cornmeal, pepper, salt, and baking powder. In a separate bowl mix the eggs, milk, shortening, and honey. Add to the dry ingredients. Add the corn, sausage, Cheddar cheese, onion, and apple. Pour into a greased 9 x 13-inch dish. Bake in a 425° oven for 20 to 25 minutes.

MAKES 12 SERVINGS.

Grandview Lodge

Grandview Lodge

809 Valley View Circle Road
Waynesville, North Carolina 28786
(800) 255-7826

With its 3,000-foot elevation, the Grandview Lodge provides its guests with something they are unlikely to find down in the flatlands—cool summer evenings. The lodge's main building dates to the late 1800s when it was part of a large farm and orchard. The fifteen guest rooms are furnished with antiques that are not just old, but comfortable and functional as well.

Grandview Chocoholic Tart

1¾ **cups all-purpose flour**
⅓ **cup unsweetened cocoa**
¼ **cup sugar**
¼ **cup shortening**
½ **cup butter or margarine**
⅓ **to ½ cup ice water**
....
12 **ounces bittersweet chocolate or**
      semisweet chocolate chips
⅔ **cup sugar**
1 **tablespoon chocolate or coffee**
      liqueur
1 **tablespoon instant coffee powder**
2 **tablespoons milk**
2 **eggs**
1 **cup coarsely chopped walnuts**

In a medium bowl, combine the flour, cocoa, and sugar. Using a pastry blender or 2 knives, cut the shortening and butter into the dry ingredients until the mixture resembles coarse meal. Add the ice water slowly, mixing with a fork. Add only enough water to gather the dough into a ball. Wrap in plastic wrap and chill. This dough is stickier than ordinary pie pastry. Roll out between 2 pieces of floured waxed paper. Line an 11-inch springform pan with pastry.

In top of a double boiler or in a heavy saucepan melt the chocolate. Stir in the remaining filling ingredients except the nuts. Pour into the prepared pastry. Sprinkle with nuts. Bake in a 375° oven for 30 to 35 minutes, until set in the center. Filling will puff up slightly and crack. Cool on a wire rack. Remove the sides of the pan. Cut into 12 or 16 pie-shaped slices. It's very rich, so a small slice is sufficient.
MAKES 12 TO 16 SERVINGS.

Grandview Marinated Pork Roast

2½ **to 3 pounds boned pork loin roast**
1 **teaspoon dry mustard**
1 **teaspoon dried thyme**
3 **cloves garlic, peeled**
1 **ounce ginger**
¾ **cup dry sherry**
¾ **cup brewed soy sauce**

Place the pork loin in a shallow pan, fat-side-up. In a cup mix the mustard and thyme together. Rub into the fat. In a food processor fitted with a steel blade, drop the garlic and ginger into the chute with the motor running, and chop finely. Add the sherry and soy sauce and pulse a few times. (Without a food processor, chop the garlic finely and grate the ginger. Place in a pint container, add sherry and soy sauce, cover with lid and shake to combine ingredients.) Pour the marinade over the meat. Cover and refrigerate at least 6 but preferably 12 hours, turning the meat 2 to 3 times.

Remove the meat from the marinade. Strain the marinade into a small saucepan. Save the strained solids for addition to the meat in the roasting pan. Heat the liquid to boiling, skimming as necessary. Remove from the heat and set aside.

Place the meat fat-side up and reserve the strained solids in a shallow pan. Roast in a preheated 325° oven to an internal temperature of 140°, about 1 hour and 15 minutes. Cover the meat and pan securely, and keep in a warm place for 30 minutes. Add the pan juices to the marinade. Boil down to thicken, removing the fat from the surface. Slice the roast thinly. Move the sliced roast to a heated platter and pour the sauce over the meat.

Note: Use a pork loin that is about 2½ inches thick.
MAKES 6 TO 8 SERVINGS.

The Old Stone Inn

900 Dolan Road
Waynesville, North Carolina 28786
(704) 456-3333

The Old Stone Inn is situated on six acres of wooded hill country at an elevation of 3,200 feet. Summers here are cool, but the rooms, with their quilts, rockers, and fireplaces, are warm and cozy. The inn is surrounded by century-old oaks, mountain laurel, dogwood, and rhododendron. The attractions of North Carolina's mountainous west are legendary. Aside from the mountains themselves, travelers may enjoy the nearby Cherokee Indian Reservation, Brevard Music Center, Biltmore Mansion, Theater at Flat Rock, and Great Smoky Mountain National Park.

Kentucky Pot Roast with Vegetables

3 **cans double-strength beef consommé**
½ **cup red wine**
2 **tablespoons Kentucky bourbon**
    Dash Tabasco sauce
2 **teaspoon Worcestershire sauce**

½ teaspoon dried thyme
½ teaspoon dried rosemary
1 teaspoon dried basil
1 teaspoon black pepper
6 (or more) cloves garlic
4 medium onions, peeled and quartered
1 2-pound chuck roast
6 medium potatoes, peeled and quartered
6 medium turnips, peeled and quartered
6 large carrots, peeled and quartered
1 tablespoon arrowroot
½ cup cold water

In a large glass or plastic dish combine the consommé, wine, bourbon, Tabasco, Worcestershire, spices, garlic, and onions. Place the chuck roast in the mixture. Cover and marinate overnight.

The next day, place the roast and marinade in a baking pan, and cover. Bake in a 300° oven for 2 hours and 30 minutes.

Remove from the oven and add the potatoes, turnips, and carrots. Return to the oven and bake another 2 hours, or until the roast may be pulled apart with a fork.

To thicken the sauce, combine 1 tablespoon of arrowroot with ½ cup of cold water and stir into a the broth.

MAKES 6 SERVINGS.

Baked Pineapple

1 20-ounce can crushed pineapple, lightly drained
½ cup sugar
1 tablespoon self-rising flour
2 tablespoons butter, melted
¼ teaspoon ground cinnamon
¼ teaspoon grated nutmeg
2 eggs, beaten
....
¾ cup shredded Cheddar cheese
1 cup corn flakes, crushed
3 tablespoons butter, melted

The Old Stone Inn

In a medium bowl combine the pineapple, sugar, flour, 2 tablespoons of butter, cinnamon, nutmeg, and eggs. Mix well and pour into a greased 1-quart baking dish. Distribute the cheese evenly over the top.

In a bowl mix the corn flakes and melted butter, and sprinkle over the top of the cheese. Bake in a 325° oven for 35 minutes.

MAKES 4 TO 6 SERVINGS.

Potato Pie

2 large potatoes
2 tablespoons olive oil
1 unbaked 10-inch pie shell
1 cup shredded Monterey Jack cheese
1 cup shredded Cheddar cheese
3 eggs
1 cup evaporated milk
1 tablespoon grated onion
1 teaspoon soy sauce
Dash Tabasco sauce

Scrub the potatoes and slice thinly. In a skillet heat the olive oil and sauté the sliced potatoes until tender. Drain on paper towels, cool, and spread evenly over the bottom of the pie shell. Sprinkle the cheeses over the potatoes. In a medium bowl combine the eggs, milk, onion, soy sauce, and Tabasco. Whisk until thoroughly blended, and pour over the cheeses. Bake in a 325° oven for 30 to 40 minutes, until set in the center and lightly browned. Let stand about 10 minutes before serving.

Note: This may be prepared in advance and refrigerated overnight. In the morning, just pop it in the oven. (It will take longer to bake, however, if it is cold.)

MAKES 8 TO 10 SERVINGS.

Scottish Pancakes

1½ cups old-fashioned oats
2 cups buttermilk
1½ teaspoons sugar
1 teaspoon baking soda
1 teaspoon salt
½ cup all-purpose flour
2 eggs, beaten

Preheat an electric griddle or frying pan to 350°. In a large bowl mix the oats and buttermilk together in a bowl and let stand for 5 minutes. In a separate bowl combine the

sugar, soda, salt, and flour. Add the dry ingredients to the oat mixture. Add the beaten eggs, mixing well. Spoon onto the well-oiled griddle (cooking spray does not work well for this). Brown 1 side, then flip once only. Remove from the griddle when golden brown.

MAKES 4 SERVINGS.

Miss Betty's Bed and Breakfast Inn

600 West Nash Street
Wilson, North Carolina 27893
(919) 243-4447

Wilson has been called the "antique capital of North Carolina," and Miss Betty's is an inn befitting such a place. A Victorian mansion in Wilson's historic district, it is a showplace of old-fashioned elegance and fine furnishings. In addition to its many antique shops, the town is also known for its eastern Carolina-style barbecue.

Apple Swirl Cake

2 cups peeled, cored, and chopped tart apples
3 tablespoons sugar
1 teaspoon ground cinnamon
2 cups sugar
1 cup oil
4 eggs
¼ cup orange juice
2 teaspoons vanilla extract
3 cups sifted all-purpose flour
1 tablespoon baking powder
½ teaspoon salt
Confectioners' sugar

In a medium bowl mix together the apples, 3 tablespoons of sugar, and cinnamon. Set aside.

In a large bowl, combine 2 cups of sugar and the oil and beat well. Add the eggs, orange juice, and vanilla. In a separate bowl sift together the flour, baking powder, and salt. Add the dry ingredients to the creamed mixture and beat until smooth. Pour one-third of the batter into a greased and floured 12-cup bundt pan, alternating with half of the apple mixture. Repeat. End with a layer of batter on top. Bake in a 325° oven for 1 hour or until a toothpick inserted in the center comes out clean.

Cool in the pan for 10 to 15 minutes. Turn out onto a wire rack or serving plate to complete cooling. Sprinkle with confectioners' sugar.

MAKES 8 SERVINGS.

Pecan Mini Muffins

- 1 *cup firmly packed light brown sugar*
- ⅓ *cup all-purpose flour*
  Pinch salt
- 1 *cup chopped pecans*
- 2 *eggs*
- ½ *teaspoon vanilla extract*

In a medium bowl mix all ingredients by hand just until moistened. Oil or spray mini muffin pans generously. Spoon in the batter. Bake in a 350° oven for 20 minutes. Remove from the pans immediately.

MAKES 2 DOZEN.

Miss Betty's

NORTH DAKOTA

*T*his North Dakota farmhouse, built in 1926, looks out over fields, woods, hills, and coulees. Much of the 300-acre farm property remains a virgin prairie with tall grasses, wildflowers, and natural springs. The house features Russian and Norwegian collectibles, reflecting the heritages of the innkeepers. The two comfortable guest rooms are furnished with antiques and family heirloom quilts. A separate cottage that once served as office for a country lawyer is also available.

Volden Farm

Danish Aebleskiver

- 2   cups cake flour
- 2   cups buttermilk
- ½   teaspoon baking soda
- 2   teaspoon baking powder
      Dash sugar
      Dash salt
- 5   seeds cardamom, crushed in mortar and pestle
- 4   eggs, separated

In a large bowl mix all ingredient, except the egg whites with an electric mixer until blended. In a separate bowl beat the egg whites until stiff but not dry. Fold the egg whites into the batter. Meanwhile, heat an Aebleskiver pan to medium-hot. Pour on a few drops of safflower oil, then pour each three-fourths full of batter. Cook until bubbly, turning with a hat pin until light brown.

Serve with various jellies and confectioners' sugar. Dip each bite first in jelly (plum and cherry are especially nice), then in sugar. Also good with marmalade and butter, melted and poured over top.

MAKES 6 TO 8 SERVINGS.

Root Veggie Soup

- 1   large potato, peeled and diced
- 1   large sweet potato, peeled and diced
- 2   parsnips, peeled and cut into chunks
- 2   carrots, peeled and cut into chunks
- 1   rutabaga, peeled and diced
- 1   large onion, chopped
- 4   cloves garlic, chopped
- ½   red bell pepper, sliced
- 1   tomato, sliced

Parsley or cilantro
- 2   tablespoons chicken bouillon granules
- 1   slice wheat bread (optional)

In a stockpot combine all ingredients. Cover with water. Cook for 1 hour. May be thickened with 1 slice of wheat bread, cubed.

MAKES 6 TO 8 SERVINGS.

Norwegian Sweet Soup (Sot Suppe)

- 2   cups pitted prunes
- 1   cup dark raisins
- ½   cup currants
- 1   cup light raisins
- 1   cup dried apricots
- 1   sliced orange, with skin
- 2   sticks cinnamon
- 2   teaspoons ground cloves
- ¼   teaspoon nutmeg

- ½   cup firmly packed brown sugar
- ¼   cup tapioca

In a stockpot combine the prunes, raisins, currants, raisins, apricots, orange, cinnamon, cloves, and nutmeg, and cover with water. Simmer for 1 hour.

Add the brown sugar and tapioca. Simmer, stirring a couple of times, for another 15 minutes. Let cool in the pan, then refrigerate. Serve warm or cold.

Note: Add orange or apple juice if desired, when serving. Serve with dollops of crème fraîche. Keeps well in the refrigerator.

MAKES 4 TO 6 SERVINGS.

Crème Fraîche

2   **cups gourmet cream or heavy cream**
2   **tablespoons buttermilk**

Mix together thoroughly and cover. Let stand at room temperature until thick, at least overnight. Refrigerate. Good for 2 weeks.
MAKES 2 CUPS.

101 Ryral Avenue
Regent, North Dakota 58650
(701) 563-4542

A modern home on the North Dakota Prairies, this B&B is the right choice for activity minded travelers. In addition to the seven guest rooms, there is a 2,000-square-foot recreation room with a swimming pool, treadmill, exercise bicycle, and suana. Volleyball, ten-nis, and basketball courts are only three blocks away. For those seeking more restful pleasures, decks on either side of the house are available for sunning, bird watching, and relaxing.

Wheat Berry Salad

1   **cup wheat soaked overnight**
1   **8-ounce package cream cheese, soft-ened**
1   **3-ounce package instant vanilla or pistachio pudding**
3   **tablespoons lemon juice**
1   **cup or more Cool Whip**
1   **teaspoon vanilla extract**
1½ **cups crushed pineapple in juice, undrained**

In a covered saucepan cook the wheat for 40 minutes. Rinse to cool. Drain. In a medium bowl stir the cream cheese to soften, and add the pudding and lemon juice. Fold in the Cool Whip and vanilla. Fold in the pineapple and wheat.

The salad will keep several days.
MAKES 4 TO 6 SERVINGS.

Crescent Taco Hot Dish

1½ **to 2 pounds hamburger**
1   **small onion, diced**
1   **15-ounce can tomato sauce**
1   **1¼-ounce package taco seasoning**
1   **10-ounce tube crescent rolls**
    Taco chips
2   **cups sour cream**
4   **cups shredded Cheddar cheese**
    Shredded lettuce
    Hot taco sauce

In a skillet brown the hamburger and onion. Add the tomato sauce and taco seasoning. Mix and simmer for 10 minutes.

Separate the tube of rolls and line a greased 9 x 13-inch pan. Sprinkle with 1½ cups of crushed taco chips. Spoon the meat mixtures over the chips. Top with sour cream. Sprinkle Cheddar cheese over the sour cream. Place 1 cup of crushed taco chips on top. Bake in a 375° oven for 25 minutes. Serve with shredded lettuce and hot taco sauce.
MAKES 6 TO 8 SERVINGS.

OHIO

Bailey House

Bailey House Bed and Breakfast

112 North Water Street
Georgetown, Ohio 45121
(513) 378-3078

During the time that Ulysses S. Grant was growing up in Georgetown, he frequently visited the Bailey home. Built in 1830 by a doctor, the Greek Revival three-story brick house has four large pillars in front and a large central hall with winding staircase. The spacious guest rooms have Federal-style mantels, woodwork, and original ash flooring, and they feature antique beds,

chests of drawers, and wash stands. Not far away is the Grant family home, centerpiece of the Georgetown National Historic District.

Apple French Toast

1   cup firmly packed brown sugar
½   cup butter, melted
2   tablespoons light corn syrup
3   large apples, cored and peeled
    Day-old French bread
3   eggs
1   cup milk
1   tablespoon vanilla extract

In a small pan combine the brown sugar, butter, and corn syrup and cook until thick, 2 to 3 minutes. Pour into a ungreased 9 x 13-inch pan. Arrange the apple slices on top. Slice the French bread into ¾-inch-thick slices. In a large bowl beat the 3 eggs, milk, and vanilla. Dip the bread in the mixture. Let the bread slices soak for 30 seconds in the milk mixture. Arrange on top of the apples. Cover and refrigerate overnight.

Bake uncovered in a 350° oven for 35 to 40 minutes.

MAKES 9 SERVINGS.

Gooey Butter Coffeecake

1   16-ounce box pound cake mix
4   eggs
½   cup butter, melted
1   8-ounce package cream cheese
4½ teaspoons vanilla extract
1   16-ounce box confectioners' sugar

In a large bowl blend the cake mix with 2 eggs and the melted butter. Pour into a 9 x 13-inch pan or 2 8-inch square pans. In a separate bowl mix the cream cheese, 2 eggs, vanilla, and confectioners' sugar (reserve 2 tablespoons). Mix well and pour over the batter in the pan. Bake in a 300° oven for 15 minutes. Sprinkle the remaining confectioners' sugar on top and bake for 25 to 30 minutes longer or until set. Cool and cut. Freezes well.

MAKES 8 TO 12 SERVINGS.

The Inn on Kelleys Island

Box 11, 317 West Lakeshore Drive
Kelleys Island, Ohio 43438
(417) 746-2258

Kelleys Island, in Lake Erie off Marblehead and Sandusky, is about as secluded and old-fashioned a place as travelers are likely to find in Ohio. Quaint shops, restaurants, and taverns abound here. The inn, built as a private home in 1876, is richly Victorian and is the perfect place to stay for those who want to explore the island on foot or with bicycles. In addition to its four *well-appointed guest rooms, it features a player piano, big comfortable sofas, a fireplace, and a glorious view of Lake Erie.*

Zucchini Bread

  3 *eggs, beaten*
  2 *cups sugar*
  1 *cup oil*
  3 *cups all-purpose flour*
  1 *teaspoon salt*
  1 *teaspoon baking powder*
 ½ *teaspoon baking soda*
  3 *teaspoons ground cinnamon*
  2 *cups grated zucchini*
  2 *teaspoons vanilla extract*
 ½ *cup chopped walnuts*

In a large bowl beat the eggs. Beat in the sugar and oil. In a separate bowl mix the flour, salt, baking powder, soda, and cinnamon. Add the dry ingredients to the sugar and oil and mix with a spoon. Stir in the zucchini, vanilla, and walnuts. Pour into 2 greased and floured 5 x 9-inch loaf pans. Bake in a 325° oven for 1 hour.

MAKES 2 LOAVES.

The Signal House

234 West Front Street
Ripley, Ohio 45167
(513) 392-1640

The Signal House

*T*his stately Ohio River home once served as an extraordinary sort of lighthouse. Abolitionist would hang a lantern in its skylight to signal former slaves escaping on the "Underground Railroad" that it was safe to cross the river. A Greek Italianate home built during the 1830s, it has twelve-foot ceilings, ornate plaster moldings, and two charming parlors. Guests may enjoy a grand view of the Ohio from any one of three broad porches.

Bourbon Slush

  3 *tea bags*
  2 *cups boiling water*
  1 *cup bourbon*
1½ *cups sugar*
  6 *cups water*
  1 *6-ounce can frozen orange juice concentrate*
  1 *6-ounce can frozen lemonade concentrate*

Steep the tea bags in the boiling water for 5 minutes. Remove the bags. In a pitcher or large container combine the tea, bourbon, sugar, 6 cups of water, frozen orange juice, and lemonade. Stir and pour into a freezer container. Freeze.

Remove from the freezer 10 minutes before serving. Spoon into glasses.

MAKES 16 CUPS.

Hot Chicken Salad

  2 *cups diced cooked chicken*
  2 *cups diced celery*
 ½ *small onion, thinly sliced*
 ½ *green bell pepper, chopped or strips*
  1 *6-ounce can sliced water chestnuts*
  2 *tablespoons chopped stuffed olives*
  2 *tablespoons lemon juice*
  1 *cup mayonnaise*
  1 *cup shredded sharp Cheddar cheese*
  1 *cup crushed corn chips*

In a 3-quart casserole combine all ingredients except the cheese and corn chips. Cover and cook in the microwave at 70% for 10 minutes. Sprinkle the cheese on top of the chicken mixture and top with corn chips. Cook at 70% power for 10 minutes.

MAKES 8 SERVINGS.

Company Pot Roast

  1 *to 2 tablespoons oil*
  1 *3-pound pot roast*
  1 *medium onion, sliced*
  2 *tablespoons sugar*
  1 *cube beef bouillon*
  1 *stick cinnamon*
1½ *cups water*
 ½ *cup dry sherry*
 ¼ *cup soy sauce*
  8 *carrots, halved lengthwise*
  4 *potatoes, peeled and halved*
4½ *teaspoons cornstarch*
 ¼ *cup cold water*

In a Dutch oven heat the oil and brown the roast and onion. Add the sugar, bouillon, cinnamon, water, sherry, and soy sauce. Cover and simmer for 2 to 3 hours or until the meat is tender. Add the carrots and potatoes, cover and simmer for 30 minutes or until the vegetables are tender. Spoon the juices over the vegetables. Thicken the juice with 4½ teaspoons of cornstarch mixed with ¼ cup cold water. Boil, stirring constantly, until thickened.

Note: If meat the becomes dry, add water and skim off the excess fat.

MAKES 5 TO 6 SERVINGS.

Allen Villa Bed and Breakfast

434 South Market Street
Troy, Ohio 45373
(513) 335-1181

*W*hen built in 1874, this was described as the most palatial residence in town, and visitors nowadays might very well use that same description. Meticulously restored, the mansion still shows off its white *marble mantles, winding staircase, and large bay windows. Guests who select one of its five guest rooms, all furnished with period antiques, can fully appreciate its charms*

Strawberry Banana Frozen Dessert

  1   8-ounce package cream cheese, softened
  ¾ cup sugar
  2   bananas, sliced
  1   10-ounce package frozen strawberries, thawed
  1   20-ounce can crushed pineapple, drained
      Chopped nuts (optional)
  1   9-ounce carton Cool Whip

In a large bowl blend together the cream cheese and sugar. In a separate bowl mix the bananas, strawberries, pineapple, and nuts thoroughly but gently, and combine with the cream cheese. Fold in the Cool Whip. Pour into a 9 x 13-inch pan and freeze.
MAKES 6 SERVINGS.

Oil Pastry Crust

  1½ cups all-purpose flour
  ½   teaspoon salt
  4½ teaspoons sugar
  ½   cup oil
  2   tablespoons milk

In a large bowl combine the flour, salt, and sugar. Add the oil and milk, and mix. Press to fit into 2 9-inch pie pan. Prick with a fork. Bake in a 400° oven for 15 to 17 minutes.
MAKES 2 9-INCH PIE CRUSTS.

Peach Glacé Pie

  5   cups sliced peaches (7 medium)
  1   cup sugar
  3   tablespoons cornstarch
  ½ cup water
  1   baked 9-inch pie shell

Mash enough of the peaches to measure 1 cup. In a 2-quart saucepan mix the sugar and cornstarch. Stir in ½ cup of water and mashed peaches gradually. Cook over medium heat, stirring constantly, until the mixture thickens and boils. Boil and stir for 1 minute. Cool.

Fill the pie shell with sliced peaches. Pour the cooked mixture over top. Refrigerate until set, at least 3 hours.

Note: To prevent discoloration, use an ascorbic acid mixture as directed on the package.
MAKES 6 TO 8 SERVINGS.

Korean (Spinach) Salad

  1   10-ounce bag fresh spinach
  1   6-ounce can water chestnuts, sliced
  1   6-ounce can bean sprouts, drained
  3   to 4 hard-boiled eggs, sliced
  4   to 5 strips bacon, cooked and crumbled

  ½ cup oil
  ¾ cup catsup
  ¾ cup minced onion
  1   tablespoon Worcestershire sauce
  ¼ cup white vinegar
  ½ cup firmly packed brown sugar

Just before serving, in a salad bowl mix the spinach, water chestnuts, bean sprouts, eggs, and bacon. In a small bowl mix the remaining ingredients. Serve the dressing with the salad.
MAKES 4 TO 6 SERVINGS.

Twice Baked Potatoes

  4   baking potatoes
  1½ teaspoons minced instant onion
  ¾ cup evaporated milk
  1   cup shredded sharp Cheddar, Colby, or Jack cheese
  ½ teaspoon salt
  2   tablespoons butter
  1   tablespoon parsley flakes

Bake the potatoes for about 1 hour. While the potatoes are baking, in a medium bowl add the onion to the milk and let stand.

Scoop out the inside of the potatoes, saving the shells. Mash the insides with the milk-onion mixture, cheese, salt, butter, and parsley. Spoon back into the shells. Place on a baking sheet. Bake in a 400° oven for about 10 minutes. These potatoes may be stored in the freezer for future use and then baked in a 400° oven for 45 minutes.
MAKES 4 SERVINGS.

Teriyaki Marinade

  ½ cup soy sauce
  ½ cup oil
  2   teaspoons sugar
  ½ cup fresh orange juice
  1   teaspoon ground ginger
  1   clove garlic, pressed

In a shallow bowl or a jar with a tight-fitting lid combine all ingredients. Use at once, or cover and refrigerate until needed.
MAKES ABOUT 1½ CUPS.

Allen Villa

Celery Seed Salad Dressing

  ⅔ cup vinegar
  1   teaspoon dry mustard
  1   teaspoon salt
  1   cup sugar
  2   cups oil
  1   teaspoon celery seed

In a blender combine all ingredients and blend until smooth.
MAKES 2¾ CUPS.

Poppy Seed Salad Dressing

  ⅔ cup vinegar
  1   teaspoon dry mustard
  1   teaspoon salt
  1   cup sugar
  2   cups oil
  1   8-ounce container sour cream
  1   teaspoon poppy seeds

In a blender combine all ingredients and blend until smooth.
MAKES ABOUT 3¾ CUPS.

Perfection Salad

- 2 6-ounce packages lime gelatin
- 4 cups hot water
- 3 cups cool water
- 2 cups shredded cabbage
- ½ cup grated carrot
- ¼ cup shredded celery
- 1 cup drained crushed pineapple
- 1 3-ounce package lime gelatin

In a large bowl mix the 6-ounce packages of lime gelatin in hot water. Stir until dissolved. Add the cool water, and stir well. Add the cabbage, carrot, celery, and pineapple. Pour into the desired dish. Refrigerate until set. Prepare the 3-ounce package of lime gelatin according to the package directions and pour it over the top of the set gelatin. Refrigerate until firm.

MAKES 6 TO 8 SERVINGS.

Lime Fluff Salad

- 2 6-ounce packages lime gelatin
- 4 cups hot water
- 2 cups cool water
- 1 cup crushed pineapple
- ⅓ cup chopped pecans (optional)
- 1 package Dream Whip
- ½ cup milk

In a large bowl stir the gelatin and hot water until dissolved. Add the cool water, pineapple, and pecans. Refrigerate until thickened.

In a separate bowl mix the Dream Whip and milk. Whip until stiff. Gradually fold in the thickened gelatin. Mix well and transfer to a 9 x 13-inch pan. Refrigerate again for a couple of hours or overnight.

MAKES 8 SERVINGS.

Orange Fluff Salad

- 2 6-ounce packages orange gelatin
- 4 cups hot water
- 2 cups cool water
- 1 cup crushed pineapple
- 1 11-ounce can mandarin oranges, drained
- 1 package Dream Whip
- ½ cup milk

In a large bowl dissolve the gelatin in hot water. Add the cool water, pineapple, and oranges. Refrigerate until thickened.

In a separate bowl mix the Dream Whip and milk. Whip until stiff. Gradually fold in the gelatin. Mix well and transfer to a 9 x 13-inch pan. Refrigerate again for a couple of hours or overnight.

MAKES 8 SERVINGS.

Carrots and Raisins

- 2 tablespoons butter or margarine
- 1½ pounds baby carrots, scraped, cut into ¼-inch diagonal slices
- ½ cup water or dry white wine
- ½ teaspoon grated nutmeg
- ⅔ cup white raisins
- 3 teaspoons firmly packed light brown sugar

In a medium skillet melt the butter. Add the carrots, water, and nutmeg. Cover and cook over low heat for 15 minutes. Stir in the raisins and brown sugar and cook for 5 minutes or until the raisins are plump and the carrots glazed.

MAKES 4 TO 6 SERVINGS.

Herb Salad Dressing

- ½ cup plain yogurt
- 1 tablespoon lemon juice
- 1 teaspoon chopped parsley
- 1 teaspoon dillweed
  - Garlic salt to taste
  - Salt to taste
  - Mayonnaise to taste

In a small bowl combine the ingredients. Pour over salad.

MAKES 4 SERVINGS.

Champagne Punch

- 1 12-ounce can frozen lemonade
- 1 12-ounce can frozen Tropicana cranberry, raspberry, strawberry drink
- 1 2-liter bottle Sprite
- 1 bottle cold dry André champagne

In a punch bowl combine all ingredients.

MAKES ABOUT 3½ QUARTS.

Hawaiian Cloud Punch

- 1 1-quart can pineapple juice
- 1 1-quart can tropical fruit juice
- 1 2-liter bottle Sprite
- 2 pints vanilla ice cream
- 2 pints orange sherbet

In a punch bowl combine all ingredients.

MAKES ABOUT 1½ GALLONS.

Pink Arctic Freeze

- 2 3-ounce packages cream cheese
- 2 tablespoons mayonnaise or salad dressing
- 2 tablespoons sugar
- 1 16-ounce can whole cranberry sauce
- 1 9-ounce can crushed pineapple, drained
- ½ cup chopped walnuts
- 1 cup heavy cream, whipped
  Lettuce leaves for garnish

In a large bowl soften the cream cheese. Blend in the mayonnaise and sugar. Add the fruit and nuts. Fold in the whipped cream. Pour into an 8½ x 4½-inch loaf pan. Freeze until firm, 6 hours or overnight.

To serve, let stand at room temperature about 15 minutes, turn out on lettuce, and slice.

MAKES 8 TO 10 SERVINGS.

OKLAHOMA

Country Inn

Route 3, Box 1925
Claremore, Oklahoma 74017
(918) 342-1894

Country antiques, weathered barn wood, iron beds, and wallpaper with rural scenes are some of the touches that make the County Inn unique and memorable. The exterior of the inn is even designed like a barn with its own grain silo. The "silo" encloses a stairway, which leads to guest rooms upstairs. Bicycles are available for a ride in the countryside. Claremore is the site of the Will Rogers Memorial, a house museum that is a popular tourist attraction.

Ham Frittata

 2 tablespoons margarine
¼ cup chopped onion
¼ cup chopped green bell pepper
 2 ounces mushrooms
10 eggs
½ cup sour cream
2¾ ounces ham, diced
1¼ cups shredded Monterey Jack cheese
1½ cups shredded Cheddar cheese

½ chicken bouillon cube
 1 tablespoon margarine
 3 tablespoons all-purpose flour
¾ cup milk
¼ cup shredded Monterey Jack cheese
¼ cup grated Parmesan cheese

1⅛ cups soft breadcrumbs
 2 tablespoons grated Parmesan cheese
 1 tablespoon chopped parsley
 3 tablespoons margarine, melted

In a skillet melt 2 tablespoons of margarine and sauté the onion, pepper, and mushrooms. In a large bowl whisk the eggs and sour cream. Add the sautéed mixture, ham, 1¼ cups of Monterey Jack and 1½ cups of Cheddar cheeses, and pour into a 9-inch glass pie plate sprayed with cooking spray. Bake in a 325° oven for 50 minutes or until set in the center and blonde in color. Cool to room temperature and refrigerate.

In a saucepan dissolve the bouillon cube in 1 tablespoon of margarine over medium heat. Slowly add the flour (will thicken). Add the milk, blending until smooth. Add ¼ cup of Monterey Jack and the Parmesan cheese and stir. The sauce should be thick. Cool and refrigerate.

In a plastic container combine the breadcrumbs, 2 tablespoons of Parmesan, parsley, and margarine. Toss lightly.

Microwave the frittata on high for 1 minute. Spread Mornay sauce over the frittata and sprinkle with crumbs. Bake in a 325° oven for 40 to 45 minutes. Crumbs should be brown. Slice and serve.

MAKES 6 SERVINGS.

Arcadian Inn

Arcadian Inn

328 East First
Edmond, Oklahoma 73034
(405) 348-6347, (800) 299-6347

The Arcadian Inn is located next to the University of Central Oklahoma, four blocks from the antique-shopping district of downtown Edmond. A striking three-story structure, this inn was built in 1908 as the home of a local medical doctor. Edmond is a suburb of Oklahoma City, which has several major tourist attractions.

Pumpkin Pancakes

1 30-ounce can Libby's Pumpkin Pie
   Mix
3 eggs
4 cups pancake mix
½ cup oil
   Water or milk, as needed for consistency

In a large bowl mix together the pumpkin, eggs, pancake mix, and oil. Add water as needed to make the right consistency for pancakes, like thick milkshake. Oil a hot griddle (350°) and ladel on pancake batter. Cook the pancakes about 7 minutes on each side. These are very moist pancakes.
MAKES 8 TO 12 SERVINGS.

Arcadian Inn
Vanilla Butter Sauce

1 egg, slightly beaten
½ cup sugar
1 cup light corn syrup
⅓ cup butter
1 tablespoon vanilla extract

In a saucepan beat the egg. Add the sugar, corn syrup, and butter. Bring the mixture to a boil. Remove the pan from the heat. Stir in the vanilla.

Delicious over Pumpkin Pancakes with chopped apples and pecans.
MAKES ABOUT 2 CUPS.

*Graham-
Carroll House*

501 North 16th Street
Muskogee, Oklahoma 74401
(918) 683-0100, (800) 878-0167

---

*T*his majestic nineteen-room Victorian Gothic oil mansion features queen-size beds, private baths, whirlpool tubs for two, antiques, and Victorian gardens. The inn offers romantic getaway packages.

Graham-Carroll House

Graham-Carroll House Punch

1 1-quart can pineapple juice
1 16-ounce package frozen whole
   strawberries (unsweetened)
2 large ripe bananas
1 12-ounce can frozen orange juice
   concentrate
4½ cups water

In an electric blender blend all ingredients. Serve in a punch bowl with ice.
MAKES ABOUT 1½ QUARTS.

*Holmberg
House*

766 DeBarr
Norman, Oklahoma 73069
(405) 321-6221

---

*T*his inn was built in 1914 as a residence by Professor Fredrik Holmberg, first dean of the College of Fine Arts of the University of Oklahoma. The inn sits just across the street from the university campus. Decorated with antiques, it has a large front porch as well as a spacious parlor.

Stuffed French Toast with Bananas, Blueberries, and Cream Cheese with Fresh Blueberry Sauce

4 large croissants, cut in half lengthwise
2 large bananas, sliced
8 ounces fresh or frozen blueberries
1 8-ounce package cream cheese,
   cubed
2 cups milk
6 eggs
¼ cup melted butter

Grease a 1½-quart casserole dish. Lay the bottom half of the croissants in the dish. Cover with sliced bananas, blueberries, and cream cheese. Place the croissant tops on. In a large bowl mix the milk, eggs, and butter. Pour over the croissants. Bake in a 350° oven for 45 to 60 minutes.

Variation: Add 1 teaspoon of maple flavoring or reduce the milk slightly and add some maple syrup or pancake syrup.
MAKES 4 SERVINGS.

Blueberry Sauce

8 ounces fresh or frozen blueberries
½ cup water
   Sugar to taste

In a small saucepan combine all ingredients and bring to a boil. Reduce the heat to a simmer and cook for 10 to 30 minutes. Stir and mash some of the blueberries. The mixture should thicken slightly.

Serve 1 to 2 tablespoons over each serving of Baked French Toast and sprinkle with a dash of confectioners' sugar.
MAKES ABOUT 1½ CUPS.

Fresh Fruit Sundae

   Chocolate sauce (fudge or regular)
½ pint washed and halved strawberries
2 large bananas, sliced
   Whipped cream (canned or homemade)
   Chopped pecans
   Maraschino cherries

In the bottom of 4 old-fashioned sundae glasses place 1½ teaspoons of chocolate sauce. Layer strawberries and bananas until slightly overfull. Top with whipped cream and sprinkle with nuts. Garnish with cherries.

MAKES 4 SERVINGS.

Herb Popovers

1   cup sifted all-purpose flour
½   teaspoon salt
1   cup milk
2   eggs
1   to 2 teaspoons chopped fresh herbs

In a medium bowl beat the flour, salt, milk, eggs, and herbs together just until smooth. Pour into well-greased popover tins (or muffin cups). Bake in a 425° oven for 35 to 40 minutes, until golden brown. Serve immediately.

MAKES 5 TO 9 POPOVERS, DEPENDING ON THE SIZE OF THE CUP.

Holmberg House

The Grandison

❧

*1841 Northwest Fifteenth
Oklahoma City, Oklahoma 73106
(405) 521-0011*

Some of the best features of this inn are the rockers on the large front porch, an ornate gazebo on the lawn, solid brass fixtures throughout, massive oak beams, and a garden with many varieties of flowers as well as fruit and nut trees. All rooms are furnished with period antiques. A recent renovation added Jacuzzi tubs, gas fireplaces, and queen/king-size beds.

Hot 'n Spicy Cinnamon Sauce

⅓   cup sugar
2   teaspoons cornstarch
    Dash salt
¼   teaspoon ground cinnamon
⅔   cup water
2   tablespoons Red Hots

In a saucepan mix all ingredients together over medium heat. Bring to a boil, stirring frequently. Serve warm over warm apple dumplings, ice cream, or a favorite dessert.

MAKES ABOUT ⅔ CUP.

Hot Fruit Compote

1   40-ounce bottle Dole Orchard Peach Juice
½   cup firmly packed brown sugar
¼   cup butter
    Ground cinnamon
    Cinnamon stick
    Grated nutmeg
1   29-ounce can sliced peaches in juice
1   15¼-ounce can chunk pineapple in juice
1   29-ounce can sliced pears in juice
2½   cups (½ 40-ounce bottle) Dole Mountain Cherry Juice
1   cup frozen black cherries
1   to 2 bananas

In a saucepan bring the peach juice, brown sugar, butter, cinnamon, cinnamon stick, and nutmeg to a boil. Add the drained peaches, pineapple, pears, and cherry juice. Reduce heat and simmer for 20 minutes. Add the frozen black cherries and simmer just until the cherries are heated. Slice the bananas into serving dishes and pour the hot fruit mixture on top.

Note: Adjust the brown sugar, butter, and spices to your taste.

MAKES 4 TO 6 SERVINGS.

Grape Ice Cream

1   cup sugar (use up to 2 cups to taste)
1   pint grape juice (or 2 cans frozen concentrate)
    Milk (enough to fill freezer)

In a large bowl dissolve the sugar in the grape juice. Pour into a 1½-gallon ice cream freezer. Add enough milk to fill the freezer and follow the manufacturer's instructions for freezing.

MAKES 1½ GALLONS.

OREGON

Cowslip's Bell

159 North Main
Ashland, Oregon 97520
(800) 888-6819 for reservations

*T*his cozy and romantic inn is named for the cowslip, a close relative of the primrose. Cowslips blooming in abundance in the spring garden are a spectacular scene that guests never forget. Continuing the floral and romantic theme, each of the four rooms at Cowlip's Bell is named for a flower mentioned in Shakespeare's plays—Gillyvor, Rosebud Suite, Love-in-Idleness, and Cuckoo-Bud.

Cheese Blintz Soufflé with Warm Blueberry Sauce

- 1 8-ounce package cream cheese
- 1 16-ounce carton ricotta cheese
- 2 egg yolks
- 1 tablespoon sugar
- 1 teaspoon vanilla extract

....

- ½ cup butter, softened
- ⅓ cup sugar

- 6 eggs
- 1 cup all-purpose flour
- 2 teaspoons baking powder
- 1½ cups plain yogurt
- ½ cup orange juice
   Warm Blueberry Sauce (recipe follows)

In a small bowl beat the cream cheese until smooth. Add the ricotta cheese, egg yolks, sugar, and vanilla. Mix thoroughly and set aside. In a separate bowl cream the butter and sugar. Add the eggs and beat well. In a third bowl mix the flour and baking powder. Add to the egg mixture alternately with the yogurt and orange juice. Stir only until moistened. Pour half of the batter into a buttered 9 x 13-inch glass baking pan. Spread cream cheese filling over the batter. Filling will be thick. Cover with the remaining batter. Bake in a 350° oven for 50 minutes or until done. It will be slightly golden on top.
MAKES 8 SERVINGS.

Warm Blueberry Sauce

- ¼ cup sugar
- 1 tablespoon all-purpose flour
   Pinch salt
- 1 cup water
- 1 teaspoon fresh lemon juice
- 1 cup blueberries
- 1½ teaspoons unsalted butter
- ¼ teaspoon ground cinnamon

In a saucepan combine the sugar, flour, salt, water, and lemon juice. Cook until the mixture thickens slightly. Add the blueberries and cook over moderate heat, stirring for 1

Cowslip's Bell

minute. Remove from the heat and add the butter. Stir until melted. Add the cinnamon and stir. Spoon over soufflé portions.
MAKES 8 SERVINGS.

Chili Cheese Egg Puff

- 10 eggs
- ½ cup all-purpose flour
- 1 teaspoon baking powder
- ½ teaspoon salt
- 2 cups cottage cheese
- 4 cups shredded Monterey Jack cheese
- ½ cup butter, melted
- 1 7-ounce can diced green chiles
   Salsa
   Sour cream

In a large bowl beat the eggs until lemon-colored. Add the flour, baking powder, salt, cottage cheese, Monterey Jack cheese, and butter. Mix until smooth. Add the chiles and stir. Pour the mixture into a buttered 9 x 13-inch glass baking pan. Bake in a 350° oven for about 40 minutes or until firm and the top is slightly browned.

Slice into 8 serving portions and serve with salsa and sour cream on the side.
MAKES 8 SERVINGS.

Hersey House

451 North Main Street
Ashland, Oregon 97520
(514) 469-8128

*O*riginally built as a residence in 1904, Hersey House has a spacious front porch and a large outdoor deck for reading, lounging, or relaxing. Guests also enjoy the elegant parlor with its restored antique Aeolian player organ. Nearby attractions include Crater Lake, the old mining town of Jacksonville, Oregon, and performances during the Oregon Shakespeare Festival in Ashland.

Quick Bread Pudding

4	*cups milk*
2	*tablespoons butter*
2	*cups quick bread (e.g. banana bread), cubed*
½	*cup sugar*
½	*teaspoon salt*
1	*teaspoon vanilla extract (or rum)*
2	*eggs*
	Whipped cream

The bread should be stale, but not hard and dry. In a saucepan scald the milk and butter. Soak the bread in milk for 5 to 10 minutes.

Add the sugar, salt, vanilla, and slightly beaten eggs, and stir until the sugar is dissolved. Pour into 8 individual ramekins. Set the dishes in a pan of hot water. Bake in a 375° oven for 1 hour or less, until a knife inserted in a center pudding comes out clean. Top with whipped cream.
MAKES 8 SERVINGS.

Nutty Apple Muffins

1½	*cups unbleached flour*
1½	*teaspoons baking powder*
¾	*teaspoon salt*
¼	*teaspoon grated nutmeg*
2	*eggs*
1	*cup sugar*
⅓	*cup canola oil*
2	*cups peeled, diced apples*
1½	*cups chopped nuts*
¼	*cup shredded sweetened coconut*
2	*tablespoons sesame seeds*
2	*tablespoons poppy seeds*

In a medium bowl combine the flour, baking powder, salt, and nutmeg. In a separate bowl beat the eggs, sugar, and oil. Add the apples, nuts, coconut, sesame seeds, and poppy seeds. Stir in the dry ingredients until just moistened.

Fill greased muffin cups three-fourths full. Bake in a 350° oven for 25 to 30 minutes.

Cool in the pan for 10 minutes before removing.
MAKES 2 DOZEN.

Minted Melon Ball Syrup

½	*cup water*
1	*cup sugar*
2	*tablespoons chopped fresh mint*

In a saucepan boil the water and sugar to dissolve. Add the mint and remove from the heat. Let stand 1 to 2 hours or overnight. Strain.

Pour over any combination of melon balls. Best if refrigerated overnight.
MAKES ABOUT 1 CUP.

Chetco River Inn

Chetco River Inn

21202 High Prairie Road
Brookings, Oregon 97415
(800) 327-2688

*T*his inn offers the wilderness-minded guest thirty-five acres of privacy and tranquility on the Chetco River in southern Oregon. Guests enjoy hiking the nature trails in the Kalmiopsis Wilderness Area nearby.

Oregon Cranberry Hazelnut Biscotti

1	*cup sugar*
½	*cup butter, softened*
3	*eggs*
¼	*cup sherry*
½	*cup dried cranberries*
½	*cup chopped hazelnuts*
1½	*teaspoons baking powder*
3	*cups all-purpose flour*

In a large bowl mix together all of the ingredients. Divide in half and pat out 2 loaves ½ x 3 x 16 inches on a greased cookie sheet. Bake in a ed 375° oven until lightly browned. Cool on the pan.

Cut into ¾-inch slices and place cut-side-down on the baking sheet.

Bake in a 375° oven for 15 to 20 minutes until the cookies are brown and crunchy. Store in an airtight container. Freezes well. If they are not baked a second time, they are a delicious soft cookie.
MAKES ABOUT 3 DOZEN.

Grilled Oregon Chenoch Salmon

½	*cup soy sauce*
½	*cup sherry*
2	*crushed cloves garlic*
¼	*cup Marionberry or blackberry jam*

In a plastic bag combine the soy sauce, sherry, garlic, and jam, and mix well. Marinate salmon steaks in the sauce no more than 30 minutes. Refrigerate while marinating.

Grill the salmon on aluminum foil over coals just until done. Baste with marinating sauce while grilling. Place a rosemary bough on the grill for added taste.

MAKES 1¼ CUPS OF MARINADE.

8505 Galloway Road
Cloverdale, Oregon 97112
(503) 965-6745

The innkeepers of this inn make it clear that Sandlake is for "lovers of privacy" and "lovers of nature." It's tucked into a quiet cove on Oregon's Pacific coast just south of Cape Lookout State Park. The inn, listed on the Oregon historic registry, was constructed as a farmhouse in 1894 from fir timbers salvaged from a shipwreck.

Sandlake Country Inn Cookies

- 2 cups butter
- 3 cups firmly packed light brown sugar
- 2 eggs
- 4 cups all-purpose flour
- 2 teaspoons baking soda

Sandlake Country Inn

- 1 tablespoon ground cinnamon
- 2 teaspoons ground ginger
- 1 teaspoon salt
- 2 teaspoons vanilla extract
- 2 cups chopped walnuts
- 3 cups chocolate chips
     Confectioners' sugar

In a large bowl cream the butter and brown sugar. Beat in the eggs.

In a separate bowl combine the flour, soda, cinnamon, ginger, and salt. Add this mixture slowly to the butter mixture. Add the vanilla and blend all well. Add the nuts and chocolate chips. Store covered in the refrigerator, baking as needed.

It is best to refrigerate the cookie dough before the first batch of baking. To bake, form the dough into 1-inch balls, roll in confectioners' sugar, and place on an ungreased cookie sheet. Bake in a 375° oven for 10 minutes. Cookies will be soft.

Cool a little, then remove from the cookie sheet.

MAKES 12 DOZEN.

Hot Spiced Cider

- 2 quarts apple cider
- ¼ cup firmly packed dark brown sugar
- ½ teaspoon ground allspice
- 1½ teaspoons whole cloves
- 2 cinnamon sticks
- ¼ cup orange juice concentrate

In a crock pot combine all of the ingredients. Cover and simmer on low for 2 to 4 hours. Strain before serving hot.

MAKES 8 SERVINGS.

Baked Apple Oatmeal

- 4 cups old-fashioned oats
- 2⅔ cups nonfat dry milk
- 3¾ cups firmly packed brown sugar
- 2 tablespoons ground cinnamon
- 1 teaspoon salt
- 2 cups chopped walnuts
- 2 cups raisins
- 2 tablespoons butter
- 2 cups apples, peeled and chopped
- 4 cups boiling water

In a large bowl combine dry the ingredients, walnuts, and raisins. Fold in the butter, apples, and boiling water. Pour into a 4-quart baking dish. Bake uncovered in a

350° oven for 30 minutes. Serve hot with milk.

MAKES 8 SERVINGS.

Buttery Raisin Scones with Walnuts

- 2 cups all-purpose flour
- 2 teaspoons baking powder
- ⅔ cup sugar
- ⅓ cup butter
- ½ cup raisins
- ¼ cup chopped walnuts
- 2 eggs
- ½ cup sour cream
- 1 teaspoon vanilla extract
- 1 teaspoon sugar

In a large bowl beat together the flour, baking powder, sugar, and butter until the mixture resembles coarse meal. Mix in the raisins and walnuts. In a separate bowl beat together the eggs, sour cream, and vanilla until blended, then add all at once to the flour mixture. Beat until blended. Do not overbeat. Spread the batter (it will be very thick) into a greased 10-inch springform pan and sprinkle the top with 1 teaspoon of sugar. Bake in a 350° oven for 25 to 30 minutes or until the top is browned and a cake tester inserted in the center comes out clean. Allow to cool, then cut into 8 wedges.

MAKES 8 SERVINGS.

240 East California Street
Jacksonville, Oregon 97530
(800) 367-1942

This inn, constructed originally as a house in 1861, was one of the six original dwellings in the gold rush town of Jacksonville. It is listed on the National Register of Historic Places. Guests are greeted by eighty-five different kinds of of roses that line the white picket fence in front of the inn. Special features include antiques, polished hardwood floors, lace curtains, and oriental rugs.

Yellow Tomato and Sage Soup with Chanterelle Mushrooms

⅓ cup olive oil
1 each carrot, peeled and diced
3 stalks celery, diced
1 jalapeño, seeded and minced
1 leek (white part only), diced
3 cloves garlic, minced
3 pounds yellow tomatoes, cored and sliced
1 tablespoon black pepper
½ teaspoon cumin
1 chipotle chile (dried smoked jalapeño)
2 tablespoons chopped fresh sage leaves
1½ teaspoons sea salt
¼ pound chanterelle mushrooms, sliced thin
Fresh sage leaves for garnish

In a saucepan heat ¼ cup of oil and sauté the carrots, celery, jalapeño, leek, and garlic for 5 minutes, stirring occasionally. Add the yellow tomatoes, black pepper, cumin, and chipotle chile. Reduce the heat to medium and cook until slightly thickened. Strain the soup through a colander or run through a food mill to remove the tomato skins and seeds. Add the chopped sage and salt. Keep the soup warm. In a sauté pan heat the remaining oil and cook the chanterelles until tender, stirring occasionally. Drain any excess oil from the mushrooms and discard. Add the cooked mushrooms to the soup. Ladle the soup into bowls and garnish with sage leaves.

MAKES 6 SERVINGS.

Wild Mushroom and Spinach Frittata

½ cup butter
1 cup coarse breadcrumbs
1 small yellow onion, chopped
1 cup sliced wild mushrooms, ¼ inch thick (shiitake, chanterelle, crimini, etc.)
¾ cup fresh spinach, cooked, stems removed

McCully House Inn

10 eggs, lightly beaten
2 teaspoons finely chopped fresh sage (or 1 teaspoon dried sage)
Salt and pepper to taste
1 cup grated Swiss or Monterey Jack cheese

In a 10-inch ovenproof skillet or sauté pan melt 2 tablespoons of butter over medium heat. Stir in the breadcrumbs and cook, stirring often, until they have absorbed the butter and are golden. Remove from the heat and set the crumbs aside. Clean the skillet

In a separate small sauté pan melt 2 tablespoons of butter over medium heat and sauté the onion until translucent. Add the wild mushrooms and cook briefly until tender. Remove from the heat and set aside.

In the clean skillet melt the remaining butter over low heat. Stir the cooked spinach into the beaten eggs and pour into the skillet. Add the sautéed onions and mushrooms and stir to distribute evenly. Add the sage. Season with salt and pepper. Cook without stirring for 2 to 3 minutes (it is important not to overcook), until the bottom has just begun to set. Tilt the skillet just a little to check. Put the skillet in a 350° oven and bake for 3 minutes. Sprinkle the cheese and the breadcrumbs evenly over the top. Bake 2 more minutes and remove from the oven. Loosen the edges and slide the frittata onto a large serving plate. Cut into wedges and serve.

MAKES 5 SERVINGS.

Chilled Peach Soup

1 cup water
½ cup sugar
¾ cup peach schnapps
3 pounds peaches, peeled and sliced
½ cup heavy cream
½ cup rum
¼ cup chopped basil leaves

In saucepan bring the water, sugar, and schnapps to a boil, stirring until the sugar is dissolved. Remove from the heat and add the peaches. Purée. Let the mixture cool and stir in the cream and rum. Chill. Garnish with basil.

MAKES 4 SERVINGS.

Sautéed Halibut with Honeydew-Hazelnut Compote and Vanilla Citrus Butter Sauce

¼ honeydew melon, diced small
1 tablespoon cilantro, minced
½ cup diced red onion
1 jalapeño, minced
½ cup hazelnuts, toasted and finely chopped
1 tablespoon sugar
1½ tablespoons lime juice
1½ tablespoons champagne vinegar
2 tablespoons hazelnut oil
1 teaspoon oriental fish sauce
....
½ vanilla bean, split lengthwise
½ cup Chardonnay
2 tablespoons orange juice
1 tablespoon lime juice
1 shallot, minced
8 whole black peppercorns
1 bay leaf
2 tablespoons heavy cream
⅓ pound unsalted butter, chilled and cubed small
....
4 halibut fillets
2 tablespoons olive oil
Salt and pepper to taste
Lemon, lime, and orange wedges for garnish

In a medium bowl combine the honeydew melon, cilantro, onion, jalapeño, hazelnuts, sugar, lime juice, vinegar, hazelnut oil, and fish sauce. Mix well and chill.

In a small heavy-bottomed saucepan combine the vanilla bean, wine, citrus juices, shallot, pepper, and bay leaf. Reduce the mixture over high heat until syrupy. Add the cream and reduce by half.

Turn down the heat to medium and quickly whisk in the butter one piece at a time until incorporated. Remove from the heat and strain. Keep warm.

Brush the halibut with olive oil and season with salt and pepper to taste. Grill the halibut to the desired doneness.

Spoon the butter sauce onto 4 plates. Top the sauce with halibut. Mound the compote over the fish. Garnish with lemon, lime, and orange wedges around the plate border and serve.

MAKES 4 SERVINGS.

Touvelle House

455 North Oregon Street, P.O. Box 1891
Jacksonville, Oregon 97530
(800) 846-8422

---

*T**he Touvelle House is a classic example of the Craftsman style of architecture, featuring broad over-hanging eaves, tapered porch posts, and shingled exterior walls. Inside the house, guests are impressed with the wood paneling, square-beamed ceilings, and built-in cabi-netry. Common areas throughout the inn—the great room, library, sunroom, and dining room—invite guests to relax and unwind. Nearby tourist attractions are the down-town Jacksonville historic district, Crater Lake, the Oregon caves, and white water rafting on the Rogue River.*

Breakfast Burst

1   *12-ounce can orange juice concen-trate*
3   *cups skim milk*
1   *banana (really ripe)*
¼   *cup vanilla extract*
½   *cup confectioners' sugar*
1½ *teaspoons ground cinnamon*
1   *cup cut-up fruit (peaches, pineapple, strawberries, pears, etc.)*

In a blender combine all of the ingredients and blend for 1 minute. May be kept for 4 days in the refrigerator, but make sure to blend before serving.

MAKES 8 TO 10 SERVINGS.

Spinach Soufflés (Vegetarian)

      French bread
1   *tablespoon Dijon mustard*
1   *10-ounce box frozen spinach, thawed*
4½ *teaspoons basil*
1   *tablespoon garlic powder*
1   *tablespoon lemon pepper*
1   *5-ounce can black olives*
2   *cups feta cheese*
2   *cups shredded Swiss cheese*
14 *eggs*
1½ *cups milk*
      Dash paprika

Spray an 8 x 11-inch baking dish with cook-ing spray. Cut up ¼-inch cubes of French bread and spread on bottom (just barely cover, not too thick). Dab Dijon mustard on the bread cubes, distributing evenly. Squeeze the water from the frozen spinach, and arrange the spinach over the bread. Sprinkle with basil, garlic powder, and lemon pepper. Slice the olives and arrange on the spinach. Crumble feta cheese over the olives. Spread Swiss cheese over the feta. In a large bowl beat the eggs and milk until mixed, and pour over the casserole. Sprinkle generously with paprika. Cover with foil and refrigerate overnight.

Bake covered with foil in a 375° oven for 30 minutes. Remove the foil and bake for 1 hour and 15 minutes.

MAKES 8 TO 10 SERVINGS.

Portland Guest House

1720 Northeast Fifteenth Avenue
Portland, Oregon 97212
(503) 282-1402

---

*B**uilt in 1890, the Portland Guest House is ideally situated for guests who want to take in all the sights and scenes of the Rose City. Many shops, restaurants, theaters, and restaurants are an easy walk from the Guest House. Attractions within an easy drive of Portland and the inn include Mount Hood, Mount St. Helens, and the beautiful beaches of Oregon's Pacific coast.*

Breakfast Cake

3   *cups all-purpose flour*
2   *cups sugar*
¾   *cup shortening*
2   *eggs*
1   *generous cup buttermilk*
1   *teaspoon baking soda*

In a large bowl mix the flour and sugar. Cut in the shortening. Remove 1 scant cup of crumbs and set aside. To the remaining mix-ture add the eggs and buttermilk with soda

Portland Guest House

added to it. Beat very well. Pour into a greased 9 x 13-inch baking pan or 2 pie plates. Sprinkle the reserved crumbs on top. Bake in a 350° oven for 35 minutes.

MAKES 8 TO 12 SERVINGS.

Swiss Bircher Muesli

1⅓ **cups regular rolled oats**
1⅓ **cups milk**
  2 **tablespoons currants, golden raisins, or chopped dry fruit**
 ¼ **teaspoon salt**
 ½ **cup chopped, toasted blanched almonds**
 ¼ **cup honey**
  2 **unpeeled tart apples, shredded**
  3 **tablespoons lemon juice**

In a medium bowl soak the rolled oats overnight in milk. Add the remaining ingredients just before serving.

Note: Garnish with apple slices and nuts. Serve with brown sugar, milk, or fruit. Fresh tasting and healthy.

MAKES 4 SERVINGS.

Gilbert Inn
❧

341 Beach Drive
Seaside, Oregon 97138
(800) 410-9770 for reservations

*A*lthough it has undergone some modernization and restoration, this inn still looks much as it did when built by Alexander Gilbert in 1892. Guest-pleasing features include the huge fireplace in the parlor and the tongue-and-groove ceilings and walls crafted from natural fir. It is decorated throughout with antiques and colorful French-print furniture. Just one block from the ocean, Gilbert Inn is within easy walking distance of Seaside's fine shops and restaurants.

Muffin-Cheese Bake

  6 **halved English muffins**
12 **frozen precooked link sausages (any flavor)**
  8 **eggs**
  4 **cups milk**
     Salt and pepper to taste
     Grated cheese (Monterey Jack or Oregon's own Tillamook Cheddar)

Spray an 11x14-inch casserole with cooking spray. Lay English muffins in the prepared casserole. Top with sausages. In a medium bowl mix the eggs, milk, salt, and pepper. Pour over the casserole. Top with grated cheese. Cover and refrigerate overnight.

Bake uncovered in a 350° oven for 45 to 50 minutes, or until browned lightly. Let set a few minutes.

MAKES 6 SERVINGS.

Gilbert Inn

PENNSYLVANIA

Churchtown Inn

2100 Main Street
Churchtown, Pennsylvania 17555
(717) 445-7794

*L*isted on the National Register of Historic Places, Churchtown Inn is a restored eighteenth-century field-stone mansion in the heart of Pennsylvania Dutch country. The leaded-glass front entrance door opens into a huge living room with a crystal chandelier. Guest rooms, some with canopy beds, are furnished with period antiques. The glass-enclosed garden room overlooks the rolling farmlands of the Amish people who live nearby. Tours of local Amish farms and communities are available. Guests may arrange with the innkeepers to have dinner at a private Amish or Mennonite home.

Granola-Oatmeal Pancakes

2 cups milk

1 cup granola
1 cup old-fashioned rolled oats
½ cup butter, melted and cooled
½ cup all-purpose flour
2 eggs, slightly beaten
2 tablespoons sugar
2 teaspoons baking powder
¼ teaspoon grated nutmeg
¼ teaspoon ground cinnamon
¼ teaspoon salt

In a large bowl combine the milk, granola, and rolled oats. Cover and refrigerate overnight.

The next morning, in a separate bowl combine the remaining ingredients. Gradually add the dry ingredients to the granola mixture. Stir until smooth. Preheat a griddle. Spoon onto a hot buttered griddle and cook until bubbles appear. Turn over and cook until done.

MAKES 6 SERVINGS.

Churchtown Inn

Stu's Creamy Scrambled Eggs

4 tablespoons butter, divided
2 tablespoons all-purpose flour

1 cup sour cream
24 eggs
¾ teaspoon salt
⅛ teaspoon pepper
   Chopped parsley
1 cup shredded Cheddar cheese
1 cup sliced ripe olives or green onions
1 cup crisp bacon bits
1 cup chopped shrimp
1 cup sour cream

In a saucepan melt 2 tablespoons of butter. Stir in the flour and cook until bubbly. Remove from the heat and blend in 1 cup of sour cream. Return to the heat until bubbly and smooth, then set aside. In a bowl beat together the eggs, salt, and pepper.

In a wide frying pan over medium-low heat melt the remaining 2 tablespoons butter. Pour in the eggs, and cook gently, lifting the cooked portion to allow the uncooked egg to flow underneath, until the eggs are softly set. Remove from the heat and gently stir in the sour cream mixture. Keep warm in a serving dish until needed.

Garnish with parsley and serve with the remaining ingredient as condiments.

MAKES 12 SERVINGS.

Cream Cheese Scrambled Eggs in Toast Cups

1 3-ounce package cream cheese, softened
¼ cup milk
4 to 6 eggs

1 teaspoon chopped chives, plus extra
    for garnish
1 teaspoon salt
2 tablespoons butter
4 slices bread, crusts removed and
    buttered

In a bowl beat the cream cheese until smooth. Gradually add the milk. Add the eggs, chives, and salt and beat with a fork or whisk until foamy. In a frying pan melt the butter. When sizzling, pour in the egg mixture. Cook over medium heat, stirring and moving the eggs from center and from the sides, until the eggs are thick and creamy.

Butter both sides of the bread. Push the bread into lightly greased muffin cups so that corners form points. Bake in a 350° oven until golden brown. Toast cups can be made ahead and reheated just before serving. Serve the eggs in the toast cups and sprinkle with more chives.

MAKES 4 SERVINGS.

Wake-Up Parfaits

3 tablespoons orange juice
2 cups fresh blackberries, raspberries,
    or blueberries
2 cups sliced bananas or peaches
1 cup homemade granola
1 cup vanilla yogurt
    Mint sprigs and edible flower blos-
    soms for garnish

In a large bowl combine the juice and fruit. In 6 wine goblets layer half the fruit, half the granola, and half the yogurt. Repeat the layers. Garnish with a sprig of fresh mint and an edible flower, such as johnny-jump-up or nasturtium. Chill until served.

MAKES 6 SERVINGS.

The Inn at Twin Linden

The Inn at Twin Linden

2092 Main Street
Churchtown, Pennsylvania 17555
(717) 445-7619

Fresh flowers in the guest rooms are a guest-pleasing amenity at this unique inn in an 1800s Lancaster County estate house. The stenciled walls and oak and antique furnishings throughout recapture the mood of the past. Guests enjoy the unique brick courtyard surrounded by a two-acre garden. Another nice touch, although thoroughly modern, is the outdoor Jacuzzi. Activities include touring the Amish farms and craft shops in the area, antique shopping, golf, tennis, and swimming.

Napoleon with Proscuitto, Chevre, and Roasted Peppers

6 roasted red bell peppers, seeded and
    sliced in half lengthwise
3 tablespoons tomato purée
1 egg
1 tablespoon water
1 to 2 sheets puff pastry
6 thin slices of prosciutto, sliced in
    half lengthwise
2/3 cup crumbled chèvre (goat cheese)
2 tablespoons fresh chopped basil

In a food processor or blender combine 6 roasted red peppers halves with the tomato purée. Process until smooth and set aside. In a cup whisk together the egg and water. Cut 6 2 x 4½-inch rectangles from the puff pastry sheets and place them on a lightly greased baking sheet. Brush the egg wash onto the tops of each rectangle. Bake in a 375° oven for 12 to 15 minutes, until puffed and golden brown. Allow to cool slightly.

Cut each rectangle in half, creating a top and bottom. Layer each bottom rectangle with 1 slice of proscuitto, crumbled goat cheese, 1 slice of roasted pepper, and another slice of prosciutto. Replace the top rectangles and place the Napoleons on a lightly greased baking sheet. Bake in a 375° oven for 8 to 10 minutes, until heated through.

In a small saucepan heat the puréed sauce until just warm. Remove the sauce from heat and stir in the basil. Divide the sauce among individual plates and set a Napoleon on each plate to serve.

MAKES 6 SERVINGS.

Lobster Corn Fricassee with Fettuccini and Chives

3/4 cup butter
2 tablespoons chopped shallots
2 cups uncooked Maine lobster meat
    in 1- to 2-inch chunks
1 tablespoon all-purpose flour
2 tablespoons lemon juice
1/2 cup dry white wine
1 cup fish stock
1 cup cooked fresh white corn
2 tablespoons fresh chopped tarragon
2 tablespoons fresh chopped chives,
    plus extra for garnish
1½ cups fresh fettuccini, cooked al
    dente and reserved

In a large saucepan melt ¼ cup of butter over moderately high heat. Reduce the heat and sauté the shallots until softened, about 3 minutes. Add the lobster meat and just cook through, 1 to 2 minutes. Sprinkle on flour and lemon juice and stir briskly. Stir in the white wine and reduce slightly, 1 to 2 minutes. Add the stock and reduce again slightly, 1 to 2 minutes. Whisk in the remaining ½ of cup butter in bits until creamy and just melted. Remove from the heat and stir in the corn and tarragon. Refresh the fettuccini briefly in boiling water if necessary and divide among 6 plates. Spoon the fricassee over the pasta and sprinkle with fresh chives.

MAKES 6 SERVINGS.

Cappuccino Crunch Pie

1 cup all-purpose flour
1/4 cup firmly packed dark brown sugar
5 tablespoons cold butter, in bits

3 tablespoons finely chopped bittersweet chocolate
½   cup chopped walnuts
1   teaspoon vanilla extract
2   teaspoons water

· ·

½   cup softened butter
1   cup firmly packed brown sugar
3   teaspoons instant coffee
1   teaspoon vanilla extract
3   ounces bittersweet chocolate,
  melted
4   eggs

· ·

2   cups heavy cream
⅓   cup confectioners' sugar
  Chocolate curls for garnish

In a medium bowl combine the flour and ¼ cup of brown sugar. With a pastry blender or in a food processor, cut in 5 tablespoons of butter until the mixture is crumbly. Stir in the 3 tablespoons of chocolate and the nuts. Mix in the vanilla and water until it just combines. With floured hands, press the mixture into a 9-inch springform pan. Bake in a 350° oven for 20 minutes. Cool completely.

In a medium bowl combine ½ cup of butter and 1 cup of brown sugar with an electric mixer, until fluffy. Add the coffee and vanilla and beat until smooth. Add 3 ounces of melted chocolate and beat until combined. Add the eggs one at a time, beating for 3 minutes after each addition. Spread the mixture into the crust. Chill at least 3 hours.

Up to 1 hour before serving, in a large bowl whip together the cream and the confectioners' sugar until stiff. Spread or pour the whipped cream onto the filling layer. Garnish with chocolate curls. Keep refrigerated until ready to serve.

MAKES 8 TO 10 SERVINGS.

R.D. 2, Box 202-A
Clearville, Pennsylvania 15535
(814) 784-3342

*T**his inn appeals to guests who are looking for a rustic hideaway in the*

country. Situated on a 126-acre farm, it allows guests enjoy fishing, swimming, or boating on the lake, watching the wildlife, exploring the one-hundred-year-old barn with its antique farm implements, and admiring the flower and herb garden. The guest house, with its old brick interior walls and ancient oak beams, is furnished with antiques to establish a pleasing country atmosphere. Guests who want the ultimate in privacy and country living may spend the night in a cozy cabin in the woods, converted from a grain storage barn.

Lemon Yogurt Bread

3   cups all-purpose flour
1   teaspoon salt
1   teaspoon baking soda
½   teaspoon baking powder
1   cup finely chopped almonds
3   eggs
1   cup oil
1¾   cups sugar
2   cups lemon yogurt
1   tablespoon lemon extract

In a medium bowl sift the dry ingredients. Add the nuts. In a separate bowl beat the eggs. Add the oil and sugar and beat well. Add the yogurt and lemon extract. Blend in the dry ingredients. Pour into 2 loaf pans or a bundt pan. Bake in a 350° oven for 1 hour.

MAKES 2 LOAVES.

Hot Cranberry Spice Punch

1   gallon cranberry cocktail
½   gallon apple juice
1   12-ounce can lemonade concentrate
4½   cups water
2   cups pineapple juice
  Lemon slices for garnish
  Spice bag made of whole nutmeg,
  cinnamon, allspice, cloves

In a large pan bring the juices and water to a boil. Add the spice bag and simmer for 3 to 4 minutes. Remove the bag. Press 2 or 3 cloves

into lemon slices for garnish. Serve from a pot or ceramic bowl.

MAKES 36 SERVINGS.

Chicken Casserole

3   cups chicken, cooked and diced
8   ounces raw macaroni
2   10½-ounce cans cream of mushroom soup
2   cups milk
2   cups grated sharp Cheddar cheese
1   1-ounce jar pimentos, chopped
¼   cup chopped green bell peppers
1   tablespoon chopped onion
1   teaspoon salt
1   teaspoon dried rosemary (2 teaspoons fresh)

In a large bowl mix all of the ingredients and refrigerate overnight. Pour into a 2-quart casserole. Bake in a 350° oven for 1 hour and 15 minutes to 1 hour and 30 minutes, or until brown.

Note: Serve with herb bread and tossed salad.

MAKES 6 SERVINGS.

P.O. Box 356
Eagles Mere, Pennsylvania 17731-0356
(800) 426-3273 for reservations

*T**his inn has been welcoming guests for more than one hundred years. It was built as an inn in 1878 to serve the craftsmen and carpenters who were building resort homes for wealthy Pennsylvanians in the mountain village of Eagles Mere. The daily room rate includes a five-course gourmet dinner as well as a full country breakfast. The common areas include a pub as well as a dining room and living room. Golf and tennis are available at the* *nearby Eagles Mere Country Club. Guests also enjoy fishing, boating, or swimming in Eagles Mere Lake.*

Eagles Mere Inn

Roquefort Soup

6 tablespoons butter
6 cups medium chopped cabbage
4½ cups medium-chopped cauliflower
4½ cups chicken broth
....
1½ cups heavy cream
1½ ounces Roquefort cheese, crumbled
    Pumpernickel or whole wheat crou-
    tons for garnish
    Chopped fresh parsley

In a stockpot melt the butter over low heat and sauté the cabbage until soft. Add the cauliflower and chicken broth, and bring to a boil. Reduce the heat to a simmer. Cover and cook for 30 minutes, until the cauliflower is soft.

Stir in the cream and Roquefort cheese. Blend in completely and heat to 180°.

In a blender purée the soup solids into a smooth pottage. Ladle into bowls and garnish with pumpernickel or whole wheat croutons spread with a dollop of Roquefort. Sprinkle with chopped fresh parsley.

MAKES 20 6-OUNCE SERVINGS.

Wild Rice Pancake

¼ cup butter
1 cup finely diced onion
¼ cup finely diced carrot
2 cups wild rice
5 cups hot chicken broth
....
¼ cup finely minced shallots
¼ cup finely minced scallions

1⅓ cups cooked wild rice
4 eggs, beaten well
⅔ cup heavy cream or crème fraîche
2⅔ cups well-cooked wild rice
    Crème fraîche with chopped fresh
    herbs for garnish

Melt the butter over medium-low heat and sauté the onion and carrot until cooked completely but not brown. Then add the rice and toss with the vegetables. Then add the hot chicken broth and cook until all the grains are open and partly fluffy.

In a blender purée the shallots, scallions, and 1⅓ cups of cooked wild rice. Add and combine the well-beaten eggs and cream. Add the well-cooked wild rice and toss together to coat the rice.

Cook on a hot greased griddle. Garnish with a dollop of crème fraîche combined with chopped fresh herbs.

MAKES 4 SERVINGS.

Crab Outer Banks

1 cup mayonnaise
2 eggs, beaten
2 tablespoons prepared mustard
½ teaspoon Worcestershire sauce
¼ heaping teaspoon sweet paprika
1 teaspoon thyme
½ teaspoon white pepper
2 cups medium-diced celery
1½ cups medium-diced scallions, mostly
    whites
2 pounds blue crab, lump backfin
    meat
⅔ cup breadcrumbs
¾ cup fine dry breadcrumbs
    Melted butter
1 8-ounce jar sauce (beurre blanc,
    Nantau, or other)
12 cooked shrimp or edible flowers
2 tablespoons capers
¼ cup finely sliced scallion greens
12 lemon wraps or crowns

In a large bowl combine the mayonnaise, eggs, mustard, Worcestershire sauce, paprika, thyme, and pepper. Combine completely with a whisk, then sprinkle celery, scallions, crab, and breadcrumbs over. Gently fold together.

Grease 12 individual baking dishes with softened butter. Sprinkle 1½ teaspoons of fine, dry breadcrumbs over the bottom of

each baking dish. Portion the crab mixture evenly into center of the baking dishes, ½-inch away from the sides. Cover the dishes with plastic wrap and refrigerate until ready to cook.

Remove the plastic wrap and sprinkle each with 1½ teaspoons of breadcrumbs and melted butter. Bake in a 350° oven for 9 to 10 minutes. Remove from the oven and place baking dishes on plates. Spoon 1½ ounces of sauce between each crab mound and the side of the dish. Garnish each crab mound with 1 shrimp, ½ teaspoon of capers, and 1 teaspoon of scallion greens. Place 1 lemon wrap or crown on each plate. Add vegetables to each plate.

MAKES 12 SERVINGS.

West Indian Rum Beef Stew

12 cups coarsely chopped onions
2½ bay leaves
6   pounds prime rib cubes, ¾-inch,
     trimmed of fat and gristle
2   tablespoons fresh pressed garlic
1   tablespoon fresh ground black pep-
     per
3   tablespoons sugar
3   green bell peppers, cut julienne
     (¼ x 2 inches)
3   red bell peppers, cut into julienne
     (¼ x 2 inches)
3   yellow bell peppers, cut into juli-
     enne (¼ x 2 inches)
6   fresh tomatoes, coarsely chopped
3   cups water
1   cup tomato paste
1   tablespoon Tabasco sauce
1   tablespoon Vietnamese sauce
1   cup stuffed olives
¾   cup Meyer's dark rum
     Chopped parsley

In a stockpot mix the onions, bay leaves, beef, garlic, pepper, sugar, peppers, and tomatoes. In a medium bowl mix the water, tomato paste, Tabasco, and Vietnamese sauce. Pour the mixture into the vegetable mixture, and cover. Bake in a 325° oven.

Just before serving or storing mix in the olives and rum.

Garnish with chopped parsley.

MAKES 18 SERVINGS.

Cold Apple and Orange Soup

3 tablespoons fresh lemon juice
6 cups apple juice
2 tablespoons sugar
3 cinnamon sticks
12 apples (Rome, Cortland, or Winesap) pared and sliced
....
1½ teaspoons vanilla extract
....
4½ cups orange juice
6 cups half and half
Apple slices
Fresh parsley

In a large cooking pot combine the lemon juice, apple juice, sugar, and cinnamon sticks. Add the pared, sliced apples. Place over medium heat and cook, covered, until the apples are tender. Remove from the heat. Remove the cinnamon sticks and then add the vanilla.

Place in a food processor and process into a purée. Then add the orange juice and half and half. Immediately chill.

Garnish with thin, unpeeled apple slices dipped in lemon juice, and tiny parsley leaves.

MAKES 30 SERVINGS.

Shady Lane

Allegheny Avenue
Eagles Mere, Pennsylvania 17731
(800) 524-1248 for reservations

This seven-guestroom inn is situated on a mountaintop in a quaint Victorian village that has been called "the town time forgot." Eagles Mere blossomed as a resort community more than one hundred years ago, and it still radiates the atmosphere of a turn-of-the-century small-town resort. There is much to do here, including boating, fishing, golf, swimming, tennis, skiing, hiking, and exploring the two rugged and mountainous state parks in the area—World's End and Rickets Glen. Unusual shops and restaurants are also plentiful in Eagles Mere.

Italian Eggs in Tomatoes

4 large ripe tomatoes
Salt and fresh ground pepper
¼ cup diced onion
1 tablespoon chopped garlic
¼ cup chopped fresh basil
2 tablespoons olive oil
4 large eggs
¼ cup grated Parmesan cheese
Parsley for garnish

Cut off a small slice from the top of the tomatoes and core tomatoes. Scoop out the pulp and reserve. Sprinkle the inside with salt and pepper. Turn upside down to drain.

In a bowl chop the reserved pulp and add onion, garlic, basil, olive oil, salt, and pepper. Scatter the mixture evenly over the bottom of a baking dish large enough to hold the tomatoes snugly. Place the tomatoes right-side up and break an egg inside each one. Sprinkle with salt, pepper, and Parmesan cheese.

Bake in a 425° oven for 20 minutes. Do not let the yolks become too firm. Garnish with parsley.

MAKES 4 SERVINGS.

Old-Fashioned Apple Cake

4 to 5 apples, peeled and chopped
2 cups sugar
¾ cup oil
½ teaspoon baking soda
1 teaspoon vanilla extract
2 eggs
2 cups all-purpose flour
1 teaspoon ground cinnamon
....
½ cup firmly packed dark brown sugar
3 tablespoons butter, softened
1 tablespoon flour
Confectioners' sugar for dusting

In a large bowl combine the apples, sugar, and oil. Add the soda, vanilla, eggs, flour, and cinnamon and mix. Grease a 9 x 13-inch baking pan and pour in the batter.

In a small bowl combine the brown sugar, butter, and flour. Mix and sprinkle over the batter. Bake in a 350° oven for 40 minutes.

Sprinkle with confectioners' sugar before serving.

MAKES 12 SERVINGS.

Coconut-Walnut Cake

1 18¼-ounce package yellow cake mix
1 3-ounce package vanilla instant pudding
4 eggs
¼ cup oil
1⅓ cups water
1 teaspoon vanilla extract
1¼ cups shredded coconut
1 cup chopped walnuts
Confectioners' sugar for dusting

In a large bowl mix the cake mix, instant pudding, eggs, oil, water, and vanilla. Mix well. Add the coconut and walnuts. Grease and flour a tube pan and pour in the batter. Bake in a 325° oven for 1 hour.

Sprinkle with confectioners' sugar before serving.

MAKES 12 SERVINGS.

Bechtel Mansion Inn

400 West King Street
East Berlin, Pennsylvania 17316
(800) 331-1108

Bechtel Mansion Inn

*B*rass chandeliers abound in this Queen Anne-style Victorian inn; they hang in the living room, the parlor, and even in one of the nine guest rooms. Other notable features are the original Brussels carpet and wallpaper in the parlor and the vertical oak and cherry shutters in the parlor and living room. The downstairs area also has a central hallway with huge double doors of etched glass. All the guest rooms are furnished with period antiques. Listed on the National Register of Historic Places (built in 1897), this inn is in Pennsylvania Dutch Country. Golf, tennis, swimming, and skiing are available nearby.

Pennsylvania Dutch Crumb Coffee Cake

- 4 *cups unsifted all-purpose flour*
- 1 *teaspoon baking powder*
- 2/3 *cup shortening*
- 1/2 *teaspoon salt*
- 2 1/2 *cups sugar*
- 2 *eggs, beaten*
- 1 1/2 *cups buttermilk*
- 1 *teaspoon baking soda*
- 1 *cup firmly packed brown sugar*
- 1/2 *cup coconut*
- 1 *teaspoon ground cinnamon*

In a large bowl blend the flour, baking powder, shortening, salt, and sugar. Reserve 1 cup of this mixture as a crumb topping for use later.

In a separate bowl mix the eggs, buttermilk, and soda together. Then blend in the remaining portion of the original dry mixture, stirring thoroughly. There will be some small lumps in the batter. Add the brown sugar, the coconut, and cinnamon to the cup of original crumb topping mixture set aside earlier. Pour the coffee cake batter mixture into 3 greased and floured 8-inch squarecake pans. Sprinkle the topping equally on top of batter in all 3 pans. Bake in a 350° oven for 35 minutes.
MAKES 12 SERVINGS.

Black Forest Coffee Cake

- 3 *eggs*
- 1 1/2 *cups sugar*
- 1/2 *cup shortening, melted*
- 1 1/2 *cups milk*
- 2 *tablespoons vanilla extract*
- 3 *cups all-purpose flour*
- 2 *teaspoons baking powder*
- 1 *cup semisweet chocolate chips*
- 1 *21-ounce can cherry pie filling*

....

- 1 *cup baking mix*
- 1/2 *cup sugar*
- 1/4 *cup butter or margarine*
- 1/2 *cup semisweet chocolate chips for garnish*

In a bowl beat the eggs; add the 1 1/2 cups of sugar, shortening, milk, and vanilla. Then add flour and baking powder. When well-mixed add 1 cup of chocolate chips. Pour into a greased 9 x 13-inch baking pan. Drop the cherry pie filling by the teaspoons in even rows into the batter.

In a small bowl combine the baking mix, 1/2 cup of sugar, and butter with a pastry blender to form loose crumbs. Sprinkle over the top of the batter. Garnish with chocolate chips. Bake in a 375° oven for 50 minutes to 1 hour, until golden brown.
MAKES 8 SERVINGS.

The Inn at Meadowbrook

R.D. 7, Box 7651
Cherry Lane Road
East Stroudsburg, Pennsylvania 18301
(800) 249-6861

*T*his inn offers sixteen guest rooms in a quiet country setting in the Pocono Mountains. The manor house, built in 1842, has large bedrooms with private bathrooms, as well as some bedrooms with bath-sharing privileges. Rooms are also available in the adjoining mill house. Nearby activities include cross-country skiing, ice skating, tennis, fishing, and swimming.

Cranberry Breakfast Casserole

- 2 *Granny Smith apples, thinly sliced with the skin on*
- 24 *ounces fresh cranberries*
- 1/2 *cup all-purpose flour*
- 1 *cup sugar*

....

- 1/2 *cup butter, melted*
- 1/2 *cup firmly packed brown sugar*
- 1/2 *cup chopped pecans*
- 1 *cup instant oatmeal*

Grease a 9 x 13-inch baking pan. In a large bowl mix the apples, cranberries, flour, and sugar together and pour into the prepared pan. In a separate bowl combine the butter, brown sugar, pecans, and oatmeal. Cover the apple-cranberry mixture with topping. Bake in a 350° oven for 45 minutes.
MAKES 8 SERVINGS.

Sour Cream Pancakes

- 4 *eggs*
- 1/2 *teaspoon salt*
- 1 *teaspoon baking soda*
- 6 *tablespoons all-purpose flour*
- 2 *tablespoons sugar*
- 2 *cups sour cream*

In a blender combine all of the ingredients in the order listed above. Blend for 30 seconds. Scrape down the sides of the blender with a spatula and blend again. Let sit for 2 or 3 minutes, then pour on a hot griddle in 3- or 4-inch circles. Flip over when bubbles appear on the top and brown the other side.
MAKES 6 SERVINGS.

Strata

- 2 *cups bread cubes*
- 1/2 *cup grated American cheese*
- 1/2 *cup grated Swiss cheese*
- 12 *eggs*
- 1 *cup heavy cream*
- 1 *teaspoon dry mustard*
- 1/2 *pound cooked sausage, crumbled*

In a well-greased 9 x 13-inch baking pan evenly spread the bread cubes. Sprinkle both cheeses over the bread. Blend the eggs, cream, and mustard together. Pour the mixture over the bread and cheese, then sprinkle the sausage over the casserole. Cover with foil and refrigerate overnight. Bake in a 350° oven for 50 minutes.

MAKES 8 SERVINGS.

Chicken and Shrimp Milano

  1 *tablespoon butter*
  1 *slice bacon, finely chopped*
  1 *clove garlic, finely chopped*
  2 *whole skinless, boneless chicken breasts, sliced into 2-inch strips*
  1 *tablespoon lemon juice*
  8 *large shrimp, peeled and deveined*
 ¼ *cup champagne*
 ½ *cup heavy cream*
     Grated Parmesan cheese

In a large pan melt the butter and sauté the bacon and garlic until the garlic is translucent. Do not brown. Add the chicken strips and lemon juice and sauté. Add the shrimp and champagne. Reduce about half of the liquid and add the cream. Sprinkle with Parmesan cheese and serve over pasta.

MAKES 4 SERVINGS.

The Inns at Doneckers

318-324 North State Street
Ephrata, Pennsylvania 17522
(717) 738-9502

*F*our separate inns within a few blocks of one another in this charming town in Lancaster County are actually included in the Inns at Doneckers. The Guesthouse, 318–324 North State Street, has twenty rooms, each individually decorated and named for a prominent person or place in the area. The Gerhart House, 287 Duke Street,

The Inns at Doneckers

with five rooms, features inlaid pine floors and native chestnut doors and trim. The 1777 House, 301 West Main Street, with ten guest rooms and two carriage house suites, features fine antiques and hand-cut stenciling. Careful restoration has retained the original stone masonry, tile flooring, and many other authentic details of this house. The Homestead, 251 North State Street, has four suites and rooms, each with fireplace and/or Jacuzzi.

Carrot Cake with Chervil

  2 *tablespoons butter*
  1 *pound young carrots, scraped and cut into slices less than ¼-inch thick*
  1 *cup chicken stock*
     Artificial sweetener equivalent to ½ teaspoon of sugar (optional)
  1 *teaspoon salt*
     Pinch pepper
  1 *teaspoon olive oil (optional)*
 ¼ *pound mushrooms, rinsed, stems trimmed, and minced*
 ½ *shallot, minced*
    ....
  2 *eggs*
  3 *tablespoons grated Swiss cheese (or Gruyère)*
  2 *tablespoons coarsely chopped fresh chervil or parsley*
  1 *teaspoon soft butter*
     Sprigs of fresh chervil or parsley Asparagus or artichoke purée)

In a saucepan heat 2 tablespoon of butter. Add the carrots, and allow to color lightly without becoming soft. Then add the chicken stock, artificial sweetener, salt, and pepper.

Simmer the carrots, covered, for 5 minutes, then uncover and cook over moderate heat for 15 minutes. The liquid should be evaporated but the carrots should not be dry.

Meanwhile, in a nonstick skillet, or a skillet greased with 1 teaspoon of olive oil, sauté the minced mushrooms and shallot.

Remove the carrots to a chopping board, and chop them coarsely with a knife. In a medium bowl beat the eggs lightly with a fork. Add the carrots, mushrooms, Swiss cheese, and chervil, and mix together gently.

With a pastry brush, very lightly butter a 1-quart mold and put in the carrot mixture. Cover the mold with the aluminum foil. Place in a pan of hot water. Bake in a 425° oven for 25 to 30 minutes, or until the carrots are completely set. Unmold it onto a platter and pour sauce in a ribbon around it. Decorate the center with the sprigs of chervil.

MAKES 4 SERVINGS.

Chocolate Decadence

 16 *ounces bittersweet chocolate, cut into pieces*
 10 *tablespoons butter*
  5 *large eggs, separated*
  1 *tablespoon all-purpose flour*
 ¼ *teaspoon cream of tartar*
  1 *teaspoon sugar*
  4 *cups heavy cream, whipped Raspberry and kiwi coulis*

Line an 8 x 2-inch round cake pan with parchment paper.

In the top of a double boiler melt the chocolate and butter, stirring occasionally until smooth. Whisk in the egg yolks and flour. Set aside.

In a large bowl beat the egg whites with cream of tartar until soft peaks form. Gradually add the sugar and beat until stiff but not dry. Fold one-fourth of the whites into the chocolate mixture to lighten, then quickly fold in the remaining whites. Pour the batter in the prepared pan. Bake in a 425° oven for 15 minutes. Remove from the oven and let cool completely in the pan. Chill for several hours.

When ready to serve, run a knife around the edge, invert, take the parchment off, and frost with whipped cream. Serve with raspberry and kiwi coulis. (Coulis is a puree of fresh fruit sauce).

Note: As the cake cools the center will sink. That's correct.

MAKES 6 TO 8 SERVINGS.

Sautéed Chicken Breast, with Gulf Shrimp and Raspberry Sauce

- 1 6-ounce boneless, skinless chicken cutlet
  Salt and pepper to taste
- 1 cup spinach leaves, trimmed and washed
- 2 teaspoons sugar
- ¼ cup water
- 2 pounds large shrimp
- ¼ cup raspberries, fresh or frozen

Season the chicken with salt and pepper. In a nonstick pan sauté the chicken for 2 minutes on each side. Place the spinach in an oven-proof dish, sprinkle with sugar, and place the sautéed chicken breast on top. Bake in a 350° oven for 15 minutes.

In the same sauté pan bring the water to boil. Cook the peeled and deveined shrimp no more than 2 minutes. Remove the shrimp and keep warm. Pour the raspberries into the shrimp cooking water. Bring to a quick simmer, and remove from the heat.

Remove the chicken and the spinach from the baking dish. Keep the spinach on the bottom and make sure not to transfer any liquid to the serving dish. Place the shrimp on top of the chicken and pour raspberry sauce over.

MAKES 1 SERVING.

Wild Mushroom Soup

- ¼ cup butter
- 10 chopped shallots
- 2 cups dry white wine
- 3 gallons rich brown stock
- 5 pounds white mushrooms, brushed, cleaned, and chopped coarsely
- ½ pound dry mixed wild mushrooms, reconstituted and coarsely-chopped
- ¼ cup chopped fresh tarragon
- 1 cup tomato paste
  Salt and pepper to taste
- ½ cup cornstarch

In a skillet melt the butter and sauté the shallots until translucent. Add the wine and reduce by half. Add the stock, mushrooms, and tarragon, and bring to a boil. Add the tomato paste, reduce the heat and simmer until the mushrooms are thoroughly cooked. Add salt and pepper to taste. Return to a boil. Mix the cornstarch with ½ cup of cold water and slowly add to the boiling soup. Cook until the soup reaches the desired thickness.

MAKES 12 SERVINGS.

Golden Pheasant Inn

≈

River Road
Erwinna, Pennsylvania 18920
(610) 294-9595

***T**his quaint inn with six guest rooms is between the Delaware River and the Pennsylvania Canal. It was built in 1857 as a mule barge stop to serve travelers and workers on the canal. One of the innkeepers, Michel Faure, a native of France, delights guests with his gourmet creations as chef de cuisine at the Golden Pheasant Inn. Nearby attractions include golf, tennis, swimming, and skiing.*

Chicken Chasseur

- 2 2½ to 3-pound chickens
  Salt and pepper to taste
  Thyme to taste
- ½ cup oil
- ¼ cup finely diced shallots or onions
- ¼ cup garlic
- ¾ pound mushrooms, thinly sliced
- ¾ cup white wine
- ½ cup brandy
- 1 pint tomatoes, peeled, seeded, and cubed
- 1 13¾-ounce can chicken broth
- ½ cup chopped parsley

Clean and disjoint the chicken. Season with salt, pepper, and thyme. In a large sauté pan heat oil. Add the chicken pieces and brown carefully on all sides. To prepare the sauce, remove the chicken and all but ¼ cup of the sauté oil, add the shallots, garlic, mushrooms, and wine. Flambé with brandy and simmer until tender.

Add the tomatoes and chicken broth. Check the seasoning. Add the chicken. Cook for 30 minutes or until tender. Cover and reduce to a simmer. Sprinkle chopped parsley over individual servings.

MAKES 8 SERVINGS.

Stuffed Clams Brittany

- 3 pounds clams
- 1 cup dry white wine (Muscadet)
- 1 shallot, chopped
- 6 clove garlic, chopped
- ½ cup parsley
  Tarragon to taste
  Basil to taste
- 1 tablespoon chopped chives
- ¼ teaspoon paprika
  Salt and pepper to taste
- ½ cup butter
- ¾ cup breadcrumbs

Wash the clams. In a large saucepan combine the wine and shallot. Cover and bring to a boil. Add the clams and cook until the clams open, about 5 minutes. Cool.

Remove 1 shell from each clam. Place the clams on a large baking sheet or large ceramic dish. Mix together the garlic, herbs, chives, paprika, salt, pepper, and butter. Place a spoonful on each clams. Sprinkle with breadcrumbs. Place under the broiler 2 to 3 minutes, or bake in a 450° oven for 4 to 5 minutes. Serve at once.

MAKES 6 SERVINGS.

Normandy Lamb Stew

- 2 tablespoons butter
- 2 tablespoons oil
- 3 pounds lamb neck or shoulder, cut into chunks
- 1 cup chopped onions
- 2 tablespoons all-purpose flour
- 2 cups stock (beef, veal, or chicken)

- 2 cloves garlic, minced
  Bouquet garni (bay leaf, thyme, parsley, leek)

Salt and pepper to taste
24   **pearl onions**
12   **baby carrots, cut into pieces**
½   **cup chopped parsley**

In a heavy casserole heat the butter and oil. Add the meat and color on all sides. Add the onions. Cook until soft. Sprinkle on the flour. Add the stock, garlic, bouquet garni, salt, and pepper. Cover and simmer for 1 hour. Add the vegetables and simmer for 30 minutes. Stir in the parsley. Serve.

MAKES 6 TO 8 SERVINGS.

Provençale Sautéed Potatoes

¼   **cup olive oil**
2   **pounds small new potatoes**
14   **cloves garlic, unpeeled**
    Salt and pepper to taste
¼   **cup chopped flat-leaf parsley**

In a flameproof casserole or heavy sauté pan warm the olive oil. Over low heat add the potatoes, garlic, salt, and pepper. Cover and cook the potatoes until tender, about 40 minutes. May be kept warm in the oven until served. Sprinkle with parsley just before serving.

MAKES 4 SERVINGS.

Breton Pound Cake

½   **cup raisins**
¼   **cup rum**
6   **large egg yolks**
2¼   **cups all-purpose flour**
1   **cup sugar**
1   **cup butter, at room temperature**
    Dash salt
2   **tablespoons chopped orange zest**

Soak the raisins in rum. Butter an 8 x 4-inch loaf pan. In a bowl beat the egg yolks. Place the flour in large bowl. Make a well in the center and add the sugar, butter, and salt. Mix.

Add the egg yolks, raisins, rum, and orange zest. Mix gently. Transfer the dough to the prepared pan. Brush the top with sprinkled sugar or egg yolk. Make a lattice design with a fork. Bake in a 350° oven for about 1 hour.

Cool. Unmold. Slice.

MAKES 1 LOAF.

Pears in Red Wine

6   **Bartlett (William) pears, halved, cored, and peeled**
    Orange zest
1   **cinnamon stick**
3   **cups red wine**
½   **cup sugar**

Place the pears in a large enameled ironware pan. Add the zest, cinnamon stick, and wine. Sprinkle with sugar. Bake in a 350° oven for approximately 30 minutes or until the pears cook. May be served for dessert hot or chilled.

MAKES 6 SERVINGS.

Butternut Squash Bisque

¼   **cup butter**
½   **cup chopped leeks**
½   **cup chopped onion**
½   **cup chopped celery**
2   **cups chopped apples**
2   **tablespoons all-purpose flour**
7   **cups chicken stock**
4   **cups peeled and diced butternut squash**
4   **cups diced potatoes**
1   **teaspoon thyme**
½   **teaspoon dried sage**
¼   **teaspoon dried rosemary**
¼   **teaspoon turmeric**
    Pinch grated nutmeg
    Salt and pepper to taste
1   **cup cider**
¼   **cup Calvados**
½   **cup light cream**
1   **cup grated Parmesan cheese**

In a large saucepan melt butter and sauté the leeks, onions, celery, and apples over medium heat for 15 minutes. Add the flour and stir until blended. Add the chicken stock and simmer for 10 minutes.

Add the squash, potatoes, and herbs. Season with salt and pepper. Cook for 20 minutes. In a food processor purée the bisque. Add the cider, Calvados, and cream. Sprinkle Parmesan cheese on each serving.

MAKES 6 TO 8 SERVINGS.

Provençale Custard

4   **cups milk**
1   **cup sugar**
4   **whole eggs plus 6 egg yolks**
¼   **cup dark rum**

Pour the milk into a saucepan over medium heat. Stir in the sugar, and stir until almost boiling. Remove the pan from the heat. In a mixing bowl whisk together the whole eggs and egg yolks. Slowly add the milk. Whisk in the rum. Pour into 6 custard cups. Place the cups in a water bath. Bake in a 300° oven for 30 to 40 minutes.

MAKES 6 SERVINGS.

Croutons

Cut bread into cubes. In a bowl toss croutons with olive oil, granulated garlic, granulated onions, cayenne, dried thyme, and dried oregano. Spread onto an ungreased baking sheet. Bake in a 350° oven, turning frequently, until browned and crisp.

Golden Pheasant Inn

Caesar Dressing

2   **tablespoons lemon juice**
1   **teaspoon Worcestershire sauce**
2   **cloves garlic**
½   **teaspoon salt**
½   **teaspoon pepper**
1   **tablespoon mustard**
1   **large egg**
6   **tablespoons olive oil**

In a bowl or blender mix all of the ingredients except the olive oil. Add the olive oil. Mix 1 minute or until smooth.

MAKES ABOUT ½ CUP.

Alsatian Lentil Soup

8   **ounces lentils**
8   **cups chicken broth**
14   **ounces chopped carrots**
14   **ounces chopped potatoes**
1   **leek, sliced**
1   **onion, sliced**

2 *cloves garlic*
½ *cup chopped parsley*
1 *bay leaf*
2 *whole cloves*
8 *peppercorns*
7 *ounces bacon (optional)*
   Salt to taste
¾ *cup cream (optional)*

In a bowl soak the lentils in water overnight.
Wash and drain the lentils. Place in a large saucepan with chicken broth, vegetables, garlic, parsley, bay leaf, cloves, peppercorns, and bacon. Simmer for 2 hours. Remove the bay leaf. Pass the soup through a food mill if desired. Season with salt. Add cream.
MAKES 6 TO 8 SERVINGS.

Arleusian Garlic Soup

2 *tablespoons butter*
¾ *cup whole cloves garlic, peeled*
1¼ *pounds potatoes, quartered*
2 *carrots, quartered*
8 *cups water*
   Salt and pepper to taste
   Cream to taste

In a large saucepan melt the butter and gently cook the garlic, stirring often, until it begins to brown. Add the remaining ingredients except the cream. Bring to a boil, cover partially, and cook gently for 1 hour. The vegetables should be soft. In a food processor purée the soup. Reheat. Add the cream.
MAKES 6 SERVINGS.

Chicken with Tarragon Vinegar

3 *tablespoons olive oil*
3 *tablespoons unsalted butter*
1 *3- to 4-pound chicken (or 4 boneless breasts)*
   Salt and pepper to taste
1 *cup white wine*
4 *shallots, minced*
1 *cup diced onions*
2 *medium tomatoes, diced*
½ *cup tarragon vinegar*
1 *bunch tarragon, minced*

In a large skillet heat the oil and butter. Season the chicken with salt and pepper. Sauté the chicken and remove from the pan. Add

the wine, shallots, onions, and tomatoes to the pan. When cooked, slowly add the vinegar. Return the chicken to the pan. Sprinkle with tarragon and cover. Cook for 3 minutes and serve.
MAKES 4 SERVINGS.

Cranberry Apricot Relish

4 *cups cranberries*
2 *cups chopped dried apricots*
1 *cup raisins*
1 *tablespoon grated orange zest*
¼ *teaspoon ground ginger*
2 *cups water*
½ *cup French brandy*
1 *cup sugar*

In a large pot combine all of the ingredients except the sugar. Bring to a boil over high heat, and simmer for 10 minutes or until the berries pop open. Remove from the heat. Add the sugar and stir until dissolved. Cool. Can be frozen.
MAKES ABOUT 2 QUARTS.

Chicken with Artichoke Hearts

4 *boneless, skinless chicken breasts*
   Salt and pepper to taste
   Flour
2 *large eggs, beaten*
   Oil
   Unsalted butter
½ *cup lemon juice*
1 *14-ounce can artichoke hearts*
1 *cup water*
1 *tablespoon chicken base*
2 *teaspoons cornstarch*
½ *cup fresh chopped parsley*

Pound the chicken breasts until thin. Season with salt and pepper. Coat with flour. Dip in beaten eggs. Coat with flour again.
In a large skillet heat the oil and butter and sauté the chicken until no longer pink inside. Add the lemon juice and artichoke hearts. In a bowl mix the water with the chicken base, cornstarch, and parsley. Add to the skillet. Bring to a simmer, and serve immediately.
MAKES 4 SERVINGS.

Stuffed Pork Chops Provençale

2 *tablespoons olive oil*
1 *cup finely chopped onion*
1 *cup chopped mushrooms*
¼ *teaspoon dried thyme*
¼ *teaspoon oregano*
¼ *teaspoon tarragon*
¼ *teaspoon marjoram*
2 *teaspoons chopped garlic*
¼ *teaspoon lemon juice*
   Salt and ground pepper to taste
   Freshly grated nutmeg to taste
1 *egg*
2 *cups dry bread cubes*
- - - - - - - - - - - - - - -
4 *double-rib pork chops, trimmed*
2 *tablespoons olive oil*
½ *cup dry white wine*
- - - - - - - - - - - - - - -
½ *cup Italian parsley, chopped*

In a frying pan warm 2 tablespoons of olive oil. Add the onion and cook gently until softened. Add the mushrooms and sauté. Add the herbs, garlic, lemon juice, salt, pepper, and nutmeg to taste. Empty into a bowl and cool. Add the egg and bread cubes. Mix. Make a pocket in each chop with a small sharp knife. Season with salt and fresh ground pepper. Stuff the chops with the mixture. In a heavy ovenproof pan sauté the chops in 2 tablespoons of olive oil until brown. Turn once. Add the wine. Cover. Bake in a 300° oven for about 25 minutes, until tender. Serve with chopped Italian parsley garnish.
MAKES 4 SERVINGS.

Garlic Mashed Potatoes

6 *large potatoes*
6 *whole cloves garlic, peeled*
   Milk
   Salt and pepper to taste

Peel the potatoes and cut into chunks. Place in a saucepan with water, garlic, and salt. Bring to a boil and cook until tender. Remove the potatoes and purée using a potato masher. Moisten with cooking liquid and milk. Season.
MAKES 6 SERVINGS.

Green Beans Niçoise

1 *pound green beans*
½ *cup olive oil*
2 *shallots, minced*
1 *clove garlic, minced*
2 *medium red tomatoes, chopped*
½ *cup chopped celery*
1 *teaspoon salt*
   Black pepper to taste
1 *cup chicken broth*
1 *teaspoon minced fresh oregano*
1 *teaspoon minced fresh basil*
1 *tablespoon chopped parsley*

In a pan cook the green beans in water until tender-crisp. Drain.

In a large saucepan heat the oil and sauté the shallots and garlic until soft. Add the tomatoes, celery, salt, pepper, and chicken broth. Simmer uncovered for 20 minutes. Add the herbs and beans.

MAKES 4 TO 6 SERVINGS.

Mushroom Soup

2 *tablespoons butter*
1 *cup chopped onion*
2 *cloves garlic, minced*
8 *ounces mushrooms, sliced*
¼ *cup all-purpose flour*
4 *cups chicken broth*
1 *tablespoon dry sherry*
⅔ *cup milk*
1½ *tablespoons chopped parsley*

In a large saucepan heat the butter over medium heat and sauté the onion and garlic. Add the mushrooms and sauté. Add the flour and stir. Blend in the chicken broth and sherry. Finish with milk. Sprinkle with parsley.

MAKES 4 SERVINGS.

Provençale Tomatoes

8 *firm garden-ripe tomatoes*
   Salt and pepper to taste
¼ *cup olive oil*
¼ *cup finely chopped parsley*
2 *cloves garlic, finely chopped*
½ *cup breadcrumbs*

Cut the tomatoes in half. Place in a gratin dish. Sprinkle with salt and pepper. In frying pan heat the olive oil and toast the parsley, garlic, and breadcrumbs together. Sprinkle on the tomatoes. Bake in a 375° oven for 15

to 20 minutes or until the tomatoes are baked and the tops are browned.

MAKES 6 TO 8 SERVINGS.

Provençale Sautéed Mushrooms

3 *tablespoons olive oil*
1 *pound fresh mushrooms, sliced*
   Salt and pepper to taste
2 *cloves garlic*
¼ *cup finely chopped parsley*
1 *lemon*

In a large frying pan heat the olive oil and sauté the mushrooms for about 4 to 5 minutes. Add the salt, pepper, garlic, and parsley, and cook for 1 minute. Remove to a serving dish. Squeeze a few drops of lemon juice on top and serve.

MAKES 4 TO 6 SERVINGS.

Leek and Potato Soup

3 *tablespoons butter*
2 *cups sliced leeks*
2 *cups sliced onions*
3 *tablespoons all-purpose flour*
2 *quarts chicken stock*
   Salt and pepper to taste
4 *cups chopped and peeled potatoes*
½ *cup heavy cream*
¼ *cup parsley or chives, chopped*

In a large skillet melt the butter and sauté the leeks and onions without browning. Blend in the flour over moderate heat for 2 minutes without browning. Add the chicken stock. Stir in the salt, pepper, and potatoes. Bring to a boil and cover. Simmer for about 40 minutes or until the vegetables are cooked. In a food processor blend the soup, if desired. Add the cream before serving. May be served hot or cold. Garnish with parsley.

MAKES 6 TO 8 SERVINGS.

Potatoes in Red Wine

3 *pounds potatoes*
3 *tablespoons butter*
¼ *cup parsley*
3 *tablespoons chopped chives*
   Salt and pepper to taste
1 *tablespoon all-purpose flour*
½ *cup beef stock*
1 *cup Beaujolais*

In a pan cook the potatoes in boiling, salted water. Peel and slice. In a casserole heat the butter. Add the parsley, chives, salt, and pepper. Blend in the flour. Add the beef stock and wine. Simmer until the consistency of cream. Add the sliced potatoes. Serve hot.

MAKES 6 TO 8 SERVINGS.

146 South Whitford Road
Exton, Pennsylvania 19341
(610) 524-1830

*O*nly a short drive from center city Philadelphia, this fifteen-guest-room inn is in an old stone house. Guests enjoy the glass-enclosed porches, which provide a good view of the formal gardens. The dining rooms feature authentic wood-burning fireplaces. Duling-Kurtz House is conveniently located to the many historic sites, museums, galleries, and theaters throughout Chester County and the surrounding area. Other nearby activities include swimming, tennis, and golf.

Lamb Chops Duling Kurtz with Risotto

3 *ounces Arborio rice*
1 *cup lamb stock/water*
2 *cups cream*
   Chopped parsley
1 *Roma tomato, diced*
....
8 *lamb chops, trimmed*
   Salt and pepper
   Flour for dusting
1½ *ounces clarified butter*
1 *clove garlic*
¼ *cup red wine*
1 *cup lamb stock or water*
1 *sprig rosemary*
2 *anchovies, minced*

In a stockpot slowly cook the rice in 1 cup of stock until done. Drain the excess stock. Add the cream, parsley, and tomato, and bring to a boil. Season and set aside.

Season the chops with salt, pepper, and flour. In a skillet sauté the lamb in clarified butter to the desired doneness. Drain the excess butter, and add the garlic. Cook slightly. Deglaze the pan with wine. Add 1 cup of stock, rosemary, and anchovies. Reduce the stock until slightly thickened.

Serve over hot risotto and garnish with asparagus tips or a favorite vegetable.

MAKES 2 SERVINGS.

*Academy
Street Bed &
Breakfast*
❧

*528 Academy Street
Hawley, Pennsylvania 18428
(717) 226-3430*

---

*T*his Victorian house-turned-inn was built in 1863 by Captain Joseph Atkinson, a Federal soldier who was wounded at the battle of Gettysburg. Situated in the Pocono Mountains, it offers seven comfortable and cozy guest rooms in a convenient location. Fishing and boating are available at nearby Lake Wallenpaupack. Other nearby recreationl activities include swimming, golf, and tennis.

Spinach Pancakes

    2 eggs
 1¼ cups milk
 1½ cups sifted all-purpose flour
    1 teaspoon baking powder
   ¼ teaspoon salt
    3 tablespoons oil
    1 10-ounce box frozen chopped
        spinach, thawed and drained well

In a food processor combine the eggs and milk. Add the flour, baking powder, and salt, and beat well. Add the oil and spinach. Heat a skillet and melt the butter. Slowly fry the pancakes until set, turn over, and cook the other side.

MAKES 8 TO 10 SERVINGS.

Rum Raisin Ricotta Tart

   ½ cup golden raisins
   ¼ cup light rum
    1 9-inch pie shell, partially baked
    1 pound ricotta cheese
    1 teaspoon vanilla extract
    2 eggs
   ⅔ cup sugar
    2 teaspoons apricot jam, melted

In a cup soak the raisins in the rum.

In a large bowl mix the Ricotta cheese and vanilla. In a separate bowl beat the eggs with the sugar. Add the cheese mixture. Drain and add the raisins. Brush the bottom of the pie shell with apricot jam and fill with cheese mixture. Bake in a 350° oven for 45 to 50 minutes.

MAKES 6 SERVINGS.

Neapolitan Vegetable Cheesecake

    3 cups packed coarsely grated
        zucchini
    1 teaspoon salt, divided
    1 tablespoon butter or margarine
    1 onion, chopped
    1 cup coarsely grated carrots
    3 tablespoons all-purpose flour
    3 cloves garlic, finely minced
   ½ teaspoon dried whole basil
   ½ teaspoon dried whole oregano
   ¼ cup packed chopped fresh parsley
 4½ teaspoons lemon juice
    4 eggs, slight beaten
    3 cups ricotta cheese
    1 8-ounce package mozzarella cheese,
        grated
   ¾ cup grated Parmesan cheese, divided
        Salt and fresh ground pepper to
        taste
   ⅓ cup fine dry breadcrumbs, divided
    4 Roma tomatoes, thinly sliced
    1 2-ounce can anchovy fillets, drained
        and rolled

In a medium bowl combine the zucchini and ½ teaspoon of salt, and stir well. Let stand 15 minutes. Drain. Roll the zucchini in paper towels to squeeze out excess moisture. Place in a bowl and set aside.

In a large skillet melt the butter and add ½ teaspoon of salt, and the onion. Sauté for 3 to 4 minutes. Add the zucchini, carrots, flour, garlic, basil, and oregano. Cook over medium heat for 5 to 6 minutes. Remove the pan from the heat and add the parsley and lemon juice.

In a large bowl combine the eggs, ricotta, mozzarella, and ⅔ cup of Parmesan, and beat well. Add the sautéed vegetable mixture, and season with salt and pepper to taste. Stir until blended well.

In the bottom of a greased 10-inch springform pan sprinkle 1 tablespoon of breadcrumbs. Pour the vegetable mixture into the pan. Bake in a 375° oven for 30 minutes.

Dredge the tomato slices in the remaining breadcrumbs. Garnish the cheesecake with the tomato slices and rolled anchovies. Reduce the oven temperature to 350° and bake for 30 minutes. Turn off the oven, open the oven door and cook in the oven for 15 minutes. Cool on a rack for 10 minutes. Serve sprinkled with the remaining Parmesan cheese.

MAKES 8 SERVINGS.

Spinach Fettuccine "Muffins"

    1 8-ounce package spinach fettuccine
 1¼ cups grated Parmesan cheese,
        divided
    1 cup crème fraîche
    1 cup ricotta cheese
    1 cup half and half
    4 eggs
    2 teaspoons salt
   ½ teaspoon white pepper

Cook the fettuccine according to the package directions, omitting salt. Drain and set aside.

Generously butter muffin cups. Sprinkle 1 teaspoon of Parmesan cheese into each cup.

In an electric blender or food processor combine ½ cup of Parmesan cheese, crème fraîche, Ricotta cheese, half and half, eggs, salt, and pepper. Cover and process until smooth.

Place 2 tablespoons of cheese mixture into each muffin cup. Fill each muffin cup with equal amounts of fettuccine. Pour the remaining cheese mixture over the fettuccine to fill each cup. Sprinkle 1 teaspoon of

Parmesan cheese over each cup, and freeze 2 hours or until firm.

Place the frozen muffin pans on the oven rack at lowest position. Bake in a 375° oven for 35 minutes (tops of muffins will be moist). Remove from the pan and serve immediately.

MAKES 18 "MUFFINS".

Bucksville House

❦

4501 Durham Road, Rte. 412
Kintnersville, Pennsylvania 18930-1610
(610) 847-8948

---

*T*he five guest rooms in Bucksville House are decorated with a mixture of antiques and country reproductions. Some rooms have fireplaces. Guests are served breakfast in front of a walk-in fireplace or in the gazebo. Tennis, golf, and swimming are available nearby. Other activities include a nearby state park, antique shopping, and art galleries.

Nutty Raisin Bran Waffles

1½	cups all-purpose flour
4	teaspoons baking powder
¾	teaspoon salt
1½	tablespoons sugar
2	cups bran cereal
3	eggs
2¼	cups milk
⅓	cup oil
½	cup chopped pecans
¾	cup raisins

In a medium bowl combine the flour, baking powder, salt, sugar, and cereal. In a separate bowl combine the eggs, milk, and oil. Add the liquid mixture to the dry ingredients, beating until smooth. Fold in the pecans and raisins. Bake on a hot waffle iron until golden.

MAKES 6 SERVINGS.

Bucksville House

Hot Spiced Cranberry Punch

¾	cup firmly packed brown sugar
1	cup water
¼	teaspoon salt
½	teaspoon ground allspice
½	teaspoon ground cinnamon
1	quart pineapple juice
2	16-ounce cans jellied cranberry sauce
3	cups water
	Peppermint sticks

In a large saucepan combine the brown sugar, 1 cup of water, salt, spices, and pineapple juice. In a bowl whip the cranberry sauce with 3 cups of water and add to the spicy mixture. Bring to a boil. Serve with peppermint sticks.

MAKES 10 CUPS.

Australian Walkabout

❦

837 Village Road
Lampeter, Pennsylvania 17537
(717) 464-0707

---

*A*n authentic Australian-style B&B in the heart of the Amish countryside, this inn is conveniently situated for guests to embark on their own walkabouts. Nearby are many fine restaurants, a nine-hole executive golf course, historic sites, farm markets, country auctions, and shopping outlets, as well as the Amish countryside. All rooms are decorated with antiques, canopy

---

and queen-size beds, and all have private baths. A two-bedroom suite is also available.

Crunchy Corn Fritters

1	cup all-purpose flour
2	eggs, beaten
½	cup milk
¼	cup creamy Italian salad dressing
¼	cup light cream
2	cups fresh or canned corn
½	cup chopped shallots
½	cup grated Cheddar cheese
	Oil

Sift the flour into a bowl. Stir in the eggs, milk, salad dressing, and cream, and beat until smooth. Stir in the corn, shallots, and Cheddar cheese.

Heat about 2 tablespoons of oil in a pan. Drop tablespoons of corn mixture into the pan and spread the mixture out slightly. Fry until golden brown on both sides.

MAKES ABOUT 30 FRITTERS.

Spinach and Salmon Roulade

1	15¼-ounce can salmon, drained
4	shallots, chopped
½	cup mayonnaise
1	tablespoon chopped chives
8¾	ounces frozen spinach, thawed and drained
¼	cup butter
⅓	cup all-purpose flour
1	cup milk
4	eggs, separated

In a large bowl combine the salmon, shallots, mayonnaise, and chives, and mix well. Set aside.

Place the spinach in a pan and cook until all of the liquid has evaporated.

In a separate bowl melt the butter and add the flour. Stir until smooth. Add the milk gradually, stirring until the mixture boils and thickens. Quickly stir in the egg yolks and spinach. Put the mixture into a large bowl. In a medium bowl beat the egg whites until soft peaks form. Fold lightly into the spinach mixture. Pour the mixture into a greased and waxed, paper-lined tin (approximately 10 x

12 inches). Bake in a 375° oven for 12 to 15 minutes or until golden brown.

Remove from the oven and turn onto a wire rack covered with a tea towel. Carefully remove the waxed paper. Spread evenly with the salmon filling. Holding the tea towel with both hands, gently roll the roulade. Slice.
MAKES 8 SERVINGS.

Lemon Cream Cheese Cake

4⅓	ounces cream cheese
8¾	ounces butter
2	teaspoons grated lemon zest
1½	cups sugar
3	eggs, beaten
1½	cups all-purpose flour

1	cup confectioners' sugar
2	teaspoons lemon juice

In a large bowl beat the cream cheese, butter, and lemon zest together until smooth. Add the sugar and beat until light and fluffy. Beat in the eggs. Stir in the flour until smooth. Spoon into a well-greased bundt pan. Bake in a 350° oven for 30 minutes. Reduce the oven temperature to 200° and bake for 30 minutes. Cool in the pan for 10 minutes, then remove.

In a small bowl combine the confectioners' sugar and lemon juice. Pour over the cooled cake.
MAKES 8 SERVINGS.

The Manor

830 Village Road, P.O. Box 416
Lancaster, Pennsylvania 17537
(712) 464-9564

This inn with a large swimming pool is on four and one-half acres of farmland in the heart of Pennsylvania Dutch country. It's an ideal country retreat for those who want a brief respite from the stresses of modern life. Relaxing activities include rocking on the front porch and sitting on the handmade Amish furniture under the shade trees. Major tourist destinations such as Gettysburg, Hershey, Chadds Ford, and Philadelphia are just a short drive away. Golf courses, fine restaurants, and dinner theaters are also close by.

Banana Blueberry Muffins

2	ripe bananas
¼	cup sugar
½	cup butter, melted
1	egg
2	cups all-purpose flour
1	teaspoon salt
1	teaspoon baking powder
1	teaspoon baking soda
1	cup buttermilk
1	cup blueberries

In a medium bowl mash the bananas. Add the sugar, melted butter, and egg. Mix well. In a separate bowl mix the flour, salt, baking powder, and soda. Add the dry ingredients to the banana mixture with the buttermilk and stir just until combined. Fold in the blueberries. Fill greased muffin cup three-fourths full. Bake in a 350° oven for 30 minutes.
MAKES 12 MUFFINS.

Eggs Mornay

1	tablespoon butter or margarine
2	tablespoons all-purpose flour
2	cups milk
½	cup shredded Cheddar cheese
½	teaspoon salt
¼	teaspoon Worcestershire sauce
¼	teaspoon prepared mustard
8	eggs
	Paprika for sprinkling

In a saucepan melt the butter. Add the flour and milk and bring to a boil. Add the Cheddar cheese, salt, Worcestershire, and mustard. Stir and cook until thickened. Pour into a 1½-quart baking dish. Break the eggs into the sauce at intervals. Sprinkle the eggs with paprika. Bake in a 350° oven for 30 minutes or until set.
MAKES 4 TO 6 SERVINGS.

Herr Farmhouse Inn

2256 Huber Drive
Manheim, Pennsylvania 17545
(717) 653-9852

Sitting on eleven and one-half acres of rolling farmland, this inn in an old farmhouse in Lancaster County reflects the true atmosphere of the Pennsylvania Dutch country. It was built in 1738 and restored with great attention to detail. Guests are impressed with the fanlights over the main entrance, the original pine floors, and the six fireplaces. In addition to visits to Amish farms and craft shops, guests can also enjoy golf, tennis, and swimming activities nearby.

Nutty Lemon Coffeecake

1	cup butter or margarine, softened
1	cup sugar
3	eggs
1	cup sour cream
1	teaspoon vanilla extract
1	teaspoon lemon extract
2½	cups all-purpose flour
2½	teaspoons baking powder
1	teaspoon baking soda
⅛	teaspoon salt

1	cup ground pecans
½	cup sugar
1	teaspoon ground cinnamon

In a large mixing bowl cream the butter and sugar. Add the eggs, one at a time, beating well after each addition. In a small bowl mix the sour cream and extracts. In a medium bowl combine the flour, baking powder, soda, and salt. Add the dry ingredients to the creamed mixture alternately with the sour cream mixture. Mix well. Spread half in a greased 9 x 13-inch baking pan. In a small bowl combine the pecans, ½ cup of sugar, and cinnamon. Sprinkle half over the batter. Carefully pour the remaining batter on top. Sprinkle with the remaining topping. Bake in a 350° oven for 30 to 35 minutes, or until a toothpick inserted in the center comes out clean.

MAKES 16 TO 20 SERVINGS.

Poppy Seed Bread

½   cup soy oil
4   eggs
1   cup boiling water
2   tablespoons poppy seeds
1   4.6-ounce package instant lemon
     pudding
1   18¼-ounce package lemon cake mix

In a large bowl mix all of the ingredients. Pour into 2 greased 9 x 5-inch loaf pans. Bake in a 350° oven for 40 to 60 minutes.

MAKES 2 LOAVES.

258 West Front Street
Marietta, Pennsylvania 17547
(717) 426-2290

***T**he River Inn is in a two-hundred-year-old house in the heart of Marietta's historic district. Guest-pleasing amenities include six fire-places, an enclosed porch, beautiful gardens, and queen-size beds in all guest rooms, which are decorated with a blend of antiques and period reproduction furniture. Bicycles are provided for guests who want to tour area sites and get some exer-cise at the same time. Other activi-ties include touring a local winery and museums, fine dining, and shopping in area antique stores.*

The River Inn

The River Inn Tea Bread

3   cups all-purpose flour
1½   teaspoons salt
1½   teaspoons baking powder
2   tablespoons poppy seeds
2¼   cups sugar
3   eggs
1½   cups milk
1⅛   cups oil
1½   teaspoons vanilla extract
1½   teaspoons almond extract
1½   teaspoons butter extract

....

¼   cup orange juice
¾   cup sugar
½   teaspoon vanilla extract
½   teaspoon almond extract
½   teaspoon melted butter

In a large bowl mix the first 11 ingredients. Pour into 2 greased 9 x 5-inch loaf pans, fill-ing the pans two-thirds full. Bake in a 350° oven for 40 to 60 minutes.

Cool for 5 minutes.

In a small bowl combine the orange juice, sugar, vanilla, almond extract, and melted butter. Glaze the warm bread.

MAKES 2 LOAVES.

Chocolate Zucchini Bread

3   eggs
1   cup oil
2   cups sugar
2   teaspoons vanilla extract
2   cups grated zucchini, with the juice
½   teaspoon salt
2½   cups all-purpose flour
½   cup unsweetened cocoa
1   teaspoon baking soda
½   teaspoon baking powder
1   teaspoon ground cinnamon
½   cups chopped nuts

In a large bowl mix the eggs, oil, sugar, and vanilla. Add the zucchini. Add the dry ingredi-

ents and nuts. Pour into 2 greased and sug-ared 9 x 5-inch loaf pans. Bake in a 350° oven for 50 minutes.

MAKES 2 LOAVES.

1605 State Street
Mertztown, Pennsylvania 19539
(610) 682-6197

***T**he innkeepers at Longswamp have a large collection of music and books which they make available to their guests. Situated on five acres, this old farmhouse was built in the 1800s, and it's still surrounded by rich farmlands in an open-country setting. It's a nice place for a week-end getaway or a nostalgic escape from modern urban pressures. In addition to large rooms in the main house, guests may also escape to two adjoining cottages and a con-verted horse stall in the barn for maximum quietness and privacy. Mertztown is close to Amish country and a major ski area. Other nearby activities include horseback riding, biking, tennis, swimming, golf, and tennis.*

Apple-Pork Sausage Patties

1½   pounds ground pork butt, with some
     fat
¼   cup unsweetened frozen apple juice
     concentrate, thawed
½   teaspoon salt
½   teaspoon pepper
⅛   teaspoon ground cayenne pepper
1   teaspoon crumbled dried whole
     dried sage

½ **teaspoon dried thyme, crumbled**
¼ **teaspoon ground allspice**

In a large bowl combine the ground pork, apple juice, salt, peppers, sage, thyme, and allspice. Mix well, using hands if necessary to blend the spices into the meat. Break off a bit of the mixture and cook in a hot skillet, then taste. Adjust the seasonings to taste. Wrap well and refrigerate for several hours or overnight to blend the flavors.

Break off pieces of the sausage, roll into 1½-inch balls, then flatten. To cook, add just enough water to the skillet to barely cover the bottom. Add several sausage patties and cook over medium-high heat, turning, until the water evaporates. Reduce the heat to low and cook until the patties are brown and crusty, 10 to 15 minutes. Drain on paper towels before serving.

Store the mixture in the refrigerator, breaking off as much as needed at any one time; use within a week. May be frozen.

Variation: Place on baking sheets and bake in a 375° oven until browned, 20 to 25 minutes.

MAKES ABOUT 22 PATTIES.

Budapest Coffee Cake

⅔ **cup firmly packed dark brown sugar**
1 **tablespoon ground cinnamon**
1 **tablespoon unsweetened cocoa**
3 **tablespoons chopped currants**
½ **cup chopped walnuts**
3 **cups sifted all-purpose flour**
4½ **teaspoons baking powder**
1½ **teaspoons baking soda**
½ **teaspoon salt**
¾ **cup butter**
2 **teaspoons vanilla extract**
1½ **cups sugar**
3 **eggs**
2 **cups sour cream**
....
2 **cups confectioners' sugar**
1 **teaspoon vanilla extract**
2 **to 3 tablespoons milk**

Butter a 10-inch bundt pan.

In a small bowl, combine the brown sugar, cinnamon, cocoa, currants, and walnuts. Mix well and set aside.

In a medium bowl combine the flour, baking powder, soda, and salt. Mix well.

In a bowl cream the butter, vanilla, and sugar until light and fluffy. Beat in the eggs, one at a time, beating well after each addition. Fold the dry ingredients into the creamed mixture alternately with the sour cream. Spread a thin layer of the batter in the bottom of the prepared pan and sprinkle generously with one-third of the nut filling. Continue to layer, finishing with the batter. If spreading the batter is difficult, drop it by small spoonfuls. Bake in a 375° oven for 55 to 60 minutes, or until a toothpick inserted in the center comes out clean. Let cool in the pan for 5 minutes, then unmold. Serve plain or glaze with vanilla icing.

In a medium bowl combine the confectioners' sugar, 1 teaspoon of vanilla, and the milk. Beat until smooth. If necessary, add a little more milk to make a glaze about the thickness of cream sauce. Drizzle over the cake while still warm, letting it run down the sides.

This cake freezes well.

MAKES 8 TO 12 SERVINGS.

Pine Hill Farm

P.O. Box 1001
Milford, Pennsylvania 18337
(717) 296-7395

Pine Hill has enough land—268 acres—to be a working farm, but it's all for the enjoyment of it's guests, who are given unhindered access to the entire estate. They can hike the fields and forests, birdwatch and cross-country ski, or picnic beside the waterfall. Comfortable rooms are available in the main house as well as the adjoining caretaker's cottage. Many guests visit nearby Water Gap National Recreation Area, where swimming, rafting, canoeing, and bicycling are popular. Several fine restaurants and antique shops are proximate in downtown historic Milford.

Eggs McLynn

12 **slices bacon, cooked and crumbled**
12 **large eggs**
 Grated Cheddar or Monterey Jack cheese
12 **toast rounds**

Spray 12 muffin cups thoroughly with cooking spray.

Crumble a rounded tablespoon of cooked bacon in the bottom or each. Add one large egg. Top with grated Cheddar or Monterey Jack or a mixture of both cheese.

Bake in a 350° oven for 12 minutes.

Remove and immediately use a mini rubber spatula around the sides of each until they twirl in the pan. Let stand for 4 to 5 minutes. Serve on toast rounds.

MAKES 12 SERVINGS.

Deep-dish Zucchini-Mozzarella Pie

3 **medium zucchinis, diced**
¾ **cup chopped scallions**
¼ **cup chopped fresh parsley**
1 **clove garlic, minced**
2½ **cups diced mozzarella cheese**
4 **beaten eggs**
1 **cup biscuit mix**
⅓ **cup grated Parmesan or Romano cheese**
½ **cup olive oil**
 Paprika for sprinkling

In a very large bowl combine all of the ingredients. Pour into a greased 2-quart casserole dish. Sprinkle with paprika. Bake in a 350° oven for 1 hour, or until browned well and the cheese is melted. Let stand for 5 minutes.

MAKES 6 TO 8 SERVINGS.

Cedar Hill Farm

Cedar Hill Farm

305 Longenecker Road
Mount Joy, Pennsylvania 17552
(717) 653-4655

Built in 1817, the stone barn and farmhouse on this working farm overlook peaceful Little Chickies Creek, named for an Indian tribe that once roamed its banks. The house, with its open winding staircase, is furnished with many family heirlooms and antiques. Breakfast is served by the walk-in fireplace where cooking for the household was done in the 1800s. Guests also enjoy the large porch with wicker furniture. Attractions within easy driving distance include Hershey Park, Gettysburg, Amish country, and Baltimore Inner Harbor.

Pennsylvania Dutch Shoofly Cake

　1　cup molasses
2¼　cups boiling water
　1　tablespoon baking soda
　4　cups all-purpose flour
　1　16-ounce box light brown sugar
　¾　cup oil

In a large bowl mix the molasses, boiling water, and soda. In a separate bowl blend the flour, brown sugar, and oil. Reserve 4 cups for topping. Set aside.

Mix the remaining dry ingredients with the liquid. Pour into an ungreased 9 x 13-inch pan and top with the crumbs. Bake in a 325° oven for 40 to 50 minutes.

MAKES 12 SERVINGS.

Cherry Crumb Squares

　¾　cup sugar
　2　cups all-purpose flour
　2　teaspoons baking powder
　½　teaspoon salt
　½　cup margarine or butter
　1　egg
　1　21-ounce can cherry pie filling

In a bowl mix the sugar, flour, baking powder, and salt. Cut in the butter. Add the egg and mix to make crumbs. Place half of the crumbs in the bottom of a greased 9 x 13-inch pan. Pour the cherries over the crumbs. Top with the remaining crumbs. Bake in a 350° oven for 30 to 35 minutes.

MAKES 8 TO 12 SERVINGS.

Baked Oatmeal

　½　cup oil
　2　eggs
　1　cup sugar
　3　cups Old-fashioned oats
　2　teaspoons baking powder
　2　teaspoons salt
　1　cup milk

In a bowl combine the oil, eggs, and sugar. Add the oatmeal, baking powder, salt, and milk. Spoon into a 1-quart casserole. Bake in a 350° oven for 45 minutes.

MAKES 4 TO 6 SERVINGS.

The Inn at Olde New Berlin

The Inn at Olde New Berlin

321 Market Street
New Berlin, Pennsylvania 17855-0390
(717) 966-0321

The five spacious guest rooms in this inn are decorated with antique furnishings and Amish quilts. The common areas have high ceilings, inviting nooks, and ornately carved woodwork. Many guests are surprised to find these amenities in a country inn, which is situated in the wooded hills and rolling farmlands of central Pennsylvania. The innkeepers call it "an uptown experience in a rural setting." Guests enjoy exploring the old city of New Berlin, population 900, with its old houses and trees and small-town friendliness. Area activities include antique shopping, canoeing, hiking, biking, and touring the Amish farms of the area.

Black Forest Trifle

　2　21-ounce cans cherry pie filling
　1　2-layer or bundt rich chocolate cake, baked, cooled, and broken into ¾-inch pieces
　　 White Chocolate Custard (recipe follows), chilled about 1 hour
1 ½　cups heavy cream
　¼　cup confectioners' sugar
　1　teaspoon vanilla extract
　1　teaspoon Kirsch

In a large strainer or colander place the cherry pie filling to remove about three-fourths of the glaze mixture. Gently run water over the cherries. (Cherries should remain lightly coated with the glaze.)

In a 3-quart glass serving bowl place half of the cake pieces. Top with half of the White

Chocolate Custard. This custard should be thin enough to minimally seep around the cake at the edges of the bowl. Spoon half of the cherries onto top of the custard. Repeat the layering of cake, custard, and cherries. Cover and refrigerate for about 4 hours.

In small bowl, whip the cream, sugar, vanilla, and Kirsch until stiff peaks form. Reserve 1 cup, then spread the remaining mixture over the trifle. Pipe reserved cream over the trifle to decorate.

MAKES 8 TO 12 SERVINGS.

White Chocolate and Cranberry Trifle

- 1   16-ounce can jellied cranberry sauce
- ¼   cup raspberry liqueur (Chambord)
- 1   12-ounce ready-to-serve pound cake or angel food cake cut into ¾-inch pieces
  - White Chocolate Custard, chilled about 1 hour (recipe follows)
- 1½   cups heavy cream
- ¼   cup confectioners' sugar
- 1   teaspoon vanilla extract
  - Chopped pistachio nuts for garnish

In a medium bowl combine the cranberry sauce and liqueur until smooth. In a 3-quart glass serving bowl place half of the cake pieces. Spoon half of the cranberry mixture onto the cake. Top with half of the white chocolate custard.

Repeat the layering of cake, cranberry mixture, and custard, saving 2 tablespoons of cranberry mixture. Cover and refrigerate for about 6 hours.

In a small bowl whip the cream, confectioners' sugar, and vanilla until stiff peaks form. Reserve 1 cup, then spread the remaining mixture over the trifle.

Pipe the reserved cranberry mixture onto the top of trifle, making a lattice or zigzag design. Pipe the remaining whipped cream onto the trifle to decorate. Sprinkle with pistachios to add final pizzazz!

MAKES 6 TO 8 SERVINGS.

White Chocolate Custard

- ½   cup sugar
- ¼   cup cornstarch
- ¼   teaspoon salt
- 4   cups milk
- 4   large egg yolks
- 6   ounces white chocolate, grated
- 2   teaspoons vanilla extract

In a saucepan, place the sugar, cornstarch, and salt. Slowly incorporate the milk with a wire whisk until smooth. Cook over medium heat, stirring constantly, until the mixture boils and thickens. Boil 1 minute, then remove the saucepan from the heat.

In a cup beat the egg yolks with a fork. Quickly stir in about ½ cup of hot milk mixture. Return all to the saucepan. Cook over medium-low heat, stirring constantly, until the mixture thickens and coats a spoon well. Remove the pan from the heat.

Stir in the white chocolate and vanilla until the mixture is smooth. Cover with plastic wrap directly touching the custard to prevent the formation of skin.

MAKES ABOUT 5½ CUPS.

Gabriel's Chestnut-Orange Stuffing

- 3   tablespoons unsalted butter
- ½   large onion, chopped
- 3   celery stalks, chopped
- 2   medium carrots, chopped
- ¾   cup coarsely chopped vacuum-packed roasted chestnuts or fresh roasted chestnuts, chopped
- ½   teaspoon dried thyme, crumbled
- ¼   teaspoon dried sage, crumbled
- 1   to 2 tablespoons orange zest
- 3   tablespoons chopped fresh parsley
- 1   tablespoon thinly sliced fresh sage leaves
- 3   cups coarse corn bread crumbs
- 1½   cups whole wheat breadcrumbs
- 1   extra-large egg
  - Salt and freshly ground pepper to taste
- ½   to ¾ cup turkey or chicken stock

In a large heavy skillet melt the butter over medium heat. Add the onion, celery, carrots, chestnuts, thyme, dried sage, and orange zest. Cook until the onion is translucent, stirring occasionally, about 10 minutes. Add the parsley and fresh sage and stir for 2 minutes. Transfer to a large bowl. Mix in the corn bread and whole wheat breadcrumbs. Mix in the egg and season with salt and pepper. Add enough stock to moisten slightly. Cool completely.

This stuffing can be used to stuff poultry or baked in a separate casserole. It retains its moisture in the casserole, yet more stock can be added, if desired.

MAKES 12 SERVINGS.

Gabriel's Stuffed Acorn Squash

- ½   acorn squash, seeded
- ¾   cup freshly chopped mixed vegetables (broccoli, cauliflower, zucchini, summer squash, snow peas, scallions)
- 4   carrot slices
- 4   mushroom slices
- ⅛   teaspoon dried basil
- ⅛   teaspoon dried oregano
- ⅛   teaspoon dried thyme
  - Pinch salt
  - Pinch pepper
- ¼   cup white wine
- ½   to 1 teaspoon lime juice
- 1   to 2 teaspoons firmly packed brown sugar
- 2   ounces Gouda cheese, grated

Steam the acorn squash in advance. Refrigerate until ready to use.

In a skillet sauté the vegetables until al dente in olive oil, butter, or light margarine. Add the herbs, seasonings, wine, and lime juice to the vegetables and simmer for 3 to 4 minutes.

Coat the inside of the acorn squash half with brown sugar. Heat in a microwave for 1 to 2 minutes, just to take off the chill of the squash. Fill with the vegetable mixture, then top with Gouda cheese. Place in a baking pan. Bake in a 350° oven for 15 minutes, or until heated through.

Note: Serve with rice, pasta, or potatoes. Garnish with fruit.

MAKES 1 SERVING.

Spring Festival Salad

- 1½   cups mixed seasonal greens (Romaine, endive, arugula, radicchio)
- 2   tablespoons dried cranberries
- 2   tablespoons raisins
- 2   tablespoons toasted sliced almonds
- 2   tablespoons crumbled Gorgonzola cheese
- 3   large grapefruit sections

Fluff mixed greens on a salad plate. Sprinkle the next 4 ingredients on top of the greens. Arrange grapefruit sections in a spiral on top of the greens. A fanned strawberry can also be added to the center of the grapefruit wedges for extra pizzazz.

Serve with any salad dressing desired. The Inn always uses a Honey Walnut Raspberry Vinaigrette, yet a more fat-free or low-cal alternative could also be enjoyed.

MAKES 1 SERVING.

Gabriel's Pear Streusel Topper

$^1/_2$ **cup butter**
1 **tablespoon lemon juice**
4 **pears, peeled, cored and sliced**
$^1/_3$ **cup firmly packed brown sugar**
$^1/_4$ **teaspoon ground cinnamon**
$^1/_8$ **teaspoon ground nutmeg**
$^1/_8$ **teaspoon ground ginger**
$^1/_4$ **cup chopped pecans**

In a large sauté pan melt the butter. Sprinkle lemon juice over the pears, then stir into the melted butter. Add the brown sugar, spices, and pecans. Cook slowly over low heat, stirring occasionally, until the pears are somewhat softened, about 5 minutes.

Serve over a Belgian waffle or draped down the center of 2 to 3 pieces of French toast.

Plate with crisp lean bacon and a festive fanned strawberry.

Makes approximately 2 cups of topping. Use $^1/_3$ cup per serving.

MAKES 6 SERVINGS.

Magnificent Minis

$^1/_2$ **cup butter**
1 **cup sugar**
2 **eggs**
2 **medium very ripe bananas, mashed**
2 **cups all-purpose flour**
1 **teaspoon baking soda**
$^1/_4$ **cup chopped pecans**
$^1/_4$ **cup mini semi-sweet chocolate chips**
$^1/_3$ **cup chopped maraschino cherries**

Butter 45 mini-muffin cups.

In a large bowl soften the butter. Add the sugar and cream together. Beat until light and fluffy. Add the eggs, one at a time, beating until smooth.

Add the bananas and beat. In a separate bowl sift the flour and sodar. Stir gently into the creamed mixture. Fold in the pecans, chocolate chips, and cherries. Pour into the prepared mini-muffin cups. Bake in a 350° oven for 20 minutes. Remove the minis from the cups and cool on a wire rack.

MAKES 45 MUFFINS.

Pineapple Hill

1324 River Road
New Hope, Pennsylvania 18938
(215) 862-1790

A sixteen-room Colonial farmhouse built in 1790 and situated on five acres provides the setting for this unusual country inn. Guests marvel at the eighteen-inch-thick walls and original woodwork in this building. Each of the four guest rooms is individually furnished with antiques, collectibles, and original artwork. All rooms are stocked with books and magazines for the reading pleasure of guests. The nearby Delaware River provides many recreational opportunities, including tubing, rafting, canoeing, and fishing.

Baked Bananas

$^1/_2$ **cup butter, melted**
3 **tablespoons lemon juice**
6 **ripe bananas, peeled**
$^1/_3$ **cup firmly packed brown sugar**

1 **teaspoon ground ginger**
1 **cup grated coconut**

Pour the melted butter and lemon juice over the bottom of a 9-inch square baking dish. Stir the butter and lemon juice together. Roll the bananas in the butter mixture. In a small bowl mix the brown sugar and ginger. Sprinkle half over the bananas. Bake in a 375° oven for 10 minutes.

Roll the bananas over and sprinkle with the remaining sugar mixture. Bake for another 5 minutes.

Sprinkle coconut over and bake for 5 minutes.

MAKES 6 SERVINGS.

Cousin Rosie's Pineapple (Hill) Bread

$^1/_2$ **cup butter, softened**
1 **cup sugar**
5 **to 10 slices bread, cubed**
4 **eggs, beaten**
1 **cup crushed pineapple (canned is fine)**
$^1/_4$ **cup cinnamon-sugar**

In a medium bowl cream together the butter and sugar and pour into a 2-quart glass baking dish. Arrange the bread, in the dish. Pour the eggs and pineapple over the bread. Sprinkle cinnamon-sugar over the top. Bake in 350° oven for 1 hour.

Cool slightly before cutting. Can be served warm or cold. (Warm is delicious!)

MAKES 6 TO 8 SERVINGS.

Lori's "Super-Chocolatey" Cookies

2 **squares semisweet chocolate**
$2^1/_2$ **cups all-purpose flour**
1 **teaspoon baking soda**
$^1/_2$ **teaspoon salt**
1 **cup butter, at room temperature**
$^1/_2$ **cup sugar**
2 **cups firmly packed light brown sugar**
2 **eggs**
2 **teaspoons vanilla extract**

6 **semisweet chocolate squares, cut into large chunks**
6 **ounces white chocolate chips**

In a small bowl melt 2 squares of chocolate in the microwave. In a medium bowl mix the flour, soda, and salt.

In a large bowl cream the butter, sugars, eggs, vanilla, and melted chocolate. Add the dry ingredients by thirds, blending. Stir the chocolate chunks and white chocolate chips into the dough. Drop the dough by rounded tablespoons 2 inches apart onto an ungreased cookie sheet. Bake in a 375° oven for 10 to 12 minutes, until slightly browned around the edges. Move from the baking sheet to racks to cool.

MAKES 4 DOZEN COOKIES.

1005 Horsham Road
North Wales, Pennsylvania 19454
(215) 362-7500

*G*uest *rooms are available in three different buildings on this estate: the stone manor house, built in 1734; the tenant farmer's cottage; and the barn, built in 1820. Two parlors in the manor house serve as common areas for guests. In many of the guest rooms, the original exposed stone walls and elaborate stenciling are still visible. Within one hour's drive are many major tourist attractions, including the historic city of Philadelphia, the Amish country of Lancaster County, Valley Forge National Park, Atlantic City casinos, and the Aquarium at Camden, New Jersey.*

Joseph Ambler Inn Surf and Turf

  2 *3-ounce lobster tails*
  1 *4-ounce tenderloin*
  ¼ *cup all-purpose flour*

  3 *whole eggs, whipped*
  2 *teaspoons clarified butter*
  1 *cup brown stock or beef broth with collagen*
  1 *teaspoon fine chopped ginger*
  ¼ *cup Piore Williams Liquor*
  2 *teaspoons butter*
  ½ *bunch red Swiss chard, chopped large*
  ¼ *head Napa cabbage, chopped large*
     Salt and pepper to taste

Remove the lobster meat from the shells. Place the tail meat between sheets of plastic wrap and pound both tails with a mallet, taking care not to tear the meat. Remove from the wrap. In a skillet cook the tenderloin until the desired temperature and hold. Place the tenderloin in between the lobster meat. Lightly flour and dip in egg, making sure it is completely covered.

Heat a pan with clarified butter until the pan is hot but not smoking. Place the lobster in the pan. Brown for 30 seconds to 1 minute. Turn and brown the other side. Remove from the pan and hold. Heat the stock, ginger, and Piore Williams and reduce by half. Spin in 2 teaspoons of butter to thicken.

Place the lobster in a baking pan. Bake in a 350° oven for 5 minutes.

In a separate pan sauté the vegetables and season with salt and pepper to taste. Sauce the bottom of a plate, place the lobster in the center of the plate, and vegetables surrounding the lobster.

MAKES 1 SERVING.

Portabella Mushroom and Crab Appetizer

  ¼ *cup mayonnaise*
  1 *teaspoon finely chopped oregano*
  1 *teaspoon finely chopped basil*
  1 *teaspoon finely chopped parsley*
  2 *teaspoons balsamic vinegar*
  ¼ *tomato, seeded and finely diced*
  2 *slices white bread, trimmed and cubed*
  4 *ounces jumbo lump crab meat*
  2 *medium portabella mushrooms, wiped clean with a dry cloth*
  ¼ *cup grated Gruyère cheese*

  ½ *cup tawny Port*
  2 *teaspoons butter*

In a small bowl combine the mayonnaise, fresh herbs, and balsamic vinegar. Add the tomatoes, bread cubes, and crab meat. Toss together. Divide and cradle the crab mixture in the underside of the portabella mushrooms. Place in an oiled baking dish. Top with the Gruyère cheese. Bake in a 400° oven for about 10 minutes or until the mushrooms are tender and the stuffing is hot all the way through.

While the mushrooms are baking, in a saucepan bring the tawny Port to a simmer in a saucepan and cook until reduced by half. Remove the pan from the heat. Add the butter and stir in with a whisk. The sauce will thicken. Pour the sauce onto 2 plates and top with mushrooms.

MAKES 2 SERVINGS.

Shrimp Medallions with Roasted Garlic Sherry Cream Sauce and Fresh Sage Rosette

  5 *to 7 large shrimp, deveined and butterflied*
  2 *large shrimp, peeled*
  1 *egg white*
     Pinch salt and pepper
     Pinch fresh minced garlic
     Clarified butter

  ½ *cup sherry*
  2 *to 3 roasted cloves garlic, puréed*
  1 *bay leaf*
  ½ *cup heavy cream*
     Salt and pepper to taste

  4 *ounces cream cheese*
     Zest of ½ lemon
  2 *fresh sage leaves, minced*
  ⅛ *teaspoon lemon juice*

     Chopped red bell pepper
     Chopped black olives
     Whole fresh sage leaves

Lay all shrimp "butterfly"-side-down with tails pointing toward you. Place parchment paper over each shrimp and pound with a mallet. The shrimp should be flat and almost transparent.

In a food processor purée 2 shrimp, the egg white, salt, pepper, and garlic. Spread a small amount of the mousse on each shrimp.

Begin to roll 1 shrimp from the tail toward the head. Place the first shrimp on top of the second and roll from tail to end to create 1 large shrimp steak.

In a skillet sauté the "steak" in clarified butter on each side over high heat. Finish cooking in a 400° oven for 8 to 10 minutes.

In a saucepan cook the sherry, roasted garlic purée, and bay leaf over high heat until reduced by half. Add the heavy cream and reduce until thick. Remove the bay leaf. Season with salt and peper to taste.

In a food processor combine the cream cheese, lemon zest, sage, and lemon juice. Process until blended.

Sauce the plate and place the shrimp steak in the center. Pipe a cream cheese rose on the plate and garnish with chopped red pepper, black olives and fresh sage.

MAKES 1 SERVING.

Roasted Duck

1 **tablespoon red wine vinegar**
1 **tablespoon Worcestershire sauce**
3 **tablespoons stale beer**

....

1 **tablespoon granulated garlic**
½ **teaspoon white pepper**
3 **tablespoons paprika**
1 **tablespoon dry mustard**

....

1 **whole duck**

....

½ **cup water**
¼ **cup apple cider**
¼ **cup raspberry vinegar**
¼ **cup ketchup**
1 **pint blackberries**
1 **tablespoon Worcestershire sauce**
½ **cup plus 1 tablespoon firmly packed brown sugar**
½ **cup strawberry preserves**
1 **teaspoon cayenne pepper**
1 **tablespoon finely chopped ginger-root**
1 **tablespoon cumin**
¼ **onion minced**
1 **tablespoon chopped garlic**
3 **tablespoons sesame oil**

....

1 **cup beef stock or 46 -ounce can beef broth with collagen**
1 **sprig fresh rosemary**
1 **tablespoon brandy**
2 **tablespoons**

In a small bowl combine the red wine vinegar, 1 tablespoon of Worcestershire sauce, and beer. In a separate bowl combine the granulated garlic, pepper, paprika, and dry mustard. Split the duck in half, and brush the wet mix on the duck. Rub the dry mix on top of the duck. Roast in a 400° oven on a rack to catch the grease. The temperature of the duck should be 165° when done.

In a saucepan combine the water, apple cider, raspberry vinegar, ketchup, blackberries, 1 tablespoon of Worcestershire sauce, brown sugar, strawberry preserves, cayenne, ginger, cumin, onion, garlic, and sesame oil. Simmer slowly until thickened, stirring frequently so the sauce does not stick or burn.

In a separate saucepan combine the beef stock, rosemary, and brandy, and reduce to half. Add 2 tablespoons of butter to thicken.

Once the blackberry barbecue sauce is thick, spoon on the duck legs, and spoon rosemary sauce on the breasts.

MAKES 4 SERVINGS.

Hickory Bridge Farm

96 Hickory Bridge Road
Orrtanna, Pennsylvania 17353
(717) 642-5261

Hickory Bridge Farm, in the foothills of the Appalachian Mountains in south central Pennsylvania, is for guests who are looking for a quiet and peaceful retreat. Rooms are available in the old farmhouse as well as in free-standing cottages on the grounds. Each of the cottage rooms contains a Franklin stove. Guests enjoy relaxing on the back porch as well as trout fishing in the streams that run through the inn property. Nearby are such attractions as a ski resort, Gettysburg National Military Park, the Totem

Pole Playhouse, golfing, swimming, tennis, and antique shopping.

Fall Harvest Ball

1 *14-ounce can Hanover Redskin kidney beans, drained*
1 *cup chopped cooked roast beef*
¼ *cup chopped onion*
¼ *cup chopped celery*
1 *tablespoon chopped green bell pepper*
1 *tablespoon chopped pimento*
2 *tablespoons pickle relish*
1 *tablespoon prepared horseradish*
½ *cup mayonnaise*
1 *8-ounce package cream cheese, softened*
¼ *cup sour cream*
½ *cup grated sharp Cheddar cheese*
1 *teaspoon paprika*
1 *cup chopped pecans*
Chopped parsley (optional) for garnish
Assorted crackers

In a mixing bowl combine all of the ingredients except the paprika and pecans. Chill the mixture for at least 2 hours.

Shape into a ball and sprinkle paprika over the surface. Roll the ball in pecans and place in a round serving platter. Garnish with parsley, if desired. Arrange assorted crackers around the edge of the ball.

MAKES 8 TO 12 SERVINGS.

Escalloped Chicken

1 *cup dry breadcrumbs*
2 *tablespoons butter*
¾ *cup chopped celery*
½ *cup chopped onion*
2 *tablespoons chopped parsley*
½ *cup margarine*
6 *cups day-old bread*
1 *teaspoon salt*
Pinch pepper
½ *to 1 teaspoon poultry seasoning*
3 *tablespoons chicken broth*
Custard Sauce (recipe follows)
1 *large stewing chicken, cooked and diced*

Cook chicken, dice and set aside. Brown dry bread crumbs in the butter and set aside. Sauté celery, onion and parsley in margarine in skillet for about 5 minutes. Cut day old bread into small pieces. Add sautéed vegetables to the bread, tossing lightly. Turn into greased 13 x 9-inch casserole dish. Cover with ½ the custard and then with the diced chicken. Pour remaining custard over top. Sprinkle with prepared bread crumbs. Bake in a 350° oven for 45 minutes.

MAKES 10 TO 12 SERVINGS.

Custard Sauce for Escalloped Chicken

- 1 **cup chicken fat or part butter or margarine**
- 1 **cup flour**
- 4 **cups chicken broth**
- 1 **cup milk**
- 1 **teaspoon salt**
- 4 **slightly beaten eggs**

In a large saucepan melt the chicken fat. Gradually blend in the flour. Add the chicken broth and milk, stirring constantly. Add the salt, stirring until the mixture becomes very thick. Blend a little of the hot mixture into the eggs and add to the remaining mixture in the saucepan. Cook for 3 to 4 minutes.

MAKES 10 TO 12 SERVINGS.

Aunt Lillian's Delicious Cookies

- 1 **cup butter or margarine**
- 1 **cup sugar**
- 1 **cup firmly packed brown sugar**
- 1 **egg**
- 1 **cup oil**
- 1 **teaspoon vanilla extract**
- 1 **teaspoon salt**
- 1 **teaspoon cream of tartar**
- 1 **teaspoon baking soda**
- 1 **cup Rice Krispies**
- 1 **cup shredded coconut**
- 1 **cup quick-cooking oatmeal**
- 3½ **cups all-purpose flour**

In a large bowl cream the butter and sugars. Add the egg. Then add the remaining ingredients and mix. Drop by spoonful onto a greased cookie sheet. Press with fork. Bake in a 350° oven for 10 to 12 minutes.

These cookies keep well in a cookie can.

MAKES 5 DOZEN.

Chocolate Crinkles

- ½ **cup oil**
- 4 **squares unsweetened chocolate, melted**
- 2 **cups sugar**
- 4 **eggs**
- 2 **teaspoons vanilla extract**
- 2 **cups all-purpose flour**
- 2 **teaspoons baking powder**
- ½ **teaspoon salt**
- 1 **cup confectioners' sugar**

In a large bowl mix the oil, chocolate, and sugar. Blend in the eggs one at a time until mixed well. Add the vanilla. Stir the flour, baking powder, and salt into the oil mixture. Chill for several hours or overnight.

Drop by teaspoonfuls into confectioners' sugar. Roll in sugar and shape into balls. Place about 2 inches apart on a greased baking sheet. Bake in a 350° oven for 10 to 12 minutes. Do not overbake!

MAKES ABOUT 6 DOZEN.

Apple-Peanut Butter Fudge

- 1 **6-ounce package semisweet chocolate pieces (1 cup)**
- ½ **10-ounce jar marshmallow cream**
- ½ **cup peanut butter**
- 1 **teaspoon vanilla extract**
- 2 **cups sugar**
- ⅔ **cup apple juice**

In a medium bowl combine the chocolate, marshmallow cream, peanut butter, and vanilla. In a buttered heavy 2-quart saucepan combine the sugar and apple juice. Cook over medium heat until the sugar dissolves and the mixture boils. Continue cooking and stirring to the soft-ball stage at 240°. Remove from the heat quickly, and add the chocolate mixture. Stir until blended. Pour into a buttered 9 x 2-inch square baking pan. Allow to cool. Cut into squares.

MAKES ABOUT 6 DOZEN SQUARES.

Grandma Martin's Peach-Pineapple Preserves

- 5 **cups finely mashed peaches**
- 2 **cups crushed pineapple (as it comes in the can)**
- 7 **cups sugar**

- 1 **6-ounce box peach gelatin**

In a saucepan mix the peaches, pineapple, and sugar together and bring to a boil. Cook for about 20 minutes. Remove from the heat and stir in the gelatin. Stir well and pour into clean jars. Seal.

MAKES ABOUT 14 HALF-PINTS.

368 Pilottown Road
Peach Bottom, Pennsylvania 17563
(717) 548-3100

---

*T*his inn offers guests the opportunity to experience life on an authentic working farm, which has been owned by different members of the same family for more than one hundred years. The common areas, as well as the guest rooms, feature such country touches as ruffled curtains, decorative stenciling, antique clocks, and a huge fieldstone fireplace. The huge, two-story house, built of native stone, contains more than thirty rooms. Guests at Pleasant Grove enjoy day trips to such attractions as Amish farms in the Lancaster area, Hershey Park, Gettysburg National Military Park, and the cities of Philadelphia, Baltimore, and Washington, D.C.

French Toast Strata Pie

- ½ **pound bulk country sausage**
- 1 **all-purpose apple, cored, pared, and thinly sliced**
- 5 **eggs**
- 2 **cups milk**
- ⅓ **cup pure maple syrup**
- ½ **teaspoon grated nutmeg**
- ½ **pound French or Italian bread, sliced**

In a large skillet cook the sausage. Remove from the skillet, drain, and crumble. Add the apple slices to the skillet. Cover and cook over medium heat for 3 minutes.

In a medium bowl beat the eggs, milk, maple syrup, and nutmeg. In a buttered 10-inch pie plate or oblong dish, arrange three-fourths of the bread slices. Top with sausage, apples, and the remaining bread. Pour the milk mixture evenly over the top. Cover and refrigerate overnight.

Bake in a 350° oven for 55 to 60 minutes.
MAKES 6 TO 8 SERVINGS.

Corned Beef Brunch

½   **cup chopped onions**
½   **cup chopped celery**
½   **cup chopped green bell pepper**
1   **tablespoon butter**
12 **slices white bread, crusts removed**
12 **ounces sliced cooked corned beef**
1   **cup (4 ounces) shredded Cheddar cheese**
3   **eggs, beaten**
1½ **cups milk**
    Salt and pepper to taste

In a skillet sauté the onions, celery, and green pepper in butter until tender. Arrange 6 bread slices in a greased 12 x 8-inch dish. Place corned beef on each slice. Then spoon on the onion mixture, sprinkle with Cheddar cheese, and top with the remaining slices of bread.

In a bowl combine the eggs, milk, salt, and pepper. Mix well and pour over the bread slices. Bake in a 350° oven for 40 minutes.
MAKES 6 TO 8 SERVINGS.

The Decoy
✌

958 Eisenberger Road
Strasburg, Pennsylvania 17579
(800) 726-2287

Only twelve miles from Lancaster is the historic town of Strasburg and The Decoy inn. This old house with five comfortable guest rooms once belonged to an Amish family,

and it's still surrounded by the lush Amish farmlands of Lancaster County. The back roads of the surrounding countryside are ideal for bicycling. Other nearby attractions include tennis, golf, and swimming.

Country Sausage Gravy

1   **pound bulk pork sausage**
1   **10½-ounce can condensed cream of chicken soup, undiluted**
1   **soup can milk**
½   **teaspoon dry mustard**
¼   **teaspoon seasoned salt**
¼   **teaspoon pepper**
1   **cup sour cream**
    Warm biscuits
    Scrambled eggs

In a skillet crumble the pork sausage and cook until brown. Drain thoroughly. Remove. In the same skillet combine the soup and milk. Add the seasonings and bring to a boil. Reduce the heat and add the sausage and sour cream. Simmer until heated through. Do not boil. Serve over warm biscuits. Serve with scrambled eggs.
MAKES 4 TO 6 SERVINGS.

Fruit Flip

5   **cups fresh or frozen mixed berries**
¼   **cup cornstarch**
½   **cup water**
1¼ **cups sugar**
1   **18¼-ounce box white or yellow cake mix**
1   **cup shreddedcoconut**
½   **cup finely chopped walnuts**
½   **cup melted margarine**

In a greased 9 x 13-inch baking pan place the mixed berries. In a small saucepan mix the cornstarch and water. Add the sugar. Cook over a medium heat, stirring constantly, until the mixture comes to a rolling boil and has a clear appearance. Pour over the fruit. Sprinkle with cake mix, then top with coconut and walnuts. Drizzle with margarine. Bake in a 350° oven for 50 to 55 minutes.

Note: This can also be made with 5 cups of fresh or frozen rhubarb, but increase the sugar to 1½ cups.
MAKES 12 SERVINGS.

Cocoa Muffins

¼   **cup melted margarine**
¼   **cup unsweetened baking cocoa**
¾   **cup applesauce**
1¼ **cups all-purpose flour**
1   **cup sugar**
¾   **teaspoon baking soda**
½   **teaspoon ground cinnamon**
¼   **teaspoon grated nutmeg**
¼   **teaspoon salt**
1   **egg**
½   **cup raisins (optional)**

In a medium bowl blend the margarine, cocoa, and applesauce. Set aside. In a large bowl combine the flour, sugar, soda, cinnamon, nutmeg, and salt. Add the cocoa mixture and egg, and blend just until moistened. Fold in the raisins. Spoon into paper-lined muffin cups. Bake in a 350° oven for 20 minutes or until done.
MAKES 12 MUFFINS.

Spicy Cider Syrup

1   **cup sugar**
3   **tablespoons all-purpose flour**
¼   **teaspoon ground cinnamon**
¼   **teaspoon grated nutmeg**
2   **cups apple cider**
2   **tablespoons lemon juice**
1   **tablespoon butter**

In a saucepan mix the sugar, flour, and spices. Stir in the cider and lemon juice. Cook, stirring constantly, until the mixture boils and thickens. Boil and stir for 1 minute. Remove the pan from the heat. Stir in the butter. Serve warm over pancakes, waffles, or bran muffins.
MAKES ABOUT 3 CUPS.

Brown Sugar Oatmeal Pancakes

1   **cup whole wheat flour**
1   **cup all-purpose flour**
1¼ **cups quick-cooking oats**
1   **teaspoon salt**
1   **teaspoon baking soda**
⅔   **cup firmly packed brown sugar**
2   **eggs**
4   **teaspoons canola oil**
2   **cups buttermilk**

In a large bowl mix the dry ingredients. In a smaller bowl whisk the eggs and oil together. Pour the egg mixture along with the buttermilk into the dry ingredients and whisk thoroughly. Pour by ¼ cup onto a hot griddle sprayed with cooking spray.

Variation: This recipe also works if you wish to substitute applesauce for the oil, for reduced fat consumption. Be sure to use cooking spray before you cook each batch of pancakes.

MAKES 4 TO 6 SERVINGS.

Citrus Yogurt Muffins

  2   **cups all-purpose flour**
  ⅔   **cup sugar**
  1   **teaspoon baking soda**
  1   **teaspoon baking powder**
  1   **cup flaked coconut**
  ¼   **cup melted butter**
  1   **egg**
      Grated zest of 1 orange
  ¾   **teaspoon vanilla extract**
  1   **8-ounce carton lemon yogurt**
  ¼   **cup lime juice**

In a large bowl combine the flour, sugar, soda, and baking powder. In a medium bowl combine the remaining ingredients. Add to the dry ingredients and stir well. Spoon into paper-lined muffin cups. Bake in a 400° oven for 20 to 25 minutes.

MAKES 1 DOZEN.

Sausage Cheese Grits Casserole

  1   **cup quick-cooking grits**
  1   **pound bulk pork sausage**
  1   **small onion, finely chopped**
  ⅓   **cup chopped green bell pepper**
  1 ½ **cups grated Cheddar cheese**

In a saucepan cook grits according to the package directions. Set aside. In a large frying pan cook the sausage. Remove the sausage when done, draining thoroughly. Pour off all but 2 tablespoons of sausage grease. In the same pan sauté the onion and green pepper until tender. Remove from the grease and drain well. Combine the grits, sausage, onion, and pepper along with 1 cup of Cheddar cheese. Spoon into a lightly greased 8-inch square baking pan. Bake in a 350° oven for 15 minutes.

Sprinkle on the remaining cheese, and return to the oven for 5 minutes or until the cheese is melted and lightly browned.

MAKES 8 SERVINGS.

Bubble Bread

  3   **10-ounce cans refrigerator biscuits**
  1   **cup sugar**
  1   **teaspoon ground cinnamon**
....
  ½   **cup margarine**
  2   **tablespoons maple syrup**

Cut the biscuits in quarters. In a small bowl combine the sugar and cinnamon. Coat the biscuit pieces with some of the cinnamon-sugar. Do 6 to 8 pieces at a time. Pile evenly into a lightly greased tube pan.

In a saucepan bring the margarine, syrup, and remaining cinnamon-sugar to a boil, stirring constantly, until the sugar is nearly melted. Pour over the biscuits. Bake in a 350° oven for 30 minutes. Invert onto a large round serving plate.

MAKES 8 SERVINGS.

Cheddar Walnut Biscuits

  2   **cups all-purpose flour**
  1   **tablespoon baking powder**
  ½   **teaspoon cream of tartar**
  ½   **cup butter or margarine**
  ½   **cup ground walnuts**
  ½   **cup shredded Cheddar cheese**
  ⅔   **cup milk**

In a food processor combine the flour, baking powder, and cream of tartar. Add the margarine and pulse until the mixture resembles coarse crumbs. Pour into a medium bowl and stir in the nuts and Cheddar cheese. Add the milk and stir just until moistened. Turn the dough out onto a lightly floured surface. Quickly knead 10 to 12 times. Pat out the dough to ½-inch thickness. Cut with a 2½-inch biscuit cutter. Place on an ungreased baking sheet. Bake in a 450° oven for 10 to 12 minutes.

MAKES APPROXIMATELY 12 BISCUITS.

The Inn at Starlight Lake

P.O. Box 27
Starlight, Pennsylvania 18461
(800) 248-2519

*H**idden away in the lake district of northeastern Pennsylvania's Appalachian Mountains is the Inn at Starlight Lake. Opened in 1909, this guest-house still has the look and feel of a turn-of-the-century resort inn, although modern amenities such as air conditioning and private baths have been added. All rooms are individually decorated with furnishings and wall hangings reminiscent of the early 1900s. Guests are pleased to learn the daily room rate includes both breakfast and dinner. This resort area specializes in outdoor recreational activities, such as canoeing, rowboating, sailing, golfing, tennis, fishing, biking, and hiking. Spring-fed Starlight Lake offers a cool but unforgettable swimming experience.*

Pecan Pie

  1   **16-ounce box dark brown sugar**
  ¼   **cup all-purpose flour**
  ½   **teaspoon salt**
  ½   **cup milk**
  1½ **teaspoons vanilla extract**
  ½   **cup melted butter**

3 eggs, beaten
1 unbaked 9-inch pie shell
1 cup pecans

In a large bowl blend the sugar, flour, and salt. Add the milk, vanilla, and melted butter. Add the beaten eggs last. Whip only until blended. Place foil around the crust. Place the pecans in the crust. Pour in the blended ingredients. Bake in a 400° oven for 45 minutes to 1 hour.

MAKES 6 TO 8 SERVINGS.

Starlight Manicotti

2½ cups milk
1½ cups all-purpose flour
4 eggs
1½ tablespoons oil
½ teaspoon salt
....

1 16-ounce carton ricotta cheese
2 cups grated Romano-Parmesan cheese
1 cup grated Provolone cheese
5 ounces cooked chopped spinach
Marinara sauce

In a bowl combine the milk, flour, eggs, oil, and salt, and beat for 3 to 5 minutes. Place 3 tablespoons of mixture into a oiled and medium-hot crêpe pan. Cook approximately 1 minute on each side. Lay aside flat to cool.

In a large bowl combine the ricotta, Romano, Provolone, and spinach, and mix until blended well. Use a 1-ounce ice cream scoop to form the mixture into balls. Place 2 cheese balls in the center of 1 crepe and roll up. Bake in a 350° oven approximately 10 minutes.

Serve with a favorite Marinara sauce.

MAKES ABOUT 20 CRÊPES.

Creamy Garlic Dressing

3 cups oil
1 cup fresh lemon juice
2 teaspoon salt
2 teaspoons paprika
2 teaspoons white pepper
9 cloves garlic
1 teaspoon sugar
1⅔ cups evaporated milk

In a large bowl combine all of the ingredients and mix lightly. Pour half of the mixture into blender and blend. Then add the other half

and blend all together. Pour into a jar with a tight-fitting lid. Keep refrigerated. It will keep well for 2 weeks.

MAKES APPROXIMATELY 6 CUPS.

Raised Dough Waffles

2 tablespoons dry active yeast
2½ cups lukewarm water (105 to 115°)
½ cup dry milk
½ cup oil
1 teaspoon salt
1 teaspoon sugar
1½ cups all-purpose flour
½ cup whole wheat flour
¼ cup wheat germ
....

2 eggs, well-beaten
Pinch baking soda
Butter, room temperature
Maple syrup

In a large mixing bowl dissolve the yeast in ½ cup of water. Let stand 5 minutes. Stir in the remaining water, dry milk, oil, salt, and sugar.

Separately add flour, whole wheat flour, and wheat germ, beating after each addition. Mix well. Cover the bowl with a tea towel and let stand in a warm place. The bowl should be large enough to allow batter to triple in volume. Allow the batter to rise at least 8 hours or overnight.

In the morning, add the eggs and soda. Mix well. Pour about one-third cup of batter into a hot waffle iron. Bake 5 to 7 minutes, or until golden brown. Repeat with the remaining batter. Serve at once with butter and syrup.

MAKES 4 TO 6 WAFFLES.

Will's Sunday Salad

½ cup tofu, blanched and crumbled
6 fresh spinach leaves, washed and trimmed
¼ green bell pepper, chopped
1 tablespoons fresh basil or 1 teaspoon dried basil
¼ teaspoon black pepper
1 scallion, chopped
3 tablespoons cider vinegar
¾ teaspoon salt
1 cup oil
....

½ head romaine lettuce
5 ounces cooked pasta
¼ cup raisins

¾ cup shredded carrots
1 cup chopped Cheddar cheese
2 ounces broccoli, broken into small flowers
2 ounces cauliflower, broken into small flowers
2 ounces mushrooms, sliced
2 ounces pine nuts, roasted (can be unroasted but not as flavorful)

In a blender or food processor combine the tofu, spinach, green pepper, basil, black pepper, scallion, vinegar, and salt. Blend until liquefied. While the machine is still running, slowly drizzle in a steady stream of oil until the dressing thickens. Refrigerated and covered, it will stay fresh for up to a week.

In a chilled salad bowl combine the remaining ingredients. Mix well. Pour 1 to 1½ cups of dressing over the mixture and blend well. Serve cold.

MAKES 4 SERVINGS.

Pace One Country Inn

P.O. Box 108
Thornton, Pennsylvania 19373
(610) 459-3702

*P*ace One is in a historically renovated stone barn from the 1740s. It has won several awards for adaptive re-use of a historic building. Six rustic and warmly decorated guest rooms are available. Guests also enjoy the cozy and rustic bar. In the heart of the Brandywine Valley, Pace One is close to Longwood Gardens, Brandywine River Museum featuring the artistic works of the Wyeth family, and golf courses and tennis courts.

Shrimp Sauté

4½ ounces Garlic Butter (recipe follows)
1 ounce spinach leaves, cleaned

1 *ounce red onion, diced*
2 *ounces tomatoes, diced*
7 *Extra large shrimp, tail on*
2 *ounce feta cheese*
5 *ounces cooked rice*

In a sauté pan over very low heat melt the Garlic Butter and sauté the spinach, onion, and tomatoes. The butter should stay creamy and should not break. Add the shrimp and sauté until done. Add half of the feta cheese just before the pan comes off the stove.

On a round plate place a bed of rice. Top with arranged shrimp, vegetables, and sauce, and crumble the remaining feta cheese over top.

MAKES 1 SERVING.

Garlic Butter

3 *pounds margarine, softened*
3 *pounds butter, softened*
1 *cup garlic in water*
2 *tablespoons salt*
4 *teaspoons black pepper*
1/3 *cup soy sauce*
2 *tablespoons granulated garlic*
4 *cups finely diced green bell peppers*
4 *cups tomatoes, diced small*
4 *cups finely diced mushrooms*

In a large bowl combine the butter and margarine. Add the garlic in water, salt, black pepper, soy sauce, and granulated garlic, and mix well with an electric mixer. Remove from the mixer. Mix in by hand the green peppers, tomatoes, and mushrooms.

MAKES 1 GALLON.

Romaine Salad

3 *cups loosely packed Romaine lettuce*
2 *ounces blue cheese, crumbled*
2 *ounces dried cranberries*
1/4 *cup Orange Raspberry Vinaigrette dressing (recipe follows)*

In a salad bowl combine and toss together all of the ingredients. Serve on chilled dinner plates.

Note: When Romaine is prepared, it should be torn, not cut. Romaine must be kept in an airtight container in the refrigerator. Romaine must be moist and crisp, not dry and limp, with no refrigerator taste.

MAKES 2 SERVINGS.

Orange Raspberry Vinaigrette

3 *cups orange juice*
1 *cup raspberry vinegar*
1 *quart olive oil*
1 *teaspoon salt*
1 *teaspoon cracked black pepper*

In a large bowl or container with a tight-fitting lid combine all of the ingredients and mix well.

MAKES 2 QUARTS.

Victorian Guest House

118 York Road, Route 6
Towanda, Pennsylvania 18848
(717) 265-6972

Situated in the Endless Mountains, this inn is a classic example of the Queen Anne Victorian style of architecture, with ornate porches and tower rooms. It was built in 1897 by an area lumber baron, who insisted on using a different wood in each room. The result is a beautiful array of paneled and beamed ceilings, trims, and wainscoting that guests are not likely to find in another inn. All ten guest rooms are furnished with antiques. The Victorian Guest House is only six blocks from the center of town with its fine restaurants and unusual shops.

Victorian Guest House

Philadelphia Sticky Buns

2 *1-pound loaves frozen bread dough*
1/2 *cup margarine*
1 *3-3/8-ounce box butterscotch pudding (not instant)*
1 *tablespoon ground cinnamon*
1/2 *cup firmly packed brown sugar*
1/3 *cup light corn syrup*
Walnuts or pecans
Cinnamon-sugar mixture (1 teaspoon cinnamon to 1/3 cup sugar)
Raisins

Thaw the bread dough. In a medium bowl melt the margarine. Add the butterscotch pudding, cinnamon, brown sugar, and corn syrup to the melted margarine. Mix well.

Grease the sides and bottom of a 9 x 13-inch glass baking dish. Spread walnuts or pecans on the bottom of the baking dish. Pour the pudding mixture evenly over the nuts. To create the bun, flatten the thawed bread dough. Sprinkle the top of the dough with the cinnamon-sugar mixture. Spread raisins on top of the dough.

Roll the dough jellyroll fashion along the long side of the dough. Pinch the ends to seal. Stretch the dough to make about a 12-inch roll. Cut into 1-inch slices and place in the prepared baking dish. Repeat the process for the second loaf of bread dough.

Bake in a 350° oven for 15 to 20 minutes, or until browned. The buns will make a hollow thump sound when done. After the buns are removed from the oven, immediately flip the buns out onto a baking tray. Scrape all of the hot syrup and nuts onto the buns. Let cool and serve.

Guests will rave over these gooey delights.

MAKES 24 BUNS.

Cream Cheese and Raspberry Coffee Cake

1 *8-ounce package cream cheese, softened*
1 *cup sugar*
1/2 *cup margarine or butter*
2 *eggs*
1/2 *teaspoon vanilla extract*
1-3/4 *cups all-purpose flour*
1 *teaspoon baking powder*
1/2 *teaspoon baking soda*

¼ teaspoon salt
¼ cup milk
½ cup raspberry preserves
Confectioners' sugar

Grease and flour a 9 x 13-inch baking pan. In a large mixing bowl beat the cream cheese, sugar, and margarine with an electric mixer until fluffy. Add the eggs one at a time, and then the vanilla. In a separate bowl sift together the flour, baking powder, soda, and salt. Add half of the dry ingredients to the cream cheese mixture and all of the milk. Beat for 2 minutes, until blended well. Add the remaining flour on low speed until blended well. Spread the mixture evenly in the prepared pan. Spoon the raspberry preserves in 8 to 10 dollops on top of the batter. With a knife swirl the preserves into the batter. Bake in a 350° oven for 30 to 35 minutes, until a toothpick inserted in the center comes out clean.

Cool slightly on a wire rack. Sprinkle lightly with confectioners' sugar.

MAKES 24 SERVINGS.

Scratch Buttermilk Biscuits

2⅔ cups all-purpose flour
4 teaspoons baking powder
¼ teaspoon baking soda
⅔ teaspoon salt
½ cup butter-flavored shortening
1 cup low-fat buttermilk

In a large bowl sift together the flour, baking powder, soda, and salt. Cut in the shortening with a pastry blender or fork until coarse crumbs form. Make a well in the center of the flour mixture and add the buttermilk. Stir quickly with a fork just until a dough forms. Turn out onto a lightly floured surface. Knead gently for 10 to 12 strokes, by flattening the dough, folding the dough in half, flatten again, fold in half again, and so on. This will give the biscuits a layered appearance. Roll the dough to about ¾ inch thick and cut with a floured biscuit cutter. Bake in a 450° oven for about 12 minutes or until brown.

MAKES ABOUT 12 BISCUITS.

Kaltenbach's Bed & Breakfast
❧

R.D. #6, Box 106-A
Stony Fork Road
Wellsboro, Pennsylvania 16901
(800) 722-4954

This unusual inn, on a seventy-two-acre farm with cows, rabbits, and sheep, offers modern conveniences in a quiet and relaxed country atmosphere. All ten guest rooms feature king- or queen-size beds with Jacuzzis and handmade quilts. Only ten miles away is north central Pennsylvania's Grand Canyon, a natural wonder that offers sporting events for the outdoors-minded, including whitewater rafting, hiking, canoeing, biking, and horseback riding. The Victorian village of Wellsboro is also a mecca for antique treasure hunters and shoppers who love unusual stores and novelty shops.

Farmer's Breakfast

½ pound bacon, cut into ½-inch pieces
1 large onion, chopped
5 large potatoes, peeled and sliced julienne
Salt and pepper to taste
3 eggs

In a large skillet sauté the bacon just until crisp. Add the onion and cook until transparent. Add the potatoes, salt, and pepper and mix well. Cover and cook until the potatoes are tender, stirring occasionally. In a small bowl beat the eggs until light and fluffy. Pour over the potato mixture. Cook, stirring constantly, until the eggs are set.

MAKES 4 SERVINGS.

Ken's Sweet Potatoes

8 medium sweet potatoes
1¼ cups firmly packed brown sugar
½ cup apple juice
½ cup water
½ cup raisins
¼ cup butter or margarine

Cook and peel the potatoes. Allow to cool. Slice and place in a greased 2½-quart baking dish. In a small saucepan combine the remaining ingredients and bring to a boil, stirring frequently. Pour over the potatoes. Bake in a 350° oven for 45 minutes, basting occasionally.

MAKES 8 SERVINGS.

Pumpkin Roll

3 eggs
1 cup sugar
⅔ cup pumpkin
1 teaspoon baking soda
1 teaspoon ground cinnamon
¾ cup all purpose flour
Confectioners' sugar
1 8-ounce package cream cheese
¼ cup butter
1 cup confectioners' sugar
1 teaspoon vanilla extract

In a medium bowl mix the eggs and sugar together. Add the pumpkin, soda, cinnamon, and flour, and mix well. Grease a cookie sheet and line with waxed paper, then grease and flour the waxed paper. Pour the batter into the prepared pan. Bake in a 350° oven for 15 minutes. This bakes very quickly, so keep an eye on it.

Remove the warm cake from the pan onto a clean teatowel covered with confectioners' sugar. Wrap up and let cool. In a medium bowl mix the cream cheese, butter, confectioners' sugar, and vanilla. Unwrap the cake and spread with the filling. Roll up like a jelly roll, wrap in aluminum foil, and keep refrigerated. Slice and serve.

MAKES 8 SERVINGS.

Golden Apple Pie

6 cups peeled and sliced Golden Delicious apples
¾ cup plus 2 teaspoons apple juice, divided
¾ cup sugar

1 teaspoon ground cinnamon
½ teaspoon apple pie spice
¼ teaspoon vanilla extract
2 tablespoons cornstarch
....
2½ cups all-purpose flour
1 teaspoon salt
1 cup cold butter or margarine
6 to 8 tablespoons ice water

In a large saucepan combine the apples, ¾ cup of apple juice, sugar, cinnamon, apple pie spice, and vanilla, and bring to a boil over medium heat, stirring occasionally. In a cup combine the cornstarch and remaining apple juice. Add to the saucepan and return to a boil, stirring constantly. Cook and stir 1 minute more or until thickened. Remove from the heat and cool to room temperature, stirring occasionally.

Meanwhile, in a large bowl combine the flour and salt. Cut in the butter until crumbly. Sprinkle with the water, 1 tablespoon at a time; and stir with a fork until the dough can be formed into a ball. Divide in half. On a lightly floured surface, roll half to fit a 9-inch pie plate. Place in the plate and add the filling. Roll the remaining pastry to fit the top of the pie. Place over the filling and seal the edges. Cut vents in the top. If desired, decorate top of pie with pastry scraps cut into small apple shapes. Bake in a 400° oven for 40 to 45 minutes, or until the crust is lightly browned and the apples are tender.

MAKES 6 TO 8 SERVINGS.

Fall Pear Pie

8 cups thinly sliced peeled pears
¾ cup sugar
¼ cup quick-cooking tapioca
¼ teaspoon grated nutmeg
   Pastry for 9-inch double-crust pie
1 egg, lightly beaten
¼ cup heavy cream (optional)

In a large bowl combine the pears, sugar, tapioca, and nutmeg. Line a pie plate with a bottom crust. Add the pear mixture. Roll out the remaining pastry to fit the top of the pie. Place over the filling and seal the edges. Cut large slits in the top. Brush with egg. Bake in a 375° oven for 55 to 60 minutes, or until the pears are tender. Remove to a wire rack. Pour cream through the slits, if desired.

MAKES 6 TO 8 SERVINGS.

Walnut Pie

½ cup butter or margarine, melted
1 cup sugar
½ cup all-purpose flour
2 eggs
1 teaspoon vanilla extract
1 cup coarsely chopped walnuts
1 cup semisweet chocolate chips
½ cup butterscotch chips
1 unbaked 9-inch pastry shell

In a medium bowl beat the butter, sugar, flour, eggs, and vanilla with an electric mixer until blended well. Stir in the nuts and chips. Pour into the pie shell. Bake in 325° oven for 1 hour, or until golden brown. Cool on a wire rack.

MAKES 6 TO 8 SERVINGS.

Maple-Glazed Ribs

3 pounds pork spareribs, cut into serving-size pieces
1 cup maple syrup
3 tablespoons orange juice concentrate
3 tablespoons ketchup
2 tablespoons soy sauce
1 tablespoon Dijon mustard
1 tablespoon Worcestershire sauce
1 teaspoon curry powder
1 clove garlic, minced
2 green onions, minced
1 tablespoon sesame seeds, toasted

Place the ribs, meaty-side-up, on a rack in a greased 9 x 13-inch baking pan. Cover the pan tightly with foil. Bake in a 350° oven for 1 hour and 15 minutes.

Meanwhile, in a saucepan combine the remaining ingredients except the sesame seeds. Bring to a boil over medium heat. Reduce the heat and simmer for 15 minutes, stirring occasionally. Drain the ribs. Remove the rack and return the ribs to the pan. Cover with sauce. Bake, uncovered, for 35 minutes, basting occasionally. Sprinkle with sesame seeds just before serving.

MAKES 6 SERVINGS.

Zesty Sloppy Jones

4 pounds ground beef
1 cup chopped onion
1 cup finely chopped green bell pepper
2 10¾-ounces cans condensed tomato soup, undiluted
1 15-ounce can thick and zesty tomato sauce
1 8-ounce can tomato sauce
¾ cup firmly packed brown sugar
¼ cup ketchup
3 tablespoons Worcestershire sauce
1 tablespoon prepared mustard
1 tablespoon dry mustard
1 teaspoon chili powder
1 teaspoon garlic salt

In a large saucepan or Dutch oven over medium heat brown the beef and onion. Add the green pepper, and cook and stir for 5 minutes. Drain. Add the remaining ingredients, and bring to a boil. Reduce the heat, cover, and simmer for 1 hour, stirring occasionally. Serve on buns.

MAKES 20 TO 25 SERVINGS.

Pork Roast Barbecue

1 3½ to 4-pound boneless rolled pork loin roast
2 cups water, divided
2 teaspoons salt, divided
1 16-ounce can tomato purée
1 tablespoon firmly packed brown sugar
1 tablespoon white vinegar
1 tablespoon Worcestershire sauce
1 teaspoon browning sauce (optional)
¼ teaspoon pepper
¼ teaspoon dry mustard
¼ teaspoon hot pepper sauce
   Sandwich buns (optional)

Place the roast in a heavy 5-quart roaster or Dutch oven. In a cup combine 1 cup of water and 1 teaspoon of salt, and pour over the meat. Cover and simmer for 2 hours.

Drain, reserving 1 cup of broth. Cool the roast for 15 minutes. Cut into thin slices and place in an 11 x 7-inch baking dish. In a 2-quart saucepan combine the tomato purée, brown sugar, vinegar, Worcestershire sauce, and browning sauce, if desired.

Add the pepper, mustard, hot pepper sauce, remaining water, salt, and reserved broth. Bring to a boil. Cook and stir for 3 minutes. Pour over the meat. Cover and refrigerate overnight, turning the meat once.

Remove from the refrigerator for 30 minutes before reheating. Bake in a 350° oven for 1 hour. Serve on buns, if desired.

MAKES 10 TO 12 SERVINGS.

Apple Crisp

  4 *cups peeled, sliced apples*
²⁄₃ *cup firmly packed brown sugar*
½ *cup all-purpose flour*
½ *cup oats*
¼ *teaspoon ground cinnamon*
½ *cup butter, softened*

Place the apples in a 1½ -quart glass baking dish. In a medium bowl mix the brown sugar, flour, oats, cinnamon, and butter. Spoon over the apples. Microwave on high for 5 minutes, or until the apples are tender, turning 1 quarter turn after 2½ minutes.

MAKES 6 SERVINGS.

Icebox Apple Pie

4½ *cups peeled, sliced baking apples*
1½ *cups water*
  1 *tablespoon butter or margarine*
¼ *teaspoon ground cinnamon*
¼ *teaspoon grated nutmeg*
  1 *3-ounce package peach, flavored gelatin*
  1 *3-ounce package cook-and-serve vanilla pudding mix*
  1 *baked 9-inch pastry shell*

································

¼ *cup graham cracker crumbs*
  1 *tablespoon butter or margarine, melted*
1½ *teaspoons sugar*

In a large saucepan combine the apples, water, butter, cinnamon, and nutmeg. Bring to a boil. Reduce the heat and simmer uncovered for 5 minutes, or until the apples are tender. Gradually stir in the gelatin and pudding and bring to a boil. Remove from the heat and let stand for 5 minutes. Pour into the pie shell.

In a small bowl combine the remaining ingredients. Sprinkle over the filling. Chill for 3 to 4 hours or until firm.

MAKES 6 TO 8 SERVINGS.

Cherry Cheesecake

1¼ *cups all purpose flour*
1/2 *cup firmly packed light brown sugar*
½ *cup butter-flavored shortening*
  1 *cup chopped walnuts, divided*
½ *cup flaked coconut*
  2 *8-ounce packages cream cheese, softened*
²⁄₃ *cup sugar*
  2 *eggs*
  2 *teaspoons vanilla extract*
  2 *21-ounce cans cherry pie filling*

In a large bowl combine the flour and brown sugar. Cut in the shortening until crumbly. Stir in half of the nuts and the coconut. Reserve ½ cup of the mixture for topping. Press the remaining mixture into a greased 9 x 13-inch baking pan. Bake in a 350° oven for 15 minutes.

In a large bowl beat the cream cheese, sugar, eggs, and vanilla. Mix with an electric mixer until smooth. Spread over the hot baked layer. Bake for 15 minutes.

Top with the cherry pie filling, spreading to the edge. In a small bowl combine the remaining nuts and reserved crumb mixture. Sprinkle over the pie filling. Bake for 15 minutes.

Let stand until cool. Chill in the refrigerator.

MAKES 9 SERVINGS.

Five Star Brownies

  3 *eggs*
  2 *cups sugar*
1½ *teaspoons vanilla extract*
½ *cup butter or , melted*
¼ *cup shortening, melted*
1½ *cups all-purpose flour*
¾ *cup baking cocoa*
1¼ *teaspoons salt*
  1 *cup chopped nuts, optional*

In a large bowl beat the eggs, sugar, and vanilla with an electric mixer until mixed well. Add the butter and shortening. In a separate bowl combine the flour, cocoa, and salt. Stir the dry ingredients into the egg mixture and mix well. Add the nuts, if desired. Line a 9 x 13-inch baking pan with foil and grease the foil. Pour the batter into the pan. Bake in a 350° oven for 30 minutes, or until a toothpick inserted in the center comes out clean.

Cool in the pan. Turn the brownies out of the pan onto a cookie sheet, and remove the foil. Place a wire rack over the brownies, turn over, and remove the cookie sheet. Cut with a star-shaped cookie cutter or into bars.

MAKES 3 DOZEN.

Chewy Oatmeal Cookies

¾ *cup butter, softened*
½ *cup sugar*
1½ *cup firmly packed brown sugar*
  2 *eggs*
  1 *teaspoon vanilla extract*
1¼ *cups all purpose flour*
  1 *teaspoon baking powder*
½ *teaspoon baking soda*
  1 *teaspoon salt*
2½ *cups old-fashioned oats*
²⁄₃ *cup nuts*
½ *cup flaked coconut*

In a large bowl cream butter, sugar, and brown sugar with an electric mixer until light and fluffy. Beat in the eggs and vanilla. Stir in the flour, baking powder, soda, and salt; and mix well. Add the oats, nuts, and coconut, and mix well. Chill for 2 hours. Roll the dough into small balls, and place on a cookie sheet. Bake in a 350° oven for 8 to 10 minutes, or until golden brown.

Remove to a wire rack to cool.

MAKES 4 DOZEN.

The Bankhouse

875 Hillsdale Road
West Chester, Pennsylvania 19382-1975
(610) 344-7388

The Bankhouse

With only two guest rooms in a quiet and peaceful setting, the Bankhouse offers the ultimate in privacy and seclusion. It's in an eighteenth-century farmhouse on a rural road just outside the quaint little town of West Chester. In addition to local shops and restaurants, guests are within an easy drive of the Amish community of Lancaster, Longwood Gardens, the Brandywine River Museum, and Brandywine Battlefield Park. Other activities such as canoeing, horseback riding, golf, and skiing are also available nearby.

Apple Bacon Cheddar Bake

3 cups sliced apples
2 tablespoons sugar
2 cups shredded Cheddar cheese
1 pound bacon, fried crisp
4 to 5 eggs
2 cups biscuit mix (or 2 cups all-purpose flour, 3 teaspoons baking powder, and ½ teaspoon salt)
2 cups milk

In a large bowl mix the apples and sugar. Lightly butter a 9 x 13-inch pan and place the apples in a row. Cover the apples with Cheddar cheese. Sprinkle with crumbled bacon. In a separate bowl beat the remaining ingredients together. Using a ladle, pour the mixture evenly over the bacon. Bake in a 375° oven for 30 to 35 minutes, or until golden brown.
MAKES 8 TO 10 SERVINGS.

Citrus Puff Crêpe

¼ cup butter
3 eggs
½ cup all-purpose flour
½ cup milk
¼ cup sugar
2 tablespoons orange juice
1 teaspoon vanilla extract

Confectioners' sugar
Juice of 1 lemon

In a 9 x 13-inch pan melt the butter. Set aside. In a large bowl combine the eggs, flour, milk, sugar, orange juice, and vanilla, and beat well. Pour into the pan. Bake in a 450° oven for 20 minutes, or until golden and puffy. Sprinkle with the juice of 1 lemon and dust with confectioners' sugar. Serve immediately.
MAKES 4 SERVINGS.

Hollileif
Bed &
Breakfast

❧

677 Durham Road
Wrightstown, Pennsylvania 18940
(215) 598-3100

Country elegant is the style of this unusual inn, which derives its name from the forty-foot holly trees that grace the entrance. Hollileif means "beloved tree." Situated on five and one-half rolling acres, Hollileif is surrounded by trees, flowers, gardens, and streams. The five guest rooms are decorated with lace, ruffles, and other country furnishings. Fresh flowers also add a memorable and romantic touch. Nearby attractions include Peddler's Village, the artist's colony of New Hope on the Delaware River, and fine restaurants and shops.

Tropical Fruit Juice

4 teaspoons sugar or 2 packets artificial sweetener
3 capfuls tropical fruit liqueur such as Key Largo (optional)

1 ripe mango, peeled
1 ripe papaya, peeled
5 to 6 ripe bananas
Fresh or frozen strawberries
Pineapple juice, orange juice, or tropical fruit juice blend such as Caribbean Splash

In a 2-quart pitcher place the sugar or sweetener, liqueur, mango, papaya and bananas. Fill the pitcher with strawberries and almost cover the fruit with juice. Refrigerate overnight.

Pour the ingredients into a blender jar and blend at high speed until smooth and thick.
MAKES 16 SERVINGS.

Peaches in Butterscotch Sauce

1 cup heavy cream
1 cup sugar
3 tablespoons butter, cut into pieces
1 teaspoon vanilla extract
2 tablespoons brandy
10 peaches, skin removed and sliced

In a saucepan scald the cream. Place the sugar in a nonstick pan on high heat. Stir constantly with a wooden spoon until it caramelizes. Reduce the heat and cook until smooth. Remove the pan from the heat. Gradually add the cream, stirring constantly. Cook over moderate heat until the lumps dissolve, if necessary. Remove from the heat. Add the butter, vanilla, and brandy. Pour into a bowl and whisk until smooth. Divide the peaches into 10 individual serving bowls, and drizzle with sauce. Store any leftover sauce in the refrigerator.
MAKES 10 SERVINGS.

Hollileif

RHODE ISLAND

*Blue Dory
Inn*

P.O. Box 488
Block Island, Rhode Island 02807
(800) 992-7290

This Victorian inn, featuring many rooms with views of the sea, is situated at the head of Crescent Beach. All guest rooms and common areas are furnished with antiques. Nearby are miles of unspoiled beaches, which offer fishing, swimming, sailing, or exploring and beach-combing among the natural dunes. Historic sites, shops, and fine restaurants are also nearby.

Blue Dory Inn

House Cookie

    2   cups butter
    4½ cups all-purpose flour
    1½ cups maple syrup
    2   cups chopped walnut
    2   cups chocolate bits (large chunks)

In a large bowl combine all ingredients. Place small balls on an ungreased cookie sheet, and depress with 3 fingers. Bake in a 350° oven for 17 to 20 minutes or until lightly browned. Do not overbake.

MAKES ABOUT 4 DOZEN.

The Richards

144 Gibson Avenue
Narragansett, Rhode Island 02882
(401) 789-7746

Built in 1884 from stone quarried on the site, this twelve-room inn was originally part of a two-hun-dred-acre estate. It was painstak-ingly restored by the Richards family and converted into an inn in 1980. Attractions available nearby include golf, tennis, and swimming.

Adirondack Flapjacks

    3   cups all-purpose flour
    3   tablespoons sugar
    3   teaspoons baking powder
    ½   teaspoon salt
    6   large eggs, room temperature, sepa-
        rated
    3   cups milk
    9   tablespoons butter, melted
        Maple syrup

In a medium bowl combine the flour, sugar, baking powder, and salt. In a separate bowl beat the egg whites until stiff peaks form. Set aside. In a large bowl beat together the milk, butter, and egg yolks. Stir in the dry ingredi-ents. Fold in the egg whites. Pour ½ cup of batter on a hot greased skillet or griddle at a time. Cook until bubbles form at the edge. Turn and cook until done, 2 to 3 minutes. Serve with heated maple syrup.

MAKES 6 TO 8 SERVINGS.

Pear Pecan Muffins

    2   cups all-purpose flour
    2   teaspoons baking powder
    ½   teaspoon baking soda
    ½   teaspoon salt
    2   eggs
    ⅓   cup butter, melted
    ½   cup milk or ½ cup pear juice
    1   large ripe pear, chopped in cubes
    ½   cup pecans
    ¼   cup chopped candied ginger

Grease or line 12 muffin cups with paper liners. In a medium bowl combine the flour, baking powder, soda, and salt. In a large bowl combine the eggs, butter, and milk, and beat well. Add the pear, pecans, and ginger. Fold in the dry ingredients. Fill muffin cups three-fourths full. Bake in a 400° oven for 20 minutes.

MAKES 1 DOZEN.

Chocolate Pancakes

1¼ cup all-purpose flour
2 tablespoons baking powder
2 tablespoons sugar
½ teaspoon salt
2 tablespoons unsweetened cocoa
1 egg
1 cup milk
2 tablespoons oil
   Orange sauce
   Toasted pecans
   Whipped cream

In a medium bowl sift together the flour, baking powder, sugar, salt, and cocoa. In a large bowl beat the egg. Add the milk and oil, and mix well. Add the dry ingredients and beat until smooth. Spoon the batter onto a hot griddle and cook until bubbles form. Turn and bake until done.

Serve with orange sauce, toasted pecans, and whipped cream.

MAKES 4 TO 6 SERVINGS.

Cliffside Inn

2 Seaview Avenue
Newport, Rhode Island 02840
(800) 845-1811

*G*uest-room amenities at Cliffside Inn include fireplaces, period antiques, and Jacuzzi whirlpool baths. The inn is only one block from the famous Cliff Walk path, minutes from the Newport harborfront with fine shops and restaurants, and two blocks from the beach. Throughout the house are

paintings by Beatrice Turner, daughter of the wealthy owners of the house at the turn of the century. She spent her life as a recluse in this house, painting thousands of oils, most of them self-portraits, until her death in 1948.

Orange Waffles with Peach Topping

4 cups all-purpose flour
6 teaspoons baking powder
¼ cup sugar
½ teaspoon salt
8 eggs
2 cups buttermilk
½ cup butter
½ cup grated orange zest
....
¼ cup butter
½ bag frozen peaches, thawed
1 cup maple syrup

In a large bowls sift together the flour, baking powder, sugar, and salt. In a medium bowl combine the eggs, buttermilk, and ½ cup of butter. Add the orange zest. Add the liquid mixture to the dry ingredients, half of the total amount at a time. Beat well after each addition until the batter is smooth. Pour about ¾ cup onto a hot greased waffle iron. Bake until golden brown.

In a saucepan melt ¼ cup of butter over medium heat. Add the peaches and maple syrup and heat through. Serve warm on top of waffles.

MAKES 6 SERVINGS.

Francis Malbone House

392 Thames Street
Newport, Rhode Island 02840
(800) 846-0392, (401) 846-0392

*T*his historic inn was built in 1760 for shipping merchant Francis Malbone. Conveniently located on New-

port's harborfront, it is lavishly decorated with antiques and period furnishings. Many rooms have working fireplaces. Other guest-pleasing features are the gardens, the library, and several parlors.

Francis Malbone House

Artichoke Squares

3 6-ounce jars marinated artichoke hearts
1 small onion, finely chopped
1 clove garlic, minced
4 eggs
⅛ teaspoon Tabasco sauce
⅛ teaspoon oregano
⅛ teaspoon pepper
2 cups grated Cheddar cheese
½ cup Italian breadcrumbs

Drain and chop the artichokes, and reserve the marinade. In a sauté pan heat half of the marinade and sauté the onion and garlic until tender. Add the chopped artichokes. In a medium bowl beat the eggs. Add the sautéed onion and garlic, and the remaining ingredients. Pour into a greased 7 x 11-inch baking dish. Bake in a 325° oven for 30 minutes.

MAKES ABOUT 8 TO 10 SERVINGS.

Blueberry-Raspberry-Strawberry Cobbler

1 pint blueberries
1 pint raspberries
1 quart strawberries
½ cup plus 1 tablespoon sugar
   Finely grated zest of 1 lemon
2 cups all-purpose flour
¼ tablespoon baking powder
1 cup softened butter
½ cup milk
1 egg

Butter a 14-inch oblong baking dish. In a large bowl combine the berries, ½ cup of sugar, and lemon zest, and toss. Spoon into the pan.

In a medium bowl mix the flour, baking powder, and 1 tablespoon of sugar. Work in the butter with fingertips until the mixture resembles coarse crumbs. In a small bowl lightly beat the milk and egg, and slowly stir into the flour. Knead lightly until a smooth dough forms. Flatten the dough over the fruit. Bake in a 425° oven for 35 to 45 minutes.

MAKES 8 TO 10 SERVINGS.

Rhode Island House

77 Rhode Island Avenue
Newport, Rhode Island 02840
(401) 848-7787

*R*hode Island House was built in 1882 as a summer house for Thomas R. Hunter. A shingle-style residence, the inn is within easy walking distance of Cliff Walk and historic Bellevue Avenue. Each guest room has a fireplace, and some have Jacuzzi tubs and private decks. Attractions in Newport include the Newport Art Museum, the Museum of Yachting, and many fine shops and restaurants.

Rhode Island House

Grape Nut Custard

  ¾ **cup Grape Nuts cereal**
  ½ **cup raisins**
  7 **eggs**
  ¾ **cup sugar**
  1 **teaspoon vanilla extract**
  1 **quart milk**
      Fresh grated nutmeg

In the bottom of a 2-quart baking dish spread the Grape Nuts to cover the bottom.

Arrange the raisins over the Grape Nuts. In a large bowl beat the eggs, sugar, vanilla, and milk. It will be lightly frothy. Add the beaten mixture to the baking dish. Grate fresh nutmeg on top.

Place the pan in a hot water bath with water halfway up the dish. Place in the center of the oven. Bake in a 350° oven for about 1 hour, or until set.

Serve warm or cold.

MAKES 8 SERVINGS.

Hermits

  1 **cup unsalted butter**
 2¼ **cups firmly packed brown sugar**
  3 **eggs**
  ⅓ **cup molasses**
  4 **cups all-purpose flour**
 1½ **teaspoons baking powder**
 1½ **teaspoons baking soda**
 1½ **teaspoons ground cinnamon**
  1 **teaspoon ground cloves**
  1 **teaspoon grated nutmeg**
  ½ **teaspoon salt**
  1 **cup raisins**
  1 **cup coarsely chopped walnuts or pecans**
  1 **egg, beaten for glazing**

Butter and flour 3 baking sheets. In a large bowl beat the butter until fluffy, then add the brown sugar and cream until light and smooth. Add the eggs, beating well after each addition. Add the molasses and beat in. In a large bowl sift together the flour, baking powder, soda, cinnamon, cloves, nutmeg, and salt. Add the dry ingredients to the liquid mixture. Stir to blend. Add the raisins and nuts, but do not overmix.

Form the dough into long log shapes by hand, shaping them 1 inch wide and placing no more than 2 per sheet. Space the logs wide apart, as they will spread while baking. Brush with beaten egg to glaze.

Bake in the center of a 375° oven for about 12 minutes, until golden. The cookies will still be quite soft. Check carefully, the timing can vary from 10 to 14 minutes, but these cookies should not be overbaked.

Cool, then slice into bars 2 inches wide. Hermits keep well stored in an airtight container.

MAKES 4 TO 5 DOZEN.

Tarte Tatin

 10 **Golden Delicious apples**
  7 **tablespoons butter**
  ½ **cup plus 3 tablespoons sugar**
  ¼ **tablespoon lemon juice or water**
      Pie pastry or puff pastry
      Whipped cream or crème fraîche

Peel, halve, and core the apples. With the cut-side down, trim off a small slice from 1 side of each apple half so it can stand on its side.

In a 10-inch ovenproof skillet heat the butter over medium heat. Add the sugar and lemon juice, and mix well.

Starting at the outside of the pan, stand the apple halves on their sides, 1 next to the other, filling the skillet tightly. Once the outer circle is complete, place 2 halves together in the center and continue to put apples around until all are tightly packed. Continue cooking over medium to medium high heat for 25 to 30 minutes. The juice from the apples will first dissolve the sugar, then evaporate, and the sugar will slowly cook to the caramel stage. When the sugar bubbling is pale brown in color, place the skillet in the upper third of a 425° oven for 5 minutes.

Remove the skillet and increase the oven temperature to 475°. Roll out the pastry, keeping it round, until it is large enough to fully cover the top of the skillet, about 12 inches. Roll up on a rolling pin and unroll it over the apples. Trim off the excess pastry. Bake in the upper third of the oven until pastry is lightly browned, about 15 to 20 minutes.

Remove the tart from the oven and run a knife around the inside edge of the skillet to make sure that the apples and pastry are not stuck to it. Hold a heat-resistant platter over the skillet, turn the skillet upside-down, and place on a counter. Slowly lift off the skillet, unmolding the tart. Smooth the top of the tart with a spatula.

Serve warm, or reheat at a later time. Serve with whipped cream or crème fraîche. **MAKES 8 SERVINGS.**

Peaches Amaretti

6   large peaches, peeled, halved, and
    pitted
2   tablespoons unsalted butter
¼   tablespoon sugar
1   egg white
1   teaspoon fresh lemon juice
2   teaspoons brandy
4   ounces Amaretti cookies, crushed
    Whipped cream
    Grated lemon zest

Lightly grease an ovenproof dish. Place the peach halves in the prepared dish cut-side up. Set aside.

In a small bowl cream together the butter and sugar. Add the egg white. This will not mix completely. Add the lemon juice and brandy, and mix well. Add the crushed cookies and combine. Mound a large dollop of this mixture in each peach cavity. Bake in a 350° oven for 20 minutes.

Serve warm with whipped cream. Spoon pan juices on each serving and top with a sprinkling of grated lemon zest. **MAKES 6 SERVINGS.**

Villa Liberté

22 Liberty Street
Newport, Rhode Island 02840
(401) 846-7444

In the center of town off historic Bellevue Avenue, Villa Liberté is a short walk to shops, restaurants, beaches, and the wharf area of historic Newport. Its spacious sunroom is a favorite place for morning coffee and sunset watching. Before it was converted into an inn in the 1980s, this building served successively as a restaurant, bar, tea room, and a "house of the evening."

Granola

2½ cups oil
2½ cups honey
5   teaspoons vanilla extract
1   cup maple syrup (the real Vermont
    kind!)
....
2   42-ounce containers quick cooking
    oats
1   14-ounce package flaked coconut
1   12-ounce jar wheat germ
1   10-ounce bag sliced almonds and/or
    slivered almonds or walnuts
1   24-ounce box Grape Nuts cereal
1   13-ounce box bran cereal (not
    flakes)
1   24-ounce box raisins
    Dried fruit such as bananas, prunes,
    etc.

In a saucepan combine the oil, honey, vanilla, and maple syrup, and heat through. In a large bowl or stock pot mix the oats, coconut, wheat germ, almonds, Grape Nuts, and bran cereal. Pour the warmed liquid over the dry mixture. Mix together thoroughly. Spray a baking sheet or cookie sheet with cooking spray. Spread the mixture the prepared pan about 2 inches thick. Bake in a 325° oven for 10 minutes, then stir. Bake 10 to 15 minutes longer. Do not overbake.

After baking, add the raisins and any other dried fruit. Cool in the pan. Stir to chop up hardened chunks. Store in gallon-size resealable bags or a tightly closed plastic container. Granola can be frozen freeze.
MAKES ABOUT 6 QUARTS.

The Captain's House

6 Tern Drive
Wakefield, Rhode Island 02879
(401) 789-0388

This unusual inn, sitting right on the waterfront with its own private wharf, calls itself a BBB & B estab-lishment—meaning bed, breakfast, boats, and bikes. Guests can use the inn's canoes or rowboats for boating. Bikes are available for exploring the shoreline. Sport-fishing outings can also be arranged on the inn's own cabin cruiser. The rooms in the Captain's House have fireplaces as well as decks with an ocean view.

Scallop Puffs St. Anne

3   tablespoons butter
1   pound bay scallops, quartered
3   cloves garlic, minced
2   teaspoons finely minced lemon zest
3   tablespoons fresh dill, chopped
2   cups grated imported Swiss cheese
2¼   cups Hellman's mayonnaise
     Fresh ground pepper to taste
     (optional)
12   dozen 1-inch bread rounds, toasted
     using a high-quality white sand-
     wich bread
     Sweet Hungarian paprika (or any
     paprika you have on hand)
     Twisted lemon slices and dill sprigs
     for garnish

In a medium saucepan melt the butter over medium-high heat. Add the quartered scallops, garlic, and lemon zest. Stirring constantly, cook the scallops for 2 to 3 minutes, until barely cooked through. Add the dill and cook 30 seconds longer. Set aside and let cool to room temperature.

In a large bowl combine the Swiss cheese, mayonnaise, pepper, and scallops, and stir well. Cover and refrigerate until ready to use.

Preheat the broiler. Place the toast rounds about ½ inch apart on a baking sheet. Top each with about 1 heaping teaspoon of scallop mixture and sprinkle with paprika. Place puffs about 5 inches from the broiler, and cook until puffed and golden brown, about 2 to 3 minutes. Keep a close eye on them because they cook quickly.

Transfer the puffs to a serving dish and garnish with lemon slices and dill sprigs. Serve them at their best while still hot. **MAKES 12 DOZEN.**

Apple Ham Breakfast Bread Pudding

1   loaf day-old Italian bread (or any good-quality light bread on hand)
2   cups milk
7   eggs
1   teaspoon salt
½   cup sugar
1   Granny Smith apple, cored, peeled, and chopped
1   cup diced ham

½   cup butter, melted
½   cup sugar
2   tablespoons real maple syrup

Grease a 9 x 12-inch pan. Soak the bread in ½ cup of milk. Place the bread in the prepared pan.

In a large bowl mix the eggs, remaining milk, salt, ½ cup of sugar, apples, and ham. Pour over the bread. Bake in a 350° oven for about 1 hour, until the egg temperature reaches 150°. It will be more custard-like if the dish is placed in a pan of water while baking.

In a small bowl whisk the melted butter and sugar until sugar is dissolved. Add the maple syrup and pour over the warm bread pudding. Serve warm.

MAKES 12 SERVINGS.

Hazelnut Cheesecake

1   cup graham cracker crumbs
¼   cup sugar
½   cup melted butter

4   8-ounce packages cream cheese, softened
5   eggs
1½   cups sugar
1   teaspoon finely grated lemon zest
1   cup hulled hazelnuts, toasted and finely chopped (see note, below)

1   cup sour cream
¼   tablespoon confectioners' sugar
1   teaspoon vanilla extract
12   whole unhulled hazelnuts for garnish

Butter the sides of a 9-inch springform pan. In a food processor crumble the graham crackers or place between waxed paper and crush with a rolling pin. Add the sugar and butter and mix with a fork. Press into the bottom of the springform pan.

In a food processor or electric mixer whip the cream cheese. Add the eggs one at a time, until the batter is thin and smooth. Add 1½ cups of sugar, lemon zest, and ground hazelnuts, and mix well. Pour the batter into the crust. Bake in a 350° oven for 1 hour to 1 hour and 30 minutes or until brown and firm.

Cool the cheesecake in a pan for at least 1 hour.

When the cheesecake is completely cooled, remove it from the pan and place on a favorite serving plate. In a small bowl combine the sour cream, confectioners' sugar, and vanilla. Spread the sour cream mixture on top of the cheesecake. To decorate the cheesecake place the whole hazelnuts around the outer edge.

Note: To hull hazelnuts, spread on a baking sheet and bake in a 225° oven for about 20 minutes. Let the hazelnuts cool for a few minutes. Rub between a folded towel to remove most of the hulls.

MAKES 12 SERVINGS.

Grandview
Bed &
Breakfast
❧

212 Shore Road
Westerly, Rhode Island 02891
(800) 447-6384 for reservations

Grandview is appropriately named because of the panoramic view of the ocean that guests enjoy from its wraparound stone porch. Watch Hill and Westerly Beaches are a short distance away. Other nearby attractions include tennis and golf.

Grandpa Red's Favorite Muffins

½   cup butter, softened
½   cup sugar
1   egg
1   teaspoon unsweetened cocoa powder
3½   teaspoon baking powder
1   teaspoon vanilla extract
½   cup shredded coconut
½   cup chocolate chips
2   cups all-purpose flour
1   cup milk
¼   cup toasted slivered almonds

Spray 12 muffin cups with cooking spray or line with paper liners. In a large bowl combine the butter, sugar, egg, cocoa, baking powder, vanilla, coconut, and chocolate chips. Add the flour and milk and stir for 10 to 15 strokes. Do not overmix. Spoon into the prepared muffin cups. Sprinkle with slivered almonds. Bake in a 400° oven for 18 to 20 minutes or until the top is lightly browned and a knife inserted in a center muffin comes out clean.

MAKES 1 DOZEN.

Apple Pancake

3   tablespoons butter
3   apples, peeled, cored, and chopped
3   tablespoons brown sugar
1   teaspoon cinnamon

2   cups baking mix
1¼   cups milk
2   eggs
2   tablespoons sugar
2   tablespoons oil

Spray a 9-inch glass pie plate with cooking spray. In a nonstick frying pan melt the butter and sauté the apples with the brown sugar and cinnamon until cooked but firm.

In a large bowl combine the baking mix, milk, eggs, sugar, and oil and mix just until blended. Pour the pancake batter into the prepared plate. Spoon the apple mixture over the top of the batter. Bake in a 375° oven for

Grandview

25 to 30 minutes, or until a knife inserted in the center comes out clean.

MAKES 4 TO 6 SERVINGS.

Woody Hill
❧

149 South Woody Hill Road
Westerly, Rhode Island 02891
(401) 322-0452

*T*his inn is in a quiet countryside setting on a hilltop, surrounded by gardens, acres of trees, and rolling hills. Its porch and large swimming pool draw rave reviews from guests who just want to get away and relax for a while. Inside, Woody Hill's country antiques, wide-board floors, and handmade quilts provide an early American atmosphere.

Pear Sauce for Waffles

¼	**cup butter or margarine**
3	**tablespoons firmly packed brown sugar**
1	**13-ounce can pears in syrup**
½	**teaspoon ground cinnamon**
½	**teaspoon cornstarch**
	Real whipped cream

In a small saucepan melt the butter. Add the brown sugar and stir until the sugar dissolves. Drain the pears, reserving ⅓ cup of syrup. In a small bowl blend the reserved syrup, cinnamon, and cornstarch. Add to the butter mixture. Blend in the pears (chopped, if desired), and cook for 5 minutes, or until thickened. Serve warm, topped with whipped cream.

MAKES ABOUT 1¼ CUPS OR 4 LARGE SERVINGS ON WAFFLES.

Easy Beef Casserole

1½	**pounds stew beef**
2	**14½-ounce cans stewed tomatoes**
1	**onion, sliced (or to taste)**
3	**or 4 stalks celery, sliced**
5	**or 6 carrots, sliced**

In a stockpot combine all ingredients, and bring to a boil. Transfer to a casserole dish and cover. Bake in a 325° oven for 3 hours and 30 minutes. May be thickened with flour and water just before serving.

Variation: Use 1 quart of homemade stewed tomatoes, and add onion and celery.

MAKES 4 SERVINGS.

Rhubarb Bars

2	**cups all-purpose flour**
1	**cup margarine, melted**
½	**cup plus 2 tablespoons confectioners' sugar**

4	**eggs, beaten**
2	**cups sugar**
½	**cup all-purpose flour**
¾	**teaspoon salt**
4	**cups diced rhubarb**

In a medium bowl combine 2 cups of flour, the margarine, and confectioners' sugar, and mix until crumbly. Pat into the bottom of a 9 x 13-inch pan. Bake in a 350° oven for 15 minutes. In a separate bowl combine the eggs, sugar, ½ cup of flour, and salt. Fold in the rhubarb. Pour the mixture over the crust. Bake in a 350° oven for 45 minutes.

MAKES 8 TO 12 SERVINGS.

Woody Hill

SOUTH CAROLINA

New Berry Inn

240 Newberry Street Southwest
Aiken, South Carolina 29801
(803) 649-2935

Located downtown in the center of the historic district of old Aiken, this inn has been welcoming guests since 1924. The large guest rooms are furnished with antiques. Several fine restaurants and shops are within easy walking distance. Golf, tennis, and swimming are available nearby.

New Berry Inn

5:30 A.M. Ham

The night before, take a center cut of 4 to 6 pounds from a precooked ham and rinse it gently. Place it in a 2-gallon covered roasting pan. Place sliced pineapple over the surface along with a sprinkling of brown sugar and a cherry in each pineapple hole. Honey can also be poured over the surface and a 12-ounce cola is added to the pan. Do not pour the cola over the surface of the ham. Cover the roasting pan and refrigerate the ham overnight.

At 5:30 A.M. the next morning, preheat the oven for 15 minutes to 325°. Place the roasting pan in the oven. Bake in a 325° oven for 15 to 20 minutes per pound with the lid on the roasting pan. Remove the pan from the oven and allow the ham to sit for 15 minutes with the lid on the pan. Remove the ham and place on a serving tray. Slice half of the ham thinly. Serve the ham with a side of pan-fried home fries, eggs to order, and toasted home-made sour dough bread.

John Rutledge House Inn

116 Broad Street
Charleston, South Carolina 29401
(800) 476-9741 for reservations

John Rutledge, one of the signers of the Declaration of Independence, built this house in downtown Charleston in 1763. The common areas of the inn feature graceful ironwork, inlaid floors, plaster moldings, and elaborately carved Italian marble fireplaces. Rooms are available in the original house or in two adjoining carriage houses. Within easy walking distance are many of historic Charleston's most popular attractions, including the famous Four Corners of Law, Street Michael's Episcopal Church, Charleston Place, the Old City Market, and the city's finest restaurants, theaters, and shops. This inn has been named a "historic hotel of America" by the National Trust for Historic Preservation.

Rhetta Walters Cucumber Sandwiches

1	medium cucumber
1/2	cup cider vinegar
1	cup water
1	8-ounce package cream cheese, softened
1/4	cup mayonnaise or salad dressing
1/4	teaspoon garlic powder
1/4	teaspoon onion salt
	Dash Worcestershire sauce

1 loaf sliced, firm textured bread
   Thinly sliced pimento-stuffed green
   olives or paprika, for garnish

Score the cucumber lengthwise with a fork. Slice thin. In a medium bowl combine the vinegar and water. Add the cucumber slices and let stand at room temperature for at least 30 minutes. Drain well.

In a medium bowl combine the cream cheese, mayonnaise, garlic powder, onion salt, and Worcestershire sauce.

Cut the bread slices into 2-inch rounds. Spread lightly with the cream cheese mixture. Top with a cucumber slice shortly before serving. Garnish with an olive slice, sprinkling of paprika, or both.

MAKES ABOUT 12 SERVINGS.

John Rutledge House Inn

Rutledge Biscuit with Hot Sherried Fruit

1 16-ounce can pineapple chunks,
   juice reserved
1 16-ounce can peaches, cut into
   chunks, juice reserved
1 16-ounce can pears, cut into chunks,
   juice reserved
½ cup firmly packed light brown sugar
¼ tablespoon ground cinnamon
½ cup cream sherry (or to taste)
¼ tablespoon cornstarch
¼ cup cold water
....
2 cups self-rising flour
¼ teaspoon baking soda
⅓ cup shortening
1 cup buttermilk

In a 2-quart saucepan combine the pineaple, peaches, and pears, and their juices. Add the brown sugar and cinnamon, and heat through. Add the sherry.

In a small bowl or cup mix the cornstarch and water. Stir the mixture into the hot fruit. Cook, stirring constantly, until thickened.

In a large bowl combine the flour and soda. Cut the shortening into the flour with a pastry blender. Add the buttermilk and mix just until combined. Turn out onto a floured surface. Knead about 5 times, or until the dough is not sticky. Pat to ¾-inch thickness and cut with a biscuit cutter. Place on a hot greased baking pan (an iron skillet is best), sides touching. Bake in a 450° oven until lightly browned.

Serve with Hot Sherried Fruit.

MAKES 6 TO 8 SERVINGS.

Rutledge House Inn's She-Crab Soup

5 tablespoons butter
½ cup finely chopped celery
⅔ teaspoon mace
¼ teaspoon white pepper
3½ cups milk
½ cup chicken stock
5 tablespoons all-purpose flour
   Salt
2 cups crab meat (see note, below)
1 cup heavy cream
¼ cup Worcestershire sauce
3 tablespoons sherry
2 hard-boiled egg yolks
   Paprika

In large sauce pan heat the butter. Add the celery, mace, and white pepper, and cook over low heat until the celery is almost transparent. While the celery is cooking, in a small pan heat the milk and chicken stock just enough to make the milk hot, without boiling. When the celery is done, add the flour to make a roux. Do not brown but heat enough to bubble for several minutes. Slowly add the milk and chicken stock to the roux. Add salt to taste. Add the crab meat, heavy cream, Worcestershire sauce, and sherry. Simmer for 30 minutes or until thickened to the appropriate consistency.

Grate the yolks. Sprinkle over the top with the paprika.

Note: "She-crabs" are a real delicacy because they have much more taste than the "He-crabs." The orange-hued eggs of she-crabs give the soup extra flavor and color. She-crabs are difficult to find in many parts of the country so white crab meat can be substi-

tuted. Hard-boiled egg yolk may be crumbled in the soup to imitate crab eggs.

MAKES 4 SERVINGS.

King's Inn at Georgetown

King's Inn at Georgetown

≈

230 Broad Street
Georgetown, South Carolina 29440
(800) 251-8805

*T*he rooms in the King's Inn are decorated individually in antiques, fabrics, and delicate laces to give each one a distinctive character. Other memorable touches are French plaster moldings, crystal chandeliers, pine floors, and triple-sash windows in the common areas. Listed on the National Register of Historic Places, this inn was built in 1825 as a residence for Benjamin King, owner of Georgetown Rice Mill. Federal troops used the mansion as a headquarters building during the Civil War.

Frosty Orange Cups

10 large oranges
2 16-ounce cans apricot halves with
   juice, chopped
1 10½-ounce can pineapple tidbits
   with juice
3 bananas, sliced
1 cup flaked coconut
1 cup sugar

1   *6-ounce can frozen orange juice*
    concentrated, thawed
¼ *tablespoon fresh lemon juice*

Cut each orange in half in a saw-tooth pattern. Remove the orange sections and reserve. Clip the membranes inside the orange shells and remove. Place the orange shells in the freezer until thoroughly chilled.

In a large bowl combine the orange sections with the remaining ingredients and mix thoroughly. Spoon the mixture into the prepared orange shells. Return to the freezer for at least 3 hours. Remove from the freezer 30 minutes before serving. Extra orange mixture may be frozen in muffin cups lined with paper liners.

MAKES 20 SERVINGS.

Fresh Fruit 'n Honey

¾ *cup mayonnaise*
½ *cup honey*
¼ *tablespoon fresh lemon juice*
½ *teaspoon almond extract*
1   *8-ounce carton vanilla yogurt*
    Fresh fruit, cut in chunks

In a medium bowl mix the mayonnaise, honey, lemon juice, and almond extract with a spoon. Fold in the yogurt. Cover and refrigerate. Serve over chunked fresh fruit.

MAKES 2 CUPS.

Pineapple Nut Tea Sandwiches

2   *cups crushed pineapple, drained*
1   *cup sugar*
1   *cup chopped nuts*
1   *8-ounce package cream cheese*
    Milk or mayonnaise
    Thinly sliced bread

In a saucepan combine the pineapple and sugar, and bring to a boil. Cook until thick, stirring constantly. Cool.

Stir in the nuts. Soften and mash the cream cheese with enough milk or mayonnaise to make a good spreading consistency. Combine with the pineapple mixture. Spread on thin bread and top as for sandwiches. Trim and cut into squares.

MAKES ABOUT 4 CUPS.

1790 House

630 *Highmarket Street*
Georgetown, South Carolina 29440
(800) 890-7432

---

*T*his inn is noted for its unique West Indies style of architecture. It was built more than two hundred years ago when Georgetown's rice planter culture was at its peak. Guest-pleasing amenities include a garden, a large drawing room with a fireplace, and a large wraparound veranda. The 1790 House is in the heart of the downtown historic district of Georgetown, which is listed on the National Register of Historic Places.

Chicken Quiche with Special Chicken Gravy

1½ *cups milk*
3   *eggs*
2   *tablespoons margarine, melted*
½ *cup baking mix*
1   *to 2 slices onion, chopped*
    Pinch dried mustard
    Pinch sage
    Pinch thyme
    Pinch marjoram
    Pinch paprika
    Salt to taste
1   *cup grated Cheddar cheese*
1   *6-ounce can white meat chicken,*
    drained and liquid reserved

....

1   *tablespoon cornstarch*
2   *to 3 tablespoons water*
2   *to 3 dashes salt*
2   *to 3 dashes paprika*
2   *to 3 dashes dried marjoram*
2   *to 3 dashes dried sage*
2   *to 3 dashes dried thyme*
2   *to 3 dashes dried mustard*
2   *to 3 dashes garlic powder*
    Parsley for garnish

In a medium bowl blend the milk, eggs, margarine, baking mix, onion, and seasonings.

Spray a 9-inch white ceramic dish with cooking spray. Pour the egg mixture into the prepared pan. Sprinkle the cheese on top, then the crumbled chicken. Bake in a 350° oven for 40 minutes, or until set.

Pour the drained liquid from the canned chicken into a small saucepan. Add the cornstarch and mix well. Heat on low heat and stir in the water, mixing continuously while it thickens. Add the salt, paprika, marjoram, sage, thyme, mustard, and garlic powder. Continue to stir and season to taste. If it is too thick, add more water as necessary. Be careful it does not stick to the pan or cook away.

Drizzle a little gravy on each slice of chicken quiche. Garnish with parsley.

MAKES 6 SERVINGS.

1790 House Southern Grits

3   *cups water*
1   *beef bouillon cube*
¾ *cup grits (5-minute quick-cooking)*
¾ *cup shredded Cheddar cheese*
    Flour
    Oil

Spray a 9-inch square glass baking dish with cooking spray. In a medium saucepan bring the water to a boil. Drop in the bouillon cube and dissolve. Add the grits and cook, stirring occasionally, until thickened. Add the cheese and stir until blended. Pour into the prepared baking dish. Refrigerate overnight.

In the morning, cut the grits into either 9 or 12 squares (depending on the size desired). Coat with flour. In an electric skillet fry the squares with a little oil until brown on all sides.

Variation: Diced Polish sausage may be added, if desired.

MAKES 9 TO 12 SERVINGS.

1790 House

1790 House Baked Apples

2 green apples
¼ cup apple juice
1 teaspoon lemon juice
¼ tablespoon margarine, melted
1 teaspoon vanilla extract
1 cinnamon stick, broken
   Lemon or vanilla yogurt
   Ground walnuts

Peel and core the apples, and slice each in half. Place in a microwave-safe dish. In a small bowl mix the next 5 ingredients together and pour over the apples. Cover and cook in a microwave on high power for 4 to 5 minutes, until fork-tender. The time varies depending on the apples.

Place each apple half in a serving dish, top with a teaspoonful of lemon or vanilla yogurt, and sprinkle with ground walnuts. Serve warm.

MAKES 4 SERVINGS.

Amaretto Glazed Fruit

2 16-ounce cans pear halves, drained
   and juice reserved
1 teaspoon cornstarch
2 tablespoons Amaretto
2 teaspoons firmly packed brown
   sugar
½ teaspoon vanilla extract
1 16-ounce can apricot halves,
   drained
1 15¼-ounce can pineapple chunks,
   drained
   Low-fat vanilla yogurt (optional)
   Chopped nuts (optional)

In a small bowl combine ⅓ cup of reserved pear juice with the cornstarch and stir until blended. Add the Amaretto, brown sugar, and vanilla. Stir well. Set aside.

Spray a large skillet with cooking spray. Add the pear and apricot halves and pineapple chunks to the warmed pan. Sauté for 2 to 3 minutes. Pour in the Amaretto mixture and cook over medium heat for a few minutes until thickened, stirring frequently. Do not overcook. Place in individual serving dishes or use as a warm side dish with a hot entrée. Top with a dollop of low-fat yogurt and/or sprinkle with finely chopped nuts.

MAKES 8 SERVINGS.

Shaw House

Shaw House

613 Cypress Court
Georgetown, South Carolina 29440
(803) 546-9663

*T*his inn, within walking distance of the downtown historical district of Georgetown, is noted for its fine library and antiques. Huge oak trees line the streets of its neighborhood, making it a haven for birdwatchers. The famed golf courses of Myrtle Beach are just a short drive away. Other nearby attractions are the beaches of Pawley's Island and the city of Charleston.

Shrimp and Rice

1 cup margarine
1 diced onion
1 diced green bell pepper
3 pounds shrimp, peeled and deveined
2 13¾-ounce cans beef consommé
2½ cups rice
1 2-ounce jar pimentos, drained
   Salt and pepper to taste

In a skillet melt the margarine and sauté the onion and green pepper until tender.

Add the shrimp and sauté until pink. Add the consommé, rice, pimentos, and seasonings. Cover and steam for 30 minutes. Do not take the lid off during steaming.

MAKES 6 TO 8 SERVINGS.

Best Meringue Cookies

1 cup sugar
3 egg whites
1 teaspoon vanilla extract
1¼ cups chopped nuts

In a large bowl combine the sugar, egg whites, and vanilla. Beat with an electric mixer for 10 minutes at high speed. Fold in the nuts. Drop by teaspoonfuls onto a greased cookie sheet. Place in a preheated 350° oven and then turn off the heat. Leave in the oven until the oven cools, or overnight.

MAKES 2 DOZEN.

Baked Cheese Grits

1 cup raw grits, cooked in 4 cups
   water
1 cup milk
4 eggs
1 cup shredded Cheddar cheese
1 8½-ounce box corn muffin mix

In a large bowl combine all of the ingredients, and mix well. Pour into a 9-inch square pan. Bake in a 350° oven for 45 minutes.

MAKES 6 SERVINGS.

Laurel Hill Plantation

8913 North Highway 17, P.O. Box 190
McClellansville, South Carolina 29458

*T*he original Laurel Hill Plantation house, built in the 1850s, was destroyed by Hurricane Hugo in 1989. This inn is a reproduction of that house, designed to reflect the romance of the past while offering modern conveniences and amenities. It is furnished with antiques that reflect the culture of South Carolina's Low Country. McClellanville is conveniently situated between Charleston, thirty miles north, and Myrtle Beach, sixty miles south.

Laurel Hill Plantation

Cranberry Poppy Seed Muffins

1¾ cups reduced-fat baking mix
½ cup sugar
½ cup skim milk
¼ cup plain nonfat yogurt
2 egg whites (or ¼ cup cholesterol-
       free egg product)
¼ tablespoon poppy seeds
1 teaspoon grated lemon peel
½ cup cranberries (fresh or frozen
       thawed)

1 tablespoons lemon juice
¼ cup confectioners' sugar

Grease 12 medium-sized muffin cups or line with paper liners.

In a large bowl combine the first 2 ingredients until the mixture is moist. Stir the cranberries into the mixture. Fill each muffin cup three-fourths full. Bake in a 400° oven for 18 to 20 minutes or until golden brown. Remove the muffins from the pan immediately.

In a small bowl combine the lemon juice and confectioners' sugar. Drizzle onto cool muffins.

MAKES 1 DOZEN.

Fruit Salad

1 16-ounce carton sour cream
2 tablespoons sugar (or brown sugar
       for a different flavor)
1 20-ounce can pineapple tidbits,
       drained (or chunks cut in half)
1 11-ounce can mandarin oranges,
       drained
1 8-ounce jar maraschino cherries,
       drained (cut in half)
1 cup shredded coconut
¼ cup chopped pecans
¼ cup seedless raisins

In a large bowl mix the sour cream and sugar until blended well. Add the fruits and mix well. Chill.

MAKES 4 SERVINGS.

Ham and Grits Quiche

½ cup water
¼ teaspoon salt
⅓ cup quick-cooking yellow grits
       (uncooked, not instant)

1 20-ounce can evaporated milk
3 large eggs
¼ teaspoon cayenne pepper
1 teaspoon hot sauce
1½ cups shredded sharp Cheddar cheese
1½ cups shopped cooked ham (country
       hams is good)

In a pan boil the water and salt. Add the grits and cook until thickened. Cover and let stand.

In a large bowl mix the milk, eggs, pepper, and hot sauce. Add some of the egg mixture to the grits and blend well. Add the remaining egg mixture, Cheddar cheese, and ham. Mix all together until blended well. Pour into a 10-inch quiche dish (or 9½-inch deep dish pie plate). Bake in a 350° oven for 35 to 45 minutes. Let stand 10 minutes before cutting into wedges.

MAKES 6 SERVINGS.

Chesterfield Inn

❧

700 North Ocean Boulevard
Myrtle Beach, South Carolina 29577
(803) 448-3177

*T**his is one of the last quaint beachfront inns left at Myrtle Beach; most of the others have been replaced by high-rise hotels and resorts. Guests enjoy the wooden oceanfront porch, with its comfortable rocking chairs, and the unforgettable view of the ocean that it offers. Inside, the same view is available from the dining room. Just a short walk away is the popular Myrtle Beach Pavilion and Amusement Park. Playing privileges are also available to guests at most of the area's fine golf courses.*

Old-Fashioned Lemon Pie

12 eggs, beaten lightly
2½ cups sugar
2½ tablespoons all-purpose flour
¾ cup lemon juice
1½ tablespoons lemon zest
½ cup melted butter
       2 unbaked 9-inch pie shells

In a large bowl beat the eggs. Blend in the other ingredients. Pour into the pie shells. Bake in a 350° oven for 30 minutes or until firm.

MAKES 12 TO 16 SERVINGS.

Pineapple-Cheese Casserole

1 cup sugar
½ cup all-purpose flour
2 cups shredded sharp Cheddar cheese
2 cups pineapple tidbits, drained
1 roll Ritz crackers
½ cup butter

In a large bowl combine all of the ingredients except the crackers and butter. Mix well. Pour into a 1½-quart casserole dish. Crumble the crackers, and sprinkle the crumbs over the casserole. Pour melted butter on top. Bake in a 350° oven until hot throughout.

MAKES 4 TO 6 SERVINGS.

Chesterfield Inn

407 71st Avenue North
Myrtle Beach, South Carolina 29572
(803) 449-5268

*T*he rooms in this Spanish Mission-style inn are individually decorated to reflect different time periods. Other amenities include an outside hot tub and heated pool, an outside gas grill, and games such as shuffle-board and Ping-Pong. Serendipity is in a quiet, secluded location, away from the noise of tourist traffic.

Serendipity Inn

Carrot Loaf

     3　cups all-purpose flour
     2　teaspoons baking soda
     2　teaspoons baking powder
    ½　teaspoon salt
     1　teaspoon ground cinnamon
     4　eggs
     2　cups sugar
    1½　cups oil
     1　teaspoon vanilla extract
     2　cups grated raw carrots
     1　cup chopped walnuts
     1　14-ounce can crushed pineapple

In a large bowl sift together the flour, soda, baking powder, salt, and cinnamon.

In a separate bowl beat together the eggs and sugar until pale yellow. Beat in the oil and vanilla. Stir in the dry ingredients. Fold in the carrots, walnuts, and pineapple.

Butter and lightly flour a 10-inch bundt pan. Pour the batter into the prepared pan. Bake in a 350° oven for 1 hour and 10 minutes, or until a toothpick inserted in the center comes out clean

MAKES 8 SERVINGS.

304 South Hampton Street
Summerville, South Carolina 29483
(803) 871-5275

A few miles inland from Charleston, this inn occupies the Blake Washington House, a national register property which was built around 1865. Guests are impressed with the unique double porches on the front of this house, providing rest-and-relaxation space for both upstairs and downstairs visitors. Other nice touches are a swimming pool, a gazebo, and bicycles for touring Summerville's tree-lined streets, which are bounded by lovely old homes.

Hot Fruit Casserole

     1　16-ounce can pear halves, drained
     1　16-ounce can sliced peaches, drained
     1　16-ounce can pineapple chunks, drained
     1　16-ounce can apricot halves, drained
    12　maraschino cherries
    ¾　cup light brown sugar
     3　teaspoons curry powder
    ⅔　cup slivered almonds
    ⅓　cup melted butter

In a 2-quart casserole combine the fruit. Add the sugar and curry. Sprinkle with nuts. Pour the butter over the mixture. Bake in a 325° oven for 1 hour.

MAKES 6 TO 8 SERVINGS.

Cheesy Grits Casserole

    1½　cups uncooked regular grits
    ½　cup butter
     3　cups grated medium-sharp Cheddar cheese
    ¼　tablespoon Worcestershire sauce
     2　teaspoons paprika, divided
     3　eggs, beaten

In a saucepan cook the grits according to the package directions. In a large bowl combine the grits, butter, and cheese, and stir until melted. Add the Worcestershire sauce and 1 teaspoon of paprika. Mix well.

In a separate bowl add a small amount of hot grits to the eggs, stirring well. Stir the egg mixture into the remaining grits. Pour into a greased 2-quart dish. Sprinkle with the remaining paprika. Cover and refrigerate overnight.

Remove from the refrigerator 15 minutes before baking. Bake in a 325° oven for 1 hour.

MAKES 8 SERVINGS.

Square Biscuits

     3　tablespoons shortening
     2　cups sifted self-rising flour
    ¾　cup milk

In a large bowl cut the shortening into the flour. Add the milk a little at a time, stirring the dough with a heavy spoon. Turn the dough onto a well-floured board and roll or pat out to ⅓-inch thickness. Cut the dough in squares with a sharp greased knife. Place on a baking sheet. Bake in a 500° oven for 10 to 12 minutes.

MAKES ABOUT 12 BISCUITS.

SOUTH DAKOTA

Skoglund Farm

Route 1, Box 45
Canova, South Dakota 57321
(605) 247-3445

*T*his inn in the village of Canova gives you an opportunity to enjoy an overnight stay on the South Dakota prairie. Just a few miles from Sioux Falls in the southeastern corner of South Dakota, it is close to such tourist attractions as the Corn Palace, Little House on the Prairie, and Prairie Village. The overnight rate includes an evening meal as well as breakfast.

Sweet and Sour Chicken

- 2 *eggs*
- ¼ *tablespoon water*
- 4 *pounds chicken, cut up*
  Oil for frying
- ¾ *cup sugar*
- ½ *cup pineapple juice*
- ½ *cup cider vinegar*
- 3 *tablespoons catsup*
- 2 *tablespoon soy sauce*
- ½ *teaspoon salt*

In a shallow dish beat the eggs with the water. Coat the chicken. In a skillet heat a small amount of oil and fry the chicken to golden brown. Place in a foil-lined pan.

In a saucepan combine the sugar, pineapple juice, vinegar, catsup, soy sauce, and salt. Bring the mixture to a boil and simmer for 5 minutes. Pour over the chicken. Bake in a 350° oven for 1 hour. Turn the chicken once during baking.

MAKES 6 TO 8 SERVINGS.

Pheasant with Wild Rice

- 1 *cup wild rice*
- 1 *10½-ounce can cream of chicken soup*
- 1 *10½-ounce can cream of mushroom soup*
- 2 *½ cups water*
- 1 *4-ounce can mushroom pieces*
- 1 *6-ounce can water chestnuts*
- 2 *pheasants, cut up, floured, and browned*
- 1 *envelope onion soup mix*

In a 2-quart baking pan mix the rice, soups, water, mushrooms, and water chestnuts. Arrange the pheasants on top and sprinkle with onion soup mix. Cover with foil. Bake in a 350° oven for 1 hour and 30 minutes, or until done.

MAKES 4 SERVINGS.

Fruit Dressing

- *Juice of 1 orange*
- *Juice of 1 lemon*
- 1 *egg*
- 1 *cup sugar*
  Whipped topping or whipped cream

In a saucepan combine the orange juice, lemon juice, egg, and sugar, and bring to a boil. Simmer until thickened. Add whipped topping or whipped cream.

Mix with fresh fruit.

MAKES 6 SERVINGS.

Johnny Cake

- 1 *egg*
- ½ *cup sugar*
- 1¾ *cup buttermilk (or sour milk)*
- 1 *teaspoon baking soda*
- 1 *cup cornmeal*
- 1 *teaspoon baking powder*
- ½ *cup melted shortening*

In a medium bowl combine the egg, sugar, buttermilk, soda, cornmeal, baking powder, and shortening. Mix well. Pour into a 9-inch square pan. Bake in a 350° oven for 30 minutes.

MAKES 6 TO 8 SERVINGS.

Custer Mansion

35 Centennial Drive
Custer, South Dakota 57730
(605) 673-3333

*L*isted on the National Register of Historic Places, Custer Mansion was built in 1891 by Senator Newton Seymour Tubbs, an early home- steader in Dakota Territory in the Black Hills. The six bedrooms, each named after a song, are furnished with antiques. Another nice touch is a guest lounge for reading or relax- ing. Nearby activities include golf- ing, tennis, skiing, and swimming.

Pumpkin Muffins Homemade with Love

1²⁄₃ **cups all-purpose flour**
  1 **teaspoon baking soda**
 ¹⁄₂ **teaspoon baking powder**
 ¹⁄₂ **teaspoon salt**
  1 **teaspoon ground cinnamon**
 ¹⁄₂ **teaspoon ground allspice**
  1 **cup solid canned pumpkin**
 ³⁄₄ **cup evaporated milk**
 ¹⁄₃ **cup oil**
  1 **cup firmly packed brown sugar**
     (packed)
  1 **egg**
  1 **cup blueberries**
 ¹⁄₄ **tablespoon all-purpose flour**
 ....
  2 **tablespoons all-purpose flour**
  2 **tablespoons sugar**
 ¹⁄₄ **teaspoon ground cinnamon**
  1 **tablespoons butter**

In a medium bowl combine the flour, soda, baking powder, salt, 1 teaspoon of cinnamon, and allspice. In a small bowl combine the pumpkin and evaporated milk until blended. In a large bowl cream the oil and brown sugar with an electric mixer. Add the egg, and beat until the mixture is fluffy.

Add the dry ingredients to the egg mixture alternately with the pumpkin mixture. Beat well after each addition. Combine the blue-

berries with 1 tablespoon of flour. Gently fold the berries into the batter.

In a small bowl combine 2 tablespoons of flour, 2 tablespoons of sugar, ¹⁄₄ teaspoon of cinnamon, and the butter. Mix until crumbly. Sprinkle the streusel topping over the batter. Bake in a 350° oven for 40 minutes, or until a toothpick inserted in a center muffin comes out clean.

MAKES 12 MUFFINS.

Oatmeal Buttermilk Pancakes

  2 **cups rolled oats**
  2 **cups buttermilk**
  2 **eggs, well-beaten**
 ¹⁄₄ **cup butter, melted and cooled**
 ¹⁄₂ **cup raisins**
 ¹⁄₂ **cup all-purpose flour**
  2 **tablespoons sugar**
  1 **teaspoon baking powder**
  1 **teaspoon baking soda**
 ¹⁄₂ **teaspoon ground cinnamon**
 ¹⁄₄ **teaspoon salt**

In a large bowl mix together the oats and but- termilk. Cover and refrigerate overnight.

Before cooking, stir in the eggs, butter, and raisins, stirring just until blended. Set aside.

In a medium bowl combine the flour, sugar, baking powder, soda, cinnamon, and salt. Add the dry ingredients to the oat mix- ture. Stir just until moistened.

Spoon ¹⁄₃ cup of batter at a time onto a lightly greased griddle over medium to high heat. Turn when bubbly.

MAKES 18 PANCAKES.

Rhubarb Coffee Cake

2¹⁄₂ **cups all-purpose flour**
  1 **teaspoon baking soda**
  1 **teaspoon baking powder**
 ¹⁄₂ **teaspoon salt**
  1 **cup firmly packed brown sugar**
 ¹⁄₄ **cup white sugar**
 ¹⁄₂ **cup oil**
  1 **egg**
  1 **teaspoon vanilla extract**
  1 **cup buttermilk**
1¹⁄₂ **cups diced rhubarb**
 ....
  2 **tablespoons melted butter**
 ¹⁄₂ **cup sugar**

  1 **teaspoon ground cinnamon**
 ¹⁄₂ **cup chopped nuts**

In a medium bowl mix the flour, soda, baking powder, and salt. Set aside.

In a large bowl cream the sugars, oil, and egg. Beat well. Add the vanilla and buttermilk, and mix well. Fold in the rhubarb. Blend in the dry ingredients just until moistened. Do not beat.

Grease 2 8-inch layer pans. Pour the batter into the pans.

In a small bowl combine the melted butter, sugar, cinnamon, and nuts, and mix until crumbly. Sprinkle the topping over the batter. Bake in a 350 to 375° oven for 25 minutes, or until done.

MAKES 12 TO 16 SERVINGS.

Breakfast Pizza

     Pastry for a 12-inch pizza
 ¹⁄₂ **pound bacon, cooked and crumbled**
  2 **cups shredded Swiss cheese**
  4 **eggs**
1¹⁄₂ **cups low-fat sour cream**
  2 **tablespoons chopped fresh parsley**

Line a pizza pan with pastry. Bake the crust in a 425° oven for 5 minutes.

Sprinkle bacon and Swiss cheese over the crust. In a medium bowl beat the eggs, sour cream, and parsley until smooth. Pour over the crust. Bake in a 400° oven for 20 to 25 minutes.

MAKES 8 SERVINGS.

HC 37, Box 1214
Lead, South Dakota 57754
(605) 584-2473

*T*he rustic-oriented and wilder- ness-minded should love this inn. It's a log house with four guest rooms, in the scenic Black Hills of South Dakota. Ski slopes are only five minutes away, and it's also close to Deadwood, the historic *gambling town. Other major tourist attractions in the area are Mount Rushmore, the Passion play, and the Homestake Gold Mine Tour. Spearfish Canyon, where the movie "Dances with Wolves" was filmed, is also nearby.*

Hash Brown-Sausage Bake

- 2 to 3 pounds sausage
  Oil
- 1 32-ounce package hash brown potatoes (or potatoes O'Brien with the onions and peppers)
- 2 10½-ounce cans cream of celery soup
- 1 10½-ounce can cream of chicken soup
- 2 cups sour cream

In a large skillet brown the sausage. Remove from the skillet and drain well. In the skillet heat a small amount of oil and cook the hash browns. Add the hash browns, soups, and sour cream to the cooked sausage. Mix well. Pour into a greased 9 x 13-inch baking pan. At this point, cover with foil and freeze for use later, if desired. Bake in a 350° oven for 1 hour.

MAKES 8 TO 12 SERVINGS.

Fresh Fruit with Vanilla Cream

- 4 cups fresh fruit
- 1 3-ounce package cream cheese, softened
- ¼ cup confectioners' sugar
- 2 to 3 tablespoons light cream
- ½ teaspoon vanilla extract

In a serving bowl or individual dessert dishes arrange the fruit.

In a small bowl whisk together the cream cheese and confectioners' sugar. Gradually add the cream and vanilla, and stir until smooth. Pour over the fruit or serve on the side.

MAKES 4 TO 6 SERVINGS.

Abend Haus Cottages and Audrie's Bed & Breakfast

23029 Thunderhead Falls Road
Rapid City, South Dakota 57702
(605) 342-7788

This country-style inn offers rooms furnished with European antiques on a five-acre estate. Accomodations range from suites in the main house to cottage-type rooms in an old powerhouse and log houses beside a creek. The inn is surrounded by thousands of acres of national forest in a secluded Black Hills setting. Major attractions in the area include Mount Rushmore, Badlands National Park, and the historic gambling town of Deadwood.

Spicy Corn Dip

- 1 8-ounce package cream cheese
- ½ cup sour cream
- 2 tablespoons finely chopped onion
- 2 tablespoons ripe olives, chopped
- ¼ tablespoon lemon juice
- 1 12-ounce can whole kernel corn, drained
- 2 or more drops Tabasco sauce, to taste

In a medium bowl blend the cream cheese and sour cream until smooth. Gently stir in the remaining ingredients. Cover and refrigerate overnight for the flavors to blend. Serve with corn chips or raw veggies.

MAKES ABOUT 3 CUPS.

Best Cobbler Ever

- ½ cup sugar
- 2 tablespoons cornstarch
- 1 1-pound 13-ounce can sliced peaches, drained, juice reserved
- 1 10½-ounce can apricot halves, drained, juice reserved
- ¼ tablespoon butter
- ½ teaspoon ground cinnamon
- ½ teaspoon grated nutmeg

- ½ cup all-purpose flour
- ½ cup sugar
- ¾ teaspoon baking powder
- ¼ teaspoon salt
- 2 tablespoons butter, softened
- 1 egg

- 1 cup heavy cream
- 2 tablespoons honey at room temperature
- ½ teaspoon ground cinnamon

In a saucepan mix together ½ cup of sugar and cornstarch. Stir in ½ cup of reserved peach and apricot juices. Cook over medium heat for 2 minutes, stirring constantly, until the mixture boils and thickens.

Remove the pan from the heat. Stir in 1 tablespoon of butter, ½ teaspoon of cinnamon, and nutmeg. Add the peaches and apricots. Spoon the fruit mixture into a 1½-quart casserole.

In a small bowl combine the flour, ½ cup of sugar, baking powder, salt, 2 tablespoons butter, and egg. Spoon over the fruit mixture. Bake in a 400° oven for 30 minutes, until golden brown.

In a medium bowl beat together the cream, honey, and ½ teaspoon cinnamon until soft peaks form. Serve over the cobbler.

MAKES 8 SERVINGS.

Fudgy Brownies

- 4 bars unsweetened baking chocolate
- ¾ cup butter or margarine
- 2 cups sugar
- 3 eggs
- ½ teaspoon vanilla extract
- 1 cup all-purpose flour
- 1 cup chopped nuts

Grease a 9 x 13-inch baking pan. In a large glass bowl combine the chocolate and butter and microwave at high for 1½ to 2 minutes, until the chocolate is melted and the mixture is smooth when stirred.

Add the sugar, stirring with a spoon until blended. Add the eggs and vanilla, and mix well. Add the flour and nuts, stirring until blended. Spread into the prepared pan. Bake in a 350° oven for 30 to 35 minutes, until a toothpick inserted in the center comes out clean. Cool.

MAKES ABOUT 24 BROWNIES.

R.R. 2, Box 52
Webster, South Dakota 57274
(605) 486-4430

***T**his inn is part of a real working farm that has been owned by members of the same family for more than a century. Many tourists find it's a good stopping point on the way to the Black Hills, about a day's drive away. Guests may explore the barns, pastures, and fields and even help with the chores if they desire.*

Old-Fashioned Oatmeal Pancakes

- 1 cup uncooked quick oats (or old-fashioned)

- 1 cup buttermilk
- 1 egg, lightly beaten
- 2 tablespoons butter or margarine, melted and cooled
- ¼ cup raisins
- ¼ cup all-purpose flour
- ¼ tablespoon sugar
- ½ teaspoon baking powder
- ½ teaspoon baking soda
- ¼ teaspoon ground cinnamon
  Dash salt
- ½ teaspoon butter flavoring

In a large bowl combine the oats and buttermilk. Cover and refrigerate for several hours or overnight.

Add the eggs, butter, and raisins, and stir just to blend. In a separate bowl sift the flour, sugar, baking powder, soda, cinnamon, and salt together. Add the dry ingredients to the oat mixture along with the butter flavoring. Stir just until moistened.

If too thick, add a few more tablespoons of buttermilk. Fry as usual for any pancake.

MAKES 4 TO 6 SERVINGS.

512 Mulberry Street
Yankton, South Dakota 57078
(605) 665-7116

***B**uilt in 1873, this inn is listed on the National Register of Historic Places. Some of its memorable exterior features are a massive, beautifully carved front door and distinctive wooden shutters. Inside, it features walnut paneling, parquet floors, high ceilings, and numerous antiques. It also has two parlors with marble fireplaces. The inn is within easy walking distance of downtown Yankton, fine restaurants, and the Missouri River.*

River attractions include fishing, boating, and enjoying the town's parks.

Applesauce Pancakes

- 2 cups baking mix
- 2 eggs
- 1 cup applesauce
- 1 teaspoon ground cinnamon
- 1 teaspoon lemon juice

In a large bowl combine all of the ingredients and mix well. Pour ¼ cup of batter at a time onto a hot greased griddle for each pancake. Cook until bubbles form, turn, and cook the other side.

MAKES 4 TO 6 SERVINGS.

Broccoli Quiche

- 5 eggs, beaten
- 1 cup half and half
- 1¼ cups grated cheese (mild Mexican or Cheddar)
- 1¼ cups finely chopped broccoli
- 1 unbaked 9-inch pie shell
- ¼ tablespoon minced onion
- ½ small green or red bell pepper, finely chopped

In a medium bowl mix together the eggs, half and half, cheese, and broccoli. Pour into the pie crust. Sprinkle the onion and pepper over the top. Use a fork to push the vegetables down. Bake in a 350° oven for 1 hour.

MAKES 6 TO 8 SERVINGS.

Mulberry Inn

TENNESSEE

Adams Hilborne

801 Vine Street
Chattanooga, Tennessee 37403
(423) 265-5000

A *small inn with ten rooms, the Adams Hilborne has sixteen-foot ceilings and ornate moldings to reflect the atmosphere of a European-style inn. It was built in 1889. Listed on the National Register of Historic Places, it is in the Fortwood historic district of old Chattanooga. Area attractions include the Tennessee Aquarium, Ruby Falls, Rock City, and the Incline Railway.*

Orange Pecan Chicken Salad

    2   cups diced cooked chicken
    ½   cup diced celery
    ¼   cup chopped red onion
    ¼   cup chopped pecans
    ¼   cup orange juice
    ¾   cup diced melon (any kind, or ¾ cup
            seedless grapes)
    ½   cup oil-and-vinegar salad dressing
            Salt and pepper to taste
    ¼   cup mayonnaise
        French dressing
        Lettuce leaves

In a large bowl combine the chicken, celery, onion, pecans, orange juice, melon, oil-and-vinegar salad dressing, salt, and pepper. In a small bowl combine the mayonnaise and mix with French dressing, just enough to moisten. Add the mayonnaise mixture to the salad chicken and serve on lettuce.

MAKES 4 SERVINGS.

Tamale Pie

    1   tablespoon butter
    1   tablespoon oil
    ······································
    1½ pounds ground beef
    ½   to 1 pound ground pork
    1   onion, chopped (sautéed until
            translucent, not brown)
    1   green bell pepper, chopped
            Chili powder to taste
    1   10½-ounce can tomato soup
    1   soup can water
    1   12-ounce can whole kernel corn
    1   cup yellow cornmeal
    2   eggs
    1   cup milk
            Salt and pepper to taste
    1   5-ounce can black olives, pitted

In a large skillet heat the butter and oil and fry the beef and pork until brown. Add the onion, green pepper, and chili powder.

In a large bowl combine the tomato soup, water, corn, and cornmeal. Stir until the lumps disappear. In a small bowl beat the eggs and milk together. Add the milk mixture to the cornmeal mixture. Add the meat and season with salt and pepper. Pour into a 2-quart casserole dish and add the black olives. Bake in a 350° oven for 1 hour.

MAKES 6 SERVINGS.

Hachland Hill Dining Inn

Hachland Hill Dining Inn

1601 Madison Street
Clarksville, Tennessee 37043
(615) 647-4084

H*achland Hill is called "a dining inn" because of its reputation for gourmet dishes, such as Oysters Rockefeller, Chateaubriand, Moroccan Leg of Lamb, and Coquilles Saint Jacques. The innkeeper, Phila Hach, is well known as a chef and cookbook author. She plans a differ-*

ent menu each day to provide a unique dining experience for her guests. Only forty-five minutes from Nashville, this inn is near activities such as tennis, golf, and swimming.

Cooking Quail and Doves

- 1   teaspoon dry mustard
- 1   teaspoon curry powder
- 1   teaspoon celery salt
- 1   teaspoon savory salt
- 1   teaspoon garlic salt
- 2   teaspoons Worcestershire sauce
- ½   cup butter, melted
     Salt and pepper to taste
- 6   quail or 12 doves
- 1   cup water
- 3   tablespoons cornstarch
- 1   4-ounce can mushrooms
     Toasted Pecan Dressing Balls (recipe follows)

In a small bowl mix the spices and seasonings with the butter. Coat the quail or doves well with the mixture. Place the quail in a roasting pan and cover well with foil. Bake in a 250° oven for 3 hours.

In a large skillet heat the pan drippings. In a small bowl combine the water and cornstarch, and mix until smooth. Add the mixture to the pan drippings and blend until smooth. Add the mushrooms. Serve with Toasted Pecan Dressing Balls.

MAKES 6 SERVINGS.

Toasted Pecan Dressing Balls

- 2   cups water
- 1   cup uncooked white rice
- 1   teaspoon salt
- ¾   cup coarsely chopped pecans
- 1   tablespoon butter
- 1   cup diced celery
- 1   tablespoon chopped onion
- 2   eggs
- 1¼ teaspoon salt
- ¼   teaspoon pepper
- ¼   cup milk

In a stockpot or saucepan bring the water to a boil and cook the rice with salt for 25 minutes.

Toast the pecans on a baking sheet in a 350° oven. In a skillet melt the butter. Add the celery and onion, and cook until tender.

Add the rice, pecans, eggs, salt, pepper, and milk. Form into dressing balls. Place the dressing balls on a greased pan. Bake in a 350° oven for about 30 minutes, until done. Cover with aluminum foil to keep moist.

Serve game surrounded with dressing balls and gravy.

MAKES 6 SERVINGS.

Mother's Holiday Ham

- 1   cooked sugar-cured ham
- 1   16-ounce can red sour pitted cherries, juice reserved
- 2   teaspoons cornstarch
- ½   teaspoon ground cinnamon
- ¼   teaspoon ground cloves
- 1   tablespoon grape jelly
- 1   tablespoon whte vinegar
- 1   teaspoon Worcestershire sauce
- ½   cup Cognac
- 1   whole orange, thinly sliced

Score the ham and place in a baking pan. In a saucepan combine the cherry juice and cornstarch. Add the remaining ingredients and cook until thick. Pour over the ham. Bake in a 325° oven for 1 hour, basting frequently.

MAKES 8 SERVINGS.

Coquille Saint Jacques (Sea Scallops)

- ½   cup dry vermouth
- 2   pounds scallops
- 2   tablespoons shallots
- ½   teaspoon salt
- ½   teaspoon black pepper
- 2   cups thick white cream sauce
     Chopped fresh parsley

In a saucepan heat the vermouth and simmer the scallops with the shallots for about 4 minutes. Remove the scallops from the juice (the scallops must not be overcooked). Add the salt, pepper, and white sauce to the scallop broth. Stir in the scallops. Divide the scallops among sea shells. Run in a 425° oven to brown. Serve with chopped fresh parsley.

MAKES ABOUT 6 SERVINGS.

Southern-fried Chicken

- 1   large fryer, cut up
     Hot water
     Seasoned flour
     Oil or shortening for frying
     Salt and pepper to taste

- 2   tablespoons all-purpose flour
- ½   cup hot water
- 1   cup heavy cream
     Salt and pepper to taste

Dip the chicken pieces in hot water. Immediately coat with seasoned flour.

Quickly place skin-side-down in a preheated skillet with ½- to ¾-inch of hot oil. Cover and fry for 5 minutes. Remove the cover and cook 4 minutes longer.

Turn the chicken, cover, and cook 5 minutes longer. Remove the cover and cook for 4 minutes, until the chicken is brown, crunchy, and done. Sprinkle with more salt and pepper, if desired. Do not overcook.

Pour off all of the drippings except 2 tablespoons. Add 2 tablespoons of flour, and stir until blended. Add ½ cup of hot water and the cream. Stir and cook until the gravy is thick. Season with salt and pepper to taste.

Note: The hot water seals in the juices and enables more flour to stick to the chicken. This gives Southern-fried chicken that special crispy character.

MAKES 4 TO 6 SERVINGS.

Sauce Bearnaise

- 2   pounds beef tenderloin

- 2   tablespoons tarragon vinegar
- 2   shallots, chopped
- 4   egg yolks
- 1   teaspoon finely chopped parsley
- 4   tablespoons melted butter
- 1   tablespoon beef bouillon
- ¼   teaspoon salt
- 1   teaspoon dried tarragon
     Bacon slices, cooked crisp

Grill the tenderloin to the desired doneness.

In a sauté pan heat the vinegar and simmer the shallots for a few minutes. Strain. Add the egg yolks one at a time to the vinegar, beating well. Add the butter slowly with the bouillon and seasonings. Stir well. Keep warm.

Serve the beef tenderloin with the Sauce Bearnaise and crisp bacon.

MAKES 6 TO 8 SERVINGS.

Phila's Crab Maryland

3   *eggs, separated*
2   *teaspoons Worcestershire sauce*
1   *teaspoon seasoned salt*
1   *teaspoon onion powder*
    Black pepper to taste
12   *ounces precooked crab meat*
6   *slices bread, broken in pieces and*
    sprinkled with garlic oil

In a medium bowl beat the egg yolks with the Worcestershire sauce, seasoned salt, onion powder, and black pepper until light. Fold in the crab meat and bread bits. Beat the egg whites until stiff. Fold the egg whites into the crab mixture. Fry like an omelet in butter. Fold over and serve immediately.

MAKES 2 SERVINGS.

Stuffed Mushrooms à la Phila

3   *strips bacon, chopped*
1   *large onion, chopped (or ¾ cup*
    spring onions)
¼   *cup butter*
2   *cups chopped mushroom stems*
2   *cups cubed soft light bread*
2   *tablespoons catsup*
1   *tablespoon Worcestershire sauce*
¼   *cup Chablis*
    Juice of 2 lemons
24   *large mushroom caps (2 to 3 inches)*
    with stems

In a skillet sauté the bacon and onion until done but not brown. Add the butter and chopped mushroom stems, and sauté for 5 minutes. Stir in the remaining ingredients, blending until the bread is thoroughly mixed with the other ingredients. Set aside until cool enough to handle.

Stuff the mushrooms and place in a baking pan. Cover. Bake in a 350° oven for 30 minutes.

MAKES 24 STUFFED MUSHROOMS.

Fried Cheese Squares

4½   *cups milk*
1   *teaspoon salt*

4   *cups all-purpose flour*
5   *cups grated Swiss cheese*
1⅓   *cups evaporated milk*
4   *eggs*
½   *cup water*
3   *cups seasoned breadcrumbs*

In a saucepan bring 4½ cups of milk and the salt to scalding. Add the flour and stir with a heavy spoon until blended. While hot add the cheese, and stir well.

When cool enough to handle, knead until smooth. Press the dough into an oiled pan and spread out to ½-inch thickness. Chill.

Cut in 1-inch squares. In a large bowl combine the evaporated milk, eggs, and water, and mix well. Dip the squares in the egg mixture. Roll in crumbs. Fry in deep fat until golden.

MAKES ABOUT 36 SQUARES.

Snapp Inn

Snapp Inn
❧

1990 Davy Crockett Park Road
Limestone, Tennessee 37681
(423) 257-2482

*T**his inn is in a Federal-style brick home that was built in 1815. Furnished with antiques, it offers guests beautiful views of the mountains from a peaceful creekside setting. Davy Crockett Birthplace State Park with its large swimming pool is nearby.*

Oatmeal Raisin Muffins

1½   *cups boiling water*
1   *cup old-fashioned oats*

1½   *cups all-purpose flour*
2   *teaspoons cinnamon*
1   *teaspoon baking powder*
1   *teaspoon baking soda*
1   *teaspoon salt*
1   *cup margarine*
1   *cup firmly packed brown sugar*
1   *cup sugar*
2   *eggs*
1   *teaspoon vanilla extract*
1   *cup chopped nuts*
1   *cup flaked coconut*
1   *cup raisins*

In a large bowl pour boiling water over the oats. Let stand for 30 minutes.

In a separate bowl stir together the flour, cinnamon, baking powder, soda, and salt. Set aside.

In a medium bowl cream the margarine with the sugars until fluffy. Beat in the eggs, one at a time, then the vanilla. Stir in the dry ingredients, oats, nuts, coconut, and raisins until blended. Spoon into muffin cups lined with greased paper liners. Bake in a 350° oven for 20 to 25 minutes.

MAKES 1 DOZEN.

Rhubarb Brown Betty

3   *cups sliced fresh or frozen rhubarb*
    (½-inch pieces)
1   *cup cubed peeled apples*
½   *cup sugar*
½   *teaspoon ground cinnamon*
½   *cup all-purpose flour*
1   *teaspoon baking powder*
¼   *teaspoon salt*
¼   *cup butter or margarine*
⅔   *cup firmly packed brown sugar*
⅔   *cup quick-cooking oats*
    Vanilla ice cream (optional)

In a large bowl combine the rhubarb and apples. Spoon into a greased 8-inch square baking dish. In a small bowl combine the sugar and cinnamon. Sprinkle over the rhubarb mixture. Set aside.

In a medium bowl combine the flour, baking powder, and salt. Cut in the butter until the mixture resembles coarse crumbs. Stir in the brown sugar and oats. Sprinkle over the rhubarb mixture. Bake in a 350° oven for 40 to 50 minutes, or until lightly browned. Serve warm or cold with a scoop of ice cream, if desired.

MAKES 6 TO 8 SERVINGS.

The Mason Place

The Mason Place Bed & Breakfast

✌

600 Commerce Street
Loudon, Tennessee 37774
(423) 458-3921

---

*T*he Mason Place is an impeccably restored 1865 plantation home situated on three acres of lawns and gardens on which Civil War bullets and artifacts are still being found. A grand entrance hall, working fireplaces, Grecian swimming pool, gazebo, and wisteria-covered arbor are but a few of the amenities available for guests to enjoy. There are five antique-filled rooms with cozy gas-log fireplaces, authentic feather beds, and en-suite baths.

Chocolate Silk Pie

- ⅓ cup butter, softened
- 1 cup confectioners' sugar
- 2½ ounces unsweetened chocolate, melted
- 1 cup crushed Ritz crackers

....

- 4 eggs, separated
- 1 cup butter, softened
- 2 cups confectioners' sugar
- 3½ ounces unsweetened chocolate, melted and cooled
- 1 teaspoon vanilla extract
- 1 cup cream, whipped

In a medium bowl beat together ⅓ cup of butter and the sugar. Add 2½ ounces of melted unsweetened chocolate, and the cracker crumbs.

In a separate bowl whisk the egg yolks lightly and set aside. In a small bowl beat the egg whites until stiff peaks form. Set aside. In the top of a double boiler over simmering water combine 1 cup of butter, the confectioners' sugar, and 3½ ounces of unsweetened chocolate, and heat until the chocolate melts. Add ½ cup of the chocolate mixture to the egg yolks, stirring to blend. Reduce the heat slightly, and pour the egg mixture back into the double boiler. Cook, stirring constantly, until the mixture thickens. Remove the pan from the heat and stir in the vanilla.

Gently fold the egg whites into the hot chocolate mixture. Allow the mixture to cool completely. Spoon the filling into the crust, and refrigerate for at least 2 hours.

Serve with fresh whipped cream.

MAKES 6 TO 8 SERVINGS.

Bourbon Pecan Cake

- 2 cups whole red candied cherries
- 2 cups white seedless raisins
- 2 cups bourbon

....

- 2 cups butter or margarine, softened
- 2 cups sugar
- 2 cups dark brown sugar, firmly packed
- 8 eggs, separated
- 5 cups sifted all-purpose flour
- 4 cups pecan halves
- 1½ teaspoons baking powder
- 1 teaspoon salt
- 2 teaspoons ground nutmeg

In a large bowl combine the cherries, raisins, and bourbon. Cover tightly and refrigerate overnight.

Drain the fruits and reserve the bourbon. In a large bowl beat the butter with an electric mixer until light and fluffy. Add the sugar and brown sugar gradually, beating at medium speed until blended well. Add the egg yolks, blending well.

In a small bowl combine ½ cup of flour with the pecans. In a large bowl stir together the remaining flour, baking powder, salt, and nutmeg. Add 2 cups of the dry ingredients to the batter, amd mix thoroughly. Add the reserved bourbon and the remaining dry

ingredients alternately, ending with the flour. Beat well after each addition.

In a large bowl beat the egg whites until stiff but not dry. Fold the egg whites gently into the batter. Add the drained fruits and floured pecans to the batter, and blend well.

Grease a 10-inch tube pan, and line with waxed paper. Pour the batter into the pan to within 1 inch of the top. Any remaining batter may be baked in a loaf pan.

Bake in a 275° oven for 4½ hours for the tube cake, and 2 hours for the loaf. Cool in the pans for 2 to 3 hours. Remove the cakes from the pans, and peel off the waxed paper. Wrap the cakes in cheesecloth saturated with bourbon, then wrap in aluminum foil or plastic wrap and store in a covered container in the refrigerator for several weeks.

MAKES 8 TO 12 SERVINGS.

Walnut Bacon

- 1 pound bacon
- ½ cup chopped walnuts
- 1 teaspoon regular flour
- ¼ cup firmly packed dark brown sugar

Arrange the slices of bacon on a broiling pan, pushing together without overlapping. In a small bowl combine the remaining ingredients. Sprinkle the mixture over the bacon. Bake in a 350° oven for 30 minutes.

MAKES 6 TO 8 SERVINGS.

Lynchburg Bed & Breakfast

✌

P.O. Box 34
Lynchburg, Tennessee 34352
(615) 759-7158

---

*I*n a home built more than one hundred years ago, this inn is furnished with period antiques. Guests enjoy relaxing on the shady front porch. Area attractions include Tims Ford Lake and State Park, Ten-

Lynchburg

nessee walking horse farms at Shel-byville, Jack Daniel Distillery in Lynchburg, and numerous antique and gift shops.

Country Sausage Muffins

½ **pound bulk pork sausage**
1 **cup all-purpose flour**
1 **cup self-rising cornmeal**
1 **2-ounce jar diced pimento, drained**
1 **8-ounce carton French onion dip**
½ **cup milk**

In a skillet brown the sausage, stirring to crumble. Drain well, and reserve 2 table-spoons of drippings.

In a medium bowl combine the flour, cornmeal, sausage, and pimento. Add the reserved drippings, onion dip, and milk. Stir and fill each greased muffin cup two-thirds full. Bake in a 425° oven for 20 to 25 min-utes or until golden brown.

MAKES 1 DOZEN.

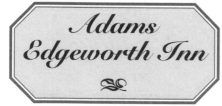

Adams Edgeworth Inn

❧

P.O. Box 343, Monteagle Assembly Monteagle, Tennessee 37356 (615) 924-4000

This inn is ideal for visitors who are looking for peace and quiet in a secluded setting. In the quaint vil-lage of Monteagle near Chat-tanooga, it was built in 1896 and is listed on the National Register of

Historic Places. Tennis, golf, and swimming are available nearby.

Omelet Bon Laboureur

6 **egg yolks, slightly beaten (or egg substitute)**
6 **egg whites, beaten stiff**
2 **pinches salt**
   Pinch chopped parsley
   Pinch tarragon
   Pinch chives
2 **tablespoons butter**

In a large bowl fold the egg whites into the beaten egg yolks with a wooden spatula. Add a little salt and a good pinch of parsley, tar-ragon, and chives. In an omelet pan melt 1 tablespoon of butter and pour the omelet mixture into the pan. Cook for 2 to 3 min-utes. Fold this foamy mass into a hot oven-proof dish. Bake in a 350° oven for 4 to 5 minutes.

Pour 1 tablespoon of melted butter over the omelet. This delicate omelet should be creamy in texture and never overcooked.

Note: Eggs are out, but herbs are in! The wonderful marriage of this bouquet of herbs is a real treat. Try to get fresh herbs if possi-ble. The difference is remarkable.

MAKES 3 TO 4 SERVINGS.

Jackie Kennedy's Austrian Strawberry Mousse

1 **quart strawberries, washed and hulled, reserve several berries for garnish**
½ **cup sugar**
½ **cup white wine (or try Cointreau)**
2 **envelopes unflavored gelatin**
½ **cup cold water**
½ **cup boiling water**
2 **cups heavy cream, whipped**

Press the berries through a fine sieve. Add the sugar and wine. Chill.

Soften the gelatin in cold water, then add the boiling water. Stir until dissolved. Cool.

In a large bowl combine the gelatin and the strawberry mixture, and beat with a rotary beater until fluffy and slightly thickened. Fold in the whipped cream.

Turn into a 2-quart oiled mold. Chill for 3 hours or longer.

Unmold onto a chilled serving platter and garnish with whole strawberries. Do not freeze.

MAKES 4 TO 6 SERVINGS.

Christopher Place Country Inn

❧

1500 Pinnacles Way Newport, Tennessee 37821 (800) 595-9441

Christopher Place, on a two-hun-dred-acre wooded site, offers all the amenities of a first-class resort—fitness gymnasium, tennis courts, sauna, hot tubs, swimming pool, and library. In addition, it's within an easy drive of the Great Smoky Mountains National Park and the mountain resort towns of Gatlin-burg and Pigeon Forge. Even the Biltmore Estate at Asheville, North Carolina, is not far away. Walking trails right on the inn property are another guest-pleasing feature.

Christopher Place Country Inn

Smoky Mountain White Bread

1 **cup pure mountain water (if you don't live in the Smoky Moun-tains, then spring water will do, but you don't know what you're missing)**
2 **tablespoons maple syrup**
2 **tablespoons butter**
3 **tablespoons powdered buttermilk**

3 cups bread flour
1 tablespoon yeast
1 teaspoon salt

In a large bowl mix all of the ingredients. Cover with a towel and let rise for several hours.

Punch down the dough, then place in a 5 x 9-inch loaf pan. Place the pan in a cold oven and let rise for about 1 hour. Bake in a 375° oven for 20 to 25 minutes.

MAKES 1 LOAF.

Beef and Wine Fettuccine

1 pound ribeye, cut into cubes
2 10½-ounce cans sliced mushrooms soup
1 jar sliced mushrooms, drained (size of jar depending on taste)
1 envelope of onion soup mix
¼ cup red wine (a burgundy is best, but any type will do)
Fettucine noodles, cooked

In a crock pot combine all of the ingredients except the noodles. Simmer on high for 1 hour, then stir.

Turn the crock pot to low and simmer for 5 to 6 hours, stirring once per hour.

Serve the beef mixture over the noodles. Great side dishes include fresh asparagus or Smoky Mountain White Bread.

MAKES 4 SERVINGS.

*Parish Patch
Farm & Inn*

❧

*1100 Cortner Road
Normandy, Tennessee 37360
(800) 876-3017*

---

*P*ositioned along the banks of the Duck River, this inn doubles as a 150-acre working farm. Guests enjoy the surrounding cornfields and green meadows where farm hands go about their daily work. Amenities include a swimming

pool, an exercise room, a terrace for resting and relaxing right on the river, and a playground for children. The cozy rooms are decorated with antiques. Fresh flowers in the rooms also add a special touch. Nashville is an hour's drive away, with major attractions such as Opryland USA theme park, the Country Music Hall of Fame, and the downtown riverfront district.

Raspberry-Apricot Pie

10 ounces frozen raspberries
1 32-ounce can apricot halves
Pastry for 1 2-crust pie
¾ cup sugar
¼ cup all-purpose flour
⅛ teaspoon salt
2 tablespoons butter
½ teaspoon almond extract

Defrost and drain the raspberries. Reserve ½ cup of juice. Place the drained apricots in the pie crust. Spoon the raspberries over the apricots and pour the juice over the top.

In a small bowl mix the sugar, flour, and salt together and sprinkle over the berries. Dot with butter and sprinkle on extract. Cover with top crust and sprinkle with sugar. Bake in a 400° oven for 50 to 60 minutes. Watch carefully.

Variation: Substitute 2½ cups of fresh blackberries and 5 fresh sliced peaches for the raspberries and apricots. Increase the sugar to 1 cup.

MAKES 6 TO 8 SERVINGS.

Whole Wheat Cinnamon Waffles

1 cup whole wheat flour
1 cup all-purpose flour
2 teaspoons sugar
4 teaspoons baking powder
1 teaspoon salt
1 teaspoon ground cinnamon
2 eggs, separated
2 cups milk
¼ cups oil

In a medium bowl sift together the flours, sugar, baking powder, salt, and cinnamon. In

a large bowl mix the egg yolks with the milk and oil. Beat the whites until stiff. Add the dry ingredients to the liquid mixture. Gently fold in the egg whites. Bake on a hot waffle iron until brown.

MAKES 4 SERVINGS.

Lemon Herb Broccoli

1 bunch broccoli
2 tablespoons butter
3 to 4 tablespoons lemon juice
1 tablespoon Dijon mustard
½ teaspoon dried marjoram, crumbled

Cut the broccoli into flowerets and steam until tender. In a saucepan melt the butter and blend in the lemon juice, mustard, and marjoram. Spoon over the broccoli.

MAKES 4 SERVINGS.

Cold Zucchini Soup

2 tablespoons butter
1 medium onion, chopped
2 13¾-ounce cans chicken broth
2 cups sliced zucchini with skin on
2 cups milk
Salt and pepper to taste

In a saucepan melt the butter and sauté the onion until yellow. Add 1 can of broth and the zucchini, and cook until tender. In a blender purée the soup until smooth. Pour back into the saucepan.

Add the remaining broth and the milk. Season with salt and pepper to taste. This can be served hot, too.

MAKES 4 TO 6 SERVINGS.

Richmont Inn

❧

*220 Winterberry Lane
Townsend, Tennessee 37882
(423) 448-6751*

---

*I*n the heart of the Great Smoky Mountains, this unusual inn is built in the style of an Appalachian cantilevered barn. The common areas *are furnished with eighteenth-century English antiques and French paintings. Each of the ten rooms is named for a prominent Appalachian personality, with furnishings that reflect mountain culture and history. Golfing privileges are available to guests at the nearby Laurel Valley Country Club.*

Other activities available in Townsend or nearby Gatlinburg and Pigeon Forge include swimming, tennis, hiking, and shopping.

Richmont Inn's Chocolate Pecan Torte

    8 large eggs, separated
    ½ cup sugar
    ⅔ cup all-purpose flour
    ½ teaspoon baking soda
    ¼ teaspoon salt
    ¾ cup ground pecans
    ⅓ cup unsweetened cocoa
    ¼ cup water
    1 teaspoon vanilla extract
    ¼ cup sugar
....
       Chocolate Frosting (recipe follows)
       Chopped pecans
       Chocolate Glaze (recipe follows)

Grease the bottoms only of 2 9-inch round cake pans. Line the bottoms of the pans with parchment paper, grease the parchment paper, and set aside. In a large bowl beat the egg yolks with an electric mixer at high speed, gradually adding ½ cup of sugar. Beat until the mixture is thick and pale yellow.

In a separate bowl combine the flour, soda, salt, pecans, and cocoa. Add the dry ingredients to the yolk mixture alternately with the water, beginning and ending with the pecan mixture. Stir in the vanilla.

Beat the egg whites at high speed with a mixer until foamy. Gradually add ¼ cup of sugar, beating until stiff peaks form. Fold the egg whites gently into the batter. Pour the batter into the prepared pans. Bake in a 375° oven for 16 to 18 minutes or until done. Cool in the pans on a wire rack for 10 minutes. Remove from the pans and allow to cool completely.

Split the cake layers in half horizontally to make 4 layers. Place 1 cake layer on a serving plate and spread 1 cup of Chocolate Frosting on top of the layer. Repeat the procedure with the second and third cake layers. Top the stack with the fourth cake layer. Spread the remaining ½ cup of frosting on the side of the cake. Gently press chopped pecans into the frosting. Spread chocolate glaze over the top immediately upon removing the pan from the heat and allow to set.

A true chocolate lover's delicacy.
MAKES 8 SERVINGS.

Chocolate Frosting

    ⅔ cup confectioners' sugar
    ⅓ cup unsweetened cocoa
    2 cups whipping cream
    1½ teaspoon vanilla extract

In a large mixing bowl combine the confectioners' sugar and cocoa. Gradually stir in the whipping cream. Add the vanilla and beat at low speed with a mixer until blended. Beat at high speed until stiff peaks form.

MAKES 3½ CUPS.

Chocolate Glaze

    2 tablespoons cocoa
    2 tablespoons water
    1 tablespoon butter
    1 cup sifted confectioners' sugar
    ¼ teaspoon vanilla extract

In a heavy stainless steel bowl combine the cocoa, water, and butter and cook over medium heat, stirring constantly, until the mixture thickens. Remove the pan from the heat, and gradually stir in the confectioners' sugar and vanilla.

MAKES ⅓ CUP.

Richmont Inn Grand Marnier Soufflé Glacé in an Orange

    4 to 5 naval oranges
   15 large egg yolks
    5 large egg whites
    2 cups sugar

    4 cups (1 quart) heavy whipping
       cream
    ¼ cup Grand Marnier
       Chocolate shavings
       Whipped cram for garnish

Cut the oranges in half and scoop out the pulp. Using a 1½-inch-wide yardstick and heavy-duty aluminum foil 18 inches wide, make 1-inch collars by folding aluminum foil around the yardstick approximately 4 or 5 times. This makes a 1½-inch band. Remove the aluminum foil from the yardstick. With a rolling pin, crease the foil and roll into a circle to form a collar. Place a collar around each orange half and apply a small piece of tape to the outside of each foil collar seam to secure.

In the top of a double boiler whip the egg yolks and whites together with the sugar and place over simmering water. Whipping constantly, bring the mixture to 165°. In a large bowl whip the cream to medium peaks. Fold the whipped cream into the egg mixture. Fold in the Grand Marnier. Place the mixture into a large piping bag and pipe into the orange halves, filling them to the top. Using a palette knife, level the top of each orange collar. Place the soufflés in the freezer for a minimum of 4 hours or overnight.

To serve, remove the collars and garnish with chocolate shavings and whipped cream. Serve tuiles or wafers sprinkled with confectioners' sugar on the side.

Variation: Pipe the soufflé mixture into ramekins or freezer-safe serving dishes wrapped with foil collars and freeze.
MAKES 8 TO 10 SERVINGS.

Frozen Strawberry Cassis Soufflé

    1 cup heavy whipping cream
    ½ quart strawberries, hulled and
       rinsed
    2 tablespoons cassis
    1¼ cups plus 2 tablespoons sugar
    3 egg whites
       Pinch salt
       Mint leaves for garnish

Lightly butter 6 3-inch ramekins and sprinkle with sugar. Using a 1½-inch-wide yardstick and heavy-duty aluminum foil 18 inches wide, make 1-inch collars by folding aluminum foil around the yardstick approximately 4 or 5 times. This makes a 1½-inch band. Remove the aluminum foil from the yardstick. With a rolling pin, crease the fold and roll into a circle to form a collar. Place the collars around the ramekins and apply a small piece of tape to the outside of each foil collar seam to secure.

In a large bowl whip the cream until soft peaks form. In a food processor puree the strawberries. Stir in the cassis and 1¼ cups of sugar. In a medium bowl beat the eggs whites and a pinch of salt until soft peaks form. Sprinkle with 2 tablespoons of sugar and beat until glossy. Fold the strawberry purée and all but ½ cup of whipped cream into the whites. Save the remaining whipped cream for piping onto the soufflés when serving. Store the cream covered in the refrigerator.

Pour the soufflé into ramekins and freeze for at least 4 hours. Upon removing the soufflé collars, use a wet knife to gently carve the edges of the soufflés, pipe whipped cream onto the tops, and garnish with a small mint leaf.

MAKES 6 SERVINGS.

Winter Fruit Casserole with Vanilla Ice Cream

- 24 candied chestnuts
- 6 apples, tornadoed (to cut in wedges so as to shape like a football -
- 6 pears, tornadoed
   Lemon juice
- 6 tablespoons butter
- ½ cup brown sugar
- 1 vanilla bean, split and scraped
- 1 cup fresh cranberries
- ½ cup dried cranberries
- ½ cup toasted almonds
....
- ½ cup plumped raisins
- 12 prunes
- 6 dried figs
- 3 ounces Cognac
   Juice of 3 oranges
   4 to 6 Brandy Snaps (recipe follows)
   Vanilla or caramel ice cream

In a saucepan poach the chestnuts in sugar syrup and set aside. Toss the apples and pears in lemon juice. In a saucepan melt the butter. Add the sugar, vanilla bean and seeds, cranberries, and raisins, and toss for 2 minutes over low heat. Add the almonds, prunes, chestnuts, figs, and cognac. Flambé. Add the orange juice and toss gently for 1 more minute. Remove the vanilla bean. Serve the warm fruit in a bowl with a doily underneath the dish. Place a Brandy Snap in the center and place a scoop of ice cream in the Brandy Snap.

A sophisticated fruit lover's treat.

MAKES 4 TO 6 SERVINGS.

Brandy Snap Cup

- 1 cup butter
- 1½ cups dark corn syrup
- ½ cup brown sugar
- 1½ cups all-purpose flour (or half cake flour and half bread flour)

In a large bowl mix all of the ingredients together. Place a sheet of parchment paper on the back of a sheet pan. Spoon out a dollop of the mixture onto the parchment. Bake in a 350° oven for approximately 7 to 8 minutes. As soon as bubbles start to form, remove the Brandy Snap from the oven and cool for 1 minute. Remove from the parchment with a palette knife and place the Brandy Snap on a cool cup shape (stainless steel timbales or espresso cups work great). Allow to cool completely until cup is set. Remove and set aside until ready for service. Repeat with the remaining batter.

MAKES 4 TO 6 SNAPS.

TEXAS

Austin's Wildflower Inn

1200 22-½ Street
Austin, Texas 78705
(512) 477-9639

With its tree-lined residential streets, stately homes and government buildings, rich history, and western-flavored cultural life, Austin is invariably a pleasant surprise for first-time visitors. Austin's Wildflower Inn is a good choice for travelers regardless of how familiar they might be with the charms of Texas' capital city. Only a few blocks from the University of Texas and the Capitol Building, it features Texas-style antique furnishings, quilts, the original oak floors, and a timeless oak in the yard.

Baked Bananas

⅓ cup butter
3 tablespoons lemon juice
6 firm, ripe bananas, peeled
1 teaspoon ground ginger
1 cup grated coconut
⅓ cup firmly packed brown sugar

In a shallow baking dish that will hold 6 bananas, spread the melted butter and lemon juice over the bottom. Stir the butter and lemon juice together until blended. Put the bananas in the dish and turn them until they are well-coated with the butter mixture. In a small bowl combine the sugar and ginger, and stir with a fork to blend. Sprinkle the sugar mixture evenly over the bananas. Bake in a 375° oven for 10 to 20 minutes, or until the butter bubbles a little. Turn the bananas over once halfway through the baking time. Sprinkle the coconut over the bananas about 5 minutes before they finish cooking.
MAKES 6 SERVINGS.

Tender Orange Muffins

1½ cups all-purpose flour
1 teaspoon baking powder
¾ teaspoon baking soda
1 teaspoon salt
1 egg
½ cup orange juice
3 tablespoons orange marmalade
½ cup sugar
6 tablespoons butter, melted
⅓ cup golden raisins

In a medium bowl mix together the flour, baking powder, soda, and salt. In a large bowl mix together the egg, orange juice, orange marmalade, and sugar until blended. Blend in melted butter. Stir the dry ingredients into the liquid mixture. Stir just until blended, and then fold in the golden raisins. Spoon the batter into greased muffin cups. Bake in a 400° oven for 12 to 18 minutes.
MAKES 1 DOZEN.

Austin's Wildflower Inn

Superb Strawberry-Banana French Toast

10 to 12 diagonal slices day-old French bread
5 eggs, lightly beaten
¾ cup milk
1 tablespoon vanilla extract
Pinch baking powder
1 16-ounce package frozen whole strawberries
3 firm bananas, sliced
1 cup sugar
1 tablespoon pumpkin pie spice
Cinnamon-sugar

In a large baking dish arrange the bread. In a medium bowl mix the eggs, milk, vanilla, and baking powder. Pour over the bread and turn each piece to coat. Cover and refrigerate overnight.

Remove the dish from the refrigerator and let sit. In a large bowl combine the strawberries, bananas, sugar, and pumpkin pie spice. Pour the strawberry mixture into a greased baking dish large enough to hold the soaked bread. Place the soaked bread on top of the strawberry-banana mixture. Sprinkle lightly with cinnamon-sugar. Bake in a 350° oven for about 30 minutes.

MAKES 4 TO 6 SERVINGS.

Honey Date Whole Wheat Muffins

    1   cup whole wheat flour
    ½   cup all-purpose flour
    ½   cup wheat germ
    2   teaspoon baking powder
    ½   teaspoon salt
    1   teaspoon ground cinnamon
    ½   teaspoon grated nutmeg
    ½   cup milk
    ½   cup honey
    ¼   cup butter, melted
    1   egg
    1   cup chopped dates
    ½   cup chopped walnuts

In a large bowl combine the flours, wheat germ, baking powder, salt, cinnamon, and nutmeg. In a small bowl combine the milk, honey, butter, and egg until blended well. Stir the liquid mixture into the dry ingredients. Fold in the dates and nuts. Spoon the batter into greased muffin cups. Bake in a 375° oven for 20 minutes.

MAKES 12 MUFFINS.

The Governor's Inn

611 West 22nd Street
Austin, Texas 78705
(800) 871-8908

This unique inn is only a few blocks from the University of Texas and the state capitol and grounds. Each of the ten guest rooms is named for a former governor. Amenities include claw-foot bathtubs in the guest rooms, a tree-shaded wraparound front porch with rockers and porch swings, and a spacious parlor. Many cultural

events such as plays and concerts, are available on the university campus. Austin's downtown Sixth Street also has many fine shops and restaurants.

Carrington's Bluff Granola

    6   cups old-fashioned oats
    1   cup wheat germ
    1   cup All-Bran cereal
    1   cup nut (your choice)
    1   cup flaked coconut
    ½   cup firmly packed brown sugar
    1   teaspoon cinnamon
    1   cup honey
    ½   cup oil

In a large bowl combine the oatmeal, wheat germ, cereal, nuts, and coconut. Add the brown sugar and cinnamon, and mix well. In a separate bowl combine the honey and oil, and heat slightly to blend (45 seconds in the microwave). Pour over the dry ingredients. Mix well. Bake in a 300° oven for 25 to 30 minutes, stirring every 10 minutes.

MAKES ABOUT 2½ QUARTS.

Aunt Betty's Toffee

    1   cup butter
    1½   cups sugar
    1   tablespoon light corn syrup
    3   tablespoons water
    1   teaspoon vanilla extract
    6   Hershey's milk chocolate bars
         Toasted almonds

In a saucepan combine the butter, sugar, corn syrup, water, and vanilla, and cook over medium to high heat, stirring occasionally, until the mixture reaches the hard-crack stage (280°). Spread in a well-greased pan. Lay the chocolate bars on top and sprinkle with toasted almonds. Allow to cool completely (refrigerate if necessary), and break into pieces.

MAKES 6 TO 8 SERVINGS.

Chris's Quiche

    1   unbaked 9-inch pie crust
    7   stripe bacon, cooked and coarsely
          chopped
    ½   cup grated Swiss cheese

    3   eggs
    1   cup half and half
    ½   teaspoon Dijon mustard
        Dash white pepper

In the bottom of the pie crust sprinkle the bacon and cheese. In a medium bowl combine the remaining ingredients, beating well. Pour the mixture over the bacon and cheese. Bake in a 350° oven for 45 to 60 minutes, until the top is golden brown.

MAKES 8 SERVINGS.

High Cotton Inn

High Cotton Inn

214 South Live Oak
Bellville, Texas 77418
(409) 865-9796

The five guest rooms in this cozy inn are furnished with period antiques. Guests enjoy the swimming pool as well as the swings on the front porch and balcony. Antique shops for unhurried browsing are nearby. Within an hour's drive of the inn are Stephen F. Austin State Park and Washington-on-the-Brazos State Park.

Shrimp Creole

    ½   cup butter
    1⅓   cups chopped green bell pepper
    1⅓   cups chopped onions
    2½   cups diced celery
    ½   cup all-purpose flour
    3   16-ounce cans tomatoes

1½   *tablespoons salt*
  Pepper to taste
2   *tablespoons firmly packed brown*
   sugar
3   *bay leaves*
8   *whole cloves*
4   *pounds fresh shrimp, peeled and*
   deveined
2   *teaspoons Worcestershire sauce*
⅛   *teaspoon Tabasco sauce*
1   *tablespoon lemon juice*
¾   *cup white wine*
  Cooked rwhite ice

In an 8-quart pot melt the butter and sauté the green pepper, onions and celery until tender. Remove the pan from the heat and add the flour. Blend well. Add the tomatoes gradually, stirring constantly. Add the salt, pepper, brown sugar, bay leaves, and cloves, and bring to a boil. Reduce the heat and simmer uncovered for 45 minutes.

Remove the bay leaves. The mixture can be refrigerate at this point if desired. Add the shrimp to the simmering thickened sauce and cook for 5 minutes. Add the Worcestershire sauce, Tabasco, lemon juice, and wine. Serve over rice.

MAKES 6 SERVINGS.

Knittel Homestead Inn
❧

520 Main, P.O. Box 132
Burton, Texas 77835
(409) 289-5102

This inn was built in three stages in the 1870s and 1880s as the home of Herman Knittel, a Prussian immigrant. One of its most distinctive features inside is the Old World free-standing staircase, which was transported by ship from Germany. The inn is furnished throughout with antiques and country-style

furniture, including the old clawfoot tubs in the guest rooms. Knittel Homestead Inn is listed on the National Register of Historic Places.

Raspberry Streusel Muffins

1   *egg*
½   *cup milk*
¼   *cup oil*
1½   *cups all-purpose flour*
½   *cup sugar*
2   *teaspoons baking powder*
½   *teaspoon salt*
1   *cup fresh raspberries, drained (or ¾*
   cup canned)

½   *cup firmly packed light brown sugar*
½   *cup chopped nuts*
2   *tablespoons all-purpose flour*
2   *teaspoons ground cinnamon*
2   *tablespoons butter, melted*

Grease 12 muffin cups or line with paper liners. In a large bowl blend the egg with a fork. Stir in the milk and oil. Blend in 1½ cups of flour, the sugar, baking powder, and salt, and stir just until moistened. The batter should be lumpy. Do not overmix. Gently fold in the berries. Fill the prepared muffin cups two-thirds full.

In a small bowl combine the brown sugar, nuts, 2 tablespoons of flour, cinnamon, and melted butter, and mix until crumbly. Sprinkle the streusel mix over the batter. Bake in a 375° oven for 20 to 25 minutes, until golden.

MAKES 1 DOZEN.

Knittel Homestead Inn

Country Home

Country Home
❧

Route 1, Box 447
Canyon, Texas 79015
(800) 664-7636

W*ith only two guest rooms and its secluded location, this inn is ideal as a retreat or getaway spot. The striking two-story living room with fireplace features an antique mantel, handmade quilts, and original paintings by the innkeeper. The living room and guest rooms are furnished with antiques. Outside, guests enjoy the porch swing or sitting in the gazebo surrounded by flowers.*

Blueberry Hot Cakes

1   *cup all-purpose flour*
4   *teaspoons baking powder*
½   *teaspoon salt*
1   *tablespoon sugar*
1   *egg*
1   *cup milk*
¼   *cup butter, melted*
  Blueberries

In a large bowl combine the flour, baking powder, salt, and sugar. In a separate bowl beat together the egg, milk, and melted butter with a fork. Add the dry ingredients to the liquid mixture. Heat a griddle until very hot and spray with cooking spray. Pour about ¼ cup of batter into the skillet for each pancake. Cook as usual. Add a few blueberries to each pancake before turning.

MAKES 4 SERVINGS.

Sausage Quiche

½ *pound sausage*
6 *eggs*
⅔ *cup milk*
1 *cup shredded Cheddar cheese*
1 *teaspoon salt*
1 *cup garlic-onion croutons*

Grease a quiche pan. In a skillet fry the crumbled sausage until brown. Drain. In a large bowl beat the eggs, milk, Cheddar cheese, and salt together. Add the sausage and pour the mixture into the prepared dish. Cover with plastic wrap and refrigerate overnight.

The next day, top the quiche with the croutons. Bake in a 325° oven for 30 minutes.
MAKES 6 SERVINGS.

Pine Colony Inn

500 Shelbyville Street
Center, Texas 75935
(409) 598-7700

*E*ast Texas hospitality is the specialty of this inn, located in an old restored hotel in the heart of the historic town of Center. The pine floors and ceiling fans throughout evoke memories of small-town friendliness and relaxed living from the past. Creations from a local artist, Woodrow Foster, adorn the walls. Fishing is available nearby in two large freshwater lakes, Toledo Bend and Lake Pinkston. Hodges Garden, the Big Thicket, and

Shreveport, Louisiana, with horse racing and riverboat gambling, are a short drive away.

Green Chili Chicken

2 *whole chickens or chicken breasts*
2 *10 ½-ounce cans cream of chicken soup*
1 *16-ounce carton sour cream*
2 *4-ounce cans chopped green chiles*
1 *bunch green onions*
4 *cups grated Cheddar cheese*
1 *5-ounce can sliced black olives*
  White rice, cooked

In a large stockpot boil the chickens in seasoned water until done. Remove the chicken and reserve the broth. Cut the chicken into serving pieces, removing the skin and bone, if desired. Place the chicken in a 2-quart casserole dish.

In a large bowl combine the chicken soup, sour cream, green chiles, and chopped green onions. Pour the mixture over the chicken pieces. Top with grated Cheddar cheese and black olives. Pour in enough broth from the chicken to make it juicy. Bake in a 350° oven for 30 minutes or until bubbly.

Serve over hot rice.
MAKES 8 SERVINGS.

Marcille's Chicken

2 *teaspoons butter*
1 *small onion, chopped*
1 *green bell pepper, chopped*
1 *to 1½ pounds chicken*
1 *8-ounce package elbow macaroni*
1 *8 ounce package cream cheese, softened*
1 *10½-ounce can cream of mushroom soup*
1 *10½-ounce can cream of chicken soup*
1 *cup water*
1 *pound Velveeta cheese, cut in strips*

In a small skillet melt the butter and sauté the onion and bell pepper until tender. Set aside.

In a stockpot boil the chicken in seasoned water until tender. Bone and chop the chicken. In a separate pot cook the macaroni to the package directions. Drain well and place in a large bowl. Add the cream cheese and stir to melt. In a saucepan heat the soups

and water together. Pour into the noodles. Add the chicken and the sautéed onion and bell pepper. Pour the mixture into a 10 x 13-inch baking dish, and top with Velveeta strips. Bake in a 350° oven until hot and bubbly.
MAKES 8 TO 10 SERVINGS.

201 Louisiana Parkway
Corpus Christi, Texas 78404
(512) 882-4123

*T*his cozy inn is appropriately named because guests can see the water and feel the breeze off Corpus Christi Bay from the four guest rooms. Within a short drive are major tourist attractions such as the USS Lexington *Floating Museum*, the Texas State Aquarium, Bay Front Plaza Convention Center, and art and science museums. Also nearby is Oleander Point, a popular sailboarding site.

Great Garlic Cheese Grits

1 *cup uncooked instant grits*
4 *cups water*
½ *cup butter (or margarine)*
1 *6-ounce roll garlic cheese*
¼ *cup shredded Cheddar cheese*
¼ *cup Worcestershire sauce*
  Pepper to taste
2 *eggs*
¼ *cup milk*
  Paprika

In a saucepan cook the grits in salted boiling water until thick, stirring occasionally, about 7 minutes.

Remove the pan from the heat and add the butter, cheeses, Worcestershire sauce, and pepper, and stir until the butter and cheese melt.

In a small bowl mix the eggs and milk together, and add to the grits mixture. Mix well and pour into a 9 x 11-inch casserole dish. Sprinkle with paprika. Bake in a 350° oven for about 30 to 40 minutes, until bubbly and slightly browned.

MAKES 6 SERVINGS.

Fruit Cups

- 1 15½-ounce can crushed pineapple
- 1 11-ounce can mandarin oranges, drained
- 1 16-ounce can sliced peaches, drained and cut
- 1 6-ounce can frozen orange juice, thawed
- 1 10-ounce small carton frozen sliced strawberrie,s thawed
- 3 bananas, sliced
- ½ lemon squeezed on bananas

Mix all together and spoon into individual small plastic cups (½ cup-cocktail size), cover with plastic wrap and freeze. Take out 1 hour before serving to defrost.

Optional: Add ½ cup berries in season (blueberries, raspberries, or blackberries.)

MAKES ABOUT 8 CUPS.

Bay Breeze

Perry's Shrimp Omelet

- 3 tablespoons butter (or margarine)
- ½ cup sliced mushrooms
- 1¾ cups frozen cooked bay shrimp, thawed
  Lemon pepper to taste
- 2 tablespoons cream cheese with chives
- 4 eggs
- ¼ cup low-fat milk

In a sauté pan melt 2 tablespoons of butter and sauté the mushrooms. Add the shrimp and sprinkle lemon pepper generously over all. Sauté for 5 minutes or until the shrimp are warm.

In a 10-inch skillet melt 1 tablespoon of butter and the cream cheese with chives. In a medium bowl whisk the eggs with the milk. When the skillet is hot, add the eggs and sprinkle generously with lemon pepper. Let the eggs cook until almost set. Add the mushroom-shrimp mixture with a slotted spoon over half of the egg mixture. Fold over the other half of the egg mixture and sprinkle with a few shrimp. Cut in half and serve.

MAKES 2 SERVINGS.

Raphael House

500 West Ennis Avenue
Ennis, Texas 75119
(214) 875-1555

*A*mong the most historic and beautiful structures in a nationally recognized historic district, the Raphael House boasts massive arches, twelve-foot ceilings, grand arches, and pocket doors. The guest rooms feature clawfoot tubs, down comforters, and English toiletries. Ennis is only thirty minutes from Dallas.

World's Greatest Chocolate Chip Cookies

- 2 cups butter
- 2 cups sugar
- 2 cups firmly packed brown sugar
- 4 eggs
- 2 tablespoons vanilla extract
- 4 cups all-purpose flour
- 5 cups oatmeal (ground fine until powder)
- 2 teaspoons baking powder

- 2 teaspoons baking soda
- 1 teaspoon salt
- 24 ounces chocolate chips
- 8 ounces grated Hershey milk chocolate bar
- 3 cups chopped nuts

In a large bowl cream together the butter, sugar, and brown sugar. Add the eggs and vanilla, and mix well. In a separate bowl combine the flour, oatmeal, baking powder, soda, and salt. Add the dry ingredients to the creamed mixture, mixing well. Fold in the chocolate chips, grated chocolate, and nuts. Roll into golf ball size cookies and place on an ungreased cookie sheet 2 inches apart. Bake in a 375° oven for 6 minutes or until done.

MAKES 9 DOZEN COOKIES.

Cream Biscuits

- 2 cups all-purpose flour
- 1 tablespoon baking powder
- 2 teaspoons sugar
- 1 teaspoon salt
- 1½ to 2 cups heavy whipping cream
  Melted butter

In a large bowl combine the flour, baking powder, sugar, and salt. Add the cream a little at a time until the dough holds together but is not too sticky. Turn onto a floured board and knead until smooth, at least 1 minute. Roll ¼ to ⅜ inch thick and cut into small circles or other small shapes. Dip in melted butter on both sides and place on a cookie sheet. Bake in a 450° oven for 10 to 12 minutes or until golden brown.

MAKES 2 DOZEN.

249 East Main Street
Fredericksburg, Texas 78624
(210) 997-8549

*T*his inn is in an old home (built in 1850) that was the first two-story

Country Cottage Inn

limestone house in the city of Fredericksburg. With a typical early Texas front porch, it also features wooden lintels over the windows and doors, hand-hewn in an elegant curve. The exposed solid-oak rafters throughout the inn were also hand cut. All eleven rooms are furnished with antiques, including one room with furniture from the birthplace of Fleet Admiral Chester W. Nimitz, who was born only two blocks away. Outside, guests enjoy the courtyard with limestone walkways and a garden with native Texas plants. The Country Cottage Inn is listed on the National Register of Historic Places.

Fresh Apple Muffins

  1   *cup oil*
  2   *cups sugar*
  3   *eggs*
  1   *teaspoon vanilla extract*
  3   *cups all-purpose flour*
  1   *teaspoon salt*
1½ *teaspoons baking soda*
 ½ *teaspoon grated nutmeg*
  1   *teaspoon ground cinnamon*
 ½ *teaspoon ground cloves*
  3   *cups diced tart apples*
  1   *cup chopped pecans or walnuts*

In a large bowl combine the oil, sugar, eggs, and vanilla. Add the flour, salt, soda, nutmeg, cinnamon, and cloves, and mix just until moistened. Fold in the apples and pecans. Spoon into greased muffin cups. Bake in a 325° oven for 25 minutes.

MAKES ABOUT 2 DOZEN.

Magnolia House

101 East Hackberry
Fredericksburg, Texas 78624
(210) 997-0306

Each of the six guest rooms at Magnolia House is uniquely decorated with antique furnishings. Fresh flowers add to the luxurious atmosphere of this inn. Outside is a custom-designed stone patio with fish pond and waterfall for the enjoyment of guests. Nearby activities include tennis, golf, and swimming. Many guests also enjoy touring the Lyndon B. Johnson National Historical Park only sixteen miles away. This attraction includes LBJ's boyhood home and the Johnson family cemetery.

Durbon Eggs

  1   *cup whipping cream*
  3   *tablespoons Grey Poupon Dijon Mustard*
  6   *eggs*
      Grated Cheddar cheese
      Dried tarragon

Spray a 9-inch square baking dish with cooking spray. In a cup or small bowl combine the cream and mustard. Pour the mixture into the prepared dish. Break the eggs into the cream mixture. Sprinkle with grated Cheddar cheese and tarragon. Bake in a 350° oven for 22 to 25 minutes.

MAKES 6 SERVINGS.

Sticky Buns

  1   *package active dry yeast*
  1   *cup warm water (105 to 115°)*
 ¼ *cup sugar*
  1   *teaspoon salt*
  1   *egg*
  2   *tablespoons butter, melted*

3½ *cups all-purpose flour*

 ½ *cup sugar*
  2   *teaspoons cinnamon*
 ¼ *to ½ cup butter, melted*

  1   *tablespoon light corn syrup*
 ½ *cup firmly packed brown sugar*
      Chopped pecans

  3   *tablespoons water*
  1   *tablespoon instant nonfat dry milk*

In a large bowl dissolve the yeast in water. Stir in ¼ cup of sugar, the salt, egg, and 2 tablespoons of butter. Add 2 cups of flour and beat until smooth. Work in the remaining 1½ cups of flour. Cover tightly and chill overnight.

In a small bowl mix ½ cup of sugar and 2 teaspoons of cinnamon.

Roll out the dough into a 9 x 15-inch rectangle. Brush with melted butter, and sprinkle with cinnamon-sugar.

In a small bowl combine the corn syrup and remaining butter and pour into a 9 x 12-inch cake pan. Sprinkle with brown sugar. Add the chopped pecans.

Roll up the dough and slice into 12 slices. Place the slices in the pan, cover, and let rise for about 1 hour in a warm oven, until doubled in bulk.

In a cup combine 3 tablespoons of water and the instant nonfat dry milk. Pour over the rolls just before baking. Bake in a 375° oven for 20 minutes.

MAKES 12 SERVINGS.

Quiche

      Croutons
 ¾ *cup grated Cheddar cheese*
 ¾ *cup grated Swiss cheese*
      Summer savory (or rosemary)
  4   *eggs*
1½ *cups half and half*
      Lemon pepper
      Mustard (optional)
 ¼ *cup chopped green bell pepper*
 ¼ *cup chopped red bell pepper*
      Green onion, chopped

Spray a quiche pan with cooking spray. Spread croutons in the bottom. Spread the Cheddar and Swiss cheeses over the croutons. Sprinkle with summer savory.

In a medium bowl beat the eggs with the half and half. Add lemon pepper, and mustard if desired. Pour the mixture over the cheeses. Sprinkle the green and red peppers and onion over the egg mixture. Bake in a 350° oven for 35 minutes.

MAKES 6 TO 8 SERVINGS.

Fruit Dip

1   *cup whipping cream*
1   *cup firmly packed light brown sugar*
1   *cup sour cream*
4   *teaspoons Kahlua*
1   *teaspoon vanilla extract*

In a medium bowl whisk all of the ingredients together.

Serve with fresh fruit, on a fresh fruit cup, or with baked pears.

MAKES 3 CUPS.

The Queen Anne

1915 Sealy Avenue
Galveston, Texas 77550
(409) 763-7088

---

*T*his inn is housed in a Queen Anne-style home built in 1905. Guest-pleasing features include antique furniture throughout, ten-foot pocket doors, stained-glass windows, and a glassed-in porch for lounging and relaxing. Guests can

The Queen Anne

ride a horse-drawn carriage to the historic Strand district for a day of shopping and strolling through the fine shops, museums, and galleries of Galveston. Nearby are Moody Gardens and Lone Star Flight Museum. Other conveniently located activities include golfing, swimming, and tennis.

Cheese Grits

4   *cups water*
1   *teaspoon salt*
1   *cup quick-cooking grits*
8   *ounces American cheese, cubed*
¼   *cup butter or margarine, softened*
2   *eggs*
½   *cup milk (approximately)*

In a large saucepan bring the water with salt to a boil. Stir the grits into the boiling water. Cover and cook for 5 minutes, stirring occasionally to insure a smooth consistency. Remove the pan from the heat. Add the American cheese and butter, and mix thoroughly until melted. Crack the eggs into a measuring cup and beat with a fork. Add enough milk to make 1 cup. Mix well and add gradually to the grits. Pour into 2 greased 9-inch pie plates. Bake in a 350° for 30 to 40 minutes.

MAKES 6 TO 8 SERVINGS.

Hazlewood House

P.O. Box 1327, 1127 Church
Galveston, Texas 77553
(409) 762-1668

---

*B*uilt originally as a residence in 1877, this cozy three-room inn features wood trim of natural cypress on the floors, ceiling, and windows. The gingerbread trim on the exterior is another interesting touch. Guests also enjoy the Jacuzzi and the swing and hammock on the

front porch. Hazlewood House is conveniently located ten blocks from the beach, the Grand 1894 Opera House, and the convention center. Golf, tennis, and swimming are also available nearby.

Nut Waffles

2   *eggs*
2   *cups all-purpose flour*
½   *cup butter, melted*
1¾   *cups milk*
1   *tablespoon firmly packed brown sugar*
4   *teaspoons baking powder*
¼   *teaspoon salt*
2   *tablespoons broken nuts*

In a medium bowl beat the eggs with a hand beater until fluffy. Beat in the flour, butter, milk, brown sugar, baking powder, and salt just until smooth.

Heat a waffle iron. Pour the batter from a cup or pitcher into the center of the waffle iron. Immediately sprinkle with nuts. Bake about 5 minutes. Remove the waffles carefully.

MAKES 4 TO 6 SERVINGS.

St. James Inn

723 Street James
Gonzales, Texas 78629
(210) 672-7066

---

*T*his inn is in an old house (built in 1914) in an old village dear to the hearts of all Texans. At Gonzales in 1835, a group of Texans now referred to as "the magnificent eighteen" fired a cannon to repel Mexican General Santa Anna's forces and began the Texas revolution. Guests enjoy visiting several sites associated with early Texas history, including Pioneer Village Living History Center and the Old

Jail Museum. Street James Inn sits right in the middle of all this history in the downtown area, surrounded by century-old pecan trees. Gonzales is one hour's drive from Austin and San Antonio.

Cream Cheese Pound Cake

- 1   cup butter
- ½   cup margarine
- 1   8-ounce package cream cheese, softened
- 3   cups sugar
- 6   eggs
- 3   cups all-purpose flour
- 1   teaspoon vanilla extract
- 1   teaspoon lemon extract

In a large bowl cream the butter, margarine, and cream cheese until light and fluffy. Gradually add the sugar. Add the eggs alternately with the flour, mixing well. Add the flavorings. Pour the batter into a well-greased tube pan. Bake in a 325° oven for 1 hour and 20 minutes, or until a toothpick inserted in the center comes out clean.

MAKES 8 SERVINGS.

Orange Apple Pancake

- 2   cups buttermilk pancake mix
- 1½   cups water
- 2   tablespoons shredded orange zest
- 1   teaspoon ground cinnamon
- 1   tablespoon butter or margarine
- 1   small red cooking apple, cored and cut into thin wedges
- ¾   cup maple syrup
- ½   cup coarsely chopped pecans

Preheat a griddle to 400° (if electric, 425°). In a medium bowl combine the pancake mix, water, orange zest, and cinnamon, and stir until fairly smooth. In a small skillet melt the butter over medium heat and cook the apple for about 4 minutes, until tender. Stir in the syrup and nuts, and heat through. Keep warm until serving.

For each pancake, pour the batter by ¼ cupfuls onto a hot, well-greased griddle. Turn the pancakes when the tops are covered with bubbles and the edges look dry. Turn only once. Top the pancakes with warm syrup mixture.

MAKES 4 SERVINGS.

Angel Biscuits

- 1   package active dry yeast
- ¼   cup warm water (105 to 115°)
- 2½   cups all-purpose flour
- ½   teaspoon baking soda
- 1   teaspoon baking powder
- 1   teaspoon salt
- ⅓   cup sugar
- ½   cup shortening
- 1   cup buttermilk

In a small bowl mix the yeast and water. Set aside. In a large bowl combine the flour, soda, baking powder, salt, and sugar. Cut in the shortening. Add the buttermilk and the yeast mixture, and blend thoroughly with a spoon. Refrigerate if desired or use immediately. (Better to make one day and use the next.)

Shape into rolls and let rise for 1 hour at room temperature.

Bake in a 375° oven for about 15 minutes, or until brown.

MAKES ABOUT 3 DOZEN.

Brown Bread or Date and Nut Bread

- 1   cup chopped dates
- 2   teaspoons baking soda
- 2   cups boiling water
- 2   tablespoons margarine
- 2   cups sugar
- 2   eggs
- 4   cups sifted all-purpose flour
- 2   teaspoons salt
- 1   cup chopped nuts

Grease 5 20-ounce cans. In a medium bow mix the dates, soda, and boiling water. Cool until lukewarm.

In a large bowl cream together the margarine, sugar, and eggs together. Stir in the date mixture. Add the flour, salt, and chopped nuts. Fill each can half full. Bake in a 350° oven for 45 minutes or until done.

MAKES 5 LOAVES.

Doyle House

205 West Doyle
Granbury, Texas 76048
(817) 573-6492

Doyle House sits on a bluff overlooking the Brazos River. On the banks of Granbury Lake, it has its own swimming pool, boat house, and fishing platform for the comfort and entertainment of guests. Each of its three guest rooms is individully decorated with period antiques. Guests enjoy visiting the nearby historic sites and fine restaurants and shops. Other nearby activities include tennis, swimming, and golf.

Ham Loaf

- 2   pounds smoked ground lean ham (not precooked)
- 1   pound ground lean pork
- 1   cup milk
- 2   eggs
- ¼   cup cracker crumbs, crushed
      Pinch sage
      Garlic cloves

In a large bowl combine all of the ingredients. Spread the mixture into a 5 x 9-inch loaf pan, firming the loaf to eliminate any air pockets. Slice the garlic and place on top of the formed loaf. Bake in a 350° oven for 1 hour to 1 hour and 30 minutes. If desired, increase the oven temperature and brown the top at the last minute. Cool slightly to slice.

Note: The loaf needs to be cold to slice thin, then grill each slice to serve.

MAKES 6 SERVINGS.

Durham House

921 Heights Boulevard
Houston, Texas 77008
(713) 868-4654

---

*L*isted on the National Register of
Historic Places, Durham House is a
classic example of a Queen Anne-
style Victorian home. It is decorated
throughout with antiques, includ-
ing claw-foot bathtubs in the guest
rooms. Other nice touches are a
spacious solarium with columns,
exterior gingerbread trim, and a
gazebo in the garden. Guests may
choose from six individually deco-
rated guest rooms. Nearby activities
include tennis, golf, and swimming.

Amorous Pears

  1   **29-ounce can pear halves in juice**
      Ground cinnamon
1½   **cups light ricotta cheese**
  3   **tablespoons sugar**
¼   **teaspoon grated nutmeg**
  3   **tablespoons orange liqueur**
½   **cup sliced almonds, toasted**

Empty the pears and juice into a shallow baking dish. Arrange the pears cut-side up.
Sprinkle each pear half with cinnamon. Bake
in a 325° oven for 20 minutes.

In a small bowl combine the ricotta, sugar,
nutmeg, and liqueur. Whip with a fork until
smooth. Refrigerate.

When the pears are warmed, remove each
with a slotted spoon and place a pear half in
each of 8 stemmed sherbet or small saucer
champagne glasses. Spoon the cheese mixture evenly over the tops of the pears. Top
each with toasted almond slices.
MAKES 8 SERVINGS.

Cranberry Apple Muffins

1½   **cups all-purpose flour**
  1   **teaspoon baking soda**
  1   **teaspoon ground cinnamon**
¼   **teaspoon salt**
  2   **large eggs**
  1   **cup firmly packed dark brown sugar**
¼   **cup oil**
  1   **teaspoon vanilla extract**
  1   **cup diced unpeeled apple**
  1   **cup fresh cranberries**
½   **cup coarsely chopped walnuts**

Grease 12 muffin cups. In a large bowl mix
the flour, soda, cinnamon, and salt. In a
medium bowl beat the eggs. Add the sugar
and beat again. Whisk in the oil and vanilla.
Stir in the apple, cranberries and walnuts.
Pour the liquid mixture over the dry ingredients and stir just until moistened. Spoon the
batter into the prepared muffin cups. Bake in
a 350° oven for 20 to 25 minutes, or until a
toothpick inserted in a center muffin comes
out clean.
MAKES 1 DOZEN.

Spicy Peach Muffins

  2   **cups all-purpose flour**
½   **cup sugar**
  2   **teaspoons baking powder**
  1   **teaspoon baking soda**
½   **teaspoon salt**
  1   **teaspoon ground cinnamon**
½   **teaspoon grated nutmeg**
      Dash ground mace
  1   **egg, beaten**
⅓   **cup oil**
⅓   **cup milk**
  1   **8-ounce carton peach yogurt**
½   **cup finely chopped dried peaches**
  2   **tablespoons sugar**
½   **teaspoon ground cinnamon**

In a large bowl combine the flour, sugar, baking powder, soda, salt, 1 teaspoon cinnamon,
nutmeg, and mace. In a separate bowl combine the egg, oil, milk, yogurt, and dried

---

peaches. Add to dry ingredients, stirring just
until dry ingredients are moistened.Spoon
into greased muffin cups. Sprinkle the top of
each muffin with the mixture of sugar and
cinnamon. Bake in a 400° oven for 20 minutes, or until a toothpick inserted in a center
muffin comes out clean. Do not overbake.
MAKES 1 DOZEN.

306 East Delta Street
Jefferson, Texas 75657
(903) 665-7322

---

*M*cKay House has fireplaces in all
seven guest rooms, all of which are
furnished with antiques. The inn
also features a garden and a porch
for the comfort and convenience of
guests. Another nice touch is the
antique pump organ in the great
room. Recreational activities avail-
able nearby include tennis, golf,
and swimming.

Peach Soup

10   **ounces frozen sliced peaches**
  1   **16-ounce carton sour cream**
¼   **cup cooking sherry**
      Milk
  6   **to 8 fresh peaches, sliced**
      Mint leaves for garnish

In a blender combine the frozen peaches,
sour cream, and sherry and blend until
smooth. Add milk until texture is creamy.
Chill overnight.

In the bottom of 8 sherbet glasses arrange
fresh sliced peaches and pour the sour cream
mixture over the top. Garnish with mint
leaves.
MAKES 8 SERVINGS.

Applesauce Bread

  2   **cups all-purpose flour**
¾   **cup sugar**

2   *teaspoons baking powder*
½   *teaspoon baking soda*
½   *teaspoon salt*
1   *teaspoon cinnamon*
½   *teaspoon grated nutmeg*
1   *cup chunky applesauce*
2   *eggs*
½   *cup oil*
½   *cup chopped nuts*
½   *cup golden raisins*
1   *tablespoon caraway seeds*

In a large mixing bowl combine the flour, sugar, baking powder, soda, salt, cinnamon, and nutmeg. Add the remaining ingredients one at a time, mixing just until moistened.

Butter and flour a 9-inch square loaf pan. Line the bottom with waxed paper, if desired. Bake in a 350° oven for about 1 hour, until a knife inserted in the center comes out clean.

Cool before cutting. Keeps well in the refrigerator.

MAKES 1 LOAF.

Joseph's Cheese Biscuits

1   *cup butter*
2   *cups grated sharp Cheddar cheese*
    Splash milk
2¼ *cups sifted self-rising flour*
1   *teaspoon salt*
1   *teaspoon ground red pepper*
    Butter
    Fruit Marmalade

In a large bowl cream together the butter and Cheddar cheese with a splash of milk. Add the flour, salt, and pepper, and mix until blended well. Spread onto a floured surface and cut out with an old snuff can (or biscuit cutter). Bake in a 450° oven for 12 to 15 minutes. Serve hot with butter and marmalade.

MAKES 2 DOZEN.

Honey Apple Pancakes

1¼ *cups all-purpose flour or whole wheat flour*
2   *teaspoons baking powder*
⅛   *teaspoon baking soda*
¼   *teaspoon salt*
¼   *teaspoon apple pie spice*
2   *eggs*
¾   *cup apple juice*
¾   *tablespoons honey*
1   *tablespoon oil*
    Apple slices and berries for garnish

In a medium bowl stir together the flour, baking powder, soda, salt, and apple pie spice, mixing well. In a small bowl stir together the egg, apple juice, honey, and oil. Add the liquid mixture all at once to the flour mixture, stirring well. The mixture will still be lumpy. Spoon the mixture onto a hot greased griddle and cook until bubbles form. Turn and cook the other side.

Garnish plate with fresh slices of apple and top with fresh berries. Wonderful!

MAKES 4 SERVINGS.

Pears Extraordinaire

6   *pears, cored*
6   *tablespoons cream cheese, softened*
6   *tablespoons honey*
¼   *teaspoon vanilla extract*
3   *tablespoons chopped walnuts*
2⅔ *tablespoons sugar*
1   *tablespoon lemon juice*
¼   *cup water*
    Raisins (optional)
    Brown sugar
    Cinnamon
    Butter
    Mint leaves for garnish

Wash and core the pears from the bottom as to stuff. In a medium bowl mix the remaining ingredients together until smooth. Stuff the mixture into the pears and sit upright in a large baking pan. Drizzle a little more honey over the pears and sprinkle with brown sugar and cinnamon. Pat with butter. Bake in a 375° oven for 30 to 45 minutes, until tender. Serve hot.

This smells as heavenly as it tastes! Wonderful in winter for a warm fruit dish.

MAKES 6 SERVINGS.

Sassy Grapefruit

6   *tablespoons amaretto*
3   *grapefruits, halved and sectioned*
6   *cherries with stems*
    Mint leaves for garnish

Pour 1 tablespoon of Amaretto over each sectioned and halved grapefruit. Place the gragepfruit in an ungreased glass baking dish. Bake in a 350° oven until the fruit is warmed throughout. Garnish each with a cherry and mint leaf on top.

MAKES 6 SERVINGS.

Pretty Lemonade

2½ *cups water*
1½ *cups sugar*
¼   *cup pesticide-free dried hibiscus flowers*
¼   *cup chopped violets (or 1 tablespoons dried lavender flowers)*
2½ *cups water*
2¼ *cups lemon juice*
½   *cup sugar*
    Fresh lavender flowers for garnish

In a medium saucepan combine 2½ cups of water, the sugar, and hibiscus flowers. Bring to a boil, stirring to dissolve the sugar. Reduce the heat and simmer for 5 minutes to extract the pink color from the hibiscus. Remove the pan from the heat. Stir in the violets. Cover and cool.

Strain the cooled herb liquid into a large pitcher or jar. Add the remaining 2½ cups of water and the lemon juice. Stir well. Add ½ cup of sugar. Chill for 2 to 3 hours before serving.

Just before serving add the ice cubes and pour into chilled glasses. Garnish with lavender flowers.

Note: If dried hibiscus flowers are not available, cook 6 large strawberries in the syrup instead. When straining the syrup after cooking, gently press the juice from the strawberries.

MAKES 6 TO 8 SERVINGS.

Pastry-wrapped Pears with Caramel Sauce

6   *large pears*
    Semisweet chocolate chips
1   *17¼-ounce package frozen puff pastry sheets*
1   *egg beaten with 1 tablespoon water*
    Caramel sauce

Peel the pears, leaving the stems intact. Cut each in half crosswise just above the thickest part of the pear. Remove the core with a melon-ball scoop or a small spoon, being careful not to break through the bottom of the pear. Fill each cavity with chocolate pieces, and replace the tops.

Thaw the pastry for 20 minutes. Unfold and roll each sheet out on a lightly floured surface to a 10 x 13-inch rectangle. Cut 6 squares from the pastry, each about 3⅓ x 3⅓ inches. Cut the remaining pastry lengthwise into ½-inch strips. Brush the strips lightly with egg mixture. Starting at the bottom, wrap the pears with pastry strips, egg-washed-side out, overlapping slightly. Leave the stem exposed at the top. Place on an ungreased baking sheet. Bake in a 425° oven for 15 minutes. Reduce the heat to 375° and bake 5 minutes longer, or until the pastry is puffed and golden brown.

Serve with a caramel sauce made with melted caramel candies and a little milk.

MAKES 6 SERVINGS.

Spiced Tea Mix

2   **cups Lipton lemon tea (green label NutraSweet)**
1   **2.3-ounce can Crystal Light orange-flavor mix**
1   **2.1-ounce can Country Time sugar-free lemonade mix**
1½   **teaspoons ground cinnamon**
1½   **teaspoons ground cloves**
8   **packages Equal or Sweet 'N Low**

In a large bowl combine all of the ingredients. Mix and add 1 level teaspoon per cup or glass. Good hot or cold.

MAKES ABOUT 2¾ CUPS OF MIX.

Warm Curried Fruit

2   **16-ounce cans chunky fruit, undrained**
1   **20-ounce can chunky pineapple, drained**
½   **cup butter**
½   **cup firmly packed brown sugar**
1   **teaspoon curry powder**
1   **teaspoon cornstarch, dissolved in water**
2   **to 3 bananas, sliced**
1   **8-ounce jar maraschino cherries, drained**
½   **cup toasted pecans, chopped**

In a large saucepan combine the fruit, pineapple, butter, brown sugar, and curry powder. Bring to a boil. Reduce the heat and simmer for 20 minutes.

Add the cornstarch, bananas, cherries, and pecans. Stir until blended well. Cover and simmer for 5 to 6 minutes.

Serve warm. Wonderful in winter.

MAKES 4 TO 6 SERVINGS.

Honeydew Joseph

½   **cup sugar**
3   **tablespoons rum**
1¼   **cups water**
2½   **cups quartered honeydew melon**
1   **tablespoon lemon juice**
    Sliced fresh strawberries
    Whole blueberries
    Mint leaves for garnish
    Whipping cream
    Cherries for garnish

In a saucepan combine the sugar, rum, and water. Bring to a boil and cook until the sugar dissolves. Boil an additional 3 minutes. Let the syrup cool.

In a blender combine the honeydew, sugar syrup, and lemon juice, and purée until smooth. Pour into an airtight container and stir well. Pour into a 9 x 13-inch pan. Freeze for 2 to 3 hours, until frozen but not solid, stirring every 30 minutes. Scrape with a fork to separate the crystals, and serve in chilled parfait glasses layering with berries. Top with mint leaves, whipping cream, and a cherry.

MAKES 4 SERVINGS.

Stillwater Inn

203 East Broadway
Jefferson, Texas 75657
(903) 665-8415

*I*n a Victorian house dating from the 1890s, this inn has a dining room with pitched ceilings, stained-glass windows, and skylights. The four guest rooms are furnished with handcrafted furniture and antiques. Also available for rustic-

minded and privacy-seeking guests is a private cottage with pine floors. Nearby activities include golf and swimming.

Grand Marnier Flan

3   **cups milk**
½   **cup heavy cream**
5   **whole eggs**
3   **egg yolks**
1   **cup sugar**
⅓   **cup Grand Marnier**
1   **teaspoon grated orange zest (optional)**
¾   **cup sugar**

In a saucepan heat the milk and cream to simmering. In a large bowl lightly beat the eggs and yolks together. Beat in 1 cup of sugar. Beat in the hot milk mixture, then add the Grand Marnier and orange zest.

In a non-ferrous pan very slowly melt ¾ cup of sugar. Stir constantly to avoid burning. When the sugar has turned light brown, allow only a few more seconds, then spoon the caramel into individual 1-cup ramekins. Pour the egg-cream mixture over the caramelized sugar and place in a water bath. Bake in a 325° oven for 45 minutes to 1 hour, or until the custards are firm and slightly brown on top.

Refrigerate 3 hours before serving.

To serve, use a thin-bladed knife to cut around the circumference of the flan. Place a suitable plate over the top and invert the flan onto the plate, shaking as necessary. The caramel will have dissolved to create an attractive topping for the dessert.

MAKES 8 SERVINGS.

Carrot Terrine

8   **large carrots, peeled**
2   **quarts water**
2   **tablespoon orange flower water (optional)**
3   **eggs**
    Salt and ground white pepper to taste

In a food processor using the continuous feed attachment or with a rotary slicer, slice the carrots into ¹⁄₁₆-inch slices. In a large pot blanch the carrots in 2 quarts of lightly salted water. Strain, returning the liquid to the pan.

Reduce the liquid by four-fifths and cool. Add the orange flower water.

Line the bottom of a 3 x 6-inch glass loaf pan with waxed paper and butter the waxed paper. In a large bowl beat the eggs, and add the reduced liquid. Add ground white pepper and salt if needed. Add the blanched carrots and transfer the mixture to the pan. Distribute evenly. Cover with buttered foil, and place in a larger pan of water. Bake in a 350° oven for 2 hours and 30 minutes. Refrigerate for several hours or overnight.

To unmold, cut around the edges with a narrow blade knife, then place in a hot water bath. Invert onto a plate and serve.

MAKES 4 TO 6 SERVINGS.

Roasted Pork Tenderloin with Dijon Mushroom Sauce

 1   *2-pound package pork tenderloins*
     Salt and pepper to taste
½   *teaspoon ground sage*
 1   *tablespoon unsalted butter*
 1   *tablespoon olive oil*
 1   *tablespoon chopped shallot*

....

¼   *cup white wine*
 2   *ounces demiglace*
 1   *cup sliced mushrooms*
 1   *cup cream*
 1   *tablespoon Dijon mustard*

....

     Chopped parsley for garnish

Season the pork with salt and pepper and rub lightly with ground sage. In a skillet over high heat, melt the butter with the olive oil. Add the shallot and sauté until the butter turns slightly brown. Carefully add the pork tenderloin and sauté on each side until lightly browned. Transfer to a large baking pan. Bake in a 450° oven for approximately 15 minutes. Turn over and cook 10 additional minutes.

After removing the pork tenderloin from the skillet, deglaze the skillet with wine. Add the shallots and demiglace. Reduce slightly. Add the mushrooms and cream. Stir in the Dijon mustard and reduce until the sauce thickens.

Pour off the grease from the pork. When the tenderloin is firm to the touch, remove and set aside.

Slice the pork tenderloin at a 45 degree angle and arrange on a plate with the other vegetables. Spoon the sauce over the pork and sprinkle with chopped parsley.

Note: Pork tenderloin is usually sold in packages of 2. If they are large (approximately 1 pound each), one package will serve 4.

MAKES 4 SERVINGS.

Dijon Mushroom Sauce

¼   *cup white wine*
¼   *cup demiglace*
 1   *cup sliced mushrooms*
 1   *tablespoon Dijon mustard*
 1   *cup cream*

After removing the pork from the skillet, deglaze the skillet with wine. Add the shallots and demiglace, and reduce slightly. Add the mushrooms and cream. Stir in the dijon mustard and reduce until the sauce thickens. Serve with the pork.

MAKES 4 SERVINGS.

Roasted Cornish Hen with Honey Cider Glaze

 4   *Cornish game hens (18 to 20 ounces each)*
     Salt and pepper to taste
 2   *tablespoons olive oil*
 1   *tablespoon unsalted butter*

....

 2   *tablespoons honey cider vinegar (or ¼ cup white wine)*
½   *cup demiglace*
 2   *tablespoons honey*

Wash and pat dry the Cornish hens. Lightly salt and pepper throughout. In a large braising pan or 2 ovenproof skillets, heat the olive oil and unsalted butter until the butter begins to brown. Place the Cornish hens in the hot skillet breast-side down. Allow to brown for 1 minute on a burner, then transfer to a 425° oven. After 20 minutes, remove the hens and pour off the excess oil. Turn breast-side-up and return to the oven for 15 minutes. Remove from the oven, pour off the oil, and finish cooking breast-side down for approximately 10 more minutes.

When degreasing and turning, it may be necessary to turn on a heating element on the stove to maintain the heat and prevent the skin from sticking to the pan.

Remove the hens from the pan and pour off the grease. Deglaze the pan with 2 tablespoons of honey cider vinegar and reduce over medium heat. Add the demiglace and honey, and cook slowly until the sauce begins to thicken. Check the seasoning and serve over the hen.

MAKES 4 SERVINGS.

Corn and Crab Chowder

½   *pound fresh crab meat (backfin or claw)*
 6   *ears fresh corn*
 2   *tablespoons butter*
½   *cup diced onion*
 3   *cups fresh chicken stock (strong)*
 2   *tablespoons light roux*
 2   *cups milk*
 1   *cup heavy cream*
     Dash cayenne pepper
     Salt and pepper to taste
     Scallions, roasted bell pepper for garnish

Pick the small pieces of shell out of the crab meat and refrigerate. Remove the corn from the cob and scrape the cob with the dull side of a knife.

In a stockpot melt the butter and sauté the onion until tender. Add the chicken stock and corn, and simmer for 15 minutes. Add the roux. Reduce the heat and stir the mixture until smooth. Add the milk, cream, and crab meat, and continue cooking over low heat for 10 minutes. Add the seasonings and garnish with chopped scallions. Roasted red bell pepper is also a delicious addition.

Variation: For Curried Corn Chowder omit crab meat and add ¼ cup of shredded carrot and 1 teaspoon of curry powder

MAKES 6 SERVINGS.

Stillwater Salad with Creamy Vinaigrette

½   *cup cream*
½   *cup milk*
 3   *cloves garlic, sliced*
 2   *heads lettuce (Bibb and red leaf)*
½   *cup chopped walnuts*
¼   *cup chopped crisp bacon*
     Creamy Vinaigrette (recipe follows)
12   *cherry tomatoes, halved*

In a sauté pan combine the cream and milk, and poach the garlic for 3 minutes. Drain. This process "tames" the strong garlic taste.

Wash the lettuce and run through a salad spinner. In a large bowl toss the lettuce with the garlic, walnuts, and bacon. Toss with Creamy Vinaigrette. Arrange on chilled plates and garnish with halved cherry tomatoes.

MAKES 6 SERVINGS.

Creamy Vinaigrette

  1   **tablespoon Dijon mustard**
  2   **egg yolks**
1½ **cups soybean oil**
  3   **tablespoons tarragon vinegar**
      Salt and pepper to taste

In a small bowl combine the mustard and egg yolks and mix lightly with a wire whisk. Slowly add the oil, beating constantly. When the mixture thickens, add the vinegar. Alternately add oil, then vinegar, until the desired creamy consistency is achieved. Season with salt and pepper to taste.

MAKES ABOUT 2 CUPS.

Gruene Mansion Inn

1275 Gruene Road
New Braunfels, Texas 78130
(210) 629-2641

Guest rooms at this inn are not in the Gruene Mansion (built in the 1870s) but in century-old barns on the mansion grounds, which have been carefully renovated and remodeled to accommodate guests. Each room combines antiques, fine fabrics, wallcoverings, and handmade furniture within a rustic setting. Old-fashioned tubs and pedestal sinks add a nice touch. Each guest room has its own private

Gruene Mansion Inn

deck overlooking the Guadalupe River. Activities available in New Braunfels include dancing Texas's oldest dancehall in the retired Community of Gruene, river sports, and fine shops and restaurants. Sea World and Fiesta Texas at San Antonio are one hour's drive away.

Eggs à la Gruene Mansion Inn

 ½ **pound American cheese, cubed**
 ½ **pound Velveeta cheese, cubed**
  1 **8-ounce carton sour cream**
  4 **ounces cream cheese**
  1 **10-ounce can Ro-tel diced tomatoes and green chiles**
  4 **whole wheat croissants**
 20 **eggs (yes, allow 5 per person in this recipe)**
 ½ **green bell pepper, diced**
    Pico de gallo (optional)

In a microwave- safe dish combine the American and Velveeta cheeses, sour cream, cream cheese, and tomatoes. Microwave or cook over a low flame until melted. Set aside but keep very hot.

Slice the croissants through the center as for a sandwich. Place on an ungreased

cookie sheet. Bake in a 350° oven for 20 minutes.

In a large bowl beat the eggs until very frothy and scramble in a large buttered skillet over medium heat. When the eggs are almost done, add the diced green pepper. Remove the croissants from the oven and place together on plates or a serving platter so they form a round base for the eggs. Pile scrambled eggs over the croissants. Pour the cheese sauce over all. Make certain the sauce is very hot and thin enough to sink to the bottom of the croissant. Serve with pico de gallo, if desired.

MAKES 4 SERVINGS.

Crêpe Cakes (Pancakes)

  2 **cups all-purpose flour**
  2 **tablespoons baking powder**
  2 **tablespoons sugar**
  1 **teaspoon salt**
  2 **cups milk**
  2 **eggs**
 ⅓ **cup oil**

  1 **21-ounce can blueberry pie filling**
  1 **16-ounce can blueberries in syrup**
  1 **teaspoon lemon juice**
    Whipped cream

In a large bowl sift the flour, baking powder, sugar, and salt together 3 times. In a separate bowl combine the milk, eggs, and oil, and beat until frothy. Pour the liquids into the flour mixture and beat with a wire whisk until smooth.

To cook, preheat a cast-iron griddle over medium heat until the griddle begins to smoke. Spray the griddle with cooking spray. Spoon the batter onto the hot griddle. When "holes" appear all through the pancakes they are ready to turn. Cook about 30 seconds each side.

The batter stays fresh in the refrigerator for 4 to 5 days.

In a saucepan combine the pie filling, blueberries in syrup, and lemon juice. Heat over medium heat until bubbly. Serve steaming hot over pancakes and top with a dollop of whipped cream.

MAKES 4 TO 6 SERVINGS.

Adams House

231 Adams Street
San Antonio, Texas 78210
(800) 666-4810

Built in 1902 in what is now known as the King William Street historic district, Adams House is a reflection of southern tradition. The four guest rooms are decorated with matched oak or walnut bedroom sets against a backdrop of fine antiques. The common areas include a piano and library for enjoyment by guests. Adams House is handy to all of San Antonio's major attractions, including Sea World, Fiesta Texas, the Alamo, Institute of Texan Cultures, and Market Square.

Caramel French Toast

    1½ cups firmly packed brown sugar
    ¾   cup butter
    ¼   cup plus 2 tablespoons corn syrup
    10 slices French bread
    4   eggs
    2½ cups milk
    1   teaspoon vanilla extract
    ¼   teaspoon salt
    3   tablespoons sugar
    1½ teaspoons ground cinnamon
    ¼   cup butter, melted

In a saucepan heat the brown sugar, ¾ cup of butter, and corn syrup, stirring constantly. Pour into a lightly greased 9 x 13-inch baking dish. Arrange bread slices over the syrup.

In a medium bowl combine the eggs, milk, vanilla, and salt. Pour over the bread slices. Refrigerate overnight.

Sprinkle sugar and cinnamon over the soaked bread, and drizzle with ¼ cup of melted butter. Bake in a 350° oven for 45 to 50 minutes.

MAKES 4 TO 6 SERVINGS.

Green Chiles Soufflé

    2   4-ounce cans chopped green chiles
    4   cups shredded Cheddar cheese
    6   eggs
    1½ cups biscuit mix
    4   cups milk
    ¾   teaspoon salt
        Fresh fruit (optional)
        Sour cream and apricot pre-
        serveves(optional)

Line a greased 9 x 13-inch baking dish with chiles. Layer the Cheddar cheese on top. In a medium bowl mix the eggs, biscuit mix, milk, and salt. Pour over the cheese and chiles. Bake in a 350° oven for 50 to 60 minutes. Serve the topping with fresh fruit or sour cream and apricot preserves.

MAKES 6 TO 8 SERVINGS.

Beckman Inn & Carriage House

≈

222 East Guenther Street
San Antonio, Texas 78204
(210) 229-1449

Beckman Inn is just across the street from the beginning point of San Antonio's famous Riverwalk. Over the years, several additions have been made to the house, which was built in 1886, to turn it into a spacious setting for a five-guest-room inn. Visitors get a favorable first impression from the rare burled-pine front door. Inside are

such memorable features as a wood mosaic floor imported from Paris, a spacious living room with fourteen-foot ceilings, and arch-shaped pocket doors. Each guest room contains an ornately carved antique Victorian bed. Beckman Inn is convenient to all of San Antonio's historic and cultural attractions in the downtown area.

Cranberry French Toast

    1   loaf French bread cut into ½-inch
        thick slices
    6   eggs
    ⅔   cup sugar
    1   teaspoon ground cinnamon
    3   cup milk
    ¼   cup firmly packed brown sugar
    ¼   cup dried cranberries
        Orange twists and grapes for garnish

Spray a 9 x 13-inch pan with cooking spray. Arrange the bread in the pan. In a large bowl mix the eggs, sugar, and cinnamon. Add the milk and pour over the bread. Sprinkle brown sugar and dried cranberries on top. Cover and refrigerate overnight. Bake in a 325° oven for 50 to 60 minutes. Garnish with a twist of orange and a grape cluster. Serve with sausage.

MAKES 6 TO 8 SERVINGS.

Dutch Pancakes
with Spicy Apples

    6   eggs
    1   cup all-purpose flour
    2   tablespoons sugar
    1   cup milk

    1   tablespoon cornstarch
    2   tablespoons cold water
    ¼   cup margarine
    ⅓   cup firmly packed brown sugar
    1   teaspoon ground cinnamon
    3   medium red apples, cored and sliced
    ½   cup light sour cream
    3   tablespoons confectioners' sugar
        Pansies or carnations for garnish

Spray a 10-inch round ovensafe skillet with cooking spray. In a medium bowl beat the eggs. Add the flour, sugar, and milk. Pour the mixture into the prepared skillet. Bake in a 400° oven for 15 minutes. Reduce the heat to 325° and bake for 40 to 45 minutes longer. Remove immediately and cut into wedges.

In a small bowl or cup combine the cornstarch and water, and mix until smooth. In a skillet melt the margarine and add the cornstarch mixture, brown sugar, and cinnamon. Cook, stirring constantly, until thickened. Add the apples and cook until tender-crisp. Spoon over the pancakes.

Combine the sour cream and confectioners' sugar. Add a dollop to each serving. Garnish with pansies or carnations. Serve with sausage.

MAKES 4 TO 6 SERVINGS.

Brackenridge House

230 Madison
San Antonio, Texas 78204
(800) 221-1412

*T*he five guest rooms of the Brackenridge House offer turn-of-the-century Texas charm, with original pine floors, double-hung windows, antique furniture, and high ceilings. Outside the house, guests may relax on the front porch, the second-floor veranda, or in the

Brackenridge House

garden area with swings, rocking chairs, and a hot tub. One-half mile south of the Alamo in the King William Street historic district, Brackenridge House is within easy walking distance of San Antonio's finest restaurants, coffee houses, antique stores, and shops.

Eggs and Artichokes

> 2 9-ounce packages frozen artichoke hearts (or 2 cans artichokes, drained)
> 1 bay leaf (optional)
> 2 10½-ounce cans cream of chicken soup
> 1 tablespoon chopped onion
> ¼ cup sherry
> 1 4-ounce can mushrooms (optional)
> 8 hard-boiled eggs, quartered
> 2 cups diced cooked ham
> 8 slices Old English cheese (or American)

In a saucepan cook the artichoke hearts as directed on the package, adding the bay leaf during cooking if desired. Drain and remove the bay leaf. In a large bowl combine the soup, onion, and sherry. Add the mushrooms, if desired. Mix well. Arrange the artichoke hearts, eggs, and ham in a 3-quart casserole. Add the soup mixture. Top with slices of cheese. Bake in a 400° oven for 25 to 30 minutes, or until the cheese is lightly browned.

MAKES 8 SERVINGS.

Orange Fluff

> 1 6-ounce can concentrated orange juice
> 1 cup milk (skim or 2%)
> 1 cup water
> 1 or 2 teaspoons vanilla extract
> ¼ cup sugar
>   Enough ice cubes to fill blender

In a blender combine all of the ingredients and whirl until smooth. Serve immediately.

MAKES 2 SERVINGS.

Yellow Rose

229 Madison
San Antonio, Texas 78204
(800) 950-9903

*T*his inn specializes in true southwestern hospitality in a very private and quiet setting. Built originally in 1879 as a residence, it has been carefully restored to its Victorian elegance for the entertainment and pleasure of guests. The Yellow Rose has five distinctively decorated guest rooms and a beautifully landscaped yard. It's convenient to downtown San Antonio's many attractions, including the Riverwalk.

Donut Muffins

> ½ cup sugar
> ⅓ cup butter
> 1 egg
> ½ cup milk
> 1½ cups all-purpose flour
> 1½ teaspoons baking powder
> ¼ teaspoon grated nutmeg
> ½ teaspoon salt
> ....
> ½ cup butter
> ½ cup sugar
> 1½ teaspoons ground cinnamon

In a large bowl cream the sugar and butter. Add the egg and milk, and mix well. Stir in the flour, baking powder, nutmeg, and salt, and mix well. Spoon into greased muffin cups. Bake in a 400° oven for 25 minutes. Remove the muffins from the pan while hot.

In a saucepan melt the butter. In a shallow dish mix the sugar and cinnamon. Roll the warm muffins in butter, then in the cinnamon-sugar. Place on a rack to cool.

MAKES 1 DOZEN.

Forgotten Cookies

 2 egg whites
 ½ teaspoon salt
 ⅔ cup sugar
 1 6-ounce package chocolate chips
 1 cup chopped nuts

In a medium bowl beat egg whites and salt until soft peaks form. Gradually add the sugar to the beaten egg whites and beat until stiff peaks form but the mixture still has a shiny luster. Fold in the chips and nuts.

Drop by teaspoonful onto a greased cookie sheet. Place in a preheated 350° oven. Close the door and immediately turn off the heat. Leave in the oven until the oven has cooled completely. Do not be tempted to open the oven door until cooled. Remove the cookies from the cookie sheet and place on a rack to cool further. Store in an airtight container after cookies are completely cooled.

Best when cooked on a dry day.
MAKES 36 COOKIES.

Winter Fruit Compote

 ½ pound dried prunes
 1   6-ounce package dried apricots
 1 stick cinnamon
 ½ lemon, thinly sliced
     Juice of 1 orange
 3 tablespoons firmly packed brown
       sugar
     Water
 ¼ cup port wine

In a 2-quart saucepan combine the prunes, apricots, cinnamon stick, lemon slices, and orange juice. Sprinkle with brown sugar. Add just enough water to barely cover the fruits. Bring to a boil. Cover, reduce the heat, and simmer for 8 to 10 minutes or until fruits are plump and tender. Stir in the port, and transfer to a glass bowl. Serve the fruits (with their liquid) warm, at room temperature, or chilled.
MAKES 4 SERVINGS.

Pflaumen Kuchen

 2 cups all-purpose flour less 1 heaping
       tablespoon
 ⅛ teaspoon baking powder
 1 egg
 ⅓ cup plus 2 scant tablespoons sugar
 1 egg

 ⅛ teaspoon baking powder
 ½ teaspoon vanilla extract
 ½ cup butter (chilled)

....

 2 16-ounce cans plums in syrup
 1 tablespoon cornstarch
 ½ teaspoon vanilla extract

In a large bowl mix the flour and baking powder. Make a well in the middle of the flour mixture and add the egg. Sprinkle the sugar and ½ teaspoon of vanilla on top. Add the chilled butter and cut in well. Mix by hand to form a ball of dough. Allow the dough to rest for 30 minutes in the refrigerator. Roll out to fit a 9-inch tart pan.

Drain the plums, and reserve the syrup. Cut the plums in half and place on the pastry, starting at the center and working out in circles. In a saucepan combine the cornstarch and ½ teaspoon of vanilla with the reserved syrup. Cook until thickened. Pour over the fruit in the tart. Bake in a 375° oven for 30 to 35 minutes or until the crust is slightly browned.
MAKES 6 TO 8 SERVINGS.

Mansion on Main
≈

802 Main Street
Texarkana, Texas 75501
(903) 792-1835

*A*ccenting the front of this inn are several ornate two-story wooden columns salvaged from the St. Louis World's Fair of 1904. These were an addition to this old house, built in 1895. In keeping with the Victorian theme of Mansion on Main, guests are provided with Victorian nightgowns and sleepshirts. All six guest rooms are furnished with period antiques. Nearby recreational activities include golf and swimming.

Gingerbread Pancakes

 1 cup all-purpose flour
 1 teaspoon sugar
 2 teaspoons baking powder
 ½ teaspoon ground ginger
 1 teaspoon ground cinnamon
 ¼ teaspoon ground allspice
 ⅛ teaspoon grated nutmeg
 ⅛ teaspoon ground cloves
 1 egg, lightly beaten
 1 cup buttermilk
 3 teaspoons melted butter or mar-
       garine
 1 teaspoon molasses
     Orange Marmalade Syrup (recipe
       follows)

In a large bowl combine the flour, sugar, baking powder, ginger, cinnamon, allspice, nutmeg, and cloves. Make a well in the center of the dry ingredients. Add the egg, buttermilk, margarine, and molasses, stirring just until moistened. Spoon about 2 teaspoons of batter into a hot, lightly greased griddle. Cook each pancake until the top is covered with bubbles and the edges look cooked. Turn and cook other side. Repeat the procedure with the remaining batter. Serve with Orange Marmalade Syrup.
MAKES 10 LARGE PANCAKES.

Orange Marmalade Syrup

 ⅔ cup maple syrup
 ⅓ cup orange marmalade

In a saucepan combine the ingredients. Bring to a boil, stirring constantly.
MAKES 1 CUP.

Bread Pudding with Amaretto Sauce

 1 loaf stale French bread
 1 12-ounce can evaporated milk
 1½ cups milk
 1 cup raisins
 1 teaspoon vanilla extract
 6 large eggs, beaten
     Splash Amaretto
     Amaretto Sauce (recipe follows)

In a large bowl combine the milks, sugar, raisins, and vanilla. Fold the eggs into the mixture, add a splash of Amaretto, and mix lightly. Plac in a well-buttered 9 x 13-inch baking dish. Bake in a 350° oven for 35 to 40 minutes.

Poke holes in the bread pudding, and pour the Amaretto Sauce over the pudding.

MAKES 8 SERVINGS.

Amaretto Sauce

½ cup unsalted butter
1 cup confectioners' sugar
¼ cup Amaretto

In a saucepan over low heat mix the butter and confectioners' sugar, stirring constantly until the mixture blends. Remove the pan from the heat, and add the Amaretto. Poke holes in the bread pudding, and pour the sauce over the pudding.

MAKES ABOUT 1½ CUPS.

Blueberry Buttermilk Oatmeal Pancakes

1¼ cups old-fashioned oatmeal (not instant)
2 cups buttermilk
2 eggs-well-beaten
1 cup all-purpose flour
1 teaspoon sugar
1 teaspoon baking soda
1 teaspoon salt
¼ cup butter, melted
1½ to 2 cups fresh or frozen blueberries
Blueberries or maple syrup
Fresh fruit for garnish

In a large bowl mix the oatmeal and buttermilk. Add the eggs. In a separate bowl combine the flour, sugar, soda, and salt. Mix the dry ingredients into the oatmeal mixture. Stir in the butter. Gently stir in the blueberries (or add 8 to 12 blueberries to each pancake after pouring the batter onto the griddle). Cook on a hot, greased griddle until golden brown.

Serve with blueberry syrup or maple syrup and any fresh fruit in season.

MAKES 12 PANCAKES.

Bed and Breakfast German Pancakes

6 large eggs
1 cup all-purpose flour
1 cup milk

1 teaspoon salt
¼ cup melted butter
½ cup confectioners' sugar
6 lemon wedges

In a large bowl beat the eggs with an electric mixer on high for 5 minutes, alternately adding the flour and milk. Add the salt. Add the melted butter. Continue to mix the ingredients for another 1 or 2 minutes.

Spray 8 individual ramekins with cooking spray. Ladle 4 ounces of batter into each baking dish. Bake in a 425° oven for 10 to 15 minutes or until brown.

Sprinkle with confectioners' sugar and squeeze lemon over the pancakes.

MAKES 8 SERVINGS.

415 South Vine Avenue
Tyler, Texas 75702
(903) 592-2221

*T**his inn was built in 1986 on the site occupied by an old mansion that had burned years earlier. Fortunately, the huge oak trees on the property escaped the fire. Guest rooms are furnished with antiques and country collectibles. A hot tub, courtyard, and game room are also provided. Several antique and craft shops are a short distance away. Attractions in the Tyler area include a zoo, two museums, and the Municipal Rose Garden. Tyler is known as "the Rose Capital of the World."*

Rosevine Inn

Vegetarian Frittata

2 teaspoons oil
3 new potatoes, cleaned and cubed
2 teaspoons olive oil or butter
1 yellow squash, cubed
1 zucchini, cubed
3 mushrooms, sliced
1 small yellow onion, chopped
4 eggs
⅓ cup milk
1 tablespoons grated Parmesan cheese
⅛ teaspoon dried oregano
Salt and pepper to taste
1 tomato, cubed
Any shredded cheese (optional)

In a 10-inch iron skillet heat 2 teaspoon of oil and cook te potatoes until done. Drain and set aside.

Spray the skillet with a cooking spray. Heat the olive oil and sauté the squash, zucchini, mushrooms, and onion until tender.

In a medium bowl beat the eggs and milk until frothy. Add the Parmesan cheese, oregano, salt, and pepper and mix well. The potatoes and tomato to the other vegetables in the skillet and stir together. Pour the egg mixture over the vegetables. Cook over medium heat, lifting the edges as the eggs cook. When the eggs are set, sprinkle cheese over the top and put under the broiler until it just starts to brown.

Garnish as desired. Cut into pie-shaped wedges and serve from the pan.

MAKES 4 TO 6 SERVINGS.

Friendship Tea

1 1-pound 2-ounce jar orange drink mix (such as Tang)
½ cup instant tea
½ teaspoon ground cloves
1 teaspoon ground cinnamon
½ cup red hots
1¼ cups sugar (less if desired)
½ cup dry lemonade mix
1 3-ounce package apricot-flavored gelatin

In a container with a tight-filling lid mix all ingredients together. Store in an airtight container. Shake well before using.

Use 2 cups of mix per crock pot to make 12 cups, or 3 teaspoon of mix with very hot water to make 1 cup.

Use 3 teaspoons of mix with very hot water to make 1 cup.

MAKES ABOUT 5 CUPS OF DRY MIX.

Homemade Ice Cream

2   boxes vanilla ice cream mix
2   cups sugar
6   eggs
1   pint whipping cream
2   12-ounce cans evaporated milk
1   quart half and half
1   Dash salt
2   teaspoons vanilla extract
    Milk to fill to the line

In a large bowl combine all ingredients and mix well. Pour into an ice cream freezer and mix until frozen. Instructions for freezing follow.

Wash all parts of the ice cream freezer before starting. Use crushed ice, the finer the better. In packing, use about 3 inches of ice in the tub, all around the container, then sprinkle about 3 ounces of table salt or 5 ounces of rock salt over the ice. Layer until the tub is filled, but not above the can. When the tub is half full, pour 1 cup of cold water over the mixture. After the tub is full, pour another cup of cold water over the salt and ice.

This is a very rich but basic recipe which can be added to easily.

Note: Preparing the ice cream mixture the day before makes a smoother ice cream and increases the yield.

MAKES 2 QUARTS.

Casa de Leona
☙

1149 Pearsall Highway 140
Uvalde, Texas 78802
(210) 278-8550

*C*asa de Leona is a Spanish hacienda with a beautifully landscaped courtyard surrounded by a seventeen-acre wilderness area along the Leona River. It's a nature lover's delight, with numerous nature trails for walking, jogging, and bird watching. The inn also has its own fishing pier. The five guest rooms include wood-burning fireplaces, and each is decorated with a different theme, combining antiques with more traditional furnishings. Area attractions include Alamo Village, Kickapoo Caverns, Fort Clark Springs, Grand Opera House of Uvalde, Fort Inge Historical Site, and Garner State Park.

Peanut Butter Pralines

1   1-pound box light brown sugar
3   tablespoons milk
3   tablespoons peanut butter
1   tablespoon butter
1   teaspoon butternut flavoring
1   cup peanuts or pecans

In a saucepan mix the light brown sugar, milk, peanut butter, butter, and butternut flavoring. Cook until the mixture reaches the soft-ball stage. Remove the pan from the heat. Beat for 1 to 2 minutes. Add the peanuts. Drop by tablespoon onto waxed paper and let cool.

MAKES ABOUT 2 DOZEN.

Tiger Butter

1   24-ounce package vanilla bark
1   cup peanut butter with peanuts
1   12-ounce package chocolate chips

Spray a 9 x 12-inch glass pan with cooking spray. In a saucepan over low heat melt the vanilla bark and peanut butter together, and mix well. Pour into the prepared pan. Sprinkle with chocolate chips. Place in a microwave for about 2 minutes or until melted. Swirl the mixture with a knife into patterns that looks like the stripes of a tiger. Cool and cut into squares.

MAKES ABOUT 2½ POUNDS.

Macadamia Chiffon Pie

½   cup firmly packed brown sugar
1   envelope unflavored gelatin
¼   teaspoon salt
1   cup milk

2   beaten egg yolks
1   teaspoon vanilla extract
2   egg whites
¼   cup firmly packed brown sugar
½   cup chopped macadamia nuts, toasted
½   cup whipping cream
1   9-inch baked pie crust
    Toasted flaked coconut (optional)

In a saucepan combine ½ cup of brown sugar, the gelatin, and salt. Stir in the milk and egg yolks. Cook over medium heat, stir until thickened. Remove the pan from the heat. Add the vanilla. Chill.

In a medium bowl beat the egg whites. Gradually add ¼ cup of brown sugar and beat until stiff peaks form. When the first mixture has chilled, add the egg whites and nuts.

In a separate bowl whip the cream and add to the gelatin mixture. Pour into the cooled pie crust and chill. Garnish with toasted coconut or leave plain.

MAKES 8 TO 10 SERVINGS.

The Round Up

10   slices bacon
6   to 8 chopped green chiles
3   to 4 green onions, chopped
1   medium tomato, chopped
¼   pound chopped, fresh mushrooms
10   eggs
5   tablespoons milk
     Black pepper to taste
     8-ounces bar longhorn cheese, grated

In a skillet fry the bacon until crisp. Drain. In the same skillet sauté the chiles, onions, tomato, and mushrooms. Crumble the bacon into the vegetables. Add the eggs, milk, and pepper; and scramble until almost done. Add the longhorn cheese, and heat until melted. Serve on toast.

MAKES 8 TO 10 SERVINGS.

Corn Waffles with Cilantro Butter

1   cup all-purpose flour
½   cup yellow cornmeal
2   tablespoons sugar
1   teaspoon baking powder
¼   teaspoon salt
1   egg

2   tablespoons melted butter
½   cup water
1   cup fresh corn
1   teaspoon vanilla extract
    Oil

....

¼   cup chopped cilantro
½   cup butter, softened

In a large bowl mix the flour, cornmeal, sugar, baking powder, and salt. In a separate large bowl whip the egg, butter, water, corn, and vanilla. Add the egg mixture to the dry ingredients and mix until just combined. Heat and grease a waffle iron. Cook the waffles according to the manufacturer's specifications.

In a small bowl whip the cilantro and butter together until smooth and creamy. Top each waffle with cilantro butter and serve with real maple syrup.

MAKES 4 SERVINGS.

Country Place

Route 1, Box 459
Wolfforth, Texas 79382
(806) 863-2030

The phrase that best describes Country Place is "a country retreat in elegant surroundings." Erected in 1992, this inn features such amenities as a swimming pool with a large deck, an outdoor hot tub, and a sunroom. All four guest rooms are lavishly furnished. The quiet country roads around this inn are ideal for walking, jogging, or biking. Nearby attractions include antique shops, wineries, golf, and swimming.

Frozen Fruit Salad

1   17-ounce can apricots, cut up
1   17-ounce can crushed pineapple
½   cup sugar
3   10-ounce packages frozen strawberries
1   6-ounce can frozen orange juice concentrate
3   tablespoons lemon juice
3   bananas, cut up

Line 6 muffin cups with paper liners. Drain the apricots and pineapple, reserving the liquid, and add enough water to make 1 cup. In a saucepan heat the liquid and sugar until the sugar dissolves. Add the remaining of ingredients. Spoon into the prepared muffin cups. Freeze until solid. Remove from the muffin pan and store in plastic freezer bags.

MAKES 6 SERVINGS.

Oatmeal-Brown Sugar Muffin

1   cup oatmeal
½   cup milk
¾   cup firmly packed brown sugar
¼   cup butter, melted
1   egg
1   cup all-purpose flour
2   teaspoons baking powder
½   cup nuts

In a large bowl mix the oatmeal, milk, and brown sugar, and let stand 5 minutes. Add the butter and egg, and blend well. Add the flour, baking powder, and nuts, and stir until mixed well. Spoon into greased muffin cups. Bake in a 400° oven for 15 minutes.

MAKES 1 DOZEN.

Country Place

Breakfast Soufflé

16   slices bread (or ½ loaf French bread)
1   pound sausage (or 2 to 3 cups chopped ham)
2   cups grated sharp Cheddar cheese
8   eggs
3   cups milk
½   teaspoon dry mustard
½   teaspoon salt
½   teaspoon Worcestershire sauce
2   cups crushed corn flakes
¼   cup butter, melted

Lightly oil a 9 x 13-inch pan. Layer the bread, meat, and Cheddar cheese in it. In a large bowl blend the eggs, milk, and seasonings together. Pour over the bread, meat, and cheese. Refrigerate overnight.

Sprinkle with corn flakes and then drizzle with butter. Set in a pan of hot water. Bake in a 350° oven for 1 hour.

MAKES 12 SERVINGS.

The Antique Rose

612 Nellius Street
Woodville, Texas 75979
(800) 386-8926

This East Texas inn is housed in a southern plantation Federal-style house that was built in 1862. All three upstairs guest rooms, located upstairs, are decorated with turn-of-the-century antiques with touches of lace and nostalgic collectibles. The old-fashioned claw-foot bathtubs add a special touch. Area attractions include antique shops, Big Thicket National Wildlife Preserve, Fain Opera House, and Heritage Village, as well as golf and swimming.

Raisin-Pecan Cinnamon Rolls

4½ to 5 cups all-purpose flour
1 package active dry yeast
1 cup milk
⅓ cup margarine or butter
⅓ cup sugar
½ teaspoon salt
3 eggs
¾ cup firmly packed brown sugar
¼ cup all-purpose flour
1 teaspoon ground cinnamon
½ cup margarine or butter
½ cup light raisins (or fresh blueberries)
½ cup chopped pecans
1 tablespoon half and half or light cream

....

1¼ cups sifted confectioners' sugar
1 teaspoon light corn syrup
½ teaspoon vanilla extract
1 to 2 tablespoons half and half or light cream

In a large bowl, combine 2¼ cups of the flour and the yeast. In a small saucepan heat the milk, ⅓ cup of margarine, ⅓ cup of sugar, and the salt just until very warm (120° to 130°) and the margarine is almost melted, stirring constantly. Add to the flour mixture. Add the eggs. Beat with an electric mixer on low speed for 30 seconds, scraping the sides of the bowl constantly. Beat on high speed for 3 minutes. Using a wooden spoon, stir in the remaining 2¼ cups of flour. Turn the dough out onto a lightly floured surface. Knead in enough of the remaining flour to make a moderately soft dough that is smooth and elastic, 3 to 5 minutes total. Shape into a ball. Place in a greased bowl, turning once. Cover; let rise in a warm place until doubled in bulk (about 1 hour).

In a medium bowl combine the brown sugar, ¼ cup of flour, and the cinnamon. Cut in the remaining margarine or butter until crumbly. Set the filling aside.

Punch the dough down. Turn onto a lightly floured surface. Cover and let rest for 10 minutes.

The Antique Rose

Roll the dough into a 12-inch square. Sprinkle the filling over the dough square. Top with raisins and pecans. Roll up jellyroll style. Pinch the edges to seal. Slice the roll into eight 1½-inch pieces. Arrange the dough pieces cut-side-up in a greased 12-inch deep-dish pizza pan or a 9 x 13-inch baking dish. Cover the dough loosely with plastic wrap, leaving room for the rolls to rise. Refrigerate the dough for 2 to 24 hours.

Uncover and let stand at room temperature for 30 minutes, (or for immediate baking, don't chill the dough, instead cover loosely. Let the dough rise in a warm place until nearly doubled, about 45 minutes).

Break any surface bubbles with a greased toothpick. Brush the dough with half and half or light cream. Bake in a 375° oven for 25 to 30 minutes or until light brown. If necessary to prevent over-browning, cover the rolls loosely with foil the last 5 to 10 minutes of baking time. Remove the rolls from the oven, and brush again with half and half or light cream. Cool for 1 minute. Carefully invert the cinnamon rolls onto a wire rack. Cool slightly. Invert again onto a serving platter.

In a bowl stir together the confectioners' sugar, corn syrup, vanilla extract, and enough half and half or light cream to make drizzling consistency. Drizzle over warm cinnamon rolls.

Variation: For Apple Cinnamon rolls, prepare as directed, except substitute 1 cup finely chopped apple for the raisins in the filling.

Note: The best part about this recipe is that the dough can be mixed and the rolls filled and shaped the night before. In the morning, just bake. Waiting for the rolls to come out of the oven is the hardest part

MAKES 8 ROLLS.

Overnight Baked Apples

4 apples (Granny Smiths are good)
Orange zest
Ground cloves
Grated nutmeg
Ground cinnamon
1 teaspoon firmly packed brown sugar
1 teaspoon butter
2 teaspoons chopped pecans
Orange juice
Sour cream

Core the apples almost to the bottom. Set the apples in a baking dish. Add a pinch of zest, cloves, nutmeg, and cinnamon to each apple. Add brown sugar and butter to each and top with pecans. Pour orange juice half way up the sides of the apples. Cover with a lid or foil. Place in an electric skillet, cover, and simmer for at least 7 hours. In the morning, serve with a dollop of sour cream.

MAKES 4 SERVINGS.

All-In-One Muffins

1¾ cups all-purpose flour
1 cup quick-cooking oatmeal
¼ cup sugar
2 teaspoons baking powder
¼ teaspoon salt
1 egg, beaten
1 cup milk
⅓ cup oil
¼ cup cooked and crumbled bacon
½ cup grated Cheddar cheese
⅓ cup chopped green bell pepper (optional)
⅓ cup onion (optional)

In a large bowl mix ingredients together. Spoon greased muffin cups. Bake in a 450° oven for 20 minutes.

MAKES 1 DOZEN.

64 South 300 East, P.O. Box 156
Monticello, Utah 84535
(800) 645-3762

The Monticello Flour Mill, built in 1933, produced flour for the community for more than thirty years. In 1989 it was renovated into the Grist Mill Inn, a unique inn with six guest rooms, a sitting room with a fireplace, and a library. Other rooms are available in the adjacent granary and a 1924 caboose on the property. Golfing, tennis, and swimming are available nearby.

Ham and Swiss Quiche

    1   unbaked 9-inch pie crust
    4   eggs
    2   cups light cream
    ½   teaspoon salt
    ⅛   teaspoon grated nutmeg
    1   cup diced cooked ham
    1   cup grated Swiss cheese

Bake the pie crust in a 425° oven for 12 minutes. This may be done the night before.

In a medium bowl whisk together the eggs, cream, salt, and nutmeg. Set aside. Spread diced ham over the bottom of the baked shell. Sprinkle Swiss cheese over the ham. Pour in the egg filling. Bake in a 425° oven for 15 minutes. Reduce the heat to 350° and bake 30 more minutes. Allow to set at least 10 minutes before serving.

MAKES 6 TO 8 SERVINGS.

English Muffin Bread

    4½ to 5 cups all-purpose flour
    2   packages active dry yeast (scant
            tablespoon)
    1   tablespoon sugar
    2   teaspoons salt
    ¼   teaspoon baking soda
    2   cups milk
    ½   cup water
        Cornmeal

In a large bowl combine 3 cups of flour, the yeast, sugar, salt, and soda. In a saucepan heat the milk and water until hot. Add the liquid mixture to the dry ingredients. Mix well and add enough flour to make a dough.

Grease 2 glass 8½ x 4½-inch, glass loaf pans, and sprinkle with cornmeal. Divide the dough into 2 equal parts. Place in loaf pans, and let rise approximately 45 minutes. Microwave each loaf separately for 6½ minutes.

Let rest 5 minutes before taking out of the pan. Slice and toast when ready to use.

MAKES 2 LOAVES.

Cinnamon Fried Apples

    4   medium cooking apples
    ⅓   cup butter
    ½   to ¾ cup sugar
    2   tablespoons cornstarch
    1½ cups water
    ¼   to ½ teaspoon ground cinnamon
    ⅛   teaspoon grated nutmeg

Peel, core, and cut the apples in half. In a 10-inch skillet melt the butter over medium heat. Stir in the sugar and cornstarch. Mix well and add the remaining ingredients. Add the apples to the sauce, cover, and cook over medium heat. Occasionally spoon the sauce over the apples as they cook.

MAKES 4 SERVINGS.

Oatmeal-Walnut Pancakes

    3   cups old-fashioned rolled oats
    2   cups all-purpose flour
    ¼   cup firmly packed brown sugar
    ½   teaspoon salt
    2   tablespoons baking powder
    1   cup chopped walnuts
    3   cups milk
    4   eggs
    ¼   cup butter, melted

In a large bowl combine the oats, flour, brown sugar, salt, baking powder, and walnuts. Set aside. In a separate bowl whisk together the milk and eggs. Pour over the dry ingredients, and mix just until combined. Add the melted butter. Spoon onto a heated, lightly oiled griddle. Cook until bubbles form on the surface, turn, and cook until golden brown. Best served with fruit syrups.

MAKES 6 SERVINGS.

Washington School Inn

Washington School Inn

❧

543 Park Avenue, P.O. Box 536
Park City, Utah 84060
(801) 649-3800

*T*his inn is located in the old Washington School, which served Park City children from 1889 until 1931. After years of idleness and neglect, the building was renovated into this unique guest house in 1985. Listed on the National Register of Historic Places, it has fifteen rooms with such amenities as hot tubs and saunas. Park City is a world-class resort city, just minutes from the skiing at Deer Valley and Wolf Mountain. Nearby are three championship golf courses.

Mexican Corn Pie (Pastel De Elote)

3   large eggs
1   cup cream-style corn
1   10-ounce package frozen corn
¼   cup finely chopped green onions
½   cup yellow cornmeal
1   cup sour cream
4   ounces Monterey Jack cheese, cut in ½-inch cubes
4   ounces sharp Cheddar cheese, cut in ½-inch cubes
1   4-ounce can chopped mild green chiles

½   teaspoon salt
¼   teaspoon Worcestershire sauce

Grease a 10-inch pie plate generously with cooking spray. In a large bowl beat the eggs. Add the remaining ingredients and stir until thoroughly mixed. Pour into the prepared pie plate. Bake in a 375° oven for 1 hour and 15 minutes.

The pie may be baked and then kept in the refrigerator for up to 3 days. Reheat the refrigerated pie in a 350° oven for about 20 minutes. The pie may also be frozen after baking and kept frozen for up to 3 months. Thaw and reheat at 350° for about 20 minutes.

MAKES 8 SERVINGS.

Pompushkas

1   cup cottage cheese
¼   cup sour cream
2   tablespoons sugar
1   teaspoon ground cinnamon
¼   teaspoon salt
1   cup all-purpose flour
2   eggs
¼   cup milk
½   cup canned or fresh blueberries (or mashed bananas)
    Maple syrup

In a large bowl combine the cottage cheese, sour cream, sugar, cinnamon, salt, flour, and eggs. Add enough milk to make the batter a little thicker consistency than pancake batter. Add blueberries or bananas to the mixture. Cook on a greased griddle until lightly brown. Serve warm with maple syrup.

MAKES 6 SERVINGS.

Harvest House

❧

29 Canyonview Drive, P.O. Box 125
Springdale, Utah 84767
(801) 772-3880

*T*his inn is less than a mile from the south entrance of Zion National Park, with its massive red rock cliffs

that appeal to tourists all year long. All four rooms in the inn have private decks for unforgettable viewing of the imposing canyon. Day hiking in the park is a favorite activity of guests. Other natural wonders within an easy drive are the North Rim of the Grand Canyon, Bryce Canyon, Cedar Breaks, and Lake Powell.

Spinach and Black Forest Ham Frittata

2   tablespoons unsalted butter
1   10-ounce box frozen chopped spinach
1   medium onion, chopped
⅓   pound smoked Black Forest ham, diced into ¼-inch pieces
8   eggs
½   cup milk
    Salt and pepper to taste
½   cup grated Cheddar cheese
¼   cup grated Parmesan cheese

Place 1 tablespoon of butter in a 10-inch glass pie plate or other similar oven-to-table dish. Set aside.

In a saucepan cook the spinach according to the package directions. Cook, drain, and squeeze as much water out of the spinach as possible. Set aside.

In a frying pan melt the remaining tablespoon of butter and sauté the onion until soft. Add the ham and sauté for 1 minute. Set aside to cool slightly.

Place the pie plate with the butter in it in the oven to melt the butter. Meanwhile, in a medium bowl whisk together the eggs, milk, and salt and pepper to taste.

Remove the pie plate from the oven. Distribute the spinach evenly over the bottom of the pie plate. Top with the ham mixture, and then sprinkle with Cheddar cheese. Gently pour the egg mixture over the cheese. Sprinkle the top with Parmesan cheese. Place the pie plate in the lower third of the oven. Bake in a 375° oven for 15 minutes. Move the pie plate to the upper third of the oven and bake for 10 minutes longer, or until the center is just set and the edges are lightly browned. Cut into wedges and serve hot or at room temperature.

MAKES 6 TO 8 SERVINGS.

Chinese Almond Cookies

> 1   *cup unsalted butter, softened*
> 1½   *cups confectioners' sugar*
> 1   *egg*
> ½   *teaspoon almond extract*
> ½   *cup yellow cornmeal*
> 1½   *cups all-purpose flour*
> ¾   *cup sliced almonds*
> ¼   *teaspoon salt*
> 1   *egg yolk, mixed with 1 teaspoon water for glaze*
>   *Whole natural almonds*

In a large bowl cream the butter and sugar with an electric mixer until smooth. Blend in the egg, then add the almond extract, cornmeal, flour, sliced almonds, and salt. Beat to mix. Wrap the dough in plastic and refrigerate until firm but not hard.

Unwrap and shape into 2 logs approximately 2 inches in diameter. Rewrap and freeze.

Line baking sheets with parchment paper or foil. Allow the dough to defrost at room temperature until it has barely thawed enough to cut, about 10 minutes. Cut the logs into generous ¼-inch round slices. Place on prepared sheets about 2 inches apart. Brush the cookies with the glaze and place an almond firmly in the center of each cookie. Bake in a 325° oven for approximately 18 to 20 minutes, or until the edges are lightly browned. Place the baking sheet on a wire rack to cool for 5 minutes. Transfer the cookies to wire racks and allow to cool completely.

MAKES 2 TO 3 DOZEN COOKIES.

Cappuccino Cookies

> 1   *cup unsalted butter, softened*
> ½   *cup firmly packed brown sugar*
> 1   *egg*
> 2   *tablespoons unsweetened cocoa*
> 1½   *teaspoons instant espresso or coffee*
> ½   *teaspoon ground cinnamon*
> ¼   *teaspoon salt*
> 1¾   *cups all-purpose flour*
> ½   *cup mini chocolate chips*

In a large bowl cream the butter and sugar with an electric mixer until smooth. Blend in the egg, then add the cocoa, espresso, cinnamon, salt, and flour. Beat to mix. Stir in the chocolate chips. Wrap the dough in plastic and refrigerate until firm but not hard. Unwrap and shape into 2 logs approximately 2 inches in diameter. Rewrap and chill until very firm.

Line baking sheets with parchment paper or foil. Cut the logs into generous ¼-inch round slices. Place on prepared sheets about 1 inch apart. Bake in a 325° oven for approximately 15 to 18 minutes, or until the cookies are barely firm to the touch. Do not overbake. Place the baking sheet on a wire rack to cool for 5 minutes. Transfer the cookies to wire racks and allow to cool completely.

MAKES 2 TO 3 DOZEN COOKIES.

Multi-Grain Pancakes

> 1   *cup all-purpose flour*
> ½   *cup whole wheat flour*
> ¼   *cup rye flour*
> ¼   *cup yellow cornmeal*
> 2   *teaspoons baking soda*
> 1   *teaspoon salt*
> 2   *tablespoons sugar*
> 2   *cups buttermilk*
> 2   *eggs*
> 6   *tablespoons unsalted butter, melted*

In a large bowl combine the flours, cornmeal, soda, salt, and sugar. Whisk together to make sure there are no lumps of baking soda. Set aside. In a separate bowl whisk together the buttermilk, eggs, and melted butter. Gradually add the wet mixture to the dry ingredients and stir until just combined.

Heat a griddle or frying pan until hot. Grease if necessary, and reduce the heat to medium low. Ladle scant ¼ cupfuls of batter onto the griddle. Cook until bubbles appear on the surface of the pancakes. Flip and cook approximately 1 minute longer.

MAKES 4 SERVINGS.

Blackberry Syrup

> 8   *cups fresh ripe blackberries*
> 1½   *cups water*
>   *Sugar*
> 1   *tablespoon lemon juice*

Pick over, rinse, and drain the berries. Place them in a large, heavy pot, and mash them with a potato masher. Add the water. Bring the mixture to a boil over medium heat. Reduce the heat to low and simmer the berries for about 10 minutes, stirring them occasionally.

Line a large sieve with 2 layers of dampened cheesecloth and set it over a bowl. Pour the berry mixture into the sieve and allow the juice to drip through. When most of the juice has passed into the bowl, press on the solids with the back of a large spoon. Do not force the pulp through the cheesecloth, just try to extract as much juice as possible. Discard the pulp. Measure the juice and pour it into a clean heavy pan. Add 1 cup of sugar for each cup of juice. Heat the mixture over medium heat, stirring until the sugar has dissolved. Increase the heat to medium-high, and boil the mixture for 2 to 3 minutes. Remove the syrup from the heat and stir in the lemon juice. If the syrup will be used within a few months, pour it into clean, dry bottles or jars and store in the refrigerator. If it is to be kept longer, pour the boiling syrup into sterilized pint canning jars and process in a water bath according to the manufacturer's directions on the jars for 15 minutes.

MAKES APPROXIMATELY 6 CUPS.

Strawberry-Rhubarb Sauce

> 2   *cups rhubarb, cut into ½-inch pieces*
> ½   *cup firmly packed brown sugar (or more to taste)*
> 1   *cup fresh strawberries, sliced*

In a heavy saucepan place the rhubarb with 2 tablespoons of water, and bring to a boil. Partially cover the pan, reduce the heat, and simmer the rhubarb for about 15 to 20 minutes until it is quite soft. Uncover and add the sugar. Cook for a few minutes longer.

Add the strawberries to the rhubarb and mix well. Turn the heat off and cover the pan. The strawberries will cook in the hot sauce in about 5 minutes. Serve warm, room temperature, or cold.

MAKES 4 SERVINGS.

Poppy Seed Banana Cake

3 cups all-purpose flour
½ teaspoon salt
1 teaspoon baking soda
1½ teaspoons baking powder
½ cup unsalted butter, softened
1 8-ounce package cream cheese, softened
1½ cups sugar
3 eggs
1 teaspoon vanilla extract
1½ cups mashed ripe bananas
¾ cup poppy seeds

Grease and flour 2 4 x 8-inch loaf pans. Set aside.

In a medium bowl sift together the flour, salt, soda, and baking powder. Set aside.

In a large bowl, beat together the butter, cream cheese, and sugar with an electric mixer until fluffy. Add the eggs one at a time, scraping down the sides of the bowl with a spatula when necessary. Add the vanilla and mashed bananas and mix well. Add the poppy seeds and with the mixer on low, gradually add the dry ingredients, and beat until just combined.

Divide the batter between the prepared pans, and smooth out the top. Bake in a 350° oven for 50 to 60 minutes or until a toothpick inserted into the center comes out clean. Remove the pans from the oven, and place on a wire rack to cool for 20 minutes. Turn the cakes out of the pans and place on wire racks to cool completely.

MAKES 2 LOAVES.

Seven Wives Inn
❧

*217 North 100 West
St. George, Utah 84770
(800) 600-3737*

***T**his inn consists of two neighboring homes in the historic district of St. George. Edwin G. Wooley, who*

built the larger house in 1873, hid polygamists in the attic after polygamy was outlawed in 1882. One of these polygamists was Benjamin F. Johnson, an ancestor of the innkeepers, who really did have seven wives; hence the name Seven Wives Inn. The house next door was built in 1883. Each house has a parlor with fireplace as well as books and games for the enjoyment of guests. All the rooms are furnished with antiques, and some have fireplaces or woodburning stoves. Nearby attractions include Zion National Park, Bryce Canyon, the North Rim of the Grand Canyon, and Lake Powell.

Sausage en Croûte

½ cup butter
3 or 4 green onions, including some tops, chopped
5 or 6 medium mushrooms, sliced
1 pound bulk sausage
¾ cup cottage cheese
1 cup all-purpose flour
3 ounces Monterey Jack cheese, grated

In a skillet melt a little butter and sauté the onions and mushrooms. In a separate skillet fry the sausage until the pink has disappeared. Refrigerate in separate containers until morning.

In a food processor mix the butter and cottage cheese until blended, leaving some pea sized butter pieces. Add the flour and turn the machine on and off until just blended. Turn out onto plastic wrap, form a ball, and wrap. Refrigerate for at least 2 hours or overnight.

Seven Wives Inn

In the morning roll out the dough, add sausage down the center, top with mushroom-onion mixture, and top with grated Monterey Jack cheese. Slash the protruding crust about 6 times and lap over the filling. Place on a cookie sheet. Bake in a 350° oven for 30 minutes or until brown.

MAKES 6 TO 8 SERVINGS.

Alison's Chicken Veronique

4 whole chicken breasts, halved and boned
2 teaspoons paprika
Salt and pepper to taste
¼ cup olive oil
2 cloves garlic, crushed
1½ cups halved green grapes
1 jalapeño pepper, finely sliced (wear gloves)
2 cups cooked rice
2 tablespoons toasted sesame seeds
Crème fraîche (see below)

Pound the chicken breasts to about ¼ inch thick. Sprinkle generously with paprika, salt, and pepper to taste. In a frying pan heat the olive oil. Add the crushed garlic and chicken breasts and brown the chicken on both sides. Transfer to a heated platter and keep warm in a 250° oven.

In a pan with the chicken juices sauté the grapes and jalapeño pepper until just warmed through. Place rice on 4 individual plates. Surround with sesame seeds. Place the chicken breasts on the rice. Top with grapes and jalapeño. Garnish with crème fraîche.

MAKES 4 SERVINGS.

Crème Fraîche

1 cup heavy cream
1 cup dairy sour cream

In a large bowl whisk the heavy cream and sour cream together. Cover loosely with plastic wrap and let stand in the kitchen or other reasonably warm spot overnight or until thickened. In cold weather this may take as long as 24 hours. Cover and refrigerate for at least 4 hours, after which the crème fraîche will be quite thick.

MAKES 2 CUPS.

VERMONT

R.R. 2, Box 2015
Arlington, Vermont 05250
(802) 375-2269

This inn and its fifty acres of farmland along the Battenkill River are part of the original land grant from King George III to the Hill family in 1775. Each of the seven guest rooms in the 1830s house is individually decorated to capture the spirit and charm of a New England farm. Rooms are also available in the 1790 guest house next door. Hill Farm Inn was one of Vermont's first country inns, and it still specializes in warm country hospitality. Nearby activities include canoeing, swimming, biking, skiing, ice skating, and trout fishing in the Battenkill River.

Hill Farm Inn

Spicy Tomato Soup

1½	cups chopped onions
3	cloves garlic minced
1	tablespoon butter, melted
1	tablespoon oil
1	teaspoon dillweed
⅛	teaspoon black pepper
6	cups tomato juice
1	tablespoon honey
1	tablespoon sour cream
1	medium fresh tomato, chopped

In a kettle combine the onions and garlic, and sauté in butter and oil for five minutes. Add the dillweed, pepper, tomato juice, and honey. Cover, and simmer for 1 hour.

Whisk in the sour cream and chopped tomato 5 minutes before serving

MAKES 7½ CUPS.

Hill Farm Inn Salad Dressing

3	cups oil
¾	cup white vinegar
¾	cup lemon juice
1	tablespoon salt
1	tablespoon sugar
½	tablespoon dry mustard
½	tablespoon granulated onion
½	tablespoon paprika
⅜	teaspoon thyme
3	cloves garlic, crushed

In a blender combine all the ingredients. Blend well. Refrigerate at least 2 hours before serving to blend flavors. Shake before using.

MAKES ABOUT 4½ CUPS.

Hearty Fruit-and-Sausage Stuffed Pork Chops

2	tablespoons olive oil
1	cup chopped onions
8	ounces sweet Italian sausage
¾	cup dried apricots
½	cup chopped parsley
2	teaspoons fennel seed
¼	cup currants
3	cloves garlic, finely minced
	Grated zest of 2 oranges
8	pork chops, double thickness if desired
2	teaspoon dried thyme
1	teaspoon black pepper
¼	teaspoon salt
	Oil
1	cup orange marmalade
½	cup Madeira
¼	cup lemon juice

Heat the oil in a large skillet, and sauté the onions approximately 10 minutes over medium heat until wilted. Add the sausage, and brown. Remove the mixture from the pan, and let cool.

Add the apricots, parsley, fennel, currants, garlic, and orange zest to sausage mixture, and stir well. Cut a pocket in each pork chop, and fill with the sausage stuffing, securing the ends with toothpicks if needed. Season the pork chops with thyme, pepper, and salt. In a skillet brown the pork chops quickly with a bit of oil. Place in a pan.

In a medium bowl stir the marmalade, Madeira, and lemon juice together, and pour half over the chops. Bake the chops in a 350° oven for 20 minutes, turning halfway through and basting with the remaining Madeira mixture as needed, until the chops are cooked to an internal temperature of 150°. Remove from the oven, and serve immediately.

MAKES 8 SERVINGS.

The Leslie Place

P.O. Box 62
Belmont, Vermont 05730
(800) 352-7439

Leslie Place, on its secluded one-hundred-acre setting, is ideal for escape-minded guests. They may hike, bike, go horseback riding, take a sleigh ride, swim, enjoy theater and fine restaurants in the area, or simply kick back and savor the view of the surrounding mountains from the gardens. Nearby are several major ski areas for which Vermont is famous.

Strawberry-Banana-Nut Crumble

  1 *cup sliced banana*
  ½ *cup sliced frozen strawberries*

  1½ *tablespoons brown sugar*
  2 *teaspoons all-purpose flour*
  2 *teaspoons chopped nuts*
  2 *teaspoons soft butter*
  ¼ *teaspoon cinnamon*

Divide the banana and strawberries between 2 greased 6-ounce custard cups.

In a small bowl mix the remaining ingredients, and sprinkle over the fruit. Bake in a 325° oven for 25 minutes until bubbly. Serve warm.

MAKES 2 SERVINGS.

The Leslie Place

Raspberry Streusel Coffee Cake

  2 *cups all-purpose flour*
  ¾ *cup sugar*
  ½ *cup milk*
  ¼ *cup butter, softened*
  1 *egg*
  2 *teaspoons baking powder*
  ½ *teaspoon salt*
  ½ *teaspoon grated nutmeg*
  1 *cup fresh raspberries (or frozen raspberries, thawed)*

  ½ *cup sugar*
  ⅓ *cup all-purpose flour*
  ½ *teaspoon ground cinnamon*
  ½ *teaspoon grated nutmeg*
  ¼ *cup butter, softened*

In a large mixing bowl combine 2 cups of flour, ¾ cup of sugar, milk, ¼ cup of butter, egg, baking powder, salt, and ½ teaspoon of nutmeg. Beat with an electric mixer at slow speed 1 to 2 minutes until mixed well. Gently fold in the berries. Spread in a greased and floured 9-inch square baking pan.

Mix together the remaining ingredients except the butter. Bake in a 375° oven for 30 to 35 minutes until done.

MAKES 9 SERVINGS.

Honey Currant Scones

 2½ *cups all-purpose flour*
  2 *teaspoons grated orange zest*
  1 *teaspoon baking powder*
  ½ *teaspoon baking soda*
  ½ *teaspoon salt*
  ½ *cup butter or margarine*
  ½ *cup currants*
  ½ *cup dairy sour cream*
  ⅓ *cup honey*
  1 *egg, slightly beaten*

In a large bowl combine the flour, orange zest, baking powder, soda, and salt, and mix well. Cut in the butter until the mixture resembles small peas. Add the currants. In a medium bowl combine the sour cream, honey, and egg, and mix well. Stir the honey mixture into the dry ingredients to form a soft dough. Knead the dough on a lightly floured surface 10 times. Shape the dough into an 8-inch square. Cut the dough into 4 squares, and cut each square diagonally into 2 triangles. Place the triangles on a greased baking sheet.

Bake in a 375° oven for 15 to 20 minutes or until golden brown. Serve warm.

MAKES 8 SCONES.

Deep-dish Apple Dessert

  1 *tablespoon all-purpose flour*
  ¼ *teaspoon salt*
  ½ *teaspoon cinnamon*
  ½ *teaspoon nutmeg*
  2 *teaspoons lemon juice*
  ⅔ *cup honey*
  4 *cups sliced, peeled tart apples*
  1 *tablespoon butter*
  1 *cup biscuit mix*
 1½ *tablespoons sugar*
  ½ *cup milk*

In a large mixing bowl combine the flour, salt, cinnamon, and nutmeg with the lemon juice and honey. Add the apples, and put in an 8-inch square pan (or 1½-quart casserole). Dot with the butter. In a separate bowl combine the biscuit mix with the sugar, and add the milk. Pour over the apples. Bake uncovered in a 425° oven for 35 to 40 minutes or until done.

MAKES 8 SERVINGS.

Molly Stark Inn

1067 East Main Street
Bennington, Vermont 05201
(802) 442-9631

*A*menities at this inn in a Queen Anne-style Victorian home (built in the 1890s) include brass beds, claw-foot tubs, hardwood floors, antique furnishings, Jacuzzis, handmade quilts, and wood-burning stoves. Major tourist attractions in the area include the historical area of old Bennington, the Norman Rockwell Exhibition, Bennington Battle Monument, summer stock theater, the Bennington Museum featuring the paintings of Grandma Moses, ski resorts, and trout fishing on the Battenkill River.

Puffed Apple Pancake (a.k.a. Dutch Apple Baby)

- 4   large eggs, slightly beaten
- 1   tablespoon vanilla extract
- ¾   cup milk

- ¾   cup all-purpose flour
- 1   apple, cored, peeled, and thinly sliced
- 2   tablespoons lemon juice
- ¼   cup brown sugar
    Cinnamon for dusting
    Maple syrup

Spray 4 ovensafe 1-cup baking dishes with cooking spray. In a medium bowl combine the eggs, vanilla, milk, and flour until just blended. The batter will be lumpy. Divide evenly among the dishes. In a separate bowl toss the apple slices with the lemon juice and sugar until coated. Arrange in the center of each dish in an attractive spoked pattern. Sprinkle the tops with cinnamon. Bake in a 425° oven for 12 to 18 minutes or until puffed and golden brown. Top with warm maple syrup and enjoy!

MAKES 4 SERVINGS.

Molly's Healthy Granola

- ¾   cup firmly packed dark brown sugar
- ½   cup plus 3 tablespoons butter
- 1   teaspoon nutmeg
- 1   teaspoon cinnamon
- 6   cups old-fashioned oats
- 2   cups sliced or slivered almonds

- ½   cup dried cherries
- ½   cup raisins
- ½   cup dried banana chips
- ½   cup golden raisins
- ¼   cup flaked coconut

In a saucepan combine the brown sugar, butter, nutmeg, and cinnamon, and simmer the mixture, stirring, for 3 minutes or until the sugar is dissolved. In a large bowl combine well the oats and almonds, and toss the mixture with the sugar mixture until coated well. Spread the mixture on a large baking sheet. Bake in the middle of a 350° oven, stirring occasionally for, 15 to 20 minutes or until it is golden. Let the granola cool, and in a bowl toss it with the fruit.

Note: The granola keeps in a airtight container for 2 weeks.

MAKES ABOUT 8 CUPS.

Smoked Salmon Quesadilla

- 1   10-inch flour tortilla
- ½   cup Boursin
- 1   ripe smoked Roma tomato (or fresh Roma tomato), diced
- 1   teaspoon chopped fresh dill
- ½   teaspoon capers
- 2   ounces smoked salmon
- 1   cup sour cream
- 1   tablespoon chopped fresh dill
- 2   tablespoons olive oil
- 1   red onion, cut in half and sliced crosswise

Bring the flour tortilla to room temperature. Spread the Boursin on half the tortilla. Top with the tomato, 1 teaspoon of dill, capers, and salmon slices. Fold the tortilla in half, and press lightly.

In a medium bowl mix together the sour cream and 1 tablespoon of dill until blended. Set aside.

In a saucepan heat the olive oil. Sauté the tortilla over medium heat until golden brown. Turn over, and brown the other side. Serve warm with the sour cream mixture and sliced red onion.

MAKES 2 SERVINGS.

The Millbrook

The Millbrook

P.O. Box 410, Route 44
Brownsville, Vermont 05037
(802) 484-7283

*B*rownsville is noted for the many grist mills that operated on the stream that meanders through the village. The Millbrook Inn is situated in the 1880s home of one of these mill operators from the past. The five guest rooms are decorated with family antiques and collectibles. With five common areas for their enjoyment, guests have plenty of room to relax and unwind. Opportunities for outdoor sports abound in this area, including hang-gliding, skiing, canoeing, golfing, biking, and hiking.

Giant Fortune Popovers

- 1   cup all-purpose flour
- 2   large eggs
- 2   tablespoons oil
- 1   cup water
    Pinch salt

Spray 6 large popover pans (or custard cups) with cooking spray, and heat in a 400° oven.

In a large bowl combine the flour, eggs, oil, water, and salt. Stir well, but do not beat. Pour the mixture into the prepared pans. Bake in a 400° oven for 40 minutes until the popovers are large and well-puffed. (Do not open the oven any more than necessary.)

Prick each popover with a sharp, narrow knife to allow the steam to escape. Insert "fortunes" or cute messages into the slit. Reduce the oven to 350°. Bake for another 20 minutes. Serve warm.

MAKES 6 POPOVERS.

Catamount Burgers

- ¼ pound thinly sliced lean ham (per person)
- ¼ pound thinly sliced extra-sharp Vermont Cheddar cheese (per person)
- Tabasco sauce to taste
- Maple syrup
- Cooking spray

Spray a baking dish with cooking spray. In a dish arrange slightly overlapping layers of ham, and then Cheddar cheese. Dot with the Tabasco sauce. Lightly pour maple syrup over the top. Bake in a 300° oven until the cheese melts. Broil the top for 2 to 3 minutes just before serving.

MAKES 1 SERVING.

The Shire Inn

❧

Main Street, P.O. Box 37
Chelsea, Vermont 05038
(802) 685-3031

Because it's free of souvenir shops and other gaudy commercial establishments, Chelsea was described by one newspaper as "vintage Vermont" and "the quintessential New England village." The Shire Inn blends perfectly with this authentic milieu. Set on twenty-three acres, the Federal-style home was built of red Vermont brick by a prominent New England family in 1832. It features a grand spiral staircase and a parlor with a wood-burning fireplace. All six guest rooms are decorated with antiques, and four have their own working fireplaces. Many of Vermont's best attractions are within an easy drive of Chelsea, including Quechee Gorge, Mount Mansfield, and the golden-domed state capitol at Montpelier.

Cheddar Ale Soup

- 10 tablespoons unsalted butter
- ½ medium onion, chopped
- 1 stalk celery, diced
- 2 carrots, diced
- ½ cup all-purpose flour
- 2 cups chicken broth
- 4 cups water
- 1 12-ounce bottle ale
- 1 cup heavy cream
- 1½ teaspoons Dijon mustard
- 2 cups shredded Cheddar cheese
- Salt and white pepper to taste

....

- 1 tablespoon butter
- ¼ medium green pepper, diced
- ¼ medium red pepper, diced

In a large pot melt the butter over medium-low heat. Add the onion, celery, and carrot, and simmer for 5 minutes or until softened. Sprinkle the flour over the vegetables, and cook for an additional 5 minutes. Add the water and chicken broth a little at a time, stirring with a whisk to incorporate the liquid fully. Add the ale, and simmer for 20 to 30 minutes. Add the cream, Dijon mustard, and Cheddar cheese, and simmer until the cheese is melted. Season with salt and white pepper to taste.

In a skillet melt 1 tablespoon of butter and sauté the peppers until just barely tender. They should be slightly crisp.

Serve the soup with a few bits of the red and green pepper sprinkled in it.

MAKES 16 ¾-CUP SERVINGS.

The Shire Inn

Lentil Soup

- 2 tablespoons unsalted butter
- 1 cup diced onion
- 1 cup diced celery
- 2 cups diced carrot
- ½ cup diced red bell pepper
- 4 cups water
- 1¾ cups red lentils, picked over
- ½ teaspoon ground allspice
- 1 teaspoon ground cumin
- 2 tablespoons chopped fresh cilantro for garnish

In a skillet melt the butter over medium heat. Add the onion, celery, carrot, and red pepper, and sauté until just tender.

Rinse the lentils. In a saucepan bring the water to a boil. Add the lentils, and skim the froth. Reduce the heat, and add the cooked vegetables, allspice, and cumin, and cook partially covered for 15 minutes. Serve the soup with chopped cilantro sprinkled on top.

MAKES 16 ¾-CUP SERVINGS.

Sea Scallops with Tomato Coulis

- 1 28-ounce can whole, peeled low-sodium tomatoes
- 1 tablespoon olive oil
- 2 tablespoons minced shallots
- 1 clove garlic, minced
- 1 teaspoon red wine vinegar
- 1 teaspoon dried crumbled basil

....

- 28 sea scallops
- 2 tablespoons clarified butter

Strain the tomatoes, reserving the juice. Seed and chop the tomatoes.

In a skillet heat the olive oil over medium low heat. Sauté the shallots and garlic until translucent. Add the tomatoes and reserved juice, and cook until reduced to a purée. Stir in the wine vinegar and basil. Cover, and keep warm over low heat.

Slice the scallops in half horizontally. In a large sauté pan melt 1 tablespoon butter over medium high heat. When the pan is hot and the butter melted, add half the scallops to the pan slowly so the pan does not cool too much. Cook the scallops briefly on each side about a total of 1½ minutes. Do not overcook! Remove the scallops, and place on 2 warm plates in a warm oven (170°). Add the remaining tablespoon of butter, and repeat the instructions with the remaining scallops. To serve, top the scallops with the coulis.

MAKES 4 SERVINGS.

Chicken Dijonaise

1	**tablespoon unsalted butter**
1	**teaspoon Dijon mustard**
1	**4-ounce chicken breast, boneless and skinless**
16	**herb croutons, ground**

In a small pan melt the butter, and stir in the mustard. Coat both sides of the chicken breast with the mustard mixture, then coat both sides with the ground croutons. Place in a glass baking dish. Bake in a 350° oven for 20 minutes.

MAKES 1 SERVING.

Individual Asparagus Quiches

1	**cup unsalted butter, room temperature**
6	**ounces cream cheese, room temperature**
2	**cups all-purpose flour**

6	**fresh asparagus spears**
2	**leeks**
2	**tablespoons unsalted butter**
3	**large eggs**
1½	**cups half and half**
1	**tablespoon chopped fresh parsley**
1	**tablespoon fresh snipped chives**
1	**teaspoon fresh snipped dill**
1	**cup shredded Gruyère cheese**
¼	**cup chopped sliced almonds**

In a large bowl combine 1 cup of butter, the cream cheese, and flour. Divide the dough in half, then each half into 4 pieces. Press each piece into the cup of a regular, ungreased muffin pan.

In a large pot steam the asparagus until al dente. Run under cool water to stop cooking, and drain on paper towels. Cut each spear in half lengthwise, then into 1 inch strips, including the tips. Set the tips aside for garnish. Using only the white part of the leeks, rinse well, and chop. In a skillet sauté the leeks in 2 tablespoons butter until soft. Set side. In a separate bowl mix the eggs, half and half, and spices together. Place into the

bottom of each crust the pieces of 1 asparagus spear, one-sixth of the Gruyère cheese, and one-sixth of the almonds. Pour about ⅓ cup of the egg mixture into each crust. Bake in a 350° oven for 25 minutes or until the crust is done and a knife inserted in the center of the quiche comes out clean.

Garnish with the reserved asparagus tips.

MAKES 6 QUICHES.

Blackberry Grapefruit Sorbet

1½	**cups sugar**
1½	**cups water**
3	**cups ruby red grapefruit juice**
1	**10-ounce bag frozen blackberries**
2	**tablespoons Triple Sec**
4	**cups water**

In a saucepan mix together the sugar and water. Cook over medium heat, stirring constantly, until the sugar is dissolved. Set aside. In a food processor place 1½ cups of the grapefruit juice and the berries, and blend until smooth. Strain the mixture into a large bowl to remove the seeds. Add the sugared water mixture, the Triple Sec, the remaining 1½ cups grapefruit juice, and 4 cups water to the blackberry grapefruit mixture. Mix well. Pour into a gallon container, and place in the freezer.

Before it has frozen solid, but when it has begun to freeze, reblend the mixture in the food processor. Then return to the gallon container and freeze.

Note: The sorbet should be smooth when frozen. It may need to be reblended if it becomes icy.

MAKES 1 GALLON.

Raspberry Sorbet

2	**cups red Burgundy wine**
¼	**cup lemon juice**
1	**cup sugar**
2	**10-ounce bags frozen raspberries**

In a saucepan over medium heat mix together the wine, lemon juice and sugar. Add the raspberries and bring to a boil. Reduce the heat and cook for 10 to 15 minutes over low heat, stirring occasionally. Cool slightly. In a food processor blend the mixture until smooth. Strain the mixture to remove the

seeds, and place in a half gallon container in the freezer. Freeze until the mixture is about three-fourths frozen. Take out of the freezer, and reblend in the food processor. Return to the container, and freeze.

Note: The sorbet should be smooth and may be reblended if it becomes icy.

MAKES ½ GALLON.

Maple Carrots

½	**cup water**
10	**baby carrots**
1	**tablespoon maple syrup**

In a sauté pan over medium-high heat the water. Add the carrots and maple syrup, and bring to a boil. As the water boils off, the carrots will sauté in the syrup. The carrots are done when lightly sautéed.

MAKES 2 SERVINGS.

Sautéed Spinach

1	**tablespoon extra virgin olive oil**
1	**medium clove garlic, minced**
1	**carrot, peeled and diced**
½	**medium onion, diced**
1	**zucchini, seeded and chopped**
¼	**cup red bell pepper, diced**
5	**cups (about 1 bag) fresh spinach, washed and stems removed**
1	**tablespoon grated Parmesan cheese**

In a large skillet heat the olive oil over medium heat. Add the garlic, and sauté for 1 minute. Add the carrot, onion, zucchini, and pepper, and sauté for 3 to 4 minutes. (The vegetables should still be crisp.) Add the spinach a handful at a time so the temperature of the skillet does not reduce too quickly. Sauté the spinach until just wilted. Sprinkle with the Parmesan cheese, and serve.

MAKES 2 SERVINGS.

Lemon Soufflé Mousse with Raspberry Sauce

2	**packages ladyfingers**
2	**8-ounce packages cream cheese, softened**
4½	**tablespoons lemon juice**
4	**teaspoons vanilla extract**
2	**cups confectioners' sugar**
2	**drops yellow food coloring**
1	**pint light whipping cream**

1 12-ounce package frozen raspberries, in syrup
1½ teaspoons cornstarch
2 tablespoons Grand Marnier

Line a deep bowl, sides and bottom, with the ladyfingers. (Plan for 2 ladyfingers per person.) In a large bowl blend together the cream cheese, lemon juice, vanilla, confectioners' sugar, and food coloring. In a separate bowl whip the cream until stiff, then fold into the cream cheese mixture. Pour over the ladyfingers, and chill overnight.

In a medium pot bring the raspberries to a boil. Remove from the heat. In a small bowl mix the cornstarch with a little water to form a paste consistency, and add to the berries along with the Grand Marnier. Stir until thickened. Place briefly over low heat if necessary.
MAKES 16 SERVINGS.

Almond Cake with Blueberry Sauce

½ cup unsalted butter, softened
8 ounces almond paste
¾ cup sugar
3 large eggs
1 tablespoon Kirsch
¼ teaspoon almond extract
¼ cup all-purpose flour
⅓ teaspoon baking powder
½ cup Crème de Cassis
1 tablespoon cornstarch
¾ cup dry white wine
1 tablespoon lemon juice
1 tablespoon unsalted butter
1½ cups wild Maine blueberries (the small ones)

Butter and flour a 9-inch round cake pan. In a large mixing bowl blend the butter and almond paste until the paste is well incorporated and the mixture has no lumps. Add the sugar, and blend. Add the eggs one at a time to the mixture, beating after each addition. Add the Kirsch and the almond extract, and mix well. Add the flour and baking powder. Blend until just mixed. Pour the mixture into the prepared cake pan. Bake in a 350° oven for 40 minutes or until a knife inserted in the center comes out clean. Invert on a rack or serving platter to cool slightly.

In a medium bowl whisk together the Cassis and cornstarch. Add the wine and lemon juice. In a medium saucepan melt 1 tablespoon butter, and stir in the Cassis mixture. Cook over medium heat, stirring constantly, until thickened and glossy. Add the berries, and continue stirring about 10 to 15 minutes until they burst. Remove from heat. Place in a glass storage container and chill.

To serve, drizzle the blueberry sauce over the cake.
MAKES 16 SERVINGS.

The Craftsbury Inn

᪾

Main Street
Craftsbury, Vermont 05826-0036
(802) 586-2848

---

*T*his inn was built around 1850 as a residence by a prominent merchant in Craftsbury. Guests are impressed by such fine details as the original birds-eye maple woodwork and china cabinets, the old embossed tin ceilings, and random-width wood floors with square nails. The foundation and porch steps are from granite that was quarried in Craftsbury. The ten guest rooms feature handmade quilts and antiques. Guests can select from many recreational activities in the area, including swimming, fly fishing, hiking, biking, canoeing, and golfing.

Butternut Squash and Apple Soup

2 tablespoons butter or margarine
1 Spanish onion, diced
2 pounds butternut squash, peeled, seeded, and cut into cubes
4 cups chicken stock
2 cups pure Vermont apple cider
¼ cup Vermont maple syrup
¼ cup heavy cream
Salt and pepper to taste

Nutmeg to taste
Cinnamon to taste

In a medium saucepan melt the butter over medium heat and sauté the onion for 3 minutes. Add the cubed squash, and sauté for 3 minutes. Add the chicken stock, apple cider, and maple syrup, and simmer, reducing to one-fourth. Strain, purée, and put back into the saucepan. Add the heavy cream, salt, pepper, nutmeg, and cinnamon to taste, and reheat.
MAKES 6 SERVINGS.

Spinach Linguine and Smoked Trout with Alfredo Sauce Appetizer

6 ounces fresh spinach linguine (or dried)
2 tablespoons oil
1 teaspoon minced garlic
½ cup heavy cream
2 ounces smoked trout
¼ cup freshly grated Parmesan cheese
Salt and pepper to taste
2 scallions, diced for garnish

In a large pot cook and cool down the linguine. In a medium saucepan on medium to high heat add the oil and garlic. Sauté for 2 minutes, and add the heavy cream, linguine, smoked trout, Parmesan cheese, salt, and pepper. Simmer, stirring frequently, until the sauce thickens. Serve garnished with the chopped scallions.
MAKES 2 SERVINGS.

The Craftsbury Inn

Poached Salmon with a Cucumber-Caper Sauce

6   cups water
2   5-ounce boneless salmon
....
¼   cup white wine
3   tablespoons cucumber, peeled, cut lengthwise, seeded, and sliced into half-moons
1   teaspoon capers
½   teaspoon of lemon juice
¼   cup heavy cream
    Fresh thyme or dill (optional)

In a large pot bring 6 cups of water to a boil. Place the salmon in the water, and cook for 10 minutes. Remove the salmon from the pot, and place on a serving platter.

In a small saucepan reduce the white wine, cucumbers, capers, lemon juice, and heavy cream until thickened. Ladle the sauce over salmon, and garnish with a sprig of fresh thyme, if desired.

MAKES 2 SERVINGS.

Pecan Cheesecake

6   8-ounce packages cream cheese
2   cups sugar
2   eggs
1   tablespoon vanilla extract
1   tablespoon ground ginger
2   cups ground pecans
    Sugar for sprinkling
1   teaspoon cinnamon

In a mixing bowl with a paddle whip the cream cheese until soft. Add the sugar, and mix 3 minutes. With the mixer on low, add the eggs one at a time, then add the vanilla and ginger, and mix.

Place parchment paper on the bottom of a springform pan, and spray the side of the pan with cooking spray to prevent sticking. Pour the mixture into the prepared pan. Spread the ground pecans on top of cheesecake, covering ¼-inch thick. Sprinkle sugar and the cinnamon on top.

Fill a roasting pan half full with hot water. Place the springform pan in the hot water bath. Bake in a 400° oven for 1 hour. Reduce to 325°, and bake for 30 minutes. Reduce to 275°, and bake for 1 hour. Remove from the oven, and cool for 6 to 10 hours.

MAKES 8 TO 10 SERVINGS.

Breast of Chicken with Maple Mustard Sauce

4   6-ounce boneless skinless chicken breasts
3   tablespoons light oil
    All-purpose flour
2   tablespoons clarified butter
½   cup finely diced shallots
⅓   cup brandy
⅓   cup white wine
1   tablespoon Worcestershire sauce
3   tablespoons Dijon mustard
3   tablespoons Vermont maple syrup
½   cup chicken stock
⅓   cup heavy cream
1   tablespoon diced scallions for garnish

On a cutting board cover the chicken with plastic, and pound firm to ¼-inch thickness. Cut each chicken breast into 3 strips. In a large sauté pan on high heat add the oil. Lightly coat the chicken pieces with flour. When the oil is hot, sauté the chicken until golden brown. Place the browned chicken on a small sheet pan. Bake in a 350° oven for 15 minutes.

Pour the excess oil from the sauté pan, and add 2 tablespoons of clarified butter to the pan. Over medium heat add the diced shallots, and stir for 30 seconds. Remove the sauté pan from the heat, and add the brandy, white wine, Worcestershire sauce, Dijon mustard, maple syrup, and chicken stock. Place the pan back on the heat, and reduce the liquids to one-fourth. Add the heavy cream, and reduce to half. The sauce should be the consistency of gravy. Pour the sauce into a serving dish.

Remove the chicken from the oven, and place in the sauce. Garnish with the chopped scallions, and serve.

MAKES 4 SERVINGS.

Silas Griffith Inn

R.R. 1, Box 66-F
Danby, Vermont 05739
(800) 545-1509

Situated in Vermont's Green Mountains, this inn was built in 1891 as a residence for his new bride by Silas Griffith, a lumber baron and one of Vermont's first millionaires. The hand-carved cherry woodwork, embossed tin ceilings, and stained glass windows capture the elegant lifestyle of the rich and famous of turn-of-the-century New England. Other amenities include a swimming pool, a large living room for use by guests, a library, and a TV room. The inn is within easy driving distance of several of Vermonts major ski resorts.

Orange-Chocolate Bars

⅓   cup margarine
⅔   cup firmly packed brown sugar
1   egg
1   cup all-purpose flour
¼   teaspoon salt
¼   teaspoon baking soda
1¼   cups quick-cooking oats
½   cup milk
1   cup chocolate chips
1½   teaspoon grated orange zest
....
1   cup confectioners' sugar
    Orange juice

Grease an 8-inch square pan with cooking spray. In a large mixing bowl beat the margarine and brown sugar until creamy. Add the egg, and beat well. In a separate bowl mix the flour, salt, soda, and oatmeal. Add the dry ingredients to the sugar mixture alternately with the milk. Add the chocolate chips and orange zest, and mix. Pour into the prepared pan. Bake in a 375° oven for 35 to 40 minutes or until done. Remove from the oven, and cool.

In a medium bowl mix 1 cup confectioners' sugar with enough orange juice to make a light frosting. Spread over the cooled bars, cut, and serve.

MAKES 6 TO 8 SERVINGS.

Multi-Grain Pancakes

1½ cups unbleached flour
1 cup whole wheat flour
1 cup quick oats
½ cup cornmeal
1 tablespoon baking powder
2 teaspoons baking soda
1 teaspoon salt
4 eggs
4 cups buttermilk
½ cup honey
½ cup margarine, melted
1 cup chopped nuts
Maple syrup

In a large bowl mix the dry ingredients. In a separate bowl beat the eggs and buttermilk. Add the honey and melted margarine. Fold into the dry ingredients, mixing well. Add the nuts.

Heat and oil a griddle. Cook as usual for pancakes. Serve with Vermont maple syrup.

MAKES 6 TO 8 SERVINGS.

Cream Scones

2 cups all-purpose flour
1 tablespoon baking powder
½ teaspoon salt
¼ cup sugar
1⅓ cups heavy cream

In a large mixing bowl combine the flour, baking powder, salt, and sugar, stirring to mix well. Using a fork, stir in the cream, and mix until the dough holds together in a rough mass. The dough will be quite sticky. Turn the dough onto a lightly floured board. Knead the dough 8 or 9 times. Pat into a circle about 10 inches across. Cut into 12 wedges, and place on a baking sheet. Bake in a 425° oven for about 15 minutes or until golden brown.

Note: Raisins or chopped apricots may also be added.

MAKES 12 SERVINGS.

Berkson Farms

R.R. 1, Box 850
Enosburg Falls, Vermont 05450
(802) 933-2522

This inn is ideal for guests who want to escape to the country. It is situated in a century-old farmhouse on a six-hundred-acre working farm. Guests are welcome to assist with the chores, including milking the cows, gathering eggs from the hen house, and collecting sap from maple trees during the spring sugar season. Numerous trails throughout the farm are provided during the winter for snowmobiling or cross-country skiing. Fishing, hunting, and swimming are also available right on the farm. Other activities nearby include golf, tennis, horseback riding, and summer theater.

Berkson's BBQ Chicken

½ cup oil
1 cup cider vinegar
1 tablespoon salt
1½ teaspoons poultry seasoning
¼ teaspoon pepper
1 egg
2 to 3 fryers, cut up

In a shallow dish combine the oil, vinegar, salt, poultry seasoning, pepper, and egg. Marinate the chicken overnight.

Grill to the desired doneness.

MAKES 6 TO 8 SERVINGS.

Berkson's Vermont Cabbage Soup

2 slices bacon, diced
2 onions, sliced
3 carrots, chopped
1 head cabbage, shredded
1 pound sliced Polish kielbasa
Chicken broth
1 potato, grated
1 teaspoon thyme
Salt and pepper to taste

In a Dutch oven fry the diced bacon until crisp. Add the onions, carrots, and cabbage, cover, and sweat. Add the kielbasa and enough chicken broth to cover. Cook over medium heat for 2 hours. Add the potato, thyme, and salt and pepper to taste. Cook 1 hour or more.

MAKES 6 SERVINGS.

Maplewood Inn

Maplewood Inn

Route 22-A South
Fair Haven, Vermont 05743
(800) 253-7729

Listed on the Vermont State Register of Historic Places, this inn (built in 1843), is a classic example of a Greek Revival-style structure. All five guest rooms are furnished with period antiques. Guests also enjoy several common rooms, including a keeping room with fireplace, a gathering room with library, and a parlor with a complimentary bar. Bicycles and canoes are provided on site. Fine shopping and restaurants are nearby. Other major Vermont tourist destinations within an easy drive are Lakes Bomoseen, St. Catherine, and Champlain; Hubbardton Battlefield; Norman Rockwell Museum; and New England Maple Museum.

Maplewood Inn Granola

- 6 *cups uncooked oats*
- 1 *cup sliced (or slivered) almonds*
- 1 *cup broken walnuts*
- 1 *cup chopped pecans*
- 1 *cup sesame seeds*
- 1 *cup shelled sunflower seeds*
- 1 *cup wheat germ*
- 1 *cup shredded coconut*
- 2/3 *cup canola oil*
- 2/3 *cup honey*
- 1/4 *cup maple syrup*
- 1 *cup raisins*
- 1 *cup dates (or a combination of any dried fruit totaling 2 cups)*

In a large bowl mix the oats, nuts, seeds, wheat germ, and coconut. In a medium saucepan heat the oil, honey, and syrup until blended. Pour over the dry ingredients, and mix well. Spread into a large baking pan(s) or deep cookie sheet. Bake in a 325° oven until lightly browned, turning and stirring every 10 minutes. (Usually cooks in 30 minutes.) Cool when done, mix, and add the dried fruit. Store in an airtight container, preferably glass. Keeps well.

Variation: Omit the pecans and use all walnuts.

MAKES ABOUT 4 QUARTS.

Sweet Potato Bread

- 1 *cup butter or margarine, softened*
- 2 *cups sugar*
- 4 *eggs*
- 2½ *cups cooked, mashed sweet potatoes*
- 3 *cups all-purpose flour*
- 2 *teaspoons baking powder*
- 1 *teaspoon baking soda*
- 1 *teaspoon cinnamon*
- ½ *teaspoon nutmeg*
- ¼ *teaspoon salt*
- 1 *teaspoon vanilla extract*
- ½ *cup flaked coconut*
- ½ *cup chopped walnuts (or pecans)*

In a large mixing bowl cream the butter. Gradually add the sugar, and beat. Add the eggs one at a time, beating after each addition. Add the sweet potatoes, and beat. In a separate bowl combine the flour, baking powder, soda, cinnamon, nutmeg, and salt. Gradually add to the sweet potato mix, beating after each addition. The batter will be stiff. Stir in the vanilla, coconut, and nuts. Pour the batter into a well-greased tube pan.

Bake in a 350° oven for 1 hour and 15 minutes or until a toothpick inserted in the center comes out clean.

Cool in the pan for 15 minutes. Remove from the pan, and let cool completely.

Note: Can also be baked in 2 standard loaf pans. Check after 50 minutes, and cook until a toothpick inserted in the center comes out clean.

MAKES 8 SERVINGS.

Spiced Pear Compote

- 3 *16-ounce cans pear slices in syrup*
- 1 *cup firmly packed brown sugar*
- ½ *teaspoon cinnamon*
- ¼ *teaspoon nutmeg*
- ¼ *teaspoon allspice*
- ¼ *cup lemon juice (or orange juice)*

Drain the syrup from pears, and reserve 1 cup syrup. In a large bowl mix the syrup with the brown sugar, spices, and fruit juice. Add the pears, and mix gently, covering the pears with syrup. Let stand overnight in the refrigerator to allow the full flavor to develop. (Two days is even better.) Serve in small compote dishes.

Note: May also be served warm. This can also be made with peaches or a combination of peaches and pears.

MAKES 6 TO 8 SERVINGS.

Silver Maple Lodge

R.R. 1, Box 8
Fairlee, Vermont 05045
(800) 666-1946

Silver Maple Lodge

*T*his old inn has been welcoming travelers since the 1920s, making it one of Vermont's oldest continuously operating country inns. Rooms are also available in an adjoining farmhouse that dates to the late 1700s. Guests may choose from eight cozy rooms in the old farmhouse or six cottages decorated with nostalgic knotty pine walls. A large wraparound screened porch is available to guests. Nearby attractions include Calvin Coolidge's birthplace, home, and grave; the Saint-Gaudens National Historic Site; Quechee Gorge ("Vermont's little Grand Canyon"); and outdoor sports such as golf, tennis, swimming, hiking, and canoeing.

Lemon Tea Bread

- 1 *cup King Arthur all-purpose flour*
- 1½ *teaspoons baking soda*
- 1½ *teaspoons baking powder*
- ¼ *teaspoon salt*
- ¼ *cup butter, softened*
- 1½ *cups sugar*
- 3 *eggs*
- 1 *tablespoon pure lemon extract*
- 1 *teaspoon pure vanilla extract*
- 1½ *cups sour cream*
  Pinch nutmeg for dusting

In a medium bowl combine the flour, soda, baking powder, and salt. Set aside. In a mixing bowl on medium speed beat the butter, sugar, eggs, and extracts for 2 minutes. Blend the sour cream into the egg mixture, then blend the flour combination into the egg mixture. Pour the batter into 2 greased 8½ x 4½-inch loaf pans. Dust with nutmeg. Bake in a 315° oven for 50 to 55 minutes or until a toothpick inserted in the center comes out clean.

MAKES 2 LOAVES.

Strawberry Swirl Coffee Cake

- ¾ *cup butter or margarine, softened*
- 1½ *cups sugar*

3 eggs
1½ teaspoons vanilla extract
3 cups King Arthur all-purpose flour
1½ teaspoons baking powder
1½ teaspoons baking soda
¼ teaspoon salt
1½ cups sour cream
 Strawberry preserves

In a large mixer bowl combine the butter, sugar, eggs, and vanilla. Beat on medium speed for 2 minutes. Mix in the flour, baking powder, soda, and salt alternately with the sour cream.

Grease 2 5 x 9-inch loaf pans. Spoon most of the batter into the pans (reserve just enough to layer the tops). Spread a thin layer of strawberry preserves onto the batter in each pan and then swirl slightly with a fork. Do not blend preserves into the batter. Cover the strawberry preserves with the reserved batter, and dust the tops lightly with sugar. Bake in a 350° oven for about 60 minutes or until a wooden pick inserted in the center comes out clean. Cool slightly in pans before removing.

MAKES 2 LOAVES.

Spicy Orange Nut Bread (Nut Tree)

1 cup ground orange zest
½ cup water
2 tablespoons sugar

2¼ cups all-purpose flour
1 cup sugar
2½ teaspoons baking powder
¾ teaspoon salt
½ teaspoon ground cinnamon
⅔ cup milk
3 tablespoons oil (or melted shortening)
2 eggs
¼ teaspoon vanilla extract
½ teaspoon orange extract
2 drops almond extract
2 drops lemon extract
¾ cup coarsely chopped walnuts
½ teaspoon cinnamon
2 tablespoons sugar

Place the orange zest in a medium saucepan, add the water and 2 tablespoons of sugar, and heat to boiling, then cover and cook over low heat 10 to 15 minutes until the zest is tender

and practically all the water is absorbed. Cool.

In a mixing bowl sift the flour, 1 cup of sugar, baking powder, and cinnamon. Add the milk, oil, eggs, vanilla, and extracts. Beat at low speed just until well mixed. Mix in the cooled orange zest and walnuts. Divide the batter evenly into 2 greased 8 x 4-inch loaf pans. Sprinkle the tops generously with a mixture of ½ teaspoon of cinnamon and 2 tablespoons of sugar. Bake in a 350° oven for 45 to 50 minutes (55 to 60 minutes for the 5 x 9 x 3 pan) until well browned and a toothpick inserted in the center comes out clean. Turn out, and cool on rack.

MAKES 2 LOAVES.

Goshen, Vermont 05733
(802) 247-6735

---

*A*t the foot of Romance Mountain in Green Mountain National Forest of Vermont lies Blueberry Hill, a restored farmhouse from the early 1800s. Guests enjoy the fresh air, freedom from noise, and open lands that surround this inn, making it ideal as a getaway spot. Each of the twelve guest rooms is furnished with antiques. Guests also enjoy strolling among the flowers in the greenhouse. Several hiking trails radiate from the inn. Lake Dunmore just down the road offers such water sports as windsurfing, boating, and swimming.

Four O'Clock Sesame French Bread

1 tablespoon butter
1 tablespoon salt
1 tablespoon sugar
2 cups boiling water
1 tablespoon active dry yeast
⅔ cup lukewarm water (105 to 115°)

6 to 6½ cups unbleached flour
1 cup toasted sesame seeds
 Oil
¼ to ½ cup yellow cornmeal
 Butter

In a large mixing bowl combine the butter, salt, sugar, and boiling water. Stir to dissolve the ingredients and let cool to lukewarm. In another bowl sprinkle the yeast over the ⅔ cup lukewarm water. Let the yeast dissolve and start to foam. Add the yeast mixture to the first liquid mixture. In a separate bowl mix together the flour and sesame seeds. Slowly add the flour mixture to the liquids, beating well after each addition.

When well combined, turn the dough out on a floured board and knead until it is smooth and elastic. Form the dough into a ball and place in an oiled ceramic or earthenware bowl. Cover it with a damp cloth, and place in a warm spot. Let the dough rise for 1 to 1½ hours or until doubled in size.

Punch the dough down, and knead into a ball. Return to the bowl, cover, and let rise again 1 hour or until doubled in size.

Brush 3 French bread pans with oil, and sprinkle the bottom with cornmeal. (If you don't have special pans, use a large cookie sheet, and prepare with oil and cornmeal.) Punch the dough down, and divide it into 3 parts. Shape each loaf by patting it into a rectangular shape, then rolling it tightly into a long loaf. Pinch the seam and ends to seal. Place the loaves seam-side down in the pans (or cookie sheet.) Cover the loaves with the damp cloth, and let rise until doubled, about 30 minutes.

Bake the loaves on the middle rack of a 400° oven for about 1 hour. (For a crisp, hard crust, brush the loaves often with cold water.) Serve the bread warm from the oven with lots of fresh butter.

MAKES 3 LOAVES

Dill-Caraway Dinner Rolls

3 cups cottage cheese
½ cup minced onion
3 tablespoons unsalted butter, melted
3 tablespoons active dry yeast
1½ cups warm water (105 to 115°)
7 cups unbleached flour
2 teaspoons salt
¼ cup sugar
3 eggs, room temperature

2 tablespoons caraway seeds
3 tablespoons dillweed

In a small pan heat the cottage cheese until warm. Set aside. In another small pan sauté the onion in the butter until it is soft and translucent. Add this to the cottage cheese.

In a small bowl stir the yeast into the warm water and wait until it gets foamy. In a large bowl combine the flour, salt, and sugar. Add the yeast, and stir well. Add the eggs one at a time, stirring well after each addition, then stir in the caraway and dill. (The dough will be moist.) Add the cottage cheese and onion, and stir until all the ingredients are well combined.

Turn the dough onto a well-floured board, and knead lightly for 5 minutes. Place the dough into a greased bowl, cover loosely with plastic wrap, and let rise in a warm place until doubled in size.

Punch the dough down, and form into about 30 rolls (or 2 loaves, if desired). Place rolls about 2 inches apart on a greased cookie sheet (or loaves in bread pans), and allow to rest for about 15 minutes until they have risen slightly. Bake in a 350° oven for 15 to 20 minutes bread for 45 to 50 minutes).

MAKES 30 ROLLS OR 2 LOAVES.

Shrimp Tartlets

Pastry for a 9-inch pie crust
1½ *cups medium shrimp, peeled, deveined, and cut in half*
½ *cup chopped green onion*
1 *tablespoon butter*
½ *pound grated Gruyère cheese (or fontina cheese)*
1 *cup mayonnaise*
4 *eggs*
1 *cup half and half*
½ *teaspoon salt*
½ *teaspoon dillweed (or 1 tablespoon minced fresh dill)*

Divide the pastry into 8 small balls. Roll out each piece in a circle and press into 8 small tartlet pans. Trim the edges, and set aside in the refrigerator while preparing the filling.

In a skillet sauté the shrimp and green onion in the butter until the shrimp just turn pink. Spread evenly over the bottom of each tartlet pan. Distribute the grated Gruyère cheese evenly over the shrimp.

In a medium bowl beat together the mayonnaise, eggs, half and half, salt, and dillweed. Pour over the mixture in the tartlet pans. Bake the tartlets in a 400° oven for 15 to 20 minutes. Remove them from the oven, let them sit for 5 minutes, then carefully remove them from their pans, and serve immediately.

MAKES 8 SERVINGS.

Pasta with Citrus Beurre Blanc

1 *pound fresh pasta*
⅓ *cup minced shallots*
½ *cup freshly squeezed lemon juice (or orange juice)*
1 *cup dry white wine*
2 *cups heavy cream*
½ *cup unsalted butter, cut into small pieces*
Salt and freshly ground black pepper to taste
Fresh parsley, minced for garnish
2 *scallions, minced for garnish*

Bring a large kettle of salted water to a full boil. (While waiting for the water to boil, prepare the sauce for the pasta.) When the water is boiling, add the pasta, and cook until al dente. Drain well.

In a small nonreactive saucepan combine the shallots, citrus juice, and wine. Cook over medium heat until reduced to about 3 tablespoons. Add the heavy cream to the reduction, and continue to reduce until there is about 1½ cups and the sauce coats the back of a wooden spoon.

Turn off the heat, and add the butter, whisking in piece by piece. Strain out the shallots, and add salt and pepper to taste. Serve over the freshly cooked pasta, and garnish with fresh parsley and scallions.

MAKES 8 SERVINGS.

Beef Tenderloin Stuffed with Basil Shallot Butter

1 *5-pound beef tenderloin, room temperature, trimmed of fat and silverskin*
1 *pound maple-cured bacon*
2 *cups unsalted butter, room temperature*
6 *to 8 shallots, minced*

1½ *cups finely chopped fresh basil leaves*
½ *cup dried basil leaves, revived in boiling water and well drained*
Salt and freshly ground white pepper to taste
Whole basil leaves and cherry tomato halves for garnish

Make sure the tenderloin is trimmed of all fat. Separate the bacon into individual strips. In a food processor fitted with a steel blade cream the butter, shallots, basil, salt, and pepper until combined well.

Trim the rounded ends of the tenderloin, reserving the end pieces. Insert a long, narrow, sharp knife into one end of the tenderloin, and twist the knife to make a hole. Repeat this procedure on the other end so that the hole extends through the center of the entire loin. Spoon the basil butter in a pastry bag with a large plain tip. Fill the tenderloin with the butter from one end, then the other. Seal on each end with the reserved trimmings. Wrap the entire tenderloin well with the bacon.

Place the beef in a large baking pan. Roast in a 425° oven for 10 minutes. Reduce the heat to 350° and roast for another 25 minutes for rare (or 35 minutes for medium). Remove the roast from the oven, and let it rest for 10 minutes before slicing. Garnish the sliced beef tenderloin with the fresh basil leaves and cherry tomato halves.

MAKES 10 SERVINGS.

Pork Tenderloin Medallions in Vermouth-Mustard Sauce

Unsalted butter
2 *pork tenderloins (about 1 pound each)*
Salt and pepper to taste
3 *tablespoons olive oil*
2 *large garlic, finely minced*
1 *tablespoon grated lemon zest*
1 *cup dry vermouth*
¼ *cup Dijon mustard*
2 *tablespoons soy sauce*

Butter a large flameproof baking dish, and set it aside. Trim the excess fat from the tenderloins. Cut into ¾-inch medallions, and season the medallions with salt and pepper.

In a heavy skillet melt the butter, add the olive oil, and heat until very hot. Add the medallions, a few at a time, and brown them on both sides. Remove the browned medallions to a buttered baking dish. In the same skillet (add more butter and oil if necessary) sauté the garlic over medium heat. When translucent, add the lemon zest, vermouth, mustard, and soy sauce. Simmer about 5 minutes, scraping the bottom of the pan well to deglaze. Pour the sauce evenly over the medallions.

Cover the baking dish tightly with foil, and place in the middle of the oven. Bake (braise) the medallions in a 325° oven for 25 to 30 minutes.

MAKES 4 TO 6 SERVINGS.

Sautéed Zucchini Fingers with Parmesan Cheese

- 2 *slender medium zucchini*
- 1 *tablespoon butter*
- 1 *tablespoon olive oil*
- 1 *clove garlic, finely minced*
- 2 *tablespoons chopped fresh basil*
  Salt and freshly ground black pepper to taste
- ½ *cup freshly grated Parmesan cheese*

Cut the zucchini in half and section into fingers approximately 2 x ½ inches. In a large skillet heat the butter and oil over medium-high heat. Add the garlic, and sauté for 1 minute. Lower the heat, and add the zucchini fingers, tossing to coat them with the garlic. Continue tossing until the fingers are lightly browned and tender but still on the crunchy side. Add the basil, season with salt and pepper, and toss in the Parmesan cheese.

Turn off the heat and cover the pan for 1 minute to give the Parmesan cheese a chance to soften. Serve immediately with an additional grinding of black pepper.

MAKES 2 SERVINGS.

Blueberry Gâteau

- ½ *cup unsalted butter, softened*
- 1 *cup sugar*
- 1 *cup unbleached all-purpose flour*
- 1 *teaspoon baking powder*
  Pinch salt
- 2 *eggs*
- 3 *cups blueberries, picked over, washed, and drained*

- 2 *tablespoons sugar*
- 2 *tablespoons freshly squeezed lemon juice*
- 1 *tablespoon unbleached flour*

Lightly butter a 9-inch springform pan. In a large bowl cream the butter with 1 cup of sugar until light and fluffy. In a separate bowl mix together 1 cup of flour, the baking powder, and salt. Beat this into the butter mixture. Beat in the eggs one at a time. Place the batter in the prepared springform pan.

In a medium bowl toss the berries with 2 tablespoons sugar, lemon juice, and 1 tablespoon of flour. Spread evenly over the top of the batter. Bake in a 350° oven for 1 hour. Cool in the pan. Remove the sides of the pan and turn onto a cake plate, berry-side up.

MAKES 6 TO 8 SERVINGS.

The Vermont Inn

The Vermont Inn

❧

HC 34, Box 37-J, Route 4
Killington, Vermont 05751
(800) 541-7795

This inn has won awards for its fine dining. Its lounge features a wood-burning stove and beautiful views of the surrounding mountains. Built originally as a farmhouse in 1840, it sits on a five-acre wooded site in the Green Mountain. Amenities include a sauna, hot tub, tennis court, swimming pool, reading room, and parlor with a fireplace. Some of the eighteen guest rooms have fireplaces.

Activities within an easy drive include golf, ice skating, horseback riding, bicycle rentals, canoeing, and summer theater.

Mussels Dijon

- 2 *dozen mussels*
- 1 *tablespoon olive oil*
- 1 *tablespoon minced garlic*
- ¼ *cup sliced Spanish onions*
- ¼ *cup white wine*
- 1 *tablespoon Dijon mustard*
- ½ *cup heavy cream*
- ½ *cup clam juice*
- 1 *loaf crusty bread*

Debeard and rinse the mussels. Heat a large sauté pan to 425°. Place the oil in the pan, and sauté the garlic and onions. Deglaze the pan with the white wine, and add the Dijon mustard. Place the mussels in the pan with the cream and clam juice. Cover with an inverted pan to create a "steamer". Reduce the heat slightly, and steam for 5 minutes. The mussels are done when the shells open and the mussels are firm. Heap the mussels in a large bowl, and pour the broth over them. Serve with crusty bread for dipping.

MAKES 2 SERVINGS.

Vermont Baked Veal

- 1 *pound veal*
- 2 *cloves garlic, minced*
- 1 *cup chopped spinach*
- ½ *cup diced shallots*
- 2 *tablespoons olive oil*
- 2 *cups shredded Cheddar cheese*
- ½ *cup cooked and diced bacon*
  Salt and pepper to taste
  Nutmeg to taste
- ½ *cup all-purpose flour*
- 4 *eggs, slightly beaten*
- ½ *cup breadcrumbs*

Cut the veal into 12 slices and pound lightly until very thin. Set aside.

In a skillet sauté the garlic, spinach, and shallots in the olive oil until soft. Remove from the heat. Add the Cheddar cheese, bacon, salt, pepper, and nutmeg, and mix until blended.

Place ¼ cup of the stuffing on a slice of veal, and roll tightly. Dredge in the flour and dip into the beaten eggs. Roll in the bread crumbs. Repeat with the remaining slices of veal. Place in a greased baking pan. Bake in a 350° oven for 15 to 20 minutes or until golden brown.

MAKES 4 SERVINGS.

Mulligatawny Soup

- 1 *tablespoon oil*
- 2 *onions, diced*
- 3 *tablespoons chopped parsley*
  Salt and pepper to taste
- 2 *carrots, sliced*
- 4 *ribs celery, with leaves*
- ½ *pound mushrooms*
- 3 *tablespoons all-purpose flour*
- 5 *chicken breasts, diced*
- 8 *cups chicken broth*
- ½ *cup cooked rice*
- 1 *cup heavy cream*

In a stockpot heat the oil and sauté the onions. Add the parsley, salt, pepper, carrots, celery, mushrooms, flour, and chicken. Add the broth and simmer for 30 minutes. Add the rice and cream.

MAKES 16 SERVINGS.

Nonfat Balsamic Vinegar

- 1½ *cups Dijon mustard*
- 2 *cups balsamic vinegar*
- ½ *cup water*
- 4 *cups orange juice*
- 2 *tablespoons honey*
- 1 *clove garlic, finely minced*
- 1½ *teaspoons fresh chives*
- 2 *teaspoons fresh parsley*
- ½ *teaspoon dry dill*
  Pinch salt
- 5 *turns freshly ground black pepper*

In a container with a tight-fitting lid combine all of the ingredients. Mix well. Cover and store in the refrigerator.

MAKES 8 CUPS.

Rabbit Hill Inn

Rabbit Hill Inn

Lower Waterford, Vermont 05848
(802) 748-5168

Rabbit Hill Inn sits on a fifteen-acre site in a quaint Vermont village overlooking the Connecticut River Valley. With its striking white exterior columns and such amenities as four-poster canopied beds, it bills itself as "an inn for romantics." Guests enjoy the gazebo, oil lamp-lit porches, and the Snooty Fox Pub. Activities available at the inn include cross-country skiing, swimming, tobogganing, hiking, fishing, and canoeing. Guests also have acces to a nearby eighteen-hole golf course.

Banana Chutney

- 2 *tablespoons shallots*
- 2 *tablespoons peanut oil*
- 3 *bananas, peeled and diced*
- 1 *cup papaya*
- ¾ *cup guava juice*
- ¼ *cup mango juice*
- 1 *tablespoon firmly packed brown sugar*
- 1 *teaspoon sugar*
- 2 *tablespoons currants*
- 1 *tablespoon curry*
- ½ *teaspoon tumeric*
- ¼ *teaspoon cumin*
- 1 *tablespoon white wine vinegar*
- 2 *tablespoons lime juice*
- ½ *teaspoon salt*
- ½ *teaspoon pepper*

In a skillet sauté the shallots in the peanut oil for 5 minutes. Add the bananas, papaya, juices, sugars, currants, curry, tumeric, and cumin to the shallots, bring to a boil, and simmer for 20 minutes. Add the vinegar, lime juice, salt, and pepper, and simmer for another 15 minutes.

MAKES 3 TO 4 CUPS.

Maple Dressing

- 2 *egg yolks*
- 2 *tablespoons prepared mustard*
- 2 *tablespoons minced garlic*
- ¼ *cup apple cider vinegar*
- ¼ *cup balsamic vinegar*
- ¾ *cup olive oil*
- ¼ *cup oil*
- ¼ *cup honey*
- ¾ *cup maple syrup*
- ½ *teaspoon salt*
- ¼ *teaspoon white pepper*

In a mixer or by hand whisk together the egg yolks and mustard until lightly thickened. Add the garlic. Add the vinegars slowly while whisking. Add the oils slowly while whisking. Add the honey and maple syrup, and whip to incorporate. Season with salt and pepper.

MAKES 4 CUPS.

Scallop Chili

- 2 *red bell peppers, halved, seeded and core removed*
- 2 *yellow bell peppers, halved, seeded and core removed*
- 2 *green bell peppers, halved, seeded and core removed*
- ½ *gallon or 4 pounds scallops*
- 3 *tablespoons olive oil*
- 1 *large onion diced*
- 1½ *tablespoons minced garlic*
- 2 *diced jalapeños*
- 1 *6-ounce can tomato paste*
- 2½ *cups fish stock*
- 1 *quart whole peeled tomatoes, crushed in the palm of the hand*
- 1 *pound dried black beans, soaked in water overnight, strained, rinsed, and cooked in fresh water until tender*
- 2 *bay leaves*
- 1 *teaspoon salt*
- 3 *teaspoons cumin*
- 2 *teaspoons diced thyme*
- 2 *teaspoons dried basil*
- ½ *teaspoon cayenne pepper*
- 2 *teaspoons chili powder*
- ½ *teaspoon red pepper flakes*

Grill the peppers until well charred. Dice when cool, and set aside. Over a very hot fire grill the scallops until rare but slightly charred.

In a sauté pan heat the olive oil. When hot, add the onions, garlic, and jalapeños. Sauté 7 to 10 minutes, then add the diced peppers and tomato paste, stirring to incorporate. Add the fish stock, crushed tomatoes, black beans, and all seasonings. Bring to a boil, and simmer 30 minutes. Add the grilled scallops, and stir to incorporate. Cook for 5 to 10 minutes, then remove from the heat. Remove the bay leaves.

Note: It is important not to overcook the scallops in either the grilling or sauté process. Overcooked scallops become rubbery and tough.

MAKES 6 TO 8 SERVINGS.

Vermont Cheddar Cheese Soup

- 6 *tablespoons unsalted butter*
- 1 *cup diced onion*
- 2 *teaspoons minced garlic*
- ½ *cup diced celery*
- ½ *cup diced carrot*
- 8 *tablespoons all-purpose flour*
- 1 *teaspoon dry mustard*
- 4 *cups chicken stock*
- 2 *cups heavy cream*
- 1½ *pounds Vermont Cheddar cheese, grated*
- 1 *teaspoon Worcestershire sauce*
  Salt and pepper to taste

In a soup pot melt the butter. When hot, add the onion, garlic, celery, and carrots. Sauté for 7 to 10 minutes. Sprinkle the flour and dry mustard on top, reduce heat, and stir constantly to incorporate for 10 minutes. Add the chicken stock 1 cup at a time, whisking to incorporate each time. Add the heavy cream, bring to a boil, and simmer for 45 minutes.

Strain into another pot. Add the Cheddar cheese and Worcestershire sauce, and whisk to incorporate and melt. If needed, return the mixture to a very low heat (or use a double boiler) to help melt the Cheddar cheese. Season with salt and pepper.

Variation: Add ham, sun-dried tomatoes, grilled chicken, or croutons.

MAKES 12 SERVINGS.

Tomato, Bean, Turkey Soup

- 2 *cups diced onions*
- 1 *cup diced green bell peppers*
- 1 *cup diced celery*
- 1 *tablespoon ground garlic*
- ¼ *cup butter*
- 8 *cups chicken stock*
- 8 *cups homemade tomato sauce (or store-bought)*
- 1 *pound dried white beans, soaked in water overnight, then cook until tender*
- 1 *tablespoon salt*
- 1 *teaspoon black pepper*
- 2 *pounds cooked, diced turkey*
- 1 *pound ham, diced*
- 1 *cup grated Parmesan cheese*
- 1 *tablespoon dried basil*

In a skillet melt the butter and sauté the onions, peppers, celery, and garlic for 10 minutes. Add the chicken stock, and bring to a boil. Add the tomato sauce, white beans, salt, and pepper. Bring to a boil, and simmer for 30 minutes. Add the diced turkey, ham, Parmesan cheese, and dried basil. Mix to incorporate. Adjust seasonings if necessary. Serve hot.

MAKES 6 TO 8 SERVINGS.

Pumpkin Cheese Cake

- 3 *eggs*
- 1 *8-ounce package cream cheese*
- ¼ *cup butter*
- 1½ *cups sugar*
- 1½ *cups canned pumpkin*
- 4 *cups all-purpose flour*
- 1 *teaspoon baking powder*
- 1 *teaspoon baking soda*
- ½ *teaspoon salt*
- ½ *cup sour cream*

In a mixing bowl blend the eggs, cream cheese, and butter. Add the sugar, and mix. Add the pumpkin, and blend well. In a separate bowl mix the flour, baking powder, soda, salt, and sour cream. Blend well, and add to the cream cheese mixture. Pour the mixture into 2 9-inch buttered cake pans. Cook in a 350° oven for 40 minutes or until a knife inserted in the center comes out clean.

MAKES 6 TO 8 SERVINGS.

Rhubarb Mustard

- 2 *cups mustard seed*
- 2 *cups water*
- ½ *cup ground mustard*
- 3 *tablespoons butter*
- 1½ *quarts rhubarb, diced*
- 1 *onion, diced*
- 1 *tablespoons garlic*
- 1⅔ *cups rice vinegar*
- ⅓ *cup balsamic vinegar*
- ½ *cup Sherry vinegar*
- ½ *cup sugar*
- 2 *teaspoons salt*

In a blender purée the mustard seed, water, and ground mustard. Set aside. In a skillet sauté the butter, rhubarb, onion, and garlic. In a medium bowl mix together the vinegars, sugar, and salt. Add the vinegar mixture to the rhubarb mixture, and simmer for 30 minutes. Add the purée, and cook for 15 minutes. Stir, and let stand 10 minutes.

MAKES 2 QUARTS.

Chilled Fruit Soup

Cranberry juice
Pineapple juice
Whipping cream
Fresh strawberries and banana slices

Mix together equal parts of the cranberry juice, pineapple juice, and whipping cream. Add the fruit. Pour into a glass bowl, and chill.

Variation: Try adding different types of tropical juices.

Spiced Fruit Soup

- 4 *cups apple cider*
- 4 *cups apple juice*
- 4 *cups heavy cream*
- ¼ *cup sugar*
- 1 *teaspoon cinnamon*
  Apple slices

In a large bowl whip together all the ingredients except the cinnamon and apple slices. Dredge the apple slices in the cinnamon, then add to the mixture. Refrigerate until adequately chilled.

MAKES APPROXIMATELY 3 QUARTS.

Raspberry-Cream Cheese Coffee Cake

- 2¼ *cups all-purpose flour*
- ¾ *cups sugar*
- ¾ *cup butter*
- ½ *teaspoon baking powder*

½ teaspoon baking soda
¼ teaspoon salt
¾ cup sour cream
2 eggs
1 teaspoon almond extract
1 8-ounce package cream cheese, softened
¼ cup sugar
½ cup raspberry preserves
½ cup sliced almonds

In a large bowl combine the flour and ¾ cup sugar. Using a pastry blender cut in the butter until coarse and crumbly. Reserve 1 cup of the crumb mixture. Add the baking powder, soda, salt, sour cream, 1 egg, and the almond extract. Blend well. Spread the batter over the bottom and 2 inches up the side of a greased and floured 10-inch springform pan.

In a medium bowl combine the cream cheese, ¼ cup sugar, and 1 egg. Blend well. Spread over the batter in the pan. Spoon the preserves evenly over the cheese filling. In a small bowl combine the reserved crumb mixture and sliced almonds. Sprinkle over the top. Bake in a 350° oven for 45 to 55 minutes.

MAKES 8 SERVINGS.

Granola Coffee Cake

2 cups all-purpose flour
½ cup granola
¾ cup white sugar
1 cup firmly packed dark brown sugar
1 teaspoon cinnamon
½ teaspoon salt
¾ cup oil
½ cup nuts
1 teaspoon baking soda
1 teaspoon baking powder
1 cup buttermilk
1 egg
1 teaspoon vanilla extract

In a large bowl mix the flour, granola, sugars, cinnamon, salt, and vegetable oil. Reserve ½ cup for topping. Add the nuts, soda, baking powder, buttermilk, egg, and vanilla. Pour into a 9 x 13-inch pan sprayed with cooking spray. Sprinkle the reserved topping over the batter. Add more nuts to topping, if desired. Bake in a 350° oven for 30 minutes.

MAKES 8 SERVINGS.

Baked Beans with Pancetta and Pecans

2½ pounds white beans
1½ pounds pancetta (or bacon), finely chopped
1 cup honey
2 cups molasses
½ pound dark brown sugar
½ cup prepared mustard
⅛ cup minced fresh garlic
3 onions, diced
2½ teaspoon salt
1 cup maple syrup
½ cup balsamic vinegar
2 cups beef stock
4 cups chopped pecans, toasted
Reserved bean water

Soak the beans in water overnight, drain, and rinse with cold water. Place in a pot, and cover with fresh water. Bring to a boil, then turn down the heat, and simmer until the beans are tender. Strain, and reserve the bean water for later use.

Place the beans in a 2- to 3-inch deep roasting pan. Add the remaining ingredients except for the pecans and bean water. Stir the ingredients thoroughly so they are evenly distributed. Add enough bean water to cover about ½-inch above the beans. Save any remaining bean water. Cover the pan with aluminum foil. Bake in a 325° oven for 5 to 6 hours. Occasionally remove the cover, and stir. Add the remaining bean water if necessary. Remove the cover for the last 45 minutes of baking.

After removing the beans from the oven, stir in the toasted pecans.

Note: This recipe will work without the balsamic vinegar and beef stock if they are not readily available. The beans will keep in the refrigerator for 7 to 10 days and get better with a little age. They also freeze very well.

MAKES 1 GALLON.

Butternut Squash and Pear Gratin

4 teaspoons salt
2 teaspoons pepper
½ tablespoon cinnamon
½ teaspoon grated nutmeg
½ teaspoon ground allspice
½ teaspoon ground cloves
2 teaspoons butter

2½ pounds butternut squash, peeled and sliced not more than ¼-inch thick
5 pears (hard, green, underripe pears work best)
4 cups heavy cream (or half and half or milk)

In a small bowl combine the spices, and set aside.

Butter the baking dish. Layer the bottom of the pan with the sliced squash, overlapping until the bottom is covered. Season evenly with one-third of the spice mix. Slice the pears, and layer them over the squash. (There is no need to overlap, but be sure to layer evenly.) Cover the pears with another layer of squash as done before. Season with half of the remaining spice mix. Add another layer of pears. Finish with the remaining sliced squash and spices.

Slowly pour 2 cups of cream over the layers so as not to disturb the layering. Press down on the layers using your hands. Pour on the remaining cream, and press down again. Cover with aluminum foil. Bake in a 350° oven for 1 hour.

Remove the foil, and continue cooking for 15 minutes or until tender when pierced with a knife.

Chill the gratin overnight so the heavy cream has a chance to solidify with the squash and pears. To serve, slice into squares, and remove from baking pan. Reheat on a cookie sheet in a 350° oven for 5 to 7 minutes.

MAKES 6 TO 8 SERVINGS.

Combes Family Inn

953 East Lake Road
Ludlow, Vermont 05149
(800) 822-8799

*T*his is a true family inn situated on fifty acres of meadows and woods in the heart of Vermont's mountain and lake region. The dining room has exposed beams and a large bay window overlooking pastures and the Okemo Mountains. The lounge is paneled in weathered barn wood, contributing to the homey, country atmosphere of the inn. Nearby attractions include the alpine slide at Bromley (especially appealing to children), Okemo Mountain Resort, Lake Rescue and Echo Lake, and several ski resorts.

Cranberry Nut Bread

- 2 cups all-purpose flour
- ½ teaspoon baking soda
- ½ teaspoon salt
- ½ teaspoon baking powder
- 1 egg
- 1 cup sugar
- 2 tablespoons shortening
  Juice and zest of 1 orange, adding enough boiling water to make ¾ cup of liquid
- 1 cup nuts
- 1 cup chopped cranberries

Grease and flour a 9 x 5-inch loaf pan. In a medium bowl sift the flour, soda, salt, and baking powder. In a large bowl beat the egg, sugar, and shortening. Add the dry ingredients alternately with the liquid. Stir in the nuts and cranberries. Pour into the prepared pan. Bake in a 325° oven for 1 hour.

Note: Orange juice may be substituted for the freshly squeezed orange.

MAKES 1 LOAF.

Ham and Cheese Pancakes

- ¾ cup yellow cornmeal
- ¾ cup all-purpose flour
- 1 teaspoon baking powder
- ¼ teaspoon baking soda
- ¼ teaspoon salt
- 1½ cups buttermilk (or sour milk)
- 3 eggs, separated
- ¼ cup melted butter
- ⅓ cup diced Vermont sharp Cheddar cheese
- ⅓ cup finely chopped ham
  Whipped butter and maple syrup

In a medium bowl blend the cornmeal, flour, baking powder, soda, and salt. In a large bowl whisk the buttermilk, egg yolks, and 1 ½ tablespoons of melted butter. Add the dry ingredients. In a separate bowl beat the egg whites until stiff, and fold in to the mixture.

In a large skillet heat 1 tablespoon melted butter. Working in batches, pour ¼ cup of batter into pan. Cook about 3 minutes per side until cakes are bubbly and golden. Add more butter to the pan as needed. Serve with whipped butter and Vermont maple syrup.

Note: For brunch use crumbled blue cheese instead of Cheddar cheese.

MAKES 4 SERVINGS.

Vermont Fiddlehead Pie

- 1 unbaked 8-inch pie crust
- 2 tablespoons olive oil
- 2 cups of coarsely chopped fiddleheads (or broccoli or zucchini)
- 1 small onion, chopped
- 1 cup shredded sharp or mild Vermont Cheddar cheese
- 4 eggs
- 1 tablespoon coarse mustard
- 2 tablespoons flour
- 1 cup evaporated milk (or half and half)

Precook the pie crust in a 350° oven (to prevent a soggy crust).

In a skillet heat the olive oil and sauté the fiddleheads and onion. Place in the precooked crust, followed by the Cheddar cheese. In a medium bowl blend the eggs, mustard, flour, and half and half, and pour into the pie crust over the other ingredients. Bake in a 350° oven for 50 minutes. The pie is cooked when a knife inserted into the center comes out clean. Let set for 5 minutes or so before cutting. Serve hot, warm, or cold.

MAKES 8 SERVINGS.

Echo Lake Inn

Echo Lake Inn
≈

Route 100 Tyson
Ludlow, Vermont 05149
(802) 228-8602

*O*ne of the historic inns of Vermont, Echo Lake has been welcoming guests since 1840. Its long heritage includes frequent visits by President Calvin Coolidge, who was born nearby. The twenty-six guest rooms range from suites to shared and family units, each individually decorated. Also available are modern condominium units in a restored cheese factory next door. Guest-pleasing amenities include a living room with a fireplace, a swimming pool, a front porch with antique rocking chairs, and a tennis court. Major ski resorts are nearby.

Pasta Trilogy

- 1 cup sour cream
- 1 cup heavy cream
  ....
- 12 large shrimp, peeled and deveined
- ½ pound fresh sea scallops
- ½ cup butter
- 3 ounces Pernod
  Meat from 1 cooked lobster, diced
  Salt and pepper to taste
- 12 ounces fresh angel hair pasta

Whisk the creams together in a small bowl. Place the crème fraîche in a covered jar in a warm area for 12 hours.

In a large sauté pan sauté the shrimp and scallops in butter. Remove when cooked through. Add the Pernod and crème fraîche to the liquid in the sauté pan. Reduce by about half or until the desired sauce consistency is reached. Return the shrimp and scallops to the pan, and add the diced lobster meat. Season with salt and pepper to taste.

In a pot cook the angel hair pasta in boiling water until al dente. Top with the trilogy mixture.

MAKES 4 SERVINGS.

Vermont Apple Soup with Curry

>   2   tablespoons butter
>   1   medium onion, chopped
>   1   pound Granny Smith apples, peeled,
>   cored, and diced
>   1   tablespoon curry powder
>   2½   cups chicken stock
>   ½   cup whipping cream
>   Salt and pepper to taste
>   Sour cream (optional)
>   Chopped fresh chives (optional)

In a large heavy saucepan melt the butter over medium heat. Add the onion, and sauté 4 minutes. Add the apples, and sauté about 3 minutes until the apples begin to soften. Add the curry powder, and cook 15 seconds. Gradually stir in the stock. Increase the heat, and simmer about 10 minutes until the apples are tender. Add the cream, and simmer 5 minutes. Season with salt and pepper. Ladle the soup into bowls. If desired, top with a dollop of sour cream, and sprinkle with chives.

Note: This can be prepared 2 hours ahead. Cover and refrigerate, then rewarm over medium heat.

MAKES 4 SERVINGS.

Scallop-Stuffed Norwegian Salmon en Papillotes

>   1   carrot
>   1   onion
>   1   stalk celery
>   4   boneless salmon fillets
>   ½   pound sea scallops
>   4   parchment sheets (12 x 16 inches)
>   Salt and pepper to taste
>   1   lemon, thinly sliced
>   4   sprigs fresh dill
>   ½   cup white wine
>   ½   cup butter

Julienne the carrot, onion, and celery, and set aside. Slice each salmon fillet lengthwise down the center about three-fourths of the way through. Insert 3 or 4 scallops. Place

each stuffed fillet centered on half of a parchment sheet. Season the fish with salt and pepper, then cover it with the julienned vegetables. Arrange 3 slices of lemon over the vegetables, top with dill, and sprinkle with white wine. Dot with butter. Fold each parchment in half over the salmon. Crimp the edges by making tight folds every inch or so all around to seal completely. Place on a baking sheet. Bake in a 350° oven for 8 to 10 minutes. Cut a cross in the top of the parchment before serving.

MAKES 4 SERVINGS.

The Governors Inn

❧

*86 Main Street
Ludlow, Vermont 05149
(802) 228-8830*

*T*his inn was built in 1890 by Vermont Governor William W. Stickney as a wedding present for his bride. Less than one mile from Okemo Mountain, it offers eight guest rooms decorated with period antiques. Oriental rugs, brass beds, and polished oak trim throughout add to the elegant and lush atmosphere of the Governor's Inn. The common areas include a foyer with a fireplace and a living room with an ornate slate fireplace. Nearby lakes and the Black River are popular scenic attractions of this region of Vermont.*

Charlie's Breakfast Porridge

>   3   cups water
>   1½   teaspoons salt
>   2   cups old-fashioned oats
>   2   eggs
>   1   cup milk
>   ¼   cup dark molasses

>   3   ounces Vermont maple syrup
>   ¼   cup firmly packed brown sugar
>   ½   teaspoon ground cinnamon
>   ¾   teaspoon grated nutmeg
>   1½   teaspoons ground ginger
>   ¼   pound golden raisins
>   ¼   cup chopped walnuts
>   Vanilla ice cream

In a saucepan boil the water and salt. Add the oats, and cook 5 minutes. Cool.

In a separate bowl combine the remaining ingredients, and add to the oatmeal. Pour into a greased 9 x 13-inch baking pan. Bake in a 350° oven for 1 hour. Serve hot with a small dab of vanilla ice cream.

MAKES 8 SERVINGS.

Graham Cracker Breakfast Cakes

>   ¾   cup all-purpose flour
>   ¾   cup graham cracker crumbs
>   1   tablespoon baking powder
>   1   tablespoon salt
>   1   cup milk
>   2   tablespoons melted butter
>   1   egg
>   ½   cup chopped pecans
>   Vanilla ice cream
>   Maple syrup

In a large mixing bowl combine the flour, graham cracker crumbs, baking powder, and salt. In a separate bowl combine the milk, butter, and egg. Add to the flour mixture, and mix well. Add the nuts. For each cake pour ¼ cup on a prepared griddle. Serve with vanilla ice cream and maple syrup.

MAKES 4 SERVINGS.

Parsnip Vichyssoise

>   2   large leeks, white parts only, halved
>   lengthwise and sliced crosswise
>   ½-inch thick
>   3   pounds parsnips, peeled, and cut
>   into chunks
>   3   medium boiling potatoes, peeled
>   and cut into chunks
>   3   large garlic cloves, crushed
>   1   large onion, halved and thinly sliced
>   2   tablespoons firmly packed light
>   brown sugar
>   1   teaspoon ground cardamom
>   3   cups chicken stock, divided
>   3   cups white wine

½ *cup unsalted butter, cut into small*
   pieces
¼ *cup fresh lemon juice*
2½ *cups half and half*   2½
   cups heavy cream
   Salt and freshly ground pepper
   Whole chives for garnish

In a large roasting pan combine the leeks, parsnips, potatoes, garlic, and onion. Sprinkle with the brown sugar and cardamom, and stir to combine. Pour 2 cups of chicken stock and the white wine over the vegetables, and dot with butter. Cover tightly with aluminum foil. Braise in a 350° oven for 2 hours until the vegetables are very tender. Lift the foil, and stir the vegetables occasionally.

Transfer the vegetables and any liquid to a large saucepan. Add 1 additional cup of chicken stock and the lemon juice, and bring to a boil. Reduce the heat, and simmer covered for 20 minutes. Working with small batches, blend the soup in a food processor or blender. (The blender will produce a more even result.) Cool, add the creams, and heat, stirring occasionally, until warmed through. Do not boil. Taste for seasoning, and serve garnished with snipped chives and chive blossoms.

MAKES 8 SERVINGS.

Our Famous Potato Soufflé

6 *cups mashed potato*
1 *8-ounce container whipped cream*
   cheese with chives
2 *eggs*
¼ *cup sour cream*
   Pinch salt
¼ *cup unsalted butter*

Butter a 1½-quart soufflé dish. In a medium mixing bowl place all the ingredients, and mix well. Pour into the prepared soufflé dish. Bake in a 400° oven for 45 minutes.

MAKES 6 TO 8 SERVINGS.

The Governor's Inn Pretty Potato Prune Pudding

2 *cups mashed white potato*
2 *cups mashed sweet potato*
2 *eggs*
2 *egg yolks*

⅓ *cup fine cornmeal*
   Salt and freshly ground white pepper
½ *cup unsalted butter*
15 *dried pitted prunes (they should be*
   fresh and soft)
Parsley for garnish
   Yellow daylillies for garnish

Butter a 1½-quart soufflé mold. Prepare the white and sweet potatoes separately. Sieve the potatoes into separate bowls with a ricer or strainer. To each of the potatoes add 1 egg and 1 egg yolk, and half of the cornmeal, salt, pepper, and butter. Set aside. Prepare the prunes by chopping them into quarters.

Spread the white potato mixture into the bottom of the mold. Arrange the prunes over the top and cover with the sweet potato mixture. Cover the pudding with a piece of buttered waxed paper, and place in a roasting pan large enough to accommodate the mold, and pour water deep enough to come about halfway up the sides around the mold. Bake in a 325° oven for 1 hour and 30 minutes. The potato is done when a toothpick inserted in the center comes out clean and is hot to the touch. Unmold the pudding on a round platter, and garnish around the base with parsley and a few yellow daylilies. Slice or scoop the pudding, and serve.

MAKES 6 TO 8 SERVINGS.

Scallop Mousse Florentine Croûte

1 *small clove garlic*
8 *ounces scallops*
1 *egg*
½ *teaspoon salt*
⅛ *teaspoon ground hot red pepper*
   Cayenne pepper
½ *cup heavy cream, chilled*
1 *teaspoon chopped fresh tarragon*
8 *sheets phyllo dough (17 x 12 inches)*
½ *cup butter, melted*
   Cornmeal
4 *cups chopped fresh spinach*
   Hollandaise sauce

In a food processor finely chop the garlic. Add the scallops, egg, salt, and pepper, and process until smooth. With the motor running, add the cream in a thin stream. Stop immediately when all the cream is added.

Transfer to a bowl, and stir in the tarragon. Refrigerate.

Cover the phyllo with damp towel. Place 1 sheet of phyllo on waxed paper. Brush with butter, and sprinkle with cornmeal. Repeat with the remaining sheets, stacking them. Spread the spinach over the phyllo. Pipe the mousse lengthwise in 2-inch strips, leaving a ½-inch border. Using the waxed paper as guide, roll up the phyllo tightly. Place on a greased baking sheet. Score in 6 equal slices. Bake in a 400° oven for 20 to 25 minutes until golden. Cut into 6 slices. Serve on a heated plate in a pool of Hollandaise sauce.

MAKES 6 SERVINGS.

Vermont Chicken with Apples

1 *tablespoon olive oil*
1 *tablespoon unsalted butter*
4 *medium-sized boneless chicken*
   breasts, cut in half at middle,
   skin on
⅓ *cup chopped shallots*
¼ *cup apple brandy (Calvados)*
¼ *teaspoon dried thyme*
¼ *teaspoon salt*
¼ *teaspoon freshly cracked pepper*
¾ *cup apple juice*
2 *Granny Smith apples, halved, cored,*
   and sliced
¾ *cup heavy cream*
   Chopped parsley for garnish

In a large sauté pan heat the olive oil and butter, and brown the chicken. Remove the chicken and drain off all but 1 tablespoon of the pan drippings. Add the shallots, and sauté until soft, scraping up some of the browned bits in the sauté pan. Return the chicken to sauté pan, and pour in the apple brandy. Carefully ignite and let the flame die down. Sprinkle the chicken with the thyme, salt, and half of the pepper. Pour the apple juice over the chicken, and bring to a boil. Lower the heat, and simmer covered for 20 minutes.

Remove the cover and place the apples on the chicken. Cover, and cook 10 minutes longer. (Chicken temperature should read 160°, and apples should be tender.) With a slotted spoon remove the chicken and apples to a serving platter, and keep warm. Pour the pan drippings into a glass measuring cup, and allow to stand a few minutes for fat to rise to the top. Remove the fat. Return the juices to the sauté pan, bring quickly to a boil, and reduce by almost half. (The sauce will begin to look like syrup.) Stir in the cream, and heat until the sauce starts to thicken. Spoon over the chicken and apples. Garnish with chopped parsley.

MAKES 4 SERVINGS.

Suprêmes de Volaille Emballe

½   large chicken breast per serving
1   16-ounce can whole berry cranberry sauce
    Butter
1   package phyllo dough, defrosted in the refrigerator

Cut each ½ chicken breast crosswise (not lengthwise). Pound each piece lightly to flatten. Place 1 tablespoon of cranberry sauce and 1 tablespoon of butter on one piece of breast, and place another breast on top. Cut the defrosted phyllo dough in half lengthwise. Brush 4 pieces with melted butter. Stack sheets of dough to make an X. Place the chicken in the center, and pull the ends up together, closing them like a beggar's purse on top. Bake in a 375° oven for 25 minutes.

MAKES 1 SERVING.

Pink Grapefruit Sorbet

2   16-ounce cans grapefruit sections
½   cup reserved grapefruit juice
¼   cup vermouth
2   tablespoons grenadine
½   cup simple syrup
4   egg whites

Drain the grapefruit, and reserve ½ cup of juice. Place the drained fruit in a food processor, and with the metal blade in place pulse 5 or 6 times. Add the remaining ingredients, including the ½ cup reserved juice, and freeze in an ice cream maker according to the manufacturer's directions.

Note: Consult an instruction cook book for instructions on how to prepare a simple syrup.

MAKES ABOUT 1 QUART.

Battenkill Inn
❧

P.O. Box 948
Manchester, Vermont 05254
(800) 441-1628

---

*F*rom the balconies of guest rooms in this Victorian farmhouse (built in the 1840s), guests can view Vermont's famous Battenkill River and Green Mountains. Some of the guest rooms also have wood-burning fireplaces. Recreational opportunities available in the area include golf, skiing, and canoeing.

Cream Cheese Roll-Ups

2   8-ounce packages cream cheese (can use low-fat or nonfat)
1   tablespoon mayonnaise (can use low-fat or nonfat)
½   package cracked peppercorn ranch Knorr's Dip Mix (or any flavor)
1   package flour tortillas (burrito size)
    Salsa

In a large bowl mix the cream cheese, mayonnaise, and dip mix together. Spread on the tortillas, roll up, and chill for a couple hours. Cut diagonally into bite-sized pieces, and serve with salsa.

Note: This can be made up to 3 days ahead of time and refrigerated until used.

MAKES 8 TO 12 SERVINGS.

Battenkill Inn

Hot Crab Dip

12   ounces cream cheese, softened
1   6-ounce can crab meat, drained
2   teaspoons prepared horseradish
    Dash Worcestershire sauce
2   tablespoons finely chopped onion
    Fresh dill (or dried)
    Parmesan cheese
    Breadcrumbs

In a large bowl combine the cream cheese, crab meat, horseradish, Worcestershire sauce, and onion. Fill a ramekin or mini soufflé dish with the mixture. Top with Parmesan cheese and breadcrumbs. Bake in a 350° oven for 30 minutes until hot throughout.

Note: Recipe may be made ahead of time and frozen before baking. Low-fat cream cheese works well in this recipe.

MAKES ABOUT 12 SERVINGS.

Battenkill Inn Brown Apple Betty

    McIntosh apples
1   16-ounce box gingersnaps
    Brown sugar to taste
    Sugar to taste
    Ground cinnamon to taste
    Allspice to taste
    Ginger to taste
    Nutmeg to taste
½   cup butter
½   cup pecan pieces

Depending on what size pan you use, core and slice enough apples to fill either a 8 x 12-inch or a 9-inch square pan. In a small bowl mix a couple of tablespoons of brown sugar and white sugar, and add the cinnamon, allspice, nutmeg and ginger to taste.

In a saucepan melt the butter. In a medium bowl crush the ginger snaps. Add the melted butter, the nuts, and a couple tablespoons of brown sugar. Layer this on top of the apple mixture. Bake in a 350° oven for approximately 45 minutes.

MAKES 6 TO 8 SERVINGS.

Orange Whiskey French Toast

1   *loaf French bread (or homemade bread)*
½   *orange, grated*
4   *large eggs*
2   *teaspoons half and half (or heavy cream or milk)*
3   *tablespoons whiskey (or orange liquor or brandy)*

Slice the bread into 1½-inch slices. In a food processor grate the orange. In a 9 x 11-inch baking dish mix the eggs, orange, milk, and whiskey together. Place the bread slices in the mixture for a couple minutes, then flip. Cook on a hot griddle for approximately 3 minutes, flip. Cook until golden brown.

Note: Grate the whole orange, and freeze the leftovers to add to muffins, pancakes or sauces for extra flavor.

Variation: Grease the bottom of a 9 x 11-inch baking dish. Arrange the bread slices on the bottom of the dish. Pour the egg mixture over the bread. Cover, and refrigerate until the mixture is soaked up by the bread (or overnight). Bake in a 350° oven for 20 minutes or until golden brown.

MAKES 6 TO 8 SERVINGS.

Sweet Potato and Cheddar Johnnycakes

¾   *cup all-purpose flour*
1½   *cups cornmeal*
5   *teaspoons baking powder*
1   *teaspoon salt*
_____
¼   *cup oil*
2   *cups peeled and grated sweet potatoes*
½   *cup diced scallions*
1   *cup chopped McIntosh apple*
_____
3   *eggs, beaten*
1½   *cups milk*
   Clarified butter
1   *apple, julienned*
   Maple syrup
   Sliced Cheddar cheese

In a large bowl mix the flour, cornmeal, baking powder, and salt. In a skillet heat the oil and sauté the sweet potatoes, scallions, and chopped apple until the sweet potato is fully cooked. Allow to cool, and add the mixture to the dry ingredients. Add the eggs and milk, and mix well. Pan-fry by spoonful in clarified butter. Serve with the julienned apple, maple syrup, and sliced Cheddar cheese.

MAKES 12 5-INCH JOHNNYCAKES.

1811 House

Route 7-A, Box 39
Manchester, Vermont 05254
(800) 432-1811

_____

Built in the 1770s, the house has operated as an inn since 1811, except for a period when it was the private residence of Mary Lincoln Isham, granddaugher of President Abraham Lincoln. This property, listed on the National Register of Historic Places, is a classic example of the Federal style of architecture from the early 1800s. The fourteen guest rooms feature such amenities as canopied beds, fireplaces, oriental rugs, fine paintings, and fireplaces. Sitting on a seven-acre lawn with flower gardens and a pond, it offers a beautiful view of Vermont's Green Mountains. Nearby activities include golf, swimming, fishing, skiing, canoeing, and fine shops and restaurants.

Chicken Diable

2   *pounds boneless, skinless chicken breasts*
¼   *cup margarine or butter*
½   *cup honey*
¼   *cup Dijon mustard*
1   *teaspoon salt*
1   *tablespoon (or more) curry powder*

Cut the chicken into strips. Wash and dry. In a shallow baking pan melt the margarine, and stir in the remaining ingredients. Roll the chicken in the mixture, and arrange in a single layer in the baking pan. Bake in a 350° oven for approximately 10 minutes, turning once, until golden in color.

Note: Use chicken tenders in place of cut chicken breasts. Good to serve with omelets, scrambled eggs, or waffles, with apple slices as garnish.

MAKES 12 SERVING.

English Toffee

1   *cup butter (not margarine)*
1   *cup sugar*
2   *tablespoons water*
4   *to 6 small milk chocolate bars*
1   *cup chopped pecans*

In a large heavy saucepan combine the butter, sugar, and water. Stir over medium heat until the ingredients are combined. Cook until the mixture reaches the hard crack stage, stirring constantly. Quickly pour the mixture onto an edged cookie sheet. Break the chocolate bars into squares, and place on the hot toffee. As soon as the chocolate softens, spread over the top, and sprinkle with the chopped nuts, pressing them into the chocolate. When cooled, break into bite-sized pieces, and store in a covered container.

MAKES ABOUT 2 POUNDS.

1811 House Soufflé

1   *loaf white sandwich bread*
   Butter or margarine, softened
1   *package Old English cheese slices*
1   *large (or 2 small) chicken breasts, skinned and cut into bite-size pieces*
8   *large eggs (or 6 jumbo)*
1   *tablespoon chopped fresh rosemary*
3   *cups milk*
   Salt and freshly ground pepper

Cut the crust from enough slices of bread to fit snugly into a 9 x 13-inch baking dish (2 layers needed). Butter one side of each bread slice, and fit half the slices, butter-side up, into the bottom of the dish. Cover the bread with cheese slices, then sprinkle the chicken evenly over the cheese. Top with the remaining bread slices, butter-side up. In a blender beat together the eggs, rosemary, milk, salt, and pepper. Carefully pour the egg mixture over the bread in the casserole, making sure all the top bread is moistened. Cover tightly with plastic wrap, and refrigerate overnight.

Bake in a 325° oven for 1 hour or until nicely puffed and browned on top. Cut into squares, and serve.

MAKES 10 SERVINGS.

Jumbo Crunchy Chocolate Chip Cookies

3½   cups all-purpose flour
 1   tablespoon baking soda
 1   teaspoon salt
½   cup butter
½   cup margarine
 1   cup firmly packed brown sugar
 1   cup sugar
 1   egg
 2   teaspoons vanilla extract
 1   cup oil
1½   cups corn flakes
1½   cups oatmeal
 1   12-ounce package chocolate chips

In a large bowl mix the flour, soda, and salt together. In a separate bowl cream the butter, margarine, and sugars well. Beat in the egg and vanilla. Stir in the flour mixture alternately with the oil until all is thoroughly mixed. Stir in the corn flakes, oatmeal, and chocolate chips. Chill the dough for approximately one hour before baking.

Drop by heaping tablespoons (or use a small ice cream scoop) onto an ungreased cookie sheet 3 inches apart (or by teaspoonfuls if smaller cookies are desired). Bake in a 350° oven for 13 to 14 minutes (for large cookies) or until golden brown. Cool on racks.

MAKES ABOUT 40 4-INCH COOKIES.

The Inn at Manchester

❧

P.O. Box 41
Manchester, Vermont 05254
(800) 273-1793

Built in 1867, this building was renovated under the auspices of the Vermont Department of Historic Preservation. The result is a guest house that blends the Victorian elegance of the past with the finest of amenities demanded by modern guests. Memorable paintings, prints, and posters hang throughout the inn, complementing the Victorian antiques. Guests enjoy beautiful views of the mountains and meadows from the pool or the spacious front porch. Other nice touches are a parlor and library. Skiing, bicycling, swimming, fishing, and canoeing are available nearby.

Chocolate Chip Coffee Cake

 2   cups all-purpose flour
½   cup sugar
 1   cup melted butter
 1   cup sour cream
 2   eggs
 2   tablespoons milk
 1   tablespoon vanilla extract
 2   teaspoons baking powder
 1   teaspoon baking soda
 6   ounces semisweet mini chocolate chips
½   cup chopped nuts (optional)
   Confectioners' sugar (optional)

Butter and flour a 10-inch tube pan. In a large bowl mix the dry ingredients together. Make a well in the center of the flour, and add the remaining ingredients 1 at a time. Add the chips and nuts, if desired, last. Turn

---

the batter into the prepared pan. Bake in a 350° oven for 45 minutes or until lightly browned on top. Sprinkle with confectioners' sugar, if desired.

Note: Best served the day after baking.

MAKES 8 SERVINGS.

Aunt Rose's Famous Date and Nut Bread

 1   teaspoon baking soda
 1   cup boiling water
 1   cup raisins (see note below)
 1   tablespoons shortening
¾   cup sugar
 1   egg
 1   teaspoon vanilla extract
½   teaspoon unsweetened cocoa
1¾   cups all-purpose flour
½   cup chopped nuts

In a medium bowl dissolve the soda in the boiling water, and soak the raisins for a half an hour. In a separate bowl cream the shortening with the sugar. Add the egg, vanilla, cocoa, and the raisin mixture. Blend in the flour. Add the nuts. Pour the batter into a 5 x 9-inch loaf pan. Bake in a 350° oven for 45 minutes.

Note: This recipe was often prepared by the innkeeper's Aunt Rose. Raisins were usually substituted for the dates, but it was always called date and nut bread. Cream cheese is delicious on this bread.

MAKES 1 LOAF.

Manchester Highlands Inn

*Highland Avenue
Manchester, Vermont 05255
(800) 743-4565*

This Victorian-style inn offers fifteen guest rooms with such special touches as antique furnishings, feather beds, down comforters, and lace curtains. Other amenities are the swimming pool and a pub. Within a few miles are the ski areas at Stratton and Bromley, as well as other popular sports activities, including golf, swimming, canoeing, tennis, and fine restaurants and shops.

Banana Walnut Pancakes à la Mode

- 1 cup all-purpose flour
- ¼ cup walnuts
  Pinch salt
- 1 teaspoon sugar
- ¼ cup wheat germ
- 1 teaspoon baking soda
- 1 very ripe banana
- 1 cup buttermilk
- 1 egg
- 1 pint maple walnut ice cream, softened
  Maple syrup

In a food processor place the flour, walnuts, salt, sugar, wheat germ, soda, and banana, and blend for about 15 seconds. Add the buttermilk and egg. Process until smooth. Cook on a hot griddle for about 3 minutes per side until the pancakes are golden. To serve, top with a small scoop of ice cream. Sprinkle with more chopped nuts, if desired, and pass around the warm Vermont maple syrup.

MAKES 4 SERVINGS.

Best Ever Kahlua Brownies

- 3 ounces unsweetened chocolate
- 6 tablespoons butter
- 1½ cups sugar
- 3 large eggs
- 3 tablespoons kahlua
- 1½ teaspoons vanilla extract
- ¾ cup unbleached flour
  Pinch salt

In a large microwave-safe bowl melt the chocolate and butter in the microwave. Add the sugar, and mix to combine. Add the eggs, kahlua, and vanilla, and mix well. Stir in the flour and salt. Pour the batter into a greased 8 x 10-inch baking pan. Bake in a preheated 350° oven for 25 minutes.

Note: For a change of pace, substitute amaretto or peppermint schnapps for the kahlua. Or, for peanut butter lovers, add ½ cup (or more) to the batter before cooking.

MAKES 8 SERVINGS.

Lemon Soufflé Pancakes

- 3 jumbo eggs (or 4 large eggs), separated
- 1 cup low-fat cottage cheese
- 1 tablespoon Vermont maple syrup
- 2 tablespoons fresh lemon juice
- 2 teaspoons lemon zest
- 2 tablespoons oil
- 2 teaspoons baking powder
- ½ cup all-purpose flour
  Pinch salt

In a food processor blend together the egg yolks, cottage cheese, syrup, lemon juice and zest, and oil. Process for 20 seconds. Add the baking powder, flour, and salt. Process for 10 seconds. In a small bowl beat the egg whites just until they hold stiff peaks. Fold the egg whites gently into the batter. Cook on a hot greased griddle for about 3 minutes per side or until golden. Serve immediately with warm Vermont maple syrup, of course.

MAKES 12 MEDIUM PANCAKES.

*Woodward Road
Mendon, Vermont 05701
(800) 752-0570*

General John Woodward built the Red Clover Inn in 1840 as a summer estate. It has thirteen guest rooms—eight in the main house and five in the carriage house—all of which offer a good view of the surrounding mountains. Other nice touches include the swimming pool, hiking paths, and cross-country skiing trails. Guests also enjoy the many recreational activities offered by this area, including golf, swimming, tennis, and skiing.

Maple Walnut Vinaigrette

- ½ cup chopped walnuts
- 1 tablespoon chopped celery leaves
- 1 teaspoon minced garlic
- 1 tablespoon minced shallots
- ¼ cup maple syrup
- ¼ cup sherry vinegar
- ½ cup cider vinegar
- ¼ cup walnut oil
- 1½ cups salad oil
  Salt and pepper to taste

In a container with a tight-fitting lid combine all the ingredients, and mix well.

MAKES ABOUT 3 CUPS.

Black and White Chocolate Macaroon Tart

- 3 cups flaked coconut
- ⅓ cup sugar (only use if coconut is unsweetened)
- 2 egg whites
- 2 tablespoons all-purpose flour

6 *ounces white chocolate*
⅔ *cup sour cream*
2 *egg yolks*
⅔ *cup heavy cream*
6 *ounces dark chocolate*
2 *tablespoons rum*

Line the bottom of a 9-inch tart pan with parchment paper or waxed paper. Combine the coconut, sugar, egg whites, and flour, and pour into the prepared tart pan. Bake in a 375° oven for 20 minutes.

In the top of a double boiler over simmering water melt the white chocolate. Combine with the sour cream, and set aside. In a separate pan over the double boiler, heat and stir the egg yolks and heavy cream until thick. Add the dark chocolate, and heat until melted. Remove from the heat, and add the rum. Spoon into the tart shell, alternating 1 dollop of white with 1 dollop of dark. When all has been added, swirl with a knife until marbled. Chill.

MAKES 6 TO 8 SERVINGS.

Couscous-stuffed Cornish Game Hens

1 *cup chicken stock*
1 *cup water*
1 *onion*
1 *stalk celery*
1 *cup mushrooms*
  Butter
1 *tablespoon fresh sage (or 1 teaspoon dried)*
2 *cups couscous*
  Salt and pepper to taste

....

4 *Cornish game hens*
1 *tablespoon thyme*
1 *tablespoon sage*
2 *tablespoons chopped garlic*
  Salt and freshly ground pepper to taste
  Juice from 1 lime

In a saucepan bring the stock and water to a boil. In a skillet sauté the vegetables in butter until tender. Add the sage and couscous, and stir to coat. Add the boiling liquid. Cover, and let sit for 5 minutes. Season with salt and pepper.

Loosen the skin on the Cornish hen breasts. In a small bowl combine the herbs and seasonings. Rub the herb mixture under the skin. Stuff the hens with the couscous fill-

ing. Place the hens in a roasting pan. Preheat the oven to 400°, then reduce to 350°. Roast approximately 45 minutes or until done.

MAKES 4 SERVINGS.

Pumpkin Bisque

2 *tablespoons butter*
1 *medium onion, chopped*
2 *stalks celery, chopped*
3 *cloves garlic, chopped*
4 *cups light vegetable stock (or light chicken stock or water)*
2 *tomatoes, chopped*
2 *bay leaves*
½ *teaspoon grated nutmeg*
2 *cups pumpkin purée*
1 *cup heavy cream*
  Salt and pepper to taste

In a stockpot melt the butter and sauté the onions, celery, and garlic. Add the stock, tomatoes, bay leaves, and nutmeg. Cook until the vegetables are very soft. Strain, and reserve the liquid.

In a food processor or blender purée the vegetables with some of the reserved liquid, and strain through a sieve. In the stockpot combine the remaining liquid, puréed vegetables, and pumpkin, and heat. Add the cream, and season with salt and pepper.

MAKES 4 TO 6 SERVINGS.

Oatmeal Cinnamon Raisin Bread

1½ *cups old-fashioned oats*
1½ *cups boiling water*
3 *tablespoons butter*
3 *tablespoons honey*
1 *tablespoon firmly packed brown sugar*
2 *teaspoons salt*
½ *cup raisins*
1 *tablespoon active dry yeast*
2 *eggs*
4 *to 5 cups unbleached flour*

....

3 *tablespoons melted butter*
1 *cup sugar combined with 2 tablespoons ground cinnamon*

In a large bowl combine the oats and boiling water. Add the butter, honey, brown sugar, salt, and raisins. Let cool until warm (about 100°) Add the yeast, eggs, and flour, and mix well.

On a lightly floured board knead the dough for 10 minutes. Place in a greased bowl, cover, and let rise until doubled in bulk. Punch down, and cut in half. Roll out each half into a rectangle. Brush with melted butter, and sprinkle with the cinnamon-sugar mixture.

Roll up, tuck in the ends, and place in greased loaf pans. Allow to rise until doubled in bulk. Bake in a 375° oven for 40 minutes. Remove from the pan, and cool on racks. Brush with additional melted butter, if desired.

MAKES 2 LOAVES.

Swift House Inn

❦

25 Stewart Lane
Middlebury, Vermont 05753
(802) 388-9925

G*uests have a choice of rooms in three different buildings at this inn: the main house, the gatehouse, or the carriage house. These rooms feature such amenities as claw-foot tubs, marble fireplaces, antiques, oversized four-poster beds, and fresh flowers. The common areas include a winding staircase, a cherry-paneled dining room, and several sitting rooms for reading or relaxing. Guests may select from many attractions in the area, including golf, biking, hiking, or fishing. Concerts, theaters, and specialty shops are within easy walking distance.*

Swift House Inn

Swift House Inn Shrimp, Chicken, Smoked Sausage Louisiana

6 *tablespoons olive oil*
1 *pound thinly sliced kielbasa*
1 *large onion, chopped*
1 *large green bell pepper, chopped*
5 *stalks celery, chopped*
4 *cloves garlic, minced*
1 *hot jalapeño pepper, seeded and minced*
1 *tablespoon dried oregano*
1 *tablespoon chili powder*
1 *tablespoon cumin*
1 *28-ounce can whole peeled tomatoes*
32 *large shrimp (2 pounds), cleaned and shelled*
4 *boneless chicken breasts, cubed*
   Salt to taste
4 *cups cooked brown rice*

In a skillet heat 2 tablespoons of oil and sauté the kielbasa in until brown. Set aside.

In a separate skillet heat 2 tablespoons of oil and sauté the onion, green pepper, and celery for 5 minutes or until soft. Add the garlic, hot pepper, oregano, chili, and cumin, and sauté 1 minute. Drain the tomatoes, reserving the liquid, and add to the vegetables with the kielbasa. Stir, adding more tomato liquid if needed.

In a skillet heat 2 tablespoons of oil and sauté the shrimp and chicken for about 5 minutes until just cooked, and stir into the kielbasa mixture. Season with salt. Serve over steamed brown rice.

Note: This can be prepared to the point of adding the shrimp and chicken and reheated to finish.

MAKES 8 SERVINGS.

Swift House Inn Poppy Seed Bread

2½ *cups sugar*
2 *cups butter, melted and cooled*
½ *cup maple syrup*
2 *cups half and half*
5 *large eggs*
2 *teaspoons vanilla extract*
¾ *cup poppy seeds*
4½ *cups all-purpose flour*
4½ *teaspoons baking powder*

In a large bowl mix the sugar, butter, maple syrup, half and half, eggs, and vanilla. Gently stir in the remaining ingredients. Do not overmix. Divide among 3 greased loaf pans. Bake in a 350° oven for 1 hour or until a toothpick inserted in the center comes out clean.

MAKES 3 LOAVES.

Hortonville Inn

Hortonville Inn

❧

R. D. 1, Box 14
Mount Holly, Vermont 05758
(802) 259-2587

G*uests enjoy the country charm and "down-home" living they find at Hortonville Inn, situated on thirteen wooded acres near the town of Mount Joy. Many old-fashioned country stores filled with native crafts and Vermont products are also available nearby for leisurely browsing. Several ski resorts are within an easy drive.*

Hot Mulled Cider

1 *gallon apple juice (or cider)*
2 *teaspoons whole cloves*
2 *or 3 cinnamon sticks, broken*
1 *cup firmly packed brown sugar*
6 *tablespoons margarine (optional)*

In a large kettle pour the apple juice, and add the cloves, cinnamon, and sugar. Heat for 30 minutes, stirring occasionally, until the sugar is melted. For extra richness, melt 6 tablespoons of margarine in the mixture.

Note: To store, let sit 1 day, then strain and discard the spices. Bottle the cider, and store in the refrigerator.

MAKES 1 GALLON.

Sherried Mushrooms

½ *cup butter*
¾ *teaspoon garlic powder*
2½ *tablespoons cooking sherry*
1 *6-ounce can mushroom stems and pieces, drained*

In a microwave-safe dish melt the butter in a microwave with the garlic powder and cooking sherry. When melted add the mushrooms, stir, and reheat until nicely warmed.

Note: Good for hors d'oeuvres

MAKES 4 SERVINGS.

Jamie's Stuffed Potato Snack

Oil
4 *potatoes*
2 *cups grated Cheddar cheese*
4 *slices bacon, cooked and crumbled*

Slice the potatoes lengthwise ½ inch from the edges. Hollow out the centers of the potatoes. In a skillet heat oil for deep frying. Drop the hollowed potatoes into the hot grease until golden brown and tender. Remove from the grease, and pat dry. Fill the hollowed potatoes with a mixture of grated Cheddar cheese and bacon pieces. Bake in a 400° oven until the cheese melts.

Note: Great as a side dish or as a snack.

MAKES 8.

Strawberry Delight Spread for Breads or Waffles

1 *tablespoon honey*
1 *cup butter, softened*
½ *cup frozen strawberries, thawed, with syrup*

In a medium bowl mix the honey and butter until soft. Gradually add the berries and juice until blended.

Note: Keeps 3 weeks in the refrigerator.

MAKES 1½ CUPS.

Brookside Farms

P.O. Box 36, Hwy. 22-A
Orwell, Vermont 05760
(802) 948-2727

*T*his unique inn—with its massive white columns reminiscent of a southern plantation mansion— reflects the neoclassic Greek Revival style of architecture. Built originally in 1789, it was enlarged in 1843. It's listed on the National Register of Historic Places. Seven guest rooms, all furnished with antiques, are available in the main house as well as the adjoining tenant house. Brookside doubles as a three-hundred-acre working farm specializing in livestock and maple syrup production. Guests have access to miles of hiking paths and cross-country skiing trails on the estate.

Hearty Buttermilk Berry Cakes Breakfast

- 1   6-ounce can frozen orange juice
- 1   42-ounce can Hawaiian pineapple juice
- 8   medium-sized strawberries
....
- 16   slices bacon
....
- 8   leaves kale, washed and drained
- 4   kiwis, halved
- 4   strawberries, halved
    Raspberries, washed and drained
....
- 2⅔   cups buttermilk
- 2   large eggs
- 3   cups all-purpose flour
- 2½   tablespoons cinnamon sugar
- 2   teaspoons baking powder
- 1½   teaspoons baking soda

- ½   teaspoon salt
- 1   cup raspberries
- 1   cup thin sliced bananas
    Confectioners' sugar
    Parsley for garnish
    Vermont maple syrup, warmed

In a pitcher combine the frozen orange juice and pineapple juice. Mix thoroughly. Serve in champagne flutes. Cut a medium-sized strawberry one-third from the bottom, and place on the rim of the glass.

Prepare the bacon, wrap it in paper towels, and set it on the rear of the stovetop.

On a dinner plate place a leaf of kale at the top. Put half a kiwi and half a strawberry in the center of the kale, and sprinkle 12 or so raspberries around the kiwi and strawberry.

In a large bowl mix the buttermilk, eggs, and flour until smooth. Add the cinnamon sugar, baking powder, soda, and salt one at a time, and mix well. Add 1 cup of raspberries and the bananas. Cook on a medium-high griddle sprayed with cooking spray. Place 4 to 5 good-sized pancakes across a plate. Sprinkle the stack with confectioners' sugar. Place 2 slices of crisp bacon on the middle of the pancake stack. Top with a sprig of parsley, and serve with the warmed syrup.

MAKES 8 SERVINGS.

Brookside Eggs with Sausage

- 8   sausage links (or patties)
- 8   leaves kale
- 2   melons, sliced into quarters, zests removed
    Berries (or 1 11-ounce can mandarin oranges, drained)
- 9   large eggs
- 1   teaspoon granulated garlic
- ¼   teaspoon dried oregano
- ¼   teaspoon dried marjoram
- ¼   teaspoon dried basil
- ½   teaspoon sesame seeds
- 1½   tablespoons chopped parsley
....
    Buttered rye toast
    Jam
    Hazelnut coffee and/or honey lemon tea

In a skillet cook the sausage, and roll in paper towel to drain. Place on the back of the stove. On a plate place a leaf of kale and ¼ slice of melon. Spoon the berries over the melon. Beat the eggs and seasonings until fluffy. Cook in a medium-hot skillet with 1 teaspoon melted butter or cooking spray. Stir frequently until fully scrambled. Place on a plate, and top with the sausage. Serve with buttered rye toast, jam, and hazelnut coffee and/or honey lemon tea.

MAKES 8 SERVINGS.

Baked Tomato and Egg Breakfast

- 4   tomatoes
- 9   eggs
- 1   teaspoon granulated garlic
- ¼   teaspoon dried oregano
- ¼   teaspoon dried marjoram
- ¼   teaspoon dried basil
- ½   teaspoon sesame seeds
- 1½   tablespoonschopped parsley
    Shredded mozzarella cheese
    Cooking spray
    Parsley for garnish
    7-grain toast

Slice off the top and stem of each tomato. Scoop out all seeds and only a bit of the pulp. In a bowl beat the eggs, garlic, oregano, marjoram, basil, sesame seeds, and chopped parsley, and pour into the tomatoes. Sprinkle with shredded mozzarella cheese. Place in a baking dish sprayed lightly with cooking spray. Bake in a 400° oven until the eggs are done. Top with parsley, and serve with 7-grain toast.

Note: This is a great dish for vegetarians.

MAKES 4 SERVINGS.

Lake St. Catherine Inn

Lake St. Catherine Inn

P.O. Box 129
Poultney, Vermont 05764
(802) 287-9347

The natural wonder that gives this inn its unique atmosphere is Lake St. Catherine, a seven-mile-long spring-fed lake in the Green Mountains of Vermont. Right outside the door of all thirty-five guest rooms is the inn's own marina, with aluminum boats, canoes, and paddleboats for the enjoyment of guests. It's the perfect vacation or getaway spot for families with children. The daily room rate includes a five-course dinner as well as breakfast. Other nearby attractions include skiing, summer theater performances, and shopping in antique stores and factory outlets.

Bananas Kahlua

```
3   tablespoons butter
1/3 cup firmly packed light brown sugar
    Pinch ground cinnamon
    Pinch grated nutmeg
1/4 cup kahlua
4   bananas
    Vanilla ice cream (or experiment
       with different flavors)
    Chopped nuts and maraschino cher-
       ries for garnish
```

In a skillet melt the butter, add the sugar, and stir until dissolved. Add cinnamon, nutmeg, and kahlua, and heat until bubbly. Add the bananas, and cook for 3 to 5 minutes until heated throughout. Place the ice cream into stemware, and top with the bananas and sauce. Garnish with the chopped nuts and cherries.
MAKES 4 SERVINGS.

Marinated Mushrooms

```
1   8-ounce carton fresh mushrooms,
       cut into fourths
    Fresh chopped basil, garlic, parsley
       and oregano (dried if fresh
       unavailable)
    Virgin olive oil (or vegetable oil)
    Red wine vinegar
    Salt and pepper to taste
..................................
    Fresh lettuce
1   red bell pepper, roasted and sliced
       for garnish
    Parsley for garnish
```

In a pan of lightly salted water place the mushrooms. Heat to boil. As soon as it comes to a boil, drain and rinse the mushrooms in cold water. In a medium bowl combine the remaining ingredients, and marinate a few hours. Serve on a bed of lettuce garnished with a slice of red pepper and a parsley sprig.
MAKES 6 SERVINGS.

Okemo Lantern Lodge

P.O. Box 247
Proctorsville, Vermont 05153
(802) 226-7770

Built in the early 1800s, this inn in the Green Mountains radiates the warmth of a traditional Victorian home, with its stained-glass windows and natural butternut woodwork. Guests can choose from ten individually decorated rooms, furnished with antiques, wicker furniture and, in some cases, canopy beds. Another nice touch is the heated swimming pool. This area of Vermont is a skiier's delight. Nearby Okemo has eleven lifts for alpine skiing and eighty-three different trails for cross-country enthusiasts.

Okemo Lantern Lodge

Dody Blueberry Pancakes

```
1 1/2 cups all-purpose flour
  2   teaspoons baking soda
  3   tablespoons sugar
  2   eggs
  1   cup milk (approximately)
      Cooking spray
      Fresh blueberries (or frozen)
```

In a large bowl mix together the dry ingredients. In a separate bowl beat the eggs and milk together. Add to the dry ingredients and stir just to remove lumps. Spray a griddle well with cooking spray. Pour the batter onto a hot griddle set at 350°.

Arrange the blueberries on the pancake batter, and cover with a bit more batter. Turn and cook the other side.

Note: If the berries are frozen, the center of the pancakes will take longer to cook.
MAKES 4 TO 6 SERVINGS.

Pasta with Three Mushroom Sauce

```
1/2 cup olive oil
  6 ounces button mushrooms
  2 portabella mushrooms
  3 cloves garlic or more
    A few ounces dried porcini mush-
       rooms, soaked in water and
       rinsed twice
1/2 cup heavy cream
  1 8-ounce package fettuccine, cooked
       (or spaghetti)
    Salt and pepper to taste
```

In a skillet heat the olive oil and sauté the button and portabella mushrooms and garlic. When cooked, add the rehydrated porcini mushrooms with some liquid, and simmer together a few minutes. Add the cream, and boil briefly. Toss with fettuccine. Season to taste.
MAKES 4 TO 6 SERVINGS.

Italian Vegetable Soup

6 tablespoons olive oil
1 onion, chopped
2 cloves garlic
1 zucchini, chopped
1 yellow squash, chopped
  A few mushroom, sliced
1 20-ounce can chicken broth (or
  homemade broth)
2 teaspoons dried basil
1 20-ounce can tomatoes, cut up
1 16-ounce can red beans
½ cup or so any small pasta
2 cups fresh spinach

In a skillet heat the olive oil and sauté the onion, garlic, zucchini, yellow squash, and mushrooms. Add the chicken broth, and simmer for a while. Add the dried basil, tomatoes, and red beans and simmer. About 15 minutes before serving, add the pasta and spinach.

MAKES 4 TO 6 SERVINGS.

The Putney Inn

❦

*P.O. Box 181, Depot Road
Putney, Vermont 05346
(800) 653-5517*

This old farmhouse-turned-inn (built in the 1790s) also served in the early 1900s as a Catholic seminary of the missionary order of the Society of St. Edmund. In 1963 it was refurbished and converted into an inn with twenty-five bedrooms. Guests enjoy its hand-hewn beams, interesting antiques, a central brick hearth in the living room, and plants and flowers both inside and outside. The Putney Inn is convenient to all of southern Vermont's historic villages and attractions.

Clam Chowder

4 pounds onions
4 pounds celery
4 pounds potatoes
1 cup plus 5 tablespoons clarified butter
1½ cups all-purpose flour
2½ cups chopped clams
1½ cups water
1½ ounces fresh basil
4½ teaspoons fresh thyme
1½ teaspoons fresh oregano
½ teaspoon freshly ground white pepper
½ teaspoon minced garlic
5½ ounces Sherry
1½ teaspoons clam base
1½ cups heavy cream

Dice the onions, celery, and potatoes. In a saucepan cook the potatoes 3 minutes. Chill, and reserve. In a skillet heat the clarified butter and sauté the onions and celery. Add the flour to make a roux. Drain the clams, and add the water and clam juice to the roux. Cook until thickened, and then simmer for 20 minutes. Add the clams, spices, Sherry, clam base, and potatoes. Simmer for 15 minutes, and taste for seasoning. Add the cream for service.

MAKES 8 SERVINGS.

Carrot Bread

2 cups oil
3 cups sugar
1½ teaspoons vanilla extract
6 cups all-purpose flour
1½ teaspoons baking powder
1½ teaspoons baking soda
¾ tablespoon ground cinnamon
¼ teaspoon nutmeg
¼ teaspoon salt
2 cups eggs, slightly beaten
1 10-ounce can crushed pineapple, slightly drained
4 cups shredded carrots
1 quart walnuts

In a large bowl blend the oil, sugar, and vanilla until creamy. Sift in the dry ingredients. Add the eggs, and blend well. Slowly add the pineapple to the mix, then add the carrots and walnuts. Spoon into 3 oiled 9 x 5-inch loaf pans. Bake in a 350° oven for 45 to 60 minutes, until a toothpick inserted in the center comes out clean.

MAKES 3 LOAVES.

Vermont Cranberry-Apple Pork Medallions on Sweet Potato Pancakes

24 3-ounce pork loin medallions, pounded to ¼-inch thick
6 tablespoons seasoned all-purpose flour
¾ cup oil
3 ounces chopped shallots
24 ounces Vermont early McIntosh apples, peeled and sliced
6 ounces sun-dried cranberries
2 ounces maple sugar
3 cups Metcalf's Hard Apple Cider
1 cup cranberry juice concentrate
¾ cup Vermont Cider Mill Apple Cider concentrate
3 cups pork demiglacé
1½ teaspoons freshly grated nutmeg
1½ teaspoons freshly ground juniper
1½ teaspoons salt
6 tablespoons chopped fresh sage
¾ cup butter

Dust the pounded pork medallions with the flour. In a skillet heat some of the oil and sauté the pork. Remove from the pan, and finish in the oven if needed, 5 minutes at most. Add the shallots and apples to the pan, add oil, and sauté 2 minutes. Add the cranberries and maple sugar to the pan, and sauté 2 minutes. Deglaze the pan with the cider, and reduce by half. Add the concentrates and demiglacé to the sauce, and simmer 2 minutes. Add the spices and salt, and simmer 2 minutes. Add the sage and butter to the sauce, and shake over heat until the butter is totally incorporated. Return the pork to the sauce for 1 minute to reheat.

MAKES 8 SERVINGS.

Apple-Maple Pancakes

1 pound apples, peeled and diced into large chunks
3 eggs
3 tablespoons butter, melted
2½ cups buttermilk
½ cup apple cider concentrate
4 cups all-purpose flour
1½ teaspoons baking soda
1 tablespoon baking powder
1 teaspoon salt
1 teaspoon ground cinnamon
½ teaspoon grated nutmeg
¾ cup maple sugar

In a saucepan poach the apples in water until tender. Refrigerate the apples until chilled.

In a large bowl whip the eggs, melted butter, buttermilk, and apple cider concentrate until blended. Mix with the chilled apples, and reserve. In a separate bowl mix all the dry ingredients. Add the dry ingredients to the wet and mix until blended well. Cook 3-ounce cakes on a flat-top griddle with butter or butter substitute until done.

MAKES 6 TO 8 SERVINGS.

Maple-Pecan Cheesecake

2 cups finely chopped gingersnaps
6 tablespoons melted butter
4 8-ounce packages cream cheese
1 cup dark firmly packed brown sugar
½ cup maple syrup
3 eggs, separated
½ cup sour cream
½ teaspoon salt
1 teaspoon vanilla extract
¾ teaspoon maple extract
1 cup chopped toasted pecans

In a medium bowl mix together the gingersnaps and butter. Press into the bottom and halfway up the sides of a 9-inch springform pan.

In a large bowl cream together the cream cheese and brown sugar until the mixture is light and fluffy. Beat in the maple syrup. Add the egg yolks 1 at a time. Beat in the sour cream, salt, vanilla, maple extract, and pecans. In a separate bowl beat the egg whites until they hold stiff peaks. Whisk one-fourth of the egg whites into the cream cheese mix. Fold in the remaining whites gently but thoroughly. Pour into the crust. Bake in a 350° oven for 1 hour. Turn off the oven, and let cool completely. Chill.

MAKES 12 TO 16 SERVINGS.

Placidia Farm

Placidia Farm

❧

R.D. 1, Box 275
Randolph, Vermont 05060
(802) 728-9883

This hand-hewn log house with only one guest room or suite is perfect for couples seeking a private getaway in the country. It's six miles out of Randolph, up a dirt road on eighty-one acres with mountain views, brook, and pond. In central Vermont, it's convenient to all of the state's many activities and tourist attractions, including skiing, summer theater, golfing, swimming, tennis, horseback riding, hiking, and tennis.

Wake-Up Parfaits

3 tablespoons orange juice
2 cups sliced bananas (or peaches)
2 cups fresh blackberries (or raspberries or blueberries)
1 cup homemade granola
1 cup vanilla yogurt
  Fresh mint for garnish
  Edible flowers

In a large bowl combine the juice and fruit. In 6 wine goblets layer half the fruit, half the granola, and half the yogurt. Repeat the layers. Garnish with a sprig of fresh mint and an edible flower, such as johnny jump-up or nasturtium. Chill until served.

MAKES 6 SERVINGS.

Yogurt Pancakes with Fresh Berries

½ cup unbleached flour
½ cup whole wheat flour
1 tablespoon sugar
1 teaspoon baking powder
½ teaspoon baking soda
¼ teaspoon salt
½ teaspoon grated nutmeg
1 egg

½ cup milk
½ cup plain yogurt
2 tablespoons oil
¾ cup fresh blackberries, raspberries, peaches
  Sliced bananas or nectarines
  Butter and maple syrup

In a large bowl combine the flours, sugar, baking powder, soda, salt, and nutmeg. In a separate bowl beat the egg with the milk and yogurt. Beat in the oil, and add the liquid mixture to the dry ingredients. Stir until just moistened. Do not overmix. Gently fold in the fruit. Bake on a hot, greased griddle until the edges are golden and bubbles rise to the surface. Turn and bake until golden.

Serve at once with butter and pure maple syrup.

MAKES 3 TO 4 SERVINGS.

Pecan-Whole Wheat Waffles

1 cup all-purpose flour
1 cup whole wheat flour
4½ teaspoons sugar
2 teaspoons baking powder
1 teaspoon baking soda
½ teaspoon salt
3 egg yolks
2 cups buttermilk
½ cup butter, melted
3 egg whites
¼ to ½ cup chopped pecans

In a medium bowl sift together the dry ingredients. Blend well with a whisk. In a large bowl blend the egg yolks well with the buttermilk and melted butter. Lightly blend the dry ingredients with the liquid ingredients until there are no lumps. In a small bowl beat the egg whites until they peak and fold them along with the pecans into the batter. Bake in a greased waffle iron until golden brown.

Serve with warm maple syrup and homemade applesauce, if desired.

MAKES 6 SERVINGS.

Fresh Blackberry Muffins

½ cup unsalted butter, room temperature
1¼ cups sugar
2 large eggs, room temperature
2 cups all-purpose flour

2 teaspoons baking powder
½ teaspoon salt
½ cup milk
2 cups fresh blackberries (or frozen, thawed and drained)
4 teaspoons sugar

Grease 12 to 16 muffin cups. In a large bowl cream the butter and 1¼ cups of sugar with an electric mixer until light. Add the eggs one at a time, beating well after each. In a small bowl sift together the flour, baking powder, and salt. Add the dry ingredients to the butter mixture alternately with the milk. Fold in the berries. Divide the batter among the prepared muffin cups. Sprinkle 4 teaspoons of sugar over the batter. Bake in a 375° oven for about 30 minutes.

Serve warm or at room temperature.

MAKES 12 TO 18 MUFFINS.

Hartness House Inn

30 Orchard Street
Springfield, Vermont 05156
(802) 885-2115

Built in 1903, this inn was origi-nally the mansion of James Hart-ness, inventor, astronomer, and governor of Vermont from 1920 to 1922. Decorated throughout with Victorian-period antiques, it also has a swimming pool, a clay tennis court, and its own network of nature trails on a thirty-two-acre site. Unique to the Hartness House is its historic observatory with a 600-power telescope and an under-ground tunnel and museum where Hartness did his inventing. On clear nights guests can scan the skies through the telescope. Within an hour's drive are some of Vermont's finest ski areas, including Stratton, Bromley, and Okemo.

Mountain Maple Poppy Dressing

4 cups mayonnaise
¾ cup maple syrup
½ cup red wine (burgundy)
¼ cup red wine vinegar
¼ cup sugar
2 tablespoons poppy seeds

In a large container with a tight-fitting lid combine all the ingredients, and mix thor-oughly.

MAKES APPROXIMATELY ½ GALLON.

The Governor's Crouton

½ cup butter
3 ½-inch slices French bread
3 1-ounce slices Vermont chèvre (goat cheese)
¼ cup sun-dried tomatoes, lightly poached to soften
2 tablespoons olive oil
1 tablespoon chopped garlic
1 small sprig fresh rosemary

Butter and lightly toast the French bread slices. Cover with goat cheese slices. Place on a buttered pie tin. Bake in a 350° oven until crisp.

While the croutons are heating, in a small pan combine the remaining ingredients, and sauté on medium heat until the garlic starts to cook. Remove from the heat. Place the crou-tons on a serving plate, and top with the tomato mixture. Serve immediately.

MAKES 1 SERVING.

Hazelnut Braised Salmon

4 8-ounce salmon fillets
2 cups finely chopped hazelnuts
¼ cup butter
½ cup water
....
1 tablespoon chopped shallots
½ cup Frangelico liquor
1 pint heavy cream
Salt and pepper to taste

Press the salmon fillets into the hazelnuts, lightly coating the fillets. Preheat a 9-inch sauté pan with butter, and sear the salmon on both sides about 30 seconds each or until light brown. Transfer to a baking dish, and

add water. Bake in a 350° oven for 10 to 15 minutes or until the salmon is firm to the touch.

In a saucepan reduce the shallots and Frangelico by half. Add the heavy cream, and reduce by half again, stirring continuously. Continue to reduce until the sauce begins to thicken. Add salt and pepper to taste. Ladle 4 tablespoons of sauce on each serving plate, place a salmon fillet on the sauce, garnish, and serve.

MAKES 4 SERVINGS.

Apple Normandy Cheesecake

3 cups graham cracker crumbs
½ cup melted butter
....
4 8-ounce packages cream cheese
2 cups sugar
8 eggs
2 teaspoons vanilla extract
2 tablespoons ground cinnamon
½ cup sifted all-purpose flour
6 tablespoons applejack brandy
2 Golden Delicious apples

In a medium bowl mix the graham cracker crumbs and butter to moisten. Pack the crumbs on the bottom of and three-fourths of the way up the sides of a 10-inch springform pan, and set aside.

In a large bowl mix the cream cheese, sugar, and vanilla with an electric mixer at medium speed until well mixed. Add the eggs one at a time until batter consistency, then add the remaining ingredients, mixing slowly. Pour into the prepared pan. Place the spring-form pan in a shallow pan of water. Bake in a 300° oven for 1 hour and 30 minutes

Peel and core the apples, and slice into half moons. Fan out on top of the cheese-cake. Bake an additional 20 to 30 minutes or until center is set. Chill overnight.

MAKES 12 TO 16 SERVINGS.

Hartness House Inn

The Brass Lantern Inn

❧

717 Maple Street
Stowe, Vermont 05672
(800) 729-2980

In a restored 1800 farmhouse and carriage barn, this inn offers nine guest rooms, each with its own identity and decor. All rooms are furnished with antiques and quilts. Most offer good views of nearby Mount Mansfield, and some have wood-burning fireplaces. The central living room for the use of all guests also has a wood-burning fireplace. The village of Stowe is a four-season resort town, offering fine restaurants, shops, and the work of craftspeople and artists.

Butternut Squash Soup

```
 2  pounds butternut squash, trimmed,
      seeded, and cleaned
 4  cups water
 1  tablespoon salt
 ¼  cup butter, melted
 ¼  cup white wine
 ½  cup diced celery
 ½  cup diced onion
 ½  cup diced green bell pepper
 1  teaspoon fresh tarragon leaves
 ½  teaspoon ground cinnamon
 ½  teaspoon grated nutmeg
 ¼  teaspoon ground cloves
 4  cups chicken stock
 ¼  cup all-purpose flour
 ¼  cup butter, melted
 ½  cup Vermont maple syrup
 ¼  cup dry Sherry
```

In a large pot with salted water place the squash, and cook approximately 40 minute until soft. Strain out the squash, reserving 2 cups of liquid and discarding the rest. In the same pot heat ¼ cup of butter and the white wine and sauté the diced vegetables for 5 minutes. Add the herbs and spices. Add the

chicken stock and 1 cup of reserved liquid. Bring to a boil, then thicken with a roux made by mixing the flour with ¼ cup of melted butter. In a blender or food processor purée the cooked squash with the remaining 1 cup of reserved liquid. Add to the pot and cook on low heat for 5 minutes, stirring often. Add the syrup and Sherry. Mix well, and serve.

MAKES 12 TO 16 SERVINGS.

Anadama Bread

```
 3½  cups water
  ¾  cup molasses
  ½  cup margarine
  1  cup cornmeal
  2  packages active dry yeast
  1  tablespoon salt
 10  cups (approximately) all-purpose
       flour
```

In a medium pot heat the water, molasses, and margarine to boiling. Stir in the cornmeal with a wire whisk, and cook for 2 minutes, stirring constantly. Set aside, and cool for approximately 45 minutes.

In a large bowl combine the yeast, salt, and 2 cups flour. Beat in the cornmeal mixture for several minutes. Add 1½ cups of flour, and beat for several more minutes. Add 5 cups of flour to form a soft dough. Knead for 5 to 10 minutes, adding more flour if needed. Shape into a ball, and place in a greased bowl. Cover with a damp cloth and let rise for 1 hour and 30 minutes.

Punch down the center with a fist, and let rest 15 minutes. Grease 2 large bread pans, roll out the dough, and place into the pans. Let rise for 45 minutes.

Bake in a 350° oven for 30 to 35 minutes. Remove immediately from pans, and cool.

MAKES 2 LOAVES.

Rhubarb Bread

```
 1½  cups firmly packed brown sugar
  ¾  cup oil
  1  egg
 2½  cups all-purpose flour
  1  cup buttermilk (or add 1 tablespoon
       vinegar to fresh milk)
  1  teaspoon salt
  1  teaspoon baking soda
  1  teaspoon ground cinnamon
  1  teaspoon vanilla extract
```

```
 2½  cups chopped rhubarb
  ½  cup walnuts or pecans (optional)
  ½  cup sugar
  1  tablespoon butter
```

In a medium bowl mix the brown sugar, oil, and egg together. Add the flour, buttermilk, salt, soda, cinnamon, and vanilla. Fold in the rhubarb and nuts, if desired. Place in 2 greased 5 x 9-inch loaf pans. Combine the sugar and butter, and sprinke over the top of the batter. Bake in a 325° oven for 1 hour.

MAKES 2 LOAVES.

Green Mountain Inn

❧

Main Street, P.O. Box 60
Stowe, Vermont 05672
(802) 253-7301

In the heart of the resort town of Stowe, known as "the ski capital of the East," is this inn with sixty-four guest rooms, built in 1833 as a private residence. It's been welcoming guests as an inn since the mid 1800s. Many of the rooms have queen-sized canopy beds, fireplaces, and Jacuzzis. Other amenities are country quilts, period antiques, stenciling, and draperies of early American design. Green Mountain Inn also has a fully equipped fitness facility and a heated outdoor pool. Other nice touches are the watercolor paintings of a local artist, Walton Blodgett, which hang throughout the common areas. This property is listed on the National Register of Historic Places.

Green Mountain Inn French Toast

¼ cup yeast
½ cup warm water (105 to 110°)
1½ cups quick oats
3 cups water
⅔ cup melted butter
1¾ tablespoons salt
¾ cup honey
7½ cups all-purpose flour
....
1 cup toasted pecans
3 8-ounce packages cream cheese
3 tablespoons confectioners' sugar
2 teaspoons fresh lemon juice
1 tablespoon vanilla extract
....
3 eggs
¼ teaspoon ground cinnamon
1 teaspoon vanilla extract
1 teaspoon Grand Marnier
Maple syrup

In a medium bowl mix the yeast and warm water, and let stand. In a large mixing bowl mix the oats, 3 cups of water, melted butter, salt, and honey. Add the yeast and water mixture. Mix together. Add the flour. Set aside to rise.

Divide the dough, and knead. Shape into loaves, and put into greased standard loaf pans. Let rise. Bake in a 325° oven for 35 minutes.

In a mixer bowl cream the pecans, cream cheese, confectioners' sugar, lemon juice, and vanilla with a paddle until light and fluffy. Place in a pastry bag and set aside.

In a medium bowl beat the eggs with the cinnamon, vanilla, and Grand Marnier. Hollow out the bread with a long knife, making a hole 1½ inches in diameter, and pipe in the cream cheese mixture. Chill for 2 hours. Slice the bread as needed, dip in the egg batter, and grill until golden. Serve with Vermont maple syrup.

Note: If desired, coat the tops of the loaves with an egg white and oats mixture before baking

MAKES 2 LOAVES.

Green Mountain Inn

Hickory-smoked Chicken and Sweet Potato Hash with Poached Eggs and Lemon Herb Beurre Blanc

Clarified butter
2 large sweet potatoes, blanched until al dente, diced
¼ cup diced onion
2 cups fresh corn
1 clove garlic, minced
¼ red bell pepper, diced
2 hickory-smoked chickens, cut in ½-inch cubes
¼ teaspoon chopped fresh rosemary
2 scallions, thinly sliced
Salt and pepper to taste
....
3 cups white wine
1 cup lemon juice
½ cup minced shallots
3 sprigs fresh thyme
8 to 10 peppercorns
....
½ cup heavy cream
1 cup butter
Chopped fresh chives or parsley
2 eggs, poached

In a hot nonstick pan heat a small amount of clarified butter and sauté the potatoes, onion, corn, garlic, and red pepper until golden. Add the chicken, rosemary, and scallions, and season with salt and pepper.

In a saucepan combine the wine, juice, shallots, thyme, and peppercorns, and reduce to a syrup. Add the heavy cream, and reduce until thick. Cube the butter, and add one piece at a time to the mixture on low heat until all are incorporated in the sauce. Strain through a fine strainer, season with salt and pepper to taste, and set aside in a warm place. Add fresh chopped chives or parsley just before serving. Serve poached eggs on the hash, and top with the herb beurre blanc.

MAKES 4 TO 6 SERVINGS.

The Siebeness Inn

3681 Mountain Road
Stowe, Vermont 05672
(800) 426-9001

*A*ll eleven guest rooms of his country-style inn are decorated with country antiques and quilts and accented with stenciling and colonial prints. Guests may enjoy the swimming pool, the outdoor hot tub, and the large fieldstone fireplace in the lounge. Besides skiing, other activities available in Stowe include horse-drawn sleigh rides, ice skating, fitness gymnasiums, shopping the quaint boutiques, and dining in the fine restaurants of this resort town.

Mor Munsen

2 cups sugar
2 cups butter or margarine, melted
4 eggs
1 teaspoon vanilla extract
2 cups all-purpose flour
½ cup currants
½ cup sliced almonds

In a large mixing bowl place the sugar. Add the butter, and mix well. Add the eggs, and mix well. Add the vanilla, then the flour, mixing well. Pour into a greased 9 x 13-inch pan. Sprinkle the currants and almonds on top. Bake in a 375° oven for about 30 minutes or until lightly brown. Cool, and cut into squares.

Note: This is a Norwegian recipe the innkeepers used to serve only during the holidays until they found that guests liked them for breakfast.

MAKES 24 SQUARES.

Mini Shoofly Pies

  1 **cup butter**
  6 **ounces cream cheese**
  1 **cup all purpose flour**
....
  2 **eggs, lightly beaten**
1½ **cups firmly packed dark brown sugar**
  2 **tablespoons milk**
  1 **teaspoon vanilla extract**
....
  ½ **cup butter or margarine**
  1 **cup sugar**
1½ **cups all-purpose flour**

In a large bowl combine 1 cup of butter, the cream cheese, and 1 cup of flour, and form into 48 little balls. Press the pastries into ungreased mini muffin cups, one ball per cup.

In a separate bowl mix the eggs, the brown sugar, the milk, and the vanilla by hand, and pour into the pastries.

In a mixer bowl combine ½ cup of butter, the sugar, and 1½ cups of all-purpose flour until the ingredients are of cornmeal consistency. Sprinkle the crumbs on top of the dough. Bake in a 375° oven for 20 minutes. Remove from the muffin cups while hot.

MAKES 48 MINI PIES.

The Siebeness Inn

Stuffed Eggplant Appetizer

    Oil
  1 **onion, thinly sliced**
  1 **28-ounce can plum tomatoes, in juice**
    Few leaves fresh basil (or 1 tablespoon dry)
    Pinch sugar

    Salt and pepper to taste
....
  1 **large eggplant**
  2 **eggs**
  ¼ **cup water**
  ½ **cup all-purpose flour**
  ½ **cup seasoned breadcrumbs**
  ½ **cup oil (or olive oil)**
....
  2 **cups ricotta cheese**
  2 **eggs**
  ¼ **cup grated Parmesan cheese**
  1 **tablespoon parsley**
    Salt and pepper to taste

In a saucepan heat a small amount of oil and sauté the onion. Chop the tomatoes, and add to the onions with the basil, sugar, and seasonings. Simmer for about 30 minutes. Slice enough thin circles of eggplant for 2 per serving (about 12). In a bowl beat the eggs with water. Dip the eggplant in the flour, then the egg mixture, then the breadcrumbs. In a skillet heat ½ cup of oil and sauté over medium heat until lightly brown. Cool on paper towels.

Pour a thin layer of tomato sauce on the bottom of a 9 x 13-inch baking pan. In a medium bowl mix the ricotta cheese, eggs, Parmesan cheese, parsley, salt, and pepper. Take an eggplant slice, place about 1 heaping tablespoon of mixture on it, and fold in half, placing it in the pan. Continue to do this with all the eggplant, laying the pieces against each other. Pour the remaining sauce over the top. Bake in a 375° oven for about 30 minutes. Serve 2 on each plate.

Note: If desired, substitute a commercial sauce for the homemade Tomato Basil Sauce.

MAKES 4 TO 6 SERVINGS.

Hyde Away Inn

❧

R.R. 1, Box 65, Route 17
Waitsfield, Vermont 05673
(802) 496-2322

T*his rustic inn is a great escape destination for guests who want to get away for a little rest and*

relaxation in the heart of Vermont's Green Mountains. It has a big outside deck for leisurely mountain viewing. Another plus is the soothing fireplace in the living room area. Nearby recreational activities include snowshoeing, skiing, tennis, and swimming.

Maple Ginger Vinaigrette

  ½ **cup minced fresh ginger**
  2 **tablespoons minced garlic**
  ½ **cup balsamic vinegar**
  ½ **cup maple syrup**
  1 **cup peanut oil**
1½ **cups water**
    Salt and pepper to taste

In a bowl combine the ginger, garlic, vinegar, and syrup. Whisk in the oil and water. Season with salt and pepper to taste.

MAKES APPROXIMATELY 1 QUART.

Hyde Away Inn Southwest Pasta

    Dried chipotles (amount depends on how spicy you want it)
  ⅓ **cup peanut oil**
....
  3 **cups heavy cream**
    Pinch salt
1¾ **cups cooked, sliced Vermont chorizo sausage**
  ½ **cup chopped scallions**
  ½ **cup chopped tomatoes**
1½ **cup cooked black beans**
  9 **large shrimp, peeled and deveined**
  4 **servings favorite pasta, cooked**
  4 **teaspoons chipotle purée**

In a bowl reconstitute the dried chipotles. In a blender combine the reconstituted chipotles and the peanut oil, and blend well.

In a saucepan combine the cream, salt, chorizo sausage, scallions, tomatoes, and black beans. Cook over medium heat until hot and the cream has reduced by one-third. Toss in the shrimp. When the shrimp are cooked, pour over pasta. Top each serving with a teaspoon of the chipotle purée.

MAKES 4 SERVINGS.

Thai Grilled Duck

- 1 cup peanut oil
- ½ cup lime juice
- 2 tablespoons soy sauce
- 3 tablespoons fresh ginger
- 3 tablespoons firmly packed brown sugar
- 2 tablespoons minced garlic
- 3 tablespoons crushed red pepper

....

- 2 16-ounce duck breasts, halved and scored
- 1 cup chopped scallions
- 1 cup chopped tomatoes
- 4 servings angel hair pasta, cooked
  Snow peas for garnish
  Red pepper for garnish

In a bowl blend the peanut oil, lime juice, soy sauce, ginger, brown sugar, garlic, and red pepper. In a glass dish marinate the duck breasts for a least 1 hour in the Thai marinade. Grill the duck to the desired temperature. Let rest.

In a saucepan combine the Thai Marinade, scallions, and tomatoes, and heat. Toss in the angel hair pasta. Once heated, place in the middle of the plate. Slice the duck into ¼-inch medallions, and fan around the pasta. Heat more Thai Marinade, and drizzle on top of the plate. Garnish with the snow peas and red pepper.

MAKES 4 SERVINGS.

The Inn at the Round Barn Farm

❧

R.R. 1, Box 247
East Warren Road
Waitsfield, Vermont 05673
(802) 496-2276

*T*he big round barn (built in 1810) on the eighty-five-acre estate that surrounds this inn is so impressive that the inn was named for it. Possibly the only guest house in the country where guests can swim in a barn, it houses a sixty-foot lap pool, that extends into a greenhouse with hibiscus and bougainvillea. Each of the eleven guest rooms in this unique inn is individually decorated, and some have fireplaces, Jacuzzis, steam showers, or canopied beds. All are richly wallpapered and have original pine floors and fresh flowers. The Inn at the Round Barn Farm has its own cross-country ski center and miles of marked trails for ski enthusiasts.

Southwestern Fiesta Cheesecake

- 4 8-ounce packages cream cheese, softened
- 3 eggs
- 2 cups grated Monterey Jack cheese,
- 2 cloves garlic, crushed
- 2 4-ounce cans green chilies, drained and chopped
  Tortilla crust

....

- 1 cup sour cream
- ½ cup salsa, drained

....

- 1 orange bell pepper
- 1 small red bell pepper
- 1 bunch scallions
- 1 small yellow bell pepper
- 1 6-ounce can black olives
- ½ red onion
- 1 tomato, peeled, seeded, and chopped
- ¼ bunch parsley (or cilantro)
- 1 4-ounce jar mild jalapeños (or green chilies)

In a food processor or mixer beat the cream cheese until fluffy. Add the eggs one at a time. Add the grated cheese, garlic, and chilies, and blend well. Pour into the prepared crust. Bake for 50 minutes or until firm. Turn the oven off, and let sit for 1 hour, or put in the refrigerator, uncovered. Let chill for 2 hours. In a medium bowl combine the sour cream and salsa, and refrigerate until chilled.

Remove the cheesecake from the pan, and divide your cheesecake into slices. Top the center with a tomato rose or green onion flowers. Spread the chilled salsa-sour cream mixture over the top of the cheesecake. Cut diamond-shaped pieces from red, yellow, and orange peppers. Form a pattern around the edge of the cheesecake. In the center place 6 to 8 green onion flowers. Place the remaining garnishes in a concentric design around the center.

Note: For a hotter version, use Jalapeño Jack in place of the Monterey Jack cheese.

MAKES 8 SERVINGS.

Curried Mango Chutney Cheesecake

- Toasted flaked coconut

....

- 4 8-ounce packages cream cheese
- 1 cup Major Grey Mango Chutney
- 2 cloves garlic, minced
- 3 scallions, heads plus ½-inch green, sliced
- 3 eggs
- 2 teaspoons curry powder
- 1 teaspoon salt

....

- 1 cup mango chutney
- 1 cup slivered almonds, toasted
- ½ cup scallions, sliced
- ½ cup toasted flaked coconut
  Edible flower (optional)

In a greased 9-inch springform pan press the toasted coconut into the bottom and sides of th e pan. In a food processor or mixer beat the cream cheese until fluffy. Add the chutney, garlic, scallions, eggs, curry, and salt. Blend well. Spoon mixture into the prepared pan. Bake in a 300° oven for 30 minutes or until firm. Turn the oven off, and let sit for 1 hour or place directly into the refrigerator, uncovered, and chill for 2 hours.

Remove from the pan and decorate. Spread the top of the cheesecake with mango chutney. Sprinkle slivered almonds around the edge of the cheesecake. Sprinkle scallions and coconut in a circular fashion around the edge of the almonds. Sprinkle more scallions in a circular fashion around edge of the first row of scallions to form 3 concentric circles. Place an edible flower in the center, or leave plain.

MAKES 4 CUPS, ABOUT 15 OR MORE SERVINGS.

Cottage Cheese Pancakes with Raspberry Maple Syrup

> 1 cup large curd Cabot cottage cheese
> ½ cup all-purpose flour
> 4 eggs
> 6 tablespoons melted butter
>
> ·····························
>
> 1 cup Vermont maple syrup (Grade B Dark Amber has the best flavor for cooking)
> ⅔ cup fresh raspberries (or frozen)
> 2 tablespoons raspberry jam

In a mixer whip the cottage cheese. Add the flour and eggs, and start the mixer again. With mixer on, add the melted butter. (This should be a thick batter.) Test a small amount of batter on a heated grill and if it is not thick enough, add a small amount of flour.

Cook the pancakes until golden, then flip, and cook for an additional minute. Do not overcook. (These pancakes are moist and should spring back to the touch.)

In a nonstick pan combine the syrup and raspberries. If using frozen raspberries heat on low until raspberries defrost, stirring occasionally. Stir in the jam to help the syrup mixture thicken. Heat until the syrup boils, then turn off the heat, and let sit. Syrup is ready to spoon over pancakes after the mixture has set for a few minutes, allowing it to thicken.

MAKES 4 SERVINGS.

Grünberg Haus

∾

R.R. 2, Box 1595
Route 100 South
Waterbury, Vermont 05676-9621
(800) 800-7760

*T*his striking three-story inn is built like an Austrian chalet, with intricately carved balconies in the Tyrolean style of architecture. All fifteen guest rooms open to a balcony that surrounds the Grunberg House, providing breathtaking views of the Green Mountains (grünberg *means "green mountain"). The central living room, with a massive fieldstone fireplace, also offers panoramic views of the mountains. Other amenities include a deck, a tennis court, an outdoor Jacuzzi, and cross-country skiing trails. Nearby recreational activities include horseback riding, tubing, canoeing, and fishing.*

Maple Poached Pears

> ½ cup Vermont maple syrup
> 2 quarts water
> 3 fresh Bosc pears
> 1 8-ounce carton vanilla yogurt
>   Grated nutmeg for garnish
> 6 sprigs mint

In a saucepan combine the maple syrup and water, and bring to a boil. Reduce the heat. Peel, halve, and core the pears. Simmer, cutside up, in the maple mixture until just tender. To serve, make a small pool of yogurt on a 6-inch serving plate, then drain a pear half, and position it in the center of the pool, cutside down. Dust with nutmeg, and garnish with a mint sprig.

MAKES 6 SERVINGS.

Vermont Cheddar Pie

> 2 cups frozen hash browns, thawed
> 1 medium onion, finely chopped
> 1 teaspoon seasoned pepper
> ⅓ cup grated Pecorino Romano cheese
> 2 teaspoons garlic powder
> ⅓ cup frozen chopped spinach, thawed
> ⅓ cup crumbled fresh feta cheese
> 1 cup grated sharp Vermont Cheddar cheese
>
> ·····························
>
> 2 eggs
> ½ cup milk
> 2 tablespoons parsley flakes
> 2 teaspoons paprika

Grease a 9-inch glass pie plate. Combine the potatoes with all but 2 tablespoons of the onion, and press the mixture into the pie plate to form a crust. Sprinkle the crust with the pepper, Romano cheese, and garlic pow-

Grünberg Haus

der, then dot with the spinach and feta cheese. Top evenly with the Cheddar cheese.

In a bowl whisk together the eggs and milk, and pour over the pie, working from the edge to the middle. Position the reserved chopped onion on top of the Cheddar cheese in the center of the pie, sprinkle the parsley flakes in a ring around the onion, then sprinkle the paprika around the parsley to make an outside ring. Bake in a 325° oven approximately 1 hour until lightly browned. Cool, cut into 6 slices, then microwave 6 to 7 minutes.

MAKES 6 SERVINGS.

Lemon Ricotta Pancakes

> ¾ cup all-purpose flour
> ½ teaspoon grated nutmeg
> 1 tablespoon sugar
> 1 teaspoon baking powder
> 1 cup ricotta cheese
> 2 eggs
> ⅔ cup milk
>   Juice and grated zest of 1 lemon
>   Confectioners' sugar for dusting
>   Vermont maple syrup

In a bowl combine the dry ingredients. In a separate bowl combine the wet ingredients, then mix with the dry ingredients. Pour approximately ¼ cup of batter onto a hot, oiled grill, and cook until golden brown, flipping once. Arrange on a warm antique platter. Dust with confectioners' sugar. Serve with maple syrup.

MAKES 6 SERVINGS.

Pear and Cheddar Omelets

> 2 eggs
> ½ eggshell water (2 tablespoons)
> 1¼ teaspoon salt
> ¼ teaspoon seasoned pepper
> 2 tablespoons butter

¼ **cup diced pears, poached in maple syrup (recipe follows)**
¼ **cup grated Vermont Cheddar cheese**

In a small bowl whisk together the eggs, water, salt, and pepper. Spray a 9-inch non-stick skillet with cooking spray, then add the butter. When butter is just melted, add the egg mixture and allow to cook until eggs start to set. Gently lift the eggs with a pliable spatula, tilting the pan to allow the uncooked mixture to flow under the cooked mixture until just about everything is cooked. Position the pear and cheese on half of the omelet, then using a pliable spatula, fold half the omelet onto the other half. Turn off the heat, and let sit a minute. To serve, using a pliable spatula gently slide the omelet out of the pan onto a plate.
MAKES 1 SERVING.

Pumpkin Apple Streusel Muffins

2½   **cups all-purpose flour**
2   **cups sugar**
1   **tablespoon pumpkin pie spice**
1   **teaspoon baking soda**
½   **teaspoon salt**
2   **eggs**
1   **cup canned pumpkin**
½   **cup oil**
2   **cups chopped McIntosh apples**

4   **teaspoons butter**
¼   **cup sugar**
½   **teaspoon ground cinnamon**

In a large bowl combine the flour, 2 cups of sugar, pumpkin pie spice, baking soda, and salt. In a separate bowl combine the eggs, pumpkin, oil, and apples, then mix with the dry ingredients just until moistened. Scoop the batter into 18 greased muffin cups.

In a small bowl cut together the butter, ¼ cup of sugar, and cinnamon until crumbly. Sprinkle over the muffins. Bake in a 350° oven for 30 to 35 minutes.
MAKES 18 MUFFINS.

Thatcher Brook Inn
❧

P.O. Box 490
Route 100 North
Waterbury, Vermont 05676
(800) 292-5911

---

*T*he two features of this inn that guests find most memorable are its long front porch and the twin gazebos that frame the main entrance. Once inside, they also enjoy the hand-carved fireplace and stairway in the living room and the library with a wood-burning fireplace. Built as a residence for a local lumber baron in 1899, Thatcher Brook Inn is listed on the Vermont Register of Historic Buildings. Conveniently located attractions include ski resorts, swimming at Lake Waterbury State Park, golf, biking, and canoeing.

Deep-dish French Toast

½   **cup butter**
1   **cup firmly packed brown sugar**
1   **tablespoon corn syrup**
2   **apples, cored and sliced**
3   **to 4 peaches, peeled and sliced**
½   **loaf French or Italian bread, sliced in ½-inch uniform pieces**
10   **eggs**
1½   **cups milk**
1   **teaspoon vanilla extract**
   Grated nutmeg and ground cinnamon to taste

Thatcher Brook Inn

In a saucepan melt the butter, add the brown sugar and corn syrup, and mix well. Bring to a boil. Pour into a 9 x 13-inch pan. Layer the fruit over the syrup mixture, and cover with the bread slices. (Fit the bread rather closely.) In a medium bowl beat the eggs, milk, and vanilla together. Pour over the top., and let sit overnight.

Bake in a 325 to 350° oven for 1 hour and 25 minutes. Season with the nutmeg and cinnamon.

Note: This recipe must be prepared the night before.
MAKES 8 TO 10 SERVINGS.

Deerhill Inn
❧

Valley View Road, P.O. Box 136
West Dover, Vermont 05356
(802) 464-3100

---

*E*verything about this inn is designed to help guests wind down and relax. The patio and lounge offer beautiful views of the surrounding Green Mountains. Guests also enjoy settling down in front of the wood-burning fireplace in the lounge, relaxing with a good book in the library, or swimming or sunning by the pool. For those who just have to get out and do something, biking, fishing, golfing, and skiing opportunities are available nearby.

Celery-Almond Soup

2   **teaspoons oil**
½   **cup chopped celery**
¼   **cup peeled and diced carrots**
¼   **cup chopped onions**
2   **tablespoons all-purpose flour**
2   **cups chicken broth**
¼   **cup shaved almonds**
¼   **cup roux (paste of melted butter and flour for thickening)**

In a saucepan heat the oil and sauté the vegetables until wilted. Add the flour, and cook for 2 minutes. Add the chicken broth, bring to a boil, then simmer vegetables about 15 minutes until tender.

In the meantime, on a sheet pan sprayed with cooking spray toast the almonds in a 400° oven until golden brown. When golden, immediately remove from the sheet pan to prevent burning. Whisk in the roux until the soup thickens. Add the almonds, reserving a few for garnishing. Serve at once.

MAKES 4 SERVINGS.

Deerhill Salad

> Red and green Boston (or Bibb) leaf
>   lettuce, for 4 people
> 4 large cherry tomatoes
>   Salad dressing

Clean and spin-dry the lettuce. Wash and core the tomatoes. Refrigerate for 1 hour. Use the whole leaf of the red-leaf lettuce to form the bed of the salad. Gradually stack the green-leaf lettuce, shiny-side up, to form the top of the salad. It should resemble a cabbage rose in bloom.

With the cherry tomato stem-side up, slice in wedges with a sharp knife, taking care not to penetrate through the bottom. The tomato will open in 4 sections to resemble a red flower in bloom. Place in the center of the salad. Top with any favorite dressing.

MAKES 4 SERVINGS.

Bruchetta

> ½ loaf Italian bread (or French)
> ½ cup olive oil to which 1 slivered
>   clove garlic has been added
> ¼ cup basil pesto
> 1 small purple eggplant
> 1 large red bell pepper, roasted,
>   peeled, and quartered
> 4 slices mozzarella cheese
> 1 cup marinara sauce, heated

Slice 4 ¾-inch thick pieces of bread from the loaf. Brush one side of each with the garlic oil. Place on a hot grill (may use a broiler) until toasted. While browning, brush the other side with the garlic oil. Turn and toast. Remove from the grill, and place on a cookie sheet. Top each with the pesto. Slice the egg-plant into ½-inch slices. Cook the eggplant in the same manner as the bread.

Remove the eggplant from the grill, and place each slice of eggplant on a slice of bread. Place 1 piece of roasted red pepper on each slice of eggplant and 1 slice of mozzarella cheese on top of each pepper. Bake in a 450° oven until the cheese melts. Remove, and serve at once on a bed of hot marinara sauce.

MAKES 4 SERVINGS.

Roasted Red Potatoes

> 4 large red bliss potatoes
>   Vegetable oil (or oil of choice)
>   Salt, pepper, rosemary, and chopped
>   garlic to taste

Cut 4 large red bliss potatoes in half crosswise. Nip or cut off the rounded end of the potato so the potato sits upright. Also bevel ¼ inch of the sliced edge of the potato. Coat the potato with the oil, and stand on end in a shallow roasting pan. Season with the salt, pepper, rosemary and chopped garlic. Roast in a 475° oven for 45 minutes to an hour or until a pointed knife passes easily through the potato.

MAKES 4 SERVINGS.

Blueberry Shortcake

> 1¾ cups all-purpose flour
>   3 tablespoons baking powder
> ¼ teaspoon salt
> ½ cup sugar
> ½ cup butter or margarine
> ¾ cup milk
> ·····································
>   2 cups fresh blueberries
> ¾ cup sugar
>   Additional blueberries
>   6 scoops vanilla ice cream
>   Whipped cream

In a medium bowl combine the flour, baking powder, salt, ½ cup of sugar, and butter. Cut the butter into the flour with a pastry knife until corn-sized nuggets appear. Stir in the milk, and mix with a wooden spoon for 30 seconds. Spread onto a well-floured board, and knead gently for 15 seconds. Roll out to ½-inch thickness, and cut into 6 3-inch circles with a biscuit cutter or jar cap. Place on a greased baking sheet. Bake in a 425° oven for 15 to 20 minutes or until golden color. Remove from the oven, and cool.

Set out 6 serving plates. In a blender combine the blueberries and sugar, and blend until puréed. Slice the biscuits in half horizontally. On each of the 6 plates pour 3 tablespoons of the blueberry purée. On top of each place the bottom half of a biscuit. Place additional blueberries, a scoop of ice cream, and whipped cream on top of the biscuit. Top with the other half of the biscuit, and garnish with more purée, blueberries, and whipped cream in a attractive manner.

MAKES 6 SERVINGS.

Grilled Lamb Loin with Kiwi in Port Wine Sauce

> 1 small onion, diced
> 1 large clove garlic, chopped
> 2 tablespoons soy sauce
> 3 tablespoons sesame oil
>   Dash Worcestershire sauce
> 1 teaspoon cracked black pepper
> 1 loin lamb, boned by the butcher
> ·····································
> 1 cup good-quality tawny Port wine
> ¼ cup chopped shallots
> 1 cup brown sauce
> ·····································
> 2 to 4 kiwi fruits

In a small bowl combine the onion and garlic with the soy sauce, sesame oil, Worcestershire sauce, and pepper. Rub the mixture on the lamb loin, and store in a covered glass pan overnight in the refrigerator.

Remove from the refrigerator 1 hour before ready to cook. Prepare a grill or broiler. Grill or broil the lamb until the desired doneness. Meanwhile, in a saucepan reduce the Port from 1 cup to ½ cup. Add the chopped shallots, and heat. Strain out the shallots, and add the brown sauce to the Port. Whisk together, and heat through.

Peel and slice the kiwi into ¼-inch thick slices. Remove the lamb loins from the grill or broiler, and let set for 5 minutes. Slice the loin diagonally into ¼-inch slices. Place the lamb and kiwi slices alternately fanned out on each of 4 serving plates. Serve with the Port wine sauce.

MAKES 4 SERVINGS.

Coldbrook Road, P.O. Box 457
Wilmington, Vermont 05363
(802) 464-3511

*T*he twenty-nine luxurious guest
rooms in this inn are housed in
three different buildings: the main
house, originally built as a farm
house in the 1800s; the wine house,
attached to the main building; and
a free-standing carriage house.
Each room is furnished lavishly
with New England antiques, and
some have working fireplaces. Hundreds of antique decoys are scattered throughout the inn complex,
symbolizing its dual role as a game
bird farm. The Hermitage also has
its own five-hundred-acre hunting
preserve, providing guests with
guides, dogs, pheasants, and par-
tridges for a unique hunting experience. Cross-country ski trails are
also scattered throughout
the property.

Maple Walnut Pie

> 1 **9-inch pie shell**
> **Egg-and-water mixture, well beaten**
> ....
> ½ **cup firmly packed dark brown sugar**
> 2 **tablespoons all-purpose flour**
> 1¼ **cups maple syrup (the darker the**
> **better)**
> 3 **tablespoons butter, melted or very**
> **soft**
> 3 **eggs**
> 1 **teaspoon vanilla extract**
> **Chopped walnut pieces**

Wash the pie shell with a mixture of beaten
egg and water. Bake in a 375° oven for 4 or 5
minutes to set. (Preparing the crust in this
manner will prevent it from becoming soggy
from the pie mixture.)

In a large bowl combine all the ingredients
except the walnuts. Pour into the egg-washed
pie crust. Top with the walnut pieces. Bake in
a 375° oven approximately 45 minutes to 1
hour until set.
MAKES 6 TO 8 SERVINGS.

Roast Goose
with Victoria Sauce on
Vegetable Nut Stuffing

> 1 **8- to 10-pound goose**
> ....
> ½ **cup butter**
> 1 **cup finely diced onion**
> 1 **cup finely diced celery**
> 1 **cup finely diced carrot**
> ½ **cup finely chopped walnuts**
> 2 **tart apples, diced ¼-inch thick**
> 1 **cup sliced mushrooms**
> 2 **bay leaves**
> ½ **teaspoon dried thyme**
> 1 **cup white wine**
> ½ **cup chicken broth**
> ½ **cup breadcrumbs**
> **Salt and pepper to taste**
> ....
> ½ **cup green grapes, halved**
> ½ **cup white Port wine**
> 1 **16-ounce can whole cranberry sauce**
> ½ **cup chicken broth**
> **Cornstarch**
> **Cold water**

Roast the goose on a rack in a 350° oven
approximately 2 to 2½ hours until the hip
juices run clear when pricked. Keep warm.

In a skillet melt the butter and sauté the
onion, celery, and carrot until soft. Add the
walnuts, apples, mushrooms, bay leaves,
thyme, and wine. Simmer approximately 10
minutes over medium heat. Add ½ cup of
chicken broth, and reduce until most of the
liquid evaporates. Remove from the heat, and
let cool slightly. Remove the bay leaves. Add
the breadcrumbs to produce a moist, cohe-
sive stuffing. Season with salt and pepper, and
keep warm.

Place a saucepan on high heat. Add the
grapes and white Port wine. Allow the alcohol
to flame off. Add the cranberry sauce and
chicken broth. Heat to a simmer. In a small
bowl dissolve about 1 tablespoon of cornstarch in 2 tablespoons of water, and thicken
the cranberry sauce mixture with the cornstarch and water mixture. Keep warm.

Portion the stuffing on dinner plates. Carve
the goose like a roast turkey, and arrange the
slices, partially overlapping, on the stuffing.
Mask with the sauce.
MAKES 4 TO 6 SERVINGS.

Cream of Chestnut Soup

> 1 **pound shelled and peeled chestnuts**
> **(buy 2 pounds)**
> 3 **sprigs parsley**
> 2 **cups full-flavored chicken stock**
> ....
> **Butter as needed**
> 1 **medium carrot, grated**
> 2 **leeks, finely minced**
> 3 **stalks celery, finely minced**
> 1 **small onion, finely minced**
> 1 **teaspoon dried tarragon**
> **Flour and butter roux**
> 1 **cup heavy cream**
> **Salt to taste**
> 1 **teaspoon paprika**
> **Dry Sherry to taste**

With a paring knife make an X-shaped slit in
the flat side of the chestnuts. Either boil the
nuts for 2 to 3 minutes, or bake on a sheet
pan in a 375° oven for 3 to 4 minutes or until
hot. (Work in small batches. The nuts have to
be peeled while still quite warm, and the oil
in the nuts will aid in releasing the shell and
brown skin if the proper temperature is
reached. Work with very warm nuts, or
return to the heat.) Using the edge of the paring knife, cut away the shell and furry skin on
the nuts. Discard any dried, shriveled, or
moldy nuts. Eighty percent of the fresh chestnuts should peel completely, like shelling
hard-boiled eggs.

In a food processor or blender with a
metal blade purée the nuts and parsley,
adding some chicken stock if necessary to
make a fine purée. Simmer with the remaining stock for 15 to 20 minutes.

In a skillet melt the butter and sauté the
vegetables until soft. Do not brown. Add the
vegetables along with the tarragon to the simmering chestnuts and stock. Simmer an additional 10 minutes. Thicken with roux in small
quantities at a time, whisking constantly. (Be
careful not to over thicken.) Cook out the
roux with each addition. Add the heavy
cream. Adjust the salt to taste. Add the
paprika, and finish with small quantity of
butter and Sherry to taste.

Note: The nuts may be done ahead of time. Store the nuts immersed in inexpensive cocktail sherry, and refrigerate covered for up to a week.
MAKES 4 SERVINGS.

Cream of Vegetable Soup

In a stockpot sauté shallots and/or onion until soft, add diced vegetables, and simmer in a gamebird stock with thyme and bay leaves. At the Hermitage Inn, the poultry stock varies with whatever gamebird carcasses are on hand. The soup is thickened with roux, the seasonings adjusted, and lastly creamed to finish.

Note: There is no recipe per se. The soups at the Hermitage Inn are like the salad dressings—du jour.

Misty Mountain Lodge

326 Stowe Hill Road
Wilmington, Vermont 05363
(802) 464-3961

*T*his small family inn with eight guest rooms is in a converted farmhouse. Guests enjoy the walking trails and cross-country ski trails on the adjoining 150-acre estate. Other amenities include a whirlpool tub and a fieldstone fireplace in the great room. Nearby activities include downhill skiing, golf, boating, and swimming.

Misty Mountain Lodge

Dandelion Jelly

> *Picked and washed dandelion blossoms*
> 1 *1¾-ounce package Sure-Jel*
> 1 *teaspoon lemon or orange extract*
> 4½ *cups sugar*

Place as many washed blossoms as will fit into a pan with 1 quart of water. Boil 3 minutes. (Boil only 3 minutes or it will turn green instead of a beautiful golden color.) Stir the flowers. Strain.

In the pan boil the liquid and extract with the Sure-Jel. Add the sugar. Boil about 3 minutes, stirring constantly. Remove from the heat, pour into jars, and seal.

Note: If one likes the taste of honey, they will like dandelion jelly.
MAKES ABOUT 3½ PINTS.

Fruit Crisp

> *Fruit of choice (even canned peaches make a nice winter treat)*
> 1 *cup sugar*
> 1 *cup all-purpose flour*
> 1 *teaspoon baking powder*
> 1 *egg*
> ⅓ *cup melted butter*

Place the fruit in bottom of a greased 8 x 12-inch pan. In a bowl mix the sugar, flour, baking powder, and egg until it reaches a crumbly consistency. Sprinkle the crumbs over fruit, and pour the melted butter over all. Bake in a 350° oven for 30 minutes or until brown and bubbly.

Note: For brunch, the innkeepers recommend serving it plain. For dinner, serve with ice cream. This should be served warm.
MAKES 6 TO 8 SERVINGS.

Cold Carrot Salad

> 1 *8-ounce can tomato sauce*
> ½ *cup sugar*
> ½ *cup wine vinegar*
> ⅓ *cup oil*
> 1 *teaspoon salt*
> 1 *teaspoon dry mustard*
> ½ *teaspoon pepper*
> 2 *pounds (about 6 cups) carrots, peeled, sliced, cooked, drained, and cooled*
> 1 *red onion, thinly sliced*
> 1 *green bell pepper, thinly sliced*

In a large bowl combine the tomato sauce, sugar, vinegar, oil, salt, mustard, and pepper. Stir until blended. Add the carrots, onion, and green pepper, and stir to mix well. Cover, and chill, preferably overnight.
MAKES 12 TO 16 SERVINGS.

Trails End

5 Trail's End Lane
Wilmington, Vermont 05363
(802) 464-2727

*I*n a secluded setting on ten acres on a quiet country road, this inn is the perfect choice for guests who are looking to get away from it all for a few days. Trail's End has an outdoor heated swimming pool, a clay tennis court, a large pond, and flower gardens. Each of the fifteen guest rooms is done in a different color scheme and is furnished with family heirlooms and antiques. Within an easy drive are two of Vermont's most popular skiing areas— Haystack and Mount Snow.

Crabbies

> ½ *cup butter or margarine, softened*
> 1 *jar Old English cheese spread*
> 1½ *teaspoons mayonnaise*
> ½ *teaspoon garlic salt*
>   *Old Bay Seasoning to taste*
> ½ *pound crab meat*
> 8 *English muffins, split in half*

In a large bowl combine the butter, cheese spread, and mayonnaise. Add the seasonings and crab meat. Spread on the muffins. Cut into quarters, and broil until hot and brown. Serve immediately.
MAKES 8 SERVINGS.

Carbonnade of Beef

> ½ *cup all-purpose flour*
> 2½ *tablespoons salt*

1   teaspoon pepper
6   pounds boneless beef chuck roast,
      sliced
5   tablespoons oil
5   tablespoons butter or margarine
8   cups thickly sliced onions
2   cloves garlic, crushed
6   sprigs parsley
2   bay leaves
1   teaspoon crushed dried thyme
2   cups beef broth
2   12-ounce cans ale (or beer)
¼   cup firmly packed light brown sugar
2   tablespoons white vinegar

In a large bowl combine the flour, 1 table-spoon of salt, and ½ teaspoon of pepper. Add the beef, and toss lightly to coat well. In a large skillet heat 4 tablespoons of oil and 4 tablespoons of butter or margarine over medium heat. Cook the beef a few slices at a time until browned. Remove the beef with a slotted spoon. Add the remaining oil and butter or margarine, and heat until melted. Add the onions and garlic, and sauté about 5 minutes until tender. Remove from the skillet.

Make a bouquet garni by placing the parsley, bay leaves, and thyme in a piece of cheesecloth. Tie to form a bag. In a 4½-quart casserole alternate layers of beef and onions. Place the bouquet garni in the center of the mixture.

In a skillet combine the beef broth, ale, sugar, vinegar, and remaining salt and pepper. Heat to boiling, stirring frequently. Pour over the beef and onions, cover the casserole. Bake in a 350° oven for 2 hours and 30 minutes. Meat should be fork-tender. Discard the bag, and skim off the fat.

MAKES 12 SERVINGS.

Noodle Carrot Toss

2   12-ounce packages medium egg noo-
       dles
¾   cup butter or margarine, melted
2   tablespoons salt
6   cups shredded carrots
¾   cup finely chopped parsley
4   eggs, slightly beaten
1¼   cups milk
¾   teaspoon pepper

In a large saucepan cook the noodles according to package directions, but cook only 4 minutes. Drain, and return to the saucepan. Add the butter or margarine, and set aside.

In a separate saucepan heat 1 inch of water and 1 tablespoon of salt to boiling. Add the carrots, and cook 2 to 3 minutes, stirring occasionally. Drain well, and add the carrots and parsley to the noodles.

In a medium bowl combine the remaining ingredients and remaining 1 tablespoon of salt. Beat until smooth. Pour over the noodles, and toss well. Pour into a well-greased casserole, and cover. Bake in a 375° oven for 40 minutes, stirring occasionally.

MAKES 12 SERVINGS.

Hungarian Goulash

6   tablespoons oil
4   pounds beef chuck, cut into 1½-inch
       cubes
2   tablespoons all-purpose flour
1   13¾-ounce can condensed beef
       bouillon
3   cups chopped red onions
6   cloves garlic, finely chopped
3   cups finely chopped peeled tomatoes
3   tablespoons Hungarian paprika
1   teaspoon salt
⅛   teaspoon pepper
     Cooked noodles

In a large skillet heat the oil, and brown the beef cubes a few at a time. As the beef cubes brown, transfer to a Dutch oven. Sprinkle the meat with flour, and toss.

To the skillet add the beef bouillon, and heat, scraping the brown bits. Add to the beef. In the skillet heat the remaining ¼ cup of oil. Cook the onions and garlic over low heat until tender. Add the onion mixture, tomatoes, paprika, salt, and pepper to the beef cubes, and stir. Bring to a boil, cover, and simmer 2 hours or until the meat is fork-tender. Skim off the fat. Serve over noodles.

MAKES 8 TO 10 SERVINGS.

VIRGINIA

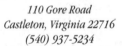

Thistle Hill Bed and Breakfast Inn

5541 Sperryville Pike
Boston, Virginia 22713
(540) 987-9142

*V*isitors to Virginia's mountainous west are often surprised by the boldness of the terrain. For instance, Old Rag Mountain near Sperryville is as rugged and craggy as any western peak. The Thistle Hill B&B is a good choice for those who wish to explore Old Rag and other lofty summits in nearby Shenandoah National Park. Also nearby are "Little" Washington (where George did his first surveying job), several highly respected wineries, and numerous historic sites such as Monticello, Montpelier, and Ashlawn. All-terrain bikes and a hot tub are available.

Thistle Hill

Thistle Hill Eggs

½ **English muffin, lightly toasted**
1 **slice tomato**
1 **egg, poached for 3½ minutes**
    Hollandaise sauce (or 1 package
        Knorr Hollandaise Mix, prepared)
2 **slices bacon, cooked crisp**
    Parsley for garnish
    Tomato wedges or fruit for garnish

Place the English muffin on a serving plate. Top with the tomato slice and the egg. Spoon Hollandaise sauce over the egg. Place crossed slices of bacon on top. Garnish with parsley and tomato wedge or fruit. Serve immediately.

Note: For a 2-egg serving use ½ of a luncheon or sandwich-size English muffin or 2 regular muffin halves. Top with 3 slices of bacon.
MAKES 1 SERVING.

Thistle Hill Tea Cakes

½ **cup butter**
½ **cup sugar**
1 **egg**
¾ **cup all-purpose flour**
....
1 **teaspoon baking powder**
½ **cup golden raisins**
⅓ **cup slivered almonds**
    Crushed corn flakes

In a medium bowl cream the butter and sugar. Add the egg and cream again. Add the flour and baking powder, mixing well. Add the raisins and almonds, and mix again. Roll

by teaspoonfuls in lightly crushed corn flakes. Bake in a 350° oven for 13 to 15 minutes.
MAKES 1½ DOZEN.

Blue Knoll Farm Bed and Breakfast

110 Gore Road
Castleton, Virginia 22716
(540) 937-5234

A 19th-century farmhouse in the foothills of Virginia's Blue Ridge Mountains, the Blue Knoll is situated on a quiet country road surrounded by rolling hills covered with cattle, grass, and wildflowers. In the area, visitors will find ample opportunities for hiking, horseback riding, shopping, and wine sampling.

Pineapple Upside-Down French Toast

¼ **cup unsalted butter**
½ **cup firmly packed dark brown sugar**
¾ **cup fresh or firmly packed (well-**
        drained) crushed pineapple

Blue Knoll Farm

Dash ground cinnamon
1½ cups milk
2 large eggs
¼ teaspoon salt
6 ¾-inch thick slices challah bread

Spray a 9 x 13-inch baking dish with cooking spray. In a saucepan melt the butter and stir in the sugar, pineapple, and cinnamon. In a shallow bowl whisk together the milk, eggs, and salt. Spread the pineapple mixture evenly across the bottom of the prepared baking dish. Dip the bread slices in the milk mixture and arrange in a single layer on top of the pineapple. Bake in a 400° oven for 20 to 25 minutes or until the bread is golden brown. Cool very briefly (1 to 2 minutes). Remove from the baking dish.

MAKES 2 TO 4 SERVINGS.

Basil Breakfast Strata

1 cup milk
½ cup dry white wine
1 day-old loaf of challah or peasant bread, cut in ½-inch thick slices
8 ounces thinly sliced proscuitto, cut or torn into pieces
4 cups grated cheese (Provolone, Swiss, or Jarlsberg)
3 ripe tomatoes, sliced
½ cup pesto
4 eggs, beaten
Salt and pepper to taste
½ cup heavy cream

In a shallow bowl mix the milk and wine. Dip the bread slices in the mixture, squeeze gently, and place the slices in a 9 x 13-inch baking dish. Cover the layer with half of the proscuitto, half of the cheese, and half of the tomato slices. Drizzle with pesto. Repeat the layers, filling the dish. Beat the eggs with salt and pepper and pour evenly over the top of

the dish. Cover with plastic wrap and refrigerate overnight.

Remove the dish from the refrigerator to warm to room temperature. Drizzle cream over the top. Bake in a 350° oven for 50 minutes or until puffy and browned.

MAKES 6 TO 8 SERVINGS.

Fresh Seasonal Fruit Topped with Raspberry Sauce

1 10-ounce package frozen raspberries, thawed and juice reserved

....

1 tablespoon fresh lemon juice
6 cups seasonal fresh fruit, cut into bite-sized cubes (fresh peaches are particularly delicious)

In a blender blend the raspberries with their juice along with the lemon juice until smooth. Strain the sauce. Divide the fruit into 6 to 8 individual bowls and serve with sauce.

MAKES 6 TO 8 SERVINGS.

Miss Molly's Inn

4141 Main Street
Chincoteague, Virginia 23336
(804) 336-6686

Built in 1886 by J.T. Rowley, known to shellfish lovers as "Clam King of the World," this charming Victorian is a Chincoteague Island landmark. For almost as long as anyone hereabouts can remember, it was the home of Miss Molly, who was Mr. Rowley's daughter. The inn, of course, is named for her, and together with its seven well appointed guest rooms, it is as gracious as the lady it celebrates.

Miss Molly's World Famous Eggs

1 tablespoon butter
½ cup finely chopped scallions, green part only
24 large eggs (use more if the eggs are small)
Louisiana Hot Sauce to taste (use lots!)
Crushed red pepper to taste
Salt and pepper, preferably freshly ground
2 cups grated sharp Cheddar cheese
Dried or fresh dill

In a skillet melt the butter and sauté the scallions. Add the eggs, hot sauce, red pepper, and salt and pepper to taste to the scallions. When almost done throw in the cheese and finish cooking the eggs. Add dill at the end, and serve more on the top of the eggs after turning them out onto a warm serving platter. Serve with hot croissants, if desired.

MAKES 8 TO 12 SERVINGS.

Miss Molly's Apple Cake (Apfelkuchen)

2 eggs
1 cup sugar
9 tablespoons margarine
1 tablespoon oil
1 teaspoon vanilla extract
2 cups self rising flour
3 very large Rome apples

In a large bowl combine the eggs, sugar, margarine, oil, and vanilla. Fold the flour into the mixture. Set aside. Peel and quarter the apples.

Butter and flour a 10-inch springform pan. Spread the batter over the bottom of the prepared pan. The batter should be stiff and will not pour. Place the apples round-side up

Miss Molly's Inn

around the edge of the pan and in the center. Score the apples deeply with a sharp knife. Bake in a 350° oven for approximately 1 hour and 15 minutes.

Note: This is a really delicious cake and beautiful to look at with the sliced apples peeping through the cake. Wonderful with whipped cream.

MAKES 12 SERVINGS.

The Bailiwick Inn

The Bailiwick Inn

4023 Chain Bridge Road
Fairfax, Virginia 22030
(703) 691-2266

*I*mmediately across from the Fairfax County Courthouse, where among other things George Washington's will is filed, stands a nineteenth century home known nowadays as the Bailiwick Inn. It's a big house, accommodating fourteen spacious guest rooms. All are individually furnished with antiques, and some have fireplaces and Jacuzzi tubs. Fairfax is one of the most historic towns in a state known for its history. One of the oldest toll roads in the nation, the "Ox Road," is now the city's main street and runs right in front of the inn. George Mason University is a few blocks away, and Manassas National Battlefield Park is a short drive into the countryside.

Roasted Red Pepper Soup

4 **large red bell peppers**

1 **medium onion, chopped**
1 **shallot, chopped**
2 **cloves garlic, chopped**

1 **teaspoon olive oil**
1 **sprig fresh thyme**
1 **bay leaf**
2 **cups chicken stock**
 Salt and pepper to taste
½ **teaspoon Tabasco sauce**

Roast the peppers over an open flame using a gas stove, broiler or grill. Turn the peppers so the skin becomes evenly charred and blackened. Place the roasted peppers in a plastic bag and let cool. Rub all the blackened skin off the peppers . Remove the seeds and chop the flesh coarsely.

In a saucepan heat the olive oil and sweat the onion, shallot, and garlic until soft and translucent. Add the red peppers and reduce any liquid they have rendered. Add the herbs, and cover with the chicken stock. Bring to a boil and simmer for 20 to 30 minutes.

Remove the herbs. In a blender purée the soup until smooth. Strain and reheat. Adjust the seasoning with salt, pepper, and Tabasco and serve.

MAKES 4 SERVINGS.

Scones

3 **cups all-purpose flour**
⅓ **cup sugar**
2½ **teaspoons baking powder**
¾ **teaspoon salt**
¾ **cup firm butter**

¾ **cup currants or chopped dates**

1 **teaspoon grated orange zest**
½ **teaspoon baking soda**
1 **cup buttermilk**

1 **tablespoon cream**
2 **tablespoons sugar**
¼ **teaspoon ground cinnamon**

In a large bowl stir together the flour, ⅓ cup of sugar, baking powder, and salt. Cut the butter into the dry ingredients with a pastry blender or 2 knives until it resembles coarse meal. Stir in the currants and orange zest. Dissolve the baking soda in the buttermilk.

Make a well in the middle of the mixture and add buttermilk all at once. Stir the mixture with fork until the dough pulls away from the side of the bowl. Gather the dough into a ball with floured hands, and turn out onto a lightly floured board. Roll out into a ½-inch thick circle. Using 1-inch to 1½-inch cutter cut into individual scones. Place 1½-inches apart on a baking sheet. Brush with cream. In a small bowl combine 2 tablespoons of sugar and the cinnamon, and sprinkle the mixture over the scones. Bake in a 425° oven for 10 minutes until lightly browned.

Serve warm with lightly whipped heavy cream and different fruit preserves.

MAKES ABOUT 2 DOZEN.

Caledonia Farm 1812

47 Dearing Road
Flint Hill, Virginia 22627
(540) 675-3693

*W*ith Virginia's Blue Ridge Mountains in the background, the Caledonia Farm glories in an extraordinarily beautiful setting of scenic pastures lined by stone fences. It has history to offer as well—the Federal-style house and companion summer kitchen were completed at about the time the War of 1812 got underway. Its two-foot-thick stone walls and thirty-two-foot beams remain intact to this day, along with the carved mantles, paneled windows, and wide pine floors. The enormous fireplace in the winter kitchen is a popular gathering place when the weather is chilly, while during warmer months the three porches allow guest to enjoy the outdoors.

Eggs Benedict Caledonia

1 package Hollandaise sauce mix
3 tablespoons lemon juice
1 English muffin, split
  Butter or margarine
2 slices Canadian bacon or ham
2 eggs
  Garnish of choice

Prepare the Hollandaise sauce according to the package directions using 3 tablespoons of lemon juice instead of the milk.

Toast or broil the muffin halves and spread with butter. Top with slices of Canadian bacon or ham. Poach the eggs 3½ minutes in cups sprayed with cooking spray. When the whites are set and yolks liquid, invert the eggs upon the awaiting muffins. Decoratively smother with Hollandaise sauce and top with a twisted sliver of lemon. Garnish the plate with fresh parsley and any house specialty such as homemade applesauce, and proudly present.

Note: The Hollandaise sauce is the key to great Eggs Benedict, and after trying a variety or recipes and mixes, Phil suggests the French or Knorr packaged sauce but replace the milk with 3 tablespoons of real lemon juice. Unlike anything else, he says, it's fool-proof, mixes well, refrigerates and is ready whenever the cook turns up the heat.

MAKES 1 SERVING.

Apple Nut Bread

2 cups all-purpose flour
¾ cup sugar

1 tablespoon baking powder
½ tablespoon baking soda
½ tablespoon ground cinnamon
1 egg
1 cup applesauce
2 tablespoons oil
1 cup chopped nuts

In a large bowl combine the flour, sugar, baking powder, soda, and cinnamon. Add the egg, oil, and applesauce, and blend well. Add the nuts. Pour the batter into a greased 5 x 9-inch loaf pan or 12 cup muffin pan. Bake in a 350° oven for 45 minutes. The bread is done when a toothpick inserted in the center comes out clean. Cool and serve.

MAKES 1 LOAF.

La Vista Plantation

4420 Guinea Station Road
Fredericksburg, Virginia 22408
(540) 898-8444

Built in 1838, this Virginia plantation home was already almost a quarter of a century old when two massive armies squared off in 1862 at nearby Fredericksburg to fight one of the bloodiest battles of the Civil War. Set against the lush countryside of Virginia's Spotsylvania County, the house reflects the Classic Revival style with high ceilings, wide heart of pine floors, acorn and oak leaf moldings, and two-story front portico. The ten-acre grounds present a fine balance of mature trees, flowering shrubs, pastures, woods, garden, and a pond stocked with bass and sunfish. There are two guest rooms, both handsomely furnished.

Morning Glory Muffins

4 cups all-purpose flour
2½ cups sugar
4 teaspoons baking soda
4 teaspoons ground cinnamon

1 teaspoon salt
2 cups oil
6 eggs, lightly beaten
4 teaspoons vanilla extract
4 cups grated, peeled apples

La Vista Plantation

---

1 cup raisins
1 cup flaked coconut
1 cup shredded carrots
1 cup chopped walnuts (optional)

In a large bowl combine the flour, sugar, baking soda, cinnamon, and salt. In a separate bowl mix the oil, eggs, and vanilla. Stir into the dry ingredients just until moistened. Fold in the apples, raisins, coconut, carrots, and nuts. Fill greased or paper-lined muffin cups two-thirds full. Bake in a 350° oven for 25 to 30 minutes or until a toothpick inserted in a center muffin comes out clean.

MAKES 3 DOZEN.

Orange Toasted Almond Muffins

2½ cups all-purpose flour
1 cup sugar
3½ teaspoons baking powder
½ teaspoon salt
¼ teaspoon almond extract
1 tablespoon grated orange zest
⅓ cup oil
¾ cup evaporated milk
½ cup water
1 egg
1 cup toasted finely chopped almonds, divided
1 cup sifted confectioners' sugar
1 to 2 tablespoon orange juice

In a large bowl combine the flour, sugar, baking powder, salt, almond extract, orange zest, oil, evaporated milk, water, and egg, and beat with an electric mixer at high speed for 30 seconds until blended. Fold in ¾ cup of chopped almonds. Spoon the batter into 18 greased or paper-lined muffin cups, filling two-thirds full. Bake in a 375° oven for 15 to 18 minutes, or until a toothpick inserted in the center comes out clean. Remove from the pan, and cool on wire rack.

In a small bowl combine the confectioners' sugar and orange juice. Spread over each muffin. Sprinkle with the remaining almonds.

MAKES 18 MUFFINS.

Creamed Virginia Country Ham

3 tablespoons butter
3 tablespoons minced onion

3 tablespoons green bell pepper
3 tablespoons all-purpose flour
2 cups milk
1 cup chopped Virginia country ham

....

1 tablespoon chopped parsley or
   chives
¼ teaspoon paprika
2 tablespoons dry sherry

In a skillet melt the butter over medium heat, and sauté the onion and green pepper until light brown. Sprinkle in the flour, and stir a few minutes. Add the milk slowly, stirring constantly. Add the ham and simmer, stirring until thickened. Remove the pan from the heat, and season with the remaining ingredients. Serve over hot buttered toast, English muffins, or corn bread or corn muffins.

MAKES 4 TO 6 SERVINGS.

Killahevlin

Killahevlin

1401 North Royal Avenue
Front Royal, Virginia 22630
(800) 847-6132

*N*amed for the Irish hamlet where its builder grew up, Killahevlin rises on the highest point in Front Royal, Virginia, which, in turn, stands in the shadow of the Blue Ridge near the northern entrance to the Shenandoah National Park. A stately, Edwardian mansion, the main building features a spacious screened veranda and a fine view of the mountains. In addition to the six lovely rooms in the mansion, there are three spacious suites in the adjacent Tower House built in 1905 as a guest cottage.

Very Berry Coffee Cake

1½ cups sifted all-purpose flour

....

1 teaspoon baking powder
¼ teaspoon salt
½ cup butter, softened
1 cup sugar
2 large eggs

....

1 teaspoon vanilla extract
3 tablespoons sour cream
⅓ cup milk
1½ cups fresh berries (or frozen,
     thawed; try a combination of
     blueberries, blackberries and
     raspberries)

....

3 tablespoons butter, softened
⅓ cup sugar
¼ cup unsifted all-purpose flour
½ teaspoon ground cinnamon

Grease a 9-inch square pan with shortening. In a medium bowl sift together 1½ cups of flour, baking powder, and salt. Set aside. In a large bowl cream ½ cup of butter and eggs with an electric mixer. Add the eggs one at a time, and beat until fluffy. Add the vanilla and sour cream, and mix well. Alternately add the dry ingredients and milk to the batter, beginning and ending with the flour. Spread half the batter into the prepared pan and smooth the top. Spread the berries (well drained) on top of the batter. Cover the berries with the remaining batter and spread the top evenly with a spatula (some berries will show through).

In a small bowl combine 3 tablespoons of butter, ⅓ cup of sugar, ¼ cup of flour, and cinnamon, and pinch with fingertips to make crumbs. Spread on top of the cake. Bake in the center of a 350° oven for 30 to 35 minutes, or longer in a glass pan, until a toothpick inserted in the center comes out clean and the cake is golden brown. Cool the cake completely in the pan on a wire rack.

Cut into squares and serve at room temperature.

MAKES 12 SERVINGS.

Fresh Banana Coffee Cake

½ cup butter, softened
1¼ cups sugar
2 eggs
1½ cups all-purpose flour
½ teaspoon baking powder
½ teaspoon baking soda
1½ teaspoons salt
2 very ripe bananas, mashed
3 tablespoons sour cream

Butter a 9-inch square cake pan. In a large bowl cream the butter and sugar until blended. Add the eggs and beat until fluffy. In a separate bowl stir together the flour, baking powder, soda, and salt. Add to the creamed mixture, along with the mashed bananas and sour cream. Mix until the batter is smooth and blended well. Pour into the prepared pan. Bake in a 350° oven for 30 to 35 minutes or until the cake feels firm to the touch. Cool the cake completely in the pan on a wire rack. Refrigerate before cutting into squares.

Serve at room temperature.

MAKES 12 SERVINGS.

Sleepy Hollow Farm

16280 Blue Ridge Turnpike
Gordonsville, Virginia 22942
(540) 832-5555

*S*ome sections of the home may have been built as far back as the eighteenth century, but most of the structure seen today dates to the 1850s. It has continued to grow and evolve over the years, but remains as it has always been, a simple farmhouse. Sleepy Hollow is located in historic Orange County at the edge of the Virginia Blue Ridge. Visitors may want to visit Montpelier, the home of James and Dolley Madison.

Sleepy Hollow Farm

In House Cookies

½   **cup margarine**
½   **cup butter**
1   **cup oil**
1   **cup sugar**
1   **cup packed dark brown sugar**
1   **egg, beaten**

1   **teaspoon vanilla extract**
3½   **cups all-purpose flour**

1   **teaspoon baking soda**

1   **teaspoon salt**
1   **cup Rice Krispies**
1   **cup flaked coconut**
1   **cup quick oats**

In a large bowl cream together the margarine, butter, oil, sugar, and brown sugar. Add the egg and vanilla, and mix well. In a separate bowl sift together the flour, soda, and salt. Add the dry ingredients to the batter. Fold in the Rice Krispies, coconut, and oats. Drop by teaspoons onto a greased foil-lined baking sheet. Bake in a 350° oven for 10 to 12 minutes.

MAKES 3 TO 4 DOZEN.

Poached Pears
with Sauce and Cream

1   **bottle spiced wine**
2   **cups cranberry juice**
1   **cup Port wine**
1   **cup orange juice**
1   **cup of brown sugar**
2   **cinnamon sticks**
2   **cloves**
    Zest of 2 oranges, thinly sliced
¼   **teaspoon ground cardamom**
8   **to 12 medium pears**
4   **to 5 tablespoons lemon juice**
    Sweetened whipped cream

In a large saucepan or stockpot combine the wine, cranberry juice, port, and orange juice. Add the brown sugar, cinnamon, cloves, orange zest, and cardamom. Bring the mixture to a simmer.

Peel and core the pears and trim the bottoms so they will stand up in the liquid mixture. In a shallow dish roll the pears in the lemon juice.

Add the pears and lemon juice to the saucepan and cover. Bring the mixture to a boil, reduce the heat, and simmer for 15 to 45 minutes until the pears are tender. The pears are done when the tines of a fork enter easily.

Transfer the pears to a serving dish. Reduce the syrup by boiling over high heat. Be careful not to burn the syrup. Add sugar to taste if necessary.

When ready to serve, place the pears in individual bowls. Heat the syrup and pour 2 tablespoons of the syrup over the pears. As a final touch, put 1 tablespoon of sweetened slightly whipped cream on top of each pear so it gently dribbles down the sides.

MAKES 8 TO 12 SERVINGS.

The
Hummingbird
Inn

❧

Wood Lane, P.O. Box 147
Goshen, Virginia 24439
(800) 397-3214

*T*he pace of life in the Shenandoah Valley country is slow, as this Goshen, Virginia, architectural marvel can testify. A unique Victo-

The Hummingbird Inn

rian Carpenter Gothic villa, it was begun in 1780 and not completed in its present form until 1853. The final product was well worth the time and the effort, however. The walls, the shutters, the rooms, the fireplaces, the antiques—everything is gorgeous here. And in the summer garden there are plenty of hummingbirds.

Lemon Chess Pie

2   **whole eggs**
4   **egg yolks**
1   **cup sugar**
4   **tablespoons butter, melted**
¼   **cup heavy cream**

1   **tablespoon flour**

1   **tablespoon yellow cornmeal**
¼   **cup lemon juice**

1   **tablespoon grated lemon zest**
1   **unbaked 9-inch pie shell**

In a large bowl beat the eggs, yolks, and sugar together with an electric mixer at high speed for 2 minutes. Add the butter and cream, and beat again at high speed for 2 minutes. Add the flour, cornmeal, lemon juice and zest, and mix well. Pour into the pie shell. Bake in a 350° oven for 45 to 60 minutes until the top is medium brown and a toothpick inserted in the center comes out clean. Allow to cool to room temperature.

Serve with whipped cream if desired.

MAKES 6 SLICES.

Baked Orange-Honey-
Cinnamon French Toast

¼   **cup butter or margarine**
4   **whole eggs (or egg substitute)**
⅓   **cup orange juice**
½   **teaspoon vanilla extract**

1   **tablespoon Curacao liqueur**
    (optional)

⅛   **teaspoon salt**
2   **pinches nutmeg**
¼   **teaspoon tarragon**
¼   **cup honey**

¾ teaspoon ground cinnamon
6 thick slices machine-made oatmeal bread (or other hearty bread)
¼ cup slivered toasted almonds

Place the butter in a 12 x 17-inch half-sheet baking pan, and place in a 375° oven to melt for about 4 minutes. While the butter is melting, in a shallow bowl combine the eggs, juice, vanilla, liqueur, salt, nutmeg, and tarragon, and mix well.

Remove the pan from the oven. Pour in the honey and sprinkle with cinnamon. Cut each slice of bread in half. Dip the bread in the egg mixture, coating both sides evenly, and drain the excess liquid. Arrange the slices on top of the honey cinnamon mixture. Bake in a 375° oven for 20 to 25 minutes until lightly brown on the upper side.

With a metal turner, invert toast onto heated plates, two half-slices per person. Sprinkle with almonds and serve with additional honey on the side. Serve with any breakfast meat, and garnish plate with banana slices, orange twists, strawberries or other fruit. Keeps well lightly covered with aluminum foil in warm oven.

MAKES 6 SERVINGS.

The Joshua Wilton House

412 South Main Street
Harrisonburg, Virginia 22801
(540) 434-4464

The Joshua Wilton House is within walking distance of one of the Shenandoah Valley's most historic towns. A beautifully restored Victorian it offers five guest bedrooms furnished with high quality antiques. The on-premises restaurant features locally grown produce. There is also a cafe featuring outdoor seating and a romantic gazebo.

Honey Macadamia Bars

Pastry for a 2-crust pie
3 cups sugar
3 cups plus 2 tablespoons butter
2 cups plus 2 tablespoons honey
1¼ cups heavy cream
4¼ cups lightly roasted, rough chopped macadamia nuts

....

1 cup heavy cream
8 ounces semisweet chocolate, finely chopped
¼ cup butter

Line a 11 x 17-inch baking pan with the pastry. Bake in a 350° oven until light golden. In a heavy-bottomed stainless steel pot combine the sugar, 3 cups plus 2 tablespoons of butter, honey, and 1¼ cups of heavy cream. Stir over medium high heat until the sugar is dissolved. Attach a candy thermometer and cook without stirring until it reaches 260°. Remove the pan from the heat and add the macadamia nuts. Stir until combined. Pour into the pre-baked pastry shell. Bake in a 350° oven for 30 minutes. Cool completely.

In a saucepan heat 1 cup of heavy cream to just below a boil. Remove the pan from the heat and add the chocolate. Allow the mixture to sit for 30 seconds. Add ¼ cup of butter and stir until smooth. Spread the glaze over the cooled candy. Cut into diamond-shaped bars.

Note: The Joshua Wilton House uses local wildflower honey in this recipe.

MAKES 16 TO 20 SERVINGS.

Pumpkin Cheesecake

2 cups ground graham cracker crumbs
¼ cup brown sugar
½ cup finely chopped pecans

....

1 teaspoon ground cinnamon
Melted butter

....

3 8-ounce packages cream cheese, softened
1 cup firmly packed dark brown sugar
1½ cups fresh pumpkin purée

....

1 teaspoon ground cinnamon

....

1 teaspoon allspice
3 eggs, room temperature
4 ounces white chocolate, melted

Butter a 10-inch springform pan. In a medium bowl combine the graham cracker crumbs, ¼ cup of brown sugar, pecans, and cinnamon with enough melted butter to bind the mixture. Press into the prepared pan. Bake in a 375° for 8 to 10 minutes.

In a large bowl beat the cream cheese and 1 cup of brown sugar until well combined. Add the pumpkin and spices. Add the eggs one at a time, then the melted chocolate. Do not overbeat. Pour the filling into the baked crust. Place the pan in a water bath. Bake in a 375° for about 45 minutes until set.

MAKES 6 TO 8 SERVINGS.

Butternut Squash and Apple Soup

¼ cup butter
1 medium onion, diced
4 tart apples, peeled, cored and cut into wedges

....

1 tablespoon chopped fresh thyme leaves
1 butternut squash, peeled, seeded, and cut in to chunks
1 quart chicken stock (or dry apple cider)
Salt, white pepper, and nutmeg to taste

In a saucepan melt the butter and slowly cook the onion for about 20 minutes or until very soft and sweet. Do not allow to color. Add the apples and thyme and cook for a few more minutes. Add the butternut squash and just cover with the stock or cider (or a combination).

Simmer until the squash is very tender. Purée with an immersion blender or transfer in batches to a food processor or blender. For an extra smooth consistency pass through a strainer with medium size holes. Season with salt, white pepper and nutmeg.

MAKES 4 TO 6 SERVINGS.

The Joshua Wilton House

Shenandoah Countryside

211 Somers Road
Luray, Virginia 22835
(540) 743-6434

*T*he Shenandoah Countryside features an outstanding view made
all the more remarkable by the
fact that a large part of what
guests see—more than forty-five
acres—is the B&B's own property. A
long, leisurely stroll through the
quaint town of Luray is
worthwhile.

Fat-free Banana-Raisin Muffins

1 cup all-purpose flour
1 cup unprocessed bran
¼ cup sugar
2 teaspoons baking powder
1 teaspoon baking soda
....
1 teaspoon ground cinnamon
¼ teaspoon salt
½ cup pitted prunes
1 tablespoon water
½ cup mashed banana (approximately
   1 medium)
....
1 teaspoon vanilla
1 8-ounce nonfat yogurt
2 large egg whites
1 cup golden raisins

In a large bowl combine the flour, bran,
sugar, baking powder, soda, cinnamon, and
salt. In a food processor blend the prunes
and water to make a thick paste. Add the
banana, vanilla, yogurt, and egg whites, and
mix well. Stir the liquid mixture into the dry
ingredients just until moistened. Fold in the
raisins. Spoon the batter into 12 muffin cups.
Bake in a 375° oven for 25 to 30 minutes.
MAKES 1 DOZEN.

Custard Filled Cornbread

1 cup all-purpose flour
¾ cup yellow cornmeal
....
1 teaspoon baking powder
½ teaspoon baking soda
2 eggs
3 tablespoons butter or margarine,
   melted
3 tablespoons sugar
½ teaspoon salt
2 cups milk
1½ teaspoons white vinegar
1 cup heavy cream (or half and half)

Grease an 8-inch square pan. Heat the pan in
a 350° oven. In a medium bowl combine the
flour, cornmeal, baking powder, and soda. In
a large bowl beat the eggs with the melted
butter. Add the sugar, salt, milk, and vinegar.
Add the dry ingredients and mix just until
moistened and the lumps are gone. Pour the
batter into the hot pan. Pour the heavy cream
in the center of the batter. Do not stir. Bake in
a 350° oven for 1 hour.

Serve warm.

Note: At Shenandoah Countryside this is
used as a shortcake base for strawberries or
rhubarb or blueberries.

MAKES 6 TO 8 SERVINGS.

The Madison House

413 Madison Street
Lynchburg, Virginia 24504
(804) 528-1503

*I*t took nine different colors of
paint to produce the rather extraordinary effect seen on the exterior of
the Madison House. With its Victorian decor, antique-filled parlors,
and library featuring books dating
back as far as the 1700s, the interior is remarkable as well. Among
the Madison's many attractions is
the high English tea served each
afternoon.

Orange Scones

3 cups all-purpose flour
¼ cup sugar
....
1 tablespoon baking powder
½ teaspoon baking soda
½ teaspoon salt
¾ cup cold butter, cut into pieces
1 cup heavy cream
¼ teaspoon orange extract
   Cream
   Butter and jam

In a large bowl combine the flour, sugar, baking powder, soda, and salt. Cut in the cold
butter until the mixture resembles coarse
meal. Add the cream and orange extract, mixing until the dry ingredients are moistened.
Shape the dough into a ball, and place on a
lightly floured surface. Roll the dough to ½-
inch thickness. Cut into 2-inch rounds with a
biscuit cutter. Place double layers of dough
on an ungreased baking sheet. Brush the tops
with cream. Bake in a 400° oven for 12 to 15
minutes.

Serve hot with butter and jam.

MAKES ABOUT 2 DOZEN.

Drop Pudding

1 cup pancake mix
1 cup milk
1 egg
   Blueberries (or raspberries, fresh or
      frozen, or cooked apples)
   Butter and maple syrup

In a small bowl combine the pancake mix,
milk, and egg. Add the blueberries and mix to
coat fruit. Divide the batter among 2
ramekins. Bake in a 450° oven for 20 minutes.

Serve hot with butter and maple syrup.

MAKES 2 SERVINGS.

Shenandoah Countryside

Shenandoah Springs

P.O. Box 770
Madison, Virginia 22727
(540) 923-4300

This country inn is surrounded by plenty of country—more than 1,000 acres of forests, meadows, shady lanes, and scenic views. The nearby lake is great for fishing, canoeing, and, in winter, ice skating. Not far away is the Jackson Ridge Wagon Trail dating to the 1800s.

Jiffy Plum Cake

¾ cup oil
3 cups sugar
3 eggs
....
1 teaspoon ground cinnamon
2 cups self-rising flour
2 4-ounce jars strained plum baby food
1 cup chopped pecans
1 cup confectioners' sugar
   Juice of 1 lemon

In a large bowl combine the oil, sugar, eggs, cinnamon, flour, and plum baby food. Fold in the pecans. Spoon into a tube pan. Bake in a 375° oven for 50 to 60 minutes.

In a small bowl combine the confectioners' sugar and lemon juice. Pour over the cake while it is still warm.
MAKES 8 SERVINGS.

Pumpkin Dip

1 8-ounce cream cheese
....
1 teaspoon ground cinnamon
1 16-ounce box confectioners' sugar
½ teaspoon ginger
1 16-ounce can pumpkin
   Gingersnaps

In a medium bowl combine the cream cheese, cinnamon, confectioners' sugar, ginger, and pumpkin. Mix together and serve with gingersnaps.
MAKES ABOUT 5 CUPS.

Broccoli Salad

1 bunch raw broccoli, cut into flowerets
½ to 1 cup raisins
10 slices bacon, cooked and crumbled
1 medium red onion (or 5 green onions), sliced
1 cup nuts
....
1 cup mayonnaise
2 teaspoons cider vinegar
¼ cup sugar

In a salad bowl combine the broccoli flowerets, raisins, bacon, onion and nuts. Toss well. In a separate bowl combine the mayonnaise, vinegar, and sugar. Pour the dressing over the salad, and toss to coat.
MAKES 4 TO 6 SERVINGS.

The Widow Kip's Country Inn

355 Orchard Drive
Mount Jackson, Virginia 22842
(540) 477-2400

This 1830s home rests on seven Shenandoah Valley acres within view of the majestic Massanutten Mountains. The inn's five guest rooms are decorated with antiques and feature their original fireplaces, locally crafted quilts, and fourposters. Two courtyard cottages are also available.

The Widow Kip's Country Inn

Apple Crisp Pancake

1 egg, beaten
¾ cup milk
¾ cup chunky applesauce
....
1 teaspoon vanilla extract
2 cups pancake mix
....
½ cup quick oats
¼ cup brown sugar
¼ cup pancake mix
2 tablespoons butter

Spray a jelly roll pan with cooking spray. In a large bowl combine the egg, milk, applesauce, vanilla, and pancake mix. Spread the mixture in the prepared pan. In a medium bowl combine the oats, brown sugar, pancake mix, and butter. Sprinkle the topping over the pancake batter. Bake in a 375° oven for 14 to 16 minutes.
MAKES 8 SERVINGS.

Apple Cinnamon Syrup

1 cup sugar
2 tablespoons cornstarch
2 teaspoons ground cinnamon
2 cups apple cider or juice
2 tablespoons lemon juice
¼ cup butter

In a saucepan combine the sugar, cornstarch, cinnamon, cider, and lemon juice. Bring the mixture to a boil. Remove the pan from the heat and add the butter.
MAKES ABOUT 3¼ CUPS.

The Hidden Inn

249 Caroline Street
Orange, Virginia 22960
(540) 672-3625

T*he Hidden Inn is appropriately named because it's perfect for those who want to escape for a weekend in the country or relax from the daily routine. Each of the ten guest rooms is individually decorated, featuring a brass or canopy bed, antiques, and a cozy handmade quilt. A museum on the life and works of James Madison, who is known as the father of the U.S. Constitution, is just a short walk away. Montpelier, several of Virginia's finest wineries, and numerous Civil War sites are nearby.*

Mushrooms in Puff Pastry

- 3 **tablespoons butter**
- 1 **pound fresh mushrooms, sliced**
- 2 **scallions, chopped**
- 4 **ounces cream cheese**
- ½ **teaspoon herbes de Provence**
- 2 **tablespoons grated Romano cheese**
- 2 **sheets puff pastry, thawed**
- 1 **egg, beaten**
  Sour cream

In a skillet melt the butter and sauté the mushrooms and scallions until tender. Drain the excess liquid. Add the cream cheese, cover, and heat over very low heat until the cheese melts. Stir the cream cheese into the mushrooms and add the herbs and Romano cheese. Place half of the mushroom mixture down the center of each pastry sheet and fold the sides in. Decorations such as hearts or leaves may be cut from extra pastry and placed on top. Brush the pastry with egg. Place on a baking sheet. Bake in a 350° oven for 20 to 30 minutes. The pastry will puff and turn golden brown.

Cut each pastry into 5 equal servings. Serve hot with a dollop of sour cream.
MAKES 10 SERVINGS.

Marinated Flank Steak Salad

- ½ **cup red wine vinegar**
- 1 **cup oil**
- 1 **cup tomato juice**
- 1 **tablespoon minced garlic**
- 1 **tablespoon crushed fresh rosemary**
  Dash hot sauce
- 1 **teaspoon pepper**
- ½ **teaspoon salt**
- 2 **tablespoons chopped fresh basil**
- 2 **pounds flank steak**

- 4 **stalks heart of palm, sliced**
- ¼ **pound fresh mushrooms, sliced**
- 2 **stalks celery, diced**
- 1 **8-ounce bottle vinaigrette dressing**
  Mixed greens
  Sliced tomato
  Monterey Jack cheese, grated

In a bowl combine the first 9 ingredients. In a shallow pan marinate the steak for 8 hours or overnight.

Broil or cook on a grill for 3½ minutes on each side until rare to medium. Slice thin on the diagonal, across the grain of the meat.

In a large bowl combine the steak slices, hearts of palm, mushrooms, and celery, and toss with the vinaigrette dressing. Serve over a bed of mixed greens with sliced tomato and Jack cheese. Serve chilled or at room temperature.
MAKES 4 SERVINGS.

Praline Mincemeat Cheesecake

- ½ **cup butter**
- 1 **cup graham cracker crumbs**
- ¼ **cup sugar**
- 2 **8-ounce packages cream cheese, softened**
- 1 **14-ounce can sweetened condensed milk**
- 1 **envelope unflavored gelatin (2½ teaspoons)**
- ¼ **cup lemon juice**
- 1⅓ **cups mincemeat**
- ½ **cup chopped pecans**

- 1 **tablespoon grated lemon zest**
- 1 **cup heavy cream, whipped**

In a saucepan melt the butter. Stir in the crumbs and sugar. Pat firmly on the bottom of a 9-inch springform pan. Chill.

In a large bowl beat the cream cheese until fluffy. Add the sweetened condensed milk, beating until smooth. In a small saucepan soften the gelatin in the lemon juice, heat, and stir until dissolved. Add the cheese mixture with the mincemeat, nuts, and zest, and mix well. Thoroughly fold in the whipped cream. Turn into the prepared crust. Chill for 3 hours or until set. Garnish with a dollop of whipped cream.
MAKES 6 TO 8 SERVINGS.

Sweet Potato Muffins

- ½ **cup margarine**
- 1 **cup sugar**
- 1 **16-ounce can sweet potatoes or yams, drained**
- 2 **large eggs**
- 1½ **cups milk**

- 1 **teaspoon lemon extract**
- 2½ **cups all-purpose flour**
- 4½ **teaspoons baking powder**
- ¾ **teaspoon grated nutmeg**
- ½ **teaspoon salt**

- 1 **teaspoon ground cinnamon**
- ½ **cup chopped walnuts**

- ¼ **cup sugar**
- 1 **tablespoon ground cinnamon**

In a large bowl cream the butter and sugar until light and fluffy. Beat in the sweet potatoes. Add the eggs and beat well. Mix in the milk and lemon extract. In a medium bowl combine the flour, baking powder, nutmeg, salt, and cinnamon. Add to the creamed mixture and mix lightly. Do not overmix. Stir in the nuts.

Spray muffin cups with cooking spray. Fill the muffin cups three-fourths full. Sprinkle with cinnamon-sugar mixture. Bake in a 400° oven for 20 to 25 minutes or until lightly browned. Cool on a rack.
MAKES 1 DOZEN.

The Ashby Inn

692 Federal Street
Paris, Virginia 22130
(540) 592-3900

*T*he Ashby Inn is a converted 1829 residence in the Virginia village of Paris near the foothills of the Blue Ridge. The inn is located near the site of the Ashby Tavern, frequented by George Washington when he was a young surveyor. Most of the inn's guest room furnishings date to the early 1800s. The original kitchen with its walnut beams and stone fireplace has been converted to a taproom. The surrounding area offers hiking along the Appalachain Trail, horse shows and races, vineyards, anitque shops, and fishing.

Ashby Inn Crab Cakes

2   **pounds picked jumbo lump crab meat**
2   **tablespoons breadcrumbs**
2   **pinches Old Bay Seasoning**

2   **large eggs**
1   **tablespoon (slightly heaping) mayonnaise**
1   **tablespoon chopped parsley**
2   **dashes Tabasco sauce**
2   **dashes lemon juice**
1   **tablespoon chopped fresh tarragon**

   Clarified butter
   Lemon–Caper Mayonnaise (recipe follows)

In a large bowl toss the crab meat with the breadcrumbs and Old Bay Seasoning. In a medium bowl vigorously whisk the eggs, mayonnaise, parsley, Tabasco, lemon juice, and tarragon. Gently mix the egg mixture into the crab mixture. Divide into 8 cakes and broil with clarified butter.

Plate, and pour butter over the top of each cake. Serve with Lemon–Caper Mayonnaise.
MAKES 6 SERVINGS.

Lemon–Caper Mayonnaise

1   **cup mayonnaise**
   Juice of 1 lemon
1½   **tablespoons chopped caper**
1½   **tablespoons chopped parsley**
   Salt and pepper to taste

In a small bowl combine all ingredients.
MAKES ABOUT 1¼ CUPS.

Warm Arborio Rice Pudding with Sun-dried Cherries and Hazelnuts

½   **cup sugar**
3½   **cups half and half**
1   **vanilla bean, split**
½   **cup aborio rice**
¼   **cup plus**
1   **tablespoon sun-dried cherries**
2   **ounces hazelnut liqueur**
½   **cup toasted hazelnuts, skins removed and lightly crushed**

In an ovenproof saucepan combine the sugar, half and half, and vanilla beans. Bring to a boil, then add the rice. Cover with foil. Bake in a 350° oven, stirring every 30 minutes, for about 1 hour and 30 minutes.

Meanwhile, in a small saucepan warm the sun-dried cherries with the hazelnut liqueur until the cherries are tender. When the rice pudding is done, add the liqueur and all but 1 tablespoon of cherries (reserved for garnish) to the pudding. Mix well. Top with the remaining cherries and toasted hazelnuts. Serve immediately
MAKES 4 TO 6 SERVINGS.

Gravlax with Mustard-Dill Sauce

2   **teaspoons crushed black peppercorns**
½   **cup sugar**
1¼   **cups coarse (kosher) salt**
1   **ounce crushed coriander seeds**
2   **ounces vodka**
1   **side fresh salmon**
   Small bunch fresh dill, rinsed and shaken dry

In a medium bowl combine the peppercorns, sugar, salt, coriander, and vodka, and rub evenly all over the fish skin-side up. Top with the dill.

Cover the dish with plastic wrap, draping it loosely over the sides. Place a plate or bowl with weights (such as a can or 2 of food) on top of the plastic covered fish and refrigerate, basting and turning the fish over every 12 hours or so, for 2 days.

Remove the weights and scrape off the dill and spices. Serve the gravlax, or wrap it tightly and store in the refrigerator for as long as 3 or 4 more days. For longer storage, place the fish in a small container just large enough to hold it, sprinkle with a little more chopped dill and a little vinegar, and cover with olive oil. It will keep in this fashion for up to 1 week.

Place the fish skin-side down on a carving board and slice across the grain in translucent thin slices. Cut on a slant and free from the skin at the base of each slice (the thinner the slice the better).

Serve with pumpernickel bread and shaved fennel and red onions marinated in a small amount of champagne vinegar and olive oil, chives, salt, and pepper.
MAKES 4 TO 6 SERVINGS.

Mustard-Dill Sauce

½   **cup Dijon mustard**
2   **teaspoons dry mustard**
6   **tablespoons sugar**
¼   **cup white vinegar**
½   **cup fresh dill**
⅔   **cup oil**
   Salt and white pepper to taste

In a food processor combine the Dijon mustard, dry mustard, sugar, vinegar, and dill. While processing, slowly add the oil. Adjust the seasoning with more sugar and/or vinegar and salt and pepper.
MAKES ABOUT 2¼ CUPS.

High Meadows Lane
Scottsville, Virginia 24590
(804) 286-2218

Scottsville, Virginia, on the James River in central Virginia was already one hundred years old when the original part of this inn was built in 1832. Two other additions were made to the complex over the years until it was renovated and opened as an inn in 1985. Listed on the National Register of Historic Places, it also has a vineyard on the property. The thirteen distinctively decorated rooms are furnished with period antiques. Guests enjoy the fifty surrounding acres of gardens, footpaths, forests, and ponds. Nearby attractions include Appomattox, Monticello, and the presidential homes of James Madison and James Monroe.

Spicy Sour Cream and Raisin Muffins

 2 **large eggs**
½ **cup sour cream**
½ **cup milk**
 2 **tablespoons instant coffee**
¾ **cup raisins**
1½ **cups all-purpose flour**
½ **cup old-fashioned oats**
½ **cup sugar**
 2 **teaspoons baking powder**
½ **teaspoon ground cinnamon**
½ **teaspoon ground cloves**
½ **teaspoon ground allspice**

Grease muffin cups. In a medium bowl combine the eggs, sour cream, milk, and instant coffee. Whisk until blended well. Stir in the raisins. Let stand 5 minutes. Stir.

In a large bowl mix the flour, oatmeal, sugar, baking powder, and spices. Add the sour cream mixture and fold in until the dry ingredients are moistened. Scoop the batter into the prepared muffin cups. Sprinkle with oatmeal flakes. Bake in a 375° oven for 20 to 25 minutes until browned.
MAKES 1 DOZEN.

Blackberry Orange Tea Bread

 5 **cups all-purpose flour**
 1 **cup sugar**
 1 **cup firmly packed light brown sugar**
 2 **tablespoons plus 1 teaspoon baking powder**
 2 **teaspoons salt**
 2 **cups blackberries**
 2 **teaspoons grated orange zest**
 2 **eggs**
2½ **cups milk**
 2 **teaspoons vanilla extract**
 6 **tablespoons oil**

In a large bowl mix the flour, sugar, brown sugar, baking powder, and salt. Add the remaining ingredients and mix gently. Pour into 2 greased loaf pans. Bake in a 350° oven for 1 hour.
MAKES 2 LOAVES.

Chicken Breast Citron

 6 **half chicken breasts deboned with skins left on**
 1 **cup lemon juice (5 lemons)**
 1 **cup lime juice (7 limes)**

¾ **cup all-purpose flour**
 2 **teaspoons paprika**
    Freshly ground pepper to taste
¾ **cup chicken stock**
 2 **tablespoons firmly packed brown sugar**
 2 **teaspoons herbes de Provence**
 1 **lemon, thinly sliced**

At least 12 hours before dinner, place the chicken breasts in a shallow dish. Combine lemon and lime juices and pour over the chicken. Marinate overnight, turning the chicken pieces occasionally.

Remove the chicken from the marinade, and reserve the remaining marinade. In a small bowl combine the flour, paprika, and

pepper. Dredge the chicken and place skin-side up in a shallow baking pan. Bake in a 350° oven for 25 minutes.

In a small saucepan place the remaining marinade. Add the stock, brown sugar, and herbs. Heat to a boil, and set aside. After 25 minutes, lay a slice of lemon on each breast and pour the sauce over. Return to the oven and bake for 20 minutes.
MAKES 6 SERVINGS.

Ratatouille Strata

 4 **slices whole wheat bread**
 6 **tablespoons olive oil**
 3 **onions, sliced**
 1 **eggplant, diced**
 1 **zucchini, diced**
 1 **green bell pepper, diced**
 5 **tomatoes, chopped**
 4 **eggs**
 2 **cups milk**
 1 **cup grated Gruyère cheese**
⅓ **cup Parmesan cheese**

In a greased 9-inch square baking dish arrange the bread. In a skillet heat the olive oil and sauté the onions and eggplant until tender but not brown. Add the zucchini and pepper and continue to sauté for 10 minutes. Finally, add the chopped tomatoes, cover, and cook for 10 minutes more. Pour the vegetable mixture evenly over the bread slices. In a medium bowl whisk the eggs and milk together, and add the grated Gruyère cheese. Pour the mixture over the bread and vegetables. Sprinkle all with Parmesan. Bake in a 350° oven for 1 hour, until set.
MAKES 9 SERVINGS AS A HOT DISH OR 18 AS A COLD ADDITION TO A BUFFET TABLE.

Chocolate Tortini

 1 **cup heavy cream, chilled**
½ **cup chocolate-flavored syrup, chilled**
¼ **cup almond macaroon or vanilla wafer crumbs**
¼ **cup plus 2 tablespoons chopped toasted almonds, divided**
¼ **cup chopped maraschino cherries**
4½ **teaspoons rum or ½ teaspoon rum extract**
    Marashino cherries for garnish

In a small bowl beat the cream until stiff. Gently fold in the chocolate syrup. Stir in the cookie crumbs, ¼ cup of chopped almonds, chopped maraschino cherries, and rum or rum extract. Divide the mixture among 4 dessert dishes and freeze until firm, about 4 hours. Just before serving, sprinkle with the remaining chopped almonds and garnish with maraschino cherries.

MAKES 4 SERVINGS.

The Manor at Taylor's Store

❧

Route 1, Box 533
Smith Mountain Lake, Virginia 24184
(540) 721-3951

*T*aylor's Store was established as a trading post in 1799. The manor house was built during the early 1800s as the focus of a prosperous tobacco plantation. The house as it appears today is a blend of several periods and styles as it has been restored and enlarged several times. Period antiques lend the house a romantic atmosphere and recall its long history. Nearby is Smith Mountain Lake, which offers boating, fishing, and swimming, while the Blue Ridge Parkway and the city of Roanoke are only about twenty minutes away by car.

Breakfast in a Cookie

½ cup canola oil
½ cup unsweetened applesauce
½ cup brown sugar
¼ cup egg substitute
1 tablespoon vanilla extract

1 tablespoon orange juice

1 tablespoon lemon juice
½ cup oat bran
½ cup seven-grain cereal
½ cup all-purpose flour
½ cup whole wheat pastry flour

1 teaspoon baking soda
½ teaspoon salt

1 teaspoon ground cinnamon

1 teaspoon ground allspice

1 teaspoon ground ginger
½ teaspoon ground cloves
3 cups old-fashioned oats
1 cup golden raisins
¼ cup unsweetened flaked coconut (optional, adds significant fat)
¼ cup chopped walnuts (optional, adds significant fat)

In a large bowl beat together the oil, applesauce, and brown sugar with an electric mixer. Add the egg substitute, vanilla, orange juice, and lemon juice, then beat again. In a separate bowl sift together the oat bran, 7-grain cereal, flours, soda, salt, and spices. Add the dry ingredients to the wet ingredients and mix well. Stir in the oats, and fold in the raisins and other optional ingredients, if desired. Drop the cookie dough by the tablespoon on ungreased cookie sheets. Bake in a 350° oven for 15 minutes or until golden. Remove the cookies from the sheet immediately and cool completely.

MAKES 3 DOZEN LARGE COOKIES.

Baked Cheese Grits

4 cups water
1 teaspoon salt
1 clove garlic, finely minced
5 tablespoons margarine
1 cup grits
½ cup low-fat sharp Cheddar cheese
½ cup egg substitute
⅓ cup skim milk

In a saucepan bring the water, salt, garlic, and margarine to a boil. Slowly pour in the grits, whisk into the water, and cook until thick. Mix in the cheese. In a small bowl beat the egg substitute and milk. Whisk the mixture into the grits. Transfer the grits to a 2-quart casserole dish or individual ramekins for baking. Bake in a 425° oven for 1 hour.

MAKES 8 TO 10 SERVINGS.

Southern Sausage Gravy

1 pound turkey sausage
½ cup margarine
⅔ cup all-purpose flour

6½ cups skim milk
½ teaspoon salt

1 teaspoon freshly ground pepper
¼ teaspoon Italian seasoning

Spray a large nonstick skillet with cooking spray. Brown the sausage in the skillet, stirring until it crumbles. Remove the sausage from the skillet, drain in a colander, and pat dry with paper towels. Wipe the pan drippings from the skillet. In the same skillet melt the margarine. Add the flour, stirring until smooth. Cook for 1 minute, stirring constantly. Gradually add the milk and cook over medium heat, stirring constantly, until thickened and bubbly. Stir in the seasonings and sausage. Cook until thoroughly heated, stirring constantly.

MAKES 8 SERVINGS.

Manor Moon Pie

8 whole wheat pita breads
½ cup low-fat yogurt cheese (or Neufchâtel)
2½ tablespoons strawberry preserves (or raspberry or peach)
2 cups egg substitute (equal to 8 eggs)
1 cup skim milk
2 teaspoons vanilla extract
2 tablespoons sugar
2 cups fresh strawberries, sliced and lightly sugared
Confectioners' sugar

Cut each pita bread in half to make 2 "pockets".

In a food processor combine the cheese and preserves until well blended. In a medium bowl mix together the egg substitute, milk, vanilla, and sugar, and stir well.

Carefully open 1 pita pocket and spread 1 tablespoon of the fruited cheese over the inside. Repeat this with each of the halves. Preheat a griddle to 350° (medium heat), spray with cooking spray or spread a small amount or margarine on the griddle to prevent sticking. Carefully dip each pita pocket in the egg batter and place it on the griddle. Cook until browned, flip, and cook until browned on the reverse side.

To serve, layer 2 of the crescent-shaped pitas just overlapping each other. Top with fresh strawberries and a sprinkle of confectioners' sugar.

MAKES 8 SERVINGS.

Heart Healthy Virginia Peanut Soup

- 2 tablespoons safflower margarine
- 2 ribs celery, chopped
- 1 medium onion, chopped
- 2 tablespoons all-purpose flour
- 2 cups chicken broth
- 2 cups skim milk
- 1 cup crunchy or smooth peanut butter (natural, freshly ground, without added oil, sugar, salt, or additives)
  Salt and pepper to taste
  Paprika

In a saucepan melt the margarine and brown the celery and onion. Add flour and chicken broth and bring to a boil. Add milk and combine well. Reduce the heat to medium low. Add the peanut butter and whisk to combine. Simmer for 5 minutes.

Ladle the soup into a blender in small batches and blend until smooth. Return it to the pan, reheat, and season with salt and pepper to taste.

Serve sprinkled with paprika.

MAKES 6 TO 8 SERVINGS.

Lee's Whole Grain Pancakes

- 1 cup stone-ground whole-grain flour
- 2 tablespoons sugar
- 2 tablespoons baking powder
....
- 1 teaspoon allspice
- ¼ teaspoon nutmeg
- 2 egg whites, whipped slightly
- 1 cup skim milk
- 2 tablespoons safflower or canola oil
  Granola, fruit, or nuts (optional)

In a medium bowl combine the flour, sugar, baking powder, allspice, and nutmeg. Add the egg whites and mix until the texture resembles cornmeal. Add the milk and oil at the same time and blend well. Allow the batter to "rise" for at least 20 minutes (this step is very important to a successful pancake!)

Spray a griddle with cooking spray. If desired sprinkle granola, fruit or nuts over the batter after it has been poured on the griddle. Cook on each side until golden.

MAKES 8 TO 10 PANCAKES OR 2 LARGE PORTIONS.

The Famous Manor Apple Puffs

- 2 pats canola margarine
- ½ cup egg substitute (2 eggs or 4 whites)
- ½ cup all-purpose flour
- ½ cup skim milk
  Dash nutmeg
- 2 apples, peeled, cored, chopped
  Sugar and cinnamon to taste
- ¼ cup chopped walnuts
- 1 tablespoon raisins
- 2 pats canola margarine
  Confectioners' sugar
  Maple syrup

In a medium bowl mix together the egg, flour, milk, and nutmeg with a whisk. In a separate bowl toss the apples with the cinnamon and sugar. Add the nuts and raisins to the chopped apples. Place a pat of margarine in each of 2 9-ounce au gratin ramekins, and put them in a 400° oven for at least 5 minutes, until the margarine melts and dishes get very hot. Carefully remove the dishes from the oven and ladle ½ cup of batter into each. Top with a generous scoop full of the apple- nut, raisin mixture. Immediately return the dishes to the oven and bake for 15 to 20 minutes or until they are puffed up and golden brown. Sprinkle with confectioners' sugar and serve immediately.

Offer Virginia maple syrup for guests to pour on top if they like, but many people find that the fruit and nut mixture adds plenty of sweetness.

MAKES 2 SERVINGS.

The Sampson Eagon Inn

❧

238 East Beverley Street
Staunton, Virginia 24401
(800) 597-9722

---

*T*he inn is located right across the street from Woodrow Wilson's birthplace in the Gospel Hill historic district of the fine, old Shenandoah

Valley town of Staunton. There are many elegantly restored Victorian homes in the area. Enlarged and remodeled repeatedly over more than a century, the inn displays elements of several architectural styles. Decorated and furnished to reflect a given period in the house's past, the five guest rooms are named after former owners.

Frank's Sugar and Spice Baked Apples

- 1⅓ cups firmly packed light brown sugar
- 1⅓ cups firmly packed dark brown sugar
- 2 teaspoons ground cinnamon
- 1 whole nutmeg, freshly grated
- ½ to 1 cup coarsely chopped pecans
....
- 4 medium Golden Delicious apples

In a medium bowl mix the sugars, spices, and nuts very thoroughly. Store in an airtight container in a dry place.

Core and peel the apples. Place each apple in an individual microwaveable ramekin. Lightly pack about 1 heaping tablespoon of sugar mixture in each apple's center and sprinkle some on the top and sides. Cover with microwaveable plastic wrap. Microwave on high for 8 minutes. The apples are ready when springy to the touch. They will also hold in a warm oven for 30 to 45 minutes.

MAKES 4 SERVINGS.

Grand Marnier Soufflé Pancakes

- 6 eggs, separated
- 2½ tablespoons sugar
- 2 cups small curd cottage cheese
- ¼ cup canola oil
- 1 cup plus 3 tablespoons unbleached all-purpose flour
- ½ teaspoon salt
- 4 teaspoons baking powder
- 5 tablespoons freshly squeezed orange juice (must be fresh)
....
- 1 tablespoon freshly grated orange zest
....

1   tablespoon Grand Marnier
¼   cup finely chopped pecans

In a large bowl beat the egg whites until stiff. In a food processor combine the egg yolks and remaining ingredients except the pecans and blend until smooth. Transfer the batter to a large bowl and let rest for at least 30 minutes.

Fold in the pecans and beaten egg whites, and cook on a hot buttered griddle being careful not to burn the cakes. The smaller the cakes, the easier they will be to burn. Use about ¼ cup of batter for each. When finished, the cakes can be held in a warm oven for a few minutes. (The texture will become a bit firmer upon standing.)

Serve with pure maple syrup or fresh strawberry sauce.

MAKES 6 SERVINGS.

Belgian Kahlua Pecan Waffles

1   cup plus
1   tablespoon unbleached flour
½   teaspoon salt
2   tablespoons sugar
2¾   teaspoons baking powder
½   teaspoon ground cinnamon
⅛   to ¼ teaspoon freshly grated nutmeg
2   eggs, room temperature, separated
½   cup butter, melted and cooled
2   tablespoons Kahlua
1½   cups milk less 2 tablespoons, at
        room temperature
⅓   to ½ cup chopped pecans

In a large bowl sift together the flour, salt, sugar, baking powder, cinnamon, and nutmeg. In a separate bowl combine the egg yolks, butter, Kahlua, and milk, and mix well. Whisk the milk mixture into the dry ingredients and beat until smooth. Let the batter rest for about 30 minutes. Beat the egg whites until stiff, not dry. Fold the egg whites, along with the pecans, gently into the batter. Bake according to the waffle iron directions.

MAKES 4 SERVINGS.

Bleu Rock Inn

≈

12567 Lee Highway
Washington, Virginia 22747
(540) 987-3190

---

*S*ituated in a renovated farmhouse on eighty rolling acres of Virginia countryside, the Bleu Rock Inn is developing a reputation for fine food and wine. Its owners also own and operate the well known La Bergerie Restaurant in Alexandria, Virginia. The inn is surrounded by vineyards, and there is a pond where guests can try their luck at catching bass, blue gill, and catfish. For those who love fresh fruit, the inn has an orchard offering succulent nectarines, peaches, apricots, and apples in season.

Asparagus Soup with Morel Coulis

1   tablespoon canola oil
1   large leek, white end only, sliced
1   small potato, peeled and diced
1   quart hot chicken stock
24   pieces jumbo asparagus, hard stems
      removed, sliced
3   to 4 large sprigs parsley, stems
      removed
      Pinch nutmeg
      Salt and fresh ground black pepper
....

1   tablespoon canola oil
1   pound morels (known as morkles in
      Rappahannock County), gently
      washed
1   teaspoon minced shallot
½   cup hot chicken stock
2   ounces crème fraîche
      Pinch cayenne
      Salt and freshly ground pepper to
      taste

In a stockpot heat 1 tablespoon of olive oil over medium heat and sweat the leeks for 6 minutes until soft (do not color). Add 1 quart of hot stock, the potatoes, and salt. Bring to a boil, and cook for 5 minutes. Add the asparagus and boil for 4 to 6 minutes until tender. In a blender purée the hot soup with parsley, nutmeg, salt, and pepper, very carefully. Cool in ice to help hold color.

In a saucepan heat 1 tablespoon of oil and sweat the morels for 3 to 4 minutes over high heat. Add the shallots, and cook for 1 minute. Add ½ cup of hot stock, bring to a boil, and cook for 4 minutes. Pour into a blender with the crème fraîche and seasonings, and purée until smooth.

Presentation: Serve cold asparagus soup in chilled cups with mushroom coulis drizzled in a design on top, or hot with mushroom coulis drizzled on top in warm soup bowls.

MAKES 4 SERVINGS.

Chicken Casserole with Fava Beans and Spring Potatoes

2   cups fresh shelled fava beans
1   tablespoon canola oil
2   button mushrooms, whole
      Salt and pepper to taste
1   cup chicken stock
2   to 3 tablespoons canola oil
1   free range chicken, cut into 10
      pieces (2 legs, 2 thighs, 2 wings
      with last joint removed, and 2
      breasts, cut in half)
12   cloves garlic, peeled but left whole
1   bay leaf
      Sprigs fresh thyme
1   pound new potatoes, rinsed and
      split in half
2   pearl onions, peeled but left whole
1   bunch scallions, minced
      Salt and freshly ground pepper to
      taste

Blanch the favas in boiling water for 1 minute. Shock in ice water and drain. Peel off the skin with a sharp paring knife and pop the beans out. Reserve.

In a sauté pan heat 1 tablespoon of oil over high heat. Toss in the mushrooms, salt, and pepper, and cook for 2 to 3 minutes. Add the stock, bring to a boil, and cook for 3 minutes. Reserve.

Salt and pepper the chicken pieces. In large cast-iron skillet heat 2 tablespoons of oil over high heat. Add chicken skin-side down and cook until golden brown. Turn the pieces over. Add the bay leaf, garlic, thyme, potatoes, and pearl onions. Transfer the pan to the oven. Roast in a 425° oven for 15 minutes. Pour in the mushrooms with stock, and roast another 25 minutes. Remove from the oven and keep warm on the stove over low heat. Add the favas and scallions, and warm for 5 minutes. Remove the bay leaf.

Present this dish in its roasting pan and serve with a light watercress salad and warm sourdough bread.

MAKES 4 SERVINGS.

P.O. Box 119
White Post, Virginia 22663
(540) 837-1375

The name leaves little doubt that this is a French-style country inn, and so it is. Guests may think they are in the South of France rather than just an hour's drive from the Washington, D.C. Beltway. The manor house, known as Mount Airy, dates to 1753. It offers ten guest rooms and three separate dining rooms, all decorated with Victorian or European antiques, fine art, and Provencale fabrics.

Poached Egg in a Nest

- 3   *tablespoons extra virgin olive oil*
  Salt and pepper to taste
- 4   *thick slices ripe tomato*
- ½   *cup pine nuts*
- 1   *tablespoon unsalted butter*
- 3   *cups washed spinach*
- 1   *cup chickory or dandelion leaves*
  Pinch fresh grated nutmeg

- ½   *teaspoon fresh chopped tarragon*
- 1   *teaspoon fresh chopped chives*
  Salt and pepper to taste
- 2   *quarts simmering water*
- 2   *tablespoons white vinegar*
....
- 1   *teaspoon salt*
- 4   *large eggs*

In a large skillet heat 2 tablespoons of olive oil over medium high heat and gently sauté the salted and peppered tomato slices. Place an individual slice on 4 plates.

Wipe the skillet clean and add a few drops of olive oil and the pine nuts. Gently toss over medium heat until golden brown. Set aside. In a clean skillet heat the remaining olive oil and butter over medium heat, and sauté the spinach and chickory, tossing gently Add the nutmeg, tarragon, and chives, and cook for 2 minutes. Season with salt and pepper to taste. Set aside.

In a non-corrosive pot combine the water, white vinegar, and 1 teaspoon of salt and bring to a simmer. Crack the eggs into a bowl, and gently pour into the simmering water. Cook for 3 minutes. While the eggs are cooking, divide the greens into 4 servings. Swirl with a fork to create a nest, and set each serving on a tomato slice. With fingertips make a hollow in the greens. Remove the eggs and place 1 in each nest. Sprinkle pine nuts around the greens and serve.

Note: L'Auberge Provençale serves this with sautéed wild mushrooms, pheasant breast, and chicken sausage with chervil, chives and nutmeg. Parma Ham is also nice if pheasant is not available. A mimosa, fresh baked croissant, saffron cottage fries and viola! Breakfast is served.

MAKES 4 SERVINGS.

Sautéed Tomato Provençale

- 2   *tablespoons olive oil*
- 4   *whole poached Italian tomatoes, skin removed*
- 1   *teaspoon chopped fresh rosemary (or fresh thyme or ½ teaspoon chopped fresh sage)*
- 4   *poached eggs*
  Salt and pepper to taste
- 4   *small sprigs fresh dill for garnish*

In a frying pan heat the oil and sauté the whole tomatoes and rosemary for 3 minutes. Remove the pan from the heat.

Cut the tomatoes lengthway almost through, to form a nest for poached egg. Place a poached egg in each tomato, season with salt and pepper to taste, and garnish with fresh dill sprigs.

MAKES 4 SERVINGS.

Lobster and Broccoli Quiche

- 1   *10 x 15 x ⅛-inch puff pastry*
- 1   *lobster tail and claws, cooked and chopped*
- ½   *head cooked broccoli, cut up*
- 1   *cup grated cheese (Parmesan or mozzarella or both)*
- 8   *eggs*
- 2   *cups heavy cream*
- 2   *cups milk*
- 1   *tablespoon chopped shallots*
- 1   *tablespoon chopped dill*
  Salt and pepper to taste

Roll out the puff pastry and place into a greased quiche pan loosely. Allow for the puff pastry to shrink around the edges, be sure to leave extra pastry to hang over edge. Cut small amounts from the corners to patch any tears. Bake in a 350° oven for exactly 3 ½ minutes. Remove the pastry from the oven, allow it to deflate, and push back into the pan. Patch any tears that might occur.

Place the chopped lobster, broccoli, and grated cheese evenly in the pastry. In a large bowl mix together thoroughly the eggs, heavy cream, milk, shallots, and dill. Season with salt and pepper to taste. Pour the custard gently into the crust over the lobster, cheese, and broccoli. Place the quiche on a baking sheet. Bake in a 350° oven for 50 to 60 minutes or until the center looks set and the top is lightly brown.

Cool before cutting. After cutting, rewarm in the oven if desired.

MAKES 6 TO 8 SERVINGS.

Hubbard Squash Soup

- ¼   *cup butter*
- 1   *leek, chopped, white part only*
- 1   *medium onion, diced*

2   cloves garlic, chopped
2   pounds Hubbard squash (or other
        winter squash) peeled, seeded,
        and chopped
1   large potato, peeled, chopped
⅛   teaspoon grated fresh nutmeg
1   quart chicken stock
1   cup heavy cream

In a 6-quart pot melt the butter and sauté the leek, onion, and garlic in butter over medium heat for 5 minutes. Add the squash, potato, and chicken stock and simmer 20 to 30 minutes until vegetables are tender. In a blender purée the soup. Strain and return to pot. Add the cream, season with salt and pepper to taste, and reheat.
MAKES 6 SERVINGS.

Warm Asparagus Salad with Balsamic Vinaigrette

1   cup walnuts
    Peanut oil

....

½   cup balsamic vinegar
2   teaspoons salt
½   tablespoon chopped shallots
½   tablespoon chopped garlic
1½ tablespoons Dijon mustard
1   cup peanut oil (use reserve from
        roasting nuts)

....

4   ounces goat cheese marinated in
        olive oil and Italian herbs
8   thin slices prosciutto, rolled
24 asparagus spears, wooden ends
        removed, blanched until tender-
        crisp

In a baking dish roast the walnuts in peanut oil in a 250° oven for 5 minutes. Remove from the oven, and drain, reserving 1 cup of oil. Allow the walnuts to cool, then chop coarsely.

In a blender combine the vinegar, salt, shallots, garlic, and Dijon mustard. Blend on low speed. With the blender running, slowly add 1 cup of peanut oil. Blend until incorporated.

Arrange the goat cheese, prosciutto, and asparagus on a cold salad plate, allowing 6 stalks of asparagus to be fanned out with the goat cheese and 2 slices of rolled proscuitto.

Drizzle with vinaigrette and garnish with chopped walnuts.
MAKES 4 SERVINGS.

Rack of Lamb

2½ racks lamb (Frenched by butcher)
        Olive oil to cover
1   bunch thyme
1   bunch sage
1   bunch rosemary
1   bunch basil
8   bay leaves
4   cloves garlic, chopped

....

1   teaspoon fresh ground black pepper
2   tablespoons oil

With a very sharp knife make shallow cuts just to break the silver skin of the lamb. Cover with olive oil, herbs, garlic, and black pepper, and allow to marinate for 24 hours if possible, in the refrigerator.

In a skillet heat the oil to very hot. Sear the racks on all sides. Remove the pan from the heat, and drain off all oil. Leave the racks in the skillet. Bake in a 350° oven for about 10 to 15 minutes or until a meat thermometer registers 140° for medium rare. Remove from the oven, and let sit for 5 minutes.

Slice between each rib, plate with Spinach Aioli Sauce (recipe follows), and serve with Petit Artichokes and Oyster Mushrooms with Cloves, Basil, Thyme and Bay Leaf (recipe follows).
MAKES 4 SERVINGS.

Spinach Aioli

1   teaspoon butter
1   10-ounce bag fresh spinach, well
        washed
1   teaspoon chopped shallots
⅛   teaspoon nutmeg
    Salt and pepper to taste
4   eggs
6   cloves garlic
2   tablespoons lemon juice
2   cups olive oil

In a skillet melt the butter and sauté the spinach, shallots, nutmeg, and salt and pepper to taste until wilted and hot.

In a blender blend the eggs, then add the garlic and shut off the blender. Add the spinach mixture, and pulse to purée the spinach. Add the lemon juice, and pulse. With the blender on, slowly add the olive oil until fully blended and smooth. Taste and season with salt and pepper as needed.

To serve with lamb, use as is for a sauce or mix with ¼ cup of cream for a smoother and creamier sauce.
MAKES 4 SERVINGS.

Petit Artichokes with Oyster Mushrooms, Cloves, Basil, Thyme and Bay Leaf

8   artichoke bottoms
3   tablespoons butter
1   tablespoon chopped shallots
2   teaspoons chopped garlic
¼   cup lemon juice
½   cup dry white wine
6   whole cloves
1   sprig thyme
1   bay leaf
    Salt and pepper to taste
1   tablespoon butter
½   pound oyster mushrooms, cleaned,
        root end discarded, clusters sepa-
        rated
1   teaspoon chopped garlic
1   teaspoon chopped shallots
    Salt and pepper to taste

In a small saucepan melt 3 tablespoons of butter and sauté the artichokes with 1 tablespoon of shallots and 2 teaspoons of garlic for 2 minutes. Add the lemon juice, wine, thyme, bay leaf, cloves, and salt and pepper. Add enough water to just cover the artichokes, and bring to a boil. Reduce the heat, and simmer for 5 minutes, just until tender. Remove the artichokes from the liquid, drain, and set aside.

In a skillet melt 1 tablespoon of butter and sauté the mushrooms with 1 teaspoon of garlic and 1 teaspoon of shallots. Season with salt and pepper. Stir often, until the mushrooms are soft. Reserve. Arrange the artichokes and mushrooms on serving plates and serve.
MAKES 4 SERVINGS.

Polenta-stuffed Quail with Applewood-smoked Bacon, Glennfiddich Sauce, and Caramelized Apples

2 medium Granny Smith apples, peeled, cored, and cubed
2 tablespoons sugar
3 cups chicken stock
  Salt and pepper to taste
1 cup polenta
4 quail, de-boned, rinsed, patted dry (hold in refrigerator)
  Flour to dust
2 tablespoons olive oil
 ....
  Glennfiddich Sauce (recipe follows)
4 strips applewood-smoked bacon, cooked

In a very hot skillet place all at once the apples and sugar, and toss for 1 to 2 minutes until brown. Set aside.

In a 1½-quart saucepan bring the chicken stock to a boil. Add the apples and season with salt and pepper to taste. Add the polenta and stir. Reduce the heat to a simmer, and stir until thick. Remove the pan from the heat, and set aside to cook. When the polenta is cold, stuff into the quails and truss. Lightly dust each quail with flour. In a skillet heat the olive oil, add the quail and brown. Drain the oil from the frying pan and discard.

Place the quail back in the frying pan. Roast in a 350° oven for 15 minutes or until the internal temperature is 150°. Serve with Glennfiddich Sauce and 1 strip of applewood smoked bacon per bird.

MAKES 4 SERVINGS.

Glennfiddich Sauce

1 teaspoon shallots, minced
1 teaspoon garlic, minced
1 tablespoon butter
1 cup cider
1 ounce Glennfiddich
1 cup demiglace or brown sauce
  Salt and pepper to taste
1 teaspoon chopped sage

In a saucepan melt the butter and sauté garlic and shallots for 1 minute. Add the cider and reduce by two-thirds. Add the Glennfiddich,

brown sauce, salt and pepper to taste, and sage. Serve with quail.

MAKES 4 SERVINGS.

Toffee Bars

1 cup unsalted butter (plus 2 tablespoons to grease pan)
1¾ cups all-purpose flour
½ cup brown sugar
½ cup sugar
1 egg yolk
1 teaspoon vanilla extract
1¾ cups all-purpose flour
  Pinch salt
¾ cup diced pecans
11 ounces Belgian dark chocolate, chopped very fine

Butter a jelly roll pan. Spread the pecans on a baking sheet. Roast in a 350° oven for 5 minutes. Reserve.

In a large bowl cream the butter with the sugars. Beat in the egg yolk and vanilla. Add the flour and salt, and blend well. Spread the batter in the prepared pan. Bake in a 350° oven for 15 to 20 minutes.

Remove the pan from the oven. While still hot, sprinkle with chocolate and spread, sprinkle with nuts all over, and press in with a sheet of waxed paper. Score into squares with sharp knife while still warm. Cool and break apart squares for serving.

MAKES 8 SERVINGS.

French Sweet Cream with Peach Basil Compote and Fresh Berries

2 tablespoons unflavored gelatin
2 tablespoons cold water
1 cup heavy cream
½ cup sugar
14 ounces crème fraîche
3 ounces mascarpone
1½ teaspoons vanilla extract
1 tablespoon fresh squeezed lemon juice
  Peach Basil Compote (recipe follows)
½ cup strawberries
½ cup blackberries

In a small bowl sprinkle the gelatin over the cold water and let stand 10 minutes.

In a large stainless steel bowl whisk together the heavy cream, sugar, creme fraiche, and mascarpone. Place the bowl over a pot of simmering water. When the cream mixture is warm, dissolve the gelatin over low heat and whisk into the cream. Continue heating the mixture, stirring occasionally, until hot, about 150°. Stir in the vanilla extract and lemon juice. Strain the custard through a fine strainer. Pour the custard into ramekins. Refrigerate the French creams for several hours until set.

To serve unmold each cream by dipping the ramekins in hot water for several seconds. Run a knife around the inside edge of each ramekin and invert onto a plate. Serve with the Peach Basil Compote and fresh berries.

MAKES 6 TO 8 SERVINGS.

Peach Basil Compote

3 cups sugar
1½ cups water
12 peaches, peeled and sliced
½ cup chopped basil
1 tablespoon sweet butter

In a saucepan bring the sugar and water to a boil, and boil for 2 minutes.

Add the sliced peaches and chopped basil and return to a boil. Add the sweet butter and stir until melted. Remove from the stove. Keep at room temperature and serve with French sweet cream.

MAKES 6 TO 8 SERVINGS.

Newport House Bed and Breakfast

710 South Henry Street
Williamsburg, Virginia 23185-4113
(804) 229-1775

---

*T*he house is a replica of a Newport, Rhode Island, home that was built in 1756 and destroyed 200 years later to make room for a

Newport House

parking lot. Built to museum standards in 1988 from a design of the famous early American architect Peter Harrison, the Newport House honors two centuries of tradition. Only a five-minute walk from Colonial Williamsburg and a five-minute drive from Jamestown, this B&B puts its guests in close touch with our nation's pre-colonial past. It is furnished with antiques and reproductions, most of which are available for sale (to guests only) upon request.

Colonial Bread

    3 cups whole wheat flour
    2 tablespoons yeast
    3 cups warm water (105 to 115°)
    ....
    3 cups bread flour
    3 cups unbleached flour
    2 tablespoons salt
       Water

In a large bowl mix the whole wheat flour with the yeast and 3 cups of warm water. Cover with damp tea towel and leave in a warm place for 8 to 12 hours.

Add the starter to the bread flour, unbleached flour, and salt. Add enough water to make a stiff dough. Knead well. Place in a bowl and cover with a moist tea towel. Let rise for 2 hours in a warm place.

Punch down and place in a baking pan (Newport House recommends a large round greased wedding-cake tin with sides made higher with 6-inch aluminum flashing. Bread in the colonial period was almost always large and round). Cover with a moist tea towel and let rise in warm place for 1 hour.

Bake in a 450° oven for 30 minutes. Remove the bread from the pan and bake in a 300° oven for another 30 minutes.
MAKES 1 LOAF.

Colonial Jonnycakes

    1   cup dark rum
    1   cup whole milk (or half and half)
    1   tablespoon dark molasses
    1   tablespoon sugar
    1   teaspoon salt
    1½   cups Jonnycake meal (see note, below)

In a large bowl combine all ingredients. Cover and let stand overnight.

In the morning, stir up well. The batter needs to be about the consistency of runny mashed potatoes, so add a little more milk if necessary. Drop about a tablespoon of the batter at a time onto a greased griddle heated to 375 to 400°. Cook a few minutes on each side until the cakes have reached a medium tan. Serve with butter and molasses on top.

Note: Jonnycake meal is a rare white flint corn found only in parts of Rhode Island and Connecticut. One source is Carpenter's Grist Mill, Inc., 35 Narragansett Avenue, Wakefield, RI, 02879. This meal must be kept in the freezer, otherwise it will quickly spoil. In the colonial period it was stored in a muslin bag suspended in a barrel of rum, but since that isn't done any more rum has been added to the recipe instead.

The word Jonnycake (note no "h" in it) is short for Journeycake, as some people used to carry then in their pockets for a snack on the road, but that isn't recommended.
MAKES 4 TO 6 SERVINGS.

Colonial Chocolate Cake Pécoul

    9   ounces semisweet chocolate (or
         chocolate chips)
    3   tablespoons water
    ½   cup plus 2 tablespoons butter,
         melted
    4   eggs
    1½   cups sugar
    3   tablespoons all-purpose flour

In a heavy saucepan melt the chocolate with 3 tablespoons of water over low heat, stirring

until smooth. Add the butter and egg yolks, stirring all the time. Add the sugar. In a medium bowl beat the egg whites until stiff, and stir them into the batter. Finally stir in the flour.

Grease and flour a 9-inch round pan. Pour the batter into the prepared pan. Bake in a 400° oven for 11 minutes. Reduce the oven temperature to 325° and bake for 20 minutes.

The cake is so gooey that it may not actually release from the pan, so it may have to be served from the pan.

Note: Pécoul is a 1769 plantation mansion (national historic monument) on the Caribbean Island of Martinique that used to be in the family.
MAKES 6 TO 8 SERVINGS.

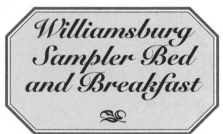

Williamsburg Sampler Bed and Breakfast

❧

922 Jamestown Road
Williamsburg, Virginia 23185
(757) 253-0398

---

*A**lthough built in 1976, America's bicentennial year, the Sampler is a faithful replica of an eighteenth century home and is well suited to the spirit of Colonial Williamsburg. The antiques, pewter, and framed samplers in the guest rooms re-create the look and feel of an early American home. The delicious, colossal morning meal here is sometimes described as a "skip lunch" breakfast.*

Sampler's Baked Colonial Pudding

    ⅓   cup cornmeal
    ½   cup molasses
         Pinch salt
    3   cups scalded milk

Williamsburg Sampler

1 egg, beaten
1 cup raisins
¼ teaspoon ground ginger
14 teaspoons ground cinnamon
¼ teaspoon nutmeg
1 cup cold milk

In a medium bowl mix well the cornmeal, molasses, and salt. In a large bowl pour the mixture over the scalded milk. Let stand 5 minutes.

Add the egg, spices, and raisins. Transfer the mixture to an 8-inch square baking dish, and place in a 275° oven. After 10 minutes, add the cold milk. Stir. Bake for 2 hours.

MAKES 6 TO 7 SERVINGS.

Williamsburg Sampler Blueberry Walnut Bread

1 pint fresh blueberries
1 cup sugar
1½ cups all-purpose flour
1 cup whole wheat flour
1 teaspoon baking powder
1 teaspoon baking soda
½ teaspoon ground cinnamon
½ teaspoon salt
5 eggs
½ cup plus 1 tablespoon oil
1 teaspoon vanilla extract
1 cup chopped walnuts

Grease and flour a 5 x 9-inch loaf pan. Put the blueberries in a bowl and sprinkle with ½ cup of the sugar. In a small bowl combine the flours, baking powder, soda, cinnamon, and salt, and stir well. In a large bowl beat the eggs, beating in the remaining sugar until the mixture thickens and is pale yellow. Stir in the oil and vanilla. Add the walnuts and flour

mixture, and stir only until moistened. Add the blueberry mixture and any liquid accumulated. Pour the batter into the prepared pan. Bake in a 350° oven for 45 minutes or until done.

MAKES 1 LOAF.

The Sampler's Colonial Potato Rolls

2 large potatoes
....
1 teaspoon salt
2 tablespoons sugar
2 tablespoons butter
1½ cups potato water
¾ cup scalded milk
1 yeast cake
7 cups sifted all-purpose flour

Peel the potatoes and boil in a pot of water for 30 minutes. Drain and reserve the water. Mash the potatoes, adding the salt, sugar, and butter and beat well. Then add the potato water and hot milk, and cool until lukewarm. Add the yeast and stir in 4 cups of the flour, beating well. Add just enough of the remaining flour to make a dough stiff enough to knead. Knead on a floured board until smooth and elastic. Brush the top with additional melted butter and place in a large greased bowl. Cover the bowl and let rise slowly for 5 hours in a warm place until the dough has doubled in bulk.

Place on a floured board and pat out to a thickness of about ½-inch (do not knead again). Pinch off small pieces and shape into small rolls. Place in greased pans and let rise until very light and more than doubled in size. Bake in a 400° oven for 20 minutes or until done.

MAKES APPROXIMATELY 48 TO 50 ROLLS.

Williamsburg Sampler's Bananas Coconut Milk

3 ripe bananas
1 can coconut milk (obtained from Chinese grocery store)
3 to 4 tablespoons firmly packed brown sugar
  Pinch salt

Peel the bananas, and cut into 3 or 4 sections and then halves.

Bring the coconut milk to a half boil. Add the brown sugar and salt, then add the bananas and cook until the bananas are half soft. Serve hot or cold.

MAKES ABOUT 3 SERVINGS.

Sampler's Green Pea Dip

¼ cup blue cheese
¼ cup milk
1 pint sour cream
1 envelope green pea soup mix
½ envelope onion soup mix
3 cloves garlic, crushed
....
1 teaspoon Worcestershire sauce

In a medium bowl combine all ingredients until blended well. Chill for 35 minutes. Serve with raw vegetables.

MAKES ABOUT 2 CUPS.

Creamy Herbs Omelet

4 eggs
1 teaspoon salt
4 tablespoons milk
⅛ teaspoon pepper
1 generous tablespoon chopped fresh herbs (parsley, chives, tarragon or any desired combinations)
1 tablespoon butter

In a medium bowl beat the eggs slightly to combine the yolks and whites. Add the milk and pepper, and herbs to taste.

In a hot 8-inch skillet melt the butter over moderate heat. Add the eggs. As the mixture cooks, draw the edges to the center to allow the uncooked portion to run underneath. The omelet is done when it is just set. To brown the bottom, hold over heat briefly, shaking the pan to prevent sticking. As soon as the omelet is set and browned, tip the pan and fold 1 side of the omelet, roll onto a hot platter, and serve at once.

MAKES 1 SERVING.

Azalea House Bed and Breakfast

551 South Main Street
Woodstock, Virginia 22664
(540) 459-3500

A gracious B&B in the heart of Virginia's lush Shenandoah Valley, the Azalea House features balcony views of the Blue Ridge, stenciled ceilings, family antiques in the guest rooms and, of course, clouds of azalea blossoms in spring. The century-old Victorian home is located in a registered Historical District, close to antiquing, hiking trails, vineyards, Civil War sites, fine restaurants, and horseback riding.

Baked Apple Pancake

- 6 **tablespoons butter**
- ⅓ **teaspoon ground cinnamon**
- ⅓ **teaspoon nutmeg**
- 2 **large Granny Smith apples cored, peeled and sliced**
- 3 **tablespoons lemon juice**
- 5 **tablespoons confectioners' sugar**

- 3 **eggs, room temperature**
- ½ **cup all-purpose flour**
- ¼ **teaspoon salt**
- ½ **cup milk**

In an ovenproof 10-inch skillet with rounded sides melt the butter. Remove 2 tablespoons of butter and set aside in a small bowl.

In a small bowl combine the cinnamon and nutmeg. In a large bowl place the apple slices with lemon juice, and toss with the sugar and half of the spice mixture. Add the apples to the butter in the skillet and cook for 4 minutes or until the apples are tender but hold their shape. In a bowl or blender combine the eggs, flour, salt, milk, 2 tablespoons of melted butter, and remaining spices. Beat until smooth. Spread the apples evenly over the bottom of the skillet, and pour the batter on top. Bake in a 425° oven for 20 minutes or until golden and puffy. Turn over on a plate after loosening the sides. Serve at once with a dusting of confectioners' sugar.

MAKES 4 TO 6 SERVINGS.

Country Breakfast Pie

- 4 **slices bacon (cut in half)**
- 2 **cups frozen hash brown potatoes with green peppers, onions and pimento slices**
- 6 **large eggs (lightly beaten)**
- ¼ **cup milk**
- ½ **teaspoon salt**
- ⅛ **teaspoon ground pepper**
- ½ **teaspoon Creole seasoning**
- ¼ **cup sliced black olives**
- 1 **cup shredded sharp Cheddar cheese**

Place the bacon in a pie plate. Microwave until crisp, and remove to cool on a paper towel. Spread the potatoes, peppers, and onions evenly in the pie plate and microwave on high for 6 to 7 minutes if frozen and 4 to 5 minutes if room temperature (thawed). In a medium bowl combine the eggs, milk, salt, pepper, and Creole seasoning, and pour over the potatoes. Bake in a 400° oven for 20 minutes or until set. Sprinkle with black olives and cheese and crumbled bacon, and return to the oven until the cheese melts. Let stand 5 minutes, then cut into wedges.

Green chilies may be added for more flavor. Salsa will add more color.

MAKES 6 TO 8 SERVINGS.

Butterscotch Pinwheel Biscuits

- 2 **cups all-purpose flour**
- 2 **teaspoons baking powder**
- ½ **teaspoon salt**
- ⅓ **cup shortening**
- ⅔ **cup milk**
- 3 **tablespoons butter, softened**
- ½ **cup firmly packed dark brown sugar**
- ½ **teaspoon ground cinnamon**

In a large bowl combine the flour, baking powder, and salt, and cut in the shortening until the mixture resembles coarse meal. Add the milk, stirring until blended. Turn onto a lightly floured surface and knead 4 or 5 times. Roll into a 12-inch square, spread with softened butter, and sprinkle with brown sugar and cinnamon. Roll up jelly roll fashion. Use a pastry cloth if desired. Pinch the seam to seal. Cut into 1-inch slices and place in greased muffin cups Bake in a 375° oven for 25 to 30 minutes or until golden brown.

MAKES ABOUT 1 DOZEN.

Azalea House

1014 North Garden
Bellingham, Washington 98225
(360) 671-7828

This Queen Anne Victorian offers ten guest rooms with splendid views of Bellingham Bay. A Steinway grand piano adorns the entryway. Seattle is ninety miles to the south, while Vancouver, British Columbia, is fifty-five miles to the north.

Peanut Butter Chocolate Chiperoos

    1   cup semisweet chocolate chips
    1   cup butter, softened
    1   cup sugar
    1   cup firmly packed dark brown sugar
    ½   cup creamy peanut butter
    2   eggs room temperature
    1   teaspoon vanilla extract
    2½ cups all-purpose flour
    1   teaspoon baking soda
    ¼   teaspoon salt
    4   ounces white chocolate chips
    4   ounces toffee chips

In the top of a double boiler over simmering water or in a microwave melt the chocolate chips, stirring until smooth. In a large bowl beat the butter until creamy. Gradually add the sugars and peanut butter and beat until well blended. Beat in the eggs and vanilla. Stir in the flour, soda, and salt. Stir in the white chocolate chips and toffee ships. Using a spatula stir in the melted chocolate to create stripes. Drop the dough by teaspoonful onto baking sheets, leaving an inch between cookies. Bake in a 350° oven for 10 to 12 minutes. Transfer to wire racks to cool.

Variation: Peanut butter with nuts can be used as well or nuts add to the batter for a crunchier taste.

MAKES ABOUT 3 DOZEN.

Oatmeal Banana Chocolate Chip Muffins

    ½   cup shortening
    1   cup sugar
    1   egg
    1   teaspoon vanilla extract
    2   ripe bananas
    1   cup cooked oatmeal
    2   cups all-purpose flour
    1   teaspoon baking powder
    ½   teaspoon baking soda
    ½   teaspoon salt
    ½   cup mini chocolate chips

In a large bowl cream together the shortening and sugar. Add the egg, vanilla, bananas, and oatmeal, and mix well. Add the flour, baking powder, soda, salt, and chocolate chips, and mix until moistened. Pour into greased muffin cups. Bake in a 350° oven for 22 minutes

MAKES 1 DOZEN.

Route 1, Box 650
Eastsound, Washington 98245
(800) 376-4914

This secluded hideaway is located on Orcas Island, perhaps the most scenic of the islands in the San Juan archipelago. The inn overlooks eighty acres of forest and farmland in Crow Valley practically in the shadow of Turtleback Mountain. Constructed in the late 1800s in the "Folk National" farmhouse style, it has been carefully renovated to accommodate seven comfortable guest rooms. The area provides ample opportunity for almost any outdoor activity. At the end of the day, guests will enjoy relaxing by the Rumford fireplace in the living room.

Ricotta Torte with Red Pepper Sauce

    1   cup milk
    2   tablespoons butter, melted

3 eggs
¾ cup unbleached flour
3 tablespoons cornmeal
   Pinch salt

....

1 bunch spinach
1 cup ricotta cheese
2 tablespoons finely chopped onion
¼ cup freshly grated Parmesan cheese
1 egg
   Pinch nutmeg
   Salt and pepper to taste

....

   Butter
   Red Pepper Sauce (recipe follows)
   Sour Cream
   Fresh oregano leaves (or basil)

In a blender combine the milk, melted butter, 3 eggs, flour, cornmeal, and a pinch of salt, and blend until smooth. Let rest for 1 hour.

In a saucepan steam the spinach in a minimum of water until tender. Dry well. In a food processor combine the spinach, ricotta, Parmesan, 1 egg, nutmeg, and salt and pepper to taste, and blend well. Set aside.

In a nonstick skillet melt a small amount of butter Add just enough batter to coat the bottom and cook for about 1 minute until the bubbles pop. Turn and brown the other side. Place the finished crêpe on a large square of foil. Spread one-fifth of the spinach filling on the crêpe. Prepare a second crêpe and again spread with spinach filling. Repeat until 5 crêpes have been spread with filling, and top with a sixth crêpe. Seal in foil. Bake in a 325° oven for about 15 minutes until heated through.

Cut into 6 wedges. Spoon Red Pepper Sauce over each wedge and garnish with a dollop of sour cream and fresh oregano or basil leaves.

MAKES 6 SERVINGS.

Turtleback Farm Inn

Red Pepper Sauce

3 red peppers
2 tablespoons olive oil
2 tablespoons butter
3 large cloves garlic, peeled and minced
2 tablespoons finely chopped onion
¼ cup sliced mushrooms
1 cup chicken stock
2 tablespoons heavy cream
   Pinch basil
   Salt and pepper to taste

Place the peppers in a baking dish. Preheat oven to Bake the peppers in a 325° oven for 15 minutes until the skins begin to blacken. Put into a plastic bag to steam for about 10 minutes. Remove from the bag and cool, peel, and seed.

In a small skillet heat the olive oil and butter, and sauté the garlic, onion, and mushrooms until tender. In a food processor combine the sautéed garlic, onions, and mushrooms with the peppers. Add the stock and process until smooth. Transfer to a small saucepan and simmer for about 5 minutes. Add the cream, a pinch of basil, and salt and pepper to taste. Keep warm until time to serve.

MAKES ABOUT 2 CUPS.

Spiced Pancakes with Savory Applesauce

3 eggs, separated
2 cups buttermilk
⅓ cup butter, melted
1 cup whole wheat flour
1 cup unbleached white flour
2 teaspoons baking powder
¾ teaspoon baking soda
½ teaspoon salt
½ teaspoon ground cinnamon
½ teaspoon grated nutmeg
½ teaspoon ground allspice

....

2 cups applesauce, preferable homemade
2 tablespoons butter
½ cup currants
1½ tablespoons lemon juice
½ cup firmly packed brown sugar

¼ teaspoon ground cinnamon (or to taste)
¼ teaspoon grated nutmeg (or to taste)
¼ teaspoon cloves (or to taste)
¼ teaspoon allspice (or to taste)

In a medium bowl beat the egg whites until stiff but not dry peaks form. In a separate bowl combine the egg yolks, buttermilk, and ⅓ cup of melted butter. Blend in the flours, baking powder, soda, salt, ½ teaspoon of cinnamon, ½ teaspoon of nutmeg, and ½ teaspoon of allspice. Fold in the egg whites. Bake on a hot griddle.

In a saucepan combine the applesauce, 2 tablespoons of butter, currants, lemon juice, brown sugar, ¼ teaspoon of cinnamon, ¼ teaspoon of nutmeg, cloves, and ¼ teaspoon of allspice, and cook over low heat until the currants are plumped and the flavors blended. Serve warm or cool with the Spiced Pancakes.

MAKES 4 SERVINGS.

Espresso Cheesecake

2 cups crushed Oreo or chocolate wafer cookies
¼ cup butter, melted

....

4 8-ounce packages cream cheese
3 eggs
½ cup sour cream
¼ cup Kahlua
¼ cup strong espresso
¾ cup firmly packed brown sugar
1 teaspoon vanilla extract
¾ teaspoon salt

In a medium bowl combine the cookie crumbs and melted butter. Press into the bottom and up the sides of a 10-inch springform pan. Set aside.

In a large bowl combine the cream cheese, eggs, sour cream, kahlua, espresso, brown sugar, vanilla, and salt. Pour the filling into the crust. Bake in a 350° oven for 1 hour. Cool completely, then chill over night before serving.

MAKES 8 SERVINGS.

Hillside House Bed and Breakfast

365 Carter Avenue
Friday, Harbor, Washington 98250
(360) 378-4730

Surrounded by firs and pristine northwestern scenery, the Hillside House is situated on an acre of land looking out toward Mount Baker, the harbor, and ferries coming and going. There are three guest rooms all benefiting from the excellent view.

Chili Brunch

- 12 **eggs**
- 1/3 **cup all-purpose flour**
- 1 **teaspoon garlic powder**
- 1 **teaspoon salt (or to taste)**
- 1 **teaspoon pepper (or to taste)**
- 4 **cups shredded Cheddar cheese**
- 2 **cups cottage cheese**
- 1 **4-ounce can mild chilies, diced**
- 1/2 **cup melted butter**

In a large bowl mix all of the above ingredients together. Pour into a greased 9 x 13-inch baking dish. Refrigerate overnight if desired. Bake in a 350° oven for 45 minutes.

Serve with a tablespoon of mild salsa and sour cream on top.

MAKES 12 SERVINGS.

Lemon Walnut Scones

- 1/2 **cup butter**
- 1/3 **cup margarine**
- 1 **tablespoon baking powder**
- 1/8 **teaspoon salt**
- 2/3 **cup sugar**
- 1 **grated lemon zest**
- 3 **cups all-purpose flour, sifted**
- 1 **egg**
- 1 **teaspoon vanilla extract**
   Milk
- 1/3 **cup chopped walnuts**

In a large bowl cream together the butter, margarine, baking powder, salt, sugar, and lemon zest. Cut the flour into the mixture. In a 1-cup measure combine the egg, vanilla, and enough milk to make 1 cup. Add the walnuts. Turn the dough onto a floured surface and knead by hand until smooth. If the dough is too wet, add a little flour. It should be loose (sticky). Scoop heaping tablespoon-size portions into a small bowl of flour, roll until covered, and place on a cookie sheet about 2 inches apart. Pat down slightly. Bake in a 400° oven for about 20 minutes until slightly brown.

MAKES 12 SCONES

Fresh Fruit Coffeecake

- 1/3 **cup butter**
- 1 **cup sugar**
- 3 **cups sifted all-purpose flour**
- 1 **tablespoon baking powder**
- 1/2 **teaspoon salt**
- 1 **cup milk**
- 2 **eggs**
- 2 **cups fresh or frozen berries or other fruit**

- 1/3 **cup butter, softened**
- 3/4 **cup brown sugar**
- 1/2 **cup all-purpose flour**
- 3/4 **teaspoon ground cinnamon**

In a large bowl combine the 1/3 cup of butter and the sugar with an electric mixer. Add 3 cups of flour, the baking powder, salt, milk, and eggs, and mix until smooth. Add the fruit. Pour into a greased 9 x 13-inch baking dish.

In a small bowl combine the brown sugar, 1/2 cup of flour, and cinnamon. Cut 1/3 cup of butter into butter into the remaining ingredients and sprinkle over the cake. Refrigerate overnight if desired. Bake in a 375° oven for 50 minutes or until done inside. Bake time will vary with type of fruit. Cool for 15 minutes before serving.

MAKES 14 SERVINGS.

Hillside House

Tucker House Bed and Breakfast

260 B Street
Friday Harbor, Washington 98250
(800) 965-0123

A restored Victorian, the Tucker House offers six nicely furnished rooms to San Juan Island visitors. Located only two blocks from the ferry landing, this B&B is only two blocks from the shops, restaurants, galleries, marinas, and Whale Museum of Friday Harbor. Tucker House offers a picket-fenced yard full of flowers, decks to lounge in the sun, and an outside hot tub to soothe tired muscles. Situated in the banana belt of the Pacific Northwest, San Juan Island has more sunshine and less rain than the U.S. mainland. Its protected harbors provide good sea kayaking opportunities, charter fishing, and other aquatic sports.

Tucker House Soufflé

- 4 **eggs**
- 1/2 **cup milk (half and half)**
- 1/8 **teaspoon dry mustard**
- 1/4 **teaspoon Italian seasoning**
- 1/8 **teaspoon seasoned salt**
- 1/2 **cup grated Cheddar cheese**

Spray 4 ramekins with cooking spray. In a blender combine the eggs, milk, dry mustard, Italian seasoning, seasoned salt, and Cheddar cheese. Pour the blended egg mixture into each ramekin. Bake in a 450° oven for 20 minutes, or until golden brown and fluffy.

Serve in the ramekin with a slice of orange and Cinnamon Bread (recipe follows).

MAKES 4 SERVINGS.

Tucker House Specialty Cinnamon Bread

  1 *package active dry yeast.*
  ⅓ *cup warm water (105 to 115°)*
  ⅔ *cup warm milk (110°)*
  1 *teaspoon salt*
  ¼ *cup butter, melted and cooled*
  ¼ *cup sugar*
  2 *eggs*
3½ *to 4 cups all-purpose flour*
  2 *tablespoons butter, melted*
  ¼ *cup sugar*
1½ *teaspoons ground cinnamon*
  3 *tablespoons melted butter*
....
  ½ *cup of powdered sugar (unsifted)*
  ½ *teaspoon of vanilla extract*
  1 *teaspoon of half and half*
  ½ *teaspoon of Grand Marnier*
  ½ *teaspoon of ground/scraped orange zest*

In a large bowl combine the yeast and warm water. Let stand until bubbly.

Stir in the milk, salt, ¼ cup of butter, and ¼ cup of sugar. Add the eggs and 2 cups of flour, and beat until smooth. Add 1½ to 2 cups of flour and beat until smooth. Turn the firm dough into a greased bowl and cover. Let rise in a warm place until double in bulk.

Turn onto a floured board and knead lightly. Add flour as necessary to get a firm, not sticky loaf. Roll out across the floured board until thin and elongated.

Brush on 2 tablespoon of melted butter. In a small bowl combine ¼ cup of sugar and the cinnamon. Sprinkle the cinnamon-sugar mixture over the dough. Roll the dough jelly roll fashion. Place the loaf in a 5 x 9-inch loaf pan. Brush the top with the remaining 3 tablespoons of melted butter. Cover and let rise again until almost doubled, 45 to 60 minutes. Bake in a 350° oven for 30 to 35 minutes. The loaf should sound hollow when tapped the top of the loaf. Turn the loaf out of the pan onto a cooling rack.

In a small bowl mix the confectioners' sugar, vanilla, half and half, Grand Marnier, and orange zest until firm, but easily spreadable. Add confectioners' sugar if necessary. Brush on a coating mixture on the top, sides, and ends while the loaf is still warm (hot not).

Serve with the Tucker House Soufflé (recipe precedes) for breakfast. Great for an evening snack too.

MAKES 1 LOAF.

Chick-a-Dee Inn at Ilwaco

Chick-a-Dee Inn at Ilwaco

120 Williams Street Northeast
P.O. Box 922
Ilwaco, Washington 98624
(360) 642-8686

*T*he Chick-a-dee had its beginning nearly seven decades ago as a Presbyterian Church. Today, it is a Country Inn and B&B with ten guest rooms tucked into the eves and dormers of the old church and furnished with a variety of antiques. Hikers and nature lovers will enjoy the twenty-eight miles of uncluttered beach that stretch out below the inn. Lighthouses mark a pair of rocky headlands at the end of the Ilwaco Peninsula. In addition there are museums, shops, fishing, sports, and a wide variety of restaurants.

Crustless Quiche in Muffin Tin

12 *eggs*
 1 *cup shredded cheese*
 ¼ *pound spinach, chopped*
 ¼ *pound mushrooms, sliced*

In a large bowl beat the eggs. Add the remaining ingredients. Pour the mixture into nonstick muffin cups. Bake in a 325° oven for 20 minutes.

Serve with fruit.

Variation: Add meats or potato.
MAKES 12 SERVINGS.

Velvet Hash

 1 *15-ounce can corned beef hash (or fresh corned beef)*
   Fresh potatoes, chopped or grated
 1 *onion, chopped*
   Fresh beets, chopped (or ½ can beets)

In a large bowl mix all of the ingredients together. In a greased skillet add the mixture and press with a spatula to flatten. Cook over medium heat until the bottom begins to crisp and brown, about 5 minutes. Turn in sections and cook until crisp and golden.

MAKES 2 SERVINGS.

Mountain Home Lodge

8201 Mountain Home Road
P.O. Box 687
Leavenworth, Washington 98826
(509) 548-7077

*P*ristine mountain scenery and vigorous outdoor activities are the big attractions here. All nine of the distinctively appointed guest rooms look out over an enchanting twenty-acre meadow toward the Stuart Range of the Cascades. The lodge is especially enchanting during the winter, when the only access is via a tracked snowcat. Cross-country skiers will love the miles of groomed trails, and the truly adventurous may want to take on the 1,700-foot sledding hill. After a long day in the snow, a plunge into one of the lodge's outdoor hot tubs can be most satisfying. Warmer weather brings hiking, mountain biking, whitewater rafting, horseback *riding, fishing, swimming, tennis and an abundance wildlife to enjoy.*

Mountain Home Granola

- 4 cups mixed flakes (oats, corn, wheat, bran)
- 1 teaspoon grated nutmeg
- 1 teaspoon ground cinnamon
- ½ cup honey
- ½ cup butter, melted
- 1 cup chopped nuts (pecan, walnut and/or sunflower seeds)
- ½ cup raisins
- ½ cup coconut

Line a baking sheet with foil. Spread the flakes in the pan and mix in the nutmeg and cinnamon. Stir the honey with the melted butter until well blended, then mix with the flakes until well coated. Bake in a 300° oven for 20 to 30 minutes, turning the cereal every 10 minutes. Be careful not to overbake. The flakes will seem a little sticky when done, but they crisp as they cool. Stir in the nuts, raisins and coconut after baking. Store in airtight container or ziploc bags in the refrigerator. Keeps 30 days.

MAKES ABOUT 5 CUPS.

Sherry Cake

- 1 18¼-ounce package yellow cake mix
- 1 6-ounce package instant vanilla pudding
- 4 eggs
- ¾ cup oil
- ¾ cup Sherry
- 1 teaspoon grated nutmeg
   Confectioners' sugar

In a large bowl combine the cake mix, pudding mix, eggs, oil, sherry, and nutmeg, and mix with an electric mixer until blended. Spoon into a greased bundt pan. Bake in a 350° oven for 45 minutes.

Cool the cake for 5 minutes. Unmold and sprinkle with sifted confectioners' sugar. Serve sliced at room temperature.

MAKES 12 TO 20 SERVINGS.

Gina's Mushroom Curry Soup

- 1 10½-ounce can condensed cream of mushroom soup
- 1 soup can milk (1¼ cups)
- 1 teaspoon curry powder
- 1 teaspoon dried onion flakes
- ⅔ to ¾ cup sliced fresh mushrooms
- 2 teaspoons lemon juice

In a saucepan combine all of the ingredients and simmer over medium heat for 5 minutes to allow the flavors to blend and the mushrooms to soften.

Can easily be doubled, tripled, etc.!

MAKES 2 SERVINGS.

Route 1, Box 1940
Lopez Island, Washington 98261
(360) 468-2253

*M*acKaye Harbor Inn was built in 1904 by the Tralnes family. In 1927, while the Tralnes were visiting relatives in Norway, their teenage children dramatically rebuilt the old farmhouse on the bay. It was the first island home to have electric lights. In the 1960s, the house was purchased and converted into a restaurant and pub. In 1985, it was completely restored and decorated to its earlier charm as one of Lopez Island's most grand and gracious homes. The inn now offers five beautiful guest rooms.

Finnish Pancake

- ¼ cup butter
- 8 eggs
- ½ teaspoon salt
- ⅔ cup all-purpose flour
- ¼ cup honey
- 2½ cups milk

In a 9 x 13-inch baking dish melt the butter in a 425° oven. In a blender combine the eggs, salt, flour, honey, and milk, alternating flour and milk last. Mix well. Pour the batter into the preheated baking dish of melted butter. Bake in a 425° oven for 20 to 25 minutes until puffed and golden.

Drizzle with hot jam or sprinkle with nutmeg or powdered sugar.

Note: This is the recipe that gets the best reviews and therefor, has become the benchmark or tradition at the Inn. It's almost like having custard for breakfast, something gently for the awakening tummy and tongue.

MAKES 6 TO 8 SERVINGS.

Glazed Apple Soufflé Omelet

- 4 golden delicious apples, sliced
- ¾ cup brown sugar
- 6 eggs separated, room temperature
- 3 tablespoons butter
- 1 tablespoon freshly squeezed lemon juice
- 1 teaspoon grated lemon zest
   Whipped cream

In a large ovenproof pan melt the butter and sauté the apples over medium heat with ¼ cup of brown sugar and the lemon juice until glazed, turning frequently. In a large bowl beat the egg whites to soft peaks. Add ¼ cup of brown sugar and beat until stiff. Beat the yolks with ¼ cup of brown sugar and the lemon zest until thick and lemon colored. Fold in the whites. Sprinkle the apples with cinnamon. Spoon the whites over the apples. Bake in a 375° oven for 15 to 20 minutes or until golden brown and set. Serve at once, flipped over, and topped with whip cream.

MAKES 4 TO 5 SERVINGS.

Dill Bread

- 2 tablespoons yeast
- ½ cup lukewarm water (105 to 115°)
- ¼ cup minced fresh dill
- 2 tablespoons butter
- 2 cups cottage cheese

4½ cups all-purpose flour
¼ cup firmly packed brown sugar
2 tablespoons minced onion
2 teaspoons salt
½ teaspoon baking soda
2 eggs

In a small bowl combine the yeast with water and set aside. In a separate small bowl mix the dill and butter together. In a large bowl combine the remaining ingredients to form a dough. Mix the bubbling yeast mixture and dill butter into the dough. Turn onto a floured board and knead for 5 minutes. The dough should be sticky. Place in a greased bowl and allow to rise until doubled.

Punch down and allow to rise again.

Punch down and form into 7 little loaves or 2 large loaves, then place in greased pans. Let rise.

Bake in a 350° oven for 45 minutes or until browned.

MAKES 7 LITTLE OR 2 LARGE LOAVES.

Summer Berry Pie

1½ cups all-purpose flour
1 tablespoon sugar
½ cup oil
1 teaspoon salt
1 tablespoon milk

    Fresh raspberries or strawberries
1 cup sugar
¼ teaspoon salt
3 tablespoons cornstarch
1½ cups water
1 3-ounce package raspberry or straw-berry gelatin

In a medium bowl combine the flour, 1 table-spoon of sugar, oil, salt, and milk, and mix well. Pat the pastry into a 9-inch pie plate. Bake in a 425° oven for 10 minutes.

Fill the cooled shell with fresh raspberries or strawberries. In a saucepan combine 1 cup of sugar, the salt, cornstarch, and water, and boil for 1 minute. Add the gelatin and boil another minute. Pour over the berries in the shell. Cool.

MAKES 6 TO 8 SERVINGS.

Bread Pudding with Whiskey Sauce

¾ cup raisins
2 tablespoons dark rum
1 pound French bread, cut into 1-inch cubes
3 cups milk (do not use low fat or nonfat)
1 cup half and half
3 eggs, beaten
2 cups sugar
3 tablespoons unsalted butter, melted
2 tablespoons vanilla extract
½ teaspoon ground cinnamon

½ cup unsalted butter
½ cup sugar
½ cup firmly packed brown sugar
1 egg
2 tablespoons whiskey

In a small bowl soak the raisins in rum for 20 minutes. Generously butter a 13 x 9-inch baking pan. In a large bowl combine the bread, milk, and half and half, and soak for 5 minutes.

In a medium bowl whisk together 3 eggs, 2 cups of sugar, 3 tablespoons of melted butter, the vanilla, and cinnamon. Pour the mixture over the bread. Add the raisins and rum. Toss to coat. Transfer to the prepared pan. Bake in a 325° oven for 1 hour and 30 minutes to 2 hours or until the top is golden brown.

In a saucepan melt ½ cup of butter with ½ cup of sugar and the brown sugar over low heat until the sugars dissolve. In a small bowl whisk 1 egg. Gradually whisk in some of the melted butter mixture. Return the mixture to the saucepan and whisk for 1 minute until smooth. Do not boil. Whisk in the whiskey. Spoon the sauce over the bread pudding.

MAKES 8 SERVINGS.

The Tudor Inn

1108 South Oak Street
Port Angeles, Washington 98362
(360) 452-3138

*T*he wooden charm of the Tudor era is apparent in this Olympic Peninsula inn. The five guest rooms provide outstanding views of the Olympic Mountains or the Straits of Juan de Fuca. The inn is in Port Angeles, the largest town on the peninsula and the terminal for ferries crossing over to Canada's Vancouver Island.

Little Egg Soufflés

3 eggs
1½ tablespoons cottage cheese
1½ teaspoons water
1 teaspoon baking powder
½ teaspoon Italian seasoning
5 to 6 drops hot sauce, such as Tabasco sauce
⅔ cup Cheddar or Swiss cheese

Grease 2 6-ounce soufflé dishes. In a small bowl beat all ingredients except the cheese with a wire whisk. Stir in the cheese and pour into the greased soufflé dishes. Bake in a 350° oven for 15 to 20 minutes or until set.

Note: The recipe can be doubled or tripled for up to 6 servings.

MAKES 2 SERVINGS.

Granola

8 cups regular oats
1 cup unsalted sunflower seeds
½ cup sesame seeds
½ cup coconut
¼ cup wheat germ
½ cup chopped nuts (walnuts or pecans)

¾ cup oil
¾ cup brown sugar
½ cup honey

In a 9 x 13-inch pan combine the oats, sunflower seeds, sesame seeds, coconut, wheat germ, and nuts, and stir to mix.

In a small saucepan combine the oil, brown sugar, and honey, and warm over low heat until mixed. Pour over the oatmeal mixture and stir well, coating the oats evenly. Bake in a 250° oven for 20 minutes. Stir and bake another 20 minutes. Stir and turn the oven off. Leave the granola in the oven for another 20 minutes. Total time in the oven is 1 hour. Store in zip-lock bags or other airtight containers. Keeps well in freezer.

MAKES ABOUT 3 QUARTS.

The James House

1238 Washington Street
Port Townsend, Washington 98368
(800) 385-1238

*T*his grand Victorian mansion was built in 1889 by Francis James who owned much of Port Townsend and selected its most scenic spot for his home. Fine western woods combined with the attention to detail typical of nineteenth-century construction combine to make this home a masterpiece. Most of the twelve guest rooms provide expansive water views, and all are furnished with period antiques.

The James House

James House Scones

9   cups all-purpopse flour
⅓   cup baking powder, less 1 tablespoon
1   cup sugar
1   tablespoon salt
⅔   cup butter
½   cups frozen blueberries
6   eggs
2¼   cups milk

In a large bowl mix together the flour, baking powder, sugar, and salt. Cut the butter into the flour mixture. Add the berries, tossing to coat. In a separate bowl beat the eggs to break down, then add the milk. Add the egg mixture to the flour, and mix just to incorporate. Overmixing will cause the berries to bleed into the dough. Turn the mixture onto a well floured board and knead into a ball. If the dough is sticky, knead in a little more flour. Flatten to about to ¾ thick. Cut the dough into triangles. Place the scones on a sheet pan and rest for 20 minutes.

Bake in a 350° oven for 15 to 20 minutes or until golden brown.

Variation: Instead of the blueberries use currants and add ¾ cup of grated orange zest.

MAKES 24 SCONES.

Fruit and Yogurt Bircher Muesli

2   cups rolled oats
   Milk to cover
⅓   cup honey
¾   cup seedless red grapes
1   cup chopped pineapple
2   pears, diced
½   banana, halved and sliced
2   cups peach yogurt
2   sweet apples, grated
   Toasted coconut

In a bowl place the oats and just cover with milk. Let stand for 15 minutes. In a large bowl toss together the grapes, pineapple, pears and banana. Stir in the yogurt. Add the honey to the oats, mixing well. Grate the apples and mix into the oats. Add the oat and apple mixture to the fruit. Serve in individual bowls topped with toasted coconut.

MAKES 12 SERVINGS.

Ravenscroft Inn

533 Quincy Street
Port Townsend, Washington 98368
(360) 385-2784

*T*he Ravenscroft Inn is a replication of an historic Charleston single house situated high on the bluff overlooking Port Townsend, the Olympic Peninsula's Victorian seaport. Several of the rooms offer commanding views of the bay and mountains. Guests may explore the Olympic National Park, walk the seven mile sand spit at Dungeness, or hike through North America's only rain forest. Port Townsend and its environs offer activities such as theater, unparalleled dining, boating, biking, fishing, kayaking, and hiking.

Blackberry Soup

2   cups fresh or frozen blackberries (or boysenberries)
⅓   cup sugar
1   tablespoon lemon juice
1   cinnamon stick
2   cups water
2   tablespoons potato starch (or cornstarch, but soup will be opaque)
   Yogurt
   Berry leaves and lemon zest for garnish

In a saucepan bring the berries, sugar, lemon juice, cinnamon stick, and 2 cups of water to a boil. Reduce the heat, cover, and simmer for 10 minutes.

Strain the mixture through cheesecloth, discarding the pulp and the cinnamon stick. Taste the strained juice and add additional sugar and lemon juice, if necessary. There should be 2 cups.

In a saucepan stir together the starch and ¼ cup of water. Cook and stir for about 2 to 3

Ravenscroft Inn

minutes until thickened and bubbly. Add the juice mixture, and cook and stir unil thickened. Do not boil. Cover the surface with clear plastic wrap. Cool, and refrigerate.

To serve, squirt yogurt from a squeeze bottle onto soup and draw a toothpick through it to create a squiggle or heart, etc. Or sprinkle with lemon zest or create a flower design with the yogurt and use a berry leaf and very thinly sliced lemon zest to add to the eye appeal.

MAKES 2 SERVINGS.

Chocolate Cheesecake Muffins

    6 *ounces cream cheese, softened*
   ¼ *cup sugar*
    1 *egg*
   ⅛ *teaspoon salt*
   ¼ *cup chocolate chips*
....
   ½ *cup chocolate chips*
  1½ *cups flour*
    1 *teaspoon soda*
   ½ *teaspoon salt*
   ½ *cup sugar*
   ⅓ *cup oil*
    1 *egg*
    1 *teaspoon vanilla extract*
    1 *cup water*
       Confectioners' sugar

In a medium bowl combine the cream cheese, ¼ cup of sugar, 1 egg, and salt, and beat until creamy. Stir in the chocolate chips. Set aside.

In the top of a double boiler over simmering water melt the chocolate chips. Stir until smooth. Remove the pan from the heat.

In a small bowl combine the flour, soda, and salt. Set aside. In a large bowl combine ½ cup of sugar, the oil, 1 egg, and the vanilla, and beat well. Stir in the chocolate. Beat in

the flour mixture alternately with the water. Fill greased muffin cups one-third full with batter. Spoon 1 tablespoon of filling onto the batter. Spoon the batter over the filling to cover, no more than two-thirds full. Bake in a 350° oven for 20 to 25 minutes or until golden brown. Cool and remove from pans. Sprinkle with confectioners' sugar.

MAKES 24 MUFFINS.

Mushroomed Eggs in Lemon Sauce

    7 *tablespoons butter*
   12 *to 16 eggs*
    2 *tablespoons minced shallots or*
       green onions
    1 *pound mushrooms, sliced*
       Salt and pepper to taste
    1 *cup grated Parmesan cheese (or mixture of Parmesan, Cheddar, and Swiss)*
....
    5 *tablespoons butter*
    6 *tablespoons all-purpose flour*
    2 *cups milk*
    1 *cup heavy cream (or half and half)*
    1 *teaspoon lemon juice (or ¼ teaspoon lemon extract)*
....
       English muffins
       Fresh parsley and slivered olives for garnish

In a large skillet melt 4 tablespoons of butter and scramble the eggs in until softly done. Remove to a greased or buttered 9 x 13-inch glass baking dish. In the skillet melt 3 tablespoons of butter and sauté the onions and mushrooms until lightly done. Spread this mixture evenly over the egg mixture and sprinkle with about one-third of the cheese.

In the same skillet melt 5 tablespoons of butter over low heat. Blend in the flour, and cook until bubbly, stirring constantly. Gradually add in a little milk until the mixture is smooth. Continue to whisk in the remaining milk. Whisk in the cream, salt, and pepper, and simmer for 4 to 5 minutes until smooth and creamy. Beat in the lemon juice.

Pour lemon sauce over the eggs and mushrooms, and top with the remaining cheese. At this point cover with aluminum foil

and refrigerate overnight if desired. Bake covered in a 375° oven for 15 to 20 minutes. If refrigerated, be sure to bring dish to room temperature before baking.

Serve over toasted, buttered English muffins, and garnish with fresh parsley and slivered olives.

MAKES 8 SERVINGS.

Prune Apricot Coffee Cake

   ¾ *cup dried apricots*
   ¾ *cup dried prunes*
   ⅔ *cup firmly packed dark brown sugar*
    1 *tablespoon all-purpose flour*
    1 *tablespoon ground cinnamon*
    2 *cups all-purpose flour*
    2 *teaspoons baking powder*
   ½ *teaspoon salt*
   ¾ *cup shortening or butter, softened*
   ¾ *cup sugar*
    2 *eggs*
    1 *teaspoon vanilla extract*
   ¾ *cup milk*
    6 *tablespoons butter, melted*
   ⅓ *cup chopped walnuts*

In a medium bowl soak the fruit in hot water to cover for 5 minutes. Omit soaking if the fruit is soft. Drain and chop fine.

Grease and flour a 9-inch tube or bundt pan. In a small bowl combine the brown sugar, 1 tablespoon of flour, and cinnamon. Set aside.

In a medium bowl sift 2 cups of flour with the baking powder and salt. Set aside.

In a large bowl beat the shortening, sugar, eggs, and vanilla with an electric mixer for 5 minutes. Beat in one-third of the dry ingredients alternately with half of the milk, repeat, and end with dry ingredients. Beat just until combined. Fold in the fruit. Turn one-third of the batter into the pan, spreading evenly. Sprinkle with one-third of the brown sugar mixture, then 2 tablespoons of melted butter. Repeat twice. Sprinkle the top with walnuts. Covered and refrigerate overnight at this point if desired. Bake in a 350° oven for 55 minutes. Allow to cool for 25 minutes before serving.

MAKES 8 SERVINGS.

Salisbury

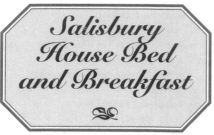

Salisbury House Bed and Breakfast

❧

750 16th Avenue East
Seattle, Washington 98112
(206) 328-8682

---

*O*nly minutes from the modern rush of downtown Seattle, this quiet B&B is situated on a tree-lined residential street. The house dates to 1904, and guest rooms still reflect its beginnings. One has a rare six-foot claw-foot tub. Public rooms are large and bright, and there is a game room, great for an evening game of chess or a morning of letter writing by the fire.

Mary's Oatmeal Pancakes

- 2 **cups rolled oats (not instant)**
- 3 **cups buttermilk**

- ½ **cup all-purpose flour**
- 1 **teaspoon baking soda**
- 1 **teaspoon baking powder**
- ¼ **teaspoon salt**
- 2 **eggs, lightly beaten**
- ¼ **cup oil**

- 3 **Golden Delicious apples**
- ⅓ **cup water**
  Sugar and ground cinnamon to taste

In a large bowl combine the oats and buttermilk, cover, and refrigerate overnight.

In a separate bowl combine the flour, soda, baking powder, and salt. Add the dry ingredients to the oat mixture. In a small bowl combine the eggs and oil. Add the egg mixture to the oatmeal mixture. Heat a griddle to 350° and cook the pancakes until golden brown. Serve with homemade chunky applesauce.

Peel, core and slice the apples. In a saucepan cook the apples with water over low heat until the apples are soft but still hold together. Add sugar and cinnamon to taste.
MAKES 4 TO 6 SERVINGS.

Cathy's Sugar Cookies

- 2 **cups butter, softened**
- 2 **cups sugar**
- 6 **ounces cream cheese, room temperature**
- 2 **egg yolks**
- 1 **teaspoon salt**
- 2 **teaspoons vanilla extract (Mexican if available)**
- 2 **teaspoons almond extract**
- 5 **cups all-purpose flour**

In a large bowl cream the butter, sugar, and cream cheese.

Beat the egg yolks lightly, and add to the butter mixture. Add the salt, vanilla, and almond extract and mix well. Mix in the flour. The dough will be heavy, use hands if necessary to blend the ingredients. Cover the bowl and refrigerate about 30 minutes.

Roll out the dough on a floured surface and cut out. Place on an ungreased cookie sheet. Bake in a 350° oven for 8 to 10 minutes. Cool on sheets of waxed paper and decorate as desired.
MAKES 4 DOZEN.

Shelburne Country Inn

❧

P.O. Box 250
Seaview, Washington 98644
(360) 642-2442

---

*E*stablished in 1896, the Shelburne has been serving travelers for just over a century. Located between the Columbia River and the Pacific Ocean on Long Beach Peninsula, the inn is surrounded by stunning scenery. The peninsula has an unspoiled, twenty-eight-mile stretch of wild coastline, the longest continuous beach in the United States. Breakfast is served family style at a large oak table in the lobby. The menu changes each morning to reflect what is fresh and in season.

Sourdough Banana Bread

- ½ **cup butter, softened**
- ½ **cup margarine, softened**
- 2 **cups sugar**
- 3 **eggs**
- 2¼ **cups mashed banana**
- 1 **cup sourdough starter**
- 1 **cup buttermilk**
- 4¼ **cups all-purpose flour**
- 2 **teaspoons salt**
- 2 **teaspoon sbaking powder**
- 1 **teaspoon baking soda**
- 1½ **cups chopped walnuts**

In a large bowl cream the butter and margarine with an electric mixer with the paddle attachment. Add the sugar and beat until light and fluffy. Then add the eggs, one at a time, beating until well blended. Stir in the mashed banana, starter, and buttermilk. In a separate bowl sift the flour with the salt, baking powder, and soda. Add the dry ingredients to the liquid mixture, and gently stir. When almost smooth, add the walnuts and stir until well blended, being careful not to overstir. Pour into 2 greased 5 x 9-inch loaf pans. Bake in a 350° oven for 1 hour and 5 minutes, or until a toothpick inserted in the center comes out clean.

Cool thoroughly before slicing.
MAKES 1 LOAF.

Raised Belgian Waffles

- *1 cup warm water (105 to 115°)*
- *2 tablespoons dry yeast*
- *4 cups milk, scalded and cooled to 100°*
- *1 cup butter, melted*
- *2 teaspoons salt*
- *2 teaspoons sugar*
- *3 cups all-purpose flour plus 1 cup whole wheat flour*
- *4 eggs, separated*
- *½ teaspoon baking soda*
- *Grated rind of 1 orange*

In a large mixing bowl sprinkle the yeast over the warm water. Let stand to dissolve for 5 minutes.

Add the milk, butter, salt, sugar, and flour to the yeast mixture and beat until smooth. Cover the bowl with plastic wrap and let stand overnight at room temperature. Just before cooking the waffles, beat in the egg yolks, baking soda, and orange zest. In a separate bowl whip the egg whites until stiff but not dry. Fold into the waffle batter until fully incorporated. The batter will be thin enough to pour. Pour ½ to ¾ cup of batter into a very hot waffle iron. Bake the waffles until golden and crisp. Serve hot with maple syrup.

MAKES 4 TO 6 SERVINGS.

Whole Wheat Date Scones

- *8 ounces pitted dates*
- *1 cup boiling water*

- *1 cup cake flour*
- *1 cup whole wheat flour*
- *2 cups all-purpose flour*
- *2 tablespoons baking powder*
- *¼ teaspoon ground cinnamon*
- *1 teaspoon salt*
- *2 tablespoons brown sugar*
- *Grated zest of 1 orange*
- *½ cup unsalted butter, chilled and cut into small pieces*
- *½ cup margarine, chilled and cut into small pieces*
- *⅓ cup chopped walnuts*
- *⅓ cup milk*

Grease a baking sheet measuring 11 x 18-inch and set aside.

Sift together three times:

In a medium bowl soak the dates in the boiling water for 5 minutes. Drain, chop, and cool.

In a large bowl sift together the flours, baking powder, cinnamon, salt, and brown sugar 3 times. Add the grated orange zest to the flour mixture. Cut in the butter and margarine with a pastry blender or the paddle attachment of a mixer on low speed. The mixture should have a fine texture when fully incorporated. Mix 2 tablespoons of the flour mixture with the drained, chopped, and cooled dates and add the chopped walnuts. Then add this mixture to the rest of the flour mixture. Lastly, with as few strokes as possible, add ⅓ cup of milk. Stir only until the mixture holds together. Divide the dough into 2 equal portions and pat each ball into a flat round about 1 inch thick. Using a large knife, cut each round into 6 equal pie-shaped wedges. Place on a greased baking sheet in the round, with small spaces between each wedge. Brush the tops with cream and sprinkle sugar atop each scone. Bake in a 450° oven toward the top of the oven for approximately 10 minutes or until the scones are a nice golden brown.

Serve hot from the oven for best results.

MAKES 12 SCONES.

Savory Baked Cheese Grits

- *3 cups cooked grits*
- *1½ cups grated % Jack cheese*
- *2 large eggs, beaten*
- *1½ cups heavy cream (or evaporated skim milk if counting calories)*
- *2 tablespoons butter, melted*
- *½ teaspoon salt*
- *½ teaspoon paprika*
- *¼ teaspoon cayenne pepper*
- *1 tablespoon chopped fresh parsley*
- *1 tablespoon chopped fresh chives*

Grease 12 standard size muffin cups. In a large bowl stir together all ingredients until mixed. Using a large spoon or ice cream scoop, divide the mixture evenly among muffin cups.

Bake in a 375° oven for 25 to 30 minutes or until just firm. Cool in pans for 10 minutes, before inverting onto a baking sheet or aluminum foil. Transfer to a serving plates, allowing 2 cups per serving.

MAKES 1 DOZEN.

Split Pea Soup

- *2 pounds smoked ham hocks*
- *Water to cover*
- *1 16-ounce bag green split peas*
- *5 cups chicken stock*
- *1 teaspoon salt*
- *1 bay leaf*
- *2 tablespoons oil*
- *3 large cloves garlic, minced*
- *1 medium yellow onion, chopped*
- *2 medium potatoes, peeled and cut into bite-sized pieces*
- *2 carrots, peeled and sliced ½-inch thick*
- *2 stalks celery, sliced ½-inch thick*
- *Water*
- *Chopped parsley*
- *Freshly ground black pepper to taste*

Rinse the ham hocks then place in a stockpot with water to cover. Bring to a boil, then simmer for 45 minutes, or until the meat separates easily from the bone. Remove from the water and allow to cool to the touch. Discard the water.

Rinse and drain the split peas, and place in the stockpot with the chicken stock, salt, and bay leaf. Bring to a boil, and simmer for 1 hour. While the peas simmer, in a sauté pan heat the oil and sauté the garlic and onion until tender and slightly browned. Add to the peas and simmer for 1 hour.

Add the potato, carrots, and celery. Add up to 2 cups more water, if necessary. Remove the ham from the bones and cut into bite-sized pieces. Add to the peas and vegetables. Continue to simmer until the vegetables are done and the ham is heated through. Remove the bay leaf. Season with freshly ground black pepper and freshly chopped parsley.

MAKES 6 SERVINGS.

WEST VIRGINIA

Highlawn Inn

304 Market Street
Berkeley Springs, West Virginia 25411
(304) 258-5700

The same warm mineral waters that once attracted Indian tribes to the Berkeley Springs area still bring droves of visitors to the town. Berkeley Springs is noted nowadays for its artisans, resorts, clubs, summer concerts, and Apple Butter Festival held each Columbus Day. A small, intimate retreat, the Victorian Highlawn Inn offers ten individually decorated and named guest rooms.

Confetti-Herb Squash

- 2 cups yellow squash, cooked, mashed, and drained
- 2 eggs, well beaten
- ½ cup undiluted evaporated milk
- ¼ cup margarine, melted
- 1 tablespoon sugar
- 1 tablespoon all-purpose flour
- ¾ cup grated Swiss cheese
    Salt and pepper to taste
- 2 tablespoons chopped fresh tarragon
- 1 tablespoons chopped fresh basil
- ½ cup chopped onions

- ¼ cup chopped red bell peppers
- ¼ cup chopped green bell peppers
    Breadcrumbs

In a large bowl combine the squash, eggs, milk, margarine, sugar, flour, Swiss cheese, salt, pepper, tarragon, basil, onions, and peppers. Mix well. Pour into a greased glass casserole. Top with breadcrumbs. Bake in a 350° oven for about 1 hour or until the center is set.

Note: This dish adapts well to being doubled, made ahead, and baked next day, or baked and frozen. Defrost and reheat covered with foil.

MAKES 6 SERVINGS.

Orange Chicken

- 6 chicken breasts, skin and bone removed
    Salt, pepper, paprika
- 1 cup chopped mixed red and green bell peppers (mixed)
- 1 large onion, chopped
- 1 cup sliced mushrooms
- 2 cups orange juice
- 1 tablespoon firmly packed dark brown sugar
- 1 cup dry sherry

Place the chicken in a shallow pan, and sprinkle with salt, pepper, and paprika. Sprinkle the peppers, onion, and mushrooms over the chicken. In a small bowl combine the orange juice, brown sugar, and sherry. Pour over the chicken. Cover with foil. Bake in a 350° oven for 2 hours. Uncover and bake until brown.

Optional: Pour the baking juices into a saucepan and add some cornstarch or arrow root to thicken. Serve over rice.

Note: The dish may be prepared, covered, and refrigerated overnight before baking.

MAKES 6 SERVINGS.

Highlawn Inn

Cottonwood Inn

Route 2, Box 61-S
Charles Town, West Virginia 25414
(800) 868-1188

In the Shenandoah Valley near Harpers Ferry, the Cottonwood Inn

Cottonwood Inn

is more than 150 years old. The restored farmhouse is reached via a small bridge over Bullskin Run on a road that passes through lush, rolling farmlands. The inn offers its guests songbirds, an extensive library, and six peaceful acres for strolls and contemplation. History buffs will want to visit the nearby Antietam Battlefield and Harpers Ferry, where the John Brown Raid initiated the violence that soon exploded into the Civil War.

Sausage Bread

1   cup shredded fresh Parmesan cheese
     (not the kind from a can!)
¼   teaspoon salt
¼   teaspoon black pepper
¼   teaspoon ground basil
¼   teaspoon garlic powder
2   eggs
1   pound ground sausage (pork or
     turkey)
1   loaf frozen white bread dough,
     thawed overnight in refrigerator

In a large bowl mix the cheese and seasonings. Add the eggs and blend well. In a skillet cook and crumble the sausage. Reserve the drippings if desired. Add the sausage to the egg and cheese mixture, and blend thoroughly. Place the dough on a large ungreased cookie sheet and press into a rectangle approximately 10 x 14 inches. This starts out seeming impossible. The dough is easier to work with when still stiff and a little cold. Avoid thin spots that will tear and leak while cooking. Stretch the dough to the length of the pan to get a long thin loaf. Form the sausage filling into a long thin loaf along the middle of the dough. Fold the outside edges of the dough over the top of the filling and press together to seal. Don't get grease or oil on the dough, or the edges will not stick together. When the loaf is well formed with no leaky spots, work sausage drippings or butter under the loaf to keep it from sticking. Bake in a 350° oven for 20 to 25 minutes or until lightly browned so the filling doesn't get dry. Slice only when needed and serve warm. Keep the sliced edges covered or they will dry out quickly.

MAKES 6 SERVINGS.

Spiced Hot Cider

1   gallon apple cider-fresh and sweet
     Zest of 1 orange
     Juice and zest of 1 lemon
⅓   cup firmly packed dark brown sugar
1   heaping teaspoon whole cloves
1   heaping teaspoon whole allspice
2   sticks cinnamon
⅓   cup Old Savannah (liquid) Cinna-
     mon Mix (or 4 sticks cinnamon)

In a saucepan combine all ingredients except the rum and bring to a boil. Simmer for 30 minutes. Keep uncovered for a great aroma. Strain out the solids and serve hot in carafes or an electric urn. Add the rum before serving, if desired.

Note: More allspice and cloves can give a spicier taste but can also make it bitter. Do not use ground spices or mixture will have too much sediment.

MAKES 1 GALLON

White Horse Bed and Breakfast

❧

*120 Fayette Avenue
Fayetteville, West Virginia 25840
(304) 574-1400*

Situated on twenty-seven acres in the center of the historic town of Fayetteville, West Virginia, the White Horse is only five minutes from the spectacular New River Gorge Bridge and exciting whitewater rafting. The mansion was built in 1906 by a county sheriff and is listed on the National Register of Historic Landmarks. The walls in the dining room are covered with a hand-painted mural from France. There are nine well-appointed guest rooms, as well as a library and sun room.

Sausage Casserole

1   pound sausage (breakfast)
1   10½-ounce can cream of mushroom
     soup
2½   cups milk
4   eggs
¾   teaspoon dry mustard
     Dash Worcestershire sauce
2   cups grated American cheese
8   slices bread, cubed

In a skillet cook the sausage until brown and drain. Set aside. In a medium bowl mix together the soup, milk, eggs dry mustard, and Worcestershire sauce. In a buttered 1-quart baking dish layer the bread, 1 cup of cheese, half of the sausage, and half of the soup mixture. Layer the remaining cheese, sausage, and soup mixture. Refrigerate overnight.

Bake in a 300° oven for 1 hour and 30 minutes.

MAKES 4 TO 6 SERVINGS.

Waffles

2   cups baking mix
1   egg
½   cup oil
1¼   cups soda water

In a large bowl combine all of the ingredients. Cook in a waffle iron for 3 minutes on high.

MAKES ABOUT 4 SERVINGS.

Tunnel Mountain Bed and Breakfast

Route 1, Box 59-1
Elkins, West Virginia 26241
(304) 636-1684

Named for the 1890 railroad tunnel that passes under the property, this B&B is located on five wooded acres surrounded by mountains, forests, and rivers. The house is finished in pine and rare wormy chestnut woodwork and is decorated throughout with antiques, collectibles, and crafts. Close by are Blackwater Falls, Canaan Valley State Park, Dolly Sods, Seneca Rocks, and Spruce Knob. West Virginia beckons to hikers, cross-country skiers, fishermen, spelunkers, white water rafters, and nearly every variety of outdoor enthusiast.

Cranberry Sour Cream Coffeecake

  ½   **cup butter**
  1   **cup sugar**
  2   **eggs**
  2   **cups all-purpose flour**
  1   **teaspoon baking soda**
  1   **teaspoon baking powder**
  ½   **teaspoon salt**
  1   **cup sour cream**

Tunnel Mountain

  1   **teaspoon almond extract**
  1   **16-ounce can whole berry cranberry sauce**
  ½   **cup chopped pecans**

....

  ¾   **cup confectioners' sugar**
  ½   **teaspoon almond extract**
  1   **to 2 tablespoons warm water**

Grease and flour a 9 x 12-inch pan. Mix the butter and sugar until fluffy. Add the eggs one at a time. In a separate bowl combine the flour, soda, baking powder, and salt. Add the dry ingredients and sour cream alternately to the butter mixture. Blend in 1 teaspoon of almond extract.The batter will be thick. Spread half of the batter in the prepared pan, then spread ½ can of whole berry sauce over the batter. Add r remaining batter and top with the rest of the cranberry sauce. Sprinkle with nuts. Bake in a 350° oven for 40 to 45 minutes.

In a small bowl mix the confectioners' sugar, almond extract, and warm water. Glaze the cake after it has cooled for 20 minutes.

MAKES 8 SERVINGS.

Red Velvet Cake

  ½   **cup butter**
  1½   **cups sugar**
  2   **eggs**
  2   **level tablespoons cocoa**
  2   **ounces red food coloring**
  ½   **teaspoon salt**
  1   **teaspoon vanilla extract**
  1   **cup buttermilk**
  1   **cup all-purpose flour**
  1½   **teaspoons baking soda**
  1   **tablespoons vinegar**
    Red Velvet Cake Icing (recipe follows)

In a large bowl cream the butter, sugar, and eggs. In a cup make a paste of cocoa and food coloring and add to the creamed mixture. In a small bowl mix the salt and vanilla with buttermilk, and add to the butter mixture alternately with the flour. In a cup mix the soda and vinegar, and fold into the cake mixture. Do not use a mixer. Pour into 2 floured and greased 9-inch round cake pans. Bake in a 350° oven for 30 minutes. Remove from the pan shortly after baking. Ice the cooled cake layers with Red Velvet Cake Icing.

MAKES 6 TO 8 SERVINGS.

Red Velvet Cake Icing

  5   **tablespoons all-purpose flour**
  1   **cup milk**
  1   **cup sugar**
  1   **cup butter**
  1   **teaspoon vanilla extract**

In a saucepan boil the flour and milk until thick. Let the mixture stand at room temperature for a few hours.

In a medium bowl beat the sugar, butter, and vanilla until smooth. Add the flour mixture and beat until fluffy. Spread on the cake.

MAKES ICING FOR 1 2-LAYER CAKE.

Hutton House

P.O. Box 88
Routes 250/219
Huttonsville, West Virginia 26273
(304) 335-6701

Built at the turn of the century, the Queen Anne Victorian Hutton House is listed on the National Register of Historic Places. Meticulously restored, it can still boast its original oak woodwork, ornate windows with twenty-nine separate panes of glass, pocket doors, wrap-around porch, winding staircase, and three-story turret. The house has a commanding view of the Tygart River Valley and the Laurel Mountains. Breakfast comes with syrup made from sugar maples on the Hutton House property.

Zucchini Frittata

  1½   **teaspoons olive oil**
  1   **tablespoon butter**
    Grated zucchini (about 3 or 3 ounces)
    Salt
  5   **to 6 shakes House of Tsang Mangolian Fire Oil**

4 **eggs**
½ **cup shredded Monterey Jack cheese**
Salsa

In an eight-inch iron skillet heat ½ tablespoon olive oil and butter. Cover the bottom of the pan with grated zucchini. Sprinkle with salt and House of Tsang Mangolian Fire Oil (this is more flavorful than hot). If the fire oil is not available just use salt and pepper.

In a small bowl lightly beat the eggs and add them to the pan. Don't stir. Cook over low heat (too high heat will incorporate too much air) until three-fourths set. Sprinkle on the Monterey Jack cheese and place under a preheated broiler. Remove when the eggs are puffed and the cheese is golden, about 4 minutes. Cut in half and place on individual plate with a tablespoon of salsa on top.

MAKES 2 SERVINGS.

Sausage Madeira

10 **to 12 inches medium-hot Italian**
sausage
3 **tablespoons butter**
¼ **cup Madeira wine**
2 **carrots, thinly sliced**
½ **medium-size onion (sweet is best),**
medium sliced

In a skillet fry the sausage thoroughly and let brown on all sides. Set aside. Pour the oil out of the pan and leave the browned bits. Deglaze the pan with the butter and wine. Cook until bubbling and reduced. Add the carrots and onion. Stir-fry over high heat until tender but still crisp. Slice the sausage, add to the pan, and heat through.

MAKES 2 TO 4 SERVINGS.

Breakfast Sorbet

1 **cantaloupe (or 1 fresh pineapple, or**
a quart of strawberries)
3 **tablespoons sugar**
3 **tablespoons half and half**
3 **tablespoons strawberry liqueur**

Peel and cut the fruit and place in a food processor. Add the sugar, half and half, and strawberry liqueur. Blend until the mixture is smooth liquid. Place in a container and freeze until hard. "Scratch" up with a fork (you don't want any lumps) and serve by either spooning the mixture into a dish or

forming balls with a melon baller or small ice cream scoop. Garnish with fresh fruit such as kiwi slices or berries in season.

MAKES 6 TO 8 SERVINGS.

Aspen Hall Inn

≈

405 Boyd Avenue
Martinsburg, West Virginia 25401
(304) 263-4385

---

*A*spen Hall is a 200-year-old lime-stone mansion situated under a canopy of giant locust trees on several acres near North Mountain. Listed on the Register of Historic Places, the mansion began as a small stone fort built by Quakers about 1750. The house seen today was completed in 1788 and enlarged in 1905. The interior retains all of its original Georgian features, including a winding, three-story staircase. One of the ornate parlors contains a grand piano. The five exceptionally large guest rooms have separate sitting rooms and lots of antiques. The dining room is a showplace for antique china.*

Plantation Cakes with Sautéed Apples and Maple Sugar

8 **teaspoons margarine**
4 **eggs**
1 **cup milk**
1 **cup all-purpose flour**
½ **teaspoon salt**
2 **large apples**
2 **tablespoons margarine**
½ **cup crushed maple sugar, per apple**

Aspen Hall Inn

Prepare 4 individual oven proof 1 cup quiche dishes by placing 2 teaspoons of margarine in the bottom of each dish and prewarming them in a 450° oven for 5 minutes.

In a medium bowl whisk the eggs with the milk. Sift in the flour and salt, and blend with a whisk. Remove the hot dishes from the oven and swirl to spread the margarine over the bottom surface of each dish. Pour in the batter and quickly return to a 400° oven for 20 minutes.

While pancakes bake, peel, core, and thickly slice one large apple for each of 2 pancakes. In a skillet melt 2 tablespoons of margarine and sauté the apples just until transparent and still holding shape. Three minutes before the pancakes come out, sprinkle the apples with crushed maple sugar. Toss gently to coat the slices. Serve on top of the pancakes.

Note: Plantation cakes are four-inch high puffs baked in the oven, similar to popovers.

MAKES 4 SERVINGS.

Fresh Peach Cobbler

5 **cups peeled and sliced peaches**
1 **cup sugar**
3 **tablespoons all-purpose flour**
¼ **teaspoon ground cinnamon**
Dash salt
....
⅓ **cup water**
1 **teaspoon vanilla extract**
½ **teaspoon orange extract**
1½ **cups all-purpose flour**
2 **teaspoons baking powder**
½ **teaspoon salt**

In a large bowl gently stir together the peaches, sugar, flour, cinnamon, and salt. Spoon into a 9 x 13-inch pan that has been greased with margarine.

In a large bowl cream the shortening and 1 cup of sugar. Add the egg. Mix in the water, vanilla, and orange extract alternately with the flour, baking powder, and salt. Spoon over the peaches.

Bake in a 350° oven for 35 minutes. This is a very nice dessert for guests on a milk-free diet.

Note: Try to get tree ripened peaches!

MAKES 8 SERVINGS.

Hampshire House 1884

&ea;

165 North Grafton
Romney, West Virginia 26757
(304) 822-7171

Dating *from 1884, the Hampshire House is situated in Romney, a sleepy hamlet on the South Branch of the Potomac River. There are six named and individually decorated guest rooms. The music room features a pump organ and the dining room is furnished with English tavern tables. Romney is the oldest town in West Virginia and is great for strolling.*

High Protein Fruit Pancakes

½   **cup yogurt (lemon, vanilla, coffee, or plain)**
¾   **cup low-fat cottage cheese**
1   **cup 2% milk**
2   **eggs**
2   **tablespoons firmly packed brown sugar or honey**
2   **tablespoons olive (or other vegetable oil)**
½   **to 1 cup chopped fruit (apples, pears, bananas, peaches, blueberries or strawberries, or all-fruit jam)**
½   **to 1 cup chopped nuts (optional)**

1   **cup whole wheat flour**
⅓   **cup wheat germ**
⅓   **cup yellow cornmeal**

1   **teaspoon baking soda**
1   **teaspoon baking powder**
½   **teaspoon salt (optional)**

In a large bowl beat the yogurt, cottage cheese, milk, eggs, brown sugar, oil, chopped fruit, and nuts.

In a separate bowl blend the dry ingredients. Add to the liquid mixture and mix well. Pour ¼ cup of batter on a hot griddle. Turn the pancakes over when bubbles appear. Take the pancakes off the griddle when steam appears. Serve with jam, syrup, or yogurt.

MAKES 20 PANCAKES.

French Omelet

3   **eggs**
2   **tablespoons water**

1   **tablespoon butter**
1   **tablespoon peanut oil**
    American, Swiss, cottage, or Parmesan cheese
    Cooked chopped bacon, ham, beef, chicken, shrimp, or crab
    Sautéed mushrooms, bell peppers, squash, spinach, onion, okra, sugar peas, etc.

In a bowl beat the eggs and water.

In a 10-inch non-stick skillet heat the butter and oil. Pour the eggs in the hot skillet when the butter stops bubbling. Lift the edges of the eggs and tilt the skillet to allow the center of the eggs to reach the bottom of the pan to cook. Sprinkle cheese, meat, and vegetables over the half of the eggs away from the skillet handle. Cook until the eggs begin to dry on top, 2 to 3 minutes. Slide the half of the of omelet with filling ingredients onto a heated plate. Fold the other half over the top. Serve with toast.

Note: Save come inside ingredients to put on top so you can tell what kind of omelet you made.

MAKES 1 SERVING.

Thomas Shepherd Inn

Thomas Shepherd Inn

&ea;

300 West German Street
P.O. Box 1162
Shepherdstown, West Virginia 25443
(304) 876-3715

At *the Thomas Shepherd Inn, guests are surrounded by reminders of the past: a 1738 grist mill that can boast the world's largest overshot water wheel, a monument to James Rumsey, inventor of an early version of the steamboat, and the Old Market House, built in 1880. All of this is near the inn in historic Shepherdstown, while only minutes away are Harpers Ferry and Antietam, the site of one of history's bloodiest battles. The inn offers seven delightfully furnished guest rooms, two formal dining rooms, and a broad porch.*

Asparagus Omelet

Basmanti rice
Tamari soy sauce
Basil leaves, fresh preferred
Parsley
Asparagus
Mushrooms, wild or cultivated
Butter
Apricots in sugar syrup
Eggs
Grated nutmeg
Oil

Prepare the rice according to the package directions. When done, add soy sauce, basil, and parsley.

In a steamer steam the asparagus until tender.

In a skillet sauté the mushrooms in butter. Add soy sauce and basil. Save 2-inch tops of asparagus and slice the remainder into 1-inch pieces. Add to the mushrooms.

In a saucepan make a sugar syrup using ½ sugar and ½ water, and simmer the apricots until tender.

In a small bowl combine the eggs, nutmeg, basil, and a bit of cold water.

In a skillet heat the oil. Make an omelet. Fill with the mushrooms and asparagus mixture.

Serve on a plate with asparagus tips on the omelet, drizzled with clarified butter. Add the rice, and apricots with sugar syrup. Garnish with a bouquet of fresh herbs and edible flowers such as basil, parsley, tarragon, nasturtiums, calendulas, etc.

MAKES 1 SERVING.

Strawberries with Citrus Sugar, Balsamic Vinegar, and Crushed Pepper

- 1 quart strawberries, sliced
- 3 tablespoons citrus sugar (see below)
- 1 tablespoon sugar
- 1 tablespoon balsamic vinegar
- ¼ teaspoon crushed peppercorns

About 45 minutes before serving, in a medium bowl mix all ingredients together.

Serve garnished with crème fraîche or whipped cream and a sprig of mint.

Citrus sugar: 1 cup sugar of combined with the zest of 1 orange and 1 lemon.

Ingredients can be added according to taste.

MAKES 6 SERVINGS.

Nectarines Poached in Rosé and Ginger

- 2 cups rosé or fruit wine
- 2 cups sugar
- 2 cups water
- 4 1-inch pieces gingerroot, sliced
- 6 nectarines, halved, pits removed
- 1 teaspoon almond flavoring
  Crème fraîche or sour cream
  Candied ginger and springs of mint

In a saucepan combine the wine, sugar, water, and ginger. Bring to a boil and simmer for about 20 minutes.

Add the nectarines and simmer on low heat until the fruit is tender, about 2 to 3 minutes.

Remove from the heat and add almond flavoring. With a slotted spoon remove the nectarines from the liquid and cool on a wire rack.

Serve at room temperature with a little of the liquid. Garnish with crème fraîche, and a few slivers of candied ginger, and a sprig of mint.

MAKES 6 SERVINGS.

Bourbon Pecan Baked Apples

- 1 cup firmly packed dark brown sugar
- 2 teaspoons lemon juice
- 1 teaspoon ground cinnamon
  Pinch ground cloves
  Pinch salt
- ⅔ cup pecan pieces
- 6 tablespoons bourbon
- 2 teaspoons vanilla extract
- 2 tablespoons butter
- 12 apples, cored

In a saucepan combine the sugar, lemon juice, cinnamon, cloves, and salt. Simmer a minute or so. Add the pecans, bourbon, vanilla and butter. Heat until butter melts. Cook a bit.

Place the apples in a baking dish and fill with the nut mixture. Brush with glaze. Bake in a 350° oven for 50 to 60 minutes, brushing with glaze occasionally.

Cool for about 10 minutes before serving. Garnish with crème fraîche.

MAKES 12 SERVINGS.

Blueberry Sour Cream Muffins

- ½ cup margarine, softened
- ¾ cup sugar
- 2 eggs
- 1½ teaspoon vanilla extract
- ¾ cup sour cream
- 2 cups all-purpose flour
- ¼ teaspoon baking soda
- ½ teaspoon salt
- 1 cup blueberries

In a large bowl cream the margarine and sugar. Beat in the eggs one at a time. Beat in the vanilla and sour cream.

In a medium bowl combine the flour, soda and salt. Stir into the butter mixture. Fold in the blueberries. Spoon into greased muffin cups and sprinkle with sugar.

Bake in a 375° oven for 23 minutes.

MAKES 1 DOZEN.

WISCONSIN

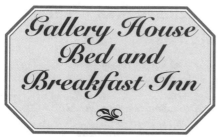

Gallery House Bed and Breakfast Inn

215 North Main Street
Alma, Wisconsin 54610
(608) 685-4975

---

*O*nly two streets wide, Alma is squeezed between the Mississippi River and a set of 500-foot-high bluffs. Steps are as important as streets for getting around in historic Alma, and many of its famed stairways have been given their own names and signs. Built in 1861, the Gallery House B&B is the oldest complete structure in Alma's historic district. Originally a mercan-

Gallery House

tile building, the inn has three cozy guest rooms and several stately common rooms decorated with antiques and a constantly expanding collection of original art and photography. The gourmet breakfast is served by candlelight in a dining room overlooking the Mississippi.

Pear Cranberry Sauce

    1 to 2 ripe pears
    1 16-ounce can whole berry cranberry
       sauce

Dice the pears into medium-sized pieces and place in a saucepan with the cranberry sauce. Cook for 5 minutes over low heat or until the pears are tender. Serve warm over French toast or pancakes.
MAKES ABOUT 3 CUPS.

Gougere au Jambon

    ½ cup water
    ¼ cup butter
    ½ cup all-purpose flour
    2 eggs, beaten
    ½ cup finely diced sharp Cheddar
       cheese
    1 tablespoon butter
    1 tablespoon all-purpose flour
    ½ cup low sodium chicken stock
       Salt and pepper to taste
    2 ounces sliced mushrooms
    2 tablespoons chopped fresh parsley
    4 ounces cooked ham, julienne strips
    3 tablespoons grated Parmesan cheese
       and fresh sourdough bread
       crumbs combined

Place the water in a small saucepan. Cut ¼ cup of butter into small pieces and add to the water. Bring slowly to a boil, making sure that the butter is completely melted before the water boils. Turn up the heat and allow to boil for at least 30 seconds. Take the pan off the heat and add the flour all at once. Stir quickly and vigorously until the mixture comes away from the sides of the pan. Spread on a plate to cool.

For the ham mixture, melt the butter in a small saucepan. Add the flour. Cook for 1 to 2 minutes until pale straw colored. Gradually whisk in the stock until smooth. Add a pinch of salt and pepper and the chopped parsley. Stir in the mushrooms and ham, and set aside.

To continue the pastry, add a pinch of pepper to the paste and return to the saucepan. Gradually add the eggs to the paste mixture. It may not be necessary to add all the egg. The mixture should be smooth and shiny and hold its shape when ready. If it is too thick, beat in a little more egg. Add the Cheddar cheese, and spoon into individual soufflé dishes, pushing the mixture up on the sides, and leaving a well in the center. Fill the center with the ham mixture and scatter the Parmesan and breadcrumb mixture on each soufflé. Bake in a 400° oven until the pastry is puffed and nicely browned. Serve immediately.
MAKES 4 TO 6 SERVINGS.

Gollmar Mansion Inn

422 3rd St.
Baraboo, Wisconsin 53913
(608) 356-9432

*T*he inn is only four blocks from the historic square of Baraboo, placing it within easy walking distance of many charming shops, galleries, and cafes. Built in 1889, the very Victorian Gollmar features hand-painted ceiling murals, bevelled glass windows, chandeliers, beaded oak woodwork, and many original antiques.

Linda's Raspberry Chocolate Chip Muffins

1 egg
1 cup milk
¼ cup safflower oil
2 cups all-purpose flour
¼ cup sugar
3 teaspoons baking powder
1 teaspoon salt
½ cup semisweet chocolate chips
½ cup raspberries

Grease 12 muffin cups. In a large bowl beat the eggs. Stir in the milk and oil. Mix in the remaining ingredients just until moistened. The batter should be lumpy. Fill muffin cups two-thirds full. Bake in a 400° oven for 20 to 25 minutes or until golden brown. Remove from the pan.
MAKES 1 DOZEN.

Gollmar Mansion Inn

Decadent French Toast

½ cup butter
1 cup firmly packed brown sugar
2 tablespoons light corn syrup
16 slices sandwich bread (oatmeal, wheat, etc.)
6 eggs
2 cups milk
2 teaspoons vanilla extract

Melt the butter in a 2-quart microwave safe dish. Add brown sugar and corn syrup. In the microwave, bring the mixture to a boil. Place the bread in the pan stacked 2 slices deep.

In a medium bowl beat the eggs, milk, and vanilla extract together and pour over the bread. Cover and refrigerate overnight.

Bake in a 350° oven for 45 minutes or until golden brown. Serve with sour cream, fruit (strawberries, blueberries, etc.), or just eat plain.
MAKES 8 SERVINGS.

Canoe Bay

W16065 Hogback Road
Chetek, Wisconsin 54728
(715) 924-4594

*I*ts architecture inspired by the work of Frank Lloyd Wright, Canoe Bay fits into its setting like a waterfall in a forest. Each of its buildings is unique: the Lodge, with its thirty-foot fieldstone fireplace; the Inn, with its classic prairie styling and deck cantilevered over a lake; and redwood Dream Cottage. Whirlpools, fireplaces, private decks, and lake views make the fourteen guest rooms as special as the buildings themselves. Two private lakes and hundreds of forested acres provide endless opportunities for spirit-lifting outdoor activities.

Fall Harvest Pasta

¼ cup raw wild rice
1¼ cups water (or chicken broth)
6 6-ounce duck or chicken breasts
2 tablespoons fines herbes
Salt and pepper to taste
¼ cup olive oil
1 16-ounce package pasta
½ cup diced onion
2 tablespoons minced garlic
1 cup shredded carrot
2 cups white wine (Chardonnay preferred)
½ cup dried cranberries

In a saucepan add rice to the water (or broth) and simmer until tender but crisp.

Season the duck with 1 tablespoon of herbs and salt and pepper. Heat 2 tablespoons oil in a heavy skillet over medium heat, and cook the duck, skin-side down, rendering until crisp. Turn the breasts over, cover the skillet, and cook another 1 to 2 minutes, until the meat is medium rare.

In a large pot add a little salt and oil to 1½ gallons of water and bring to a boil. Cook the pasta. While the pasta cooks, in a skillet sauté the onions, garlic, carrot, remaining herbs, and cooked wild rice in 2 tablespoons of oil, until the onions are translucent. Add the wine to the sauté, and reduce by one-third.

Drain the pasta and return to its pot. Add the sauce, and toss. Season to taste with salt and pepper and apportion to six pre-warmed plates. Slice the duck breasts ⅛-inch thick (skins on); fan slices over plates of pasta. Garnish with dried cranberries.

Note: The wild rice, duck, and pasta can be prepared ahead of time. To serve, reheat pasta in boiling water one minute. Reheat the duck by slicing the cold breast and warming for 2 minutes in a 350° oven.
MAKES 6 SERVINGS.

Chef Bruno's New Potato Salad

2 pounds whole new potatoes
8 ounces bacon, uncooked
½ onion, finely chopped
2 cloves garlic, peeled and chopped
2 tablespoons capers
1 tablespoon leaf tarragon
¼ cup olive oil
Salt and pepper to taste

In a large pot boil the potatoes until easily pierced by a fork. Drain and cool.

When the potatoes have cooled, chop into ½-inch pieces (leave the skin on).

In large saucepan sauté the chopped bacon. Discard half of the grease. Add the onion and garlic to the pan, and sauté for 2 minutes. Transfer the contents of the pan to a large bowl and add the remaining ingredients to the bowl. Toss well.

Serve chilled.

MAKES 10 SERVINGS.

Flourless Chocolate Almond Torte

½	cup butter
⅔	cup sugar
3	eggs
4	ounces semisweet chocolate, melted
½	cup finely ground almonds

4	ounces semi-sweet chocolate, finely chopped
⅓	cup heavy cream

2	8-ounce packages frozen raspberries, with juice
½	cup sugar
¼	cup water

Fresh raspberries

In a large bowl beat the butter and sugar with an electric mixer until light and fluffy. With the mixer running, add the eggs one at a time, followed by the melted chocolate. Add the almonds and mix well.

Grease an 8-inch cake pan, then line the pan with parchment paper. Grease and flour the parchment liner in the pan. Pour the mixture into the prepared cake pan. Bake in a 375° oven for 30 minutes or until a cake tester (or toothpick) inserted halfway between the center and edge of the pan comes out with larger wet chunks. Cool completely on a countertop for at least 2 hours before serving.

In a small saucepan bring the cream to a boil. Remove the pan from the heat. Add the chocolate and stir until smooth and the chocolate pieces have melted.

Do not refrigerate, unless you won't be serving until the next day. After refrigerating, allow three hours on a countertop before serving.

In a separate saucepan combine the raspberries, ½ cup of sugar, and water, and bring to a boil. Strain the sauce to remove seeds. Refrigerate until ready to serve.

On a chilled dinner plate, set a piece of the torte. Pour the sauces on either side of the slice. Add a dollop of freshly whipped cream, perhaps fresh raspberries, and serve.

MAKES 12 SERVINGS.

Courthouse Square

Courthouse Square Bed and Breakfast
❧

210 East Polk Street
Crandon, Wisconsin 54520
(715) 478-2549

---

*T*he Courthouse Square is situated on the shores of Surprise Lake, yet coveniently in the heart of town. The guest rooms inspire lingering relaxation, each facing the lake or the park across the street. In spring and summer stroll by the lake, enjoy the gardens and the birds at the many feeders, take a bike ride or walk through town, feed the deer, or relax on the porch. Visit the many antique and gift shops in the area. In autum enjoy the changing fall foliage. Enjoy the tranquility of winter; miles of trails just moments away, downhill skiing a short drive away.

Cherry Bread

¼	cup shortening
1	cup lightly packed brown sugar
1	beaten egg
2	cups all-purpose flour
2	teaspoons baking powder
½	teaspoon salt
⅔	cup milk
⅓	cup syrup from maraschino cherries
½	cup drained red maraschino cherries, chopped
½	cup almonds, chopped (optional)

In a large bowl mix all the ingredients. Pour into a greased 5 x 9-inch loaf pan. Let stand for 20 minutes. Bake in a 350° oven for 55 to 60 minutes.

MAKES 1 LOAF.

Courthouse Square Strawberry Blintz

1	8-ounce package cream cheese
1	6-ounce carton ricotta cheese
2	egg yolks
1	tablespoon sugar
½	teaspoon almond extract

1	cup all-purpose flour
2	teaspoons baking powder
1½	cups vanilla yogurt
½	cup orange juice
½	teaspoon vanilla extract
½	cup butter, softened
⅓	cup sugar
5	eggs
2	egg whites

1	quart fresh strawberries, washed, trimmed, and sliced
	Sugar to taste
	Whipped cream

In a medium bowl beat the cream cheese until smooth. Add the ricotta, egg yolks, sugar, and almond extract. Mix thoroughly and set aside.

In a small bowl combine the flour and baking powder and set aside. In another small bowl combine the yogurt, orange juice, and vanilla. In a large bowl cream the butter and sugar. Add the eggs and egg whites, and beat until mixed well. Add the flour and yogurt mixtures alternately to the egg mixture. Pour half of the batter into a greased 9 x 13-inch glass baking dish. Gently add the ricotta filling, spreading over the batter base. Top with the remaining batter, gently covering the filling to the side of the dish. Bake in a 350° oven for 45 to 50 minutes or until golden brown.

Cut into 8 servings. Place each serving on a plate, cover with fresh strawberries, sweetened to taste, and garnish with a dollop of whipped cream.

MAKES 8 SERVINGS.

Eagle Centre House

❧

*W370 S9590 Highway 67
Eagle, Wisconsin 53119
(414) 363-4700*

*T*he Eagle Centre House is a replica of an 1846 Greek Revival-style stagecoach inn. Built on a high point overlooking the surrounding terrain, it stands at the center of sixteen secluded acres in the scenic Kettle Moraine. The nineteenth-century feeling of the inn is enhanced by the carefully gathered antiques that fill bedrooms and common areas alike. Second floor rooms feature whirlpool baths.

Cherry Cordial

> 2 **parts cherries, pitted**
> 2 **parts sugar**
> 1 **part alcohol, gin or vodka**

Cover and steep for 6 weeks, stirring weekly. Strain. Serve the liqueur at tea time or after dinner.

The fruit may be used in pancakes with the liqueur as the syrup. The fruit may also be used as a garnish.

Baked Eggs À la Kathriene

> 12 **eggs**
> **Salt and pepper to taste**
> **Thyme to taste**
> **Cheddar cheese**

Break the eggs into the greased nonstick muffin cups. Sprinkle with salt, white pepper, and thyme. Bake in a 350° oven for 10 to 15 minutes. Top with a pinch of grated Cheddar cheese, melt, and serve.

MAKES 1 DOZEN.

Brennan Manor

❧

*1079 Everett Road
Eagle River, Wisconsin 54521
(715) 479-7353*

*G*uests are welcomed at the front door of this English Tudor-style inn by a genuine suit of armor. Inside, they will discover hand-carved woodwork, arched windows, balconies, and a thirty-foot stone fireplace in the great room. All guest rooms upstairs lead to an open balcony overlooking this impressive great room. The grounds include two stone patios, sweeping lawns leading to the lake, and a private swimming area. Nearby attractions include the world's largest chain of freshwater lakes, golfing, biking, water skiing, and sailing.

Brennan Manor

Pennsylvania Dutch Egg Bread

> 3 **slices stale breadcrusts removed**
> ¼ **cup melted butter**
> 6 **eggs**
> ¼ **teaspoon salt**
> **Pinch pepper**

Cut the bread into ½-inch cubes. In a skillet melt the butter. Add the bread cubes and heat until the bread cubes are crisp and golden brown.

In a small bowl beat the eggs lightly to mix the yolks and whites. Stir in salt and pepper. Pour the egg mixture over the bread cubes and continue cooking until the eggs are set. Turn over when the bottom is brown (as with an omelet). Let the other side brown and serve immediately.

MAKES 4 TO 6 SERVINGS.

Brennan Manor Rice Muffins

> 1 **cup all-purpose flour**
> 1 **tablespoon sugar**
> ½ **teaspoon salt**
> ½ **teaspoon baking powder**
> ½ **cup milk**
> 1 **egg**
> 1 **cup boiled rice**
> 2 **tablespoons melted shortening**

In a small bowl sift the flour, sugar, salt, and baking powder. In a large bowl beat the eggs, milk, and drained cooked rice. Stir in the shortening and add the dry ingredients. Stir until moistened. Spoon the batter into buttered muffin pans. Bake in a 425° oven for 20 minutes.

MAKES 1 DOZEN.

Lemonade Drops

> 1 **6-ounce can frozen lemonade concentrate**
> 1 **cup shortening**
> 1 **cup sugar**
> 2 **eggs**
> 3 **cups all-purpose flour**
> 1 **teaspoon baking soda**
> **Pinch salt**

Thaw the frozen lemonade. Set aside half for topping (3 ounces). In a large bowl cream the shortening and sugar well. Add the eggs. In a medium bowl sift the flour, soda and salt. Alternately add the flour mixture and lemonade to the batter.

Drop by teaspoons onto a greased cookie sheet. Bake in a 375° oven for 10 minutes. While still warm, brush the tops of the cookies with the reserved lemonade and sprinkle the tops with sugar.

MAKES ABOUT 3 DOZEN.

Eagle Harbor Inn

❦

9914 Water Street
Ephraim, Wisconsin 54211
(414) 854-2121

A *collection of houses gathered into a village beside the waters of Green Bay, the Eagle Harbor Inn offers nine B&B rooms and thirty-two suites. The inn provides access to the scenic wonders and year-round outdoor activities that have made Door County, Wisconsin famous. It also offers a beautifully equipped fitness room, sauna, indoor pool, and outdoor grills and picnic seating throughout the resort.*

Whole-Grain Chocolate Chip Muffins

1½ *cups raisins*
¼ *cup buttermilk*
....
1 *cup all-purpose flour*
2 *cups whole wheat flour*
3 *teaspoons cinnamon*
4 *teaspoons baking soda*
½ *teaspoon salt*
....
3 *bananas (ripe and mashed)*
¾ *cup butter*
3 *eggs*
....

1 *cup water (hot)*
1 *cup walnuts (chopped)*
1½ *cups brown sugar*
3½ *cups rolled oats*
½ *cup wheat germ*
1 *cup chocolate chips*

In a small bowl plump the raisins in the hot water, and set aside. In a large bowl combine the flours, cinnamon, soda, and salt. In a small bowl cream the bananas and butter. Add the egg. In a separate bowl combine the buttermilk and walnuts. Add the banana mixture and the walnuts and buttermilk to the dry ingredients. In a medium bowl combine the brown sugar, oats, wheat germ, and chocolate chips. Add the mixture to the batter, and mix until combined. Spoon into greased muffin cups. Bake in a 350° oven for 20 minutes.

MAKES 3 DOZEN.

Nedd's Apple Cake

3 *cups unbleached flour*
1 *tablespoon baking powder*
½ *teaspoon salt*
4 *large Granny Smith apple,s peeled*
    and sliced (or tart apples)
¼ *cup sugar*
2 *teaspoons ground cinnamon*
4 *large eggs*
1 *cup oil*
1¾ *cups sugar*
½ *cup fresh orange juice*
2 *teaspoons vanilla*

In a medium bowl combine the flour, baking powder, and salt. In a separate bowl combine the apples, ¼ cup of sugar, and cinnamon. In a large bowl mix the eggs, oil, 1 ¾ cups sugar, orange juice, and vanilla. Add the dry ingredients to the egg mixture and stir until blended. Layer the cake batter and apple mixture in a greased 9 x 13-inch pan. Bake in a 350° oven for 50 to 60 minutes.

MAKES 8 SERVINGS.

Door County Dried Cherry Granola

3 *cups rye flakes*
6 *cups rolled oats*
6 *cups barley flakes*
6 *cups wheat flakes*
3 *cups wheat bran*

1½ *cups safflower oil*
2 *cups honey*
2 *teaspoons ground cinnamon*
2 *cups Door County dried cherries*

In a large bowl combine the rye flakes, rolled oats, barley flakes, wheat flakes, and wheat bran. In a medium saucepan heat the safflower oil and honey until dissolved. Mix all ingredients except the cinnamon and cherries together until the flakes are well coated. Spread the granola out onto baking sheets. Bake in a 350° oven until golden. Don't forget to turn the granola half way through the baking process. When the granola is cool sprinkle with cinnamon. Add the cherries.

MAKES ABOUT 7 QUARTS.

Lamp Post Inn

❦

408 South Main Street
Fort Atkinson, Wisconsin 53538
(414) 563-6561

E *very room in this charming inn has its own antique phonograph for the listening pleasure of guests. Another interesting touch is the antique Victorian pump organ in the parlor. Situated in downtown Fort Atkinson, Lamp Post Inn has three rooms, all furnished with antiques. Nearby attractions are Aztalan State Park and Museum, Fort Koshkonong, and Kettle Moraine State Forest trails. The area*

Lamp Post Inn

offers golfing, swimming, tennis, horseback riding, skiing, fishing, and biking.

Sweet Puff Pancake

Fresh fruit (strawberries, peaches or
  raspberries are best).
2 tablespoons butter
½ cup all-purpose flour
⅓ cup sugar
½ cup milk
3 large eggs
  Whipped cream

Sprinkle the fruit with sugar and let sit overnight.

In a skillet melt the butter over low heat. In a small bowl whisk the flour, sugar, milk, and eggs. Pour into a skillet and cook over medium heat for 1 minute. Immediately bake in a 425° oven for about 8 minutes or until very puffy and beginning to brown. Remove from the oven and top with fresh fruit and whipped cream.

MAKES 2 SERVINGS.

*Cabin
at Trail's End*

≫

Route 2, Box 84-A
Kendall, Wisconsin 54638
(608) 427-3870

Guests who want to get away and unwind will find this inn in the scenic hills of west central Wisconsin a real delight. Situated on eighty secluded acres, it specializes in wildlife and native wildflowers. Each of the guest rooms features a king-size bed with feather pillows and a down comforter, as well as a cedar sauna. Nearby attractions include biking, canoeing, skiing, and shopping at small-town antique shops.

Breakfast Souffle Roll

¼ cup butter
½ cup all-purpose flour
¼ teaspoon pepper
2 cups milk
6 egg whites
¼ teaspoon cream of tartar
6 egg yolks
6 ounces thinly sliced ham
6 ounces thinly sliced Swiss cheese

Line a 10 x 15-inch pan with foil, grease and lightly flour. Line a slightly larger pan with foil, and grease generously.

In a medium saucepan melt the butter. Stir in the flour and pepper. Add the milk all at once. Cook and stir until thickened and bubbly. Remove from the heat. Cool slightly.

In a large bowl whip the egg whites with the cream of tartar into stiff peaks. In a medium bowl beat the egg yolks. Slowly stir the thickened mixture into the egg yolks.

Fold a little of the beaten whites into the yolk mixture. Fold the yolk mixture into the remaining beaten egg whites. Spread in the prepared 10 x 15-inch pan. Bake in a 375° oven for about 20 minutes or until the soufflé is puffed and slightly set and a knife inserted in the center comes out clean.

Immediately loosen the soufflé from the baking sheet. Place the larger foil-lined pan over the soufflé. Invert the soufflé onto a larger pan. Carefully peel off the foil.

Place the ham and cheese in a thin layer on top of the soufflé. Use foil on the pan to lift and help roll up soufflé from the short side. Cool, wrap in foil, and chill up to 24 hours.

Before serving, cover the soufflé with foil and heat in a 375° oven for about 40 minutes or until heated through. Transfer to a warm platter.

MAKES 8 SERVINGS.

Cream Cheese Roll

3 eggs
1 cup sugar
⅓ cup water
1 teaspoon vanilla
1 cup cake flour (or ¾ cup all-purpose
  flour)
1 teaspoon baking powder
¼ teaspoon salt

....

1 8-ounce package cream cheese
½ cup confectioners' sugar, sifted
½ teaspoon vanilla
2 cups sliced fresh fruit

Line a 10 x 15-inch jelly roll pan with foil or waxed paper. Grease the waxed paper.

In a medium bowl beat the eggs for about 5 minutes or until very thick and lemon colored. Gradually beat in the sugar. On a low speed, blend in water and vanilla. Gradually add flour, baking powder and salt, beating just until the batter is smooth. Pour into a pan. Bake in a 375° oven for 12 to 15 minutes or until a wooden pick inserted in the center comes out clean.

Loosen the cake from the pan. Invert on a towel sprinkled with confectioner's sugar. Carefully remove the foil. While hot, roll the cake and towel from a narrow end. Cool on a wire rack.

In a small bowl beat the cream cheese, confectioners sugar, and vanilla.

Unroll the cake, remove the towel, and spread the cake with the cream cheese mixture. Arrange fruit on top and roll up the cake. Sprinkle with confectioners' sugar.

Note: At the Cabin at Trails End, the favorite fruit for this dessert is wild blackberries that grow throughout the wooded acreage.

MAKES 4 TO 6 SERVINGS.

Poached Apples

6 medium apples
⅔ cup packed brown sugar
¾ cup water
1 teaspoon nutmeg
1 teaspoon cinnamon
1 tablespoon lemon juice
  Vanilla yogurt

Peel, core, and cut the apples into wedges. Set aside.

In a medium saucepan combine the brown sugar, water, nutmeg, cinnamon, and lemon juice. Bring to a boil. Add the apples. Return to boiling, then reduce the heat. Cover and simmer for 5 to 8 minutes or until the apples are tender. Cool slightly.

Divide the apples and syrup into 6 individual bowls. Spoon the vanilla yogurt on top. Serve at once.

MAKES 6 SERVINGS.

4134 Ridge Road
Kewaskum, Wisconsin 53040
(414) 626-4853

*T*his inn is best described as a "country get-away." It's an old brick farmhouse (built in the mid 1800s) on a nine-acre tree farm. The spacious grounds include a garden and numerous fruit trees. The three rooms are furnished with period antiques. Within minutes of Country Ridge are many recreational opportunities, including golfing, bowling, boating, fishing, swimming, biking, hiking, art galleries, and craft shops.

Heavenly Baked Eggs

    1   pound sliced bacon
    1⅓ cups cottage cheese
    1   teaspoon salt
    14 eggs
    4   ounces mushrooms
    1   teaspoon pepper

In a skillet cook the bacon until crisp, drain, and discard all but 2 tablespoons of drippings. Crumble the bacon. In a large bowl, lightly beat the eggs and add the bacon, bacon drippings, cottage cheese, salt, pepper, and mushrooms. Pour into a greased 9 x 11-inch baking dish. Bake uncovered in a 350° oven for 40 to 45 minutes or until a knife inserted near the center comes out clean.

Let stand for 5 minutes before serving.
MAKES 8 SERVINGS.

Fruit Dip

    2   tablespoons butter
    2   tablespoons all-purpose flour
    ¾ cup sugar
    ⅔ cup pineapple juice
    2   beaten eggs
    1   8-ounce carton whipped topping

In a saucepan melt the butter. Add the flour and pineapple juice, and cook until boiling. Remove the pan from the heat and add the eggs and sugar. Cook until the mixture is thick. Remove from the heat and cool.

Fold in the whipped topping and chill.

Use as a dip with fresh fruit or line a cookie sheet with 8 croissants, rolled thin, baked and cooled. Spread the dip on top and arrange the fruit.
MAKES 8 SERVINGS.

Route 2, Box 121
La Farge, Wisconsin 54639
(608) 625-4492

*T*ucked away in the hills of Kickapoo Valley in Southwestern Wisconsin, this B&B is named for one of America's loveliest and best loved wildflowers. Guests enjoy their evenings and breakfasts in a secluded cottage facing woods, fields, and orchards. The cottage is located on a working farm with plenty of livestock, and there is abundant wildlife such as owls, hawks, deer, pheasant, and song birds.

Lemon-Spice Puffs

    1   package active dry yeast
    ¼ cup water
    2   eggs, beaten
    ¾ cup scalded milk
    6   tablespoons sugar
    1   teaspoon salt
    5   tablespoons shortening
    1   tablespoon grated lemon peel
    1   teaspoon lemon juice
    3   cups all-purpose flour
    1   tablespoon sugar
    1   teaspoon ground cinnamon

In a small bowl soften the yeast in the warm water. Add the beaten eggs. To the scalded milk add 6 tabelspoons of sugar, the salt, shortening, lemon peel, and juice. Cool to lukewarm. Add the egg-yeast mixture. Add the flour 1 cup at a time, beating until the mixture is smooth. Cover and let rise until doubled.

Stir down the dough. Fill greased muffin cups half full. Sprinkle with a mixture of 1 tablespoon of sugar and the cinnamon. Cover and let rise.

Bake in a 375° oven for 20 minutes or until a toothpick inserted in a center puff comes out clean..
MAKES 18 PUFFS.

Trillium Rice Muffins

    1¾ cups unbleached flour
    ¼ cup brown rice flour
    4   teaspoons baking powder
    ½ teaspoon salt
    ¼ cup honey
    2   tablespoons melted butter
    1   cup whole milk
    1   egg, beaten
    ½ cup cooked brown rice

In a medium bowl sift together the flours, baking powder, and salt. In a small saucepan melt together the honey, butter, and milk, and stir in the beaten egg. Pour the liquid mixture into the dry ingredients and stir together. Fold in the cooked rice. Spoon into greased muffin cups. Bake in a 350° for 15 to 20 minutes or until a toothpick inserted in a center muffin comes out clean.
MAKES 1 DOZEN.

Banana Dream Muffins

    2¼ cups unbleached flour
    ½ teaspoon salt
    2   teaspoons baking powder
    ½ teaspoon ground cinnamon
    ½ cup melted butter
    2   cups firmly packed brown sugar
    2   large eggs
    2   large, extra ripe bananas (peeled
          and mashed)
    1   teaspoon vanilla
    1   cup fresh blueberries

In a large bowl sift together the flour, salt, baking powder, and cinnamon. In a separate bowl, mix the butter and brown sugar. Stir in the eggs, then add the bananas. Stir in the vanilla. Pour the liquid mixture into the dry ingredients and stir together. Fold in the blueberries. Spoon the batter into greased muffin cups. Bake in a 350° oven for 25 to 30 minutes or until a toothpick inserted in a center muffin comes out clean.

MAKES 18 TO 20 MEDIUM-SIZED MUFFINS.

The Geneva Inn
❧

N2009 State Road 120
Lake Geneva, Wisconsin 53147
(414) 248-5680

---

*G*uests at the waterfront Geneva *Inn may chose from nine unique rooms, each individually decorated to reflect the charm of an old-fashioned English inn. Most rooms provide a sweeping view of Lake Geneva. Specially made quilts, robes, and complementary cognac and chocolates at bedtime add to the luxurious feeling of the accommodations. The private marina makes it easier to enjoy the lake or, if desired, to arrive by boat.*

Pan-fried Cornmeal-crusted Catfish, with Cucumber-Yogurt Coulis, Pineapple Salsa, and Couscous

¼ **cup plain yogurt**
¼ **cup sour cream**
½ **cup peeled, seeded and diced cucumber**
1½ **teaspoon minced garlic**
1½ **teaspoon chopped shallot**
1½ **teaspoon chopped parsley**

....

½ **cup diced pineapple**
1 **tablespoon chopped green onion**
1½ **teaspoon chopped cilantro**

....

1¾ **cups chicken stock**
1 **tablespoon each finely diced carrot**
1 **tablespoon finely diced celery**
1 **tablespoon finely diced onion**
1 **tablespoon finely diced red bell pepper**
1 **tablespoon finely diced yellow bell pepper**
1 **cup couscous**
1 **tablespoon finely chopped mint**

....

1 **to 2 tablespoons clarified butter**
4 **6-ounce portions catfish**
1½ **cups cornmeal**

In a food processor combine the yogurt, sour cream, cucumber, garlic shallot, parsley, and pulse for 5 seconds. Chill.

In a small bowl combine the pineapple, onion, and cilantro, and mix well.

Combine all ingredients

In a saucepan bring the chicken stock to a boil. Add the carrot, celery, onion, and peppers, and simmer for 3 minutes. Add the couscous, stir, and cover. Turn off the heat and let sit for 10 minutes. Add the mint and fluff with a fork.

In a sauté pan heat the with clarified butter. Dredge the catfish in cornmeal and sauté until golden brown on each side, approximately 2 minutes per side.

To assemble, spoon some of the cucumber-yogurt sauce on the plate and place one serving of catfish on top. Top with some salsa and serve with the couscous.

MAKES 4 SERVINGS.

Raspberry Vinaigrette

3 **eggs**
¼ **cup oil**
5 **ounces walnut oil**

The Geneva Inn

½ **bottle raspberry vinegar**
1 **16-ounce jar melba sauce**
1 **cup honey**
2 **teaspoons ground peppercorns**

In a blender place the eggs and add just enough oil to cover the blades. Purée this mixture, then slowly add the walnut oil and raspberry vinegar, alternating until both are used. Then add the melba sauce and blend until smooth. To finish, add the honey and ground pepper and blend.

MAKES ABOUT 5 CUPS.

Hungarian Gulyas Soup

1 **pound beef tips, browned**
3 **medium onions, peeled and chopped**
1 **bunch of celery, chopped medium dice**
5 **cups beef stock or broth**
4 **cups water**
1 **tablespoon caraway seeds**
   Salt and white pepper to taste
2 **16 ounce cans tomatoes, broken up**
4 **potatoes peeled and diced**
¼ **cup fresh parsley, chopped fine for garnish**
   Sour cream for garnish

In a saucean bring the stock and water to a boil. Add the chopped onions, celery, canned tomatoes, caraway seeds, salt and pepper to the stock.

Add the browned beef tips and diced potatoes, and simmer for 45 minutes or until the meat is fork tender. Ladle into bowls and top with sour cream and parsley.

MAKES 4 SERVINGS.

Hot Crab and Artichoke Dip

1 **8-ounce package cream cheese, softened**
½ **cup sour cream**
2 **tablespoons salad dressing**
1 **tablespoon lemon juice**
1¼ **teaspoons Worcestershire sauce**
½ **teaspoon dry mustard**
   Pinch garlic salt
1 **tablespoon milk**
¼ **cup grated Cheddar cheese**
   Paprika

1 8-ounce can Maryland crabmeat, cartilage removed
1 can artichoke hearts, drained and chopped

In a large bowl mix the cream cheese, sour cream, salad dressing, lemon juice, Worcestershire sauce, mustard and garlic salt until smooth. Add enough milk to make the mixture creamy. Stir in 2 tablespoons of the grated cheese. Fold the crab meat and artichoke hearts into the cream cheese mixture.

Pour into a greased 1-quart casserole. Top with the remaining cheese. Bake in a 325° oven for about 30 minutes or until the mixture is bubbly and browned on top. Sprinkle the top with paprika.

MAKES 6 TO 8 SERVINGS.

French Apple and Walnut Tarts

½ cup soft butter
½ cup sugar
2 large eggs
¾ cup all-purpose flour blended with ½ teaspoon baking powder
2 tablespoons milk
½ cup walnuts, coarsely chopped
....
4 to 5 apples
2 to 3 tablespoons butter, melted
Confectioners' sugar

In a medium bowl beat the butter until light and fluffy. Gradually beat in the sugar. Add the eggs one at a time, beating until smooth. Fold in the flour blended with baking powder. Stir in the milk and chopped walnuts. Set aside. Butter 6 to 8 individual tart tins or large muffin cups. Divide the batter mixture evenly between them. Peel, quarter, and core apples. Cut each quarter into thin, even slices. Stand the apple slices in batter rounded-side up, pressing down lightly so they are all level. Brush with butter. Bake in a 375° oven for 25 minutes or until golden brown. Cook for 3 to 5 minutes. Gently lift from the pans. Just before serving, dust with confectioners' sugar.

MAKES 6 TO 8 TARTS.

Annie's Bed and Breakfast
❧

2117 Sheridan Drive
Madison, Wisconsin 53704
(608) 244-2224

*A*nnie's is a rustic cedar shake and stucco house in a quiet neighborhood overlooking a beautiful valley view of Warner Park. Only one block from Lake Mendota, it is surrounded by tall green spruces and extensive gardens. There are two antique-filled suites, each with two bedrooms and, in a separate room, a whirlpool bath with mirrors, plants, and music.

Cranberry Apple Breakfast Pudding

4 cups skim milk
½ cup brown sugar
½ teaspoon salt
2 tablespoons butter
....
1 cup fresh cranberries
¼ cup firmly packed brown sugar
....
½ box golden seedless raisins
2 cups old-fashioned oats
4 to 5 large Red Delicious apples, cored, thinly sliced, not peeled
1 cup chopped nuts (pecans, walnuts, or almonds)

Annie's

In a microwave-save bowl heat the milk, brown sugar, salt, and butter for about 5 minutes on high or until very hot but not boiling.

In a small bag shake the cranberries with ¼ cup of brown sugar. Add in order the raisins, oats, and apples. Add the cranberries and nuts. Mix well. Pour into a buttered stoneware bowl. Bake in a 350° oven for 30 minutes.

Stir to integrate the fruit throughout. Serve in a bowl with a dollop of caramel sauce or/and sweetened sour cream and cinnamon.

MAKES 8 SERVINGS.

Annie's Breakfast Cookies

5 cups skim milk
8 beaten eggs
½ cup light oil
1 12-ounce box golden seedless raisins
¼ cup firmly packed brown sugar
5½ cups old-fashioned oats
....
2 heaping cups whole wheat flour
2 tablespoons baking powder
1 teaspoon salt
....
4 large bananas, cut up (or 1 quart fresh blueberries, or 1 package chocolate chips)
1½ cups chopped nuts (pecans, cashews, walnuts or almonds)

In a large bowl combine the milk, eggs, oil, raisins, brown sugar, and oats. Mix well, then add the flour, baking powder, and salt. Let the mixture soak for 2 minutes before proceeding. Carefully add the bananas, taking care not to break the fruit. Lastly, add the nuts.

Oil the grill well and heat to about 300° as these need to cook rather slowly so they don't burn. Spread ¼ cup of batter into a "cookie" on the grill. Watch carefully. Turn once. "Cookie" will be nice and thick, no more than four inches in diameter. This recipe will made 44 "cookies". Serve 2 to a plate. They freeze very well and are easy to serve at a later date. Just spread them lightly with soft butter as for a piece of toast, and heat them on high in the microwave only until hot. When they are ready, the butter will melt.

MAKES 44 "COOKIES."

Canterbury Inn

Canterbury Inn

❦

315 West Gorham at State
Madison, Wisconsin 53703
(608) 258-8899

---

*T*he inn is housed in Madison's
historic Jacobson Building
completed in 1924. It features a
whimsical entryway with promenade overlooking the atrium of a
bookstore. Each of the six guest
rooms are named for one of the pilgrim travelers in the Canterbury
Tales. The downtown location
provides easy access to numerous
shops, restaurants, coffeehouses,
and the University of
Wisconsin campus.

Tuscany Vegetable Soup

- ½ cup olive oil
- 2 tablespoons minced garlic
- 1 cup zucchini, thinly sliced length-
     wise and cut into half moons
- 1 cup tomatoes, removed seeds and
     dice
- 1 green bell pepper diced
- 2 stalks (not bunches) of celery diced
- 1 medium onion, finely diced
- 1 cup spinach, stems removed, torn
     into small pieces
....
- 1 cup all-purpose flour
- ¼ cup tomato paste
- ¼ cup lemon juice
- ½ cup white wine

- 1 quart vegetable stock
- 1 tablespoon dried basil
- 1 tablespoon dried oregano
- 1 tablespoon garlic powder
- 1 teaspoon white pepper
....
- ½ cup fresh basil, chopped
- ¼ cup fresh parsley, chopped

In a stock pot heat the olive oil and sauté the
minced garlic, zucchini, tomatoes, pepper,
celery, onion, and spinach. When tender, stir
in the flour. Add the tomato paste, liquids,
and dry herbs, and simmer until thickened.
   Stir in the fresh herbs and serve.
MAKES 4 TO 6 SERVINGS.

Fresh Ginger Carrot Soup

- ½ cup butter
- 1 quart carrots, peeled and diced
- 1 tablespoon minced gingerroot
- 1 tablespoon minced garlic
- 1 teaspoon white pepper
....
- 1 cup all-purpose flour
- 1 cup white wine
- 2 cups vegetable stock
- 1 cup heavy cream
    Fresh parsley chopped for garnish
    Salt to taste

In a saucepan melt the butter and sauté the
diced carrots along with the ginger, garlic,
and pepper. When the carrots are tender, but
not overdone, remove the pan from the heat.
Add the flour. Puré the carrot mixture in a
food processor. Return the mixture to the
stove. Over low heat whisk in the wine, stock,
and cream. Simmer until thickened. Serve
with parsley garnish.
MAKES 4 TO 6 SERVINGS.

The Johnson Inn

❦

231 West North Street
Plainfield, Wisconsin 54966
(715) 335-4383

White pillars, the deep green of
shade trees and beds of domestic
and wild flowers welcome visitors to
The Johnson Inn, with a sense of the
peace and charm of small town
America in the 1800s. The house
features tall ceilings with medallions, carved oak paneling and
woodwork, fireplaces and open
stairways, and beautiful birch flooring. Guests may choose from The
Sherman Safari Room, which was
once the upstairs sleeping porch,
the Rothermel Room with wicker
and lace, the more formal Walker
Room, or the charm of the smaller
Hall Room.

Chocolate Doughnuts

- ¼ cup butter
- 1¼ cups sugar
- 1½ ounces chocolate, melted
- 1 cup buttermilk
- 2 eggs well eaten
- 4 cups all-purpose flour
- 1 teaspoon baking soda
- 1 teaspoon cinnamon
- 1½ teaspoons ground vanilla extract

In a large bowl mix the butter and sugar. Add
the melted chocolate, eggs, and buttermilk.
Add the dry ingredients. Chill the dough.
   Cut the dough into doughnuts. Fry in hot
oil (375°). Frost with chocolate icing.
MAKES 2 DOZEN.

French Doughnuts (Sugar-Free)

- 1 cup water
- ½ cup butter
- 1 cup all-purpose flour
- 4 eggs

In a deep-fryer preheat the oil to 350°. In a
saucepan bring the water to a boil. Add the
butter to the boiling water and return to a
boil. Stir until the mixture leaves the sides of
the pan. Remove the pan from the heat. Beat
in the eggs one at a time. Drop the dough by
teaspoons in hot oil. Roll in sugar.

The Johnson Inn

The same recipe doubles for cream puffs. Just bake in a 400° oven on an ungreased cookie sheet for 40 to 45 minutes. Fill with any filling desired, such as sugar-free pudding and whipped topping.

MAKES 24 SERVINGS.

Lamb's Inn Bed and Breakfast
❧

Route 2, Box 144
Richland Center, Wisconsin 53581
(608) 585-4301

The Lamb's Inn Bed and Breakfast is located just three miles outside Richland Center, in a special hidden valley, below Sunset Apple Orchard. The 1800s farmhouse has been completely renovated to appear as it did when Albert Misslich brought his bride to the farm. Everything about this old-fashioned family farm is created to help guests unwind from today's fast-paced life. All four bedrooms have king or queen beds, private baths, bedside lights for reading, and the home has central air.

Gramma's Bread Pudding

8 *cups milk, scalded*
¼ *cup raisins*
9 *eggs*
2 *tablespoons vanilla extract*

1½ *teaspoons salt*
2 *tablespoons cornstarch*
1½ *cups sugar*
5 *cups cubed day-old bread*

In a large bowl combine the milk, raisins, eggs, and vanilla. In a small bowl combine the salt, cornstarch, and sugar. Add the dry ingredients to the milk mixture. Butter a 9 x 13-inch pan. Place the cubed bread in a pan, and add the above ingredients. Sprinkle with cinnamon and nutmeg. Place the pan in a waterbath. Bake in a 350° oven for 1 hour or until the center is firm. Serve warm with whipped cream.

MAKES 8 SERVINGS.

Lamb's Inn Quiche

2 *cups all-purpose flour*
1 *teaspoon salt*
¾ *cup shortening*
¼ *cup cold water*
....
12 *eggs*
1½ *cups sour cream*
1½ *cups milk*
1 *teaspoon salt*
1 *teaspoon basil*
1 *medium onion, diced and cooked in microwave, 1 to 2 minutes until soft*
1 *pound bacon cooked until crisp and crumbled*
1 *cup Cheddar cheese*
1 *cup Swiss, Co-Jack, mozzarella or any choice*
Broccoli, fresh tomatoes or mushrooms (optional)

In a large bowl combine the flour, salt, and shortening. Cut together with a pastry blender until the size of peas. Add the cold water and work together until the particles stick together. Handle only as necessary. Divide the pastry dough into 2 parts. Roll out and place in 2 9-inch pie plates. Bake in a 350° oven for 10 minutes.

Our guests enjoy fresh tomatoes and mushroom with the cheese. This recipe makes. Recipe can easily be cut in half for one quiche.

In a large bowl combine the eggs, sour cream, milk, salt, and basil. Sprinkle the remaining ingredients in the pie shells. Pour the egg mixture over the fillings. Bake in a

350° oven for 1 hour or until knife inserted in the center comes out clean.

MAKES 2 LARGE QUICHES, 12 TO 16 SERVINGS.

Just-N-Trails Bed and Breakfast
❧

Route 1, Box 274
Sparta, Wisconsin 54656
(608) 269-4522

Situated on a farm, this B&B places its guests well out into the Wisconsin countryside. The guest rooms are scattered among an old granary, a carriage house, a pair of log cabins, and a 1920s-era midwestern farmhouse. Adventurers will find plenty to do and see hereabouts. They can bike the Elroy-Sparta or Great River Trails, canoe the La Crosse River, ski or snow tube the slopes behind the farm, or browse Amish craft shops.

Blueberry Ricotta Cheese Streusel Coffeecake

2⅓ *cups all-purpose flour*
1½ *cups sugar*
1 *teaspoon salt*
½ *cup oil*
....
2 *teaspoons baking powder*
¾ *cup milk*
2 *eggs*
1 *teaspoon almond flavoring*
1 *cup blueberries, fresh or frozen*
....
1 *cup nonfat ricotta cheese*
1 *egg*
2 *tablespoons sugar*
1 *tablespoon lemon juice*
....
½ *cup ground pecans*
⅓ *cup brown sugar*
1 *teaspoon cinnamon*

In a large bowl combine the flour, 1 ½ cups of sugar, salt, and oil, and mix until crumbly. Reserve 1 cup of crumbs for topping. To the remaining crumbs add the baking powder, milk, 2 eggs, and 1 teaspoon of almond flavoring, and blend well. Add the blueberries. Pour into a sprayed or greased 9 x 13-inch pan. In a medium bowl combine the ricotta, 1 egg, ½ cup of sugar, and lemon juice, and spread over the first layer. In a separate bowl combine the reserved topping, the pecans, brown sugar, and cinnamon. Sprinkle over the ricotta layer. Bake in a 350° oven for 45 minutes to 1 hour or until the topping is golden brown and springs back from touch.

The ricotta cheese makes this very delicately textured and tasty.

MAKES 8 SERVINGS.

Berry Pizza

    3   cups all-purpose flour
    ¾   cup confectioners' sugar
    ¾   cup butter
....
    ⅔   cup sugar
   16   ounces nonfat cream cheese
    2   eggs
    2   tablespoons lemon juice
....
    1   cup sugar
    ¼   cup cornstarch
    1   12-ounces can frozen fruit punch
        concentrate
....
    8   strawberries, cut in half
   16   blueberries
    1   kiwi, sliced and quartered

In a large bowl combine the flour and confectioners' sugar. Cut in the butter. Pat into a 10 x 15-inch pan. Bake in a 350 ° oven for 10 minutes until light golden brown. Cool.

In a small food processor combine ⅔ cup of sugar, the cream cheese, eggs, and lemon juice until creamy without lumps. Spread over the cooled crust. Bake in a 250° oven for 10 to 15 minutes until the cheese mixture looks dull.

In a glass dish mix 1 cup of sugar and the cornstarch, and blend in the juice. Microwave until the mixture thickens like pie filling. Pour over the cheese layer. Cut the pizza into 16 pieces. Place one piece of each of the three fruits on each slice.

MAKES 16 SERVINGS.

The Franklin Victorian
❧

220 East Franklin Street
Sparta, Wisconsin 54656
(608) 269-3894

This Victorian mansion took several years to build during the late 1890s, and still has plenty to show for all that effort. Hardwood maple floors, leaded windows, filigreed brass light fixtures, ceramic tile fireplaces, an open staircase, and a magnificent sunset stained glass window remind visitors that this house was once at the center of social life in Sparta. The owners have furnished the old house with just the right combination of antiques and comfortable contemporary pieces.

Red Flannel Hash Skillet

    1   medium sweet onion, chopped
    1   clove garlic, crushed (optional)
    1   medium green bell pepper, chopped
    1   medium red bell pepper, chopped
....
    2   15-ounce cans corn beef hash
....
    8   large eggs
    2   medium Roma tomatoes, each cut
        into 16 wedges
    2   cups medium Cheddar cheese, grated
    1   teaspoon seasoned salt
    1   teaspoon black pepper
    ¼   cup mixed spices (chives, sweet
        basil, parsley, oregano, red pep-
        per)

In a medium bowl combine the onion, garlic, green pepper, and red pepper. Mix them together in a bowl and set aside.

In a large mixing bowl combine the corn beef and one-fourth of the vegetable mixture. Mix well.

Spray the sides and bottoms of 8 #3 cast iron skillets with cooking spray. Add hash mixture to each pan, Dividing evenly among the 8 skillets. Spread over the bottoms and up the sides of the pans.

Divide the vegetable mixture evenly over the hash in each pan.

Make a depression in the center of each pan of hash. Break 1 egg into each depression. Sprinkle shredded cheese over each pan. Sprinkle with spices, then put tomato wedges around each egg in spoke fashion. Bake in a 300° oven for approximately 20 to 25 minutes or until the eggs are done.

MAKES 8 SERVINGS.

Snickerdoodle

    ½   cup butter
    2   cups sugar
    2   eggs, separated
    ¼   teaspoon salt
    1   cup milk
    3   cups all-purpose flour
    2   teaspoons baking powder
    3   teaspoons confectioners' sugar
    1   teaspoon ground cinnamon

In a large bowl cream the butter and sugar together. Add the egg yolks and salt, and mix thoroughly. In a separate bowl sift together the flour and baking powder. Add the milk and flour alternately. In a medium bowl beat the egg whites until fluffy but not stiff and add to the batter. Beat well. Spread in the prepared 9 x 13-inch pan. Sift the confectioners' sugar and cinnamon over the top. Bake in a 350° oven for about 30 minutes.

MAKES 12 SERVINGS.

Veggie Oven Pancake

    1   tablespoon margarine
    ½   cup all-purpose flour
    ½   cup milk
    2   eggs, slightly beaten
    ¼   teaspoon salt
    2   tablespoons margarine
    2   cups broccoli florets
    1   cup red onion, cut in 1 inch pieces
    1   cup green bell pepper, cut in 1 inch
        pieces
    1   cup ripe tomato, cut in 1 inch pieces
    ¼   teaspoon salt
    ¼   teaspoon pepper
 1½   cups shredded Cheddar cheese

In a 9-inch pan melt 1 tablespoon of margarine in the oven for 2 to 3 minutes. Meanwhile, in a small bowl stir together the flour, milk, eggs, and ¼ teaspoon of salt.Pour into the pie pan with the melted butter. Bake in a 425° oven for 12 to 15 minutes or until golden.

Meanwhile, in a 10-inch skillet melt 2 tablespoons of margarine. Add the vegetables, salt, and pepper. Cook over medium heat, stirring constantly, until crisp tender (approximately 12 to 15 minutes).

Sprinkle ½ cup of Cheddar cheese in the bottom of the baked pancake. Top with the vegetables. Sprinkle with 1 cup of cheese. Return to the oven and bake for 5 to 7 minutes until the cheese melts.

MAKES 6 TO 8 SERVINGS.

The Scofield House Bed and Breakfast

908 Michigan Street
Sturgeon Bay, Wisconsin 54235
(414) 743-7727

The high Victorian Scofield House was built in 1902 and shows its heritage inside and out. The common rooms reflect the Victorian penchant for fancy, while the six guest rooms are intimate and romantic. The tip of the peninsula is less than an hour's drive. Spend the day touring its small villages.

The Scofield House

Scofield House Egg-Cheese-Sausage Strata

  2 **pounds bulk pork sausage**
  1 **10½-ounce can cream of mushroom soup**
  1 **cup sour cream (or sour half and half)**
  4 **whole English muffins (sourdough, whole wheat or plain)**
  1 **pound grated Monterey Jack cheese**
  6 **eggs (extra large or jumbo)**
     Finely grated green pepper (optional)
     Paprika

Brown and drain the sausage. In a medium bowl mix the soup and sour cream. Crumble the muffins into a greased 8 x 12-inch pan. In a separate bowl mix the eggs and milk together. Layer half of the sausage, half of the cheese mixture, and half of the soup mixture on top of the crumbled muffins. Repeat the layers, ending with the soup mixture, and smooth with a spatula. Pour the milk and egg mixture over all. Sprinkle the top with paprika. Poke with a sharp knife to absorb the liquid and let stand in the refrigerator overnight or cover with plastic wrap and foil, and freeze.

If frozen, thaw first, and remove the plastic and foil. Bake uncovered in a 350° oven for 1 hour. Cut into squares after "resting" 5 minutes.

MAKES 8 TO 10 SERVINGS.

Lemon-Raspberry Streusel Muffins

  2 **cups unbleached all-purpose flour**
1½ **cups sugar**
  2 **teaspoons baking powder**
  ½ **teaspoon baking soda**
  ½ **teaspoon salt**
  1 **8 ounce carton lemon yogurt**
  1 **teaspoon lemon peel**
  ½ **cup canola oil**
  2 **eggs**
  1 **cup fresh or frozen raspberries (unthawed)**
....
  ⅓ **cup sugar**
  ¼ **cup all-purpose flour**
  2 **tablespoons butter**

In a large bowl combine 2 cups of flour, ½ cup of sugar, the baking powder, baking

soda, and salt, and mix well. In a small bowl combine the yogurt, oil, lemon peel, and eggs. Mix well. Add the liquid mixture to the dry ingredients, and stir just until moistened. Gently stir in the raspberries.

Spray 12 regular or 36 mini muffin cups with cooking spray. In a small bowl combine ⅓ cup of sugar and ¼ cup of flour. Cut in the butter until crumbly. Sprinkle over the muffins. Bake in a 400° oven for 15 to 18 minutes for mini muffins; 18 to 20 minutes for regular muffins.

MAKES 3 DOZEN MINI OR 1 DOZEN REGULAR.

White Lace Inn

16 North Fifth Avenue
Sturgeon Bay, Wisconsin 84235
(414) 743-1105

The inn is only two blocks from the center of the homey lakeside town of Sturgeon Bay with its small cafes, shops, and interesting architecture. Built in 1903, the inn is a perfect match for this turn-of-the-century town. Consisting of three Victorian homes with long, inviting porches, floral wallpapers, and antiques, it offers nineteen comfortable guest rooms. Sturgeon Bay is located in Door County, known for its many historic lighthouses, two of which are located in the town itself not far from the inn.

Cherry Almond Cream Cheese Muffins

  6 **cups all-purpose flour**
  2 **cups sugar**
  3 **tablespoons baking powder**
  1 **teaspoon cinnamon**
....
1½ **cups butter, melted**
1½ **cups milk**
  6 **eggs, beat**
1½ **to 2 teaspoons almond extract**

1 **8-ounce package cream cheese, softened in the microwave**
5 **cups rinsed frozen cherries**

....

Cinnamon-sugar
1 **cup chopped walnuts**

In a large bowl sift together the flour, sugar, baking powder, and cinnamon. In a separate large bowl blend the butter, milk, eggs, and almond extract. Add the cream cheese and mix well. Fold in the frozen cherries. Scoop with an ice cream scoop into muffin cups lined with paper liners. Sprinkle with cinnamon-sugar, and walnuts if desired. Bake in a 425° oven for 15 to 20 minutes.

MAKES 1 DOZEN.

Creamy Old Fashioned Rice Pudding

1 **pound medium grain white rice**
  Water
1½ **cups half and half**
1½ **cups sugar**
4 **eggs**
4 **teaspoons vanilla extract**
¼ **to ½ cup golden raisins**

In a pan soak the rice in hot water for 10 minutes. Drain. Repeat.

Add enough hot water to cover ¾ to 1 inch above the rice, cover, and cook over low heat. Stir every 10 minutes until the water is absorbed, usually 30 minutes.

Add 1 cup of half and half and the sugar to the rice and cook over low to medium heat, stirring every 10 minutes for about 30 minutes.

Add the eggs and ½ cup of half and half (or up to 1 cup of half and half) and the vanilla. Add to the cooled rice or add the rice to the egg mixture a spoonful at a time. Cook for 10 more minutes or until absorbed.

Add the raisins and cook uncovered for 10 minutes.

Remove from the heat and cool.

MAKES 6 TO 8 SERVINGS.

White Lace Inn Chocolate Heath Bar Cookies

2 **cups butter**
2 **cups sugar**
2 **cups firmly packed brown sugar**

White Lace Inn

4 **eggs**
3 **teaspoons vanilla extract**

....

4½ **cups all-purpose flour**
2 **teaspoons baking soda**
2 **teaspoons baking powder**

....

7 **cups old fashioned oats**
1 **large chopped Hershey bar**
6 **large chopped Heath bar**
1 **cup chopped nuts**

In a large bowl cream the butter, sugar, and brown sugar. Beat in the eggs and vanilla. In a separate bowl combine the flour, soda, and baking powder. Add the dry ingredients to the creamed mixture. Stir in the oats, candy, and nuts. Drop by spoonful onto a greased baking sheet. Bake in a 375° oven for 8 to 10 minutes (underbake).

MAKES ABOUT 6 DOZEN.

Fruit Soup

6 **to 8 cups apple cider**
1 **lemon, washed, sliced in half lengthwise, then sliced very thin**
1 **or 2 oranges, washed, sliced in half lengthwise, then sliced very thin**
½ **box golden raisins**
2 **sticks cinnamon**
1 **teaspoon ground cinnamon**
1 **teaspoon ground allspice**
¼ **teaspoon ground ground cloves**
1 **6-pound 10-ounce can sliced peaches**
1 **6-pound 10-ounce can can sliced pears**
1 **pound cherries**

In a stockpot combine the apple cider, lemon, oranges, raisins, cinnamon, allspice, and cloves. Simmer gently for about 20 minutes.

Add the peaches and pears, and simmer gently for another 15 to 20 minutes.

Add the cherries and let sit for 15 minutes before putting in the refrigerator.

Note: White Lace Inn serves fruit soup warmed up in the winter months and chilled with fresh spearmint sprigs in the summer.

MAKES 8 TO 10 SERVINGS.

Rosenberry Inn

511 Franklin Street
Wausau, Wisconsin 54403
(715) 842-5733

A historic home built in 1908 by Judge Marvin Rosenberry, the inn features beautiful stained-glass windows, wide halls, and a carved oak stairway. The neighborhood stretches out in long blocks lined by other historic and architecturally significant residences. The inn is within easy walking distance of downtown shops, art dealers, and cafes. Not far away is the Leigh Yawkey Woodson Art Museum with its respected wildlife art collections.

Almond Sour Cream Fruit Topping

2 **cups sour cream**
⅓ **cup firmly packed brown sugar**
⅜ **teaspoon almond extract (or to taste)**

In a medium bowl blend all of the ingredients and spoon over sliced fresh fruit.

MAKES 2 ⅓ CUPS.

Apple Crisp

4 **pounds (Cortland, Macintosh, etc.) apples**
1½ **tablespoons lemon juice**
⅓ **cup sugar**
¾ **teaspoon cinnamon**
¼ **teaspoon nutmeg**

Rosenberry Inn

1   cup all-purpose flour
3   cups rolled oats
1½ cups firmly packed brown sugar
1   teaspoon salt
1   cup butter, melted

Peel, core and slice the apples. Sprinkle with lemon juice, sugar, cinnamon, and nutmeg. Mix well. Spread in the bottom of a 9 x 13-inch baking dish. In a large bowl combine the flour, rolled oats, brown sugar, salt, and butter. Spread evenly over the apples. Bake in a 350° oven for 30 minutes.

Can be served warm with whipped cream or ice cream.

MAKES 8 SERVINGS.

Pancake Puff

1   cup water
½   cup butter or margarine
½   teaspoon grated orange peel
1   cup pancake mix
4   eggs
    Fruit Cocktail Topping or Buttery
    Peach Topping

In a large saucepan bring the water, butter, and orange peel to a boil. Add the pancake mix, stirring vigorously until the mixture leaves the sides of the pan and forms a ball. Remove the pan from the heat. Add the eggs one at a time, beating well after each addition. Spread evenly on the bottom and sides of 2 greased 9-inch pie plates. Bake in a 400° oven for 15 minutes or until golden. Serve with Fruit Cocktail Topping or Buttery Peach Topping.

MAKES 8 SERVINGS.

Fruit Cocktail Topping for Pancake Puff

1   cup sour cream
1   tablespoon honey

1   teaspoon grated orange peel
½   teaspoon cinnamon
1   16-ounce can fruit cocktail, drained

In a medium bowl mix all ingredients together and chill well before serving.

MAKES ABOUT 3 CUPS.

Buttery Peach Topping for Pancake Puff

1   16-ounce can sliced cling peaches
2   tablespoons butter
1   tablespoon fresh orange juice
1   teaspoon grated orange peel
2   teaspoons cornstarch
⅛   teaspoon nutmeg

In in a saucepan combine all ingredients and boil for 2 minutes.

MAKES ABOUT 2 CUPS.

Rosenberry Berry Baked Pancake

3   eggs slightly beaten
¾   cups all-purpose flour
¾   cups milk
1   cup fresh or frozen berries (blueber-
    ries, raspberries, tart cherries,
    etc., or sliced apples)
½   tablespoon sugar
½   teaspoon ground cinnamon
3   tablespoons butter

In a 9-inch deep dish pie pan melt the butter. Whisk the eggs, flour, and milk together. Pour into the prepared pie pan. Add the berries, spreading evenly. Mix the sugar and cinnamon together and sprinkle over the top of the egg mixture. Bake in a 375° oven for 20 to 25 minutes or until puffed and golden in color.

MAKES 4 TO 6 SERVINGS.

Jesse's Wolf River Lodge

Jesse's Wolf River Lodge

N2119 Taylor Road
White Lake, Wisconsin 54491
(715) 882-2182

B*uilt from native hemlock logs in 1929, this rustic lodge has played host to trout fisherman and other outdoor enthusiasts for more than two-thirds of a century. Canoers, kayakers, rafters, and cross-country skiers gather here to enjoy the wilds. Handmade quilts and braided rugs add warmth to the eight antique-filled guest rooms.*

Queen Anne's Honey Bread

4   cups milk
4   cups water
1   12-ounce can evaporated milk
1½   cups instant mashed potatoes
1½   cups honey
8   tablespoons yeast
13   cups bread flour
13   cups whole wheat flour
9   eggs
¼   cup salt
1½   cups oil

In a saucepan heat the water, milk, and evaporated milk to 135°. Add the potatoes, honey, and yeast, and let set for 5 minutes.

In a huge bowl combine the flours. Add the eggs, salt, and oil, and mix well with an electric mixer with a hook.

Add the potato mixture, and mix well. Cover and let rise to double in bulk. Form into 12 loaves. Place in greased loaf pans. Bake in a 350° oven for 30 minutes.

MAKES 12 LOAVES.

Crêpe Suzette

      3 eggs
      1 teaspoon salt
      1 tablespoon oil
      1 cup all-purpose flour
    1½ cups milk
      1 tablespoon oil
         Strawberry jam
         Confectioners' sugar

In a medium bowl beat the eggs, salt, oil, and flour with half the milk until smooth. Add the remaining milk. Heat an 8-inch heavy fry pan with sloping sides (or a crêpe pan) on high heat. Coat the bottom of the pan with 1 tablespoon of oil. Pour off the excess oil. Coat the bottom of the pan with about ⅓ cup of crêpe batter. Fry one side until lightly browned. Flip the pancake and cook about 30 seconds. Remove from the pan and keep warm. Repeat the process to make additional pancakes.

Spread each pancake with homemade strawberry jam. Roll up and sprinkle with confectioners' sugar.

MAKES 10 PANCAKES.

The Historic Bennett House

825 Oak Street
Wisconsin Dells, Wisconsin 53965
(608) 254-2500

*T*he Historic Bennett House, built in 1863, is located one block from downtown Wisconsin Dells. Decorated in soft rose and antique white, it is relaxing and welcoming. Warm and inviting in its casual elegance, the spacious living room is a great place for conversation, looking at original Bennett Stereoscopic views, looking at interesting books or browsing through magazines, some featuring the Bennett House. In cool weather feel the warmth of the fireplace or just take time out to rest between sight seeing. In summer the rear screened porch awaits. White wicker swing, love seat and chairs, flowers and the sound of a fountain nearby lull guests into total relaxation. After a fun-filled day or maybe for a rest between activities, the comfortable guest bedroom awaits. Choose one of three; The Wing, The English Room, or The Garden Room.

Happy Hour Mini Cheese Balls

      1 cup minced dried beef
      1 8-ounce package cream cheese
      1 tablespoon French dressing
      1 teaspoon chopped onion
      1 tablespoon chopped pimento-stuffed
         olives
    ½ teaspoon Worcestershire sauce

In a medium bowl combine the dried beef, cream cheese, French dressing, onin, olives, and Worcestershirc sauce. Mix well. Shape into small balls with greased hands. Chill. Serve with a pretzel stick in each.

MAKES ABOUT 12 SERVINGS.

Bennett's River Sunrise

      4 English muffins
    12 eggs (hard cooked)
      1 cup mayonnaise (Hellman's)
         Salt and pepper to taste
      2 to 3 slicing tomatoes
      1 cup grated Cheddar cheese (medium)
    ½ pound sliced honey ham
         Dillweed (optional)

Using a fork, open the muffins, making 8 pieces. Set aside.

Peel the eggs and place in a mixing bowl. Use a pastry blender to chop the eggs. Add salt and pepper to taste and the mayonnaise, stir together, and set aside.

Slice the tomatoes into 8 slices.

Assemble by placing honey ham on each muffin, add a slice of tomato, and top with a scoop of egg mixture. Sprinkle grated Cheddar cheese over all.

Place under the broiler until the cheese melts and bubbles. Sprinkle with dill.

Serve with a slice of cantaloupe and a large strawberry.

MAKES 4 SERVINGS.

Minestrone

      1 cup dried white beans
    ½ cup kidney beans
    12 cups water
    ½ pound salami, diced
      2 cups chopped celery
      2 14-ounce cans diced tomatoes
      1 cup cubed turnip
    ¼ cup chopped parsley
      1 teaspoon crushed basil (or dry
         leaves)
      1 16-ounce can tomato sauce
      1 13¾-ounce can beef consommé
      6 cups shredded white cabbage
      2 large zucchini, sliced
    ½ to 1 cup small spiral macaroni
         Salt and pepper to taste

In a large kettle cover the beans with 4 cups of water and bring to a boil. Cover and cook for 2 minutes. In a Dutch oven brown thc salami and celery. Stir in the beans and liquid, tomatoes, turnip, parsley, basil, and remaining 8 cups of water.

Add the tomato sauce and beef consommé. Cover and simmer for 2 hours to 2 hours and 30 minutes. Stir in the cabbage and zucchini, and cook 30 minutes more. Bring the soup to a boil and stir in the spiral macaroni. Serve with fresh ground Parmesan sprinkled on top.

This soup freezes well.

MAKES 6 SERVINGS.

Split-Pea Vegetable Soup (Low-Fat)

      2 large potatoes with skins, cut into
         chunks
      3 or 4 large carrots, sliced
      3 or 4 stalks of celery, chopped
      1 medium onion, chopped
      1 cup dry split peas
      8 to 10 cups water
      1 tablespoon butter

Salt and pepper to taste
1 *10 ½-ounce can split pea soup*
1 *small head cabbage (white)*

In a stockpot bring the water to a boil. Add the cut-up vegetables, split peas, butter, salt, and pepper. Cover and boil gently for 30 minutes. Add the split pea soup. Cut up the cabbage and add to the soup. Cook for 30 minutes.

Serve with Ritz crackers.

MAKES 6 SERVINGS.

Spectacular Carrot Cake

1½ *cups oil*
2 *cups sugar*
3 *eggs*
2¼ *cups all-purpose flour*
2 *teaspoons ground cinnamon*
2 *teaspoons baking soda*
1 *teaspoon salt*
2 *teaspoons vanilla extract*
2 *cups shredded carrots*
2 *cups flaked coconut*
1 *cup chopped walnuts*
1 *8-ounce can crushed pineapple*

....

3 *cups confectioners' sugar*
1 *8-ounce package cream cheese, softened*
1 *teaspoon lemon extract*

In a large bowl cream the oil, sugar and eggs together. In a separate bowl sift the flour, cinnamon, baking soda, and salt together. Add with the remaining ingredients to the oil mixture, and blend well. Pour into a well-greased 9 x 13-inch cake pan. Bake in a 350° oven for 50 to 60 minutes.

In a medium bowl combine the confectioners' sugar, cream cheese, and lemon extract and mix until smooth. If too thick for spreading, add hot water, 1 teaspoon at a time. Spread on the cooled cake.

MAKES 8 SERVINGS.

The Historic Bennett House

WYOMING

Spahn's Bighorn Mountain Bed and Breakfast

P.O. Box 579
Big Horn, Wyoming 82833
(307) 674-8150

*T*his B&B offers sweeping views of the Wyoming sky and mountains. Perched like a bird of prey in the tall pines at the edge of the Big Horn Mountains, it is a rustic, though comfortable log retreat likely to please any fresh air enthusiast. The main house has a three-story living room, enormous open fireplace, and a broad, hexagonal deck and two guest rooms in the main house. There are also a pair of separate cabins about a five minute drive from the main house.

Barbecued Buffalo Sandwiches

  2 pounds ground buffalo
  1 medium onion, chopped
  1 14-ounces bottle catsup
  ½ cup water
  ¼ cup chopped celery
  ⅛ cup lemon juice
  1 tablespoon brown sugar
  ½ tablespoon Worcestershire sauce
  ½ tablespoon salt
  1 teaspoon vinegar
  ¼ teaspoon dry mustard

In a heavy skillet cook and stir the buffalo and onion until the buffalo is brown and tender. Stir in the remaining ingredients, and heat to boiling. Reduce the heat, cover, and simmer for 30 minutes. Serve on toasted wheat buns.

MAKES 4 TO 6 SERVINGS.

Buffalo Burgundy

2½ pounds buffalo stew meat
  1 10½-ounce can mushroom soup
  1 cup burgundy
  1 package onion soup mix
    Cooked rice

In a 1½-quart casserole dish combine the buffalo meat, soup, burgundy, and onion soup mix. Cover. Bake in a 300° oven for 3 hours.

Serve over rice. Beef may be substituted if buffalo is unavailable. Serve with spinach salad.

MAKES 4 TO 6 SERVINGS.

Fresh Spinach Salad

  1 package fresh spinach
  1 20-ounce can bean sprouts, drained
      and rinsed
  8 slices bacon, cooked and crumbled
  3 hard-boiled eggs, diced

  1 cup oil
  ⅓ cup sugar
  ⅓ cup catsup
  ¼ cup vinegar
  1 teaspoon Worcestershire sauce
    Salt to taste

In a salad bowl combine the spinach, bean sprouts, bacon, and eggs. In a small bowl

Spahn's Bighorn Mountain

combine the oil, sugar, catsup, vinegar, Worcestershire sauce, and salt to taste. Pour over the salad.

MAKES 4 SERVINGS.

A. Drummond's Ranch

399 Happy Jack Road
Cheyenne/Laramie, Wyoming 82007
(307) 634-6042

*L*ooking south toward the towering Colorado Rockies, the ranch sits on 120 Wyoming acres beside a scenic state park and 55,000 acre National Forest. The carriage house loft has a private deck, hot tub, gas fireplace, steam sauna, and stocked pantry. Hunting, fishing, hiking, biking, and climbing are just outside the door. Guests may bring their horse or pet.

Spinach with Garlic and Strawberries

- 2 **tablespoons butter (or olive oil)**
- 2 **bunches spinach, washed and chopped**
- 2 **cloves garlic, finely chopped**
- 4 **to 6 strawberries, washed sliced**

In a large skillet melt the butter. Add the spinach and cook for about 1 to 2 minutes until limp, stirring occasionally. Add the garlic and stir. Garnish the cooked spinach with berries.

Strange? Yes, but lovely to look at and tasty to eat!

MAKES 4 TO 6 SERVINGS.

A. Drummond's Ranch

Raspberry Salad Dressing

- ¼ **cup strong brewed tea**
- 3 **tablespoons olive oil**
- 2 **tablespoons apple cider vinegar**
- 1 **tablespoon raspberry preserves**
- 1½ **tablespoons Dijon mustard**
- ¼ **cup chopped chives**

In a jar with a tight-fitting lid combine all of the ingredients.

MAKES ABOUT 1 CUP.

Graham Crackers

- 2 **cups whole wheat flour**
- 1 **cup all-purpose flour**
- 1 **teaspoon baking powder**
- ½ **teaspoon baking soda**
- ¼ **teaspoon salt**
- ½ **cup shortening**
- ½ **cup packed brown sugar**
- ¼ **cup honey**
- 1 **teaspoon vanilla extract**
- ½ **cup milk**

In a medium bowl mix together the flours, baking powder, soda, and salt. In a large bowl beat together everything else but the milk. Add the milk and flour mixture alternately to the second mixture. Mix well. Form into a ball and refrigerate about 2 hours. Divide the dough into fourths. On a floured surface, roll out each quarter to a 15 x 5-inch rectangle. Cut that rectangle into 6 2½ x 5-inch rectangles. Make a crease across the center of each of the smaller rectangles, and prick with a fork. Place on a greased baking sheet. Bake in a 350° oven for 10 to 15 minutes.

MAKES 2 DOZEN.

Adventurers' Country Bed and Breakfast

3803 I-80 South Service Road
Cheyenne, Wyoming 82001
(307) 632-4087

*T*his B&B is on the 102-acre Raven Cry Ranch near Cheyenne in the southeastern corner of Wyoming. There are four large guest rooms decorated in comfortable western style. During the summer the ranch offers a number of "Horseback Adventures" that take riders on week-long treks into the Medicine Bow Mountains.

Devonshire Cream

- 1 **cup heavy cream**
- ½ **cup confectioners' sugar**
- 1½ **teaspoons vanilla extract**
- 1 **cup sour cream**
- 5 **tablespoons amaretto liquor**

In a large, chilled bowl beat the heavy cream, confectioners' sugar, and vanilla until soft peaks form. Beat in the sour cream, blending well. Add the Amaretto liquor, folding in. Refrigerate in a covered container. Serve as a topping for fruit, or pile it on scones.

MAKES 2 CUPS.

Carrot-Raisin Muffins

- 1½ **cups sugar (or less)**
- 1 **cup oil**
- 3 **large eggs, beaten**
- 2 **teaspoons vanilla extract**
- 1 **7-ounce can crushed pineapple, with juice**
- 2 **cups plus 2 tablespoons all-purpose flour**
- 2 **teaspoons baking soda**
- 1½ **teaspoons cinnamon**
- 1 **teaspoon salt**
- 2 **cups grated carrots**
- 1 **cup raisins**
- 1 **cup chopped nuts (optional)**

In a medium bowl mix the ingredients and add the pineapple. In a large bowl combine the flour, soda, cinnamon, and salt. Add the egg mixture and mix just until moistened. The batter will be thick. Add 2 cups of grated carrots, 1 cup of raisins, and 1 cup chopped nuts, if desired. Fill greased muffin cups ¾ full. Bake in a 375° oven for 15 to 20 minutes.

MAKES 2 DOZEN SMALL OR REGULAR MUFFINS OR 1 DOZEN TEXAS SIZE.

Swiss Cheese and Vegetable Quiche

- 1 cup shredded Swiss cheese
- 1 small tomato, diced
- 1 small onion, diced
- 1 small green pepper, diced
- 1 yellow squash, chopped
- 4 eggs, beaten
- 1 teaspoon Dijon mustard
- 1 teaspoon seasoned salt, or less, if desired
- 1 cup half and half
  Pastry for 1 9-inch crust

Line a quiche pan with the pastry. Layer Swiss cheese, tomato, pepper, onion, and squash in the crust. In a small bowl blend the eggs, mustard, salt, and half and half. Pour the egg mixture into the pie crust. Bake in a 350° oven for 40 to 50 minutes or until a knife inserted 1-inch from the center comes out clean.

MAKES 6 SERVINGS.

Porch Swing Bed and Breakfast

712 East 20th Street
Cheyenne, Wyoming 82001
(307) 778-7182

*T*his authentically restored and furnished 1907 registered historic home offers guests a full breakfast served on the back porch in summer and by the dining room fire in cold weather. The Porch Swing is within walking distance of the downtown shopping area, museums and restaurants. Cheyenne is surrounded by ranches, farmland, and roads that lead west to mountain parks for hiking, fishing, bicycling, or cross-country skiing.

Garden Frittata

- 2 tablespoons butter
- ½ cup onion, chopped
- 2 cloves garlic, pressed
- 1 cup spinach, broccoli or mushrooms, finely chopped
- ½ teaspoon basil
- ½ teaspoon thyme
- 6 eggs
- 1 cup Swiss cheese (optional)
- ½ cup grated Parmesan
- 1 teaspoon salt
- ¼ teaspoon pepper
- ½ cup heavy cream or sour cream
- 1 cup milk
- 1 cup torn bread
  Dash Tabasco sauce

In a large bowl combine all of the ingredients, reserving ½ cup of Swiss cheese and ¼ cup of Parmesan. Pour into an 8-inch pan (or something comparable). Sprinkle the reserved ingredients on top of the frittata. Bake in a 350° oven for 30 to 40 minutes.

MAKES 6 SERVINGS.

German Dutch Pancake

- 3 eggs
- ¾ cup unbleached all-purpose flour
- ¾ cup milk
- ¼ teaspoon salt
- ½ teaspoon vanilla extract
- 1½ tablespoons butter
  Swiss Honey Butter (recipe follows)

Heat a cast iron skillet in a 500° oven. Melt the butter in the hot skillet. In a blender combine the eggs, flour, milk, salt, and vanilla, and blend. Reduce the heat to 400°, pour the batter into the preheated skillet. Bake in a 400° oven for 20 minutes. Slip onto a heated platter (or serve in the skillet). Cut into pie shaped wedges and serve immediately.

Serve with Swiss Honey Butter.

MAKES 4 SERVINGS.

Swiss Honey Butter

- ½ cup butter
- ½ cup honey
- ½ cup heavy cream
- 1 teaspoon vanilla extract

In a small bowl cream the butter with the honey. Slowly add the heavy cream, beating constantly until the mixture is fluffy. Add the vanilla. Spoon over hot pancakes.

MAKES 1½ CUPS.

Grits Soufflé with Ham Sauce

- 8 cups boiling water
- 1 teaspoon salt
- 2 cups grits
- ¼ cup butter
- 1 roll garlic cheese (or ½ cup processed cheese spread and 2 garlic cloves minced)
- 2 tablespoons sherry
- 1 tablespoon Tabasco sauce
- 2 tablespoons Worcestershire
- 2 eggs, well beaten

- 2 tablespoons butter
- 3 tablespoons all-purpose flour
- 1 13¾-ounce can beef or vegetable broth
- ½ cup chopped mushrooms
- ½ cup slivered almonds
- 2 cups chopped ham
- ½ cup chopped stuffed green olives
- ½ cup sherry
- 1 tablespoon worcestershire
  Cayenne pepper to taste

In a stockpot combine and stir the water, salt, and grits. Cook according to the directions on the grits package. Remove the pan from the heat and add the butter, cheese, sherry, Tabasco, Worcestershire, and eggs. Pour into a 9 x 13-inch pan. Bake in a 350° oven for 1 hour.

In a saucepan combine the butter, flour, and broth and cook until thickened. Add the remaining ingredients, and simmer for 10 minutes. Serve over grits.

MAKES 6 TO 8 SERVINGS.

Yeast Waffles

- 1 package active dry yeast
- 1¼ cups warm water (105 to 115°)
- 1½ cups unbleached all-purpose flour
- ¼ cup lukewarm milk
- 3 tablespoons butter, melted
- 1½ tablespoons honey
- 1 teaspoon salt
- 2 eggs
  Fresh strawberries

In a large bowl dissolve the yeast in warm water. Mix in the flour, cover with plastic wrap, and let stand at room temperature overnight.

The next morning, mix together the lukewarm milk, honey, melted butter, salt, and eggs. Stir the milk mixture into the flour/yeast mixture about 15 minutes before baking. Cook in a waffle iron until the desired color is reached. Serve with fresh strawberries and pure maple syrup.

Note: The dough will rise during the night. Use a bowl large enough so that the mixture won't rise over the top.

MAKES 4 TO 6 SERVINGS.

Biscotti (Italian Anise Cookies)

½ cup butter, softened
1½ cups sugar
½ teaspoon salt
    Zest of 1 medium orange
    Zest of 1 medium lemon, finely
        grated
1 tablespoon anise seed
3 eggs, slightly beaten
3 cups unbleached all-purpose flour
2½ teaspoons baking powder
½ teaspoon baking soda
1 cup coarsely chopped toasted
        almonds
1 6-ounce bag semisweet chocolate
        chips, mint or regular

In a large bowl beat the butter, sugar, salt, orange zest, lemon zest, and anise seed until light. Add the eggs and beat well. Stir in the flour, baking powder, soda, and nuts. Mix well. Divide the dough in half or thirds. Shape into logs about 1½ inches in diameter. Place the logs 4 inches apart on a greased baking sheet. Bake in a 325° oven for 25 minutes.

Remove the pan from the oven. Reduce the heat to 275°. Cut the logs into ¾-inch slices. Lay the slices cut-side down, 1½-inches apart on baking sheets.

Bake an additional 40 minutes, or until very dry. Cool.

If desired, frost with melted semisweet chocolate chips on one side of each cookie. Freezes well.

MAKES ABOUT 4 DOZEN.

Rhubarb Crisp

1 cup unbleached all-purpose flour
¾ cup oatmeal
1 teaspoon ground cinnamon
1 cup firmly packed brown sugar
½ cup butter, melted
1 cup sugar
1 cup water
3 tablespoons cornstarch
1 teaspoon vanilla extract
4 cups sliced rhubarb

In a medium bowl combine the flour, oatmeal, cinnamon, and brown sugar. Press half the mixture into an 8-inch square pan. In a saucepan combine and cook the sugar, water, cornstarch, and vanilla until thick. Remove from the heat, add the rhubarb, and mix well. Spread the filling on the pressed oatmeal mixture and top with the other half of the dry mixture. Bake in a 350° oven for 1 hour. Great hot with ice cream.

MAKES 6 SERVINGS.

Hunter Peak Ranch

⁀

P.O. Box 1731, Painter Route
Cody, Wyoming 82414
(307) 587-3711

---

*T*he ranch places its guests within easy reach of the Chief Joseph Scenic Highway, Beartooth Plateau, Upper Sunlight Creek, and Yellowstone National Park. Accommodations include housekeeping cabins and suites equipped with all the necessary amenities. The main lodge has a library, a big central hall, and a large dining room. Every conceivable variety of outdoor activity, including constructive loafing, is possible in the area. Rugged backcountry pack trips are also available.

Greek Vegetables

4 Roma tomatoes
    Raw vegetables (potatoes, Zucchini,
        onions, green, red, and yellow
        bell peppers, carrots, squash, cel-
        ery, mushrooms, cabbage), sliced
        or diced
½ cup white rice
½ cup brown rice
2 tablespoons wine vinegar
1 cube beef or chicken bouillon
1 teaspoon hot sauce
    Salt and pepper to taste
    Shredded cheese

Oil a 9 x 13-inch pan. Dice 2 tomatoes, and spread in the bottom of the prepared pan. Over the tomatoes sprinkle the raw vegetables. Add the white and brown rice. Layer additional vegetables. Top with 2 more diced tomatoes.

In a 1 cup measure, pour the wine vinegar, bouillon cube, hot sauce (more or less to taste), salt, and pepper, and add water to make 1 cup. Mix and pour over the mixture in the pan. Cover. Bake in a 350° oven for 1 hour and 30 minutes.

Uncover, add the shredded cheese (a combination of favorites work well). Bake an additional 30 minutes.

MAKES 8 TO 10 SERVINGS.

Gooseberry/Cherry Pie

2 cups green gooseberries
2 cups sweet red cherries
1½ cups sugar
¾ cup whole wheat flour
1 tablespoon cinnamon
1 9-inch pie shell

½ cup old-fashioned oats
⅓ cup whole wheat flour
⅓ cup brown sugar
1 teaspoon cinnamon
¼ cup margarine

In a large bowl combine the gooseberries, cherries, sugar, ¾ cup of whole wheat flour, and cinnamon. Spoon the mixture into the pie shell. Bake in a 350° oven for 45 minutes.

In a small bowl combine the oats, ⅓ cup of whole wheat flour, brown sugar, 1 teaspoon of cinnamon, and margarine. Remove the crisp from the oven and sprinkle with the mixture. Return to the oven and bake until the topping is golden.

MAKES 6 SERVINGS.

The Wildflower Inn

The Wildflower Inn

❧

P. O. Box 3724
Jackson, Wyoming 83001
(307) 733-4710

Situated on three beautiful acres covered with aspens, cottonwoods, and wildflowers, the inn has five sunny guestrooms. A delicious mountain breakfast is served in the dining room or—weather permitting—on the deck overlooking the pond. Guests can enjoy nearby skiing, tennis, golf, fishing, climbing, hiking, rafting, biking, restaurants, and shopping, or lounging, and relaxing in the solarium, complete with a hot tub.

Wildflower Inn Oatmeal Pancakes

- 2 *cups old-fashioned oatmeal*
- 2 *cups buttermilk*
- 2 *eggs, lightly beaten*
- ¼ *cup butter or margarine, melted and cooked*
- ½ *cup all-purpose flour*
- 2 *tablespoons sugar*
- 1 *teaspoon baking powder*
- 1 *teaspoon baking soda*
- ¼ *teaspoon salt*

In a large bowl combine the oats and buttermilk, and soak for about 15 minutes. Add the eggs and butter. Stir well. Add the flour, sugar, baking powder, soda, and salt. Stir gently. Ladle with a ¼ cup measuring cup onto a medium hot grill. Cook until golden on each size.

Serve with warm maple syrup.

MAKES 4 SERVINGS.

Fantastic Buttermilk Pancakes

- 1 *egg*
- 1 *cup buttermilk*
- 1 *cup sour cream*
- 1 *teaspoon baking powder*
- 1 *teaspoon baking soda*
- 1 *cup all-purpose flour*

Mix all ingredients together gently. Let sit for 10 minutes while the batter rises. Very important. Lightly oil a medium hot grill. I use a ¼ cup measuring cup.

Serve with warm maple syrup or homemade jam. Don't let them float off the plate!

Note: The lightest, most delicious buttermilk pancakes ever...

MAKES 4 SERVINGS.

Cornmeal Pancakes

- 2 *cups yellow cornmeal*
- 1 *cup all-purpose flour*
- 1 *tablespoon sugar*
- 1 *teaspoon salt*
- 1 *teaspoon baking soda*
- 1 *teaspoon baking powder*
- 2 *cups buttermilk or plain yogurt*
- ½ *cup milk*
- ¼ *cup oil*
- 2 *large eggs*

In a large bowl mix the cornmeal, flour, sugar, salt, soda, and baking powder together. Add the buttermilk, milk, oil, and eggs. Stir until all ingredients are incorporated. Let sit for 5 to 10 minutes. Cook on a medium hot grill.

This recipe is wonderful with the addition of fresh blueberries. Gently stir 1 to 2 cups of fresh blueberries into the batter.

MAKES 8 SERVINGS.

Raspberry Muffins

- 1½ *cups all-purpose flour*
- ¼ *cup sugar*
- ¼ *cup firmly packed brown sugar*
- 2 *teaspoons baking powder*
- ¼ *teaspoon cinnamon*
- 1 *egg, lightly beaten*
- ½ *cup milk*
- ½ *cup butter, melted*

....

- 1¼ *cups fresh raspberries*
    Cinnamon-sugar

In a large bowl combine the flour, sugar, brown sugar, baking powder, and cinnamon. Add the egg, milk, and butter, and mix just until moistened. Fill greased muffin cups two-thirds full. Sprinkle the tops lightly with cinnamon sugar.

Bake in a 350° oven for 20 to 25 minutes until lightly brown and done to the touch.

MAKES 1 DOZEN.

Buckwheat Waffles

- 1½ *cups buckwheat flour*
- 1½ *cups all-purpose flour*
- ¼ *cup sugar*
- 4 *teaspoons baking powder*
- 1½ *teaspoons baking soda*
- 1 *teaspoon salt*
- 6 *eggs*
- 3 *cups buttermilk*
- 1 *cup butter, melted and cooled*

In a large bowl combine the flours, sugar, baking powder, soda, and salt. In a separate bowl beat the eggs, buttermilk and butter together until well combined. Add the liquid mixture to the dry ingredients amd mix until just blended. Cook on a hot waffle iron until they stop steaming and are brown and crisp. Watch out when opening the lid, they might just float away! Serve with fresh strawberries and warm maple syrup.

MAKES 4 SERVINGS.

Apple Museli

- 1 *cup old-fashioned rolled oats*
- ¾ *cup apple juice*
- 2 *tablespoons vanilla yogurt*
- ⅓ *cup sliced almonds*
- ⅓ *cup diced fresh apple*

Chill until very cold, about 30 minutes or so.
MAKES 2 SERVINGS.

Orange Museli

> 1 cup old-fashioned rolled oats
> 1 cup orange juice
> 1 teaspoon lemon juice
> ¼ cup raisins
> ¼ cup chopped nuts
> 3 cups chopped fresh fruit
> 1 cup plain yogurt
>   Brown sugar or honey to taste

Chill and serve with a dollop of cold vanilla
yogurt or whipped cream.
MAKES 4 SERVINGS.

Super Oatmeal

> 2 cups old-fashioned rolled oats
> 4 cups milk
> ¼ teaspoon salt
> 1 fresh nectarine or peach, peeled and
>   diced
> 1 apple, cored and diced
> 1 banana, diced

In a saucepan combine all of the ingredients
and let soak for 5 minutes or so. Simmer
slowly over low heat, stirring often. Cook
until thickened and tender, about 10 to 15
minutes.
MAKES 6 SERVING.

Scrambled Eggs with Smoked Salmon in Potato Nests

> 1 pound baking potatoes, peeled and
>   shredded
> 1 large egg white
> 1 teaspoon salt
> 1 teaspoon fresh ground pepper
> 20 extra large eggs
> ¼ cup diced, roasted red pepper
> ½ cup smoked salmon from the west
>   coast
>   Salt and freshly ground pepper to
>   taste

Spray 8 muffin cups with cooking spray.
  Mix ingredients together and divide among
the tins. Shape around sides and bottoms of
tins evenly. Bake the nests in a 375° oven for

25 to 35 minutes until brown and crisp. Cool
for a few minutes and remove to a wire rack
while finishing the eggs.
  In a large bowl beat the eggs. In a large
skillet (or 2 skillets) scramble the eggs. Just
before completion, fold in the red pepper,
smoked salmon, salt, and fresh ground pepper to taste.
  Fill each potato cup heaping with scrambled eggs, and top with a small dollop of sour
cream. Serve immediately with homemade
whole grain toast, grilled grapefruit halves
with brown sugar, cold fresh orange juice,
and fragrant French roast coffee. (A spoonful
of caviar on top of the sour cream would be a
real treat!)
MAKES 8 SERVINGS.

Warm Orange Omelet Souffle with Strawberries

> 9 egg whites
> 9 tablespoons sugar
> 9 egg yolks
> 3 tablespoons all-purpose flour
> ½ teaspoon freshly grated orange peel
> ....
> 6 tablespoons butter
> ½ cup orange juice
> 3 tablespoons sugar
> ¼ teaspoon freshly grated orange peel
> ....
> 2 tablespoons butter
> 2 tablespoons sugar
> ½ teaspoon freshly grated orange peel
> ½ cup orange juice
> 3 cups sliced fresh strawberries

In a large bowl beat the egg whites until
foamy. Gradually add the sugar and continue
beating until the whites are stiff.
  In a separate bowl beat the egg yolks with
the flour and orange peel until thick and light
yellow. Gently fold the yolk mixture into the
beaten egg whites. Set aside.
  In a 12-inch ovenproof frying pan melt 6
tablespoons of butter. Add ½ cup of orange
juice, 3 tablespoons of sugar, and ¼ teaspoon
of orange peel. Cook until bubbling, remove
from the heat, and gently slide large spoonfuls of the egg mixture onto the hot sauce.
Bake in a 350° oven for 10 to 15 minutes
until set around the edges and slightly creamy
in the middle. While this is baking, prepare
the strawberries.

In a separate frying pan combine 2 tablespoons of butter, 2 tablespoons of sugar, ½
teaspoon of orange peel, and ½ cup of
orange juice, and heat until bubbling.
Remove the pan from the heat, and stir in the
strawberries.
  Serve the omelet soufflé at once. Spoon
down into the bottom of the pan to scoop out
the orange sauce and serve on plates with
warm strawberries on top and a dab of sour
cream.
MAKES 4 SERVINGS.

The Alpine House
∾

P.O. Box 20245
Jackson Hole, Wyoming 83001
(307) 739-1570

---

*T*he Alpine House is owned and
operated by Hans and Nancy John-
stone, a pair of Winter Olympic ath-
letes who have chosen to make the
ski country of western Wyoming
their home. Guest rooms are light,
airy, and comfortably furnished. A
number of packages including
lodging and backcountry ski
adventures are available.

Alpine House Linzer Torte

> ½ cup plus 2 tablespoons butter
> ½ cup sugar
> 1 egg
> 1 teaspoon baking powder
> ¼ teaspoon ground cinnamon
> ¼ teaspoon ground cloves
> 1½ cups all-purpose flour
> ¾ cup ground hazelnuts or almonds
> ½ cup raspberry jam

In a medium bowl beat the butter with an
electric mixer until softened. Add the sugar,
egg, baking powder, and spices. Beat until
mixed well. Stir in the flour and almonds by
hand, do not use electric mixer. Form into a

ball, wrap in plastic wrap, and chill for about 1 hour.

Divide the chilled dough in half, keeping one half refrigerated. On a lightly floured board, flatten the dough by hand and then roll into 10-inch circle. Wrap the circle around the rolling pin and place on an ungreased 9-inch tart pan with a removable bottom. Gently press the dough into a pan and ½-inch up the sides.

On a lightly floured board, roll out the remaining dough and cut into lattice strips. Weave the strips over the bottom crust to form a lattice top. Press the ends of the strips into the rim of the bottom crust and trim the ends. Spoon a teaspoon of raspberry jam into each section of lattice. Bake in a 350° oven for 25 to 20 minutes or the until crust is golden brown. Cool in a pan on a wire rack. Remove the sides of the pan and place on a nice serving plate. Sprinkle well with confectioners' sugar once completely cool.

MAKES 6 TO 8 SERVINGS.

Grand Teton Coffee Cake

> 2 **cups butter, softened**
> 2 **cups firmly packed brown sugar**
> 4 **eggs**
> 2 **teaspoons vanilla extract**
> 4 **cups all-purpose flour**
> 2 **teaspoons baking powder**
> 2½ **teaspoons baking soda**
> 1½ **teaspoons cardamom**
> ½ **teaspoon salt**
> 2 **cups sour cream or plain yogurt**
>
> ¼ **cup brown sugar**
> 1 **tablespoon cinnamon**
> ½ **cup chopped walnuts**
>   **Confectioners' sugar**

In a large bowl cream together the butter and sugar until fluffy. Add the eggs and vanilla extract, and beat well. In a separate bowl sift together the flour, soda, baking powder, cardamom, and salt. Alternately add the flour mixture and sour cream to the butter mixture and mix until just blended. Do not overmix!

Create the streusel mixture by blending all 3 ingredients. Spoon ⅓ of the cake batter into a greased bundt pan, half of the streusel mixture, then one-third of the batter, the remaining streusel mix, then the remaining batter. Bake in a 350° oven for 1 hour to 1 hour and 30 minutes until brown on top. Sprinkle with confectioners' sugar when completely cool.

MAKES 8 SERVINGS.

Wolf Hotel
❧

101 East Bridge, P.O. Box 1298
Saratoga, Wyoming 82331
(307) 326-5525

---

*T*he Wolf Hotel opened in 1893 with a gala masquerade ball. For years the hotel served as a key stop for the Walcott Stage Line. Rooms are quaint and furnished with original dressers and iron beds. Downstairs, there is a saloon.

Black Bean Soup

> 2 **cups dried black beans**
>
> 8 **cups cold water**
> ½ **pound cooked ham, cubed (optional)**
> 1 **beef bouillon cube**
> 1 **chicken bouillon cube**
> 1 **green bell pepper, finely chopped**
> 1 **small onion, chopped**
> ¾ **cup chopped celery**
> ¾ **cup diced carrot**
> 1 **bay leaf**
> ¼ **teaspoon cumin**
> ¼ **teaspoon cilantro**
> 2 **cloves garlic, crushed**
> 2 **tablespoons olive oil**
> 1 **to 2 dried Habañero peppers, whole**
>   **(or ½ to 1 fresh, finely diced**
>   **Habañero pepper)**
>   **Salt and pepper to taste**
> ¼ **cup dry sherry**

Pick over and wash the beans. In a large kettle or stockpot cover the beans with water and soak overnight. Drain the beans and add 8 cups of cold water, cover and simmer for one hour and 30 minutes. Add the remaining ingredients except the sherry, and simmer until the beans and vegetables are tender.

Add the sherry and cook for 10 minutes to allow the flavors to blend.

Remove the Habañero if dried pepper is used.

MAKES 8 TO 10 SERVINGS.

Judd's Sailor Soup

> 1 **pound dried small white beans**
> 2 **quarts cold water**
> 2 **to 3 pounds smoked ham hocks**
> 2 **cloves garlic, crushed**
>   **Salt and pepper to taste**
> 2 **teaspoons cider vinegar**
> 1 **bay leaf**
> 2 **tablespoons bacon drippings**
> 1 **small onion, chopped**

In a large stock pot or kettle wash the beans and cover with cold water. Bring to a boil, reduce the heat, and boil gently for 2 minutes. Remove from the heat, cover, and let stand for 1 hour. Do not drain. Add the ham hocks, garlic, salt, pepper, vinegar, and bay leaf. Return to the heat and simmer for approximately 2 hours and 30 minutes.

Remove the ham hocks, cut the meat from the bone, and return the meat to the soup. In a skillet melt the bacon drippings and add the onion, cooking until lightly browned. Add the onion to the soup. Simmer for 30 minutes, or until the meat and beans are tender. Remove the bay leaf.

Note: If ham base is available, use a heaping tablespoon to increase the flavor.

MAKES 8 SERVINGS.

Wolf Hotel

CANADA

Situated on a 3,800-acre grain farm, Anola's provides all the space anyone would ever likely need to stretch their legs and arms. There are two guest rooms in the main farmhouse and a separate accommodation in a nearby honeymoon cottage. An on-site museum includes a collection of western Canadian antiques and memorabilia.

Anola's Granola

 6 cups rolled oats
 2 cups triticale flakes (available at a healthfood stores or bulk food stores)
 2 cups barley flakes (available at a healthfood stores or bulk food stores)
 1 cup rye flakes (available at a health-food stores or bulk food stores)
 1 cup wheat flakes (available at a healthfood stores or bulk food stores)
 ½ cup flax (available at a healthfood stores or bulk food stores)
 1½ cups wheat germ, unroasted
 1 cup natural bran
 1 cup unsweetened coconut
 1 cup firmly packed brown sugar
 ½ cup sesame seeds
 ½ cup sunflower seeds
 ½ cup slivered almonds
 1 tablespoon cinnamon
 ....

 ¾ cup canola oil or olive oil
 1½ cups water
 ½ cup honey
 1 tablespoon vanilla extract
 1½ cups raisins

In a large bowl or plastic container mix the triticale, barley, rye, and wheat flakes. Add the flax, wheat germ, bran, coconut, brown sugar, sesame seeds, almonds, and cinnamon. In a glass bowl combine the oil, water, honey, and vanilla extract, and stir together. Microwave the liquids on high for 2 minutes.

Pour the warm liquid over the dry ingredients and mix well. Divide the mixture onto 3 cookie sheets. Bake in a 300° oven for 30 minutes. Every 10 minutes rotate the cookie sheets in the oven and stir each pan. (If overbaked, the granola tends to get dark because of the honey.) Remove from the oven and add ½ cup of raisins to each cookie sheet. Cool.

Store in airtight containers. Place the granola in the freezer and then it is always fresh.
MAKES ABOU T 23 CUPS.

Rhubarb Pecan Muffins

 2 cups barley flour
 ¾ cup sugar
 1½ teaspoons baking soda
 1 teaspoon salt
 ¾ cup chopped pecans
 1 egg
 ¼ cup canola oil
 2 teaspoons grated orange peel
 ¾ cup orange juice
 1½ cups finely chopped rhubarb (cranberries may be substituted)
 ....

 ½ cup quick-cooking oats
 ½ cup firmly packed brown sugar
 ¼ cup finely chopped pecans
 ¼ cup butter, melted
 ¼ teaspoon ground cinnamon
 ¼ teaspoon ground ginger

In a large bowl combine the barley flour, sugar, soda, salt, and ¾ cup of pecans. Add the oil, orange peel, orange juice, and rhubarb, and stir just until moistened. Fill 12 lightly greased muffin cups.

In a small bowl combine the oats, brown sugar, ¼ cup of pecans, butter, cinnamon, and ginger. Sprinkle the topping over the batter. Bake in a 375° oven for 20 to 25 minutes.

MAKES 1 DOZEN.

Dickens Inn

Dickens Inn

R.R. #1
Cochrane, Alberta TOL OWO
Canada
(403) 932-3945

The Dickens Inn is centrally located between Banff and Calgary, placing its guests within easy reach of some of western Canada's most popular destinations. For instance, the Canadian Olympic Park is less that half an hour's drive, the Sunshine Ski Village about ninely minutes away, and Lake Louise about two hours away. Open year-round, the Victorian inn offers three guest rooms with four-poster beds in a country setting with magnificent views of the Canadian Rockies.

Egg & Ham Casserole

12 to 14 large eggs
    Salt and pepper to taste
2 cups grated Cheddar cheese
3 medium potatoes, grated (raw)
1 pound cooked ham, cubed small

In a large bowl scramble the eggs and season with salt and pepper. Add the cheese, potatoes, and ham, and mix well. Pour into a greased 9 x 12-inch baking dish. Bake in a 350° oven for 45 to 50 minutes. Cut into 6 pieces and garnish the plate with fresh fruit slices.

Variations: Try substituting sausage or bacon for the ham and add any other ingredients desired (onion, celery, mushrooms, tomatoes, etc.).
MAKES 6 SERVINGS.

Belgian Waffles

2 eggs, separated
1½ cups milk
2 cups all-purpose flour
4 teaspoons baking powder
1 teaspoon salt
1 tablespoon sugar
2 tablespoons butter or margarine , melted

In a small bowl beat the egg whites until stiff, but not dry. Set aside.

In a large bowl beat the egg yolks until thick and creamy. Continue beating while adding the milk. In a separate bowl mix the flour, baking ppwder, salt, and sugar together, and gradually add to the milk mixture. Beat until smooth.

Fold in the stiffly beaten egg whites and melted butter. Pour approximately 1 cup of batter onto a hot waffle maker. Bake for about 3 minutes until golden. Repeat with the remaining batter.

Dust each waffle lightly with icing sugar. Serve with butter and warm fruit and maple syrups.
MAKES 4 SERVINGS.

Black Cat Guest Ranch

Box 6267
Hinton, Alberta T7V 1X6
Canada
(403) 865-3084, (800) 859-6840

Hidden away in a forest on the eastern slope of the Canadian Rocky Mountains, the Black Cat Guest Ranch is a year-round retreat offer-

ing sixteen guest rooms and extraordinary views. During warm weather months, guest can enjoy hiking, horseback riding, fishing, and sightseeing. Winter brings opportunities for cross-country skiing and snowshoeing.

Yorkshire Pudding

3 eggs
1 cup milk
2 tablespoons margarine, melted
1 cup all-purpose flour
½ teaspoon salt

In a medium bowl beat the eggs. Add the remaining ingredients. Set aside for at least 2 hours before cooking. The batter should be thin like farm cream. Do not refrigerate the batter, it should get to room temperature.

Grease 12 muffin cups and pour the batter in. Bake in a 375° oven for 40 minutes.
MAKES 1 DOZEN.

Solomon Granola

7 cups uncooked large flake oats
1 cup wheat germ
½ cup sunflower seeds
1 cup large flake coconut
¼ cup brown sugar
½ teaspoon salt
½ cup liquid honey
½ cup hot water
½ cup oil
   Soft raisins (optional)

In a large bowl mix the oats, wheat germ, sunflower seeds, and coconut. In a separate bowl mix the remaining ingredients. Pour over the dry ingredients and stir well. Spread in shallow pans. Bake in a 300°oven for about 1 hour. Stir every 10 minutes. Soft raisins may be added after it is cooked.
MAKES ABOUT 3 QUARTS.

Inn at the Ranch

Inn at the Ranch

❧

Box 562
Smoky Lake, Alberta T0A 3C0
Canada
(403) 656-2474

*T*he inn is on the 7,000-acre B&E Ranch. There are four guest rooms at the ranch house as well as a spacious dining room and library available to visitors. Your hosts will prepare a picnic lunch for you to take to historic Fort Victoria or on an exploratory drive along the old Victoria Trail used more than a century ago by Indians and fur traders.

Cranberry Pie

1¾ *cups sugar, divided*
 ½ *cup nuts*
 3 *cups fresh/frozen cranberries*
 ½ *cup chopped pecans*
 1 *cup all purpose flour*
 2 *eggs*
 ½ *cup margarine, melted*

Generously grease a 10-inch pie plate. Sprinkle with ¾ cup of sugar and the nuts. Add the cranberries. In a medium bowl beat the eggs well, gradually adding 1 cup of sugar, and beat until thoroughly mixed. Add the flour and melted butter. Beat well.

Pour the batter over the cranberries. Bake in a 350° oven for 1 hour.

Invert onto a serving plate. Serve with ice cream or whipped cream or whipped topping.
MAKES 6 TO 8 SERVINGS.

Cheese Cookies

 ½ *cup butter*
 2 *cups grated Cheddar cheese*
 1 *cup all-purpose flour*
 3 *tablespoons onion soup*

In a large bowl mix all ingredients together and knead until thoroughly mixed. Roll into a log. Wrap in waxed paper and chill.

Slice ¼-inch thick and place on an ungreased cookie sheet.

Bake in a 325° oven for 10 to 15 minutes.

Freezes well cooked or uncooked. Serve as an hors d'oeuvres.
MAKES ABOUT 3 DOZEN.

Cranberry Coconut Muffins

 1 *cup cranberries*
 2 *cups all-purpose flour*
 2 *eggs*
 ¾ *cup sugar*
 ¼ *cup oil*
 1 *teaspoon vanilla extract*
 1 *teaspoon baking soda*
 1 *tablespoon baking powder*
 ¼ *teaspoon ground cinnamon*
 ¼ *teaspoon salt*
1¼ *cups buttermilk*
 ¾ *cup coconut*

In a small bowl coat the cranberries with ½ cup of flour. In a large bowl beat the eggs until foamy. Add the sugar, oil, and vanilla. In a medium bowl combine the remaining flour, baking soda, baking powder, cinnamon, and salt. Add the dry ingredients to the batter alternately with the buttermilk. Mix in the cranberries and coconut. Bake in a 400° oven for 18 to 20 minutes.
MAKES 18 MUFFINS.

Bison Burger

 2 *pounds ground bison*
1½ *teaspoon salt*
 1 *teaspoon Worcestershire sauce*
 ½ *teaspoon garlic powder*
 1 *egg*
 ½ *teaspoon pepper*
 1 *tablespoon dry mustard*
 1 *teaspoon cumin*
 1 *teaspoon powdered onion*

In a large bowl combine all the ingredients and form into patties. Barbecue on a grill or broil or fry at medium heat for 5 minutes on one side, and flip over and cook 5 minutes on the other side. Serve hot on a toasted bun with desired condiments.

Variation: Use the above recipe, omitting the egg, then stir-fry and add a jar of spaghetti sauce to serve over noodles.
MAKES 4 SERVINGS.

Norwood Bed and Breakfast

❧

201 Norwood Court
Wetaskiwin, Alberta T9A 3P2
Canada
(403) 352-7880

*T*his B&B offers old-fashioned country hospitality. There are two guest rooms furnished with antiques, one of them in Victorian style. A sitting room, library, and Jacuzzi are available for guests' enjoyment. In the Wetaskiwin area are the Reynolds-Alberta Museum, Canada's Aviation Hall of Fame, the Alberta Central Railroad Museum, and a variety of special shops and tea houses.

Sourdough Starter

 1 *cup milk*
 1 *cup all-purpose flour*
 ¼ *cup sugar*

In a medium bowl mix all of the ingredients well and let stand at room temperature for 48 hours.

Feed after every use by adding 1 cup of milk, 1 cup of flour, and ¼ cup sugar.

Applesauce Sourdough Doughnuts

2⅔ cups all-purpose flour
1½ teaspoons baking powder
½ teaspoon baking soda
1 teaspoon salt
½ teaspoon grated nutmeg
½ teaspoon ground cinnamon
¼ cup buttermilk
½ cup starter
2 tablespoons shortening
½ cup sugar
2 egg yolks
½ teaspoon vanilla extract
½ cup applesauce

In a large bowl combine all the ingredients. Mix and knead well. Roll out and cut into doughnuts. Let stand until doubled.

In a deep fryer heat oil to 390° and fry the doughnuts until golden.

Variation: Use 1 whole egg instead of 2 egg yolks, no vanilla, and add ¼ teaspoon of mace instead.

MAKES 2 DOZEN.

Rolled Biscuits Sourdough

1 cup starter
2 tablespoons oil
1 cup all-purpose flour
2 teaspoon baking powder
½ teaspoon baking soda
½ teaspoon salt

In a large bowl mix the starter and oil. In a separate bowl sift together the flour, baking powder, soda, salt, and add to the starter and oil. Roll the mixture on a floured board until ½-inch thick. Cut biscuits, place on a baking sheet, and let rise for 15 minutes.

Bake in a 425° oven for 10 to 12 minutes.

MAKES ABOUT 1 DOZEN.

Chocolate Cake Sourdough

½ cup starter
1 cup water
¼ cup nonfat dry milk
1½ cups all-purpose flour
....

1 cup sugar
½ cup shortening
1 teaspoon vanilla extract
1½ teaspoons soda
1 teaspoon cinnamon
½ teaspoon salt
2 eggs
3 semi-sweet chocolate squares melted

In a medium bowl mix the starter, water, dry milk, and flour, cover with plastic wrap, and let stand for 2 to 3 hours until bubbly.

In a separate bowl cream together the sugar, shortening, vanilla, soda, cinnamon, and salt. Add the eggs one at a time, beating well after each addition. Add the starter mixture and mix well. Pour into 3 9-inch round pans or 1 9 x 13-inch pan. Bake in a 350° oven for 25 to 30 minutes.

MAKES 8 SERVINGS.

Amish Waffle Batter

1 cup all-purpose flour
1 cup sifted cake flour
1½ cups milk
2½ teaspoons baking powder
2 eggs, well beaten
5 tablespoons butter
1 teaspoon vanilla extract
....

1⅔ cups water
⅔ cup sugar
2 tablespoons white corn syrup
8 ounces frozen raspberries
2 drops red food coloring
2 tablespoons cornstarch
1 3-ounce box raspberry gelatin
8 ounces frozen blueberries

In a large bowl combine the flours, milk, baking powder, eggs, butter, and vanilla in order just until smooth. Bake in a hot waffle iron.

In a saucepan combine the water, sugar, corn syrup, coloring, and cornstarch and cook over medium heat until thickened. Remove the pan from the heat, add the gelatin, and stir until dissolved. Let cool. Add the berries. Serve warm over waffles with a scoop of vanilla ice cream or whipped topping.

MAKES 4 SERVINGS.

Raspberry Kuchen

1 egg, well beaten
½ cup sugar
½ cup milk
2 tablespoons oil
1 cup all-purpose flour
2 teaspoon baking powder
1 cup fresh raspberries
....
½ cup all-purpose flour
½ cup sugar
3 tablespoons butter

In a medium bowl combine the egg, ½ cup of sugar, milk, and oil, and mix well. In a separate bowl sift together the flour and baking powder. Stir the dry ingredients into the egg mixture.

Pour into a greased 8-inch pan. Sprinkle raspberries over the batter. In a small bowl combine ½ cup of flour and ½ cup of sugar. Cut in the butter until the mixture resembles coarse crumbs. Sprinkle the topping over the raspberries. Bake in a 375° oven for 25 to 30 minutes or until a toothpick inserted in the center comes out clean.

MAKES 16 SQUARES.

Chocolate-Dipped Fruit

1 cup semisweet chocolate chips
1 to 2 tablespoons shortening
1 6-ounce package dried apricots
1 pint fresh strawberries

In a saucepan melt the chocolate chips and shortening over low heat, stirring constantly until smooth. Spear the fruit with toothpicks into chocolate. Place on waxed paper or stick the toothpicns into a block of styrofoam until hardened.

After set, arrange on a serving plate and enjoy.

MAKES ABOUT 6 TO 8 SERVINGS.

Two Hour Bread or Buns

3 cups hot water
½ cup sugar
6 tablespoons light olive oil
1 teaspoon salt
2 eggs (or egg substitute)
2 tablespoons fast rising instant yeast
2 teaspoons whole wheat flour
7 to 8 cups all-purpose flour

In a large bowl combine the hot water, sugar, oil, eggs, yeast, and whole wheat flour with a wooden spoon. Add 7 to 8 cups of flour to get it past the stick stage. After it can no longer be stirred with a spoon, turn the dough onto a floured surface and knead it. Cover the lightly oiled bowl with a tea towel and let rise for 15 minutes. Punch down, knead, and let rise twice more.

Divide the risen dough into 4 equal parts and shape into loaves. Place in a lightly oiled loaf pans. Let rise for about 30 minutes until doubled. Bake in a 350° oven for 25 minutes.

Note: This can also be made into buns or cinnamon buns. Or use only white flour for a light weight bread or buns.

MAKES 4 LOAVES.

Helens Bed and Breakfast
❧

302 East Fifth Street
North Vancouver, British Columbia V7L 1L1
Canada
(604) 985-4869

A Victorian home in North Vancouver, Helens is just across the inlet from one of North America's most dynamic cities and busiest harbors. The B&B offers antique decor, elegant dining, and a view of the Vancouver cityscape.

High Energy Muffins

- ½ **cup whole wheat flour**
- ½ **cup soy flour**
- ½ **cup wheat germ**
- ⅓ **cup nonfat dry milk**
- 1 **teaspoon salt**
- 1 **cup milk**
- 3 **teaspoons baking powder**
- 3 **tablespoons firmly packed brown sugar**
- ⅓ **cup chopped nuts**
- ⅓ **teaspoon ground mace**
- 3 **tablespoons oil**
- 1 **egg**

In a large bowl combine all the ingredients and mix just until moistened. Fill greased muffin cups. Bake in a 350° oven for 20 minutes.

MAKES 1 DOZEN.

Zucchini Pancakes

- 2 **cup grated zucchini**
- 1 **cup grated carrots**
- ½ **cup grated onion**
- 2 **eggs**
- 1 **teaspoon salt**
- 1 **teaspoon baking powder**
  Chopped parsley
  Pepper
- 1 **cup all-purpose flour**

In a large bowl combine all of the ingredients, and mix well. In a large skillet heat a little oil. Spoon ½ ladle of batter into the hot skillet and cook on both sides.

Hint: To prevent the pancakes from sticking, rub a raw potato over the griddle.

MAKES 4 TO 6 SERVINGS.

Microwave Cranberry Relish

- 1 **16-ounce package fresh cranberries**
- 1 **medium orange, chopped**
- 1 **lime, chopped**
- 2 **tablespoons ginger, finely chopped**
- 1 **cup sugar**
- ¼ **cup water**

In a 10-cup microwave-safe bowl combine combine the cranberries, orange, lime, ginger, sugar, and water, and microwave uncovered on high for 13 minutes, stirring 4 times.

Pour into jars and seal. This will last 1 year.

MAKES ABOUT 4 HALF-PINTS.

Laburnum Cottage

Laburnum Cottage Bed & Breakfast
❧

1388 Terrace Avenue
North Vancouver, British Columbia V7R 1B4
Canada
(604) 988-4877

T his charming home is set in an English garden surrounded by virgin forest and has a richly Victorian feeling. Yet it is only fifteen minutes from the bustle of downtown Vancouver or Horseshoe Bay. Vancouver and the surrounding mountains offer an unusual combination of wilderness and big city attractions.

Cherry Nut Loaf

- 1 **cup brown sugar**
- ¼ **cup butter**
- 1 **egg, beaten**
- 1 **6-ounce jar maraschino cherries**
- 2 **cups all-purpose flour**
- 2 **teaspoons baking powder**
- ½ **teaspoon salt**

In a large bowl combine the brown sugar, butter, and egg. Pour the juice from the cherries in a cup and fill with milk. Add the liquid mixture to the batter. In a separate bowl sift together the flour, baking powder, and salt. Add the dry ingredients to the batter, and fold in the cherries cut in half. Add the nuts. Mix well and pour into a greased 5 x 9-inch loaf pan. Let stand 20 minutes before baking. Bake in a 350° oven for 45 minutes.

MAKES 1 LOAF.

Cheese Soda Bread

- 3 **cups all-purpose flour**
- 3 **teaspoons baking powder**
- 1 **teaspoon baking soda**
- 1 **teaspoon salt**
- 1 **cup whole wheat flour**

¼ cup shortening
1¾ cups buttermilk
1 medium egg
2 cups grated old Cheddar cheese

In a large bowl combine the flour, baking powder, baking soda, and salt. Add the whole wheat flour and blend lightly with a fork. Add the shortening and cut in finely. Measure the buttermilk, add the egg, and beat together with a fork. Add to the dry ingredients along with the cheese and stir gently just to blend. Turn out on a floured surface and knead gently about 10 times. Do not overknead.

Shape into a round and place on a greased baking sheet. Press the top down slightly to level and cut a cross ½-inch deep with a sharp knife to allow for expansion and even baking. Bake in a 375° oven for about 1 hour or until well browned.

Serve warm or cold. Best eaten the day it is made.

MAKES 1 LOAF.

Captain's Passage

1510 Beddis Road
Salt Spring Island, British Columbia V8K 2E3
Canada
(604) 537-9469

Relax in the spacious, comfortable rooms with private baths and entrances, and wonderful ocean views of other islands and marine traffic, close enough to hear the water. Enjoy the variety of birds, animals, and marine life, walk to one of Salt Spring's best beaches, or read. The combination of hospitality, comfort, and privacy makes this unique bed and breakfast an ideal getaway.

Captain's Passage

British Columbia Peach Pancakes

2½ cups all-purpose flour
6 teaspoons baking powder
2 tablespoons sugar
1 teaspoon salt
1½ cups milk (or one-third peach juice)
4 eggs
¼ cup butter, melted
1 16-ounce can chopped peaches (or equivalent fresh)
½ cup raisins soaked in rum (optional)
 Cinnamon to taste

In a large bowl combine the flour, baking powder, sugar, and salt. Add the eggs and butter, and slowly add enough milk to achieve a thick batter. Add the In a skillet heat a small amount of butter and ladle the batter into the skillet. Cook until golden on each side. Serve with fruit or maple syrup.

MAKES 6 SERVINGS.

Hastings House

160 Upper Ganges Road
Salt Spring Island, British Columbia V8K 2S2
Canada
(604) 537-2362

The Hasting House is a wonder for those who love the woody half-timbered Tudor style, but it has much more to offer than architec-

ture. On British Columbia's Salt Spring Island, the inn is set on a thirty-acre seaside estate. Giant stone or brick fireplaces, heavy ceiling timbers, and classic furnishings provide a rich, manor house atmosphere. The views through the many-paned windows are of garden, forest, and sea. The Hastings is widely known for its food.

Sockeye Salmon Tartar with Basil Oil

12 ounces (300 g) cleaned sockeye salmon fillets
2 ounces (50 g) smoked salmon
1 tablespoon Dijon mustard
1 teaspoon catsup
1 teaspoon red wine vinegar
1 egg yolk
2 anchovies
2 tablespoons chopped shallots
2 tablespoons chopped capers
1 teaspoon lemon juice
1 teaspoon cognac
 Salt and pepper to taste
 Tabasco sauce to taste
 Worcestershire sauce to taste
 Cayenne pepper to taste
 Basil oil
¼ cup (50 g) chopped basil leaves
½ cup (100 ml) extra virgin olive oil

Coarsely chop the salmon and the smoked salmon. Add the mustard, catsup, red wine vinegar, egg yolk, anchovies, shallots, capers, lemon juice, cognac, salt, pepper, Tabasco, Worcestershire, and cayenne to taste, and mix well. Season to taste. In a blender purée the basil and olive oil. Arrange the tartar on a plate. Drizzle with the basil oil.

Serve with toast or potato pancakes and champagne.

MAKES 4 SERVINGS.

Salt Roasted Duck and Blackberries

1 whole duck
2 ounces (60 g) coarse salt
½ bunch parsley
2 cloves garlic
1 medium onion, cut in pieces

⅔   *cup (120 g) sugar*
⅓   *cup (100 ml) red wine vinegar*
⅔   *cup (200 ml) duck sauce*
⅔   *cup (200 g) blackberries*
  Salt and pepper to taste
  Tabasco sauce to taste

Rub the inside and outside of the duck with salt. Stuff with parsley, garlic, and cut onion. Place on a roasting rack in a 350° oven for 2 hours and 30 minutes or until nice and crispy.

In a saucepan caramelize the sugar. Add the vinegar and duck stock, and cook for about 20 minutes. Add the blackberries and simmer for 15 minutes. Season with salt, pepper, and Tabasco to taste.

MAKES 4 SERVINGS.

Venison Loin with Sesame Crust

1   *tablespoon chopped fresh thyme*
1   *tablespoon chopped fresh parsley*
1   *tablespoon chopped fresh basil*
1   *tablespoon chopped fresh sage*
3   *tablespoons sesame seeds*
1½   *pounds (600 g) cleaned venison loin*
  Salt and pepper to taste
2   *tablespoons Dijon mustard*
2   *tablespoons grape seed oil*

In a small bowl mix the chopped herbs with the sesame seeds. Season the venison loin with salt and pepper, brush with mustard, and coat with the herb-sesame mixture. In a skillet Hheat the grape seed oil until very hot, and roast the meat on both sides.

Reduce the heat, cook slowly, and glaze for 5 to 6 minutes. Set the meat aside, and allow to rest a few minutes.

MAKES 4 SERVINGS.

The Old Farmhouse

The Old Farmhouse Bed and Breakfast

❧

1077 North End Road
Salt Spring Island, British Columbia V8K 1L9
Canada
(604) 537-4113

Settled among tall trees, orchards, and meadows, this recently restored century-old Heritage farmhouse is on Salt Spring Island. Guest rooms lead to carefully tended gardens with herbs, overstuffed flower beds, and towering fir trees. The Farmhouse is known for its food, and guests are invited to visit the kitchen.

Poached Eggs on Polenta with Bearnaise Sauce

4   *cups water*
1½   *cups cornmeal*
½   *teaspoon salt*
3   *teaspoons salt*
3   *tablespoons butter*
....
1   *cup butter*
3   *egg yolks*
¼   *cup white wine vinegar*
¼   *cup white wine*
1   *shallot, chopped*
1   *teaspoon butter*
1   *teaspoon pepercorns*
  Salt and pepper to taste
  Pinch cayenne pepper
  Fresh tarragon
....
  Water
¼   *cup vinegar*
6   *eggs*

In a stockpot bring 4 cups of water to a boil. Very slowly add the cornmeal, stir vigorously, and simmer for 15 minutes. Stir in the butter, and spread the polenta on a flat surface. Let cool. Cut out circles with a cookie cutter. In a large frying pan melt a little bit of butter and sauté the polenta on both sides. Keep warm.

In a saucepan clarify the butter. Set aside. In a small saucepan combine the vinegar, wine, shallot, peppercorns, and butter. Place on high heat and reduce to 3 tablespoons of liquid. Cool, and strain into a bowl. Add the 3 egg yolks, and place the bowl over simmering water. The bowl must not touch the water. With a wire whisk, slowly add the clarified butter 1 tablespoon at a time. Take care to keep the water under the bowl from being too hot, or the sauce will curdle. Season with salt, pepper, cayenne, and tarragon.

In a large pot bring an inch of water to a boil. Add the vinegar. Break the eggs one at a time into a cup and slide into the water. Poach for 3 minutes.

Place the warm polenta on a dinner plate. Place the poached eggs on the polenta, and pour some Bearnaise sauce over the egg. Place under the broiler for about 2 minutes.

MAKES ABOUT 6 SERVINGS.

Weston Lake Inn

❧

813 Beaver Point Road
Salt Spring Island, British Columbia V8K 1X9
Canada
(250) 653-4311

Guests enjoy a fine view of landscaped gardens, woodlands, pastures, and serene Weston Lake. The inn is a country home offering three tastefully appointed guest rooms with private baths, down duvets, loveseats, and plenty of fresh flowers. On Salt Spring Island, it places guests in the center of one of Canada's best-loved retreats.

Blueberry-Yogurt Bran Muffins

2   cups yogurt
2   teaspoons baking soda
....

1   cup blueberries
1   tablespoon all-purpose flour
....

1½   cups packed brown sugar
2   eggs
1   cup oil
2   cups bran
2   teaspoons vanilla extract
....

2   cups all-purpose flour
4   teaspoons baking powder
½   teaspoon salt

In a medium bowl combine the yogurt and soda. Set aside. In a medium bowl toss the blueberries with 1 tablespoon of flour and set aside. In a large bowl mix the brown sugar, eggs, and oil until fluffy. Add the bran and vanilla. In a separate bowl sift the flour, baking powder, and salt. Add to the sugar mixture alternately with the yogurt. Fold in the blueberries. Pour into greased muffin cups. Bake in a 350° oven for 25 to 30 minutes.

MAKES 15 LARGE MUFFINS.

Three-Cheese Scones

1   egg
1   egg yolk
½   cup light cream
½   cup shredded Swiss cheese
½   cup shredded old Cheddar cheese
¼   cup freshly grated Parmesan cheese
2   cups all-purpose flour
4   teaspoons baking powder
½   teaspoon salt
¼   cup butter
....

1   egg white
    Grated Parmesan cheese

In a small bowl beat the egg, egg yolk, and cream lightly with a fork until blended. In a large bowl mix the cheeses. In a food processor mix the flour, baking powder, and salt. Add the cold butter, and process until coarse. Add the contents of the food processor to the cheeses, tossing together. Add the egg mixture all at once, stirring with a fork. Press into a ball and knead gently on a floured surface no more than 10 times. Roll into a circle

½-inch thick. Score into 8 or 12 triangles, brush with egg white, and sprinkle with Parmesan. Bake in a 425° oven for 12 to 15 minutes.

MAKES 8 TO 12 TRIANGLES.

Borthwick Country Manor

❧

9750 Ardmore Drive, R.R. 2
Sidney, British Columbia V8L 5H5
Canada
(604) 656-9498

---

*A*n English Tudor manor on the scenic Saanich Peninsula, the Borthwick offers meticulously landscaped gardens, an outdoor hot tub, and a nearby beach. Only minutes away are the world famous Butchart Gardens, Victoria Butterfly Gardens, and the old London-like town of Victoria.

Bran Scones

1   cup milk
1   egg
1   cup Post 100% Bran Cereal
1¾   cups all-purpose flour
3   tablespoons sugar
1   tablespoon baking powder
⅓   cup butter

In a medium bowl blend the milk, egg, and bran cereal. Set aside. In a large bowl mix the flour, sugar, and baking powder. Cut in the butter until crumbly. Add the cereal mixture, mixing until moistened. Turn onto a lightly floured surface, and knead 10 to 12 times. Divide in half. Pat each into a 6-inch circle. Place on an ungreased baking sheet, and score each into 6 or 8 wedges. Bake in a 425° oven for 15 minutes or until golden brown.

MAKES 16 SMALL SCONES.

Johnson House

Johnson House

❧

2278 West 34th Avenue
Vancouver, British Columbia V6M 1G6
Canada
(604) 266-4175

A restored 1920s Craftsman-style home, the Johnson House is furnished throughout with antiques. There are also delightful collections of hobby horses, coffee grinders, morning glory Victrolas, clocks, and toys. The main floor has French doors, cottage windows, and a big, homey living room with fireplace. The guest rooms are romantically furnished and offer views of the city skyline or mountains.

Whole Wheat-Oatmeal Pancakes

1   cup whole wheat unbleached flour
1   cup quick-cooking rolled oats
1   teaspoon baking powder
1   teaspoon baking soda
3   tablespoons sugar
1   teaspoon salt
....

2   eggs
4   tablespoons oil
2   cups buttermilk
2   teaspoons vanilla extract

In a large bowl combine the flour, oats, baking powder, soda, sugar, and salt. In a separate bowl combine the eggs, oil, buttermilk, and vanilla, and beat with a fork. Add the liquid to the dry ingredients and mix until just blended. Let sit 5 minutes. Cook on a lightly buttered griddle. Serve with real maple syrup or fruit syrup.

MAKES 4 SERVINGS.

Healthy Apple-Spice Muffins

1½ cups firmly packed brown or
     demarra sugar
⅔ cup oil
1 large egg
2 teaspoons vanilla extract
1⅛ cups buttermilk
2 teaspoons apple cider vinegar
....
1¼ cups unbleached whole wheat flour
1¼ cups unbleached white flour
1½ teaspoons baking soda
2 teaspoons cinnamon
1 teaspoon nutmeg
½ teaspoon salt
2½ cups chopped apple (leave the skin
     on)
½ cup walnuts or pecans

Grease or spray muffin cups with cooking spray. In a medium bowl combine the sugar and oil. Add the egg, vanilla, buttermilk, and vinegar, and mix well. In a large bowl combine the flours, soda, cinnamon, nutmeg, and salt. Add the liquid mixture and stir just until moistened. Fold in the apple and walnuts. Pour into the prepared muffin cups. Bake in a 325° oven for 30 minutes.

MAKES 15 TO 18 MUFFINS.

Beaconsfield Inn

❧

998 Humboldt Street
Victoria, British Columbia V8V 2Z8
Canada
(604) 384-4044

*F*ew cities are more British in flavor than Victoria, the capital of British Columbia. With its formal

Beaconsfield Inn

gardens, lamppost flower baskets, quaint pubs, and penchant for afternoon tea, the city makes visitors think they are in London. The Beaconsfield Inn places guests in the heart of this gracious old Victorian town. It is only one block from Beacon Hill Park and four blocks from the bustling waterfront. Like Victoria itself, the inn turns back the clock with its polished-panel Edwardian-era interior. Guest rooms feature goose-down comforters, claw-foot tubs, Jacuzzis, skylights, and English antiques.

Cheese, Apple, Amaretto Omelet

2 tablespoons butter
3 tablespoons sugar
1 apple, peeled, cored, thinly sliced
1 tablespoons amaretto liqueur (or ½
     teaspoon almond extract)
1½ tablespoons cream cheese, softened
....
4 eggs, at room temperature
2 tablespoons cream or milk
     Dash salt and pepper
2 teaspoons butter

In a skillet melt the butter and add the sugar. SautÈ the apples until tender. Stir in the amaretto and remove the pan from the heat. Cover and set aside to keep warm.

In a medium bowl beat together the eggs, cream, salt, and pepper. Melt 1 teaspoon of butter in a hot omelet pan. Pour half of the egg mixture into the pan. When the eggs have set, cover with half the apple mixture. Top with half the cream cheese and continue cooking for 1 minutes. Cut the omelet in half

and fold or roll, and slide out of the pan onto a heated serving dish. Repeat with the remaining ingredients to make a second omelet. Serve each immediately.

MAKES 4 SERVINGS.

Mushroom Shrimp Croissants

4 large croissants
¼ cup butter
8 eggs
¼ cup milk
1 tablespoon minced fresh dill
½ cup finely chopped mushrooms
⅓ cup shrimp (or finely chopped
     cooked spinach, drained)
½ cup shredded Monterey Jack cheese

Warm the croissants in a 225° oven for 5 to 10 minutes.

In a medium skillet melt the butter. In a large bowl beat the eggs and milk. Add the dill, mushrooms, and shrimp. Pour into the skillet and scramble until creamy. Remove the croissants from the oven and slice lengthwise about three-fourths of the way through. Fill the croissants with the egg mixture, and sprinkle with cheese. Broil the croissants open-face just until the cheese melts. Serve immediately.

MAKES 4 SERVINGS.

Swallow Hill Farm

❧

4910 William Head Road
Victoria, British Columbia V9B 5T7
Canada
(604) 474-4042

Swallow Hill Farm

Guests enjoy spectacular mountain and ocean views at this four-acre farm. They can also watch for deer, hawks, seals, eagles, otters, and other wildlife that frequent the area. While it is way out in the country, the Swallow Hill offers plenty of creature comforts such as featherbeds, duvets, and sumptuous breakfasts.

Yummy Ginger Cookies

    4   cups all-purpose flour
    2   teaspoons baking soda
    2   teaspoons ground cinnamon
    2   teaspoons ground cloves
    2   teaspoons ground ginger
 1 1/2 cups margarine or butter
    2   cups sugar
    2   eggs
   1/2 cup molasses

In a medium bowl combine the flour, baking soda, cinnamon, cloves, and ginger. Set aside. In a large bowl beat the margarine, sugar, eggs, and molasses. Add the dry ingredients and mix well. Roll out the dough for cut cookies or spoon out onto a cookie sheet. Bake in a 375° oven for 8 to 10 minutes.

MAKES ABOUT 4 DOZEN.

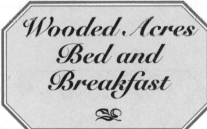

Wooded Acres
Bed and
Breakfast

4907 Rocky Point Road, R.R. #2
Victoria, British Columbia V9B 5B4
Canada
(604) 478-8172

*T**hree wooded acres shelter this B&B, which offers a pair of well-appointed suites to Vancouver Island visitors. The rural setting is peaceful, but guests are close*

enough to Victoria to enjoy all its British-style charm.

Banana Chocolate Chip Muffins

    2   cups all-purpose flour
    2   teaspoons baking powder
   1/2 teaspoon salt
        Pinch cream of tartar
   1/2 cup butter
    1   cup sugar
    2   eggs
   1/2 cup milk
    1   teaspoon vanilla extract
    1   banana, mashed
   1/2 cup miniature chocolate chips

In a large bowl combine the flour, baking powder, salt, and cream of tartar. Mix dry Make a well in the center. In a medium bowl cream the butter. Add the sugar and mix well. Beat in the eggs one at a time, and add the milk and vanilla. Blend in the banana. Pour the liquid ingredients into the well. Stir just until moistened. Add the banana and chocolate chips, and mix quickly. Bake in a 400° oven for 20 to 25 minutes.

MAKES 9 LARGE MUFFINS.

Wooded Acres

Apple Strudel Bake

    6   apples, sliced
 1 1/4 cups sugar
    2   teaspoons cinnamon
        Pinch of salt
        ....
 2 1/2 cups all-purpose flour
    2   teaspoons sugar
   1/2 teaspoon salt
    1   cup shortening
    2   egg yolks
        Cold milk
  Raisins or dried cranberries

In a large bowl combine the apples, sugar, cinnamon, and a pinch of salt. In a separate bowl combine the flour, sugar, and salt. Cut in the shortening and mix as for pastry

In a cup beat the egg yolks. Add the cold milk to make 2/3 cup. Mix into the crust a little at a time as for pastry. Be gentle for a tender crust. Gently press a good 1/2 portion of the dough into an 11 x 14-inch cookie sheet. The crust is quite "short" and a little difficult to roll. Remember to be gentle.

Crumble 2 cups of bran flakes over the crust, and a handful or raisins or dried cranberries if desired. Spread the apple mix over the bran flakes. Top with the remaining crust. Beat 2 egg whites until frothy, and spread over the crust. Bake in a 400° oven for 25 minutes or until the apples are tender.

MAKES 6 SERVINGS.

Golden Dreams

6412 Easy Street
Whistler, British Columbia, V0N 1B6
Canada
(800) 668-7055

*T**his small, cozy inn offers guests a change to "get away from it all" in the setting of a small mountain village. The three guest rooms are individually decorated to reflect Aztec, Victorian, and Oriental themes. Guests particularly enjoy the beautiful views of the surrounding mountains. Golden Dreams is conveniently located to Whistler Village as well as golfing, tennis, swimming, and skiing activities.*

Delightful Blueberry Custard

    3   tablespoons butter
    8   eggs
   1/2 teaspoon salt
   2/3 cups all-purpose flour
    1   cup fresh or frozen blueberries

¼ *cup honey*
2½ *cups milk*
1 *teaspoon vanilla extract*
   Hot jam or maple syrup for driz-
      zling
   Nutmeg and confectioners' sugar for
      sprinkling

In a large baking dish or 9 x 13-inch pan melt the butter. In a blender combine the eggs, salt, flour, honey, milk, and vanilla. Pour into the preheated baking dish of melted butter and sprinkle with blueberries. Bake in a 425° oven for 20 to 15 minutes until puffed and golden.

Drizzle with hot jam or maple syrup. Sprinkle with nutmeg and confectioners' sugar. In the summer, garnish with fresh raspberries and mint from the garden.

MAKES 6 TO 8 SERVINGS.

Banana Poppy Seed Pancakes

3 *cups whole wheat flour*
2 *teaspoons baking powder*
2 *teaspoons baking soda*
1 *teaspoon salt*
½ *cup firmly packed brown sugar*
½ *teaspoon nutmeg*
4 *eggs*
2 *cups milk*
1 *teaspoon vanilla extract*
2 *bananas*
¼ *cup poppy seeds*
   Confectioners' sugar
   Flavored yogurt

In a large bowl combine the dry ingredients (even the night before to save time!). In a blender whirl up the wet ingredients. Quarter the bananas lengthwise and then chop into pieces, add these and the poppy seeds to the dry ingredients. Fold in the liquid mixture to form an even batter.

Fry about 3 tablespoons of batter on a nonstick electric griddle, turning once. Be creative on the size and the extras that you have on hand. (Chocolate chips, toasted almonds, coconut, sunflower seeds, raisins etc.)

Serve sprinkled with confectioners' sugar and a generous slathering of flavored yogurt. Garnish with fresh or frozen strawberries and top with toasted almonds.

MAKES 4 TO 6 SERVINGS.

Dorrington Bed and Breakfast

❧

13851 19A Avenue
White Rock, British Columbia V4A 9M2
Canada
(604) 535-4408

***T**he Dorrington offers a pampering, seven-hundred-square-foot suite with canopied bed, fireplace, Jacuzzi, and warmed marble. A second suite is equally luxurious but not quite so large. Only five minutes away is the White Rock Beach promenade where couples can stroll and enjoy a cappuccino at a sidewalk café.*

Tea Scones

3 *cups all-purpose flour*
½ *cup sugar*
4 *teaspoon baking powder*
½ *teaspoon salt*
½ *cup butter or margarine*
1 *tablespoons orange or lemon rind*
½ *cup raisins or currants*
2 *eggs*
   Milk

In a large bowl mix the flour, sugar, baking powder, and salt together. Cut in the butter to make a crumb-like mixture. Stir in the orange rind and raisins.

In a 1-cup measuring cup beat the eggs. Add milk to measure 1 cup. Stir lightly into the dry mixture to form a soft dough. Roll out the dough to ½-inch thickness. Cut in rounds with a cutter. Place on a lightly greased cookie sheet. Bake in a 450° oven for 15 minutes.

Serve with butter, strawberry jam and Devon Cream.

MAKES ABOUT 1 DOZEN.

Morning B&B Saver

16 *slices white bread, with crusts*
      removed
   Slices Canadian back bacon or ham
   Slices sharp Cheddar cheese
6 *eggs*
½ *teaspoon salt*
½ *teaspoon pepper*
½ *to 1 teaspoon dry mustard*
¼ *cup minced onion*
¼ *cup green pepper, finely chopped*
1 *to 2 teaspoon Worcestershire Sauce*
3 *cups whole milk*
   Dash Tabasco sauce
½ *cup butter*
   Crushed Special K or Corn Flakes

In a buttered 9-inch glass baking dish place 8 pieces of bread. Add bread pieces to cover the dish entirely. Cover the bread with thin slices of back bacon. Lay slices of Cheddar cheese on top of the bacon and then cover with slices of bread to make it like a sandwich. In a medium bowl beat the eggs with salt and pepper. Add the dry mustard, onion, green pepper, Worcestershire sauce, milk, and Tabasco.

Pour over the sandwiches, cover, and refrigerate overnight.

In the morning, melt the butter and pour over the top.

Cover with the crushed Special K or Corn Flakes.

Bake uncovered in a 350° oven for 1 hour. Let sit for 10 minutes before serving.

Serve with fresh cup-up fruit and salsa.

MAKES 6 SERVINGS.

Mecklenburgh Inn

❧

78 Queen Street
Chester, Nova Scotia B0J 1J0
Canada
(902) 275-4638

***L**ocated in the heart of the renowned seaside village of Chester, the inn dates to 1890. Guests can enjoy wandering the village's his-*

toric streets and browsing through its craft shops and boutiques. Halifax, with its active nightlife and bustling harbor, is about forty-five minutes away by car.

Mecklenburgh Inn

Eggs Benedict with a Twist

> 1   **cup heavy cream**
> 4   **ounces Gorgonzola cheese**
> 8   **eggs**
> 1   **pound salmon**
>   **White wine**
>   **Bouquet garni**
> 4   **English muffins**

In a medium bowl whip the cream to a soft consistency. Whip in the softened gorgonzola cheese.

In a large pan poach the salmon in simmering water with white wine and a bouquet garni. Poach the eggs to the desired doneness. Toast the muffins. Arrange the salmon on the muffins. Top with poached eggs. Pour the gorgonzola mixture over the eggs. Serve with hash browns.

MAKES 4 SERVINGS.

Mecklenburgh Omelets

> 4   **eggs**
>   **Salt and pepper to taste**
>   **Fresh basil to taste**
> 2   **tablespoons butter**
> ½   **cup chopped marinated artichokes**
> ¼   **cup chopped sundried tomatoes**
> ½   **cup shredded asiago cheese**
> ¼   **cup chopped scallions**

In a medium bowl whip the eggs with salt, pepper and fresh basil. In an omelet pan melt 1 tablespoon of butter. Add half of the egg mixture, and cook until it begins to set. Sprinkle the remaining ingredients on top.

Slide the omelet pan under the broiler until the cheese is brown and the mixture puffs up. Repeat the procedure for the second omelet. Don't fold them over. Serve open-faced.

MAKES 2 SERVINGS.

The Old Rectory Bed and Breakfast

❦

R.R. #1
Port Williams, Nova Scotia B0P 1T0
Canada
(902) 542-1815

---

*T**he Old Rectory offers three guest rooms, home-cooked breakfasts, and a relaxed atmosphere. All around the home are tall trees and orchards. Enjoy the apple harvest, birdwatching, hiking, or agate and amythest collecting.*

Fruit Duff

> 2   **tablespoons butter**
> 1   **cup all-purpose flour**
> ½   **cup sugar**
>   **Pinch salt**
> ⅔   **cup milk**
> 2   **cups chopped fruit or berries**

In a 6- to 7-inch cast iron frying pan pan melt the butter. In a medium bowl mix the dry ingredients. Add the milk and stir to make a batter. Spoon over the melted butter. Top with fruit. Bake in a 350° oven for 30 minutes,

MAKES 4 SERVINGS.

Maritime Brown Bread

> 1½   **cup cornmeal**
> 1½   **cups oatmeal**
> 3   **tablespoons salt**
> 5   **tablespoons vegetable oil**
> 4   **cups boiling water**
> 4   **cup cold water**
> 1½   **cups molasses**
> 3   **tablespoons yeast**

In a large bowl combine the cornmeal, oats, salt, and oil. Add the boiling water. Cool some. Add the cold water and molasses. Sprinkle the yeast on top. Let the mixture stand for 10 to 15 minutes. Stir and add flour to knead. Knead for 10 minutes. Let the dough rise. Shape into loaves and let rise again.

Bake in a 325° oven for 50 to 60 minutes.

MAKES 2 LOAVES.

Salmon River House

❦

9931 #7 Highway
Salmon River Bridge, Nova Scotia B0J 1P0
Canada
(902) 889-3353, (800) 565-3353

---

*S**et back in the woods on cliffs above the Salmon River, this B&B is a favorite of sportsmen. This is no rustic lodge, however, but a quiet retreat with a library and all the comforts one could ask. The six guest rooms feature distinctive country decor. Boating, hiking, fishing, hunting, beachcombing, dining, and a quaint "Craft Cottage" are all offered on site.*

Chicken Crêpes Acadienne

> ¼   **cup butter or lite margarine**
> ½   **cup sliced fresh mushrooms**
> 2   **cups white sauce**
> 1   **cup chicken broth or chicken stock**
> ½   **cup lite mayonnaise**
> ¼   **cup cream (optional)**
> 2   **cups diced cooked chicken**
> ¼   **cup grated Swiss cheese**

In a large skillet melt the butter and lightly sautè the mushrooms. Add half of the white sauce and all remaining ingredients except the Swiss cheese. Heat over low to medium

Salmon River House

heat until thickened and bubbly. Spoon into crepes and fold over.

Mix the Swiss cheese into the remaining white sauce, and heat thoroughly.

Pour over the crêpes, and garnish with chopped chives or fresh parsley.

MAKES 6 TO 8 CRÊPES.

French Crêpe Batter

  2 *eggs*
1¼ *cups milk*
  1 *cup all-purpose flour*
  2 *tablespoons oil*

In an electric blender combine the eggs and milk, and blend for 1 minute.

With the blender running slowly, add the flour and continue to blend 1 more minute. Add the vegetable oil and blend for 2 minutes.

The batter may be used immediately, but for best results let stand 1 hour before using.

This batter is excellent for use with an electric crêpe maker, or may be used by pouring a little in a large skillet and titling in a circular motion to coat the pan with a very thin layer. Cook until golden brown.

MAKES 6 TO 8 SERVINGS.

Poached Atlantic Salmon

  4 *salmon steaks 1-inch thick*
  1 *bay leaf*
  1 *carrot, pared and sliced*
  1 *small leek, thinly sliced*
  1 *teaspoon lemon juice*
  1 *sprig fresh parsley*

  1 *small zucchini, julienned*
 ½ *red pepper, julienned*
  1 *bunch fresh asparagus tips (or broccoli)*
 ¼ *pound fresh mushrooms, cleaned and sliced*
  1 *tablespoon lemon juice*
 ½ *cup white wine*

  1 *tablespoons butter*
     Salt and pepper to taste
     Lemon slices and mandarin orange segments for garnish

In a large pot place the fish, add the bay leaf, carrot, leek, 1 teaspoon of lemon juice, and parsley. Add cold water to cover the salmon and bring to a boil over medium heat. Turn the fish over, and let stand for 4 to 5 minutes in hot liquid over low heat.

Meanwhile, in a separate pan combine the remaining vegetables, lemon juice, wine and butter. Cover and cook over medium heat for 3 minutes. Remove the vegetables from the wine liquid and set aside. Continue cooking the liquid over high heat for 4 to 5 minutes to reduce and thicken slightly. Remove the bay leaf. Correct the seasoning with salt and pepper to taste.

Remove the salmon steaks from the poaching liquid and remove the skin. Arrange on a serving plate with julienned vegetables and pour wine liquid over all. Garnish with a lemon slice and mandarin orange segments.

MAKES 4 SERVINGS.

Benmiller Inn
❧

R.R. #4
Goderich, Ontario N0G 1H0
Canada
(519) 524-2191

---

*T*he Benmiller began as a woolen mill in the 1830s. It consists of four buildings offering a total of forty-seven uniquely decorated guest rooms. Located at the edge of the Lake Huron's famed Bruce Peninsula, Goderich offers hiking, skiing, watersports, golf, and beaches. Stratford's famous Shakespearean Festival Theatre is nearby.

Chamber's Farmed Rabbit

  1 *rabbit*

     Olive oil
  1 *onion, roughly cut*
 ½ *carrot, roughly cut*
  1 *celery stalk, roughly cut*
  1 *bulb garlic, cut in half*
  2 *bay leaves*
  3 *peppercorns*
 ½ *bunch fresh thyme*
  4 *cups stock made from rabbit carcass*
  2 *cups white wine*
  1 *cup 35% cream*
     Juice of 1 lime

Remove the hind legs from the rabbit and separate the tenderloin from the forelegs. Use the forelegs and ribs to make the stock. Portion the tenderloin in 4-inch pieces using a cleaver to cut across the spine.

In a stock pot sauté the onion, celery, carrot, garlic, thyme, bay leaves, and peppercorns in enough olive oil that the vegetables to not stick. Season with salt and pepper. When the vegetables become translucent, add the hind legs and allow to sauté for a couple of minutes.

Add the wine and stock to the pot and bring the liquid to a simmer. Cover and braise in a 350° oven for 1 hour and 30 minutes or until the legs are very tender. Remove the rabbit legs carefully from the liquid. Reduce the remaining liquid until a thick sauce forms. Add 1 cup of 35% cream and the lime juice. Simmer for 5 minutes. Pass the liquid through a strainer.

In a heated pan add enough oil to coat the pan lightly. Add the tenderloins of the rabbit. Rotate evenly until the meat is nicely browned on all sides and thoroughly cooked. Warm the legs in rabbit stock until they are heated through, then coat the skin with Pommery mustard. Pour the sauce over the rabbit and serve with vegetables.

MAKES 2 SERVINGS.

Grilled Salmon Fillets with Purée of Shrimp, Coconut, and the Essence of Curry

  6 *6- to 7-ounce portions salmon fillets*
     Butter

4 white cooking onions, diced
2 carrots, thinly sliced
750 ml Zinfandel
4 14-ounce cans coconut milk
1 litre 35% cream
24 black tiger shrimp, shelled and deveined
3 tablespoons milk curry powder
2 teaspoon turmeric
1 banana, sliced

Preheat a grill or barbecue on high, cover.

In a saucepan heat a small amount of butter and sautÈ the onions and carrots until the onions become translucent. Stir in the curry powder and turmeric. Add the Zinfandel and reduce by three-fourths.

Add the shrimp and banana, and cook until the shrimp turns red. In a food processor purée until the mixture is relatively smooth and the shrimp are broken down. Use a blender if an even smoother consistency is desired, Reheat and serve,

Grill the salmon fillets. Using a quality food release spray, spray fillets on one side, then spray the grilling area. Lay sprayed-side down on the prepared area. Before turning the fillet spray the salmon a second time. The salmon is ready to be flipped when the color changes around the outside of the fillet. It is not ready to be flipped if it still sticks to the grill.

Accompany the dish with flavored potato purées and sautéed julienne vegetables.

Pool sauce on a deep plate. Center a large quenelle of potato puree, topped with sautÈed julienne vegetables. Lay 1 portion of grilled salmon on top of vegetables.

MAKES 6 PORTIONS.

Stone Maiden Inn

❧

123 Church Street
Stratford, Ontario N5A 2R3
Canada
(519) 271-7129

Built in 1872 as a private residence, the Victorian Stone Maiden has been welcoming visitors to

Stratford for over a century. It has served as a boarding house and hotel since the early 1900s. Restored to its original elegance, it is now a charming 15-room B&B in the heart of historic Stratford. From May through October, Stratford hosts the annual Shakespearian Festival in honor of the well known Bard of Stratford (England).

Stone Maiden Breakfast Casserole

1 pound line sausage (pork or beef)
10 slices whole wheat bread, cubed
2 cups shredded Cheddar cheese
5 eggs
¾ teaspoon dry mustard
1½ cups milk
1 10½-ounce can mushroom soup
½ soup can milk

Grease a 9 x 13-inch metal or glass pan. In a skillet brown the sausage, and cut into small slices. Scatter the bread in the bottom of the pan, and top with cheese and sausage pieces.

In a medium bowl whisk the eggs, mustard, and 1½ cups of milk together. Pour over the layers. Cover and refrigerate overnight.

In a medium bowl mix the mushroom soup and ½ can of milk together and pour over the casserole. Bake uncovered in a 300° oven for 1 hour.

MAKES 6 TO 8 SERVINGS.

Decadent French Toast

2 tablespoons corn syrup
1 cup firmly packed brown sugar
5 tablespoons margarine or butter
16 (approximately) slices wheat sandwich bread, crusts removed
5 eggs
1½ cups milk
1 teaspoon vanilla extract
½ cup sour cream
1½ cups fresh strawberries, hulled (or 1 10-ounce package unsweetened frozen berries, partially thawed)

In a heavy saucepan combine the corn syrup, brown sugar, and margarine, and heat, stirring constantly until bubbly.

Pour the syrup into a buttered 9 x 13-inch glass or metal pan. Nestle the bread slices into the syrup in the pan, making 2 overlapping layers. Cut the bread to fit into the corners and edges. In a large bowl mix the eggs, milk, and vanilla together and pour over the bread, covering well. Cover and refrigerate overnight.

Bake in a 350° oven for 45 minutes.

To serve, loosen the edges of the bread from the pan sides with a knife, and invert the pan onto a serving plate so the caramel is on top. Cut into serving portions and top each with a tablespoon of sour cream and some berries. Serve immediately.

MAKES 6 TO 8 SERVINGS.

The Inn at Bay Fortune

❧

Souris R.R. #4
Bay Fortune, Prince Edward Island C0A 2B0
Canada
(902) 687-3745

Prince Edward Island is, perhaps, not as widely know as it should be for its scenic beauty, bucolic villages, and warm sea water— warmer, in fact, than any north of the Carolinas. Sitting on 46-acres facing Bay Fortune, the Inn at Bay Fortune allows its guests to enjoy all the island's charms while living and eating in grand style. There are several top-flight golf courses nearby, and Charlottetown, less than an hour away, has a very active night life.

Reuben Bread Pudding with Maple Onion Jam

2 cups milk
2 tablespoon Dijon mustard
½ teaspoon salt
½ teaspoon pepper

3 *eggs*
2 *egg yolks*
8 *ounces rye bread, cut into ½-inch*
cubes
6 *ounces corned beef, cut into ½-inch*
cubes
½ *teaspoon ground caraway*
2 *ounces sauerkraut*
¼ *cup chopped chives*
....

Maple Onion Jam (recipe follows)

In a saucepan simmer the milk, Dijon, caraway, salt, and pepper. Remove the pan from the heat.

In a large bowl whisk the eggs and egg yolks together. Slowly add the milk mixture and continue to whisk.

Bake the cubed bread in a 350° oven for 15 to 20 minutes until completely toasted and golden brown.

Combine the corned beef with the egg and milk mixture and the toasted bread cubes, sauerkraut and chives. Let the mixture rest for 20 minutes.

Divide the batter into 6 ramekins that have been sprayed with cooking spray. Place the ramekins in a water bath half the pudding depth. Bake in a 350° oven for 45 minutes until the edges puff and the center sets. Serve with Maple Onion Jam.

Note: It may also be baked in one large baking dish and served at the table. Adjust the baking time accordingly.

MAKES 6 SERVINGS.

Maple Onion Jam

2 *large yellow onions, peeled and*
sliced
3 *tablespoons olive oil*
½ *cup maple syrup*
¼ *teaspoon salt*

In a skillet slowly caramelize the onions in oil until they are a deep golden brown. Gradually lower the heat as the onions cook. This step must be done with patience as it is the recipe key. When the onions are brown, not burned, add the maple syrup and simmer for 5 minutes. Remove from the heat and add the salt. Serve warm.

MAKES 6 SERVINGS.

Island Blue Mussel and Sweet Potato Chowder

5 *pounds Island Blue Mussels*
1 *pound onions, chopped*
¼ *cup butter*
4 *cloves garlic*
2 *pounds sweet potatoes, shredded*
8 *ounces carrot, shredded*
3 *cups milk*
3 *cups heavy cream*
2 *bay leaves*

In a large pot with a tight-fitting lid place the mussels and ¼ cup of water. Place over high heat, cover, and steam until the shells open wide. Discard any that won't open. Remove the meat and set aside. Reserve the steaming liquid and some shells for garnish.

In a stockpot melt the butter and sweat the onions for 10 minutes. Add the garlic and sweat for 5 more minutes. Add the sweet potatoes, carrot, milk, and cream, and simmer for 30 minutes or until the vegetables are soft. Transfer the mixture to a blender and purée, or strain through a fine mesh strainer. Return to the pot. Add the mussel juice and thin to the desired consistency. Bring back to heat, add the mussels, and serve.

MAKES 6 SERVINGS.

Ripplecove Inn
❧

700 Ripplecove Road
Ayer's Cliff, Québec J0B 1C0
Canada
(819) 838-4296

Established in 1945 as a summer resort and fishing lodge, the Ripplecove Inn is now an all-season resort offering a heated pool, two private beaches, and a full range of winter and summer activities. There are twenty-five designer-decorated guest rooms, many with whirlpool baths and fireplace. The country

French cuisine can be enjoyed at tables overlooking magnificent Lake Massawippi.

Onion and Champagne Soup

2 *tablespoons butter*
6 *onions, chopped*
1 *liter water*
Egg yolks
8 *ounces (200 g) creamy Camembert*
1 *bottle champagne*
1 *teaspoon Armagnac*
8 *ounces porto*
Salt and pepper
Cayenne pepper
1 *bay leaf*

Brown the onions in the butter and add the water, let boil for 10 minutes.

Add the champagne, bring to a small boil. Add the camembert and mix with a wooden spoon. Mix together the egg yolks and the porto then add them to the soup.

Keep in a double boiler, and before serving add the Armagnac.

MAKES 6 TO 8 SERVINGS.

Fillet of Trout with Rose Petal Sauce

2 *tablespoons plus 2 teaspoon ground*
almonds
¼ *cup cornstarch*
2 *tablespoons sugar*
½ *cup rose petals (red)*
1 *cup lobster broth*
Pinch saffron
Salt to taste
Ginger to taste
4 *trout fillets*
Salt and pepper
Butter

In a baking pan bake the trout in the oven for 10 min, with butter on top and bottom, add salt and pepper. Mix the cornstarch with 2 tablespoons of lobster broth. Then add to the rest of the broth the sugar, saffron, and 2 tablespoons of almonds. Bring to a boil, mix until the sauce thickens. Mash the rose petals and the rest of the almonds to become a paste, then add it to the sauce and bring to a boil. Add the ginger and the salt.

Check the seasoning and serve with trout.

MAKES 4 SERVINGS.

Frozen Chocolate and Mocha Mousse

>   7 *ounces (200 g) dark chocolate, melted*
>   4 *teaspoons Tia Maria*
>   4 *eggs, separated*
>   1 *cup thickened cream*
>
> ....
>
>   12 *ounces melted white chocolate*
>   ¾ *cup butter, melted*
>   2 *teaspoons Tia Maria*
>   3 *eggs, separated*
>   ⅔ *cup thickened cream*
>
> ....
>
>   1 *cup hazelnut praline*
>   1 *cup thickened cream*
>   1 *ounces Tia Maria*

Line a 5 x 9-inch loaf pan with plastic wrap.

In a large bowl combine the chocolate, 4 teaspoons of liqueur, and 4 egg yolks, and stir until smooth. In a small bowl whip 1 cup of cream until soft peaks form, then fold into the chocolate mixture. Pour half of the chocolate mixture into the prepared pan. Freeze for several hours or until firm.

In a large bowl combine the white chocolate, butter, 2 teaspoons of liqueur, and 3 egg yolks. Stir until smooth. Fold in the whipped cream and the egg whites as done for the dark layer. Top the dark layer with the white chocolate and freeze until firm.

Add the rest of the dark chocolate and freeze for several hours.

In a heatproof bowl stir the praline over hot water until pourable. Gradually stir in the cream and liqueur. Refrigerate until cool. Pour sauce over each serving of mousse.

MAKES 6 SERVINGS.

124 Rue St. Raphael
Cap-à-L'Aigle, Charlevoix, Québec G0T 1B0
Canada
(418) 665-4431

A charming country inn in the heart of the quaint Charlevoix region, La Pinsonnière offers twenty-seven distinctively decorated guest rooms. The elegance of the inn is enhanced by original artwork and artistic dining experiences. The inn is near the most southerly strip of tundra in Canada, and the wildlife viewing here is extraordinary. The nearby Saguenay Park is noted for its breathtaking fjord and many whale species.

Rabbit in Sage and Wild Mushroom Sauce

>   ⅓ *cup unsalted butter*
>   1 *young rabbit with liver, cut into serving pieces*
>   5 *morel mushrooms, sliced*
>   2 *shallots, peeled and minced*
>   ½ *cup dry white wine*
>   2 *tablespoons brandy*
>   2 *tablespoons chopped fresh sage*
>   1 *cup rabbit or chicken stock*
>   ½ *cup heavy cream*
>   *Salt and freshly ground pepper to taste*
>   *Rabbit liver, if included with rabbit pieces*

Wash the rabbit pieces and pat dry. Reserve the liver.

About one half hour before serving, in a heavy skillet melt 3 tablespoons of the butter, and sautÈ the rabbit over medium heat until partially cooked and beginning to brown. Place the pieces in a lightly oiled 9 x 13-inch pan. Bake in a 325° oven for 30 minutes.

During the final 10 minutes of baking, heat the morels and shallots gently in the same pan that browned the rabbit. Cover and cook over low heat until the shallots are translucent but not browned. Add the wine, brandy, and sage. Increase the heat and reduce the sauce to one-third its original volume.

Pour in the stock and reduce again to one-third of its volume.

Whisk the cream into the wine stock. Remove the skillet from the heat and whisk in the remaining butter (cut into small bits) one piece at a time. Season with salt and pepper. Keep the sauce warm but do not boil.

Sauté the liver in 1 tablespoon butter until just pink on the inside.

To serve, place the rabbit on a heated serving platter, cover with the sauce and garnish with the liver that has been sliced across the grain.

MAKES 4 SERVINGS.

La Pinsonniere Floating Island

>   2 *cups milk*
>   2 *cups water*
>   ½ *cup sugar*
>   2 *vanilla beans*
>   8 *egg whites (save yolks and use in creme anglaise below)*
>   ½ *cup sugar*
>   *Pinch salt*
>   *Fresh raspberries*
>   *Crème Anglaise (recipe follows)*

In a large saucepan, bring the milk, water, sugar, and vanilla beans to a boil. Turn down the heat and allow to simmer.

In a large bowl beat the egg whites with a pinch of salt until soft peaks form. Add the sugar and keep beating until the peaks are stiff. Using 2 teaspoons, form the egg white mixture to 8 egg like shapes. Poach in the simmering liquid for 3 minutes on each side. Carefully remove the egg white "islands" with a strainer and drain on paper towels. Serve "floating" on a puddle of Crème Anglaise, garnished with fresh raspberries.

MAKES 8 SERVINGS.

Crème Anglaise

>   8 *egg yolks*
>   ½ *cup sugar*
>   1 *quart milk*
>   1 *vanilla bean, split*

In a large saucepan beat the egg yolks until sticky, about 1 minutes. Gradually beat in the sugar. In a separate pan heat the milk with the vanilla bean.

Slowly beat in the hot vanilla milk by droplets. Cook over moderately low heat until the sauce is thick enough to coat a spoon. Do not let the sauce come to a simmer or the egg yolks will curdle. Remove the vanilla bean before serving.

Serve warm or cool.

MAKES 1 QUART.

Scallop Salad with Cantal Cheese

> *Mixed salad greens such as oak leaf, red leaf or Boston lettuce*
> *Lemon juice vinaigrette*
> 4 *ounces Cantal cheese, shaved or grated*
> 12 *sea scallops*
> 2 *tablespoons olive oil*
> 2 *teaspoons heavy cream*
> 2 *chopped shallots*
> 1 *tablespoon white wine vinegar*

Wash and drain the lettuce. Pat dry on paper towels. Season the greens with a lemon juice vinaigrette. Set aside.

In a skillet heat the olive oil over medium high heat. When the oil is almost smoking, add the scallops and toss for about 3 minutes until brown on the outside but still rare on the inside.

Add the chopped shallots to the scallops, cook for 1 minute, and deglaze the pan with the white wine vinegar. Add the cream, and reduce over heat for 30 seconds. Remove the pan from the heat.

Arrange seasoned greens in the middle of plates. Sprinkle with cheese shavings. Place warm scallops on top.

MAKES 4 SERVINGS.

Westwind

Manitou Beach, Saskatchewan S0K 4T0
Canada
(306) 946-3821

Manitou Beach is world renowned for its high density mineral water, believed by many to relieve a variety of ailments. The Westwind is a good choice for those who want to sample the waters. There are four well-appointed guest rooms. And if the water won't fix you up, the country breakfast at the Westwind probably will.

Tomato Flan

> *Pastry for 1 10-inch pie*
> *Thinly sliced tomatoes*
> 2 *cups chopped ham (or salami, or other sausage) -layer over tomatoes*
> 6 *ounces of cheddar cheese (sliced) on top of ham*
> 8 *to 10 crustless slices French bred (thin) to cover cheese*
> ½ *cup whipping cream*
> 1 *cup sour cream (commercial)*
> 8 *eggs*
> *Salt and pepper to taste*
> *Nutmeg*
> *Paprika*
> *Butter*

Place the pie crust in a large quiche pan or flan pan. Arrange thinly sliced tomatoes to cover the crust. Layer the ham over the tomatoes. In a large bowl beat the cream, sour cream, and eggs. Season with salt, pepper and a pinch of nutmeg. Pour over the ham. Sprinkle with paprika and dot with butter. Bake in a 400° oven for 30 to 40 minutes, until firm and golden.

MAKES 10 SERVINGS.

Onion Flan

> 1 *teaspoon yeast*
> 1 *teaspoon sugar*
> ½ *cup lukewarm water (105 to 115°)*
> ....
> 1 *cup all-purpose flour*
> 1 *teaspoon salt*
> 1 *egg*
> ....
> 1 *cup bacon, chopped*
> 1 *cup sliced onions (in rings)*
> ⅓ *cup sliced Cheddar cheese*

In a small bowl mix the yeast, sugar, and warm water, and leave in warm place for 15 minutes until frothy.

In a large bowl mix the flour and salt, and make a well in the center. Add the yeast mixture and egg, and mix well. Turn the dough onto a floured surface and knead until smooth and elastic. Cover and let rise in a warm place for 45 minutes to 1 hour. Roll out and line a greased quiche or flan pan. Let rise for 15 minutes.

In a skillet brown the bacon and then sautÈ the onions until soft. Drain. Cover the flan base with onions and bacon. Arrange the cheese slices on top. Bake in a 400° oven for 30 to 35 minutes. May be reheated at 300 ° for 30 to 40 minutes.

MAKES 4 TO 6 SERVINGS.

Latimer on Oxford

37 Oxford Street West
Moose Jaw, Saskatchewan S6H 2N2
Canada
(306) 692-5481

Built in 1911, the house combines Greek Revival design with the quality craftsmanship of early Canadian construction. Ten Corinthian columns support the front balconies, while a solid oak door opens to welcome guests into the beautifully appointed interior. There are many period antiques. Moose Jaw is now home to a multimillion-dollar mineral spring spa.

Rusk (a type of Scottish Bun)

> 1 *yeast cake*
> ¼ *cup lukewarm water (95°)*
> ¼ *cup butter*
> ¼ *cup sugar*
> 1 *teaspoon salt*
> 1 *pint scalded milk*

3   *cups all-purpose flour*

2   *eggs, well beaten*

3   *cups all-purpose flour*

1   *slightly beaten egg white diluted*
        with a little cold water
        Sugar

In a small bowl dissolve the yeast cake in the warm water and set aside.

Dissolve the butter, sugar, and salt in the scalded milk. When the milk mixture is lukewarm add the yeast cake and 3 cups of the flour. Cover and let rise.

Punch the dough down and then add the eggs and enough of the flour to make a stiff batter. Knead the dough until smooth and elastic. Cover again and allow to rise.

Form the dough into rolls or buns of any shape. Let rise again.

Bake in a 425° oven for 35 to 40 minutes. Before removing the buns from the oven brush the tops with a slightly beaten egg white which has been diluted with a little cold water. Sprinkle the tops of the buns with sugar.

MAKES 12 TEXAS BUNS OR A LOT OF APPETIZER TEASERS.

Moose Jaw Minuet

16   *slices of bread, crusts removed*

6   *to 8 slices black forest ham or good*
       quality ham

¼   *to ½ pound grated Canadian Old*
       Cheddar cheese or equivalent

6   *eggs*

3   *cups milk*
       Salt and pepper to taste

1   *teaspoon dry mustard*

¼   *cup onion, finely chopped*

2   *teaspoon Worcestershire sauce*
       Dash of Tabasco sauce

¼   *cup margarine*

1   *cup crushed Special K or Corn Flakes*
       cereal

In the bottom of a 9 x 13-inch pan arrange 8 slices of bread. Top with the ham, cheese, and the remaining 8 slices of bread.

In a large bowl beat the eggs and milk together. Add the salt, pepper, mustard, onion, Worcestershire sauce, and Tabasco sauce to the egg mixture and continue to beat. Carefully pour the egg mixture over the bread mixture. Cover the pan and let stand overnight in the refrigerator.

In a saucepan melt the margarine and pour in the cereal. Sprinkle on top of the bread mixture. Bake in a 350° oven for 1 hour. Take the pan out of the oven and let stand for 10 minutes.

MAKES 8 SERVINGS.

INDEX

B

C

ℋ

N

O

𝒬

ℛ

S